Ninth Edition

DECISION SUPPORT AND BUSINESS INTELLIGENCE SYSTEMS

Efraim Turban

University of Hawaii

Ramesh Sharda

Oklahoma State University

Dursun Delen

Oklahoma State University

With contributions by

Jay E. Aronson

The University of Georgia

Ting-Peng Liang

National Sun Yat-sen University

David King

JDA Software Group, Inc.

Prentice Hall

Boston   Columbus   Indianapolis   New York   San Francisco   Upper Saddle River
Amsterdam   Cape Town   Dubai   London   Madrid   Milan   Munich   Paris   Montreal   Toronto
Delhi   Mexico City   Sao Paulo   Sydney   Hong Kong   Seoul   Singapore   Taipei   Tokyo

Editorial Director: Sally Yagan
Editor in Chief: Eric Svendsen
Executive Editor: Bob Horan
Editorial Project Manager: Kelly Loftus
Editorial Assistant: Jason Calcano
Director of Marketing: Patrice Jones
Senior Marketing Manager: Anne Fahlgren
Marketing Assistant: Melinda Jensen
Senior Managing Editor: Judy Leale
Senior Production Project Manager:
   Karalyn Holland
Senior Operations Supervisor: Arnold Vila
Operations Specialist: Ilene Kahn

Art Director: Jane Conte
Cover Designer: Bruce Kenselaar
Manager, Rights and Permissions: Shannon Barbe
Manager, Cover Visual Research & Permissions:
   Karen Sanatar
Cover Art: Getty Images, Inc.
Media Project Manager: Lisa Rinaldi
Full-Service Project Management:
   Sharon Anderson/BookMasters, Inc.
Composition: Integra
Printer/Binder: Hamilton Printing Co.
Cover Printer: Lehigh-Phoenix Color/Hagerstown
Text Font: 10/12 Garamond

Credits and acknowledgments borrowed from other sources and reproduced, with permission, in this textbook appear on appropriate page within text.

Microsoft® and Windows® are registered trademarks of the Microsoft Corporation in the U.S.A. and other countries. Screen shots and icons reprinted with permission from the Microsoft Corporation. This book is not sponsored or endorsed by or affiliated with the Microsoft Corporation.

Many of the designations by manufacturers and seller to distinguish their products are claimed as trademarks. Where those designations appear in this book, and the publisher was aware of a trademark claim, the designations have been printed in initial caps or all caps.

Library of Congress Cataloging-in-Publication Data

Turban, Efraim.
   Decision support and business intelligence systems/Efraim Turban, Ramesh Sharda, Dursun Delen.—9th ed.
     p. cm.
   Rev. ed. of: Decision support and business intelligence systems/Efraim Turban . . . [et al.]. 8th ed. c2007.
   Includes bibliographical references and index.
   ISBN 978-0-13-610729-3
   1. Management—Data processing.   2. Decision support systems.   3. Expert systems (Computer science)
   4. Business intelligence.   I. Sharda, Ramesh.   II. Delen, Dursun.   III. Title.   IV. Title: Decision support
   and business intelligence systems.
HD30.2.T87 2011
658.4'030285—dc22

2009040368

10 9 8 7 6 5 4 3 2

Prentice Hall
is an imprint of

PEARSON

www.pearsonhighered.com

ISBN 10:   0-13-610729-X
ISBN 13: 978-0-13-610729-3

Dedicated to our spouses and children with love

—The Authors

ABOUT THE AUTHORS

Efraim Turban (M.B.A., Ph.D., University of California, Berkeley) is a visiting scholar at the Pacific Institute for Information System Management, University of Hawaii. Prior to this, he was on the staff of several universities, including City University of Hong Kong; Lehigh University; Florida International University; California State University, Long Beach; Eastern Illinois University; and the University of Southern California. Dr. Turban is the author of more than 100 refereed papers published in leading journals, such as *Management Science, MIS Quarterly,* and *Decision Support Systems.* He is also the author of 20 books, including *Electronic Commerce: A Managerial Perspective* and *Information Technology for Management.* He is also a consultant to major corporations worldwide. Dr. Turban's current areas of interest are Web-based decision support systems, social commerce and collaborative decision making.

Ramesh Sharda (M.B.A., Ph.D., University of Wisconsin–Madison) is director of the Institute for Research in Information Systems (IRIS), ConocoPhillips Chair of Management of Technology, and a Regents Professor of Management Science and Information Systems in the Spears School of Business Administration at Oklahoma State University (OSU). More than 100 papers describing his research have been published in major journals, including *Management Science, Information Systems Research, Decision Support Systems,* and *Journal of MIS.* He cofounded the AIS SIG on Decision Support Systems and Knowledge Management (SIGDSS). Dr. Sharda serves on several editorial boards, including those of *INFORMS Journal on Computing, Decision Support Systems,* and *ACM Transactions on Management Information Systems.* His current research interests are in decision support systems, collaborative applications, and technologies for managing information overload. Dr. Sharda is also a cofounder of iTradeFair.com, a company that produces virtual trade fairs.

Dursun Delen (Ph.D, Oklahoma State University) is an Associate Professor of Management Science and Information Systems in the Spears School of Business at Oklahoma State University (OSU). Prior to his appointment as an assistant professor at OSU in 2001, he worked for Knowledge Based Systems Inc., in College Station, Texas, as a research scientist for 5 years, during which he led a number of decision support and other information systems research projects funded by federal agencies such as the Department of Defense, NASA, the National Institute of Standards and Technology (NIST), and the Department of Energy. His research has appeared in major journals, including *decision support systems, communications of the ACM, computers and operations research, computers in industry, journal of production operations management, Artificial Intelligence in Medicine,* and *Expert Systems with Applications,* among others. With Professor David Olson he recently published a book on advanced data mining techniques. He is an associate editor for the International *Journal of RF Technologies: Research and Applications* and serves on the editorial boards of the *Journal of Information and Knowledge Management, International Journal of Intelligent Information Technologies, Journal of Emerging Technologies in Web Intelligence,* and *International Journal of Service Sciences.* His research and teaching interests are in decision support systems, data and text mining, knowledge management, business intelligence, and enterprise modeling.

BRIEF CONTENTS

PART I   **Decision Support and Business Intelligence**   **1**

    Chapter 1   Decision Support Systems and Business Intelligence   2

PART II   **Computerized Decision Support**   **37**

    Chapter 2   Decision Making, Systems, Modeling, and Support   38

    Chapter 3   Decision Support Systems Concepts, Methodologies, and Technologies: An Overview   70

    Chapter 4   Modeling and Analysis   135

Part III   **Business Intelligence**   **189**

    Chapter 5   Data Mining for Business Intelligence   190

    Chapter 6   Artificial Neural Networks for Data Mining   241

    Chapter 7   Text and Web Mining   286

    Chapter 8   Data Warehousing   326

    Chapter 9   Business Performance Management   374

PART IV   **Collaboration, Communication, Group Support Systems, and Knowledge Management**   **419**

    Chapter 10   Collaborative Computer-Supported Technologies and Group Support Systems   420

    Chapter 11   Knowledge Management   471

PART V   **Intelligent Systems**   **529**

    Chapter 12   Artificial Intelligence and Expert Systems   530

    Chapter 13   Advanced Intelligent Systems   580

PART VI   **Implementing Decision Support Systems and Business Intelligence**   **633**

    Chapter 14   Management Support Systems: Emerging Trends and Impacts   634

CONTENTS

Preface xvi

Part I   Decision Support and Business Intelligence   1

Chapter 1 Decision Support Systems and Business Intelligence   2

1.1   Opening Vignette: Norfolk Southern Uses Business Intelligence for Decision Support to Reach Success   3

1.2   Changing Business Environments and Computerized Decision Support   5

1.3   Managerial Decision Making   7

1.4   Computerized Support for Decision Making   9

1.5   An Early Framework for Computerized Decision Support   11
   ▶ APPLICATION CASE 1.1 Giant Food Stores Prices the Entire Store   14

1.6   The Concept of Decision Support Systems (DSS)   16
   ▶ APPLICATION CASE 1.2 A DSS for Managing Inventory at GlaxoSmithKline   16

1.7   A Framework for Business Intelligence (BI)   18
   ▶ APPLICATION CASE 1.3 Location, Location, Location   21
   ▶ APPLICATION CASE 1.4 Alltel Wireless: Delivering the Right Message, to the Right Customers, at the Right Time   23

1.8   A Work System View of Decision Support   25

1.9   The Major Tools and Techniques of Managerial Decision Support   26
   ▶ APPLICATION CASE 1.5 United Sugars Corporation Optimizes Production, Distribution, and Inventory Capacity with Different Decision Support Tools   27

1.10   Plan of the Book   28
   ▶ APPLICATION CASE 1.6 The Next Net   30

1.11   Resources, Links, and the Teradata University Network Connection   30
   Chapter Highlights   31   •   Key Terms   32
   Questions for Discussion   32   •   Exercises   33
      ▶ END OF CHAPTER APPLICATION CASE Vodafone Uses Business Intelligence to Improve Customer Growth and Retention Plans   34
   References   35

Part II   Computerized Decision Support   37

Chapter 2 Decision Making, Systems, Modeling, and Support   38

2.1   Opening Vignette: Decision Modeling at HP Using Spreadsheets   39

2.2   Decision Making: Introduction and Definitions   41

2.3   Models   44

2.4   Phases of the Decision-Making Process   45

2.5   Decision Making: The Intelligence Phase   48
   ▶ APPLICATION CASE 2.1 Making Elevators Go Faster!   48

2.6   Decision Making: The Design Phase   50

■ **TECHNOLOGY INSIGHTS 2.1** The Difference Between a Criterion and a Constraint   51

■ **TECHNOLOGY INSIGHTS 2.2** Are Decision Makers Really Rational?   52

2.7   Decision Making: The Choice Phase   58

2.8   Decision Making: The Implementation Phase   58

2.9   How Decisions Are Supported   59

■ **TECHNOLOGY INSIGHTS 2.3** Decision Making in the Digital Age   61

▶ **APPLICATION CASE 2.2** Advanced Technology for Museums: RFID Makes Art Come Alive   63

2.10 Resources, Links, and the Teradata University Network Connection   64

Chapter Highlights   65   •   Key Terms   65
Questions for Discussion   65   •   Exercises   66

▶ **End of Chapter Application Case** Decisions and Risk Management (!) That Led to the Subprime Mortgage Crisis   67

References   68

Chapter 3 Decision Support Systems Concepts, Methodologies, and Technologies: An Overview   70

3.1   Opening Vignette: Decision Support System Cures for Health Care   71

3.2   Decision Support System Configurations   74

3.3   Decision Support System Description   75

▶ **APPLICATION CASE 3.1** A Spreadsheet-Based DSS Enables Ammunition Requirements Planning for the Canadian Army   76

3.4   Decision Support System Characteristics and Capabilities   77

3.5   Decision Support System Classifications   79

▶ **APPLICATION CASE 3.2** Expertise Transfer System to Train Future Army Personnel   81

3.6   Components of Decision Support Systems   85

3.7   The Data Management Subsystem   89

▶ **APPLICATION CASE 3.3** Pacific Sunwear Tracks Business Performance   90

■ **TECHNOLOGY INSIGHTS 3.1** The Capabilities of a Relational DBMS in a DSS   92

■ **TECHNOLOGY INSIGHTS 3.2** The 10 Essential Ingredients of Data (Information) Quality Management   94

3.8   The Model Management Subsystem   96

▶ **APPLICATION CASE 3.4** SNAP DSS Helps OneNet Make Telecommunications Rate Decisions   98

■ **TECHNOLOGY INSIGHTS 3.3** Major Functions of an MBMS   100

3.9   The User Interface (Dialog) Subsystem   100

■ **TECHNOLOGY INSIGHTS 3.4** Next Generation of Input Devices   104

3.10 The Knowledge-Based Management Subsystem   105

▶ **APPLICATION CASE 3.5** IAP Systems' Intelligent DSS Determines the Success of Overseas Assignments and Learns from the Experience   106

3.11 The Decision Support System User   106

3.12 Decision Support System Hardware   107

3.13 A DSS Modeling Language: Planners Lab   108

▶ **APPLICATION CASE 3.6** Nonprofits Use Planners Lab as a Decision-Making Tool   109

3.14 Resources, Links, and the Teradata University Network Connection   125
Chapter Highlights   126   •   Key Terms   127
Questions for Discussion   128   •   Exercises   128
▶ **END OF CHAPTER APPLICATION CASE** Spreadsheet Model-Based Decision Support for Inventory Target Setting at Procter & Gamble   132
References   133

Chapter 4   Modeling and Analysis   135

4.1 Opening Vignette: Model-Based Auctions Serve More Lunches in Chile   136

4.2 Management Support Systems Modeling   139
▶ **APPLICATION CASE 4.1** Lockheed Martin Space Systems Company Optimizes Infrastructure Project-Portfolio Selection   140
▶ **APPLICATION CASE 4.2** Forecasting/Predictive Analytics Proves to be a Good Gamble for Harrah's Cherokee Casino and Hotel   142

4.3 Structure of Mathematical Models for Decision Support   145

4.4 Certainty, Uncertainty, and Risk   147

4.5 Management Support Systems Modeling with Spreadsheets   149
▶ **APPLICATION CASE 4.3** Showcase Scheduling at Fred Astaire East Side Dance Studio   150

4.6 Mathematical Programming Optimization   152
▶ **APPLICATION CASE 4.4** Spreadsheet Model Helps Assign Medical Residents   152
■ **TECHNOLOGY INSIGHTS 4.1** Linear Programming   154

4.7 Multiple Goals, Sensitivity Analysis, What-If Analysis, and Goal Seeking   157

4.8 Decision Analysis with Decision Tables and Decision Trees   161
▶ **APPLICATION CASE 4.5** Decision Analysis Assists Doctor in Weighing Treatment Options for Cancer Suspects and Patients   164

4.9 Multicriteria Decision Making with Pairwise Comparisons   165
▶ **APPLICATION CASE 4.6** Multicriteria Decision Support for European Radiation Emergency Support System   166

4.10 Problem-Solving Search Methods   168
▶ **APPLICATION CASE 4.7** Heuristic-Based DSS Moves Milk in New Zealand   170

4.11 Simulation   171
▶ **APPLICATION CASE 4.8** Improving Maintenance Decision Making in the Finnish Air Force Through Simulation   171
▶ **APPLICATION CASE 4.9** Simulation Applications   176

4.12 Visual Interactive Simulation   177

4.13 Quantitative Software Packages and Model Base Management   179

4.14 Resources, Links, and the Teradata University Network Connection   180
Chapter Highlights   181   •   Key Terms   182
Questions for Discussion   182   •   Exercises   183

▶ **END OF CHAPTER APPLICATION CASE** HP Applies Management Science Modeling to Optimize Its Supply Chain and Wins a Major Award   185
References   187

Part III Business Intelligence   189

Chapter 5 Data Mining for Business Intelligence   190

5.1   Opening Vignette: Data Mining Goes to Hollywood!   191

5.2   Data Mining Concepts and Applications   194

▶ **APPLICATION CASE 5.1** Business Analytics and Data Mining Help 1-800-Flowers Excel in Business   195

■ **TECHNOLOGY INSIGHTS 5.1** Data in Data Mining   197

▶ **APPLICATION CASE 5.2** Law Enforcement Organizations Use Data Mining to Better Fight Crime   199

▶ **APPLICATION CASE 5.3** Motor Vehicle Accidents and Driver Distractions   203

5.3   Data Mining Applications   204

▶ **APPLICATION CASE 5.4** A Mine on Terrorist Funding   206

5.4   Data Mining Process   207

▶ **APPLICATION CASE 5.5** Data Mining in Cancer Research   213

5.5   Data Mining Methods   216

▶ **APPLICATION CASE 5.6** Highmark, Inc., Employs Data Mining to Manage Insurance Costs   222

5.6   Data Mining Software Tools   228

▶ **APPLICATION CASE 5.7** Predicting Customer Churn—A Competition of Different Tools   231

5.7   Data Mining Myths and Blunders   233
Chapter Highlights   234   •   Key Terms   235
Questions for Discussion   235   •   Exercises   236

▶ **END OF CHAPTER APPLICATION CASE** Data Mining Helps Develop Custom-Tailored Product Portfolios for Telecommunication Companies   238
References   239

Chapter 6 Artificial Neural Networks for Data Mining   241

6.1   Opening Vignette: Predicting Gambling Referenda with Neural Networks   242

6.2   Basic Concepts of Neural Networks   245

■ **TECHNOLOGY INSIGHTS 6.1** The Relationship Between Biological and Artificial Neural Networks   247

▶ **APPLICATION CASE 6.1** Neural Networks Help Reduce Telecommunications Fraud   248

6.3   Learning in Artificial Neural Networks   253

▶ **APPLICATION CASE 6.2** Neural Networks Help Deliver Microsoft's Mail to the Intended Audience   254

6.4   Developing Neural Network–Based Systems   259

■ **TECHNOLOGY INSIGHTS 6.2** ANN Software   263

6.5   Illuminating the Black Box of ANN with Sensitivity Analysis   264

▶ **APPLICATION CASE 6.3** Sensitivity Analysis Reveals Injury Severity Factors in Traffic Accidents   266

6.6   A Sample Neural Network Project   267

6.7 Other Popular Neural Network Paradigms 270

6.8 Applications of Artificial Neural Networks 274

▶ **APPLICATION CASE 6.4 Neural Networks for Breast Cancer Diagnosis 276**
Chapter Highlights 277 • Key Terms 277
Questions for Discussion 278 • Exercises 278

▶ **END OF CHAPTER APPLICATION CASE Coors Improves Beer Flavors with Neural Networks 282**
References 284

Chapter 7 Text and Web Mining 286

7.1 Opening Vignette: Mining Text for Security and Counterterrorism 287

7.2 Text Mining Concepts and Definitions 289

■ **TECHNOLOGY INSIGHTS 7.1 Text Mining Lingo 290**

▶ **APPLICATION CASE 7.1 Text Mining for Patent Analysis 291**

7.3 Natural Language Processing 292

▶ **APPLICATION CASE 7.2 Text Mining Helps Merck to Better Understand and Serve Its Customers 294**

7.4 Text Mining Applications 296

▶ **APPLICATION CASE 7.3 Mining for Lies 297**

▶ **APPLICATION CASE 7.4 Flying Through Text 301**

7.5 Text Mining Process 302

▶ **APPLICATION CASE 7.5 Research Literature Survey with Text Mining 309**

7.6 Text Mining Tools 312

7.7 Web Mining Overview 312

7.8 Web Content Mining and Web Structure Mining 314

▶ **APPLICATION CASE 7.6 Caught in a Web 315**

7.9 Web Usage Mining 316

7.10 Web Mining Success Stories 318

▶ **APPLICATION CASE 7.7 Web Site Optimization Ecosystem 319**
Chapter Highlights 321 • Key Terms 322
Questions for Discussion 322 • Exercises 323

▶ **END OF CHAPTER APPLICATION CASE HP and Text Mining 323**
References 325

Chapter 8 Data Warehousing 326

8.1 Opening Vignette: DirecTV Thrives with Active Data Warehousing 327

8.2 Data Warehousing Definitions and Concepts 328

▶ **APPLICATION CASE 8.1 Enterprise Data Warehouse Delivers Cost Savings and Process Efficiencies 331**

8.3 Data Warehousing Process Overview 333

▶ **APPLICATION CASE 8.2 Data Warehousing Supports First American Corporation's Corporate Strategy 333**

8.4 Data Warehousing Architectures 335

8.5 Data Integration and the Extraction, Transformation, and Load (ETL) Processes 342

▶ **APPLICATION CASE 8.3 BP Lubricants Achieves BIGS Success 342**

8.6   Data Warehouse Development   346

▶ **APPLICATION CASE 8.4** Things Go Better with Coke's Data Warehouse   347

▶ **APPLICATION CASE 8.5** HP Consolidates Hundreds of Data Marts into a Single EDW   350

■ **TECHNOLOGY INSIGHTS 8.1** Hosted Data Warehouses   352

▶ **APPLICATION CASE 8.6** A Large Insurance Company Integrates Its Enterprise Data with AXIS   357

8.7   Real-Time Data Warehousing   359

▶ **APPLICATION CASE 8.7** Egg Plc Fries the Competition in Near-Real-Time   360

■ **TECHNOLOGY INSIGHTS 8.2** The Real-Time Realities of Active Data Warehousing   363

8.8   Data Warehouse Administration and Security Issues   364

■ **TECHNOLOGY INSIGHTS 8.3** Ambeo Delivers Proven Data Access Auditing Solution   365

8.9   Resources, Links, and the Teradata University Network Connection   365

Chapter Highlights   367   •   Key Terms   367
Questions for Discussion   367   •   Exercises   367

▶ **END OF CHAPTER APPLICATION CASE** Continental Airlines Flies High with Its Real-Time Data Warehouse   369

References   371

Chapter 9   Business Performance Management   374

9.1   Opening Vignette: Double Down at Harrah's   375

9.2   Business Performance Management (BPM) Overview   377

9.3   Strategize: Where Do We Want to Go?   379

9.4   Plan: How Do We Get There?   382

9.5   Monitor: How Are We Doing?   383

▶ **APPLICATION CASE 9.1** Discovery-Driven Planning: The Coffee Wars   385

9.6   Act and Adjust: What Do We Need to Do Differently?   387

9.7   Performance Measurement   390

▶ **APPLICATION CASE 9.2** Expedia.com's Customer Satisfaction Scorecard   393

9.8   BPM Methodologies   395

■ **TECHNOLOGY INSIGHTS 9.1** BSC Meets Six Sigma   402

9.9   BPM Technologies and Applications   404

9.10   Performance Dashboards and Scorecards   408

Chapter Highlights   411   •   Key Terms   412
Questions for Discussion   412   •   Exercises   413

▶ **END OF CHAPTER APPLICATION CASE** Tracking Citywide Performance   414

References   416

Part IV   Collaboration, Communication, Group Support Systems, and Knowledge Management   419

Chapter 10   Collaborative Computer-Supported Technologies and Group Support Systems   420

10.1   Opening Vignette: Procter & Gamble Drives Ideation with Group Support Systems   421

10.2   Making Decisions in Groups: Characteristics, Process, Benefits, and Dysfunctions   423

■ **TECHNOLOGY INSIGHTS 10.1** Benefits of Working in Groups and Dysfunctions of the Group Process **425**

10.3 Supporting Groupwork with Computerized Systems **426**

▶ **APPLICATION CASE 10.1** GSS Boosts Innovation in Crime Prevention **427**

■ **TECHNOLOGY INSIGHTS 10.2** Unsupported Aspects of Communication **430**

10.4 Tools for Indirect Support of Decision Making **431**

▶ **APPLICATION CASE 10.2** Catalyst Maintains an Edge with WebEx **433**

10.5 Integrated Groupware Suites **436**

▶ **APPLICATION CASE 10.3** Wimba Extends Classrooms at CSU, Chico **440**

10.6 Direct Computerized Support for Decision Making: From Group Decision Support Systems to Group Support Systems **441**

■ **TECHNOLOGY INSIGHTS 10.3** Modeling in Group Decision Making: EC11 for Groups **443**

▶ **APPLICATION CASE 10.4** Collaborative Problem Solving at KUKA **444**

▶ **APPLICATION CASE 10.5** Eastman Chemical Boosts Creative Processes and Saves $500,000 with Groupware **445**

10.7 Products and Tools for GDSS/GSS and Successful Implementation **448**

■ **TECHNOLOGY INSIGHTS 10.4** The Standard GSS Process **449**

10.8 Emerging Collaboration Tools: From VoIP to Wikis **453**

■ **TECHNOLOGY INSIGHTS 10.5** VoIP System Helps Increase Productivity and Enhance Learning Experiences at the State University of New York **453**

10.9 Collaborative Efforts in Design, Planning, and Project Management **456**

▶ **APPLICATION CASE 10.6** CPFR Initiatives at Ace Hardware and Sears **461**

10.10 Creativity, Idea Generation, and Computerized Support **462**
Chapter Highlights **465** • Key Terms **466**
Questions for Discussion **466** • Exercises **467**

▶ **END OF CHAPTER APPLICATION CASE** Dresdner Kleinwort Wasserstein Uses Wiki for Collaboration **468**
References **469**

Chapter 11 Knowledge Management 471

11.1 Opening Vignette: MITRE Knows What It Knows Through Knowledge Management **472**

11.2 Introduction to Knowledge Management **474**

▶ **APPLICATION CASE 11.1** KM at Consultancy Firms **477**

▶ **APPLICATION CASE 11.2** Cingular Calls on Knowledge **480**

11.3 Organizational Learning and Transformation **481**

▶ **APPLICATION CASE 11.3** NASA Blends KM with Risk Management **483**

11.4 Knowledge Management Activities **485**

11.5 Approaches to Knowledge Management **486**

▶ **APPLICATION CASE 11.4** Texaco Drills for Knowledge **488**

■ **TECHNOLOGY INSIGHTS 11.1** KM: A Demand-Led Business Activity **490**

11.6 Information Technology (IT) In Knowledge Management **493**

11.7 Knowledge Management Systems Implementation **498**

▶ **APPLICATION CASE 11.5** Knowledge Management: You Can Bank on It at Commerce Bank **501**

11.8 Roles of People in Knowledge Management 504

▶ **APPLICATION CASE 11.6** Online Knowledge Sharing at Xerox 506

■ **TECHNOLOGY INSIGHTS 11.2** Seven Principles for Designing Successful COP 508

11.9 Ensuring the Success of Knowledge Management Efforts 509

■ **TECHNOLOGY INSIGHTS 11.3** MAKE: Most Admired Knowledge Enterprises 510

▶ **APPLICATION CASE 11.7** The British Broadcasting Corporation Knowledge Management Success 511

▶ **APPLICATION CASE 11.8** How the U.S. Department of Commerce Uses an Expert Location System 512

■ **TECHNOLOGY INSIGHTS 11.4** Six Keys to KM Success for Customer Service 513

■ **TECHNOLOGY INSIGHTS 11.5** KM Myths 516

▶ **APPLICATION CASE 11.9** When KMS Fail, They Can Fail in a Big Way 517

■ **TECHNOLOGY INSIGHTS 11.6** Knowledge Management Traps 518

*Chapter Highlights 520 • Key Terms 521
Questions for Discussion 521 • Exercises 522*

▶ **END OF CHAPTER APPLICATION CASE** Siemens Keeps Knowledge Management Blooming with ShareNet 523

References 524

Part V Intelligent Systems 529

Chapter 12 Artificial Intelligence and Expert Systems 530

12.1 Opening Vignette: A Web-Based Expert System for Wine Selection 531

12.2 Concepts and Definitions of Artificial Intelligence 532

▶ **APPLICATION CASE 12.1** Intelligent System Beats the Chess Grand Master 533

12.3 The Artificial Intelligence Field 535

■ **TECHNOLOGY INSIGHTS 12.1** Artificial Intelligence Versus Natural Intelligence 537

▶ **APPLICATION CASE 12.2** Automatic Speech Recognition in Call Centers 539

▶ **APPLICATION CASE 12.3** Agents for Travel Planning at USC 541

12.4 Basic Concepts of Expert Systems 542

■ **TECHNOLOGY INSIGHTS 12.2** Sample Session of a Rule-Based ES 545

▶ **APPLICATION CASE 12.4** Expert System Helps in Identifying Sport Talents 546

12.5 Applications of Expert Systems 546

▶ **APPLICATION CASE 12.5** Sample Applications of ES 547

12.6 Structure of Expert Systems 550

▶ **APPLICATION CASE 12.6** A Fashion Mix-and-Match Expert System 552

12.7 Knowledge Engineering 553

■ **TECHNOLOGY INSIGHTS 12.3** Difficulties in Knowledge Acquisition 555

12.8 Problem Areas Suitable for Expert Systems 564

▶ **APPLICATION CASE 12.7** Monitoring Water Quality with Sensor-Driven Expert Systems 565

12.9 Development of Expert Systems 566

12.10 Benefits, Limitations, and Critical Success Factors of Expert Systems   569

12.11 Expert Systems on the Web   572

▶ **APPLICATION CASE 12.8** Banner with Brains: Web-Based ES for Restaurant Selection   573

▶ **APPLICATION CASE 12.9** Rule-Based System for Online Consultation   573

■ **TECHNOLOGY INSIGHTS 12.4** Automated and Real-Time Decision Systems   574

Chapter Highlights   575   •   Key Terms   576
Questions for Discussion   576   •   Exercises   577

▶ **END OF CHAPTER APPLICATION CASE** Business Rule Automation at Farm Bureau Financial Services   577

References   578

Chapter 13   Advanced Intelligent Systems   580

13.1 Opening Vignette: Machine Learning Helps Develop an Automated Reading Tutoring Tool   581

13.2 Machine-Learning Techniques   582

13.3 Case-Based Reasoning   585

▶ **APPLICATION CASE 13.1** A CBR System for Optimal Selection and Sequencing of Songs   590

13.4 Genetic Algorithms and Developing GA Applications   593

▶ **APPLICATION CASE 13.2** Genetic Algorithms Schedule Assembly Lines at Volvo Trucks North America   600

■ **TECHNOLOGY INSIGHTS 13.1** Genetic Algorithm Software   600

13.5 Fuzzy Logic and Fuzzy Inference Systems   601

13.6 Support Vector Machines   606

13.7 Intelligent Agents   613

■ **TECHNOLOGY INSIGHTS 13.2** Intelligent Agents, Objects, and ES   617

13.8 Developing Integrated Advanced Systems   622

▶ **APPLICATION CASE 13.3** International Stock Selection   623

▶ **APPLICATION CASE 13.4** Hybrid ES and Fuzzy Logic System Dispatches Trains   625

Chapter Highlights   625   •   Key Terms   626
Questions for Discussion   627   •   Exercises   627

▶ **END OF CHAPTER APPLICATION CASE** Improving Urban Infrastructure Management with Case-Based Reasoning   628

References   629

Part VI   Implementing Decision Support Systems and Business Intelligence   633

Chapter 14   Management Support Systems: Emerging Trends and Impacts   634

14.1 Opening Vignette: Coca-Cola's RFID-Based Dispenser Serves a New Type of Business Intelligence   635

14.2 RFID and New BI Application Opportunities   636

14.3 Reality Mining   641

14.4 Virtual Worlds   644

■ **TECHNOLOGY INSIGHTS 14.1** Second Life as a Decision Support Tool   645

14.5 The Web 2.0 Revolution   649

14.6 Virtual Communities   650

14.7 Online Social Networking: Basics and Examples   653

▶ **APPLICATION CASE 14.1** Using Intelligent Software and Social Networking to Improve Recruiting Processes   656

14.8 Cloud Computing and BI   658

14.9 The Impacts of Management Support Systems: An Overview   659

14.10 Management Support Systems Impacts on Organizations   661

14.11 Management Support Systems Impacts on Individuals   664

14.12 Automating Decision Making and the Manager's Job   665

14.13 Issues of Legality, Privacy, and Ethics   667

14.14 Resources, Links, and the Teradata University Network Connection   671

Chapter Highlights   671   •   Key Terms   672

Questions for Discussion   672   •   Exercises   672

▶ **END OF CHAPTER APPLICATION CASE** Continental Continues to Score with Data Warehouse   674

References   675

Glossary   678

Index   691

Online Chapters

Chapter 2 Online Files

W2.1   The MMS Running Case

Chapter 3 Online Files

W3.1   Databases

W3.2   Major Capabilities of the UIMS

Chapter 4 Online Files

W4.1   Influence Diagrams

W4.2   Linear Programming Optimization: The Blending Problem

W4.3   Lindo Example: The Product-mix Model

W4.4   Lingo Example: The Product-mix Model

W4.5   Links to Excel Files of Section 4.9

Chapter 5 Online Files

W5.1   Credit Risk

W5.2   Movie Train

W5.3   Movie Test

Chapter 6 Online Files

W6.1   The Forest CoverType Dataset

Chapter 9 Online Files

W9.1   Portfolio of Options

W9.2   Effective Performance Measurement

W9.3   Influence Problems with Dashboard Displays

PREFACE

We are experiencing major growth in the use of computer-based decision support. Companies such as IBM, Oracle, Microsoft, and others are creating new organizational units focused on analytics that help businesses become more effective and efficient in their operations. As more and more decision makers become computer and Web literate, they are using more computerized tools to support their work. The field of decision support systems (DSS)/business intelligence (BI) is evolving from its beginnings as primarily a personal-support tool and is quickly becoming a shared commodity across organizations.

The purpose of this book is to introduce the reader to these technologies, which we call, collectively, *management support systems (MSS)*. The core technology is BI. In some circles, it is also referred to as *analytics*. We use these terms interchangeably. This book presents the fundamentals of the techniques and the manner in which these systems are constructed and used.

Most of the specific improvements made in this ninth edition concentrate on three areas: BI, data mining, and automated decision support (ADS). Despite the many changes, we have preserved the comprehensiveness and user friendliness that have made the text a market leader. We have also reduced the book's size by eliminating generic material and by moving material to the Web site. Finally, we present accurate and updated material that is not available in any other text. We first describe the changes in the ninth edition and return to expanding on the objectives and coverage later in the Preface.

WHAT'S NEW IN THE NINTH EDITION?

With the goal of improving the text, this ninth edition makes several enhancements to the major changes in the eighth edition. The last edition transformed the book from the traditional DSS to BI and fostered the tight linkage with the Teradata University Network (TUN). These changes have been retained. The new edition has many timely additions, and dated content has been deleted. The following major specific changes have been made:

- *New chapters.* The following chapters have been added:

  Chapter 7, "Text and Web Mining." This new chapter explores two of the most popular business analytics tools in a comprehensive, yet easy-to-understand, way. The chapter provides a wide variety of Application Cases to make the subject interesting and appealing to the intended audience. [85% new material]

  Chapter 14, "management support systems: emerging trends and impacts." This chapter examines several new phenomena that are already changing or are likely to change decision support technologies and practices—RFID, virtual worlds, cloud computing, social networking, Web 2.0, virtual communities, and so on. It also updates some coverage from the last edition on individual/organizational/societal impacts of computerized decision support. [80% new material]

- *Streamlined coverage.* We have made the book shorter by keeping the most commonly used content. We also reduced the preformatted online content so that the book does not appear too dependent on this content. Instead, we will use a Web site to provide updated content and links on a regular basis. We reduced the number of references in each chapter. Specifically, we streamlined the introductory coverage of business intelligence and data mining by deleting Chapter S and instead putting some of that content in Chapter 1. With this change, the reader can get an overview of the overall content through Chapter 1—both decision support and BI technologies. This overview can prepare a student to begin thinking about a term project in either area (should the instructor require it) right from the beginning of the term. The details of DSS are examined in Chapters 2 through 4, and BI topics begin with Chapter 5. We deleted the chapters that were available as online chapters with the last edition and incorporated some of that content into this edition.

- *New author team.* This edition includes one new author and an expanded role for an author from the last edition. Building upon the excellent content that has been prepared by the authors of the previous edition (Turban, Aronson, Liang, and Sharda), this edition was revised primarily by Ramesh Sharda and Dursun Delen. Both Ramesh and Dursun have worked extensively in DSS and data mining and have industry as well as research experience. Dave King (JDA Systems), a coauthor of *The Strategy Gap* (a book on corporate performance management) contributed Chapter 9, "Business Performance Management."

- *All new figures for PowerPoint.* Although the figures in the print edition have been retained from previous editions and new figures added for the new content, all the figures have been redrawn in color and are available through the image library for use in PowerPoint presentations.

- *A live update Web site.* Adopters of the textbook will have access to a Web site that will include links to news stories, software, tutorials, and even YouTube videos related to topics covered in the book.

- *Revised and updated content.* Almost all of the chapters have new opening vignettes and closing cases that are based on recent stories and events. For example, the closing case at the end of Chapter 2 asks the students to apply Simon's decision-making phases to better understand the current economic conditions caused by the subprime mortgage mess in the United States. In addition, Application Cases throughout the book have been updated to include recent examples of applications of a specific technique/model. New Web site links have been added throughout the book. We also deleted many older product links and references. Finally, most chapters have new exercises, Internet assignments, and discussion questions throughout.

Other specific changes made to the ninth edition are summarized next:

- Chapter 3 includes a major DSS software section to introduce The Planners Lab software. This software builds upon a DSS software tool that was very popular in the 1980s and 1990s. The PC-based version of the software is available for free to academics. The chapter includes a concise introduction to this software and several exercises to help students learn to use the DSS builder software. This section was contributed by Dr. Jerry Wagner of University of Nebraska-Omaha and the founder of Planners Lab.

- Chapter 4 brings back a brief coverage of analytic hierarchy process (AHP) and also introduces some free/inexpensive pairwise ratings software that the students can use. In addition, all the Microsoft Excel–related coverage has been updated to work with Microsoft Excel 2007.

- Chapter 5 presents an in-depth, comprehensive discussion of data mining. The presentation of the material in this chapter follows a methodical approach that corresponds to the standardized process used for data-mining projects. Compared to the corresponding chapter in the eighth edition, this chapter has been entirely rewritten to make it an easy-to-use digest of information for data mining. Specifically, it excludes text and Web mining (which are covered in a separate chapter) and significantly expands on data-mining methods and methodologies.

- Chapter 6 provides detailed coverage on artificial neural networks (ANN) and their use in managerial decision making. The most popular ANN architectures are described in detail; their differences as well as their uses for different types of decision problems are explained. A new section on the explanation of ANN models via sensitivity analysis has been added to this chapter.

- Chapter 7 is a mostly new chapter, as described earlier.

- Chapters 8 and 10 through 13 have been updated to include new Technology Insights, Application Cases, and updated text, as appropriate. For example, Chapter 13 now includes coverage of newer techniques, such as fuzzy inference systems, support vector machines, and intelligent agents.
- Chapter 9 is a new chapter that combines material from multiple chapters in the previous edition. Besides streamlining and updating the coverage through a new opening vignette, a new closing case, and discussions throughout, it includes new sections on key performance indicators (KPI), operational metrics, Lean Six Sigma, payoff of Six Sigma, and a section on BPM architecture.
- Chapter 14 is a mostly new chapter, as described earlier.

We have retained many of the enhancements made in the last edition and updated the content. These are summarized next:

- **_Links to TeradataUniversityNetwork (TUN)._** Most chapters include links to TUN (**teradatauniversitynetwork.com**). The student side of the Teradata site (Teradata Student Network [TSN]; **teradatastudentnetwork.com**) mainly includes assignments for students. A visit to TSN allows students to read cases, view Web seminars, answer questions, search material, and more.
- **_Fewer boxes, better organized._** We reduced the number of boxes by more than 50 percent. Important material was incorporated in the text. Only two types of boxes now exist: Application Cases and Technology Insights.
- **_Book title._** We retained the changed title of the book—_Decision Support and Business Intelligence Systems._
- **_Software support._** The TUN Web site provides software support at no charge. It also provides links to free data mining and other software. In addition, the site provides exercises in the use of such software.

OBJECTIVES AND COVERAGE

Organizations can now easily use intranets and the Internet to deliver high-value performance-analysis applications to decision makers around the world. Corporations regularly develop distributed systems, intranets, and extranets that enable easy access to data stored in multiple locations, collaboration, and communication worldwide. Various information systems applications are integrated with one another and/or with other Web-based systems. Some integration even transcends organizational boundaries. Managers can make better decisions because they have more accurate information at their fingertips.

Today's decision support tools utilize the Web for their analysis, and they use graphical user interfaces that allow decision makers to flexibly, efficiently, and easily view and process data and models by using familiar Web browsers. The easy-to-use and readily available capabilities of enterprise information, knowledge, and other advanced systems have migrated to the PC and personal digital assistants (PDAs). Managers communicate with computers and the Web by using a variety of handheld wireless devices, including mobile phones and PDAs. These devices enable managers to access important information and useful tools, communicate, and collaborate. Data warehouses and their analytical tools (e.g., online analytical processing [OLAP], data mining) dramatically enhance information access and analysis across organizational boundaries.

Decision support for groups continues to improve, with major new developments in groupware for enhancing collaborative work, anytime and anywhere. Artificial intelligence methods are improving the quality of decision support and have become embedded in many applications, ranging from automated pricing optimization to intelligent Web search engines. Intelligent agents perform routine tasks, freeing up time that decision makers can devote to important work. Developments in wireless technologies, organizational learning, and knowledge management deliver an entire organization's expertise on the solution of problems anytime and anywhere.

BI, DSS, and expert systems (ES) courses and portions of courses are recommended jointly by the association for computing machinery (ACM), the Association for Information Systems (AIS), and the Association of Information Technology Professionals (AITP, formerly DPMA). This course is designed to present the decision support and artificial intelligence components of the model curriculum for information systems; it actually covers more than the curriculum recommends. The text also covers the decision support and artificial intelligence components of the Master of Science Information Systems (MSIS) 2000 Model Curriculum draft (see **acm.org/education/curricula.html#MSIS2000**). Another objective is to provide practicing managers with the foundations and applications of BI, group support systems (GSS), knowledge management, ES, data mining, intelligent agents, and other intelligent systems.

The theme of this revised edition is BI and analytics for enterprise decision support. In addition to traditional decision support applications, this edition expands the reader's understanding of the world of the Web by providing examples, products, services, and exercises and by discussing Web-related issues throughout the text. We highlight Web intelligence/Web analytics, which parallel BI/business analytics (BA) for e-commerce and other Web applications. The book is supported by a Web site (**pearsonhighered.com/ turban**), which provides some online files. We will also provide links to software tutorials through a special section of the Web site.

THE SUPPLEMENT PACKAGE: PRENHALL.COM/TURBAN

A comprehensive and flexible technology-support package is available to enhance the teaching and learning experience. The following instructor and student supplements are available on the book's Web site, **pearsonhighered.com/turban**:

- *Instructor's Manual.* The Instructor's Manual includes learning objectives for the entire course and for each chapter, answers to the questions and exercises at the end of each chapter, and teaching suggestions (including instructions for projects). The Instructor's Manual is available on the secure faculty section of **pearsonhighered .com/turban**.
- *Test Item File and TestGen Software.* The Test Item File is a comprehensive collection of true/false, multiple-choice, fill-in-the-blank, and essay questions. The questions are rated by difficulty level, and the answers are referenced by book page number. The Test Item File is available in Microsoft Word and in the computerized form of Prentice Hall TestGen. TestGen is a comprehensive suite of tools for testing and assessment. It allows instructors to easily create and distribute tests for their courses, either by printing and distributing through traditional methods or by online delivery via a local area network (LAN) server. TestGen features wizards that assist in moving through the program, and the software is backed with full technical support. Both the Test Item File and testgen software are available on the secure faculty section of **pearsonhighered.com/turban**.
- *PowerPoint slides.* PowerPoint slides are available that illuminate and build on key concepts in the text. Faculty can download the PowerPoint slides from **pearsonhighered.com/turban**.
- *Materials for your online course.* Pearson Prentice Hall supports our adopters using online courses by providing files ready for upload into Blackboard course management systems for testing, quizzing, and other supplements. Please contact your local Pearson representative for further information on your particular course. In addition, a blog site will include continuous updates to each chapter including links to new material and related software. It will be available through the text web site.

ACKNOWLEDGMENTS

Many individuals have provided suggestions and criticisms since the publication of the first edition of this book. Dozens of students participated in class testing of various chapters, software, and problems and assisted in collecting material. It is not possible to name everyone who participated in this project, but our thanks go to all of them. Certain individuals made significant contributions, and they deserve special recognition.

First, we appreciate the efforts of those individuals who provided formal reviews of the first through ninth editions (school affiliations as of the date of review):

Robert Blanning, Vanderbilt University
Ranjit Bose, University of New Mexico
Warren Briggs, Suffolk University
Lee Roy Bronner, Morgan State University
Charles Butler, Colorado State University
Sohail S. Chaudry, University of Wisconsin–La Crosse
Kathy Chudoba, Florida State University
Wingyan Chung, University of Texas
Woo Young Chung, University of Memphis
Paul "Buddy" Clark, South Carolina State University
Pi'Sheng Deng, California State University–Stanislaus
Joyce Elam, Florida International University
Kurt Engemann, Iona College
Gary Farrar, Jacksonville University
George Federman, Santa Clara City College
Jerry Fjermestad, New Jersey Institute of Technology
Joey George, Florida State University
Paul Gray, Claremont Graduate School
Orv Greynholds, Capital College (Laurel, Maryland)
Martin Grossman, Bridgewater State College
Ray Jacobs, Ashland University
Leonard Jessup, Indiana University
Jeffrey Johnson, Utah State University
Jahangir Karimi, University of Colorado Denver
Saul Kassicieh, University of New Mexico
Anand S. Kunnathur, University of Toledo
Shao-ju Lee, California State University at Northridge
Yair Levy, Nova Southeastern University
Hank Lucas, New York University
Jane Mackay, Texas Christian University
George M. Marakas, University of Maryland
Dick Mason, Southern Methodist University
Nick McGaughey, San Jose State University
Ido Millet, Pennsylvania State University–Erie
Benjamin Mittman, Northwestern University
Larry Moore, Virginia Polytechnic Institute and State University
Simitra Mukherjee, Nova Southeastern University
Marianne Murphy, Northeastern University
Peter Mykytyn, Southern Illinois University
Natalie Nazarenko, SUNY College at Fredonia
Souren Paul, Southern Illinois University
Joshua Pauli, Dakota State University

Roger Alan Pick, University of Missouri–St. Louis
W. "RP" Raghupaphi, California State University–Chico
Loren Rees, Virginia Polytechnic Institute and State University
David Russell, Western New England College
Steve Ruth, George Mason University
Vartan Safarian, Winona State University
Glenn Shephard, San Jose State University
Jung P. Shim, Mississippi State University
Meenu Singh, Murray State University
Randy Smith, University of Virginia
James T.C. Teng, University of South Carolina
John VanGigch, California State University at Sacramento
David Van Over, University of Idaho
Paul J.A. van Vliet, University of Nebraska at Omaha
B. S. Vijayaraman, University of Akron
Howard Charles Walton, Gettysburg College
Diane B. Walz, University of Texas at San Antonio
Paul R. Watkins, University of Southern California
Randy S. Weinberg, Saint Cloud State University
Jennifer Williams, University of Southern Indiana
Steve Zanakis, Florida International University
Fan Zhao, Florida Gulf Coast University

Several individuals contributed material to the text or the supporting material. For this edition, we acknowledge the contributions of Dave King (JDA Software Group, Inc.) and Jerry Wagner (University of Nebraska–Omaha). Barbara Wixom wrote the opening vignette for Chapter 1 to illustrate the special relationship of this book to Teradata University Connection. Peter Horner, Editor of *OR/MS Today* allowed us to reuse new application stories from *OR/MS Today* as opening vignette and closing cases for Chapter 4. Dan Power (**Dssresources.com** and University of Northern Iowa) permitted us to use information from his column on virtual worlds. Major contributors for the previous editions include Mike Goul (Arizona State University), whose contributions were included in Chapter S of the eighth edition, Leila A. Halawi (Bethune-Cookman College) who provided material for the chapter on data warehousing, and Christy Cheung (Hong Kong Baptist University) who contributed to the chapter on knowledge management, Linda Lai (Macau Polytechnic University of China), Dave King (JDA Software Group, Inc.), Lou Frenzel, an independent consultant whose books *Crash Course in Artificial Intelligence and Expert Systems* and *Understanding of Expert Systems* (both published by Howard W. Sams, New York, 1987) provided material for the early editions; Larry Medsker (American University), who contributed substantial material on neural networks; and Richard V. McCarthy (Quinnipiac University), who performed major revisions in the seventh edition.

Third, the book benefited greatly from the efforts of many individuals who contributed advice and interesting material (such as problems), gave feedback on material, or helped with class testing. These individuals are Warren Briggs (Suffolk University), Frank DeBalough (University of Southern California), Mei-Ting Cheung (University of Hong Kong), Alan Dennis (Indiana University), George Easton (San Diego State University), Janet Fisher (California State University, Los Angeles), David Friend (Pilot Software, Inc.), Paul Gray (Claremont Graduate School), Mike Henry (OSU), Dustin Huntington (Exsys, Inc.), Subramanian Rama Iyer (Oklahoma State University), Angie Jungermann (Oklahoma State University), Elena Karahanna (The University of Georgia), Katie Murray (OSU), Mike McAulliffe (The University of Georgia), Chad Peterson (The University of Georgia), Neil Rabjohn (York University), Jim Ragusa (University of Central Florida), Elizabeth Rivers, Alan

Rowe (University of Southern California), Steve Ruth (George Mason University), Linus Schrage (University of Chicago), Antonie Stam (University of Missouri), Ron Swift (NCR Corp.), Merril Warkentin (Northeastern University), Paul Watkins (The University of Southern California), Ben Mortagy (Claremont Graduate School of Management), Dan Walsh (Bellcore), Richard Watson (The University of Georgia), and the many other instructors and students who have provided feedback.

Fourth, several vendors cooperated by providing development and/or demonstration software: Axiom (Little Rock, Arkansas), CACI Products Company (LaJolla, California), California Scientific Software (Nevada City, California), Cary Harwin of Catalyst Development (Yucca Valley, California), Demandtec (San Carlos, California), DS Group, Inc. (Greenwich, Connecticut), Expert Choice, Inc. (Pittsburgh, Pennsylvania), Nancy Clark of Exsys, Inc. (Albuquerque, New Mexico), Jim Godsey of GroupSystems, Inc. (Broomfield, Colorado), Raimo Hämäläinen of Helsinki University of Technology, Gregory Piatetsky-Shapiro of KDNuggets.com, Logic Programming Associates (UK), Gary Lynn of NeuroDimension Inc. (Gainesville, Florida), Palisade Software (Newfield, New York), Jerry Wagner of Planners Lab (Omaha, Nebraska), Promised Land Technologies (New Haven, Connecticut), Salford Systems (La Jolla, California), Sense Networks (New York, New York), Gary Miner of Statsoft, Inc. (Tulsa, Oklahoma), Ward Systems Group, Inc. (Frederick, Maryland), Idea Fisher Systems, Inc. (Irving, California), and Wordtech Systems (Orinda, California).

Fifth, special thanks to the Teradata University Network and especially to Hugh Watson, Michael Goul, Executive Director; Barb Wixom, Associate Director; Susan Baxley, Program Director; and Mary Gros, Teradata, a division of NCR, and a liaison between Teradata and the academic community, for their encouragement to tie this book with TUN and for providing useful material for the book.

Sixth, many individuals helped us with administrative matters and editing, proofreading, and preparation. The project began with Jack Repcheck (a former Macmillan editor), who initiated this project with the support of Hank Lucas (New York University). Judy Lang collaborated with all of us, provided editing, and guided us during the entire project through the eighth edition.

Finally, the Prentice Hall team is to be commended: Executive Editor Bob Horan, who orchestrated this project; our editorial project manager Kelly Loftus, who kept us on the timeline; Kitty Jarrett, who copyedited the manuscript; and the production team, Karalyn Holland at Prentice Hall, and the staff at GGS Book Services, who transformed the manuscript into a book.

We would like to thank all these individuals and corporations. Without their help, the creation of this book would not have been possible. Ramesh and Dursun want to specifically acknowledge the contributions of previous coauthors Jay Aronson and T. P. Liang whose original contributions constitute significant components of the book.

E.T.

R.S.

D.D.

---

[1]Note that Web site URLs are dynamic. As this book went to press, we verified that all the cited Web sites were active and valid. Web sites to which we refer in the text sometimes change or are discontinued because companies change names, are bought or sold, merge, or fail. Sometimes Web sites are down for maintenance, repair, or redesign. Most organizations have dropped the initial "www" designation for their sites, but some still use it. If you have a problem connecting to a Web site that we mention, please be patient and simply run a Web search to try to identify the new site. Most times, the new site can be found quickly. We apologize in advance for this inconvenience.

Decision Support and Business Intelligence

LEARNING OBJECTIVES FOR PART I

1 Understand the complexity of today's business environment

2 Understand the foundations and key issues of managerial decision making

3 Recognize the difficulties in managerial decision making today

4 Learn the major frameworks of computerized decision support: decision support systems (DSS) and business intelligence (BI)

This book deals with a collection of computer technologies that support managerial work—essentially, decision making. These technologies have had a profound impact on corporate strategy, performance, and competitiveness. These techniques are also strongly connected to the Internet, intranets, and Web tools, as shown throughout the book. In Part I, we provide an overview of the whole book in one chapter. We cover several topics in this chapter. The first topic is managerial decision making and its computerized support; the second is frameworks for decision support. We then introduce business intelligence. We also provide brief coverage of the tools used and their implementation, as well as a preview of the entire book.

Decision Support Systems and Business Intelligence

LEARNING OBJECTIVES

1 Understand today's turbulent business environment and describe how organizations survive and even excel in such an environment (solving problems and exploiting opportunities)

2 Understand the need for computerized support of managerial decision making

3 Understand an early framework for managerial decision making

4 Learn the conceptual foundations of the decision support systems (DSS[1]) methodology

5 Describe the business intelligence (BI) methodology and concepts and relate them to DSS

6 Describe the concept of work systems and its relationship to decision support

7 List the major tools of computerized decision support

8 Understand the major issues in implementing computerized support systems

The business environment (climate) is constantly changing, and it is becoming more and more complex. Organizations, private and public, are under pressures that force them to respond quickly to changing conditions and to be innovative in the way they operate. Such activities require organizations to be agile and to make frequent and quick strategic, tactical, and operational decisions, some of which are very complex. Making such decisions may require considerable amounts of relevant data, information, and knowledge. Processing these, in the framework of the needed decisions, must be done quickly, frequently in real time, and usually requires some computerized support.

This book is about using business intelligence as computerized support for managerial decision making. It concentrates both on the theoretical and conceptual foundations of decision support, as well as on the commercial tools and techniques that are available. This introductory chapter provides more details

---

[1] The acronym *DSS* is treated as both singular and plural throughout this book. Similarly, other acronyms, such as *MIS* and *GSS*, designate both plural and singular forms.

of these topics as well as an overview of the book. This chapter has the following sections:

1.1 Opening Vignette: Norfolk Southern Uses Business Intelligence for Decision Support to Reach Success
1.2 Changing Business Environments and Computerized Decision Support
1.3 Managerial Decision Making
1.4 Computerized Support for Decision Making
1.5 An Early Framework for Computerized Decision Support
1.6 The Concept of Decision Support Systems (DSS)
1.7 A Framework for Business Intelligence (BI)
1.8 A Work System View of Decision Support
1.9 The Major Tools and Techniques of Managerial Decision Support
1.10 Plan of the Book
1.11 Resources, Links, and the Teradata University Network Connection

1.1 OPENING VIGNETTE: NORFOLK SOUTHERN USES BUSINESS INTELLIGENCE FOR DECISION SUPPORT TO REACH SUCCESS

There are four large freight railroads in the United States, and Norfolk Southern is one of them. Each day, the company moves approximately 500 freight trains across 21,000 route miles in 22 eastern states, the District of Columbia, and Ontario, Canada. Norfolk Southern manages more than $26 billion in assets and employs over 30,000 people.

For more than a century, the railroad industry was heavily regulated, and Norfolk Southern and its predecessor railroads made money by managing their costs. Managers focused on optimizing the use of railcars to get the most production out of their fixed assets. Then, in 1980, the industry was partially deregulated, which opened up opportunities for mergers and allowed companies to charge rates based on service and enter into contracts with customers. On-time delivery became an important factor in the industry.

Over time, Norfolk Southern responded to these industry changes by becoming a "scheduled railroad." This meant that the company would develop a fixed set of train schedules and a fixed set of connections for cars to go between trains and yards. In this way, managers could predict when they could get a shipment to a customer.

Norfolk Southern has always used a variety of sophisticated systems to run its business. Becoming a scheduled railroad, however, required new systems that would first use statistical models to determine the best routes and connections to optimize railroad performance, and then apply the models to create the plan that would actually run the railroad operations. These new systems were called TOP, short for Thoroughbred Operating Plan; TOP was deployed in 2002.

Norfolk Southern realized that it was not enough to run the railroad using TOP—it also had to monitor and measure its performance against the TOP plan. Norfolk Southern's numerous systems generate millions of records about freight records, railcars, train GPS information, train fuel levels, revenue information, crew management, and historical tracking records. Unfortunately, the company was not able to simply tap into this data without risking significant impact on the systems' performance.

Back in 1995, the company invested in a 1-terabyte Teradata data warehouse, which is a central repository of historical data. It is organized in such a way that the data is easy to access (using a Web browser) and can be manipulated for decision support. The warehouse data comes from the systems that run the company (i.e., source systems), and once the data is moved from the source systems to the warehouse users can access and use the data without risk of impacting operations.

In 2002, the data warehouse became a critical component of TOP. Norfolk Southern built a TOP dashboard application that pulls data from the data warehouse and then graphically depicts actual performance against the trip plan for both train performance and connection performance. The application uses visualization technology so that field managers can more easily interpret the large volumes of data (e.g., there were 160,000 weekly connections across the network). The number of missed connections has decreased by 60 percent since the application was implemented. And, in the past 5 years, railcar cycle time has decreased by an entire day, which translates into millions of dollars in annual savings.

Norfolk Southern has an enterprise data warehouse, which means that once data is placed in the warehouse, it is available across the company, not just for a single application. Although train and connection performance data is used for the TOP application, the company has been able to leverage that data for all kinds of other purposes. For example, the Marketing Department has developed an application called accessNS, which was built for Norfolk Southern customers who want visibility into Norfolk Southern's extensive transportation network. Customers want to know where their shipments are "right now"—and at times they want historical information: Where did my shipment come from? How long did it take to arrive? What were the problems along the route?

accessNS allows more than 14,500 users from 8,000 customer organizations to log in and access predefined and custom reports about their accounts at any time. Users can access current data, which is updated hourly, or they can look at data from the past 3 years. accessNS provides alerting and RSS feed capabilities; in fact, 4,500 reports are pushed to users daily. The self-service nature of accessNS has allowed Norfolk Southern to give customers what they want and also reduce the number of people needed for customer service. In fact, without accessNS, it would take approximately 47 people to support the current level of customer reporting.

Departments across the company—from Engineering and Strategic Planning to Cost and Human Resources—use the enterprise data warehouse. One interesting internal application was developed by Human Resources. Recently, the department needed to determine where to locate its field offices in order to best meet the needs of Norfolk Southern's 30,000+ employees. By combining employee demographic data (e.g., zip codes) with geospatial data traditionally used by the Engineering Group, Human Resources was able to visually map out the employee population density, making it much easier to optimize services offices locations.

Today, the Norfolk Southern data warehouse has grown to a 6-terabyte system that manages an extensive amount of information about the company's vast network of railroads and shipping services. Norfolk Southern uses the data warehouse to analyze trends, develop forecasting schedules, archive records, and facilitate customer self-service. The data warehouse provides information to over 3,000 employees and over 14,000 external customers and stakeholders.

Norfolk Southern was the first railroad to offer self-service business intelligence, and its innovation is setting an example that other railroads have followed. The company was also one of the first railroads to provide a large variety of historical data to external customers.

Questions for the Opening Vignette

1. How are information systems used at Norfolk Southern to support decision making?
2. What type of information is accessible through the visualization applications?
3. What type of information support is provided through accessNS?
4. How does Norfolk Southern use the data warehouse for HR applications?
5. Can the same data warehouse be used for business intelligence and optimization applications?

What We Can Learn from This Vignette

This vignette shows that data warehousing technologies can offer a player even in a mature industry the ability to attain competitive advantage by squeezing additional efficiency from its operations. Indeed, in many cases, this may be the major frontier to explore. Getting more out of a company's assets requires more timely and detailed understanding of its operations, and the ability to use that information to make better decisions. We will see many examples of such applications throughout this book.

Additional resources about this vignette are available on the Teradata University Network, which is described later in the chapter. These include other papers and a podcast titled "Norfolk Southern Uses Teradata Warehouse to Support a Scheduled Railroad."

Source: Contributed by Professors Barbara Wixom (University of Virginia), Hugh Watson (University of Georgia), and Jeff Hoffer (University of Dayton).

1.2 CHANGING BUSINESS ENVIRONMENTS AND COMPUTERIZED DECISION SUPPORT

The opening vignette illustrates how a global company excels in a mature but competitive market. Companies are moving aggressively to computerized support of their operations. To understand why companies are embracing computerized support, including business intelligence, we developed a model called the *Business Pressures–Responses–Support model*, which is shown in Figure 1.1.

The Business Pressures–Responses–Support Model

The Business Pressures–Responses–Support model, as its name indicates, has three components: Business pressures that result from today's business climate, responses (actions taken) by companies to counter the pressures (or to take advantage of the opportunities available in the environment), and computerized support that facilitates the monitoring of the environment and enhances the response actions taken by organizations.

THE BUSINESS ENVIRONMENT The environment in which organizations operate today is becoming more and more complex. This complexity creates opportunities on the one hand and problems on the other. Take globalization as an example. Today, you can easily find suppliers and customers in many countries, which means you can buy cheaper materials and sell more of your products and services; great opportunities exist. However, globalization also means more and stronger competitors. Business environment factors can be divided into four major categories: *markets, consumer demands, technology, and societal*. These categories are summarized in Table 1.1.

  Note that the *intensity* of most of these factors increases with time, leading to more pressures, more competition, and so on. In addition, organizations and departments within organizations face decreased budgets and amplified pressures from top managers to increase performance and profit. In this kind of environment, managers must respond quickly, innovate, and be agile. Let's see how they do it.

ORGANIZATIONAL RESPONSES: BE REACTIVE, ANTICIPATIVE, ADAPTIVE, AND PROACTIVE Both private and public organizations are aware of today's business environment and pressures. They use different actions to counter the pressures. Vodafone

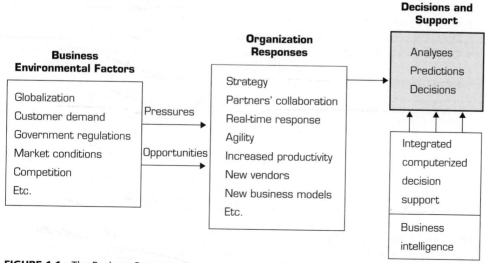

FIGURE 1.1 The Business Pressures–Responses–Support Model

TABLE 1.1 Business Environment Factors That Create Pressures on Organizations

Factor	Description
Markets	Strong competition
	Expanding global markets
	Booming electronic markets on the Internet
	Innovative marketing methods
	Opportunities for outsourcing with IT support
	Need for real-time, on-demand transactions
Consumer demands	Desire for customization
	Desire for quality, diversity of products, and speed of delivery
	Customers getting powerful and less loyal
Technology	More innovations, new products, and new services
	Increasing obsolescence rate
	Increasing information overload
	Social networking, Web 2.0 and beyond
Societal	Growing government regulations and deregulation
	Workforce more diversified, older, and composed of more women
	Prime concerns of homeland security and terrorist attacks
	Necessity of Sarbanes-Oxley Act and other reporting-related legislation
	Increasing social responsibility of companies
	Greater emphasis on sustainability

New Zealand Ltd (Krivda, 2008), for example, turned to BI to improve communication and to support executives in its effort to retain existing customers and increase revenue from these customers (see case at the end of this chapter). Managers may take other actions, including the following:

- Employ strategic planning.
- Use new and innovative business models.
- Restructure business processes.
- Participate in business alliances.
- Improve corporate information systems.
- Improve partnership relationships.
- Encourage innovation and creativity.
- Improve customer service and relationships.
- Move to electronic commerce (e-commerce).
- Move to make-to-order production and on-demand manufacturing and services.
- Use new IT to improve communication, data access (discovery of information), and collaboration.
- Respond quickly to competitors' actions (e.g., in pricing, promotions, new products and services).
- Automate many tasks of white-collar employees.
- Automate certain decision processes, especially those dealing with customers.
- Improve decision making by employing analytics.

Many, if not all, of these actions require some computerized support. These and other response actions are frequently facilitated by computerized DSS.

CLOSING THE STRATEGY GAP One of the major objectives of computerized decision support is to facilitate closing the gap between the current performance of an organization and its desired performance, as expressed in its mission, objectives, and goals, and the strategy to achieve them. In order to understand why computerized support is needed and how it is provided, especially for decision-making support, let's look at managerial decision making.

Section 1.2 Review Questions

1. List the components of and explain the Business Pressures–Responses–Support model. *P. 5. Figure 1.1.*
2. What are some of the major factors in today's business environment? *P6. Table 1.1*
3. What are some of the major response activities that organizations take? *p*

1.3   MANAGERIAL DECISION MAKING

Management is a process by which organizational goals are achieved by using resources. The resources are considered inputs, and attainment of goals is viewed as the output of the process. The degree of success of the organization and the manager is often measured by the ratio of outputs to inputs. This ratio is an indication of the organization's *productivity*, which is a reflection of the *organizational and managerial performance*.

The level of productivity or the success of management depends on the performance of managerial functions, such as planning, organizing, directing, and controlling. To perform their functions, managers are engaged in a continuous process of making decisions. Making a decision means selecting the best alternative from two or more solutions.

The Nature of Managers' Work

Mintzberg's (2008) classic study of top managers and several replicated studies suggest that managers perform 10 major roles that can be classified into three major categories: *interpersonal, informational,* and *decisional* (see Table 1.2).

To perform these roles, managers need information that is delivered efficiently and in a timely manner to personal computers (PCs) on their desktops and to mobile devices. This information is delivered by networks, generally via Web technologies.

In addition to obtaining information necessary to better perform their roles, managers use computers directly to support and improve decision making, which is a key task that is part of most of these roles. Many managerial activities in all roles revolve around decision making. *Managers, especially those at high managerial levels, are primarily decision makers.* We review the decision-making process next but will study it in more detail in the next chapter.

The Decision-Making Process

For years, managers considered decision making purely an art—a talent acquired over a long period through experience (i.e., learning by trial-and-error) and by using intuition. Management was considered an art because a variety of individual styles could be used in approaching and successfully solving the same types of managerial problems. These styles were often based on creativity, judgment, intuition, and experience rather than on systematic quantitative methods grounded in a scientific approach. However, recent research suggests that companies with top managers who are more focused on persistent work (almost dullness) tend to outperform those with leaders whose main strengths are interpersonal communication skills (Kaplan et al., 2008; Brooks, 2009). It is more important to emphasize methodical, thoughtful, analytical decision making rather than flashiness and interpersonal communication skills.

不同职位：

TABLE 1.2 Mintzberg's 10 Managerial Roles

Role	Description
Interpersonal	
Figurehead	Is symbolic head; obliged to perform a number of routine duties of a legal or social nature
Leader	Is responsible for the motivation and activation of subordinates; responsible for staffing, training, and associated duties
Liaison 联络人	Maintains self-developed network of outside contacts and informers who provide favors and information
Informational	
Monitor	Seeks and receives a wide variety of special information (much of it current) to develop a thorough understanding of the organization and environment; emerges as the nerve center of the organization's internal and external information
Disseminator	Transmits information received from outsiders or from subordinates to members of the organization; some of this information is factual, and some involves interpretation and integration
Spokesperson	Transmits information to outsiders about the organization's plans, policies, actions, results, and so forth; serves as an expert on the organization's industry
Decisional	
Entrepreneur	Searches the organization and its environment for opportunities and initiates improvement projects to bring about change; supervises design of certain projects
Disturbance handler	Is responsible for corrective action when the organization faces important, unexpected disturbances
Resource allocator	Is responsible for the allocation of organizational resources of all kinds; in effect, is responsible for the making or approval of all significant organizational decisions
Negotiator	Is responsible for representing the organization at major negotiations

Sources: Compiled from H. A. Mintzberg, *The Nature of Managerial Work*. Prentice Hall, Englewood Cliffs, NJ, 1980; and H. A. Mintzberg, *The Rise and Fall of Strategic Planning*. The Free Press, New York, 1993.

Managers usually make decisions by following a four-step process (we learn more about these in Chapter 2):

1. Define the problem (i.e., a decision situation that may deal with some difficulty or with an opportunity).
2. Construct a model that describes the real-world problem.
3. Identify possible solutions to the modeled problem and evaluate the solutions.
4. Compare, choose, and recommend a potential solution to the problem.

To follow this process, one must make sure that sufficient alternative solutions are being considered, that the consequences of using these alternatives can be reasonably predicted, and that comparisons are done properly. However, the environmental factors listed in Table 1.1 make such an evaluation process difficult for the following reasons:

- Technology, information systems, advanced search engines, and globalization result in more and more alternatives from which to choose.
- Government regulations and the need for compliance, political instability and terrorism, competition, and changing consumer demands produce more uncertainty, making it more difficult to predict consequences and the future.

- Other factors are the need to make rapid decisions, the frequent and unpredictable changes that make trial-and-error learning difficult, and the potential costs of making mistakes.
- These environments are growing more complex every day. Therefore, making decisions today is indeed a complex task.

Because of these trends and changes, it is nearly impossible to rely on a trial-and-error approach to management, especially for decisions for which the factors shown in Table 1.1 are strong influences. Managers must be more sophisticated; they must use the new tools and techniques of their fields. Most of those tools and techniques are discussed in this book. Using them to support decision making can be extremely rewarding in making effective decisions. In the following section, we look now at why we need computer support and how it is provided.

Section 1.3 Review Questions

1. Describe the three major managerial roles, and list some of the specific activities in each. *P.8 Table 1.2*
2. Why have some argued that management is the same as decision making?
3. Describe the four steps managers take in making a decision. *P.8 four-step process*

1.4 COMPUTERIZED SUPPORT FOR DECISION MAKING

From traditional uses in payroll and bookkeeping functions, computerized systems are now penetrating complex managerial areas ranging from the design and management of automated factories to the application of artificial intelligence methods to the evaluation of proposed mergers and acquisitions. Nearly all executives know that information technology is vital to their business and extensively use information technologies, especially Web-based ones.

Computer applications have moved from transaction processing and monitoring activities to problem analysis and solution applications, and much of the activity is done with Web-based technologies. BI tools such as data warehousing, data mining, online analytical processing (OLAP), dashboards, and the use of the Web for decision support are the cornerstones of today's modern management. Managers must have high-speed, networked information systems (wireline or wireless) to assist them with their most important task: making decisions. Let's look at why and how computerized systems can help.

Why We Use Computerized Decision Support Systems

Today's computerized systems possess capabilities that can facilitate decision support in a number of ways, including the following:

- ***Speedy computations.*** A computer enables the decision maker to perform many computations quickly and at a low cost. Timely decisions are critical in many situations, ranging from a physician in an emergency room to a stock trader on the trading floor. With a computer, thousands of alternatives can be evaluated in seconds. Furthermore, the benefits-to-cost ratio of computers and the speed of executions are constantly increasing.
- ***Improved communication and collaboration.*** Many decisions are made today by groups whose members may be in different locations. Groups can collaborate and communicate readily by using Web-based tools. Collaboration is especially important along the supply chain, where partners—all the way from vendors to customers—must share information.
- ***Increased productivity of group members.*** Assembling a group of decision makers, especially experts, in one place can be costly. Computerized support can

improve the collaboration process of a group and enable its members to be at different locations (saving travel costs). In addition, computerized support can increase the productivity of staff support (e.g., financial and legal analysts). Decision makers can also increase their productivity by using software optimization tools that help determine the best way to run a business (see Chapter 4).

- **_Improved data management._**   Many decisions involve complex computations. Data for these can be stored in different databases anywhere in the organization and even possibly at Web sites outside the organization. The data may include text, sound, graphics, and video, and they can be in foreign languages. It may be necessary to transmit data quickly from distant locations. Computers can search, store, and transmit needed data quickly, economically, securely, and transparently.

- **_Managing giant data warehouses._**   Large data warehouses, like the one operated by Wal-Mart, contain terabytes and even petabytes of data. Computers can provide extremely great storage capability for any type of digital information, and this information can be accessed and searched very rapidly. Special methods, including parallel computing, are available to organize, search, and mine the data. The costs related to data warehousing are declining.

- **_Quality support._**   Computers can improve the quality of decisions made. For example, more data can be accessed, more alternatives can be evaluated, forecasts can be improved, risk analysis can be performed quickly, and the views of experts (some of whom are in remote locations) can be collected quickly and at a reduced cost. Expertise can even be derived directly from a computer system using artificial intelligence methods (discussed in Part III and also Chapter 12). With computers, decision makers can perform complex simulations, check many possible scenarios, and assess diverse impacts quickly and economically.

- **_Agility support._**   Competition today is based not just on price but also on quality, timeliness, customization of products, and customer support. In addition, organizations must be able to frequently and rapidly change their mode of operation, reengineer processes and structures, empower employees, and innovate in order to adapt to their changing environments. Decision support technologies such as intelligent systems can empower people by allowing them to make good decisions quickly, even if they lack some knowledge.

- **_Overcoming cognitive limits in processing and storing information._**   According to Simon (1977), the human mind has only a limited ability to process and store information. People sometimes find it difficult to recall and use information in an error-free fashion due to their cognitive limits. The term **cognitive limits** indicates that an individual's problem-solving capability is limited when a wide range of diverse information and knowledge is required. Computerized systems enable people to overcome their cognitive limits by quickly accessing and processing vast amounts of stored information (see Chapter 2).

- **_Using the Web._**   Since the development of the Internet and Web servers and tools, there have been dramatic changes in how decision makers are supported. Most important, the Web provides (1) access to a vast body of data, information, and knowledge available around the world; (2) a common, user-friendly graphical user interface (GUI) that is easy to learn to use and readily available; (3) the ability to effectively collaborate with remote partners; and (4) the availability of intelligent search tools that enable managers to find the information they need quickly and inexpensively.

- **_Anywhere, anytime support._**   Using wireless technology, managers can access information anytime and from anyplace, analyze and interpret it, and communicate with those involved.

These and other capabilities have been driving the use of computerized decision support since the late 1960s, but especially since the mid-1990s. Next, we present an early framework for decision support.

Section 1.4 Review Questions

1. How have the capabilities of computing evolved over time? Web-based technologies
2. List some capabilities of computing that can facilitate managerial decision making. p.9 - p.10
3. How can a computer help overcome the cognitive limits of humans?
4. Why is the Web considered so important for decision support?

1.5 AN EARLY FRAMEWORK FOR COMPUTERIZED DECISION SUPPORT

An early framework for computerized decision support includes several major concepts that are used in forthcoming sections and chapters of this book. Gorry and Scott-Morton created and used this framework in the early 1970s, and the framework then evolved into a new technology called DSS.

The Gorry and Scott-Morton Classical Framework

Gorry and Scott-Morton (1971) proposed a framework that is a 3-by-3 matrix, as shown in Figure 1.2. Two dimensions are the degree of structuredness and the types of control.

DEGREE OF STRUCTUREDNESS The left side of Figure 1.2 is based on Simon's (1977) idea that decision-making processes fall along a continuum that ranges from highly structured (sometimes called *programmed*) to highly unstructured (i.e., *nonprogrammed*)

	Type of Control		
Type of Decision	**Operational Control**	**Managerial Control**	**Strategic Planning**
Structured	**1** Accounts receivable Accounts payable Order entry	**2** Budget analysis Short-term forecasting Personnel reports Make-or-buy	**3** Financial management Investment portfolio Warehouse location Distribution systems
Semistructured	**4** Production scheduling Inventory control	**5** Credit evaluation Budget preparation Plant layout Project scheduling Reward system design Inventory categorization	**6** Building a new plant Mergers & acquisitions New product planning Compensation planning Quality assurance HR policies Inventory planning

Unstructured	**7**
	Buying software
	Approving loans
	Operating a help desk
	Selecting a cover for
	  a magazine
		8
		Negotiating
		Recruiting an executive
		Buying hardware
		Lobbying
			9
			R & D planning
			New tech development
			Social responsibility
			  planning

FIGURE 1.2 Decision Support Frameworks

decisions. Structured processes are routine and typically repetitive problems for which standard solution methods exist. *Unstructured processes* are fuzzy, complex problems for which there are no cut-and-dried solution methods. Simon also described the decision-making process with a three-phase process of *intelligence, design,* and *choice.* Later, a fourth phase was added: *implementation* (see Chapter 2). The four phases are defined as follows:

1. ***Intelligence.*** This phase involves searching for conditions that call for decisions.
2. ***Design.*** This phase involves inventing, developing, and analyzing possible alternative courses of action (solutions).
3. ***Choice.*** This phase involves selecting a course of action from among those available.
4. ***Implementation.*** This phase involves adapting the selected course of action to the decision situation (i.e., problem solving or opportunity exploiting).

The relationships among the four phases are shown in Figure 1.3. We will discuss these phases in more detail in Chapter 2.

An **unstructured problem** is one in which none of the four phases described in Figure 1.3 is structured.

In a **structured problem**, all phases are structured. The procedures for obtaining the best (or at least a good enough) solution are known. Whether the problem involves finding an appropriate inventory level or choosing an optimal investment strategy, the objectives are clearly defined. Common objectives are cost minimization and profit maximization.

Semistructured problems fall between structured and unstructured problems, having some structured elements and some unstructured elements. Keen and Scott-Morton (1978) mentioned trading bonds, setting marketing budgets for consumer products, and performing capital acquisition analysis as semistructured problems.

TYPES OF CONTROL The second half of the Gorry and Scott-Morton framework (refer to Figure 1.2) is based on Anthony's (1965) taxonomy, which defines three broad categories

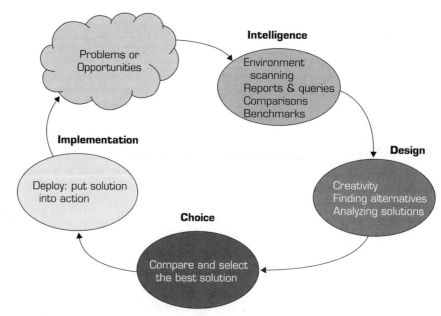

FIGURE 1.3 The Steps of Decision Support

that encompass all managerial activities: *strategic planning*, which involves defining long-range goals and policies for resource allocation; *management control*, the acquisition and efficient use of resources in the accomplishment of organizational goals; and *operational control*, the efficient and effective execution of specific tasks.

THE DECISION SUPPORT MATRIX   Anthony's and Simon's taxonomies are combined in the nine-cell decision support matrix shown in Figure 1.2. The initial purpose of this matrix was to suggest different types of computerized support to different cells in the matrix. Gorry and Scott-Morton suggested, for example, that for *semistructured decisions* and *unstructured decisions,* conventional management information systems (MIS) and management science (MS) tools are insufficient. Human intellect and a different approach to computer technologies are necessary. They proposed the use of a supportive information system, which they called a *DSS*.

Note that the more structured and operational control-oriented tasks (such as those in cells 1, 2, and 4) are usually performed by lower-level managers, whereas the tasks in cells 6, 8, and 9 are the responsibility of top executives or highly trained specialists.

Computer Support for Structured Decisions

Computers have supported structured and some semistructured decisions, especially those that involve operational and managerial control, since the 1960s. Operational and managerial control decisions are made in all functional areas, especially in finance and production (i.e., operations) management.

Structured problems, which are encountered repeatedly, have a high level of structure. It is therefore possible to abstract, analyze, and classify them into specific categories. For example, a make-or-buy decision is one category. Other examples of categories are capital budgeting, allocation of resources, distribution, procurement, planning, and inventory control decisions. For each category of decision, an easy-to-apply prescribed model and solution approach have been developed, generally as quantitative formulas. This approach is called *management science.*

MANAGEMENT SCIENCE   The **management science (MS)** approach (also called the **operations research [OR]** approach) says that in solving problems managers should follow the four-step systematic process described in Section 1.3. Therefore, it is possible to use a *scientific approach* to automating portions of managerial decision making.

The MS process adds a new step 2 to the process described in Section 1.3 so that the steps are as follows:

1. Define the problem (i.e., a decision situation that may deal with some difficulty or with an opportunity).
2. Classify the problem into a standard category.
3. Construct a model that describes the real-world problem.
4. Identify possible solutions to the modeled problem and evaluate the solutions.
5. Compare, choose, and recommend a potential solution to the problem.

MS is based on mathematical modeling (i.e., algebraic expressions that describe problems). Modeling involves transforming a real-world problem into an appropriate prototype structure (model). Computerized methodologies can find solutions to the standard category models quickly and efficiently (see Chapter 4). Some of these, such as linear programming, are deployed directly over the Web.

AUTOMATED DECISION MAKING   A relatively new approach to supporting decision making is called **automated decision systems (ADS)**, sometimes also known as *decision* *automation systems* (DAS; see Davenport and Harris, 2005). An ADS is a rule-based system that provides a solution, usually in one functional area (e.g., finance, manufacturing), to a specific repetitive managerial problem, usually in one industry (e.g., to approve or not to approve a request for a loan, to determine the price of an item in a store). Application Case 1.1 shows an example of applying automated decision systems to a problem that every organization faces—how to price its products or services.

APPLICATION CASE 1.1

Giant Food Stores Prices the Entire Store

Giant Food Stores, LLC, a regional U.S. supermarket chain based in Carlisle, Pennsylvania, had a narrow Every Day Low Price strategy that it applied to most of the products in its stores. The company had a 30-year-old pricing and promotion system that was very labor intensive and that could no longer keep up with the pricing decisions required in the fast-paced grocery market. The system also limited the company's ability to execute more sophisticated pricing strategies.

Giant was interested in executing its pricing strategy more consistently based on a definitive set of pricing rules (pricing rules in retail might include relationships between national brands and private-label brands, relationships between sizes, ending digits such as "9," etc.). In the past, many of the rules were kept on paper, others were kept in people's heads, and some were not documented well enough for others to understand and ensure continuity. The company also had no means of reliably forecasting the impact of rule changes before prices hit the store shelves.

Giant Foods worked with DemandTec to deploy a system for its pricing decisions. The system is able to handle massive amounts of point-of-sale and competitive data to model and forecast consumer demand, as well as automate and streamline complex rules-based pricing schemes. It can handle large numbers of price changes, and it can do so without increasing staff. The system allows Giant Foods to codify pricing rules with "natural language" sentences rather than having to go through a technician. The system also has forecasting capabilities. These capabilities allow Giant Foods to predict the impact of pricing changes and new promotions before they hit the shelves. Giant Foods decided to implement the system for the entire store chain.

The system has allowed Giant Foods to become more agile in its pricing. It is now able to react to competitive pricing changes or vendor cost changes on a weekly basis rather than when resources become available. Giant's productivity has doubled because it no longer has to increase staff for pricing changes. Giant now focuses on "maintaining profitability while satisfying its customer and maintaining its price image."

Source: "Giant Food Stores Prices the Entire Store with DemandTec," DemandTec, **demandtec.com** (accessed March 26, 2009).

ADS initially appeared in the airline industry, where they were called *revenue* (or *yield) management* (or revenue optimization) systems. Airlines use these systems to dynamically price tickets based on actual demand. Today, many service industries use similar pricing models. In contrast with management science approaches, which provide a model-based solution to generic structured problems (e.g., resource allocation, inventory level determination), ADS provide rule-based solutions. The following are examples of business rules: "If only 70% of the seats on a flight from Los Angeles to New York are sold 3 days prior to departure, offer a discount of x to nonbusiness travelers," "If an applicant owns a house and makes over $100,000 a year, offer a $10,000 credit line," and "If an item costs more than $2,000, and if your company buys it only once a year, the purchasing agent does not need special approval." Such rules, which are based on experience or derived through data mining, can be combined with mathematical models to form solutions that can be automatically and instantly applied to problems (e.g., "Based

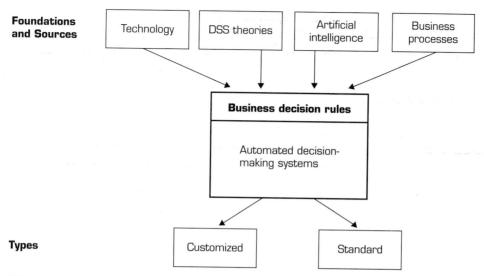

FIGURE 1.4 Automated Decision-Making Framework

on the information provided and subject to verification, you will be admitted to our university"), or they can be provided to a human, who will make the final decision (see Figure 1.4). ADS attempt to automate highly repetitive decisions (in order to justify the computerization cost), based on business rules. ADS are mostly suitable for frontline employees who can see the customer information online and frequently must make quick decisions. For further information on ADS, see Davenport and Harris (2005).

Computer Support for Unstructured Decisions

Unstructured problems can be only partially supported by standard computerized quantitative methods. It is usually necessary to develop customized solutions. However, such solutions may benefit from data and information generated from corporate or external data sources (see Part III and Chapter 12). Intuition and judgment may play a large role in these types of decisions, as may computerized communication and collaboration technologies (see Chapter 10), as well as knowledge management (see Chapter 11).

Computer Support for Semistructured Problems

Solving semistructured problems may involve a combination of standard solution procedures and human judgment. MS can provide models for the portion of a decision-making problem that is structured. For the unstructured portion, a DSS can improve the quality of the information on which the decision is based by providing, for example, not only a single solution but also a range of alternative solutions, along with their potential impacts. These capabilities help managers to better understand the nature of problems and thus to make better decisions.

In Chapter 2, we provide a detailed description of how decisions are supported during the major phases of decision making: intelligence, design, choice, and implementation.

Section 1.5 Review Questions

1. What are structured, unstructured, and semistructured decisions? Provide two examples of each.
2. Define *operational control*, *managerial control*, and *strategic planning*. Provide two examples of each.

3. What are the nine cells of the decision framework? Explain what each is for.
4. How can computers provide support for making structured decisions?
5. Define *automated decision systems (ADS)*.
6. How can computers provide support to semistructured and unstructured decisions?

1.6 THE CONCEPT OF DECISION SUPPORT SYSTEMS (DSS)

In the early 1970s, Scott-Morton first articulated the major concepts of DSS. He defined **decision support systems (DSS)** as "interactive computer-based systems, which help decision makers utilize *data* and *models* to solve unstructured problems" (Gorry and Scott-Morton, 1971). The following is another classic DSS definition, provided by Keen and Scott-Morton (1978):

> Decision support systems couple the intellectual resources of individuals with the capabilities of the computer to improve the quality of decisions. It is a computer-based support system for management decision makers who deal with semistructured problems.

Note that the term *decision support system*, like *management information system* (MIS) and other terms in the field of IT, is a content-free expression (i.e., it means different things to different people). Therefore, there is no universally accepted definition of DSS. (We present additional definitions in Chapter 3.) Actually, DSS can be viewed as a *conceptual methodology*—that is, a broad, umbrella term. However, some view DSS as a narrower, specific decision support application.

DSS as an Umbrella Term

The term *DSS* can be used as an umbrella term to describe any computerized system that supports decision making in an organization. An organization may have a knowledge management system to guide all its personnel in their problem solving. Another organization may have separate support systems for marketing, finance, and accounting; a supply-chain management (SCM) system for production; and several expert systems for product repair diagnostics and help desks. DSS encompasses them all.

Application Case 1.2 demonstrates some of the major characteristics of the DSS framework. The problem to be solved was unstructured, but the initial analysis was based on the decision maker's structured definition of the situation, using an MS approach. The DSS was built using data available from corporate data sources. The development platform was a spreadsheet. The DSS provided a quick what-if analysis (see Chapter 4). Furthermore, the DSS was flexible and responsive enough to allow managerial intuition and judgment to be incorporated into the analysis.

APPLICATION CASE 1.2

A DSS for Managing Inventory at GlaxoSmithKline

GlaxoSmithKline (GSK) is a global pharmaceutical company. The company sells products in hundreds of product categories—prescription drugs, over-the-counter medicines, oral health care products, nutritional health drinks, among others. In this highly competitive retail market, it is important to have enough product quantity on hand to provide a high service level to customers, but excess inventory costs money, so developing an optimal inventory policy is essential in achieving a decent profit. GSK wanted to evaluate its inventory policies and develop a new policy, if necessary.

GSK collects all of its sales and demand information through the supply chain planning system. From this system, it extracted the historical forecast and demand, month-end inventory, production lot size, and lead time information. GSK developed a model that takes these inputs and estimates the safety stock (measured in weeks forward carryover [WFC], which is the number of weeks of estimated demand capacity). The model can determine how changes in the safety stock affect the customer service level.

The entire model was built using a spreadsheet tool (Microsoft Excel). The Excel-based DSS enables the company to evaluate many what-if situations. Because of the stochastic nature of demand for many products, the model includes a simulation feature, which allows the company to analyze the impact of uncertainty in demand on the optimal safety stock level. Managers have found the DSS to be very helpful in making inventory decisions.

Source: J. Shang, P. R. Tadikamalla, L. J. Kirsch, L. Brown, "A Decision Support System for Managing Inventory at GlaxoSmithKline," *Decision Support Systems,* Vol. 46, No. 1, 2008, pp. 1–13.

How can a thorough risk analysis, like the one in Application Case 1.2, be performed so quickly? How can the judgment factors be elicited, quantified, and worked into a model? How can the results be presented meaningfully and convincingly to the executive? What are what-if questions? How can the Web be used to access and integrate appropriate data and models? We provide answers to these questions in Chapters 3 and 4. The DSS concepts introduced in Chapter 3 provide considerable insights to software vendors that develop decision support tools, to builders that construct specific decision support applications, and to users.

DSS AS A SPECIFIC APPLICATION Although *DSS* usually refers to the umbrella term, some use it in a narrower scope to refer to a process for building customized applications for unstructured or semistructured problems. Others use the term *DSS* to refer to the DSS application itself.

THE ARCHITECTURE OF DSS The DSS methodology recognizes the need for data to solve problems. These data can come from many sources, including the Web (see Chapter 5). Every problem that has to be solved and every opportunity or strategy to be analyzed requires some data. Data are the first component of the DSS architecture (see Figure 1.5). Data related to a specific situation are manipulated by using models (see Chapters 3 and 4). These models, which are the second component of the DSS architecture, can be standard (e.g., an Excel function) or customized. Some systems have a knowledge (or intelligence) component. This is the third component of the DSS architecture. Users are the vital fourth component of the architecture. Interfacing with the system via a user interface is the fifth component of the DSS architecture.

When creating a DSS, it is important to plan the system and then purchase (or build) the components and "glue" them together. In many DSS, the components are standards and can be purchased. But in other situations, especially unstructured ones, it is necessary to custom build some or all of the components. The details of the major components are provided in Chapter 3.

TYPES OF DSS There are many types of DSS, each with different objectives. The two major types are the *model-oriented DSS*, in which quantitative models are used to generate a recommended solution to a problem, and *data-oriented DSS*, which support ad

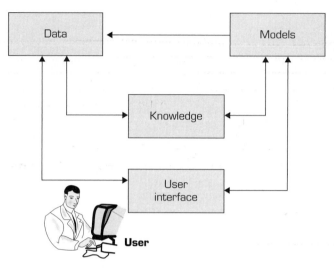

FIGURE 1.5 High-Level Architecture of a DSS

hoc reporting and queries. For details and other types, see Chapter 3 and the Special Interest Group on Decision Support, Knowledge and Data Management Systems (SIGDSS) Web site at **sigs.aisnet.org/sigdss**.

Evolution of DSS into Business Intelligence

In the early days of DSS, managers let their staff do some supportive analysis by using DSS tools. As PC technology advanced, a new generation of managers evolved—one that was comfortable with computing and knew that technology can directly help make intelligent business decisions faster. New tools such as OLAP, data warehousing, data mining, and intelligent systems, delivered via Web technology, added promised capabilities and easy access to tools, models, and data for computer-aided decision making. These tools started to appear under the names BI and *business analytics* in the mid-1990s. We introduce these concepts next, and relate the DSS and BI concepts in the following sections.

Section 1.6 Review Questions

1. Provide two definitions of *DSS*. P.16
2. Describe *DSS* as an umbrella term. P.16
3. Describe the architecture of DSS. P.17
4. How is the term *DSS* used in the academic world?

1.7 A FRAMEWORK FOR BUSINESS INTELLIGENCE (BI)

The decision support concepts presented in Sections 1.5 and 1.6 have been implemented incrementally, under different names, by many vendors that have created tools and methodologies for decision support. As the enterprise-wide systems grew, managers were able to access user-friendly reports that enabled them to make decisions quickly. These systems, which were generally called executive information systems (EIS), then began to offer additional visualization, alerts, and performance measurement capabilities. By 2006, the major *commercial* products and services appeared under the umbrella term business intelligence (BI).

Definitions of BI

Business intelligence (BI) is an umbrella term that combines architectures, tools, databases, analytical tools, applications, and methodologies (see Turban et al., 2008). It is, like DSS, a content-free expression, so it means different things to different people. Part of the confusion about BI lies in the flurry of acronyms and buzzwords that are associated with it (e.g., business performance management [BPM]). BI's major objective is to enable interactive access (sometimes in real time) to data, to enable manipulation of data, and to give business managers and analysts the ability to conduct appropriate analysis. By analyzing historical and current data, situations, and performances, decision makers get valuable insights that enable them to make more informed and better decisions. The process of BI is based on the *transformation* of data to information, then to decisions, and finally to actions.

A Brief History of BI

The term *BI* was coined by the Gartner Group in the mid-1990s. However, the concept is much older; it has its roots in the MIS reporting systems of the 1970s. During that period, reporting systems were static, two dimensional, and had no analytical capabilities. In the early 1980s, the concept of *executive information systems (EIS)* emerged. This concept expanded the computerized support to top-level managers and executives. Some of the capabilities introduced were dynamic multidimensional (ad hoc or on-demand) reporting, forecasting and prediction, trend analysis, drill-down to details, status access, and critical success factors. These features appeared in dozens of commercial products until the mid-1990s. Then the same capabilities and some new ones appeared under the name BI. Today, a good BI-based enterprise information system contains all the information executives need. So, the original concept of EIS was transformed into BI. By 2005, BI systems started to include *artificial intelligence* capabilities as well as powerful analytical capabilities. Figure 1.6 illustrates the

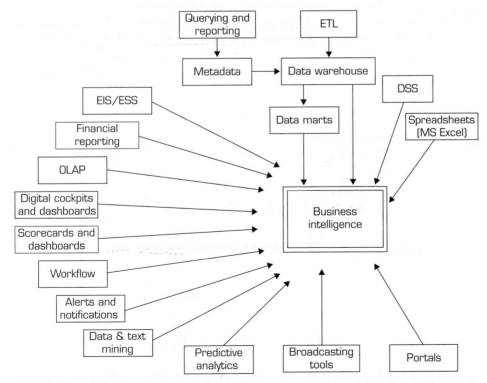

FIGURE 1.6 Evolution of Business Intelligence (BI)

various tools and techniques that may be included in a BI system. It illustrates the evolution of BI as well. The tools shown in Figure 1.6 provide the capabilities of BI. The most sophisticated BI products include most of these capabilities; others specialize in only some of them. We will study several of these capabilities in more detail in Chapters 5 through 9.

The Architecture of BI

A BI system has four major components: a *data warehouse*, with its source data; *business analytics*, a collection of tools for manipulating, mining, and analyzing the data in the data warehouse; *business performance management (BPM)* for monitoring and analyzing performance; and a *user interface* (e.g., a dashboard). The relationship among these components is illustrated in Figure 1.7. We will discuss these in detail in Chapters 5 through 9.

Notice that the data warehousing environment is mainly the responsibility of technical staff, whereas the analytical environment (also known as *business analytics*) is the realm of business users. Any user can connect to the system via the user interface, such as a browser, and top managers may use the BPM component and also a dashboard.

Some business analytics and user interface tools are introduced briefly in Section 1.9 and in Chapter 9. However, one set of tools, *intelligent systems* (see Chapters 12 and 13), can be viewed as a futuristic component of BI.

DATA WAREHOUSING The data warehouse and its variants are the cornerstone of any medium-to-large BI system. Originally, the data warehouse included only historical data that were organized and summarized, so end users could easily view or manipulate data and information. Today, some data warehouses include current data as well, so they can provide real-time decision support (see Chapter 8).

BUSINESS ANALYTICS End users can work with the data and information in a data warehouse by using a variety of tools and techniques. These tools and techniques fit into two major categories:

1. ***Reports and queries.*** Business analytics include static and dynamic reporting, all types of queries, discovery of information, multidimensional view, drill-down to details, and so on. These are presented in Chapter 9. These reports are also related to BPM (introduced next).

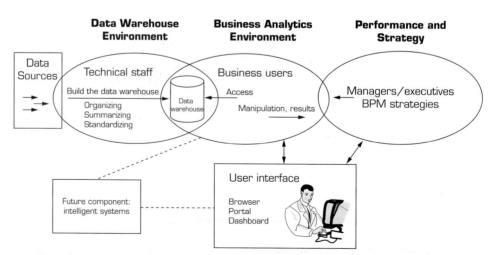

FIGURE 1.7 A High-Level Architecture of BI *Source*: Based on W. Eckerson, *Smart Companies in the 21st Century: The Secrets of Creating Successful Business Intelligent Solutions.* The Data Warehousing Institute, Seattle, WA, 2003, p. 32, Illustration 5.

2. ***Data, text, and Web mining and other sophisticated mathematical and statistical tools.*** Data mining (described further in Chapters 5 through 8) is a process of searching for unknown relationships or information in large databases or data warehouses, using intelligent tools such as neural computing, predictive analytics techniques, or advanced statistical methods (see Chapter 6). As discussed further in Chapter 7, mining can be done on Web data as well. Two examples of useful applications of data mining follow:

EXAMPLE 1

National Australia Bank uses data mining to aid its predictive marketing. The tools are used to extract and analyze data stored in the bank's Oracle database. Specific applications focus on assessing how competitors' initiatives are affecting the bank's bottom line. The data mining tools are used to generate market analysis models from historical data. The bank considers initiatives to be crucial to maintaining an edge in the increasingly competitive financial services marketplace.

EXAMPLE 2

FAI Insurance Group uses its data mining to reassess the relationship between historical risk from insurance policies and the pricing structure used by its underwriters. The data analysis capabilities allow FAI to better serve its customers by more accurately assessing the insurance risk associated with a customer request. Through the use of neural networks and linear statistics, the analysts comb the data for trends and relationships.

Application Case 1.3 describes the application of another BI technique—cluster analysis.

APPLICATION CASE 1.3

Location, Location, Location

Hoyt Highland Partners is a marketing intelligence firm that assists health care providers with growing their patient base. The firm also helps determine the best locations for the health care provider's practices. Hoyt Highland Partners was working with an urgent care clinic client. The urgent care clinic faced increased competition from other urgent care operators and convenient care clinics. The clinic needed to decide if it should move its location or change marketing practices to increase its income. To help with this decision, Hoyt Highland identified, using Acxiom's PersonicX system, where the most concentrated areas of the clinic's target audience were located.

Acxiom's PersonicX categorizes every U.S. household into one of 70 segments and 21 life-stage groups. The placement is based on specific consumer behavior as well as demographic characteristics. The information includes consumer surveys outlining behaviors and attitudes and location characteristics for important markets. Hoyt Highland used PersonicX to determine which clusters were well represented in the urgent care clinic database and which clusters provide the operator with the highest return-on-investment (ROI) potential.

Using the software's geospatial analysis capability, Hoyt Highland found that 80% of the clinic's patients lived within a 5-mile radius of a clinic location. It also found that young families were well represented, but that singles and seniors were underrepresented. In addition, it found that proximity is a top factor in the choice of an urgent care clinic. This analysis helped the clinic to determine that the best course of action was to change its marketing focus rather than to move its clinics. Today, the clinic focuses its marketing toward patients who live within a 5-mile radius of a clinic location and toward young families.

Source: "Location, Location, Location," Acxiom, **acxiom.com** (accessed March 26, 2009).

BUSINESS PERFORMANCE MANAGEMENT Business performance management **(BPM)**, which is also referred to as **corporate performance management (CPM)**, is an emerging portfolio of applications and methodology that contains evolving BI architecture and tools in its core. BPM extends the monitoring, measuring, and comparing of sales, profit, cost, profitability, and other performance indicators by introducing the concept of management and feedback. It embraces processes such as planning and forecasting as core tenets of a business strategy. In contrast with the traditional DSS, EIS, and BI, which support the bottom-up extraction of information from data, BPM provides a top-down enforcement of corporate-wide strategy. BPM is the topic of Chapter 9 and is usually combined with the *balanced scorecard methodology* and dashboards.

The User Interface: Dashboards and Other Information Broadcasting Tools

Dashboards (which resemble automobile dashboards) provide a comprehensive visual view of corporate performance measures (also known as key performance indicators), trends, and exceptions. They integrate information from multiple business areas. Dashboards present graphs that show actual performance compared to desired metrics; thus, a dashboard presents an at-a-glance view of the health of the organization. In addition to dashboards, other tools that broadcast information are corporate portals, digital cockpits, and other visualization tools (see Chapter 9). Many visualization tools, ranging from multidimensional cube presentation to virtual reality, are integral parts of BI systems. Recall that BI emerged from EIS, so many visual aids for executives were transformed to BI software. Also, technologies such as geographical information systems (GIS) play an increasing role in decision support.

Styles of BI

The architecture of BI depends on its applications. MicroStrategy Corp. distinguishes five styles of BI and offers special tools for each. The five styles are report delivery and alerting; enterprise reporting (using dashboards and scorecards); cube analysis (also known as slice-and-dice analysis); ad-hoc queries; and statistics and data mining.

The Benefits of BI

As illustrated by the opening vignette, the major benefit of BI to a company is the ability to provide accurate information when needed, including a real-time view of the corporate performance and its parts. Such information is a must for all types of decisions, for strategic planning, and even for survival.

Thompson (2004) reported the following to be the major benefits of BI, based on the results of a survey:

- Faster, more accurate reporting (81%)
- Improved decision making (78%)
- Improved customer service (56%)
- Increased revenue (49%)

Notice that many of the benefits of BI are *intangible*. This is why, according to Eckerson (2003), so many executives *do not* insist on a rigorous cost-justification for BI projects. Thompson (2004) also noted that the most common application areas of BI are general reporting, sales and marketing analysis, planning and forecasting, financial consolidation, statutory reporting, budgeting, and profitability analysis.

An interesting data mining application using *predictive analytics tools* (discussed further in Chapters 5 through 7) is described in Application Case 1.4.

APPLICATION CASE 1.4

Alltel Wireless: Delivering the Right Message, to the Right Customers, at the Right Time

In April 2006, Alltel Wireless launched its "My Circle" campaign and revolutionized (now merged with Verizon) the cell phone industry. For the first time, customers could have unlimited calling to any 10 numbers, on any network, for free. To solidify the impact of the "My Circle" campaign in a time of rising wireless access rates, Alltel saw a need for a centralized, data-focused solution to increase the number of new customers and to enhance relationships with existing customers.

Through Acxiom's PersonicX segmentation system (**acxiom.com**), Alltel was able to cluster its data on U.S. households based on specific consumer behavior and demographic characteristics. This enriched Alltel's customer and prospect data by providing better insight into buying behavior and customer subscription lifecycle events. With these analytical techniques, Alltel could inform specific customer segments about opportunities that would enhance their wireless experience, such as text messaging bundles and ringtone downloads. Additionally, Alltel could now target new customers who had a greater likelihood to activate a subscription through lower cost Web and call center channels.

By automating its customer lifecycle management with Acxiom's BI software suite, Alltel was able to manage more than 300 direct marketing initiatives per year, increase customer additions by 265%, increase return on investment by 133%, and create ongoing business value of over $30 million.

Source: "Customer Lifecycle Management," Acxiom, **acxiom.com** (accessed March 26, 2009).

The Origins and Drivers of BI

Where did modern approaches to data warehousing (DW) and BI come from? What are their roots, and how do those roots affect the way organizations are managing these initiatives today? Today's investments in information technology are under increased scrutiny in terms of their bottom-line impact and potential. The same is true of DW and the BI applications that make these initiatives possible.

Organizations are being compelled to capture, understand, and harness their data to support decision making in order to improve business operations. Legislation and regulation (e.g., the Sarbanes-Oxley Act of 2002) now require business leaders to document their business processes and to sign off on the legitimacy of the information they rely on and report to stakeholders. Moreover, business cycle times are now extremely compressed; faster, more informed, and better decision making is therefore a competitive imperative. Managers need the *right information* at the *right time* and in the *right place*. This is the mantra for modern approaches to BI.

Organizations have to work smart. Paying careful attention to the management of BI initiatives is a necessary aspect of doing business. It is no surprise, then, that organizations are increasingly championing BI. The opening vignette discussed a BI success story at Norfolk Southern. You will hear about more BI successes and the fundamentals of those successes in Chapters 5 through 9. Examples of typical applications of BI are provided in Table 1.3.

The DSS–BI Connection   DSS VS. BI

By now, you should be able to see some of the similarities and differences between DSS and BI. First, their architectures are very similar because BI evolved from DSS. However, BI implies the use of a data warehouse, whereas DSS may or may not have such a feature. BI is therefore more appropriate for large organizations (because data warehouses are expensive to build and maintain), but DSS can be appropriate to any type of organization.

TABLE 1.3 Business Value of BI Analytical Applications

Analytic Application	Business Question	Business Value
Customer segmentation	What market segments do my customers fall into, and what are their characteristics?	Personalize customer relationships for higher satisfaction and retention.
Propensity to buy	Which customers are most likely to respond to my promotion?	Target customers based on their need to increase their loyalty to your product line. Also, increase campaign profitability by focusing on the most likely to buy.
Customer profitability	What is the lifetime profitability of my customer?	Make individual business interaction decisions based on the overall profitability of customers.
Fraud detection	How can I tell which transactions are likely to be fraudulent?	Quickly determine fraud and take immediate action to minimize cost.
Customer attrition	Which customer is at risk of leaving?	Prevent loss of high-value customers and let go of lower-value customers.
Channel optimization	What is the best channel to reach my customer in each segment?	Interact with customers based on their preference and your need to manage cost.

Source: A. Ziama and J. Kasher, *Data Mining Primer for the Data Warehousing Professional*. Teradata, Dayton, OH, 2004.

Second, most DSS are constructed to *directly* support specific decision making. BI systems, in general, are geared to provide accurate and timely information, and they support decision support *indirectly*. This situation is changing, however, as more and more decision support tools are being added to BI software packages.

Third, BI has an executive and strategy orientation, especially in its BPM and dashboard components. DSS, in contrast, is oriented toward analysts.

Fourth, most BI systems are constructed with commercially available tools and components that are fitted to the needs of organizations. In building DSS, the interest may be in constructing solutions to very unstructured problems. In such situations, more programming (e.g., using tools such as Excel) may be needed to customize the solutions.

Fifth, DSS methodologies and even some tools were developed mostly in the academic world. BI methodologies and tools were developed mostly by software companies. (See Zaman, 2005, for information on how BI has evolved.)

Sixth, many of the tools that BI uses are also considered DSS tools. For example, data mining and predictive analysis are core tools in both areas.

Although some people equate DSS with BI, these systems are not, at present, the same. It is interesting to note that some people believe that DSS is a part of BI—one of its analytical tools. Others think that BI is a special case of DSS that deals mostly with reporting, communication, and collaboration (a form of data-oriented DSS). Another explanation (Watson, 2005) is that BI is a result of a continuous revolution and, as such, DSS is one of BI's original elements. In this book, we separate DSS from BI. However, we point to the DSS–BI connection frequently.

MANAGEMENT SUPPORT SYSTEMS (MSS)   Due to the lack of crisp and universal definitions of DSS and BI, some people refer to DSS and BI, as well as their tools, either independently or in combination, as **management support systems (MSS)**. MSS is a broad enough concept to be viewed as a technology that supports managerial tasks in general and decision making in particular. In this book, we use *MSS* when the nature of the technology involved is not clear, and we use it interchangeably with the combined term *DSS/BI*.

In addition to the major frameworks of decision support presented so far, we need to look at a new proposed framework—the *work system*—which we present next.

Section 1.7 Review Questions

1. Define *BI*. P. 19
2. List and describe the major components of BI. P.20 Architecture of BI
3. List and describe the major tangible and intangible benefits of BI.
4. What are the major similarities and differences of DSS and BI? P. 23 -25
5. Define *MSS*.

1.8 A WORK SYSTEM VIEW OF DECISION SUPPORT

Claiming that the revolutionary DSS agenda is now "ancient history," Alter (2004), a DSS pioneer, suggested a new approach to managerial decision support. Alter dropped the word *systems* from DSS, focusing on *decision support,* which he defines as the use of any plausible computerized or noncomputerized means for improving decision making in a particular repetitive or nonrepetitive business situation in a particular organization.

By adding noncomputerized means, Alter expanded the landscape of decision support to include nontechnical decision-improvement interventions and strategies. To cope with the possibility of a huge field with many disciplines, Alter postulated that decision support may come from the different aspects of *work systems*. He defined a **work system** as a system in which human participants and/or machines perform a business process, using information, technology, and other resources, to produce products and/or services for internal or external customers. A work system operates within a surrounding environment, often using shared infrastructure, and sometimes within a conscious strategy for the organization or work system. Furthermore, Alter postulated that a work system usually has nine elements. Each of these elements can be varied or modified in order to provide better organizational performance, decision quality, or business process efficiency. The following are the nine elements, along with some possible sources of improvements:

1. **Business process.** Variations in the process rationale, sequence of steps, or methods used for performing particular steps
2. **Participants.** Better training, better skills, higher levels of commitment, or better real-time or delayed feedback
3. **Information.** Better information quality, information availability, or information presentation
4. **Technology.** Better data storage and retrieval, models, algorithms, statistical or graphical capabilities, or computer interaction
5. **Product and services.** Better ways to evaluate potential decisions
6. **Customers.** Better ways to involve customers in the decision process and to obtain greater clarity about their needs
7. **Infrastructure.** More effective use of shared infrastructure, which might lead to improvements
8. **Environment.** Better methods for incorporating concerns from the surrounding environment
9. **Strategy.** A fundamentally different operational strategy for the work system

The work system concept is interesting, and it has considerably expanded the field of managerial decision support. Much more research is needed before this concept can be used as a guide to both the academic and practical worlds.

Now that you are familiar with the major frameworks of the field, we can look at its major tools.

Section 1.8 Review Questions

1. What is Alter's definition of *decision support*? P.25
2. Define *work system*. P.25
3. List the nine elements of a work system. 1-9 P.25.
4. Explain how decision making can be improved by changing an element of a work system.

1.9 THE MAJOR TOOLS AND TECHNIQUES OF MANAGERIAL DECISION SUPPORT

How DSS/BI is implemented depends on which tools are used.

The Tools and Techniques

A large number of tools and techniques have been developed over the years to support managerial decision making. Some of them appear under different names and definitions. The major computerized tool categories are summarized in Table 1.4. Full descriptions are provided in other chapters of this book, as shown in Table 1.4.

TABLE 1.4 Computerized Tools for Decision Support

Tool Category	Tools and Their Acronyms	Chapter in the Book
Data management	Databases and database management system (DBMS)	3, 8
	Extraction, transformation, and load (ETL) systems	8
	Data warehouses (DW), real-time DW, and data marts	8
Reporting status tracking	Online analytical processing (OLAP)	9
	Executive information systems (EIS)	2
Visualization	Geographical information systems (GIS)	9
	Dashboards	9
	Information portals	9
	Multidimensional presentations	9
Business analytics	Optimization	4
	Data mining, Web mining, and text mining	6, 7
	Web analytics	7
Strategy and performance management	Business performance management (BPM)/Corporate performance management (CPM)	9
	Business activity management (BAM)	9
	Dashboards and scorecards	9
Communication and collaboration	Group decision support systems (GDSS)	10
	Group support systems (GSS)	10
	Collaborative information portals and systems	10
Social networking	Web 2.0	3, 10, 14
Knowledge management	Knowledge management systems (KMS)	11
	Expert locating systems	11
Intelligent systems	Expert systems (ES)	12
	Artificial neural networks (ANN)	6
	Fuzzy logic	13
	Genetic algorithms	13
	Intelligent agents	13
	Automated decision systems (ADS)	3, 12

The Tools–Web Connection

All these tools are available today either solely as Web-based versions or in both Web-based and non-Web-based formats. The relationships between these tools and the Web can be viewed as a two-way street. In the following chapters, we provide more details on the tools–Web connection.

Hybrid Support Systems

The objective of computerized decision support, regardless of its name or nature, is to assist management in solving managerial or organizational problems (and assess opportunities and strategies) faster and better than possible without computers. To attain this objective, a support system may use several of the tools and techniques mentioned in Table 1.4 in what is known as a **hybrid (integrated) support system**. Every type of tool has certain capabilities and limitations. By integrating several tools, we can improve decision support because one tool can provide advantages where another is weak (see Chapter 14).

Machine repair provides a useful example of a hybrid support system. A repair technician diagnoses a problem and identifies the best tools to make the repair. Although only one tool may be sufficient, it is often necessary to use several tools to improve results. Sometimes there may be no standard tools. In such a case, special tools must be developed, such as a ratchet tip at the end of a screwdriver handle, or a screwdriver blade at the end of a ratchet wrench to reach into hard-to-reach places. The managerial decision-making process described in Application Case 1.5 illustrates the combined use of several decision support technologies in solving a single enterprise-wide problem.

APPLICATION CASE 1.5

United Sugars Corporation Optimizes Production, Distribution, and Inventory Capacity with Different Decision Support Tools

United Sugars Corporation, headquartered in Bloomington, Minnesota, is a grower-owned cooperative that sells and distributes sugar products for its member companies. United has a 25 percent U.S. market share and sales of more than $1 billion annually. When the United States Sugar Corporation in southern Florida joined the cooperative, United Sugars decided to revise its marketing and distribution plans to gain access to new markets and serve existing ones more efficiently. Improvements in managing the supply chain and in the supply chain's design were in order.

A strategic model was developed to identify the minimum-cost solutions for packaging, inventory, and distribution. The company's enterprise resource planning (ERP) system (and a legacy database system) provided data for several mathematical models (see Chapter 4). This first model contained about 1 million decision variables and more than 250,000 relationships.

A Web-based GIS graphically displays reports and optimal solutions. A map of the United States indicates the locations of plants, warehouses, and customers. Each one is a hotspot that links to additional information about the solutions.

This model is also used to schedule production and distribution. Results are uploaded into the ERP to support operational decisions. The results of the strategic model drive the generation of subsequent models for inventory analysis. These models simulate a variety of inventory situations, through what-if analyses, and help analysts reduce the overall inventory. Results are displayed in a variety of formats in a Web browser.

This hybrid decision support system consists of several optimization and simulation models, an ERP, and Web interfaces.

Sources: Compiled from M. D. Cohen, C. B. Charles, and A. L. Medaglia, "Decision Support with Web-Enabled Software," *Interfaces*, Vol. 31, No. 2, 2001, and "U.S. Sugar in the News," **unitedsugars.com** (accessed July 2006).

A hybrid approach is often related to a problem-solving approach that uses several tools in different ways, such as the following:

- Use each tool independently to solve different aspects of the problem.
- Use several loosely integrated tools. This mainly involves transferring data from one tool to another for further processing.
- Use several tightly integrated tools. From the user's standpoint, the tool appears as a unified system.

In addition to performing different tasks in the problem-solving process, tools can support each other. For example, an expert system (ES) can enhance the modeling and data management of a DSS. A neural computing system or a group support system (GSS) can support the knowledge acquisition process in building an ES. ES and artificial neural networks play an increasingly important role in enhancing other decision support technologies by making them "smarter." The components of such systems may also include MS, statistics, and a variety of other computer-based tools. For details, see Chapter 14.

Emerging Technologies and Technology Trends

A number of emerging technologies directly and indirectly influence DSS. As technology advances, the speed of computation increases, leading to greater computational capability, while the physical size of the computer decreases. Every few years, there is a several-factor change in these parameters. Some specific technologies to watch are presented in Chapter 14.

Section 1.9 Review Questions

1. List the nine major categories of decision support tools. P.26 Chart

? **2.** In what ways can the Web facilitate the use of these tools?

3. What is a hybrid system? What are its benefits? P.27

1.10   PLAN OF THE BOOK

The 14 chapters of this book are organized into seven parts, as shown in Figure 1.8.

Part I: Decision Support and Business Intelligence

In Chapter 1, we have provided an introduction, definitions, and an overview of decision support systems and business intelligence.

Part II: Computerized Decision Support

Chapter 2 describes the process and methodologies of managerial decision making. Chapter 3 provides an overview of DSS and its major components. Chapter 4 describes the topic of (mathematical) modeling and analysis. It describes both structured models and modeling tools. It also describes how unstructured problems can be modeled.

Part III: Business Intelligence

BI includes several distinct components. We begin by focusing on applications and the process of data mining and analytics in Chapter 5. Chapter 6 describes some of the technical details of the algorithms of data mining, including neural networks. Chapter 7 describes the emerging application of text and Web mining. Then, in Chapter 8,

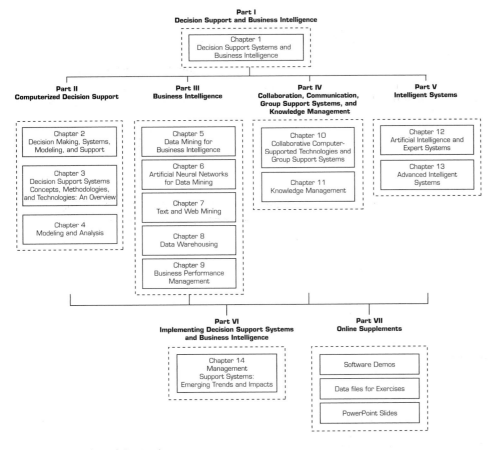

FIGURE 1.8 Plan of the Book

we focus on data warehouses, which are necessary for enabling analytics and performance measurement. Chapter 9 discusses BPM, dashboards, scorecards, and related topics.

Part IV: Collaboration, Communication, Group Support Systems, and Knowledge Management

In this part, Chapter 10 deals with the support provided to groups working either in the same room or at different locations, especially via the Web. Chapter 11 is an in-depth discussion of knowledge management (KM) systems, which are enterprise-level support systems that manage the knowledge needed for decision support.

Part V: Intelligent Systems

The fundamentals of artificial intelligence and ES are the subject of Chapter 12. Advanced intelligent systems, including genetic algorithms, fuzzy logic, and hybrids, are the subject of Chapter 13. Chapter 14 attempts to integrate all the material covered here and concludes with a discussion of emerging trends, such as how the ubiquity of cell phones, GPS devices, and wireless PDAs is resulting in the creation of massive new databases. A new breed of data mining and BI companies is emerging to analyze these new databases and create a much better and deeper understanding of customers' behaviors and movements. This has even been given a new name—reality mining. Application Case 1.6 highlights one such example. We will learn about this application and several others in Chapter 14.

APPLICATION CASE 1.6

The Next Net

Sense Networks is one of many companies developing applications to better understand customers' movements. One of its applications analyzes data on the movements of almost 4 million cell phone users. The data come from GPS, cell phone towers, and local Wi-Fi hotspots. The data are anonymized, but are still linked together. This linkage enables data miners to see clusters of customers getting together at specific locations (bars, restaurants) at specific hours. Clustering techniques can be used to identify what types of "tribes" these customers belong to—business travelers, "young travelers," and so on. By analyzing data at this level of detail, customer profiles can be built at a very fine level.

Besides the conventional use of the information to target customers with better precision and appropriate offers, such systems may someday be helpful in studying crime and the spread of disease. Other companies that are developing techniques for performing similar analyses include Google, Kinetics, and Nokia.

Source: Compiled from S. Baker, "The Next Net," *BusinessWeek*, March 2009, pp. 42–46.

1.11 RESOURCES, LINKS, AND THE TERADATA UNIVERSITY NETWORK CONNECTION

The use of this chapter and most other chapters in this book can be enhanced by the tools described in the following sections.

Resources and Links

We recommend the following major resources and links:

- The Data Warehousing Institute (**tdwi.org**)
- Information Management (**information-management.com**)
- The OLAP Report (**olapreport.com**)
- DSS Resources (**dssresources.com**)
- Information Technology Toolbox (**businessintelligence.ittoolbox.com**)
- Business Intelligence Network (**b-eye-network.com**)
- AIS World (**isworld.org**)
- Microsoft Enterprise Consortium (**enterprise.waltoncollege.uark.edu/mec**)

Cases

All major MSS vendors (e.g., MicroStrategy, Microsoft, Oracle, IBM, Hyperion, Cognos, Exsys, SAS, FICO, Business Objects, SAP, Information Builders) provide interesting customer success stories. Academic-oriented cases are available at Harvard Business School Case Collection (**hbsp.harvard.edu/b01/en/academic/edu_home.jhtml**), Business Performance Improvement Resource (**bpir.com**), Idea Group Publishing (**idea-group.com**), Ivy League Publishing (**ivylp.com**), KnowledgeStorm (**knowledgestorm.com**), and other sites. Miller's *MIS Cases* (2005) contains simple cases, using spreadsheet and database exercises, that support several of the chapters in this book.

Vendors, Products, and Demos

Most vendors provide software demos of their products and applications. Information about products, architecture, and software is available at **dssresources.com**.

Periodicals

We recommend the following periodicals:

- *Decision Support Systems*
- *CIO Insight* (**cioinsight.com**)
- *Technology Evaluation* (**technologyevaluation.com**)
- *Baseline Magazine* (**baselinemag.com**)
- *Business Intelligence Journal* (**tdwi.org**)

Additional References

Additional selected references are provided in the online files for some chapters.

The Teradata University Network Connection

This book is tightly connected with the free resources provided by Teradata University Network (TUN; see **teradatauniversitynetwork.com**).

The TUN portal is divided into two major parts: one for students and one for faculty. This book is connected to the TUN portal via a special section at the end of each chapter. That section includes appropriate links for the specific chapter, pointing to relevant resources. In addition, we provide hands-on exercises, using software and other material (e.g., cases), at TUN.

The Book's Web Site

This book's Web site, **pearsonhighered.com/turban**, contains supplemental textual material organized as Web chapters that correspond to the printed book's chapters. The topics of these chapters are listed in the online chapter table of contents.[2]

Chapter Highlights

- The business environment is becoming complex and is rapidly changing, making decision making more difficult.
- Businesses must respond and adapt to the changing environment rapidly by making faster and better decisions.

- The time frame for making decisions is shrinking, whereas the global nature of decision making is expanding, necessitating the development and use of computerized DSS.
- The rate of computerization is increasing rapidly, and so is its use for managerial decision support.

---

[2] As this book went to press, we verified that all the cited Web sites were active and valid. However, URLs are dynamic. Web sites to which we refer in the text sometimes change or are discontinued because companies change names, are bought or sold, merge, or fail. Sometimes Web sites are down for maintenance, repair, or redesign. Many organizations have dropped the initial "www" designation for their sites, but some still use it. If you have a problem connecting to a Web site that we mention, please be patient and simply run a Web search to try to identify the possible new site. Most times, you can quickly find the new site through one of the popular search engines. We apologize in advance for this inconvenience.

- MSS are technologies designed to support managerial work. They can be used independently or in combination.
- Computerized support for managers is often essential for the survival of an organization.
- An early decision support framework divides decision situations into nine categories, depending on the degree of structuredness and managerial activities. Each category is supported differently.
- Structured repetitive decisions are supported by standard quantitative analysis methods, such as MS, MIS, and rule-based automated decision support.
- DSS use data, models, and sometimes knowledge management to find solutions for semistructured and some unstructured problems.
- Automated decision support is provided today in many industries to find solutions to repetitive decisions (such as item pricing) based on business rules.
- BI methods utilize a central repository called a data warehouse that enables efficient data mining, OLAP, BPM, and data visualization.

- BI architecture includes a data warehouse, business analytics tools used by end users, and a user interface (such as a dashboard).
- Many organizations use BPM systems to monitor performance, compare it to standards and goals, and show it graphically (e.g., using dashboards) to managers and executives.
- Data mining is a tool for discovering information and relationships in a large amount of data.
- All MSS technologies are interactive and can be integrated together and with other computer-based information systems (CBIS) into hybrid support systems.
- Web technology and the Internet, intranets, and extranets play a key role in the development, dissemination, and use of MSS.
- The work system is a new concept in decision support that broadens the field to include non-computerized methods combined with computerized ones.

Key Terms

automated decision
   system (ADS) *13*
business intelligence
   (BI) *19*
business performance
   management (BPM)
   (or corporate
   performance

management
   [CPM]) *22*
cognitive limits *10*
dashboard *22*
data mining *21*
decision support system
   (DSS) *16*

hybrid (integrated)
   support system *27*
management science
   (MS) (or operations
   research [OR]) *13*
management support
   system (MSS) *24*

semistructured
   problem *12*
structured problem *12*
unstructured problem *12*
work system *25*

Questions for Discussion

1. Give examples for the content of each cell in Figure 1.2.
2. Survey the literature from the past 6 months to find one application each for DSS, BI, and intelligent systems. Summarize the applications on one page and submit it with the exact sources.
3. Observe an organization with which you are familiar. List three decisions it makes in each of the following categories: strategic planning, management control (tactical planning), and operational planning and control.

4. Compare and contrast MS with ADS.
5. Which organizational responses can be considered reactive and which can be considered proactive?
6. Discuss how a wireless system can improve decision making.
7. Discuss the importance of ADS.
8. Distinguish BI from DSS.

Exercises

TERADATA STUDENT NETWORK (TSN) AND OTHER HANDS-ON EXERCISES

1. Go to **teradatastudentnetwork.com**. Using the registration your instructor provides, log on and learn the content of the site. Prepare a list of all materials available there. You will receive assignments related to this site. Prepare a list of 20 items in the site that you think could be beneficial to you.

2. Enter the TUN site and select "cases, projects and assignments." Then select the case study: "Harrah's High Payoff from Customer Information." Answer the following questions about this case:
   a. What information does the data mining generate?
   b. How is this information helpful to management in decision making? (Be specific.)
   c. List the types of data that are mined.
   d. Is this a DSS or BI application? Why?

3. Go to **teradatastudentnetwork.com** and find the paper titled "Data Warehousing Supports Corporate Strategy at First American Corporation" (by Watson, Wixom, and Goodhue). Read the paper and answer the following questions:
   a. What were the drivers for the DW/BI project in the company?
   b. What strategic advantages were realized?
   c. What operational and tactical advantages were achieved?
   d. What were the critical success factors (CSF) for the implementation?

TEAM ASSIGNMENTS AND ROLE-PLAYING

1. Write a 5- to 10-page report describing how your company or a company you are familiar with currently uses computers and information systems, including Web technologies, in decision support. In light of the material in this chapter, describe how a manager could use such support systems if they were readily available. Which ones are available to you and which ones are not?

2. Design a computerized system for a brokerage house that trades securities, conducts research on companies, and provides information and advice to customers (such as "buy," "sell," and "hold"). In your design, clearly distinguish the tools you plan to use. Be sure to discuss input and output information. Assume that the brokerage company is a small one with only 20 branches in four different cities.

3. Find information on the proactive use of computers versus transaction processing systems (TPS) to support ad hoc decisions. Each member of the group should choose an application in a different industry (e.g., retail, banking, insurance, food). Be sure to include the impacts of the Web/Internet. Summarize the findings and point out the similarities and differences of the applications. Use as sources companies that employ students, trade magazines, Internet newsgroups, and vendor Web sites. Finally, prepare a class presentation on your findings.

4. Go to **fico.com**, **ilog.com**, and **pega.com**. View the demos at these sites. Prepare a list of ADS by industry and by functional area. Specify what types of decisions are automated.

INTERNET EXERCISES

1. Search the Internet for material regarding the work of managers, the need for computerized support, and the role DSS play in providing such support. What kind of references to consulting firms, academic departments, and programs do you find? What major areas are represented? Select five sites that cover one area and report your findings.

2. Explore the public areas of **dssresources.com**. Prepare a list of its major available resources. You might want to refer to this site as you work through the book.

3. Go to **fico.com**. Use the information there to identify five problems in different industries and five problems in different functional areas that can be supported by ADS.

4. Go to **sap.com** and **oracle.com**. Find information on how ERP software helps decision makers. In addition, examine how these software products use Web technology and the Web itself. Write a report based on your findings.

5. Go to **intelligententerprise.com**. For each topic cited in this chapter, find some interesting developments reported on the site, and prepare a report.

6. Go to **cognos.com** and **businessobjects.com**. Compare the capabilities of the two companies' BI products in a report.

7. Go to **microsoft.com**. Examine its BI offerings.

8. Go to **oracle.com**. Check out its BI offerings. How do Oracle's BI offerings relate to its ERP software?

9. Go to **microstrategy.com**. Find information on the five styles of BI. Prepare a summary table for each style.

10. Go to **oracle.com** and click the Hyperion link under Applications. Determine what the company's major products are. Relate these to the support technologies cited in this chapter.

END OF CHAPTER APPLICATION CASE

Vodafone Uses Business Intelligence to Improve Customer Growth and Retention Plans

The Problem

Vodafone New Zealand Ltd., a subsidiary of the U.K.–based telecommunications giant, had achieved tremendous success in New Zealand. Starting from a very small base, the company quickly attained more than 50% market share. However, as the mobile phone industry began to reach maturity, Vodafone's market share stagnated at about 56% and the total number of customers leveled off. To make matters worse, other competitors emerged, the cost of compliance with government regulations began to increase, and the revenue per customer also lagged. The company had to refocus its strategy of retaining and increasing revenue from the current customers. John Stewart, senior manager of customer analytics for Vodafone New Zealand, said, "Now that we have all of these customers, we need to answer new questions: How do we increase our profit margins? How do we add revenue streams from these customers? And how do we keep them as customers?" Vodafone needed to make better decisions based on real-time knowledge of its market, customers, and competitors. According to reporter Cheryl Krivda, "Vodafone needed to make a wholesale shift to analytical marketing, using business intelligence (BI) that could rapidly provide fact-based decision support. The goal: to help the company deliver the right message to the appropriate customers when they wanted it, using the preferred channel."

Solution

First, Vodafone formed a customer knowledge and analysis department to conduct analysis, modeling, market research, and competitive intelligence. John Stewart was the manager of this unit. Vodafone implemented an enterprise data warehouse (EDW) to obtain a single view of all of the information in the organization. EDW permits a well-integrated view of all of the organization's information to allow generation of predefined or ad hoc queries and reports, online analytical processing, and predictive analysis (Chapter 9). The company also developed its analytical team by hiring modeling specialists. In addition to the Teradata data warehouse platform, many other software tools, such as KXEN, SAS, and SPSS, were also used to build models and generate insights.

With the Teradata EDW platform and all the relevant tools in place, employees from Vodafone's sales and marketing department are now able to perform analyses and achieve better customer-offer optimization, campaign effectiveness analysis, and customer service. Stewart believes that the new tools give Vodafone the ability to develop "holistic insights." He says,

> As a team, we're leaning over one another's shoulders, asking questions and providing support. In the process, we learn from each other, which helps us deliver greater value in the insights we put out to the business. When you bring all of these sources of knowledge and information together, you can uncover the deeper insights about our customers.

One application of the EDW is a trigger-based marketing campaign. In the past, manual intervention was required to initiate a marketing campaign. With the new platform, Vodafone can automatically initiate a marketing offer based on a customer's recent activity.

Results

Perhaps the biggest benefit of the EDW is that the analysts can spend more time generating insights than managing data. "Now we can get campaigns to the customer more efficiently and effectively," says Stewart. "That's not to say we send out wave after wave of campaigns, though. It's increasingly targeted and refined in terms of who we campaign to, and the relevance to the customer is greater, too."

The system also provides better information to decision makers to support the decision-making process. Vodafone is developing an application to optimize both revenue and prioritization of customer offers. The goal is "to get the best possible return . . . from the process of campaigning and contacting customers." Without divulging specifics, it appears that the company is on its way to achieving these goals.

Source: Compiled from C. D. Krivda, "Dialing Up Growth in a Mature Market," *Teradata Magazine*, March 2008, pp. 1–3.

Questions for the Case

1. What were the challenges for Vodafone New Zealand?
2. How did it address these issues?
3. List the tools used by Vodafone's applications.
4. What benefits are being derived from this initiative?
5. What can we learn from this case?

References

Acxiom. "Location, Location, Location." **acxiom.com** (accessed March 26, 2009).

Alter, S. (2004, December). "A Work System View of DSS in Its Fourth Decade." *Decision Support Systems.*

Anthony, R. N. (1965). *Planning and Control Systems: A Framework for Analysis.* Cambridge, MA: Harvard University Graduate School of Business.

Baker, S. (2009). "The Next Net." *BusinessWeek,* March 9, 2009, pp. 42–46.

Brooks, D. (2009, May 18). "In Praise of Dullness." *New York Times,* **nytimes.com/2009/05/19/opinion/19 brooks.html** (accessed June 2, 2009).

Cohen, M. D., C. B. Charles, and A. L. Medaglia. "Decision Support with Web-Enabled Software." *Interfaces,* Vol. 31, No. 2, 2001.

Davenport, T. H., and J. G. Harris. (2005, Summer). "Automated Decision Making Comes of Age." *MIT Sloan Management Review,* Vol. 46, No. 4, pp. 83–89.

DemandTec. "Giant Food Stores Prices the Entire Store with DemandTec," **demandtec.com** (accessed March 26, 2009).

Eckerson, W. (2003). *Smart Companies in the 21st Century: The Secrets of Creating Successful Business Intelligent Solutions.* Seattle, WA: The Data Warehousing Institute.

Gorry, G. A., and M. S. Scott-Morton. (1971). "A Framework for Management Information Systems." *Sloan Management Review,* Vol. 13, No. 1, pp. 55–70.

Kaplan, S. N., M. M. Klebanov, and M. Sorensen. (2008, July). "Which CEO Characteristics and Abilities Matter?" Swedish Institute for Financial Research Conference on the Economics of the Private Equity Market; AFA 2008 New Orleans Meetings Paper. Available at SSRN: **ssrn.com/abstract= 972446** (accessed June 2, 2009).

Keen, P. G. W., and M. S. Scott-Morton. (1978). *Decision Support Systems: An Organizational Perspective.* Reading, MA: Addison-Wesley.

Krivda, C. D. (2008, March). "Dialing Up Growth in a Mature Market." *Teradata Magazine,* pp. 1–3.

Miller, M. L. (2005). *MIS Cases,* 3rd ed. Upper Saddle River, NJ: Prentice Hall.

Mintzberg, H. A. (1980). *The Nature of Managerial Work.* Englewood Cliffs, NJ: Prentice Hall.

Mintzberg, H. A. (1993). *The Rise and Fall of Strategic Planning.* New York: The Free Press.

Shang, J., P. R. Tadikamalla, L. J. Kirsch, and L. Brown. (2008, December). "A Decision Support System for Managing Inventory at GlaxoSmithKline." *Decision Support Systems,* Vol. 46, No. 1, pp. 1–13.

Simon, H. (1977). *The New Science of Management Decision.* Englewood Cliffs, NJ: Prentice Hall.

Thompson, O. (2004, October). "Business Intelligence Success, Lessons Learned." **technologyevaluation.com** (accessed June 2, 2009).

Turban, E., R. Sharda, J. E. Aronson, and D. King. (2008). *Business Intelligence: A Managerial Approach.* Upper Saddle River, NJ: Prentice Hall.

United Sugars. "U.S. Sugar in the News." **unitedsugars.com** (accessed June 2, 2009).

Watson, H. (2005, Winter). "Sorting Out What's New in Decision Support." *Business Intelligence Journal.*

Zaman M. (2005, January). "Business Intelligence: Its Ins and Outs." **technologyevaluation.com** (accessed June 2, 2009).

Ziama, A., and J. Kasher. (2004). *Data Mining Primer for the Data Warehousing Professional.* Dayton, OH: Teradata.

Computerized Decision Support

LEARNING OBJECTIVES FOR PART II

1 Understand the conceptual foundations of decision making

2 Understand Simon's four phases of decision making: intelligence, design, choice, and implementation

3 Understand the concept of rationality and its impact on decision making

4 Understand the foundations, definitions, and capabilities of decision support systems (DSS) and business intelligence (BI)

5 Describe DSS components and technology levels

6 Describe the various types of DSS and explain their use

7 Explain the importance of databases and database management

8 Explain the importance of models and model management

In Part II, we concentrate on decision making, the decision support methodology, technology components, and development. Throughout, we highlight the major impacts of the Internet on DSS. Chapter 2 contains an overview of the conceptual foundations of decision making, the reason that all DSS are developed. Chapter 3 provides an overview of DSS: its characteristics, structure, uses, and types. Some of the major components of DSS are presented in Chapter 4.

Decision Making, Systems, Modeling, and Support

LEARNING OBJECTIVES

1 Understand the conceptual foundations of decision making

2 Understand Simon's four phases of decision making: intelligence, design, choice, and implementation

3 Recognize the concepts of rationality and bounded rationality and how they relate to decision making

4 Differentiate between the concepts of making a choice and establishing a principle of choice

5 Learn how DSS support for decision making can be provided in practice

6 Understand the systems approach

Our major focus in this book is the support of decision making through computer-based information systems. The purpose of this chapter is to describe the conceptual foundations of decision making and how support is provided. This chapter includes the following sections:

2.1 Opening Vignette: Decision Modeling at HP Using Spreadsheets
2.2 Decision Making: Introduction and Definitions
2.3 Models
2.4 Phases of the Decision-Making Process
2.5 Decision Making: The Intelligence Phase
2.6 Decision Making: The Design Phase
2.7 Decision Making: The Choice Phase
2.8 Decision Making: The Implementation Phase
2.9 How Decisions Are Supported
2.10 Resources, Links, and the Teradata University Network Connection

2.1 OPENING VIGNETTE: DECISION MODELING AT HP USING SPREADSHEETS

HP is a major manufacturer of computers, printers, and many industrial products. Its vast product line leads to many decision problems. Olavson and Fry have worked on many spreadsheet models for assisting decision makers at HP and have identified several lessons from both their successes and their failures when it comes to constructing and applying spreadsheet-based tools. They define a *tool* as "a reusable, analytical solution designed to be handed off to nontechnical end users to assist them in solving a repeated business problem."

When trying to solve a problem, HP developers consider the three phases in developing a model. The first phase is problem framing, where they consider the following questions in order to develop the best solution for the problem:

- Will analytics solve the problem?
- Can an existing solution be leveraged?
- Is a tool needed?

The first question is important because the problem may not be of an analytic nature, and therefore a spreadsheet tool may not be of much help in the long run without fixing the nonanalytical part of the problem first. For example, many inventory-related issues arise because of the inherent differences between the goals of marketing and supply chain groups. Marketing likes to have the maximum variety in the product line, whereas supply chain management focuses on reducing the inventory costs. This difference is partially outside the scope of any model. Coming up with nonmodeling solutions is important as well. If the problem arises due to "misalignment" of incentives or unclear lines of authority or plans, no model can help. Thus, it is important to identify the root issue.

The second question is important because sometimes an existing tool may solve a problem that then saves time and money. Sometimes modifying an existing tool may solve the problem, again saving some time and money, but sometimes a custom tool is necessary to solve the problem. This is clearly worthwhile to explore.

The third question is important because sometimes a new computer-based system is not required to solve the problem. The developers have found that they often use analytically derived decision guidelines instead of a tool. This solution requires less time for development and training, has lower maintenance requirements, and also provides simpler and more intuitive results. That is, after they have explored the problem deeper, the developers may determine that it is better to present decision rules that can be easily implemented as guidelines for decision making rather than asking the managers to run some type of a computer model. This results in easier training, better understanding of the rules being proposed, and increased acceptance. It also typically leads to lower development costs and reduced time for deployment.

If a model has to be built, the developers move on to the second phase—the actual design and development of the tools. Adhering to five guidelines tends to increase the probability that the new tool will be successful. The first guideline is to develop a prototype as quickly as possible. This allows the developers to test the designs, demonstrate various features and ideas for the new tools, get early feedback from the end users to see what works for them and what needs to be changed, and test adoption. Developing a prototype also prevents the developers from overbuilding the tool and yet allows them to construct more scalable and standardized software applications later. Additionally, by developing a prototype developers can stop the process once the tool is "good enough," rather than building a standardized solution that would take longer to build and be more expensive.

The second guideline is to "build insight, not black boxes." The HP spreadsheet model developers believe that this is important, because oftentimes just entering some data and receiving a calculated output is not enough. The users need to be able to think of alternative scenarios, and the tool does not support this if it is a "black box" that only provides one recommendation. They argue that a tool is best only if it provides information to help make and support decisions rather than just give the answers. They also believe that an interactive tool helps the users to understand the problem better, therefore leading to more informed decisions.

The third guideline is to "remove unneeded complexity before handoff." This is important, because as a tool becomes more complex it requires more training and expertise, more data, and more recalibrations. The risk of bugs and misuse also increases. Sometimes it is best to study the problem, begin modeling and analysis, and then start shaping the program into a simple-to-use tool for the end user.

The fourth guideline is to "partner with end users in discovery and design." By working with the end users the developers get a better feel of the problem and a better idea of what the end users want. It also increases the end users' ability to use analytic tools. The end users also gain a better understanding of the problem and how it is solved using the new tool. Additionally, including the end users in the development process enhances the decision makers' analytical knowledge and capabilities. By working together, their knowledge and skills complement each other in the final solution.

The fifth guideline is to "develop an Operations Research (OR) champion." By involving end users in the development process, the developers create champions for the new tools who then go back to their departments or companies and encourage their coworkers to accept and use them. The champions are then the experts on the tools in their areas and can then help those being introduced to the new tools. Having champions increases the possibility that the tools will be adopted into the businesses successfully.

The final stage is the handoff, when the final tools that provide complete solutions are given to the businesses. When planning the handoff, it is important to answer the following questions:

- Who will use the tool?
- Who owns the decisions that the tool will support?
- Who else must be involved?
- Who is responsible for maintenance and enhancement of the tool?
- When will the tool be used?
- How will the use of the tool fit in with other processes?
  - Does it change the processes?
  - Does it generate input into those processes?
- How will the tool impact business performance?
- Are the existing metrics sufficient to reward this aspect of performance?
- How should the metrics and incentives be changed to maximize impact to the business from the tool and process?

By keeping these lessons in mind, developers and proponents of computerized decision support in general and spreadsheet-based models in particular are likely to enjoy greater success.

Questions for the Opening Vignette

1. What are some of the key questions to be asked in supporting decision making through DSS?
2. What guidelines can be learned from this vignette about developing DSS?
3. What lessons should be kept in mind for successful model implementation?

What We Can Learn from This Vignette

This vignette relates to providing decision support in a large organization:

- Before building a model, decision makers should develop a good understanding of the problem that needs to be addressed.
- A model may not be necessary to address the problem.
- Before developing a new tool, decision makers should explore reuse of existing tools.
- The goal of model building is to gain better insight into the problem, not just to generate more numbers.
- Implementation plans should be developed along with the model.

Source: Based on T. Olavson and C. Fry, "Spreadsheet Decision-Support Tools: Lessons Learned at Hewlett-Packard," *Interfaces,* Vol. 38, No. 4, July/August 2008, pp. 300–310.

2.2 DECISION MAKING: INTRODUCTION AND DEFINITIONS

We are about to examine how decision making is practiced and some of the underlying theories and models of decision making. You will also learn about the various traits of decision makers, including what characterizes a good decision maker. Knowing this can help you to understand the types of decision support tools that managers can use to make more effective decisions. In the following sections, we discuss various aspects of decision making.

Characteristics of Decision Making

In addition to the characteristics presented in the opening vignette, decision making may involve the following:

- Groupthink (i.e., group members accept the solution without thinking for themselves) can lead to bad decisions.
- Decision makers are interested in evaluating what-if scenarios.
- Experimentation with a real system (e.g., develop a schedule, try it, and see how well it works) may result in failure.
- Experimentation with a real system is possible only for one set of conditions at a time and can be disastrous.
- Changes in the decision-making environment may occur continuously, leading to invalidating assumptions about a situation (e.g., deliveries around holiday times may increase, requiring a different view of the problem).
- Changes in the decision-making environment may affect decision quality by imposing time pressure on the decision maker.
- Collecting information and analyzing a problem takes time and can be expensive. It is difficult to determine when to stop and make a decision.
- There may not be sufficient information to make an intelligent decision.
- Too much information may be available (i.e., information overload).

Ultimately, we want to help decision makers make better decisions (e.g., see Churchman, 1982). However, making better decisions does not necessarily mean making decisions more quickly. The fast-changing business environment often requires faster decisions, which may actually be detrimental to decision quality. One study asked managers which areas suffered most when fast decision making was required (Horgan, 2001). The areas that managers identified as suffering the most from fast decision making included personnel/human resources (27%), budgeting/finance (24%), organizational structuring (22%), quality/productivity (20%), information technology (IT) selection and installation (17%), and process improvement (17%).

To determine how real decision makers make decisions, we must first understand the process and the important issues involved in decision making. Then we can understand appropriate methodologies for assisting decision makers and the contributions information systems can make. Only then can we develop DSS to help decision makers.

This chapter is organized based on the three key words that form the term *DSS*: *decision*, *support*, and *systems*. A decision maker should not simply apply IT tools blindly. Rather, the decision maker gets support through a rational approach that simplifies reality and provides a relatively quick and inexpensive means of considering various alternative courses of action to arrive at the best (or at least a very good) solution to the problem.

A Working Definition of *Decision Making*

Decision making is a process of choosing among two or more alternative courses of action for the purpose of attaining one or more goals. According to Simon (1977), managerial decision making is synonymous with the entire management process. Consider the important managerial function of planning. Planning involves a series of decisions: What should be done? When? Where? Why? How? By whom? Managers set goals, or plan; hence, planning implies decision making. Other managerial functions, such as organizing and controlling, also involve decision making.

Decision Making and Problem Solving

A problem occurs when a system does not meet its established goals, does not yield the predicted results, or does not work as planned. Problem solving may also deal with identifying new opportunities. Differentiating the terms **decision making** and **problem solving** can be confusing. One way to distinguish between the two is to examine the phases of the decision process (see Chapter 1): (1) intelligence, (2) design, (3) choice, and (4) implementation. Some consider the entire process (phases 1–4) as problem solving, with the choice phase as the real decision-making process. Others view phases 1–3 as formal decision making, ending with a recommendation, with problem solving additionally including the actual implementation of the recommendation (phase 4). Note that a problem may include situations in which a person must decide which opportunity to exploit.

In this book, we use the terms *decision making* and *problem solving* interchangeably.

Decision-Making Disciplines

Decision making is directly influenced by several major disciplines, some of which are behavioral and some of which are scientific in nature. We must be aware of how their philosophies can affect our ability to make decisions and provide support. Behavioral disciplines include anthropology, law, philosophy, political science, psychology, social psychology, and sociology. Scientific disciplines include computer science, decision analysis, economics, engineering, the hard sciences (e.g., biology, chemistry, physics), management science/operations research, mathematics, and statistics.

Each discipline has its own set of assumptions about reality and methods. Each also contributes a unique, valid view of how people make decisions. Finally, a lot of variation exists as to what constitutes a successful decision in practice. For example, Crainer (2002) discussed the "75 greatest management decisions ever made." All of them were successful for a number of reasons, some serendipitous. Other great decisions, such as building the Great Wall of China, made good sense at the time (Crainer considered it a success) but actually failed in practice because of bad managerial practices. Other decisions eventually failed as well.

An important characteristic of management support systems (MSS) is their emphasis on the **effectiveness**, or "goodness," of the decision produced rather than on the computational efficiency of obtaining it; this is usually a major concern of a transaction processing system. Most Web-based DSS are focused on improving decision effectiveness. **Efficiency** may be a by-product.

Decision Style and Decision Makers

In the following sections, we examine the notion of decision style and specific aspects about decision makers.

DECISION STYLE   **Decision style** is the manner by which decision makers think and react to problems. This includes the way they perceive a problem, their cognitive responses, and how values and beliefs vary from individual to individual and from situation to situation. As a result, people make decisions in different ways. Although there is a general process of decision making, it is far from linear. People do not follow the same steps of the process in the same sequence, nor do they use all the steps. Furthermore, the emphasis, time allotment, and priorities given to each step vary significantly, not only from one person to another, but also from one situation to the next. The manner in which managers make decisions (and the way they interact with other people) describes their decision style. Because decision styles depend on the factors described earlier, there are many decision styles. Personality temperament tests are often used to determine decision styles. Because there are many such tests, it is important to try to equate them in determining decision style. However, the various tests measure somewhat different aspects of personality, so they cannot be equated.

Researchers have identified a number of decision-making styles. These include heuristic and analytic styles. One can also distinguish between autocratic versus democratic styles. Another style is consultative (with individuals or groups). Of course, there are many combinations and variations of styles. For example, a person can be analytic and autocratic, or consultative (with individuals) and heuristic.

For a computerized system to successfully support a manager, it should fit the decision situation as well as the decision style. Therefore, the system should be flexible and adaptable to different users. The ability to ask what-if and goal-seeking questions provides flexibility in this direction. A Web-based interface using graphics is a desirable feature in supporting certain decision styles. If an MSS is to support varying styles, skills, and knowledge, it should not attempt to enforce a specific process. Rather, it should help decision makers use and develop their own styles, skills, and knowledge.

Different decision styles require different types of support. A major factor that determines the type of support required is whether the decision maker is an individual or a group. Individual decision makers need access to data and to experts who can provide advice, whereas groups additionally need collaboration tools. Web-based MSS can provide support to both.

A lot of information is available on the Web about cognitive styles and decision styles (e.g., see Birkman International, Inc., **birkman.com**; Keirsey Temperament Sorter and Keirsey Temperament Theory, **keirsey.com**). Many personality/temperament tests are available to help managers identify their own styles and those of their employees. Identifying an individual's style can help establish the most effective communication patterns and ideal tasks for which the person is suited.

DECISION MAKERS   Decisions are often made by individuals, especially at lower managerial levels and in small organizations. There may be conflicting objectives even for a sole decision maker. For example, when making an investment decision an individual investor may consider the rate of return on the investment, liquidity, and safety as objectives. Finally, decisions may be fully automated (but only after a human decision maker decides to do so!).

This discussion of decision making focuses in large part on an individual decision maker. Most major decisions in medium-sized and large organizations are made by groups. Obviously, there are often conflicting objectives in a group decision-making setting. Groups can be of variable size and may include people from different departments or from different organizations. Collaborating individuals may have different cognitive styles, personality types, and decision styles. Some clash, whereas others are mutually enhancing. Consensus can be a difficult political problem. Therefore, the process of decision making by a group can be very complicated. Computerized support can greatly enhance group decision making. Computer support can be provided at a broad level, enabling members of whole departments, divisions, or even entire organizations to collaborate online. Such support has evolved over the past few years into enterprise information systems (EIS) and includes group support systems (GSS), enterprise resource management (ERM)/enterprise resource planning (ERP), supply chain management (SCM), knowledge management systems (KMS), and customer relationship management (CRM) systems.

Section 2.2 Review Questions

1. What are the various aspects of decision making? P. 41
2. Why is decision making so complex in today's business environment?
3. Identify similarities and differences between individual and group decision making.
4. Compare decision making and problem solving. Determine whether it makes sense to distinguish between the two.
5. Define *decision style* and describe why it is important to consider in the decision-making process.

2.3 MODELS[1]

A major characteristic of a DSS and many BI tools (notably those of business analytics) is the inclusion of at least one model. The basic idea is to perform the DSS analysis on a model of reality rather than on the real system. A *model* is a simplified representation or abstraction of reality. It is usually simplified because reality is too complex to describe exactly and because much of the complexity is actually irrelevant in solving a specific problem. Models can represent systems or problems with various degrees of abstraction. They are classified, based on their degree of abstraction, as iconic, analog, or mathematical.

Iconic (Scale) Models

An **iconic model**, also called the *scale model*—the least abstract type of model—is a physical replica of a system, usually on a different scale from the original. An iconic model may be three-dimensional, such as a model of an airplane, a car, a bridge, or a production line. Photographs are two-dimensional iconic models.

Analog Models

An **analog model** behaves like the real system but does not look like it. It is more abstract than an iconic model and is a symbolic representation of reality. Models of this type are usually two-dimensional charts or diagrams. They can be physical models, but the shape of the model differs from that of the actual system. The following are some examples of analog models:

- Organization charts that depict structure, authority, and responsibility relationships
- Maps on which different colors represent objects, such as bodies of water or mountains
- Stock market charts that represent the price movements of stocks
- Blueprints of a machine or a house
- Animations, videos, and movies

Mental Models

Decision makers sometimes develop mental models, especially in time-pressure situations (e.g., when airplane pilots consider whether to fly). **Mental models** are descriptive representations of decision-making situations that people form in their heads and think about. Their thought processes work through scenarios to consider the utility of and risks involved in each potential alternative. Typically, mental models are used when there are mostly qualitative factors in the decision-making problem. Mental models help frame the decision-making situation, a topic of cognition theory (see Shoemaker and Russo, 2004).

---

[1] Caution: Many students and professionals view models strictly as those of "data modeling" in the context of systems analysis and design. Here, we consider analytical models such as those of linear programming, simulation, and forecasting.

The methodology provided by cognitive maps can be used in practice to explicate a mental model of an individual or to develop a group consensus.

Mathematical (Quantitative) Models

The complexity of relationships in many organizational systems cannot be represented by icons or analogically because such representations would soon become cumbersome and using them would be time-consuming. Therefore, more abstract models are described mathematically. Most DSS analyses are performed numerically with mathematical or other quantitative models.

The Benefits of Models

An MSS uses models for the following reasons:

- Manipulating a model (changing decision variables or the environment) is much easier than manipulating a real system. Experimentation is easier and does not interfere with the organization's daily operations.
- Models enable the compression of time. Years of operations can be simulated in minutes or seconds of computer time.
- The cost of modeling analysis is much lower than the cost of a similar experiment conducted on a real system.
- The cost of making mistakes during a trial-and-error experiment is much lower when models are used than with real systems.
- The business environment involves considerable uncertainty. With modeling, a manager can estimate the risks resulting from specific actions.
- Mathematical models enable the analysis of a very large, sometimes infinite, number of possible solutions. Even in simple problems, managers often have a large number of alternatives from which to choose.
- Models enhance and reinforce learning and training.
- Models and solution methods are readily available on the Web.
- Many Java applets (and other Web programs) are available to readily solve models.

Advances in computer graphics, especially through Web interfaces and their associated object-oriented programming languages, have led to an increased tendency to use iconic and analog models to complement MSS mathematical modeling. For example, visual simulation combines all three types of models. We defer our detailed discussion on models until Chapter 4.

Section 2.3 Review Questions

1. Describe the different categories of models. *Iconic Models, Analog Models, Mental Models, Mathematical*
2. How can mathematical models provide the benefits listed in this section? *numerically*
3. How can mental models be utilized in decision making involving many qualitative factors? *line 5 P.44*
4. How can modern IT tools help synthesize qualitative and quantitative factors in decision making?

2.4 PHASES OF THE DECISION-MAKING PROCESS

It is advisable to follow a systematic decision-making process. Simon (1977) said that this involves three major phases: intelligence, design, and choice. He later added a fourth phase, implementation. Monitoring can be considered a fifth phase—a form of feedback. However, we view monitoring as the *intelligence phase* applied to the *implementation phase*. Simon's model is the most concise and yet complete characterization of rational decision making. A conceptual picture of the decision-making process is shown in Figure 2.1.

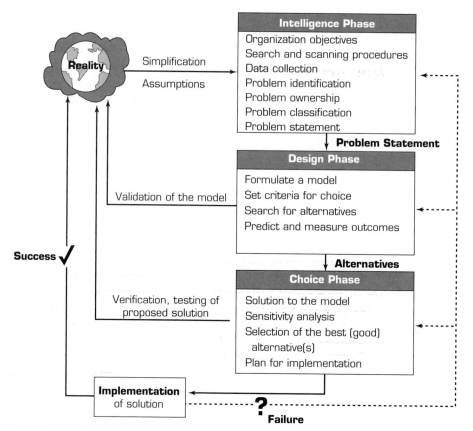

FIGURE 2.1 The Decision-Making/Modeling Process

There is a continuous flow of activity from intelligence to design to choice (see the bold lines in Figure 2.1), but at any phase, there may be a return to a previous phase (feedback). Modeling is an essential part of this process. The seemingly chaotic nature of following a haphazard path from problem discovery to solution via decision making can be explained by these feedback loops.

The decision-making process starts with the **intelligence phase**; in this phase, the decision maker examines reality and identifies and defines the problem. *Problem ownership* is established as well. In the **design phase**, a model that represents the system is constructed. This is done by making assumptions that simplify reality and writing down the relationships among all the variables. The model is then validated, and criteria are determined in a principle of choice for evaluation of the alternative courses of action that are identified. Often, the process of model development identifies alternative solutions and vice versa.

The **choice phase** includes selection of a proposed solution to the model (not necessarily to the problem it represents). This solution is tested to determine its viability. When the proposed solution seems reasonable, we are ready for the last phase: implementation of the decision (not necessarily of a system). Successful implementation results in solving the real problem. Failure leads to a return to an earlier phase of the process. In fact, we can return to an earlier phase during any of the latter three phases. The decision-making situations described in the opening vignette and the MMS running case (in Online File W2.1) follow Simon's four-phase model, as do almost all other decision-making situations. Web impacts on the four phases, and vice versa, are shown in Table 2.1.

TABLE 2.1 Simon's Four Phases of Decision Making and the Web

Phase	Web Impacts	Impacts on the Web
Intelligence	Access to information to identify problems and opportunities from internal and external data sources	Identification of opportunities for e-commerce, Web infrastructure, hardware and software tools, etc.
	Access to artificial intelligence methods and other data mining methods to identify opportunities	Intelligent agents, which reduce the burden of information overload
	Collaboration through group support systems (GSS) and knowledge management systems (KMS)	Smart search engines
	Distance learning, which can provide knowledge to add structure to problems	
Design	Access to data, models, and solution methods	Brainstorming methods (e.g., GSS) to collaborate in Web infrastructure design
	Use of online analytical processing (OLAP), data mining, and data warehouses	Models and solutions of Web infrastructure issues
	Collaboration through GSS and KMS	
	Similar solutions available from KMS	
Choice	Access to methods to evaluate the impacts of proposed solutions	Decision support system (DSS) tools, which examine and establish criteria from models to determine Web, intranet, and extranet infrastructure
		DSS tools, which determine how to route messages
Implementation	Web-based collaboration tools (e.g., GSS) and KMS, which can assist in implementing decisions	Decisions implemented on browser and server design and access, which ultimately determined how to set up the various components that have evolved into the Internet
	Tools, which monitor the performance of e-commerce and other sites, including intranets, extranets, and the Internet	

Note that there are many other decision-making models. Notable among them is the Kepner-Tregoe method (Kepner and Tregoe, 1998), which has been adopted by many firms because its tools are readily available from Kepner-Tregoe, Inc. (**kepner-tregoe.com**; also see Bazerman, 2005). We have found that these alternative models, including the Kepner-Tregoe method, readily map into Simon's four-phase model.

Even though ultimately a human decision maker is responsible for every decision, automated systems have evolved to help businesses make decisions more productively and consistently. A complication in the business environment is that decisions often must be made frequently and rapidly, utilizing online information. Typically, these problems are highly structured. The insurance industry was one of the first to adopt such automated decision-making (ADM) technology. It uses ADM in underwriting, but utilizes rules-based technology. For details on ADM decision making, see Davenport (2004) and Indart (2005).

We next turn to a detailed discussion of the four phases illustrated by the MMS running case described in Online File W2.1. Note that Online File W2.1 has four distinct parts, corresponding to Simon's four phases of decision making.

Section 2.4 Review Questions

1. List and briefly describe Simon's four phases of decision making. *P.46*
2. Why is a fifth phase, evaluation, not necessary? *fourth & fifth kinda same*
3. What can cause a problem to exist in decision making? *the first phase*

2.5 DECISION MAKING: THE INTELLIGENCE PHASE

Intelligence in decision making involves scanning the environment, either intermittently or continuously. It includes several activities aimed at identifying problem situations or opportunities. It may also include monitoring the results of the implementation phase of a decision-making process. (See the MMS running case situations in Online File W2.1.1.)

Problem (or Opportunity) Identification

The intelligence phase begins with the identification of organizational goals and objectives related to an issue of concern (e.g., inventory management, job selection, lack of or incorrect Web presence) and determination of whether they are being met. Problems occur because of dissatisfaction with the status quo. Dissatisfaction is the result of a difference between what people desire (or expect) and what is occurring. In this first phase, a decision maker attempts to determine whether a problem exists, identify its symptoms, determine its magnitude, and explicitly define it. Often, what is described as a problem (e.g., excessive costs) may be only a symptom (i.e., measure) of a problem (e.g., improper inventory levels). Because real-world problems are usually complicated by many interrelated factors, it is sometimes difficult to distinguish between the symptoms and the real problem, as described in the MMS running case in Online File W2.1.1. New opportunities and problems certainly may be uncovered while investigating the causes of symptoms. For example, Application Case 2.1 describes a classic story of recognizing the correct problem.

APPLICATION CASE 2.1
Making Elevators Go Faster!

This story has been reported in numerous places and has almost become a classic example to explain the need for problem identification. Ackoff (as cited in Larson, 1987) described the problem of managing complaints about slow elevators in a tall hotel tower. After trying many solutions for reducing the complaint: staggering elevators to go to different floors, adding operators, and so on, the management determined that the real problem was not about the *actual* waiting time but rather the *perceived* waiting time. So the solution was to install full-length mirrors on elevator doors on each floor. As Hesse and Woolsey (1975) put it, "the women would look at themselves in the mirrors and make adjustments, while the men would look at the women, and before they knew it, the elevator was there." By reducing the perceived waiting time, the problem went away. Baker and Cameron (1996) give several other examples of distractions, including lighting, displays, and so on, that organizations use to reduce perceived waiting time. If the real problem is identified as *perceived* waiting time, it can make a big difference in the proposed solutions and their costs. For example, full-length mirrors probably cost a whole lot less than adding an elevator!

Sources: Based on J. Baker and M. Cameron, "The Effects of the Service Environment on Affect and Consumer Perception of Waiting Time: An Integrative Review and Research Propositions," *Journal of the Academy of Marketing Science,* Vol. 24, September 1996, pp. 338–349; R. Hesse and G. Woolsey, *Applied Management Science: A Quick and Dirty Approach,* SRA Inc., Chicago, 1975; R. C. Larson, "Perspectives on Queues: Social Justice and the Psychology of Queuing," *Operations Research,* Vol. 35, No. 6, November/December 1987, pp. 895–905.

The existence of a problem can be determined by monitoring and analyzing the organization's productivity level. The measurement of productivity and the construction of a model are based on real data. The collection of data and the estimation of future data are among the most difficult steps in the analysis. The following are some issues that may arise during data collection and estimation and thus plague decision makers:

- Data are not available. As a result, the model is made with, and relies on, potentially inaccurate estimates.
- Obtaining data may be expensive.
- Data may not be accurate or precise enough.
- Data estimation is often subjective.
- Data may be insecure.
- Important data that influence the results may be qualitative (soft).
- There may be too many data (i.e., information overload).
- Outcomes (or results) may occur over an extended period. As a result, revenues, expenses, and profits will be recorded at different points in time. To overcome this difficulty, a present-value approach can be used if the results are quantifiable.
- It is assumed that future data will be similar to historical data. If this is not the case, the nature of the change has to be predicted and included in the analysis.

When the preliminary investigation is completed, it is possible to determine whether a problem really exists, where it is located, and how significant it is. A key issue is whether an information system is reporting a problem or only the symptoms of a problem. For example, in the MMS running case (see Online File W2.1), sales are down; there is a problem, but the situation, no doubt, is symptomatic of the problem. Also, as suggested in the opening vignette, it is critical to know the real problem. Sometimes it may be a problem of perception, incentive mismatch, or organizational processes rather than a poor decision model.

Problem Classification

Problem classification is the conceptualization of a problem in an attempt to place it in a definable category, possibly leading to a standard solution approach. An important approach classifies problems according to the degree of structuredness evident in them. This ranges from totally structured (i.e., programmed) to totally unstructured (i.e., unprogrammed), as described in Chapter 1.

Problem Decomposition

Many complex problems can be divided into subproblems. Solving the simpler subproblems may help in solving a complex problem. Also, seemingly poorly structured problems sometimes have highly structured subproblems. Just as a semistructured problem results when some phases of decision making are structured whereas other phases are unstructured, so when some subproblems of a decision-making problem are structured with others unstructured, the problem itself is semistructured. As a DSS is developed and the decision maker and development staff learn more about the problem, it gains structure. Decomposition also facilitates communication among decision makers. Decomposition is one of the most important aspects of the analytical hierarchy process (AHP is discussed in Chapter 4; see Bhushan and Rai, 2004; Forman and Selly, 2001; Saaty, 2001; and **expertchoice.com**), which helps decision makers incorporate both qualitative and quantitative factors into their decision-making models. In the MMS running case (see Online File W2.1), several aspects need to be investigated: advertising, sales, new car acquisition, and so on. Each of these is a subproblem that interacts with the others.

Problem Ownership

In the intelligence phase, it is important to establish problem ownership. A problem exists in an organization only if someone or some group takes on the responsibility of attacking it and if the organization has the ability to solve it. The assignment of authority to solve the problem is called **problem ownership**. For example, a manager may feel that he or she has a problem because interest rates are too high. Because interest rate levels are determined at the national and international levels, and most managers can do nothing about them, high interest rates are the problem of the government, not a problem for a specific company to solve. The problem companies actually face is how to operate in a high—interest-rate environment. For an individual company, the interest rate level should be handled as an uncontrollable (environmental) factor to be predicted.

When problem ownership is not established, either someone is not doing his or her job or the problem at hand has yet to be identified as belonging to anyone. It is then important for someone to either volunteer to own it or assign it to someone. This was done, very clearly, in the MMS running case (see Online File W2.1.1).

The intelligence phase ends with a formal problem statement.

Section 2.5 Review Questions

1. What is the difference between a problem and its symptoms? P.48
2. Why is it important to classify a problem? P.49
3. What is meant by *problem decomposition*? P.49
4. Why is establishing problem ownership so important in the decision-making process? P.50

2.6 DECISION MAKING: THE DESIGN PHASE

The design phase involves finding or developing and analyzing possible courses of action. These include understanding the problem and testing solutions for feasibility. A model of the decision-making problem is constructed, tested, and validated. (See the MMS running case in Online File W2.1.2.)

Modeling involves conceptualizing a problem and abstracting it to quantitative and/or qualitative form (see Chapter 4). For a mathematical model, the variables are identified, and their mutual relationships are established. Simplifications are made, whenever necessary, through assumptions. For example, a relationship between two variables may be assumed to be linear even though in reality there may be some nonlinear effects. A proper balance between the level of model simplification and the representation of reality must be obtained because of the cost–benefit trade-off. A simpler model leads to lower development costs, easier manipulation, and a faster solution but is less representative of the real problem and can produce inaccurate results. However, a simpler model generally requires fewer data, or the data are aggregated and easier to obtain.

The process of modeling is a combination of art and science. As a science, there are many standard model classes available, and, with practice, an analyst can determine which one is applicable to a given situation. As an art, creativity and finesse are required when determining what simplifying assumptions can work, how to combine appropriate features of the model classes, and how to integrate models to obtain valid solutions. In the MMS running case (see Online Files W2.1.1 through W2.1.4), the problem at hand was very vague: The MMS team investigated the data to develop an understanding that was more of a mental model of the situation, as teams are wont to do in such a situation. Models were indeed used and tested, but they were not described in the MMS running case. Models have **decision variables** that describe the alternatives from among which a manager must choose (e.g., how many cars to deliver to a specific rental agency, how to advertise at specific times, which Web server to buy or lease), a result variable or a set of result variables (e.g., profit, revenue, sales) that describes the objective or goal of the decision-making problem, and uncontrollable variables or parameters (e.g., economic conditions) that describe the environment. The process of modeling involves determining the (usually mathematical, sometimes symbolic) relationships among the variables. These topics are discussed in Chapter 4.

Selection of a Principle of Choice

A **principle of choice** is a criterion that describes the acceptability of a solution approach. In a model, it is a result variable. Selecting a principle of choice is not part of the choice phase but involves how a person establishes decision-making objective(s) and incorporates the objective(s) into the model(s). Are we willing to assume high risk, or do we prefer a low-risk approach? Are we attempting to optimize or satisfice? It is also important to recognize the difference between a criterion and a constraint (see Technology Insights 2.1). Among the many principles of choice, normative and descriptive are of prime importance.

Normative Models

Normative models are models in which the chosen alternative is demonstrably the best of all possible alternatives. To find it, the decision maker should examine all the alternatives and prove that the one selected is indeed the best, which is what the person would normally want. This process is basically **optimization.** In operational terms, optimization can be achieved in one of three ways:

1. Get the highest level of goal attainment from a given set of resources. For example, which alternative will yield the maximum profit from an investment of $10 million?
2. Find the alternative with the highest ratio of goal attainment to cost (e.g., profit per dollar invested) or maximize productivity.
3. Find the alternative with the lowest cost (or smallest amount of other resources) that will meet an acceptable level of goals. For example, if your task is to select hardware for an intranet with a minimum bandwidth, which alternative will accomplish this goal at the least cost?

TECHNOLOGY INSIGHTS 2.1   The Difference Between a Criterion and a Constraint

Many people new to the formal study of decision making inadvertently confuse the concepts of criterion and constraint. Often, this is because a criterion may imply a constraint, either implicit or explicit, thereby adding to the confusion. For example, there may be a distance criterion that the decision maker does not want to travel too far from home. However, there is an implicit constraint that the alternatives from which he selects must be within a certain distance from his home. This constraint effectively says that if the distance from home is greater than a certain amount, then the alternative is not feasible—or, rather, the distance to an alternative must be less than or equal to a certain number (this would be a formal relationship in some models; in the model in this case, it reduces the search, considering fewer alternatives). This is similar to what happens in some cases when selecting a university, where schools beyond a single day's driving distance would not be considered by most people, and, in fact, the utility function (criterion value) of distance can start out low close to home, peak at about 70 miles (about 100 km)—say, the distance between Atlanta (home) and Athens, Georgia—and sharply drop off thereafter.

Normative decision theory is based on the following assumptions of rational decision makers:

- Humans are economic beings whose objective is to maximize the attainment of goals; that is, the decision maker is rational. (More of a good thing [revenue, fun] is better than less; less of a bad thing [cost, pain] is better than more.)
- For a decision-making situation, all viable alternative courses of action and their consequences, or at least the probability and the values of the consequences, are known.
- Decision makers have an order or preference that enables them to rank the desirability of all consequences of the analysis (best to worst).

Kontoghiorghes et al. (2002) described the rational approach to decision making, especially as it relates to using models and computing.

Are decision makers really rational? See Technology Insights 2.2 and Schwartz (1998, 2004) for anomalies in rational decision making. Though there may be major anomalies in the presumed rationality of financial and economic behavior, we take the view that they could be caused by incompetence, lack of knowledge, multiple goals being framed inadequately, misunderstanding of a decision maker's true expected utility, and time-pressure impacts. For more on rationality, see Gharajedaghi (2006).

There are other anomalies, often caused by time pressure. For example, Stewart (2002) described a number of researchers working with intuitive decision making. The idea of "thinking with your gut" is obviously a heuristic approach to decision making. It works well for firefighters and military personnel on the battlefield. One critical aspect of decision making in this mode is that many scenarios have been thought through in advance. Even when a situation is new, it can quickly be matched to an existing one on-the-fly, and a reasonable solution can be obtained (through *pattern recognition*). Luce et al. (2004) described how emotions affect decision making, and Pauly (2004) discussed inconsistencies in decision making.

We believe that irrationality is caused by the factors listed previously. For example, Tversky et al. (1990) investigated the phenomenon of preference reversal, which is a known problem in applying the AHP to problems. Also, some criterion or preference may be omitted from the analysis. Ratner et al. (1999) investigated how variety can cause individuals to choose less-preferred options, even though they will enjoy them less. But we maintain that variety clearly has value, is part of a decision maker's utility, and is a criterion and/or constraint that should be considered in decision making.

TECHNOLOGY INSIGHTS 2.2   Are Decision Makers Really Rational?

Some researchers question the concept of rationality in decision making. There are countless cases of individuals and groups behaving irrationally in real-world and experimental decision-making situations. For example, suppose you need to take a bus to work every morning, and the bus leaves at 7:00 A.M. If it takes you 1 hour to wake up, prepare for work, and get to the bus stop, you should therefore always awaken at or before 6:00 A.M. However, sometimes (perhaps many times) you may sleep until 6:30, knowing that you will miss breakfast and not perform well at work. Or you may be late and arrive at the bus stop at 7:05, hoping that the bus will be late, too. So, why are you late? Multiple objectives and hoped-for goal levels may lead to this situation. Or your true expected utility for being on time might simply indicate that you should go back to bed most mornings!

In the MMS running case in Online File W2.1.2, rationality prevailed. Maximizing profit was clearly the principle of choice.

Suboptimization 次优化，次最佳化）

By definition, optimization requires a decision maker to consider the impact of each alternative course of action on the entire organization because a decision made in one area may have significant effects (positive or negative) on other areas. Consider, for example, a marketing department that implements an electronic commerce (e-commerce) site. Within hours, orders far exceed production capacity. The production department, which plans its own schedule, cannot meet demand. It may gear up for as high demand as possible. Ideally and independently, the department should produce only a few products in extremely large quantities to minimize manufacturing costs. However, such a plan might result in large, costly inventories and marketing difficulties caused by the lack of a variety of products, especially if customers start to cancel orders that are not met in a timely way. This situation illustrates the sequential nature of decision making (see Borges et al., 2002; and Sun and Giles, 2001).

A systems point of view assesses the impact of every decision on the entire system. Thus, the marketing department should make its plans in conjunction with other departments. However, such an approach may require a complicated, expensive, time-consuming analysis. In practice, the MSS builder may close the system within narrow boundaries, considering only the part of the organization under study (the marketing and/or production department, in this case). By simplifying, the model then does not incorporate certain complicated relationships that describe interactions with and among the other departments. The other departments can be aggregated into simple model components. Such an approach is called **suboptimization**.

If a suboptimal decision is made in one part of the organization without considering the details of the rest of the organization, then an optimal solution from the point of view of that part may be inferior for the whole. However, suboptimization may still be a very practical approach to decision making, and many problems are first approached from this perspective. It is possible to reach tentative conclusions (and generally usable results) by analyzing only a portion of a system, without getting bogged down in too many details. After a solution is proposed, its potential effects on the remaining departments of the organization can be tested. If no significant negative effects are found, the solution can be implemented.

Suboptimization may also apply when simplifying assumptions are used in modeling a specific problem. There may be too many details or too many data to incorporate into a specific decision-making situation, and so not all of them are used in the model. If the solution to the model seems reasonable, it may be valid for the problem and thus be adopted. For example, in a production department, parts are often partitioned into A/B/C inventory categories. Generally, A items (e.g., large gears, whole assemblies) are expensive (say, $3,000 or more each), built to order in small batches, and inventoried in low quantities; C items (e.g., nuts, bolts, screws) are very inexpensive (say, less than $2) and ordered and used in very large quantities; and B items fall in between. All A items can be handled by a detailed scheduling model and physically monitored closely by management; B items are generally somewhat aggregated, their groupings are scheduled, and management reviews these parts less frequently; and C items are not scheduled but are simply acquired or built based on a policy defined by management with a simple economic order quantity (EOQ) ordering system that assumes constant annual demand. The policy might be reviewed once a year. This situation applies when determining all criteria or modeling the entire problem becomes prohibitively time-consuming or expensive.

Suboptimization may also involve simply bounding the search for an optimum (e.g., by a heuristic) by considering fewer criteria or alternatives or by eliminating large portions of the problem from evaluation. If it takes too long to solve a problem, a good-enough solution found already may be used and the optimization effort terminated.

Descriptive Models 解述的

Descriptive models describe things as they are or as they are believed to be. These models are typically mathematically based. Descriptive models are extremely useful in DSS for investigating the consequences of various alternative courses of action under different configurations of inputs and processes. However, because a descriptive analysis checks the performance of the system for a given set of alternatives (rather than for all alternatives), there is no guarantee that an alternative selected with the aid of descriptive analysis is optimal. In many cases, it is only satisfactory.

模仿 Simulation is probably the most common descriptive modeling method. **Simulation** is the imitation of reality and has been applied to many areas of decision making. Computer and video games are a form of simulation: An artificial reality is created, and the game player lives within it. Virtual reality is also a form of simulation because the environment is simulated, not real. A common use of simulation is in manufacturing. Again, consider the production department of a firm with complications caused by the marketing department. The characteristics of each machine in a job shop along the supply chain can be described mathematically. Relationships can be established based on how each machine physically runs and relates to others. Given a trial schedule of batches of parts, it is possible to measure how batches flow through the system and to use the statistics from each machine. Alternative schedules may then be tried and the statistics recorded until a reasonable schedule is found. Marketing can examine access and purchase patterns on its Web site. Simulation can be used to determine how to structure a Web site for improved performance and to estimate future purchases. Both departments can therefore use primarily experimental modeling methods.

Classes of descriptive models include the following:

- Complex inventory decisions
- Environmental impact analysis
- Financial planning
- Information flow
- Markov analysis (predictions)
- Scenario analysis
- Simulation (alternative types)
- Technological forecasting
- Waiting-line (queuing) management

A number of nonmathematical descriptive models are available for decision making. One is the cognitive map (see Eden and Ackermann, 2002; and Jenkins, 2002). A cognitive map can help a decision maker sketch out the important qualitative factors and their causal relationships in a messy decision-making situation. This helps the decision maker (or decision-making group) focus on what is relevant and what is not, and the map evolves as more is learned about the problem. The map can help the decision maker understand issues better, focus better, and reach closure. One interesting software tool for cognitive mapping is Decision Explorer from Banxia Software Ltd. (**banxia.com**; try the demo).

Another descriptive decision-making model is the use of narratives to describe a decision-making situation. A *narrative* is a story that helps a decision maker uncover the important aspects of the situation and leads to better understanding and framing. This is extremely effective when a group is making a decision, and it can lead to a more common viewpoint, also called a *frame*. Juries in court trials typically use narrative-based approaches in reaching verdicts (see Allan, Frame, and Turney, 2003; Beach, 2005; and Denning, 2000).

Good Enough, or Satisficing

According to Simon (1977), most human decision making, whether organizational or individual, involves a willingness to settle for a satisfactory solution, "something less than the best." When **satisficing**, the decision maker sets up an aspiration, a goal, or a desired level of performance and then searches the alternatives until one is found that achieves this level. The usual reasons for satisficing are time pressures (e.g., decisions may lose value over time), the ability to achieve optimization (e.g., solving some models could take a really long time, and recognition that the marginal benefit of a better solution is not worth the marginal cost to obtain it (e.g., in searching the Internet, you can look at only so many Web sites before you run out of time and energy). In such a situation, the decision maker is behaving rationally, though in reality he or she is satisficing. Essentially, satisficing is a form of suboptimization. There may be a best solution, an optimum, but it would be difficult, if not impossible, to attain it. With a normative model, too much computation may be involved; with a descriptive model, it may not be possible to evaluate all the sets of alternatives. *why?*

Related to satisficing is Simon's idea of *bounded rationality*. Humans have a limited capacity for rational thinking; they generally construct and analyze a simplified model of a real situation by considering fewer alternatives, criteria, and/or constraints than actually exist. Their behavior with respect to the simplified model may be rational. However, the rational solution for the simplified model may not be rational for the real-world problem. Rationality is bounded not only by limitations on human processing capacities, but also by individual differences, such as age, education, knowledge, and attitudes. Bounded rationality is also why many models are descriptive rather than normative. This may also explain why so many good managers rely on intuition, an important aspect of good decision making (see Stewart, 2002; and Pauly, 2004).

Because rationality and the use of normative models lead to good decisions, it is natural to ask why so many bad decisions are made in practice. Intuition is a critical factor that decision makers use in solving unstructured and semistructured problems. The best decision makers recognize the trade-off between the marginal cost of obtaining further information and analysis versus the benefit of making a better decision. But sometimes decisions must be made quickly, and, ideally, the intuition of a seasoned, excellent decision maker is called for. When adequate planning, funding, or information is not available, or when a decision maker is inexperienced or ill trained, disaster can strike.

Developing (Generating) Alternatives

A significant part of the model-building process is generating alternatives. In optimization models (such as linear programming), the alternatives may be generated automatically by the model. In most MSS situations, however, it is necessary to generate alternatives manually. This can be a lengthy process that involves searching and creativity, perhaps utilizing electronic brainstorming in a GSS. It takes time and costs money. Issues such as when to stop generating alternatives can be very important. Too many alternatives can be detrimental to the process of decision making. A decision maker may suffer from information overload. Cross (2001) described a new initiative for administrators in higher-education institutions to handle information overload: The National Learning Infrastructure Initiative (NLII) Institute Readiness Program (READY) provides a way to organize and communicate information about the incorporation of technology into higher education. The Web-based READY portal filters through large amounts of information to select only relevant items for alternative selection. Generating alternatives is heavily dependent on the availability and cost of information and requires expertise in the problem area. This is the least formal aspect of problem solving. Alternatives can be generated and evaluated using heuristics. The generation of alternatives from either individuals or groups can be supported by electronic brainstorming software in a Web-based GSS.

Note that the search for alternatives usually occurs after the criteria for evaluating the alternatives are determined. This sequence can ease the search for alternatives and reduce the effort involved in evaluating them, but identifying potential alternatives can sometimes aid in identifying criteria. Identifying criteria and alternatives proved difficult in the online MMS running case (see Online File W2.1.2). The analysts first had to identify the many problems. After the problems were identified, years of experience and access to information through the CLAUDIA portal made it easy for the team to develop obvious solutions and establish their value to the bottom line.

The outcome of every proposed alternative must be established. Depending on whether the decision-making problem is classified as one of certainty, risk, or uncertainty, different modeling approaches may be used (see Drummond, 2001; and Koller, 2000). These are discussed in Chapter 4.

Measuring Outcomes

The value of an alternative is evaluated in terms of goal attainment. Sometimes an outcome is expressed directly in terms of a goal. For example, profit is an outcome, profit maximization is a goal, and both are expressed in dollar terms. An outcome such as customer satisfaction may be measured by the number of complaints, by the level of loyalty to a product, or by ratings found through surveys. Ideally, a decision maker would want to deal with a single goal, but in practice, it is not unusual to have multiple goals (see Barba-Romero, 2001; and Koksalan and Zionts, 2001). When groups make decisions, each group participant may have a different agenda. For example, executives might want to maximize profit, marketing might want to maximize market penetration, operations might want to minimize costs, and stockholders might want to maximize the bottom line. Typically, these goals conflict, so special multiple-criteria methodologies have been developed to handle this. One such method is the AHP.

Risk

All decisions are made in an inherently unstable environment. This is due to the many unpredictable events in both the economic and physical environments. Some risk (measured as probability) may be due to internal organizational events, such as a valued employee quitting or becoming ill, whereas others may be due to natural disasters, such as a hurricane. Aside from the human toll, one economic aspect of Hurricane Katrina was that the price of a gallon of gasoline doubled overnight due to uncertainty in the port capabilities, refining, and pipelines of the southern United States. What can a decision maker do in the face of such instability?

In general, people have a tendency to measure uncertainty and risk badly. Purdy (2005) said that people tend to be overconfident and have an illusion of control in decision making. The results of experiments by Adam Goodie at the University of Georgia indicate that most people are overconfident most of the time (Goodie, 2004) This may explain why people often feel that one more pull of a slot machine will definitely pay off.

However, methodologies for handling extreme uncertainty do exist. For example, Yakov (2001) described a way to make good decisions based on very little information, using an information gap theory and methodology approach. Aside from estimating the potential utility or value of a particular decision's outcome, the best decision makers are capable of accurately estimating the risk associated with the outcomes that result from making each decision. Thus, one important task of a decision maker is to attribute a level of risk to the outcome associated with each potential alternative being considered. Some decisions may lead to unacceptable risks in terms of success and can therefore be discarded or discounted immediately.

In some cases, some decisions are assumed to be made under conditions of certainty simply because the environment is assumed to be stable. Other decisions are made under conditions of uncertainty, where risk is unknown. Still, a good decision maker can make working estimates of risk. Also, the process of developing BI/DSS involves learning more about the situation, which leads to a more accurate assessment of the risks.

Scenarios 方案

A **scenario** is a statement of assumptions about the operating environment of a particular system at a given time; that is, it is a narrative description of the decision-situation setting. A scenario describes the decision and uncontrollable variables and parameters for a specific modeling situation. It may also provide the procedures and constraints for the modeling.

Scenarios originated in the theater, and the term was borrowed for war gaming and large-scale simulations. Scenario planning and analysis is a DSS tool that can capture a whole range of possibilities. A manager can construct a series of scenarios (i.e., what-if cases), perform computerized analyses, and learn more about the system and decision-making problem while analyzing it. Ideally, the manager can identify an excellent, possibly optimal, solution to the model of the problem.

Scenarios are especially helpful in simulations and what-if analyses. In both cases, we change scenarios and examine the results. For example, we can change the anticipated demand for hospitalization (an input variable for planning), thus creating a new scenario. Then we can measure the anticipated cash flow of the hospital for each scenario.

Scenarios play an important role in MSS because they:

- Help identify opportunities and problem areas
- Provide flexibility in planning
- Identify the leading edges of changes that management should monitor
- Help validate major modeling assumptions
- Allow the decision maker to explore the behavior of a system through a model
- Help to check the sensitivity of proposed solutions to changes in the environment, as described by the scenario

Possible Scenarios

There may be thousands of possible scenarios for every decision situation. However, the following are especially useful in practice:

- The worst possible scenario
- The best possible scenario
- The most likely scenario
- The average scenario

The scenario determines the context of the analysis to be performed. Scenarios were used in the MMS running case (see Online File W2.1.2) in establishing the value of each alternative.

Errors in Decision Making

The model is a critical component in the decision-making process, but a decision maker may make a number of errors in its development and use. Validating the model before it is used is critical. Gathering the right amount of information, with the right level of precision and accuracy, to incorporate into the decision-making process is also critical. Sawyer (1999) described "the seven deadly sins of decision making," most of which are behavior or information related.

Section 2.6 Review Questions

1. Define *optimization* and contrast it with *suboptimization*. P.51 & P51
2. Compare the normative and descriptive approaches to decision making. P.51 & P34.
3. Define *rational decision making*. What does it really mean to be a rational decision maker?
4. Why do people exhibit bounded rationality when solving problems? P. 35
5. Define *scenario*. How is a scenario used in decision making? P.57
6. Some "errors" in decision making can be attributed to the notion of decision making from the gut. Explain what is meant by this and how such errors can happen.

2.7 DECISION MAKING: THE CHOICE PHASE

Choice is the critical act of decision making. The choice phase is the one in which the actual decision and the commitment to follow a certain course of action are made. The boundary between the design and choice phases is often unclear because certain activities can be performed during both of them and because the decision maker can return frequently from choice activities to design activities (e.g., generate new alternatives while performing an evaluation of existing ones). The choice phase includes the search for, evaluation of, and recommendation of an appropriate solution to a model. A solution to a model is a specific set of values for the decision variables in a selected alternative. In the MMS running case (see Online File W2.1.2), choices were evaluated as to their viability and profitability. A choice was made to correct data errors and to move a specific number of cars from one set of locations to another. The advertising plan was modified, and new data and features were to be added to the firm's DSS.

Note that solving a model is not the same as solving the problem the model represents. The solution to the model yields a recommended solution to the problem. The problem is considered solved only if the recommended solution is successfully implemented.

Solving a decision-making model involves searching for an appropriate course of action. Search approaches include **analytical techniques** (i.e., solving a formula), **algorithms** (i.e., step-by-step procedures), heuristics (i.e., rules of thumb), and blind searches (i.e., shooting in the dark, ideally in a logical way). These approaches are examined in Chapter 4.

Each alternative must be evaluated. If an alternative has multiple goals, they must all be examined and balanced against each other. **Sensitivity analysis** is used to determine the robustness of any given alternative; slight changes in the parameters should ideally lead to slight or no changes in the alternative chosen. **What-if analysis** is used to explore major changes in the parameters. Goal seeking helps a manager determine values of the decision variables to meet a specific objective. All this is discussed in Chapter 4.

Section 2.7 Review Questions

1. Explain the difference between a principle of choice and the actual choice phase of decision making.
2. Why do some people claim that the choice phase is the point in time when a decision is really made?
3. How can sensitivity analysis help in the choice phase?

2.8 DECISION MAKING: THE IMPLEMENTATION PHASE

In *The Prince*, Machiavelli astutely noted some 500 years ago that there was "nothing more difficult to carry out, nor more doubtful of success, nor more dangerous to handle, than to initiate a new order of things." The implementation of a proposed solution to a problem is, in effect, the initiation of a new order of things or the introduction of change. And change must be managed. User expectations must be managed as part of change management.

The definition of *implementation* is somewhat complicated because implementation is a long, involved process with vague boundaries. Simplistically, the **implementation phase** involves putting a recommended solution to work, not necessarily implementing a computer system. Many generic implementation issues, such as resistance to change, degree of support of top management, and user training, are important in dealing with MSS. In the MMS running case (see Online File W2.1.4), implementation was a little fuzzy. Some decisions were pilot tested by the people responsible for those aspects of decision making before the decision was implemented nationally. Essentially for MMS, implementation involved updating computer systems, testing models and scenarios for impacts, and physically moving the cars from some locations to others. The computer system updates ideally should involve some kind of formal information system development approach, while the actual implementation of the decision may not.

Implementation is covered in detail in later chapters. The decision-making process, though conducted by people, can be improved with computer support, which is the subject of the next section.

Section 2.8 Review Questions

 1. Define *implementation*.
 2. How can a DSS support the implementation of a decision?

2.9   HOW DECISIONS ARE SUPPORTED

In Chapter 1, we discussed the need for computerized decision support and briefly described some decision aids. Here we relate specific MSS technologies to the decision-making process (see Figure 2.2). Databases, data marts, and especially data warehouses are important technologies in supporting all phases of decision making, particularly when accessed via Web-based interfaces. They provide the data that drive decision making.

Support for the Intelligence Phase

The primary requirement of decision support for the intelligence phase is the ability to scan external and internal information sources for opportunities and problems and to interpret what the scanning discovers. Web tools and sources are extremely useful for environmental

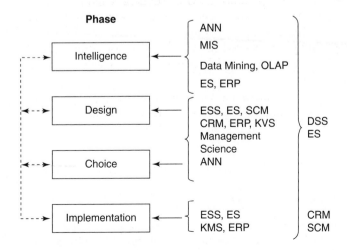

FIGURE 2.2   DSS Support

scanning. Web browsers provide useful front ends for a variety of tools, from OLAP to data mining and data warehouses. Data sources can be internal or external. Internal sources may be accessible via a corporate intranet. External sources are many and varied.

Decision support/BI technologies can be very helpful. For example, a data warehouse can support the intelligence phase by continuously monitoring both internal and external information, looking for early signs of problems and opportunities through a Web-based enterprise information portal (also called a dashboard), as in the MMS running case (see Online File W2.1.2). Similarly, (automatic) data (and Web) mining (which may include expert systems [ES], CRM, genetic algorithms, neural networks, and other ADM systems) and (manual) OLAP also support the intelligence phase by identifying relationships among activities and other factors. Geographic information systems (GIS) can be utilized either as stand-alone systems or integrated with these systems so that a decision maker can determine opportunities and problems in a spatial sense. These tools are often described as business analytics (BA) or Web analytics applications. These relationships can be exploited for competitive advantage (e.g., CRM identifies classes of customers to approach with specific products and services). A KMS can be used to identify similar past situations and how they were handled. GSS can be used to share information and for brainstorming. As seen in Chapter 14, even cell phone and GPS data can be captured to create a micro-view of customers and their habits. The Internet provides consistent, familiar interface tools via portals and access to critical, often fuzzy information necessary to identify problems and opportunities. Finally, visualization systems and tools, typically embedded within many of these packages, can be utilized to present results in formats that assist decision makers in identifying opportunities and problems.

Another aspect of identifying internal problems and capabilities involves monitoring the current status of operations. When something goes wrong, it can be identified quickly and the problem can be solved. Tools such as business activity monitoring (BAM), business process management (BPM), and product life-cycle management (PLM) provide such capability to decision makers.

ES, in contrast, can render advice regarding the nature of a problem, its classification, its seriousness, and the like. ES can advise on the suitability of a solution approach and the likelihood of successfully solving the problem. One of the primary areas of ES success is interpreting information and diagnosing problems. This capability can be exploited in the intelligence phase. Even intelligent agents can be used to identify opportunities.

Another area of support is reporting. Both routine and ad hoc reports can aid in the intelligence phase. For example, regular reports can be designed to assist in the problem-finding activity by comparing expectations with current and projected performance. Web-based OLAP tools are excellent at this task. So are visualization tools and electronic document management systems.

Much of the information used in seeking new opportunities is qualitative, or soft. This indicates a high level of unstructuredness in the problems, thus making DSS quite useful in the intelligence phase.

The Internet and advanced database technologies have created a glut of data and information available to decision makers—so much that it can detract from the quality and speed of decision making. Fortunately, intelligent agents and other artificial intelligence tools can lessen the burden. Technology Insights 2.3 describes some of the issues that managers are grappling with in the digital age of decision making.

Support for the Design Phase

The design phase involves generating alternative courses of action, discussing the criteria for choices and their relative importance, and forecasting the future consequences of using various alternatives. Several of these activities can use standard models provided

TECHNOLOGY INSIGHTS 2.3   Decision Making in the Digital Age

Kepner-Tregoe, Inc. (**kepner-tregoe.com**) surveyed managers and workers across the United States to determine how they cope with the need for faster decision making and how companies are balancing the requirement for speed with the concomitant need for quality.

Decision makers are under pressure to keep up, but in the process they often sacrifice the quality of decision making. Digital-age decision makers are not making the most of what is available. They are often unable to gather sufficient information, they do a poor job of sharing that information, and they fail to involve the right people in the decision process. The following are Kepner-Tregoe's key findings:

- ***More decisions are being made in less time.*** Both managers and workers must make more decisions in the same or less time. Sixty-five percent of workers and 77 percent of managers said that they must make more decisions every day. At the same time, most also agreed that the amount of time they have to make decisions has either decreased or stayed the same.

- ***Respondents are missing opportunities.*** Despite the pressure to make speedy decisions, nearly 75 percent of workers and 80 percent of managers said they miss opportunities because they don't make decisions quickly enough. Most agreed that decisions are frequently not implemented in a timely manner.

- ***Many feel as if they are losing the race.*** When asked to compare the speed of their organization's decision making to that of rivals, only one-quarter of workers and fewer than one-third of managers said they are moving faster than their competition.

- ***Many barriers to speed are human.*** Workers and managers closely agreed that the need for multiple approvals is the most frequently encountered barrier. Other common roadblocks mentioned are organizational politics, changing priorities, and getting people to agree up front on what they want a decision to accomplish.

- ***IT clearly has a widespread influence.*** When asked specifically where IT has become the most important source of information for decision making, both workers and managers listed budgeting/finance, purchasing, and customer service, followed closely by daily product management, quality/productivity, personnel/human resources, and process improvement.

- ***Sources of information are constantly changing.*** When asked where they get the information on which they base their decisions today (compared to three years ago), both workers and managers described a major shift from real to virtual sources. The most dramatic change was in the increased use of e-mail. Most also agreed not only that the quantity of information has increased, but that the quality of the information has increased as well.

- ***Decision-making amnesia is rampant.*** Organizations are not very effective at preserving their decision-making experiences. Of those who said that their organizations have a system in place to house decision criteria, 77 percent of workers and 82 percent of managers said they couldn't assess the utility of their databases.

Sources: Modified from D. K. Wessel, "Decision Making in the Digital Age," *DM Review 2002 Resource Guide*, Vol. 12, No. 12, December 2001; and material from Kepner-Tregoe, Inc., **kepner-tregoe.com** (accessed July 2009).

by a DSS (e.g., financial and forecasting models, available as applets). Alternatives for structured problems can be generated through the use of either standard or special models. However, the generation of alternatives for complex problems requires expertise that can be provided only by a human, brainstorming software, or an ES. OLAP and data mining software are quite useful in identifying relationships that can be used in models (see the MMS running case in Online File W2.1.2). Most DSS have quantitative analysis capabilities, and an internal ES can assist with qualitative methods as well as with the expertise required in selecting quantitative analysis and forecasting models. A KMS should certainly be consulted to determine whether such a problem has been encountered before or whether there are experts on hand who can provide quick understanding and answers. CRM systems, revenue management systems (as in the MMS running case), ERP, and SCM systems software are useful in that they provide models of business processes that can test assumptions and scenarios. If a problem requires brainstorming to help identify important issues and options, a GSS may prove helpful. Tools that provide cognitive mapping can also help. All these tools can be accessed via the Web. Cohen et al. (2001) described several Web-based tools that provide decision support, mainly in the design phase, by providing models and reporting of alternative results. Each of their cases has saved millions of dollars annually by utilizing these tools. Web-based DSS are helping engineers in product design as well as decision makers solving business problems.

Support for the Choice Phase

In addition to providing models that rapidly identify a best or good-enough alternative, a DSS can support the choice phase through what-if and goal-seeking analyses. Different scenarios can be tested for the selected option to reinforce the final decision. Again, a KMS helps identify similar past experiences; CRM, ERP, and SCM systems are used to test the impacts of decisions in establishing their value, leading to an intelligent choice. An ES can be used to assess the desirability of certain solutions as well as to recommend an appropriate solution. If a group makes a decision, a GSS can provide support to lead to consensus.

Support for the Implementation Phase

This is where "making the decision happen" occurs. The DSS benefits provided during implementation may be as important as or even more important than those in the earlier phases. DSS can be used in implementation activities such as decision communication, explanation, and justification.

Implementation-phase DSS benefits are partly due to the vividness and detail of analyses and reports. For example, one chief executive officer (CEO) gives employees and external parties not only the aggregate financial goals and cash needs for the near term, but also the calculations, intermediate results, and statistics used in determining the aggregate figures. In addition to communicating the financial goals unambiguously, the CEO signals other messages. Employees know that the CEO has thought through the assumptions behind the financial goals and is serious about their importance and attainability. Bankers and directors are shown that the CEO was personally involved in analyzing cash needs and is aware of and responsible for the implications of the financing requests prepared by the finance department. Each of these messages improves decision implementation in some way. In the MMS running case (see Online File W2.1), team members had access to information in order to make decisions, and they also had information about the results of the decisions.

BAM, BPM, PLM, KMS, EIS, ERP, CRM, and SCM are all useful in tracking how well an implementation is working. GSS is useful for a team to collaborate in establishing implementation effectiveness. For example, a decision might be made to get rid of unprofitable customers. An effective CRM can identify classes of customers to get rid of, identify the impact of doing so, and then verify that it really worked that way.

All phases of the decision-making process can be supported by improved communication through collaborative computing via GSS and KMS. Computerized systems can facilitate communication by helping people explain and justify their suggestions and opinions.

Decision implementation can also be supported by ES. An ES can be used as an advisory system regarding implementation problems (such as handling resistance to change). Finally, an ES can provide training that may smooth the course of implementation.

Impacts along the value chain, though reported by an EIS through a Web-based enterprise information portal, are typically identified by BAM, BPM, SCM, and ERP systems. CRM systems report and update internal records, based on the impacts of the implementation. These inputs are then used to identify new problems and opportunities—a return to the intelligence phase.

New Technology Support for Decision Making

Web-based systems have clearly influenced how decision making is supported. With the development of mobile commerce (m-commerce), more and more personal devices (e.g., personal digital assistants [PDAs], cell phones, tablet computers, laptop computers) can access information sources, and users can respond to systems with information updates, collaboration efforts, and decisions. This is especially important for salespeople, who can be more effective if they can access their CRM while on the road and then enter orders. Constant access to corporate data, inventory and otherwise, can only help them in their work. Overall, wireless devices are taking on greater importance in the enterprise, generally by accessing specialized Web servers that provide data and communication directly to m-commerce devices.

Application Case 2.2 gives an example of RFID technology in use at a museum.

APPLICATION CASE 2.2

Advanced Technology for Museums: RFID Makes Art Come Alive

Museums are not known for utilizing state-of-the-art technology in general. However, some are now using high-tech devices to understand their visitors (customers) to determine what they want to see (demand) and when. Visitors using handheld devices at several of the Smithsonian museums can view maps; access interactive lists of exhibits; get help locating specific items; find schedules of guided tours; see video clips and pictures, including some of items not on the floor; instant message (IM) other visitors; and obtain information about others in their group. The Smithsonian hopes that this system, called SIguide, will produce a better museum experience for visitors and allow them to spend their time effectively. It can also promote various underutilized exhibits, essentially advertising them to an appropriate audience based on interest detected by the system. Through location-tracking technology, the system can track demand for specific exhibits or types of exhibits, and the Smithsonian can make better decisions about future exhibits.

The Cleveland Museum of Art is taking its tracking technology a step further by using radio frequency identification (RFID) tags. The system collects detailed information about visitors' use of the exhibits and helps determine individual versus group behavior to identify high-demand exhibits. It can also track viewing and movement patterns through the museum, ultimately leading to an experience personalized for each visitor.

The Museum of Natural History in Aarhus, Denmark, has put RFID tags next to an exhibit of 50 stuffed birds. Visitors carry a PDA to access the text, quizzes, and audio and video clips that are stored in them. Some museums are even tagging their collections with RFID to track them internally.

Sources: Based on C. Lindquist, "Magical History Tour," *CIO,* July 15, 2005; S. Hsi and H. Fait, "RFID Enhances Visitors' Museum Experience at the Exploratorium," *Communications of the ACM,* Vol. 48, No. 9, September 2005, pp. 60–65; and F. Khan, "Museum Puts Tags on Stuffed Birds," *RFID Journal,* September 7, 2004.

Section 2.9 Review Questions

1. Describe how DSS/BI technologies and tools can aid in each phase of decision making.
2. Describe how new technologies can provide decision-making support.

2.10 RESOURCES, LINKS, AND THE TERADATA UNIVERSITY NETWORK CONNECTION

The use of this chapter and most other chapters in this book can be enhanced by the tools described in the following sections.

Resources and Links

We recommend looking at the following resources and links for further reading and explanations:

- The Data Warehousing Institute (**tdwi.org**)
- *CIO* magazine (**cio.com**)
- DSS Resources (**dssresources.com**)

Cases

All major BI/BA vendors (e.g., MicroStrategy, Teradata, Oracle, IBM, Fair Isaac, SAP, Information Builders, Expert Choice) provide interesting customer success stories on BI/BA technology use. Because these technologies are ultimately utilized in decision making, there are always aspects of the decision-making process described in the story. Look at the vendors' Web sites for cases. Cases are also available at the Teradata University Network (**teradatauniversitynetwork.com**). Specifically, consider "Harrah's High Payoff from Customer Information" and "Whirlpool." Academic-oriented cases are available at the Harvard Business School Case Collection: **hbsp.harvard.edu/product/cases**.

Vendors, Products, and Demos

There are many online sources for online decision making. Many vendors are listed in Chapter 4. However, to get started, consider the Expert Choice package (**expertchoice.com**).

Periodicals

We recommend the following periodicals:

- *Decision Support Systems* (**elsevier.com**)
- *CIO* (**cio.com**)
- *CIO Insight* (**cioinsight.com**)
- *Baseline Magazine* (**baselinemag.com**)

The Teradata University Connection

Teradata University Network.com (TUN) (**teradatastudentnetwork.com**, for students) provides a wealth of material related to decision making, mostly through BI tools that include data warehouses, data marts, visualization, OLAP, data mining, and other forms of business analytics. The site provides cases, articles, exercises, and software.

Chapter Highlights

- Managerial decision making is synonymous with the whole process of management.
- Human decision styles need to be recognized in designing MSS.
- Individual and group decision making can both be supported by MSS.
- Problem solving is also opportunity evaluation.
- A model is a simplified representation or abstraction of reality.
- Models are used extensively in MSS; they can be iconic, analogical, or mathematical.
- Decision making involves four major phases: intelligence, design, choice, and implementation.
- In the intelligence phase, the problem (opportunity) is identified, classified, and decomposed (if needed), and problem ownership is established.
- In the design phase, a model of the system is built, criteria for selection are agreed on, alternatives are generated, results are predicted, and a decision methodology is created.

- There is a trade-off between model accuracy and cost.
- Rationality is an important assumption in decision making. Rational decision makers can establish preferences and order them consistently.
- In the choice phase, alternatives are compared, and a search for the best (or a good-enough) solution is launched. Many search techniques are available.
- In implementing alternatives, a decision maker should consider multiple goals and sensitivity-analysis issues.
- Satisficing is a willingness to settle for a satisfactory solution. In effect, satisficing is suboptimizing. Bounded rationality results in decision makers satisficing.
- Computer systems, especially those that are Web based, can support all phases of decision making by automating many of the required tasks or by applying artificial intelligence.

Key Terms

algorithm *58*
analog model *44*
analytical techniques *58*
choice phase *46*
decision making *42*
decision style *42*
decision variable *50*
descriptive model *54*
design phase *46*
effectiveness *42*
efficiency *42*
iconic model *44*
implementation phase *59*
intelligence phase *46*
mental model *44*
normative model *51*
optimization *51*
principle of choice *51*
problem ownership *50*
problem solving *42*
satisficing *55*
scenario *57*
sensitivity analysis *58*
simulation *54*
suboptimization *53*
what-if analysis *58*

Questions for Discussion

1. Why is intuition still an important aspect of decision making?
2. Define *efficiency* and *effectiveness*, and compare and contrast the two.
3. Why is it important to focus on the effectiveness of a decision, not necessarily the efficiency of making a decision?
4. What are some of the measures of effectiveness in a toy manufacturing plant, a restaurant, an educational institution, and the U.S. Congress?
5. Even though implementation of a decision involves change, and change management is very difficult, explain how change management has *not* changed very much in thousands of years. Use specific examples throughout history.
6. Despite the advances in ADM methods and tools, why should we still insist that a human being be responsible for every decision?
7. Why should all information system development projects focus on some aspect of decision making in practice?
8. Your company is considering opening a branch in China. List typical activities in each phase of the decision (intelligence, design, choice, implementation) of whether to open a branch.
9. You are about to sell your car. What principles of choice are you most likely to use in deciding whether to offer or reject offers? Explain.
10. You are about to buy a car. Using Simon's four-phase model, describe your activities at each step.
11. The use of scenarios is popular in computerized decision making. Why? For what types of decisions is this technique most appropriate?

12. Explain, through an example, the support given to decision makers by computers in each phase of the decision process.
13. Some experts believe that the major contribution of DSS is to the implementation of a decision. Why is this so?

14. Most managers are capable of using the telephone without understanding or even considering the electrical and magnetic theories involved. Why is it necessary for managers to understand MSS tools to use them wisely?

Exercises

TERADATA STUDENT NETWORK (TSN) AND OTHER HANDS-ON EXERCISES

1. Choose a case at TSN or use the case that your instructor chooses. Describe in detail what decisions were to be made in the case and what process was actually followed. Be sure to describe how technology assisted or hindered the decision-making process and what the decision's impacts were.
2. Most companies and organizations have downloadable demos or trial versions of their software products on the Web so that you can copy and try them out on your own computer. Others have online demos. Find one that provides decision support, try it out, and write a short report about it. Include details about the intended purpose of the software, how it works, and how it supports decision making.
3. Early in the chapter, we mention the Great Wall of China as a major blunder. Investigate it. Study the history of the Great Wall. Look up why it was constructed, how it was done, how long it took, and similar facts. Why did it fail to meet its primary objective? Identify four other equally major blunders and explain what happened in each case.
4. According to Bennis and Nanus (2003), "Managers are people who do things right and leaders are people who do the right thing. The difference may be summarized as activities of vision and judgment—effectiveness—versus activities of mastering routines—efficiency." (Also see Baron and Padwa, 2000.) Explain how this view relates to decision making, managers, executives, and systems.
5. Comment on Simon's (1977) philosophy that managerial decision making is synonymous with the whole process of management. Does this make sense? Explain. Use a real-world example in your explanation.
6. Consider a situation in which you have a preference about where you go to college: You want to be not too far away from home and not too close. Why might this situation arise? Explain how this situation fits with rational decision-making behavior.
7. When you were looking for a college program, somehow you were able to decide on going where you are now. Examine your decision-making process and describe it in a report. Explain how you eliminated the many thousands of programs around the world and then in your own country or region. What criteria were important? What was your final set of alternatives? How did you decide among them? Compare your results with those of others in the class.

8. You are about to buy a car. What criteria are important? What specific choices do you have, and how will you limit your choices? Go to Expert Choice, Inc. (**expertchoice .com**) to learn about the AHP and structure your problem within its framework. Does this make intuitive sense? Explain why it does or does not.
9. Stories about suboptimization issues abound in some formerly centrally planned national economies in which the output of factories was measured by seemingly useful measures, with unexpected and disastrous results. Specifically, a ball-bearing factory's output was measured by the total weight of the ball bearings produced, so the plant manager decided to produce one very large ball bearing each month. There was a shoe factory where output was measured by the number of left shoes, so the plant manager decided to make only left shoes to double the factory's official output. Explain in detail how the measure of the result variable (output) of a subsystem can contribute to bad decisions that lead to suboptimized results for the entire system and what the consequences might be. Think in terms of what it means to establish a principle of choice. This is not unique to centrally planned economies but can happen in any organization. Give an example from your personal or professional life in which this happened.
10. According to H. L. Mencken, "There is always an easy solution to every human problem—neat, plausible and wrong" ("The Divine Afflatus," *New York Evening Mail*, Nov. 16, 1917; later published in *Prejudices: Second Series*, 1920; and *A Mencken Chrestomathy*, 1949). Explain this statement in the light of the decision-making material in this chapter and examples with which you are familiar.

TEAM ASSIGNMENTS AND ROLE-PLAYING

1. Interview a person who has recently been involved in making a business decision. Try to identify the following:
   a. The scope of the problem solved.
   b. The people involved in the decision. (Explicitly identify the problem owners.)
   c. Simon's phases. (You may have to ask specific questions, such as how the problem was identified.)
   d. The alternatives (choices) and the decision chosen.
   e. How the decision was implemented.
   f. How computers were used to support the decision making or why they were not used.
   Produce a detailed report, describing an analysis of this information, and clearly state how closely this real-world

decision-making process compares to Simon's suggested process. Clearly identify how computers were used or explain why they were not used in this situation.

2. Develop a cognitive map of the decision-making problem of selecting a job or a university program, using Decision Explorer from Banxia Software, Ltd. (**banxia.com**). Describe your thought processes and how you developed the map.

3. Watch the movie *12 Angry Men* (1957), starring Henry Fonda. Comment on the group decision-making process that the jury followed. Explain how this is a demonstration of group decision making. Does it fit into Simon's four-phase model? Explain why or why not, citing examples from the movie.

4. Watch the movie *The Bachelor* (1999), starring Chris O'Donnell. In it, a man must marry by a deadline to inherit $100 million. There are many alternatives, but the criteria are quite fuzzy. Watch the scene toward the end of the movie where about 1,000 brides converge on a church and want to know what the criteria are. Explain how the main character describes his criteria and what they are. Explain why they are quite vague. Explain what his criteria really are. Given enough time, compare your answers to Piver (2000).

5. Have everyone in your group individually make a list of the factors they considered when selecting a place to live (or alternatively, the program of study in which you are enrolled) and approximately how much weight (percentage) they individually put on each factor. Determine which and how many of the factors were common. Using a common list of factors, have each individual weight them. Discuss within the group why certain factors were important and others were not. Take an average of the factors' weights and see if anyone's factor weights were close. Write up your results in a report, indicating how these factors affect this type of decision making.

INTERNET EXERCISES

1. Search the Internet for material on managerial decision making. What general classes of materials can you identify in a sample of 10 sites?

2. Many colleges and universities post their course catalogs, course descriptions, and syllabi on the Web. Examine a sample of 10 courses in at least 4 different disciplines within a business school. Compare their topical material and identify how each course relates to decision making. What is the major focus of these courses? What percentage of them includes computerized support? In which departments are they typically found?

3. Search the Internet for companies and organizations that provide computerized support for managerial decision making. (Hint: Search for *business intelligence*.) Take a sample of five software vendors and characterize their products, based on specific functional market area (e.g., marketing, manufacturing, insurance, transportation), level of managerial support (e.g., strategic, tactical, operational, transactional), type of computerized tool (e.g., DSS, data mining, BI, OLAP, EIS, ES, Artificial Neural Networks [ANN], cluster analysis), and how they utilize Web technologies. Take a sample of 10 nonvendors (e.g., consultants). What kinds of support do they provide?

4. Access a DSS/BI software vendor's Web site (select one or use the one your instructor selects). Select a success story of the software or use the one your instructor selects. Describe in detail what decisions were to be made and what process was actually followed. Be sure to describe how technology assisted (or hindered) the decision-making process and what the decision's impacts were.

END OF CHAPTER APPLICATION CASE

Decisions and Risk Management (!) That Led to the Subprime Mortgage Crisis

The U.S. financial markets have experienced a storm unseen since the Great Depression (some say worse than that). Losses in the financial sector wiped out much of the liquidity in the U.S. credit industry, further affecting companies' ability to borrow and continue operations. The ensuing recession has had a staggering effect on the world economy, leading to millions of job losses and causing national governments to intervene to keep the world financial systems from collapsing altogether. Because our objective in this book is to understand and learn about computer-supported decision making, we will not dig deep into financial aspects of what led to the subprime mortgage crisis. Many of the following Web sites do a good job of explaining or illustrating what happened. Review the material at the following sites (and thousands of others like these):

- **www.businesspundit.com/sub-prime/** (Caution: some people may find a few words offensive.)
- E. L. Andrews, "My Personal Credit Crisis," **nytimes.com/2009/05/17/magazine/17fore**

closure-t.html?_r=1&ref=magazine&page-wanted=print
- **en.wikipedia.org/wiki/Subprime_mortgage_crisis**
- **bestwaytoinvest.com/subprime-meltdown**
- **investopedia.com/articles/07/subprime-overview.asp**

Read as many of these stories as you can. They paint a picture of a complete disregard for risk, irrational assumptions, lying, pure and simple greed, and follow-the-crowd mentality (groupthink). It will be a good learning experience to discuss the crisis in context of the decision-making model described in this chapter.

Questions for the Case

1. Apply principles of the intelligence phase of Simon's decision-making model, and discuss major problems that led to the subprime mortgage crisis.
2. Given what has already taken place, reapply the intelligence phase principles to determine the *current* state of the problem.
3. What can you recommend about the crisis now? Apply design and choice phase principles to guide you.
4. What issues will you have to keep in mind as you move your proposed solutions to implementation?

References

Allan, N., R. Frame, and I. Turney. (2003). "Trust and Narrative: Experiences of Sustainability." *The Corporate Citizen*, Vol. 3, No. 2.

Baker, J., and M. Cameron. (1996, September). "The Effects of the Service Environment on Affect and Consumer Perception of Waiting Time: An Integrative Review and Research Propositions." *Journal of the Academy of Marketing Science*, Vol. 24, pp. 338–349.

Barba-Romero, S. (2001, July/August). "The Spanish Government Uses a Discrete Multicriteria DSS to Determine Data Processing Acquisitions." *Interfaces*, Vol. 31, No. 4, pp. 123–131.

Baron, D., and L. Padwa. (2000). *Moses on Management*. New York: Pocket Books.

Bazerman, M. H. (2005). *Judgment in Managerial Decision Making*, 6th ed. New York: Wiley.

Beach, L. R. (2005). *The Psychology of Decision Making: People in Organizations*, 2nd ed. Thousand Oaks, CA: Sage.

Bennis, W., and B. Nanus. (2003). *Leaders: Strategies for Taking Charge*. New York: HarperBusiness Essentials.

Bhushan, N., and K. Rai. (2004). *Strategic Decision Making: Applying the Analytic Hierarchy Process*. Heidelberg: Springer-Verlag.

Borges, M. R. S., J. A. Pino, and C. Valle. (2002, July 4–7). "On the Implementation and Follow-up of Decisions." *Proceedings of DSIage 2002*, Cork, Ireland.

Churchman, C. W. (1982). *Prediction and Optimal Decision*. Westport, CT: Greenwood Publishing Group.

Cohen, M.-D., C. B. Charles, and A. L. Medaglia. (2001, March/April). "Decision Support with Web-Enabled Software." *Interfaces*, Vol. 31, No. 2, pp. 109–129.

Crainer, S. (2002). *The 75 Greatest Management Decisions Ever Made: . . . And 21 of the Worst*. New York: MJF Books.

Cross, V. (2001, May/June). "Ready for Some Decision Making Help?" *EDUCAUSE Review*, Vol. 36, No. 3.

Davenport, T. (2004, October 1). "Decision Evolution." *CIO*.

Denning, S. (2000). *The Springboard: How Storytelling Ignites Action in Knowledge-Era Organizations*. Burlington, MA: Butterworth-Heinemann.

Drummond, H. (2001). *The Art of Decision Making: Mirrors of Imagination, Masks of Fate*. New York: Wiley.

Eden, C., and F. Ackermann. (2002). "Emergent Strategizing." In A. Huff and M. Jenkins (eds.). *Mapping Strategic Thinking*. Thousand Oaks, CA: Sage Publications.

Forman, E. H., and M. A. Selly. (2001). *Decision by Objectives*. Singapore: World Scientific Publishing Co.

Gharajedaghi, J. (2006). *Systems Thinking: Managing Chaos and Complexity: A Platform for Designing Business Architecture*, 2nd ed. Woburn, MA: Butterworth-Heinemann.

Goodie, A. (2004, Fall). "Goodie Studies Pathological Gamblers' Risk-Taking Behavior." *The Independent Variable*. Athens, GA: The University of Georgia, Institute of Behavioral Research. Available at **ibr.uga.edu/publications/fall2004.pdf**.

Hesse, R., and G. Woolsey. (1975). *Applied Management Science: A Quick and Dirty Approach*. Chicago: SRA Inc.

Horgan, D. J. (2001, November 15). "Management Briefs: Decision Making: Had We But World Enough and Time." *CIO*.

Hsi, S., and H. Fait. (2005, September). "RFID Enhances Visitors' Museum Experience at the Exploratorium." *Communications of the ACM*, Vol. 48, No. 9, pp. 60–65.

Indart, B. (2005, Summer). "Navigating the Decision Making Process Through Automation." *Business Intelligence Journal*, Vol. 10, No. 3.

Jenkins, M. (2002). "Cognitive Mapping." In D. Partington (ed.). *Essential Skills for Management Research*. Thousand Oaks, CA: Sage Publications.

Kepner, C., and B. Tregoe. (1998). *The New Rational Manager*. Princeton, NJ: Kepner-Tregoe.

Khan, F. (2004, September 7). "Museum Puts Tags on Stuffed Birds." *RFID Journal*.

Koksalan, M., and S. Zionts (eds.). (2001). *Multiple Criteria Decision Making in the New Millennium*. Heidelberg: Springer-Verlag.

Koller, G. R. (2000). *Risk Modeling for Determining Value and Decision Making*. Boca Raton, FL: CRC Press.

Kontoghiorghes, E. J., B. Rustem, and S. Siokos. (2002). *Computational Methods in Decision Making, Economics and Finance*. Boston: Kluwer.

Larson, R. C. (1987, November/December). "Perspectives on Queues: Social Justice and the Psychology of Queueing." *Operations Research*, Vol. 35, No. 6, pp. 895–905.

Lindquist, C. (2005, July 15). "Magical History Tour." *CIO*.

Luce, M. F., J. W. Payne, and J. R. Bettman. (2004). "The Emotional Nature of Decision Trade-offs." In S. J. Hoch, H. C. Kunreuther, and R. E. Gunther (eds.). *Wharton on Making Decisions*. New York: Wiley.

Olavson, T., and C. Fry. (2008, July/August). "Spreadsheet Decision-Support Tools: Lessons Learned at Hewlett-Packard." *Interfaces*, Vol. 38, No. 4, pp. 300–310.

Pauly, M. V. (2004). "Split Personality: Inconsistencies in Private and Public Decisions." In S. J. Hoch, H. C. Kunreuther, and R. E. Gunther (eds.). *Wharton on Making Decisions*. New York: Wiley.

Piver, S. (2000). *The Hard Questions: 100 Essential Questions to Ask Before You Say "I Do."* New York: J.P. Tarcher.

Purdy, J. (2005, Summer). "Decisions, Delusions, & Debacles." *UGA Research Magazine*.

Ratner, R. K., B. E. Kahn, and D. Kahneman. (1999, June). "Choosing Less-Preferred Experiences for the Sake of Variety." *Journal of Consumer Research*, Vol. 26, No. 1.

Saaty, T. L. (2001). *Decision Making for Leaders: The Analytic Hierarchy Process for Decisions in a Complex World*, new ed. Pittsburgh: RWS Publications.

Sawyer, D. C. (1999). *Getting It Right: Avoiding the High Cost of Wrong Decisions*. Boca Raton, FL: St. Lucie Press.

Schwartz, H. (1998). *Rationality Gone Awry? Decision Making Inconsistent with Economic and Financial Theory*. Westport, CT: Praeger.

Schwartz, H. (2004). *The Paradox of Choice*. New York: HarperCollins.

Shoemaker, P. J. H., and J. E. Russo. (2004). "Managing Frames to Make Better Decisions." In S. J. Hoch, H. C. Kunreuther, and R. E. Gunther (eds.). *Wharton on Making Decisions*. New York: Wiley.

Simon, H. (1977). *The New Science of Management Decision*. Englewood Cliffs, NJ: Prentice Hall.

Stewart, T. A. (2002, November). "How to Think with Your Gut." *Business 2.0*.

Sun, R., and C. L. Giles. (2001, July/August). "Sequence Learning: From Recognition and Prediction to Sequential Decision Making." *IEEE Intelligent Systems*.

Tversky, A., P. Slovic, and D. Kahneman. (1990, March). "The Causes of Preference Reversal." *American Economic Review*, Vol. 80, No. 1.

Wessel, D. K. (2001, December). "Decision Making in the Digital Age." *DM Review 2002 Resource Guide*, Vol. 12, No. 12.

Yakov, B.-H. (2001). *Information Gap Decision Theory: Decisions Under Severe Uncertainty*. New York: Academic Press.

CHAPTER

3

Decision Support Systems Concepts, Methodologies, and Technologies: An Overview

LEARNING OBJECTIVES

1 Understand possible decision support system (DSS) configurations

2 Understand the key differences and similarities between DSS and BI systems

3 Describe DSS characteristics and capabilities

4 Understand the essential definition of DSS

5 Understand important DSS classifications

6 Understand DSS components and how they integrate

7 Describe the components and structure of each DSS component: the data management subsystem, the model management subsystem, the user interface (dialog)

subsystem, the knowledge-based management subsystem, and the user

8 Explain Internet impacts on DSS and vice versa

9 Explain the unique role of the user in DSS versus management information systems (MIS)

10 Describe DSS hardware and software platforms

11 Become familiar with a DSS development language

12 Understand current DSS issues

In Chapter 1, we introduced DSS and stressed its support in the solution of complex managerial problems. In Chapter 2, we presented the methodology of decision making. In this chapter, we show how DSS superiority is achieved by examining its capabilities, structure, and classifications in the following sections:

3.1 Opening Vignette: Decision Support System Cures for Health Care
3.2 Decision Support System Configurations
3.3 Decision Support System Description
3.4 Decision Support System Characteristics and Capabilities
3.5 Decision Support System Classifications
3.6 Components of Decision Support Systems
3.7 The Data Management Subsystem
3.8 The Model Management Subsystem
3.9 The User Interface (Dialog) Subsystem

3.10 The Knowledge-Based Management Subsystem
3.11 The Decision Support System User
3.12 Decision Support System Hardware
3.13 A DSS Modeling Language: Planners Lab
3.14 Resources, Links, and the Teradata University Network Connection

3.1 OPENING VIGNETTE: DECISION SUPPORT SYSTEM CURES FOR HEALTH CARE

The Problem

Avantas is an Omaha, Nebraska-based company recognized for proven best-practice work strategies for the health industry. These work strategies were developed to deliver immediate margin recovery and long-term financial savings by focusing on those areas in which health care organizations can realize continual and quantifiable improvement by creating value with regard to staffing and scheduling activities. Blending state-of-the-art technology and sound business processes, Avantas creates a precise balance of labor supply to patient demand across the client enterprise, regardless of the hospital's size or geographic location.

Avantas works with a variety of hospital systems to better manage their nursing resources. In this specific situation, Avantas worked with a client to help improve staffing decisions. The client needed to decide whether the five-hospital system needed to hire additional temporary staff to cover staffing demands during the upcoming flu season, a time of high patient volume. The five hospitals are located in the same metropolitan area. This particular exercise focused on the inpatient units (general medical/surgical and intensive care units) at each hospital.

This particular application of Planners Lab™ addressed staffing needs of a hospital system during a typical high-demand period. Typically, the flu season strains hospitals' nursing resources. Not only do the hospitals need more nurses to handle the increase in patients, but the nurses also have an increased rate of unplanned absences due to the flu. This can cause major staffing problems for a hospital, including the possibility of turning away patients. In an effort to better prepare for the increased demand. The hospital system decided to look at current staffing and forecasted hiring levels to prepare for any potential weeks or days when staffing could be critically low. This high-demand time generally begins in January and continues through the end of March. The problem was analyzed at the end of October, allowing time for adjustments before patient volumes increased.

Solution

Decision makers in this case were the hospital system's CFO, the chief nursing executive, unit managers, and the human resources director. They wanted to adopt an easy-to-use tool. Avantas decided to use Planners Lab after previous attempts at analyzing this situation in Excel. Planners Lab offered an easy-to-use alternative to Excel to create "what-if" scenarios.

The hospital system's human resource staff had established short-term hiring goals to increase the number of nurses on staff. They had to keep in mind that these nurses would need at least 12 weeks of orientation before they would be available to take patients without assistance. The model also considered the current turnover rate. Another variable that could be adjusted was the number of temporary nurses contracted to work during the high-volume period. These variables could be adjusted to better accommodate the approaching high-demand time. The hospital system needed a software tool that would make it easy to adjust these variables and view the effects of its decisions.

The model is structured on a biweekly basis in order to incorporate the number of hours worked by core and contingency staff, with a lag of 12 weeks for training new hires. The basic model includes each hospital within the health system, a node for the entire health system, a node for human resource variables, and a node for different adjustments to explain the behavior of new hires. The variables within this model are primarily quantitative and include the following:

- Total hours demanded for 2009 flu season
- Total hours from 2008 flu season

- Total hours from 2008 flu season after new hires
- Gap between hours demanded and actual hours from 2008
- Gap between hours demanded and actual hours from 2008 after new hires
- Total required hires to meet demand
- Total remaining hires to meet demand after new hires

In terms of complexity, the model is straightforward and uses few advanced functions within the Planners Lab program. However, if the model had been completed in Excel, it would have easily made a 30-hour project a 160-hour project in terms of the advanced Excel techniques and expertise needed, such as macro programming. Furthermore, the plain-English assumptions in the Planners Lab model are easily explained to others.

The following example shows how this model can be interpreted, changed, and applied by analyzing the impact of recruiters on the number of new hires. The analysis initially assumed that there were six resident nurse (RN) recruiters who were projected to recruit six individuals per week. Only a few of these new recruits actually make it past the interview stage of the hiring process, which lowers the net number of recruits after turnover is considered. Consequently, if the number of new recruits is less than the turnover, the vacancy rate increases and each hospital faces staffing problems. Figure 3.1 shows the desired vacancy rate versus the projected vacancy rate.

Thus, with all other assumptions holding true, the vacancy rate will be higher than desired, meaning that contingency resources will be needed to help staff the hospitals. Contingency resources include the following types of staff; agency nurses, core staff working overtime, traveling nurses, and other float resources in the hospitals. Contingency resources are more expensive than core staff, so the goal is to reach the desired turnover rate to limit use of these resources.

What happens if the number of hospital recruiters is increased from 6 to 12? Figure 3.2 illustrates such a change.

By changing the assumption from 6 recruiters to 12, one can project that toward the end of January the desired vacancy rate is reached and the need for contingency resources is averted. Other variables, including the Number of Average Recruits per Recruiter per Week, Actual Employment Ratio of New Recruits, Total Resident Nurse (RN) Staff, Current Resident Nurse (RN) Openings, and even the Desired Vacancy Rate, can be adjusted to reach desired scenarios as well.

Without increasing the number of recruiters to 12, the desired vacancy rate would not be achieved in the next 3 months. However, the primary concern was to determine if the hospital system would have enough staff to treat the approaching high-demand flu season. In Figure 3.3, we

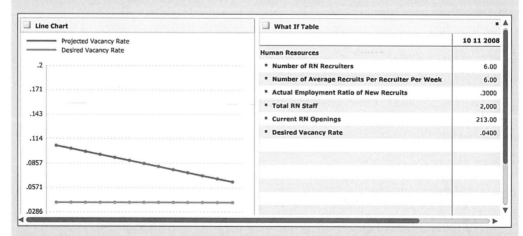

FIGURE 3.1   Projected Vacancy Rate Versus Desired Vacancy Rate

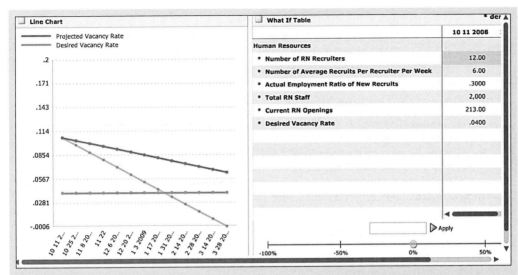

FIGURE 3.2   Projected Vacancy Rate Versus Desired Vacancy Rate "What-if" Scenario with Six Additional RN Recruiters

can see how the additional hires made by the hospital system impacted the total actual hours worked versus the number of hours demanded during the 2009 flu season. The figure shows that the current hiring effort will provide enough staff for most of the flu season to treat the forecasted level of patients with the current levels of contingency resources being utilized. Temporary staff will be needed for a few weeks in the early part of the year, but additional short-term contracts are all that will be necessary.

Results

The hospital system's final decision was that current hiring goals were sufficient to address the upcoming high-demand time. Short-term hiring goals were continually monitored and adjusted if it appeared they were not attainable. The hospital system continued to use the Planners Lab model on a weekly basis to update the hiring goals with the actual hires as they became available. Planners were also able to identify two or three periods of time when staffing was too low, and extra efforts were made to bring on additional staff members in advance of those times.

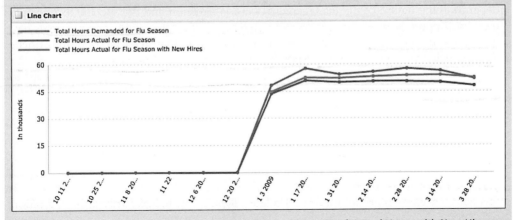

FIGURE 3.3   Demanded Hours Versus Total Actual Hours Versus Total Actual Hours with New Hires

The Planners Lab model provided the information the decision makers needed to make informed decisions on how to proceed. In the past, these decisions would have been made in the dark, because the decision makers did have time to create a complicated spreadsheet. The Planners Lab model was ideal because it was easy to understand and maintain.

Questions for the Opening Vignette

1. Why would this decision involve senior executives in an organization?
2. What types of decision parameters were used in making this decision?
3. What other modeling tools could be used for developing a model?
4. Besides the parameters considered by the modelers in this case study, what other situations could a staffing projection model include?
5. Why is this model a good example of a DSS?

What We Can Learn from This Vignette

A key component of DSS is the ability to visualize the results. It is important for executives to visualize the results of modifying assumptions, as discussed in this example.

Oftentimes, decision makers are forced to make a decision without understanding their true options. This is the reality of business decisions that have to be made in a timely manner. When deadlines are short and analytical resources are tight, companies are left with limited options to thoroughly understand the decisions they need to make.

In this example, decision makers were able to quickly use the Planners Lab tool to set up a DSS to model the complex scenario they faced. Not only did this save the hospital system money, because it required few resources to generate the analysis, but, more important, it enabled the executives to make informed decisions on how to proceed with confidence. Without this tool, a decision could have been made to bring on a number of expensive temporary nurse contracts, which the model showed was not necessary. This is an example of a DSS application. In this chapter, we will see many other related DSS applications. We will also learn to build a DSS using the Planners Lab software employed in this vignette.

Source: This vignette was adapted from a case study contributed by Dr. G. R. Wagner, Julie Kiefer, and Tadd Wood.

3.2 DECISION SUPPORT SYSTEM CONFIGURATIONS

Decision support can be provided in many different configurations. These configurations depend on the nature of the management-decision situation and the specific technologies used for support, as described in Chapter 1 (see Figure 1.2). Decision support systems have three basic components (each with several variations) that are typically deployed online: data, models, and a user interface. Knowledge is an optional component. Each component is managed by software that is either commercially available or must be programmed for the specific task.

The manner in which these components are assembled defines their major capabilities and the nature of the support provided. For example, models are emphasized in a model-oriented DSS. Such models can be customized with a spreadsheet or a programming language or can be provided by standard algorithm-based tools that include linear programming. Similarly, in a data-oriented DSS, a database and its management play the major roles. Both of these types of DSS were used in the opening vignette. In this chapter, we explore all these and related topics, but first we revisit the definitions of a DSS.

Section 3.2 Review Questions

1. List and describe the three major components of DSS. P. 74.
2. Explain how subjective data can be utilized in a DSS in light of the situations described in the opening vignette.
3. Models play a key role in DSS. Why? Explain how models exist in spreadsheet packages such as Excel.

3.3 DECISION SUPPORT SYSTEM DESCRIPTION

The early definitions of a DSS identified it as a system intended to support managerial decision makers in semistructured and unstructured decision situations. DSS were meant to be adjuncts to decision makers, extending their capabilities but not replacing their judgment. They were aimed at decisions that required judgment or at decisions that could not be completely supported by algorithms. Not specifically stated but implied in the early definitions was the notion that the system would be computer based, would operate interactively online, and preferably would have graphical output capabilities, now simplified via Web servers and browsers.

Early definitions of DSS were open to several interpretations. Soon, several other definitions appeared that caused considerable disagreement as to what a DSS really is. For details, see Alter (1980), Bonczek et al. (1980), Keen (1980), Little (1970), and Moore and Chang (1980).

A DSS Application

A DSS is typically built to support the solution of a certain problem or to evaluate an opportunity. This is a key difference between DSS and BI applications. In a very strict sense, **business intelligence (BI)** systems monitor situations and identify problems and/or opportunities, using analytic methods. Reporting plays a major role in BI; the user generally must identify whether a particular situation warrants attention, and then analytical methods can be applied. Again, although models and data access (generally through a data warehouse) are included in BI, DSS typically have their own databases and are developed to solve a specific problem or set of problems. They are therefore called **DSS applications**.

Formally, a DSS is an approach (or methodology) for supporting decision making. It uses an interactive, flexible, adaptable computer-based information system (CBIS) especially developed for supporting the solution to a specific nonstructured management problem. It uses data, provides an easy user interface, and can incorporate the decision maker's own insights. In addition, a DSS includes models and is developed (possibly by end users) through an interactive and iterative process. It supports all phases of decision making and may include a knowledge component. Finally, a DSS can be used by a single user on a PC or can be Web based for use by many people at several locations.

Later in this chapter we explore the various DSS configurations. However, it is beneficial first to deal with the characteristics and capabilities of DSS. We present these next.

Figure 3.4 shows a typical Web-based DSS architecture. This DSS structure utilizes models in BI work. Processing is distributed across several servers in solving large analytical problems. This multitiered architecture uses a Web browser to run programs on an application server. The server accesses data to construct one or more models. Data may also be provided by a data server that optionally extracts data from a data warehouse or a legacy mainframe system. When the user requires that the model be optimized, the model, populated with the data, is transferred to an optimization server. The optimization server accesses additional data from the data server, if needed, solves the problem, and provides the solution directly to the user's Web browser. Generated solution reports, which the application server may massage to make readable by

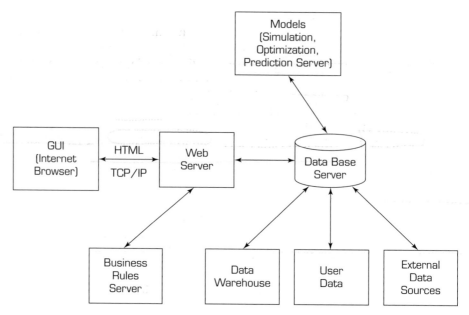

FIGURE 3.4 Multitiered Architecture for Incorporating Optimization, Simulation, and Other Models into Web-Based DSS *Sources:* Based on Delen, D., R. Sharda, and P. Kumar, "Movie Forecast Guru: A Web-Based DSS for Hollywood Managers," *Decision Support Systems,* vol. 43, 2007, pp. 1151–1170; and M. D. Cohen, C. B. Kelly, and A. L. Medaglia, "Decision Support with Web-Enabled Software," *Interfaces,* Vol. 31, No. 2, 2001, pp. 109–129.

managers, may be sent directly to appropriate parties via e-mail or may be made available through another Web portal as part of this enterprise information system (EIS). DSS may also run in stand-alone mode, usually through a spreadsheet or a modeling language, as in Application Case 3.1.

APPLICATION CASE 3.1

A Spreadsheet-Based DSS Enables Ammunition Requirements Planning for the Canadian Army

The Canadian Army offers various training courses throughout the year, which it divides into three semesters. The Army needed a program to help determine an accurate budget for buying ammunitions for the training courses, because in the past it was budgeting around $60 million and only spending around $40 million.

The developers of the new DSS, called the Ammunition Requirements Calculator (ARC), used an Excel spreadsheet at the Army's request. The Army uses 250 types of ammunition, runs around 120 courses, and has multiple sessions of various courses. Thus, a large model was required.

A combination of templates and Visual Basic for Applications (VBA) was used to create the model. VBA allowed creation of a user-friendly interface to enable easy input and button-click access to corresponding macros. To calculate the new budgets, all the user has to do is enter the number of sections of each course for each semester using the Section Training Plan (STP) that the Army creates manually when it decides what courses it wants to offer each semester for a year. The spreadsheet then calculates the number of rounds of each type of ammunition needed for each course. The Army and the developers agreed upon a 5 percent risk level. Additionally, by using VBA macro codes in creating the model, users are able to easily add and delete courses as well as change course priorities.

With this model, the difference between the estimated budget and the actual expenditures has decreased. In addition, it now takes Army staffers less time to create the budget. For example, in fiscal year 2002–2003 there was a $24 million slippage (how much the budget was overestimated compared to the actual expenditure). In fiscal year 2003–2004 this dropped to a $9 million slippage, and in fiscal year 2004–2005 it was down to $1.3 million in slippage. Additionally, any change to the plan now only takes moments to recalculate, whereas earlier a change to the plan took weeks of effort. Finally, the developers of the DSS claim that, to date, they had not heard of a single shortage of ammunition for the training courses since the Army implemented the ARC.

Source: Based on: W. J. Hurley and M. Balez, "A Spreadsheet Implementation of an Ammunition Requirements Planning Model for the Canadian Army," *Interfaces,* Vol. 38, No. 4 July/August 2008, pp. 271–280.

Section 3.3 Review Questions

1. Why do people attempt to narrow the definition of DSS?
2. Give your own definition of *DSS*. Compare it to the definitions in question 1.
3. Explain how the system described in Application Case 3.1 is a DSS. Use the definition from question 2.

3.4 DECISION SUPPORT SYSTEM CHARACTERISTICS AND CAPABILITIES

Because there is no consensus on exactly what a DSS is, there is obviously no agreement on the standard characteristics and capabilities of DSS. The capabilities in Figure 3.5 constitute an ideal set, some members of which are described in the definitions of DSS and illustrated in the opening vignette.

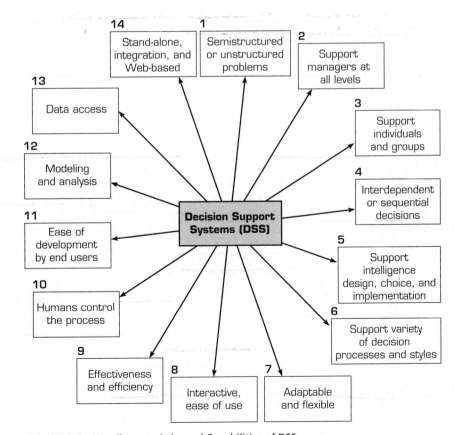

FIGURE 3.5 Key Characteristics and Capabilities of DSS

The term *BI* is not quite synonymous with *DSS*, but the two terms are often used interchangeably in practice. We differentiate the two in that DSS are generally built to solve a specific problem and include their own database(s), whereas BI applications focus on reporting and identifying problems by scanning data extracted from a data warehouse. Both systems generally include analytical tools, although BI systems with such tools are typically called *business analytics systems*. Both DSS and BI applications have become tightly aligned with Web implementations in terms of data and model access from servers and browsers as clients to run the system, although some may run locally as a spreadsheet or another modeling language (refer to Application Case 3.1).

Business analytics (BA) implies the use of models and data to improve an organization's performance or competitive posture. In business analytics, the focus is on the use of models, even if they are buried deeply inside the system. Although extremely effective, advanced models are rarely utilized in BI. (That is changing gradually, as we will see in later chapters.) This is because few managers, and even analysts, understand how and when to apply appropriate models to describe and analyze a particular situation. Data mining and OLAP (online analytical processing) systems have models embedded in them, but they are still not well understood in practice.

Web analytics is an approach to using business analytics tools on real-time Web information to assist in decision making. Most of these applications are related to electronic commerce (e-commerce), especially in CRM, but some have been initiated in product development and supply chain management (SCM).

Finally, the term **predictive analytics** describes the business analytics method of forecasting problems and opportunities rather than simply reporting them as they occur. Predictive analytics utilizes advanced forecasting and simulation models.

The key characteristics and capabilities of DSS (as shown in Figure 3.5) are:

1. Support for decision makers, mainly in semistructured and unstructured situations, by bringing together human judgment and computerized information. Such problems cannot be solved (or cannot be solved conveniently) by other computerized systems or through use of standard quantitative methods or tools. Generally, these problems gain structure as the DSS is developed. Even some structured problems have been solved by DSS.
2. Support for all managerial levels, ranging from top executives to line managers.
3. Support for individuals as well as groups. Less-structured problems often require the involvement of individuals from different departments and organizational levels or even from different organizations. DSS support virtual teams through collaborative Web tools. DSS have been developed to support individual and group work, as well as to support individual decision making and groups of decision makers working somewhat independently.
4. Support for interdependent and/or sequential decisions. The decisions may be made once, several times, or repeatedly.
5. Support in all phases of the decision-making process: intelligence, design, choice, and implementation.
6. Support for a variety of decision-making processes and styles.
7. The decision maker should be reactive, able to confront changing conditions quickly, and able to adapt the DSS to meet these changes. DSS are flexible, so users can add, delete, combine, change, or rearrange basic elements. They are also flexible in that they can be readily modified to solve other, similar problems.
8. User-friendliness, strong graphical capabilities, and a natural language interactive human–machine interface can greatly increase the effectiveness of DSS. Most new DSS applications use Web-based interfaces.

9. Improvement of the effectiveness of decision making (e.g., accuracy, timeliness, quality) rather than its efficiency (e.g., the cost of making decisions). When DSS are deployed, decision making often takes longer, but the decisions are better.

10. The decision maker has complete control over all steps of the decision-making process in solving a problem. A DSS specifically aims to support, not to replace, the decision maker.

11. End users are able to develop and modify simple systems by themselves. Larger systems can be built with assistance from information system (IS) specialists. Spreadsheet packages have been utilized in developing simpler systems. OLAP and data mining software, in conjunction with data warehouses, enable users to build fairly large, complex DSS.

12. Models are generally utilized to analyze decision-making situations. The modeling capability enables experimentation with different strategies under different configurations. In fact, the models make a DSS different from most MIS.

13. Access is provided to a variety of data sources, formats, and types, including GIS, multimedia, and object-oriented data.

14. The DSS can be employed as a stand-alone tool used by an individual decision maker in one location or distributed throughout an organization and in several organizations along the supply chain. It can be integrated with other DSS and/or applications, and it can be distributed internally and externally, using networking and Web technologies.

These key DSS characteristics and capabilities allow decision makers to make better, more consistent decisions in a timely manner, and they are provided by the major DSS components, which we will describe after discussing various ways of classifying DSS (next).

Section 3.4 Review Questions

1. List the key characteristics and capabilities of DSS.
2. Describe how providing support to a workgroup is different from providing support to group work. Explain why it is important to differentiate these concepts.
3. What kinds of DSS can end users develop in spreadsheets?
4. Why is it so important to include a model in a DSS?

3.5 DECISION SUPPORT SYSTEM CLASSIFICATIONS

DSS applications have been classified in several different ways (see Power, 2002; Power and Sharda, 2009). The design process, as well as the operation and implementation of DSS, depends in many cases on the type of DSS involved. However, remember that not every DSS fits neatly into one category. Most fit into the classification provided by the Association for Information Systems Special Interest Group on Decision Support Systems (AIS SIGDSS). We discuss this classification first, followed by other well-known classifications that more or less fit into the former's classification set.

The AIS SIGDSS Classification for DSS

The AIS SIGDSS (**sigs.aisnet.org/SIGDSS/**) has adopted a concise classification scheme for DSS that was proposed by Power (2002). It includes the following categories:

- Communications-driven and group DSS (GSS)
- Data-driven DSS
- Document-driven DSS
- Knowledge-driven DSS, data mining, and management ES applications
- Model-driven DSS

There may also be hybrids that combine two or more categories. These are called compound DSS. We discuss the major categories next.

COMMUNICATIONS-DRIVEN AND GROUP DSS Communications-driven and Group DSS (GSS) include DSS that use computer, collaboration, and communication technologies to support groups in tasks that may or may not include decision making. Essentially, all DSS that support any kind of group work fall into this category. They include those that support meetings, design collaboration, and even supply chain management. Knowledge management systems (KMS) that are developed around communities that practice collaborative work also fall into this category. We discuss these in more detail in later chapters.

DATA-DRIVEN DSS Data-driven DSS are primarily involved with data and processing them into information and presenting the information to a decision maker. Many DSS developed in OLAP and data mining software systems fall into this category. There is minimal emphasis on the use of mathematical models.

In this type of DSS, the database organization, often in a data warehouse, plays a major role in the DSS structure. Early generations of database-oriented DSS mainly used the *relational* database configuration. The information handled by relational databases tends to be voluminous, descriptive, and rigidly structured. A database-oriented DSS features strong report generation and query capabilities. Indeed, this is primarily the current application of the tools marked under the BI umbrella. The chapters on data warehousing and business performance management (BPM) describe several examples of this category of DSS.

DOCUMENT-DRIVEN DSS Document-driven DSS rely on knowledge coding, analysis, search, and retrieval for decision support. They essentially include all DSS that are text based. Most KMS fall into this category. These DSS also have minimal emphasis on utilizing mathematical models. For example, a system that we built for the U.S. Army's Defense Ammunitions Center falls in this category. The main objective of document-driven DSS is to provide support for decision making using documents in various forms: oral, written, and multimedia.

KNOWLEDGE-DRIVEN DSS, DATA MINING, AND MANAGEMENT EXPERT SYSTEMS APPLICATIONS These DSS involve the application of knowledge technologies to address specific decision support needs. Essentially, all artificial intelligence–based DSS fall into this category. When symbolic storage is utilized in a DSS, it is generally in this category. ANN and ES are included here. Because the benefits of these *intelligent DSS* or *knowledge-based DSS* can be large, organizations have invested in them. These DSS are utilized in the creation of *automated decision-making systems*, as described in Chapter 2. The basic idea is that rules are used to automate the decision-making process. These rules are basically either an ES or structured like one. This is important when decisions must be made quickly, as in many e-commerce situations.

MODEL-DRIVEN DSS The major emphases of DSS that are primarily developed around one or more (large-scale/complex) optimization or simulation models typically include significant activities in model formulation, model maintenance, model management in distributed computing environments, and what-if analyses. Many large-scale applications fall into this category. Notable examples include those used by Procter & Gamble (Farasyn et al., 2008), HP (Olavson and Fry, 2008), and many others.

The focus of such systems is on using the model(s) to optimize one or more objectives (e.g., profit). The most common end-user tool for DSS development is Microsoft Excel. Excel includes dozens of statistical packages, a linear programming package (Solver), and many financial and management science models. We will study these in more detail in the next chapter. Specific tools are available for developing financial planning models. We will learn to use one such language in Section 3.13.

6) **COMPOUND DSS** A compound, or hybrid, DSS includes two or more of the major categories described earlier. Often, an ES can benefit by utilizing some optimization, and clearly a data-driven DSS can feed a large-scale optimization model. Sometimes documents are critical in understanding how to interpret the results of visualizing data from a data-driven DSS.

An emerging example of a compound DSS is a product offered by WolframAlpha (**wolframalpha.com**). It compiles knowledge from outside databases, models, algorithms, documents, and so on to provide answers to specific questions. For example, it can find and analyze current data for a stock and compare it with other stocks. It can also tell you how many calories you will burn when performing a specific exercise or the side effects of a particular medicine. Although it is in early stages as a collection of knowledge components from many different areas, it is a good example of a compound DSS in getting its knowledge from many diverse sources and attempting to synthesize it.

APPLICATION CASE 3.2

Expertise Transfer System to Train Future Army Personnel

The Expertise Transfer System (ETS) is a knowledge-transfer system developed at Oklahoma State University. The ETS is designed to capture the knowledge of experienced personnel potentially leaving an organization and those who have been recently deployed to the field. This knowledge is captured on video, converted into units of actionable knowledge called "nuggets," and presented to users in a number of learning-friendly views. ETS begins with an audio/video recorded interview between a subject matter expert (SME) and a "knowledge harvester." Once the videos are recorded, the meat of the ETS process takes place. First, the digital audio/video (A/V) files are converted to text. Currently, this is accomplished with human transcriptionists, but promising results have been obtained using voice-recognition (VR) technologies for transcription, and someday most of the transcription will be automated. Second, the transcriptions are parsed into small units and organized into knowledge nuggets (KN). Simply put, a KN is a significant experience the interviewee had during his or her career. Third, the KNs are incorporated into the ETS. The KN text is linked back to the portion of the A/V interview from which it was harvested. The result is a searchable 30- to 60-second video clip (with captions) of the KN. Finally, additional features are added to the KNs to make them easy to find, more user friendly, and more effective in the classroom.

The ETS offers many KN features for the user. A summary page provides the user with the title or "punchline" of the KN, the interviewee's name and deployment information, and a bulleted-list summary of the KN. Clicking a video link takes users to the KN video clip; clicking a transcript link provides a complete transcript of the nugget. A causal map function gives the user an opportunity to see and understand the interviewee's thought processes as he or she describes the situation captured by the nugget. Related links provide users with a list of regulatory guidance associated with the KN, and a link to related nuggets lists all KNs within the same knowledge domain. Information is also provided about the interviewee, recognized subject matter experts in the KN domain, and supporting images related to the nugget. Each page also includes capabilities for users to rate the KN, make comments about it, and suggest their own tags, to make future searching faster and easier. This brings Web 2.0 concepts of user participation to knowledge management.

One of the primary objectives of the ETS is to quickly capture knowledge from the field and incorporate it into future training. This is accomplished with the My URL feature. This function enables course developers and instructors to use ETS to create a URL that can be passed directly into course curriculum and lesson plans. When an instructor clicks the URL it brings him or her directly to the KN. As such, the "war story" captured in the nugget becomes the course instructor's war story and provides a real-world decision-making or problem-solving scenario right in the classroom. An example of the ETS implemented for the Defense Ammunition Center can be accessed through **dac-etf.iris.okstate.edu**.

Sources: Based on our own documents and S. Iyer, R. Sharda, D. Biros, J. Lucca, and U. Shimp, "Organization of Lessons Learned Knowledge: A Taxonomy of Implementation," *International Journal of Knowledge Management*, Vol. 5, No. 3 (2009).

Holsapple and Whinston's Classification

Holsapple and Whinston (2000) classified DSS into the following six frameworks: text-oriented DSS, database-oriented DSS, spreadsheet-oriented DSS, solver-oriented DSS, rule-oriented DSS, and compound DSS. Essentially, these frameworks readily map into the AIS SIGDSS categories:

- The *text-oriented* DSS are the same as the document-driven DSS.
- The *database-oriented* DSS are the data-driven DSS of the AIS SIGDSS.
- The *spreadsheet-oriented DSS* are generally another form of model-driven DSS in which the functions and add-in programs of the spreadsheet are used to create and manage the models. Because packages such as Excel can include a rudimentary DBMS or can readily interface with one, they can handle some properties of a database-oriented DSS, especially the manipulation of descriptive knowledge.
- The *solver-oriented DSS* map directly into the model-driven DSS.
- The *rule-oriented DSS* include most knowledge-driven DSS, data mining, and management ES applications.
- The *compound DSS* integrates two or more of those cited above and is defined the same as by the SIGDSS.

Alter's Output Classification

Alter's (1980) classification is based on the "degree of action implication of system outputs," or the extent to which system outputs can directly support (or determine) the decision. According to this classification, there are seven categories of DSS (see Table 3.1). The first two types are data oriented, performing data retrieval or analysis; the third deals both with data and models. The remaining four are model oriented, providing simulation capabilities, optimization, or computations that suggest an answer. Clearly, these correspond to the AIS SIGDSS data-driven and model-driven categories, along with compound DSS.

Other DSS Categories

Several other important categories of DSS include (1) institutional and ad hoc DSS; (2) personal, group, and organizational support; (3) individual support system versus GSS; and (4) custom-made systems versus ready-made systems. We discuss these next.

INSTITUTIONAL AND AD HOC DSS Institutional DSS (see Donovan and Madnick, 1977) deal with decisions of a recurring nature. A typical example is a portfolio management system (PMS), which has been used by several large banks for supporting investment decisions. An institutionalized DSS can be developed and refined as it evolves over a number of years, because the DSS is used repeatedly to solve identical or similar problems. It is important to remember that an institutional DSS may not be used by everyone in an organization; it is the *recurring nature of the decision-making problem* that determines whether a DSS is institutional versus ad hoc.

Ad hoc DSS deal with specific problems that are usually neither anticipated nor recurring. Ad hoc decisions often involve strategic planning issues and sometimes management control problems. Justifying a DSS that will be used only once or twice is a major issue

TABLE 3.1 Characteristics of Different Classes of Decision Support Systems

Orientation	Category	Type of Operation	Type of Task	User	Usage Pattern	Time
Data	File drawer systems	Access data items	Operational	Nonmanagerial line personnel	Simple inquiries	Irregular
	Data analysis systems	Ad hoc analysis of data files	Operational analysis	Staff analyst or managerial line personnel	Manipulation and display of data	Irregular or periodic
Data or models	Analysis information systems	Ad hoc analysis involving multiple databases and small models	Analysis, planning	Staff analyst	Programming special reports, developing small models	Irregular, on request
Models	Accounting models	Standard calculations that estimate future results on the basis of accounting definitions	Planning, budgeting	Staff analyst or manager	Input estimates of activity; receive estimated monetary results as output	Periodic (e.g., weekly, monthly, yearly)
	Representational models	Estimating consequences of particular actions	Planning, budgeting	Staff analyst	Input possible decision; receive estimated results as output	Periodic or irregular (ad hoc) analysis
	Optimization models	Calculating an optimal solution to a combinatorial problem	Planning, resource allocation	Staff analyst	Input constraints and objectives; receive answer	Periodic or irregular (ad hoc) analysis
	Suggestion models	Performing calculations that generate a suggested decision	Operational	Nonmanagerial line personnel	Input a structured description of the decision situation; receive a suggested decision as output	Daily or periodic

Source: Condensed from Alter (1980), pp. 90–91.

in DSS development. Countless ad hoc DSS applications have evolved into institutional DSS. Either the problem recurs and the system is reused or others in the organization have similar needs that can be handled by the formerly ad hoc DSS.

PERSONAL, GROUP, AND ORGANIZATIONAL SUPPORT   The support given by DSS can be separated into three distinct, interrelated categories (Hackathorn and Keen, 1981): personal support, group support, and organizational support.

Personal Support   Here the focus is on an individual user performing an activity in a discrete task or decision. The task is fairly independent of other tasks.

Group Support   The focus here is on a group of people, all of whom are engaged in separate but highly interrelated tasks. An example is a typical finance department in which one DSS can serve several employees working on the preparation of a budget. If the use of an ad hoc DSS spreads, it becomes a group support DSS. *Caution:* This is not the same as a GSS that provides collaboration and communication capabilities to a group working together.

Organizational Support   Here the focus is on organizational tasks or activities involving a sequence of operations, different functional areas, possibly different locations, and massive resources. This may also be considered enterprise-wide support. The opening vignette contains several examples of this level of support.

INDIVIDUAL DSS VERSUS A GROUP SUPPORT SYSTEM   Several DSS researchers and practitioners (e.g., Keen, 1980) have pointed out that the fundamental model of a DSS—the lonely decision maker striding down the hall at high noon—is true only for minor decisions. In most organizations, be they public, private, Japanese, European, American, or other, most major decisions are made collectively and cooperatively.

Working in a group can be a complicated process, and it can be supported by computers in what is called a **group support system (GSS)**. Originally, GSS were designed to operate with all participants in the same room (i.e., a decision room) at the same time (e.g., same time/same place situation). Currently, GSS are deployed over the Web and are designed to operate in anytime/anyplace mode. These include courseware (e.g., course management software), such as the Blackboard distance-learning system, which provides support to all individuals and groups involved in a course. As a content management system, it provides support to the group of students taking the course. In addition, it functions as a GSS through its discussion lists, e-mail feature, and virtual classroom. Perhaps the best example of collaboration in this mode is the wiki technology (e.g., **wikipedia.org**) that has become so common. Another example is Microsoft SharePoint. We will learn more about these in Chapter 10.

Custom-Made Systems Versus Ready-Made Systems

Many DSS are custom made for individual users and organizations (e.g., the system in the opening vignette). However, a comparable problem may exist in similar organizations. For example, hospitals, banks, and universities share many similar problems. Similarly, certain nonroutine problems in a functional area (e.g., finance, accounting) can repeat themselves in the same functional area of different areas or organizations. Therefore, it makes sense to build generic DSS that can be used (sometimes with modifications) in several organizations. Such DSS are called *ready-made* and are sold by various vendors (e.g., Cognos, MicroStrategy, Teradata). Essentially, the database, models, interface, and other support features are built in: Just add an organization's data and logo. The major OLAP and data mining vendors provide DSS templates for a variety of functional areas, including finance, real estate, marketing, and accounting. The number of ready-made DSS continues to increase because of their flexibility and low cost. They are typically developed using Internet technologies for database access and communications, and Web browsers for interfaces. They also readily incorporate OLAP and other easy-to-use DSS generators.

One complication in terminology results when an organization develops an institutional system but, because of its structure, uses it in an ad hoc manner. An organization can build a large data warehouse but then use OLAP tools to query it and perform ad hoc analysis to solve nonrecurring problems. The DSS exhibits the traits of ad hoc and institutional systems and also of custom and ready-made systems. Several ERP, CRM, knowledge management (KM), and SCM companies offer DSS applications online. These kinds of systems can be viewed as ready-made, although typically they require modifications (sometimes major) before they can be used effectively.

Section 3.5 Review Questions

1. List the DSS classifications of the AIS SIGDSS.
2. Define *document-driven DSS.*
3. Compare Holsapple and Whinston's classification with the AIS SIGDSS classification.
4. List the capabilities of institutional DSS and ad hoc DSS.
5. Define the term *ready-made DSS.*

3.6 COMPONENTS OF DECISION SUPPORT SYSTEMS

A DSS application can be composed of a data management subsystem, a model management subsystem, a user interface subsystem, and a knowledge-based management subsystem. We show these in Figure 3.6.

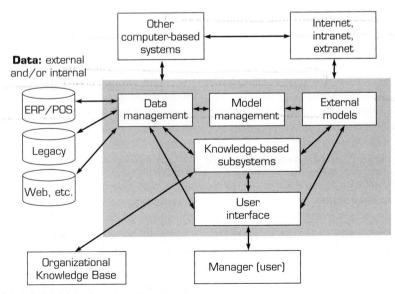

FIGURE 3.6 Schematic View of DSS

The Data Management Subsystem

The data management subsystem includes a database that contains relevant data for the situation and is managed by software called the **database management system (DBMS)**.[1] The data management subsystem can be interconnected with the corporate **data warehouse**, a repository for corporate relevant decision-making data. Usually, the data are stored or accessed via a database Web server.

The Model Management Subsystem

The model management subsystem is a software package that includes financial, statistical, management science, or other quantitative models that provide the system's analytical capabilities and appropriate software management. Modeling languages for building custom models are also included. This software is often called a **model base management system (MBMS)**. This component can be connected to corporate or external storage of models. Model solution methods and management systems are implemented in Web development systems (such as Java) to run on application servers.

The User Interface Subsystem

The user communicates with and commands the DSS through the user interface subsystem. The user is considered part of the system. Researchers assert that some of the unique contributions of DSS are derived from the intensive interaction between the computer and the decision maker. The Web browser provides a familiar, consistent graphical user interface (GUI) structure for most DSS. For locally used DSS, a spreadsheet also provides a familiar user interface.

The Knowledge-Based Management Subsystem

The knowledge-based management subsystem can support any of the other subsystems or act as an independent component. It provides intelligence to augment the decision maker's own. It can be interconnected with the organization's knowledge repository (part of a knowledge management system [KMS]), which is sometimes called the **organizational knowledge base**. Knowledge may be provided via Web servers. Many artificial intelligence methods have been implemented in Web development systems such as Java and are easy to integrate into the other DSS components.

By definition, a DSS must include the three major components—DBMS, MBMS, and user interface. The knowledge-based management subsystem is optional, but it can provide many benefits by providing intelligence in and to the three major components. As in any other MIS, the user may be considered a component of DSS.

How the DSS Components Integrate

The components just described form the DSS application system, which can be connected to a corporate intranet, to an extranet, or to the Internet. Typically, the components communicate via Internet technology. Web browsers typically provide the user interface. The schematic view of a DSS and the components shown in Figure 3.6 provide a basic

---

[1] *DBMS* is used as both singular and plural (*system* and *systems*), as are many other acronyms in this text.

TABLE 3.2   **Overall Capabilities of DSS**

<table>
<tr><td colspan="4" align="center">*General Capabilities*</td></tr>
<tr><td>**User Interface**</td><td>**Data**</td><td>**Models**</td><td>**Knowledge**</td></tr>
<tr>
<td>Easy to use
For routine use and modification and construction of DSS</td>
<td>Access to a variety of data sources, types, and formats for a variety of problems and contexts</td>
<td>Access to a variety of analysis capabilities with some suggestion or guidance available</td>
<td>Access to a variety of artificial intelligence tools to provide intelligence to the other three components and to provide mechanisms for problem solving directly</td>
</tr>
<tr><td colspan="4" align="center">*Component Capabilities*</td></tr>
<tr><td>**User Interface**</td><td>**Data**</td><td>**Models**</td><td>**Knowledge**</td></tr>
<tr>
<td>A consistent GUI, usually via a Web client
Variety of user input devices
Variety of output formats and devices
Variety of flexible dialog styles
Support communication among users and with developer
Support knowledge of users (documentation)
Capture, store, analyze (and track) dialogs
Flexible and adaptive dialog support
Integrates DSS components</td>
<td>Variety of data forms and types
Data extraction, capture, and integration, especially into local, multi-dimensional data cubes
Data access function:
a. Retrieval/query
b. Report/display
c. User/efficient data handling
Database management function on both clients and servers
Variety of logical data views available
Data documentation
Tracking of data usage
Flexible and adaptive data support</td>
<td>Library of models to constitute a model base:
a. Many types
b. Maintain, catalog, integrate
c. Canned (preprogrammed) library
Model building facility
Model manipulation and use facility
Model base management functions
Model documentation
Tracking of model usage
Flexible and adaptive model support</td>
<td>Library of artificial intelligence
Techniques to assist users in:
a. The user interface
b. The database
c. The model base
Assistance directly in decision making
Enables automated decision making
Symbolic reasoning capabilities directly for decision making
Improved decision making through more accurate tools, such as expert systems (ES) and artificial neural networks</td>
</tr>
</table>

Source: Based on R. H. Sprague and E. Carlson, *Building Effective Decision Support Systems*, Prentice Hall, Englewood Cliffs, NJ, 1982, p. 313. Reprinted by permission of Prentice Hall.

understanding of the general structure of a DSS. In Table 3.2, we show a summary of DSS capabilities, broken down by components. It will be useful to refer to this table as you read the rest of the chapter.

In Table 3.3, we provide a sampling of the impacts of the Web on DSS components and vice versa. These impacts have been substantial because improvements in the Internet have had a major effect on how we access, use, and think of DSS. Next, we present a more detailed look at each component; additional details are also provided in later chapters.

TABLE 3.3 DSS Components and Web Impacts

DSS Component	Web Impacts	Impacts on the Web
Database management system (DBMS)	Database servers provide data directly	A means to conduct e-commerce, m-commerce, and u-commerce (transactions must be stored and acted upon)
	Consistent, friendly graphical user interface (GUI)	Customer tracking and use imply cross-selling, up-selling, and help system access, which impact Web traffic
	Provides for a direct mechanism to query databases	Database Web servers store data about the Web for analysis, using models to determine effectiveness and efficiency (via Web intelligence and Web analytics)
	Provides a consistent communication channel for data, information, and knowledge	
	Connections to data via portable devices (PDA, cell phones, etc.)	
	Connections to data warehouses	
	Connections to internal and external data sources	
	Data access through mobile-commerce (m-commerce) and universal commerce (u-commerce, also known as ultimate-commerce and ubiquitous-commerce) devices	
	Direct access by customers	
	Intranets and extranets	
	Web-based development tools	
	New programming languages and systems	
	Proliferation of database use throughout organizations, which made enterprise-wide systems feasible	
	Access to information about databases	
Model base management system (MBMS)	Access to models and solution methods implemented as Java applets and other Web development systems	Improved infrastructure design and updates
	Use of models by untrained managers (and analysts) because they are so easy to use	Models and solutions of Web infrastructure issues
	Access to Web-based artificial intelligence tools to suggest models and solution methods in DSS	Models of Web message routing improve performance
	Access to information about models	Forecasting models predict viability of hardware and software choices
User interface dialog System	Web browsers provide a flexible, consistent, and familiar DSS GUI	Initial GUIs and the computer mouse helped define how Web browsers work
	Access to information about user interfaces	Users have an expectation of how they will access data, information, models, etc.
	Experimental user interfaces are tested, distributed, and used via the Web	Speech recognition and generation are deployed over the Web
	New interfaces are readily available	New graphical-oriented display mechanisms are deployed over the Web
	Artificial intelligence–based tools communicate directly with users via Web-based interface tools	

(continued)

TABLE 3.3   Continued

DSS Component	Web Impacts	Impacts on the Web
Knowledge-based management system (KBMS)	Access to artificial intelligence methods Access to information about artificial intelligence methods Access to knowledge Web-based artificial intelligence tools deployed as Java applets or as other Web development system tools Artificial intelligence–based tools readily run and provide access to customers directly (help desks, newscasts, etc.)	Artificial intelligence methods readily handle network design issues and message routing ES diagnose problems and workarounds for failures in Internet communication, hardware, and software in servers and clients ES and intelligent agents diagnose hardware problems and recommend specific repairs Intelligent search engines learn user patterns Intelligent agents readily monitor Internet performance and alert IT staff when problems arise or are predicted to arise
User	User attitudes and expectations are strongly influenced by Web tools and access Users expect ready access and 100% reliability of information, other sources, and other users	The proliferation of the Web and access has increased commercial development via and on the Web E-commerce proliferation led to the need for fast servers, clients, and communication channels

Section 3.6 Review Questions

1. List the major components of DSS and briefly define each.
2. Briefly explain how the Web is utilized in each major component of a DSS.
3. How can a knowledge-based component help each of the other DSS components?
4. Describe the basic structure of a DSS and its components.

3.7   THE DATA MANAGEMENT SUBSYSTEM

The data management subsystem is composed of the following elements:

- DSS database
- DBMS
- Data directory
- Query facility

These elements are shown schematically in Figure 3.7 (in the shaded area). The figure also shows the interaction of the data management subsystem with the other parts of the DSS, as well as its interaction with several data sources. A brief discussion of these elements and their function follows; extensive further discussion is provided in Online File W3.1 and in Chapter 5. In Application Case 3.3, the primary focus of the DSS is on the database.

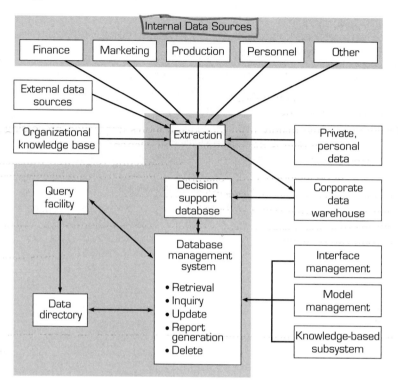

FIGURE 3.7   Structure of the Data Management Subsystem

APPLICATION CASE 3.3

Pacific Sunwear Tracks Business Performance

Pacific Sunwear is a specialty retailer offering casual fashion styles under its own brand and other brands, such as Hurley, Fox, Roxy, Quiksilver, and several others. The company wanted a system to determine which styles, colors, and sizes were selling at which stores in order to make inventory and purchasing decisions quickly and efficiently. The company built a Netezza data warehouse and used MicroStrategy's BI reporting platform. Using software from MicroStrategy and QuantiSense, the company now has dashboards to track store and product performance. The BI platform's prebuilt

and ad hoc reporting capabilities enable Pacific Sunwear staff to make better decisions with regard to store management, operations, merchandizing, planning, and so on. Managers can track stock outs or overstocks to plan future purchases as well as promotional offerings. The company is now planning to make this information available on mobile devices. It has made a big difference in the company's financial performance.

Source: Based on "Pacific Sunwear: Tracking Business Trends with BI," *Apparel*, June 2009, **apparelmag.com** (accessed June 16, 2009).

The Database

A **database** is a collection of interrelated data organized to meet the needs and structure of an organization that can be used by more than one person for more than one application. We provide the fundamentals of databases here and extensive details in Online File W3.1.

Several configurations for a database are possible. In many DSS instances, data are imported from the data warehouse or a legacy mainframe database system through a database Web server. For other DSS applications, a special database is constructed, as needed.

Several databases can be used in one DSS application, depending on the data sources. Generally, users expect to utilize a Web browser for access, and database Web servers deliver the data, regardless of the source. The data in a DSS database, as shown in Figure 3.7, are extracted from internal and external data sources, as well as from personal data belonging to one or more users. The extraction results go to the specific application's database or to the corporate data warehouse (see Chapter 5), if it exists. In the latter case, it can be used for other applications.

Internal data come mainly from the organization's transaction processing system. A typical example of such data is the monthly payroll. Depending on the needs of the DSS, operational data from functional areas, such as marketing (e.g., Web transactions from e-commerce), might be included. Other examples of internal data are machine maintenance scheduling and budget allocations, forecasts of future sales, costs of out-of-stock items, and future hiring plans. Internal data can be made available through Web browsers over an *intranet*, an internal Web-based system. Currently, data warehouses also contain internal data for the purpose of analysis.

External data include industry data, market research data, census data, regional employment data, government regulations, tax rate schedules, and national economic data. These data can come from government agencies, trade associations, market research firms, econometric forecasting firms, and the organization's own efforts to collect external data. Like internal data, external data can be maintained in the DSS database or accessed directly when the DSS is used. External data are provided, in many cases, over the *Internet* (e.g., from computerized online services or as picked up by search engines). For example, the U.S. National Weather Service and U.S. Census readily provide data, as do many other government, university, and private sources.

Private data can include guidelines used by specific decision makers and assessments of specific data and/or situations.

Data Organization

Should a DSS have a stand-alone database? It depends. In small, ad hoc DSS, data can be entered directly into models, sometimes extracted directly from larger databases. In large organizations that use extensive amounts of data, such as Wal-Mart, AT&T, and American Airlines, data are organized in a data warehouse and used when needed. Note that a data warehouse is a large store of nonvolatile, cleansed, standard-formatted data. It is not used for transaction processes, but for analysis. Transactions are aggregated and loaded into the data warehouses.

Although some DSS access transaction data from a transaction-processing system (TPS), typically those data are offloaded into another source (such as a data warehouse or other type of large DBMS) so that the analysis software will not interfere with the TPS and vice versa. (This aspect will become clear in the discussion on data warehousing in Chapter 5.)

Some large DSS have their own fully integrated, multiple-source DSS databases. A separate DSS database need not be physically separate from the corporate database. They can be stored together physically for economic reasons. Respicio et al. (2002) described a spreadsheet-oriented DSS for production planning and scheduling. This DSS has a separate database, essentially in an Excel spreadsheet, populated with data extracted from a legacy database. Updates to the legacy database based on the DSS solutions are uploaded. A DSS database can also share a DBMS with other systems.

A DSS database can include multimedia objects (e.g., pictures, maps, sounds). Object-oriented databases in eXtensible Markup Language (XML) exist and are used in DSS. These are becoming more important as mobile commerce (m-commerce) applications are deployed because XML is becoming the standard data translation method for m-commerce devices (e.g., PDAs, cell phones, notebook computers, tablet computers). The XML format is also used for standard Web browser access to data.

Data Extraction

To create or load a DSS database or a data warehouse, it is often necessary to capture data from several sources. This operation is called **extraction**. It basically consists of the importing of files, summarization, standardization filtration, and condensation of data; this process is known also as *extraction, transformation, and load (ETL)*. Extraction also occurs when the user produces reports from data in the DSS database.

Integration from disparate sources is a key part of this process. The data for the warehouse are extracted from internal and external sources (see Chapter 5). The extraction process is frequently managed by a DBMS. OLAP and data mining systems have the capability to extract data directly from all these systems, as well as from Web sources stored as HTML and XML documents, and transform them into a format suitable for analysis. To some degree, even spreadsheet systems such as Excel have this capability.

The extraction process is not trivial. MIS professionals generally structure this process so that users need not deal with its complicated details. Much effort is required to structure the extraction process properly. To extract needed data, an exact query must typically be made to several related data tables that may span several independent databases. The pieces to be extracted must be integrated so that a useful DSS database results.

The Database Management System

A database is created, accessed, and updated by a DBMS. Most DSS are built with a standard commercial relational DBMS that provides the capabilities described in Technology Insights 3.1. DBMS are often purchased from major vendors (e.g., IBM, Microsoft, Oracle), but there is a growing trend to utilize low-cost, open-source alternatives, such as MySQL (**mysql.com**). An effective database and its management can support many managerial activities; some typical examples are general navigation among records, support for creating and maintaining a diverse set of data relationships, and report generation. However, the real power of a DSS occurs when data are integrated with the decision-making model(s).

TECHNOLOGY INSIGHTS 3.1   The Capabilities of a Relational DBMS in a DSS

The relational DBMS in a DSS supports the following activities:

- Capture or extract data for inclusion in a DSS database
- Update (i.e., adds, deletes, edits, changes) data records and files
- Interrelate data from different sources
- Retrieve data from the database for queries and reports (e.g., using SQL via the Web)
- Provide comprehensive data security (e.g., protection from unauthorized access and recovery capabilities)
- Handle personal and unofficial data so that users can experiment with alternative solutions, based on their own judgment
- Perform complex data manipulation tasks based on queries
- Track data use within the DSS
- Manage data through a data dictionary

The Query Facility

In building and using DSS, it is often necessary to access, manipulate, and query data. The **query facility** performs these tasks. It accepts requests for data from other DSS components (refer to Figure 3.7), determines how the requests can be filled (consulting the data directory if necessary), formulates the detailed requests, and returns the results to the issuer of the request. The query facility includes a special query language (e.g., SQL). Programming languages (e.g., .NET and Java) and other systems utilize SQL query structures directly as well. Important functions of a DSS query system are selection and manipulation operations (e.g., the ability to follow a computer instruction, such as "Search for all sales in the Southeast Region during June 2006 and summarize sales by salesperson"). Although it is transparent to the user, this is a critical activity. All the user may see is a screen with a simple request for data, and following the click of a button, the user gets the results neatly formatted in a table in a dynamic HTML (or other Web-structured) page displayed on the screen.

The Directory

The data **directory** is a catalog of all the data in a database. It contains data definitions, and its main function is to answer questions about the availability of data items, their source, and their exact meaning. The directory is especially appropriate for supporting the intelligence phase of the decision-making process by helping to scan data and identify problem areas or opportunities. The directory, like any other catalog, supports the addition of new entries, deletion of entries, and retrieval of information about specific objects. All the database elements have been implemented on database Web servers that respond to Web browser screens. The Web has dramatically changed the way we access, use, and store data. Next we touch on some important database and DBMS issues— some of which are general, and some that pertain specifically to DSS.

Key Database and Database Management System Issues

Although many issues affect databases and are caused by databases, here we focus on four important ones that affect DSS dramatically: data quality, data integration, scalability, and security. These are also discussed, in part, in Online File W3.1.

DATA QUALITY   A key issue in data management is data quality. As we discussed in Chapter 2, decision makers (specifically executives and managers) generally do not feel that they get the data and information they really need to do their work.

Poor quality data, which leads to poor quality information, leads directly to waste. The data cannot be trusted, and therefore neither can any analysis based on them. The old adage "garbage in/garbage out" (GIGO) applies. With poor data, processes will fail or simply perform badly. For example, given inaccurate data in a CRM system, customers may be contacted many times, clustered into incorrect groupings, and so on, leading to missed sales opportunities and unhappy customers. The main notion underlying poor data quality is that it leads to waste (see English, 2002, 2005; "Getting Clean," 2004; and Gonzales, 2004). Waste in manufacturing leads to scrap and rework. English (2005) indicated that some 10 to 20 percent of operating revenue is used to pay for information scrap and rework (e.g., updates to prevent bad decisions). According to a TDWI report (Erickson, 2002), in the United States alone, firms routinely lose over $600 billion per year due to poor data quality.

Data quality is of interest to professionals from many areas: data mining, customer relationship management, supply chain management, and so on. If you can't be sure of the quality and consistency of the data that is used to make decisions, you can't be sure about the decisions you make. See Technology Insights 3.2 for details on how to tackle data quality at the enterprise level.

Data cleanup (e.g., validation and verification) tools differ from those utilized in data cleansing for data warehousing. Tools for cleansing and matching data are available from Firstlogic Inc., Group 1 Software Inc., Trillium Software, DataFlux Corp., and others.

DATA INTEGRATION A single version of the truth is ultimately what decision makers want from their information systems. Data and information are all over the place in most organizations. When it comes time to develop any enterprise system, or even a single DSS, data must be gathered from disparate sources and integrated into that single version of the truth so that everyone is on the same page. The U.S. Department of Homeland Security has experienced expensive disasters in terms of its attempts to integrate data from its semi-independent, siloed agencies (see details in Online File W3.1). Initially, enterprise information portals were utilized to bring data together and present it as a unified whole; however, it is critical to create a true master view of the data. It is possible for one person's portal to access what is believed to be similar data from a different source than that for another person's portal. The two individuals think they have the same data in front of them, but they do not. Just as with data quality issues, a careful analysis of all data, their sources, and precision and accuracy must be mapped into a set of metadata that can be used to create a single version of the truth.

TECHNOLOGY INSIGHTS 3.2   The 10 Essential Ingredients of Data (Information) Quality Management

Because poor data (and consequently information) quality can lead to disastrous results and significant expense, it is important to understand how to manage data in a quality manner by design. Here are Larry English's top 10 suggestions:

1. Understand that data quality is a business problem, not only a systems problem. Solve it as a business process, not just a systems process. Poor data quality affects the entire business and its operations. Some issues impacting poor quality occur as the result of business processes (e.g., data entry).
2. Focus on information customers and suppliers, not just data. Quality improvement of the data is the key.
3. Focus on all components of information and data, including their definition, content, and presentation.
4. Implement data/information quality management processes, not just software to handle them.
5. Measure data accuracy in addition to validity.
6. Measure real costs, not just the percentage, of poor quality data/information; also measure their results.
7. Emphasize process improvement and preventive maintenance, not just data cleansing.
8. Improve processes (and hence data quality) at the source.
9. Provide quality training to managers and information producers. Educate them as to the impacts of poor data quality and how to improve it.
10. Actively transform the culture to one that values data quality.

Sources: Adapted from L. English, "IQ and Muda," *DM Review*, Vol. 15, No. 9, September 2005, pp. 40–46; and L. English, "The Essentials of Information Quality Management," *DM Review*, Vol. 12, No. 9, September 2002, pp. 36–44.

Integration issues generally become critical when implementing an EIS such as a CRM. Information about customers may be scattered throughout several databases, but customers expect to be treated as if there is a single organization reaching them. Also, when migrating to a new system, integration becomes key. Even when attempting to integrate content into a content management system, major problems occur. For example, York International migrated some 8,000 engineering documents from one CMS to the enterprise standard CMS over a weekend, but it took months to deal with access and security problems. Middleware, such as products from ECI Services, can help by scanning documents and identifying problems and applying solutions (see Raden, 2005; and Siluer, 2005). For database integration, enterprise information integration (EII) products, such as DB2 Information Integrator, Oracle XML Data Synthesis, Informatica Integration Competency Center, and even XML standardization can help.

SCALABILITY   Large databases (and data warehouses) present major scalability problems. As the size of the data to be stored and accessed increases, processing times and storage space also grow, sometimes dramatically. The Internet is clearly the main driving force for applications, especially across the enterprise. The physical sciences, biological sciences, medicine, and engineering are growing in importance in terms of the size of databases and types of analyses being performed. Genetics provides a ready example in terms of the kinds and size of data needed for genome projects. The pharmaceutical industry needs large-scale databases not only for processing forms for approval, but also for analysis and prediction of the effectiveness of new compounds. In addition to the two major directions, there will be major changes in traditional DBMS areas, including data models, access methods, query processing algorithms, concurrency control, recovery, query languages, and user interfaces to DBMS. Finally, related technologies (e.g., data mining) are maturing. Clearly, new storage technologies and search mechanisms need to be and are continually being developed. For example, part of the storage issue can be solved by carefully splitting data up and having them span multiple disk drives, perhaps each with access by several processors. Multiprocessor clusters, symmetric multiprocessing (SMP) systems, and massively parallel processing (MPP) hardware systems with appropriate parallel processing software can provide effective parallel search and access capabilities.

DATA SECURITY   One key issue that DBMS is supposed to handle by its very nature is data security. The consequences of unauthorized access to unsecured data can be extremely detrimental to the financial well-being of an organization. In some cases, data security is required by confidentiality laws (e.g., in medicine, law enforcement). In some situations, unauthorized access extends to modifying data in place or destroying it. Data must be protected from unauthorized access through security measures such as ID and password protection. It is also important to identify exactly who has access to and why they have access to specific sets of data and to what level an individual is allowed to change the data in the system. Finally, data can be encrypted so that even in the case of unauthorized access the viewed data is scrambled and unintelligible.

Section 3.7 Review Questions

1. Why does a DSS generally include its own database?
2. Describe the similarities and differences among internal, external, and private data.
3. Describe the components of a DBMS: the query facility, the directory, and the data.
4. What are the major functions (capabilities) of a DBMS?
5. What is extraction? P 92.
6. What is the function of a query facility?
7. What is the function of a directory?

3.8 THE MODEL MANAGEMENT SUBSYSTEM

The model management subsystem of a DSS is composed of the following elements:

- Model base
- MBMS
- Modeling language
- Model directory
- Model execution, integration, and command processor

These elements and their interfaces with other DSS components are shown in Figure 3.8. The following sections define and describe the function of each of these elements.

The Model Base

A **model base** contains routine and special statistical, financial, forecasting, management science, and other quantitative models that provide the analysis capabilities in a DSS. The ability to invoke, run, change, combine, and inspect models is a key DSS capability that differentiates it from other CBIS. The models in the model base can be divided into four major categories: strategic, tactical, operational, and analytical. In addition, there are model building blocks and routines.

Strategic models are used to support top managers' strategic planning responsibilities. Potential applications include devising an e-commerce venture, developing corporate objectives, planning for mergers and acquisitions, selecting a plant location, analyzing environmental impact, and creating a nonroutine capital budget. An example of a DSS strategic model is that of Southwest Airlines (Songini, 2002). Southwest used its system to create accurate financial forecasts so that it could identify strategic opportunities. A large-scale linear programming model is at the heart of Southwest's POP DSS, which allows executives of the company to plan large, expensive equipment needs as many years ahead as needed. FedEx's Web-based ISIS DSS is used in making strategic decisions.

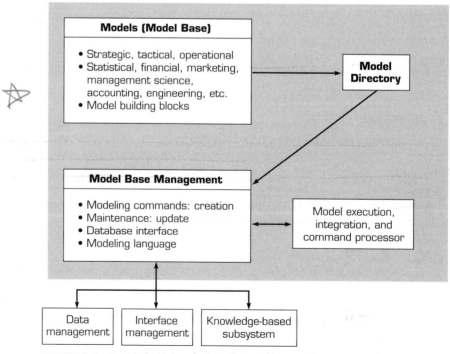

FIGURE 3.8 Structure of the Model Management Subsystem

Tactical models are used mainly by middle managers to assist in allocating and controlling the organization's resources. Examples of tactical models include those for Web server selection, labor requirement planning, sales promotion planning, plant-layout determination, and routine capital budgeting. Tactical models are usually applicable only to an organizational subsystem, such as the accounting department. Their time horizons vary from 1 month to less than 2 years. Some external data are needed, but the greatest requirements are for internal data.

Operational models are used to support the day-to-day working activities of the organization. Typical decisions involve e-commerce transaction acceptance (e.g., purchases), approval of personal loans by a bank, production scheduling, inventory control, maintenance planning and scheduling, and quality control. Operational models mainly support first-line managers' decision making with a daily to monthly time horizon. These models normally use only internal data.

An excellent example of an operational model is the one developed by a large U.S. national bank with hundreds of branches (the officers of the bank wish it to remain anonymous). The bank developed an artificial neural network (ANN) model (for a development cost of about $300,000) to determine whether specific loan applicants should be given loans. The system's accurate predictions allowed the bank to hold back on hiring additional loan officers, saving the bank some $200,000 in its first year of operation.

Analytical models are used to perform analysis on data. They include statistical models, management science models, data mining algorithms, financial models, and more. Sometimes they are integrated with other models, such as strategic planning models. Humana Corp. uses analytical models to determine benefit classes for health care.

The foundations of *business analytics* (including predictive analytics) encompass all these analytical models. Typically, business analytics tools are Web based, hence the term *Web analytics.* These tools may readily be applied to Web systems; one example of their use is for administering and monitoring e-commerce. Business analytics software is generally easy to use.

The models in the model base can also be classified by functional areas (e.g., financial models, production control models) or by discipline (e.g., statistical models, management science allocation models). The number of models in a DSS can vary from a few to several hundred. Models in DSS are basically mathematical; that is, they are expressed by formulas. These formulas can be preprogrammed using DSS development tools such as Excel. They can be written in a spreadsheet and stored for future use, or they can be programmed for only one use.

Model Building Blocks and Routines

In addition to strategic, tactical, and operational models, the model base can contain **model building blocks** and routines. Examples of the software elements used to build computerized models include a random-number-generator routine, a curve- or line-fitting routine, a present-value computational routine, and regression analysis. Such building blocks can be used in several ways. They can be used on their own for such applications as data analysis. They can also be used as components of larger models. For example, a present-value component can be part of a make-or-buy model. Some of these building blocks are used to determine the values of variables and parameters in a model, as in the use of regression analysis to create trend lines in a forecasting model. Building blocks are available in DSS commercial development software, such as the functions and add-ins of Excel, and in the general modeling structures of OLAP and data mining software. The implementation of model solution methods directly in Java and other Web development systems has simplified access and integration of models. In Section 3.13, you will learn about a model building language called Planners Lab.

Model Components for Building DSS

At a higher level than building blocks, it is important to consider the different types of models and solution methods needed in the DSS. Often at the start of development, there is some sense of the model types to be incorporated, but this may change as more is learned about the decision problem. Some DSS development systems include a wide variety of components (e.g., Analytica from Lumina Decision Systems), whereas others have a single one (e.g., Lindo). Often, the results of one type of model component (e.g., forecasting) are used as input to another (e.g., production scheduling). In some cases, a modeling language is a component that generates input to a solver, whereas in other cases, the two are combined. Models can be classified in many different ways. A common way to classify the models for decision making is on the basis of whether the model inputs are assumed to be known with certainty (deterministic) or are to be uncertain (probabilistic). Typical deterministic modeling components include those for linear programming and its specializations (e.g., network programming, integer programming) and its generalizations (e.g., nonlinear programming), modeling languages (e.g., AMPL, GAMS), PERT and CPM charts (typically embedded in project management software), dynamic programming, and so on. On the probabilistic side, typical modeling components include those for forecasting (i.e., predictive analytics), Markov modeling, queuing, simulation, and so on. Others that can be treated either deterministically or probabilistically include vehicle routing and scheduling and production planning, which each contain a number of modeling components. These components are typically embedded directly into OLAP and data mining software.

Modeling Tools

Because DSS deal with semistructured or unstructured problems, it is often necessary to customize models, using programming tools and languages. Some examples of these are .NET Framework languages, C++, and Java. OLAP software may also be used to work with models in data analysis. Even languages for simulation such as Arena and statistical packages such as those of SPSS offer modeling tools developed through the use of a proprietary programming language. For small and medium-sized DSS or for less complex ones, a spreadsheet (e.g., Excel) is usually used. We will use Excel for many key examples in this book. Application Case 3.4 describes a spreadsheet-based DSS.

APPLICATION CASE 3.4
SNAP DSS Helps OneNet Make Telecommunications Rate Decisions

Telecommunications network services to educational institutions and government entities are typically provided by a mix of private and public organizations. Many states in the United States have one or more state agencies that are responsible for providing network services to schools, colleges, and other state agencies. One example of such an agency is OneNet in Oklahoma. OneNet is a division of the Oklahoma State Regents for Higher Education and operated in cooperation with the Office of State Finance.

Usually agencies such as OneNet operate as an enterprise-type fund. They must recover their costs through billing their clients and/or by justifying appropriations directly from the state legislatures. This cost recovery should occur through a pricing mechanism that is efficient, simple to implement, and equitable. This pricing model typically needs to recognize many factors: convergence of voice, data, and video traffic on the same infrastructure; diversity of user base in terms of educational institutions, state agencies, and so on; diversity of applications in use by state clients, from e-mail to videoconferences, IP telephoning, and distance learning; recovery of current costs, as well as planning for upgrades and future developments; and leverage the shared infrastructure to enable further economic development and collaborative work across the state that leads to innovative uses of OneNet.

These considerations led to the development of a spreadsheet-based model. The system, SNAP-DSS, or Service Network Application and Pricing

(SNAP)-based DSS, was developed in Microsoft Excel 2007 and used the VBA programming language.

The SNAP-DSS offers OneNet the ability to select the rate card options that best fit the preferred pricing strategies by providing a real-time, user-friendly, graphical user interface. In addition, the SNAP-DSS not only illustrates the influence of the changes in the pricing factors on each rate card option, but also allows the user to analyze various rate card options in different scenarios using different parameters. This model has been used by OneNet financial planners to gain insights into their customers and analyze many what-if scenarios of different rate plan options.

Source: Based on: J. Chongwatpol and R. Sharda, "SNAP: A DSS to Analyze Network Service Pricing for State Networks," *Decision Support Systems,* forthcoming (2010).

The Model Base Management System

MBMS software has four main functions:

- Model creation, using programming languages, DSS tools and/or subroutines, and other building blocks
- Generation of new routines and reports
- Model updating and changing
- Model data manipulation

The MBMS is capable of interrelating models with the appropriate linkages through a database (see Technology Insights 3.3).

The Model Directory

The role of the model directory is similar to that of a database directory. It is a catalog of all the models and other software in the model base. It contains model definitions, and its main function is to answer questions about the availability and capability of the models.

Model Execution, Integration, and Command

The following activities are usually controlled by model management. *Model execution* is the process of controlling the actual running of the model. *Model integration* involves combining the operations of several models when needed (e.g., directing the output of one model, say forecasting, to be processed by another one, say a linear programming planning model) or integrating the DSS with other applications. Portucel Industrial (a major Portuguese paper producer) uses a DSS that contains six integrated models: three capacity planning and scheduling models, two cutting plan models, and one demand forecasting model (see Respicio et al., 2002).

An interesting question for a DSS might be which models should be used for what situations. Such model selection cannot be done by the MBMS because it requires expertise and therefore is done manually. This is a potential automation area for a knowledge component to assist the MBMS. Another interesting, more subtle, question is what method should be used to solve a particular problem in a specific model class. For example, an assignment problem (say assigning 10 jobs to 10 people) is a type of transportation problem, which is a type of network flow problem, which is a type of linear programming problem, which is a type of mathematical optimization problem. Special solution methods are generally more efficient when dealing with more specialized structures. In other words, special methods for solving an assignment problem should work better than applying transportation problem

---

TECHNOLOGY INSIGHTS 3.3   Major Functions of an MBMS

The following are the major functions of an MBMS:

- Creates models easily and quickly, either from scratch or from existing models or from the building blocks
- Allows users to manipulate models so that they can conduct experiments and sensitivity analyses ranging from what-if to goal-seeking analyses
- Stores, retrieves, and manages a wide variety of different types of models in a logical and integrated manner
- Accesses and integrates the model building blocks
- Catalogs and displays the directory of models for use by several individuals in the organization
- Tracks model data and application use
- Interrelates models with appropriate linkages with the database and integrates them within the DSS
- Manages and maintains the model base with management functions analogous to those in database management: store, access, run, update, link, catalog, and query
- Uses multiple models to support problem solving

---

algorithms to it, and so on. But this is not always true. And to complicate matters, there may be many ways to solve a specific problem, depending on its characteristics. Again, there is potential for the knowledge component to assist in selecting an appropriate solution method.

In the late 1990s, the elements of the MBMS migrated to Web-based systems, deployed as Java applets or modules of other Web development systems.

Section 3.8 Review Questions

1. Models are classified as strategic, tactical, or operational. What is the purpose of such a classification? Give an example of each type of model.
2. List some of the major functions of an MBMS.
3. Compare the features and structure of an MBMS to those of a DBMS.
4. Why is model selection for DSS difficult?
5. How can a knowledge component assist in model selection?

3.9 THE USER INTERFACE (DIALOG) SUBSYSTEM

The term **user interface** covers all aspects of communication between a user and the DSS or any MSS. It includes not only the hardware and software but also factors that deal with ease of use, accessibility, and human–machine interactions. Some MSS experts feel that the user interface is the most important component because it is the source of many of the power, flexibility, and ease-of-use characteristics of MSS. Others believe that the user interface is the system from the user's standpoint because it is the only part of the system that the user sees.

A difficult user interface is one of the major reasons managers do not use computers and quantitative analyses as much as they could, given the availability of these technologies. The Web browser has been recognized as an effective DSS GUI because it is flexible, user friendly, and a gateway to almost all sources of necessary information and data. Essentially, Web browsers have led to the development of portals and dashboards, which front end many DSS.

Management of the User Interface Subsystem

The user interface subsystem is managed by software called the **user interface management system (UIMS)**. The UIMS is composed of several programs that provide the capabilities listed in Online File W3.2. The UIMS is also known as the *dialog generation and management system.*

The User Interface Process

The user interface process for an MSS is shown schematically in Figure 3.9. The user interacts with the computer via an action language processed by the UIMS. It enables the user to interact with the model management and data management subsystems. In advanced systems, the user interface component includes a natural language processor or can use standard **objects** (e.g., pull-down menus, buttons) through a **graphical user interface (GUI)**.

DSS User Interfaces

Actual DSS (and data, information, and knowledge) access is provided through Web browsers, including voice input and output, portable devices, and direct-sensing devices (mainly for input). We discuss these next, along with some speculation as to the future of interfaces.

DSS are typically accessed via Web-browser technology (or at least a similar-looking screen). Essentially, the Web browser provides a portal or dashboard to access the system. Even when a customized user interface is developed, it typically is a GUI. Web-browser technologies have changed our expectations of how software should look and feel. Many DSS provide drill-down capabilities (to look into data for the source of problems) and a traffic light display (i.e., green = OK, red = problems, yellow = problem brewing).

A DSS is used on the Web in several ways. First, users can go on the intranet and activate ready-made DSS applications. All they need do is enter some data or specify dates and other information. The DSS is then run, and the users can see the results. Second, they can get online advice and help on how to use the DSS applications. Third,

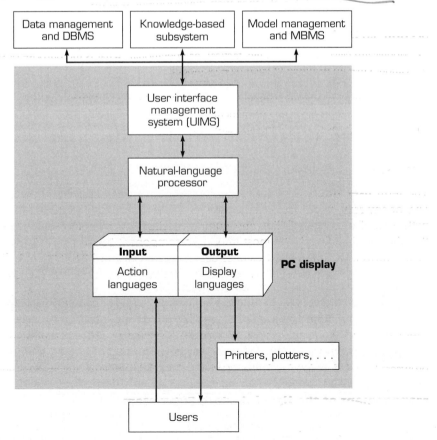

FIGURE 3.9 Schematic View of the User Interface System

they can communicate with others regarding the interpretation of the DSS results. Finally, they can collaborate in implementing solutions generated by the DSS model.

Web tools provide communication and collaboration capabilities for group support systems (GSS) and KMS, as well as for content management systems, EIS, CRM, and SCM. Given that Web browsers are the typical user access path for DSS and data, most major software vendors, especially those providing database access, provide portals or dashboards, which allow access to data and methods to solve problems—essentially DSS.

IBM's WebSphere portal (**ibm.com/websphere**) lets employees access information and business processes in a comfortable format, leading to collaboration and faster and better decision making. This includes IBM's e-commerce and SCM applications. The WebSphere portal provides capabilities that allow an organization to connect everyone involved in its supply chain (vendors through customers) together so that collaboration is smooth and effective. EIS ranging from SCM to knowledge management can effectively be accessed though the Microsoft Digital Dashboard and IBM WebSphere portal. Many other companies offer similar capabilities, including **correlate.com** for linking of various types of knowledge assets, Microsoft's SharePoint portal platform, and so on.

A variety of portable devices has been made Web-ready, including notebook and tablet PCs, PDAs, pocket PCs (another type of PDA), and cell phones. Many of these devices include technology to tap directly into the Web. They allow either handwritten input or typed input from internal or external keyboards. Some DSS user interfaces utilize natural-language input (i.e., text in a human language) so that the users can easily express themselves in a meaningful way. Because of the fuzzy nature of human language, it is fairly difficult to develop software to interpret it. However, these packages increase in accuracy every year, and they will ultimately lead to accurate input, output, and language translators (e.g., look into research at Carnegie Mellon University's Language Technologies Institute at **lti.cs.cmu.edu**).

Cell phone inputs through SMS are becoming more common for at least some consumer DSS-type applications. For example, one can send an SMS request for search on any topic to GOOGL (46645). It is most useful in locating nearby businesses, addresses, or phone numbers, but it can also be used for many other decision support tasks. For example, users can find definitions of words by entering the word "define" followed by a word, such as "define extenuate." Some of the other capabilities include:

- Translations: "Translate thanks in Spanish."
- Price lookups: "Price 32GB iPhone."
- Calculator: Although you would probably just want to use your phone's built-in calculator function, you can send a math expression as an SMS for an answer.
- Currency conversions: "10 usd in euros."
- Sports scores and game times: Just enter the name of a team ("NYC Giants"), and Google SMS will send the most recent game's score and the date and time of the next match.

This type of SMS-based search capability is also available for other search engines, including Yahoo! and Microsoft's new search engine Bing.

With the emergence of Apple's iPhone as a leading smartphone, many companies are developing iPhone applications to provide purchasing-decision support. For example, Amazon.com's iPhone application allows a user to take a picture of any item in a store (or wherever) and send it to Amazon.com. Amazon.com's graphics-understanding algorithm tries to match the image to a real product in its databases and sends the user a page similar to Amazon.com's product info pages, allowing users to perform price comparisons in real time.

Voice input for these devices and PCs is common and fairly accurate (but not perfect). When voice input with accompanying speech-recognition software (and readily available text-to-speech software) is used, verbal instructions with accompanied actions and outputs can be invoked. These are readily available for DSS and are incorporated into the portable devices described earlier. An example of voice inputs that can be used for a general purpose DSS is Google's 411 service. Besides being accessible through SMS, it can also be accessed through a phone number. (Admittedly, it is currently U.S. centric for now.) A user calls 1-800-GOOG-411 and speaks the information on the caller's location and the type of information being sought. For example, a user can give her zip code and say "pizza delivery." Google provides the search results and can even place a call to a business. This consumer-centric technology is also finding business uses. For example, Alltel, a cell phone company that is now part of Verizon, offers customers the capability of having their phone messages converted into text e-mails and sent to their e-mail inboxes.

Finally, as far as DSS and data access devices go, personal music players such as iPods and other MP3 players can display data, pictures, and video (via podcasting), thus making them capable of displaying portal information and effectively giving them access to a DSS.

In addition to text-to-speech capabilities, gestures are important for human understanding. Visit **ananova.com** to see an example of an artificial newscaster and **alicebot.org** for an example of natural-language text processing with speech-output capabilities. When you activate Alice, she will keep a close watch on the mouse indicator on the screen. The voice-capable Alice Silver Edition won the prestigious Loebner Prize in 2004. It is possible to use speech-generation (e.g., text-to-speech) technology with or without an animated character. SitePal (**sitepal.com**) provides animated characters that include facial gestures for Web sites for a small monthly fee. Other such software is available for free (e.g., from NaturalSoft Ltd. at **naturalreaders.com**; the paid version has more features). And Microsoft's Agent technology provides both voice-input and speech-generation from text.

Recent efforts in business process management (BPM) have led to inputs directly from physical devices for analysis via DSS. For example, radio frequency identification (RFID) chips can record data from sensors in railcars or in process products in a factory. Data from these sensors (e.g., recording an item's status) can be downloaded at key locations and immediately transmitted to a database or data warehouse, where they can be analyzed and decisions can be made concerning the status of the items being monitored. Wal-Mart and Best Buy are developing this technology in their SCM, and such *sensor networks* are also being used effectively by other firms.

Several user interface developments are under way in terms of software and hardware. On the software side, scientists are constantly developing improvements in voice recognition, natural-language processing in both directions, voice input (speech recognition), voice output (speech-to-text), and language translation. These may or may not include gestures for input and output. In addition, virtual reality technology can be used for data display, allowing a decision maker to "fly" over a landscape that represents the data being analyzed, for example. Artificial intelligence methodologies and technologies directly affect these improvement efforts. For example, scientists at the University of London's Goldsmiths College and at Cornell University are developing systems that attempt to make computers recognize and respond to users' emotions and even help users understand their own emotions better following their interaction with computational devices. Scientists at Cornell are also developing methods for letting computers deal with human ambiguity in a meaningful way. See Anthes (2006) for some initial details.

On the hardware side, the quality and size of visual output displays are physically limited by the size of molecules. Even so, displays are getting better and better, especially in PDAs and mobile phones. Videoconferencing systems are becoming more immersive. Indeed, all such developments are now described under the umbrella term *telepresence*. The reader is encouraged to visit the corresponding Wikipedia page at (**en.wikipedia.org/ wiki/Telepresence**) to keep abreast of developments in this area. With many large companies entering the telepresence arena, we are even more likely to see major developments in enabling decision support through video and telepresence. Finally, see Technology Insights 3.4 for an introduction to other developments in user input devices.

DSS Developments

We conclude the sections on the three major DSS components with information on some recent technology and methodology developments that affect DSS and decision making. Many developments in DSS components are the result of new developments in hardware and software computer technology, data warehousing, data mining, OLAP, Web technologies, integration of technologies, and DSS application to various and new functional areas. There is also a clear link between hardware and software capabilities and improvements in DSS. Hardware continues to shrink in size while increasing in speed and other capabilities. The sizes of databases and data warehouses have increased dramatically. Data warehouses now provide hundreds of petabytes of sales data for retail organizations and content for major news networks.

As Web tools, both on the browser and server sides, and Java and other development systems improve, so will the interface and data and model access capabilities of DSS.

TECHNOLOGY INSIGHTS 3.4   Next Generation of Input Devices

The last few years have seen exciting developments in user interfaces. Perhaps the most common example of the evolving user interfaces is the iPhone's multitouch interface that allows a user to zoom, pan, and scroll through a screen just with the use of a finger. These changes are almost revolutionary from the previous generation of touch-screen computing interfaces that were available in the first part of this decade as touch tablets and pen-based input devices. The success of iPhone has spawned many other developments of similar user interfaces from other providers such as Palm (Palm Pre).

Microsoft Surface (see **microsoft.com/surface** and **en.wikipedia.org/wiki/Microsoft_Surface**) is an example of the next generation of such platforms available in larger-screen applications. It does not require touch, but instead processes inputs based on hand gestures and real-world objects. It has a 360-degree user interface and can recognize an object and track its movements. It is multitouch and multiuser. Users can interact with the platform by touching or dragging their fingertips or by placing and moving objects. Surface can respond to 52 touches at a time.

In the last few years, gaming devices have evolved significantly to be able to receive and process gesture-based inputs. In 2007, Nintendo introduced the Wii game platform, which is able to process motions and gestures. This controller has led to the development of games that are far more realistic and immersive in nature. Other game platforms, such as Microsoft's Xbox360 and Sony's PSP3, also offer capabilities along these lines through vibrating handsets.

The next generation of these technologies is in the form of mind-reading platforms. A company called Emotiv (**en.wikipedia.org/wiki/Emotiv**) made big news in early 2008 with a promise to deliver a game controller that a user would be able to control by thinking about it. These technologies are to be based on electroencephalography, the technique of reading and processing the electrical activity at the scalp level as a result of specific thoughts in the brain. The technical details are available on Wikipedia (**en.wikipedia.org/wiki/Electroencephalography**) and the Web. Although Emotiv has not yet released a consumer product, its potential is significant for many other DSS-type applications. Many other companies are developing similar technologies. A list of some of Emotiv's competitors and their technical approaches is available at **en.wikipedia.org/wiki/Emotiv#Competitors**.

User interfaces are going to change significantly in the next few years. Their first use will probably be in gaming and consumer applications, but the business and DSS applications won't be far behind.

Sources: Various Wikipedia sites and the company Web sites provided in the feature.

However, scalability, as discussed earlier, remains a problem. However, parallel processing hardware and software technologies have made major inroads in solving the scalability issue.

We expect to see more seamless integration of DSS components as they adopt Web technologies, especially XML. These Web-based technologies have become the center of activity in developing DSS. Web-based DSS have reduced technological barriers and have made it easier and less costly to make decision-relevant information and model-driven DSS available to managers and staff users in geographically distributed locations, especially through mobile devices.

Artificial intelligence continues to make inroads in improving DSS. Faster, intelligent search engines are an obvious outcome. There are many others, especially in interface use. Intelligent agents promise to improve the interface in areas as diverse as direct natural-language processing and creating facial gestures. Artificial intelligence solutions can readily be incorporated into or used as a DSS.

DSS are becoming more embedded in or linked to most ES. Similarly, a major area to expect improvements in DSS is in GSS in supporting collaboration at the enterprise level. This is true even in the educational arena. Almost every new area of information systems involves some level of decision-making support. Thus, DSS, either directly or indirectly, has impacts on CRM, SCM, ERP, KM, PLM, BAM, BPM, and other EIS. As these systems evolve, the active decision-making component that utilizes mathematical, statistical, or even descriptive models increases in size and capability, although it may be buried deep within the system.

Finally, different types of DSS components are being integrated more frequently. For example, GIS are readily integrated with other, more traditional, DSS components and tools for improved decision making.

Section 3.9 Review Questions

1. What is the major purpose of a user interface system?
2. Describe the user interface process.
3. What are the major functions of a UIMS?
4. Describe why Web tools are typically used for DSS interfaces.
5. List four new developments in user interfaces.
6. List four new developments in DSS, other than user interface developments.

3.10 THE KNOWLEDGE-BASED MANAGEMENT SUBSYSTEM

Many unstructured and even semistructured problems are so complex that their solutions require expertise. This can be provided by an ES or another intelligent system. Therefore, advanced DSS are equipped with a component called a knowledge-based management sub-system. This component can supply the required expertise for solving some aspects of the problem and provide knowledge that can enhance the operation of other DSS components. Knowledge components may be provided by ES, neural networks, intelligent agents, fuzzy logic, case-based reasoning systems, and so on. Knowledge-based ES and mathematical modeling can be integrated in several ways, including knowledge-based aids that support parts of the decision process not handled by mathematics (e.g., selecting a model class or solution methodology); intelligent decision modeling systems to help with developing, applying, and managing model libraries; and decision analytic ES to integrate uncertainty into the decision-making process. The knowledge component consists of one or more intelligent systems.

Like database and model management software, knowledge-based management software provides the necessary execution and integration of the intelligent system. Caution: A KMS is typically a text-oriented DSS; not a knowledge-based management system. A DSS that includes such a component is called an intelligent DSS, a DSS/ES, an expert-support system, an active DSS, or a knowledge-based DSS (see Application Case 3.5 for an example that includes both an ES and an ANN in a Web-based package written in Java). Most data mining applications include intelligent systems, such as ANN and rule-induction methods for ES, to search for potentially profitable patterns in data. Many OLAP systems include ANN and data-induction tools that extract rules for ES (e.g., KnowledgeSEEKER from Angoss Software Corp., **angoss.com**).

APPLICATION CASE 3.5

IAP Systems' Intelligent DSS Determines the Success of Overseas Assignments and Learns from the Experience

Overseas assignments for managers and executives can be an exciting adventure for the entire family, or they can be disastrous. If an assignment is a failure, the cost of replacing the manager and the impact on his or her family can cost well over $250,000. Many companies (e.g., Coca-Cola) require employees to have overseas assignments before they can move into high executive positions.

The critical issue is to be able to predict whether a specific assignment will be a good or bad experience for the manager and his or her family. Enter intelligent DSS. The International Assignment Profile (IAP) is a new, state-of-the-art method for use in ex-pat preparation (or selection) that collects important comprehensive information about the family and compares their answers to known conditions in the anticipated international location. IAP increases the human and business success of international assignments by spotting key issues and pinpointing the weak links or problems that could compromise an international relocation or assignment while there is still time to plan and prevent problems.

IAP's goals include the following:

• Better preparation for transfer
• Faster adjustment to international locations

• Significant reduction in compromised assignments
• No failed assignments

IAP is written in Exsys Corvid, a Web-based ES shell (**exsys.com**). Through feedback from past assignments, ANN learns emerging patterns. IAP uses modern technology and artificial intelligence to assist companies in making more accurate, less stressful foreign placements and international relocations. The employee and his or her spouse complete the IAP interview process on the Web or on their computers. The system analyzes the information, detects and isolates critical patterns that might jeopardize the business purpose of the relocation, and produces a report for planning and problem prevention. IAP produces a detailed list of exactly what issues need to be resolved and what planning needs to be done to ensure success. When the entire family is happy, the assignment succeeds. For a large firm, using IAP can readily save millions of dollars per year.

Sources: Based on: International Assignment Profile Systems, Inc., **iapsystems.com** (accessed June 3, 2009); and Exsys, Inc., **exsys.com** (accessed June 3, 2009).

Section 3.10 Review Questions

1. List the various knowledge-based tools that can comprise a knowledge-based management system.
2. What capabilities does a knowledge-based management system provide to DSS either in total or to each component?

3.11 THE DECISION SUPPORT SYSTEM USER

The person faced with a decision that an MSS is designed to support is called the *user*, the *manager*, or the *decision maker*. However, these terms fail to reflect the heterogeneity that exists among the users and usage patterns of MSS (see Alter, 1980). There are differences in the positions users occupy, their cognitive preferences and abilities, and their ways of arriving at a decision (i.e., decision styles). The user can be an individual or a group, depending on who is responsible for the decision. The user, although not listed as a major component of DSS, by definition provides the *human intellect*. The user, as the person or people primarily responsible for making the decision, provides expertise in guiding the development and use of a DSS. This intellectual capability is critical to the system's success and proper use. If the main user of a DSS is replaced by another, less knowledgeable, user (in terms of the decision-making problem and environment), the DSS will generally be less effective.

An MSS has two broad classes of users: managers and staff specialists. Staff specialists, such as financial analysts, production planners, and market researchers, outnumber managers by about three to two, and they use computers much more than managers. When designing an MSS, it is important to know who will actually have hands-on use of it. In general, managers expect systems to be more user-friendly than do staff specialists. Staff specialists tend to be more detail oriented, are more willing to use complex systems in their day-to-day work, and are interested in the computational capabilities of the MSS. That is why the first users of OLAP were staff specialists.

Often, staff analysts are the intermediaries between managers and the MSS. An **intermediary** allows a manager to benefit from a DSS without actually having to use the keyboard. Several types of intermediaries reflect different support for the manager:

- **Staff assistants** have specialized knowledge about management problems and some experience with decision support technology.
- **Expert tool users** are skilled in the application of one or more types of specialized problem-solving tools. An expert tool user performs tasks that the problem solver does not have the skill or training to perform.
- **Business (system) analysts** have a general knowledge of the application area, a formal business administration education (not in computer science), and considerable skill in using DSS construction tools.
- **Facilitators (in a GSS)** control and coordinate the use of software to support the work of people working in groups. The facilitator is also responsible for conducting workgroup sessions.

Within the categories of managers and staff specialists, there are important subcategories that influence MSS design. For example, managers differ by organizational level, functional area, educational background, and need for analytic support. Staff specialists differ with respect to education, functional area, and relationship to management. Today's users are typically very hands-on oriented, in both creating and using DSS, although they may need help from analysts in initially setting up access to needed data.

Section 3.11 Review Questions

1. List and describe the two broad classes of DSS users.
2. List and describe the four types of DSS intermediaries.
3. Why are most users typically very hands-on in their DSS usage patterns?

3.12 DECISION SUPPORT SYSTEM HARDWARE

DSS have evolved simultaneously with advances in computer hardware and software technologies. Hardware affects the functionality and usability of the MSS. The choice of hardware can be made before, during, or after the design of the MSS software, but it is often determined by what is already available in the organization.

Typically, MSS run on standard hardware. The major hardware options are the organization's servers, mainframe computers with legacy DBMS, workstations, personal computers, or client/server systems. Distributed DSS run on various types of networks, including the Internet, intranets, and extranets. Access may be provided for mobile devices, including notebook PCs, tablet PCs, PDAs, and cell phones. This portability has become critical for deploying decision-making capability in the field, especially for salespersons and technicians.

The de facto DSS hardware standard is a Web server through which the DBMS provides data accessed from existing databases on the server, data warehouses, or legacy databases. Users access the DSS by using client PCs (or mobile devices) on which Web browsers are running. Models are provided directly through packages running either on the server, the mainframe, or some external system, or even on the client PC.

The power and capabilities of the World Wide Web have a dramatic impact on DSS. The Web can be used for collecting both external and internal (intranet) data for a DSS database. The Web can be used for communication and collaboration among DSS builders, users, and management. In addition, the Web can be used to download DSS software, use DSS applications provided by the company, or buy online from application service providers (ASPs). All major database vendors (e.g., IBM, Microsoft, Oracle, Sybase) provide Web capabilities by running directly on Web servers. Data warehouses and even legacy systems running on mainframes or ported to small RISC workstations can be accessed through Web technologies. Typically, models are solved on fast machines, but they are also run on Web servers, either running in the background or accessed from other systems, such as mainframes.

Optimization, simulation, statistics systems, and ES currently run in Java. These developments simplify access to data, models, and knowledge, and they simplify their integration. EIS/portals and OLAP systems provide powerful tools with which to develop DSS applications, generally via Web tools. New software development tools, such as Java, PHP, and the .NET Framework, automatically provide powerful onscreen objects (e.g., buttons, text boxes) for interfacing with databases and models. These readily open up direct access to the Web for the DSS developer. In many ways, this simplifies the developer's tasks, especially by providing common development tools and a common interface structure through Web browser technologies. A relatively recent open source platform is Ruby on Rails (**rubyonrails.org**).

Section 3.12 Review Questions

1. Why are DSS hardware and software choices often based on a firm's existing systems?
2. List potential PCs and mobile devices that decision makers could use to connect to a DSS.
3. List the potential hardware options for DSS implementation.
4. List the reasons the Web is utilized for DSS development and deployment.

3.13 A DSS MODELING LANGUAGE: PLANNERS LAB

As mentioned earlier, DSS can be developed with traditional programming languages or spreadsheets. Developing a model in a programming language such as Java requires programming expertise, but most business users today are comfortable using spreadsheets. Thus, many DSS today are built using spreadsheets because the end users are familiar with the look and feel of a spreadsheet. However, using a spreadsheet for modeling a problem of any significant size presents problems with documentation and error diagnosis. It is very difficult to determine or understand nested, complex relationships in spreadsheets created by someone else. This makes it difficult to modify a model built by someone else. A related issue is the increased likelihood of errors creeping into the formulas. With all the equations appearing in the form of cell references, it is challenging to figure out where an error might be. These issues were addressed in an early generation of DSS development software that was available on mainframe computers in the 1980s. One such product, Planners Lab, has been developed for today's computing environment and applications. This software is introduced and explained in this section. (Most of the material in this section has been adapted from materials contributed by Dr. Gerald Wagner.) Application Case 3.6 describes some applications of Planners Lab.

APPLICATION CASE 3.6
Nonprofits Use Planners Lab as a Decision-Making Tool

The Charles Drew Health Center (CDHC), located in North Omaha, Nebraska, has traditionally provided services to the residents of North Omaha. With a shift in population, CDHC was looking at the possibility of starting a satellite clinic. CDHC's goals were to increase the number of patients and increase awareness of the health center to the greater Omaha area. The new clinic would ideally be located near public transportation and be in an area of diverse socioeconomic status containing individuals who have chronic illnesses. CDHC contracted with the Community Development Consulting Group to use Planners Lab to determine the best location for its satellite clinic.

Input data included population data based on zip code, demographic and behavioral information of the area, and the number of providers in the area. Three zip codes were analyzed. The CDHC provided financial information for the model. Demographic information was obtained online based on the current demographics of the main CDHC, with the realization that they may not be the same at the new location. Information on the shift of Omaha residents was obtained through interviews with the Omaha Housing Authority. Additional information was provided by the Iowa Nebraska Primary Care Association. In order to use the model as a template, a growth rate of 5 percent was assumed and expenses were estimated.

The Community Development Consulting Group's model for the CDHC was designed as a template to be utilized in analyzing various areas for a satellite office. The model also has the ability to analyze information for building a new Community Health Center. It is extremely easy to add additional areas to analyze. The model can be used as a template by any health care facility in the nation to make location decisions.

Community Development Consulting Group has built models for several other nonprofit organizations. For example, Camp Fire USA in Omaha has a vision of following the Hull House model in Chicago (**hullhouse.org**). This would mean greatly expanding the number and kind of services offered. Expansion also entailed adding a significant amount of space, which meant negotiating for additional surrounding land. A Planners Lab model provided Camp Fire decision makers and the Board of Directors with a tool to simulate alternative scenarios.

Lutheran Family Services of Nebraska has a portfolio of about 30 programs of varying size and importance. It wanted a tool to evaluate future program investment and budgeting as well as maintenance, expansion, and possible elimination of individual programs. A Planners Lab model was created to perform a portfolio analysis similar to the well-known Boston Consulting Group matrix. The executive team was surveyed to assign weights to multiple factors for both "achievability" and "importance." Weights were collected for the following qualitative factors: core competencies, competitive advantage, sustainability, brand, impact on community, independence, client need for service, government regulations, and direct competition. These weights were combined for the horizontal axis in the portfolio matrix. Several different quantitative variables were used for the vertical axis, including total expenses and net margin.

The Open Door Mission of Omaha had successfully completed a capital campaign and was ready for facility expansion. A Planners Lab model was created that took into account the various services provided by the Open Door Mission, space requirements for each, and future client growth. Nearly 60 variables were involved in the model, including clinic square footage, industrial washer dryer square footage, meals per day, and ratio of men to medical staff.

Source: Contributed by Dr. G. R. Wagner and his students. Additional information on these applications including the complete models is available at **plannerslab.com**.

In the early days of DSS, one highly successful software product was the Interactive Financial Planning System (IFPS) from Execucom Systems Corporation in Austin, Texas. Execucom was founded by Dr. Gerald Wagner, who is also the founder of the Planners Lab. IFPS had a modeling language similar to that of the Planners Lab. During its era, IFPS was the dominant software package for financial planning. More than 1,500 corporations and government agencies along with more than 250 universities used IFPS.

Planners Lab is a good example of a DSS building tool. The software is free to academic institutions and can be downloaded from **plannerslab.com**. Planners Lab includes the following components: (1) an easy-to-use algebraically oriented model-building language and (2) an easy-to-use state-of-the-art option for visualizing model output, such as answers to What If and Goal Seek questions to analyze results of changes in assumptions. The combination of these components enables business managers and analysts to build, review, and challenge the assumptions that underlie decision-making scenarios.

Planners Lab makes it possible for the decision makers to "play" with assumptions to reflect alternative views of the future. Every Planners Lab model is an assemblage of assumptions about the future. Assumptions may come from databases of historical performance, market research, and the decision makers' minds, to name a few sources. Most assumptions about the future come from the decision makers' accumulated experiences in the form of opinions.

The resulting collection of equations is a Planners Lab model that *tells a readable story for a particular scenario*. Planners Lab lets decision makers describe their plans in their own words and with their own assumptions. The product's raison d'être is that a simulator should facilitate a conversation with the decision maker in the process of describing business assumptions. All assumptions are described in English equations (or the user's native language).

The best way to learn how to use Planners Lab is to launch the software and follow along. The software can be downloaded at **plannerslab.com**. A tutorial is downloaded with the software. See Courtney (2008) for another tutorial.

Generating Assumptions

Before looking at an example, note that the development of every Planners Lab model involves three steps. First, name/define the time periods. Second, outline the model. Third, develop the equations that contain the data and assumptions for the model.

The actual hands-on Planners Lab model builder is most likely a financial analyst, business analyst, or executive assistant. The model builder works closely with decision makers to capture their opinions for the model logic. We now describe a typical scenario.

The VP of Finance has a decision to make regarding investment in a new R&D project. He calls a meeting with his Planners Lab analyst, the VP of R&D, and others who can contribute to solving his problem. They meet in a room equipped with a video projector; the analyst has a laptop computer. The VP of Finance gives his impression of the problem at hand. Others do the same. All have seen the Planners Lab in action before, so they know where they are headed (i.e., giving their opinions about assumptions). The analyst now acts like a meeting recorder (not a facilitator or leader). As each person discusses his or her views of the assumptions, the analyst captures them in the Planners Lab software. For example, the VP of R&D says, "I think this investment will require $450,000 over 3 years." This causes the analyst to ask, "Can we refine that a little? Can we break it down into specific costs such as people, space, and equipment costs?" As the decision makers continue to think out loud, the analyst continues to capture the assumptions, and the model-building process is now in progress. The assumptions will resemble something like this:

COLUMNS 2010, 2011, 2012

Salary per employee = 95000

People cost = Number of employees × Salary per employee

Number of employees = 2, 4, 6

Square feet per employee = 150

Space cost per square foot = 24

Space cost = Space cost per square foot × Square feet per employee × Number of employees

Total cost = People cost + Space cost

Figure 3.10 shows how this appears in a Planners Lab model. Even without training, anyone can understand it. The planning horizon is 3 years. There will be two employees in 2010, four in 2011, and six in 2012. People costs are computed from the number of employees multiplied by individual salaries, which average $95,000. Space cost is computed at the rate of $24 (per square foot), multiplied by 150 (square feet per employee), multiplied by the number of employees. Variables can be named anything and spelled any way. Assumptions can be entered in any order, any words used, and computations can be defined in any way.

Planners Lab Tutorial Example

The Planners Lab program starts with a welcome screen for the user to create a new model or to open a saved model that may be stored locally or on the network. To create

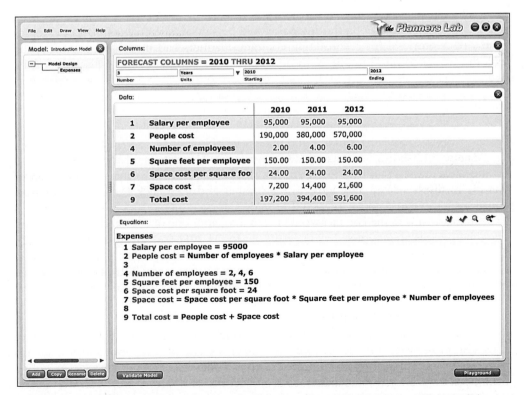

FIGURE 3.10 An Example of a Model Showing Time Periods, Assumptions, Data as Plain-English Equations, and a Results Table

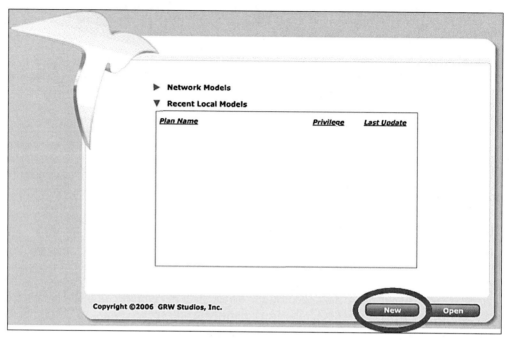

FIGURE 3.11   Initial Screen at Startup

a new model, the user has two options: (1) click the New button (see Figure 3.11) or (2) go to the File menu and choose New.

After clicking the New button, the software is ready to develop a new model from scratch. The example used in this tutorial would be similar to what might be a model for preparing a proposal for a consulting contract. Planners Lab model equations can be exported to Microsoft Word (how to do that is explained later) and equations for the entire model are also presented. It would be good to look at these now as a reference.

The Planners Lab menu is located at the top of the window and has five categories: File, Edit, Draw, View, and Help. Due to space limitations, many menu features will not be discussed. The user should simply "play around" with the available options; most likely those not discussed will be intuitive and understandable.

Figure 3.12 shows the Data table (see arrow 1). This data is for the node displayed on the stage. Data for other nodes are not displayed. The Data table can be open or closed. To display data, click View in the toolbar and then click Data table. To show equations for multiple nodes, press the Ctrl key and click the nodes.

In this example, the contract would begin in quarter one of 2010 and last for 2 years. The time periods are expressed as Q1 2010 out to Q4 2011 (see arrow 2 in Figure 3.12). There is flexibility in how to define time periods. Examples of other options would be Q1–Q8, Quarter 1–Quarter 8, and Quarter 1 2010 out to Quarter 8 2011. The general rule of thumb when using Planners Lab is to define things in the way that makes the most sense.

The model outline is in the left window (see arrow 3 in Figure 3.12). This hierarchical tree is an outline to define the pieces in a model. It is like a book outline or table of contents. Breaking up a model into chunks makes the model easier to maintain and also easier to explain to others. The tree is made up of nodes and subnodes. Users can define the tree however they want and call nodes and subnodes whatever they want. Of course, the users may not want to break up the model into pieces and just put all the assumptions into one node.

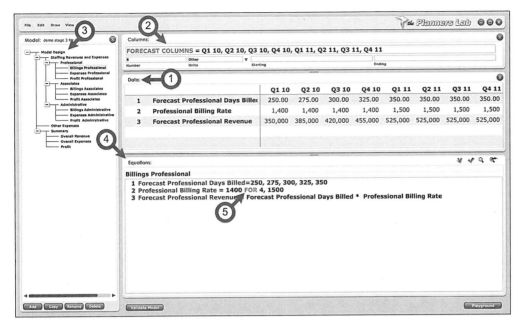

FIGURE 3.12 Model Outline (Left Window) and Highlighted Reserved Words

In this example the "level 1" nodes are *Professional, Associates,* and *Administrative.* This means that three types of people are involved in this proposal. Again, users can name things whatever they want. For example, "Professional" might have been named "Seniors." Although the software does not care what things are called, it is important that their spelling and case be consistent.

Within each level 1 node are subnodes for billings, expenses, and profit. Again, the model can be laid out in any way; nothing is predetermined. The same variable name(s) can be used in more than one node.

The next step is to add equations for each node in the tree (see arrow 4 in Figure 3.12). The variables on the left-hand side of equations are in red.

One rule of thumb is that if the data/assumptions change from one time period to another, they are separated by commas. For example, *Forecast Professional Days Billed* is expected to be 250 in the first time period, 275 in the next time period, 300 in the next time period, 325 in the next, and then 350. Another rule of thumb is that the last thing that appears in an equation is used for all remaining time periods. Thus, the value of 350 is used for quarters 5, 6, 7, and 8.

The next equation is for *Professional Billing Rate.* Notice the word **FOR** (see arrow 5 in Figure 3.12). The software calls this a keyword or a reserved word. Keywords have a specific purpose and meaning to simplify modeling. In this case, it means just what would be expected. The *Professional Billing Rate* is 1,400 for four time periods and then 1,500 for all remaining time periods. A list of the most frequently used keywords is included later in this section. Additional information on keywords can be found at **plannerslab.com** and through the software's Help command.

Look at the subnode *Expenses Professional* and notice the word **IN** in the equation (see arrow 1 in Figure 3.13). This is the way to refer to variables in another node. In this case, it is saying that *Forecast Professional Income* is equal to *Professional Person Salary Per Day* multiplied by *Forecast Professional Days Billed,* as defined in the node *Billings Professional.* As is the case throughout, just read the equations in a logical manner and

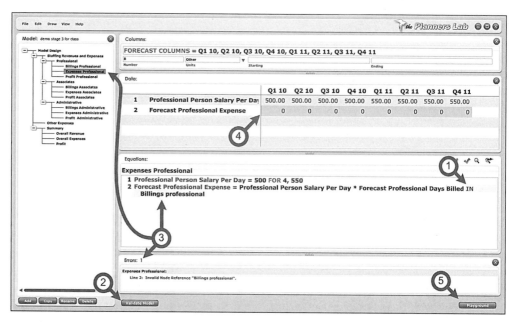

FIGURE 3.13 Validate Model Option with Errors Highlighted

they will probably make sense. The meaning of the rest of the nodes and their equations should be clear.

To check for modeling errors, click the Validate button (see arrow 2 in Figure 3.13). The software lets the user know of any errors (see arrow 3 in Figure 3.13). In the model tree, node(s) that have errors are highlighted in orange. Within the equations for that node, the errors are highlighted yellow, and below the equations is a window with a description of the error(s). In the example, the reference to the variable *Billings Professional* has "professional" without capitalization. Because variables in Planners Lab are case sensitive, this is an error. With a little practice, finding and correcting errors is very easy. The most common errors are consistency errors. Variables don't have to be spelled correctly, but they have to be consistent.

Note in Figure 3.13 that values for *Forecast Professional Expense* in the data table are zero (see arrow 4 in Figure 3.13). That is because the equations for that node are not shown on the stage.

Before moving on to the results, let's make some changes to the model to include risk or uncertainty. Thus far in the example there has been no explicit recognition of the possibility of uncertainty. For example, *Forecast Professional Days Billed* was assumed to be 250 in time period one. It is more likely that the number will not be exactly 250. That is easy to handle in Planners Lab by using Monte Carlo simulation.

For this example, the probability distribution used is the triangular distribution. The three items that define the triangular distribution are values for least, most probable, and most. The keyword to use is **TRIRAND** (see Figure 3.14). In Planners Lab, this is reflected as **TRIRAND** (least value, most probable value, most value), and for our example this could be **TRIRAND** (225, 250, 300). This simply means that *Forecast Professional Days Billed* could be as low as 225, is most likely going to be 250, but could go as high as 300. The value of doing this will be obvious when we examine the results.

To see the results, click the Playground button (see arrow 5 in Figure 3.13). The word *playground* was chosen because this is a place to play with assumptions. After clicking the

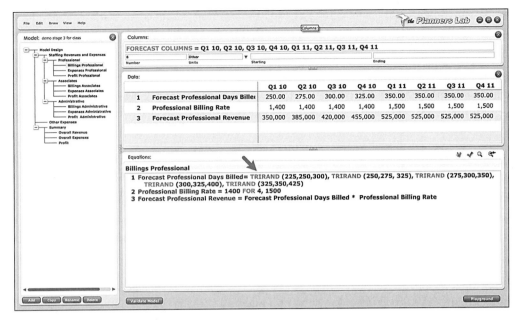

FIGURE 3.14 Monte Carlo Simulation with TRIRAND

Playground button, note the row of charting icons (see arrow 1 in Figure 3.15). Chart icons are discussed in detail later in this tutorial.

Throughout the software, drag-and-drop technology is used. To get a line chart, drag the Line Chart icon into the open window and then decide what to display in the Line Chart. The open window is called the *stage*. As an example, click the *Billings Professional* node. Note that variables are categorized automatically as either Goal or What If variables (see arrow 2 in Figure 3.15). What If variables impact Goal variables, and Goal variables

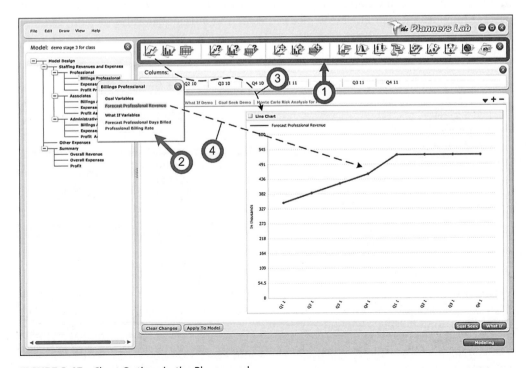

FIGURE 3.15 Chart Options in the Playground

impact no other variables. In this case, *Professional Billing Rate* is one variable that affects *Forecast Professional Revenue.* The What If variables are the ones to play with to determine their impact on a Goal variable, such as profit.

For a line chart, drag the Line Chart icon onto the stage (see number 3 in Figure 3.15). At this point, the chart is empty. To display data for *Forecast Professional Revenue,* drag that variable name on top of the empty chart (see number 4 in Figure 3.15), drop it, and the data is displayed. Any combination of charts can be chosen, and any data can be charted following the same process. Each chart type is summarized and explained later.

Figure 3.16 depicts some examples of charts that might be used for this model. Number 1 is a line chart, number 2 shows the corresponding bar chart, and number 3 is a table with selected variables. Number 4 is a Monte Carlo Risk Analysis graph. Each chart type is explained later in this tutorial. Any number of charts can be placed on the stage, but of course too many charts are confusing and the charts become too small. This layout of charts on the stage is called a "dashboard." It is a living dashboard. As a What If analysis is performed on a variable, the effect ripples through all charts affected by the change.

Any number of dashboards can be created, and each dashboard can contain any number of charts. To create a new dashboard, click the "+" symbol (see arrow 1 in Figure 3.17). Individual dashboards can be given any name (see arrow 2 in Figure 3.17). By clicking the tabs, the user can change the view from one dashboard to another. Useful Planners Lab features include the What If and Goal Seek charts. These enable the user to simulate the effects of changes in selected What If variables. Notice that some of the chart types have a question mark; this means the data in them is editable. These are for asking the What If questions (see number 3 in Figure 3.17).

Figure 3.17 shows changes in the What If variable *Professional Billing Rate* (see number 4). This is simply done by grabbing a specific data point or an entire line for the base case, dragging it to where it is wanted, and dropping it. The effect of the change on a Goal variable, such as *Profit,* is shown (see number 5). The lighter line shows that the What If variable (*Professional Billing Rate*) increased about 14 percent. The impact of the change on the Goal variable (*Profit*) is shown instantly as the lighter line for the Goal variable of *Profit.* The increase is about 44 percent. When the user moves the mouse pointer over a data point, a text box appears with

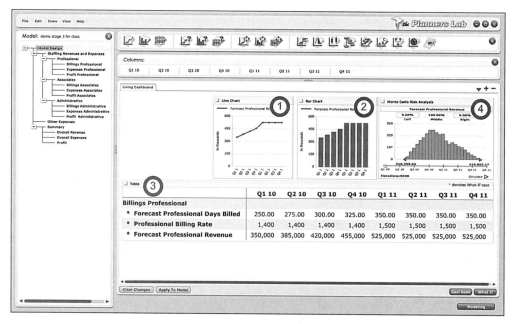

FIGURE 3.16   A Stage in the Playground with Several Chart Types

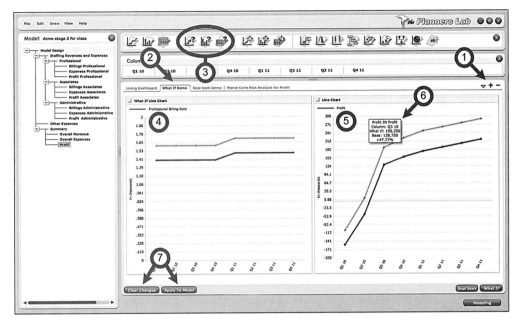

FIGURE 3.17   Charts for What If Analysis

the base case and the What If case (see arrow 6 in Figure 3.17). If the user wants to change the base case data to the new What If data, this can be accomplished by clicking the Apply To Model button (see arrow 7 in Figure 3.17). The changes can be reversed by choosing the Clear Changes button (see arrow 7). All changes are accumulated until one of these two buttons is clicked. A What If scenario can be saved by choosing Open Scenario List in the File menu, selecting Create New, and then naming it.

Figure 3.18 depicts a Goal Seek scenario. Suppose, the user wants to determine changes necessary in the variable *Professional Person Salary Per Day* to increase the

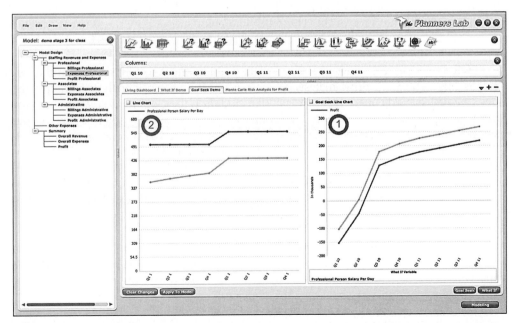

FIGURE 3.18   Goal Seeking to Determine Changes Needed in a What If Variable to Achieve Desired Result in a Goal Variable

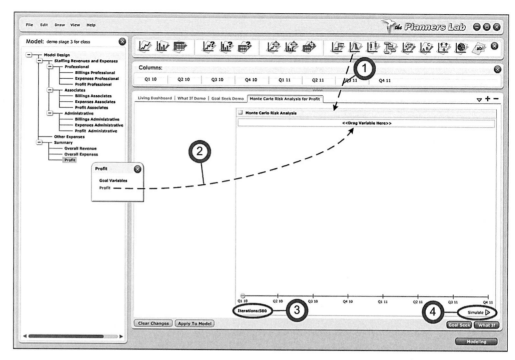

FIGURE 3.19 Monte Carlo Simulation Start Options

company's profit by about $50,000 in each period. The Goal Seek chart is the one with the "target graphic" in the icon bar. Drag and drop the Goal variable *Profit* and the What If variable *Professional Person Salary Per Day* onto the empty Goal Seek chart (see number 1 in Figure 3.18). Create a separate line chart that displays the What If variable. Drag the Goal line to increase profit by about $150,000 and drop it. The lighter line represents the goal wanted for profit. The other line chart shows how the What If variable needs to change in order to achieve the profit goal. The lighter color lines are the What If cases and the darker ones are the base cases.

Before leaving this section of the tutorial, it is important to further explain the risk analysis chart. To create a risk analysis chart, drag-and-drop the risk analysis icon onto the stage (the bell shaped curve). Here we will drag-and-drop the Goal variable *Profit* onto the chart. Any Goal variable can be used, but only one variable can be used at a time. In our example, the user has chosen the desired number of Monte Carlo iterations (number 3, Figure 3.19). The default is 500. Clicking the Simulate button (number 4, Figure 3.19) runs the simulation.

The results in Figure 3.20 show the results of 500 iterations for quarter one of 2011. To see another quarter, move the slider to another quarter. In this example, we want to see a 95 percent confidence interval. Therefore, 2.5 percent was put in each tail by clicking the "Right" and "Left" text boxes and placing 2.5 in each. The result is that we have reason to believe with 95 percent confidence that profit in this quarter will be between $242,339.05 and $255,221.86. Note the left and right arrows by the left- and rightmost bars. Those can be grabbed and moved to wherever wanted to show percent chances of being greater than and/or less than values indicated.

Another chart type is shown in Figure 3.21. The Variable Tree chart (see number 1) can be especially useful for two purposes. One is for debugging (i.e., Are the variables related as expected?). The other purpose is for easily explaining to someone what

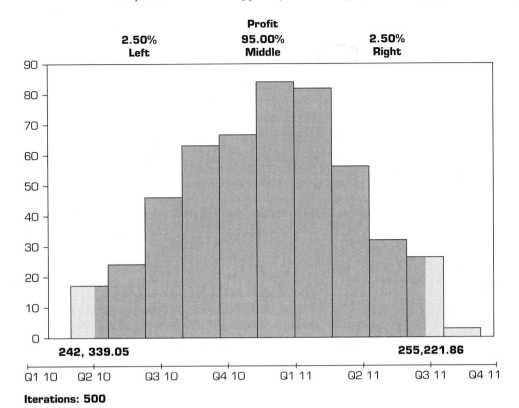

FIGURE 3.20   Example of Risk Analysis Using Monte Carlo Simulation

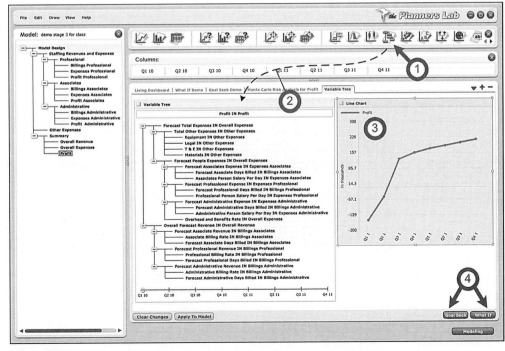

FIGURE 3.21   Using the Variable Tree to See Relationships Among Variables in the Model

variables affect what. To create a Variable Tree chart we drag the Variable Tree icon onto the stage and drag on a Goal variable (see number 2). A Goal variable needs to be provided, and in this case *Profit* is used. Clicking all of the "+" signs opens all of the relationships (they are already opened in this figure). This display is a clear and understandable way to see how variables in the model are related to *Profit*.

In this example, a line chart has also been dragged onto the stage and *Profit* shown (see number 3). At this point another Planners Lab feature will be shown that has been available all along but not described. Note the two buttons called Goal Seek and What If in the bottom right-hand corner (see number 4). Rather than drag and drop data points in a chart or changing values in a What If table, the user can edit the equations directly in the window that will open when one of these is clicked. For example, click the What If button and see the new window open at the bottom of the screen in Figure 3.22 (see number 1). What If variables can be dragged into this window from the model outline or directly from the Variable Tree. In this case, we drag *Professional Billing Rate* from the Variable Tree into the window (see number 2). It is instantly shown as *Professional Billing Rate* **IN** *Billings Professional* = 1,400 **FOR** 4, 1,500. This equation can now be edited, such as changing the 1,400 to 1,800 and the 1,500 to 1,600 (see number 3). Clicking the See Results button (see number 4) shows how this affects the *Profit* line chart (see number 5). This method of performing a What If analysis is more powerful than what was described previously in this tutorial. Goal Seek can be done in a similar manner with a Goal variable and a What If variable.

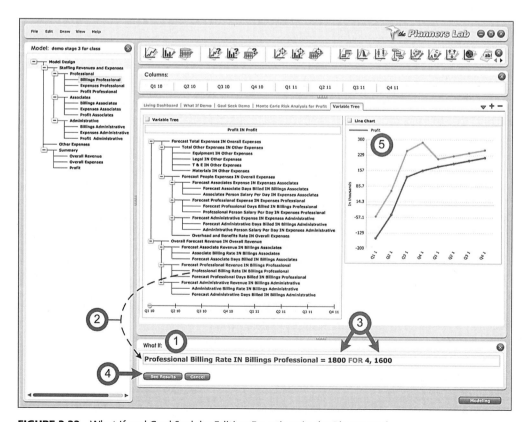

FIGURE 3.22   What If and Goal Seek by Editing Equations in the Playground

Summary of Planners Lab Charts

Figure 3.23 summarizes key charts in Planners Lab. Before getting into explanations, it is possible to customize the charts. Note that in the upper-left-hand corner next to the chart type name is a square that looks like a button. Clicking the square shows the available options. The options vary among chart types. Options include changing colors of lines or bars, showing bars vertically or horizontally, and so on. Space will not be used here to explain each option, but how to use these features should be self-explanatory.

LINE CHART Line charts show data points as a line for selected variables. Line charts are useful for recognizing trends or outliers in time series data. What If line charts have lighter lines around them to differentiate those from "normal" line charts. Time periods are on the horizontal axis, and the scale for the selected variable is on the vertical axis. By default, all time periods are displayed when a chart is first displayed. However, the user can grab and drag out of the window any time period(s) displayed. Just grab the time period label and drag it off. Likewise, the user can grab any variable and drag it off the stage. Just grab the variable name in the legend or the line in the chart and drag it off the stage.

WHAT IF LINE CHART Similar to a line chart, the What If line chart graphs the selected variables for each time period as a line. In this case, only What If variables can be selected. The What If line chart allows the user to create a what-if scenario by dragging single data points in the graph to a different level or by dragging the entire line.

GOAL SEEK LINE CHART The Goal Seek line chart graphs one selected Goal variable. Besides the Goal variable, the user also provides a What If variable by dragging a selection into the designated area in the chart. Now, the user can set a desired value for the Goal variable, and the program will determine what changes in the What If variable are required to reach this goal.

BAR CHART Like a line chart, the bar chart depicts the values of selected Goal variables and/or What If variables for all time periods. The time periods are on the horizontal axis, and the scale for the selected variables are on the vertical axis.

WHAT IF BAR CHART What If bar charts only allow What If variables. To change the value of a what-if variable, click on the top end of a bar for a time period and move it to the desired level. Note that only the lighter colored part of the bar can be moved, because this represents the what-if case. The darker part remains at the actual values to

	Line Chart		What If Line Chart		Goal Seek Line Chart
	Bar Chart		What If Bar Chart		Goal Seek Bar Chart
	Table		What If Table		Goal Seek Table
	Impact Analysis		Risk Analysis		Variable Tree
	Pie Chart		Sticky Note		

FIGURE 3.23 Key Charts Planners Lab

serve as a reference point. Multiple bars can be moved at one time with Ctrl-click or Shift-click.

TABLE   A table allows the user to display data for selected variables. Rather than dragging and dropping one variable at a time, an entire node can be dragged on top of the table and all variables in a node will be displayed. This is also true for other chart types. However, other chart types usually can only contain a few variables. The table does not have that concern.

WHAT IF TABLE   What If tables are an alternative to What If bar and line charts. This form of performing a What If analysis is probably the most useful. With the What If table, the user can pinpoint an *exact value,* which is difficult if dragging and dropping line charts or bar charts.

GOAL SEEK TABLE   Goal Seek tables are comparable to Goal Seek bar and line charts. The form of a table is very useful when the user intends to choose an exact value for a what-if variable, which is not always possible in line or bar charts.

IMPACT ANALYSIS   With an Impact Analysis, the user can determine the numerical impact what-if variables have on a chosen Goal variable. The inputs are a Goal variable and What If variables. Using a slider, the user can choose a percentage change to apply to all the What If variables. The impacts on the Goal variable (percentage change) are displayed. These impacts are for each What If variable, independent of all others.

RISK ANALYSIS   This chart is the basis for explicitly reflecting risk or uncertainty in an output variable as affected by uncertainty in input variables. The two risk analysis functions in Planners Lab are **TRIRAND** and **NORRAND**.

VARIABLE TREE   The Variable Tree shows a dependency tree of a selected Goal variable, which means a hierarchical depiction of all What If variables that have an impact on the Goal variable. This is very useful to quickly and easily see relationships between variables, such as when debugging a model.

PIE CHART   A Pie Chart shows the percentage distribution of several variables averaged across all time periods.

STICKY NOTE   Sticky notes are useful to place notes anywhere on the dashboard. Simply drag a note to where it is wanted and type in text. This can be useful for annotation of data and in presentations.

Frequently Used Planners Lab Keywords

COMMENT   **COMMENT** allows users to insert comments into a model. It is handy for adding explanatory comments. Here is a simple example:

```
Growth Rate = 1.2, PREVIOUS * 1.02
COMMENT this is based upon what we have seen in the past.
```

FOR   The keyword **FOR** is a shortcut for repeating values across time periods (columns). The following are typical examples:

```
Price = 10, 12 FOR 2, 15
```

This means that *Price* is $10 in period one, then $12 for two time periods, and then $15 for the remaining two time periods.

```
Hourly charge = 20, 22, 24 FOR 3
```

This could have been written as

```
Hourly charge = 10, 22, 24, 24, 24
```

but the word **FOR** is a shortcut. This could also been written simply as

```
Hourly charge = 20, 22, 24
```

Because 24 is the last term in the equation, it is used for all remaining time periods.

THRU The keyword **THRU** is a shortcut to designate one variable name through another variable name. See its use with the keyword **SUM**.

SUM The keyword **SUM** does just what you would expect—it sums numbers. Here is an example:

```
Revenue from product A = 10
Revenue from product B = 15
Revenue from product C = 25
Revenue all products = SUM (Revenue from product A THRU Revenue from
  product C)
```

TOTAL The keyword **TOTAL** again does what you might expect—it totals numbers. In Planners Lab, the **TOTAL** keyword totals the values associated with all instances of a variable name in a model or in a range of nodes in a model. Consider the following example:

```
Corporate Profit = TOTAL (Product Profit)
```

This totals all data associated with the variable *Product Profit* in all nodes within the model.

Another option is to specify a variable name in selected nodes. Here is an example:

```
Profit from trees = TOTAL (Profit IN Tree type 1 THRU Profit IN Tree
  type 4)
```

NPV **NPV** is used to compute net present value. **NPV** is normally used to determine the value of some project investment (e.g., installing new equipment or constructing a new building). This is like the inside out of your savings account. Say you put money into an account at some interest rate, such as 10 percent. The beginning principal gains interest at the rate of 10 percent per year. If you put in $100 on January 1, you have $110 on December 31. You leave it all in the savings account and then on December 31 of the next year your total is $110 multiplied by 1.10, and so on.

With **NPV,** you want to do the reverse. Rather than taking the beginning amount and growing it by some interest rate, you take future cash flows and discount them back to today's value. In time period one, you take the cash flow at the end of period one and divide it by 1 plus the discount rate. With **NPV**, you provide a discount rate, such as 0.10. The discount rate then is sort of like an interest rate. In time period two, that period's cash flow is divided by the square of one plus the discount rate. Each year's **NPV** is summed together, and the final number is the present value over the life of a project. The total of each year's NPV is the amount of dollars the project is worth above and beyond that discount rate.

A simple example is as follows:

```
Net present value = NPV (Initial investment, Cash flow, Discount rate).
```

The variables *Initial investment, Cash flow,* and *Discount rate* are those described in your model. *Cash flow* is the difference between money coming in and money going out in each time period.

IRR   **IRR** is used to compute the internal rate of return. It is closely related to net present value. **IRR** finds that discount rate where **NPV** is equal to zero. A simple example is as follows:

```
Internal rate of return = IRR (Initial investment, Cash flow)
```

The discount rate could be the amount you could earn in a safe savings account. So if IRR is greater than that, it might be worth taking the risk to earn more.

TREND   **TREND** is used for forecasting the time series of a variable by using simple linear regression, where time periods are the "independent" variable. Here is an example:

```
Money used = 1000, 1500, 2000, TREND
```

In this example, there is a clear straight line increase in *Money used* each time period. Usually it is not so obvious, but there will always be a "best fit" line through the data points. The **TREND** function uses that "best fit" line to estimate the data for the remaining time periods.

FORECAST   **FORECAST** is another kind of simple linear regression. It is the "workhorse" for forecasting when one variable is dependent upon another variable. Rather than using time as an independent variable, as with **TREND**, one variable is forecast as a "function" of another variable. Here is an example assuming a six-column model:

```
Unit price = 295, 275, 300, 325, 350, 400
Units sold = 47000, 59000, 50700, FORECAST (Unit price)
```

Unit price for the six time periods is 295, 275, 300, 325, 350, and 400. The software then computes the relationship (correlation) between *Unit price* and *Units sold* in the first three time periods. Using this information, it computes *Units sold* for the remaining three periods based on *Unit price* in the last three periods.

COL   The **COL** keyword is used in special column equations when referring to and performing the operations on the column statements or to access a particular column in an equation. Here is an example:

```
Year = SUM (COL Jan THRU COL Dec)
```

In the example, the forecast columns are specified as Jan THRU Dec (i.e., months).

IN   The **IN** keyword is used to refer to a variable that exists outside of the current node for use in equations. Here is an example:

```
"Node A" has equations:
  b = 2
  q = 8
```

```
"Node B" has equations:
  a = 5
  b = 6
Total = 20 + a IN Node A·(b IN Node A + b IN Node B + q IN
Node A / 4)
```

MOVAVG   The **MOVAVG** function calculates the moving average over the last three periods. This is often used for forecasting purposes. Here is an example:

```
Sales = 200, 400, 600
Average Sales = MOVAVG (Sales)
```

PREVIOUS   The **PREVIOUS** keyword is used in an equation when the value of the variable in one column is derived from that of a previous column. This keyword is probably the one most often used. A column offset specifies how far back to retrieve a previous value. If no column offset is specified, then 1 is used. If **PREVIOUS** is used with a variable name after it, that variable's value in the previous column will be used. If no value is available, then zero will be used. Here is an example:

```
Sales = 17000, 20000, PREVIOUS * 1.07
(or)
Sales = 17000, 20000, PREVIOUS 2 * 1.07 Sales ratio = 5, 6, 7
Sales = 10000, PREVIOUS Sales ratio * 2000
(or)
Sales = 10000, PREVIOUS 2 Sales ratio * 2000
```

OTHER LESS OFTEN USED KEYWORDS   Many other functions are available within Planners Lab. We will not describe them here, but they can be looked up online or under the software's Help feature. Other interesting keywords include: **BCRATIO, CEILING, FLOOR, FUTURE, IF . . . THEN . . . ELSE, LN, MATRIX, MAX, MIN, POWER, ROUND, STDEV,** and several others.

3.14   RESOURCES, LINKS, AND THE TERADATA UNIVERSITY NETWORK CONNECTION

The use of this chapter and most other chapters in this book can be enhanced by the tools described in the following sections.

Resources and Links

We recommend looking at the following resources and links for further reading and explanations:

- The Data Warehousing Institute (**tdwi.org**)
- The OLAP Report (**olapreport.com**)
- DSS Resources (**dssresources.com**)

Cases

All major MSS vendors (e.g., MicroStrategy, Microsoft, Oracle, IBM, Hyperion, Cognos, Exsys, Fair Isaac, SAP, Information Builders) provide interesting customer success stories. Academic-oriented cases are available at the Harvard Business School Case Collection (**hbsp.harvard.edu/products/cases.html**), Business Performance Improvement Resource (**bpir.com**), Idea Group Publishing (**idea-group.com**), Ivy League Publishing (**ivylp.com**), ICFAI Center for Management Research (**icmr.icfai.org/casestudies/icmr_case_studies.htm**), KnowledgeStorm (**knowledgestorm.com**), and other sites. For additional case resources, see Teradata University Network (**teradatauniversitynetwork.com**).

Miller's *MIS CASES*

All the cases in Miller's *MIS Cases* (2009) involve decision making and can be utilized. The spreadsheet cases are all essentially model-driven DSS, and the database cases are all data-driven DSS.

Periodicals

We recommend the following periodicals:

- *Advisor* (**advisor.com**)
- *Baseline Magazine* (**baselinemag.com**)
- *Business Intelligence Journal* (**tdwi.org**)
- *CIO* (**cio.com**)
- *CIO Insight* (**cioinsight.com**)
- *Computerworld* (**computerworld.com**)
- *Decision Support Systems* (**elsevier.com**)
- *eWEEK* (**eweek.com**)
- *InfoWeek* (**infoweek.com**)
- *InfoWorld* (**infoworld.com**)
- *Management Information Systems Quarterly (MIS Quarterly)* (**misq.org**)
- *Technology-Evaluation* online magazine (**technologyevaluation.com**)

The Teradata University Connection

Teradata University Network (TUN) (**teradatastudentnetwork.com**, for students) provides a wealth of information and cases on DSS; however, it is typically termed as BI. All cases and white papers that involve aspects of decision making are DSS-relevant pieces.

Chapter Highlights

- There are several definitions of *DSS*.
- A DSS is designed to support complex managerial problems that other computerized techniques cannot. DSS is user oriented, and it uses data and models.
- DSS are generally developed to solve specific managerial problems, whereas BI systems typically report status, and, when a problem is discovered, their analysis tools are utilized by decision makers.
- DSS can provide support in all phases of the decision-making process and to all managerial levels for individuals, groups, and organizations.
- DSS is a user-oriented tool. Many applications can be developed by end users, often in spreadsheets.

- DSS can improve the effectiveness of decision making, decrease the need for training, improve management control, facilitate communication, save effort by the users, reduce costs, and allow for more objective decision making.
- The AIS SIGDSS classification of DSS includes communications-driven and group DSS (GSS), data-driven DSS, document-driven DSS, knowledge-driven DSS, data mining and management ES applications, and model-driven DSS. Several other classifications map into this one.
- Several useful classifications of DSS are based on why they are developed (institutional vs. ad hoc), what level within the organization they support (personal, group, or organizational), whether they support individual work or group work (individual DSS vs. GSS), and how they are developed (custom vs. ready-made).
- A modeling language such as the Planners Lab can be a powerful tool for developing DSS that are easy to understand.
- The major components of a DSS are a database and its management, a model base and its management, and a user-friendly interface. An intelligent (knowledge-based) component can also be included. The user is also considered to be a component of a DSS.
- The components of DSS are typically deployed and integrated via Internet technologies. Web browsers are typically used as user interfaces.
- Data warehouses, data mining, and OLAP have made it possible to develop DSS quickly and easily.

- The data management subsystem usually includes a DSS database, a DBMS, a data directory, and a query facility.
- Data are extracted from several sources, internal and external.
- The DBMS provides many capabilities to the DSS, ranging from storage and retrieval to report generation.
- The model base includes standard models and models specifically written for the DSS.
- Custom-made models can be written in programming languages, in special modeling languages, and in Web-based development systems (e.g., Java, the .NET Framework).
- The user interface (or dialog) is of utmost importance. It is managed by software that provides the needed capabilities. Web browsers commonly provide a friendly, consistent DSS GUI.
- The user interface capabilities of DSS have moved into small, portable devices, including PDAs, mobile telephones, and even MP3 players.
- The DSS is supplemented by the user's intellectual capabilities. The user is knowledgeable about the problem being solved.
- A DSS can be used directly by managers (and analysts), or it can be used by intermediaries.
- DSS applications are typically developed, delivered, and run on the Web. It is convenient to distribute them to remote locations.

Key Terms

ad hoc DSS *82*
analytical model *97*
business (system)
   analyst *107*
business analytics
   (BA) *78*
business intelligence
   (BI) *75*
data warehouse *86*
database *90*
database management
   system (DBMS) *86*

directory *93*
DSS application *75*
expert tool
   user *107*
extraction *92*
facilitator (in a GSS) *107*
graphical user interface
   (GUI) *101*
group support system
   (GSS) *84*
institutional DSS *82*
intermediary *107*

model base *96*
model base
   management
   system (MBMS) *86*
model building blocks
   97
object *101*
operational models *97*
organizational
   knowledge base *86*
predictive analytics *78*
query facility *93*

staff assistant *107*
strategic models *96*
tactical models *97*
user interface *100*
user interface
   management system
   (UIMS) *100*

Questions for Discussion

1. Review the major characteristics and capabilities of DSS. How do each of them relate to the major components of DSS?
2. List some internal data and external data that could be found in a DSS for a university's admissions office.
3. Explain how poor data quality can lead to bad decisions.
4. Why is it so important for an organization to make data quality a key organizational issue?
5. Why is it so important to have a single version of the truth when it comes to data integration for decision making? Give or find an example of when not having a single version of the truth in believed data integration led to problems for an organization.
6. Why is scalability an important database issue?
7. Why is data security an important database issue?
8. Provide a list of possible strategic, tactical, and operational models for a university, a restaurant, and a chemical plant.
9. Review the models described in the situations described in the opening vignette, the End of Chapter Application Case, and the other Application Cases for this chapter. Compare and contrast what they are and how they are used. Explain how this illustrates the difficulty in model management as compared with that of database management.
10. Show the similarities between DBMS and MBMS. What is common to both and why? What are the differences and why?
11. Why was DSS the first MIS ever defined as requiring a computer?
12. Why does a DSS need a DBMS, a model management system, and a user interface, but not necessarily a knowledge-based management system?
13. Why might the user be considered a component of a DSS?
14. Why do managers use intermediaries? Will they continue to use them in the future? Why or why not? Would you? Why or why not?
15. Why are DSS typically developed on an organization's existing hardware and software?
16. Why are DSS typically developed and deployed with Web-based technology? Discuss the potential benefits that a DSS application can derive from the Web in terms of both developers and users.
17. What are the benefits and the limitations of the AIS SIGDSS classification for DSS?
18. Compare an individual DSS to a group DSS. How are they similar? How are they different?
19. How has the Web affected the components of DSS and vice versa?
20. Compare a custom-made DSS with a ready-made DSS. Describe and discuss the advantages and disadvantages of each.
21. Search for a ready-made DSS. What type of industry is its market? Explain why it is a ready-made DSS.

Exercises

TERADATA STUDENT NETWORK (TSN) AND OTHER HANDS-ON EXERCISES

1. Explore **teradatastudentnetwork.com**. In a report, describe at least three interesting DSS applications and three interesting DSS areas (e.g., CRM, SCM) that you have discovered there.
2. Examine Daniel Power's DSS Resources site at **dssre sources.com**. Take the Decision Support Systems Web Tour (**dssresources.com/tour/index.html**). Explore other areas of the Web site.
3. On the Web, locate free speech-input software and try speech input. In a report, describe your experience. Try to find someone with a strong accent to use it as well as someone with a fairly neutral accent. What happens? Would you use this package on a regular basis? Why or why not?
4. On the Web, locate a free text-to-speech software package and try it. In a report, describe your experience. Describe several good applications of this software package.
5. On the Web, locate a free language-translation software package (text-to-text) and try it. (Note: Some of these are readily available running on Web servers.) Among other tests, try translating something with many idioms into

another language and then back to the first language. Compare the initial text to the final version. Is it understandable? In a report, describe your experience.

6. On the Web, find a DSS software vendor with download-able demo software. Download the software, install it, and test it. Report your findings to the class and demonstrate the software's capabilities.
7. Camp Fire USA is a national organization with local community outreach programs. One program is for after-school programs for first through fifth grade students. They now have one school and are considering expansion into one or two additional schools. The two additional schools being considered are Buffett and Gates. Camp Fire has obtained a grant in the amount of $125,000 per year for 3 years to extend to one or more additional schools.

   Your assignment is to create a Planners Lab model to analyze various scenarios and then make a recommendation of what Camp Fire might do. Starting assumptions are as given below. Try to arrive at a defensible recommendation to offer programs at both schools and do that within Camp Fire's ability to cover costs in the amount of

$125,000 per year. You are free to make changes in assumptions to achieve this goal if your changes are rational and reasonably supported. Assumptions include the following:

a. The staff to student ratio is 1 staff member for each 10 students.

b. The salary for a staff member is $30,000 per year.

c. For Buffett, miscellaneous costs are estimated to be $10,000 per year. For Gates, they are $5,000.

d. There are estimated to be 30 student prospects at Buffett and 20 at Gates.

e. The Gates school board has agreed to donate $15,000 if Camp Fire will host its program at its school.

Assumptions	2009	2010	2011
COMMENT Camp Fire USA assumptions			
Expansion funds	125,000	125,000	125,000
Staff to student ratio	0.1	0.1	0.1
Staff salary	30,000	30,000	30,000
COMMENT Buffett school assumptions			
Number of Buffett students	30	30	30
Number of Buffett required staff	3	3	3
Buffett required staff cost	90,000	90,000	90,000
Buffett misc costs	10,000	10,000	10,000
Buffett donation	0	0	0
Cost to add Buffett	100,000	100,000	100,000
Balance of expansion funds if add Buffett	25,000	25,000	25,000
COMMENT Gates school assumptions			
Number of Gates students	20	20	20
Number of Gates required staff	2	2	2
Gates required staff cost	60,000	60,000	60,000
Gates misc costs	5,000	5,000	5,000
Gates donation	15,000	15,000	15,000
Cost to add Gates	50,000	50,000	50,000
Balance of expansion funds if add Gates	75,000	75,000	75,000

8. **Pedro's Tree Trimming Business.** Pedro is developing a business plan and an application for financing for a tree-trimming business that he intends to start. He will run the service for 5 years and then dissolve it. He has developed the following information on various aspects of this business:

- **Truck costs:** Pedro plans on buying two new Ford F-150 trucks for the business, which can be purchased for $24,000 each. This cost includes taxes and fees at purchase. The resale value for a truck after 5 years is estimated at $8,000. The following describes the annual operating costs for a single truck: Annual insurance cost

is $1,200 and annual license and inspection fees are $100. Maintenance cost is $400 in the first year and increases by $200 in each subsequent year. The cost of repairs is zero for the first 2 years and will be $200 in the third year. In subsequent years, the cost will grow by $200 per year.

- **Fuel costs:** Fuel costs are $0.15/mile. In addition to job mileage, each truck will be driven 2,000 miles a year. The round trip to each job averages 20 miles.

- **Shredders:** In addition to trucks, Pedro must purchase wood shredders. He needs one shredder that costs $5,000. The shredder must be replaced at the beginning of the third year for a cost of $5,000. Shredders have no resale value.

- **Labor:** Each job requires two trimmers for an 8-hour day and $50 in supplies. Tree trimmers earn $15 an hour. The workers are hired hourly. Overhead (office, phone, secretary, etc.) for running the business is 40 percent of the trimmer labor cost. Pedro will be the manager with an annual salary of $30,000.
- **Demand:** The demand for service is expected to be 250 jobs per year. The fee per job is $650.

Based on this information, develop a model to project financial statements for Pedro's Tree Trimming. The bank usually wishes to see the following components for financial performance on an annual basis and over the 5-year period: total revenue, total costs, profits, and annual cash flow. The cash flow can also be used to develop a net present value of the investment. Use a discount rate of 15 percent (0.15). With Planners Lab software's graphics facilities, it is easy to present results in graphical form. Submit a copy of your model and financial projections in tabular as well as graphical form. (Acknowledgment: This exercise is adapted from an exercise prepared by Prof. Paul Jensen of University of Texas-Austin.)

9. Develop a Planners Lab model of the "bailout" loan that the federal government recently made to General Motors. One of the provisions of the loan agreement was that GM must produce a plan by March showing a positive net present value using "reasonable" assumptions. If it does not, it may be required to repay the loans immediately. The time frame for the NPV calculation is not given, but GM must provide pro forma financial statements out to 2014, so that is the time horizon we will use.

Assume that you are the analyst who was asked to build a model for this bailout decision back in mid-2008. A summary of GM's income statements for 2006 and 2007 and estimated results for 2008 using reports for the first three quarters are provided. This data is in an Excel spreadsheet that can be imported into the Planners Lab to start the development of your model, as described later. All the data is in millions of dollars, so a figure of $500 is actually $500 million and $13,400 is $13.4 billion.

GM was expected to get loans totaling $13.4 billion at 5 percent per year, and these must be repaid by December 29 of 2011. Loans are actually to be repaid quarterly, but we are going to assume annual payments in the amount of $4.921 billion per year from 2009–2011. GM must also reduce executive compensation and eliminate perks such as corporate jets. It cannot declare new dividends as long as it owes money to the government.

In addition to these requirements, the Bush administration suggested several other "targets" that GM should attempt to achieve, but these are not strict requirements. These targets are summarized in the following table, along with the way you should treat them in your Planners Lab model. To get started, read the following about the terms for the loans:

- **en.wikipedia.org/wiki/Automotive_industry_crisis_of_2008**
- **autonews.com/article/20081219/ANA02/812199997**

Build a model to estimate financial performance of the bailout decision.

GM Should Attempt to:	Assumption in PL Model
Be financially viable, which means it must be able to show a positive net present value using reasonable assumptions.	No time period is given for the net present value calculations, but elsewhere in the terms document it is stated that pro forma financial statements must be provided up to 2014, so that is the time frame we will use. It will be based on net gain or loss and a discount rate of 10%.
	Variable name: *Net Present Value*
	Node: *Net revenue*
Repay loans totaling $13.4 billion with an interest rate of 5% payable quarterly and a maturity date of December 29, 2011.	Assume annual payments, not quarterly. The annual payments will be $4.921 billion per year from 2009 to 2011.
	Variable name: *Bailout Loan Payment*
	Node: *Costs and expenses*
Accept limits on executive compensation and eliminate perks, such as corporate jets.	Assume this reduces selling, general, and administrative expense by $250 million per year, starting in 2009.
	Variable name: *Reduction in Perks Expense*
	Node: *Costs and expenses*
Not issue new dividends while they owe government debt.	Starting in 2009 dividends will be zero, saving about $600 million per year until the debt is repaid December 29, 2011.
	Variable name: *Reduction in Dividends*
	Node: *Costs and expenses*

GM Should Attempt to:	Assumption in PL Model
Reduce debts by two-thirds via a debt for equity exchange; that is, get bondholders to trade bonds for stock.	Reduce interest expense by two-thirds, not including the bailout loan. This will be modeled by reducing operating expenses by about $1 billion a year. Variable name: *Reduction in Interest Expense* Node: *Costs and expenses*
Make one-half of the voluntary employees beneficiary association (VEBA) payments in the form of stock. VEBA is the retirement fund that will be administered by the UAW. Payments start in 2010.	GM's payments are expected to be about $600 million per year, so this will still result in a net increase in expenses of about $300 million in 2010 and after, instead of the $600 million it would have been otherwise. Variable name: *Reduction in VEBA Payments* Node: *Costs and expenses*
Eliminate the jobs bank.	This is likely to happen. It's hard to figure out what GM's share is with the data, but assume it is about $400 million per year. Variable name: *Elimination of Jobs Bank* Node: *Costs and expenses*
Implement work rules and wages that are competitive with transplant auto manufacturers (U.S. operations of Toyota and Honda) by December 31, 2009.	This is perhaps the key variable, because it affects the cost of vehicles sold. Most provisions will be resisted by the UAW, but something has to give. See how much the *Automotive Cost of Sales Rate* has to be reduced to get to a positive NPV, given the other savings. The UAW says they are already competitive and that labor is only 10% of the vehicle cost. Toyota and Honda pay about $40–45 per hour. Some say GM pays $70–75 (see the Wikipedia entry on the U.S. auto crisis). Variable name: *Automotive Cost of Sales Rate* (This is already defined and is the percentage of auto cost relative to sales in dollars. For 2006, it was 95.7%. For 2009 assume it is 90%.)

This exercise was contributed by Prof. Jim Courtney, Louisiana Tech.

TEAM ASSIGNMENTS AND ROLE-PLAYING

1. In groups of no more than five students each, consider how each of you decided into which university or program you wanted to enroll. Each member should write down on a piece of paper two lists: (1) the important factors (criteria) that you considered and (2) the specific universities or programs you considered. As a group, consider what factors you had in common and which ones were different. Do the same for the specific universities or programs. Describe where each of you got your information for this problem. Also, think about what types of software you could have used (a DSS) to help you in the decision-making process. Write up your results in a report.

INTERNET EXERCISES

1. Search the Internet for literature and information about DSS and its relationship to BI, business analytics, and predictive analytics. Describe what you find.

2. Identify a DSS software vendor. Obtain information about its products. Write up your findings about its products in a report.

3. On the Internet, identify a course syllabus and materials for a DSS/BI/business analytics course at another college or university. Compare the course description to that of your own course. Repeat this assignment, using a DSS/BI/business analytics course syllabus from a university in another country. Use **isworld.org**.

4. Search the Web for capabilities of mobile devices (e.g., PDAs, cells phones) and describe how decision makers can utilize them effectively.

5. Perform a Web search and report on the current status of data security. What tools exist and what features do they have? Can any of them be called DSS? Why or why not?

END OF CHAPTER APPLICATION CASE

Spreadsheet Model-Based Decision Support for Inventory Target Setting at Procter & Gamble

Procter & Gamble (P&G) is a large, diversified, multinational consumer products company. Its modeling and decision support group was asked to create global inventory models. P&G has needed "scientific" models to help it control its inventory since the mid-1980s when it implemented Distribution Requirements Planning (DRP). P&G needed an easy way to establish reliable safety stock levels at both the item and location levels. This safety stock is needed to allow for uncertainty in demand as well as the uncertainty in production during the time when replenishments would be delivered.

The original solution was created using Lotus 1-2-3, but over the years the company has developed a suite of global inventory models using Excel. When developing the spreadsheet models, the company kept two goals in mind: "educate supply chain planners on various types, roles, and root causes of inventories in supply chains and provide a quick method for setting safety stock within a DRP framework." The latest model, in addition to growing into a global inventory model, also provides a mechanism for the central support group to train users and assist those who have questions. The inventory components in the models include: cycle stocks, safety stocks, frozen stocks, and anticipation stocks.

Most of P&G's models use a continuous review policy. Continuous review policy, as the name implies, means that inventory levels are monitored continually. When inventory goes below a set order point, the company reorders up to a set amount using an order quantity (number of items per unit) or a multiple of the order quantity. The models have been developed to accommodate the demand and production situation that P&G faces. Examples of these issues in the models include:

1. Modeling of normal and gamma distributions for demands or forecast errors
2. Recognition of a two-tier distribution network: customers receive replenishments directly from the plant or through a local distribution center
3. Pull and push policies

4. Integration of forecast bias in the safety stock calculation
5. Automatic pooling of demands across shipping points
6. Replenishment intervals (shipping calendar) to effectively address replenishments across many items

The modelers at P&G employed Monte Carlo simulations (which we learn a bit more about in the next chapter) in spreadsheets to evaluate different inventory policies by analyzing the policy's impact on the customer-service levels. These model simulations enable decision makers to identify the best inventory setting policies.

Over the years, P&G has made numerous improvements to its spreadsheet models and has released 10 versions in 20 years. Some of the improvements to the models include separating the various types of data, such as input, calculations, and results, by grouping and formatting differently; putting all pertinent data on the same screen; using color coding and highlights to designate both mandatory and optional fields; drawing attention to obvious mistakes, such as negative numbers where a negative is impossible or abnormally high or low numbers from what is expected in that field; and using fewer graphs, and then only when they make understanding the results easier.

Additionally, the company made an improvement using a safety factor that is automatically calculated to determine how many standard deviations of demand are kept as safety stock to ensure the target fill rate. Previous versions of the models required time-consuming manual entry of safety factors that had to be looked up, which limited flexibility and accuracy. Computation of the safety factor uses parameters such as a target fill rate, reaction times, lot size, forecast error, and type of probability distribution. Using these factors, the function uses a binary search to automatically calculate the safety factor. The system is utilized by hundreds of supply chain planners, incorporates well-documented work processes, and integrates a formal release process.

Success of this DSS has resulted in P&G developing other related systems, such as a Raw and Packing Materials Inventory Model; an Extended Inventory Model, which is able to model more intricate distribution networks; and a Retailer Inventory Model, which can calculate inventory at the store shelves level. These models use common terminology and are built using functions from a common function library that extends the statistical functions in Excel with user-defined inventory management functions that are written in Visual Basic for Applications.

An interesting system development issue is that the company uses very few macros. Users are located all over the world and speak different languages and own various computer systems, and macros do not necessarily translate from one computer system to another very well.

Finally, the company upgrades its systems every 18 to 24 months and announces the upgrades via the P&G intranet site. Users can do self-training on the upgrades through the computer or attend training seminars in person. User manuals are provided with the upgrades.

This case demonstrates a decision support model that can be developed using commercially available tools. Of course, significant expertise needed to develop the underlying mathematical models. The case also touches upon the need for systems developers to be aware of the unique needs of a global, diversified company in terms of diversity of languages, systems in use, and so on.

Questions for the Case

1. Describe the benefits of the developed inventory decision systems in use at P&G.
2. What other inputs might be relevant in building inventory decision models?
3. Would it be better for this DSS to be available as a Web-based DSS?
4. What lessons can you learn from studying this case?

Source: Based on I. Farasyn, K. Perkoz, and W. Van de Velde, "Spreadsheet Models for Inventory Target Setting at Procter and Gamble," *Interfaces*, Vol. 38, No. 4, July/August 2008, pp. 241–250.

References

Alter, S. L. (1980). *Decision Support Systems: Current Practices and Continuing Challenges.* Reading, MA: Addison-Wesley.

Anthes, G. H. (2006, January 23). "Computer to User: You Figure It Out." *Computerworld*, Vol. 40, No. 4, p. 24.

Bonczek, R. H., C. W. Holsapple, and A. B. Whinston. (1980). "The Evolving Roles of Models in Decision Support Systems." *Decision Sciences*, Vol. 11, No. 2, pp. 337–356.

Chongwatpol, J., and R. Sharda. (2010, forthcoming). "SNAP: A DSS to Analyze Network Service Pricing for State Networks," *Decision Support Systems*.

Courtney, J. F. (2008). "Software Review: The Planners Lab Modelling and Visualisation System." *International Journal of Applied Decision Sciences*, Vol. 1, No. 1.

Donovan, J. J., and S. E. Madnick. (1977). "Institutional and Ad Hoc DSS and Their Effective Use." *Data Base*, Vol. 8, No. 3, pp. 79–88.

English, L. (2002, September). "The Essentials of Information Quality Management." *DM Review*, Vol. 12, No. 9.

English, L. (2005, September). "IQ and Muda." *DM Review*, Vol. 15, No. 9, pp. 40–46.

Erickson, W. (2002). *Data Quality and the Bottom Line.* **tdwi.org** (accessed June 17, 2009).

Farasyn, I., K. Perkoz, and W. Van de Velde. (2008, July/August). "Spreadsheet Models for Inventory Target Setting at Procter and Gamble." *Interfaces*, Vol. 38, No. 4, pp. 241–250.

"Getting Clean: Strategic Technology: Data Management." (2004, August). *CIO Insight*, No. 42, pp. 72–77.

Gonzales, M. L. (2004, June 1). "The Architecture of Enterprise Data Quality." *Intelligent Enterprise*, Vol. 7, No. 9, p. 17.

Hackathorn, R. D., and P. G. W. Keen. (1981, September). "Organizational Strategies for Personal Computing in Decision Support Systems." *MIS Quarterly*, Vol. 5, No. 3, pp. 21–27.

Holsapple, C. W., and A. B. Whinston. (2000). *Decision Support Systems: A Knowledge-Based Approach.* Cambridge, MA: Thomson Learning.

Hurley, W. J., and M. Balez. (2008, July/August). "A Spreadsheet Implementation of an Ammunition Requirements Planning Model for the Canadian Army." *Interfaces*, Vol. 38, No. 4, pp. 271–280.

Iyer, S., R. Sharda, D. Biros, J. Lucca, and U. Shimp. (2009). "Organization of Lessons Learned Knowledge: A Taxonomy of Implementation." *International Journal of Knowledge Management*, Vol. 5, No. 3.

Keen, P. G. W. (1980, Fall). "Adaptive Design for Decision Support Systems." *Data Base*, Vol. 12, Nos. 1 and 2, pp. 15–25.

Little, J. D. C. (1970, April). "Models and Managers: The Concept of a Decision Calculus." *Management Science*, Vol. 16, No. 8, pp. 466–485.

Miller, M. L. (2005). *MIS Cases*, 3rd ed. Upper Saddle River, NJ: Prentice Hall.

Moore, J. H., and M. G. Chang. (1980, Fall). "Design of Decision Support Systems." *Data Base*, Vol. 12, Nos. 1 and 2, pp. 8–14.

Olavson, T., and C. Fry. (2008, July/August). "Spreadsheet Decision-Support Tools: Lessons Learned at Hewlett-Packard." *Interfaces,* Vol. 38, No. 4, pp. 300–310.

"Pacific Sunwear: Tracking Business Trends with BI." (2009, June). *Apparel.* **apparelmag.com/ME2/dirmod.asp? sid=&nm=&type=MultiPublishing&mod=PublishingTit les&mid=CD746117C0BB4828857A1831CE707DBE&tie r=4&id=137DDFAE6B5A48529AA49EDC5212969A** (accessed June 16, 2009).

Power, D. J. (2002). *Decision Making Support Systems: Achievements, Trends and Challenges.* Hershey, PA: Idea Group Publishing.

Power, D. J., and R. Sharda. (2009). "Decisions Support Systems." In S.Y. Nof (Ed.), *Springer Handbook of Automation.* New York: Springer-Verlag.

Raden, N. (2005, October). "Start Making Sense." *Intelligent Enterprise*, Vol. 8, No. 10, pp. 25–31.

Respicio, A., M. E. Captivo, and A. J. Rodrigues. (2002, July 4–7). "A DSS for Production Planning and Scheduling in the Paper Industry." *Proceedings of DSI Age 2002*, Cork, Ireland.

Siluer, B. (2005, October). "Content: The Other Half of the Integration Problem." *Intelligent Enterprise*, Vol. 8, No. 10, pp. 33–37.

Songini, M. L. (2002, July 15). "Southwest Expands Business Tools' Role." *Computerworld*, Vol. 36, No. 29, p. 6.

Sprague, R. H., and E. Carlson. (1982). *Building Effective Decision Support Systems.* Englewood Cliffs, NJ: Prentice Hall.

4

Modeling and Analysis

LEARNING OBJECTIVES

1 Understand the basic concepts of management support system (MSS) modeling

2 Describe how MSS models interact with data and the user

3 Understand some different, well-known model classes

4 Understand how to structure decision making with a few alternatives

5 Describe how spreadsheets can be used for MSS modeling and solution

6 Explain the basic concepts of optimization, simulation, and heuristics, and when to use them

7 Describe how to structure a linear programming model

8 Understand how search methods are used to solve MSS models

9 Explain the differences among algorithms, blind search, and heuristics

10 Describe how to handle multiple goals

11 Explain what is meant by sensitivity analysis, what-if analysis, and goal seeking

12 Describe the key issues of model management

In this chapter, we describe the model base and its management, one of the major components of decision support systems (DSS). We present this material with a note of caution: Modeling can be a very difficult topic and is as much an art as a science. The purpose of this chapter is not necessarily for you to *master the topics* of modeling and analysis. Rather, the material is geared toward *gaining familiarity* with the important concepts as they relate to DSS and their use in decision making. It is important to recognize that the modeling we discuss here is only cursorily related to the concepts of data modeling. You should not confuse the two. We walk through some basic concepts and definitions of modeling before introducing the influence diagram (see Online File W4.1), which can aid a decision maker in sketching a model of a situation and even solving it. We next introduce the idea of modeling directly in spreadsheets. We then discuss the structure and application of some successful time-proven models and methodologies: optimization, decision analysis, decision trees, analytic hierarchy process, search methods, heuristic programming, and simulation.

This chapter includes the following sections:

4.1 Opening Vignette: Model-Based Auctions Serve More Lunches in Chile
4.2 Management Support Systems Modeling
4.3 Structure of Mathematical Models for Decision Support
4.4 Certainty, Uncertainty, and Risk
4.5 Management Support Systems Modeling with Spreadsheets
4.6 Mathematical Programming Optimization
4.7 Multiple Goals, Sensitivity Analysis, What-If Analysis, and Goal Seeking
4.8 Decision Analysis with Decision Tables and Decision Trees
4.9 Multicriteria Decision Making with Pairwise Comparisons
4.10 Problem-Solving Search Methods
4.11 Simulation
4.12 Visual Interactive Simulation
4.13 Quantitative Software Packages and Model Base Management
4.14 Resources, Links, and the Teradata University Network Connection

4.1 OPENING VIGNETTE: MODEL-BASED AUCTIONS SERVE MORE LUNCHES IN CHILE

Problem

Economists love to say that there is no such thing as a free lunch. But the Chilean government agency responsible for school grants, Junta Nacional de Auxilio Escolar y Becas (JUNAEB), is an exception to the rule. During the school year, JUNAEB provides breakfast and lunch for 2 million children in primary and secondary public schools. In a developing country where about 14 percent of children under the age of 18 live below the poverty line, many students depend on these free meals as a key source of nutrition.

In 1980, JUNAEB began assigning catering contracts to companies through competitive auctions. At first, only three companies submitted bids, but this number rose to 30 during the 1990s and remains close to that level today.

Given the volume of meals it procures, JUNAEB has always had significant bargaining power over vendors. However, until the late 1990s, JUNAEB awarded contracts based on subjective, and quite rudimentary, criteria, making it easy for bidders to exert inappropriate pressures on JUNAEB officials. Vendors lacked incentives to reduce costs and inefficiencies, and JUNAEB wound up paying a high price for low-quality products.

In 1997, JUNAEB's board asked a team of academics to design and implement a new mechanism for auctioning its school meals service. This mechanism assigns bids in a single-round, sealed-bid combinatorial auction and is based on an integer linear programming model. The new model was implemented for the first time that year and has been updated and enhanced since then. It represents an interesting long-term application of management science support (MSS) modeling.

Solution

For the purposes of the auction, Chile is divided into approximately 120 school districts, or territorial units (TUs). JUNAEB holds auctions for school catering services in one-third of these districts every year, awarding 3-year contracts. The auction process begins when JUNAEB contacts and registers potential vendors. The agency then evaluates the companies from a managerial, technical, and financial point of view and eliminates those that don't meet minimum reliability standards. Qualifying vendors are classified according to two characteristics: (1) their financial and operating capacity and (2) their technical and managerial competence.

After the companies are classified, JUNAEB publishes a call to tender with the rules for bidding. Potential vendors submit their bids through an online system. Each bid includes a technical project for meal service and its price. The technical project must meet regulations established by JUNAEB, such as nutritional and hygiene requirements. In this way, meal plans are standardized.

Vendors that satisfy these conditions remain in the bidding process and compete on price, through their respective bids. A bid can cover anywhere from 1 to 12 TUs, depending on the vendor's classification. Vendors can submit as many bids as they want; each bid is accepted or rejected in its entirety. When JUNAEB accepts a company's bid, the company must provide all meal services in the corresponding TUs.

Because JUNAEB allows companies to submit bids that cover multiple TUs, vendors can take advantage of economies of scale. The shared use of infrastructure in neighboring regions, volume discounts, and efficiencies in transportation and staffing all contribute to the economies of scale. Firms generally submit many bids, ranging from bids that cover just one TU to those that cover a package of TUs. The ability to submit bids on various groupings of TUs defines the combinatorial character of this auction—and makes identifying the optimal solution much more difficult.

Each bid includes prices for the various catering services that JUNAEB provides in the corresponding TUs. Furthermore, JUNAEB asks companies to quote alternatives to these services, such as improvements to the nutritional quality of the meals. Vendors also quote prices for different levels of demand, thereby reducing the risk the vendors would face if they provide fewer meals because of unforeseen events, such as teacher strikes. Firms can also offer discounts if the real demand turns out to be higher than anticipated.

The new model's objective is to select a combination of bids that supply all of the TUs at a minimum cost. The performance of vendors based on JUNAEB's evaluations, or their quality index, is also a factor in awarding contracts. Other constraints include:

- ***Limits on the number of vendors supplying a region.*** Having too few vendors increases the risk of supply interruptions, whereas having too many can make management more difficult.
- ***A maximum award per vendor.*** This is calculated as a function of other contracts held by the vendor, its quality index, and its financial and operating capacity.
- ***Minimum prices.*** A phenomenon known as "winner's curse" occurs when the firm that bids the lowest price is found to have underestimated its costs, raising the possibility of losses or even financial ruin. To avoid this, unrealistically low bids are eliminated.

Furthermore, various scenarios, such as different food structures and demand levels, are considered. By combining all of the possible variations, more than 700 scenarios were generated for analysis. In practice, the decision maker will be interested in evaluating no more than 200 of them.

To find the optimal assignment for each scenario, the problem is formulated as an integer linear programming model. A binary decision variable for each bid is defined, where the decision is either to accept the bid or reject it. Other auxiliary binary variables that correspond to the restrictions limiting the number of firms in each region and the number of firms in the winning assignment are also included.

Not surprisingly, the difficulty of solving combinatorial bidding models is one of the main impediments to their broader use. Solving this model can be a challenging task. A real instance of the problem contains about 90,000 binary variables, so the model has to be solved efficiently. The JUNAEB Contract Award Commission was able to evaluate these scenarios along with the quality and robustness of their solutions. For example, the model allows JUNAEB to analyze the performance of the optimal solution when the demand level is 100 percent and compare this to the performance when demand is 80 percent.

It is important to note that the commission selects the scenario to be considered for the award, but the optimization model provides the specific solution. The entire process including data processing, administrative tasks, legal procedures, and analysis of scenarios is usually completed in no more than 10 days.

Results

The use of an optimization model in the bidding process to award school meal contracts in Chile, along with other managerial advances at JUNAEB, has yielded significant social benefits. For example, a comparison of the 1999 auction (which used the new model) and the 1995 auction (carried out under the old process) found substantial improvements in the nutritional quality of the meals, the meal-service infrastructure, and the labor conditions of the food handlers. Although these improvements increased total costs by 24 percent (in real terms), the average price of a meal rose by only 0.76 percent. In all, the new model saved the government about $40 million a year, or the cost of feeding 300,000 children.

Using mathematical modeling to assign contracts allowed JUNAEB to reap significant savings for the following reasons:

- The new process is objective and transparent, providing few opportunities for vendors to put pressure on decision makers.
- The process is impartial and reliable. It forces companies to compete and to increase productivity. Participating vendors have improved their management, enhanced the quality of their services, and cut their prices, and they still manage to make profits. In fact, a survey by JUNAEB compared the companies' average profit on sales before and after the model was introduced. The results showed profits increased from 3.2 percent to 4.9 percent. Average return on equity also rose, climbing from 28 percent to 38 percent, reflecting the vendors' higher rate of investment.
- By allowing companies to make bids that cover multiple TUs, vendors can take advantage of economies of scale.
- In every scenario, JUNAEB is able to get the lowest-cost bid combination that meets all of its restrictions. This would be nearly impossible to accomplish manually. If the agency attempted to do so and made an assignment just 2 percent more costly than the optimal solution, it would overspend by $10 million, the equivalent of providing food to 40,000 children.

The clearest evidence of the model's success is its continued use. JUNAEB introduced the model in 1997 and has applied it ever since. To date, the Chilean government has awarded more than $2 billion of contracts using the combinatorial auction methodology. In 2002, this work received the IFORS Prize for Operational Research in Development, awarded by the International Federation of Operational Research Societies to the best application of operational research in developing countries.

Questions for the Opening Vignette

1. What decision problem does the Chilean agency face?
2. Would a decision process that does not use a model be able to accommodate the desired goals?
3. What other approaches could you use to make these decisions?
4. What other applications of this type of auction model can you envision?

What We Can Learn from This Vignette

OR/MS Today features stories about the successful use of management science support models. This vignette describes an interesting application of one type of model—the auction model. Auction models are used everywhere. Perhaps the most common example of an auction model is eBay, which has made auctions a practical application for many buyers and sellers. Another application of model-based auctions that you may be familiar with is the process that Google and other search engines use for determining prices for sponsored advertisements to be shown when certain keywords are entered as search terms.

This vignette illustrates that the power of management science modeling can extend beyond private-sector applications and can assist the government in decision making. In developing countries, state-run social programs often account for the bulk of the national budget. The success of this case shows that sophisticated decision-making tools can help. Small changes in these programs can lead to enormous savings, and these savings can lead to tangible improvements in quality of life, such as meals for schoolchildren. The vignette also indicates the international nature of success of such models.

We are about to discuss some details about analytical models, how they are solved, and how they can be used in DSS to assist managers in decision making. Before turning to the details, in the next section, we initially describe a few more lessons that other organizations have faced and solved by using models.

Source: Adapted from J. Catalán, R. Epstein, M. Guajardo, D. Yung, L. Henriquez, C. Martínez, and G. Weintraub, "No Such Thing as a Free Lunch?" *OR/MS Today*, April 2009, **lionhrtpub.com/orms/orms-4-09/frlunch.html** (accessed June 2009). (Reproduced and edited with permission from *OR/MS Today* and the authors.)

4.2 MANAGEMENT SUPPORT SYSTEMS MODELING

Many readily accessible applications describe how the models incorporated in DSS contribute to organizational success. These include Pillowtex (see ProModel, 2009), Fiat (see ProModel, 2006), Procter & Gamble (see Camm et al., 1997), and others. Although we do not describe these actual cases, we do discuss some modeling lessons from these organizations next.

Simulation models can enhance an organization's decision-making process and enable it to see the impact of its future choices. Fiat (see ProModel, 2006) saves $1 million annually in manufacturing costs through simulation. The 2002 Winter Olympics (Salt Lake City, Utah) used simulation to design security systems and bus transportation for most of the venues. This predictive technology enabled the Salt Lake Organizing Committee to model and test a variety of scenarios, including security operations, weather, and transportation-system design, in its highly variable and complex vehicle-distribution network. Savings of over $20 million per year were realized. Even companies under financial stress need to invest in such solutions to squeeze more efficiency out of their limited resources. Maybe even more so. Pillowtex, a $2 billion company that manufactures pillows, mattress pads, and comforters, had filed for bankruptcy and needed to reorganize its plants to maximize net profits from the company's operations. It employed a simulation model to develop a new lean manufacturing environment that would reduce the costs and increase throughput. The company estimated that the use of this model resulted in over $12 million savings immediately. (See **promodel.com**.)

Lessons from Modeling at Procter & Gamble

Modeling is a key element in most DSS and a necessity in a model-based DSS. There are many classes of models, and there are often many specialized techniques for solving each one. Simulation is a common modeling approach, but there are several others. For example, consider the optimization approach Procter & Gamble (P&G) took in redesigning its distribution system (see Camm et al., 1997). P&G's DSS for its North America supply-chain redesign includes several models:

- A generating model (based on an algorithm) to make transportation-cost estimates. This model is programmed directly into the DSS.
- A demand-forecasting model (statistics based).
- A distribution center location model. This model uses aggregated data (a special modeling technique) and is solved with a standard linear/integer optimization package.
- A transportation model (i.e., a specialization of a linear programming model) to determine the best shipping option from product sources to distribution centers (fed to it from the previous model) and hence to customers. This model is solved using commercial software and is loosely integrated with the distribution location model. These two problems are solved sequentially. The DSS must interface with commercial software and integrate the models.
- A financial and risk simulation model that takes into consideration some qualitative factors that require important human judgment.
- A geographical information system (GIS; effectively a graphical model of the data) for a user interface.

The P&G situation demonstrates that a DSS can be composed of several models—some standard and some custom built—used collectively to support strategic decisions in the company. It further demonstrates that some models are built directly into the DSS software development package, some need to be constructed externally to the DSS software, and others can be accessed by the DSS when needed. Sometimes, a massive effort is necessary to assemble or estimate reasonable model data; in the case of P&G, about

500 employees were involved over the course of about a year. In addition, the models must be integrated, models may be decomposed and simplified, sometimes a suboptimization approach is appropriate, and, finally, human judgment is an important aspect of using models in decision making.

Lessons from Additional Modeling Applications

As is evident from the situations described in the preceding section, modeling is not a simple task. For further information, see Stojkovic and Soumis (2001), which describes a model for scheduling airline flights and pilots; Gabriel et al. (2001), which describes a model for the U.S. national energy-economic situation; and Teradata (2003), which describes how Burlington Northern Santa Fe Corporation optimizes railcar performance through **mathematical (quantitative) models** (a system of symbols and expressions representing a real situation) embedded in its OLAP tool. The model developer must balance the model's simplification and representation requirements so that it will capture enough of reality to make it useful for the decision maker.

Applying models to real-world situations can save millions of dollars or generate millions of dollars in revenue. At American Airlines, models were used extensively in SABRE through the American Airlines Decision Technologies (AADT) Corp. AADT pioneered many new techniques and their application, including management. For example, optimizing the altitude ascent and descent profile for its planes saved several million dollars per week in fuel costs. AADT saved hundreds of millions of dollars annually in the early 1980s, and its incremental revenues eventually exceeded $1 billion annually, outpacing the revenue of the airline itself (see Horner, 2000; Mukherjee, 2001; and Smith et al., 2001). Christiansen et al. (2009) describe the applications of such models in shipping company operations. They describe applications of TurboRouter, a DSS for ship routing and scheduling. They claim that over the course of just a 3-week period, a company used this model to better utilize its fleet, generating additional profit of $1–2 million in just a short time. We provide another example of a model application in Application Case 4.1.

APPLICATION CASE 4.1

Lockheed Martin Space Systems Company Optimizes Infrastructure Project-Portfolio Selection

The Lockheed Martin Space Systems Company is located in Denver, Colorado, occupies 5,500 acres and 37 buildings (the majority of which were built before 1970), and produces products meant for space travel. Lockheed Martin needed an efficient model to help it optimize its project selection for the company's infrastructure. The Facility Operations and Services (FO&S) group was in charge of making the selection of what infrastructure projects would be addressed during the fourth quarter of each year from a list that normally numbered around 300 with a budget of around $10 million. This method was time consuming, because up to 20 people had to attend three to five meetings during the third quarter of each year in order to make the decisions. Additionally, each person had

knowledge of different areas of improvement, which made it difficult to come to decisions and led to hours of negotiation and intradepartmental tension. Thus, selections were based on qualitative information and were often suboptimal. Therefore, Lockheed Martin decided to develop a DSS based on multi-attribute utility theory that would facilitate project selection.

An Excel spreadsheet was used to develop the optimization model because of its familiarity to all the managers and ease of use. The DSS had three stages. The first stage used multi-attribute utility theory to determine a numeric value for each project through a swing-weighting technique, whereby the most vital attributes for maintenance and infrastructure modernization were combined in a utility function. The numeric values were determined by defining the attributes by "best and worst levels," having the departments rank what they wanted altered from worst to best, assigning 100 points to projects with the most-needed improvements as compared to zero points to projects that were not hurt by going from the most needed rank to a lesser rank, and using the range of 0–100 to normalize raw weights. The second stage used a Bayesian approach on the financial data collected from the projects completed in the previous 5 years to develop estimates of mean and variance for spending on earlier projects. A "chance constraint" kept the project selections within the budget with a small probability for overruns. The third stage estimated the mean and variance of project costs and duration.

Although the costs of improvements are fairly easy to determine, the payoffs are not as easy to estimate because infrastructure projects return profits indirectly. Five attributes were identified as being the most important in helping the company make a profit. The regulatory attribute encompassed state and federal regulations. The modernization attribute addressed how well the facility was set up to take

care of business and employee requirements. The risk attribute rated the threat of damage that the facility presented to the flight hardware. The infrastructure attribute dealt with the "deterioration of building systems." Finally, the business attribute addressed whether a project enhanced the probability of winning contracts.

The Excel model was executed using Premium Solver. The model had 267 0/1 decision variables and 2 constraints. The model contained six worksheets: one worksheet of data inputs and model outputs once Premium Solver had run; two worksheets addressing sensitivity analysis; and three worksheets containing the model parameters. Additionally, a mandate column was added to the spreadsheet for projects that carryover from year to year and that require funds from the budget to pay for them. An exclude column was also added.

In the end, this model improved the project selection process by helping the company to better use budgetary funds and also by "reducing carryover costs, and increasing overall utility to the departments."

Source: Based on C. Z. Gurgur and C. T. Morley, "Lockheed Martin Space Systems Company Optimizes Infrastructure Project-Portfolio Selection," *Interfaces,* Vol. 38, No. 4, July/August 2008, pp. 251–262.

Current Modeling Issues

We next discuss some major modeling issues, such as problem identification and environmental analysis, variable identification, forecasting, the use of multiple models, model categories (or appropriate selection), model management, and knowledge-based modeling.

IDENTIFICATION OF THE PROBLEM AND ENVIRONMENTAL ANALYSIS   We discussed problem and environmental analysis in depth in Chapter 2. One very important aspect of it is **environmental scanning and analysis**, which is the monitoring, scanning, and interpretation of collected information. No decision is made in a vacuum. It is important to analyze the scope of the domain and the forces and dynamics of the environment. A decision maker needs to identify the organizational culture and the corporate decision-making processes (e.g., who makes decisions, degree of centralization). It is entirely possible that environmental factors have created the current problem. BI/business analytics (BA) tools can help identify problems by scanning for them. The problem must be understood and everyone involved should share the same frame of understanding, because the problem will ultimately be represented by the model in one form or another. Otherwise, the model will not help the decision maker.

VARIABLE IDENTIFICATION   Identification of a model's variables (e.g., decision, result, uncontrollable) is critical, as are the relationships among the variables. Influence diagrams, which are graphical models of mathematical models, can facilitate the identification process. A more general form of an influence diagram, a cognitive map, can help a decision maker develop a better understanding of a problem, especially of variables and their interactions.

FORECASTING (PREDICTIVE ANALYTICS) **Forecasting** is predicting the future. This form of predictive analytics is essential for construction and manipulating models, because when a decision is implemented the results usually occur in the future. Whereas DSS are typically designed to determine what will be, traditional MIS report what is or what was. There is no point in running a what-if (sensitivity) analysis on the past, because decisions made then have no impact on the future. Forecasting is getting easier as software vendors automate many of the complications of developing such models. For example, SAS (**sas.com**) has a High Performance Forecasting system that incorporates its predictive analytics technology, ideally for retailers. This software is more automated than most other forecasting packages.

E-commerce has created an immense need for forecasting and an abundance of available information for performing it. E-commerce activities occur quickly, yet information about purchases is gathered and should be analyzed to produce forecasts. Part of the analysis involves simply predicting demand; however, forecasting models can use product life cycle needs and information about the marketplace and consumers to analyze the entire situation, ideally leading to additional sales of products and services. As seen in Chapter 1 Application Case 1.1, such information can be used to set prices and promotion plans.

Many organizations have accurately predicted demand for products and services, using a variety of qualitative and quantitative methods. But until recently, most companies viewed their customers and potential customers by categorizing them into only a few, time-tested groupings. Today, it is critical not only to consider customer characteristics, but also to consider how to get the right product(s) to the right customers at the right price at the right time in the right format/packaging. The more accurately a firm does this, the more profitable the firm is. In addition, a firm needs to recognize when not to sell a particular product or bundle of products to a particular set of customers. Part of this effort involves identifying lifelong customer profitability. These customer relationship management (CRM) system and revenue management system (RMS) approaches rely heavily on forecasting techniques, which are typically described as *predictive analytics.* These systems attempt to predict who their best (i.e., most profitable) customers (and worst ones as well) are and focus on identifying products and services at appropriate prices to appeal to them. We describe an effective example of such forecasting at Harrah's Cherokee Casino and Hotel in Application Case 4.2.

APPLICATION CASE 4.2
Forecasting/Predictive Analytics Proves to Be a Good Gamble for Harrah's Cherokee Casino and Hotel

Harrah's Cherokee Casino and Hotel uses a revenue management (RM) system to optimize its profits. The system helps Harrah's attain an average 98.6 percent occupancy rate 7 days a week all year, with the exception of December, and a 60 percent gross revenue profit margin. One aspect of the RM system is providing its customers with Total Rewards cards, which track how much money each customer gambles. The system also tracks reservations and overbookings , with the exception of those made through third parties such as travel agencies. The RM system calculates the opportunity cost of saving rooms for possible customers who gamble more than others, because gambling is Harrah's main source of revenue. Unlike the traditional method of company employees only tracking the "big spenders," the RM system also tracks the "mid-tier" spenders. This has helped increase the company's profits. Only customers who gamble over a certain dollar amount are recommended by the RM system to be given rooms at the hotel; those who spend less may be given complimentary rooms at nearby hotels in order to keep the bigger spenders close by. The RM system also tracks which gaming machines are most popular so that management can place them strategically throughout the casino in order to encourage customers to gamble more money. Additionally, the system helps track the success of different marketing projects and incentives.

The casino collects demand data, which are then used by a forecasting algorithm with several components: smoothed values for base demand, demand trends, annual and day-of-the-week seasonality, and special event factors. The forecasts are used by overbooking and optimization models for inventory-control

recommendations. The booking recommendation system includes a linear program (to be introduced later in the chapter). The model updates the recommendations for booking a room periodically or when certain events demand it. The bid-price model is updated or optimized after 24 hours have passed since the last optimization, when five rooms have been booked since the last optimization, or when the RM analyst manually starts a new optimization. The model is a good example of the process of forecasting demand and then using this information to employ a model-based DSS for making optimal decisions.

Source: Based on R. Metters, C. Queenan, M. Ferguson, L. Harrison, J. Higbie, S. Ward, B. Barfield, T. Farley, H. A. Kuyumcu, and A. Duggasani, "The 'Killer Application' of Revenue Management: Harrah's Cherokee Casino & Hotel," *Interfaces*, Vol. 38, No. 3, May/June 2008, pp. 161–175.

MULTIPLE MODELS A DSS can include several models (sometimes dozens), each of which represents a different part of the decision-making problem. For example, the P&G supply chain DSS includes a location model to locate distribution centers, a product-strategy model, a demand-forecasting model, a cost-generation model, a financial- and risk-simulation model, and even a GIS model. Some of the models are standard and built in to DSS development generators and tools. Others are standard but are not available as built-in functions. Instead, they are available as freestanding software that can interface with a DSS. Nonstandard models must be constructed from scratch. The P&G models were integrated by the DSS, and the problem had multiple goals. Even though cost minimization was the stated goal, there were other goals, as is shown by the way the managers took political and other criteria into consideration when examining solutions before making a final decision.

MODEL CATEGORIES Table 4.1 classifies DSS models into seven groups and lists several representative techniques for each category. Each technique can be applied to either a **static** or a **dynamic model**, which can be constructed under assumed environments of certainty, uncertainty, or risk. To expedite model construction, we can use special decision analysis systems that have modeling languages and capabilities embedded in them. These include spreadsheets, data mining systems, OLAP systems, and modeling languages that help an analyst build a model. We will introduce one of these systems later in the chapter.

MODEL MANAGEMENT Models, like data, must be managed to maintain their integrity, and thus their applicability. Such management is done with the aid of model base management systems (MBMS), which are analogous to database management systems (DBMS).

KNOWLEDGE-BASED MODELING DSS uses mostly quantitative models, whereas expert systems use qualitative, knowledge-based models in their applications. Some knowledge is necessary to construct solvable (and therefore usable) models. We defer the description of knowledge-based models until later chapters.

TABLE 4.1 Categories of Models

Category	Process and Objective	Representative Techniques
Optimization of problems with few alternatives	Find the best solution from a small number of alternatives	Decision tables, decision trees, analytic hierarchy process
Optimization via algorithm	Find the best solution from a large number of alternatives, using a step-by-step improvement process	Linear and other mathematical programming models, network models
Optimization via an analytic formula	Find the best solution in one step, using a formula	Some inventory models
Simulation	Finding a good enough solution or the best among the alternatives checked, using experimentation	Several types of simulation
Heuristics	Find a good enough solution, using rules	Heuristic programming, expert systems
Predictive models	Predict the future for a given scenario	Forecasting models, Markov analysis
Other models	Solve a what-if case, using a formula	Financial modeling, waiting lines

CURRENT TRENDS IN MODELING One recent trend in modeling involves the development of model libraries and solution technique libraries. Some of these codes can be run directly on the owner's Web server for free, and others can be downloaded and run on an individual's PC, Unix machine, or server. The availability of these codes means that powerful optimization and simulation packages are available to decision makers who may have only experienced these tools from the perspective of classroom problems. For example, the Mathematics and Computer Science Division at Argonne National Laboratory (Argonne, Illinois) maintains the NEOS Server for Optimization at **neos.mcs.anl.gov/neos/index.html**. You can find links to other sites by clicking the Resources link at **informs.org**, the Web site of the Institute for Operations Research and the Management Sciences (INFORMS). A wealth of modeling and solution information is available from INFORMS. The Web site for one of INFORMS' publications, *OR/MS Today*, at **lionhrtpub.com/ORMS.shtml** includes links to many categories of modeling software. We will learn about some of these shortly.

There is a clear trend toward developing and using Web tools and software to access and even run software to perform modeling, optimization, simulation, and so on. This has, in many ways, simplified the application of many models to real-world problems. However, to use models and solution techniques effectively, it is necessary to truly gain experience through developing and solving simple ones. This aspect is often overlooked. Another trend, unfortunately, involves the lack of understanding of what models and their solutions can do in the real world. Organizations that have key analysts who understand how to apply models indeed apply them very effectively. This is most notably occurring in the revenue management area, which has moved from the province of airlines, hotels, and automobile rental to retail, insurance, entertainment, and many other areas. CRM also uses models, but they are often transparent to the user. With management models, the amount of data and model sizes are quite large, necessitating the use of data warehouses to supply the data and parallel computing hardware to obtain solutions in a reasonable time frame.

There is a continuing trend toward making MSS models completely transparent to the decision maker. For example, **multidimensional analysis (modeling)** involves data analysis in several dimensions. In multidimensional analysis (modeling) and some other cases, data are generally shown in a spreadsheet format, with which most decision makers are familiar. Many decision makers accustomed to slicing and dicing data cubes are now using OLAP systems that access data warehouses. Although these methods may make modeling palatable, they also eliminate many important and applicable model classes from consideration, and they eliminate some important and subtle solution interpretation aspects. Modeling involves much more than just data analysis with trend lines and establishing relationships with statistical methods.

There is also a trend to build a model of a model to help in its analysis. An **influence diagram** is a graphical representation of a model; that is, it is a model of a model. Some influence diagram software packages are capable of generating and solving the resultant model. We describe influence diagrams in depth in Online File W4.1.

Section 4.2 Review Questions

1. List three lessons learned from modeling. P. 140
2. List and describe the major issues in modeling. P. 141
3. What are the major types of models used in DSS? Quantitative models. P. 143
4. Why are models not used in industry as frequently as they should or could be?
5. What are the current trends in modeling? P. 144

4.3 STRUCTURE OF MATHEMATICAL MODELS FOR DECISION SUPPORT

In the following sections, we present the topics of MSS mathematical models (e.g., mathematical, financial, engineering). These include the components and the structure of models.

The Components of Decision Support Mathematical Models

All models are made up of four basic components (see Figure 4.1): result (or outcome) variables, decision variables, uncontrollable variables (and/or parameters), and intermediate result variables. Mathematical relationships link these components together. In nonquantitative models, the relationships are symbolic or qualitative. The results of decisions are determined based on the decision made (i.e., the values of the decision variables), the factors that cannot be controlled by the decision maker (in the environment), and the relationships among the variables. The modeling process involves identifying the variables and relationships among them. Solving a model determines the values of these and the result variable(s).

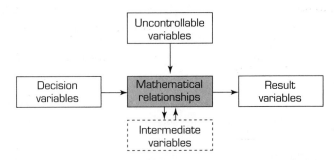

FIGURE 4.1 The General Structure of a Quantitative Model

RESULT (OUTCOME) VARIABLES **Result (outcome) variables** reflect the level of effectiveness of a system; that is, they indicate how well the system performs or attains its goal(s). These variables are outputs. Examples of result variables are shown in Table 4.2. Result variables are considered *dependent variables*. Intermediate result variables are sometimes used in modeling to identify intermediate outcomes. In the case of a dependent variable, another event must occur first before the event described by the variable can occur. Result variables depend on the occurrence of the decision variables and the uncontrollable variables.

DECISION VARIABLES **Decision variables** describe alternative courses of action. The decision maker controls the decision variables. For example, for an investment problem, the amount to invest in bonds is a decision variable. In a scheduling problem, the decision variables are people, times, and schedules. Other examples are listed in Table 4.2.

UNCONTROLLABLE VARIABLES, OR PARAMETERS In any decision-making situation, there are factors that affect the result variables but are not under the control of the decision maker. Either these factors can be fixed, in which case they are called **uncontrollable variables**, or **parameters**, or they can vary, in which case they are called *variables*. Examples of factors are the prime interest rate, a city's building code, tax regulations, and utilities costs (others are shown in Table 4.2). Most of these factors are uncontrollable because they are in and determined by elements of the system environment in which the decision maker works. Some of these variables limit the decision maker and therefore form what are called the *constraints* of the problem.

TABLE 4.2 Examples of the Components of Models

Area	Decision Variables	Result Variables	Uncontrollable Variables and Parameters
Financial investment	Investment alternatives and amounts	Total profit, risk	Inflation rate
		Rate of return on investment (ROI)	Prime rate
			Competition
		Earnings per share	
		Liquidity level	
Marketing	Advertising budget	Market share	Customer's income
	Where to advertise	Customer satisfaction	Competitor's actions
Manufacturing	What and how much to produce	Total cost	Machine capacity
		Quality level	Technology
	Inventory levels	Employee satisfaction	Materials prices
	Compensation programs		
Accounting	Use of computers	Data processing cost	Computer technology
	Audit schedule	Error rate	Tax rates
			Legal requirements
Transportation	Shipments schedule	Total transport cost	Delivery distance
	Use of smart cards	Payment float time	Regulations
Services	Staffing levels	Customer satisfaction	Demand for services

INTERMEDIATE RESULT VARIABLES   **Intermediate result variables** reflect intermediate outcomes in mathematical models. For example, in determining machine scheduling, spoilage is an intermediate result variable, and total profit is the result variable (i.e., spoilage is one determinant of total profit). Another example is employee salaries. This constitutes a decision variable for management: It determines employee satisfaction (i.e., intermediate outcome), which, in turn, determines the productivity level (i.e., final result).

The Structure of MSS Mathematical Models

The components of a quantitative model are linked together by mathematical (algebraic) expressions—equations or inequalities.

A very simple financial model is

$$P = R - C$$

where P = profit, R = revenue, and C = cost. This equation describes the relationship among the variables. Another well-known financial model is the simple present-value cash flow model, where P = present value, F = a future single payment in dollars, i = interest rate (percentage), and n = number of years. With this model, it is possible to determine the present value of a payment of $100,000 to be made 5 years from today, at a 10 percent (0.1) interest rate, as follows:

$$P = 100,000 / (1 + 0.1)^5 = 62,092$$

We present more interesting and complex mathematical models in the following sections.

Section 4.3 Review Questions

1. What is a decision variable? P.146 .
2. List and briefly discuss the three major components of linear programming.
3. Explain the role of intermediate result variables. P.147

4.4 CERTAINTY, UNCERTAINTY, AND RISK[1]

Part of Simon's decision-making process described in Chapter 2 involves evaluating and comparing alternatives; during this process, it is necessary to predict the future outcome of each proposed alternative. Decision situations are often classified on the basis of what the decision maker knows (or believes) about the forecasted results. We customarily classify this knowledge into three categories (see Figure 4.2), ranging from complete knowledge to complete ignorance:

- Certainty
- Risk
- Uncertainty

When we develop models, any of these conditions can occur, and different kinds of models are appropriate for each case. Next, we discuss both the basic definitions of these terms and some important modeling issues for each condition.

---

[1] Some parts of the original versions of Sections 4.4, 4.6, 4.8, and 4.11 were adapted from Turban and Meredith (1994).

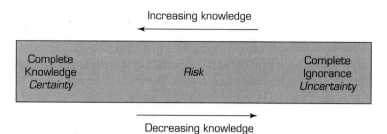

FIGURE 4.2 The Zones of Decision Making

Decision Making Under Certainty

In decision making under **certainty**, it is *assumed* that complete knowledge is available so that the decision maker knows exactly what the outcome of *each course of action* will be (as in a deterministic environment). It may not be true that the outcomes are 100 percent known, nor is it necessary to really evaluate *all* the outcomes, but often this assumption simplifies the model and makes it tractable. The decision maker is viewed as a perfect predictor of the future because it is assumed that there is only one outcome for each alternative. For example, the alternative of investing in U.S. Treasury bills is one for which there is complete availability of information about the future return on the investment if it is held to maturity. A situation involving decision making under certainty occurs most often with structured problems with short time horizons (up to 1 year). Certainty models are relatively easy to develop and solve, and they can yield optimal solutions. Many financial models are constructed under assumed certainty, even though the market is anything but 100 percent certain.

Decision Making Under Uncertainty

In decision making under **uncertainty**, the decision maker considers situations in which several outcomes are possible for each course of action. In contrast to the risk situation, in this case, the decision maker does not know, or cannot estimate, the probability of occurrence of the possible outcomes. Decision making under uncertainty is more difficult than decision making under certainty because there is insufficient information. Modeling of such situations involves assessment of the decision maker's (or the organization's) attitude toward risk (see Nielsen, 2003).

Managers attempt to avoid uncertainty as much as possible, even to the point of assuming it away. Instead of dealing with uncertainty, they attempt to obtain more information so that the problem can be treated under certainty (because it can be "almost" certain) or under calculated (i.e., assumed) risk. If more information is not available, the problem must be treated under a condition of uncertainty, which is less definitive than the other categories.

Decision Making Under Risk (Risk Analysis)

A decision made under **risk**[2] (also known as a *probabilistic* or *stochastic* decision-making situation) is one in which the decision maker must consider several possible

---

[2] Our definitions of the terms *risk* and *uncertainty* were formulated by F. H. Knight of the University of Chicago in 1933. Other, comparable definitions also are in use.

outcomes for each alternative, each with a given probability of occurrence. The long-run probabilities that the given outcomes will occur are assumed to be known or can be estimated. Under these assumptions, the decision maker can assess the degree of risk associated with each alternative (called *calculated* risk). Most major business decisions are made under assumed risk. **Risk analysis** (i.e., calculated risk) is a decision-making method that analyzes the risk (based on assumed known probabilities) associated with different alternatives. Risk analysis can be performed by calculating the expected value of each alternative and selecting the one with the best expected value.

Section 4.4 Review Questions

1. Define what it means to perform decision making under assumed certainty, risk, and uncertainty.
2. How can decision-making problems under assumed certainty be handled?
3. How can decision-making problems under assumed uncertainty be handled?
4. How can decision-making problems under assumed risk be handled?

4.5 MANAGEMENT SUPPORT SYSTEMS MODELING WITH SPREADSHEETS

Models can be developed and implemented in a variety of programming languages and systems. These range from third-, fourth-, and fifth-generation programming languages to computer-aided software engineering (CASE) systems and other systems that automatically generate usable software. (For example, influence diagram software typically generates and sometimes solves usable models; see Online File W4.1.) We focus primarily on *spreadsheets* (with their add-ins), modeling languages, and transparent data analysis tools. Previous chapters (see Application Case 3.1 and Technology Insights 4.1, for example) have introduced spreadsheet-based modeling.

With their strength and flexibility, spreadsheet packages were quickly recognized as easy-to-use implementation software for the development of a wide range of applications in business, engineering, mathematics, and science. Spreadsheets include extensive statistical, forecasting, and other modeling and database management capabilities, functions, and routines. As spreadsheet packages evolved, add-ins were developed for structuring and solving specific model classes. Among the add-in packages, many were developed for DSS development. These DSS-related add-ins include Solver (Frontline Systems Inc., **solver.com**) and What's*Best!* (a version of Lindo, from Lindo Systems, Inc., **lindo.com**) for performing linear and nonlinear optimization; Braincel (Jurik Research Software, Inc., **jurikres.com**) and NeuralTools (Palisade Corp., **palisade.com**) for artificial neural networks; Evolver (Palisade Corp.) for genetic algorithms; and @RISK (Palisade Corp.) for performing simulation studies. Comparable add-ins are available for free or at a very low cost. (Conduct a Web search to find them; new ones are added to the marketplace on a regular basis.)

The spreadsheet is clearly the most popular *end-user modeling tool* (see Figure 4.3) because it incorporates many powerful financial, statistical, mathematical, and other functions. Spreadsheets can perform model solution tasks such as linear programming and regression analysis. The spreadsheet has evolved into an important tool for analysis, planning, and modeling (see Farasyn et al., 2008; Hurley and Balez, 2008; and Ovchinnikov and Milner, 2008). Application Case 4.3 describes an interesting application of a spreadsheet-based optimization model in a small business.

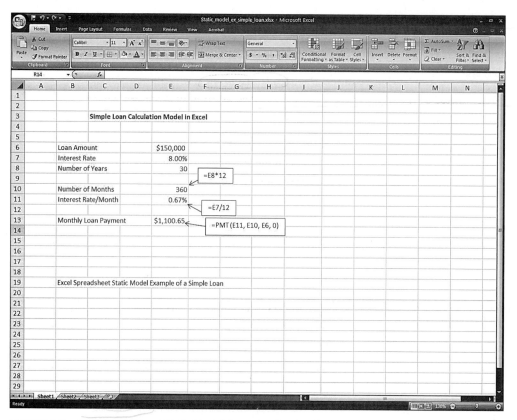

FIGURE 4.3 Excel Spreadsheet Static Model Example of a Simple Loan Calculation of Monthly Payments

APPLICATION CASE 4.3

Showcase Scheduling at Fred Astaire East Side Dance Studio

The Fred Astaire East Side Dance Studio in New York City presents two ballroom showcases a year. The studio wanted a cheap, user-friendly, and quick computer program to create schedules for its showcases that involved heats lasting around 75 seconds and solos lasting around 3 minutes. The program was created using an integer programming optimization model in Visual Basic and Excel. The employees just have to enter the students' names, the types of dances the students want to participate in, the teachers the students want to dance with, how many times the students want to do each type of dance, what times the students are unavailable, and what times the teachers are unavailable. This is entered into an Excel spreadsheet. The program then uses guidelines provided by the business to design the schedule. The guidelines include: a dance type not being performed twice in a row if possible, a student participating in each quarter of the showcase in order to keep him/her active throughout, all participants in each heat performing the same type of dance (with a maximum of seven couples per heat), eliminating as many one-couple heats as possible, each student and teacher only being scheduled once per heat, and allowing students and teachers to dance multiple times per dance type if desired. A two-step heuristic method was used to help minimize the number of one-couple heats. In the end, the program cut down the time the employees spent creating the schedule and allowed for changes to be calculated and made quickly as compared to when made manually. For the summer 2007 show-case, the system scheduled 583 heat entries, 19 dance types, 18 solo entries, 28 students, and 8 teachers. This combination of Microsoft Excel and Visual Basic enabled the studio to use a model-based decision support system for a problem that could be time consuming to solve.

Source: Based on M. A. Lejeune and N. Yakova, "Showcase Scheduling at Fred Astaire East Side Dance Studio," Interfaces, Vol. 38, No. 3, May/June 2008, pp. 176–186.

Other important spreadsheet features include what-if analysis, goal seeking, data management, and programmability (i.e., macros). With a spreadsheet, it is easy to change a cell's value and immediately see the result. Goal seeking is performed by indicating a target cell, its desired value, and a changing cell. Extensive database management can be performed with small datasets, or parts of a database can be imported for analysis (which is essentially how OLAP works with multidimensional data cubes; in fact, most OLAP systems have the look and feel of advanced spreadsheet software after the data are loaded). Templates, macros, and other tools enhance the productivity of building DSS.

Most spreadsheet packages provide fairly seamless integration because they read and write common file structures and easily interface with databases and other tools. Microsoft Excel is the most popular spreadsheet package. In Figure 4.4, we show a simple loan calculation model in which the boxes on the spreadsheet describe the contents of the

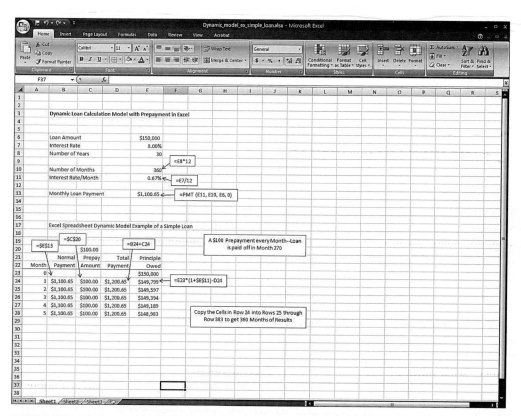

FIGURE 4.4 Excel Spreadsheet Dynamic Model Example of a Simple Loan Calculation of Monthly Payments and the Effects of Prepayment

cells, which contain formulas. A change in the interest rate in cell E7 is immediately reflected in the monthly payment in cell E13. The results can be observed and analyzed immediately. If we require a specific monthly payment, we can use goal seeking (see Section 4.7) to determine an appropriate interest rate or loan amount.

Static or dynamic models can be built in a spreadsheet. For example, the monthly loan calculation spreadsheet shown in Figure 4.3 is static. Although the problem affects the borrower over time, the model indicates a single month's performance, which is replicated. A dynamic model, in contrast, represents behavior over time. The loan calculations in the spreadsheet shown in Figure 4.4 indicate the effect of prepayment on the principal over time. Risk analysis can be incorporated into spreadsheets by using built-in random-number generators to develop simulation models (see Section 4.11).

Spreadsheet applications for models are reported regularly. A special issue of *Interfaces* (2008) described many such actual applications. We will learn how to use a spreadsheet-based optimization model in the next section.

Section 4.5 Review Questions

1. What is a spreadsheet?
2. What is a spreadsheet add-in? How can add-ins help in DSS creation and use?
3. Explain why a spreadsheet is so conducive to the development of DSS.

4.6 MATHEMATICAL PROGRAMMING OPTIMIZATION

The basic idea of optimization was introduced in Chapter 2. **Linear programming (LP)** is the best-known technique in a family of optimization tools called *mathematical programming*; in LP, all relationships among the variables are linear. It is used extensively in DSS (see Application Case 4.4). LP models have many important applications in practice. These include supply chain management, product mix decisions, routing, and so on. Special forms of the models can be used for specific applications. For example, Application Case 4.4 describes a spreadsheet model that was used to create a schedule for medical interns.

APPLICATION CASE 4.4

Spreadsheet Model Helps Assign Medical Residents

Fletcher Allen Health Care (FAHC) is a teaching hospital that works with the University of Vermont's College of Medicine. In this particular case, FAHC employs 15 residents with hopes of adding 5 more in the diagnostic radiology program. Each year the chief radiology resident is required to make a year-long schedule for all of the residents in radiology. This is a time-consuming process to do manually because there are many limitations on when each resident is and is not allowed to work. During the weekday working hours, the residents work with certified radiologists, but nights, weekends, and holidays are all staffed by residents only. The residents are also required to take the "emergency rotations," which involve taking care of the radiology needs of the emergency room, which is often the busiest on weekends. The radiology program is a 4-year program, and there are different rules for the work schedules of the residents for each year they are there. For example, first- and fourth-year residents cannot be on call on holidays, second-year residents cannot be on call or assigned ER shifts during 13-week blocks when they are assigned to work in Boston, third-year residents must work one ER rotation during only one of the major winter holidays (Thanksgiving or Christmas/New Year's). Also, first-year residents cannot be on call until after January 1, and fourth-year residents cannot be on call after December 31, and so on. The goal that the various chief residents have each year is to give each person the maximum number of days between on-call days as is possible. Manually, only 3 days between on-call days was the most a chief resident had been able to accomplish.

In order to create a more efficient method of creating a schedule, the chief resident worked with an MS class of MBA students to develop a spreadsheet model to create the schedule. To solve this multiple-objective decision-making problem, the class used a constraint method made up of two stages. The first stage was to use the spreadsheet created in Excel as a calculator and to not use it for optimizing. This allowed the creators "to measure the key metrics of the residents' assignments, such as the number of days worked in each category." The second stage was an optimization model, which was layered on the calculator spreadsheet.

Assignment constraints and the objective were added. The Solver engine in Excel was then invoked to find a feasible solution. The developers used Premium Solver by Frontline and the Xpress MP Solver engine by Dash Optimization to solve the yearlong model. Finally, using Excel functions, the developers converted the solution for a yearlong schedule from zeros and ones to an easy-to-read format for the residents. In the end, the program could solve the problem of a schedule with 3 to 4 days in between on calls instantly and with 5 days in between on calls (which was never accomplished manually).

Source: Based on A. Ovchinnikov and J. Milner, "Spreadsheet Model Helps to Assign Medical Residents at the University of Vermont's College of Medicine," *Interfaces,* Vol. 38, No. 4, July/August 2008, pp. 311–323.

Mathematical Programming

Mathematical programming is a family of tools designed to help solve managerial problems in which the decision maker must allocate scarce resources among competing activities to optimize a measurable goal. For example, the distribution of machine time (the resource) among various products (the activities) is a typical allocation problem. LP allocation problems usually display the following characteristics:

- A limited quantity of economic resources is available for allocation.
- The resources are used in the production of products or services.
- There are two or more ways in which the resources can be used. Each is called a *solution* or a *program.*
- Each activity (product or service) in which the resources are used yields a return in terms of the stated goal.
- The allocation is usually restricted by several limitations and requirements, called *constraints.*

The LP allocation model is based on the following rational economic assumptions:

- Returns from different allocations can be compared; that is, they can be measured by a common unit (e.g., dollars, utility).
- The return from any allocation is independent of other allocations.
- The total return is the sum of the returns yielded by the different activities.
- All data are known with certainty.
- The resources are to be used in the most economical manner.

Allocation problems typically have a large number of possible solutions. Depending on the underlying assumptions, the number of solutions can be either infinite or finite. Usually, different solutions yield different rewards. Of the available solutions, at least one is the best, in the sense that the degree of goal attainment associated with it is the highest (i.e., the total reward is maximized). This is called an **optimal solution**, and it can be found by using a special algorithm.

Linear Programming

Every LP problem is composed of *decision variables* (whose values are unknown and are searched for), an *objective function* (a linear mathematical function that relates the decision variables to the goal, measures goal attainment, and is to be optimized), *objective function coefficients* (unit profit or cost coefficients indicating the contribution to the objective of one unit of a decision variable), *constraints* (expressed in the form of linear inequalities or equalities that limit resources and/or requirements; these relate the variables through linear relationships), *capacities* (which describe the upper and sometimes lower limits on the constraints and variables), and *input/output (technology) coefficients* (which indicate resource utilization for a decision variable). See Technology Insights 4.1, also see Online File W4.2 for another example problem.

The LP Product-Mix Model Formulation

MBI Corporation, which manufactures special-purpose computers, needs to make a decision: How many computers should it produce next month at the Boston plant? MBI is considering two types of computers: the CC-7, which requires 300 days of labor and $10,000 in materials, and the CC-8, which requires 500 days of labor and $15,000 in materials. The profit contribution of each CC-7 is $8,000, whereas that of each CC-8 is $12,000. The plant has a capacity of 200,000 working days per month, and the material budget is $8 million per month. Marketing requires that at least 100 units of the CC-7 and at least 200 units of the CC-8 be produced each month. The problem is to maximize the company's profits by determining how many units of the CC-7 and how many units of the CC-8 should be produced each month. Note that in a real-world environment, it could possibly take months to obtain the data in the problem statement, and while gathering the data the decision maker would no doubt uncover facts about how to structure the model to be solved. Web-based tools for gathering data can help.

Modeling in LP: An Example

A standard LP model can be developed for the MBI Corporation problem just described. As discussed in Technology Insights 4.1, the LP model has three components: decision variables, result variables, and uncontrollable variables (constraints).

TECHNOLOGY INSIGHTS 4.1   Linear Programming

LP is perhaps the best-known optimization model. It deals with the optimal allocation of resources among competing activities. The allocation problem is represented by the model described here.

The problem is to find the values of the decision variables X_1, X_2, and so on, such that the value of the result variable Z is maximized, subject to a set of linear constraints that express the technology, market conditions, and other uncontrollable variables. The mathematical relationships are all linear equations and inequalities. Theoretically, any allocation problem of this type has an infinite number of possible solutions. Using special mathematical procedures, the LP approach applies a unique computerized search procedure that finds a best solution(s) in a matter of seconds. Furthermore, the solution approach provides automatic sensitivity analysis.

The decision variables are as follows:

$$X_1 = \text{units of CC-7 to be produced}$$
$$X_2 = \text{units of CC-8 to be produced}$$

The result variable is as follows:

$$\text{Total profit} = Z$$

The objective is to maximize total profit:

$$Z = 8{,}000X_1 + 12{,}000X_2$$

The uncontrollable variables (constraints) are as follows:

$$\text{Labor constraint: } 300X_1 + 500X_2 \leq 200{,}000 \text{ (in days)}$$
$$\text{Budget constraint: } 10{,}000X_1 + 15{,}000X_2 \leq 8{,}000{,}000 \text{ (in dollars)}$$
$$\text{Marketing requirement for CC-7: } X_1 \geq 100 \text{ (in units)}$$
$$\text{Marketing requirement for CC-8: } X_2 \geq 200 \text{ (in units)}$$

This information is summarized in Figure 4.5.

The model also has a fourth, hidden component. Every LP model has some internal intermediate variables that are not explicitly stated. The labor and budget constraints may each have some slack in them when the left-hand side is strictly less than the right-hand side. This slack is represented internally by slack variables that indicate excess resources available. The marketing requirement constraints may each have some surplus in them when the left-hand side is strictly greater than the right-hand side. This surplus is represented internally by surplus variables indicating that there is some room to adjust the right-hand sides of these constraints. These slack and surplus variables are intermediate. They can be of great value to a decision maker because LP solution methods use them in establishing sensitivity parameters for economic what-if analyses.

The product-mix model has an infinite number of possible solutions. Assuming that a production plan is not restricted to whole numbers—which is a reasonable assumption in a monthly production plan—we want a solution that maximizes total profit: an optimal solution. Fortunately, Excel comes with the add-in Solver, which can readily obtain an optimal (best) solution to this problem. We enter these data directly

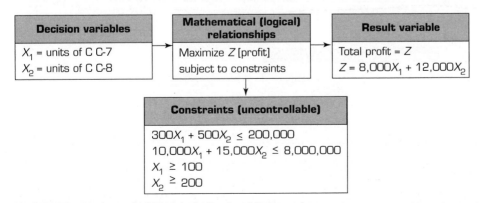

FIGURE 4.5 Mathematical Model of a Product-Mix Example

into an Excel spreadsheet, activate Solver, and identify the goal (by setting Target Cell equal to Max), decision variables (by setting By Changing Cells), and constraints (by ensuring that Total Consumed elements is less than or equal to Limit for the first two rows and is greater than or equal to Limit for the third and fourth rows). Also, in Options, we activate the boxes Assume Linear Model and Assume Non-negative, and then we solve the problem. Next, we select all three reports—Answer, Sensitivity, and Limits—to obtain an optimal solution of $X_1 = 333.33$, $X_2 = 200$, Profit = \$5,066,667, as shown in Figure 4.6. Solver produces three useful reports about the solution. Try it.

The evaluation of the alternatives and the final choice depend on the type of criteria selected. Are we trying to find the best solution? Or will a good-enough result be sufficient? (See Chapter 2.)

LP models (and their specializations and generalizations) can be specified directly in a number of user-friendly modeling systems. Two of the best known are Lindo and Lingo (Lindo Systems, Inc., **lindo.com**; demos are available). Lindo is an LP and integer programming system. Models are specified in essentially the same way that they are defined algebraically. Based on the success of Lindo, the company developed Lingo, a modeling language that includes the powerful Lindo optimizer and extensions for solving nonlinear problems. Lindo and Lingo models and solutions of the product-mix model are provided in Online Files W4.2, W4.3, and W4.4, respectively.

The uses of mathematical programming, especially of LP, are fairly common in practice. There are standard computer programs available. Optimization functions are available in many DSS integrated tools, such as Excel. Also, it is easy to interface other optimization software with Excel, DBMS, and similar tools. Optimization models are often included in decision support implementations, as shown in Application Cases 4.2 and 4.3. More details

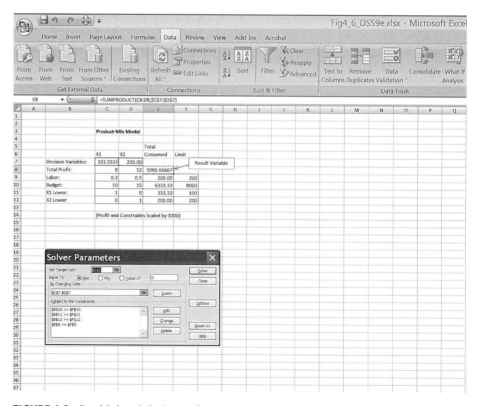

FIGURE 4.6 Excel Solver Solution to the Product-Mix Example

on LP, a description of another classic LP problem called the *blending problem*, and an Excel spreadsheet formulation and solution are described in Online File W4.2. A list of related Excel files is in Online File W4.5.

The most common optimization models can be solved by a variety of mathematical programming methods, including the following:

- Assignment (best matching of objects)
- Dynamic programming
- Goal programming
- Investment (maximizing rate of return)
- Linear and integer programming
- Network models for planning and scheduling
- Nonlinear programming
- Replacement (capital budgeting)
- Simple inventory models (e.g., economic order quantity)
- Transportation (minimize cost of shipments)

Section 4.6 Review Questions

1. List and explain the assumptions involved in LP.
2. List and explain the characteristics of LP.
3. Describe an allocation problem.
4. Define the product-mix problem.
5. Define the blending problem.
6. List several common optimization models.

4.7 MULTIPLE GOALS, SENSITIVITY ANALYSIS, WHAT-IF ANALYSIS, AND GOAL SEEKING

The search process described earlier in this chapter is coupled with evaluation. Evaluation is the final step that leads to a recommended solution.

Multiple Goals

The analysis of management decisions aims at evaluating, to the greatest possible extent, how far each alternative advances managers toward their goals. Unfortunately, managerial problems are seldom evaluated with a single simple goal, such as profit maximization. Today's management systems are much more complex, and one with a single goal is rare. Instead, managers want to attain *simultaneous goals*, some of which may conflict. Different stakeholders have different goals. Therefore, it is often necessary to analyze each alternative in light of its determination of each of several goals (see Koksalan and Zionts, 2001).

For example, consider a profit-making firm. In addition to earning money, the company wants to grow, develop its products and employees, provide job security to its workers, and serve the community. Managers want to satisfy the shareholders and at the same time enjoy high salaries and expense accounts, and employees want to increase their take-home pay and benefits. When a decision is to be made—say, about an investment project—some of these goals complement each other, whereas others conflict. Kearns (2004) described how the analytic hierarchy process (AHP), which we will introduce in Section 4.9, combined with integer programming, addressed multiple goals in evaluating IT investments.

Many quantitative models of decision theory are based on comparing a single measure of effectiveness, generally some form of utility to the decision maker. Therefore, it is usually necessary to transform a multiple-goal problem into a single-measure-of-effectiveness problem before comparing the effects of the solutions. This is a common method for handling multiple goals in an LP model.

Certain difficulties may arise when analyzing multiple goals:

- It is usually difficult to obtain an explicit statement of the organization's goals.
- The decision maker may change the importance assigned to specific goals over time or for different decision scenarios.
- Goals and subgoals are viewed differently at various levels of the organization and within different departments.
- Goals change in response to changes in the organization and its environment.
- The relationship between alternatives and their role in determining goals may be difficult to quantify.
- Complex problems are solved by groups of decision makers, each of whom has a personal agenda.
- Participants assess the importance (priorities) of the various goals differently.

Several methods of handling multiple goals can be used when working with MSS. The most common ones are:

- Utility theory
- Goal programming
- Expression of goals as constraints, using LP
- A points system

Sensitivity Analysis

A model builder makes predictions and assumptions regarding input data, many of which deal with the assessment of uncertain futures. When the model is solved, the results depend on these data. **Sensitivity analysis** attempts to assess the impact of a change in the input data or parameters on the proposed solution (i.e., the result variable).

Sensitivity analysis is extremely important in MSS because it allows flexibility and adaptation to changing conditions and to the requirements of different decision-making situations, provides a better understanding of the model and the decision-making situation it attempts to describe, and permits the manager to input data in order to increase the confidence in the model. Sensitivity analysis tests relationships such as the following:

- The impact of changes in external (uncontrollable) variables and parameters on the outcome variable(s)
- The impact of changes in decision variables on the outcome variable(s)
- The effect of uncertainty in estimating external variables
- The effects of different dependent interactions among variables
- The robustness of decisions under changing conditions

Sensitivity analyses are used for:

- Revising models to eliminate too-large sensitivities
- Adding details about sensitive variables or scenarios
- Obtaining better estimates of sensitive external variables
- Altering a real-world system to reduce actual sensitivities
- Accepting and using the sensitive (and hence vulnerable) real world, leading to the continuous and close monitoring of actual results

The two types of sensitivity analyses are automatic and trial-and-error.

AUTOMATIC SENSITIVITY ANALYSIS   Automatic sensitivity analysis is performed in standard quantitative model implementations such as LP. For example, it reports the range within which a certain input variable or parameter value (e.g., unit cost) can vary without having any significant impact on the proposed solution. Automatic sensitivity analysis is usually limited to one change at a time, and only for certain variables. However, it is very powerful because of its ability to establish ranges and limits very fast (and with little or no additional computational effort). For example, automatic sensitivity analysis is part of the LP solution report for the MBI Corporation product-mix problem described earlier. Sensitivity analysis is provided by both Solver and Lindo. Sensitivity analysis could be used to determine that if the right-hand side of the marketing constraint on CC-8 could be decreased by one unit, then the net profit would increase by $1,333.33. This is valid for the right-hand side decreasing to zero. For details, see Hillier and Lieberman (2005) and Taha (2006).

TRIAL-AND-ERROR SENSITIVITY ANALYSIS   The impact of changes in any variable, or in several variables, can be determined through a simple trial-and-error approach: You change some input data and solve the problem again. When the changes are repeated several times, better and better solutions may be discovered. Such experimentation, which is easy to conduct when using appropriate modeling software, such as Excel, has two approaches: what-if analysis and goal seeking.

What-If Analysis

What-if analysis is structured as *What will happen to the solution if an input variable, an assumption, or a parameter value is changed?* Here are some examples:

- What will happen to the total inventory cost if the cost of carrying inventories increases by 10 percent?
- What will be the market share if the advertising budget increases by 5 percent?

With the appropriate user interface, it is easy for managers to ask a computer model these types of questions and get immediate answers. Furthermore, they can perform multiple cases and thereby change the percentage, or any other data in the question, as desired. The decision maker does all this directly, without a computer programmer.

Figure 4.7 shows a spreadsheet example of a what-if query for a cash flow problem. (You can link to the Excel file for Figure 4.7 from Online File W4.5.) When the user changes the cells containing the initial sales (from 100 to 120) and the sales growth rate (from 3% to 4% per quarter), the program immediately recomputes the value of the annual net profit cell (from $127 to $182). At first, initial sales were 100, growing at 3 percent per quarter, yielding an annual net profit of $127. Changing the initial sales cell to 120 and the sales growth rate to 4 percent causes the annual net profit to rise to $182. What-if analysis is common in expert systems. Users are given the opportunity to change their answers to some of the system's questions, and a revised recommendation is found.

Goal Seeking

Goal seeking calculates the values of the inputs necessary to achieve a desired level of an output (goal). It represents a backward solution approach. The following are some examples of goal seeking:

- What annual R&D budget is needed for an annual growth rate of 15 percent by 2009?
- How many nurses are needed to reduce the average waiting time of a patient in the emergency room to less than 10 minutes?

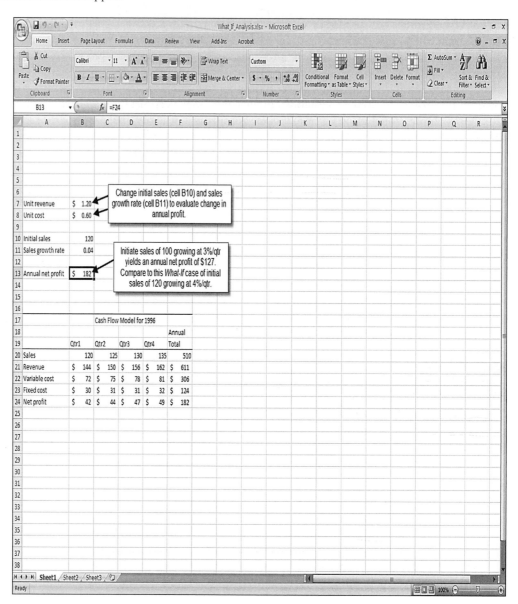

FIGURE 4.7   Example of a What-If Analysis Done in an Excel Worksheet

An example of goal seeking is shown in Figure 4.8. For example, in a financial planning model in Excel, the internal rate of return is the interest rate that produces a net present value (NPV) of zero. Given a stream of annual returns in Column E, we can compute the net present value of planned investment. By applying goal seeking, we can determine the internal rate of return where the NPV is zero. The goal to be achieved is NPV equal to zero, which determines the internal rate of return (IRR) of this cash flow, including the investment. We set the NPV cell to the value 0 by changing the interest rate cell. The answer is 38.77059 percent. (You can link to the Excel files and its resultant solution for Figure 4.8 from Online File W4.5.)

COMPUTING A BREAK-EVEN POINT BY USING GOAL SEEKING   Some modeling software packages can directly compute break-even points, which is an important application of

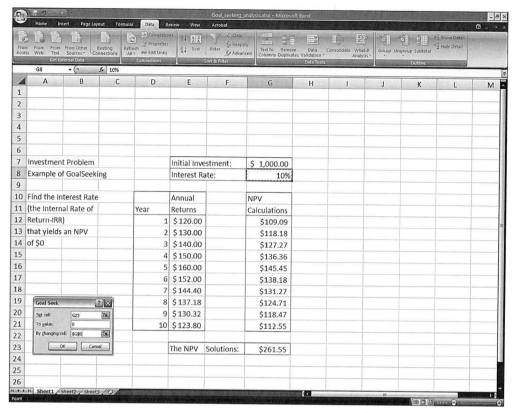

FIGURE 4.8 Goal-Seeking Analysis

goal seeking. This involves determining the value of the decision variables (e.g., quantity to produce) that generate zero profit.

In many general applications programs, it can be difficult to conduct sensitivity analysis because the prewritten routines usually present only a limited opportunity for asking what-if questions. In a DSS, the what-if and the goal-seeking options must be easy to perform.

Section 4.7 Review Questions

1. List some difficulties that may arise when analyzing multiple goals.
2. List the reasons for performing sensitivity analysis.
3. Explain why a manager might perform what-if analysis.
4. Explain why a manager might use goal seeking.

4.8 DECISION ANALYSIS WITH DECISION TABLES AND DECISION TREES

Decision situations that involve a finite and usually not too large number of alternatives are modeled through an approach called **decision analysis** (see Arsham, 2006a, 2006b; and Decision Analysis Society, **decision-analysis.society.informs.org**). Using this approach, the alternatives are listed in a table or a graph, with their forecasted contributions to the goal(s) and the probability of obtaining the contribution. These can be evaluated to select the best alternative.

Single-goal situations can be modeled with *decision tables* or *decision trees*. Multiple goals (criteria) can be modeled with several other techniques, described later in this chapter.

Decision Tables

Decision tables conveniently organize information and knowledge in a systematic, tabular manner to prepare it for analysis. For example, say that an investment company is considering investing in one of three alternatives: bonds, stocks, or certificates of deposit (CDs). The company is interested in one goal: maximizing the yield on the investment after one year. If it were interested in other goals, such as safety or liquidity, the problem would be classified as one of *multicriteria decision analysis* (see Koksalan and Zionts, 2001).

The yield depends on the state of the economy sometime in the future (often called the *state of nature*), which can be in solid growth, stagnation, or inflation. Experts estimated the following annual yields:

- If there is solid growth in the economy, bonds will yield 12 percent, stocks 15 percent, and time deposits 6.5 percent.
- If stagnation prevails, bonds will yield 6 percent, stocks 3 percent, and time deposits 6.5 percent.
- If inflation prevails, bonds will yield 3 percent, stocks will bring a loss of 2 percent, and time deposits will yield 6.5 percent.

The problem is to select the one best investment alternative. These are assumed to be discrete alternatives. Combinations such as investing 50 percent in bonds and 50 percent in stocks must be treated as new alternatives.

The investment decision-making problem can be viewed as a *two-person game* (see Kelly, 2002). The investor makes a choice (i.e., a move), and then a state of nature occurs (i.e., makes a move). Table 4.3 shows the payoff of a mathematical model. The table includes *decision variables* (the alternatives), *uncontrollable variables* (the states of the economy; e.g., the environment), and *result variables* (the projected yield; e.g., outcomes). All the models in this section are structured in a spreadsheet framework.

If this were a decision-making problem under certainty, we would know what the economy will be and could easily choose the best investment. But that is not the case, so we must consider the two situations of uncertainty and risk. For uncertainty, we do not know the probabilities of each state of nature. For risk, we assume that we know the probabilities with which each state of nature will occur.

TREATING UNCERTAINTY Several methods are available for handling uncertainty. For example, the *optimistic approach* assumes that the best possible outcome of each alternative

TABLE 4.3 Investment Problem Decision Table Model

Alternative	State of Nature (Uncontrollable Variables)		
	Solid Growth (%)	Stagnation (%)	Inflation (%)
Bonds	12.0	6.0	3.0
Stocks	15.0	3.0	−2.0
CDs	6.5	6.5	6.5

will occur and then selects the best of the best (i.e., stocks). The *pessimistic approach* assumes that the worst possible outcome for each alternative will occur and selects the best of these (i.e., CDs). Another approach simply assumes that all states of nature are equally possible. (See Clemen and Reilly, 2000; Goodwin and Wright, 2000; and Kontoghiorghes et al., 2002.) Every approach for handling uncertainty has serious problems. Whenever possible, the analyst should attempt to gather enough information so that the problem can be treated under assumed certainty or risk.

TREATING RISK The most common method for solving this risk analysis problem is to select the alternative with the greatest expected value. Assume that experts estimate the chance of solid growth at 50 percent, the chance of stagnation at 30 percent, and the chance of inflation at 20 percent. The decision table is then rewritten with the known probabilities (see Table 4.4). An expected value is computed by multiplying the results (i.e., outcomes) by their respective probabilities and adding them. For example, investing in bonds yields an expected return of 12(0.5) + 6(0.3) + 3(0.2) = 8.4 percent.

This approach can sometimes be a dangerous strategy because the utility of each potential outcome may be different from the value. Even if there is an infinitesimal chance of a catastrophic loss, the expected value may seem reasonable, but the investor may not be willing to cover the loss. For example, suppose a financial advisor presents you with an "almost sure" investment of $1,000 that can double your money in one day, and then the advisor says, "Well, there is a .9999 probability that you will double your money, but unfortunately there is a .0001 probability that you will be liable for a $500,000 out-of-pocket loss." The expected value of this investment is as follows:

$$0.9999 \ (\$2,000 - \$1,000) + .0001 \ (-\$500,000 - \$1,000) = \$999.90 - \$50.10$$
$$= \$949.80$$

The potential loss could be catastrophic for any investor who is not a billionaire. Depending on the investor's ability to cover the loss, an investment has different expected utilities. Remember that the investor makes the decision only *once*.

Decision Trees

An alternative representation of the decision table is a decision tree (for examples, see Mind Tools Ltd., **mindtools.com**). A **decision tree** shows the relationships of the problem graphically and can handle complex situations in a compact form. However, a decision tree can be cumbersome if there are many alternatives or states of nature. TreeAge Pro (TreeAge Software Inc., **treeage.com**) and PrecisionTree (Palisade Corp.,

TABLE 4.4 Decision Under Risk and Its Solution

Alternative	Solid Growth .50 (%)	Stagnation, .30 (%)	Inflation, .20 (%)	Expected Value (%)
Bonds	12.0	6.0	3.0	8.4 (maximum)
Stocks	15.0	3.0	−2.0	8.0
CDs	6.5	6.5	6.5	6.5

APPLICATION CASE 4.5

Decision Analysis Assists Doctor in Weighing Treatment Options for Cancer Suspects and Patients

Professor Victor Grann of Columbia University's School of Public Health wanted to analyze the value of new genetic tests for the detection of various cancers. This is an important issue, because there is no point in paying for a test if the results do not lead the patient to undergo treatment to mitigate the problem. Also, if a patient does begin a new treatment after the genetic testing, what effect does it have on the patient's longevity and the quality of life? This can be viewed as a decision tree problem: whether to test for a gene or not; resulting scenarios of positive or negative test results; and, if positive, the likelihood of success of a selected treatment. This is exactly the type of modeling decision trees can address.

Professor Grann has built several decision tree models to analyze similar decision-making scenarios using TreeAge software. In one of his first models,

he showed that a woman testing positive for breast cancer could, on average, extend her life by several years if she accepted the recommended treatment of a preventive mastectomy and a surgery to remove her ovaries. Newer models take into account the results of more recent clinical trials, which help in updating the probabilities of specific scenarios. Professor Grann argues that these models can help in determining whether a specific test or treatment is cost-effective in terms of increasing a patient's survival rate and/or quality of life. He has built many other decision tree models and has run simulations to help make such decisions.

Source: Based on TreeAge Software, Inc., "Dr. Victor Grann Uses Decision Analysis to Weigh Treatment Options for Patients at High Risk of Developing Cancer," 2009, **treeage.com/resources/includes/Grann_cs.pdf** (accessed July 2009).

palisade.com) include powerful, intuitive, and sophisticated decision tree analysis systems. These vendors also provide excellent examples of decision trees used in practice. We describe how an expert in medicine evaluates various genetic tests via decision trees in Application Case 4.5.

A simplified investment case of **multiple goals** (a decision situation in which alternatives are evaluated with several, sometimes conflicting, goals) is shown in Table 4.5. The three goals (criteria) are yield, safety, and liquidity. This situation is under assumed certainty; that is, only one possible consequence is projected for each alternative; the more complex cases of risk or uncertainty could be considered. Some of the results are qualitative (e.g., low, high) rather than numeric.

See Clemen and Reilly (2000), Goodwin and Wright (2000), and Decision Analysis Society (**faculty.fuqua.duke.edu/daweb/**) for more on decision analysis. Although doing

TABLE 4.5 Multiple Goals

Alternative	Yield (%)	Safety	Liquidity
Bonds	8.4	High	High
Stocks	8.0	Low	High
CDs	6.5	Very high	High

so is quite complex, it is possible to apply mathematical programming directly to decision-making situations under risk. We discuss several other methods of treating risk later in the book. These include simulation, certainty factors, and fuzzy logic.

Section 4.8 Review Questions

1. What is a decision table?
2. What is a decision tree?
3. How can a decision tree be used in decision making?
4. Describe what it means to have multiple goals.

4.9 MULTICRITERIA DECISION MAKING WITH PAIRWISE COMPARISONS

Multicriteria (goal) decision making was introduced in Chapter 2. One of the most effective approaches is to use weights based on decision-making priorities. However, soliciting weights (or priorities) from managers is a complex task, as is calculation of the weighted averages needed to choose the best alternative. The process is complicated further by the presence of qualitative variables. One method of multicriteria decision making is the analytic hierarchy process developed by Saaty (1996, 1999) (also see **expertchoice.com** and this book's Web site).

The Analytic Hierarchy Process

The **analytic hierarchy process (AHP)**, developed by Thomas Saaty (1995, 1996), is an excellent modeling structure for representing *multicriteria* (multiple goals, multiple objectives) *problems*—with sets of criteria and alternatives (choices)—commonly found in business environments. The decision maker uses AHP to decompose a decision-making problem into relevant criteria and alternatives. The AHP separates the analysis of the criteria from the alternatives, which helps the decision maker to focus on small, manageable portions of the problem. The AHP manipulates quantitative and qualitative decision-making criteria in a fairly structured manner, allowing a decision maker to make trade-offs quickly and "expertly."

Expert Choice (**expertchoice.com**; a demo is available directly on its Web site) is an excellent commercial implementation of the AHP. A problem is represented as an inverted tree with a goal node at the top. All the weight of the decision is in the goal (1.000). Directly beneath and attached to the goal node are the criteria nodes. These are the factors that are important to the decision maker. The goal is decomposed into criteria, to which 100 percent of the weight of the decision from the goal is distributed. To distribute the weight, the decision maker conducts pairwise comparisons of the criteria: first criterion to second, first to third, . . . , first to last; then, second to third, . . . , second to last; . . . ; and then the next-to-last criterion to the last one. This establishes the importance of each criterion; that is, how much of the goal's weight is distributed to each criterion (how *important* each criterion is). This objective method is performed by internally manipulating matrices mathematically. The manipulations are transparent to the user because the operational details of the method are *not* important to the decision maker. Finally, an inconsistency index indicates how consistent the comparisons were, thus identifying inconsistencies, errors in judgment, or simply errors. The AHP method is consistent with decision theory.

The decision maker can make comparisons verbally (e.g., one criterion is moderately more important than another), graphically (with bar and pie charts), or numerically (with a *matrix*—comparisons are scaled from 1 to 9). Students and business professionally prefer graphical and verbal approaches over matrices (based on an informal sample).

Beneath each criterion are the same sets of choices (alternatives) in the simple case described here. Like the goal, the criteria decompose their weight into the choices, which capture 100 percent of the weight of each criterion. The decision maker performs a pairwise comparison of choices in terms of *preferences,* as they relate to the specific criterion under consideration. Each set of choices must be pairwise compared as they relate to each criterion. Again, all three modes of comparison are available, and an inconsistency index is derived for each set and reported.

Finally, the results are synthesized and displayed on a bar graph. The choice with the most weight is the correct choice. However, under some conditions the correct decision may not be the right one. For example, if there are two "identical" choices (e.g., if you are selecting a car for purchase and you have two identical cars), they may split the weight and neither will have the most weight. Also, if the top few choices are very close, there may be a missing criterion that could be used to differentiate among these choices.

Expert Choice also has a sensitivity analysis module. A group version called Comparium Teamtime synthesizes the results of a group of decision makers using the same model. This version can work on the Web.

Overall, the AHP as implemented in Expert Choice attempts to derive a decision maker's preference (utility) structure in terms of the criteria and choices and helps him or her to make an expert choice.

In addition to Expert Choice, other software packages allow for weighting of pairwise choices. For example, Web-HIPRE (**hipre.hut.fi**), an adaptation of AHP and several other weighting schemes, enables a decision maker to create a decision model, enter pairwise preferences, and analyze the optimal choice. These weightings can be computed using AHP as well as other techniques. It is available as a Java applet on the Web so it can be easily located and run online, free for noncommercial use. To run Web-HIPRE, one has to access the site and leave a Java applet window running. The user can enter a problem by providing the general labels for the decision tree at each node level and then entering the problem components. After the model has been specified, the user can enter pairwise preferences at each node level for criteria/subcriteria/alternatives. Once that is done, the appropriate analysis algorithm can be used to determine the model's final recommendation. The software can also perform sensitivity analysis to determine which criteria/subcriteria play a dominant role in the decision process. Finally, the Web-HIPRE can also be employed in group mode. Application Case 4.6 describes an application of Web-HIPRE in developing plans for managing disasters related to nuclear and radiation accidents.

APPLICATION CASE 4.6

Multicriteria Decision Support for European Radiation Emergency Support System

Environmental emergencies such as nuclear or radiation accidents are a major potential threat anywhere in the world, but even more so in Europe, with so many large population centers located relatively close together. Nuclear accidents have vast impacts, but are fortunately rare. However, their infrequency means that there are few data points for future learning and advance preparation. In addition, the problem has multiple objectives, because different constituencies (general population, government, politicians, technical personnel, environmentalists, first responders, etc.) have different goals when dealing with such a crisis.

To prepare for such emergency situations, the European Commission asked researchers to develop a system called Real-time Online Decision Support System (RODOS). RODOS provides reports about possible accidents and their potential impacts and enables evaluation of measures taken to a possible crisis. An analyzing system (ASY) projects the impact of an accident across an area and over time. A countermeasure system (CSY) simulates effects of different countermeasure plans in terms of benefits and costs across different objectives. The third component (ESY) allows decision makers to rank the various countermeasure plans and then determine the best course of action. For this third component, Web-HIPRE, a multi-attribute decision-making tool, was

used. Web-HIPRE allowed the problem to be structured into criteria and alternatives. Each of these was linked to Web pages that explained the details of the criteria/subcriteria/alternatives.

The model was used for eliciting group preferences at workshops on decision analysis of countermeasure and remediation strategies after an accidental release of radiation. These workshops were treated as training exercises. RODOS was introduced to participants at a workshop in Germany. The participants were given a hypothetical scenario and were asked to apply the model for realistic decision making. The participants considered the RODOS model to be very useful for training purposes and as a tool to perform sensitivity analysis of available options.

Source: Based on J. Geldermann, V. Bertsch, M. Treitz, S. French, K. N. Papamichail, and R. P. Hämäläinen, "Multicriteria Decision Support and Evaluation of Strategies for Nuclear Remediation Management," *Omega*, Vol. 37, No. 1, February 2009, pp. 238–251.

Another software product, ChoiceAnalyst, also is available for decision making in pairwise mode. It is a multicriteria decision-making tool and is not based on AHP. The following information was contributed by Cary Harwin, who developed the software. ChoiceAnalyst takes a direct approach, using a gradient-free derivative and probability and statistics to generate a sampling using a confidence level and confidence interval (whose default is a model option) and a ranking calculation. A global minima is iteratively found that best satisfies the decision maker and criteria weights along with the paired preference weight matrix. The number of iterations to reach convergence depends on the particular model involved.

ChoiceAnalyst can break down complex problems into a simple series of pairwise comparisons by considering one criterion at a time. Only three screens need to be filled to build a decision model (Figure 4.9). The user simply lists the possible choices, provides the criteria that the choices should be judged on, and enters a weight reflecting the importance of each criterion. Finally, the user lists the decision makers and assigns them weights if they carry a different value of knowledge or experience for the decision at hand.

ChoiceAnalyst then presents a random pair of choices, considering the listed criterion. The user simply selects which is better (and by about how much) based on the current criterion. Once all of the pairings have been evaluated, ChoiceAnalyst calculates and presents the results, which also can be provided in a PDF report. A trial copy of the software is available at **choiceanalyst.com**.

Section 4.9 Review Questions

1. What is analytic hierarchy process?
2. What steps are needed in applying AHP?
3. What are the differences between AHP software and software such as ChoiceAnalyst?

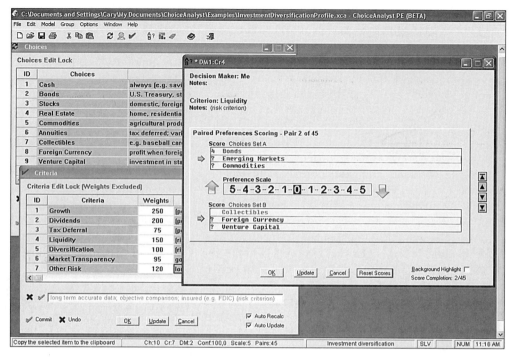

FIGURE 4.9   ChoiceAnalyst Screen

4.10   PROBLEM-SOLVING SEARCH METHODS

We next turn to several well-known search methods used in the choice phase of problem solving. These include analytical techniques, algorithms, blind searching, and heuristic searching.

The choice phase of problem solving involves a search for an appropriate course of action (among those identified during the design phase) that can solve the problem. Several major search approaches are possible, depending on the criteria (or criterion) of choice and the type of modeling approach used. These search approaches are shown in Figure 4.10. For normative models, such as mathematical programming-based ones, either an analytical approach is used or a complete, exhaustive enumeration (comparing the outcomes of all the alternatives) is applied. For descriptive models, a comparison of a limited number of alternatives is used, either blindly or by employing heuristics. Usually the results guide the decision maker's search.

Analytical Techniques

Analytical techniques use mathematical formulas to derive an optimal solution directly or to predict a certain result. Analytical techniques are used mainly for solving structured problems, usually of a tactical or operational nature, in areas such as resource allocation or inventory management. Blind or heuristic search approaches are generally employed to solve more complex problems.

Algorithms

Analytical techniques may use algorithms to increase the efficiency of the search. An algorithm is a step-by-step search process for obtaining an optimal solution (see

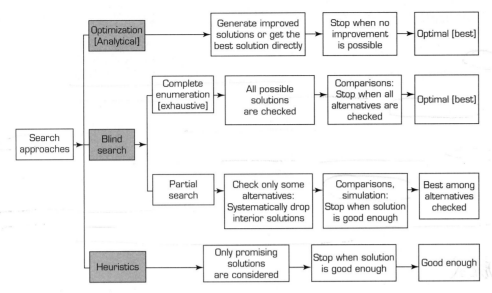

FIGURE 4.10 Formal Search Approaches

Figure 4.11). (Note: There may be more than one optimum, so we say *an* optimal solution rather than *the* optimal solution.) Solutions are generated and tested for possible improvements. An improvement is made whenever possible, and the new solution is subjected to an improvement test, based on the principle of choice (i.e., objective value found). The process continues until no further improvement is possible. Most mathematical programming problems are solved by using efficient algorithms. Web search engines use algorithms to speed up searches and produce accurate results. Google's search algorithms are so good that Yahoo! pays millions of dollars annually to use them.

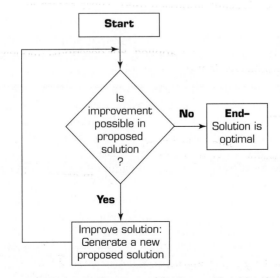

FIGURE 4.11 The Process of Using an Algorithm

Blind Searching

In conducting a search, a description of a desired solution may be given. This is called a *goal*. A set of possible steps leading from initial conditions to the goal is called the *search steps*. Problem solving is done by searching through the possible solutions. The first of these search methods is blind searching. The second is heuristic searching.

Blind search techniques are arbitrary search approaches that are not guided. There are two types of blind searches: a *complete enumeration*, for which all the alternatives are considered and therefore an optimal solution is discovered; and an *incomplete*, or partial, search, which continues until a good-enough solution is found. The latter is a form of suboptimization.

There are practical limits on the amount of time and computer storage available for blind searches. In principle, blind search methods can eventually find an optimal solution in most search situations, and, in some situations, the scope of the search can be limited; however, this method is not practical for solving very large problems because too many solutions must be examined before an optimal solution is found.

Heuristic Searching

For many applications, it is possible to find rules to guide the search process and reduce the number of necessary computations through heuristics. **Heuristics** are the informal, judgmental knowledge of an application area that constitute the rules of good judgment in the field. Through domain knowledge, they guide the problem-solving process. **Heuristic programming** is the process of using heuristics in problem solving. This is done via heuristic search methods, which often operate as algorithms but limit the solutions examined either by limiting the search space or stopping the method early. Usually, rules that have either demonstrated their success in practice or are theoretically solid are applied in heuristic searching. In Application Case 4.7, we provide an example of a DSS in which the models are solved using heuristic searching. A similar system was developed for Waste Management of Delaware (see Dignan, 2004).

APPLICATION CASE 4.7
Heuristic-Based DSS Moves Milk in New Zealand

A major New Zealand dairy company had some 350 client farmers served by 12 tankers over two shifts. Because of its rising client base and rising milk collection costs, the company decided to improve its milk tanker scheduling by implementing a heuristic-based DSS. The vehicle schedulers, who had previously set up schedules manually, estimated milk supply by supplier (which varies seasonally and daily); operated the tanker fleet within location, budget, and other constraints; and attempted (among several goals) to minimize the cost per kilogram of milk delivered to the company's factories.

This complex (in a theoretical and practical sense) routing problem is very difficult to solve to optimality in a reasonable time, so the company developed a model-based DSS called FleetManager.

A heuristic search approach was implemented. The model's objective function and constraints take into consideration the experience and preferences of the expert schedulers. The development team worked closely with schedulers and other experts in modeling the situation. The vehicle-routing models were solved by the Gillet and Miller Sweep Heuristic to create trial solutions, which the schedulers then examined via a graphical user interface. The schedulers were then able to adjust solutions based on additional knowledge as to their practicality. Output screens of the system can be found at **orms-today.com**.

Since implementing FleetManager, the company's collection costs have decreased by more than 30 percent, schedule development time has decreased by more than 50 percent, and client complaints have decreased by more than 60 percent. Intangible benefits include a morale boost among schedulers, who now have time to deal with unanticipated complications in the schedule. The heuristic methodology of the DSS developed for this New Zealand dairy company could be applied to almost any complex delivery system.

Sources: Modified and condensed from C. Basnet and L. Foulds, "Fleet Manager Milks Efficiency Out of Dairy Company," *OR/MS Today*, Vol. 32, No. 6, December 2005, pp. 36–42; and B. Gillet and L. Miller, "A Heuristic Algorithm for the Vehicle Dispatch Problem," *Operations Research*, Vol. 22, No. 2, March/April 1974, pp. 340–349.

Section 4.10 Review Questions

1. What is a search approach?
2. List the different problem-solving search methods.
3. What are the practical limits to blind searching?
4. How are algorithms and heuristic search methods similar? How are they different?

4.11 SIMULATION

Simulation is the appearance of reality. In MSS, simulation is a technique for conducting experiments (e.g., what-if analyses) with a computer on a model of a management system.

Typically, real decision-making situations involve some randomness. Because DSS deals with semistructured or unstructured situations, reality is complex, which may not be easily represented by optimization or other models but can often be handled by simulation. Simulation is one of the most commonly used DSS methods. See Application Case 4.8 and Seila et al. (2003).

APPLICATION CASE 4.8

Improving Maintenance Decision Making in the Finnish Air Force Through Simulation

The Finnish Air Force wanted to gain efficiency in its maintenance system in order to keep as many aircraft as possible safely available at all times for training, missions, and other tasks, as needed. A discrete event simulation program similar to those used in manufacturing was developed to accommodate workforce issues, task times, material handling delays, and the likelihood of equipment failure.

The developers had to consider aircraft availability, resource requirements for international operations, and the periodic maintenance program. The information for normal conditions and conflict conditions was input into the simulation program because the maintenance schedule could be altered from one situation to another.

The developers had to estimate some information due to confidentiality, especially with regards to conflict scenarios (no data of battle-damage probabilities was available). They used several methods to acquire and secure data, such as asking experts in aircraft maintenance fields at different levels for their opinions and designing a model that allowed the confidential data to be input into the system. Also, the simulations were compared to actual performance data to make sure the simulated results were accurate.

The maintenance program was broken into three levels:

1. The organizational level, in which the fighter squadron takes care of preflight checks, turn-around checks (which occur when an aircraft returns), and other minor repairs at the main command airbase in normal conditions
2. The intermediate level, in which more complicated periodic maintenance and failure repairs

are taken care of at the air command repair shop at the main airbase in normal conditions

3. The depot-level, in which all major periodic maintenance is taken care of and is located away from the main airbase

During conflict conditions, the system is decentralized from the main airbase. The maintenance levels just described may continue to do the exact same repairs, or periodic maintenance may be eliminated. Additionally, depending on need, supplies, and capabilities, any of the above levels may take care of any maintenance and repairs needed at any time during conflict conditions.

The simulation model was implemented using Arena software based on the SIMAN language and involved using a graphical user interface (GUI) that was executed using Visual Basic for Applications (VBA). The input data included simulation parameters and the initial system state: characteristics of the air commands, maintenance needs, and flight operations; accumulated flight hours; and the location of each aircraft. Excel spreadsheets were used for data input and output. Additionally, parameters of some of the input data were estimated from statistical data or based on information from subject matter experts. These included probabilities for time between failures, damage sustained during a single-flight mission, the duration of each type of periodic maintenance, failure repair, damage repair, the times between flight missions, and the duration of a mission. This simulation model was so successful that the Finnish Army, in collaboration with the Finnish Air Force, has now devised a simulation model for the maintenance for some of its new transport helicopters.

Source: Based on V. Mattila, K. Virtanen, and T. Raivio, "Improving Maintenance Decision Making in the Finnish Air Force Through Simulation," *Interfaces*, Vol. 38, No. 3, May/June 2008, pp. 187–201.

Major Characteristics of Simulation

Simulation is not strictly a type of model; models generally *represent* reality, whereas simulation typically *imitates* it. In a practical sense, there are fewer simplifications of reality in simulation models than in other models. In addition, simulation is a technique for *conducting experiments*. Therefore, it involves testing specific values of the decision or uncontrollable variables in the model and observing the impact on the output variables. At DuPont, decision makers had initially chosen to purchase more railcars; however, an alternative involving better scheduling of the existing railcars was developed, tested, and found to have excess capacity, and it ended up saving money.

Simulation is a *descriptive* rather than a *normative* method. There is no automatic search for an optimal solution. Instead, a simulation model describes or predicts the characteristics of a given system under different conditions. When the values of the characteristics are computed, the best of several alternatives can be selected. The simulation process usually repeats an experiment many times to obtain an estimate (and a variance) of the overall effect of certain actions. For most situations, a computer simulation is appropriate, but there are some well-known manual simulations (e.g., a city police department simulated its patrol car scheduling with a carnival game wheel).

Finally, simulation is normally used only when a problem is too complex to be treated using numerical optimization techniques. **Complexity** in this situation means either that the problem cannot be formulated for optimization (e.g., because the assumptions do not hold), that the formulation is too large, that there are too many interactions among the variables, or that the problem is stochastic in nature (i.e., exhibits risk or uncertainty).

Advantages of Simulation

Simulation is used in MSS for the following reasons:

- The theory is fairly straightforward.
- A great amount of *time compression* can be attained, quickly giving a manager some feel as to the long-term (1- to 10-year) effects of many policies.

- Simulation is descriptive rather than normative. This allows the manager to pose what-if questions. Managers can use a trial-and-error approach to problem solving and can do so faster, at less expense, more accurately, and with less risk.
- A manager can experiment to determine which decision variables and which parts of the environment are really important, and with different alternatives.
- An accurate simulation model requires an intimate knowledge of the problem, thus forcing the MSS builder to constantly interact with the manager. This is desirable for DSS development because the developer and manager both gain a better understanding of the problem and the potential decisions available.
- The model is built from the manager's perspective.
- The simulation model is built for one particular problem and typically cannot solve any other problem. Thus, no generalized understanding is required of the manager; every component in the model corresponds to part of the real system.
- Simulation can handle an extremely wide variety of problem types, such as inventory and staffing, as well as higher-level managerial functions, such as long-range planning.
- Simulation generally can include the real complexities of problems; simplifications are not necessary. For example, simulation can use real probability distributions rather than approximate theoretical distributions.
- Simulation automatically produces many important performance measures.
- Simulation is often the only DSS modeling method that can readily handle relatively unstructured problems.
- Some relatively easy-to-use simulation packages (e.g., Monte Carlo simulation) are available. These include add-in spreadsheet packages (e.g., @RISK), influence diagram software, Java-based (and other Web development) packages, and the visual interactive simulation systems to be discussed shortly.

Disadvantages of Simulation

The primary disadvantages of simulation are as follows:

- An optimal solution cannot be guaranteed, but relatively good ones are generally found.
- Simulation model construction can be a slow and costly process, although newer modeling systems are easier to use than ever.
- Solutions and inferences from a simulation study are usually not transferable to other problems because the model incorporates unique problem factors.
- Simulation is sometimes so easy to explain to managers that analytic methods are often overlooked.
- Simulation software sometimes requires special skills because of the complexity of the formal solution method.

The Methodology of Simulation

Simulation involves setting up a model of a real system and conducting repetitive experiments on it. The methodology consists of the following steps, as shown in Figure 4.12:

1. **Define the problem.**   We examine and classify the real-world problem, specifying why a simulation approach is appropriate. The system's boundaries, environment, and other such aspects of problem clarification are handled here.
2. **Construct the simulation model.**   This step involves determination of the variables and their relationships, as well as data gathering. Often the process is described by using a flowchart, and then a computer program is written.
3. **Test and validate the model.**   The simulation model must properly represent the system being studied. Testing and validation ensure this.

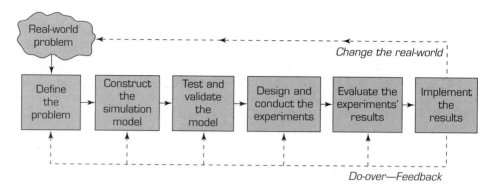

FIGURE 4.12 The Process of Simulation

4. ***Design the experiment.*** When the model has been proven valid, an experiment is designed. Determining how long to run the simulation is part of this step. There are two important and conflicting objectives: accuracy and cost. It is also prudent to identify typical (e.g., mean and median cases for random variables), best-case (e.g., low-cost, high-revenue), and worst-case (e.g., high-cost, low-revenue) scenarios. These help establish the ranges of the decision variables and environment in which to work and also assist in debugging the simulation model.

5. ***Conduct the experiment.*** Conducting the experiment involves issues ranging from random-number generation to result presentation.

6. ***Evaluate the results.*** The results must be interpreted. In addition to standard statistical tools, sensitivity analyses can also be used.

7. ***Implement the results.*** The implementation of simulation results involves the same issues as any other implementation. However, the chances of success are better because the manager is usually more involved with the simulation process than with other models. Higher levels of managerial involvement generally lead to higher levels of implementation success.

Many simulation packages are Web ready. They are typically developed along the lines of the DSS architecture shown in Figure 3.4, where a user connects to the main server through a Web browser. This server connects to optimization servers and database servers, and the optimization and database servers in turn may connect to data warehouses, which populate the models.

Simulation Types

In the following sections, we describe the major types of simulation: probabilistic simulation, time-dependent and time-independent simulation, object-oriented simulation, and visual simulation.

PROBABILISTIC SIMULATION In probabilistic simulation, one or more of the independent variables (e.g., the demand in an inventory problem) are probabilistic. They follow certain probability distributions, which can be either discrete distributions or continuous distributions:

- *Discrete distributions* involve a situation with a limited number of events (or variables) that can take on only a finite number of values.
- *Continuous distributions* are situations with unlimited numbers of possible events that follow density functions, such as the normal distribution.

The two types of distributions are shown in Table 4.6. Probabilistic simulation is conducted with the aid of a technique called Monte Carlo simulation, which DuPont used.

TABLE 4.6 Discrete Versus Continuous Probability Distributions

Daily Demand	Discrete Probability	Continuous Probability
5	.10	Daily demand is normally distributed with a mean of 7 and a standard deviation of 1.2.
6	.15	
7	.30	
8	.25	
9	.20	

TIME-DEPENDENT VERSUS TIME-INDEPENDENT SIMULATION *Time-independent* refers to a situation in which it is not important to know exactly when the event occurred. For example, we may know that the demand for a certain product is three units per day, but we do not care *when* during the day the item is demanded. In some situations, time may not be a factor in the simulation at all, such as in steady-state plant control design. However, in waiting-line problems applicable to e-commerce, it is important to know the precise time of arrival (to know whether the customer will have to wait). This is a *time-dependent* situation.

OBJECT-ORIENTED SIMULATION There have been some advances in the area of developing simulation models by using the object-oriented approach. SIMPROCESS (CACI Products Company, **caciasl.com**) is an object-oriented process modeling tool that lets the user create a simulation model by using screen-based objects (e.g., metro cars). Unified Modeling Language (UML) is a modeling tool that was designed for object-oriented and object-based systems and applications. Because UML is object oriented, it could be used in practice for modeling complex, real-time systems. UML is particularly well suited for modeling. A *real-time system* is a software system that maintains an ongoing, timely interaction with its environment; examples include many DSS and information and communication systems (see Selic, 1999). Also, Java-based simulations are essentially object oriented.

VISUAL SIMULATION The graphical display of computerized results, which may include animation, is one of the most successful developments in computer–human interaction and problem solving. We describe this in the next section.

Simulation Software

Hundreds of simulation packages are available for a variety of decision-making situations. Most run as Web-based systems, and newer implementation packages are Java based. Many online demonstrations of simulations are written in Java. PC software packages include Analytica (Lumina Decision Systems, **lumina.com**) and the Excel add-ins Crystal Ball (Decisioneering, **decisioneering.com**) and @RISK (Palisade Corp., **palisade.com**). Web-based systems include WebGPSS (GPSS, **webgpss.com**), and SIMUL8 (SIMUL8 Corp., **SIMUL8.com**). A major commercial size software for simulation is Arena (**arenasimulation.com**).

Simulation Examples

Saltzman and Mehrotra (2001) used a simulation approach to analyze a call center. Jovanovic (2002) determined how to schedule tasks in distributed systems via simulation. This is important when managing grid computer networks. Dronzek (2001) used simulation to improve critical care in a military hospital. He analyzed proposed changes in a health care system, using simulation modeling to determine the impact of potential changes without disrupting the established process of care or disturbing staff, patients, or the facility. Credit Suisse First Boston uses an ASP simulation system to predict the risk and reward potential of investments (see Dembo et al., 2000).

General Motors (see Stackpole, 2005; Gallagher, 2002; Gareiss, 2002; and Witzerman, 2001) delays constructing physical models of automobiles until late in the design process because simulation (e.g., crash tests, wind-tunnel tests) is less expensive and produces more accurate results in testing new products. Witzerman (2001) described how GM's paint shop robots are simulated for improved performance. The simulation tools in use today by GM are very effective and have led to major improvements. It now takes only 18 months to develop a new vehicle, down from 48 months. Engineering productivity is way up, as is quality. In Application Case 4.9, we provide several additional examples of simulation applications, including those for e-learning systems.

APPLICATION CASE 4.9
Simulation Applications

Simulation applications vary widely. Some are in scientific disciplines, others are in business, and yet others are, essentially, video/computer games. The following is a sampler of several simulation applications:

- **E-learning.** Tacit skill training is expensive, and if people can experience walkthroughs without one-on-one human interaction, the savings can be dramatic. For example, the U.S. Department of Agriculture (USDA) developed a Web-based simulation system to provide more than 400 geographically dispersed federal employees training on how to use the PeopleSoft 8.0 human resource management system. The cost of developing e-learning simulations, even with custom video, can be less than $20,000. Humana, Inc., used simulation to train 150 top executives in navigating complex change initiatives. Business simulations have been used for decades at leading colleges of business (e.g., the Carnegie Mellon Tepper School of Business).

- **Production scenarios.** Agilent's California Semiconductor Test division simulates supply-side production scenarios to coordinate sourcing for new product launches, to keep excess and obsolete inventory (caused by engineering changes) low, and to respond quickly to new orders. One clear benefit has been a reduction of 30 to 40 percent in the inventory of most components, with some reductions as high as 60 percent.

- **IT/software products.** CNA Financial Corp. uses simulation tools from iRise, Inc., to determine how potential software system requirements will work out. The simulations bring products to life and show business users how they will function in practice. In this way, the firm can communicate requirements from business users to software developers more accurately, which, in turn, shortens the requirements cycle. This is critical when development is offshored (i.e., outsourced to a firm in another country). Serena developed its ProcessView Composer software to simulate, visualize, and prototype business processes and application requirements. This has greatly reduced rework due to flawed requirements.

- **Web applications.** In a manner similar to CNA, Wachovia Corp. uses iRise simulation tools in a user design laboratory to simulate Web applications before their release to internal users.

- **Military battles.** The U.S. military conducts battle simulations running on high-powered graphics engines and supercomputers using software based largely on that developed for the entertainment industry (video and computer games). These systems simulate a training environment that reflects the stress and uncertainty of battle situations. For example, flight simulators save many hours of flight training time. By including artificial intelligence capabilities, characters in the simulations can even reason on their own.

- ***Pharmaceutical development.*** Pharmaceutical firms simulate how drugs interact with the human body, down to the DNA level, thus accurately predicting their impacts. Savings are realized in the testing phases if potential compounds prove ineffective in the computer simulation. Pharmaceutical development simulations run on high-powered parallel computers.
- ***Product design.*** Even simple products can benefit from simulation. Earlier in this section, we described how General Motors uses simulations in new product design and manufacturing. Even the aerodynamics of Pringles chips have been analyzed using simulation methods to determine how air flows around their unique double-saddle shape. The problem

was that the shape of the chip caused it to fly off the manufacturer's conveyer belt if the belt was running too fast. Based on information found through simulation, the shape of the chip was redesigned.

Sources: Modified and abstracted from T. Hoffman, "Simulations Revitalize E-Learning," *Computerworld*, August 4, 2003, pp. 26–27; S. Boehle, "The Next Generation of E-Learning," *Training*, January 2005, pp. 23–31; R. Michel, "Decision Support Smoothes Semiconductor Test Division's Outsourced Model," *Manufacturing Business Technology*, June 2005, p. 30; H. Havenstein, "App Simulation in Demand," *Computerworld*, June 27, 2005, pp. 1, 77; D. Verton, "Simulating Fallujah," *Computerworld*, January 31, 2005, p. 28; "Million-Atom Biology Simulation Could Improve Drug Development," *Computerworld*, November 14, 2005, p. 39; P. Arena, S. Rhody, and M. Stavrianos, "The Truth About Facts," *DM Review*, January 2006, pp. 30–34; and D. Briody, "The Flight of the Pringle," *CIO Insight*, August 2005, p. 22.

Section 4.11 Review Questions

1. List the characteristics of simulation. P.172
2. List the advantages and disadvantages of simulation. P.172 -173
3. List and describe the steps in the methodology of simulation. P.173
4. List and describe the types of simulation. P.174

4.12 VISUAL INTERACTIVE SIMULATION

We next examine methods that show a decision maker a representation of the decision-making situation in action as it runs through scenarios of the various alternatives. These powerful methods overcome some of the inadequacies of conventional methods and help build trust in the solution attained because they can be visualized directly.

Conventional Simulation Inadequacies

Simulation is a well-established, useful, descriptive, mathematics-based method for gaining insight into complex decision-making situations. However, simulation does not usually allow decision makers to see how a solution to a complex problem evolves over (compressed) time, nor can decision makers interact with the simulation (which would be useful for training purposes and teaching). Simulation generally reports statistical results at the end of a set of experiments. Decision makers are thus not an integral part of simulation development and experimentation, and their experience and judgment cannot be used directly. If the simulation results do not match the intuition or judgment of the decision maker, a *confidence gap* in the results can occur.

Visual Interactive Simulation

Visual interactive simulation (VIS), also known as **visual interactive modeling (VIM)** and *visual interactive problem solving*, is a simulation method that lets decision makers see what the model is doing and how it interacts with the decisions made, as they are made. The technique has been used with great success in operations management DSS. The user can employ his or her knowledge to determine and try different decision strategies while interacting with the model. Enhanced learning, about both the problem and the impact of the alternatives tested, can and does occur. Decision makers also contribute to model validation. Decision makers who use VIS generally support and trust their results.

VIS uses animated computer graphic displays to present the impact of different managerial decisions. It differs from regular graphics in that the user can adjust the decision-making process and see the results of the intervention. A visual model is a graphic used as an integral part of decision making or problem solving, not just as a communication device. VIS displays the effects of different decisions in graphic form on a computer screen, as was done through the GIS in the P&G supply chain redesign through optimization. Some people respond better than others to graphical displays, and this type of interaction can help managers learn about the decision-making situation. For example, Swisher et al. (2001) applied an object-oriented visual simulation to examining the functioning of a physician clinic environment within a physician network to provide high-quality, cost-effective health care in a family practice. The simulation system identified the most important input factors that significantly affected performance. These inputs, when properly managed, led to lower costs and higher service levels. Many Java-based VIS demonstrations run directly on the Internet.

VIS can represent static or dynamic systems. Static models display a visual image of the result of one decision alternative at a time. Dynamic models display systems that evolve over time, and the evolution is represented by animation. The latest visual simulation technology has been coupled with the concept of virtual reality, where an artificial world is created for a number of purposes, from training to entertainment to viewing data in an artificial landscape. For example, the U.S. military uses VIS systems so that ground troops can gain familiarity with terrain or a city in order to very quickly orient themselves. Pilots also use VIS to gain familiarity with targets by simulating attack runs. The VIS software can also include GIS coordinates.

Visual Interactive Models and DSS

VIM in DSS has been used in several operations management decisions. The method consists of priming (like priming a water pump) a visual interactive model of a plant (or company) with its current status. The model then runs rapidly on a computer, allowing managers to observe how a plant is likely to operate in the future.

Waiting-line management (queuing) is a good example of VIM. Such a DSS usually computes several measures of performance for the various decision alternatives (e.g., waiting time in the system). Complex waiting-line problems require simulation. VIM can display the size of the waiting line as it changes during the simulation runs and can also graphically present the answers to what-if questions regarding changes in input variables.

The VIM approach can also be used in conjunction with artificial intelligence. Integration of the two techniques adds several capabilities that range from the ability to build systems graphically to learning about the dynamics of the system. High-speed parallel computers such as those made by Silicon Graphics, Inc., and HP make large-scale, complex, animated simulations feasible in real time. (For example, the movie *Toy Story* and its sequel were essentially long VIM applications.) These systems, especially those developed for the military and the videogame industry, have "thinking" characters who can behave with a relatively high level of intelligence in their interactions with users.

General-purpose commercial dynamic VIS software is readily available. For several excellent videos of real VIS applications, examine the results of the Orca Visual Simulation Environment (VSE; Orca Computer Inc., **orcacomputer.com**). The Orca VSE allows for easy implementation and testing of these systems. Other VIS software programs are GPSS/PC (Minuteman Software, **minutemansoftware.com**) and VisSim

(Visual Solutions, Inc., **vissim.com**). For information about simulation software, see the Society for Modeling and Simulation International (**scs.org**) and the annual software surveys at *OR/MS Today* (**orms-today.com**).

Section 4.12 Review Questions

1. Define *visual simulation* and compare it to conventional simulation.
2. Describe the features of VIS (i.e., VIM) that make it attractive for decision makers.
3. How can VIS be used in operations management?
4. How is an animated film like a VIS application?

4.13 QUANTITATIVE SOFTWARE PACKAGES AND MODEL BASE MANAGEMENT

Quantitative software packages are preprogrammed (sometimes called ready-made) models and optimization systems that sometimes serve as building blocks for other quantitative models. A variety of these is readily available for inclusion in DSS as major and minor modeling components; in addition, some complete packages can be considered ready-made DSS. The latter tend to be developed and sold for a very specific application, whereas the former may be used as vehicles with which to develop models. We discuss these briefly next.

The Excel spreadsheet system has hundreds of models, ranging from functions to add-in packages (e.g., Solver). For data that can be dropped into a spreadsheet, Excel has many of the capabilities needed to produce usable results for many decision-making situations.

OLAP systems are essentially collections of optimization, simulation, statistical, and artificial intelligence packages that access large amounts of data for analysis. Some OLAP packages, such as those from SAS and SPSS, were initially developed for analysis, and data management capabilities were added, whereas others, such as the Oracle Financials Suite, evolved from DBMS to which modeling capabilities were added. Data mining software, such as that from MicroStrategy (**microstrategy.com**; also available from **teradatauniversitynetwork.com**) and Megaputer PolyAnalyst (**megaputer.com**), contain models and solution methods that can be activated either automatically or directly by the user. We will of course be learning about many data mining techniques and software starting with the next chapter.

Traditional statistical packages and management science packages are also available for model construction and solution. For a comprehensive resource directory of these types of systems, see *OR/MS Today* (**orms-today.com**). Revenue management systems (RMS) focus on identifying the right product for the right customer at the right price in the right channel. Similar in idea to CRM, RMS focus mainly on competing based on price and time. Airlines have used such systems (sometimes called *yield management systems*) to determine the right price for each airline seat on each flight. These systems are also available for retail operations, entertainment venues, and many other industries. RMS typically involve determining customer behavior and using sophisticated economics and optimization models to set prices and the quantities of products or services available for that price at every given time.

Model Base Management

Now that you are aware of the different model classes and solution methods, you need to realize that it is important, especially in large-scale DSS for use at the enterprise level, to manage the models and their solutions. This is the job of a **model base management system (MBMS)**, a software package that theoretically has capabilities similar to those of a DBMS—to manage, manipulate, and run the models embedded in the DSS. There are also **relational model base management systems (RMBMS)** and **object-oriented model base management systems (OOMBMS)** that provide the capabilities of the MBMS, paralleling the concepts of RDBMS and OODBMS, respectively.

Model management is an extremely difficult task because unlike databases—of which there may be three very common databases plus two more deployed in practice—there are hundreds of model classes and many different solution algorithms that can be used within each class. Plus, models are used in a variety of different ways in different organizations. Consequently, MBMS are generally unique for each type of problem being solved. We cannot manage statistical models in the same way as simulation models or optimization models.

Section 4.13 Review Questions

1. Explain how a spreadsheet system such as Excel can be used in DSS modeling.
2. Explain why OLAP is a kind of modeling system.
3. Identify three classes of models and list two kinds of problems each can solve.
4. List the reasons model management is difficult.

4.14 RESOURCES, LINKS, AND THE TERADATA UNIVERSITY NETWORK CONNECTION

The use of this chapter and most other chapters in this book can be enhanced by the tools described in the following sections.

Resources and Links

We recommend looking at the following resources and links for further reading and explanations:

- The INFORMS Web site (**informs.org**) includes Michael Trick's optimization pages. Be sure to look at the Resources link at **informs.org**. A wealth of modeling and solution information is available from INFORMS, including its journals.
- *OR/MS Today* (**orms-today.com**) has many important modeling and analysis software system reviews. They are updated regularly and are available online. It also publishes excellent, model-based DSS applications regularly.
- COIN-OR (**coin-or.org**) is open source software for operations research (and management science) professionals.
- The Mathematics and Computer Science Division at Argonne National Laboratory in Argonne, Illinois, maintains the NEOS Server for Optimization at **neos.mcs .anl. gov/neos/index.html**. The NEOS Guide offers the Java-based Simplex Tool, which demonstrates the workings of the simplex method on small user-entered problems and is especially useful for educational purposes.
- See H. Arsham's Modeling & Simulation Resources page at **home.ubalt.edu/ntsbarsh/ Business-stat/RefSim.htm** and the Decision Science Resources page at **home .ubalt. edu/ntsbarsh/Business-stat/Refop.htm** for a wealth of information.
- See the Decision Analysis Society (**decision-analysis.society.informs.org/**) for resources on decision analysis.
- See the Decision Resources Pages at **dssresources.com**.

Cases

Major optimization and simulation vendors provide success stories on their Web sites. See Lindo Systems, Inc. (**lindo.com**), as an example. Academic-oriented cases and sample problems are available from links from the Linear Programming FAQs at **faqs.org/faqs/ linear-programming-faq**, the Business Performance Improvement Resource (**bpir.com**),

Information Global (formerly Idea Group Publishing; **igi-pub.com/Index.asp**), Ivy League Publishing (**ivylp.com**), and other sites. For additional case resources, see Teradata University Network (**teradatauniversitynetwork.com**).

Miller's MIS CASES

All the cases in Miller's *MIS Cases* (2005) involve decision making in some way. The spreadsheet cases are all essentially model-driven DSS, and the database cases are all data-driven DSS.

Vendors, Products, and Demos

The best source for information about modeling and solution method packages and systems is the "OR/MS Today Software Surveys" published in *OR/MS Today*. These include software for LP, statistical analysis, forecasting, decision analysis, vehicle routing, supply chain management (SCM), spreadsheet add-ins, and nonlinear programming. Complete surveys, including full vendor contact information, are freely accessible from **orms-today.com**. Other information can be readily reached from the INFORMS Resources page at **informs.org**, as well as from the many excellent INFORMS publications, such as *Management Science*, *Interfaces*, and *Operations Research*. Extensive examples and success stories are readily available at vendor Web sites.

Periodicals

We recommend the following periodicals:

- *Decision Sciences* (**decisionsciences.org**)
- *Decision Support Systems* (**elsevier.com**)
- *Interfaces* (**informs.org**)
- *Management Science* (**informs.org**)
- *Operations Research* (**informs.org**)
- *OR/MS Today* (**orms-today.com**)

The Teradata University Network Connection

At the Teradata University Network Web site (**teradatauniversitynetwork.com**), we recommend a specific case, report, and software, along with their accompanying questions. These include the Continental Airlines case; the report by Wayne Erickson, "The Rise of Analytic Applications: Build or Buy?"; and the MicroStrategy software with the three questions in "AdVent Technology: Using the MicroStrategy Sales Analytic Model Assignment."

Chapter Highlights

- Models play a major role in DSS because they are used to describe real decision-making situations. There are several types of models.
- Models can be static (i.e., a single snapshot of a situation) or dynamic (i.e., multiperiod).
- Analysis is conducted under assumed certainty (which is most desirable), risk, or uncertainty (which is least desirable).

- Influence diagrams graphically show the interrelationships of a model. They can be used to enhance the use of spreadsheet technology.
- Influence diagram software can be used to generate and solve a model.
- Spreadsheets have many capabilities, including what-if analysis, goal seeking, programming, database management, optimization, and simulation.

- Decision tables and decision trees can model and solve simple decision-making problems.
- Mathematical programming is an important optimization method.
- LP is the most common mathematical programming method. It attempts to find an optimal allocation of limited resources under organizational constraints.
- The major parts of an LP model are the objective function, the decision variables, and the constraints.
- Multicriteria decision-making problems are difficult but not impossible to solve.
- The AHM (e.g., Expert Choice software) is a leading method for solving multicriteria decision-making problems.
- What-if and goal seeking are the two most common methods of sensitivity analysis.
- Heuristic programming involves problem solving using general rules or intelligent search.
- Simulation is a widely used DSS approach that involves experimentation with a model that represents the real decision-making situation.

- Simulation can deal with more complex situations than optimization, but it does not guarantee an optimal solution.
- VIS/VIM allows a decision maker to interact directly with a model and shows results in an easily understood manner.
- Many DSS development tools include built-in quantitative models (e.g., financial, statistical) or can easily interface with such models.
- MBMS perform tasks analogous to those performed by DBMS.
- Unlike DBMS, there are no standard MBMS because of the many model classes, their use, and the varied techniques for solving them.
- Artificial intelligence techniques can be effectively used in MBMS.
- The Web has had a profound impact on models and model management systems, and vice versa.
- Web application servers provide model management capabilities to DSS.

Key Terms

analytic hierarchy process (AHP) *165*
certainty *148*
complexity *172*
decision analysis *161*
decision table *162*
decision tree *163*
decision variable *146*
dynamic models *143*
environmental scanning and analysis *141*
forecasting *142*
goal seeking *159*
heuristic programming *170*

heuristics *170*
influence diagram *145*
intermediate result variable *147*
linear programming (LP) *152*
mathematical (quantitative) model *140*
mathematical programming *153*
model base management system (MBMS) *179*
multidimensional analysis (modeling) *145*

multiple goals *164*
object-oriented model base management system (OOMBMS) *180*
optimal solution *153*
parameter *146*
quantitative software package *179*
relational model base management system (RMBMS) *180*
result (outcome) variable *146*
risk *148*

risk analysis *149*
sensitivity analysis *158*
simulation *171*
static models *143*
uncertainty *148*
uncontrollable variable *146*
visual interactive modeling (VIM) *177*
visual interactive simulation (VIS) *177*
what-if analysis *159*

Questions for Discussion

1. What is the relationship between environmental analysis and problem identification?
2. Explain the differences between static and dynamic models. How can one evolve into the other?
3. What is the difference between an optimistic approach and a pessimistic approach to decision making under assumed uncertainty?
4. Explain why solving problems under uncertainty sometimes involves assuming that the problem is to be solved under conditions of risk.

5. Excel is probably the most popular spreadsheet software for PCs. Why? What can we do with this package that makes it so attractive for modeling efforts?
6. Explain how OLAP provides access to powerful models in a spreadsheet structure.
7. Explain how decision trees work. How can a complex problem be solved by using a decision tree?
8. Explain how LP can solve allocation problems.
9. What are the advantages of using a spreadsheet package to create and solve LP models? What are the disadvantages?

10. What are the advantages of using an LP package to create and solve LP models? What are the disadvantages?

11. What is the difference between decision analysis with a single goal and decision analysis with multiple goals (i.e., criteria)? Explain in detail the difficulties that may arise when analyzing multiple goals.

12. Explain how multiple goals can arise in practice.

13. Compare and contrast what-if analysis and goal seeking.

14. Describe the general process of simulation.

15. List some of the major advantages of simulation over optimization and vice versa.

16. What are the advantages of using a spreadsheet package to perform simulation studies? What are the disadvantages?

17. Compare the methodology of simulation to Simon's four-phase model of decision making. Does the methodology of simulation map directly into Simon's model? Explain.

18. Many computer games can be considered visual simulation. Explain why.

19. Explain why VIS is particularly helpful in implementing recommendations derived by computers.

20. There are hundreds of DBMS packages on the market. Explain why there are no packages for MBMS.

21. Does Simon's four-phase decision-making model fit into most of the modeling methodologies described? Explain.

Exercises

TERADATA STUDENT NETWORK (TSN) AND OTHER HANDS-ON EXERCISES

1. Explore **teradatastudentnetwork.com** and determine how models are used in the BI cases and papers. Specifically, solve the three problems listed earlier, in the section "The Teradata University Network Connection."

2. Each group in the class should access a different online Java-based Web simulation system (especially those systems from visual interactive simulation vendors) and run it. Write up your experience and present it to the class.

3. Each group in the class should access a different online Java-based optimization system and run it. Write up your experience and present it to the class.

4. Go to **orms-today.com** and access the article "The 'Sound' Science of Scheduling" by L. Gordon and E. Erkut from *OR/MS Today*, Vol. 32, No. 2, April 2005. Describe the overall problem, the DSS developed to solve it, and the benefits.

5. Investigate via a Web search how models and their solutions are used by the U.S. Department of Homeland Security in the "war against terrorism." Also investigate how other governments or government agencies are using models in their missions.

6. Read M. S. Sodhi, "Breast Cancer and O.R.," *OR/MS Today*, Vol. 32, No. 6, 2005, p. 14. Consider the problem of accurately diagnosing diseases such as breast cancer and how modeling and simulation can help improve accuracy. Investigate this topic and write a detailed report. Include in your report real-world modeling and simulation efforts.

7. Read S. Boehle, "Simulations: The Next Generation of E-Learning," *Training*, Vol. 42, No. 1, January 2005, pp. 22–31. Investigate and write a report about the types of systems that have been deployed for the development of e-learning simulations and what kinds of e-learning systems have been developed in them. Try one out and include your experience in your report.

TEAM ASSIGNMENTS AND ROLE-PLAYING

1. People do not like to wait in line. Many models have been developed and solved for waiting-line models to assist organizations such as banks, theme parks, airports (for security, ticket counters, and gate counters), fast-food outlets, movie theaters, and post offices. These models are known as *queuing models*. Look into organizations that have applied these models and their associated solution methodologies in practice and investigate what kinds of goals and specific decision variables these models incorporate. Visit some organizations where queuing occurs and observe the behavior of the customers and servers. If possible, run a demo of some software and/or create and solve a queuing model. Also investigate behavioral issues about these problems. These behavioral issues often lead to information about how people waiting in line interpret their experience and are more important than the actual waiting time. (You may also find information about how theme parks handle this as a revenue management problem.) Write up your results in a report. (This exercise was inspired by B. Hendrick, "Bottom Line: Folks Hate to Wait," *The Atlanta Journal-Constitution*, February 13, 2006, pp. A1, A6.)

2. Create the spreadsheet models shown in Figures 4.3 and 4.4.

   a. What is the effect of a change in the interest rate from 8 percent to 10 percent in the spreadsheet model shown in Figure 4.3?

   b. For the original model in Figure 4.3, what interest rate is required to decrease the monthly payments by 20 percent? What change in the loan amount would have the same effect?

   c. In the spreadsheet shown in Figure 4.4, what is the effect of a prepayment of $200 per month? What prepayment would be necessary to pay off the loan in 25 years instead of 30 years?

3. As a class, build a predictive model. Everyone in the class should write his or her weight, height, and gender on a piece of paper (no names please!). If the sample is too small (you need about 20–30 students), add more students from another class.

a. Create a regression (causal) model for height versus weight for the whole class and one for each gender. If possible, use a statistical package (e.g., SPSS) and a spreadsheet (e.g., Excel) and compare their ease of use. Produce a scatter plot of the three sets of data.

b. Based on your plots and regressions, do the relationships appear to be linear? How accurate were the models (e.g., how close to 1 is the value of R^2)?

c. Does weight cause height, does height cause weight, or does neither really cause the other? Explain.

d. How can a regression model like this be used in building or aircraft design? Diet? Food selection? A longitudinal study (e.g., over 50 years) to determine whether students are getting heavier and not taller or vice versa?

4. It has been argued in a number of venues that a higher education level indicates a greater average income. The question for a college student might therefore be "Should I stay in school?"

a. Using publicly available U.S. Census data for the 50 states and Washington, DC, develop a linear regression model (causal forecasting) to see whether this relationship is true. (Note that some data massaging may be necessary.) How high was the R^2 value (a measure of quality of fit)? Create a scatter plot of the data.

b. Does the relationship appear to be linear? If not, check a statistics book and try a nonlinear function. How well does the nonlinear function perform?

c. Which five states have the highest average incomes, and which five states have the highest average education levels? From this study, do you believe that a higher average education level tends to cause a higher average income? Explain.

d. If you have studied (or will study) neural networks, using the same data, build a neural network prediction model and compare it to your statistical results.

5. Set up spreadsheet models for the decision table models from Section 4.6 and solve them.

6. Solve the MBI product-mix problem described in this chapter, using either Excel's Solver or a student version of an LP solver, such as Lindo or Win QSB. Lindo is available from Lindo Systems, Inc., at **lindo.com**; others are also available—search the Web. Examine the solution (output) reports for the answers and sensitivity report. Did you get the same results as reported in this chapter? Try the sensitivity analysis outlined in the chapter; that is, lower the right-hand side of the CC-8 marketing constraint by 1 unit, from 200 to 199. What happens to the solution when you solve this modified problem? Eliminate the CC-8 lower-bound constraint entirely (this can be done easily by either deleting it in Solver or setting the lower limit to zero) and re-solve the problem.

What happens? Using the original formulation, try modifying the objective function coefficients and see what happens.

7. *Software demonstration.* Each group should review, examine, and demonstrate in class a different state-of-the-art DSS software product. The specific packages depend on your instructor and the group interests. You may need to download a demo from a vendor's Web site, depending on your instructor's directions. Be sure to get a running demo version, not a slide show. Do a half-hour in-class presentation, which should include an explanation of *why the software is appropriate* for assisting in decision making, a *hands-on demonstration* of selected important capabilities of the software, and your *critical evaluation* of the software. Try to make your presentation interesting and instructive to the whole class. The main purpose of the class presentation is for class members to see as much state-of-the-art software as possible, both in breadth (through the presentations by other groups) and in depth (through the experience you have in exploring the ins and outs of one particular software product). Write a 5- to 10-page report on your findings and comments regarding this software. Include screenshots in your report. Would you recommend this software to anyone? Why or why not?

8. *Expert Choice software familiarity.* Have a group meeting and discuss how you chose a place to live when you relocated to start your college program (or relocated to where you are now). What factors were important for each individual then, and how long ago was it? Have the criteria changed? As a group, identify the five to seven most important criteria used in making the decision. Using the current group members' living arrangements as choices, develop an Expert Choice model that describes this decision-making problem. Do not put your judgments in yet. You should each solve the Expert Choice model independently. Be careful to keep the inconsistency ratio less than 0.1. How many of the group members selected their current home using the software? For those who did, was it a close decision, or was there a clear winner? If some group members did not choose their current homes, what criteria made the result different? (In this decision-making exercise, you should not consider spouses or parents, even those who cook really well, as part of the home.) Did the availability of better choices that meet their needs become known? How consistent were your judgments? Do you think you would really prefer to live in the winning location? Why or why not? Finally, average the results for all group members (by adding the synthesized weights for each choice and dividing by the number of group members). This is one way Expert Choice works. Is there a clear winner? Whose home is it, and why did it win? Were there any close second choices? Turn in your results in a summary report (up to two typed pages), with copies of the individual Expert Choice runs.

INTERNET EXERCISES

1. Search the Internet for literature and information about DSS and its relationship to BI, BA, and predictive analytics. Describe what you find.
2. Use TreeAge Pro decision tree software and then describe how it works and what kinds of problems can be solved with it.
3. Explore decision analysis software vendor Web sites. Identify the purpose of the package(s) that the vendor offers and the organizations that have had successes with them.
4. Go to **baselinemag.com** and access the online articles by M. Duvall, "Billy Beane: What MBAs Can Learn from MLB," May 20, 2004; D. F. Carr, "Gotcha! Weigh Your Human-Resources Software Options with Care," May 14, 2004; and M. Duvall, "Roadblock: Getting Old-Line Managers to Think in New Ways," May 14, 2004. Describe the concepts of how models can be applied in industry in the same manner that the Boston Red Sox and Oakland Athletics used them.

END OF CHAPTER APPLICATION CASE

HP Applies Management Science Modeling to Optimize Its Supply Chain and Wins a Major Award

HP's ground-breaking use of operations research not only enabled the high-tech giant to successfully transform its product portfolio program and return $500 million over a 3-year period to the bottom line, it also earned HP the coveted 2009 Edelman Award from INFORMS for outstanding achievement in operations research. "This is not the success of just one person or one team," said Kathy Chou, Vice President of Worldwide Commercial Sales at HP, in accepting the award on behalf of the winning team. "It's the success of many people across HP who made this a reality, beginning several years ago with mathematics and imagination and what it might do for HP."

To put HP's product portfolio problem into perspective, consider these numbers: HP generates more than $135 billion annually from customers in 170 countries by offering tens of thousands of products supported by the largest supply chain in the industry. You want variety? How about 2,000 laser printers and more than 20,000 enterprise servers and storage products. Want more? HP offers more than 8 million configure-to-order combinations in its notebook and desktop product line alone.

The something-for-everyone approach drives sales, but at what cost? At what point does the price of designing, manufacturing, and introducing yet another new product, feature, or option exceed the additional revenue it is likely to generate? Just as important, what are the costs associated with too much or too little inventory for such a product, not to mention additional supply chain complexity, and how does all of that impact customer satisfaction? According to Chou, HP didn't have good answers to any of those questions before the Edelman award–winning work.

"While revenue grew year over year, our profits were eroded due to unplanned operational costs,"

Chou said in HP's formal Edelman presentation. "As product variety grew, our forecasting accuracy suffered, and we ended up with excesses of some products and shortages of others. Our suppliers suffered due to our inventory issues and product design changes. I can personally testify to the pain our customers experienced because of these availability challenges." Chou would know. In her role as VP of Worldwide Commercial Sales, she's "responsible and on the hook" for driving sales, margins, and operational efficiency.

Constantly growing product variety to meet increasing customer needs was the HP way—after all, the company is nothing if not innovative—but the rising costs and inefficiency associated with managing millions of products and configurations "took their toll," Chou said, "and we had no idea how to solve it."

Compounding the problem, Chou added, was HP's "organizational divide." Marketing and sales always wanted more—more SKUs, more features, more configurations—and for good reason. Providing every possible product choice was considered an obvious way to satisfy more customers and generate more sales.

Supply chain managers, however, always wanted less. Less to forecast, less inventory, and less complexity to manage. "The drivers (on the supply chain side) were cost control," Chou said. "Supply chain wanted fast and predictable order cycle times. With no fact-based, data-driven tools, decision-making between different parts of the organization was time-consuming and complex due to these differing goals and objectives."

By 2004, HP's average order cycle times in North America were nearly twice that of its competition, making it tough for the company to be competitive despite its large variety of products. Extensive variety, once considered a plus, had become a liability.

It was then that the Edelman prize–winning team—drawn from various quarters both within the organization (HP Business Groups, HP Labs, and HP Strategic Planning and Modeling) and out (individuals from a handful of consultancies and universities) and armed with operations research thinking and methodology—went to work on the problem. Over the next few years, the team: (1) produced an analytically driven process for evaluating new products for introduction, (2) created a tool for prioritizing existing products in a portfolio, and (3) developed an algorithm that solves the problem many times faster than previous technologies, thereby advancing the theory and practice of network optimization.

The team tackled the product variety problem from two angles: prelaunch and postlaunch. "Before we bring a new product, feature or option to market, we want to evaluate return on investment in order to drive the right investment decisions and maximize profits," Chou said. To do that, HP's Strategic Planning and Modeling Team (SPaM) developed "complexity return on investment screening calculators" that took into account downstream impacts across the HP product line and supply chain that were never properly accounted for before.

Once a product is launched, variety product management shifts from screening to managing a product portfolio as sales data become available. To do that, the Edelman award–winning team developed a tool called revenue coverage optimization (RCO) to analyze more systematically the importance of each new feature or option in the context of the overall portfolio.

The RCO algorithm and the complexity ROI calculators helped HP improve its operational focus on key products, while simultaneously reducing the complexity of its product offerings for customers. For example, HP implemented the RCO algorithm to rank its Personal Systems Group offerings based on the interrelationship between products and orders. It then identified the "core offering," which is composed of the most critical products in each region. This core offering represented about 30 percent of the ranked product portfolio. All other products were classified as HP's "extended offering."

Based on these findings, HP adjusted its service level for each class of products. Core offering products are now stocked in higher inventory levels and are made available with shorter lead times, and extended offering products are offered with longer lead times and are either stocked at lower levels or

not at all. The net result: lower costs, higher margins, and improved customer service.

The RCO software algorithm was developed as part of HP Labs' "analytics" theme, which applies mathematics and scientific methodologies to help decision making and create better-run businesses. Analytics is one of eight major research themes of HP Labs, which last year refocused its efforts to address the most complex challenges facing technology customers in the next decade.

"Smart application of analytics is becoming increasingly important to businesses, especially in the areas of operational efficiency, risk management and resource planning," says Jaap Suermondt, director, Business Optimization Lab, HP Labs. "The RCO algorithm is a fantastic example of an innovation that helps drive efficiency with our businesses and our customers."

In accepting the Edelman Award, Chou emphasized not only the company-wide effort in developing elegant technical solutions to incredibly complex problems, but also the buy-in and cooperation of managers and C-level executives and the wisdom and insight of the award-winning team to engage and share their vision with those managers and executives. "For some of you who have not been a part of a very large organization like HP, this might sound strange, but it required tenacity and skill to bring about major changes in the processes of a company of HP's size," Chou said. "In many of our business [units], project managers took the tools and turned them into new processes and programs that fundamentally changed the way HP manages its product portfolios and bridged the organizational divide."

Questions for the Case

1. Describe the problem that a large company such as HP might face in offering many product lines and options.
2. Why is there a possible conflict between marketing and operations?
3. Summarize your understanding of the models and the algorithms.
4. Perform an online search to find more details of the algorithms.
5. Why would there be a need for such a system in an organization?
6. What benefits did HP derive from implementation of the models?

Source: Adapted with permission, P. Horner, "Less Is More for HP," *OR/MS Today,* Vol. 36, No. 3, June 2009, pp. 40–44.

References

Arena, P., S. Rhody, and M. Stavrianos. (2006, January). "The Truth About Facts." *DM Review*, pp. 30–34.

Arsham, H. (2006a). *Modeling and Simulation Resources.* **home.ubalt.edu/ntsbarsh/Business-stat/RefSim.htm** (accessed June 19, 2009).

Arsham, H. (2006b). *Decision Science Resources.* **home.ubalt.edu/ntsbarsh/Business-stat/Refop.htm** (accessed June 19, 2009).

Basnet, C., and L. Foulds. (2005, December). "Fleet Manager Milks Efficiency Out of Dairy Company." *OR/MS Today*, Vol. 32, No. 6, pp. 36–42.

Boehle, S. (2005, January). "The Next Generation of E-Learning." *Training*, pp. 23–31.

Briody, D. (2005, August). "The Flight of the Pringle." *CIO Insight*, p. 22.

Camm, J. D., T. E. Chorman, F. A. Dill, J. R. Evans, D. J. Sweeney, and G. W. Wegryn. (1997, January/February). "Blending OR/MS, Judgment, and GIS: Restructuring P&G's Supply Chain," *Interfaces*, Vol. 27, No. 1, pp. 128–142.

Catalán, J., R. Epstein, M. Guajardo, D. Yung, L. Henriquez, C. Martínez, and G. Weintraub. (2009, April). "No Such Thing as a Free Lunch?" *OR/MS Today*. **lionhrtpub.com/orms/orms-4-09/frlunch.html** (accessed June 2009).

Christiansen, M., K. Fagerholt, G. Hasle, A. Minsaas, and B. Nygreen. (2009, April). "Maritime Transport Optimization: An Ocean of Opportunities." *OR/MS Today*, Vol. 36, No. 2, pp. 26–31.

Clemen, R. T., and T. Reilly. (2000). *Making Hard Decisions with Decision Tools Suite.* Belmont, MA: Duxbury Press.

Dembo, R., A. Aziz, D. Rosen, and M. Zerbs. (2000). *Mark-to-Future: A Framework for Measuring Risk and Reward.* Toronto: Algorithmics Publications.

Dignan, L. (2004, August). "Waste Not." Case 130, *Baseline*.

Dronzek, R. (2001, November). "Improving Critical Care." *IIE Solutions*, Vol. 33, pp. 42–47.

Farasyn, I., K. Perkoz, and W. Van de Velde. (2008, July/August). "Spreadsheet Models for Inventory Target Setting at Procter and Gamble." *Interfaces*, Vol. 38, No. 4, pp. 241–250.

Gabriel, S. A., A. S. Kydes, and P. Whitman. (2001, January/February). "The National Energy Modeling System: A Large-Scale Energy-Economic Equilibrium Model." *Operations Research*, Vol. 49, No. 1, pp. 14–25.

Gallagher, S. (2002, November). "Grand Test Auto." *Baseline*, No. 12.

Gareiss, R. (2002, December 2). "Chief of the Year: Ralph Szygenda." *Information Week*.

Geldermann, J., V. Bertsch, M. Treitz, S. French, K. N. Papamichail, and R. P. Hämäläinen. (2009, February). "Multi-criteria Decision Support and Evaluation of Strategies for Nuclear Remediation Management." *Omega*, Vol. 37, No. 1, pp. 238–251.

Gillet, B., and L. Miller. (1974, March/April). "A Heuristic Algorithm for the Vehicle Dispatch Problem." *Operations Research*, Vol. 22, No. 2, pp. 340–349.

Goodwin, P., and G. Wright. (2000). *Decision Analysis for Management Judgment*, 2nd ed. New York: Wiley.

Gurgur, C. Z., and C. T. Morley. (2008, July/August). "Lockheed Martin Space Systems Company Optimizes Infrastructure Project-Portfolio Selection." *Interfaces*, Vol. 38, No. 4, pp. 251–262.

Havenstein, H. (2005, June 27). "App Simulation in Demand." *Computerworld*, pp. 1, 77.

Hendrick, B. (2006, February 13). "Bottom Line: Folks Hate to Wait." *Atlanta Journal-Constitution*, pp. A1, A6.

Hillier, F. S., and G. J. Lieberman. (2005). *Introduction to Operations Research*, 8th ed. New York: McGraw-Hill.

Hoffman, T. (2003, August 4). "Simulations Revitalize E-Learning." *Computerworld*, pp. 26–27.

Horner, P. (2000, June). "The SABRE Story." *OR/MS Today*, Vol. 27, No. 3, pp. 46–47.

Horner, P. (2009, June). "Less Is More for HP." *OR/MS Today*, Vol. 36, No. 3, pp. 40–44.

Hurley, W. J., and M. Balez. (2008, July/August). "A Spreadsheet Implementation of an Ammunition Requirements Planning Model for the Canadian Army." *Interfaces*, Vol. 38, No. 4, pp. 271–280.

Jovanovic, N. (2002, September). "Task Scheduling in Distributed Systems by Work Stealing and Mugging: A Simulation Study." *Journal of Computing and Information Technology*, Vol. 10, No. 3.

Kearns, G. S. (2004, January–March). "A Multi-Objective, Multi-Criteria Approach for Evaluating IT Investments: Results from Two Case Studies." *Information Resources Management Journal*, Vol. 17, No. 1, pp. 37–62.

Kelly, A. (2002). *Decision Making Using Game Theory: An Introduction for Managers.* Cambridge, UK: Cambridge University Press.

Koksalan, M., and S. Zionts (eds.). (2001). *Multiple Criteria Decision Making in the New Millennium.* Berlin: Springer-Verlag.

Kontoghiorghes, E. J., B. Rustem, and S. Siokos. (2002). *Computational Methods in Decision Making, Economics, and Finance.* Boston: Kluwer.

Lejeune, M. A., and N. Yakova. (2008, May/June). "Showcase Scheduling at Fred Astaire East Side Dance Studio." *Interfaces*, Vol. 38, No. 3, pp. 176–186.

Mattila, V., K. Virtanen, and T. Raivio. (2008, May/June). "Improving Maintenance Decision Making in the Finnish Air Force Through Simulation." *Interfaces*, Vol. 38, No. 3, pp. 187–201.

Metters, M., C. Queenan, M. Ferguson, L. Harrison, J. Higbie, S. Ward, B. Barfield, T. Farley, H. A. Kuyumcu, and A. Duggasani. (2008, May/June). "The 'Killer Application' of Revenue Management: Harrah's Cherokee Casino & Hotel." *Interfaces*, Vol. 38, No. 3, pp. 161–175.

Michel, R. (2005, June). "Decision Support Smoothes Semiconductor Test Division's Outsourced Model." *Manufacturing Business Technology*, p. 30.

Miller, M. L. (2005). *MIS Cases*, 3rd ed. Upper Saddle River, NJ: Prentice Hall.

"Million-Atom Biology Simulation Could Improve Drug Development." (2005, November 14). *Computerworld*, p. 39.

Mukherjee, A. (2001, August 9–11). "Advanced Decision Support Tools in Airline Scheduling, Planning and Operations." *Proceedings of the PRISM Symposium*, West Lafayette, IN.

Nielsen, K. (ed.). (2003). *Uncertainty in Economic Decision Making: Ambiguity Mental Models and Institutions.* Northampton, MA: Edward Elgar.

Ovchinnikov, A., and J. Milner. (2008, July/August). "Spreadsheet Model Helps to Assign Medical Residents at the University of Vermont's College of Medicine." *Interfaces,* Vol. 38, No. 4, pp. 311–323.

ProModel. (2006, March). *Fiat Case.* **promodel.com** (accessed June 2009).

ProModel. (2009). *Throughput, Cycle Time and Bottleneck Analysis with ProModel Simulation Solutions for Manufacturing.* **promodel.com** (accessed July 2009).

Saaty, T. L. (1995). *Decision Making for Leaders: The Analytic Hierarchy Process for Decisions in a Complex World.* Revised ed. Pittsburgh, PA: RWS Publishers.

Saaty, T. L. (1996). *Decision Making for Leaders,* Vol. II. Pittsburgh, PA: RWS Publishers.

Saaty, T. L. (1999). *The Brain: Unraveling the Mystery of How It Works (The Neural Network Process).* Pittsburgh, PA: RWS Publishers.

Saltzman, R. M., and V. Mehrotra. (2001, May/June). "A Call Center Uses Simulation to Drive Strategic Change." *Interfaces*, Vol. 31, No. 3, pp. 87–101.

Seila, A., V. Ceric, and P. Tadikamalla. (2003). *Applied Simulation Modeling.* Pacific Grove, CA: Duxbury Press.

Selic, B. (1999, October). "Turning Clockwise: Using UML in the Real-Time Domain." *Communications of the ACM*, Vol. 42, No. 10, pp. 46–54.

Smith, B. C., D. P. Gunther, B. V. Rao, and R. M. Ratliff. (2001, March/April). "E-Commerce and Operations Research in Airline Planning, Marketing, and Distribution." *Interfaces*, Vol. 31, No. 2, pp. 37–55.

Stackpole, B. (2005, May 15). "Virtually Flawless?" *CIO*.

Stojkovic, M., and F. Soumis. (2001, September). "An Optimization Model for the Simultaneous Operational Flight and Pilot Scheduling Problem." *Management Science*, Vol. 47, No. 9, pp. 1290–1305.

Swisher, J. R., S. H. Jacobson, J. B. Jun, and O. Balci. (2001). "Modeling and Analyzing a Physician Clinic Environment Using Discrete-Event (Visual) Simulation." *Computers & Operations Research.* Vol. 28, No. 2, pp. 105–125.

Taha, H. (2006). *Operations Research: An Introduction*, 8th ed. Upper Saddle River, NJ: Prentice Hall.

Teradata. (2003). *Burlington Northern Santa Fe.* **teradatalibrary.com/pdf/eb3082.pdf** (accessed June 19, 2009).

TreeAge Software, Inc. (2009). "Dr. Victor Grann Uses Decision Analysis to Weigh Treatment Options for Patients at High Risk of Developing Cancer." **treeage.com/resources/includes/Grann_cs.pdf** (accessed July 2009).

Verton, D. (2005, January 31). "Simulating Fallujah." *Computerworld*, p. 28.

Witzerman, J. P. (2001, August 9–11). "Using Robotic Simulation to Support General Motors Paint Shops." *Proceedings of the PRISM Symposium*, West Lafayette, IN.

P A R T

III

Business Intelligence

LEARNING OBJECTIVES FOR PART III

1 Learn the role of business analytics (BA) and data mining (DM) in Business Intelligence (BI)

2 Learn the process and methods for conducting data mining projects

3 Learn the role and capabilities of artificial neural networks (ANN) for data mining

4 Understand the contemporary variations to data mining, including text mining and Web mining

5 Gain familiarity with the process, methods and applications of text and Web mining

6 Learn about data warehousing and data marts

7 Gain familiarity with different trends in data visualization

8 Learn about business performance management (BPM) and its implementation methodologies

5

Data Mining for Business Intelligence

LEARNING OBJECTIVES

1 Define data mining as an enabling technology for business intelligence

2 Understand the objectives and benefits of business analytics and data mining

3 Recognize the wide range of applications of data mining

4 Learn the standardized data mining processes

5 Understand the steps involved in data preprocessing for data mining

6 Learn different methods and algorithms of data mining

7 Build awareness of the existing data mining software tools

8 Understand the pitfalls and myths of data mining

Generally speaking, data mining is a way to develop business intelligence from data that an organization collects, organizes, and stores. A wide range of data mining techniques are being used by organizations to gain a better understanding of their customers and their own operations and to solve complex organizational problems. In this chapter, we study data mining as an enabling technology for business intelligence, learn about the standard processes of conducting data mining projects, understand and build expertise in the use of major data mining techniques, develop awareness of the existing software tools, and explore common myths and pitfalls of data mining.

5.1 Opening Vignette: Data Mining Goes to Hollywood!
5.2 Data Mining Concepts and Applications
5.3 Data Mining Applications
5.4 Data Mining Process
5.5 Data Mining Methods
5.6 Data Mining Software Tools
5.7 Data Mining Myths and Blunders

5.1 OPENING VIGNETTE: DATA MINING GOES TO HOLLYWOOD!

Predicting box-office receipts (i.e., financial success) of a particular motion picture is an interesting and challenging problem. According to some domain experts, the movie industry is the "land of hunches and wild guesses" due to the difficulty associated with forecasting product demand, making the movie business in Hollywood a risky endeavor. In support of such observations, Jack Valenti (the longtime president and CEO of the Motion Picture Association of America) once mentioned that ". . . no one can tell you how a movie is going to do in the marketplace . . . not until the film opens in darkened theatre and sparks fly up between the screen and the audience." Entertainment industry trade journals and magazines have been full of examples, statements, and experiences that support such a claim.

Like many other researchers who have attempted to shed light on this challenging real-world problem, Ramesh Sharda and Dursun Delen have been exploring the use of data mining to predict the financial performance of a motion picture at the box office before it even enters production (while the movie is nothing more than a conceptual idea). In their highly publicized prediction models, they convert the forecasting (or regression) problem into a classification problem; that is, rather than forecasting the point estimate of box-office receipts, they classify a movie based on its box-office receipts in one of nine categories, ranging from "flop" to "blockbuster," making the problem a multinomial classification problem. Table 5.1 illustrates the definition of the nine classes in terms of the range of box-office receipts.

Data

Data was collected from variety of movie-related databases (e.g., ShowBiz, IMDb, IMSDb, AllMovie, etc.) and consolidated into a single dataset. The dataset for the most recently developed models contained 2,632 movies released between 1998 and 2006. A summary of the independent variables along with their specifications is provided in Table 5.2. For more descriptive details and justification for inclusion of these independent variables, the reader is referred to Sharda and Delen (2007).

TABLE 5.1 Movie Classification Based on Receipts

Class No.	1	2	3	4	5	6	7	8	9
Range (in millions of dollars)	<1 (Flop)	>1 <10	>10 <20	>20 <40	>40 <65	>65 <100	>100 <150	>150 <200	>200 (Blockbuster)

TABLE 5.2 Summary of Independent Variables

Independent Variable	Number of Values	Possible Values
MPAA Rating	5	G, PG, PG-13, R, NR
Competition	3	High, Medium, Low
Star value	3	High, Medium, Low
Genre	10	Sci-Fi, Historic Epic Drama, Modern Drama, Politically Related, Thriller, Horror, Comedy, Cartoon, Action, Documentary
Special effects	3	High, Medium, Low
Sequel	1	Yes, No
Number of screens	1	Positive integer

Methodology

Using a variety of data mining methods, including neural networks, decision trees, support vector machines, and three types of ensembles, Sharda and Delen developed the prediction models. The data from 1998 to 2005 were used as training data to build the prediction models, and the data from 2006 was used as the test data to assess and compare the models' prediction accuracy. Figure 5.1 shows a screenshot of SPSS's PASW Modeler (formerly Clementine data mining tool) depicting the process map employed for the prediction problem. The upper-left side of the process map shows the model development process, and the lower-right corner of the process map shows the model assessment (i.e., testing or scoring) process (more details on PASW Modeler tool and its usage can be found on the book's Web site).

Results

Table 5.3 provides the prediction results of all three data mining methods as well as the results of the three different ensembles. The first performance measure is the percent correct classification rate, which is called *bingo*. Also reported in the table is the *1-Away* correct classification rate (i.e., within one category). The results indicate that SVM performed the best among the individual prediction models, followed by ANN; the worst of the three was the CART decision tree algorithm. In general, the ensemble models performed better than the individual predictions models, of which the fusion algorithm performed the best. What is probably more important to decision makers, and standing out in the results table, is the significantly low standard deviation obtained from the ensembles compared to the individual models.

Conclusion

The researchers claim that these prediction results are better than any reported in the published literature for this problem domain. Beyond the attractive accuracy of their prediction results of the box-office receipts, these models could also be used to further analyze (and potentially

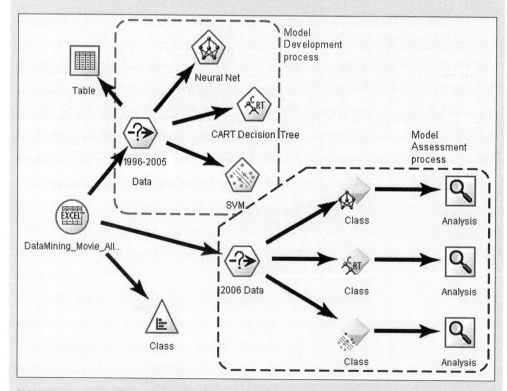

FIGURE 5.1 Process-Flow Screenshot for the Box-Office Prediction System *Source:* Used with permission from SPSS.

TABLE 5.3   Tabulated Prediction Results for Individual and Ensemble Models

Performance Measure	Prediction Models					
	Individual Models			Ensemble Models		
	SVM	ANN	C&RT	Random Forest	Boosted Tree	Fusion (Average)
Count (Bingo)	192	182	140	189	187	**194**
Count (1-Away)	104	120	126	121	104	**120**
Accuracy (% Bingo)	55.49%	52.60%	40.46%	54.62%	54.05%	**56.07%**
Accuracy (% 1-Away)	85.55%	87.28%	76.88%	89.60%	84.10%	**90.75%**
Standard deviation	0.93	0.87	1.05	0.76	0.84	**0.63**

optimize) the decision variables in order to maximize the financial return. Specifically, the parameters used for modeling could be altered using the already trained prediction models in order to better understand the impact of different parameters on the end results. During this process, which is commonly referred to as *sensitivity analysis*, the decision maker of a given entertainment firm could find out, with a fairly high accuracy level, how much value a specific actor (or a specific release date, or the addition of more technical effects, etc.) brings to the financial success of a film, making the underlying system an invaluable decision aid.

Questions for the Opening Vignette

1. Why should Hollywood decision makers use data mining?
2. What are the top challenges for Hollywood managers? Can you think of other industry segments that face similar problems?
3. Do you think the researchers used all of the relevant data to build prediction models?
4. Why do you think the researchers chose to convert a regression problem into a classification problem?
5. How do you think these prediction models can be used? Can you think of a good production system for such models?
6. Do you think the decision makers would easily adapt to such an information system?
7. What can be done to further improve the prediction models explained in this case?

What We Can Learn from This Vignette

The entertainment industry is full of interesting and challenging problems for decision makers. Making the right decisions to manage large amounts of money is critical to success (or mere survival) of many companies in this marketplace. Data mining is a prime candidate for better management of this data-rich, knowledge-poor business environment. The study described in the opening vignette clearly illustrates the power of data mining in predicting and explaining the financial outlook of a motion picture, which most still think is a form of art and hence cannot be forecasted. In this chapter, you will see a wide variety of data mining applications solving complex problems in a variety of industries where the data can be used to leverage competitive business advantage.

Sources: R. Sharda and D. Delen, "Predicting Box-Office Success of Motion Pictures with Neural Networks," *Expert Systems with Applications,* Vol. 30, 2006, pp. 243–254; D. Delen, R. Sharda, and P. Kumar, "Movie Forecast Guru: A Web-based DSS for Hollywood Managers," *Decision Support Systems,* Vol. 43, No. 4, 2007, pp. 1151–1170.

5.2 DATA MINING CONCEPTS AND APPLICATIONS

In an interview with *Computerworld* magazine in January 1999, Dr. Arno Penzias (Nobel laureate and former chief scientist of Bell Labs) identified data mining from organizational databases as a key application for corporations of the near future. In response to *Computerworld*'s age-old question of "What will be the killer applications in the corporation?" Dr. Penzias replied: "Data mining." He then added, "Data mining will become much more important and companies will throw away nothing about their customers because it will be so valuable. If you're not doing this, you're out of business." Similarly, in an article in *Harvard Business Review* Thomas Davenport (2006) argued that the latest strategic weapon for companies is analytical decision making, providing examples of companies such as Amazon.com, Capital One, Marriott International, and others that have used analytics to better understand their customers and optimize their extended supply chains to maximize their returns on investment while providing the best customer service. This level of success is highly dependent on a company understanding its customers, vendors, business processes, and the extended supply chain very well.

A large component of this understanding comes from analyzing the vast amount of data that a company collects. The cost of storing and processing data has decreased dramatically in the recent past, and, as a result, the amount of data stored in electronic form has grown at an explosive rate. With the creation of large databases, the possibility of analyzing the data stored in them has emerged. The term *data mining* was originally used to describe the process through which previously unknown patterns in data were discovered. This definition has since been stretched beyond those limits by some software vendors to include most forms of data analysis in order to increase sales with the popularity of the data mining label. In this chapter, we accept the original definition of data mining.

Although the term *data mining* is relatively new, the ideas behind it are not. Many of the techniques used in data mining have their roots in traditional statistical analysis and artificial intelligence work done since the early part of 1980s. Why, then, has it suddenly gained the attention of the business world? Following are some of most pronounced reasons:

- More intense competition at the global scale driven by customers' ever-changing needs and wants in an increasingly saturated marketplace.
- General recognition of the untapped value hidden in large data sources.
- Consolidation and integration of database records, which enables a single view of customers, vendors, transactions, etc.
- Consolidation of databases and other data repositories into a single location in the form of a data warehouse.
- The exponential increase in data processing and storage technologies.
- Significant reduction in the cost of hardware and software for data storage and processing.
- Movement toward the de-massification (conversion of information resources into nonphysical form) of business practices.

Data generated by the Internet is increasing rapidly in both volume and complexity. Large amounts of genomic data are being generated and accumulated all over the world. Disciplines such as astronomy and nuclear physics create huge quantities of data on a regular basis. Medical and pharmaceutical researchers constantly generate and store data that can then be used in data mining applications to identify better ways to accurately diagnose and treat illnesses and to discover new and improved drugs.

On the commercial side, perhaps the most common use of data mining has been in the finance, retail, and health care sectors. Data mining is used to detect and reduce fraudulent activities, especially in insurance claims and credit card use (Chan et al., 1999); to identify customer buying patterns (Hoffman, 1999); to reclaim profitable customers

(Hoffman, 1998); to identify trading rules from historical data; and to aid in increased profitability using market-basket analysis. Data mining is already widely used to better target clients, and with the widespread development of e-commerce, this can only become more imperative with time. See Application Case 5.1 for information on how 1-800-Flowers has used business analytics and data mining to excel in business.

APPLICATION CASE 5.1

Business Analytics and Data Mining Help 1-800-Flowers Excel in Business

1-800-Flowers is one of the best-known and most-successful brands in the gift-retailing business. For more than 30 years, the New York–based company has been providing customers around the world with the freshest flowers and finest selection of plants, gift baskets, gourmet foods, confections, and plush stuffed animals for every occasion. Founded by Jim McCann in 1976, 1-800-Flowers has quickly become the leader in direct-order e-commerce after opening its own Web site more than 14 years ago.

Problem

As successful as it has been, like many other companies involved in e-commerce, 1-800-Flowers needed to make decisions in real time to increase retention, reduce costs, and keep its best customers coming back for more again and again. As the business has grown from one flower shop to an online gift retailer serving more than 30 million customers, it has needed to stay ahead of the competition by being the best that it can be.

Solution

Strongly believing in the value of close customer relationships, 1-800-Flowers wanted to better understand its customers' needs and wants by analyzing every piece of data that it had about them. 1-800-Flowers decided to use SAS data mining tools to dig deep into its data assets to discover novel patterns about its customers and turn that knowledge into business transactions.

Results

According to McCann, business analytics and data mining tools from SAS have enabled 1-800-Flowers to grow its business regardless of the conditions of the larger economy. At a time when other retailers are struggling to survive, 1-800-Flowers has seen revenues grow, nearly doubling in the last 5 years.

Specific benefits of the analysis were as follows:

- ***More efficient marketing campaigns.*** 1-800-Flowers has drastically reduced the time it takes to segment customers for direct mailing. "It used to take 2 or 3 weeks—now it takes 2 or 3 days," says Aaron Cano, Vice President of Customer Knowledge Management. "That leaves us time to do more analysis and make sure we're sending relevant offers."
- ***Reduced mailings, increased response rates.*** The company has been able to significantly reduce marketing mailings while increasing response rates and be much more selective about TV and radio advertisements.
- ***Better customer experience.*** When a repeat customer logs on to 1-800-Flowers.com, the Web site immediately shows selections that are related to that customer's interests. "If a customer usually buys tulips for his wife, we show him our newest and best tulip selections," Cano says.
- ***Increased repeat sales.*** The company's best customers are returning more often because 1-800-Flowers knows who the customer is and what he or she likes. The company makes the shopping experience easy and relevant and markets to customers at the point of contact.

As a result of using business analytics and data mining, 1-800-Flowers reduced its operating expenses, increased the retention rate of its best customer segment to more than 80 percent, attracted 20 million new customers, and grew the overall repeat business from less than 40 percent to greater than 50 percent (a 10-basis-point increase in repeat sales across all brands translates into $40 million additional revenue for the business).

Sources: "SAS Helps 1-800-Flowers.com Grow Deep Roots with Customers," **sas.com/success/1800flowers.html** (accessed on May 23, 2009); "Data Mining at 1-800-Flowers," **kdnuggets.com /news/2009/n10/3i.html** (accessed on May 26, 2009).

Definitions, Characteristics, and Benefits

Simply defined, **data mining** is a term used to describe discovering or "mining" knowledge from large amounts of data. When considered by analogy, one can easily realize that the term *data mining* is a misnomer; that is, mining of gold from within rocks or dirt is referred to as "gold" mining rather than "rock" or "dirt" mining. Therefore, data mining perhaps should have been named "knowledge mining" or "knowledge discovery." Despite the mismatch between the term and its meaning, *data mining* has become the choice of the community. Many other names that are associated with data mining include *knowledge extraction, pattern analysis, data archaeology, information harvesting, pattern searching,* and *data dredging.*

Technically speaking, data mining is a process that uses statistical, mathematical, and artificial intelligence techniques to extract and identify useful information and subsequent knowledge (or patterns) from large sets of data. These patterns can be in the form of business rules, affinities, correlations, trends, or prediction models (see Nemati and Barko, 2001). Most literature defines data mining as "the nontrivial process of identifying valid, novel, potentially useful, and ultimately understandable patterns in data stored in structured databases," where the data are organized in records structured by categorical, ordinal, and continuous variables (Fayyad et al., 1996). In this definition, the meanings of the key term are as follows:

- *Process* implies that data mining comprises many iterative steps.
- *Nontrivial* means that some experimentation-type search or inference is involved; that is, it is not as straightforward as a computation of predefined quantities.
- *Valid* means that the discovered patterns should hold true on new data with sufficient degree of certainty.
- *Novel* means that the patterns are not previously known to the user within the context of the system being analyzed.
- *Potentially useful* means that the discovered patterns should lead to some benefit to the user or task.
- *Ultimately understandable* means that the pattern should make business sense that leads to user saying "mmm! It makes sense; why didn't I think of that" if not immediately, at least after some post processing.

Data mining is not a new discipline, but rather a new definition for the use of many disciplines. Data mining is tightly positioned at the intersection of many disciplines, including statistics, artificial intelligence, machine learning, management science, information systems, and databases (see Figure 5.2). Using advances in all of these disciplines, data mining strives to make progress in extracting useful information and knowledge from large databases. It is an emerging field that has attracted much attention in a very short time.

The following are the major characteristics and objectives of data mining:

- Data are often buried deep within very large databases, which sometimes contain data from several years. In many cases, the data are cleansed and consolidated into a data warehouse.
- The data mining environment is usually a client-server architecture or a Web-based information systems architecture.
- Sophisticated new tools, including advanced visualization tools, help to remove the information ore buried in corporate files or archival public records. Finding it involves massaging and synchronizing the data to get the right results. Cutting-edge data miners are also exploring the usefulness of soft data (i.e., unstructured text stored in such places as Lotus Notes databases, text files on the Internet, or enterprise-wide intranets).
- The miner is often an end user, empowered by data drills and other power query tools to ask ad hoc questions and obtain answers quickly, with little or no programming skill.
- Striking it rich often involves finding an unexpected result and requires end users to think creatively throughout the process, including the interpretation of the findings.

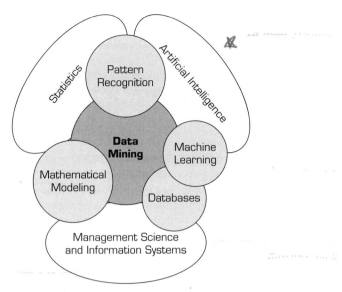

FIGURE 5.2 Data Mining as a Blend of Multiple Disciplines

- Data mining tools are readily combined with spreadsheets and other software development tools. Thus, the mined data can be analyzed and deployed quickly and easily.
- Because of the large amounts of data and massive search efforts, it is sometimes necessary to use parallel processing for data mining.

A company that effectively leverages data mining tools and technologies can acquire and maintain a strategic competitive advantage. Data mining offers organizations an indispensable decision-enhancing environment to exploit new opportunities by transforming data into a strategic weapon. See Nemati and Barko (2001) for a more detailed discussion on the strategic benefits of data mining.

TECHNOLOGY INSIGHTS 5.1   Data in Data Mining

Data refers to a collection of facts usually obtained as the result of experiences, observations, or experiments. Data may consist of numbers, words, images, and so on as measurements of a set of variables. Data are often viewed as the lowest level of abstraction from which information and knowledge are derived.

At the highest level of abstraction, one can classify data as categorical or numeric. The categorical data can be subdivided into nominal or ordinal data, whereas numeric data can be subdivided into interval or ratio. Figure 5.3 shows a simple taxonomy of data in data mining.

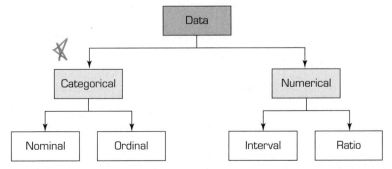

FIGURE 5.3 A Simple Taxonomy of Data in Data Mining

- **Categorical data** represent the labels of multiple classes used to divide a variable into specific groups. Examples of categorical variables include race, sex, age group, and educational level. Although the latter two variables may also be considered in a numerical manner by using exact values for age and highest grade completed, it is often more informative to categorize such variables into a relatively small number of ordered classes. The categorical data may also be called discrete data implying that it represents a finite number of values with no continuum between them. Even if the values used for the categorical (or discrete) variables are numeric, these numbers are nothing more than symbols and do not imply the possibility of calculating fractional values.
- **Nominal data** contain measurements of simple codes assigned to objects as labels, which are not measurements. For example, the variable *marital status* can be generally categorized as (1) single, (2) married, and (3) divorced. Nominal data can be represented with binomial values having two possible values (e.g., yes/no, true/false, good/bad), or multinomial values having three or more possible values (e.g., brown/green/blue, white/black/Latino/Asian, single/married/divorced).
- **Ordinal data** contain codes assigned to objects or events as labels that also represent the rank order among them. For example, the variable *credit score* can be generally categorized as (1) low, (2) medium, or (3) high. Similar ordered relationships can be seen in variables such as age group (i.e., child, young, middle-aged, elderly) and educational level (i.e., high school, college, graduate school). Some data mining algorithms, such as *ordinal multiple logistic regression,* take into account this additional rank order information to build a better classification model.
- **Numeric data** represent the numeric values of specific variables. Examples of numerically valued variables include age, number of children, total household income (in US dollars), travel distance (in miles), and temperature (in Fahrenheit degrees). Numeric values representing a variable can be integer (taking only whole numbers) or real (taking also the fractional number). The numeric data may also be called continuous data, implying that the variable contains continuous measures on a specific scale that allows insertion of interim values. Unlike a discrete variable, which represents finite, countable data, a continuous variable represents scalable measurements, and it is possible for the data to contain an infinite number of fractional values.
- **Interval data** are variables that can be measured on interval scales. A common example of interval scale measurement is temperature on the Celsius scale. In this particular scale, the unit of measurement is 1/100 of the difference between the melting temperature and the boiling temperature of water in atmospheric pressure; that is, there is not an absolute zero value.
- **Ratio data** include measurement variables commonly found in the physical sciences and engineering. Mass, length, time, plane angle, energy, and electric charge are examples of physical measures that are ratio scales. The scale type takes its name from the fact that measurement is the estimation of the ratio between a magnitude of a continuous quantity and a unit magnitude of the same kind. Informally, the distinguishing feature of a ratio scale is the possession of a nonarbitrary zero value. For example, the Kelvin temperature scale has a nonarbitrary zero point of absolute zero, which is equal to −273.15 degrees Celsius. This zero point is nonarbitrary, because the particles that comprise matter at this temperature have zero kinetic energy.
- Other data types include date/time, unstructured text, image, and audio. These data types need to be converted into some form of categorical or numeric representation before they can be processed by data mining algorithms. Data can also be classified as static or dynamic (i.e., temporal or time-series).

Some data mining methods are particular about the data types they can handle. Providing them with incompatible data types may lead to incorrect models or (more often) halt the model development process. For example, some data mining methods need all of the variables (both input as well as output) represented as numerically valued variables (e.g., neural networks, support vector machines, logistic regression). The nominal or ordinal variables are converted into numeric representations using some type of *1-of-N* pseudo variables (e.g., a categorical variable with three unique values can be transformed into three pseudo variables with binary values—1 or 0). Because this process may increase the number of variables, one should be cautious about the effect of such representations, especially for the categorical variables that have large numbers of unique values.

Similarly, some data mining methods, such as ID3 (a classic decision tree algorithm) and rough sets (a relatively new rule induction algorithm), need all of the variables represented as categorically valued variables. Early versions of these methods required the user to discretize numeric variables into categorical representations before they could be processed by the algorithm. The good news is that most implementations of these algorithms in widely available software tools accept a mix of numeric and nominal variables and internally make the necessary conversions before processing the data.

APPLICATION CASE 5.2

Law Enforcement Organizations Use Data Mining to Better Fight Crime

In the midst of these unfavorable economic conditions, police departments all over the world are facing difficult times in fighting crimes with continually shrinking resources along with fewer leads, a larger number of cases, and increasingly more complicated crimes. At a police department in the United Kingdom, investigators find that these challenges limit the cases they can tackle. A high volume of cases without definite leads—such as house burglaries and vehicle thefts that lack clear evidence—are often filed away until new evidence is found. Therefore, the challenge for the police department was to determine a way to quickly and easily find patterns and trends in unsolved criminal cases.

Each electronic case file at the police department contains physical descriptions of the thieves as well as their modus operandi (MO). Whereas many cases lacking evidence were previously filed away, the department is now re-examining them and doing it more quickly than ever before. In PASW Modeler (formerly Clementine), the data modeler uses two Kohonen neural network models to cluster similar physical descriptions and MOs and then combines clusters to see whether groups of similar physical descriptions coincide with groups of similar MOs. If a good match is found and the perpetrators are known for one or more of the offenses, it is possible that the unsolved cases were committed by the same individuals.

The analytical team further investigates the clusters, using statistical methods to verify the similarities' importance. If clusters indicate that the same criminal may be at work, the department is likely to reopen

and investigate the other crimes. Or, if the criminal is unknown but a large cluster indicates the same offender, the leads from these cases can be combined and the case reprioritized. The department is also investigating the behavior of prolific repeat offenders with the goal of identifying crimes that seem to fit their behavioral pattern. The department hopes that the PASW Modeler will enable it to reopen old cases and make connections with known perpetrators.

Another police department in the United States is facing similar challenges: lack of sufficient resources coupled with an increasing number of criminal cases. In order to produce sustainable solutions to a wide range of crime and community disorders, the department is pursuing a community-oriented policing philosophy, which is a holistic approach requiring collaborative partnerships between citizens and community agencies and careful analysis of information surrounding the criminal cases. The underlying process aims to find long-term solutions to crimes by identifying their root causes, educating the community on the extent of the problems, and then working with the community to develop collaborative solutions that effectively address these causes. The main challenge was to convince the community that their involvement is necessary for any solution to be effective.

Using PASW statistical analysis and a data mining software tool, the police department conducted extensive data analysis to discover the variables strongly associated with the criminal cases, as well as assess citizen satisfaction with community policing. The results of this analysis presented compelling evidence that community involvement coupled with intelligent data analysis are necessary ingredients in developing effective long-term solutions in the midst of economic difficulties.

Police departments around the globe are enhancing their crime-fighting techniques with innovative twenty-first-century approaches of applying data mining technology to prevent criminal activity. Success stories can be found on Web sites of major data mining tool and solution providers (e.g., SPSS, SAS, StatSoft, Salford Systems). as well as the major consultancy companies.

Sources: Based on C. McCue "Connecting the Dots: Data Mining and Predictive Analytics in Law Enforcement and Intelligence Analysis," *Police Chief Magazine,* Vol. 70, No. 10, October 2003; "Police Department Fights Crime with SPSS Inc. Technology," **spss.com/success/pdf/WMPCS-1208.pdf** (accessed July 25, 2009); "North Carolina Law Enforcement Agency Identifies Crime Areas and Secures Community Involvement," **spssshowcase.co.uk/success/pdf/CMPDCS-0109.pdf** (accessed on September 14, 2009).

How Data Mining Works

Using existing and relevant data, data mining builds models to identify patterns among the attributes presented in the dataset. Models are the mathematical representations (simple linear relationships and/or complex highly nonlinear relationships) that identify the patterns among the attributes of the objects (e.g., customers) described in the dataset. Some of these patterns are explanatory (explaining the interrelationships and affinities among the attributes), whereas others are predictive (foretelling future values of certain attributes). In general, data mining seeks to identify four major types of patterns:

1. *Associations* find the commonly co-occurring groupings of things, such as beer and diapers going together in market-basket analysis.
2. *Predictions* tell the nature of future occurrences of certain events based on what has happened in the past, such as predicting the winner of the Super Bowl or forecasting the absolute temperature of a particular day.
3. *Clusters* identify natural groupings of things based on their known characteristics, such as assigning customers in different segments based on their demographics and past purchase behaviors.
4. *Sequential relationships* discover time-ordered events, such as predicting that an existing banking customer who already has a checking account will open a savings account followed by an investment account within a year.

These types of patterns have been *manually* extracted from data by humans for centuries, but the increasing volume of data in modern times has created a need for more automatic approaches. As datasets have grown in size and complexity, direct manual data analysis has increasingly been augmented with indirect, automatic data processing tools that use sophisticated methodologies, methods, and algorithms. The manifestation of such evolution of automated and semiautomated means of processing large datasets is now commonly referred to as *data mining*.

Generally speaking, data mining tasks can be classified into three main categories: prediction, association, and clustering. Based on the way in which the patterns are extracted from the historical data, the learning algorithms of data mining methods can be classified as either supervised or unsupervised. With supervised learning algorithms, the training data includes both the descriptive attributes (i.e., independent variables or decision variables) as well as the class attribute (i.e., output variable or result variable). In contrast, with unsupervised learning the training data includes only the descriptive attributes. Figure 5.4 shows a simple taxonomy for data mining tasks, along with the learning methods, and popular algorithms for each of the data mining tasks.

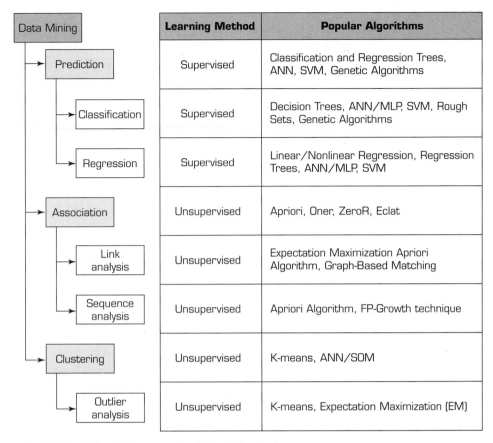

Learning Method	Popular Algorithms
Supervised	Classification and Regression Trees, ANN, SVM, Genetic Algorithms
Supervised	Decision Trees, ANN/MLP, SVM, Rough Sets, Genetic Algorithms
Supervised	Linear/Nonlinear Regression, Regression Trees, ANN/MLP, SVM
Unsupervised	Apriori, Oner, ZeroR, Eclat
Unsupervised	Expectation Maximization Apriori Algorithm, Graph-Based Matching
Unsupervised	Apriori Algorithm, FP-Growth technique
Unsupervised	K-means, ANN/SOM
Unsupervised	K-means, Expectation Maximization (EM)

FIGURE 5.4 A Simple Taxonomy for Data Mining Tasks

PREDICTION **Prediction** is commonly referred to as the act of telling about the future. It differs from simple guessing by taking into account the experiences, opinions, and other relevant information in conducting the task of foretelling. A term that is commonly associated with prediction is *forecasting*. Even though many believe that these two terms are synonymous, there is a subtle but critical difference between the two. Whereas prediction is largely experience and opinion based, forecasting is data and model based. That is, in order of increasing reliability, one might list the relevant terms as *guessing, predicting, and forecasting,* respectively. In data mining terminology, *prediction* and *forecasting* are used synonymously, and the term *prediction* is used as the common representation of the act. Depending on the nature of what is being predicted, prediction can be named more specifically as classification (where the predicted thing, such as tomorrow's forecast, is a class label such as "rainy" or "sunny") or regression (where the predicted thing, such as tomorrow's temperature, is a real number, such as "65°F").

CLASSIFICATION **Classification**, or supervised induction, is perhaps the most common of all data mining tasks. The objective of classification is to analyze the historical data stored in a database and automatically generate a model that can predict future behavior. This induced model consists of generalizations over the records of a training dataset, which help distinguish predefined classes. The hope is that the model can then be used to predict the classes of other unclassified records and, more important, to accurately predict actual future events.

Common classification tools include neural networks and decision trees (from machine learning), logistic regression and discriminant analysis (from traditional statistics), and emerging tools such as rough sets, support vector machines, and genetic algorithms. Statistics-based classification techniques (e.g., logistic regression and discriminant analysis) have received their share of criticism—that they make unrealistic assumptions about the data, such as independence and normality—which limit their use in classification-type data mining projects.

Neural networks (see Chapter 6 for a more detailed coverage of this popular machine learning algorithm) involve the development of mathematical structures (somewhat resembling the biological neural networks in the human brain) that have the capability to learn from past experiences presented in the form of well-structured datasets. They tend to be more effective when the number of variables involved is rather large and the relationships among them are complex and imprecise. Neural networks have disadvantages as well as advantages. For example, it is usually very difficult to provide a good rationale for the predictions made by a neural network. Also, neural networks tend to need considerable training. Unfortunately, the time needed for training tends to increase exponentially as the volume of data increases, and, in general, neural networks cannot be trained on very large databases. These and other factors have limited the applicability of neural networks in data-rich domains.

Decision trees classify data into a finite number of classes based on the values of the input variables. Decision trees are essentially a hierarchy of if-then statements and are thus significantly faster than neural networks. They are most appropriate for categorical and interval data. Therefore, incorporating continuous variables into a decision tree framework requires *discritization*; that is, converting continuous valued numerical variables to ranges and categories.

A related category of classification tools is rule induction. Unlike with a decision tree, with rule induction the if-then statements are induced from the training data directly, and they need not be hierarchical in nature. Other, more recent techniques such as SVM, rough sets, and genetic algorithms are gradually finding their way into the arsenal of classification algorithms and are covered in more detail in Chapter 13 as part of the discussion on advanced intelligent systems.

CLUSTERING **Clustering** partitions a collection of things (e.g., objects, events, etc. presented in a structured dataset) into segments (or natural groupings) whose members share similar characteristics. Unlike in classification, in clustering the class labels are unknown. As the selected algorithm goes through the dataset, identifying the commonalities of things based on their characteristics, the clusters are established. Because the clusters are determined using a heuristic-type algorithm, and because different algorithms may end up with different sets of clusters for the same dataset, before the results of clustering techniques are put to actual use it may be necessary for an expert to interpret, and potentially modify, the suggested clusters. After reasonable clusters have been identified, they can be used to classify and interpret new data.

Not surprisingly, clustering techniques include optimization. The goal of clustering is to create groups so that the members within each group have maximum similarity and the members across groups have minimum similarity. The most commonly used clustering techniques include *k*-means (from statistics) and self-organizing maps (from machine learning), which is a unique neural network architecture developed by Kohonen (1982).

Firms often effectively use their data mining systems to perform market segmentation with cluster analysis. Cluster analysis is a means of identifying classes of items so that items in a cluster have more in common with each other than with items in other clusters. It can be used in segmenting customers and directing appropriate marketing products to the segments at the right time in the right format at the right price. Cluster analysis is also used to identify natural groupings of events or objects so that a common set of characteristics of these groups can be identified to describe them. Application Case 5.3 describes how cluster analysis was combined with other data mining techniques to identify the causes of accidents.

APPLICATION CASE 5.3

Motor Vehicle Accidents and Driver Distractions

Driver distraction is at center stage in highway safety. A study published in 1996 by the National Highway Traffic Safety Administration (NHTSA) concluded that roughly 25 to 30 percent of the injuries caused by car crashes were due to driver distraction. In 1999, according to the Fatality Analysis Reporting System (FARS) developed by the National Center for Statistics and Analysis (NCSA), 11 percent of fatal crashes (i.e., 4,462 fatalities) were due to driver inattention.

A study was conducted to extract the patterns of distraction factors at traffic accidents. Data mining was used to draw the correlations and associations of factors from the crash datasets provided by FARS. Three data mining techniques (Kohonen-type neural networks, decision trees, and multilayer perceptron-type neural networks) were used to find different combinations of distraction factors that correlated with and potentially explained the high accident rates. The Kohonen-type neural network identified natural clusters and revealed patterns of input variables in the collection of data. Decision trees explored and classified the effect of each incident on successive events and also suggested the relationship between inattentive drivers and physical/mental conditions. Finally, a multilayer perceptron-type neural network model was trained and tested to discover the relationships between inattention and other driver-related factors in these traffic crashes. Clementine from SPSS was used to mine the data obtained from the FARS database for all three model types.

The prediction and exploration model identified 1,255 drivers who were involved in accidents in which inattention was one of the leading driver factors that led to a crash. Rear, head-on, and angled collisions, among other various output variables, were among the factors that had significant impact on the occurrence of crashes and their severity.

Sources: W. S. Tseng, H. Nguyen, J. Liebowitz, and W. Agresti, "Distractions and Motor Vehicle Accidents: Data Mining Application on Fatality Analysis Reporting System (FARS) Data Files," *Industrial Management & Data Systems,* Vol. 105, No. 9, January 2005, pp. 1188–1205; and J. Liebowitz, "New Trends in Intelligent Systems," Presentation made at University of Granada, **docto-si.ugr.es/seminario2006/presentaciones/jay.ppt** (accessed May 2009).

ASSOCIATIONS   **Associations**, or *association rule learning in data mining,* is a popular and well-researched technique for discovering interesting relationships among variables in large databases. Thanks to automated data-gathering technologies such as bar code scanners, the use of association rules for discovering regularities among products in large-scale transactions recorded by point-of-sale systems in supermarkets has become a common knowledge-discovery task in the retail industry. In the context of the retail industry, association rule mining is often called *market-basket analysis.*

Two commonly used derivatives of association rule mining are **link analysis** and **sequence mining**. With link analysis, the linkage among many objects of interest is discovered automatically, such as the link between Web pages and referential relationships among groups of academic publication authors. With sequence mining, relationships are examined in terms of their order of occurrence to identify associations over time. Algorithms used in association rule mining include the popular Apriori (where frequent itemsets are identified) and FP-Growth, OneR, ZeroR, and Eclat.

VISUALIZATION AND TIME-SERIES FORECASTING   Two techniques often associated with data mining are *visualization* and *time-series forecasting*. Visualization can be used in conjunction with other data mining techniques to gain a clearer understanding of underlying relationships. With time-series forecasting, the data are a series of values of the same variable that is captured and stored over time. These data are then used to develop models to extrapolate the future values of the same phenomenon.

HYPOTHESIS- OR DISCOVERY-DRIVEN DATA MINING   Data mining can be hypothesis driven or discovery driven. **Hypothesis-driven data mining** begins with a proposition by the user, who then seeks to validate the truthfulness of the proposition. For example, a marketing manager may begin with the following proposition: "Are DVD player sales related to sales of television sets?"

Discovery-driven data mining finds patterns, associations, and other relationships hidden within datasets. It can uncover facts that an organization had not previously known or even contemplated.

Section 5.2 Review Questions

1. Define *data mining*. Why are there many different names and definitions for data mining?
2. What recent factors have increased the popularity of data mining?
3. Is data mining a new discipline? Explain.
4. What are some major data mining methods and algorithms?
5. What are the key differences between the major data mining methods?

5.3   DATA MINING APPLICATIONS

Data mining has become a popular tool in addressing many complex businesses issues. It has been proven to be very successful and helpful in many areas, some of which are shown by the following representative examples. The goal of many of these business data mining applications is to solve a pressing problem or to explore an emerging business opportunity in order to create a sustainable competitive advantage.

- *Customer relationship management.*   Customer relationship management (CRM) is the new and emerging extension of traditional marketing. The goal of CRM is to create one-on-one relationships with customers by developing an intimate understanding of their needs and wants. As businesses build relationships with their customers over time through a variety of transactions (e.g., product inquiries, sales, service requests, warranty calls), they accumulate tremendous amounts of data. When combined with demographic and socioeconomic attributes, this information-rich data can be used to (1) identify most likely responders/ buyers of new products/services (i.e., customer profiling); (2) understand the roots causes of customer attrition in order to improve customer retention (i.e., churn analysis); (3) discover time-variant associations between products and services to maximize sales and customer value; and (4) identify the most profitable customers and their preferential needs to strengthen relationships and to maximize sales.
- *Banking.*   Data mining can help banks with the following: (1) automating the loan application process by accurately predicting the most probable defaulters; (2) detecting fraudulent credit card and online-banking transactions; (3) identifying ways to maximize customer value by selling them products and services that they are most likely to buy; and (4) optimizing the cash return by accurately forecasting the cash flow on banking entities (e.g., ATM machines, banking branches).
- *Retailing and logistics.*   In the retailing industry, data mining can be used to (1) predict accurate sales volumes at specific retail locations in order to determine correct inventory levels; (2) identify sales relationships between different products (with market-basket analysis) to improve the store layout and optimize sales promotions; (3) forecast consumption levels of different product types (based on seasonal and environmental conditions) to optimize logistics and hence maximize sales; and (4) discover interesting patterns in the movement of products (especially for the

products that have a limited shelf life because they are prone to expiration, perishability, and contamination) in a supply chain by analyzing sensory and RFID data.

- ***Manufacturing and production.***   Manufacturers can use data mining to (1) predict machinery failures before they occur through the use of sensory data (enabling what is called *condition-based maintenance*); (2) identify anomalies and commonalities in production systems to optimize manufacturing capacity; and (3) discover novel patterns to identify and improve product quality.

- ***Brokerage and securities trading.***   Brokers and traders use data mining to (1) predict when and how much certain bond prices will change; (2) forecast the range and direction of stock fluctuations; (3) assess the effect of particular issues and events on overall market movements; and (4) identify and prevent fraudulent activities in securities trading.

- ***Insurance.***   The insurance industry uses data mining techniques to (1) forecast claim amounts for property and medical coverage costs for better business planning; (2) determine optimal rate plans based on the analysis of claims and customer data; (3) predict which customers are more likely to buy new policies with special features; and (4) identify and prevent incorrect claim payments and fraudulent activities.

- ***Computer hardware and software.***   Data mining can be used to (1) predict disk drive failures well before they actually occur; (2) identify and filter unwanted Web content and e-mail messages; (3) detect and prevent computer network security bridges; and (4) identify potentially unsecure software products.

- ***Government and defense.***   Data mining also has a number of military applications. It can be used to (1) forecast the cost of moving military personnel and equipment; (2) predict an adversary's moves and hence develop more successful strategies for military engagements; (3) predict resource consumption for better planning and budgeting; and (4) identify classes of unique experiences, strategies, and lessons learned from military operations for better knowledge sharing throughout the organization.

- ***Travel industry (airlines, hotels/resorts, rental car companies).***   Data mining has a variety of uses in the travel industry. It is successfully used to (1) predict sales of different services (seat types in airplanes, room types in hotels/resorts, car types in rental car companies) in order to optimally price services to maximize revenues as a function of time-varying transactions (commonly referred to as *yield management*); (2) forecast demand at different locations to better allocate limited organizational resources; (3) identify the most profitable customers and provide them with personalized services to maintain their repeat business; and (4) retain valuable employees by identifying and acting on the root causes for attrition.

- ***Health care.***   Data mining has a number of health care applications. It can be used to (1) identify people without health insurance and the factors underlying this undesired phenomenon; (2) identify novel cost-benefit relationships between different treatments to develop more effective strategies; (3) forecast the level and the time of demand at different service locations to optimally allocate organizational resources; and (4) understand the underlying reasons for customer and employee attrition.

- ***Medicine.***   Use of data mining in medicine should be viewed as an invaluable complement to traditional medical research, which is mainly clinical and biological in nature. Data mining analyses can (1) identify novel patterns to improve survivability of patients with cancer; (2) predict success rates of organ transplantation patients to develop better donor-organ matching policies; (3) identify the functions of different genes in the human chromosome (known as genomics); and (4) discover the relationships between symptoms and illnesses (as well as illnesses and successful treatments) to help medical professionals make informed and correct decisions in a timely manner.

- *Entertainment industry.* Data mining is successfully used by the entertainment industry to (1) analyze viewer data to decide what programs to show during prime time and how to maximize returns by knowing where to insert advertisements; (2) predict the financial success of movies before they are produced to make investment decisions and to optimize the returns; (3) forecast the demand at different locations and different times to better schedule entertainment events and to optimally allocate resources; and (4) develop optimal pricing policies to maximize revenues.
- *Homeland security and law enforcement.* Data mining has a number of homeland security and law enforcement applications. Data mining is often used to (1) identify patterns of terrorist behaviors (see Application Case 5.4 for a recent example of use of data mining to track funding of terrorists' activities); (2) discover crime patterns (e.g., locations, timings, criminal behaviors, and other related attributes) to help solve criminal cases in a timely manner; (3) predict and eliminate potential biological and chemical attacks to the nation's critical infrastructure by analyzing special-purpose sensory data; and (4) identify and stop malicious attacks on critical information infrastructures (often called *information warfare*).
- *Sports.* Data mining was used to improve the performance of National Basketball Association (NBA) teams in the United States. The NBA developed Advanced Scout, a PC-based data mining application that coaching staff use to discover interesting patterns in basketball game data. The pattern interpretation is facilitated by allowing the user to relate patterns to videotape. See Bhandari et al. (1997) for details.

APPLICATION CASE 5.4
A Mine on Terrorist Funding

The terrorist attack on the World Trade Center on September 11, 2001, underlined the importance of open source intelligence. The USA PATRIOT Act and the creation of the U.S. Department of Homeland Security (DHS) heralded the potential application of information technology and data mining techniques to detect money laundering and other forms of terrorist financing. Law enforcement agencies have been focusing on money laundering activities via normal transactions through banks and other financial service organizations.

Law enforcement agencies are now focusing on international trade pricing as a terrorism funding tool. International trade has been used by money launderers to move money silently out of a country without attracting government attention. This transfer is achieved by overvaluing imports and undervaluing exports. For example, a domestic importer and foreign exporter could form a partnership and overvalue imports, thereby transferring money from the home country, resulting in crimes related to customs fraud, income tax evasion, and money laundering. The foreign exporter could be a member of a terrorist organization.

Data mining techniques focus on analysis of data on import and export transactions from the U.S. Department of Commerce and commerce-related entities. Import prices that exceed the upper quartile import prices and export prices that are lower than the lower quartile export prices are tracked. The focus is on abnormal transfer prices between corporations that may result in shifting taxable income and taxes out of the United States. An observed price deviation may be related to income tax avoidance/evasion, money laundering, or terrorist financing. The observed price deviation may also be due to an error in the U.S. trade database.

Data mining will result in efficient evaluation of data, which, in turn, will aid in the fight against terrorism. The application of information technology and data mining techniques to financial transactions can contribute to better intelligence information.

Sources: J. S. Zdanowic, "Detecting Money Laundering and Terrorist Financing via Data Mining," *Communications of the ACM,* Vol. 47, No. 5, May 2004, p. 53; and R. J. Bolton, "Statistical Fraud Detection: A Review," *Statistical Science,* Vol. 17, No. 3, January 2002, p. 235.

Section 5.3 Review Questions

1. What are the major application areas for data mining?
2. Identify at least five specific applications of data mining and list five common characteristics of these applications.
3. What do you think is the most prominent application area for data mining? Why?
4. Can you think of other application areas for data mining not discussed in this section? Explain.

5.4 DATA MINING PROCESS

In order to systematically carry out data mining projects, a general process is usually followed. Based on best practices, data mining researchers and practitioners have proposed several processes (workflows or simple step-by-step approaches) to maximize the chances of success in conducting data mining projects. These efforts have led to several standardized processes, some of which (a few of the most popular ones) are described in this section.

One such standardized process, arguably the most popular one, Cross-Industry Standard Process for Data Mining—**CRISP-DM**—was proposed in the mid-1990s by a European consortium of companies to serve as a nonproprietary standard methodology for data mining (CRISP-DM, 2009). Figure 5.5 illustrates this proposed process, which is a sequence of six steps that starts with a good understanding of the business and the need for the data mining project (i.e., the application domain) and ends with the deployment of the solution that satisfied the specific business need. Even though these steps are sequential in nature, there is usually a great deal of backtracking. Because the data mining is driven by experience and experimentation, depending on the problem situation and the knowledge/experience of the analyst, the whole process can be very iterative

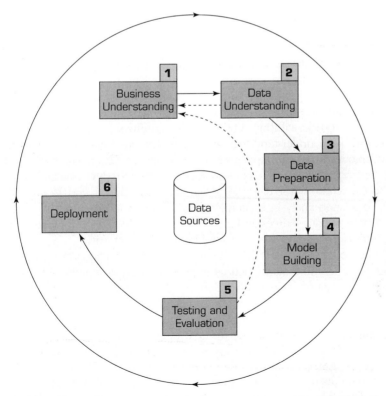

FIGURE 5.5 The Six-Step CRISP-DM Data Mining Process *Source:* Adapted from CRISP-DM.org.

(i.e., one should expect to go back and forth through the steps quite a few times) and time consuming. Because latter steps are built on the outcome of the former ones, one should pay extra attention to the earlier steps in order not to put the whole study on an incorrect path from the onset.

Step 1: Business Understanding

The key element of any data mining study is to know what the study is for. Answering such a question begins with a thorough understanding of the managerial need for new knowledge and an explicit specification of the business objective regarding the study to be conducted. Specific goals such as "What are the common characteristics of the customers we have lost to our competitors recently?" or "What are typical profiles of our customers, and how much value does each of them provide to us?" are needed. Then a project plan for finding such knowledge is developed that specifies the people responsible for collecting the data, analyzing the data, and reporting the findings. At this early stage, a budget to support the study should also be established, at least at a high level with rough numbers.

Step 2: Data Understanding

A data mining study is specific to addressing a well-defined business task, and different business tasks require different sets of data. Following the business understanding, the main activity of the data mining process is to identify the relevant data from many available databases. Some key points must be considered in the data identification and selection phase. First and foremost, the analyst should be clear and concise about the description of the data mining task so that the most relevant data can be identified. For example, a retail data mining project may seek to identify spending behaviors of female shoppers who purchase seasonal clothes based on their demographics, credit card transactions, and socioeconomic attributes. Furthermore, the analyst should build an intimate understanding of the data sources (e.g., where the relevant data are stored and in what form; what the process of collecting the data is—automated versus manual; who the collectors of the data are and how often the data are updated) and the variables (e.g., What are the most relevant variables? Are there any synonymous and/or homonymous variables? Are the variables independent of each other—do they stand as a complete information source without overlapping or conflicting information?).

In order to better understand the data, the analyst often uses a variety of statistical and graphical techniques, such as simple statistical summaries of each variable (e.g., for numeric variables the average, minimum/maximum, median, standard deviation are among the calculated measures, whereas for categorical variables the mode and frequency tables are calculated), correlation analysis, scatterplots, histograms, and box plots. A careful identification and selection of data sources and the most relevant variables can make it easier for data mining algorithms to quickly discover useful knowledge patterns.

Data sources for data selection can vary. Normally, data sources for business applications include demographic data (such as income, education, number of households, and age), sociographic data (such as hobby, club membership, and entertainment), transactional data (sales record, credit card spending, issued checks), and so on.

Data can be categorized as quantitative and qualitative. Quantitative data is measured using numeric values. It can be discrete (such as integers) or continuous (such as real numbers). Qualitative data, also known as categorical data, contains both nominal and ordinal data. Nominal data has finite nonordered values (e.g., gender data, which has two values: male and female). Ordinal data has finite ordered values. For example, customer credit ratings are considered ordinal data because the ratings can be excellent, fair, and bad.

Quantitative data can be readily represented by some sort of probability distribution. A probability distribution describes how the data is dispersed and shaped. For instance, normally distributed data is symmetric and is commonly referred to as being a bell-shaped curve. Qualitative data may be coded to numbers and then described by frequency distributions. Once the relevant data are selected according to the data mining business objective, data preprocessing should be pursued.

Step 3: Data Preparation

The purpose of data preparation (or more commonly called *data preprocessing*) is to take the data indentified in the previous step and prepare it for analysis by data mining methods. Compared to the other steps in CRISP-DM, data preprocessing consumes the most time and effort; most believe that this step accounts for roughly 80 percent of the total time spent on a data mining project. The reason for such an enormous effort spent on this step is the fact that real-world data is generally incomplete (lacking attribute values, lacking certain attributes of interest, or containing only aggregate data), noisy (containing errors or outliers), and inconsistent (containing discrepancies in codes or names). Figure 5.6 shows the four main steps needed to convert the raw real-world data into minable datasets.

In the first phase of data preprocessing, the relevant data is collected from the identified sources (accomplished in the previous step—Data Understanding—of the CRISP-DM process), the necessary records and variables are selected (based on an intimate understanding of the data the unnecessary sections are filtered out), and the records coming from multiple data sources are integrated (again, using the intimate understanding of the data the synonyms and homonyms are to be handled properly).

In the second phase of data preprocessing, the data is cleaned (this step is also known as data scrubbing). In this step, the values in the dataset are identified and dealt

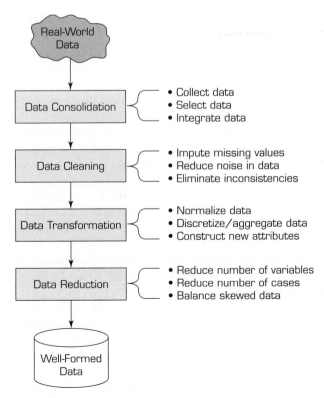

FIGURE 5.6 Data Preprocessing Steps

with. In some cases, missing values are an anomaly in the dataset, in which case they need to be imputed (filled with a most probable value) or ignored; in other cases, the missing values are a natural part of the dataset (e.g., the *household income* field is often left unanswered by people who are in the top income tier). In this step, the analyst should also identify noisy values in the data (i.e., the outliers) and smooth them out. Additionally, inconsistencies (unusual values within a variable) in the data should be handled using domain knowledge and/or expert opinion.

In the third phase of data preprocessing, the data is transformed for better processing. For instance, in many cases the data is normalized between a certain minimum and maximum for all variables in order to mitigate the potential bias of one variable (having large numeric values, such as for household income) dominating other variables (such as *number of dependents* or *years in service,* which may potentially be more important) having smaller values. Another transformation that takes place is discritization and/or aggregation. In some cases, the numeric variables are converted to categorical values (e.g., low, medium, high); in other cases a nominal variable's unique value range is reduced to a smaller set using concept hierarchies (e.g., as opposed to using the individual states with 50 different values, one may chose to use several regions for a variable that shows location) in order to have a dataset that is more amenable to computer processing. Still, in other cases one might choose to create new variables based on the existing ones in order to magnify the information found in a collection of variables in the dataset. For instance, in an organ transplantation dataset one might choose to use a single variable showing the blood-type match (1: match, 0: no-match) as opposed to separate multinominal values for the blood type of both the donor and the recipient. Such simplification may increase the information content while reducing the complexity of the relationships in the data.

The final phase of data preprocessing is data reduction. Even though data miners like to have large datasets, too much data is also a problem. In the simplest sense, one can visualize the data commonly used in data mining projects as a flat file consisting of two dimensions: variables (the number of columns) and cases/records (the number of rows). In some cases (e.g., image processing and genome projects with complex microarray data), the number of variables can be rather large, and the analyst must reduce the number down to a manageable size. Because the variables are treated as different dimensions that describe the phenomenon from different perspectives, in data mining this process is commonly called *dimensional reduction.* Even though there is not a single best way to accomplish this task, one can use the findings from previously published literature; consult domain experts; run appropriate statistical tests (e.g., principle component analysis or independent component analysis); and, more preferably, use a combination of these techniques to successfully reduce the dimensions in the data into a more manageable and most relevant subset.

With respect to the other dimension (i.e., the number of cases), some datasets may include millions or billions of records. Even though computing power is increasing exponentially, processing such a large number of records may not be practical or feasible. In such cases, one may need to sample a subset of the data for analysis. The underlying assumption of sampling is that the subset of the data will contain all relevant patterns of the complete dataset. In a homogenous dataset, such an assumption may hold well, but real-world data is hardly ever homogenous. The analyst should be extremely careful in selecting a subset of the data that reflects the essence of the complete dataset and is not specific to a subgroup or subcategory. The data is usually sorted on some variable, and taking a section of the data from the top or bottom may lead to a biased dataset on specific values of the indexed variable; therefore, one should always try to randomly select the records on the sample set. For skewed data, straightforward random sampling may not be sufficient, and stratified sampling (a proportional representation of different subgroups in the data is represented in the sample dataset) may be required. Speaking of skewed data; it is a good practice to balance the highly skewed data by either oversampling the less represented or under sampling the more represented classes. Research has shown that balanced datasets tends to produce better prediction models than unbalanced ones (Wilson and Sharda, 1994).

The essence of data preprocessing is summarized in Table 5.4, which maps the main phases (along with their problem descriptions) to a representative list of tasks and algorithms.

TABLE 5.4 **A Summary of Data Preprocessing Tasks and Potential Methods**

Main Task	Subtasks	Popular Methods
Data consolidation	Access and collect the data	SQL queries, software agents, Web services.
	Select and filter the data	Domain expertise, SQL queries, statistical tests.
	Integrate and unify the data	SQL queries, domain expertise, ontology-driven data mapping.
Data cleaning	Handle missing values in the data	Fill-in missing values (imputations) with most appropriate values (mean, median, min/max, mode, etc.); recode the missing values with a constant such as "ML"; remove the record of the missing value; do nothing.
	Identify and reduce noise in the data	Identify the outliers in data with simple statistical techniques (such as averages and standard deviations) or with cluster analysis; once identified either remove the outliers or smooth them by using binning, regression, or simple averages.
	Find and eliminate erroneous data	Identify the erroneous values in data (other than outliers), such as odd values, inconsistent class labels, odd distributions; once identified, use domain expertise to correct the values or remove the records holding the erroneous values.
Data transformation	Normalize the data	Reduce the range of values in each numerically valued variable to a standard range (e.g., 0 to 1 or −1 to +1) by using a variety of normalization or scaling techniques.
	Discretize or aggregate the data	If needed, convert the numeric variables into discrete representations using range or frequency-based binning techniques; for categorical variables reduce the number of values by applying proper concept hierarchies.
	Construct new attributes	Derive new and more informative variables from the existing ones using a wide range of mathematical functions (as simple as addition and multiplication or as complex as a hybrid combination of log transformations).
Data reduction	Reduce number of attributes	Principle component analysis, independent component analysis, Chi-square testing, correlation analysis, and decision tree induction.
	Reduce number of records	Random sampling, stratified sampling, expert–knowledge-driven purposeful sampling.
	Balance skewed data	Oversample the less represented or under sample the more represented classes.

Step 4: Model Building

In this step, various modeling techniques are selected and applied to an already prepared dataset in order to address the specific business need. The model-building step also encompasses the assessment and comparative analysis of the various models built. Because there is not a universally known *best* method or algorithm for a data mining task, one should use a variety of viable model types along with a well-defined experimentation and assessment strategy to identify the "best" method for a given purpose. Even for a single method or algorithm, a number of parameters need to be calibrated to obtain optimal results. Some methods may have specific requirements on the way that the data is to be formatted; thus stepping back to the data preparation step is often necessary.

Depending on the business need, the data mining task can be of a prediction (either classification or regression), an association, or a clustering type. Each of these data mining tasks can use a variety of data mining methods and algorithms. Some of these data mining methods were explained earlier in this chapter, and some of the most popular algorithms, including decision trees for classification, *k*-means for clustering, and the Apriori algorithm for association rule mining, are described later in this chapter.

Step 5: Testing and Evaluation

In step 5, the developed models are assessed and evaluated for their accuracy and generality. This step assesses the degree to which the selected model (or models) meets the business objectives and, if so, to what extent (i.e., do more models need to be developed and assessed). Another option is to test the developed model(s) in a real-world scenario if time and budget constraints permit. Even though the outcome of the developed models is expected to relate to the original business objectives, other findings that are not necessarily related to the original business objectives but that might also unveil additional information or hints for future directions often are discovered.

The testing and evaluation step is a critical and challenging task. No value is added by the data mining task until the business value obtained from discovered knowledge patterns is identified and recognized. Determining the business value from discovered knowledge patterns is somewhat similar to playing with puzzles. The extracted knowledge patterns are pieces of the puzzle that need to be put together in the context of the specific business purpose. The success of this identification operation depends on the interaction among data analysts, business analysts, and decision makers (such as business managers). Because data analysts may not have the full understanding of the data mining objectives and what they mean to the business and the business analysts and decision makers may not have the technical knowledge to interpret the results of sophisticated mathematical solutions, interaction among them is necessary. In order to properly interpret knowledge patterns, it is often necessary to use a variety of tabulation and visualization techniques (e.g., pivot tables, cross tabulation of findings, pie charts, histograms, box plots, scatterplots).

Step 6: Deployment

Development and assessment of the models is not the end of the data mining project. Even if the purpose of the model is to have a simple exploration of the data, the knowledge gained from such exploration will need to be organized and presented in a way that the end user can understand and benefit from. Depending on the requirements, the deployment phase can be as simple as generating a report or as complex as implementing a repeatable data mining process across the enterprise. In many cases, it is the customer, not the data analyst, who carries out the deployment steps. However, even if the analyst will not carry out the deployment effort, it is important for the customer to understand up front what actions need to be carried out in order to actually make use of the created models.

The deployment step may also include maintenance activities for the deployed models. Because everything about the business is constantly changing, the data that reflect the business activities also are changing. Over time, the models (and the patterns embedded within them) built on the old data may become obsolete, irrelevant, or misleading. Therefore, monitoring and maintenance of the models are important if the data mining results are to become a part of the day-to-day business and its environment. A careful preparation of a maintenance strategy helps to avoid unnecessarily long periods of incorrect usage of data mining results. In order to monitor the deployment of the data mining result(s), the project needs a detailed plan on the monitoring process, which may not be a trivial task for complex data mining models.

APPLICATION CASE 5.5

Data Mining in Cancer Research

According to the American Cancer Society, approximately 1.5 million new cancer cases will be diagnosed in 2009. Cancer is the second most common cause of death in the United States and in the world, exceeded only by cardiovascular disease. This year, 562,340 Americans are expected to die of cancer—more than 1,500 people a day—accounting for nearly 1 of every 4 deaths.

Cancer is a group of diseases generally characterized by uncontrolled growth and spread of abnormal cells. If the growth and/or spread is not controlled, it can result in death. Even though the exact reasons are not known, cancer is believed to be caused by both external factors (e.g., tobacco, infectious organisms, chemicals, and radiation) and internal factors (e.g., inherited mutations, hormones, immune conditions, and mutations that occur from metabolism). These causal factors may act together or in sequence to initiate or promote carcinogenesis. Cancer is treated with surgery, radiation, chemotherapy, hormone therapy, biological therapy, and targeted therapy. Survival statistics vary greatly by cancer type and stage at diagnosis.

The 5-year relative survival rate for all cancers diagnosed in 1996–2004 is 66 percent, up from 50 percent in 1975–1977. The improvement in survival reflects progress in diagnosing certain cancers at an earlier stage and improvements in treatment. Further improvements are needed to prevent and treat cancer.

Even though cancer research has traditionally been clinical and biological in nature, in recent years data-driven analytic studies have become a common complement. In medical domains where data- and analytics-driven research have been applied successfully, novel research directions have been identified to further advance the clinical and biological studies. Using various types of data, including molecular, clinical, literature-based, and clinical-trial data, along with suitable data mining tools and techniques, researchers have been able to identify novel patterns, paving the road toward a cancer-free society.

In one study, Delen (2009) used three popular data mining techniques (decision trees, artificial neural networks, and support vector machines) in conjunction with logistic regression to develop prediction models for prostate cancer survivability. The dataset contained around 120,000 records and 77 variables. A k-fold cross-validation methodology was used in model building, evaluation, and comparison. The results showed that support vector models are the most accurate predictor (with a test set accuracy of 92.85%) for this domain, followed by artificial neural networks and decision trees. Furthermore, using a sensitivity–analysis-based evaluation method, the study also revealed novel patterns related to prognostic factors of prostate cancer.

In a related study, Delen et al. (2006) used two data mining algorithms (artificial neural networks and decision trees) and logistic regression to develop prediction models for breast cancer survival using a large dataset (more than 200,000 cases). Using a *10*-fold cross-validation method to measure the unbiased estimate of the prediction models for performance comparison purposes, the results indicated that the decision tree (C5 algorithm) was the best predictor, with 93.6 percent accuracy on the holdout sample (which was the best prediction accuracy reported in the literature); followed by artificial neural networks, with 91.2 percent accuracy; and logistic regression, with 89.2 percent accuracy. Further analysis of prediction models revealed prioritized importance of the prognostic factors, which can then be used as basis for further clinical and biological research studies.

These examples (among many others in the medical literature) show that advanced data mining techniques can be used to develop models that possess a high degree of predictive as well as explanatory power. Although data mining methods are capable of extracting patterns and relationships hidden deep in large and complex medical databases, without the cooperation and feedback from the medical experts their results are not of much use. The patterns found via data mining methods should be evaluated by medical professionals who have years of experience in the problem domain to decide whether they are logical, actionable, and novel to warrant new research directions. In short, data mining is not to replace medical professionals and researchers, but to complement their invaluable efforts to provide data-driven new research directions and to ultimately save more human lives.

Sources: D. Delen, "Analysis of Cancer Data: A Data Mining Approach," *Expert Systems*, Vol. 26, No. 1, 2009, pp. 100–112; J. Thongkam, G. Xu, Y. Zhang, and F. Huang, "Toward Breast Cancer Survivability Prediction Models Through Improving Training Space," *Expert Systems with Applications*, 2009, *in press*; D. Delen, G. Walker, and A. Kadam, "Predicting Breast Cancer Survivability: A Comparison of Three Data Mining Methods," *Artificial Intelligence in Medicine*, Vol. 34, No. 2, 2005, pp. 113–127.

Other Data Mining Standardized Processes and Methodologies

In order to be applied successfully, a data mining study must be viewed as a process that follows a standardized methodology rather than as a set of automated software tools and techniques. In addition to CRISP-DM, there is another well-known methodology developed by the SAS Institute, called SEMMA (2009). The acronym **SEMMA** stands for "sample, explore, modify, model, and assess."

Beginning with a statistically representative sample of the data, SEMMA makes it easy to apply exploratory statistical and visualization techniques, select and transform the most significant predictive variables, model the variables to predict outcomes, and confirm a model's accuracy. A pictorial representation of SEMMA is given in Figure 5.7.

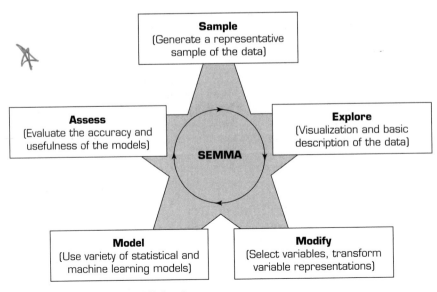

FIGURE 5.7 SEMMA Data Mining Process

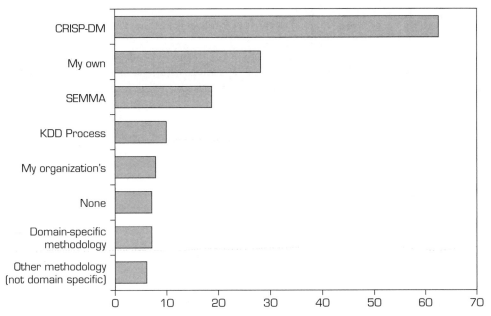

FIGURE 5.8 Ranking of Data Mining Methodologies/Processes *Source:* Used with permission from **kdnuggets.com**.

By assessing the outcome of each stage in the SEMMA process, the model developer can determine how to model new questions raised by the previous results, and thus proceed back to the exploration phase for additional refinement of the data; that is, as with CRISP-DM, SEMMA is driven by a highly iterative experimentation cycle. The main difference between CRISP-DM and SEMMA is that CRISP-DM takes a more comprehensive approach—including understanding of the business and the relevant data—to data mining projects, whereas SEMMA implicitly assumes that the data mining project's goals and objectives along with the appropriate data sources have been identified and understood.

Some practitioners commonly use the term **knowledge discovery in databases (KDD)** as a synonym for data mining. Fayyad et al. (1996) defined *knowledge discovery in databases* as a process of using data mining methods to find useful information and patterns in the data, as opposed to data mining, which involves using algorithms to identify patterns in data derived through the KDD process. KDD is a comprehensive process that encompasses data mining. The input to the KDD process consists of organizational data. The enterprise data warehouse enables KDD to be implemented efficiently because it provides a single source for data to be mined. Dunham (2003) summarized the KDD process as consisting of the following steps: data selection, data preprocessing, data transformation, data mining, and interpretation/evaluation. Figure 5.8 shows the polling results for the question of "What main methodology are you using for data mining?" (conducted by **kdnuggets.com** in August 2007).

Section 5.4 Review Questions

1. What are the major data mining processes?
2. Why do you think the early phases (understanding of the business and understanding of the data) take the longest in data mining projects?
3. List and briefly define the phases in the CRISP-DM process.
4. What are the main data preprocessing steps? Briefly describe each step and provide relevant examples.
5. How does CRISP-DM differ from SEMMA?

5.5 DATA MINING METHODS

A variety of methods are available for performing data mining studies, including classification, regression, clustering, and association. Most data mining software tools employ more than one technique (or algorithm) for each of these methods. This section describes the most popular data mining methods and explains their representative techniques.

Classification

Classification is perhaps the most frequently used data mining method for real-world problems. As a popular member of the machine-learning family of techniques, classification learns patterns from past data (a set of information—traits, variables, features—on characteristics of the previously labeled items, objects, or events) in order to place new instances (with unknown labels) into their respective groups or classes. For example, one could use classification to predict whether the weather on a particular day will be "sunny," "rainy," or "cloudy." Popular classification tasks include credit approval (i.e., good or bad credit risk), store location (e.g., good, moderate, bad), target marketing (e.g., likely customer, no hope), fraud detection (i.e., yes, no), and telecommunication (e.g., likely to turn to another phone company, yes/no). If what is being predicted is a class label (e.g., "sunny," "rainy," or "cloudy") the prediction problem is called a classification, whereas if it is a numeric value (e.g., temperature such as 68°F), the prediction problem is called a **regression**.

Even though clustering (another popular data mining method) can also be used to determine groups (or class memberships) of things, there is a significant difference between the two. Classification learns the function between the characteristics of things (i.e., independent variables) and their membership (i.e., output variable) through a supervised learning process where both types (input and output) of variables are presented to the algorithm; in clustering, the membership of the objects is learned through an unsupervised learning process where only the input variables are presented to the algorithm. Unlike classification, clustering does not have a supervising (or controlling) mechanism that enforces the learning process; instead, clustering algorithms use one or more heuristics (e.g., multidimensional distance measure) to discover natural groupings of objects.

The most common two-step methodology of classification-type prediction involves model development/training and model testing/deployment. In the model development phase, a collection of input data, including the actual class labels, is used. After a model has been trained, the model is tested against the holdout sample for accuracy assessment and eventually deployed for actual use where it is to predict classes of new data instances (where the class label is unknown). Several factors are considered in assessing the model, including the following:

- **Predictive accuracy.** The model's ability to correctly predict the class label of new or previously unseen data. Prediction accuracy is the most commonly used assessment factor for classification models. To compute this measure, actual class labels of a test dataset are matched against the class labels predicted by the model. The accuracy can then be computed as the *accuracy rate,* which is the percentage of test dataset samples correctly classified by the model (more on this topic is provided later in the chapter).
- **Speed.** The computational costs involved in generating and using the model, where faster is deemed to be better.
- **Robustness.** The model's ability to make reasonably accurate predictions, given noisy data or data with missing and erroneous values.

		True Class	
		Positive	Negative
Predicted Class	Positive	True Positive Count (TP)	False Positive Count (FP)
	Negative	False Negative Count (FN)	True Negative Count (TN)

FIGURE 5.9 A Simple Confusion Matrix for Tabulation of Two-Class Classification Results

- ***Scalability.*** The ability to construct a prediction model efficiently given a rather large amount of data.
- ***Interpretability.*** The level of understanding and insight provided by the model (e.g., how and/or what the model concludes on certain predictions).

Estimating the True Accuracy of Classification Models

In classification problems, the primary source for accuracy estimation is the *confusion matrix* (also called a *classification matrix* or a *contingency table*). Figure 5.9 shows a confusion matrix for a two-class classification problem. The numbers along the diagonal from the upper left to the lower right represent correct decisions, and the numbers outside this diagonal represent the errors.

Table 5.5 provides equations for common accuracy metrics for classification models.

When the classification problem is not binary, the confusion matrix gets bigger (a square matrix with the size of the unique number of class labels), and accuracy metrics become limited to *per class accuracy rates* and the *overall classifier accuracy*.

$$(True\ Classification\ Rate)_i = \frac{(True\ Classification)_i}{\sum_{i=1}^{n}(False\ Classification)_i}$$

TABLE 5.5 Common Accuracy Metrics for Classification Models

Metric	Description
$True\ Positive\ Rate = \frac{TP}{TP + FN}$	The ratio of correctly classified positives divided by the total positive count (i.e., hit rate or recall)
$True\ Negative\ Rate = \frac{TN}{TN + FP}$	The ratio of correctly classified negatives divided by the total negative count (i.e., false alarm rate)
$Accuracy = \frac{TP + TN}{TP + TN + FP + FN}$	The ratio of correctly classified instances (positives and negatives) divided by the total number of instances
$Precision = \frac{TP}{TP + FP}$	The ratio of correctly classified positives divided by the sum of correctly classified positives and incorrectly classified positives
$Recall = \frac{TP}{TP + FN}$	Ratio of correctly classified positives divided by the sum of correctly classified positives and incorrectly classified negatives

$$(\textit{Overall Classifier Accuracy})_i = \frac{\sum_{i=1}^{n}(\textit{True Classification})_i}{\textit{Total Number of Cases}}$$

Estimating the accuracy of a classification model (or classifier) induced by a supervised learning algorithm is important for the following two reasons: First, it can be used to estimate its future prediction accuracy, which could imply the level of confidence one should have in the classifier's output in the prediction system. Second, it can be used for choosing a classifier from a given set (identifying the "best" classification model among the many trained). The following are among the most popular estimation methodologies used for classification-type data mining models.

SIMPLE SPLIT The **simple split** (or holdout or test sample estimation) partitions the data into two mutually exclusive subsets called a *training set* and a *test set* (or *holdout set*). It is common to designate two-thirds of the data as the training set and the remaining one-third as the test set. The training set is used by the inducer (model builder), and the built classifier is then tested on the test set. An exception to this rule occurs when the classifier is an artificial neural network. In this case, the data is partitioned into three mutually exclusive subsets: training, validation, and testing. The validation set is used during model building to prevent overfitting (more on artificial neural networks can be found in Chapter 6). Figure 5.10 shows the simple split methodology.

The main criticism of this method is that it makes the assumption that the data in the two subsets are of the same kind (i.e., have the exact same properties). Because this is a simple random partitioning, in most realistic datasets where the data are skewed on the classification variable, such an assumption may not hold true. In order to improve this situation, stratified sampling is suggested, where the strata become the output variable. Even though this is an improvement over the simple split, it still has a bias associated from the single random partitioning.

K-FOLD CROSS-VALIDATION In order to minimize the bias associated with the random sampling of the training and holdout data samples in comparing the predictive accuracy of two or more methods, one can use a methodology called **k-fold cross-validation**. In k-fold cross-validation, also called *rotation estimation,* the complete dataset is randomly split into k mutually exclusive subsets of approximately equal size. The classification model is trained and tested k times. Each time it is trained on all but one fold and then tested on the remaining single fold. The cross-validation estimate of the overall accuracy

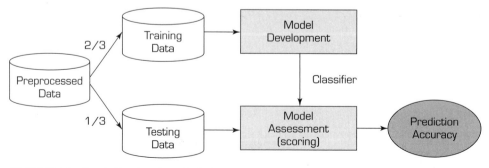

FIGURE 5.10 Simple Random Data Splitting

of a model is calculated by simply averaging the k individual accuracy measures, as shown in the following equation:

$$CVA = \frac{1}{k} \sum_{i=1}^{k} A_i$$

where CVA stands for cross-validation accuracy, k is the number of folds used, and A is the accuracy measure (e.g., hit-rate, sensitivity, specificity) of each fold.

ADDITIONAL CLASSIFICATION ASSESSMENT METHODOLOGIES   Other popular assessment methodologies include the following:

- ***Leave-one-out.***   The leave-one-out method is similar to the k-fold cross-validation where the k takes the value of 1; that is, every data point is used for testing once on as many models developed as there are number of data points. This is a time-consuming methodology, but sometimes for small datasets it is a viable option.
- ***Bootstrapping.***   With **bootstrapping,** a fixed number of instances from the original data is sampled (with replacement) for training and the rest of the dataset is used for testing. This process is repeated as many times as desired.
- ***Jackknifing.***   Similar to the leave-one-out methodology; with jackknifing the accuracy is calculated by leaving one sample out at each iteration of the estimation process.
- ***Area under the ROC curve.***   The **area under the ROC curve** is a graphical assessment technique where the true positive rate is plotted on the Y-axis and false positive rate is plotted on the X-axis. The area under the ROC curve determines the accuracy measure of a classifier: A value of 1 indicates a perfect classifier whereas 0.5 indicates no better than random chance; in reality, the values would range between the two extreme cases. For example, in Figure 5.11 A has a better classification performance than B, while C is not any better than random chance of flipping a coin.

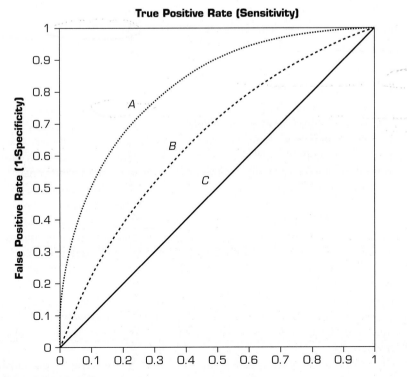

FIGURE 5.11 Sample ROC Curve

CLASSIFICATION TECHNIQUES   A number of techniques (or algorithms) are used for classification modeling, including the following:

- **Decision tree analysis.**   Decision tree analysis (a machine-learning technique) is arguably the most popular classification technique in the data mining arena. A detailed description of this technique is given in the following section.
- **Statistical analysis.**   Statistical techniques were the primary classification algorithm for many years until the emergence of machine-learning techniques. Statistical classification techniques include logistic regression and discriminant analysis, both of which make the assumptions that the relationships between the input and output variables are linear in nature, the data is normally distributed, and the variables are not correlated and are independent of each other. The questionable nature of these assumptions has led to the shift toward machine-learning techniques.
- **Neural networks.**   These are among the most popular machine-learning techniques that can be used for classification-type problems. A detailed description of this technique is presented in Chapter 6.
- **Case-based reasoning.**   This approach uses historical cases to recognize commonalities in order to assign a new case into the most probable category.
- **Bayesian classifiers.**   This approach uses probability theory to build classification models based on the past occurrences that are capable of placing a new instance into a most probable class (or category).
- **Genetic algorithms.**   The use of the analogy of natural evolution to build directed-search-based mechanisms to classify data samples.
- **Rough sets.**   This method takes into account the partial membership of class labels to predefined categories in building models (collection of rules) for classification problems.

A complete description of all of these classification techniques is beyond the scope of this book, thus only several of the most popular ones are presented here.

DECISION TREES   Before describing the details of **decision trees,** we need to discuss some simple terminology. First, decision trees include many input variables that may have an impact on the classification of different patterns. These input variables are usually called *attributes*. For example, if we were to build a model to classify loan risks on the basis of just two characteristics—income and a credit rating—these two characteristics would be the attributes and the resulting output would be the *class label* (e.g., low, medium, or high risk). Second, a tree consists of branches and nodes. A *branch* represents the outcome of a test to classify a pattern (on the basis of a test) using one of the attributes. A *leaf node* at the end represents the final class choice for a pattern (a chain of branches from the root node to the leaf node which can be represented as a complex if-then statement).

The basic idea behind a decision tree is that it recursively divides a training set until each division consists entirely or primarily of examples from one class. Each nonleaf node of the tree contains a *split point,* which is a test on one or more attributes and determines how the data are to be divided further. Decision tree algorithms, in general, build an initial tree from the training data such that each leaf node is pure, and they then prune the tree to increase its generalization, and hence the prediction accuracy on test data.

In the growth phase, the tree is built by recursively dividing the data until each division is either pure (i.e., contains members of the same class) or relatively small. The basic idea is to ask questions whose answers would provide the most information, similar to what we may do when playing the game "Twenty Questions."

The split used to partition the data depends on the type of the attribute used in the split. For a continuous attribute A, splits are of the form value(A) < x, where x is some "optimal" split value of A. For example, the split based on income could be "Income < 50000." For the categorical attribute A, splits are of the form value(A) belongs to x, where x is a subset of A. As an example, the split could be on the basis of gender: "Male versus Female."

A general algorithm for building a decision tree is as follows:

1. Create a root node and assign all of the training data to it.
2. Select the *best* splitting attribute.
3. Add a branch to the root node for each value of the split. Split the data into mutually exclusive (nonoverlapping) subsets along the lines of the specific split and mode to the branches.
4. Repeat the steps 2 and 3 for each and every leaf node until the stopping criteria is reached (e.g., the node is dominated by a single class label).

Many different algorithms have been proposed for creating decision trees. These algorithms differ primarily in terms of the way in which they determine the splitting attribute (and its split values), the order of splitting the attributes (splitting the same attribute only once or many times), the number of splits at each node (binary versus ternary), the stopping criteria, and the pruning of the tree (pre- versus postpruning). Some of the most well-known algorithms are ID3 (followed by C4.5 and C5 as the improved versions of ID3) from machine learning, classification and regression trees (CART) from statistics, and the chi-squared automatic interaction detector (CHAID) from pattern recognition.

When building a decision tree, the goal at each node is to determine the attribute and the split point of that attribute that best divides the training records in order to purify the class representation at that node. To evaluate the goodness of the split, some splitting indices have been proposed. Two of the most common ones are the Gini index and information gain. The Gini index is used in CART and SPRINT (Scalable PaRallelizable Induction of Decision Trees) algorithms. Versions of information gain are used in ID3 (and its newer versions, C4.5 and C5).

The **Gini index** has been used in economics to measure the diversity of a population. The same concept can be used to determine the purity of a specific class as a result of a decision to branch along a particular attribute or variable. The best split is the one that increases the purity of the sets resulting from a proposed split. Let us briefly look into a simple calculation of Gini index:

If a dataset S contains examples from n classes, the Gini index is defined as

$$gini(S) = 1 - \sum_{j=1}^{n} p_j^2$$

where p_j is a relative frequency of class j in S. If a dataset S is split into two subsets, S_1 and S_2, with sizes N_1 and N_2, respectively, the Gini index of the split data contains examples from n classes, and the Gini index is defined as

$$gini_{split}(S) = \frac{N_1}{N} gini(S_1) + \frac{N_2}{N} gini(S_2)$$

The attribute/split combination that provides the smallest $gini_{split}(S)$ is chosen to split the node. In such a determination, one should enumerate all possible splitting points for each attribute.

Information gain is the splitting mechanism used in ID3, which is perhaps the most widely known decision tree algorithm. It was developed by Ross Quinlan in 1986, and since then he has evolved this algorithm into the C4.5 and C5 algorithms. The basic idea behind ID3 (and its variants) is to use a concept called *entropy* in place of the Gini index. **Entropy** measures the extent of uncertainty or randomness in a dataset. If all the data in a subset belong to just one class, there is no uncertainty or randomness in that dataset; so the entropy is zero. The objective of this approach is to build subtrees so that the entropy of each final subset is zero (or close to zero). Let us also look at the calculation of the information gain.

Assume that there are two classes, P (positive) and N (negative). Let the set of examples S contain p counts of class P and n counts of class N. The amount of information needed to decide if an arbitrary example in S belongs to P or N is defined as

$$I(p, n) = -\frac{p}{p + n} \log_2 \frac{p}{p + n} - \frac{n}{p + n} \log_2 \frac{n}{p + n}$$

Assume that using attribute A a set S will be partitioned into sets $\{S_1, S_2, \ldots, S_v\}$. If S_i contains p_i examples of P and n_i examples of N, the entropy, or the expected information needed to classify objects in all subtrees S_i, is

$$E(A) = \sum_{i=1}^{v} \frac{p_i + n_i}{p + n} I(p_i, n_i)$$

Then, the information that would be gained by branching on attribute A would be

$$Gain(A) = I(p, n) - E(A)$$

These calculations are repeated for each and every attribute, and the one with the highest information gain is selected as the splitting attribute. The basic ideas behind these splitting indices are rather similar to each other but the specific algorithmic details vary. A detailed definition of ID3 algorithm and its splitting mechanism can be found in Quinlan (1986).

APPLICATION CASE 5.6

Highmark, Inc., Employs Data Mining to Manage Insurance Costs

Highmark, Inc., based in Pittsburgh, Pennsylvania, has a long tradition of providing access to affordable, quality health care to its members and communities. Highmark was formed in 1996 by the merger of two Pennsylvania licensees of the Blue Cross and Blue Shield Association: Pennsylvania Blue Shield (now Highmark Blue Shield) and a Blue Cross plan in western Pennsylvania (now Highmark Blue Cross Blue Shield). Highmark is currently one of the largest health insurers in the United States.

Data in Managed Care Organizations

The amount of data floating around in managed care organizations such as Highmark is vast. These data, often considered to be occupying storage space and viewed as a menace to be dealt with, have recently been recognized as a source of new knowledge. Data mining tools and techniques provide practical means for analyzing patient data and unraveling mysteries that can lead to better managed care at lower costs—a mission that most managed care companies are trying to achieve.

Each day, managed care companies receive millions of data items about their customers, and each piece of information updates the case history of each member. Companies have become aware of the usefulness of the data at their disposal and use analytic software tools to extract patient clusters that are more costly than average to treat. Earlier efforts at using computer technology in order to extract patient-related actionable information were limited in establishing a connection between two different diseases. For example, the software tool could scan through the data and report that diabetics or people suffering from coronary heart diseases were the most expensive to treat. However, these reporting-based software tools were inefficient in finding why these patients were getting sick or why some patients were more adversely affected by certain diseases than others. Data mining tools can solve some of these problems by analyzing multidimensional information and generating succinct relationships and correlations among different diseases and patient profiles.

Managed care organizations are inundated with data, and some of the companies do not want to add to the complexity by adding data mining applications. They may want to scan data for various reasons but are unable to decide why or how to analyze their data. Things are becoming brighter for patients as well as companies, however, because health insurance regulations are clearing the way for efficient data and structuring analysis.

The Need for Data Mining

Market pressures are driving managed care organizations to become more efficient, and hence to take data mining seriously. Customers are demanding more and better service, and competitors are becoming relentless, all of which are leading to the design and delivery of more customized products in a timely manner.

This customization brings us to the originating point of why and where the major portions of medical costs are occurring. Many organizations have started to use data mining software to predict who is more likely to fall sick and who is more likely to be the most expensive to treat. A look into the future has enabled organizations to filter out their costly patients and lower their Medicare costs by using preventive measures. Another important application of predictive studies is the management of premiums. An employer group that has a large number of employees falling in a higher cost bracket would see its rates increase.

Based on the historical data, predictive modeling might be able to foretell which patients are more likely to become a financial burden for the company. For example, a predictive modeling application might rate a diabetic patient as a high risk of increased medical costs, which by itself might not be actionable information. However, data mining implementation at Highmark draws a relationship between a diabetic patient and other patient- and environment-related parameters; that is, a patient with a specific cardiac condition might be at high risk of contracting diabetes. This relationship is drawn because the cardiac medication could lead the patient to developing diabetes later in life. Highmark officials testify to this fact by saying that they would not have monitored the patients for the cardiac medication and might not have drawn a relationship between the cardiac medication and diabetes. Medical research has been successful in codifying many of the complexities associated with patient conditions. Data mining has laid the foundation for better detection and proper intervention programs.

Sources: Condensed from G. Gillespie, "Data Mining: Solving Care, Cost Capers," *Health Data Management*, November 2004, **findarticles.com/p/articles/mi_km2925/is_200411/ ai_n8622737** (accessed May 2009); and "Highmark Enhances Patient Care, Keeps Medical Costs Down with SAS," **sas.com/ success/highmark.html** (accessed April 2006).

Cluster Analysis for Data Mining

Cluster analysis is an essential data mining method for classifying items, events, or concepts into common groupings called *clusters*. The method is commonly used in biology, medicine, genetics, social network analysis, anthropology, archaeology, astronomy, character recognition, and even in MIS development. As data mining has increased in popularity, the underlying techniques have been applied to business, especially to marketing. Cluster analysis has been used extensively for fraud detection (both credit card and e-commerce fraud) and market segmentation of customers in contemporary CRM systems. More applications in business continue to be developed as the strength of cluster analysis is recognized and used.

Cluster analysis is an exploratory data analysis tool for solving classification problems. The objective is to sort cases (e.g., people, things, events) into groups, or clusters, so that the degree of association is strong among members of the same cluster and weak among members of different clusters. Each cluster describes the class to which its members belong. An obvious one-dimensional example of cluster analysis is to establish score ranges into which to assign class grades for a college class. This is similar to the cluster analysis problem that the U.S. Treasury faced when establishing new tax brackets in the 1980s. A fictional example of clustering occurs in J. K. Rowling's *Harry Potter* books. The Sorting Hat determines to which House (e.g., dormitory) to assign first-year students at the Hogwarts School. Another example involves determining how to seat guests at a wedding. As far as data mining goes, the importance of cluster analysis is that it may reveal associations and structures in data that were not previously apparent but are sensible and useful once found.

Cluster analysis results may be used to:

- Identify a classification scheme (e.g., types of customers)
- Suggest statistical models to describe populations
- Indicate rules for assigning new cases to classes for identification, targeting, and diagnostic purposes
- Provide measures of definition, size, and change in what were previously broad concepts
- Find typical cases to label and represent classes
- Decrease the size and complexity of the problem space for other data mining methods
- Identify outliers in a specific domain (e.g., rare-event detection)

DETERMINING THE OPTIMAL NUMBER OF CLUSTERS Clustering algorithms usually require one to specify the number of clusters to find. If this number is not known from prior knowledge, it should be chosen in some way. Unfortunately, there is not an optimal way of calculating what this number is supposed to be. Therefore, several different heuristic methods have been proposed. The following are among the most commonly referenced ones:

- Look at the percentage of variance explained as a function of the number of clusters; that is, choose a number of clusters so that adding another cluster would not give much better modeling of the data. Specifically, if one graphs the percentage of variance explained by the clusters, there is a point at which the marginal gain will drop (giving an angle in the graph), indicating the number of clusters to be chosen.
- Set the number of clusters to $(n/2)^{1/2}$, where n is the number of data points.
- Use the Akaike Information Criterion (AIC), which is a measure of the goodness of fit (based on the concept of entropy) to determine the number of clusters.
- Use Bayesian information criterion (BIC), which is a model-selection criterion (based on maximum likelihood estimation) to determine the number of clusters.

ANALYSIS METHODS Cluster analysis may be based on one or more of the following general methods:

- Statistical methods (including both hierarchical and nonhierarchical), such as *k*-means, *k*-modes, and so on.
- Neural networks (with the architecture called self-organizing map, or SOM)
- Fuzzy logic (e.g., fuzzy *c*-means algorithm)
- Genetic algorithms

Each of these methods generally works with one of two general method classes:

- **Divisive.** With divisive classes, all items start in one cluster and are broken apart.
- **Agglomerative.** With agglomerative classes, all items start in individual clusters, and the clusters are joined together.

Most cluster analysis methods involve the use of a **distance measure** to calculate the closeness between pairs of items. Popular distance measures include Euclidian distance (the ordinary distance between two points that one would measure with a ruler) and Manhattan distance (also called the rectilinear distance, or taxicab distance, between two points). Often, they are based on true distances that are measured, but this need not be so, as is typically the case in IS development. Weighted averages may be used to establish these distances. For example, in an IS development project, individual modules of the system may be related by the similarity between their inputs, outputs, processes, and the specific data used. These factors are then aggregated, pairwise by item, into a single distance measure.

K-MEANS CLUSTERING ALGORITHM   The *k*-means algorithm (where *k* stands for the pre-determined number of clusters) is arguably the most referenced clustering algorithm. It has its roots in traditional statistical analysis. As the name implies, the algorithm assigns each data point (customer, event, object, etc.) to the cluster whose center (also called *centroid*) is the nearest. The center is calculated as the average of all the points in the cluster; that is, its coordinates are the arithmetic mean for each dimension separately over all the points in the cluster. The algorithm steps are listed below and shown graphically in Figure 5.12:

> **Initialization step:**   Choose the number of clusters (i.e., the value of *k*).

> **Step 1**   Randomly generate *k* random points as initial cluster centers.
> **Step 2**   Assign each point to the nearest cluster center.
> **Step 3**   Recompute the new cluster centers.

> **Repetition step:**   Repeat steps 2 and 3 until some convergence criterion is met (usually that the assignment of points to clusters becomes stable).

Association Rule Mining

Association rule mining is a popular data mining method that is commonly used as an example to explain what data mining is and what it can do to a technologically less savvy audience. Most of you might have heard the famous (or infamous, depending on how to look at it) relationship discovered between the sales of beer and diapers at grocery stores. As the story goes, a large supermarket chain (maybe Wal-Mart, maybe not; there is no consensus on which supermarket chain it was) did an analysis of customers'

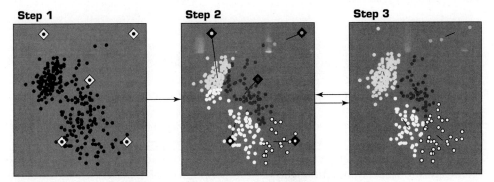

FIGURE 5.12   Graphical Illustration of the Steps in *k*-means Algorithm

buying habits and found a statistically significant correlation between purchases of beer and purchases of diapers. It was theorized that the reason for this was that fathers (presumably young men) were stopping off at the supermarket to buy diapers for their babies (especially on Thursdays), and since they could no longer go down to the sports bar as often, would buy beer as well. As a result of this finding, the supermarket chain is alleged to have placed the diapers next to the beer, resulting in increased sales of both.

In essence, association rule mining aims to find interesting relationships (affinities) between variables (items) in large databases. Because of its successful application to business problems, it is commonly called a *market-basket analysis*. The main idea in market-basket analysis is to identify strong relationships among different products (or services) that are usually purchased together (show up in the same basket together, either a physical basket at a grocery store or a virtual basket at an e-commerce Web site). For instance, market-basket analysis may find a pattern like, "If a customer buys lap-top computer and virus protection software, he/she also buys extended service plan 70 percent of the time." The input to market-basket analysis is the simple point-of-sale transaction data, where a number of products and/or services purchased together (just like the content of a purchase receipt) are tabulated under a single transaction instance. The outcome of the analysis is invaluable information that can be used to better understand customer-purchase behavior in order to maximize the profit from business transactions. A business can take advantage of such knowledge by (1) putting the items next to each other to make it more convenient for the customers to pick them up together and not forget to buy one when buying the others (increasing sales volume); (2) promoting the items as a package (do not put one on sale if the other(s) are on sale); and (3) placing them apart from each other so that the customer has to walk the aisles to search for it, and by doing so potentially seeing and buying other items.

Applications of market-basket analysis include cross-marketing, cross-selling, store design, catalog design, e-commerce site design, optimization of online advertising, product pricing, and sales/promotion configuration. In essence, market-basket analysis helps businesses infer customer needs and preferences from their purchase patterns. Outside the business realm, association rules are successfully used to discover relationships between symptoms and illnesses, diagnosis and patient characteristics and treatments (to be used in medical DSS), and genes and their functions (to be used in genomics projects), among others.

A good question to ask with respect to the patterns/relationships that association rule mining can discover is "Are all association rules interesting and useful?" In order to answer such a question, association rule mining uses two common metrics: **support** and **confidence**. Before defining these terms, let's get a little technical by showing what an association rule looks like:

$$X \Rightarrow Y \ [S\%, \ C\%]$$

$$\{\text{Laptop Computer, Antivirus Software}\} \Rightarrow \{\text{Extended Service Plan}\} \ [30\%, 70\%]$$

Here, X (products and/or service; called the *left-hand side, LHS,* or the antecedent) is associated with Y (products and/or service; called the *right-hand side, RHS,* or *consequent*). S is the support, and C is the confidence for this particular rule. The support (S) of a rule is the measure of how often these products and/or services (i.e., LHS + RHS = Laptop Computer, Antivirus Software, and Extended Service Plan) appear together in the same transaction; that is, the proportion of transactions in the dataset that contain all of the products and/or services mentioned in a specific rule. In this example, 30 percent of all transactions in the hypothetical store database had all three products present in a single sales ticket. The confidence of a rule is the measure of how often the products and/or services on the RHS (consequent) go together with the products and/or services on the LHS (antecedent); that is, the proportion of transactions that include LHS while also including the RHS. In other words, it is the conditional probability of finding the RHS of the rule present in transactions where the LHS of the rule already exists.

Several algorithms are available for generating association rules. Some well-known algorithms include Apriori, Eclat, and FP-Growth. These algorithms only do half the job, which is to identify the frequent itemsets in the database. Once the frequent itemsets are identified, they need to be converted into rules with antecedent and consequent parts. Determination of the rules from frequent itemsets is a straight-forward matching process, but the process may be time consuming with large transaction databases. Even though there can be many items on each section of the rule, in practice the consequent part usually contains a single item. In the following section, one of the most popular algorithms for identification of frequent itemsets is explained.

APRIORI ALGORITHM   The **Apriori algorithm** is the most commonly used algorithm to discover association rules. Given a set of itemsets (e.g., sets of retail transactions, each listing individual items purchased), the algorithm attempts to find subsets that are common to at least a minimum number of the itemsets (i.e., complies with a minimum support). Apriori uses a bottom-up approach, where frequent subsets are extended one item at a time (a method known as *candidate generation,* whereby the size of frequent subsets increases from one-item subsets to two-item subsets, then three-item subsets, etc.), and groups of candidates at each level are tested against the data for minimum support. The algorithm terminates when no further successful extensions are found.

As an illustrative example, consider the following. A grocery store tracks sales transactions by SKU (stock-keeping unit) and thus knows which items are typically purchased together. The database of transactions, along with the subsequent steps in identifying the frequent itemsets, is shown in Figure 5.13. Each SKU in the transaction database corresponds to a product, such as "1 = butter," "2 = bread," "3 = water," and so on. The first step in Apriori is to count up the frequencies (i.e., the supports)

Raw Transaction Data

Transaction No	SKUs (Item No)
1	1, 2, 3, 4
1	2, 3, 4
1	2, 3
1	1, 2, 4
1	1, 2, 3, 4
1	2, 4

One-Item Itemsets

Itemset (SKUs)	Support
1	3
2	6
3	4
4	5

Two-Item Itemsets

Itemset (SKUs)	Support
1, 2	3
1, 3	2
1, 4	3
2, 3	4
2, 4	5
3, 4	3

Three-Item Itemsets

Itemset (SKUs)	Support
1, 2, 4	3
2, 3, 4	3

FIGURE 5.13   Identification of Frequent Itemsets in Apriori Algorithm

of each item (one-item itemsets). For this overly simplified example, let us set the minimum support to 3 (or 50%; meaning an itemset is considered to be a frequent itemset if it shows up in at least 3 out of 6 transactions in the database). Because all of the one-item itemsets have at least 3 in the support column, they are all considered frequent itemsets. However, had any of the one-item itemsets not been frequent, they would not have been included as a possible member of possible two-item pairs. In this way, Apriori *prunes* the tree of all possible itemsets. As Figure 5.13 shows, using one-item itemsets, all possible two-item itemsets are generated and the transaction database is used to calculate their support values. Because the two-item itemset {1, 3} has a support less than 3, it should not be included in the frequent itemsets that will be used to generate the next-level itemsets (three-item itemsets). The algorithm seems deceivingly simple, but only for small datasets. In much larger datasets, especially those with huge amounts of items present in low quantities and small amounts of items present in big quantities, the search and calculation become a computationally intensive process.

Section 5.5 Review Questions

1. Identify at least three of the main data mining methods.
2. Give examples of situations in which classification would be an appropriate data mining technique. Give examples of situations in which regression would be an appropriate data mining technique.
3. List and briefly define at least two classification techniques.
4. What are some of the criteria for comparing and selecting the best classification technique?
5. Briefly describe the general algorithm used in decision trees.
6. Define *Gini index*. What does it measure?
7. Give examples of situations in which cluster analysis would be an appropriate data mining technique.
8. What is the major difference between cluster analysis and classification?
9. What are some of the methods for cluster analysis?
10. Give examples of situations in which association would be an appropriate data mining technique.

5.6 DATA MINING SOFTWARE TOOLS

Many software vendors provide powerful data mining tools. Examples of these vendors include SPSS (PASW Modeler, formerly known as Clementine), SAS (Enterprise Miner), StatSoft (Statistica Data Miner), Salford (CART, MARS, TreeNet, RandomForest), Angoss (KnowledgeSTUDIO, KnowledgeSeeker), and Megaputer (PolyAnalyst). As can be seen, most of the more popular tools are developed by the largest statistical software companies (SPSS, SAS, and StatSoft). Most of the business intelligence tool vendors (e.g., IBM Cognos, Oracle Hyperion, SAP Business Objects, Microstrategy, Teradata, and Microsoft) also have some level of data mining capabilities integrated into their software offerings. These BI tools are still primarily focused on multidimensional modeling and data visualization and are not considered to be direct competitors of the data mining tool vendors.

In addition to these commercial tools, several open source and/or free data mining software tools are available online. Probably the most popular free (and open source) data mining tool is **Weka**, which is developed by a number of researchers from the University Waikato in New Zealand (the tool can be downloaded from **cs.waikato.ac.nz/ml/weka/**). Weka includes a large number of algorithms for different data mining tasks and has an intuitive user interface. Another recently released,

TABLE 5.6 Selected Data Mining Software

Product Name	Web Site (URL)
Clementine	spss.com/Clementine
Enterprise Miner	sas.com/technologies/bi/analytics/index.html
Statistica	statsoft.com/products/dataminer.htm
Intelligent Miner	ibm.com/software/data/iminer
PolyAnalyst	megaputer.com/polyanalyst.php
CART, MARS, TreeNet, RandomForest	salford-systems.com
Insightful Miner	insightful.com
XLMiner	xlminer.net
KXEN (Knowledge eXtraction ENgines)	kxen.com
GhostMiner	fqs.pl/ghostminer
Microsoft SQL Server Data Mining	microsoft.com/sqlserver/2008/data-mining.aspx
Knowledge Miner	knowledgeminer.net
Teradata Warehouse Miner	ncr.com/products/software/teradata_mining.htm
Oracle Data Mining (ODM)	otn.oracle.com/products/bi/9idmining.html
Fair Isaac Business Science	fairisaac.com/edm
DeltaMaster	bissantz.de
iData Analyzer	infoacumen.com
Orange Data Mining Tool	ailab.si/orange/
Zementis Predictive Analytics	zementis.com

free (for noncommercial use) data mining tool is **RapidMiner** (developed by Rapid-I; it can be downloaded from **rapid-i.com**). Its graphically enhanced user interface, employment of a rather large number of algorithms, and incorporation of a variety of data visualization features set it apart from the rest of the free tools. The main difference between commercial tools, such as Enterprise Miner, PASW, and Statistica, and free tools, such as Weka and RapidMiner, is computational efficiency. The same data mining task involving a rather large dataset may take a whole lot longer to complete with the free software, and in some cases it may not even be feasible (i.e., crashing due to the inefficient use of computer memory). Table 5.6 lists a few of the major products and their Web sites.

A suite of business intelligence capabilities that has become increasingly more popular for data mining studies is **Microsoft's SQL Server**, where data and the models are stored in the same relational database environment, making model management a considerably easier task. The **Microsoft Enterprise Consortium** serves as the worldwide source for access to Microsoft's SQL Server 2008 software suite for academic purposes—teaching and research. The consortium has been established to enable universities around the world to access enterprise technology without having to maintain the necessary hardware and software on their own campus. The consortium provides a wide range of business intelligence development tools (e.g., data mining, cube building, business reporting) as well as a number of large, realistic datasets from Sam's Club, Dillard's, and Tyson Foods. A screenshot that shows development of a decision tree for churn analysis in SQL Server 2008 Business Intelligence Development Suite is shown in Figure 5.14. The Microsoft Enterprise

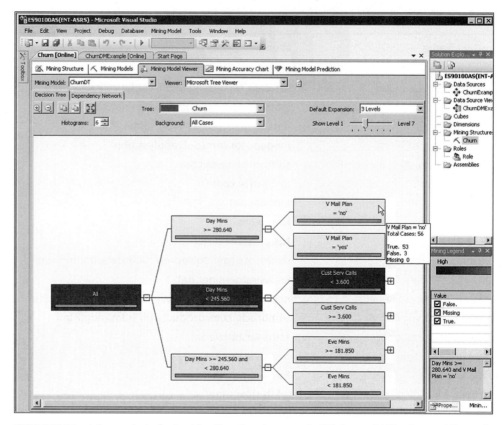

FIGURE 5.14 A Screenshot of a Decision Tree Development in SQL Server 2008 *Source:* Microsoft Enterprise Consortium and Microsoft SQL Server 2008.

Consortium is free of charge and can only be used for academic purposes. The Sam M. Walton College of Business at the University of Arkansas hosts the enterprise system and allows consortium members and their students to access these resources using a simple remote desktop connection. The details about becoming a part of the consortium along with easy-to-follow tutorials and examples can be found at **enterprise waltoncollege.uark.edu/mec/**.

A May 2009 survey by **kdnuggets.com** polled the data mining community on the following question: "What data mining tools have you used for a real project (not just for evaluation) in the past 6 months?" In order to make the results more representative, votes from tool vendors were removed. In previous years, there was a very strong correlation between the use of SPSS Clementine and SPSS Statistics as well as **SAS Enterprise Miner** and SAS Statistics, thus the votes for these two tool families were grouped together. In total, 364 unique votes were counted toward the rankings. The most popular tools were **SPSS PASW Modeler** (formerly Clementine), RapidMiner, SAS Enterprise Miner, and Microsoft Excel. Compared to poll results in previous years (see 2008 data at **kdnuggets.com/polls/2008/data-mining-software-tools-used.htm**), among commercial tools SPSS PASW Modeler, StatSoft Statistica, and SAS Enterprise Miner showed the most growth; among the free tools, RapidMiner and Orange showed the most growth. The results are shown in Figure 5.15.

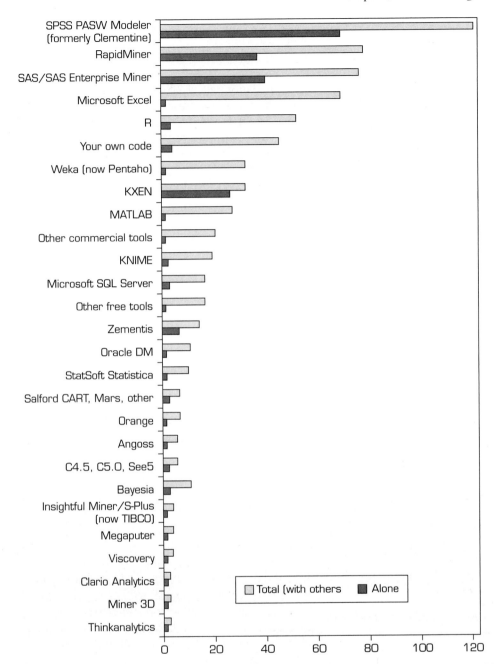

FIGURE 5.15 Popular Data Mining Software Tools (Poll Results) *Source:* Used with permission of **kdnuggets.com**.

APPLICATION CASE 5.7

Predicting Customer Churn—A Competition of Different Tools

In 2003, the Duke University/NCR Teradata Center sought to identify the best predictive modeling techniques to help manage a vexing problem for wireless telecommunications providers: customer churn. Although other industries are also faced with customers who defect to competitors, at the retail level, wireless customers switch service providers at a rate of about 25 percent per year, or 25 per month. In the early 1990s when new subscriber growth rates were in the 50 percent range, telecommunications companies were tempted to focus on new customer acquisition rather than on customer retention. However, in a new era of slower growth rates—as low as 10 percent—it is becoming clear that customer retention is vital to overall profitability.

The key to customer retention is predicting which customers are most at risk of defecting to a competitor and offering the most valuable incentives to stay. To execute such a strategy effectively, one must be able to develop highly accurate predictions—churn scorecards—so that the retention effort is focused on the relevant customers.

The Data

The data were provided by a major wireless telecommunications company using its own customer records for the second half of 2001. Account summary data was provided for 100,000 customers who had been with the company for at least 6 months. To assist in the modeling process, churners (those who left the company by the end of the following 60 days) were oversampled so that one-half of the sample consisted of churners and the other half were customers remaining with the company at least another 60 days. A broad range of 171 potential predictors was made available, spanning all the types of data a typical service provider would routinely have. Predictor data included:

- *Demographics:* Age, location, number and ages of children, etc.
- *Financials:* Credit score, credit card ownership
- *Product details:* Handset price, handset capabilities, etc.
- *Phone usage:* Number and duration of various categories of calls, etc.

Evaluation Criteria

The data were provided to support predictive modeling development. Participants (a mix of data mining software companies, university research centers, other non-profits and consultancy companies)

were asked to use their best models to predict the probability of churn for two different groups of customers: a "current" sample of 51,306 drawn from the latter half of 2001 and a "future" sample of 100,462 customers drawn from the first quarter of 2002. Predicting "future" data is generally considered more difficult because external factors and behavioral patterns may change over time. In the real world, predictive models are always applied to future data, and the tournament organizers wanted to reproduce a similar context.

Each contestant in the tournament was asked to rank the current and future score samples in descending order by probability of churn. Using the actual churn status available to the tournament organizers, two performance measures were calculated for each predictive model: the overall Gini index and the lift in the top decile. The two measures were calculated for the two samples, current and future, so that there were four performance scores available for every contestant. Evaluation criteria are described in detail in a number of locations, including the tournament Web site. The top-decile lift is the easiest to explain: It measures the number of actual churners captured among the customers ranked most likely to churn by a model.

The Results

Contestants were free to develop a separate model for each measure if they wished to try to optimize their models both to either the time period, the evaluation criterion, or both. Salford Systems was declared the winner in all categories. Salford Systems used its TreeNet software to create the model. TreeNet is an innovative form of boosted decision tree analysis that is well known for building accurate classification models. Across all the entries, the judges found that decision trees and logistic regression methods were generally the best at predicting churn, though they acknowledged that not all methodologies were adequately represented in the competition.

Salford's TreeNet models captured the most churners across the board and discovered which of the 171 possible variables were most important for predicting churn. In the top 10 percent of customers, TreeNet found 35 to 45 percent more churners than the competition average, and three times more than would be found in a random sample. For companies with large subscriber bases, this could translate to the identification of thousands more potential churners each month. Targeting these customers with an appropriate retention campaign could save a company millions of dollars each year.

Sources: Salford Systems, "The Duke/NCR Teradata Churn Modeling Tournament," **salford-systems.com/churn.php** (accessed April 20, 2009); and W. Yu, D. N. Jutla, and S. C. Sivakumar, "A Churn-Strategy Alignment Model for Managers in Mobile Telecom," *Proceedings of the Communication Networks and Services Research Conference*, IEEE Publications, 2005, pp. 48–53.

Section 5.6 Review Questions

1. What are the most popular commercial data mining tools?
2. Why do you think the most popular tools are developed by statistics companies?
3. What are the most popular free data mining tools?
4. What are the main differences between commercial and free data mining software tools?
5. What would be your top five selection criteria for a data mining tool? Explain.

5.7 DATA MINING MYTHS AND BLUNDERS

Data mining is a powerful analytical tool that enables business executives to advance from describing the nature of the past to predicting the future. It helps marketers find patterns that unlock the mysteries of customer behavior. The results of data mining can be used to increase revenue, reduce expenses, identify fraud, and locate business opportunities, offering a whole new realm of competitive advantage. As an evolving and maturing field, data mining is often associated with a number of myths, including the following (Zaima, 2003):

Myth	Reality
Data mining provides instant, crystal-ball-like predictions.	Data mining is a multistep process that requires deliberate, proactive design and use.
Data mining is not yet viable for business applications.	The current state-of-the-art is ready to go for almost any business.
Data mining requires a separate, dedicated database.	Because of advances in database technology, a dedicated database is not required, even though it may be desirable.
Only those with advanced degrees can do data mining.	Newer Web-based tools enable managers of all educational levels to do data mining.
Data mining is only for large firms that have lots of customer data.	If the data accurately reflect the business or its customers, a company can use data mining.

Data mining visionaries have gained enormous competitive advantage by understanding that these myths are just that: myths.

The following 10 data mining mistakes are often made in practice (Skalak, 2001; Shultz, 2004), and you should try to avoid them:

1. Selecting the wrong problem for data mining.
2. Ignoring what your sponsor thinks data mining is and what it really can and cannot do.

3. Leaving insufficient time for data preparation. It takes more effort than is generally understood.
4. Looking only at aggregated results and not at individual records. IBM's DB2 IMS can highlight individual records of interest.
5. Being sloppy about keeping track of the data mining procedure and results.
6. Ignoring suspicious findings and quickly moving on.
7. Running mining algorithms repeatedly and blindly. It is important to think hard about the next stage of data analysis. Data mining is a very hands-on activity.
8. Believing everything you are told about the data.
9. Believing everything you are told about your own data mining analysis.
10. Measuring your results differently from the way your sponsor measures them.

Section 5.7 Review Questions

1. What are the most common myths about data mining?
2. What do you think are the reasons for these myths about data mining?
3. What are the most common data mining mistakes? How can they be minimized and/or eliminated?

Chapter Highlights

- Data mining is the process of discovering new knowledge from databases.
- Data mining can use simple flat files as data sources or it can be performed on data in data warehouses.
- There are many alternative names and definitions for data mining.
- Data mining is at the intersection of many disciplines, including statistics, artificial intelligence, and mathematical modeling.
- Companies use data mining to better understand their customers and optimize their operations.
- Data mining applications can be found in virtually every area of business and government, including health care, finance, marketing, and homeland security.
- Three broad categories of data mining tasks are prediction (classification or regression), clustering, and association.
- Similar to other information systems initiatives, a data mining project must follow a systematic project management process to be successful.
- Several data mining processes have been proposed: CRISP-DM, SEMMA, KDD, etc.
- CRISP-DM provides a systematic and orderly way to conduct data mining projects.
- The earlier steps in data mining projects (i.e., understanding the domain and the relevant data)

consume most of the total project time (often more than 80% of the total time).
- Data preprocessing is essential to any successful data mining study. Good data leads to good information; good information leads to good decisions.
- Data preprocessing includes four main steps: data consolidation, data cleaning, data transformation, and data reduction.
- Classification methods learn from previous examples containing inputs and the resulting class labels, and once properly trained they are able to classify future cases.
- Clustering partitions pattern records into natural segments or clusters. Each segment's members share similar characteristics.
- Data mining can be hypothesis driven or discovery driven. Hypothesis-driven data mining begins with a proposition by the user. Discovery-driven data mining is a more open-ended expedition.
- A number of different algorithms are commonly used for classification. Commercial implementations include ID3, C4.5, C5, CART, and SPRINT.
- Decision trees partition data by branching along different attributes so that each leaf node has all the patterns of one class.
- The Gini index and information gain (entropy) are two popular ways to determine branching choices in a decision tree.

- The Gini index measures the purity of a sample. If everything in a sample belongs to one class, the Gini index value is zero.
- Several assessment techniques can measure the prediction accuracy of classification models, including simple split, *k*-fold cross-validation, bootstrapping, and area under the ROC curve.
- Cluster algorithms are used when the data records do not have predefined class identifiers (i.e., it is not known to what class a particular record belongs).
- Cluster algorithms compute measures of similarity in order to group similar cases into clusters.
- The most commonly used similarity measure in cluster analysis is a distance measure.
- The most commonly used clustering algorithms are *k*-means and self-organizing maps.

- Association rule mining is used to discover two or more items (or events or concepts) that go together.
- Association rule mining is commonly referred to as market-basket analysis.
- The most commonly used association algorithm is Apriori, whereby frequent itemsets are identified through a bottom-up approach.
- Association rules are assessed based on their support and confidence measures.
- Many commercial and free data mining tools are available.
- The most popular commercial data mining tools are SPSS PASW and SAS Enterprise Miner.
- The most popular free data mining tools are Weka and RapidMiner.

Key Terms

Apriori algorithm *227*	decision tree *220*	*k*-fold cross-validation *218*	prediction *201*
area under the ROC curve *219*	discovery-driven data mining *204*	knowledge discovery in databases (KDD) *215*	RapidMiner *229*
association *203*	distance measure *225*	link analysis *203*	ratio data *198*
bootstrapping *219*	entropy *222*	Microsoft Enterprise Consortium 229	regression *216*
categorical data *198*	Gini index *221*	Microsoft SQL Server 229	SAS Enterprise Miner *230*
classification *201*	hypothesis-driven data mining *204*	nominal data *198*	SEMMA *214*
clustering *202*	information gain *221*	numeric data *198*	sequence mining *203*
confidence *226*	interval data *198*	ordinal data *198*	simple split *217*
CRISP-DM *207*			SPSS PASW Modeler *230*
data mining *196*			support *226*
			Weka *228*

Questions for Discussion

1. Define *data mining*. Why are there many names and definitions for data mining?
2. What are the main reasons for the recent popularity of data mining?
3. Discuss what an organization should consider before making a decision to purchase data mining software.
4. Distinguish data mining from other analytical tools and techniques.
5. Discuss the main data mining methods. What are the fundamental differences among them?
6. What are the main data mining application areas? Discuss the commonalities of these areas that make them a prospect for data mining studies.
7. Why do we need a standardized data mining process? What are the most commonly used data mining processes?

8. Discuss the differences between the two most commonly used data mining process.
9. Are data mining processes a mere sequential set of activities?
10. Why do we need data preprocessing? What are the main tasks and relevant techniques used in data preprocessing?
11. Discuss the reasoning behind the assessment of classification models.
12. What is the main difference between classification and clustering? Explain using concrete examples.
13. Moving beyond the chapter discussion, where else can association be used?
14. What are the most common myths and mistakes about data mining?

Exercises

TERADATA STUDENT NETWORK (TSN) AND OTHER HANDS-ON EXERCISES

1. Visit **teradatastudentnetwork.com**. Identify cases about data mining. Describe recent developments in the field.

2. Go to **teradatastudentnetwork.com** or a URL provided by your instructor. Locate Web seminars related to data mining. In particular, locate a seminar given by C. Imhoff and T. Zouqes. Watch the Web seminar. Then answer the following questions:

   a. What are some of the interesting applications of data mining?

   b. What types of payoffs and costs can organizations expect from data mining initiatives?

3. For this exercise, your goal is to build a model to identify inputs or predictors that differentiate risky customers from others (based on patterns pertaining to previous customers) and then use those inputs to predict new risky customers. This sample case is typical for this domain.

   The sample data to be used in this exercise are in Online File W5.1 in the file **CreditRisk.xlsx**. The dataset has 425 cases and 15 variables pertaining to past and current customers who have borrowed from a bank for various reasons. The dataset contains customer-related information such as financial standing, reason for the loan, employment, demographic information, and the outcome or dependent variable for credit standing, classifying each case as good or bad, based on the institution's past experience.

   Take 400 of the cases as training cases and set aside the other 25 for testing. Build a decision tree model to learn the characteristics of the problem. Test its performance on the other 25 cases. Report on your model's learning and testing performance. Prepare a report that identifies the decision tree model and training parameters, as well as the resulting performance on the test set. Use any decision tree software. (This exercise is courtesy of StatSoft, Inc., based on a German dataset from **ftp.ics.uci.edu/pub/machine-learning-databases/statlog/german** renamed CreditRisk and altered.)

4. For this exercise, you will replicate (on a smaller scale) the box-office prediction modeling explained in the opening vignette. Download the training dataset from Online File W5.2, **MovieTrain.xlsx**, which has 184 records and is in Microsoft Excel format. Use the data description given in the opening vignette to understand the domain and the problem you are trying to solve. Pick and choose your independent variables. Develop at least three classification models (e.g., decision tree, logistic regression, neural networks). Compare the accuracy results using 10-fold cross-validation and percentage split techniques, use confusion matrices, and comment on the outcome. Test the models you have developed on the test set (see Online File W5.3, **MovieTest.xlsx,** 29 records). Analyze the results with different models and come up with the best classification model, supporting it with your results.

TEAM ASSIGNMENTS AND ROLE-PLAYING

1. Examine how new data-capture devices such as radio frequency identification (RFID) tags help organizations accurately identify and segment their customers for activities such as targeted marketing. Many of these applications involve data mining. Scan the literature and the Web and then propose five potential new data mining applications of RFID technology. What issues could arise if a country's laws required such devices to be embedded in everyone's body for a national identification system?

2. Interview administrators in your college or executives in your organization to determine how data warehousing, data mining, OLAP, and visualization BI/DSS tools could assist them in their work. Write a proposal describing your findings. Include cost estimates and benefits in your report.

3. A very good repository of data that has been used to test the performance of many machine-learning algorithms is available at **ics.uci.edu/~mlearn/ MLRepository.html**. Some of the datasets are meant to test the limits of current machine-learning algorithms and to compare their performance with new approaches to learning. However, some of the smaller datasets can be useful for exploring the functionality of any data mining software or the software that is available as companion software with this book, such as Statistica Data Miner. Download at least one dataset from this repository (e.g., Credit Screening Databases, Housing Database) and apply decision tree or clustering methods, as appropriate. Prepare a report based on your results. (Some of these exercises may even be proposed as semester-long projects for term papers, for example.)

4. Consider the following dataset, which includes three attributes and a classification for admission decisions into an MBA program:

GMAT	GPA	Quantitative GMAT Score (percentile)	Decision
650	2.75	35	No
580	3.50	70	No
600	3.50	75	Yes
450	2.95	80	No
700	3.25	90	Yes
590	3.50	80	Yes
400	3.85	45	No
640	3.50	75	Yes
540	3.00	60	?
690	2.85	80	?
490	4.00	65	?

a. Using the data shown, develop your own manual expert rules for decision making.

b. Use the Gini index to build a decision tree. You can use manual calculations or a spreadsheet to perform the basic calculations.

c. Use an automated decision tree software program to build a tree for the same data.

INTERNET EXERCISES

1. Visit the AI Exploratorium at **cs.ualberta.ca/~aixplore/**. Click the Decision Tree link. Read the narrative on basketball game statistics. Examine the data and then build a decision tree. Report your impressions of the accuracy of this decision tree. Also, explore the effects of different algorithms.

2. Survey some data mining tools and vendors. Start with **fairisaac.com** and **egain.com**. Consult **dmreview .com** and identify some data mining products and service providers that are not mentioned in this chapter.

3. Find recent cases of successful data mining applications. Visit the Web sites of some data mining vendors and look for cases or success stories. Prepare a report summarizing five new case studies.

4. Go to vendor Web sites (especially those of SAS, SPSS, Cognos, Teradata, StatSoft, and Fair Isaac) and look at success stories for BI (OLAP and data mining) tools. What do the various success stories have in common? How do they differ?

5. Go to **statsoft.com**. Download at least three white papers on applications. Which of these applications may have used the data/text/Web mining techniques discussed in this chapter?

6. Go to **sas.com**. Download at least three white papers on applications. Which of these applications may have used the data/text/Web mining techniques discussed in this chapter?

7. Go to **spss.com**. Download at least three white papers on applications. Which of these applications may have used the data/text/Web mining techniques discussed in this chapter?

8. Go to **teradata.com**. Download at least three white papers on applications. Which of these applications may have used the data/text/Web mining techniques discussed in this chapter?

9. Go to **fairisaac.com**. Download at least three white papers on applications. Which of these applications may have used the data/text/Web mining techniques discussed in this chapter?

10. Go to **salfordsystems.com**. Download at least three white papers on applications. Which of these applications may have used the data/text/Web mining techniques discussed in this chapter?

11. Go to **rulequest.com**. Download at least three white papers on applications. Which of these applications may have used the data/text/Web mining techniques discussed in this chapter?

12. Go to **kdnuggets.com**. Explore the sections on applications as well as software. Find names of at least three additional packages for data mining and text mining.

END OF CHAPTER APPLICATION CASE

Data Mining Helps Develop Custom-Tailored Product Portfolios for Telecommunication Companies

Background

The consulting group argonauten360° helps businesses build and improve successful strategies for customer relationship management (CRM). The company uses Relevanz-Marketing to create value by facilitating dialogue with relevant customers. Its clients include, among many others, BMW, Allianz, Deutsche Bank, Gerling, and Coca-Cola.

The Problem

As a leading consulting company to the telecommunications industry (as well as others), argonauten360° applies effective advanced analytic technologies for client scoring, clustering, and life-time-value computations as a routine part of its daily work. The requirements for flexible and powerful analytic tools are demanding, because each project typically presents a new and specific set of circumstances, data scenarios, obstacles, and analytic challenges. Therefore, the existing toolset needed to be augmented with effective, cutting-edge, yet flexible, data mining capabilities. Another critical consideration was for the solution to yield quick return on investment. The solution had to be easy to apply, with a fast learning curve, so that analysts could quickly take ownership of even the most advanced analytic procedures.

The Solution

The company needed a unified, easy-to-use set of analytical tools with a wide range of modeling capabilities and straightforward deployment options. Having to learn different tools for different modeling tasks has significantly hindered the efficiency and effectiveness of the company's consultants, causing it to lean toward a unified solution environment with capabilities ranging from data access on any medium (e.g., databases, online data repositories, text documents, XML files) to deployment of sophisticated data mining solutions on a wide range of BI systems.

After 12 months of evaluating a wide range of data mining tools, the company chose Statistica Data Miner (by StatSoft, Inc.) because (according to company executives) it provided the ideal combination of features to satisfy most every analyst's needs and requirements with user-friendly interfaces.

An Example of an Innovative Project

In Europe, so-called "call-by-call" services are very popular with cell phone users as well as with regular phone users. Such plans have no (or very low) charges for basic service, but bill for the actual air time that is used. It is a very competitive business, and the success of the call-by-call telecommunications provider depends greatly on attractive per-minute calling rates. Rankings of those rates are widely published, and the key is to be ranked somewhere in the top-five lowest-cost providers while maintaining the best possible margins. Because of the competitive environment created by this situation, popular wisdom holds that "there is virtually no price elasticity in this market (to allow providers to charge even the smallest extra margin without losing customers); and even if such price elasticity existed, it certainly could not be predicted." However, the argonauten360° consultants analyzed the available data with Statistica's data mining tool and proved that popular wisdom is wrong! Indeed, their successful analyses won argonauten360° the business of a leading provider of call-by-call services.

The Analysis

The analysis was based on data describing minute-by-minute phone traffic. Specifically, the sale of minutes of airtime over a 1-year period was analyzed. To obtain the best possible discrimination, 20 ensembles of different types of models were developed for estimation purposes. Each model employed a regression-type mathematical representation function for predicting the long-term trends; individual models were then combined at a higher level meta-model. All specific time intervals (time "zones") were carefully modeled, identifying each zone with particular price sensitivity and competitive pressures.

Results After 2 Months

Prior to the application of the models derived via data mining, heuristic "expert-opinions" were used to forecast the expected volume of minutes (of airtime) for the following 2 months. By using Statistica Data Miner, the accuracy of these prognoses improved significantly, while the error rate was cut in half. Given the enormous volume of minute-to-minute calling traffic (airtime), this was deemed to be a dramatically pleasing result, thus providing clear proof for the efficacy and potential benefits of advanced analytic strategies when applied to problems of this type.

Implementing the Solution at the Customer Site

The call-by-call provider now uses this solution for predicting and simulating optimal cellular (airtime) rates. The system was installed by argonauten360° as a complete turn-key ("push-of-the-button") solution. Using this solution, the call-by-call provider can now predict with much greater accuracy the demand (for airtime) in a highly price-sensitive and competitive market and offer the "correct" rates, thus enjoying a key competitive advantage.

In a second phase, this system will be further improved with a "dashboard-like" system that automatically compares predictions with observed data. This system will ensure that, when necessary, argonauten360° can update the estimates of model parameters to adjust to the dynamic marketplace. Hence, without acquiring any analytic know-how, the call-by-call provider now has access to a reliable implementation of a sophisticated demand-forecasting and rate-simulation system—something previously considered impossible. This is an excellent example of a successful application of data mining technologies to help the company gain competitive advantage in a highly competitive business environment.

Questions for the Case

1. Why do you think that consulting companies are more likely to use data mining tools and techniques? What specific value proposition do they offer?
2. Why was it important for argonauten360° to employ a comprehensive tool that has all modeling capabilities?
3. What was the problem that argonauten360° helped solve for a call-by-call provider?
4. Can you think of other problems for telecommunication companies that are likely to be solved with data mining?

Source: StatSoft, "The German Consulting Company argonauten360° Uses Statistica Data Miner to Develop Effective Product Portfolios Custom-Tailored to Their Customers," **statsoft.com/company/success_stories/pdf/argonauten360. pdf** (accessed on May 25, 2009).

References

Bhandari, I., E. Colet, J. Parker, Z. Pines, R. Pratap, and K. Ramanujam. (1997). "Advanced Scout: Data Mining and Knowledge Discovery in NBA Data." *Data Mining and Knowledge Discovery,* Vol. 1, No. 1, pp. 121–125.

Buck, N. (December 2000/January 2001). "Eureka! Knowledge Discovery." *Software Magazine.*

Chan, P. K., W. Phan, A. Prodromidis, and S. Stolfo. (1999). "Distributed Data Mining in Credit Card Fraud Detection." *IEEE Intelligent Systems,* Vol. 14, No. 6, pp. 67–74.

CRISP-DM. (2009). Cross-Industry Standard Process for Data Mining (CRISP-DM). **crisp-dm.org**.

Davenport, T. H. (2006, January). "Competing on Analytics." *Harvard Business Review.*

Delen, D., R. Sharda, and P. Kumar. (2007). "Movie Forecast Guru: A Web-based DSS for Hollywood Managers." *Decision Support Systems,* Vol. 43, No. 4, pp. 1151–1170.

Dunham, M. (2003). *Data Mining: Introductory and Advanced Topics.* Upper Saddle River, NJ: Prentice Hall.

Fayyad, U., G. Piatetsky-Shapiro, and P. Smyth. (1996). "From Knowledge Discovery in Databases." *AI Magazine,* Vol. 17, No. 3, pp. 37–54.

Hoffman, T. (1998, December 7). "Banks Turn to IT to Reclaim Most Profitable Customers." *Computerworld.*

Hoffman, T. (1999, April 19). "Insurers Mine for Age-Appropriate Offering." *Computerworld.*

Kohonen, T. (1982). "Self-organized Formation of Topologically Correct Feature Maps." *Biological Cybernetics,* Vol. 43, No. 1, pp. 59–69.

Nemati, H. R., and C. D. Barko. (2001). "Issues in Organizational Data Mining: A Survey of Current Practices." *Journal of Data Warehousing,* Vol. 6, No. 1, pp. 25–36.

Quinlan, J. R. (1986). "Induction of Decision Trees." *Machine Learning,* Vol. 1, pp. 81–106.

SEMMA. (2009). "SAS's Data Mining Process: Sample, Explore, Modify, Model, Assess." **sas.com/offices/europe/uk/technologies/analytics/datamining/miner/semma.html** (accessed August 2009).

Sharda, R., and Delen, D. (2006). "Predicting Box-office Success of Motion Pictures with Neural Networks." *Expert Systems with Applications,* Vol. 30, pp. 243–254.

Shultz, R. (2004, December 7). "Live from NCDM: Tales of Database Buffoonery." **directmag.com/news/ncdm-12-07-04/index.html** (accessed April 2009).

Skalak, D. (2001). "Data Mining Blunders Exposed!" *DB2 Magazine,* Vol. 6, No. 2, pp. 10–13.

StatSoft. (2006). "Data Mining Techniques." **statsoft.com/textbook/stdatmin.html** (accessed August 2006).

Wilson, R., and R. Sharda. (1994). "Bankruptcy Prediction Using Neural Networks." *Decision Support Systems,* Vol. 11, pp. 545–557.

Zaima, A. (2003). "The Five Myths of Data Mining." *What Works: Best Practices in Business Intelligence and Data Warehousing,* Vol. 15, the Data Warehousing Institute, Chatsworth, CA, pp. 42–43.

Artificial Neural Networks for Data Mining

LEARNING OBJECTIVES

1 Understand the concept and definitions of artificial neural networks (ANN)

2 Know the similarities and differences between biological and artificial neural networks

3 Learn the different types of neural network architectures

4 Learn the advantages and limitations of ANN

5 Understand how backpropagation learning works in feedforward neural networks

6 Understand the step-by-step process of how to use neural networks

7 Appreciate the wide variety of applications of neural networks

Neural networks have emerged as advanced data mining tools in cases where other techniques may not produce satisfactory predictive models. As the term implies, neural networks have a biologically inspired modeling capability but are essentially statistical modeling tools. In this chapter, we study the basics of neural networks, different types of neural network architectures, some specific applications, and the process of implementing a neural network project.

6.1 Opening Vignette: Predicting Gambling Referenda with Neural Networks
6.2 Basic Concepts of Neural Networks
6.3 Learning in Artificial Neural Networks
6.4 Developing Neural Network–Based Systems
6.5 Illuminating the Black Box of ANN with Sensitivity Analysis
6.6 A Sample Neural Network Project
6.7 Other Popular Neural Networks Paradigms
6.8 Applications of Artificial Neural Networks

6.1   OPENING VIGNETTE: PREDICTING GAMBLING REFERENDA WITH NEURAL NETWORKS

Desperate for new income and employment opportunities, as well as the need to introduce resilience into the local economy, many communities now offer a variety of incentives for new tourism businesses. One example can be found in the strong support for the abolition of laws that prohibit gambling. A vast majority of the states have placed ballots to legalize different types of gambling, some of them more than once. Proponents of legalized gambling argue that the expansion of gambling-tourism can create significant positive long-term sociocultural (e.g., better living conditions, more leisure opportunities, stronger cultural identity) and economic benefits (improved job opportunities, more disposable income, increased tax revenue, and more) for many communities.

Although many consider legalized gambling to be vital to the regeneration and revitalization of inner cities and economically depressed areas, attempts to legalize gambling have generally been met with caution or resistance. The lack of support for legalization of gambling originates from both perceived and actual ethical concerns. Opponents of gambling argue that such activities defy religious beliefs and work ethics; invite political corruption, swindling, money laundering, and organized crime; erode traditional family and societal values and responsibilities; and instigate irresponsible behavior. In addition, gambling may produce negative fiscal externalities, such as increased state expenditures on public welfare and police protection. Local communities react to gambling via three methods: (1) by judicially prohibiting the activity through the court of law, (2) by judicially legalizing the activity and controlling it through regulatory licensing laws, and (3) by overlooking the politically controversial issue.

Despite the existence of substantial literature on gambling and lottery adoption, either from a behavioral standpoint or from a socioeconomic viewpoint, the literature on the prediction of gambling-ballot outcomes seems to be deficient. In order to fill this gap, Sirakaya et al. (2005) used artificial neural networks (ANN) to gain an in-depth understanding of the factors affecting both legalization and prohibition of gambling. Their results have been shown to be superior when compared to other forecasting techniques used in analyzing gambling-related datasets.

In order to identify factors that may have an effect on determining a gambling ballot outcome, the researchers studied previously conducted and published studies, interviewed experts in the gaming industry, and investigated the theoretical foundation developed with behavioral studies. After much deliberation, the variables potentially affecting voting behavior were consolidated and synthesized.

Data

The data for the study was collected using both primary and secondary data collection techniques. Primary data related to gambling ballot outcomes (yes/no votes on gambling propositions) were obtained from all 50 state-election offices. Secondary data was compiled from a variety of sources: county-level religious data containing information about the number of churches and church members; other county-level data, such as population estimates, age, personal income, ethnicity, gender, poverty level, and education, were extracted from the U.S. Census Bureau and state data centers. The dataset included 1,287 records, each representing a county's voting outcome from a past ballot. After going through variable identification and dimensional reduction analysis, the researchers settled on the following list of variables to be used in their ANN models:

- Ballot Type I (Gambling versus Wagering, a binary variable)
- Percent population voted (real-valued numeric variable)
- Medium family income (integer-valued numeric variable)
- Percent population church members (real-valued numeric variable)
- Percent population male (real-valued numeric variable)
- Poverty level (real-valued numeric variable)
- Unemployment rate (real-valued numeric variable)
- Percent population minority—non-White percentage (real-valued numeric variable)
- Percent population older than 45 (real-valued numeric variable)
- Metropolitan statistical area (yes/no, a binary variable)

The dependent variable was the *ballot outcome* having the values of yes (i.e., majority of the people in county said "yes" to legalized gambling) and no (i.e., majority of the people in county said "no" to legalized gambling).

Solution

The researchers chose to use a multilayered perceptron (MLP) neural network architecture (i.e., feedforward neural network with backpropagation learning algorithm) because of its reputation as an excellent predictor for this type of classification problem. Figure 6.1 shows the schematic representation of the neural network model structure used for the study. As Figure 6.1 illustrates, information flows from left to right in a feedforward neural network, starting from the input data and going through the weights of the hidden neurons, ultimately creating the output. At that moment, the output is compared against the actual outcome of the same event and the difference (error or delta) is propagated back to the network to adjust the neural weights (backpropagation learning) so that the next time the same or a similar event is presented to the network, the error will be smaller.

The following procedure was followed to develop the ANN model:

1. The data was validated for missing and null values. Records with missing and/or null values were removed from the dataset.
2. Records (rows) in the dataset were randomized among themselves in order to have a truly random dataset where any part of the dataset would represent the behavior of the whole dataset.
3. The randomized dataset (1,287 records) was split into three separate data files: (1) training data, (2) cross-validation data, and (3) testing data. Because the records were randomized before the splitting, it is safe to say that each dataset represented the general behavior of the model individually. A common practice is to split a dataset into three parts using the following percentages: 60 percent for training (773 observations), 20 percent for cross-validation (257 observations), and 20 percent for testing (257 observations). To optimize the predictive power of the neural network model, both the cross-validation and the training

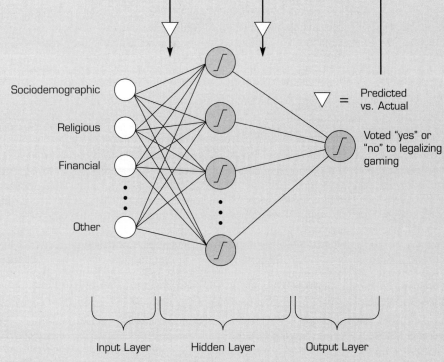

FIGURE 6.1 Schematic Representation of the Neural Network Model

datasets were used simultaneously. Once the predictive power of the training model reached the optimal level, the neural network weights were saved for the testing data.

4. Sensitivity analysis was performed to determine the cause-and-effect relationship between the inputs and outputs of a trained neural network model.

Results

The purpose of this study was to develop and test models that can be used as predictors of community support, or lack thereof, for commercial gaming. Specifically, the study examined the role of the factors that contribute to legalization and/or probation of gambling activities using artificial neural networks. Model-1 (predicting "no" votes) correctly predicted 201 out of 257 counties that would vote against gaming. Model-2 (predicting "yes" votes) correctly predicted 198 out of 257 counties that would vote for gaming.

On average, the ANN model predicted the voting outcome with 82 percent accuracy (correctly predicting four out of every five counties) on the test dataset (data that the ANN has not seen during model building process). Using sensitivity analysis on the trained neural network model, the researchers identified the most important variables in predicting gaming ballot outcomes. The most dominant variables were the county's religious inclination (i.e., percent church membership), the county's ethnic diversity (i.e., percent minority), and whether the county was classified as a Metropolitan Statistical Area (MSA) by the U.S. Census. Contrary to conventional wisdom, a county's financial characteristics (i.e., medium family income, poverty level, unemployment rate) and age distribution (i.e., percentage over 45) were not found to be significant factors in determining ballot outcomes.

Policy makers and the gaming industry could use the findings of this study (and/or similar studies) to predict which communities will pass a gambling initiative and which will strongly oppose it. The factors identified can be used as predictors for targeting those communities with high acceptance probabilities so as to effectively utilize resources to promote gambling and to avoid potential conflicts that may arise between the gaming industry and communities.

Questions for the Opening Vignette

1. Why is it important to study public opinion toward legalized gambling?
2. What factors might be used to predict public opinion toward gaming/gambling activities? Can you think of factors that are not mentioned in this case study?
3. What are the potential benefits and shortcomings of gaming/gambling for a county?
4. Why do you think ANN excels in analyzing this type of social choice problem?
5. What were the outcomes of the study? Who can use these results? How can the results be used?
6. Search the Internet to locate two additional cases that use ANN to predict public opinion.

What We Can Learn from This Vignette

As you will see in this chapter, neural networks can be applied in a wide range of areas, from standard business problems of assessing customer needs to understanding and enhancing security to improving health care and medicine. This vignette illustrates an innovative application of neural networks to predict public opinion, which most experts believe is an unpredictable phenomenon. In fact, conventional wisdom suggests that predicting the outcome of a public opinion poll is a hopeless effort, and the accuracy of such a model would not be any better than flipping a coin (i.e., random chance). However, the vignette shows that if ample effort is put forth to identify the potential factors there is very little (if anything) that cannot be predicted and analyzed with data mining techniques in general and neural networks in particular. As illustrated in the vignette, artificial neural network are not only good at predicting the outcome of complex social events, but they also are capable of revealing the underlying dynamics.

Sources: E. Sirakaya, D. Delen, and H-S. Choi, "Forecasting Gaming Referenda," *Annals of Tourism Research,* Vol. 32, No. 1, 2005, pp. 127–149; D. Delen and E. Sirakaya, "Determining the Efficacy of Data-Mining Methods in Predicting Gaming Ballot Outcomes," *Journal of Hospitality & Tourism Research,* Vol. 30, No. 3, 2006, pp. 313–332.

6.2 BASIC CONCEPTS OF NEURAL NETWORKS

Neural networks represent a brain metaphor for information processing. These models are biologically inspired rather than an exact replica of how the brain actually functions. Neural networks have been shown to be very promising systems in many forecasting and business classification applications due to their ability to "learn" from the data, their nonparametric nature (i.e., no rigid assumptions), and their ability to generalize. **Neural computing** refers to a pattern-recognition methodology for machine learning. The resulting model from neural computing is often called an **artificial neural network (ANN)** or a **neural network**. Neural networks have been used in many business applications for pattern recognition, forecasting, prediction, and classification. Neural network computing is a key component of any data mining tool kit. Applications of neural networks abound in finance, marketing, manufacturing, operations, information systems, and so on. Therefore, we devote this chapter to developing a better understanding of neural network models, methods, and applications.

The human brain possesses bewildering capabilities for information processing and problem solving that modern computers cannot compete with in many aspects. It has been postulated that a model or a system that is enlightened and supported by the results from brain research, with a structure similar to that of biological neural networks, could exhibit similar intelligent functionality. Based on this bottom-up approach, ANN (also known as *connectionist models, parallel distributed processing models, neuromorphic systems,* or simply *neural networks*) have been developed as biologically inspired and plausible models for various tasks.

Biological neural networks are composed of many massively interconnected **neurons**. Each neuron possesses **axons** and **dendrites**, fingerlike projections that enable the neuron to communicate with its neighboring neurons by transmitting and receiving electrical and chemical signals. More or less resembling the structure of their biological counterparts, ANN are composed of interconnected, simple processing elements called artificial neurons. When processing information, the processing elements in an ANN operate concurrently and collectively, similar to biological neurons. ANN possess some desirable traits similar to those of biological neural networks, such as the abilities to learn, to self-organize, and to support fault tolerance.

Coming along a winding journey, ANN have been investigated by researchers for more than half a century. The formal study of ANN began with the pioneering work of McCulloch and Pitts in 1943. Inspired by the results of biological experiments and observations, McCulloch and Pitts (1943) introduced a simple model of a binary artificial neuron that captured some of the functions of biological neurons. Using information-processing machines to model the brain, McCulloch and Pitts built their neural network model using a large number of interconnected artificial binary neurons. From these beginnings, neural network research became quite popular in the late 1950s and early 1960s. After a thorough analysis of an early neural network model (called the **perceptron**, which used no hidden layer) as well as a pessimistic evaluation of the research potential by Minsky and Papert in 1969, interest in neural networks diminished.

During the past two decades, there has been an exciting resurgence in ANN studies due to the introduction of new network topologies, new activation functions, and new learning algorithms, as well as progress in neuroscience and cognitive science. Advances in theory and methodology have overcome many of the obstacles that hindered neural network research a few decades ago. Evidenced by the appealing results of numerous studies, neural networks are gaining in acceptance and popularity. In addition, the desirable features in neural information processing make neural networks attractive for solving complex problems. ANN have been applied to numerous complex problems in a variety of application settings. The successful use of neural network applications has inspired renewed interest from industry and business.

Biological and Artificial Neural Networks

The human brain is composed of special cells called *neurons*. These cells do not die and replenish when a person is injured (all other cells reproduce to replace themselves and then die). This phenomenon may explain why humans retain information for an extended period of time and start to lose it when they get old—as the brain cells gradually start to die. Information storage spans sets of neurons. The brain has anywhere from 50 billion to 150 billion neurons, of which there are more than 100 different kinds. Neurons are partitioned into groups called *networks*. Each network contains several thousand highly interconnected neurons. Thus, the brain can be viewed as a collection of neural networks.

The ability to learn and to react to changes in our environment requires intelligence. The brain and the central nervous system control thinking and intelligent behavior. People who suffer brain damage have difficulty learning and reacting to changing environments. Even so, undamaged parts of the brain can often compensate with new learning.

A portion of a network composed of two cells is shown in Figure 6.2. The cell itself includes a **nucleus** (the central processing portion of the neuron). To the left of cell 1, the dendrites provide input signals to the cell. To the right, the axon sends output signals to cell 2 via the axon terminals. These axon terminals merge with the dendrites of cell 2. Signals can be transmitted unchanged, or they can be altered by synapses. A **synapse** is able to increase or decrease the strength of the connection between neurons and cause excitation or inhibition of a subsequent neuron. This is how information is stored in the neural networks.

An ANN emulates a biological neural network. Neural computing actually uses a very limited set of concepts from biological neural systems (see Technology Insights 6.1). It is more of an analogy to the human brain than an accurate model of it. Neural concepts usually are implemented as software simulations of the massively parallel processes involved in processing interconnected elements (also called artificial neurons, or *neurodes*) in a network architecture. The artificial neuron receives inputs analogous to the electrochemical impulses that dendrites of biological neurons receive from other neurons. The output of the artificial neuron corresponds to signals sent from a biological neuron over its axon. These artificial signals can be changed by weights in a manner similar to the physical changes that occur in the synapses (see Figure 6.3).

Several ANN paradigms have been proposed for applications in a variety of problem domains. Perhaps the easiest way to differentiate among the various neural models is on the basis of how they structurally emulate the human brain, the way they process information, and how they learn to perform their designated tasks.

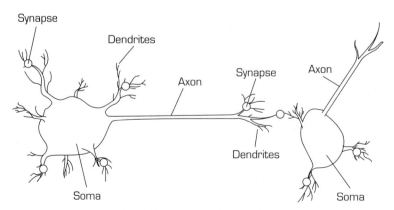

FIGURE 6.2 Portion of a Biological Neural Network: Two Interconnected Cells/Neurons

TECHNOLOGY INSIGHTS 6.1 **The Relationship Between Biological and Artificial Neural Networks**

The following list shows some of the relationships between biological and artificial networks.

Biological	Artificial
Soma	Node
Dendrites	Input
Axon	Output
Synapse	Weight
Slow	Fast
Many neurons (10^9)	Few neurons (a dozen to hundreds of thousands)

Sources: L. Medsker and J. Liebowitz, *Design and Development of Expert Systems and Neural Networks,* Macmillan, New York, 1994, p. 163; and F. Zahedi, *Intelligent Systems for Business: Expert Systems with Neural Networks,* Wadsworth, Belmont, CA, 1993.

Because they are biologically inspired, the main processing elements of a neural network are individual neurons, analogous to the brain's neurons. These artificial neurons receive the information from other neurons or external input stimuli, perform a transformation on the inputs, and then pass on the transformed information to other neurons or external outputs. This is similar to how it is presently thought that the human brain works. Passing information from neuron to neuron can be thought of as a way to activate, or trigger, a response from certain neurons based on the information or stimulus received.

Zahedi (1993) explored a dual role for ANN. One role is to borrow concepts from the biological world to improve the design of computers. ANN technology is used for complex information processing and machine intelligence. A second role is for neural networks to be used as simple biological models to test hypotheses about "real" biological neuronal information-processing systems. Of course, in the context of data mining and business analytics, we are interested in the use of neural networks for machine learning and information processing.

How information is processed by a neural network is inherently a function of its structure. Neural networks can have one or more layers of neurons. These neurons can be highly or fully interconnected, or only certain layers can be connected. Connections between neurons have an associated weight. In essence, the "knowledge" possessed by the network

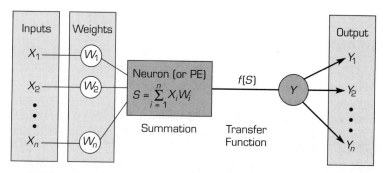

FIGURE 6.3 Processing Information in an Artificial Neuron

is encapsulated in these interconnection weights. Each neuron calculates a weighted sum of the incoming neuron values, transforms this input, and passes on its neural value as the input to subsequent neurons. Typically, although not always, this input/output transformation process at the individual neuron level is performed in a nonlinear fashion.

APPLICATION CASE 6.1

Neural Networks Help Reduce Telecommunications Fraud

The Forum of International Irregular Network Access (FIINA) estimates that telecommunications fraud results in a loss of $55 billion per year worldwide. South Africa's largest telecommunications operator was losing over $37 million per year to fraud. Subscription fraud—in which a customer provides fraudulent details or gives valid details and then disappears—was the company's biggest cause of revenue leakage. By the time the telecommunications provider is alerted to the fraud, the fraudster has already moved on to other victims. Other types of fraud include phone card manipulation, which involves tampering and cloning phone cards, and clip-on fraud, whereby a fraudster clips on to customers' telephone lines and then sell calls to overseas destinations for a fraction of normal rates.

Minotaur, developed by Neural Technologies (**neuralt.com**), was implemented to prevent fraud. Minotaur uses a hybrid mixture of intelligent systems and traditional computing techniques to provide customer subscription and real-time call-monitoring fraud detection. It processes data from numerous fields, such as event data records (e.g., switch/CDR, SS#7, IPDRs, PIN/authentication) and customer data (e.g., billing and payment, point of sale, provisioning), using a multistream analysis capacity. Frauds are detected on several levels, such as on an individual basis by using specific knowledge about the subscriber's usage, and on a global basis, using generic knowledge about subscriber usage and known fraud patterns.

Minotaur's neural capability means it learns from experience, making use of adaptive feedback to keep up-to-date with changing fraud patterns. A combination of call/network data and subscriber information is profiled and then processed using intelligent neural, rule-based, and case-based techniques. Probable frauds are identified, collected into cases, and tracked to completion by means of a powerful and flexible workflow-based operational process.

In the first 3 months following installation of Minotaur:

- The average fraud loss per case was reduced by 40 percent.
- Fraud detection time was reduced by 83 percent.
- The average time taken to analyze suspected fraud cases was reduced by 75 percent.
- The average detection hit rate was improved by 74 percent.

The combination of neural, rule-based, and case-based technologies provides a fraud detection rate superior to that of conventional systems. Furthermore, the multistream analysis capability makes it extremely accurate.

Sources: "Combating Fraud: How a Leading Telecom Company Solved a Growing Problem," **neuralt.com/iqs/dlsfa.list/dlcpti.7/downloads.html** (accessed February 2009); P. A. Estévez, M. H. Claudio, and C. A. Perez, "Prevention in Telecommunications Using Fuzzy Rules and Neural Networks," **cec.uchile.cl/~pestevez/RI0.pdf** (accessed May 2009).

Elements of ANN

A neural network is composed of **processing elements** that are organized in different ways to form the network's structure. The basic processing unit is the neuron. A number of neurons are then organized into a network. Neurons can be organized in a number of different ways; these various network patterns are referred to as *topologies*. One popular approach, known as the feedforward-backpropagation paradigm (or simply **backpropagation**), allows all neurons to link the output in one layer to the input of the next layer, but it does not allow any feedback linkage (Haykin, 2009). Backpropagation is the most commonly used network paradigm.

PROCESSING ELEMENTS   The processing elements (PE) of an ANN are artificial neurons. Each neuron receives inputs, processes them, and delivers a single output, as shown in Figure 6.3. The input can be raw input data or the output of other processing elements. The output can be the final result (e.g., 1 means yes, 0 means no), or it can be input to other neurons.

NETWORK STRUCTURE   Each ANN is composed of a collection of neurons that are grouped into layers. A typical structure is shown in Figure 6.4. Note the three layers: input, intermediate (called the hidden layer), and output. A **hidden layer** is a layer of neurons that takes input from the previous layer and converts those inputs into outputs for further processing. Several hidden layers can be placed between the input and output layers, although it is common to use only one hidden layer. In that case, the hidden layer simply converts inputs into a nonlinear combination and passes the transformed inputs to the output layer. The most common interpretation of the hidden layer is as a feature-extraction mechanism; that is, the hidden layer converts the original inputs in the problem into a higher-level combination of such inputs.

   Like a biological network, an ANN can be organized in several different ways (i.e., topologies or architectures); that is, the neurons can be interconnected in different ways. When information is processed, many of the processing elements perform their computations at the same time. This **parallel processing** resembles the way the brain works, and it differs from the serial processing of conventional computing.

Network Information Processing

Once the structure of a neural network is determined, information can be processed. We now present the major concepts related to network information processing.

INPUT   Each input corresponds to a single attribute. For example, if the problem is to decide on approval or disapproval of a loan, attributes could include the applicant's income level, age, and home ownership status. The numeric value, or representation, of an attribute is the input to the network. Several types of data, such as text, pictures, and voice, can be used as inputs. Preprocessing may be needed to convert the data into meaningful inputs from symbolic data or to scale the data.

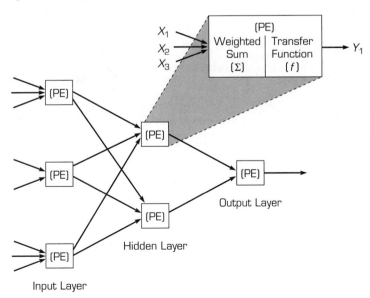

FIGURE 6.4   Neural Network with One Hidden Layer

OUTPUTS   The output of a network contains the solution to a problem. For example, in the case of a loan application, the output can be *yes* or *no*. The ANN assigns numeric values to the output, such as 1 for "yes" and 0 for "no." The purpose of the network is to compute the output values. Often, postprocessing of the output is required because some networks use two outputs: one for "yes" and another for "no." It is common to round the outputs to the nearest 0 or 1.

CONNECTION WEIGHTS   **Connection weights** are the key elements of an ANN. They express the relative strength (or mathematical value) of the input data or the many connections that transfer data from layer to layer. In other words, weights express the relative importance of each input to a processing element and, ultimately, the output. Weights are crucial in that they store learned patterns of information. It is through repeated adjustments of weights that a network learns.

SUMMATION FUNCTION   The **summation function** computes the weighted sums of all the input elements entering each processing element. A summation function multiplies each input value by its weight and totals the values for a weighted sum Y. The formula for n inputs in one processing element (see Figure 6.5a) is:

$$Y = \sum_{i=1}^{n} X_i W_i$$

For the *j*th neuron of several processing neurons in a layer (see Figure 6.5b), the formula is:

$$Y_j = \sum_{i=1}^{n} X_i W_{ij}$$

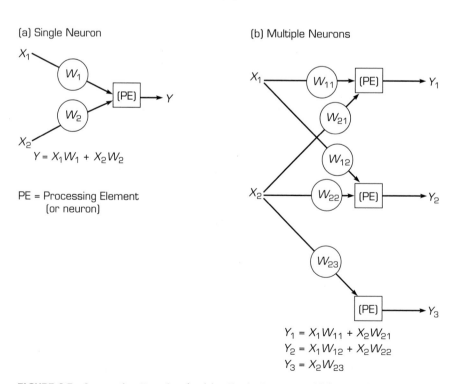

(a) Single Neuron

$$Y = X_1 W_1 + X_2 W_2$$

PE = Processing Element
(or neuron)

(b) Multiple Neurons

$$Y_1 = X_1 W_{11} + X_2 W_{21}$$
$$Y_2 = X_1 W_{12} + X_2 W_{22}$$
$$Y_3 = X_2 W_{23}$$

FIGURE 6.5   Summation Function for (a) a Single Neuron and (b) Several Neurons

TRANSFORMATION (TRANSFER) FUNCTION   The summation function computes the internal stimulation, or activation level, of the neuron. Based on this level, the neuron may or may not produce an output. The relationship between the internal activation level and the output can be linear or nonlinear. The relationship is expressed by one of several types of **transformation (transfer) functions**. The transformation function combines (i.e., adds up) the inputs coming into a neuron from other neurons/sources and then produces an output based on the transformation function. Selection of the specific function affects the network's operation. The **sigmoid (logical activation) function** (or *sigmoid transfer function*) is an S-shaped transfer function in the range of 0 to 1, and it is a popular as well as useful nonlinear transfer function:

$$Y_T = \frac{1}{\left(1 + e^{-Y}\right)}$$

where Y_T is the transformed (i.e., normalized) value of Y (see Figure 6.6).

The transformation modifies the output levels to reasonable values (typically between 0 and 1). This transformation is performed before the output reaches the next level. Without such a transformation, the value of the output becomes very large, especially when there are several layers of neurons. Sometimes a threshold value is used instead of a transformation function. A **threshold value** is a hurdle value for the output of a neuron to trigger the next level of neurons. If an output value is smaller than the threshold value, it will not be passed to the next level of neurons. For example, any value of 0.5 or less becomes 0, and any value above 0.5 becomes 1. A transformation can occur at the output of each processing element, or it can be performed only at the final output nodes.

HIDDEN LAYERS   Complex practical applications require one or more hidden layers between the input and output neurons and a correspondingly large number of weights. Many commercial ANN include three and sometimes up to five layers, with each containing 10 to 1,000 processing elements. Some experimental ANN use millions of processing elements. Because each layer increases the training effort exponentially and also increases the computation required, the use of more than three hidden layers is rare in most commercial systems.

Neural Network Architectures

There are several neural network architectures (models and/or algorithms; see Haykin, 2009). The most common ones include feedforward (with backpropagation), associative

Summation function: $Y = 3(0.2) + 1(0.4) + 2(0.1) = 1.2$

Transfer function: $Y_T = 1/(1 + e^{-1.2}) = 0.77$

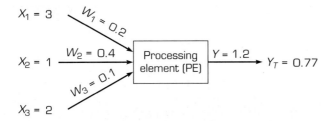

FIGURE 6.6   Example of ANN Transfer Function

memory, recurrent networks, Kohonen's self-organizing feature maps, and Hopfield networks. The feedforward network architecture (with backpropagation) is shown in Figure 6.4. Figure 6.7 shows a pictorial representation of a recurrent neural network architecture. Notice that in this architecture the connections are not unidirectional; there are many connections in every direction between the neurons, creating a chaotic-looking connection structure, which some experts believe better mimics the way biological neurons are structured in the human brain. Some of the other network architectures will be shown and briefly explained later in the chapter.

Ultimately, the architecture of a neural network model is driven by the task it is intended to address. For instance, neural network models have been used as classifiers, as forecasting tools, and as general optimizers. As shown later in this chapter, neural network classifiers are typically multilayer models in which information is passed from one layer to the next, with the ultimate goal of mapping an input to the network to a specific category, as identified by an output of the network. A neural model used as an optimizer, in contrast, can be a single layer of neurons, highly interconnected, and can compute neuron values iteratively until the model converges to a stable state. This stable state represents an optimal solution to the problem under analysis.

Finally, how a network is trained to perform its desired task is another identifying model characteristic. Neural network learning can occur in either a supervised or an unsupervised mode. With **supervised learning**, a sample training set is used to "teach" the network about its problem domain. This training set of exemplar cases (input and the desired output) is iteratively presented to the neural network. The output of the network in its present form is calculated and compared to the desired output. The **learning algorithm** is the training procedure that an ANN uses. The learning algorithm used determines how the neural interconnection weights are corrected due to differences in the actual and desired output for a member of the training set. Updating of the network's interconnection weights continues until the training algorithm's stopping criteria are met (e.g., all cases must be correctly classified within a certain tolerance level).

Alternatively, with **unsupervised learning** the network does not try to learn a target answer. Instead, the neural network learns a pattern through repeated exposures.

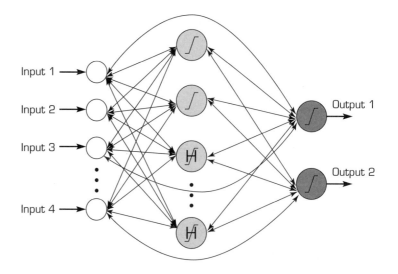

*H indicates a "hidden" neuron without a target output

FIGURE 6.7 A Recurrent Neural Network Architecture

This kind of learning can be envisioned as a neural network self-organizing or clustering its neurons related to the specific task.

Multilayer, feedforward neural networks are a class of models that show promise in classification and forecasting problems. As the name implies, these models structurally consist of multiple layers of neurons. Information is passed through the network in one direction, from the input layers of the network, through one or more hidden layers, toward the output layer of neurons. Neurons of each layer are connected only to the neurons of the subsequent layer.

Section 6.2 Review Questions

1. What is an ANN?
2. Explain the following terms: *neuron, axon,* and *synapse.*
3. How do weights function in an ANN?
4. What is the role of the summation function?
5. What is the role of the transformation function?

6.3 LEARNING IN ARTIFICIAL NEURAL NETWORKS

An important consideration in an ANN is the use of an appropriate learning algorithm (or training algorithm). Learning algorithms specify the process by which a neural network learns the underlying relationship between inputs and outputs, or just among the inputs. Hundreds of learning algorithms have been developed. ANN learning algorithms can also be classified as supervised and unsupervised (see Figure 6.8).

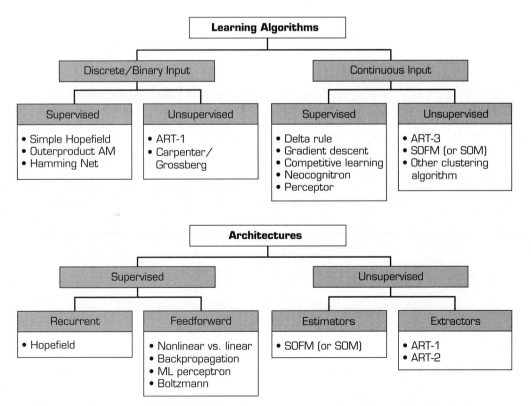

FIGURE 6.8 Taxonomy of ANN Learning Algorithms and Architectures *Source:* Based on L. Medsker and J. Liebowitz, *Design and Development of Expert Systems and Neural Computing,* Macmillan, New York, 1994, p. 166.

Supervised learning uses a set of inputs for which the appropriate (i.e., desired) outputs are known. For example, a dataset of loan applications with the success or failure of borrowers to repay their loans has a set of input parameters and presumed known outputs. With one type of supervised learning, the difference between the desired and actual outputs is used to correct the weights of the neural network. A variation of this approach simply acknowledges for each input trial whether the output is correct as the network adjusts weights in an attempt to achieve the correct results. Examples of this type of learning are backpropagation and the Hopfield network (Hopfield, 1982). Application Case 6.2 describes an application of supervised learning at Microsoft for improving the response rate of target mailings to potential customers.

APPLICATION CASE 6.2

Neural Networks Help Deliver Microsoft's Mail to the Intended Audience

Microsoft, the world leader in computer software, used BrainMaker neural network software from California Scientific (**calsci.com**) to maximize returns on direct mail. Every year, Microsoft sends approximately 40 million pieces of direct mail to 8.5 million registered customers, encouraging them to upgrade their software or to buy related products. Generally, the first mailing includes everyone in the database. The key is to direct the second mailing only to those who are most likely to respond.

Several variables were fed into the BrainMaker neural network to get productive results. The first step was to identify the variables that were relevant and to eliminate the variables that did not cause any effect. The following were some of the significant variables:

- *Recency.* Calculated in number of days, this is the last time a customer bought and registered a product. It is likely that the more recently a customer has bought something, the more likely it is that he or she will buy again the same or similar product.
- *First date to file.* This is the date of a customer's initial purchase and is a measure of loyalty. Chances are high that a customer will buy again if he or she has been loyal over time.
- *The number of products bought and registered.* This is the total number of products a customer has bought and registered.
- *The value of the products bought and registered.* This is calculated at the standard reselling price.

- *The number of days between the time the product came out and when it was purchased.* Research has shown that people who tend to buy things as soon as they are available are the key individuals to be reached.

Several other personal characteristics were also added and scored with yes/no responses.

Data was collected from seven or eight campaigns so that it was varied and represented all aspects of the business, including both Mac and Windows and high- and low-priced products. The customer-response information was converted to a format that the network could use, and yes/no responses were transformed to numeric data. Minimums and maximums were set on certain variables. Initially, the network was trained with 25 variables.

The neural network was tested on data from 20 different campaigns with known results not used during training. The results showed repeated and consistent savings. The use of BrainMaker to target customers on an average mailing resulted in a 35 percent cost savings for Microsoft. Before Microsoft began using BrainMaker, an average mailing had a response rate of 4.9 percent. With BrainMaker, the response rate to direct mailings increased to 8.2 percent.

Sources: California Scientific, "Maximize Returns on Direct Mail with BrainMaker Neural Networks Software," **calsci.com/ DirectMail.html** (accessed August 2009); and G. Piatesky-Shapiro, "ISR: Microsoft Success Using Neural Network for Direct Marketing," **kdnuggets.com/news/94/n9.txt** (accessed May 2009).

With unsupervised learning, only input stimuli are shown to the network. The network is **self-organizing**; that is, it organizes itself internally so that each hidden processing element responds strategically to a different set of input stimuli (or groups of stimuli). No knowledge is supplied about which classifications (i.e., outputs) are correct, and those that the network derives may or may not be meaningful to the network developer (this is useful for cluster analysis). However, the number of categories into which a network classifies the inputs can be controlled by setting model parameters. A person must examine the final categories to assign meaning and determine the usefulness of the results. Examples of this type of learning are **adaptive resonance theory (ART)** (i.e., a neural network architecture that is aimed at being brainlike in unsupervised mode) and Kohonen's self-organizing feature maps (i.e., neural network models for machine learning).

As mentioned earlier, many different and distinct neural network paradigms have been proposed for various decision-making domains. A neural model that has been shown appropriate for classification problems (e.g., bankruptcy prediction) is the feedforward multilayered perceptron. Multilayered networks have continuously valued neurons (i.e., processing elements), are trained in a supervised manner, and consist of one or more layers of nodes (i.e., hidden nodes) between the input and output nodes. A typical feedforward neural network is shown in Figure 6.4. Input nodes represent where information is presented to the network, output nodes provide the neural network's "decision," and the hidden nodes via the interconnection weights contain the proper mapping of inputs to outputs (i.e., decisions).

The backpropagation learning algorithm is the standard way of implementing supervised training of feedforward neural networks. It is an iterative gradient-descent technique designed to minimize an error function between the actual output of the network and its desired output, as specified in the training dataset. Adjustment of the interconnection weights, which contain the mapping function per se, starts at the output node where the error measure is initially calculated and is then propagated back through the layers of the network, toward the input layer. More details are included in the following section.

The General ANN Learning Process

In supervised learning, the learning process is inductive; that is, connection weights are derived from existing cases. The usual process of learning involves three tasks (see Figure 6.9):

1. Compute temporary outputs.
2. Compare outputs with desired targets.
3. Adjust the weights and repeat the process.

When existing outputs are available for comparison, the learning process starts by setting the connection weights. These are set via rules or at random. The difference between the actual output (Y or Y_T) and the desired output (Z) for a given set of inputs is an error called delta (in calculus, the Greek symbol delta, Δ, means "difference").

The objective is to minimize delta (i.e., reduce it to 0 if possible), which is done by adjusting the network's weights. The key is to change the weights in the right direction, making changes that reduce delta (i.e., error). We will show how this is done later.

Information processing with an ANN consists of attempting to recognize patterns of activities (i.e., pattern recognition). During the learning stages, the interconnection weights change in response to training data presented to the system.

Different ANN compute delta in different ways, depending on the learning algorithm being used. Hundreds of learning algorithms are available for various situations and configurations, some of which are discussed later in this chapter.

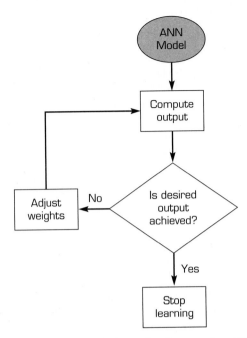

FIGURE 6.9 Supervised Learning Process of an ANN

How a Network Learns

Consider a single neuron that learns the inclusive OR operation—a classic problem in symbolic logic. The two input elements are X_1 and X_2. If either or both of them have a positive value, the result is also positive. This can be shown as follows:

	Inputs		
Case	X_1	X_2	**Desired Results**
1	0	0	0
2	0	1	1 (positive)
3	1	0	1 (positive)
4	1	1	1 (positive)

The neuron must be trained to recognize the input patterns and classify them to give the corresponding outputs. The procedure is to present the sequence of the four input patterns to the neuron so that the weights are adjusted after each iteration (using feedback of the error found by comparing the estimate to the desired result). This step is repeated until the weights converge to a uniform set of values that allows the neuron to classify each of the four inputs correctly. The results shown in Table 6.1 were produced in Excel. In this simple example, a threshold function is used to evaluate the summation of input values. After calculating outputs, a measure of the error (i.e., delta) between the output and the desired values is used to update the weights, subsequently reinforcing the correct results. At any step in the process, for a neuron j we have:

$$\text{delta} = Z_j - Y_j$$

TABLE 6.1 Example of Supervised Learning[a]

Step	X_1	X_2	Z	Initial Weights W_1	W_2	Y	Delta	Final Weights W_1	W_2
1	0	0	0	0.1	0.3	0	0.0	0.1	0.3
	0	1	1	0.1	0.3	0	1.0	0.1	0.5
	1	0	1	0.1	0.5	0	1.0	0.3	0.5
	1	1	1	0.3	0.5	1	0.0	0.3	0.5
2	0	0	0	0.3	0.5	0	0.0	0.3	0.5
	0	1	1	0.3	0.5	0	0.0	0.3	0.7
	1	0	1	0.3	0.7	0	1.0	0.5	0.7
	1	1	1	0.5	0.7	1	0.0	0.5	0.7
3	0	0	0	0.5	0.7	0	0.0	0.5	0.7
	0	1	1	0.5	0.7	1	0.0	0.5	0.7
	1	0	1	0.5	0.7	0	1.0	0.7	0.7
	1	1	1	0.7	0.7	1	0.0	0.7	0.7
4	0	0	0	0.7	0.7	0	0.0	0.7	0.7
	0	1	1	0.7	0.7	1	0.0	0.7	0.7
	1	0	1	0.7	0.7	1	0.0	0.7	0.7
	1	1	1	0.7	0.7	1	0.0	0.7	0.7

[a] Parameters: alpha = 0.2; threshold = 0.5; output is zero if the sum ($W_1 * X_1 + W_2 * X_2$) is not greater than 0.5.

where Z and Y are the desired and actual outputs, respectively. Then, the updated weights are:

$$W_i(\text{final}) = W_i(\text{initial}) + \text{alpha} \times \text{delta} \times X_i$$

where alpha is a parameter that controls how fast the learning takes place. This is called a **learning rate**. The choice of the learning rate parameter can have an impact on how fast (and how correctly) a neural network learns. A high value for the learning rate can lead to too much correction in the weight values, which causes the algorithm to just go back and forth among possible weight values, never reaching the optimal values, which may lie somewhere in between the endpoints. Too low a learning rate may slow the learning process and may lead to sub-optimal weight values. In practice, a neural network analyst will try many different learning rates to achieve the optimal learning.

Most implementations of the learning process also include a counterbalancing parameter called **momentum** to balance the learning rate. Essentially, whereas the purpose of the learning rate is to correct for the error, momentum is aimed at slowing the learning process. Many of the software programs available for neural networks can automatically select these parameters for the user or let the user experiment with many different combinations of such parameters.

As shown in Table 6.1, each calculation uses one of the X_1 and X_2 pairs and the corresponding value for the OR operation, along with the initial values, W_1 and W_2, of the neuron's weights. Initially, the weights are assigned random values, and the learning rate, alpha, is set low. Delta is used to derive the final weights, which then become the initial weights in the next iteration (i.e., row).

The initial values of weights for each input are transformed using the equation shown earlier to assign the values to the next input (i.e., row). The threshold value (0.5) sets the output Y to 1 in the next row if the weighted sum of inputs is greater than 0.5; otherwise, Y is set to 0. In the first step, two of the four outputs are incorrect (delta = 1), and a consistent set of weights has not been found. In subsequent steps, the learning algorithm improves the results until it finally produces a set of weights that give the correct results ($W_1 = W_2 = 0.7$ in step 4 of Table 6.1). Once determined, a neuron with these weights can quickly perform the OR operation.

In developing an ANN, an attempt is made to fit the problem characteristic to one of the known learning algorithms. Many variants of learning algorithms exist, but the core concepts behind all of them are similar.

Backpropagation

Backpropagation (short for *back-error propagation*) is the most widely used supervised learning algorithm in neural computing (Principe et al., 2000). It is very easy to implement. A backpropagation network includes one or more hidden layers. This type of network is considered feedforward because there are no interconnections between the output of a processing element and the input of a node in the same layer or in a preceding layer. Externally provided correct patterns are compared with the neural network's output during (supervised) training, and feedback is used to adjust the weights until the network has categorized all the training patterns as correctly as possible (the error tolerance is set in advance).

Starting with the output layer, errors between the actual and desired outputs are used to correct the weights for the connections to the previous layer (see Figure 6.10). For any output neuron j, the error (delta) = $(Z_j - Y_j)$ (df/dx), where Z and Y are the desired and actual outputs, respectively. Using the sigmoid function, $f = [1 + \exp(-x)]^{-1}$, where x is proportional to the sum of the weighted inputs to the neuron, is an effective way to compute the output of a neuron in practice. With this function, the derivative of the sigmoid function $df/dx = f(1 - f)$ and the error is a simple function of the desired and actual outputs. The factor $f(1 - f)$ is the logistic function, which serves to keep the error correction well bounded. The weights of each input to the jth neuron are then changed in proportion to this calculated error. A more complicated expression can be derived to work backward in a similar way from the output neurons through the hidden layers to calculate the corrections to the associated weights of the inner neurons. This complicated method is an iterative approach to solving a nonlinear optimization problem that is very similar in meaning to the one characterizing multiple-linear regression.

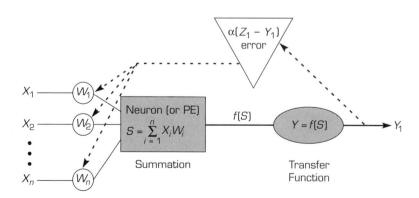

FIGURE 6.10 Backpropagation of Error for a Single Neuron

The learning algorithm includes the following procedures:

1. Initialize weights with random values and set other parameters.
2. Read in the input vector and the desired output.
3. Compute the actual output via the calculations, working forward through the layers.
4. Compute the error.
5. Change the weights by working backward from the output layer through the hidden layers.

This procedure is repeated for the entire set of input vectors until the desired output and the actual output agree within some predetermined tolerance. Given the calculation requirements for one iteration, a large network can take a very long time to train; therefore, in one variation, a set of cases is run forward and an aggregated error is fed backward to speed up learning. Sometimes, depending on the initial random weights and network parameters, the network does not converge to a satisfactory performance level. When this is the case, new random weights must be generated, and the network parameters, or even its structure, may have to be modified before another attempt is made. Current research is aimed at developing algorithms and using parallel computers to improve this process. For example, genetic algorithms (described in Chapter 13) can be used to guide the selection of the network parameters in order to maximize the desired output. In fact, most commercial ANN software tools are now using GA to help users "optimize" the network parameters.

Section 6.3 Review Questions

1. Briefly describe backpropagation.
2. What is the purpose of a threshold value in a learning algorithm?
3. What is the purpose of a learning rate and momentum?
4. How does error between actual and predicted outcomes affect the value of weights in neural networks?
5. Search the Internet to identify other learning algorithms for feedforward neural networks.

6.4 DEVELOPING NEURAL NETWORK–BASED SYSTEMS

Although the development process of ANN is similar to the structured design methodologies of traditional computer-based information systems, some phases are unique or have some unique aspects. In the process described here, we assume that the preliminary steps of system development, such as determining information requirements, conducting a feasibility analysis, and gaining a champion in top management for the project, have been completed successfully. Such steps are generic to any information system.

As shown in Figure 6.11, the development process for an ANN application includes nine steps. In step 1, the data to be used for training and testing the network are collected. Important considerations are that the particular problem is amenable to a neural network solution and that adequate data exist and can be obtained. In step 2, training data must be identified, and a plan must be made for testing the performance of the network.

In steps 3 and 4, a network architecture and a learning method are selected. The availability of a particular development tool or the capabilities of the development personnel may determine the type of neural network to be constructed. Also, certain problem types have demonstrated high success rates with certain configurations (e.g., multilayer feedforward neural networks for bankruptcy prediction, as described in the next section). Important considerations are the exact number of neurons and the number of layers. Some packages use genetic algorithms to select the network design.

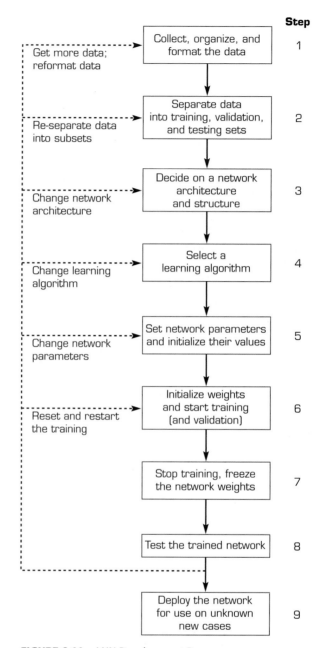

FIGURE 6.11 ANN Development Process

There are several parameters for tuning the network to the desired learning-performance level. Part of the process in step 5 is the initialization of the network weights and parameters, followed by the modification of the parameters as training-performance feedback is received. Often, the initial values are important in determining the efficiency and length of training. Some methods change the parameters during training to enhance performance.

Step 6 transforms the application data into the type and format required by the neural network. This may require writing software to preprocess the data or performing these operations directly in an ANN package. Data storage and manipulation techniques and processes must be designed for conveniently and efficiently retraining the neural network, when needed. The application data representation and ordering often influence the efficiency and possibly the accuracy of the results.

In steps 7 and 8, training and testing are conducted iteratively by presenting input and desired or known output data to the network. The network computes the outputs and adjusts the weights until the computed outputs are within an acceptable tolerance of the known outputs for the input cases. The desired outputs and their relationships to input data are derived from historical data (i.e., a portion of the data collected in step 1).

In step 9, a stable set of weights is obtained. Now the network can reproduce the desired outputs, given inputs such as those in the training set. The network is ready for use as a stand-alone system or as part of another software system where new input data will be presented to it and its output will be a recommended decision.

In the following sections, we examine these steps in more detail.

Data Collection and Preparation

The first two steps in the ANN development process involve collecting data and separating them into a training set and a testing set. The training cases are used to adjust the weights, and the testing cases are used for network validation. The data used for training and testing must include all the attributes that are useful for solving the problem. The system can only learn as much as the data can tell. Therefore, collection and preparation of data are the most critical steps in building a good system.

In general, the more data used the better. Larger datasets increase processing time during training but improve the accuracy of the training and often lead to faster convergence to a good set of weights. For a moderately sized dataset, typically 80 percent of the data are randomly selected for training and 20 percent are selected for testing. For small datasets, typically all the data are used for training and testing. For large datasets, a sufficiently large sample is taken and treated like a moderately sized dataset.

For example, say a bank wants to build a neural network–based system in order to use clients' financial data to determine whether they may go bankrupt. The bank needs to first identify what financial data may be used as inputs and how to obtain them. Five attributes may be useful inputs: (1) working capital/total assets, (2) retained earnings/total assets, (3) earnings before interest and taxes/total assets, (4) market value of equity/total debt, and (5) sales/total sales. The output is a binary variable: bankruptcy or not.

Selection of Network Structure

After the training and testing datasets are identified, the next step is to design the structure of the neural networks. This includes the selection of a **topology** and determination of (1) input nodes, (2) output nodes, (3) number of hidden layers, and (4) number of hidden nodes. The multilayer feedforward topology is often used in business applications, although other network models are beginning to find some business use as well.

The design of input nodes must be based on the attributes of the dataset. In the example of predicting bankruptcy, for example, the bank might choose a three-layer structure that includes one input layer, one output layer, and one hidden layer. The input layer contains five nodes, each of which is a variable, and the output layer contains a node with 0 for bankrupt and 1 for safe. Determining the number of hidden nodes is tricky. A few heuristics have been proposed, but none of them is unquestionably the best. A typical approach is to choose the average number of input and output nodes. In the previous case, the hidden node may be set to $(5 + 1)/2 = 3$. Figure 6.12 shows an MLP ANN structure for the box-office prediction problem.

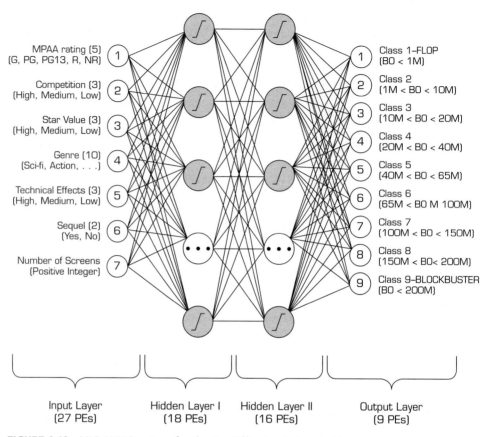

FIGURE 6.12   MLP ANN Structure for the Box-Office Prediction Problem

Learning Algorithm Selection

After the network structure is chosen, we need to find a learning algorithm to identify a set of connection weights that best cover the training data and have the best predictive accuracy. For the feedforward topology we chose for the bankruptcy-prediction problem, a typical approach is to use the backpropagation algorithm. Because many commercial packages are available on the market, there is no need to implement the learning algorithm by ourselves. Instead, we can choose a suitable commercial package to analyze the data. Technology Insights 6.2 summarizes information on the different types of neural network software packages that are available.

Network Training

Training of ANN is an iterative process that starts from a random set of weights and gradually enhances the fitness of the network model and the known dataset. The iteration continues until the error sum is converged to below a preset acceptable level. In the backpropagation algorithm, two parameters, learning rate and momentum, can be adjusted to control the speed of reaching a solution. These determine the ratio of the difference between the calculated value and the actual value of the training cases. Some software packages may have their own parameters in their learning heuristics to speed up the learning process. It is important to read carefully when using this type of software.

How are neural networks implemented in practice? After the analyst/developer has conducted enough tests to ascertain that a neural network can do a good job for the application, the network needs to be implemented in the existing systems. A number of

TECHNOLOGY INSIGHTS 6.2 ANN Software

Many tools are available for developing neural networks (see this book's Web site and the resource lists at PC AI, **pcai.com**). Some of these tools function like expert system shells. They provide a set of standard architectures, learning algorithms, and parameters, along with the ability to manipulate the data. Some development tools can support up to several dozen network paradigms and learning algorithms.

Neural network implementations are also available in most of the comprehensive data mining tools, such as the SAS Enterprise Miner, PASW Modeler (formerly Clementine), and Statistica Data Miner. Weka is an open source collection of machine-learning algorithms for data mining tasks, and it includes neural network capabilities. Weka can be downloaded from **cs.waikato.ac.nz/~ml/weka**. Statistica is available on a trial basis to adopters of this book.

Many specialized neural network tools enable the building and deployment of a neural network model in practice. Any listing of such tools would be incomplete. Online resources such as Wikipedia (**en.wikipedia.org/wiki/Artificial_neural_network**), Google's or Yahoo!'s software directory, and the vendor listings on **pcai.com** are good places to locate the latest information on neural network software vendors. Some of the vendors that have been around for a while and have reported industrial applications of their neural network software include California Scientific (BrainMaker), NeuralWare, NeuroDimension Inc., Ward Systems Group (Neuroshell), and Megaputer. Again, the list can never be complete.

Some ANN development tools are spreadsheet add-ins. Most can read spreadsheet, database, and text files. Some are freeware or shareware. Some ANN systems have been developed in Java to run directly on the Web and are accessible through a Web browser interface. Other ANN products are designed to interface with expert systems as hybrid development products.

Developers may instead prefer to use more general programming languages, such as C++, or a spreadsheet to program the model and perform the calculations. A variation on this is to use a library of ANN routines. For example, hav.Software (**hav.com**) provides a library of C++ classes for implementing stand-alone or embedded feedforward, simple recurrent, and random-order recurrent neural networks. Computational software such as MATLAB also includes neural network–specific libraries.

---

neural network shells can generate code in C++, Java, or Visual Basic that can be embedded in another system that can access source data or is called directly by a graphical user interface for deployment, independently of the development system. Or, after training an ANN in a development tool, given the weights, network structure, and transfer function, one can easily develop one's own implementation in a third-generation programming language such as C++. Most of the ANN development packages as well as data mining tools can generate such code. The code can then be embedded in a stand-alone application or in a Web server application.

Some data conversion may be necessary in the training process. This includes (1) changing the data format to meet the requirements of the software, (2) normalizing the data scale to make the data more comparable, and (3) removing problematic data. When the training dataset is ready, it is loaded into the package, and the learning procedure is executed. Depending on the number of nodes and the size of the training dataset, reaching a solution may take from a few thousand to millions of iterations.

Testing

Recall that in step 2 of the development process shown in Figure 6.11 the available data are divided into training and testing datasets. When the training has been completed, it is necessary to test the network. Testing (step 8) examines the performance of the derived network model by measuring its ability to classify the testing data correctly. **Black-box testing** (i.e., comparing test results to historical results) is the primary approach for verifying that inputs produce the appropriate outputs. Error terms can be used to compare results against known benchmark methods.

The network is generally not expected to perform perfectly (zero error is difficult, if not impossible, to attain), and only a certain level of accuracy is really required. For example, if 1 means nonbankrupt and 0 means bankrupt, then any output between 0.1 and 1 might indicate a certain likelihood of nonbankrupty. The neural network application is usually an alternative to another method that can be used as a benchmark against which to compare accuracy. For example, a statistical technique such as multiple regression or another quantitative method may be known to classify inputs correctly 50 percent of the time.

The neural network implementation often improves on this. For example, Liang (1992) reported that ANN performance was superior to the performance of multiple discriminant analysis and rule induction. Ainscough and Aronson (1999) investigated the application of neural network models in predicting retail sales, given a set of several inputs (e.g., regular price, various promotions). They compared their results to those of multiple regression and improved the adjusted R^2 (correlation coefficient) from .5 to .7. If the neural network is replacing manual operations, performance levels and speed of human processing can be the standard for deciding whether the testing phase is successful.

The test plan should include routine cases as well as potentially problematic situations. If the testing reveals large deviations, the training set must be reexamined, and the training process may have to be repeated (some "bad" data may have to be omitted from the input set).

Note that we cannot equate neural network results exactly with those found using statistical methods. For example, in stepwise linear regression, input variables are sometimes determined to be insignificant, but because of the nature of neural computing, a neural network uses them to attain higher levels of accuracy. When they are omitted from a neural network model, its performance typically suffers.

Implementation of an ANN

Implementation (i.e., deployment) of an ANN solution (step 9) often requires interfaces with other computer-based information systems and user training. Ongoing monitoring and feedback to the developers are recommended for system improvements and long-term success. It is also important to gain the confidence of users and management early in the deployment to ensure that the system is accepted and used properly.

Section 6.4 Review Questions

1. List the nine steps in conducting a neural network project.
2. What are some of the design parameters for developing a neural network?
3. Describe different types of neural network software available today.
4. How are neural networks implemented in practice when the training/testing is complete?
5. What parameters may need to be adjusted in the neural network training process?

6.5 ILLUMINATING THE BLACK BOX OF ANN WITH SENSITIVITY ANALYSIS

Neural networks have been used as an effective tool for solving highly complex real-world problems in a wide range of application areas. Even though ANN have been proven in many problem scenarios to be superior predictors and/or cluster identifiers (compared to their traditional counterparts), in some applications there exists an additional need to know "how it does what it does." ANN are typically thought of as black boxes, capable of solving complex problems but lacking the explanation of their capabilities. This phenomenon is commonly referred to as the "black-box" syndrome.

It is important to be able to explain a model's "inner being"; such an explanation offers assurance that the network has been properly trained and will behave as desired once deployed in a business intelligence environment. Such a need to "look under the hood" might be attributable to a relatively small training set (as a result of the high cost of data acquisition) or a very high liability in case of a system error. One example of such an application is the deployment of airbags in automobiles. Here, both the cost of data acquisition (crashing cars) and the liability concerns (danger to human lives) are rather significant. Another representative example for the importance of explanation is loan-application processing. If an applicant is refused for a loan, he or she has the right to know why. Having a prediction system that does a good job on differentiating good and bad applications may not be sufficient if it does not also provide the justification of its predictions.

A variety of techniques has been proposed for analysis and evaluation of trained neural networks. These techniques provide a clear interpretation of how a neural network does what it does; that is, specifically how (and to what extent) the individual inputs factor into the generation of specific network output. Sensitivity analysis has been the front runner of the techniques proposed for shedding light into the "black-box" characterization of trained neural networks.

Sensitivity analysis is a method for extracting the cause-and-effect relationships among the inputs and the outputs of a trained neural network model. In the process of performing sensitivity analysis, the trained neural network's learning capability is disabled so that the network weights are not affected. The basic procedure behind sensitivity analysis is that the inputs to the network are systematically perturbed within the allowable value ranges and the corresponding change in the output is recorded for each and every input variable (Principe et al., 2000). Figure 6.13 shows a graphical illustration of this process. The first input is varied between its mean plus-and-minus a user-defined number of standard deviations (or for categorical variables, all of its possible values are used) while all other input variables are fixed at their respective means (or modes). The network output is computed for a user-defined number of steps above and below the mean. This process is repeated for each input. As a result, a report is generated to summarize the variation of each output with respect to the variation in each input. The generated report often contains a column plot (along with numeric values presented on the x-axis), reporting the relative sensitivity values for each input variable. A representative example of sensitivity analysis on ANN models is provided in Application Case 6.3.

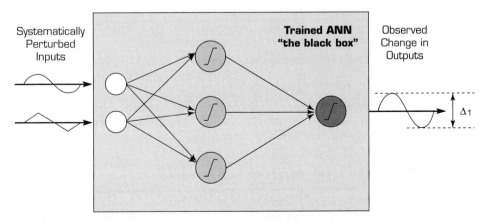

FIGURE 6.13　A Figurative Illustration of Sensitivity Analysis on an ANN Model

APPLICATION CASE 6.3

Sensitivity Analysis Reveals Injury Severity Factors in Traffic Accidents

According to the National Highway Traffic Safety Administration, over 6 million traffic accidents claim more than 41,000 lives each year in the United States. Causes of accidents and related injury severity are of special interest to traffic-safety researchers. Such research is aimed not only at reducing the number of accidents but also the severity of injury. One way to accomplish the latter is to identify the most profound factors that affect injury severity. Understanding the circumstances under which drivers and passengers are more likely to be severely injured (or killed) in an automobile accident can help improve the overall driving safety situation. Factors that potentially elevate the risk of injury severity of vehicle occupants in the event of an automotive accident include demographic and/or behavioral characteristics of the person (e.g., age, gender, seatbelt usage, use of drugs or alcohol while driving), environmental factors and/or roadway conditions at the time of the accident (e.g., surface conditions, weather or light conditions, the direction of impact, vehicle orientation in the crash, occurrence of a rollover), as well as technical characteristics of the vehicle itself (e.g., vehicle's age, body type).

In an exploratory data mining study, Delen et al. (2006) used a large sample of data—30,358 police-reported accident records obtained from the General Estimates System of the National Highway Traffic Safety Administration—to identify which factors become increasingly more important in escalating the probability of injury severity during a traffic crash. Accidents examined in this study included a geographically representative sample of multiple-vehicle collision accidents, single-vehicle fixed-object collisions, and single-vehicle noncollision (rollover) crashes.

Contrary to many of the previous studies conducted in this domain, which have primarily used regression-type generalized linear models where the functional relationships between injury severity and crash-related factors are assumed to be linear (which is an oversimplification of the reality in most real-world situations), Delen and his colleagues decided to go in a different direction. Because ANN are known to be superior in capturing highly nonlinear complex relationships between the predictor variables (crash factors) and the target variable (severity level of the injuries), they decided to use a series of ANN models to estimate the significance of the crash factors on the level of injury severity sustained by the driver.

From a methodological standpoint, they followed a two-step process. In the first step, they developed a series of prediction models (one for each injury severity level) to capture the in-depth relationships between the crash-related factors and a specific level of injury severity. In the second step, they conducted sensitivity analysis on the trained neural network models to identify the prioritized importance of crash-related factors as they relate to different injury severity levels. In the formulation of the study, the five-class prediction problem was decomposed into a number of binary classification models in order to obtain the granularity of information needed to identify the "true" cause-and-effect relationships between the crash-related factors and different levels of injury severity.

The results revealed considerable differences among the models built for different injury severity levels. This implies that the most influential factors in prediction models highly depend on the level of injury severity. For example, the study revealed that the variable seatbelt use was the most important determinant for predicting higher levels of injury severity (such as incapacitating injury or fatality), but it was one of the least significant predictors for lower levels of injury severity (such non-incapacitating injury and minor injury). Another interesting finding involved gender: The drivers' gender was among the significant predictors for lower levels of injury severity, but it was not among the significant factors for higher levels of injury severity, indicating that more serious injuries do not depend on the driver being a male or a female. Yet another interesting and somewhat intuitive finding of the study indicated that age becomes an increasingly more significant factor as the level of injury severity increases, implying that older people are more likely to incur severe injuries (and fatalities) in serious automobile crashes than younger people.

Source: D. Delen, R. Sharda, and M. Bessonov, "Identifying Significant Predictors of Injury Severity in Traffic Accidents Using a Series of Artificial Neural Networks," *Accident Analysis and Prevention*, Vol. 38, No. 3, 2006, pp. 434–444.

Review Questions for Section 6.5

1. What is the so-called "black-box" syndrome?
2. Why is it important to be able to explain an ANN's model structure?
3. How does sensitivity analysis work?
4. Search the Internet to find other ANN explanation methods.

6.6 A SAMPLE NEURAL NETWORK PROJECT

We next describe a typical application of neural networks to predict bankruptcy of companies using the same data and a similar experimental design as used by Wilson and Sharda (1994). For comparative purposes, the performance of neural networks is contrasted with logistic regression.

The Altman (1968) study has been used as the standard of comparison for many bankruptcy classification studies using discriminant analysis and logistic regression; follow-up studies have identified several other attributes to improve prediction performance. We use the same financial ratios as in Altman's study, realizing that more sophisticated inputs to the neural network model should only enhance its performance. These ratios are as follows:

X_1: Working capital/total assets

X_2: Retained earnings/total assets

X_3: Earnings before interest and taxes/total assets

X_4: Market value of equity/total debt

X_5: Sales/total assets

In step 1, we collected the relevant data. The sample, which was obtained from *Moody's Industrial Manuals,* consisted of firms that either were in operation or went bankrupt between 1975 and 1982. The sample included 129 firms, 65 of which went bankrupt during the period and 64 nonbankrupt firms matched on industry and year. Data for the bankrupt firms was obtained from the final financial statements issued before bankruptcy. Thus, the prediction of bankruptcy was to be made about 1 year in advance.

In step 2, we divided the dataset into a training set and a testing set. Because the determination of the split may affect experimental findings, a resampling procedure can be used to create many different pairs of training and testing sets, which also ensures that there is no overlap in the composition of the matched training and testing sets. For example, a training set of 20 patterns can be created by randomly setting 20 records from the collected set. A set of 20 other patterns/records can be created as a test set.

In addition, the results of this (and any other) study could be affected by the proportion of nonbankrupt firms to bankrupt firms in both the training and testing sets; that is, the population of all firms contains a certain proportion of firms on the verge of bankruptcy. This base rate may have an impact on a prediction technique's performance in two ways. First, a technique may not work well when the firms of interest (i.e., those that are bankrupt) constitute a very small percentage of the population (i.e., a low base rate). This would be due to a technique's inability to identify the features necessary for classification. Second, there are differences in base rates between training samples and testing samples. If a classification model is built using a training sample with a certain base rate, does the model still work when the base rate in the test population is different? This issue is important for one more reason: If a classification model based on a certain base rate works across other proportions, it may be possible to build a model using a higher proportion of cases of interest than actually occur in the population.

To study the effects of this proportion on the predictive performance of the two techniques, we created three proportions (or base rates) for the testing set composition while holding the composition of the training set fixed at a 50/50 base rate. The first factor level (or base rate) could be a 50/50 proportion of bankrupt to nonbankrupt cases, the second level could be an 80/20 proportion (80% nonbankrupt, 20% bankrupt), and the third level could be an approximate 90/10 proportion. We did not know the actual proportion of firms going bankrupt, but believed the 80/20 and 90/10 cases would be close.

Within each of the three different testing set compositions, 20 different training–testing set pairs were generated via Monte Carlo resampling from the original 129 firms. Thus, a total of 60 distinct training–testing dataset pairs were generated from the original data. In each case, the training set and test set pairs contained unique firms (i.e., no overlap was allowed). This restriction provided a stronger test of a technique's performance.

To summarize, neural networks and logistic regression models were developed using training sets of equal proportions of firms to determine the classification function but were evaluated with test sets containing 50/50, 80/20, and 90/10 base rates. (The dataset used here is available at this book's Web site.)

Steps 3 through 6 involved preparing for the neural network experiment. We could have used any neural network software package that implements the aforementioned backpropagation training algorithm to construct and test trained neural network models. We had to decide on the size of the neural network, including the number of hidden layers and the number of neurons in the hidden layer. For example, one possible structure was to use 5 input neurons (1 for each financial ratio), 10 hidden neurons, and 2 output neurons (1 indicating a bankrupt firm and the other indicating a nonbankrupt firm). Figure 6.14 illustrates this network configuration. Neural output values ranged from 0 to 1. The output node BR indicates a firm classified as likely to go bankrupt, and the node NBR, not so.

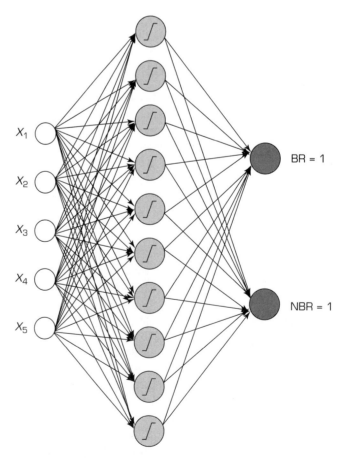

FIGURE 6.14 A Typical ANN Model for Bankruptcy Prediction

A user of a neural network has two difficult decisions to make in the training process (step 6): At what point has the neural network appropriately learned the relationships, and what is the threshold of error with regard to determining correct classifications of the test set? Typically, these issues are addressed by using training tolerances and testing tolerances that state the acceptable levels of variance for considering classifications as "correct."

Step 7 is the actual neural network training. In training the networks in this example, a heuristic backpropagation algorithm was used to ensure convergence (i.e., all firms in the training set are classified correctly). The training set was presented to the neural network software repeatedly until the software sufficiently learned the relationship between the attributes of the cases and whether a firm was distressed. Then, to accurately assess the prediction efficacy of the network, the holdout sample (i.e., test set) was presented to the network and the number of correct classifications was noted (step 8).

In determining correct classifications, a testing threshold of 0.49 was used. Thus, the output node with a value over 0.5 was used to assess whether the network provided a correct classification. Cases in which both output neurons provided output levels either less than 0.5 or greater than 0.5 were automatically treated as misclassifications.

To compare the performance of the neural network against classical statistical techniques, a logistic regression approach was implemented via SYSTAT, a statistical software package. Table 6.2 represents the average percentage of correct classifications provided by the two different techniques when evaluated by the 20 holdout samples for each of the three different test set base rates. When the testing sets contained an equal number of the two cases, neural networks correctly classified 97.5 percent of the holdout cases, whereas logistic regression was correct 93.25 percent of the time. Similarly, when the testing set comprised 20,070 bankrupt firms, neural networks classified at a 95.6 percent correct rate, whereas logistic regression correctly classified at a 92.2 percent rate.

A nonparametric test, the Wilcoxon test for paired observations, was undertaken to assess whether the correct classification percentages for the two techniques were significantly different. Those instances where statistically significant differences were found are indicated in Table 6.2 by footnotes. In general, neural networks performed significantly better than logistic regression.

Table 6.2 also illustrates the correct percentages of bankrupt firm predictions and nonbankrupt firm predictions. In the prediction of bankrupt cases, neural networks predicted significantly better than logistic regression for test sets of equal proportion, at the same percentage when the ratio was 80/20 and a little worse (although not significantly) for 90/10 test sets. The neural networks clearly outperformed the logistic regression model in the prediction of the nonbankrupt firms.

TABLE 6.2 Performance Comparison of Neural Networks and Logistic Regression

| | Test Proportions | | | | | |
| | 50/50 | | 80/20 | | 90/10 | |
Criteria	NN	LR	NN	LR	NN	LR
Overall percentage of correct classification	97.5[a]	93.25	95.6[a]	92.2	95.68[b]	90.23
Bankrupt firm classification success rate	97.0[a]	91.90	92.0	92.0	92.5	95.0 (P = .282)
Nonbankrupt firm classification success rate	98.0[a]	95.5	96.5[a]	92.25	96.0[b]	89.75

[a]$P < .01$; [b]$P < .05$.

A number of studies in the recent past have investigated the performance of neural networks in predicting business failure. Typically, these studies have compared neural network performance to that of traditional statistical techniques such as discriminant analysis and logistic regression. In addition, some recent studies have compared neural networks to other artificial intelligence techniques, such as decision trees, support vector machines, rough sets, and a variety of rule-induction systems. The purpose of this section was to illustrate how a neural network project can be carried out to predict bankruptcy, not necessarily to argue that neural networks do a better job at prediction in this problem domain.

Section 6.6 Review Questions

1. What parameters can be used to predict failure of a firm?
2. How were data divided between training and test sets for this experiment?
3. Explain what is meant by resampling in this context? How was resampling used for this problem?
4. What were the network parameters for this neural network experiment?
5. How was an output converted to bankrupt or nonbankrupt?
6. How did the neural network model compare with a logistic regression model in this experiment?

6.7 OTHER POPULAR NEURAL NETWORK PARADIGMS

The MLP-based neural networks thus far described in this chapter are just one specific type of neural network. Literally hundreds of different neural networks have been proposed. Many are variants of the MLP model; they just differ in their implementations of input representation, the learning process, output processing, and so on. However, other types of neural networks are quite different from the MLP model. Some of these are introduced later in this chapter. These other variants include radial basis function networks, probabilistic neural networks, generalized regression neural networks, and support vector machines. Many online resources describe the details of these types of neural networks. A good resource is the e-book at the StatSoft, Inc., Web site (**statsoft.com/textbook/stathome .html**). Even though the MLP is the most popular ANN architecture, it is helpful to examine some of the other varieties. The next subsection introduces two of the other popular neural network architectures: Kohonen's self-organizing feature maps and Hopfield networks.

Kohonen's Self-Organizing Feature Maps

First introduced by the Finnish professor Teuvo Kohonen, **Kohonen's self-organizing feature maps** (Kohonen networks or SOM, in short) are among the most popular data mining architectures. SOM provide a way to represent multidimensional data in much lower dimensional spaces, usually one or two dimensions. This process of reducing the dimensionality of vectors is essentially a data compression technique and is known as *vector quantisation*. Additionally, the Kohonen technique creates a network that stores information in such a way that any topological relationships within the training set are maintained.

One of the most interesting aspects of SOM is that they learn to classify data without supervision. In supervised training techniques, such as backpropagation, the training data consists of vector pairs—an input vector and a target vector. With this approach, an input vector is presented to the network (typically a multilayer feedforward network), and the output is compared with the target vector. If they differ, the weights of the network are altered slightly to reduce the error in the output. This is repeated many times and with many sets of vector pairs until the network gives the desired output. In contrast, a SOM requires no target vector. A SOM learns to classify the training data without any external supervision whatsoever.

Before getting into the details of the technique, it is often helpful to forget most everything you may already know about neural networks. If you try to think of SOM in terms of neurons, activation functions, and feedforward/recurrent connections, you will likely become confused rather quickly. So, temporarily forget all that knowledge you have gained from the previous sections of this chapter and get ready to embark on a new neural network paradigm.

SOM NETWORK ARCHITECTURE   In order to keep it simple and easy to understand, we will use a two-dimensional SOM. The network is created from a two-dimensional lattice of "nodes," each of which is fully connected to the input layer. Figure 6.15 illustrates a very small Kohonen network of 4 × 4 nodes connected to the input layer (with three inputs), representing a two-dimensional vector.

In the lattice, each node has a specific topological position (an x, y coordinate in the lattice) and has a vector of weights of the same dimension as the input vectors; that is, if the training data consists of vectors, V, of n dimensions (e.g., V_1, V_2, V_3, . . ., V_n), then each node in the lattice will contain a corresponding weight vector, W, of n dimensions (W_1, W_2, W_3, . . ., W_n).

THE SOM LEARNING ALGORITHM   Unlike many other types of neural networks, a target output does not need to be specified. Instead, during the training process the node weights are matched against the input vector. The node on the lattice that most closely resembles the input vector (and its surrounding area of nodes, "the neighborhood") is selectively optimized to more closely resemble the data for the class of which the input vector is a member. From an initial distribution of random weights, and over many iterations, the SOM eventually settles into a map of stable zones. Each zone is effectively a feature classifier, so you can think of the graphical output as a type of feature map of the input space. Any new, previously unseen input vectors presented to the network will stimulate nodes in the zone with similar weight vectors.

Training in SOM occurs in the following steps and over many iterations (details on the algorithm are also available at **ai-junkie.com/ann/som/som3.html**):

1. Each node's weights are initialized.
2. A vector is chosen from the set of training data and presented to the lattice.
3. Every node is examined to calculate which one's weight most resembles the input vector. The winning node, commonly known as the Best Matching Unit (BMU), is identified.

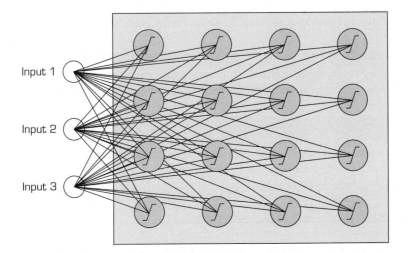

FIGURE 6.15   A 4 × 4 Kohonen (SOM) Network Structure

4. The radius of the neighborhood of the BMU is now calculated. This is a value that starts large, typically set to the "radius" of the lattice, but diminishes each step. Any nodes found within this radius are deemed to be inside the BMU's neighborhood.

5. Each neighboring node's (the nodes found in step 4) weights are adjusted to make them more like the input vector. The closer a node is to the BMU, the more its weights are altered.

6. Repeat steps 2 through 5 for N iterations or until other stopping criteria are reached.

The mathematical details of these steps can be found in Haykin (2009), and will not be given herein.

APPLICATIONS OF SOM SOM are commonly used as *visualization identification*. They can make it easy for humans to "see" relationships among vast amounts of diverse data items (e.g., multidimensional structured or unstructured data such as images, audio recordings, and text documents). With regards to image recognition, SOM can help find similar two- or three-dimensional pictures from a large collection of images in a database, which can be very useful to law enforcement agencies in identifying criminals via automated face recognition. Furthermore, the technology may also help in identifying child pornography from a collection of images on a confiscated computer drive or on a Web site. Other applications of SOM include:

- Bibliographic classification (**edpsciences.org/articles/aas/pdf/1998/10/ds1464.pdf**)
- Image-browsing systems (**cis.hut.fi/picsom/**)
- Medical diagnosis
- Interpretation of seismic activity
- Speech recognition (this is what Kohonen initially used this architecture for)
- Data compression
- Separating sound sources (**cis.hut.fi/projects/ica/cocktail/cocktail_en.cgi**)
- Environmental modeling
- Vampire classification! (**hut.fi/~jslindst/vtes/**)

Hopfield Networks

The Hopfield network is another interesting neural network architecture, first introduced by John Hopfield (1982). He demonstrated in a series of research articles in the early 1980s how highly interconnected networks of nonlinear neurons can be extremely effective in solving complex computational problems. These networks were shown to provide novel and quick solutions to a family of problems stated in terms of a desired objective subject to a number of constraints.

One of the major advantages of Hopfield neural networks, which are gaining popularity in solving optimization or mathematical programming problems, is the fact that their structure can be realized on an electronic circuit board, possibly on a VLSI (very large-scale integration) circuit, to be used as an online solver with a parallel-distributed process. The structure of a Hopfield network utilizes three common methods—penalty functions, Lagrange multipliers, and primal and dual methods—to construct an energy function. When the energy function reaches a steady state, an optimal solution of the problem is believed to be obtained. Hopfield networks have been successfully used to solve all three types of mathematical problems: linear, nonlinear, and mixed integer (Wen et al., 2009).

Architecturally, a general Hopfield network is represented as a single large layer of neurons with total interconnectivity; that is, each neuron is connected to every other neuron within the network (see Figure 6.16). In addition, the output of each neuron may depend on its own previous values. One use of Hopfield networks has

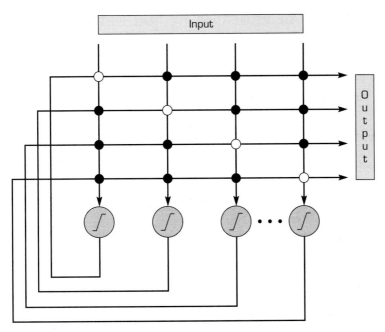

FIGURE 6.16   A Simple Hopfield Network

been in solving the classic traveling salesman problem (TSP). In this problem, each neuron in the network represents the desirability of a city n being visited in position m of a TSP tour. Interconnection weights are specified to represent the constraints of feasible solutions to the TSP (e.g., forcing a city to appear in a tour only once). An energy function is specified, which represents the objective of the model (e.g., minimize total distance in the TSP tour), and is used in determining when to stop the neural network evolution with the best possible solution. The network starts with random neuron values and, using the stated interconnection weights, the neuron values are updated iteratively over time. Gradually, the neuron values stabilize, evolving into a final state (as driven by the global energy function) that represents a solution to the problem. At this point in the network evolution, the value of neuron (n, m) represents whether city n should be in location m of the TSP tour. Although Hopfield and Tank (1985) and others have claimed great success in solving the TSP, further research has shown that those claims were somewhat premature in terms of finding "the global" optimum solution. Nonetheless, this novel approach to solving a classic optimization problem offers promise for solving a wide range of complex optimization problems, especially because Hopfield networks take advantage of the inherent parallelism of the neural structure.

Hopfield networks are distinct from feedforward networks because the neurons are highly interconnected, weights between neurons tend to be fixed, and there is no training, per se. The complexity and challenge in using a Hopfield network for optimization problems is in the correct specification of the interconnection weights and the identification of the proper global energy function to drive the network evolution process.

Section 6.7 Review Questions

1. List some of the different types of neural networks.
2. What is one key difference between an MLP network and a Kohonen network?
3. What is another name for a Kohonen network?
4. Briefly describe a Hopfield network.

6.8 APPLICATIONS OF ARTIFICIAL NEURAL NETWORKS

Because of their ability to model real-world complex problems, researchers and practitioners have found many uses for ANN. Many of these uses have led to solutions for problems previously believed to be unsolvable. At the highest conceptual level, common uses of neural networks can be classified into four general classes (somewhat resembling the general groupings of tasks addressed by data mining):

1. **Classification.**   A neural network can be trained to predict a categorical (i.e., class-label) output variable. In a mathematical sense, this involves dividing an n-dimensional space into various regions and given a point in the space one should be able to determine to which region it belongs. This idea has been used in many real-world applications of **pattern recognition**, where each pattern is transformed into a multidimensional point and classified into a certain group, each of which represents a known pattern. Types of ANN used for this task include feedforward networks (such as MLP with backpropagation learning), radial basis functions, and probabilistic neural networks.

2. **Regression.**   A neural network can be trained to predict an output variable whose values are of numeric (i.e., real or integer numbers) type. If a network fits well in modeling a known sequence of values, it can be used to predict future results. An obvious example of the regression task is stock market index predictions. Types of ANN used for this task include feedforward networks (such as MLP with backpropagation learning) and radial basis functions.

3. **Clustering.**   Sometimes a dataset is so complicated that there is no obvious way to classify the data into different categories. ANN can be used to identify special features of these data and classify them into different categories without prior knowledge of the data. This technique is useful in identifying natural grouping of things for commercial as well as scientific problems. Types of ANN used for this task include Adaptive Resonance Theory (ART) networks and SOM.

4. **Association.**   A neural network can be trained to "remember" a number of unique patterns so that when a distorted version of a particular pattern is presented the network associates it with the closest one in its memory and returns the original version of that particular pattern. This can be useful for restoring noisy data and identifying objects and events where the data is noisy or incomplete. Types of ANN used for this task include Hopfield networks.

ANN have been applied in many domains. A survey of their applications in finance can be found in Wallace (2008) and Fadlalla and Lin (2001). Many attempts have been made to use neural networks to predict and understand financial markets. Collard (1990) stated that his neural network model for commodity training resulted in significantly higher profits over other trading strategies. Kamijo and Tanigawa (1990) used a neural network to chart and understand Tokyo Stock Exchange data. They found that the model beat a "buy and hold" strategy. Finally, Fishman et al. (1991) developed a neural model using a variety of economic indicators to predict percentage change in the S&P 500 five days ahead. The authors claim that the model was more accurate in its predictions than alleged experts in the field using the same indicators. Although some of these early neural network studies claimed some level of success in predicting certain features of financial markets, the notion of the unpredictable nature of the markets still stands.

Neural networks have been successfully trained to determine whether loan applications should be approved (Gallant, 1988). It has also been shown that neural networks can predict mortgage applicant solvency better than mortgage writers (Collins et al., 1988). Predicting rating of corporate bonds and attempting to forecast their profitability is another area where neural networks have been successfully applied (see Dutta and Shakhar, 1988; and Surkan and Singleton, 1990). Neural networks outperformed regression analysis and other mathematical modeling tools in predicting bond rating and profitability. The main conclusion reached was that neural networks provided a more general framework for connecting financial information of a firm to the respective bond rating.

Another interesting area where neural networks have been successfully applied is in sports prediction. In a recent study, Loeffelholz et al. (2009) examined the use of neural networks as a tool for predicting the success of basketball teams in the National Basketball Association (NBA). They used statistics for 620 NBA games to train a number of different neural network models, including feedforward, radial basis, probabilistic, and generalized regression neural networks. They also investigated which subset of features used to train the neural networks were the most salient ones for prediction. They compared the results obtained from these networks to predictions made by numerous basketball experts. The best networks were able to correctly predict the winning team 74.33 percent of the time (on average), as compared to the experts who were correct only 68.67 percent of the time.

In another sports-related study, Iyer and Sharda (2009) explored the use of neural networks to rate and select the best combination cricket players for a competition. Using data from 1985 onward until the 2006–2007 season, they trained and tested numerous neural networks to construct a model that accurately predicted cricketers' near-future performance based on their recent-past accomplishments. They compared the predictions of their neural network models against the actual performance of the same cricketers in the World Cup 2007. Their results showed that neural networks can indeed provide accurate predictions and hence can be used as an invaluable decision support tool in the team selection process.

Fraud prevention is another successfully utilized area of neural network applications in business. Chase Manhattan Bank has successfully used neural networks in dealing with credit card fraud (Rochester, 1990), with the neural network models outperforming traditional regression approaches. Also, neural networks have been used in the validation of bank signatures to prevent fraudulent bank transactions (see Francett, 1989; and Mighell, 1989). These networks identified forgeries significantly better than any human expert.

Another important application of neural networks is in time-series forecasting. Several studies have attempted to use neural networks for time-series prediction. Examples include Fozzard et al. (1989), Tang et al. (1991), and Hill et al. (1994). The general conclusion is that neural networks appear to do at least as well as (if not better than) their statistical counterpart, the Box-Jenkins forecasting technique.

A new and prosperous area of application for neural networks is in the field of health care and medicine. Because of their ability to capture and represent highly complex relationships, neural networks are being used to discover patterns in large health care, medical, and biological datasets. In a recently published study, Das et al. (2009) claim to have developed an effective diagnosis system for heart diseases based on artificial neural networks. Using the Cleveland Heart Disease Database, they showed that neural networks can diagnose heart diseases with impressive 89 percent classification accuracy.

In another recent study, Güler et al. (2009) used artificial neural networks to develop a diagnostic system to detect the severity of traumatic brain injuries. They found a significant similarity between classifications made by neurologists and the ANN system output for normal, mild, moderate, and severe brain injuries. Automating such a high-level expertise-requiring classification problem could lead to more rapid decision making and corresponding actions to save human lives. See Application Case 6.4 for an example of how ANN are used to better diagnose breast cancer.

Because neural networks have been a subject of intense study since the late 1980s, there have been many interesting applications of them. You can do a simple Web search to find plenty of recent examples in addition to the ones listed in this chapter. Some other noteworthy applications include live intrusion tracking (see Thaler, 2002), Web content filtering (Lee et al., 2002), exchange rate prediction (Davis et al., 2001), and hospital bed allocation (Walczak et al., 2002).

APPLICATION CASE 6.4

Neural Networks for Breast Cancer Diagnosis

ANN have proven to be a useful tool in pattern recognition and classification tasks in diverse areas, including clinical medicine. Despite the wide applicability of ANN, the large amount of data required for training makes them an unsuitable classification technique when the available data are scarce. Magnetic resonance spectroscopy (MRS) plays a pivotal role in the investigation of cell biochemistry and provides a reliable method for detection of metabolic changes in breast tissue. The scarcity of MRS data and the complexity of interpretation of relevant physiological information impose extra demands that prohibit the applicability of most statistical and machine-learning techniques developed.

Knowledge-based artificial neural networks (KBANN) help to prevail over such difficulties and complexities. A KBANN combines knowledge from a domain, in the form of simple rules, with connectionist learning. This combination trains the network through the use of small sets of data (as is typical of medical diagnosis tasks). The primary structure is based on the dependencies of a set of known domain rules, and it is necessary to refine those rules through training.

The KBANN process consists of two algorithms. One is the Rules-to-Network algorithm, in which the main task is the translation process between a knowledge base containing information about a domain theory and the initial structure of a neural network. This algorithm maps the structure of an approximately correct domain theory, with all the rules and their dependencies, into a neural network structure. The defined network is then trained using the backpropagation learning algorithm.

Feedback mechanisms, which inhibit or stimulate the growth of normal cells, control the division and replacement of cells in normal tissues. In the case of tumors, that process is incapable of controlling the production of new cells, and the division is done without any regard to the need for replacement, disturbing the structure of normal tissue. Changes observed in phospholipid metabolite concentrations, which are associated with differences in cell proliferation in malignant tissues, have served as the basic inputs for the identification of relevant features present in malignant or cancerous tissues but not in normal tissues. The abnormal levels of certain phospholipid characteristics are considered indicators of tumors. These include several parameters, such as PDE, PME, Pi, PCr, γATP, αATP, and βATP. KBANN produced an accurate tumor classification of 87 percent from a set of 26, with an average pattern error of 0.0500 and a standard deviation of 0.0179.

Source: M. Sordo, H. Buxton, and D. Watson, "A Hybrid Approach to Breast Cancer Diagnosis," in *Practical Applications of Computational Intelligence Techniques*, Vol. 16, L. Jain and P. DeWilde (eds.), Kluwer, Norwell, MA, 2001. **acl.icnet.uk/PUBLICATIONS/sordo/chapter2001.pdf** (accessed May 2009).

In general, ANN are suitable for problems whose inputs are both categorical and numeric, and where the relationships between inputs and outputs are not linear or the input data are not normally distributed. In such cases, classical statistical methods may not be reliable enough. Because ANN do not make any assumptions about the data distribution, their power is less affected than traditional statistical methods when the data are not properly distributed. Finally, there are cases in which the neural networks simply provide one more way of building a predictive model for the situation at hand. Given the ease of experimentation using the available software tools, it is certainly worth exploring the power of neural networks in any data modeling situation.

Section 6.8 Review Questions

1. List some applications of neural networks in accounting and finance.
2. What are some sports applications of neural networks?
3. How have neural networks been used in health care?
4. What are some applications of neural networks in information security?
5. Conduct a Web search to identify homeland security applications of neural networks.

Chapter Highlights

- Neural computing involves a set of methods that emulate the way the human brain works. The basic processing unit is a neuron. Multiple neurons are grouped into layers and linked together.
- In a neural network, the knowledge is stored in the weight associated with each connection between two neurons.
- Backpropagation is the most popular paradigm in business applications of neural networks. Most business applications are handled using this algorithm.
- A backpropagation-based neural network consists of an input layer, an output layer, and a certain number of hidden layers (usually one). The nodes in one layer are fully connected to the nodes in the next layer. Learning is done through a trial-and-error process of adjusting the connection weights.
- Each node at the input layer typically represents a single attribute that may affect the prediction.
- Neural network learning can occur in supervised or unsupervised mode.
- In supervised learning mode, the training patterns include a correct answer/classification/forecast.
- In unsupervised learning mode, there are no known answers. Thus, unsupervised learning is used for clustering or exploratory data analysis.
- The usual process of learning in a neural network involves three steps: (1) compute temporary outputs based on inputs and random weights, (2) compute outputs with desired targets, and (3) adjust the weights and repeat the process.

- The delta rule is commonly used to adjust the weights. It includes a learning rate and a momentum parameter.
- Developing neural network–based systems requires a step-by-step process. It includes data preparation and preprocessing, training and testing, and conversion of the trained model into a production system.
- Neural network software is available to allow easy experimentation with many models. Neural network modules are included in all major data mining software tools. Specific neural network packages are also available. Some neural network tools are available as spreadsheet add-ins.
- After a trained network has been created, it is usually implemented in end-user systems through programming languages such as C++, Java, and Visual Basic. Most neural network tools can generate code for the trained network in these languages.
- Many neural network models beyond backpropagation exist, including radial basis functions, support vector machines, Hopfield networks, and Kohonen's self-organizing maps.
- Neural network applications abound in almost all business disciplines as well as in virtually all other functional areas.
- Business applications of neural networks included finance, bankruptcy prediction, time-series forecasting, and so on.
- New applications of neural networks are emerging in health care, security, and so on.

Key Terms

adaptive resonance theory (ART) 255
artificial neural network (ANN) 245
axon 245
backpropagation 248
black-box testing 264
connection weight 250
dendrite 245
hidden layer 249

Kohonen's self-organizing feature map 270
learning algorithm 252
learning rate 257
momentum 257
neural computing 245
neural network 245
neuron 245
nucleus 246

parallel processing 249
pattern recognition 274
perceptron 245
processing element (PE) 248
self-organizing 255
sigmoid (logical activation) function 251
summation function 250

supervised learning 252
synapse 246
threshold value 251
topology 261
transformation (transfer) function 251
unsupervised learning 252

Questions for Discussion

1. Compare artificial and biological neural networks. What aspects of biological networks are not mimicked by artificial ones? What aspects are similar?
2. The performance of ANN relies heavily on the summation and transformation functions. Explain the combined effects of the summation and transformation functions and how they differ from statistical regression analysis.
3. ANN can be used for both supervised and unsupervised learning. Explain how they learn in a supervised mode and in an unsupervised mode.
4. Explain the difference between a training set and a testing set. Why do we need to differentiate them? Can the same set be used for both purposes? Why or why not?

5. Say that a neural network has been constructed to predict the creditworthiness of applicants. There are two output nodes: one for yes (1 = yes, 0 = no) and one for no (1 = no, 0 = yes). An applicant receives a score of 0.83 for the "yes" output node and a 0.44 for the "no" output node. Discuss what may have happened and whether the applicant is a good credit risk.
6. Everyone would like to make a great deal of money on the stock market. Only a few are very successful. Why is using an ANN a promising approach? What can it do that other decision support technologies cannot do? How could it fail?

Exercises

TERADATA STUDENT NETWORK (TSN) AND OTHER HANDS-ON EXERCISES

1. Go to the Teradata Student Network Web site (**teradata studentnetwork.com**) or the URL given by your instructor. Locate Web seminars related to data mining and neural networks. Specifically, view the seminar given by Professor Hugh Watson at the SPIRIT2005 conference at Oklahoma State University, then answer the following questions:
   a. Which real-time application at Continental Airlines may have used a neural network?
   b. What inputs and outputs can be used in building a neural network application?
   c. Given that Continental's data mining applications are in real time, how might Continental implement a neural network in practice?
   d. What other neural network applications would you propose for the airline industry?
2. Go to the Teradata Student Network Web site (**teradata studentnetwork.com**) or the URL given by your instructor. Locate the Harrah's case. Read the case and answer the following questions:

   a. Which of the Harrah's data applications are most likely implemented using neural networks?
   b. What other applications could Harrah's develop using the data it is collecting from its customers?
   c. What are some concerns you might have as a customer at this casino?
3. This exercise relates to the bankruptcy-prediction problem discussed in this chapter. The bankruptcy-prediction problem can be viewed as a problem of classification. The dataset you will be using for this problem includes five ratios that have been computed from the financial statements of real-world firms. These five ratios have been used in studies involving bankruptcy prediction. The first sample includes data on firms that went bankrupt and firms that didn't. This will be your training sample for the neural network. The second sample of 10 firms also consists of some bankrupt firms and some non-bankrupt firms. Your goal is to train a neural network, using the first 20 data, and then test its performance on the other 10 data. (Try to analyze the new cases yourself manually before you run the neural network and see how well you do.) The following tables show the training sample and test data you should use for this exercise.

Training Sample						
Firm	WC/TA	RE/TA	EBIT/TA	MVE/TD	S/TA	BR/NB
1	0.1650	0.1192	0.2035	0.8130	1.6702	1
2	0.1415	0.3868	0.0681	0.5755	1.0579	1
3	0.5804	0.3331	0.0810	1.1964	1.3572	1
4	0.2304	0.2960	0.1225	0.4102	3.0809	1
5	0.3684	0.3913	0.0524	0.1658	1.1533	1
6	0.1527	0.3344	0.0783	0.7736	1.5046	1
7	0.1126	0.3071	0.0839	1.3429	1.5736	1

(continued)

8	0.0141	0.2366	0.0905	0.5863	1.4651	1
9	0.2220	0.1797	0.1526	0.3459	1.7237	1
10	0.2776	0.2567	0.1642	0.2968	1.8904	1
11	0.2689	0.1729	0.0287	0.1224	0.9277	0
12	0.2039	−0.0476	0.1263	0.8965	1.0457	0
13	0.5056	−0.1951	0.2026	0.5380	1.9514	0
14	0.1759	0.1343	0.0946	0.1955	1.9218	0
15	0.3579	0.1515	0.0812	0.1991	1.4582	0
16	0.2845	0.2038	0.0171	0.3357	1.3258	0
17	0.1209	0.2823	−0.0113	0.3157	2.3219	0
18	0.1254	0.1956	0.0079	0.2073	1.4890	0
19	0.1777	0.0891	0.0695	0.1924	1.6871	0
20	0.2409	0.1660	0.0746	0.2516	1.8524	0

			Test Data			
Firm	**WC/TA**	**RE/TA**	**EBIT/TA**	**MVE/TD**	**S/TA**	**BR/NB**
A	0.1759	0.1343	0.0946	0.1955	1.9218	?
B	0.3732	0.3483	−0.0013	0.3483	1.8223	?
C	0.1725	0.3238	0.1040	0.8847	0.5576	?
D	0.1630	0.3555	0.0110	0.3730	2.8307	?
E	0.1904	0.2011	0.1329	0.5580	1.6623	?
F	0.1123	0.2288	0.0100	0.1884	2.7186	?
G	0.0732	0.3526	0.0587	0.2349	1.7432	?
H	0.2653	0.2683	0.0235	0.5118	1.8350	?
I	0.1070	0.0787	0.0433	0.1083	1.2051	?
J	0.2921	0.2390	0.0673	0.3402	0.9277	?

Describe the results of the neural network prediction, including software, architecture, and training information. Submit the trained network file(s) so that your instructor can load and test your network.

4. The purpose of this exercise is to develop a model to predict forest cover type using a number of cartographic measures. The given dataset (Online File W6.1) includes four wilderness areas found in the Roosevelt National Forest of northern Colorado. A total of 12 cartographic measures were utilized as independent variables; seven major forest cover types were used as dependent variables. The following table provides a short description of these independent and dependent variables:

Number	Name	Description
		Independent Variables
1	Elevation	Elevation in meters
2	Aspect	Aspect in degrees azimuth
3	Slope	Slope in degrees
4	Horizontal_Distance_To_Hydrology	Horizontal distance to nearest surface-water features

(continued)

5	Vertical_Distance_To_Hydrology	Vertical distance to nearest surface-water features
6	Horizontal_Distance_To_Roadways	Horizontal distance to nearest roadway
7	Hillshade_9am	Hill shade index at 9 A.M., summer solstice
8	Hillshade_Noon	Hill shade index at noon, summer solstice
9	Hillshade_3pm	Hill shade index at 3 P.M., summer solstice
10	Horizontal_Distance_To_Fire_Points	Horizontal distance to nearest wildfire ignition points
11	Wilderness_Area (4 binary variables)	Wilderness area designation
12	Soil_Type (40 binary variables)	Soil type designation

Number		Dependent Variable
1	Cover_Type (7 unique types)	Forest cover type designation

Note: More details about the dataset (variables and observations) can be found in the online file.

This is an excellent example for a multiclass classification problem. The dataset is rather large (with 581,012 unique instances) and feature rich. As you will see, the data is also raw and skewed (unbalanced for different cover types). As a model builder, you are to make necessary decisions to preprocess the data and build the best possible predictor. Use your favorite tool to build the models and document the details of your actions and experiences in a written report. Use screenshots within your report to illustrate important and interesting findings. You are expected to discuss and justify any decision that you make along the way.

The reuse of this dataset is unlimited with retention of copyright notice for Jock A. Blackard and Colorado State University.

TEAM ASSIGNMENTS AND ROLE-PLAYING

1. Consider the following set of data that relates daily electricity usage as a function of outside high temperature (for the day):

Temperature, X	Kilowatts, Y
46.8	12,530
52.1	10,800
55.1	10,180
59.2	9,730
61.9	9,750
66.2	10,230
69.9	11,160
76.8	13,910
79.7	15,110
79.3	15,690
80.2	17,020
83.3	17,880

a. Plot the raw data. What pattern do you see? What do you think is really affecting electricity usage?
b. Solve this problem with linear regression $Y = a + bX$ (in a spreadsheet). How well does this work? Plot your results. What is wrong? Calculate the sum-of-the-squares error and R^2.
c. Solve this problem by using nonlinear regression. We recommend a quadratic function, $Y = a + b_1X + b_2X^2$. How well does this work? Plot your results. Is anything wrong? Calculate the sum-of-the-squares error and R^2.
d. Break up the problem into three sections (look at the plot). Solve it using three linear regression models— one for each section. How well does this work? Plot your results. Calculate the sum-of-the-squares error and R^2. Is this modeling approach appropriate? Why or why not?
e. Build a neural network to solve the original problem. (You may have to scale the X and Y values to be between 0 and 1.) Train it (on the entire set of data) and solve the problem (i.e., make predictions for each of the original data items). How well does this work? Plot your results. Calculate the sum-of-the-squares error and R^2.
f. Which method works best and why?

2. Build a real-world neural network. Using demo software downloaded from the Web (e.g., NeuroSolutions at **neurodimension.com** or another site), identify real-world data (e.g., start searching on the Web at **ics.uci.edu/~mlearn/MLRepository.html** or use data from an organization with which someone in your group has a contact) and build a neural network to make predictions. Topics might include sales forecasts, predicting success in an academic program (e.g., predict GPA from high school rating and SAT scores; being careful to look out for "bad" data, such as GPAs of 0.0), or housing prices; or survey the class for weight, gender, and height and try to predict height based on the other two factors. You could also use

U.S. Census data on this book's Web site or at **census .gov**, by state, to identify a relationship between education level and income. How good are your predictions? Compare the results to predictions generated using standard statistical methods (regression). Which method is better? How could your system be embedded in a DSS for real decision making?

3. For each of the following applications, would it be better to use a neural network or an expert system? Explain your answers, including possible exceptions or special conditions.
   a. Diagnosis of a well-established but complex disease
   b. Price-lookup subsystem for a high-volume merchandise seller
   c. Automated voice-inquiry processing system
   d. Training of new employees
   e. Handwriting recognition

4. Consider the following dataset, which includes three attributes and a classification for admission decisions into an MBA program:

GMAT	GPA	Quantitative GMAT	Decision
650	2.75	35	NO
580	3.50	70	NO
600	3.50	75	YES
450	2.95	80	NO
700	3.25	90	YES
590	3.50	80	YES
400	3.85	45	NO
640	3.50	75	YES
540	3.00	60	?
690	2.85	80	?
490	4.00	65	?

   a. Using the data given here as examples, develop your own manual expert rules for decision making.
   b. Build a decision tree using SPRINT (Gini index). You can build it by using manual calculations or use a spreadsheet to perform the basic calculations.
   c. Build another decision tree, using the entropy and information gain (ID3) approach. You can use a spreadsheet calculator for this exercise.
   d. Although the dataset here is extremely small, try to build a little neural network for it.
   e. Use automated decision tree software (e.g., See5; download a trial version from **rule-quest.com**) to build a tree for these data.
   f. Report the predictions on the last three observations from each of the five classification approaches.
   g. Comment on the similarity and differences of the approaches. What did you learn from this exercise?

5. You have worked on neural networks and other data mining techniques. Give examples of where each of these has been used. Based on your knowledge, how would you differentiate among these techniques? Assume that a few years from now you come across a situation in which neural network or other data mining techniques could be used to build an interesting application for your organization. You have an intern working with you to do the grunt work. How will you decide whether the application is appropriate for a neural network or for another data mining model? Based on your homework assignments, what specific software guidance can you provide to get your intern to be productive for you quickly? Your answer for this question might mention the specific software, describe how to go about setting up the model/neural network, and validate the application.

INTERNET EXERCISES

1. Explore the Web sites of several neural network vendors, such as California Scientific Software (**calsci.com**), NeuralWare (**neuralware.com**), and Ward Systems Group (**wardsystems.com**), and review some of their products. Download at least two demos and install, run, and compare them.

2. A very good repository of data that has been used to test the performance of neural network and other machine-learning algorithms can be accessed at **ics.uci.edu/ ~mlearn/MLRepository.html**. Some of the datasets are really meant to test the limits of current machine-learning algorithms and compare their performance against new approaches to learning. However, some of the smaller datasets can be useful for exploring the functionality of the software you might download in Internet Exercise 1 or the software that is available at StatSoft.com (i.e., Statistica Data Miner with extensive neural network capabilities). Download at least one dataset from the UCI repository (e.g., Credit Screening Databases, Housing Database). Then apply neural networks as well as decision tree methods, as appropriate. Prepare a report on your results. (Some of these exercises could also be completed in a group or may even be proposed as semester-long projects for term papers and so on.)

3. Go to **calsci.com** and read about the company's various business applications. Prepare a report that summarizes the applications.

4. Go to **nd.com**. Read about the company's applications in investment and trading. Prepare a report about them.

5. Go to **nd.com**. Download the trial version of Neurosolutions for Excel and experiment with it, using one of the datasets from the exercises in this chapter. Prepare a report about your experience with the tool.

6. Go to **neoxi.com**. Identify at least two software tools that have not been mentioned in this chapter. Visit Web

sites of those tools and prepare a brief report on the tools' capabilities.

7. Go to **neuroshell.com**. Look at Gee Whiz examples. Comment on the feasibility of achieving the results claimed by the developers of this neural network model.

8. Go to **easynn.com**. Download the trial version of the software. After the installation of the software, find the sample file called Houseprices.tvq. Retrain the neural network and test the model by supplying some data. Prepare a report about your experience with this software.

9. Visit **statsoft.com**. Download at least three white papers of applications. Which of these applications may have used neural networks?

10. Go to **neuralware.com**. Prepare a report about the products the company offers.

END OF CHAPTER APPLICATION CASE

Coors Improves Beer Flavors with Neural Networks

Coors Brewers Ltd., based in Burton-upon-Trent, Britain's brewing capital, is proud of having the United Kingdom's top beer brands, a 20 percent share of the market, years of experience, and some of the best people in the business. Popular brands include Carling (the country's bestselling lager), Grolsch, Coors Fine Light Beer, Sol, and Korenwolf.

Problem

Today's customer has a wide variety of options regarding what he or she drinks. A drinker's choice depends on various factors, including mood, venue, and occasion. Coors' goal is to ensure that the customer chooses a Coors brand no matter what the circumstances are.

According to Coors, creativity is the key to long-term success. To be the customer's choice brand, Coors needs to be creative and anticipate the customer's ever so rapidly changing moods. An important issue with beers is the flavor; each beer has a distinctive flavor. These flavors are mostly determined through panel tests. However, such tests take time. If Coors could understand the beer flavor based solely on its chemical composition, it would open up new avenues to create beer that would suit customer expectations.

The relationship between chemical analysis and beer flavor is not clearly understood yet. Substantial data exist on the chemical composition of a beer and sensory analysis. Coors needed a mechanism to link those two together. Neural networks were applied to create the link between chemical composition and sensory analysis.

Solution

Over the years, Coors Brewers Ltd. has accumulated a significant amount of data related to the final product analysis, which has been supplemented by sensory data provided by the trained in-house testing panel. Some of the analytical inputs and sensory outputs are shown in the following table:

Analytical Data: Inputs	Sensory Data: Outputs
Alcohol	Alcohol
Color	Estery
Calculated bitterness	Malty
Ethyl acetate	Grainy
Isobutyl acetate	Burnt
Ethyl butyrate	Hoppy
Isoamyl acetate	Toffee
Ethyl hexanoate	Sweet

A single neural network, restricted to a single quality and flavor, was first used to model the relationship between the analytical and sensory data. The neural network was based on a package solution supplied by NeuroDimension, Inc. (**nd.com**). The neural network consisted of an MLP architecture with two hidden layers. Data were normalized within the network, thereby enabling comparison between the results for the various sensory outputs. The neural network was trained (to learn the relationship between the inputs and outputs) through the presentation of many combinations of relevant input/output combinations. When there was no observed improvement in the network error in the last 100 epochs, training was automatically terminated. Training was carried out 50 times to ensure that a considerable mean network error could be calculated for comparison purposes. Prior to each training run, a different training and cross-validation dataset was presented by randomizing the source data records, thereby removing any bias.

This technique produced poor results, due to two major factors. First, concentrating on a single product's quality meant that the variation in the data was pretty low. The neural network could not extract useful relationships from the data. Second, it was probable that only one subset of the provided inputs would have an impact on the selected beer flavor. Performance of the neural network was affected by "noise" created by inputs that had no impact on flavor.

A more diverse product range was included in the training range to address the first factor. It was more challenging to identify the most important analytical inputs. This challenge was addressed by using a software switch that enabled the neural network to be trained on all possible combinations of inputs. The switch was not used to disable a significant input; if the significant input were disabled, we could expect the network error to increase. If the disabled input was insignificant, then the network error would either remain unchanged or be reduced due to the removal of noise. This approach is called an *exhaustive search* because all possible combinations are evaluated. The technique, although conceptually simple, was computationally impractical with the numerous inputs; the number of possible combinations was 16.7 million per flavor.

A more efficient method of searching for the relevant inputs was required. A genetic algorithm (see Chapter 13 for a detailed description of genetic algorithms) was the solution to the problem. A genetic algorithm was able to manipulate the different input switches in response to the error term from the neural network. The objective of the genetic algorithm was to minimize the network error term. When this minimum was reached, the switch settings would identify the analytical inputs that were most likely to predict the flavor.

Results

After determining what inputs were relevant, it was possible to identify which flavors could be predicted more skillfully. The network was trained using the relevant inputs previously identified multiple times. Before each training run, the network data were randomized to ensure that a different training and cross-validation dataset was used. Network error was recorded after each training run. The testing set used for assessing the performance of the trained network contained approximately 80 records out of the sample data. The neural network accurately predicted a few flavors by using the chemical inputs. For example, "burnt" flavor was predicted with a correlation coefficient of 0.87.

Today, a limited number of flavors are being predicted by using the analytical data. Sensory response is extremely complex, with many potential interactions and hugely variable sensitivity thresholds. Standard instrumental analysis tends to be of gross parameters, and for practical and economical reasons, many flavor-active compounds are simply not measured. The relationship of flavor and analysis can be effectively modeled only if a large number of flavor-contributory analytes are considered. What is more, in addition to the obvious flavor-active materials, mouth-feel and physical contributors should also be considered in the overall sensory profile. With further development of the input parameters, the accuracy of the neural network models will improve.

Questions for the Case

1. Why is beer flavor important to Coors' profitability?
2. What is the objective of the neural network used at Coors?
3. Why were the results of Coors' neural network initially poor, and what was done to improve the results?
4. What benefits might Coors derive if this project is successful?
5. What modifications would you make to improve the results of beer flavor prediction?

Sources: C. I. Wilson and L. Threapleton, "Application of Artificial Intelligence for Predicting Beer Flavours from Chemical Analysis," *Proceedings of the 29th European Brewery Congress*, Dublin, Ireland, May 17–22, 2003, **neurosolutions.com/resources/apps/beer.html** (accessed May 2009); R. Nischwitz, M. Goldsmith, M. Lees, P. Rogers, and L. MacLeod, "Developing Functional Malt Specifications for Improved Brewing Performance," The Regional Institute Ltd., **regional.org.au/au/abts/1999/nischwitz.htm** (accessed May 2009).

References

Ainscough, T. L., and J. E. Aronson. (1999). "A Neural Networks Approach for the Analysis of Scanner Data." *Journal of Retailing and Consumer Services,* Vol. 6.

Altman, E. I. (1968). "Financial Ratios, Discriminant Analysis and the Prediction of Corporate Bankruptcy." *Journal of Finance,* Vol. 23.

California Scientific. "Maximize Returns on Direct Mail with BrainMaker Neural Networks Software." **calsci.com/DirectMail.html** (accessed August 2009).

Collard, J. E. (1990). "Commodity Trading with a Neural Net." *Neural Network News,* Vol. 2, No. 10.

Collins, E., S. Ghosh, and C. L. Scofield. (1988). "An Application of a Multiple Neural Network Learning System to Emulation of Mortgage Underwriting Judgments." *IEEE International Conference on Neural Networks,* Vol. 2, pp. 459–466.

Das, R., I. Turkoglu, and A. Sengur. (2009). "Effective Diagnosis of Heart Disease Through Neural Networks Ensembles." *Expert Systems with Applications,* Vol. 36, pp. 7675–7680.

Davis, J. T., A. Episcopos, and S. Wettimuny. (2001). "Predicting Direction Shifts on Canadian–U.S. Exchange Rates with Artificial Neural Networks." *International Journal of Intelligent Systems in Accounting, Finance and Management,* Vol. 10, No. 2.

Delen, D., and E. Sirakaya. (2006). "Determining the Efficacy of Data-Mining Methods in Predicting Gaming Ballot Outcomes." *Journal of Hospitality & Tourism Research,* Vol. 30, No. 3, pp. 313–332.

Delen, D., R. Sharda, and M. Bessonov. (2006). "Identifying Significant Predictors of Injury Severity in Traffic Accidents Using a Series of Artificial Neural Networks." *Accident Analysis and Prevention,* Vol. 38, No. 3, pp. 434–444.

Dutta, S., and S. Shakhar. (1988, July 24–27). "Bond-Rating: A Non-Conservative Application of Neural Networks." *Proceedings of the IEEE International Conference on Neural Networks,* San Diego, CA.

Estévez, P. A., M. H. Claudio, and C. A. Perez. "Prevention in Telecommunications Using Fuzzy Rules and Neural Networks." **cec.uchile.cl/~pestevez/RI0.pdf** (accessed May 2009).

Fadlalla, A., and C. Lin. (2001). "An Analysis of the Applications of Neural Networks in Finance." *Interfaces,* Vol. 31, No. 4.

Fishman, M., D. Barr, and W. Loick. (1991, April). "Using Neural Networks in Market Analysis." *Technical Analysis of Stocks and Commodities.*

Fozzard, R., G. Bradshaw, and L. Ceci. (1989). "A Connectionist Expert System for Solar Flare Forecasting." In D. S. Touretsky (ed.), *Advances in Neural Information Processing Systems,* Vol. 1. San Mateo, CA: Kaufman.

Francett, B. (1989, January). "Neural Nets Arrive." *Computer Decisions.*

Gallant, S. (1988, February). "Connectionist Expert Systems." *Communications of the ACM,* Vol. 31, No. 2.

Güler, I., Z. Gökçil, and E. Gülbandilar. (2009). "Evaluating Traumatic Brain Injuries Using Artificial Neural Networks." *Expert Systems with Applications,* Vol. 36, pp. 10424–10427.

Haykin, S. S. (2009). *Neural Networks and Learning Machines,* 3rd ed. Upper Saddle River, NJ: Prentice Hall.

Hill, T., T. Marquez, M. O'Connor, and M. Remus. (1994). "Neural Network Models for Forecasting and Decision Making." *International Journal of Forecasting,* Vol. 10.

Hopfield, J. (1982, April). "Neural Networks and Physical Systems with Emergent Collective Computational Abilities." *Proceedings of National Academy of Science,* Vol. 79, No. 8.

Hopfield, J. J., and D. W. Tank. (1985). "Neural Computation of Decisions in Optimization Problems." *Biological Cybernetics,* Vol. 52.

Iyer, S. R., and R. Sharda. (2009). "Prediction of Athletes' Performance Using Neural Networks: An Application in Cricket Team Selection." *Expert Systems with Applications,* Vol. 36, No. 3, pp. 5510–5522.

Kamijo, K., and T. Tanigawa. (1990, June 7–11). "Stock Price Pattern Recognition: A Recurrent Neural Network Approach." *International Joint Conference on Neural Networks,* San Diego.

Lee, P. Y., S. C. Hui, and A. C. M. Fong. (2002, September/October). "Neural Networks for Web Content Filtering." *IEEE Intelligent Systems.*

Liang, T. P. (1992). "A Composite Approach to Automated Knowledge Acquisition." *Management Science,* Vol. 38, No. 1.

Loeffelholz, B., E. Bednar, and K. W. Bauer. (2009). "Predicting NBA Games Using Neural Networks." *Journal of Quantitative Analysis in Sports,* Vol. 5, No. 1.

McCulloch, W. S., and W. H. Pitts. (1943). "A Logical Calculus of the Ideas Imminent in Nervous Activity." *Bulletin of Mathematical Biophysics,* Vol. 5.

Medsker, L., and J. Liebowitz. (1994). *Design and Development of Expert Systems and Neural Networks.* New York: Macmillan, p. 163.

Mighell, D. (1989). "Back-Propagation and Its Application to Handwritten Signature Verification." In D. S. Touretsky (ed.), *Advances in Neural Information Processing Systems.* San Mateo, CA: Kaufman.

Minsky, M., and S. Papert. (1969). *Perceptrons.* Cambridge, MA: MIT Press.

Neural Technologies. "Combating Fraud: How a Leading Telecom Company Solved a Growing Problem." **neuralt.com/iqs/dlsfa.list/dlcpti.7/downloads.html**.

Nischwitz, R., M. Goldsmith, M. Lees, P. Rogers, and L. MacLeod. "Developing Functional Malt Specifications for Improved Brewing Performance." The Regional Institute Ltd., **regional.org.au/au/abts/1999/nischwitz.htm** (accessed May 2009).

Piatesky-Shapiro, G. "ISR: Microsoft Success Using Neural Network for Direct Marketing," **kdnuggets.com/news/94/n9.txt** (accessed May 2009).

Principe, J. C., N. R. Euliano, and W. C. Lefebvre. (2000). *Neural and Adaptive Systems: Fundamentals Through Simulations.* New York: Wiley.

Rochester, J. (ed.). (1990, February). "New Business Uses for Neurocomputing." *I/S Analyzer.*

Sirakaya, E., D. Delen, and H-S. Choi. (2005). "Forecasting Gaming Referenda." *Annals of Tourism Research,* Vol. 32, No. 1, pp. 127–149.

Sordo, M., H. Buxton, and D. Watson. (2001). "A Hybrid Approach to Breast Cancer Diagnosis." In L. Jain and P. DeWilde (eds.), *Practical Applications of Computational Intelligence Techniques,* Vol. 16. Norwell, MA: Kluwer.

Surkan, A., and J. Singleton. (1990). "Neural Networks for Bond Rating Improved by Multiple Hidden Layers." *Proceedings of the IEEE International Conference on Neural Networks,* Vol. 2.

Tang, Z., C. de Almieda, and P. Fishwick. (1991). "Time-Series Forecasting Using Neural Networks vs. Box-Jenkins Methodology." *Simulation,* Vol. 57, No. 5.

Thaler, S. L. (2002, January/February). "AI for Network Protection: LITMUS:—Live Intrusion Tracking via Multiple Unsupervised STANNOs." *PC AI.*

Walczak, S., W. E. Pofahi, and R. J. Scorpio. (2002). "A Decision Support Tool for Allocating Hospital Bed Resources and Determining Required Acuity of Care." *Decision Support Systems,* Vol. 34, No. 4.

Wallace, M. P. (2008, July). "Neural Networks and Their Applications in Finance." *Business Intelligence Journal,* pp. 67–76.

Wen, U-P., K-M. Lan, and H-S. Shih. (2009). "A Review of Hopfield Neural Networks for Solving Mathematical Programming Problems." *European Journal of Operational Research,* Vol. 198, pp. 675–687.

Wilson, C. I., and L. Threapleton. (2003, May 17–22). "Application of Artificial Intelligence for Predicting Beer Flavours from Chemical Analysis." *Proceedings of the 29th European Brewery Congress,* Dublin, Ireland. **neurosolutions.com/resources/apps/beer.html** (accessed May 2009).

Wilson, R., and R. Sharda. (1994). "Bankruptcy Prediction Using Neural Networks." *Decision Support Systems,* Vol. 11.

Zahedi, F. (1993). *Intelligent Systems for Business: Expert Systems with Neural Networks.* Belmont, CA: Wadsworth.

CHAPTER

7

Text and Web Mining

LEARNING OBJECTIVES

1 Describe text mining and understand the need for text mining

2 Differentiate between text mining and data mining

3 Understand the different application areas for text mining

4 Know the process of carrying out a text mining project

5 Understand the different methods to introduce structure to text-based data

6 Describe Web mining, its objectives, and its benefits

7 Understand the three different branches of Web mining

8 Understand Web content mining, Web structure mining, and Web log mining

This chapter provides a rather comprehensive overview of text mining and Web mining as they relate to business intelligence and decision support systems. Both Web mining and text mining are essentially the derivatives of data mining. Because text data and Web traffic data are increasing in volume an order of magnitude more than the data in structured databases, it is important to know some of the techniques used to process large amounts of unstructured data.

- 7.1 Opening Vignette: Mining Text for Security and Counterterrorism
- 7.2 Text Mining Concepts and Definitions
- 7.3 Natural Language Processing
- 7.4 Text Mining Applications
- 7.5 Text Mining Process
- 7.6 Text Mining Tools
- 7.7 Web Mining Overview
- 7.8 Web Content Mining and Web Structure Mining
- 7.9 Web Usage Mining
- 7.10 Web Mining Success Stories

7.1 OPENING VIGNETTE: MINING TEXT FOR SECURITY AND COUNTERTERRORISM

Imagine that you are a decision maker in a hostage situation at an American embassy. You are trying to understand, "Who is in charge of the terrorists?" "What is the reason behind this terrorist attack?" and "Is their group likely to attack other embassies?" Even though you have access to all kinds of information sources, you are hardly ever in a position to exploit such vast amounts of information effectively and efficiently for better decision making. How can computers help this process, which relies on accurate and timely intelligence in the midst of a crisis? The Genoa[1] project, part of DARPA's (Defense Advanced Research Projects Agency) total information awareness program, seeks to provide advanced tools and techniques to rapidly analyze information related to a current situation to support better decision making. Specifically, Genoa provides knowledge discovery tools to better "mine" relevant information sources for discovery of patterns in the form of actionable information (i.e., relevant knowledge nuggets).

One of the challenges Genoa faced was to make it easy for the end user to take the knowledge discovered by the analytics tools and embed it in a concise and useful form in an intelligence product. MITRE, a nonprofit innovative research organization chartered to work in the public interest (**mitre.org**), has been tasked with developing text mining–based software system to address this challenge. This system would allow the user to select various text mining tools and, with a few mouse clicks, assemble them to create a complex filter that fulfills whatever knowledge discovery function is currently needed. Here, a filter is a tool that takes input information and turns it into a more abstract and useful representation. Filters can also weed out irrelevant parts of the input information.

For example, in response to the crisis situation discussed earlier, an analyst might use text mining tools to discover important nuggets of information in a large collection of news sources. This use of text mining tools can be illustrated by looking at TopCat, a system developed by MITRE that identifies different topics in a collection of documents and displays the key "players" for each topic. TopCat uses association rule mining technology to identify relationships among people, organizations, locations, and events (shown with P, O, L, and E, respectively, in Figure 7.1). Grouping these relationships creates topic clusters such as the three shown in Figure 7.1, which are built from 6 months of global news from several print, radio, and video sources—over 60,000 news stories in all.

This tool enables an analyst to discover, say, an association between people involved in a bombing incident, such as "McVeigh and Nichols belong to a common organization!" which gives a starting point for further analysis, This, in turn, can lead to new knowledge that can be

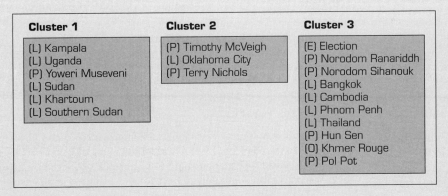

FIGURE 7.1 Topics Derived from Clustering 60,000 News Stories   *Source:* Mitre Corporation, **www.mitre.org** (accessed May 20, 2009).

---

[1] The Genoa project was started in 1997 and converted into Genoa II in 2003. The parent program, Total Information Awareness, was transitioned into a program called Topsail in 2003, both of which were highly criticized as being government-led spying programs that invaded privacy and human rights.

leveraged in the analytical model to help predict whether a particular terrorist organization is likely to strike elsewhere in the next few days. Similarly, the third topic reveals the important players in an election in Cambodia. This discovered information can be leveraged to help predict whether the situation in Cambodia is going to explode into a crisis that may potentially affect U.S. interests in that region.

Now, suppose the user wants to know more about the people in the last topic (the election in Cambodia). Instead of reading thousands of words of text from a number of articles on the topic, the analyst can compose a topic-detection filter with a biographical summarization filter (like the ones included in TopCat) that gather facts about key persons from the topic's articles. The result of such a composition would produce a short, to-the-point summary of the topic.

The summarization filter, developed with DARPA funding, identifies and aggregates descriptions of people from a collection of documents by means of an efficient syntactic analysis, the use of a thesaurus, and some simple natural language processing techniques. It also extracts from these documents salient sentences related to these people by weighting sentences based on the presence of the names of people as well as the location and proximity of terms in a document, their frequency, and their correlations with other terms in the document collection.

The summarization filter in TopCat can also perform a similar function for MITRE's Broadcast News Navigator, which applies this capability to continuously collected broadcast news in order to extract named entities and keywords and to identify the interesting transcripts and sentences that contain them. The summarization filter includes a parameter to specify the target length or the reduction rate, allowing summaries of different lengths to be generated. For example, allowing a longer summary would mean that facts about other people (e.g., Pol Pot) would also appear in the summary.

This example illustrates how mining a text collection using contemporary knowledge discovery tools such as the TopCat summarization filter can reveal important associations at varying levels of detail. The component-based approach employed in implementing TopCat allowed these filters to be easily integrated into intelligence products such as automated intelligence reporting and briefing tools and dashboards. These summarization filters can be connected to a specific region on a Web page of a *briefing book*, which can be shared across a community of collaborating analysts. When a document or a folder of documents is dropped onto a region connected to a filter, the filter processes the textual data and the information in the form of a textual summary or graphical visualization appears in that region.

Questions for the Opening Vignette

1. How can text mining be used in a crisis situation?
2. What is Genoa project? What is the motivation behind projects like Genoa?
3. What is TopCat? What does TopCat do?
4. What is a summarization filter?
5. Comment on the future of text mining tools for counterterrorism.

What We Can Learn from This Vignette

Text mining tools have been part of national intelligence initiatives such as the information awareness program for decades. In this vignette, DARPA and MITRE teamed up to develop capabilities to automatically filter text-based information sources to generate actionable information in a timely manner. They followed component-based architectures so that parts and pieces of this complex system can be revised, used, and reused independent of the rest of the information system. Using association, classification, and clustering analysis, these text-based document analysis tools illustrate the power of knowledge extraction from volumes of news articles. What has been achieved in the intelligence field is a good indicator of what can potentially be accomplished with the use of knowledge discovery tools and techniques in the near future.

Sources: MITRE Corporation, **mitre.org** (accessed on May 20, 2009); J. Mena, *Investigative Data Mining for Security and Criminal Detection,* Elsevier Science. Burlington, MA, 2003.

7.2 TEXT MINING CONCEPTS AND DEFINITIONS

The information age that we are living in is characterized by the rapid growth in the amount of data and information collected, stored, and made available in electronic media. A vast majority of business data are stored in text documents that are virtually unstructured. According to a study by Merrill Lynch and Gartner, 85 to 90 percent of all corporate data is captured and stored in some sort of unstructured form (McKnight, 2005). The same study also stated that this unstructured data is doubling in size every 18 months. Because knowledge is power in today's business world, and knowledge is derived from data and information, businesses that effectively and efficiently tap into their text data sources will have the necessary knowledge to make better decisions, leading to a competitive advantage over those businesses that lag behind. This is where the need for text mining fits into the big picture of today's businesses.

Text mining (also known as *text data mining* or *knowledge discovery in textual databases*) is the semi-automated process of extracting patterns (useful information and knowledge) from large amounts of unstructured data sources. Remember that data mining is the process of identifying valid, novel, potentially useful, and ultimately understandable patterns in data stored in structured databases, where the data are organized in records structured by categorical, ordinal, or continuous variables. Text mining is the same as data mining in that it has the same purpose and uses the same processes, but with text mining the input to the process is a collection of unstructured (or less structured) data files such as Word documents, PDF files, text excerpts, XML files, and so on. In essence, text mining can be thought of as a process (with two main steps) that starts with imposing structure on the text-based data sources followed by extracting relevant information and knowledge from this structured text-based data using data mining techniques and tools.

The benefits of text mining are obvious in the areas where very large amounts of textual data are being generated, such as law (court orders), academic research (research articles), finance (quarterly reports), medicine (discharge summaries), biology (molecular interactions), technology (patent files), and marketing (customer comments). For example, the free-form text-based interactions with customers in the form of complaints (or praises) and warranty claims can be used to objectively identify product and service characteristics that are deemed to be less than perfect and can be used as input to better product development and service allocations. Likewise, market outreach programs and focus groups generating large amounts of data. By not restricting product or service feedback to a codified form, customers can present, in their own words, what they think about a company's products and services. Another area where the automated processing of unstructured text has had a lot of impact is in electronic communications and e-mail. Text mining not only can be used to classify and filter junk e-mail, but it can also be used to automatically prioritize e-mail based on importance level as well as generate automatic responses (Weng and Liu, 2004). Following are among the most popular application areas of text mining:

- *Information extraction.* Identification of key phrases and relationships within text by looking for predefined sequences in text via pattern matching.
- *Topic tracking.* Based on a user profile and documents that a user views, text mining can predict other documents of interest to the user.
- *Summarization.* Summarizing a document to save time on the part of the reader.
- *Categorization.* Identifying the main themes of a document and then placing the document into a predefined set of categories based on those themes.
- *Clustering.* Grouping similar documents without having a predefined set of categories.

- *Concept linking.* Connects related documents by identifying their shared concepts and, by doing so, helps users find information that they perhaps would not have found using traditional search methods.
- *Question answering.* Finding the best answer to a given question through knowledge-driven pattern matching.

See Technology Insights 7.1 for explanations of some of the terms and concepts used in text mining. Application Case 7.1 describes the use of text mining in patent analysis.

TECHNOLOGY INSIGHTS 7.1   Text Mining Lingo

The following list describes some commonly used text mining terms:

- *Unstructured data (versus structured data).*   Structured data has a predetermined format. It is usually organized into records with simple data values (categorical, ordinal, and continuous variables) and stored in databases. In contrast, **unstructured data** does not have a predetermined format and is stored in the form of textual documents. In essence, the structured data is for the computers to process while the unstructured data is for humans to process and understand.
- *Corpus.*   In linguistics, a **corpus** (plural *corpora*) is a large and structured set of texts (now usually stored and processed electronically) prepared for the purpose of conducting knowledge discovery.
- *Terms.*   A *term* is a single word or multiword phrase extracted directly from the corpus of a specific domain by means of natural language processing (NLP) methods.
- *Concepts.*   *Concepts* are features generated from a collection of documents by means of manual, statistical, rule-based, or hybrid categorization methodology. Compared to terms, concepts are the result of higher level abstraction.
- *Stemming.*   **Stemming** is the process of reducing inflected words to their stem (or base or root) form. For instance, *stemmer, stemming, stemmed* are all based on the root *stem.*
- *Stop words.*   **Stop words** (or *noise words*) are words that are filtered out prior to or after processing of natural language data (i.e., text). Even though there is no universally accepted list of stop words, most natural language processing tools use a list that includes articles (*a, am, the, of,* etc.), auxiliary verbs (*is, are, was, were,* etc.), and context-specific words that are deemed not to have differentiating value.
- *Synonyms and polysemes.*   Synonyms are syntactically different words (i.e., spelled differently) with identical or at least similar meanings (e.g., *movie, film,* and *motion picture*). In contrast, **polysemes**, which are also called *homonyms*, are syntactically identical words (i.e., spelled exactly the same) with different meanings (e.g., *bow* can mean "to bend forward," "the front of the ship," "the weapon that shoots arrows," or "a kind of tied ribbon").
- *Tokenizing.*   A *token* is a categorized block of text in a sentence. The block of text corresponding to the token is categorized according to the function it performs. This assignment of meaning to blocks of text is known as **tokenizing**. A token can look like anything; it just needs to be a useful part of the structured text.
- *Term dictionary.*   A collection of terms specific to a narrow field that can be used to restrict the extracted terms within a corpus.
- *Word frequency.*   The number of times a word is found in a specific document.
- *Part-of-speech tagging.*   The process of marking up the words in a text as corresponding to a particular part of speech (such as nouns, verbs, adjectives, adverbs, etc.) based on a word's definition and the context in which it is used.
- *Morphology.*   A branch of the field of linguistics and a part of natural language processing that studies the internal structure of words (patterns of word-formation within a language or across languages).
- *Term-by-document matrix (occurrence matrix).*   A common representation schema of the frequency-based relationship between the terms and documents in tabular format where

terms are listed in rows, documents are listed in columns, and the frequency between the terms and documents is listed in cells as integer values.

- **Singular-value decomposition (latent semantic indexing).** A dimensionality reduction method used to transform the term-by-document matrix to a manageable size by generating an intermediate representation of the frequencies using a matrix manipulation method similar to principle component analysis.

APPLICATION CASE 7.1

Text Mining for Patent Analysis

A patent is a set of exclusive rights granted by a country to an inventor for a limited period of time in exchange for a disclosure of an invention (note that the procedure for granting patents, the requirements placed on the patentee, and the extent of the exclusive rights vary widely from country to country). The disclosure of these inventions is critical to future advancements in science and technology. If carefully analyzed, patent documents can help identify emerging technologies, inspire novel solutions, foster symbiotic partnerships, and enhance overall awareness of business' capabilities and limitations.

Patent analysis is the use of analytical techniques to extract valuable knowledge from patent databases. Countries or groups of countries that maintain patent databases (e.g., U.S., European Union, Japan) add tens of millions of new patents each year. It is nearly impossible to efficiently process such enormous amounts of semi-structured data (patent documents usually contain partially structured and partially textual data). Patent analysis with semi-automated software tools is one way to ease the processing of these very large databases.

A Representative Example of Patent Analysis

Eastman Kodak employs more than 5,000 scientists, engineers, and technicians around the world. During the twentieth century, these knowledge workers and their predecessors claimed nearly 20,000 patents, putting the company among the top 10 patent holders in the world. Being in the business of constant change, the company knows that success (or mere survival) depends on its ability to apply more than a century's worth of knowledge about imaging science and technology to new uses and to secure those new uses with patents.

Appreciating the value of patents, Kodak not only generates new patents but also analyzes those created by others. Using dedicated analysts and state-of-the-art software tools (including specialized text mining tools from ClearForest Corp.), Kodak continuously digs deep into various data sources (patent databases, new release archives, and product announcements) in order to develop a holistic view of the competitive landscape. Proper analysis of patents can bring companies like Kodak a wide range of benefits:

- It enables competitive intelligence. Knowing what competitors are doing can help a company to develop countermeasures.
- It can help the company make critical business decisions, such as what new products, product lines, and/or technologies to get into or what mergers and acquisitions to pursue.
- It can aid in identifying and recruiting the best and brightest new talent, those whose names appear on the patents that are critical to the company's success.
- It can help the company to identify the unauthorized use of its patents, enabling it to take action to protect its assets.
- It can identify complementary inventions to build symbiotic partnerships or to facilitate mergers and/or acquisitions.
- It prevents competitors from creating similar products and it can help protect the company from patent infringement lawsuits.

Using patent analysis as a rich source of knowledge and a strategic weapon (both defensive as well as offensive), Kodak not only survives but excels in its market segment defined by innovation and constant change.

Sources: P. X. Chiem, "Kodak Turns Knowledge Gained About Patents into Competitive Intelligence," *Knowledge Management,* 2001, pp. 11–12; Y-H. Tsenga, C-J. Linb, and Y-I. Linc, "Text Mining Techniques for Patent Analysis," *Information Processing & Management,* Vol. 43, No. 5, 2007, pp. 1216–1247.

Section 7.2 Questions

1. What is text mining? How does it differ from data mining?
2. Why is the popularity of text mining as a BI tool increasing?
3. What are some popular application areas of text mining?

7.3 NATURAL LANGUAGE PROCESSING

Some of the early text mining applications used a simplified representation called *bag-of-words* when introducing structure to a collection of text-based documents in order to classify them into two or more predetermined classes or to cluster them into natural groupings. In the bag-of-words model, text, such as a sentence, paragraph, or complete document, is represented as a collection of words, disregarding the grammar or the order in which the words appear. The bag-of-words model is still used in some simple document classification tools. For instance, in spam filtering an e-mail message can be modeled as an unordered collection of words (a bag-of-words) that is compared against two different predetermined bags. One bag is filled with words found in spam messages and the other is filled with words found in legitimate e-mails. Although some of the words are likely to be found in both bags, the "spam" bag will contain spam-related words such as *stock, Viagra,* and *buy* much more frequently than the legitimate bag, which will contain more words related to the user's friends or workplace. The level of match between a specific e-mail's bag-of-words and the two bags containing the descriptors determines the membership of the e-mail as either spam or legitimate.

Naturally, we (humans) do not use words without some order or structure. We use words in sentences, which have semantic as well as syntactic structure. Thus, automated techniques (such as text mining) need to look for ways to go beyond the bag-of-words interpretation and incorporate more and more semantic structure into their operations. The current trend in text mining is toward including many of the advanced features that can be obtained using natural language processing.

It has been shown that the bag-of-word method may not produce good enough information content for text mining tasks (e.g., classification, clustering, association). A good example of this can be found in evidence-based medicine. A critical component of evidence-based medicine is incorporating the best available research findings into the clinical decision-making process, which involves appraisal of the information collected from the printed media for validity and relevance. Several researchers from University of Maryland developed evidence assessment models using a bag-of-words method (Lin and Demner, 2005). They employed popular machine-learning methods along with more than half a million research articles collected from MEDLINE (Medical Literature Analysis and Retrieval System Online). In their models, they represented each abstract as a bag-of-words, where each stemmed term represented a feature. Despite using popular classification methods with proven experimental design methodologies, their prediction results were not much better than simple guessing, which may indicate that the bag-of-words is not generating a good enough representation of the research articles in this domain; hence, more advanced techniques such as natural language processing are needed.

Natural language processing (NLP) is an important component of text mining and is a subfield of artificial intelligence and computational linguistics. It studies the problem of "understanding" the natural human language, with the view of converting depictions of human language (such as textual documents) into more formal representations (in the form of numeric and symbolic data) that are easier for computer programs to manipulate. The goal of NLP is to move beyond syntax-driven text manipulation (which is often called "word counting") to a true understanding and processing of natural language that considers grammatical and semantic constraints as well as the context.

The definition and scope of the word "understanding" is one of the major discussion topics in NLP. Considering that the natural human language is vague and that a true understanding of meaning requires extensive knowledge of a topic (beyond what is in the words, sentences, and paragraphs), will computers ever be able to understand natural language the same way and with the same accuracy that humans do? Probably not! NLP has come a long way from the days of simple word counting, but it has an even longer way to go to really understanding natural human language. The following are just a few of the challenges commonly associated with the implementation of NLP:

- *Part-of-speech tagging.* It is difficult to mark up terms in a text as corresponding to a particular part of speech (such as nouns, verbs, adjectives, adverbs, etc.), because the part of speech depends not only on the definition of the term but also on the context within which it is used.
- *Text segmentation.* Some written languages, such as Chinese, Japanese, and Thai, do not have single-word boundaries. In these instances, the text-parsing task requires the identification of word boundaries, which is often a difficult task. Similar challenges in speech segmentation emerge when analyzing spoken language, because sounds representing successive letters and words blend into each other.
- *Word sense disambiguation.* Many words have more than one meaning. Selecting the meaning that makes the most sense can only be accomplished by taking into account the context within which the word is used.
- *Syntactic ambiguity.* The grammar for natural languages is ambiguous; that is, multiple possible sentence structures often need to be considered. Choosing the most appropriate structure usually requires a fusion of semantic and contextual information.
- *Imperfect or irregular input.* Foreign or regional accents and vocal impediments in speech and typographical or grammatical errors in texts make the processing of the language an even more difficult task.
- *Speech acts.* A sentence can often be considered an action by the speaker. The sentence structure alone may not contain enough information to define this action. For example, "Can you pass the class?" requests a simple yes/no answer, whereas "Can you pass the salt?" is a request for a physical action to be performed.

It is a longstanding dream of the artificial intelligence community to have algorithms that are capable of automatically reading and obtaining knowledge from text. By applying a learning algorithm to parsed text, researchers from Stanford University's NLP lab have developed methods that can automatically identify the concepts and relationships between those concepts in the text. By applying a unique procedure to large amounts of text, their algorithms automatically acquire hundreds of thousands of items of world knowledge and use them to produce significantly enhanced repositories for WordNet. WordNet is a laboriously hand-coded database of English words, their definitions, sets of synonyms, and various semantic relations between synonym sets. It is a major resource for NLP applications, but it has proven to be very expensive to build and maintain manually. By automatically inducing knowledge into WordNet, the potential exists to make WordNet an even greater and more comprehensive resource for NLP at a fraction of the cost.

One prominent area where the benefits of NLP are already being harvested is in customer relationship management (CRM). Broadly speaking, the goal of CRM is to maximize customer value by better understanding and effectively responding to their actual and perceived needs. An important area of CRM, where NLP is making a significant impact, is sentiment analysis. Sentiment analysis is a technique used to detect favorable and unfavorable opinions toward specific products and services using a large numbers of textual data sources (customer feedback in the form of Web postings). See Application Case 7.2 for an example of the successful application of text mining to CRM.

APPLICATION CASE 7.2

Text Mining Helps Merck to Better Understand and Serve Its Customers

Merck Sharp & Dohme (MSD) is a global, research-driven pharmaceutical company based in Germany that is dedicated to solving the world's health care needs. Established in 1891, MSD discovers, develops, manufactures, and markets vaccines and medicines to address challenging health care needs.

As one of the world's largest pharmaceutical manufacturers, MSD relies heavily on the input it gets from doctors to better help the patients they serve. The expected outcome is better care for patients who are afflicted with illnesses such as AIDS, osteoporosis, heart failure, migraine headaches, and asthma, among many others.

Realizing the importance of knowledge discovery, many years ago MSD developed an analytics program that uses data and text mining applications to better leverage its data and information assets. MSD uses text mining technology from SPSS to analyze information it collects from a variety of sources and then uses that information to create effective programs that best address physician and patient needs.

Challenge

Like any other profession, the people working in the health care industry have an array of beliefs and opinions. That's where the challenge comes in for MSD: It must get a firm grasp on what doctors are saying in the field and then pass that information on to its product development teams so it can create better drugs and effective marketing campaigns for those drugs. Considering the range of MSD's target audience, such a task is anything but simple. On one end of the spectrum are the "pioneer" doctors who are very open to new insights and research results and fairly quickly turn scientific findings into practice. At the other end of the scale are the "conservative personality" doctors who follow traditional practices and want to do everything by the book, spend a lot of time researching treatment options, and base their opinions on the thorough study of specialist articles or exchanges with colleagues. To be successful, MSD had to find the right way to approach all types of doctors. However, first it had to identify the various groups. To do so, MSD needed to use all available information from various sources, including internal data and data from external providers.

Solution

MSD decided to use text mining and quantitative analysis tools from SPSS to get a better understanding of the data collected from the surveys, some of which were conducted at various communications seminars, and then provide that valuable information to the marketing team. Some of the characteristics measured in these surveys included the number of years a doctor had been established, the number of patients a doctor serves, along with questions that led to open-ended textual responses. Once the necessary data was obtained, special analytics were used to gain further insight into the data with regard to their significance and correlation among the wide range of characteristics. MSD also used the collected data for profiling purposes. The analytic tools allowed MSD to allocate doctors to a number of typologies. By segmenting doctors based on measures introduced by the marketing department, MSD decides which action catalog best characterizes the relevant target groups.

Results

For MSD, text mining—the analysis of unstructured, textual data—is indispensable. The text mining functionality is based on the natural grammatical analysis of text. It does not depend solely on keyword search, but analyzes the syntax of language and "understands" the content. By doing so, it discovers indispensible knowledge needed to improve the company's competitive position.

MSD works with the Gesellschaft für Konsumforschung panel (Association for Consumer Research, GfK), which uses the daily "diary" entries of doctors on the panel to learn which pharmaceutical representatives have visited them, what product communications were conveyed, and whether they will include these products in the range of drugs they prescribe in the future. Text mining analyses of the product conversations noted by the doctors reveal speech patterns that accompany various prescribing behaviors. This enables MSD to optimize its products and marketing campaigns and to improve its sales representatives' communication skills. Thanks to SPSS and its text mining tools, MSD knows which properties of and information about its drugs are particularly well understood in conversations with the doctors and when the terms used in its marketing campaigns need to be refined.

Source: SPSS, "Merck Sharp & Dohme," **http:// www.spss. com/success/template_view.cfm?Story_ID=185** (accessed May 15, 2009).

Sentiment analysis offers enormous opportunities for various applications. For instance, it would provide powerful functionality for competitive analysis, marketing analysis, and detection of unfavorable rumors for risk management. A sentiment analysis approach developed by researchers at IBM seeks to extract sentiments associated with polarities of positive or negative for specific subjects (e.g., products or services) from a collection of documents (Kanayama and Nasukawa, 2006). The main issues in sentiment analysis are to identify how sentiments are expressed in texts and whether the expressions indicate positive (favorable) or negative (unfavorable) opinions toward the subject. In order to improve the accuracy of the sentiment analysis, it is important to properly identify the semantic relationships between the sentiment expressions and the subject. By applying semantic analysis with a syntactic parser and sentiment lexicon, IBM's system achieved high precision (75–95%, depending on the data) in finding sentiments within Web pages and news articles.

NLP has successfully been applied to a variety of tasks via computer programs to automatically process natural human language that previously could only be done by humans. Following are among the most popular of these tasks:

- *Information retrieval.* The science of searching for relevant documents, finding specific information within them, and generating metadata as to their contents.
- *Information extraction.* A type of information retrieval whose goal is to automatically extract structured information, such as categorized and contextually and semantically well-defined data from a certain domain, using unstructured machine-readable documents.
- *Named-entity recognition.* Also known as *entity identification* and *entity extraction*, this subtask of information extraction seeks to locate and classify atomic elements in text into predefined categories, such as the names of persons, organizations, locations, expressions of times, quantities, monetary values, percentages, and so on.
- *Question answering.* The task of automatically answering a question posed in natural language; that is, producing a human-language answer when given a human-language question. To find the answer to a question, the computer program may use either a prestructured database or a collection of natural language documents (a text corpus such as the World Wide Web).
- *Automatic summarization.* The creation of a shortened version of a textual document by a computer program that contains the most important points of the original document.
- *Natural language generation.* Systems convert information from computer databases into readable human language.
- *Natural language understanding.* Systems convert samples of human language into more formal representations that are easier for computer programs to manipulate.
- *Machine translation.* The automatic translation of one human language to another.
- *Foreign language reading.* A computer program that assists a nonnative language speaker to read a foreign language with correct pronunciation and accents on different parts of the words.

- *Foreign language writing.* A computer program that assists a nonnative language user in writing in a foreign language.
- *Speech recognition.* Converts spoken words to machine-readable input. Given a sound clip of a person speaking, the system produces a text dictation.
- *Text-to-speech.* Also called *speech synthesis*, a computer program automatically converts normal language text into human speech.
- *Text proofing.* A computer program reads a proof copy of a text in order to detect and correct any errors.
- *Optical character recognition.* The automatic translation of images of handwritten, typewritten, or printed text (usually captured by a scanner) into machine-editable textual documents.

The success and popularity of text mining depends greatly on advancements in NLP in both generation as well as understanding of human languages. NLP enables the extraction of features from unstructured text so that a wide variety of data mining techniques can be used to extract knowledge (novel and useful patterns and relationships) from it. In that sense, simply put, text mining is a combination of NLP and data mining.

Section 7.3 Review Questions

1. What is natural language processing?
2. How does NLP relate to text mining?
3. What are some of the benefits and challenges of NLP?
4. What are the most common tasks addressed by NLP?

7.4 TEXT MINING APPLICATIONS

As the amount of unstructured data collected by organizations increases, so does the value proposition and popularity of text mining tools. Many organizations are now realizing the importance of extracting knowledge from their document-based data repositories through the use of text mining tools. Following are only a small subset of the exemplary application categories of text mining.

Marketing Applications

Text mining can be used to increase cross-selling and up-selling by analyzing the unstructured data generated by call centers. Text generated by call-center notes as well as transcriptions of voice conversations with customers can be analyzed by text mining algorithms to extract novel, actionable information about customers' perceptions toward a company's products and services. Additionally, blogs, user reviews of products at independent Web sites, and discussion board postings are a gold mine of customer sentiments. This rich collection of information, once properly analyzed, can be used to increase satisfaction and the overall lifetime value of the customer (Coussement and Van den Poel, 2008).

Text mining has become invaluable for customer relationship management. Companies can use text mining to analyze rich sets of unstructured text data, combined with the relevant structured data extracted from organizational databases, to predict customer perceptions and subsequent purchasing behavior. Coussement and Van den Poel (2009) successfully applied text mining to significantly improve the ability of a model to predict customer churn (i.e., customer attrition) so that those customers identified as most likely to leave a company are accurately identified for retention tactics.

Ghani et al. (2006) used text mining to develop a system capable of inferring implicit and explicit attributes of products to enhance retailers' ability to analyze product databases. Treating products as sets of attribute–value pairs rather than as atomic entities can potentially boost the effectiveness of many business applications, including demand forecasting, assortment optimization, product recommendations, assortment comparison across retailers and manufacturers, and product supplier selection. The proposed system allows a business to represent its products in terms of attributes and attribute values without much manual effort. The system learns these attributes by applying supervised and semi supervised learning techniques to product descriptions found on retailers' Web sites.

Security Applications

One of the largest and most prominent text mining applications in the security domain is probably the highly classified ECHELON surveillance system. As rumor has it, ECHELON is assumed to be capable of identifying the content of telephone calls, faxes, e-mails, and other types of data, intercepting information sent via satellites, public switched telephone networks, and microwave links.

In 2007, EUROPOL developed an integrated system capable of accessing, storing, and analyzing vast amounts of structured and unstructured data sources in order to track transnational organized crime. Called the Overall Analysis System for Intelligence Support (OASIS), this system aims to integrate the most advanced data and text mining technologies available in today's market. The system has enabled EUROPOL to make significant progress in supporting its law enforcement objectives at the international level (EUROPOL, 2007).

The U.S. Federal Bureau of Investigation (FBI) and the Central Intelligence Agency (CIA), under the direction of the Department for Homeland Security, are jointly developing a supercomputer data and text mining system. The system is expected to create a gigantic data warehouse along with a variety of data and text mining modules to meet the knowledge-discovery needs of federal, state, and local law enforcement agencies. Prior to this project, the FBI and CIA each had its own separate databases, with little or no interconnection.

Another security-related application of text mining is in the area of **deception detection**. Applying text mining to a large set of real-world criminal (person-of-interest) statements, Fuller et al. (2008) developed prediction models to differentiate deceptive statements from truthful ones. Using a rich set of cues extracted from the textual statements, the model predicted the holdout samples with 70 percent accuracy, which is believed to be a significant success considering that the cues are extracted only from textual statements (no verbal or visual cues are present). Furthermore, compared to other deception-detection techniques, such as polygraph, this method is nonintrusive and widely applicable to not only textual data, but also (potentially) to transcriptions of voice recordings. A more detailed description of text-based deception detection is provided in Application Case 7.3.

APPLICATION CASE 7.3
Mining for Lies

Driven by advancements in Web-based information technologies and increasing globalization, computer-mediated communication continues to filter into everyday life, bringing with it new venues for deception. The volume of text-based chat, instant messaging, text messaging, and text generated by online communities of practice is increasing rapidly. Even e-mail continues to grow in use. With the massive growth of text-based communication, the potential for people to deceive others through computer-mediated communication has also grown, and such deception can have disastrous results.

Unfortunately, in general, humans tend to perform poorly at deception-detection tasks. This phenomenon is exacerbated in text-based communications. A large part of the research on deception detection (also known as *credibility assessment*) has involved face-to-face meetings and interviews. Yet, with the growth of text-based communication, text-based deception-detection techniques are essential.

Techniques for successfully detecting deception—that is, lies—have wide applicability. Law enforcement can use decision support tools and techniques to investigate crimes, conduct security screening in airports, and monitor communications of suspected terrorists. Human resources professionals might use deception detection tools to screen applicants. These tools and techniques also have the potential to screen e-mails to uncover fraud or other wrongdoings committed by corporate officers. Although some people believe that they can readily identify those who are not being truthful, a summary of deception research showed that, on average, people are only 54 percent accurate in making veracity determinations (Bond and DePaulo, 2006). This figure may actually be worse when humans try to detect deception in text.

Using a combination of text mining and data mining techniques, Fuller et al. (2008) analyzed person-of-interest statements completed by people involved in crimes on military bases. In these statements, suspects and witnesses are required to write their recollection of the event in their own words. Military law enforcement personnel searched archival data for statements that they could conclusively identify as being truthful or deceptive. These decisions were made on the basis of corroborating evidence and case resolution. Once labeled as truthful or deceptive, the law enforcement personnel removed identifying information and gave the statements to the research team. In total, 371 usable statements were received for analysis. The text-based deception detection method used by Fuller et al. (2008) was based on a process known as *message feature mining*, which relies on elements of data and text mining techniques. A simplified depiction of the process is provided in Figure 7.2.

First, the researchers prepared the data for processing. The original handwritten statements had to be transcribed into a word processing file. Second, features (i.e., cues) were identified. The researchers identified 31 features representing categories or types of language that are relatively independent of the text content and that can be readily analyzed by automated means. For example, first-person pronouns such as *I* or *me* can be identified without analysis of the surrounding text. Table 7.1 lists the categories and an example list of features used in this study.

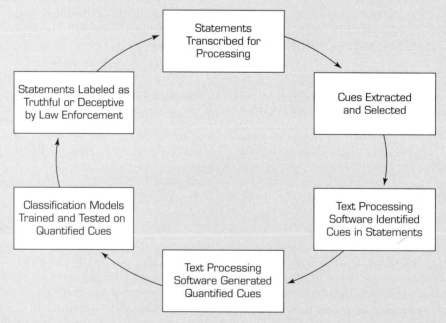

FIGURE 7.2 Text-Based Deception-Detection Process   *Source:* C. M. Fuller, D. Biros, and D. Delen, "Exploration of Feature Selection and Advanced Classification Models for High-Stakes Deception Detection," in *Proceedings of the 41st Annual Hawaii International Conference on System Sciences (HICSS),* January 2008, Big Island, HI, IEEE Press, pp. 80–99.

TABLE 7.1 Categories and Examples of Linguistic Features Used in Deception Detection

Number	Construct (Category)	Example Cues
1	Quantity	Verb count, noun-phrase count, etc.
2	Complexity	Average number of clauses, average sentence length, etc.
3	Uncertainty	Modifiers, modal verbs, etc.
4	Nonimmediacy	Passive voice, objectification, etc.
5	Expressivity	Emotiveness
6	Diversity	Lexical diversity, redundancy, etc.
7	Informality	Typographical error ratio
8	Specificity	Spatiotemporal information, perceptual information, etc.
9	Affect	Positive affect, negative affect, etc.

The features were extracted from the textual statements and input into a flat file for further processing. Using several feature-selection methods along with 10-fold cross-validation, the researchers compared the prediction accuracy of three popular data mining methods. Their results indicated that neural network models performed the best, with 73.46 percent prediction accuracy on test data samples; decision trees performed second best, with 71.60 percent accuracy; and logistic regression was last, with 67.28 percent accuracy.

The results indicate that automated text-based deception detection has the potential to aid those who must try to detect lies in text and can be successfully applied to real-world data. The accuracy of these techniques exceeded the accuracy of most other deception-detection techniques even though it was limited to textual cues.

Sources: C. M. Fuller, D. Biros, and D. Delen, "Exploration of Feature Selection and Advanced Classification Models for High-Stakes Deception Detection," in *Proceedings of the 41st Annual Hawaii International Conference on System Sciences (HICSS)*, 2008, Big Island, HI, IEEE Press, pp. 80–99; C. F. Bond and B. M. DePaulo, "Accuracy of Deception Judgments," *Personality and Social Psychology Reports*, Vol. 10, No. 3, 2006, pp. 214–234.

Biomedical Applications

Text mining holds great potential for the medical field in general and biomedicine in particular for several reasons. First, the published literature and publication outlets (especially with the advent of the open source journals) in the field are expanding at an exponential rate. Second, compared to most other fields, the medical literature is more standardized and orderly, making it a more "minable" information source. Finally, the terminology used in this literature is relatively constant, having a fairly standardized ontology. What follows are a few exemplary studies where text mining techniques were successfully used in extracting novel patterns from biomedical literature.

Experimental techniques such as DNA microarray analysis, serial analysis of gene expression (SAGE), and mass spectrometry proteomics, among others, are generating large amounts of data related to genes and proteins. As in any other experimental approach, it is necessary to analyze this vast amount of data in the context of previously known information about the biological entities under study. The literature is a particularly valuable source of information for experiment validation and interpretation. Therefore, the development of automated text mining tools to assist in such interpretation is one of the main challenges in current bioinformatics research.

Knowing the location of a protein within a cell can help to elucidate its role in biological processes and to determine its potential as a drug target. Numerous location-prediction systems are described in the literature; some focus on specific organisms, whereas others attempt to analyze a wide range of organisms. Shatkay et al. (2007) proposed a comprehensive system that uses several types of sequence- and text-based features to predict the location of proteins. The main novelty of their system lies in the way in which it selects its text sources and features and integrates them with sequence-based features. They tested the system on previously used datasets and on new datasets devised specifically to test its predictive power. The results showed that their system consistently beat previously reported results.

Chun et al. (2006) described a system that extracts disease–gene relationships from literature accessed via MEDLINE. They constructed a dictionary for disease and gene names from six public databases and extracted relation candidates by dictionary matching. Because dictionary matching produces a large number of false positives, they developed a method of machine learning–based named entity recognition (NER) to filter out false recognitions of disease/gene names. They found that the success of relation extraction is heavily dependent on the performance of NER filtering and that the filtering improved the precision of relation extraction by 26.7 percent, at the cost of a small reduction in recall.

Figure 7.3 shows a simplified depiction of a multilevel text analysis process for discovering gene–protein relationships (or protein–protein interactions) in the biomedical literature (Nakov et al., 2005). As can be seen in this simplified example that uses a simple sentence from biomedical text, first (at the bottom three levels) the text is tokenized using **part-of-speech tagging** and shallow-parsing. The tokenized terms (words) are then matched (and interpreted) against the hierarchical representation of the domain ontology to derive the gene–protein relationship. Application of this method (and/or some variation of it) to the biomedical literature offers great potential to decode the complexities in the Human Genome Project.

Academic Applications

The issue of text mining is of great importance to publishers who hold large databases of information requiring indexing for better retrieval. This is particularly true in scientific disciplines, in which highly specific information is often contained within written text. Initiatives have been launched, such as *Nature*'s proposal for an Open Text Mining Interface (OTMI) and the National Institutes of Health's common Journal Publishing Document Type Definition (DTD), that would provide semantic cues to machines to answer specific queries contained within text without removing publisher barriers to public access.

Academic institutions have also launched text mining initiatives. For example, the National Centre for Text Mining, a collaborative effort between the Universities of Manchester and Liverpool, provides customized tools, research facilities, and advice on text mining to the academic community. With an initial focus on text mining in the biological and biomedical sciences, research has since expanded into the social sciences. In the United States, the School of Information at the University of California, Berkeley, is developing a program called BioText to assist bioscience researchers in text mining and analysis.

As described in this section, text mining has a wide variety of applications in a number of different disciplines. See Application Case 7.4 for an example of how the aviation industry is using text mining of air incident reports to increase safety.

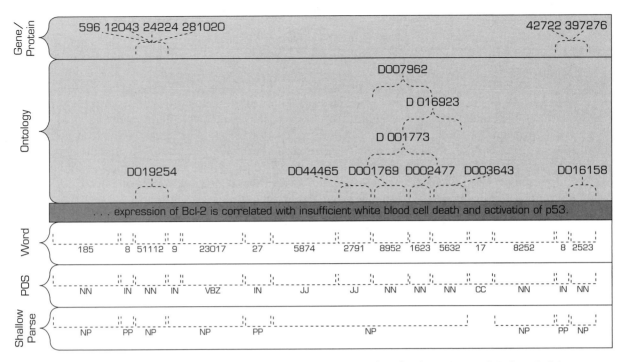

FIGURE 7.3 Multilevel Analysis of Text for Gene–Protein Interaction Identification *Source:* P. Nakov, A. Schwartz, B. Wolf, and M. A. Hearst, "Supporting Annotation Layers for Natural Language Processing," *Proceedings of the Association for Computational Linguistics (ACL),* interactive poster and demonstration sessions, 2005, Ann Arbor, Michigan, pp. 65–68.

APPLICATION CASE 7.4

Flying Through Text

Text mining has proven to be a valuable tool in extracting organizational knowledge from written documents stored in digitized form. Analysts are using text mining software to focus on key problem areas through pattern identification. For example, companies in the airline industry can apply text mining to incident reports to increase the quality of organizational knowledge. They can study mechanical, organizational, and behavioral problems in a timely manner through the use of text mining.

Airlines operate with a thorough and systematic analysis of operations. An incident report is prepared whenever an event occurs that might lead to a problem. Text mining techniques can be used to automatically identify key issues from the masses of

incident reports. The huge databases that airlines maintain have limited human interpretation, and the terminology appears different to a computer than to a human.

Aer Lingus (**aerlingus.com**) examined incident reports generated from January 1998 through December 2003 to find possible patterns and correlations. Aer Lingus used Megaputer's PolyAnalyst (**megaputer.com**), a comprehensive data and text mining software. The goal of the study was to develop a process that investigators could regularly use to identify patterns and associations with regards to incident type, location, time, and other details.

The most frequently occurring terms were identified in the incident reports. PolyAnalyst carries a lexicon of terms that is not complete but that provides a valuable starting point for text analysis. It can also generate a list of key terms (or their semantic equivalents) occurring in the data. A report called a frequent-terms report is created, which contains the terms identified and their frequency. The objective is to identify interesting clusters. A narrative summary includes a set of terms that divide the narrative descriptions into meaningful groups. For example, the key term *spillage* can be associated with four other key terms: *food, fuel, chemical,* and *toilet*. From the key terms, *food* is semantically related to *coffee, tea,* and *drink*. Thus, *food*

becomes the category node, and the different food products reported as spilled are matched to *food*.

Text mining of airline incident reports can identify underlying root causes that may lead to safety improvements. Text mining can also be used with a large set of incident reports data to validate predetermined theories and commonsense sense knowledge as well as harvesting and adding new patterns to the knowledge base.

Source: J. Froelich, S. Ananyan, and D. L Olson, "Business Intelligence Through Text Mining," *Business Intelligence Journal,* Vol. 10, No. 1, 2005, pp. 43–50.

Section 7.4 Review Questions

1. List and briefly discuss some of the text mining applications in marketing.
2. How can text mining be used in security and counterterrorism?
3. What are some promising text mining applications in biomedicine?

7.5 TEXT MINING PROCESS

In order to be successful, text mining studies should follow a sound methodology based on best practices. A standardized process model is needed similar to CRISP-DM, which is the industry standard for data mining projects (see Chapter 5). Even though most parts of CRISP-DM are also applicable to text mining projects, a specific process model for text mining would include much more elaborate data preprocessing activities. Figure 7.4 depicts a high-level context diagram of a typical text mining process (Delen and Crossland, 2008). This context diagram presents the scope of the process, emphasizing its interfaces with the larger environment. In essence, it draws boundaries around the specific process to explicitly identify what is included (and excluded) from the text mining process.

As the context diagram indicates, the input (inward connection to the left edge of the box) into the text-based knowledge discovery process is the unstructured as well as structured data collected, stored, and made available to the process. The output (outward extension from the right edge of the box) of the process is the context-specific knowledge that can be used for decision making. The controls, also called the *constraints* (inward connection to the top edge of the box), of the process include software and hardware limitations, privacy issues, and the difficulties related to processing of the text that is presented in the form of natural language. The mechanisms (inward connection to the bottom edge of the box) of the process include proper techniques, software tools, and domain expertise. The primary purpose of text mining (within the context of knowledge discovery) is to process unstructured (textual) data (along with structured data, if relevant to the problem being addressed and available) to extract meaningful and actionable patterns for better decision making.

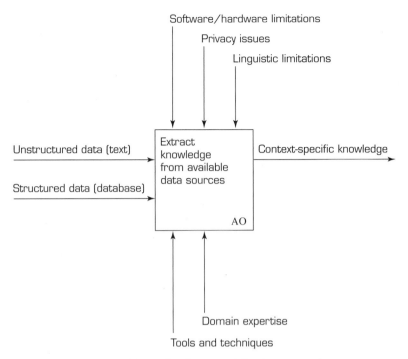

FIGURE 7.4 Context Diagram for the Text Mining Process

At a very high level, the text mining process can be broken down into three consecutive tasks, each of which has specific inputs to generate certain outputs (see Figure 7.5). If, for some reason, the output of a task is not that which is expected, a backward redirection to the previous task execution is necessary.

Task 1: Establish the Corpus

The main purpose of the first task activity is to collect all of the documents related to the context (domain of interest) being studied. This collection may include textual documents, XML files, e-mails, Web pages, and short notes. In addition to the readily available textual data, voice recordings may also be transcribed using speech-recognition algorithms and made a part of the text collection.

Once collected, the text documents are transformed and organized in a manner such that they are all in the same representational form (e.g., ASCII text files) for computer processing. The organization of the documents can be as simple as a collection of digitized text excerpts stored in a file folder or it can be a list of links to a collection of Web pages in a specific domain. Many commercially available text mining software tools could accept these as input and convert them into a flat file for processing. Alternatively, the flat file can be prepared outside the text mining software and then presented as the input to the text mining application.

Task 2: Create the Term–Document Matrix

In this task, the digitized and organized documents (the corpus) are used to create the **term–document matrix (TDM)**. In the TDM, rows represent the documents and columns represent the terms. The relationships between the terms and documents are

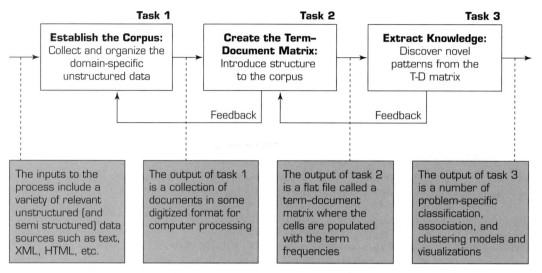

FIGURE 7.5 The Three-Step Text Mining Process

characterized by indices (i.e., a relational measure that can be as simple as the number of occurrences of the term in respective documents). Figure 7.6 is a typical example of a TDM.

The goal is to convert the list of organized documents (the corpus) into a TDM where the cells are filled with the most appropriate indices. The assumption is that the essence of a document can be represented with a list and frequency of the terms used in that document. However, are all terms important when characterizing documents? Obviously, the answer is "no." Some terms, such as articles, auxiliary verbs, and terms

Documents \ Terms	Investment Risk	Project Management	Software Engineering	Development	SAP	. . .
Document 1	1			1		
Document 2		1				
Document 3			3		1	
Document 4		1				
Document 5			2	1		
Document 6	1			1		
. . .						

FIGURE 7.6 A Simple Term–Document Matrix

used in almost all of the documents in the corpus, have no differentiating power and therefore should be excluded from the indexing process. This list of terms, commonly called *stop terms* or *stop words*, is specific to the domain of study and should be identified by the domain experts. On the other hand, one might choose a set of predetermined terms under which the documents are to be indexed (this list of terms is conveniently called *include terms* or *dictionary*). Additionally, synonyms (pairs of terms that are to be treated the same) and specific phrases (e.g., "Eiffel Tower") can also be provided so that the index entries are more accurate.

Another filtration that should take place to accurately create the indices is *stemming*, which refers to the reduction of words to their roots so that, for example, different grammatical forms or declinations of a verb are identified and indexed as the same word. For example, stemming will ensure that *modeling* and *modeled* will be recognized as the word *model*.

The first generation of the TDM includes all of the unique terms identified in the corpus (as its columns), excluding the ones in the stop term list; all of the documents (as its rows); and the occurrence count of each term for each document (as its cell values). If, as is commonly the case, the corpus includes a rather large number of documents, then there is a very good chance that the TDM will have a very large number of terms. Processing such a large matrix might be time consuming and, more important, might lead to extraction of inaccurate patterns. At this point, one has to decide the following: (1) What is the best representation of the indices? and (2) How can we reduce the dimensionality of this matrix to a manageable size?

REPRESENTING THE INDICES   Once the input documents are indexed and the initial word frequencies (by document) computed, a number of additional transformations can be performed to summarize and aggregate the extracted information. The raw term frequencies generally reflect on how salient or important a word is in each document. Specifically, words that occur with greater frequency in a document are better descriptors of the contents of that document. However, it is not reasonable to assume that the word counts themselves are proportional to their importance as descriptors of the documents. For example, if a word occurs one time in document *A*, but three times in document *B*, then it is not necessarily reasonable to conclude that this word is three times as important a descriptor of document *B* as compared to document *A*. In order to have a more consistent TDM for further analysis, these raw indices need to be normalized. As opposed to showing the actual frequency counts, the numerical representation between terms and documents can be normalized using a number of alternative methods. The following are a few of the most commonly used normalization methods (StatSoft, 2009):

- *Log frequencies.*   The raw frequencies can be transformed using the log function. This transformation would "dampen" the raw frequencies and how they affect the results of subsequent analysis.

$$f(wf) = 1 + \log(wf) \qquad \text{for } wf > 0$$

  In the formula, *wf* is the raw word (or term) frequency and $f(wf)$ is the result of the log transformation. This transformation is applied to all of the raw frequencies in the TDM where the frequency is greater than zero.

- *Binary frequencies.*   Likewise, an even simpler transformation can be used to enumerate whether a term is used in a document.

$$f(wf) = 1 \qquad \text{for } wf > 0$$

The resulting TDM matrix will contain only 1s and 0s to indicate the presence or absence of the respective words. Again, this transformation will dampen the effect of the raw frequency counts on subsequent computations and analyses.

• ***Inverse document frequencies.*** Another issue that one may want to consider more carefully and reflect in the indices used in further analyses is the relative document frequencies (*df*) of different terms. For example, a term such as *guess* may occur frequently in all documents, whereas another term, such as *software,* may appear only a few times. The reason is that one might make *guesses* in various contexts, regardless of the specific topic, whereas *software* is a more semantically focused term that is only likely to occur in documents that deal with computer software. A common and very useful transformation that reflects both the specificity of words (document frequencies) as well as the overall frequencies of their occurrences (term frequencies) is the so-called **inverse document frequency** (Manning and Schutze, 2009). This transformation for the *i*th word and *j*th document can be written as:

$$idf(i, j) = \begin{cases} 0 & if\ wf_{ij} = 0 \\ (1 + \log(wf_{ij}))\log\dfrac{N}{df_i} & if\ wf_{ij} \geq 1 \end{cases}$$

In this formula, N is the total number of documents, and df_i is the document frequency for the *i*th word (the number of documents that include this word). Hence, it can be seen that this formula includes both the dampening of the simple-word frequencies via the log function (described above) and a weighting factor that evaluates to 0 if the word occurs in all documents [i.e., $\log(N/N = 1) = 0$], and to the maximum value when a word only occurs in a single document [i.e., $\log(N/1) = \log(N)$]. It can easily be seen how this transformation will create indices that reflect both the relative frequencies of occurrences of words, as well as their semantic specificities over the documents included in the analysis. This is the most commonly used transformation in the field.

REDUCING THE DIMENSIONALITY OF THE MATRIX Because the TDM is often very large and rather sparse (most of the cells filled with zeros), another important question is "How do we reduce the dimensionality of this matrix to a manageable size?" Several options are available for managing the matrix size:

• A domain expert goes through the list of terms and eliminates those that do not make much sense for the context of the study (this is a manual, labor-intensive process).
• Eliminate terms with very few occurrences in very few documents.
• Transform the matrix using singular value decomposition.

Singular value decomposition (SVD), which is closely related to principal components analysis, reduces the overall dimensionality of the input matrix (number of input documents by number of extracted terms) to a lower dimensional space, where each consecutive dimension represents the largest degree of variability (between words and documents) possible (Manning and Schutze, 1999). Ideally, the analyst might identify the two or three most salient dimensions that account for most of the variability (differences) between the words and documents, thus identifying the latent semantic space that organizes the words and documents in the analysis. Once such dimensions are identified, the underlying "meaning" of what is contained (discussed or described) in the documents has been extracted. Specifically, assume that matrix A represents an $m \times n$ term occurrence matrix where m is the number of input documents and n is the number of terms selected for analysis. The SVD computes the $m \times r$ orthogonal matrix U, $n \times r$ orthogonal matrix V, and $r \times r$ matrix D, so that $A = UDV'$ and r is the number of eigen values of $A'A$.

Task 3: Extract the Knowledge

Using the well-structured TDM, and potentially augmented with other structured data elements, novel patterns are extracted in the context of the specific problem being addressed. The main categories of knowledge extraction methods are classification, clustering, association, and trend analysis. A short description of these methods follows.

CLASSIFICATION Arguably the most common knowledge discovery topic in analyzing complex data sources is the classification (or categorization) of certain objects. The task is to classify a given data instance into a predetermined set of categories (or classes). As it applies to the domain of text mining, the task is known as *text categorization*, where for a given set of categories (subjects, topics, or concepts) and a collection of text documents the goal is to find the correct topic (subject or concept) for each document using models developed with a training data set that included both the documents and actual document categories. Today, automated text classification is applied in a variety of contexts, including automatic or semiautomatic (interactive) indexing of text, spam filtering, Web page categorization under hierarchical catalogs, automatic generation of metadata, detection of genre, and many others.

The two main approaches to text classification are knowledge engineering and machine learning (Feldman and Sanger, 2007). With the knowledge-engineering approach, an expert's knowledge about the categories is encoded into the system either declaratively or in the form of procedural classification rules. With the machine-learning approach, a general inductive process builds a classifier by learning from a set of reclassified examples. As the number of documents increases at an exponential rate and as knowledge experts become harder to come by, the popularity trend between the two is shifting toward the machine-learning approach.

CLUSTERING **Clustering** is an unsupervised process whereby objects are classified into "natural" groups called *clusters*. Compared to categorization, where a collection of pre-classified training examples is used to develop a model based on the descriptive features of the classes in order to classify a new unlabeled example, in clustering the problem is to group an unlabelled collection of objects (e.g., documents, customer comments, Web pages) into meaningful clusters without any prior knowledge.

Clustering is useful in a wide range of applications, from document retrieval to enabling better Web content searches. In fact, one of the prominent applications of clustering is the analysis and navigation of very large text collections, such as Web pages. The basic underlying assumption is that relevant documents tend to be more similar to each other than to irrelevant ones. If this assumption holds, the clustering of documents based on the similarity of their content improves search effectiveness (Feldman and Sanger, 2007):

- *Improved search recall.* Clustering, because it is based on overall similarity as opposed to the presence of a single term, can improve the recall of a query-based search in such a way that when a query matches a document its whole cluster is returned.
- *Improved search precision.* Clustering can also improve search precision. As the number of documents in a collection grows, it becomes difficult to browse through the list of matched documents. Clustering can help by grouping the documents into a number of much smaller groups of related documents, ordering them by relevance, and returning only the documents from the most relevant group (or groups).

The two most popular clustering methods are scatter/gather clustering and query-specific clustering:

- ***Scatter/gather.*** This document browsing method uses clustering to enhance the efficiency of human browsing of documents when a specific search query cannot be formulated. In a sense, the method dynamically generates a table of contents for the collection and adapts and modifies it in response to the user selection.
- ***Query-specific clustering.*** This method employs a hierarchical clustering approach where the most relevant documents to the posed query appear in small tight clusters that are nested in larger clusters containing less similar documents, creating a spectrum of relevance levels among the documents. This method performs consistently well for document collections of realistically large sizes.

ASSOCIATION A formal definition and detailed description of **association** was provided in the chapter on data mining (Chapter 5). The main idea in generating association rules (or solving market-basket problems) is to identify the frequent sets that go together.

In text mining, associations specifically refer to the direct relationships between concepts (terms) or sets of concepts. The concept set association rule $A \Rightarrow C$, relating two frequent concept sets A and C, can be quantified by the two basic measures of support and confidence. In this case, confidence is the percentage of documents that include all the concepts in C within the same subset of those documents that include all the concepts in A. Support is the percentage (or number) of documents that include all the concepts in A and C. For instance, in a document collection the concept "Software Implementation Failure" may appear most often in association with "Enterprise Resource Planning" and "Customer Relationship Management" with significant support (4%) and confidence (55%), meaning that 4 percent of the documents had all three concepts represented together in the same document and of the documents that included "Software Implementation Failure," 55 percent of them also included "Enterprise Resource Planning" and "Customer Relationship Management."

Text mining with association rules was used to analyze published literature (news and academic articles posted on the Web) to chart the outbreak and progress of bird flu (Mahgoub et al., 2008). The idea was to automatically identify the association among the geographic areas, spreading across species, and countermeasures (treatments).

TREND ANALYSIS Recent methods of trend analysis in text mining have been based on the notion that the various types of concept distributions are functions of document collections; that is, different collections lead to different concept distributions for the same set of concepts. It is therefore possible to compare two distributions that are otherwise identical except that they are from different subcollections. One notable direction of this type of analyses is having two collections from the same source (such as from the same set of academic journals) but from different points in time. Delen and Crossland (2008) applied trend analysis to a large number of academic articles (published in the three highest-rated academic journals) to identify the evolution of key concepts in the field of information systems.

As described in this section, a number of methods are available for text mining. Application Case 7.5 describes the use of a number of different techniques in analyzing a large set of literature.

APPLICATION CASE 7.5

Research Literature Survey with Text Mining

Researchers conducting searches and reviews of relevant literature face an increasingly complex and voluminous task. In extending the body of relevant knowledge, it has always been important to work hard to gather, organize, analyze, and assimilate existing information from the literature, particularly from one's home discipline. With the increasing abundance of potentially significant research being reported in related fields, and even in what are traditionally deemed to be nonrelated fields of study, the researcher's task is ever more daunting, if a thorough job is desired.

In new streams of research, the researcher's task may be even more tedious and complex. Trying to ferret out relevant work that others have reported may be difficult, at best, and perhaps even near impossible if traditional, largely manual reviews of published literature are required. Even with a legion of dedicated graduate students or helpful colleagues, trying to cover all potentially relevant published work is problematic.

Many scholarly conferences take place every year. In addition to extending the body of knowledge of the current focus of a conference, organizers often desire to offer additional mini-tracks and workshops. In many cases, these additional events are intended to introduce the attendees to significant streams of research in related fields of study and to try to identify the "next big thing" in terms of research interests and focus. Identifying reasonable candidate topics for such mini-tracks and workshops is often subjective rather than derived objectively from the existing and emerging research.

In a recent study, Delen and Crossland (2008) proposed a method to greatly assist and enhance the efforts of the researchers by enabling a semi-automated analysis of large volumes of published literature through the application of text mining. Using standard digital libraries and online publication search engines, the authors downloaded and collected all of the available articles for the three major journals in the field of management information systems: *MIS Quarterly* (MISQ), *Information Systems Research* (ISR), and the *Journal of Management Information Systems* (JMIS). In order to maintain the same time interval for all three journals (for potential comparative longitudinal studies), the journal with the most recent starting date for its digital publication availability was used as the start time for this study (i.e., JMIS articles have been digitally available since 1994). For each article, they extracted the title, abstract, author list, published keywords, volume, issue number, and year of publication. They then loaded all of the article data into a simple database file. Also included in the combined dataset was a field that designated the journal type of each article for likely discriminatory analysis. Editorial notes, research notes, and executive overviews were omitted from the collection. Table 7.2 shows how the data was presented in a tabular format.

In the analysis phase, they chose to use only the abstract of an article as the source of information extraction. They chose not to include the keywords listed with the publications for two main reasons: (1) under normal circumstances, the abstract would already include the listed keywords, and therefore inclusion of the listed keywords for the analysis would mean repeating the same information and potentially giving them unmerited weight; and (2) the listed keywords may be terms that authors would like their article to be associated with (as opposed to what is really contained in the article), therefore potentially introducing unquantifiable bias to the analysis of the content.

The first exploratory study was to look at the longitudinal perspective of the three journals (i.e., evolution of research topics over time). In order to conduct a longitudinal study, they divided the 12-year period (from 1994 to 2005) into four 3-year periods for each of the three journals. This framework led to 12 text mining experiments with 12 mutually exclusive datasets. At this point, for each of the 12 datasets they used text mining to extract the most descriptive terms from these collections of articles represented by their abstracts. The results were tabulated and examined for time-varying changes in the terms published in these three journals.

As a second exploration, using the complete dataset (including all three journals and all four periods), they conducted a clustering analysis. Clustering is arguably the most commonly used text mining technique. Clustering was used in this study

TABLE 7.2 Tabular Representation of the Fields Included in the Combined Dataset

Journal	Year	Author(s)	Title	Vol/No	Pages	Keywords	Abstract
MISQ	2005	A. Malhotra, S. Gossain, and O. A. El Sawy	Absorptive capacity configurations in supply chains: Gearing for partner-enabled market knowledge creation	29/1	145–187	knowledge management supply chain absorptive capacity interorganizational information systems configuration approaches	The need for continual value innovation is driving supply chains to evolve from a pure transactional focus to leveraging interorganization partnerships for sharing
ISR	1999	D. Robey and M. C. Boudtreau	Accounting for the contradictory organizational consequences of information technology: Theoretical directions and methodological implications		165–185	organizational transformation impacts of technology organization theory research methodology intraorganiza-tional power electronic communication misimplementation culture systems	Although much contemporary thought considers advanced information technologies as either determinants or enablers of radical organizational change, empirical studies have revealed incon-sistent findings to support the deterministic logic implicit in such arguments. This paper reviews the contradictory
JMIS	2001	R. Aron and E. K. Clemons	Achieving the optimal balance between investment in quality and investment in self-promotion for information products		65–88	information products internet advertising product positioning signaling signaling games	When producers of goods (or services) are confronted by a situation in which their offerings no longer perfectly match consumer preferences, they must determine the extent to which the advertised features of

to identify the natural groupings of the articles (by putting them into separate clusters) and then to list the most descriptive terms that characterized those clusters. They used singular value decomposition to reduce the dimensionality of the term-by-document matrix and then an expectation-maximization algorithm to create the clusters. They conducted several experiments to identify the *optimal* number of clusters, which turned out to be nine. After the construction of the nine clusters, they analyzed the content of those clusters from two perspectives: (1) representation of the journal type (see Figure 7.7) and (2) representation of time. The idea was to explore the potential differences and/or commonalities among the three journals and potential changes in the emphasis on those clusters; that is, to answer questions such as "Are there clusters that represent different research themes specific to a single journal?" and "Is there a time-varying characterization of those clusters?" They discovered and discussed several interesting patterns using tabular and graphical representation of their findings (for further information see Delen and Crossland, 2008).

Source: D. Delen and M. Crossland, "Seeding the Survey and Analysis of Research Literature with Text Mining," *Expert Systems with Applications,* Vol. 34, No. 3, 2008, pp. 1707–1720.

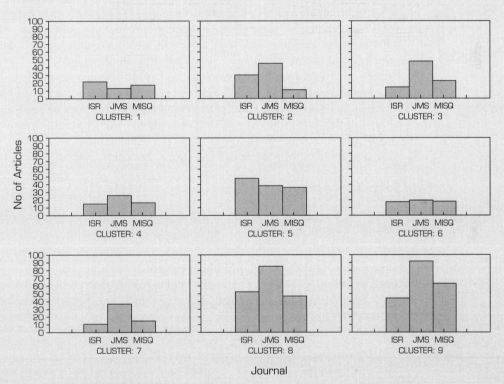

FIGURE 7.7 Distribution of the Number of Articles for the Three Journals Over the Nine Clusters   *Source:* D. Delen and M. Crossland, "Seeding the Survey and Analysis of Research Literature with Text Mining," *Expert Systems with Applications* Vol. 34, No. 3, 2008, pp. 1707–1720.

Section 7.5 Review Questions

1. What are the main steps in the text mining process?
2. What is the reason for normalizing word frequencies? What are the common methods for normalizing word frequencies?
3. What is singular value decomposition? How is it used in text mining?
4. What are the main knowledge extraction methods from corpus?

7.6 TEXT MINING TOOLS

As the value of text mining is being realized by more and more organizations, the number of software tools offered by software companies and nonprofits is also increasing. Following are some of the popular text mining tools, which we classify as commercial software tools and free software tools.

Commercial Software Tools

The following are some of the most popular software tools used for text mining. Note that many companies offer demonstration versions of their products on their Web sites.

1. ClearForest offers text analysis and visualization tools.
2. IBM Intelligent Miner Data Mining Suite, now fully integrated into IBM's InfoSphere Warehouse software, includes data and text mining tools.
3. Megaputer Text Analyst offers semantic analysis of free-form text, summarization, clustering, navigation, and natural language retrieval with search dynamic refocusing.
4. SAS Text Miner provides a rich suite of text processing and analysis tools.
5. SPSS Text Mining for Clementine extracts key concepts, sentiments, and relationships from call-center notes, blogs, e-mails, and other unstructured data and converts it to a structured format for predictive modeling.
6. The Statistica Text Mining engine provides easy-to-use text mining functionally with exceptional visualization capabilities.
7. VantagePoint provides a variety of interactive graphical views and analysis tools with powerful capabilities to discover knowledge from text databases.
8. The WordStat analysis module from Provalis Research analyzes textual information such as responses to open-ended questions, interviews, etc.

Free Software Tools

Free software tools, some of which are open source, are available from a number of nonprofit organizations:

1. GATE is a leading open source toolkit for text mining. It has a free open source framework (or SDK) and graphical development environment.
2. LingPipe is a suite of Java libraries for the linguistic analysis of human language.
3. S-EM (Spy-EM) is a text classification system that learns from positive and unlabeled examples.
4. Vivisimo/Clusty is a Web search and text-clustering engine.

Section 7.6 Review Questions

1. What are some of the most popular text mining software tools?
2. Why do you think most of the text mining tools are offered by statistics companies?
3. What do you think are the pros and cons of choosing a free text mining tool over a commercial tool?

7.7 WEB MINING OVERVIEW

The World Wide Web (or for short, Web) serves as an enormous repository of data and information on virtually everything one can conceive. The Web is perhaps the world's largest data and text repository, and the amount of information on the Web is growing rapidly every day. A lot of interesting information can be found online: whose homepage is linked to which other pages, how many people have links to a specific Web page, and how a particular site is organized. In addition, each visitor to a Web site, each search on a search engine, each click on a link, and each transaction on an e-commerce site creates additional data. Although unstructured textual data in the form of Web pages coded in

HTML or XML is the dominant content of the Web, the Web infrastructure also contains hyperlink information (connections to other Web pages) and usage information (logs of visitors' interactions with Web sites), all of which provide rich data for knowledge discovery. Analysis of this information can help us make better use of Web sites and also aid us in enhancing relationships and value for the visitors to our own Web sites.

However, according to Han and Kamber (2006), the Web also poses great challenges for effective and efficient knowledge discovery:

- ***The Web is too big for effective data mining.*** The Web is so large and growing so rapidly that it is difficult to even quantify its size. Because of the sheer size of the Web, it is not feasible to set up a data warehouse to replicate, store, and integrate all of the data on the Web, making data collection and integration a challenge.

- ***The Web is too complex.*** The complexity of a Web page is far greater than a page in a traditional text document collection. Web pages lack a unified structure. They contain far more authoring style and content variation than any set of books, articles, or other traditional text-based document.

- ***The Web is too dynamic.*** The Web is a highly dynamic information source. Not only does the Web grow rapidly, but its content is constantly being updated. Blogs, news stories, stock market results, weather reports, sports scores, prices, company advertisements, and numerous other types of information are updated regularly on the Web.

- ***The Web is not specific to a domain.*** The Web serves a broad diversity of communities and connects billions of workstations. Web users have very different backgrounds, interests, and usage purposes. Most users may not have good knowledge of the structure of the information network and may not be aware of the heavy cost of a particular search that they perform.

- ***The Web has everything.*** Only a small portion of the information on the Web is truly relevant or useful to someone (or some task). It is said that 99 percent of the information on the Web is useless to 99 percent of Web users. Although this may not seem obvious, it is true that a particular person is generally interested in only a tiny portion of the Web, whereas the rest of the Web contains information that is uninteresting to the user and may swamp desired results. Finding the portion of the Web that is truly relevant to a person and the task being performed is a prominent issue in Web-related research.

These challenges have prompted many research efforts to enhance the effectiveness and efficiency of discovering and using data assets on the Web. A number of index-based Web search engines constantly search the Web and index Web pages under certain keywords. Using these search engines, an experienced user may be able to locate documents by providing a set of tightly constrained keywords or phrases. However, a simple keyword-based search engine suffers from several deficiencies. First, a topic of any breadth can easily contain hundreds or thousands of documents. This can lead to a large number of document entries returned by the search engine, many of which are marginally relevant to the topic. Second, many documents that are highly relevant to a topic may not contain the exact keywords defining them. Compared to keyword-based Web search, Web mining is a prominent (and more challenging) approach that can be used to substantially enhance the power of Web search engines because Web mining can identify authoritative Web pages, classify Web documents, and resolve many ambiguities and subtleties raised in keyword-based Web search engines.

Web mining (or Web data mining) is the process of discovering intrinsic relationships (i.e., interesting and useful information) from Web data, which are expressed in the form of textual, linkage, or usage information. The term *Web mining* was first used by Etzioni (1996); today, many conferences, journals, and books focus on Web data mining. It is a continually evolving area of technology and business practice. Figure 7.8 presents the three main areas of Web mining: Web content, Web structure, and Web usage mining.

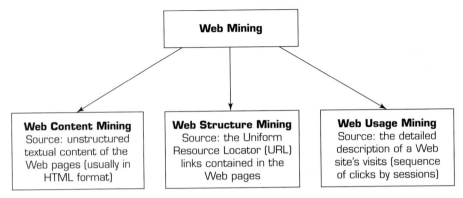

FIGURE 7.8   The Three Main Areas of Web Mining

Section 7.7 Review Questions

1. What are some of the main challenges the Web poses for knowledge discovery?
2. What is Web mining? How does it differ from regular data mining?
3. What are the three main areas of Web mining?

7.8   WEB CONTENT MINING AND WEB STRUCTURE MINING

Web content mining refers to the extraction of useful information from Web pages. The documents may be extracted in some machine-readable format so that automated techniques can generate some information about the Web pages. **Web crawlers** are used to read through the content of a Web site automatically. The information gathered may include document characteristics similar to what is used in text mining, but it may include additional concepts, such as the document hierarchy. Web content mining can also be used to enhance the results produced by search engines. For example, Turetken and Sharda (2004) described a visualization system that takes the results of a search from a search engine such as Google, reads the top 100 documents, clusters those documents by processing them using IBM's Intelligent Text Miner, and then presents the results in a graphical format.

In addition to text, Web pages also contain hyperlinks pointing one page to another. Hyperlinks contain a significant amount of hidden human annotation that can potentially help to automatically infer the notion of *authority*. When a Web page developer includes a link pointing to another Web page, this can be regarded as the developer's endorsement of the other page. The collective endorsement of a given page by different developers on the Web may indicate the importance of the page and may naturally lead to the discovery of authoritative Web pages (Miller, 2005). Therefore, the vast amount of Web linkage information provides a rich collection of information about the relevance, quality, and structure of the Web's contents, and thus is a rich source for Web mining.

A search on the Web to obtain information on a specific topic usually returns a few relevant, high-quality Web pages and a larger number of unusable Web pages. Use of an index based on authoritative pages (or some measure of it) will improve the search results and ranking of relevant pages. The idea of authority (or **authoritative pages**) stems from earlier information retrieval work using citations among journal articles to evaluate the impact of research papers (Miller, 2005). Though that was the origination of the idea, there are significant differences between the citations in research articles and hyperlinks on Web pages. First, not every hyperlink represents an endorsement (some links are created for navigation purposes and some are for paid advertisement). While this is true, if the majority of the hyperlinks are of endorsement type, then the collective opinion will still prevail. Second, for commercial and competitive interests, one authority will rarely have its Web page point to rival authorities in the same domain. For example, Microsoft may prefer not to include links on its Web pages to Apple's Web sites, because this may be regarded as endorsement of its competitor's authority. Third, authoritative pages are seldom particularly descriptive. For example, the main Web page of Yahoo! may not contain the explicit self-description that it is in fact a Web search engine.

The structure of Web hyperlinks has led to another important category of Web pages called a **hub**. A hub is one or more Web pages that provide a collection of links to authoritative pages. Hub pages may not be prominent and only a few links may point to them; however, they provide links to a collection of prominent sites on a specific topic of interest. A hub could be a list of recommended links on an individual's homepage, recommended reference sites on a course Web page, or a professionally assembled resource list on a specific topic. Hub pages play the role of implicitly conferring the authorities on a narrow field. In essence, a close symbiotic relationship exists between good hubs and authoritative pages; a good hub is good because it points to many good authorities, and a good authority is good because it is being pointed to by many good hubs. Such relationships between hubs and authorities make it possible to automatically retrieve high-quality content from the Web.

The most popular publicly known and referenced algorithm used to calculate hubs and authorities is **hyperlink-induced topic search (HITS)**. It was originally developed by Kleinberg (1999) and has since been improved on by many researchers. HITS is a link-analysis algorithm that rates Web pages using the hyperlink information contained within them. In the context of Web search, the HITS algorithm collects a base document set for a specific query. It then recursively calculates the hub and authority values for each document. To gather the base document set, a root set that matches the query is fetched from a search engine. For each document retrieved, a set of documents that points to the original document and another set of documents that is pointed to by the original document are added to the set as the original document's neighborhood. A recursive process of document identification and link analysis continues until the hub and authority values converge. These values are then used to index and prioritize the document collection generated for a specific query.

Web structure mining is the process of extracting useful information from the links embedded in Web documents. It is used to identify authoritative pages and hubs, which are the cornerstones of the contemporary page-rank algorithms that are central to popular search engines such as Google and Yahoo! Just as links going to a Web page may indicate a site's popularity (or authority), links within the Web page (or the compete Web site) may indicate the depth of coverage of a specific topic. Analysis of links is very important in understanding the interrelationships among large numbers of Web pages, leading to a better understanding of a specific Web community, clan, or clique. Application Case 7.6 describes a project that used both Web content mining and Web structure mining to better understand how U.S. extremist groups are connected.

APPLICATION CASE 7.6

Caught in a Web

We normally search for answers to our problems outside of our immediate environment. Often, however, the trouble stems from within. In taking action against global terrorism, domestic extremist groups often go unnoticed. However, domestic extremists pose a significant threat to U.S. security because of the information they possess, as well as their increasing ability, through the use of the Internet, to reach out to extremist groups around the world.

Keeping tabs on the content available on the Internet is difficult. Researchers and authorities need superior tools to analyze and monitor the activities of extremist groups. Researchers at the University of Arizona, with support from the Department of Homeland Security and other agencies, have developed a Web mining methodology to find and analyze Web sites operated by domestic extremists in order to learn about these groups through their use of the Internet. Extremist groups use the Internet to communicate, to access private messages, and to raise money online.

The research methodology begins by gathering a superior-quality collection of relevant extremist and terrorist Web sites. Hyperlink analysis is performed, which leads to other extremist and terrorist Web sites. The interconnectedness with other Web sites is crucial in estimating the similarity of the objectives of various groups. The next step is content analysis, which further codifies these Web sites based on various attributes, such as communications, fund raising, and ideology sharing, to name a few.

Based on link analysis and content analysis, researchers have identified 97 Web sites of U.S. extremist and hate groups. Oftentimes, the links between these communities do not necessarily represent any cooperation between them. However, finding numerous links between common interest groups helps in clustering the communities under a common banner. Further research using data mining to automate the process has a global aim, with the goal of identifying links between international hate and extremist groups and their U.S. counterparts.

Source: Y. Zhou, E. Reid, J. Qin, H. Chen, and G. Lai, "U.S. Domestic Extremist Groups on the Web: Link and Content Analysis," *IEEE Intelligent Systems*, Vol. 20, No. 5, September/October 2005, pp. 44–51.

Section 7.8 Review Questions

1. What is Web content mining? How does it differ from text mining?
2. Define *Web structure mining,* and differentiate it from Web content mining.
3. What are the main goals of Web structure mining?
4. What are hubs and authorities? What is the HITS algorithm?

7.9 WEB USAGE MINING

Web usage mining is the extraction of useful information from data generated through Web page visits and transactions. Masand et al. (2002) state that at least three types of data are generated through Web page visits:

1. Automatically generated data stored in server access logs, referrer logs, agent logs, and client-side cookies
2. User profiles
3. Metadata, such as page attributes, content attributes, and usage data

Analysis of the information collected by Web servers can help us better understand user behavior. Analysis of this data is often called **clickstream analysis**. By using the data and text mining techniques, a company might be able to discern interesting patterns from the clickstreams. For example, it might learn that 60 percent of visitors who searched for "hotels in Maui" had searched earlier for "airfares to Maui." Such information could be useful in determining where to place online advertisements. Clickstream analysis might also be useful for knowing *when* visitors access a site. For example, if a company knew that 70 percent of software downloads from its Web site occurred between 7 and 11 P.M., it could plan for better customer support and network bandwidth during those hours. Figure 7.9 shows the process of extracting knowledge from clickstream data and how the generated knowledge is used to improve the process, improve

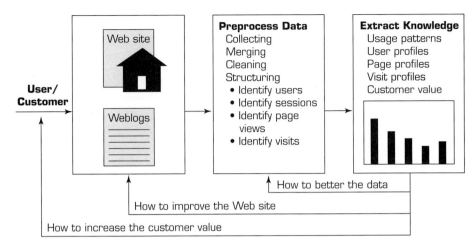

FIGURE 7.9 Extraction of Knowledge from Web Usage Data

the Web site, and, most important, increase the customer value. Nasraoui (2006) listed the following applications of Web mining:

1. Determine the lifetime value of clients.
2. Design cross-marketing strategies across products.
3. Evaluate promotional campaigns.
4. Target electronic ads and coupons at user groups based on user access patterns.
5. Predict user behavior based on previously learned rules and users' profiles.
6. Present dynamic information to users based on their interests and profiles.

Amazon.com provides a good example of how Web usage history can be leveraged dynamically. A registered user who revisits Amazon.com is greeted by name. This is a simple task that involves recognizing the user by reading a cookie (i.e., a small text file written by a Web site on the visitor's computer). Amazon.com also presents the user with a choice of products in a personalized store, based on previous purchases and an association analysis of similar users. It also makes special "Gold Box" offers that are good for a short amount of time. All these recommendations involve a detailed analysis of the visitor as well as the user's peer group developed through the use of clustering, sequence pattern discovery, association, and other data and text mining techniques.

Table 7.3 lists some of the more popular Web mining products.

Section 7.9 Review Questions

1. Define Web usage mining.
2. In an e-commerce environment, what are the potential applications of Web usage mining?
3. What is a clickstream? Why is it important in Web usage mining?
4. What types of information do Web servers collect when users visit a Web page and engage in an interactive activity?
5. Identify value-added features developed by major e-commerce sites that may be based on Web usage mining.

TABLE 7.3 Web Usage Mining Software

Product Name	Description	URL
Angoss Knowledge WebMiner	Combines ANGOSS Knowledge STUDIO and clickstream analysis	**angoss.com**
ClickTracks	Visitor patterns can be shown on Web site	**clicktracks.com**
LiveStats from DeepMetrix	Real-time log analysis, live demo on site	**deepmetrix.com**
Megaputer WebAnalyst	Data and text mining capabilities	**megaputer.com/products/wm.php3**
MicroStrategy Web Traffic Analysis Module	Traffic highlights, content analysis, and Web visitor analysis reports	**microstrategy.com/Solutions/Applications/WTAM**
SAS Web Analytics	Analyzes Web site traffic	**sas.com/solutions/webanalytics/**
SPSS Web Mining for Clementine	Extraction of Web events	**spss.com/web_mining_for_clementine**
WebTrends	Data mining of Web traffic information.	**webtrends.com**
XML Miner	A system and class library for mining data and text expressed in XML, using fuzzy logic expert system rules	**scientio.com**

7.10 WEB MINING SUCCESS STORIES

Ask.com (**ask.com**) is a well-known search engine. Ask.com believes that a fundamental component of its success lies in its ability to consistently provide better search results. However, determining the quality of search results is impossible to measure accurately using strictly quantitative measures such as click-through rate, abandonment, and search frequency; additional quantitative and qualitative measures are required. By regularly surveying its audience, Ask.com uses a mix of qualitative and quantitative measures as the basis of key performance indicators, such as "Percent of Users Saying They Found What They Were Looking For," "Percent of Users Likely to Use the Site Again," and "Rated Usefulness of Search Results," in addition to open-ended custom questions evaluating the user experience. By integrating quantitative and qualitative data, Ask.com was able to validate the move to its "Ask 3D" design, despite the fact that in testing purely quantitative measures showed no difference in performance between the old and new designs.

Scholastic.com (**scholastic.com**) is an online bookstore specializing in educational books for children. It discovered that some visitors failed to make a purchase. The critical questions were "What went wrong?" "Why didn't these visitors make a purchase?" and, ultimately, "How can we win these customers back?" Further analysis of the data showed that part of the reason was that the site didn't carry the titles they were looking for. For example, shoppers were seeking backlist titles they read decades ago and assumed Scholastic would still have them. In this case, the company leveraged Voice of Customer data to identify specific titles people sought that were out of print. This Web-based data quantified the amount of unmet market demand and its impact on future purchase behavior. Scholastic began carrying older titles on its Web site and implemented a feature that allowed the customer to sign up to receive an e-mail when an out-of-stock book became available. Of the e-mails sent, about 35 percent of recipients purchased the book.

St. John Health System is a health care system with 8 hospitals, 125 medical locations, and over 3,000 physicians. Its CRM database has over 1.1 million patients. St. John's Web site tracks satisfaction data along with transactions, such as online registration for health assessments and scheduling of physician visits, to determine how many new patients the Web site is responsible for driving into the health system. St. John has seen a 15 percent increase in new patients and a return on investment of four-to-one on funds spent on improving Web site satisfaction, despite a highly competitive health care market and a declining consumer population. This success has turned the heads of the whole organization, which now embraces online customer satisfaction as a key performance indicator with multifaceted value. St. John uses data from the Web site to monitor the success of advertising programs that drive people to the Web site, to prioritize and fund cross-departmental projects that address satisfaction improvement, and to keep the voice of the customer at the center of corporate business decisions.

Forward-thinking companies like Ask.com, Scholastic, and St. John Health System are actively using Web mining systems to answer critically important questions of "Who?" "Why?" and "How?" As documented, the benefit of integrating these systems effectively and efficiently can be significant, both in terms of incremental financial growth and increasing customer loyalty and satisfaction.

Given the continual shift of advertising dollars, resources, and, most important, customers into the online channel, the belief is that executives who aggressively pursue a more holistic view of their customers using Web mining techniques will have a substantial advantage over those who continue to base their analyses on intuitions, gut feelings, and wild guesses. Application Case 7.7 presents a detailed view of Web optimization efforts.

APPLICATION CASE 7.7

Web Site Optimization Ecosystem

It seems that just about everything on the Web can be measured—every click can be recorded, every view can be captured, and every visit can be analyzed—all in an effort to continually and automatically optimize the online experience. Unfortunately, the notions of "infinite measurability" and "automatic optimization" in the online channel are far more complex than most realize. The assumption that any single application of Web mining techniques will provide the necessary range of insights required to understand Web site visitor behavior is deceptive and potentially risky. Ideally, a holistic view to customer experience is needed that can only be captured using both quantitative and qualitative data. Forward-thinking companies, like the ones discussed in this section (i.e., Ask.com, Scholastic.com, and St. John Health System) have already taken steps toward capturing and analyzing a holistic view of the customer experience, which has led to significant gains, both in terms of incremental financial growth and increasing customer loyalty and satisfaction.

According to Peterson (2008), the inputs for Web site optimization efforts can be classified along two axes describing the nature of the data and how that data can be used. On one axis are data and information; data being primarily quantitative and information being primarily qualitative. On the other axis are measures and actions; measures being reports, analysis, and recommendations all designed to drive actions, the actual changes being made in the ongoing process of site and marketing optimization. Each quadrant created by these dimensions leverages different technologies and creates different outputs, but much like a biological ecosystem, each technological niche interacts with the others to support the entire online environment (see Figure 7.10).

Most believe that the Web site optimization ecosystem is defined by the ability to log, parse, and report on the clickstream behavior of site visitors. The underlying technology of this ability is generally referred to as **Web analytics**. Although Web analytics tools provide invaluable insights, understanding visitor behavior is as much a function of qualitatively determining interests and intent as it is quantifying clicks from page to page. Fortunately there are two

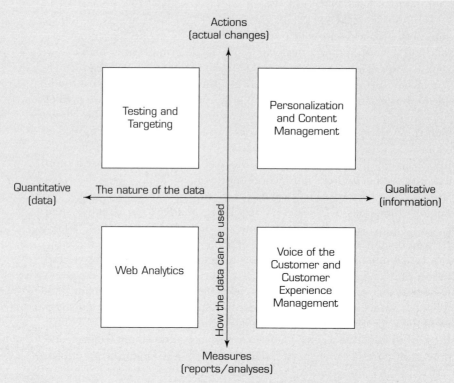

FIGURE 7.10 Two-dimensional View of the Inputs for Web Site Optimization *Source:* E. T. Peterson, *The Voice of Customer: Qualitative Data as a Critical Input to Web Site Optimization* (2008), **foreseeresults.com/Form_peterson_WebAnalstics.html** (accessed on May 22, 2009).

other classes of applications designed to provide a more qualitative view of online visitor behavior designed to report on the overall user experience and report direct feedback given by visitors and customers: **customer experience management (CEM)** and **voice of customer (VOC)**:

- Web analytics applications focus on "where and when" questions by aggregating, mining, and visualizing large volumes of data, by reporting on online marketing and visitor acquisition efforts, by summarizing page-level visitor interaction data, and by summarizing visitor flow through defined multistep processes.

- Voice of customer applications focus on "who and how" questions by gathering and reporting direct feedback from site visitors, by benchmarking against other sites and offline channels, and by supporting predictive modeling of future visitor behavior.

- Customer experience management applications focus on "what and why" questions by detecting Web application issues and problems, by tracking

and resolving business process and usability obstacles, by reporting on site performance and availability, by enabling real-time alerting and monitoring, and by supporting deep diagnosis of observed visitor behavior.

All three applications are needed to have a complete view of the visitor behavior where each application plays a distinct and valuable role. Web analytics, CEM, and VOC applications form the foundation of the Web site optimization ecosystem that supports the online business's ability to positively influence desired outcomes (a pictorial representation of this process view of the Web site optimization ecosystem is given in Figure 7.11). These similar-yet-distinct applications each contribute to a site operator's ability to recognize, react, and respond to the ongoing challenges faced by every Web site owner. Fundamental to the optimization process is measurement, gathering data and information that can then be transformed into tangible analysis, and recommendations for improvement using Web mining tools and techniques. When used properly, these applications

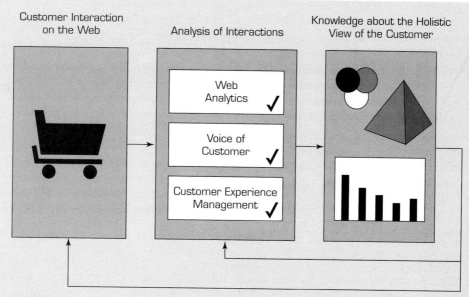

FIGURE 7.11 A Process View to Web Site Optimization Ecosystem

allow for convergent validation—combining different sets of data collected for the same audience to provide a richer and deeper understanding of audience behavior. The convergent validation model—one where multiple sources of data describing the same population are integrated to increase the depth and richness of the resulting analysis—forms the framework of the Web site optimization ecosystem. On one side of the spectrum are the primarily qualitative inputs from VOC applications; on the other side are the primarily quantitative inputs from CEM bridging the gap by

supporting key elements of data discovery. When properly implemented, all three systems sample data from the same audience. The combination of these data—either through data integration projects or simply via the process of conducting good analysis—supports far more actionable insights than any of the ecosystem members individually.

Source: E. T. Peterson, "The Voice of Customer: Qualitative Data as a Critical Input to Web Site Optimization," 2008, **foreseeresults.com/Form_Epeterson_WebAnalytics.html** (accessed on May 22, 2009).

Section 7.10 Review Questions

1. Why do we need Web mining?
2. In your own words, what are the pros and cons of Web mining?
3. What are the common characteristics of Web mining success stories?

Chapter Highlights

- Text mining is the discovery of knowledge from unstructured (mostly text based) data sources. Given that a great deal of information is in text form, text mining is one of the fastest growing branches of the business intelligence field.
- Companies use text mining and Web mining to better understand their customers by analyzing their feedbacks left on Web forms, blogs, and wikis.
- Text mining applications are in virtually every area of business and government, including marketing, finance, health care, medicine, and homeland security.

- Text mining uses natural language processing to induce structure into the text collection and then uses data mining algorithms such as classification, clustering, association, and **sequence discovery** to extract knowledge from it.
- Successful application of text mining requires a structured methodology similar to the CRISP-DM methodology in data mining.
- Text mining is closely related to information extraction, natural language processing, and document summarization.

- Text mining entails creating numeric indices from unstructured text and then applying data mining algorithms to these indices.
- Web mining can be defined as the discovery and analysis of interesting and useful information from the Web, about the Web, and usually using Web-based tools.
- Web mining can be viewed as consisting of three areas: Web content mining, Web structure mining, and Web usage mining.
- Web content mining refers to the automatic extraction of useful information from Web pages. It may be used to enhance search results produced by search engines.
- Web structure mining refers to generating interesting information from the links included in Web pages.

This is used in Google's page rank algorithm to order the display of pages, for example.
- Web structure mining can also be used to identify the members of a specific community and perhaps even the roles of the members in the community.
- Web usage mining refers to developing useful information through analysis of Web server logs, user profiles, and transaction information.
- Web usage mining can assist in better CRM, personalization, site navigation modifications, and improved business models.
- Text and Web mining are emerging as critical components of the next generation of business intelligence tools to enabling organizations to compete successfully.

Key Terms

association *308*	hubs *315*	sentiment analysis *293*	trend analysis *308*
authoritative pages *314*	hyperlink-induced topic	sequence discovery *321*	unstructured data *290*
classification *307*	search (HITS) *315*	singular value	voice of customer
clickstream analysis *316*	inverse document	decomposition *306*	(VOC) *320*
clustering *307*	frequency *306*	stemming *290*	Web analytics *319*
corpus *290*	natural language	stop words *290*	Web content mining *314*
customer experience	processing *292*	term–document matrix	Web crawler *314*
management	part-of-speech	(TDM) *303*	Web mining *313*
(CEM) *320*	tagging *300*	text mining *289*	Web structure mining *315*
deception detection *297*	polyseme *290*	tokenizing *290*	Web usage mining *316*

Questions for Discussion

1. Explain the relationship among data mining, text mining, and Web mining.
2. What should an organization consider before making a decision to purchase text mining and/or Web mining software?
3. Discuss the differences and commonalities between text mining and Web mining.
4. In your own words, define text mining and discuss its most popular applications.
5. Discuss the similarities and differences between the data mining process (e.g., CRISP-DM) and the three-step, high-level text mining process explained in this chapter.
6. What does it mean to induce structure into the text-based data? Discuss the alternative ways of inducing structure into text-based data.
7. What is the role of natural language processing in text mining? Discuss the capabilities and limitations of NLP in the context of text mining.
8. List and discuss three prominent application areas for text mining. What is the common theme among the three application areas you chose?
9. Discuss the relationship between Web mining and Web analytics.
10. What are the three main areas of Web mining? Discuss the differences and commonalities among these three areas.
11. What is Web content mining? How does it differ from text mining? Discuss and justify your answers with concrete examples.
12. What is Web structure mining? What are authoritative pages and hubs? How do they relate to Web structure mining?
13. Discuss the expected benefits of Web structure mining. Provide examples from real-world applications that you are familiar with.
14. What is Web usage mining? Draw a picture of the Web usage mining process and explain/discuss the major steps in the process.
15. Provide two exemplary business applications of Web usage mining; discuss their usage and business value.

Exercises

TERADATA STUDENT NETWORK (TSN) AND OTHER HANDS-ON EXERCISES

1. Visit **teradatastudentnetwork.com**. Identify cases about text and Web mining. Describe recent developments in the field. If you cannot find enough cases at the Teradata University network Web site, broaden your search to other Web-based resources.
2. Go to **teradatastudentnetwork.com** or locate white papers, Web seminars, and other materials related to text mining and/or Web mining. Synthesize your findings into a short written report.
3. Browse the Web and your library's digital databases to identify articles that make the natural linkage between text/Web mining and contemporary business intelligence systems.

TEAM ASSIGNMENTS AND ROLE-PLAYING

1. Examine how textual data can be captured automatically using Web-based technologies. Once captured, what are the potential patterns that you can extract from these unstructured data sources?
2. Interview administrators in your college or executives in your organization to determine how text mining and Web mining could assist them in their work. Write a proposal describing your findings. Include a preliminary cost/benefits analysis in your report.
3. Go to your library's online resources. Learn how to download attributes of a collection of literature (journal articles) in a specific topic. Download and process the data using a methodology similar to the one explained in Application Case 7.5.

INTERNET EXERCISES

1. Survey some text mining tools and vendors. Start with **clearforest.com** and **megaputer.com**. Also consult with **dmreview.com** and identify some text mining products and service providers that are not mentioned in this chapter.
2. Find recent cases of successful text mining and Web mining applications. Try text and Web mining software vendors and consultancy firms and look for cases or success stories. Prepare a report summarizing five new case studies.
3. Go to **statsoft.com**. Select Downloads and download at least three white papers on applications. Which of these applications may have used the data/text/Web mining techniques discussed in this chapter?
4. Go to **sas.com**. Download at least three white papers on applications. Which of these applications may have used the data/text/Web mining techniques discussed in this chapter?
5. Go to **spss.com**. Download at least three white papers on applications. Which of these applications may have used the data/text/Web mining techniques discussed in this chapter?
6. Go to **teradata.com**. Download at least three white papers on applications. Which of these applications may have used the data/text/Web mining techniques discussed in this chapter?
7. Go to **fairisaac.com**. Download at least three white papers on applications. Which of these applications may have used the data/text/Web mining techniques discussed in this chapter?
8. Go to **salfordsystems.com**. Download at least three white papers on applications. Which of these applications may have used the data/text/Web mining techniques discussed in this chapter?
9. Go to **kdnuggets.com**. Explore the sections on applications as well as software. Find names of at least three additional packages for data mining and text mining.

END OF CHAPTER APPLICATION CASE
HP and Text Mining

Hewlett-Packard Company (HP), founded in 1939 by William R. Hewlett and David Packard, is headquartered in Palo Alto, California. The company provides products, technologies, solutions, and services to individuals, small and medium-sized businesses, and large enterprises on a global basis. HP also offers management software solutions that enable enterprise customers to manage their IT infrastructure, operations, applications, IT services, and business processes, as well as carrier-grade platforms for various applications. Some of HP's popular product categories are commercial and consumer personal computers, workstations, handheld computing devices, inkjet printers, laser printers, digital entertainment systems, calculators and related accessories, software and services, digital photography and entertainment, graphics, imaging and printer supplies for printer hardware, printing supplies, scanning devices, and network infrastructure products, including Ethernet switch products. Retailers form the distribution channel of the company. The company also sells through distribution partners, original equipment manufacturers, and systems integrators.

Text Mining

Customers of HP communicate with the company through millions of e-mails. Structured data analysis is effective in finding out parameters such as from whom, when, where, and how the messages originated. A wealth of information would be available if mining techniques could find out why these e-mails were sent. One of the common interaction points between the customer and the company is the call center. HP is impressed by the business insights that could be culled from communications, such as word documents, e-mails, and other sources. The combination of the structured and unstructured data can create a tremendous potential for companies to find valuable business insights.

System

The standard tools that HP previously used could not report useful information from customer-related communications. Now, HP uses SAS Institute's Text Miner to uncover analytical insights from customer-related data in call center applications and then standardizes those insights. HP implemented Text Miner to combine structured data and text data to produce a hybrid structured/unstructured data set that is stored in a Microsoft SQL Server database with an Analysis Services OLAP engine. The system, today, encompasses 300,000 text documents and is roughly 50 gigabytes in size, covering an 18-month period and three call centers.

HP implemented Executive Viewer, a Web-based tool developed by Temtec (**temtec.com**) that enables HP to augment the OLAP cubes with predictive modeling, loyalty scores, and customer differentiations created by SAS Enterprise Miner.

Process

Various concepts, such as products used, call frequency, and common customer issues, are used to aggregate text data; the result is consolidated into probabilistic text clusters. This consolidated cluster is then combined with the structured data from third-party providers. HP can now combine and analyze structured data such as revenue with customer desires, attitudes, and needs.

Text analysis is challenging due to dimensionality and data dispersal. Different customer databases contain different structured information that could be integrated without much difficulty. The challenge lies in combining the structured data with unstructured data from text. SAS Text Miner uses a technique called singular value decomposition. Text mining software includes a prebuilt dictionary of words and synonym lists; it is an overwhelming task for the organization to customize the text information generated in its business environments. Text data are available at various sources that are outside the realms of traditional data warehousing. Some of the largest challenges that SAS Text Miner faces are customer activity at the HP Web site as well as finding insights into the businesses of HP's customers.

In addition to the major application of text mining, SAS Text Miner could be used proactively on customer Web sites to generate insights into the customer needs that HP could satisfy. The tool could also be used to analyze multiple suppliers/vendors with various numbers and descriptions in text.

Results

SAS Text Miner was successfully able to develop standard data definitions and product classification models with more than 80 percent accuracy. The system is now being used to support HP in contributing to the top line through improved cross-selling, targeted marketing, customer retention, and better anticipation of customer needs. The information generated from structured/unstructured data now supports multiple business users in various departments.

Questions for the Case

1. What is the practical application of text mining?
2. How do you think text mining techniques could be used in other businesses?
3. What were HP's challenges in text mining? How were they overcome?
4. In what other areas, in your opinion, can HP use text mining?

Sources: M. Hammond, "BI Case Study: What's in a Word? For Hewlett-Packard, It's Customer Insight," *Business Intelligence Journal*, Vol. 9, No. 3, Summer 2004, pp. 48–51; and B. Beal, "Text Mining: A Golden Opportunity for HP," *SearchCRM.com*, June 6, 2005, **searchdatamanagement.techtarget.com/ originalContent/0,289142,sid91_gci1136611,00.html** (accessed November 2008).

References

Chun, H. W., Y. Tsuruoka, J. D. Kim, R. Shiba, N. Nagata, and T. Hishiki. (2006). "Extraction of Gene-Disease Relations from Medline Using Domain Dictionaries and Machine Learning." *Proceedings of the 11th Pacific Symposium on Biocomputing,* pp. 4–15.

Cohen, K. B., and L. Hunter. (2008). "Getting Started in Text Mining." *PLoS Compututional Biology,* Vol. 4, No. 1, pp. 1–10.

Coussement, K., and D. Van Den Poel. (2008). "Improving Customer Complaint Management by Automatic Email Classification Using Linguistic Style Features as Predictors." *Decision Support Systems,* Vol. 44, No. 4, pp. 870–882.

Coussement, K., and D. Van Den Poel. (2009). "Improving Customer Attrition Prediction by Integrating Emotions from Client/Company Interaction Emails and Evaluating Multiple Classifiers." *Expert Systems with Applications,* Vol. 36, No. 3, pp. 6127–6134.

Delen, D., and M. Crossland. (2008). "Seeding the Survey and Analysis of Research Literature with Text Mining." *Expert Systems with Applications,* Vol. 34, No. 3, pp. 1707–1720.

Etzioni, O. (1996). "The World Wide Web: Quagmire or Gold Mine?" *Communications of the ACM,* Vol. 39, No. 11, pp. 65–68.

EUROPOL. (2007). "EUROPOL Work Program 2007." **state watch.org/news/2006/apr/europol-work-programme-2007.pdf** (accessed October 2008).

Feldman, R., and J. Sanger. (2007). *The Text Mining Handbook: Advanced Approaches in Analyzing Unstructured Data.* Boston: ABS Ventures.

Fuller, C. M., D. Biros, and D. Delen. (2008). "Exploration of Feature Selection and Advanced Classification Models for High-Stakes Deception Detection." *Proceedings of the 41st Annual Hawaii International Conference on System Sciences (HICSS),* Big Island, HI: IEEE Press, pp. 80–99.

Ghani, R., K. Probst, Y. Liu, M. Krema, and A. Fano. (2006). "Text Mining for Product Attribute Extraction." *SIGKDD Explorations,* Vol. 8, No. 1, pp. 41–48.

Han, J., and M. Kamber. (2006). *Data Mining: Concepts and Techniques,* 2nd ed. San Francisco: Morgan Kaufmann.

Kanayama, H., and T. Nasukawa. (2006). "Fully Automatic Lexicon Expanding for Domain-oriented Sentiment Analysis, EMNLP: Empirical Methods in Natural Language Processing." **trl.ibm.com/projects/textmining/takmi/sentiment_analysis_e.htm**.

Kleinberg, J. (1999). "Authoritative Sources in a Hyperlinked Environment." *Journal of the ACM,* Vol. 46, No. 5, pp. 604–632.

Lin, J., and D. Demner-Fushman. (2005). "'Bag of Words' Is Not Enough for Strength of Evidence Classification." *AMIA Annual Symposium Proceedings,* pp. 1031–1032. **pubmedcentral.nih.gov/articlerender.fcgi?artid=1560897**.

Mahgoub, H., D. Rösner, N. Ismail, and F. Torkey. (2008). "A Text Mining Technique Using Association Rules Extraction." *International Journal of Computational Intelligence,* Vol. 4, No. 1, pp. 21–28.

Manning, C. D., and H. Schutze. (1999). *Foundations of Statistical Natural Language Processing.* Cambridge, MA: MIT Press.

Masand, B. M., M. Spiliopoulou, J. Srivastava, and O. R. Zaïane. (2002). "Web Mining for Usage Patterns and Profiles." *SIGKDD Explorations,* Vol. 4, No. 2, pp. 125–132.

McKnight, W. (2005, January 1). "Text Data Mining in Business Intelligence." *Information Management Magazine.* **information-management.com/issues/20050101/1016487-1.html** (accessed May 22, 2009).

Miller, T. W. (2005). *Data and Text Mining: A Business Applications Approach.* Upper Saddle River, NJ: Prentice Hall.

Nakov, P., A. Schwartz, B. Wolf, and M. A. Hearst. (2005). "Supporting Annotation Layers for Natural Language Processing." *Proceedings of the ACL,* interactive poster and demonstration sessions, Ann Arbor, MI. Association for Computational Linguistics, pp. 65–68.

Nasraoui, O., M. Spiliopoulou, J. Srivastava, B. Mobasher, and B. Masand. (2006). "WebKDD 2006: Web Mining and Web Usage Analysis Post-Workshop Report." *ACM SIGKDD Explorations Newsletter,* Vol. 8, No. 2, pp. 84–89.

Peterson, E. T. (2008). "The Voice of Customer: Qualitative Data as a Critical Input to Web Site Optimization." **foreseeresults.com/Form_Epeterson_WebAnalytics .html** (accessed May 22, 2009).

Shatkay, H., A. Höglund, S. Brady, T. Blum, P. Dönnes, and O. Kohlbacher. (2007). "SherLoc: High-Accuracy Prediction of Protein Subcellular Localization by Integrating Text and Protein Sequence Data." *Bioinformatics,* Vol. 23, No. 11, pp. 1410–1417.

SPSS. "Merck Sharp & Dohme." **spss.com/success/template_view.cfm?Story_ID=185** (accessed May 15, 2009).

StatSoft. (2009). *Statistica Data and Text Miner User Manual.* Tulsa, OK: StatSoft, Inc.

Turetken, O., and R. Sharda. (2004). "Development of a Fisheye-based Information Search Processing Aid (FISPA) for Managing Information Overload in the Web Environment." *Decision Support Systems,* Vol. 37, No. 3, pp. 415–434.

Weng, S. S., and C. K. Liu. (2004) "Using Text Classification and Multiple Concepts to Answer E-mails." *Expert Systems with Applications,* Vol. 26, No. 4, pp. 529–543.

Zhou, Y., E. Reid, J. Qin, H. Chen, and G. Lai. (2005). "U.S. Domestic Extremist Groups on the Web: Link and Content Analysis." *IEEE Intelligent Systems,* Vol. 20, No. 5, pp. 44–51.

Data Warehousing

LEARNING OBJECTIVES

1 Understand the basic definitions and concepts of data warehouses

2 Understand data warehousing architectures

3 Describe the processes used in developing and managing data warehouses

4 Explain data warehousing operations

5 Explain the role of data warehouses in decision support

6 Explain data integration and the extraction, transformation, and load (ETL) processes

7 Describe real-time (active) data warehousing

8 Understand data warehouse administration and security issues

The concept of data warehousing has been around since the late 1980s. This chapter provides the foundation for an important type of database, called a *data warehouse*, which is primarily used for decision support and provides improved analytical capabilities. We discuss data warehousing in the following sections:

8.1 Opening Vignette: DirecTV Thrives with Active Data Warehousing
8.2 Data Warehousing Definitions and Concepts
8.3 Data Warehousing Process Overview
8.4 Data Warehousing Architectures
8.5 Data Integration and the Extraction, Transformation, and Load (ETL) Processes
8.6 Data Warehouse Development
8.7 Real-Time Data Warehousing
8.8 Data Warehouse Administration and Security Issues
8.9 Resources, Links, and the Teradata University Network Connection

8.1 OPENING VIGNETTE: DIRECTV THRIVES WITH ACTIVE DATA WAREHOUSING

As an example of how an interactive data warehousing and business intelligence product can spread across the enterprise, consider the case of DirecTV. Using software solutions from Teradata and GoldenGate, DirecTV developed a product that integrates its data assets in near real time throughout the enterprise. The company's data warehouse director, Jack Gustafson, has said publically that the product has paid for itself over and over again through its continuous use. For DirecTV, a technical decision to install a real-time transactional data management solution has delivered business benefits far beyond the technical ones originally anticipated.

DirecTV, which is known for its direct television broadcast satellite service, has been a regular contributor to the evolution of TV with its advanced HD programming, interactive features, digital video recording services, and electronic program guides. Employing more than 13,000 people across the United States and Latin America, DirecTV's 2008 revenues reached $20 billion, with total subscriber numbers approaching 50 million.

Problem

Midst of a continuing rapid growth, DirecTV faced the challenge of dealing with high transactional data volumes created by an escalating number of daily customer calls. Accommodating such a large data volume, along with rapidly changing market conditions, was one of DirecTV's key challenges. Several years ago, the company began looking for a better solution to providing the business side with daily reports on its call-center activities. Management wanted reports that could be used in many ways, including measuring and maintaining customer service, attracting new customers, and preventing customer churn. Equally important, the technical group at DirecTV wanted to reduce the resource load that its current data management system imposed on its CPUs.

Even though an early implementation of the data warehouse was addressing the company's needs fairly well, as business continued to grow its limitations became clear. Before the active data warehouse solution, the data was pulled from the server every night in batch mode, a process that was taking too long and straining the system. A daily batch-data upload to the data warehouse had long been (and for many companies, still is) the standard procedure. If the timeliness of the data is not a part of your business competitiveness, such a daily upload procedure may very well work for your organization. Unfortunately, this was not the case for DirecTV. Functioning within a highly dynamic consumer market, with a very high call volume to manage, DirecTV's business users needed to access the data from customer calls in a timely fashion.

Solution

Originally, the goal of the new data warehouse system was to send fresh data to the call center at least daily, but once the capabilities of the integrated solutions became apparent, that goal dropped to fresh data every 15 minutes. "We [then] wanted data latency of less than 15 minutes across the WAN running between different cities," Gustafson explains.

A secondary goal of the project was to simplify changed data capture to reduce the amount of maintenance required from developers. Although data sourcing across multiple platforms was not part of the initial requirement, that changed once DirecTV saw the capabilities of the GoldenGate integration system. GoldenGate allows the integration of a range of data management systems and platforms. At DirecTV, that included Oracle, the HP NonStop platform, an IBM DB2 system, and the Teradata data warehouse. "With GoldenGate, we weren't tied to one system," Gustafson says. "That also appealed to us. We're sourcing out of call logs, but we're also sourcing out of NonStop and other data sources. We thought, if we're going to buy a tool to do this, we want it to work with all the platforms we support."

Results

As the capabilities of the system became increasingly clear, its potential benefits to the business also became apparent. "Once we set it up, a huge business benefit [turned out to be] that it allowed us to measure our churn in real time," Gustafson says. "We said, 'Now that we have all these reports in real time, what can we do with them?'" One answer was to use the data to immediately reduce churn by targeting specific customers. With fresh data at their fingertips, call center sales personnel were able to contact a customer who had just asked to be disconnected and make a new sales offer to retain the customer just hours later the same day. Once the IT group set up the necessary reporting tools, sales campaigns could target specific customers for retention and prioritize them for special offers. That sort of campaign has clearly worked: "Our churn has actually gone down since we've implemented this program," Gustafson says. "Analysts are just raving about how great we're doing compared to our competitors in this area. A lot of it comes down to using this real-time copy to do analysis on customers, and to [make a fresh] offer to them the same day."

The system has also been set up to log customer service calls, reporting back constantly on technical problems that are reported in the field. That allows management to better evaluate and react to field reports, improving service and saving on dispatching technicians. Real-time call-center reports can also be produced to help manage the center's workload based on daily information on call volumes. Using that data, management can compare daily call volumes with historical averages for exception reporting.

In another business-centric use that was not originally anticipated, the company is using real-time operational reports for both order management and fraud detection. With access to real-time order information on new customers, fraud management experts can examine the data, and then use that information to weed out fraudulent orders. "That saves us rolling a truck, which drives [labor] and product costs down," Gustafson points out.

Questions for the Opening Vignette

1. Why is it important for DirecTV to have an active data warehouse?
2. What were the challenges DirecTV faced on its way to having an integrated active data warehouse?
3. Identify the major differences between a traditional data warehouse and an active data warehouse, such as the one implemented at DirecTV.
4. What strategic advantage can DirecTV derive from the real-time system as opposed to a traditional information system?
5. Why do you think large organizations like DirecTV cannot afford not to have a capable data warehouse?

What We Can Learn from This Vignette

The opening vignette illustrates the strategic value of implementing an active data warehouse, along with its supporting BI methods. DirecTV was able to leverage its data assets spread throughout the enterprise to be used by knowledge workers wherever and whenever they are needed. The data warehouse integrated various databases throughout the organization into a single, in-house enterprise unit to generate a single version of the truth for the company, putting all employees on the same page. Furthermore, the data was made available in real time to the decision makers who needed it, so they could use it in their decision making, ultimately leading to a strategic competitive advantage in the industry. The key lesson here is that a real-time, enterprise-level active data warehouse combined with a strategy for its use in decision support can result in significant benefits (financial and otherwise) for an organization.

Sources: L. L. Briggs, "DirecTV Connects with Data Integration Solution," *Business Intelligence Journal,* Vol. 14, No. 1, 2009, pp. 14–16; "DirecTV Enables Active Data Warehousing with GoldenGate's Real-Time Data Integration Technology," *Information Management Magazine,* January 2008; **directv.com**.

8.2 DATA WAREHOUSING DEFINITIONS AND CONCEPTS

Using real-time data warehousing in conjunction with DSS and BI tools is an important way to conduct business processes. The opening vignette demonstrates a scenario in which a real-time active data warehouse supported decision making by analyzing large amounts of data from various sources to provide rapid results to support critical processes. The single version of the truth stored in the data warehouse and provided in an easily digestible form expands the boundaries of DirecTV's innovative business processes. With real-time data flows, DirecTV can view the current state of its business and quickly identify problems, which is the first and foremost step toward solving them analytically. In addition, customers can obtain real-time information on their subscriptions, TV services, and other account information, so the system also provides a significant competitive advantage over competitors.

Decision makers require concise, dependable information about current operations, trends, and changes. Data are often fragmented in distinct operational systems, so managers often make decisions with partial information, at best. Data warehousing cuts through this obstacle by accessing, integrating, and organizing key operational data in a form that is consistent, reliable, timely, and readily available, wherever and whenever needed.

What Is a Data Warehouse?

In simple terms, a **data warehouse (DW)** is a pool of data produced to support decision making; it is also a repository of current and historical data of potential interest to managers throughout the organization. Data are usually structured to be available in a form ready for analytical processing activities (i.e., online analytical processing [OLAP], data mining, querying, reporting, and other decision support applications). A data warehouse is a subject-oriented, integrated, time-variant, nonvolatile collection of data in support of management's decision-making process.

Characteristics of Data Warehousing

A common way of introducing data warehousing is to refer to its fundamental characteristics (see Inmon, 2005):

- *Subject oriented.* Data are organized by detailed subject, such as sales, products, or customers, containing only information relevant for decision support. Subject orientation enables users to determine not only how their business is performing, but why. A data warehouse differs from an operational database in that most operational databases have a product orientation and are tuned to handle transactions that update the database. Subject orientation provides a more comprehensive view of the organization.
- *Integrated.* Integration is closely related to subject orientation. Data warehouses must place data from different sources into a consistent format. To do so, they must deal with naming conflicts and discrepancies among units of measure. A data warehouse is presumed to be totally integrated.
- *Time variant (time series).* A warehouse maintains historical data. The data do not necessarily provide current status (except in real-time systems). They detect trends, deviations, and long-term relationships for forecasting and comparisons, leading to decision making. Every data warehouse has a temporal quality. Time is the one important dimension that all data warehouses must support. Data for analysis from multiple sources contains multiple time points (e.g., daily, weekly, monthly views).
- *Nonvolatile.* After data are entered into a data warehouse, users cannot change or update the data. Obsolete data are discarded, and changes are recorded as new data.

These characteristics enable data warehouses to be tuned almost exclusively for data access. Some additional characteristics may include the following:

- *Web based.* Data warehouses are typically designed to provide an efficient computing environment for Web-based applications.
- *Relational/multidimensional.* A data warehouse uses either a relational structure or a multidimensional structure. A recent survey on multidimensional structures can be found in Romero and Abelló (2009).

- **Client/server.** A data warehouse uses the client/server architecture to provide easy access for end users.
- **Real time.** Newer data warehouses provide real-time, or active, data access and analysis capabilities (see Basu, 2003; and Bonde and Kuckuk, 2004).
- **Include metadata.** A data warehouse contains metadata (data about data) about how the data are organized and how to effectively use them.

Whereas a data warehouse is a repository of data, data warehousing is literally the entire process (see Watson, 2002). Data warehousing is a discipline that results in applications that provide decision support capability, allows ready access to business information, and creates business insight. The three main types of data warehouses are data marts, operational data stores (ODS), and enterprise data warehouses (EDW). In addition to discussing these three types of warehouses next, we also discuss metadata.

Data Marts

Whereas a data warehouse combines databases across an entire enterprise, a **data mart** is usually smaller and focuses on a particular subject or department. A data mart is a subset of a data warehouse, typically consisting of a single subject area (e.g., marketing, operations). A data mart can be either dependent or independent. A **dependent data mart** is a subset that is created directly from the data warehouse. It has the advantages of using a consistent data model and providing quality data. Dependent data marts support the concept of a single enterprise-wide data model, but the data warehouse must be constructed first. A dependent data mart ensures that the end user is viewing the same version of the data that is accessed by all other data warehouse users. The high cost of data warehouses limits their use to large companies. As an alternative, many firms use a lower-cost, scaled-down version of a data warehouse referred to as an *independent data mart*. An **independent data mart** is a small warehouse designed for a strategic business unit (SBU) or a department, but its source is not an EDW.

Operational Data Stores

An **operational data store (ODS)** provides a fairly recent form of customer information file (CIF). This type of database is often used as an interim staging area for a data warehouse. Unlike the static contents of a data warehouse, the contents of an ODS are updated throughout the course of business operations. An ODS is used for short-term decisions involving mission-critical applications rather than for the medium- and long-term decisions associated with an EDW. An ODS is similar to short-term memory in that it stores only very recent information. In comparison, a data warehouse is like long-term memory because it stores permanent information. An ODS consolidates data from multiple source systems and provides a near-real-time, integrated view of volatile, current data. The exchange, transfer, and load (ETL) processes (discussed later in this chapter) for an ODS are identical to those for a data warehouse. Finally, **oper marts** (see Imhoff, 2001) are created when operational data needs to be analyzed multidimensionally. The data for an oper mart come from an ODS.

Enterprise Data Warehouses (EDW)

An **enterprise data warehouse (EDW)** is a large-scale data warehouse that is used across the enterprise for decision support. It is the type of data warehouse that DirecTV developed, as described in the opening vignette. The large-scale nature provides integration of data from many sources into a standard format for effective BI and decision support applications. EDW are used to provide data for many types of DSS, including CRM, supply-chain management (SCM), business performance management (BPM), business activity monitoring (BAM), product lifecycle management (PLM), revenue management, and sometimes even knowledge management systems (KMS). Application Case 8.1 shows the enormous benefits a large company can realize from EDW, if it is designed and implemented correctly.

APPLICATION CASE 8.1
Enterprise Data Warehouse Delivers Cost Savings and Process Efficiencies

Founded in 1884 in Dayton, Ohio, the NCR Corporation is now a $5.6 billon NYSE-listed company providing technology solutions worldwide in the retail, financial, insurance, communications, manufacturing, and travel and transportation industries. NCR solutions include store automation and automated teller machines, consulting services, media products, and hardware technology.

When acquired by AT&T in 1991, NCR operated on an autonomous country- and product-centric structure, in which each country made its own decisions about product and service offerings, marketing, and pricing and developed its own processes and reporting norms. Under the country model, dozens of different financial and operational applications were required to capture the total results of the company, by no means an enterprise solution.

In 1997, when NCR was spun off on its own again, company operations were losing substantial amounts of money every day. The spin-off provided NCR with the much-needed funds to engage in the deep process changes required to maintain and strengthen its competitive position in the global market and to undertake the transformation to a truly global enterprise.

The goal was to move from a primarily hardware-focused and country-centric organizational model to an integrated, solution-oriented business structure with a global focus. To do this, NCR needed to globalize, centralize, and integrate its vast store of information resources. Only then could it gain effective control over the necessary business changes. NCR's EDW initiative was critical to the company's successful transformation and would be vital to the successful deployment of a new worldwide, single-instance, enterprise resource planning (ERP) system planned for several years later.

NCR Finance and Worldwide Customer Services (WCS) led the drive for implementation of the EDW. Business teams from Finance and WCS, Financial Information Delivery (FID), and Global Information Systems (GIS), respectively, worked closely with the EDW team to ensure that IT understood the business requirements for the new structure. The Teradata system was chosen for its scalability, its flexibility to support unstructured queries and high numbers of concurrent users, and its relatively low maintenance costs.

The enormous potential of the EDW spread throughout the company, driving organizational and process changes in Finance, where the financial close cycle was reduced from 14 days to 6 and worldwide reporting integrity standards were established; in WCS, where individual customer profitability profiles and improvement plans were made possible; and in Sales and Marketing, Operations and Inventory Management, and Human Resources. ERP operational standardization and a dramatic improvement in the business of serving its customers mean that NCR is poised for the future. Internally and externally, NCR has become a global solution provider, supported by global business processes.

The returns have already been superb. Not only has the EDW project proved to be more than self-funding at the project cost level, but revenue generation is around the corner. Some of the benefits include $100 million in annual savings in inventory-carrying costs, a $200 million sustainable reduction in accounts receivable, a $50 million reduction in annual finance costs, and $22 million in cost savings over the first 5 years of the EDW implementation for WCS.

There is still much to be done and significant value to be realized by the project. Beyond cost savings and process efficiencies, the strategy going forward is to use the EDW to drive growth.

Although the EDW project was not undertaken as a profit-producing opportunity, it was self-funding. The cost savings far exceeded the expense of implementation. As the EDW matures, growth-focused goals are developing, and the EDW will drive profits in the future. The quantified benefits of the EDW speak for themselves. There are many more benefits of a qualitative nature. A sampling of both follows.

Qualitative Benefits

- Reduced financial close cycle from 14 days to 6
- Heightened reporting integrity to corporate standards
- Created individual customer profitability profiles and improvement plans
- Provided consistent worldwide reporting processes
- Improved on-time delivery
- Decreased obsolescence due to enhanced inventory management

Quantified Benefits

- $50 million reduction in annual finance controllership costs
- $200 million sustainable reduction in accounts receivable, which translates into $20 million per year savings in accounts receivable carrying costs
- $100 million sustainable reduction in finished inventory, which, in turn, equals a $10 million per year savings in inventory carrying costs
- $22 million cost savings over the first 5 years of the EDW implementation for WCS, including automation of the SLA reporting to customers, headcount savings, and lower customer maintenance costs
- $10 million for improved supply chain management
- $6.1 million net present value of cost reductions over 5 years as a result of reducing headcount from the finance and auditing (F&A) reporting function
- $3.5 million reduction in telecommunications costs
- $3 million in savings through the reduction of ERP transition costs
- $1.7 million saved on report development costs in the rollout from Oracle 10.7 and 11 to 11i, for reports that do not have to be custom written for Oracle

Source: Teradata, "Enterprise Data Warehouse Delivers Cost Savings and Process Efficiencies," **teradata.com/t/resources/ case-studies/NCR-Corporation-eb4455/** (accessed June 2009).

Metadata

Metadata are data about data (e.g., see Sen, 2004; and Zhao, 2005). Metadata describe the structure of and some meaning about data, thereby contributing to their effective or ineffective use. Mehra (2005) indicated that few organizations really understand metadata, and fewer understand how to design and implement a metadata strategy. Metadata are generally defined in terms of usage as technical or business metadata. Pattern is another way to view metadata. According to the pattern view, we can differentiate between syntactic metadata (i.e., data describing the syntax of data), structural metadata (i.e., data describing the structure of the data), and semantic metadata (i.e., data describing the meaning of the data in a specific domain).

We next explain traditional metadata patterns and insights into how to implement an effective metadata strategy via a holistic approach to enterprise metadata integration. The approach includes ontology and metadata registries; enterprise information integration (EII); extraction, transformation, and load (ETL); and service-oriented architectures (SOA). Effectiveness, extensibility, reusability, interoperability, efficiency and performance, evolution, entitlement, flexibility, segregation, user interface, versioning, versatility, and low maintenance cost are some of the key requirements for building a successful metadata-driven enterprise.

According to Kassam (2002), business metadata comprise information that increases our understanding of traditional (i.e., structured) data. The primary purpose of metadata should be to provide context to the reported data; that is, it provides enriching information that leads to the creation of knowledge. Business metadata, though difficult to provide efficiently, release more of the potential of structured data. The context need not be the same for all users. In many ways, metadata assist in the conversion of data and information into knowledge. Metadata form a foundation for a metabusiness architecture (see Bell, 2001). Tannenbaum (2002) described how to identify metadata requirements. Vaduva and Vetterli (2001) provided an overview of metadata management for data warehousing. Zhao (2005) described five levels of metadata management maturity: (1) ad hoc, (2) discovered, (3) managed, (4) optimized, and (5) automated. These levels help in understanding where an organization is in terms of how and how well it uses its metadata.

The design, creation, and use of metadata—descriptive or summary data about data—and its accompanying standards may involve ethical issues. There are ethical considerations involved in the collection and ownership of the information contained in metadata, including privacy and intellectual property issues that arise in the design, collection, and dissemination stages (for more, see Brody, 2003).

Section 8.2 Review Questions

1. What is a data warehouse?
2. How does a data warehouse differ from a database?
3. What is an ODS?
4. Differentiate among a data mart, an ODS, and an EDW.
5. Explain the importance of metadata.

8.3 DATA WAREHOUSING PROCESS OVERVIEW

Organizations, private and public, continuously collect data, information, and knowledge at an increasingly accelerated rate and store them in computerized systems. Maintaining and using these data and information become extremely complex, especially as scalability issues arise. In addition, the number of users needing to access the information continues to increase as a result of improved reliability and availability of network access, especially the Internet. Working with multiple databases, either integrated in a data warehouse or not, has become an extremely difficult task requiring considerable expertise, but it can provide immense benefits far exceeding its cost (see the opening vignette and Application Case 8.2).

APPLICATION CASE 8.2

Data Warehousing Supports First American Corporation's Corporate Strategy

First American Corporation changed its corporate strategy from a traditional banking approach to one that was centered on CRM. This enabled First American to transform itself from a company that lost $60 million in 1990 to an innovative financial services leader a decade later. The successful implementation of this strategy would not have been possible without its VISION data warehouse, which stores information about customer behavior, such as products used, buying preferences, and client-value positions. VISION provides:

- Identification of the top 20 percent of profitable customers
- Identification of the 40 to 50 percent of unprofitable customers

- Retention strategies
- Lower-cost distribution channels
- Strategies to expand customer relationships
- Redesigned information flows

Access to information through a data warehouse can enable both evolutionary and revolutionary change. First American Corporation achieved revolutionary change, moving itself into the "sweet 16" of financial services corporations.

Sources: Adapted from B. L. Cooper, H. J. Watson, B. H. Wixom, and D. L. Goodhue, "Data Warehousing Supports Corporate Strategy at First American Corporation," *MIS Quarterly,* Vol. 24, No. 4, 2000, pp. 547–567; and B. L. Cooper, H. J. Watson, B. H. Wixom, and D. L. Goodhue, "Data Warehousing Supports Corporate Strategy at First American Corporation," SIM International Conference, Atlanta, August 15–19, 1999.

Many organizations need to create data warehouses—massive data stores of time-series data for decision support. Data are imported from various external and internal resources and are cleansed and organized in a manner consistent with the organization's needs. After the data are populated in the data warehouse, data marts can be loaded for a specific area or department. Alternatively, data marts can be created first, as needed, and then integrated into an EDW. Often, though, data marts are not developed, but data are simply loaded onto PCs or left in their original state for direct manipulation using BI tools.

In Figure 8.1, we show the data warehouse concept. The following are the major components of the data warehousing process:

- ***Data sources.*** Data are sourced from multiple independent operational "legacy" systems and possibly from external data providers (such as the U.S. Census). Data may also come from an OLTP or ERP system. Web data in the form of Web logs may also feed a data warehouse.
- ***Data extraction.*** Data are extracted using custom-written or commercial software called ETL.
- ***Data loading.*** Data are loaded into a staging area, where they are transformed and cleansed. The data are then ready to load into the data warehouse.
- ***Comprehensive database.*** Essentially, this is the EDW to support all decision analysis by providing relevant summarized and detailed information originating from many different sources.
- ***Metadata.*** Metadata are maintained so that they can be assessed by IT personnel and users. Metadata include software programs about data and rules for organizing data summaries that are easy to index and search, especially with Web tools.
- ***Middleware tools.*** Middleware tools enable access to the data warehouse. Power users such as analysts may write their own SQL queries. Others may employ a managed query environment, such as Business Objects, to access data. There are many front-end applications that business users can use to interact with data stored in the data repositories, including data mining, OLAP, reporting tools, and data visualization tools.

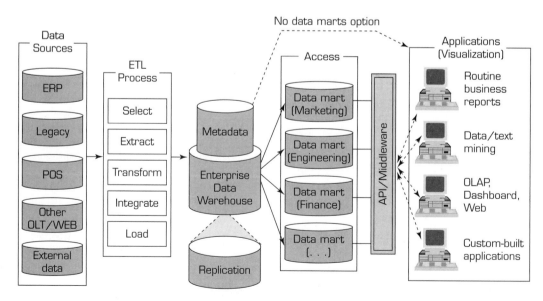

FIGURE 8.1 A Data Warehouse Framework and Views

Section 8.3 Review Questions

1. Describe the data warehousing process.
2. Describe the major components of a data warehouse.
3. Identify the role of middleware tools.

8.4 DATA WAREHOUSING ARCHITECTURES

There are several basic architectures for data warehousing. Two-tier and three-tier architectures are common (see Figures 8.2 and 8.3), but sometimes there is simply one tier. Hoffer et al. (2007) distinguished among these architectures by dividing the data warehouse into three parts:

1. The data warehouse itself, which contains the data and associated software
2. Data acquisition (back-end) software, which extracts data from legacy systems and external sources, consolidates and summarizes them, and loads them into the data warehouse
3. Client (front-end) software, which allows users to access and analyze data from the warehouse (a DSS/BI/business analytics [BA] engine)

In a three-tier architecture, operational systems contain the data and the software for data acquisition in one tier (i.e., the server), the data warehouse is another tier, and the third tier includes the DSS/BI/BA engine (i.e., the application server) and the client (see Figure 8.2). Data from the warehouse are processed twice and deposited in an additional multidimensional database, organized for easy multidimensional analysis and presentation, or replicated in data marts. The advantage of the three-tier architecture is its separation of the functions of the data warehouse, which eliminates resource constraints and makes it possible to easily create data marts.

In a two-tier architecture, the DSS engine physically runs on the same hardware platform as the data warehouse (see Figure 8.3). Therefore, it is more economical than the three-tier structure. The two-tier architecture can have performance problems for large data warehouses that work with data-intensive applications for decision support.

Much of the common wisdom assumes an absolutist approach, maintaining that one solution is better than the other, despite the organization's circumstances and unique needs. To further complicate these architectural decisions, many consultants and software vendors focus on one portion of the architecture, therefore limiting their capacity and motivation to assist an organization through the options based on its needs. But these aspects are being questioned and analyzed. For example, Ball (2005) provided decision criteria for organizations that plan to implement a BI application and have already determined their need for multidimensional data marts but need help determining the appropriate tiered architecture. His criteria revolve around forecasting needs for space and speed of access (see Ball, 2005, for details).

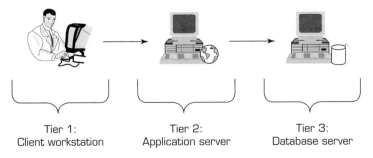

Tier 1:
Client workstation

Tier 2:
Application server

Tier 3:
Database server

FIGURE 8.2 Architecture of a Three-Tier Data Warehouse

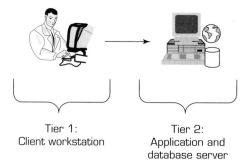

Tier 1:
Client workstation

Tier 2:
Application and
database server

FIGURE 8.3 Architecture of a Two-Tier Data Warehouse

Data warehousing and the Internet are two key technologies that offer important solutions for managing corporate data. The integration of these two technologies produces Web-based data warehousing. In Figure 8.4, we show the architecture of Web-based data warehousing. The architecture is three tiered and includes the PC client, Web server, and application server. On the client side, the user needs an Internet connection and a Web browser (preferably Java enabled) through the familiar graphical user interface (GUI). The Internet/intranet/extranet is the communication medium between clients and servers. On the server side, a Web server is used to manage the inflow and outflow of information between client and server. It is backed by both a data warehouse and an application server. Web-based data warehousing offers several compelling advantages, including ease of access, platform independence, and lower cost.

The Vanguard Group moved to a Web-based, three-tier architecture for its enterprise architecture to integrate all its data and provide customers with the same views of data as internal users (Dragoon, 2003). Likewise, Hilton migrated all its independent client/server systems to a three-tier data warehouse, using a Web design enterprise system. This change involved an investment of $3.8 million (excluding labor) and affected 1,500 users. It increased processing efficiency (speed) by a factor of six. When it was deployed, Hilton expected to save $4.5 million to $5 million annually. Finally, Hilton experimented with Dell's clustering (i.e., parallel computing) technology to enhance scalability and speed (see Anthes, 2003).

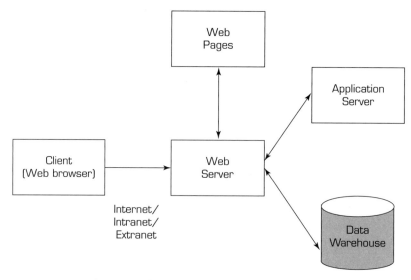

FIGURE 8.4 Architecture of Web-Based Data Warehousing

Web architectures for data warehousing are similar in structure to other data warehousing architectures, requiring a design choice for housing the Web data warehouse with the transaction server or as a separate server(s). Page-loading speed is an important consideration in designing Web-based applications; therefore, server capacity must be planned carefully.

Several issues must be considered when deciding which architecture to use. Among them are the following:

- *Which database management system (DBMS) should be used?* Most data warehouses are built using relational database management systems (RDBMS). Oracle (Oracle Corporation, **oracle.com**), SQL Server (Microsoft Corporation, **microsoft.com/sql/**), and DB2 (IBM Corporation, **306.ibm.com/software/data/db2/**) are the ones most commonly used. Each of these products supports both client/server and Web-based architectures.

- *Will parallel processing and/or partitioning be used?* Parallel processing enables multiple CPUs to process data warehouse query requests simultaneously and provides scalability. Data warehouse designers need to decide whether the database tables will be partitioned (i.e., split into smaller tables) for access efficiency and what the criteria will be. This is an important consideration that is necessitated by the large amounts of data contained in a typical data warehouse. A recent survey on parallel and distributed data warehouses can be found in Furtado (2009). Teradata (**teradata.com**) has successfully adopted and often commented on its novel implementation of this approach.

- *Will data migration tools be used to load the data warehouse?* Moving data from an existing system into a data warehouse is a tedious and laborious task. Depending on the diversity and the location of the data assets, migration may be a relatively simple procedure or (in contrary) a months-long project. The results of a thorough assessment of the existing data assets should be used to determine whether to use migration tools, and if so, what capabilities to seek in those commercial tools.

- *What tools will be used to support data retrieval and analysis?* Often it is necessary to use specialized tools to periodically locate, access, analyze, extract, transform, and load necessary data into a data warehouse. A decision has to be made on (i) developing the migration tools in-house, (ii) purchasing them from a third-party provider, or (iii) using the ones provided with the data warehouse system. Overly complex, real-time migrations warrant specialized third-party ETL tools.

Alternative Architectures

Data warehouse architecture design viewpoints can be generally categorized into enterprise-wide data warehouse design and data mart design (Golfarelli and Rizzi, 2009). In Figure 8.5 (parts a–e), we show some alternatives to the basic architectural design types that are neither pure EDW nor pure DM, but in between or beyond the traditional architectural structures. Notable new ones include hub-and-spoke and federated architectures. The five architectures shown in Figure 8.5 (parts a–e) are proposed by Ariyachandra and Watson (2006b). Previously, in an extensive study, Sen and Sinha (2005) identified 15 different data warehousing methodologies. The sources of these methodologies are classified into three broad categories: core-technology vendors, infrastructure vendors, and information-modeling companies.

The data warehousing literature provides additional discussions about a variety of architectures, such as independent data marts, data mart bus architecture with linked dimensional data marts, and federated data marts (see Ariyachandra and Watson, 2005,

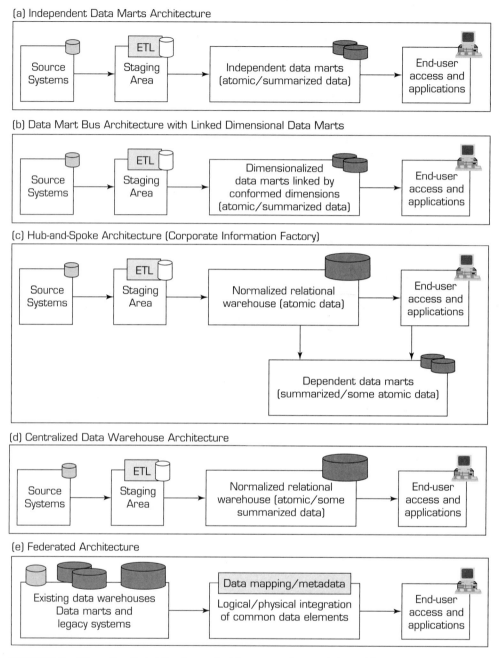

FIGURE 8.5 Alternative Data Warehouse Architectures *Source:* Adapted from T. Ariyachandra and H. Watson, "Which Data Warehouse Architecture Is Most Successful?" *Business Intelligence Journal*, Vol. 11, No. 1, First Quarter, 2006, pp. 4–6.

2006a); see Figure 8.6. In independent data marts, the marts are developed to operate independently of each other. Thus, they have inconsistent data definitions and different dimensions and measures, making it difficult to analyze data across the marts (i.e., it is difficult, if not impossible, to get to the "one version of the truth"). In a hub-and-spoke architecture, attention is focused on building a scalable and maintainable infrastructure; it is developed in an iterative way, subject area by subject area, and dependent data marts are developed. A centralized data warehouse is similar to the hub-and-spoke architecture

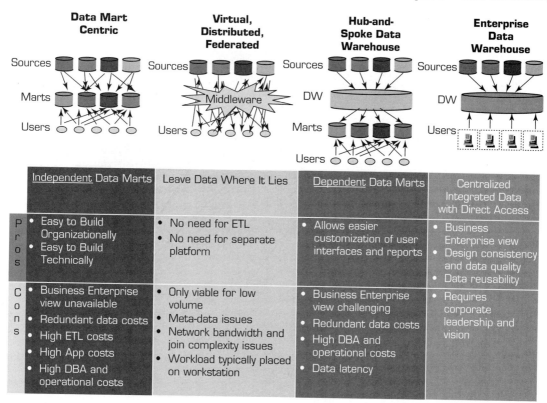

	Independent Data Marts	Leave Data Where It Lies	Dependent Data Marts	Centralized Integrated Data with Direct Access
Pros	• Easy to Build Organizationally • Easy to Build Technically	• No need for ETL • No need for separate platform	• Allows easier customization of user interfaces and reports	• Business Enterprise view • Design consistency and data quality • Data reusability
Cons	• Business Enterprise view unavailable • Redundant data costs • High ETL costs • High App costs • High DBA and operational costs	• Only viable for low volume • Meta-data issues • Network bandwidth and join complexity issues • Workload typically placed on workstation	• Business Enterprise view challenging • Redundant data costs • High DBA and operational costs • Data latency	• Requires corporate leadership and vision

FIGURE 8.6 Alternative Architectures for Data Warehousing Efforts *Source:* Based on W. Eckerson, "Four Ways to Build a Data Warehouse," *What Works: Best Practices in Business Intelligence and Data Warehousing,* Vol. 15, The Data Warehousing Institute, Chatsworth, CA, June 2003, pp. 46–49. Used with permission.

except that there are no dependent data marts. The central data warehouses architecture, which is advocated mainly by Teradata Corp., advises using data warehouses without any data marts (see Figure 8.7). This centralized approach provides users with access to all data in the data warehouse instead of limiting them to data marts. In addition, it reduces the amount of data the technical team has to transfer or change, therefore simplifying data management and administration.

The federated approach is a concession to the natural forces that undermine the best plans for developing a perfect system. It uses all possible means to integrate analytical resources from multiple sources to meet changing needs or business conditions. Essentially, the federated approach involves integrating disparate systems. In a federated architecture, existing decision support structures are left in place, and data are accessed from those sources as needed. The federated approach is supported by middleware vendors that propose distributed query and join capabilities. These eXtensible Markup Language (XML)–based tools offer users a global view of distributed data sources, including data warehouses, data marts, Web sites, documents, and operational systems. When users choose query objects from this view and press the submit button, the tool automatically queries the distributed sources, joins the results, and presents them to the user. Because of performance and data quality issues, most experts agree that federated approaches work well to supplement data warehouses, not replace them (see Eckerson, 2005).

Ariyachandra and Watson (2005) identified 10 factors that potentially affect the architecture selection decision:

1. Information interdependence between organizational units
2. Upper management's information needs

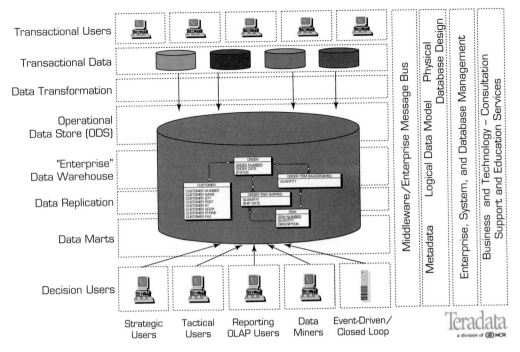

FIGURE 8.7 Teradata Corp.'s Enterprise Data Warehouse   *Source:* Teradata Corporation (teradata.com). Used with permission.

3. Urgency of need for a data warehouse
4. Nature of end-user tasks
5. Constraints on resources
6. Strategic view of the data warehouse prior to implementation
7. Compatibility with existing systems
8. Perceived ability of the in-house IT staff
9. Technical issues
10. Social/political factors

These factors are similar to many success factors described in the literature for information systems projects and DSS and BI projects. Technical issues, beyond providing technology that is feasibly ready for use, is important, but often not as important as behavioral issues, such as meeting upper management's information needs and user involvement in the development process (a social/political factor). Each data warehousing architecture has specific applications for which it is most (and least) effective and thus provides maximal benefits to the organization. However, overall, the data mart structure seems to be the least effective in practice See Ariyachandra and Watson (2006a) for some additional details.

Which Architecture Is the Best?

Ever since data warehousing became a critical part of modern enterprises, the question of which data warehouse architecture is the best has been a topic of regular discussion. The two gurus of the data warehousing field, Bill Inmon and Ralph Kimball, are at the heart of this discussion. Inmon advocates the hub-and-spoke architecture (e.g., the Corporate Information Factory), whereas Kimball promotes the data mart bus architecture with conformed dimensions. Other architectures are possible, but these two options are fundamentally different approaches, and each has strong advocates. To shed light on this controversial question, Ariyachandra and Watson (2006b) conducted an empirical study. To collect the data, they used a Web-based survey targeted at individuals involved in data warehouse implementations. Their survey included questions about the respondent, the respondent's company, the company's data warehouse, and the success of the data warehouse architecture.

In total, 454 respondents provided usable information. Surveyed companies ranged from small (less than $10 million in revenue) to large (in excess of $10 billion). Most of the companies were located in the United States (60%) and represented a variety of industries, with the financial services industry (15%) providing the most responses. The predominant architecture was the hub-and-spoke architecture (39%), followed by the bus architecture (26%), the centralized architecture (17%), independent data marts (12%), and the federated architecture (4%). The most common platform for hosting the data warehouses was Oracle (41%), followed by Microsoft (19%) and IBM (18%). The average (mean) gross revenue varied from $3.7 billion for independent data marts to $6 billion for the federated architecture.

They used four measures to assess the success of the architectures: (1) information quality, (2) system quality, (3) individual impacts, and (4) organizational impacts. The questions used a seven-point scale, with the higher score indicating a more successful architecture. Table 8.1 shows the average scores for the measures across the architectures.

As the results of the study indicate, independent data marts scored the lowest on all measures. This finding confirms the conventional wisdom that independent data marts are a poor architectural solution. Next lowest on all measures was the federated architecture. Firms sometimes have disparate decision-support platforms resulting from mergers and acquisitions, and they may choose a federated approach, at least in the short run. The findings suggest that the federated architecture is not an optimal long-term solution. What is interesting, however, is the similarity of the averages for the bus, hub-and-spoke, and centralized architectures. The differences are sufficiently small that no claims can be made for a particular architecture's superiority over the others, at least based on a simple comparison of these success measures.

They also collected data on the domain (e.g., varying from a subunit to company-wide) and the size (i.e., amount of data stored) of the warehouses. They found that the hub-and-spoke architecture is typically used with more enterprise-wide implementations and larger warehouses. They also investigated the cost and time required to implement the different architectures. Overall, the hub-and-spoke architecture was the most expensive and time-consuming to implement.

Section 8.4 Review Questions

1. What are the key similarities and differences between a two-tiered architecture and a three-tiered architecture?
2. How has the Web influenced data warehouse design?
3. List the alternative data warehousing architectures discussed in this section.

TABLE 8.1 Average Assessment Scores for the Success of the Architectures

	Independent Data Marts	Bus Architecture	Hub-and-Spoke Architecture	Centralized Architecture (No Dependent Data Marts)	Federated Architecture
Information Quality	4.42	5.16	5.35	5.23	4.73
System Quality	4.59	5.60	5.56	5.41	4.69
Individual Impacts	5.08	5.80	5.62	5.64	5.15
Organizational Impacts	4.66	5.34	5.24	5.30	4.77

4. What issues should be considered when deciding which architecture to use in developing a data warehouse? List the 10 most important factors.
5. Which data warehousing architecture is the best? Why?

8.5 DATA INTEGRATION AND THE EXTRACTION, TRANSFORMATION, AND LOAD (ETL) PROCESSES

Global competitive pressures, demand for return on investment (ROI), management and investor inquiry, and government regulations are forcing business managers to rethink how they integrate and manage their businesses. A decision maker typically needs access to multiple sources of data that must be integrated. Before data warehouses, data marts, and BI software, providing access to data sources was a major, laborious process. Even with modern Web-based data management tools, recognizing what data to access and providing them to the decision maker are nontrivial tasks that require database specialists. As data warehouses grow in size, the issues of integrating data grow as well.

The business analysis needs continue to evolve. Mergers and acquisitions, regulatory requirements, and the introduction of new channels can drive changes in BI requirements. In addition to historical, cleansed, consolidated, and point-in-time data, business users increasingly demand access to real-time, unstructured, and/or remote data. And everything must be integrated with the contents of an existing data warehouse (see Devlin, 2003). Moreover, access via PDAs and through speech recognition and synthesis is becoming more commonplace, further complicating integration issues (see Edwards, 2003). Many integration projects involve enterprise-wide systems. Orovic (2003) provided a checklist of what works and what does not work when attempting such a project. Properly integrating data from various databases and other disparate sources is difficult. But when it is not done properly, it can lead to disaster in enterprise-wide systems such as CRM, ERP, and supply-chain projects (see Nash, 2002). Also see Dasu and Johnson (2003).

Data Integration

Data integration comprises three major processes that, when correctly implemented, permit data to be accessed and made accessible to an array of ETL and analysis tools and data warehousing environment: data access (i.e., the ability to access and extract data from any data source), data federation (i.e., the integration of business views across multiple data stores), and change capture (based on the identification, capture, and delivery of the changes made to enterprise data sources). See Sapir (2005) for details. See Application Case 8.3 for an example of how BP Lubricant benefits from implementing a data warehouse that integrates data from many sources. Some vendors, such as SAS Institute, Inc., have developed strong data integration tools. The SAS enterprise data integration server includes customer data integration tools that improve data quality in the integration process. The Oracle Business Intelligence Suite assists in integrating data as well.

APPLICATION CASE 8.3

BP Lubricants Achieves BIGS Success

BP Lubricants established the BIGS program following recent merger activity to deliver globally consistent and transparent management information. As well as timely business intelligence, BIGS provides detailed, consistent views of performance across functions such as finance, marketing, sales, and supply and logistics.

BP is one of the world's largest oil and petrochemicals groups. Part of the BP plc group, BP Lubricants is an established leader in the global automotive lubricants market. Perhaps best known for its Castrol brand of oils, the business operates in over 100 countries and employs 10,000 people. Strategically, BP Lubricants is concentrating on further improving its customer focus and increasing its effectiveness in automotive markets. Following recent merger activity, the company is undergoing transformation to become more effective and agile and to seize opportunities for rapid growth.

Challenge

Following recent merger activity, BP Lubricants wanted to improve the consistency, transparency, and accessibility of management information and business intelligence. In order to do so, it needed to integrate data held in disparate source systems, without the delay of introducing a standardized ERP system.

Solution

BP Lubricants implemented the pilot for its Business Intelligence and Global Standards (BIGS) program, a strategic initiative for management information and business intelligence. At the heart of BIGS is Kalido, an adaptive enterprise data warehousing solution for preparing, implementing, operating, and managing data warehouses.

Kalido's federated enterprise data warehousing solution supported the pilot program's complex data integration and diverse reporting requirements. To adapt to the program's evolving reporting requirements, the software also enabled the underlying information architecture to be easily modified at high speed while preserving all information. The system integrates and stores information from multiple source systems to provide consolidated views for:

- *Marketing.* Customer proceeds and margins for market segments with drill down to invoice-level detail

- *Sales.* Sales invoice reporting augmented with both detailed tariff costs and actual payments
- *Finance.* Globally standard profit and loss, balance sheet, and cash flow statements—with audit ability; customer debt management supply and logistics; consolidated view of order and movement processing across multiple ERP platforms

Benefits

By improving the visibility of consistent, timely data, BIGS provides the information needed to assist the business in identifying a multitude of business opportunities to maximize margins and/or manage associated costs. Typical responses to the benefits of consistent data resulting from the BIGS pilot include:

- Improved consistency and transparency of business data
- Easier, faster, and more flexible reporting
- Accommodation of both global and local standards
- Fast, cost-effective, and flexible implementation cycle
- Minimal disruption of existing business processes and the day-to-day business
- Identifies data quality issues and encourages their resolution
- Improved ability to respond intelligently to new business opportunities

Sources: Kalido, "BP Lubricants Achieves BIGS, Key IT Solutions," **keyitsolutions.com/asp/rptdetails/report/95/cat/1175/** (accessed August 2009); Kalido, "BP Lubricants Achieves BIGS Success," **kalido.com/collateral/Documents/English-US/CS-BP%20BIGS.pdf** (accessed August 2009); and BP Lubricant homepage, **bp.com/lubricanthome.do** (accessed August 2009).

A major purpose of a data warehouse is to integrate data from multiple systems. Various integration technologies enable data and metadata integration:

- Enterprise application integration (EAI)
- Service-oriented architecture (SOA)
- Enterprise information integration (EII)
- Extraction, transformation, and load (ETL)

Enterprise application integration (EAI) provides a vehicle for pushing data from source systems into the data warehouse. It involves integrating application functionality and is focused on sharing functionality (rather than data) across systems, thereby enabling flexibility and reuse. Traditionally, EAI solutions have focused on enabling application reuse at the application programming interface (API) level. Recently, EAI is accomplished by using SOA coarse-grained services (a collection of business processes or functions) that are well defined and documented. Using Web services is a specialized way of implementing an SOA. EAI can be used to facilitate data acquisition directly into a near-real-time data warehouse or to deliver decisions to the OLTP systems. There are many different approaches to and tools for EAI implementation.

Enterprise information integration (EII) is an evolving tool space that promises real-time data integration from a variety of sources, such as relational databases, Web services, and multidimensional databases. It is a mechanism for pulling data from source systems to satisfy a request for information. EII tools use predefined metadata to populate views that make integrated data appear relational to end users. XML may be the most important aspect of EII because XML allows data to be tagged either at creation time or later. These tags can be extended and modified to accommodate almost any area of knowledge (see Kay, 2005).

Physical data integration has conventionally been the main mechanism for creating an integrated view with data warehouses and data marts. With the advent of EII tools (see Kay, 2005), new virtual data integration patterns are feasible. Manglik and Mehra (2005) discussed the benefits and constraints of new data integration patterns that can expand traditional physical methodologies to present a comprehensive view for the enterprise.

We next turn to the approach for loading data into the warehouse: ETL.

Extraction, Transformation, and Load

At the heart of the technical side of the data warehousing process is **extraction, transformation, and load (ETL)**. ETL technologies, which have existed for some time, are instrumental in the process and use of data warehouses. The ETL process is an integral component in any data-centric project. IT managers are often faced with challenges because the ETL process typically consumes 70 percent of the time in a data-centric project.

The ETL process consists of extraction (i.e., reading data from one or more databases), transformation (i.e., converting the extracted data from its previous form into the form in which it needs to be so that it can be placed into a data warehouse or simply another database), and load (i.e., putting the data into the data warehouse). Transformation occurs by using rules or lookup tables or by combining the data with other data. The three database functions are integrated into one tool to pull data out of one or more databases and place them into another, consolidated database or a data warehouse.

ETL tools also transport data between sources and targets, document how data elements (e.g., metadata) change as they move between source and target, exchange metadata with other applications as needed, and administer all runtime processes and operations (e.g., scheduling, error management, audit logs, statistics). ETL is extremely important for data integration as well as for data warehousing. The purpose of the ETL process is to load the warehouse with integrated and cleansed data. The data used in ETL processes can come from any source: a mainframe application, an ERP application, a CRM tool, a flat file, an Excel spreadsheet, or even a message queue. In Figure 8.8, we outline the ETL process.

The process of migrating data to a data warehouse involves the extraction of data from all relevant sources. Data sources may consist of files extracted from OLTP databases, spreadsheets, personal databases (e.g., Microsoft Access), or external files. Typically, all the input files are written to a set of staging tables, which are designed to facilitate the load process. A data warehouse contains numerous business rules that define such things as

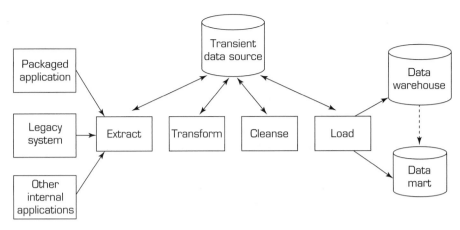

FIGURE 8.8 The ETL Process

how the data will be used, summarization rules, standardization of encoded attributes, and calculation rules. Any data quality issues pertaining to the source files need to be corrected before the data are loaded into the data warehouse. One of the benefits of a well-designed data warehouse is that these rules can be stored in a metadata repository and applied to the data warehouse centrally. This differs from an OLTP approach, which typically has data and business rules scattered throughout the system. The process of loading data into a data warehouse can be performed either through data transformation tools that provide a GUI to aid in the development and maintenance of business rules or through more traditional methods, such as developing programs or utilities to load the data warehouse, using programming languages such as PL/SQL, C++, or .NET Framework languages. This decision is not easy for organizations. Several issues affect whether an organization will purchase data transformation tools or build the transformation process itself:

- Data transformation tools are expensive.
- Data transformation tools may have a long learning curve.
- It is difficult to measure how the IT organization is doing until it has learned to use the data transformation tools.

In the long run, a transformation-tool approach should simplify the maintenance of an organization's data warehouse. Transformation tools can also be effective in detecting and scrubbing (i.e., removing any anomalies in the data). OLAP and data mining tools rely on how well the data are transformed.

As an example of effective ETL, Motorola, Inc., uses ETL to feed its data warehouses. Motorola collects information from 30 different procurement systems and sends them to its global SCM data warehouse for analysis of aggregate company spending (see Songini, 2004).

Solomon (2005) classified ETL technologies into four categories: sophisticated, enabler, simple, and rudimentary. It is generally acknowledged that tools in the sophisticated category will result in the ETL process being better documented and more accurately managed as the data warehouse project evolves.

Even though it is possible for programmers to develop software for ETL, it is simpler to use an existing ETL tool. The following are some of the important criteria in selecting an ETL tool (see Brown, 2004):

- Ability to read from and write to an unlimited number of data source architectures
- Automatic capturing and delivery of metadata
- A history of conforming to open standards
- An easy-to-use interface for the developer and the functional user

Performing extensive ETL may be a sign of poorly managed data and a fundamental lack of a coherent data management strategy. Karacsony (2006) indicated that there is a direct correlation between the extent of redundant data and the number of ETL processes. When data are managed correctly as an enterprise asset, ETL efforts are significantly reduced, and redundant data are completely eliminated. This leads to huge savings in maintenance and greater efficiency in new development while also improving data quality. Poorly designed ETL processes are costly to maintain, change, and update. Consequently, it is crucial to make the proper choices in terms of the technology and tools to use for developing and maintaining the ETL process.

A number of packaged ETL tools are available. Database vendors currently offer ETL capabilities that both enhance and compete with independent ETL tools. SAS acknowledges the importance of data quality and offers the industry's first fully integrated solution that merges ETL and data quality to transform data into strategic valuable assets. Other ETL software providers include Microsoft, Oracle, IBM, Informatica, Embarcadero, and Tibco. For additional information on ETL, see Golfarelli and Rizzi (2009), Karaksony (2006), and Songini (2004).

Section 8.5 Review Questions

1. Describe data integration.
2. Describe the three steps of the ETL process.
3. Why is the ETL process so important for data warehousing efforts?

8.6 DATA WAREHOUSE DEVELOPMENT

A data warehousing project is a major undertaking for any organization and is more complicated than a simple, mainframe selection and implementation project because it comprises and influences many departments and many input and output interfaces and it can be part of a CRM business strategy. A data warehouse provides several benefits that can be classified as direct and indirect. Direct benefits include the following:

- End users can perform extensive analysis in numerous ways.
- A consolidated view of corporate data (i.e., a single version of the truth) is possible.
- Better and more-timely information is possible. A data warehouse permits information processing to be relieved from costly operational systems onto low-cost servers; therefore, many more end-user information requests can be processed more quickly.
- Enhanced system performance can result. A data warehouse frees production processing because some operational system reporting requirements are moved to DSS.
- Data access is simplified.

Indirect benefits result from end users using these direct benefits. On the whole, these benefits enhance business knowledge, present competitive advantage, improve customer service and satisfaction, facilitate decision making, and help in reforming business processes, and therefore they are the strongest contributions to competitive advantage. (For a discussion of how to create a competitive advantage through data warehousing, see Parzinger and Frolick, 2001.) For a detailed discussion of how organizations can obtain exceptional levels of payoffs, see Watson et al. (2002). Given the potential benefits that a data warehouse can provide and the substantial investments in time and money that such a project requires, it is critical that an organization structure its data warehouse project to maximize the chances of success. In addition, the organization must, obviously, take costs into consideration. Kelly (2001) described a ROI approach that considers benefits in the categories of keepers (i.e., money saved by improving traditional decision support functions); gatherers (i.e., money saved due to automated collection and dissemination of information); and users (i.e., money saved or gained from decisions made using the data warehouse). Costs include those related to hardware, software, network bandwidth, internal development, internal support, training, and external consulting. The net present value (NPV) is calculated over the expected life of the data warehouse. Because the benefits are broken down approximately as 20 percent for keepers, 30 percent for gatherers, and 50 percent for users, Kelly indicated that users should be involved in the development process, a success factor typically mentioned as critical for systems that imply change in an organization.

Application Case 8.4 provides an example of a data warehouse that was developed and delivered intense competitive advantage for the Hokuriku (Japan) Coca-Cola Bottling Company. The system was so successful that plans are under way to expand it to encompass the more than 1 million Coca-Cola vending machines in Japan.

APPLICATION CASE 8.4

Things Go Better with Coke's Data Warehouse

In the face of competitive pressures and consumer demand, how does a successful bottling company ensure that its vending machines are profitable? The answer for Hokuriku Coca-Cola Bottling Company (HCCBC) is a data warehouse and analytical software implemented by Teradata Corp. HCCBC built the system in response to a data warehousing system developed by its rival, Mikuni. The data warehouse collects not only historical data but also near-real-time data from each vending machine (viewed as a store) that could be transmitted via wireless connection to headquarters. The initial phase of the project was deployed in 2001. The data warehouse approach provides detailed product information, such as time and date of each sale, when a product sells out, whether someone was short-changed, and whether the machine is malfunctioning. In each case, an alert is triggered, and the vending machine immediately reports it to the data center over a wireless transmission system. (Note that Coca-Cola in the United States has used modems to link vending machines to distributors for over a decade.)

In 2002, HCCBC conducted a pilot test and put all its Nagano vending machines on a wireless network to gather near-real-time point of sale (POS) data from each one. The results were astounding because they accurately forecasted demand and identified problems quickly. Total sales immediately increased 10 percent. In addition, due to the more accurate machine servicing, overtime and other costs decreased 46 percent. In addition, each salesperson was able to service up to 42 percent more vending machines.

The test was so successful that planning began to expand it to encompass the entire enterprise (60,000 machines), using an active data warehouse. Eventually, the data warehousing solution will ideally expand across corporate boundaries into the entire Coca-Cola Bottlers network so that the more than 1 million vending machines in Japan will be networked, leading to immense cost savings and higher revenue.

Sources: Adapted from K. D. Schwartz, "Decisions at the Touch of a Button," *Teradata Magazine,* **teradata.com/t/page/ 117774/index.html** (accessed June 2009); K. D. Schwartz, "Decisions at the Touch of a Button," *DSS Resources,* March 2004, pp. 28–31, **dssresources.com/cases/coca-colajapan/ index.html** (accessed April 2006); and Teradata Corp., "Coca-Cola Japan Puts the Fizz Back in Vending Machine Sales," **teradata.com/t/page/118866/index.html** (accessed June 2009).

Clearly defining the business objective, gathering project support from management end users, setting reasonable time frames and budgets, and managing expectations are critical to a successful data warehousing project. A data warehousing strategy is a blueprint for the successful introduction of the data warehouse. The strategy should describe where the company wants to go, why it wants to go there, and what it will do when it gets there. It needs to take into consideration the organization's vision, structure, and culture. See Matney (2003) for the steps that can help in developing a flexible and efficient support strategy. When the plan and support for a data warehouse are established, the organization needs to examine data warehouse vendors. (See Table 8.2 for a sample list of vendors; also see The Data Warehousing Institute [**twdi.com**] and *DM Review* [**dmreview.com**].) Many vendors provide software demos of their data warehousing and BI products.

Data Warehouse Vendors

McCloskey (2002) cited six guidelines that need to be considered when developing a vendor list: financial strength, ERP linkages, qualified consultants, market share, industry experience, and established partnerships. Data can be obtained from trade shows and corporate Web sites, as well as by submitting requests for specific product information.

TABLE 8.2 Sample List of Data Warehousing Vendors

Vendor	Product Offerings
Computer Associates (**cai.com**)	Comprehensive set of data warehouse (DW) tools and products
DataMirror (**datamirror.com**)	DW administration, management, and performance products
Data Advantage Group (**dataadvantagegroup.com**)	Metadata software
Dell (**dell.com**)	DW servers
Embarcadero Technologies (**embarcadero.com**)	DW administration, management, and performance products
Business Objects (**businessobjects.com**)	Data cleansing software
Harte-Hanks (**harte-hanks.com**)	Customer relationship management (CRM) products and services
HP (**hp.com**)	DW servers
Hummingbird Ltd. (**hummingbird.com**)	DW engines and exploration warehouses
Hyperion Solutions (**hyperion.com**)	Comprehensive set of DW tools, products, and applications
IBM (**ibm.com**)	DW tools, products, and applications
Informatica (**informatica.com**)	DW administration, management, and performance products
Microsoft (**microsoft.com**)	DW tools and products
Oracle (including People Soft and Siebel) (**oracle.com**)	DW, ERP, and CRM tools, products, and applications
SAS Institute (**sas.com**)	DW tools, products, and applications
Siemens (**siemens.com**)	DW servers
Sybase (**sybase.com**)	Comprehensive set of DW tools and applications
Teradata (**teradata.com**)	DW tools, products, and applications

Van den Hoven (1998) differentiated three types of data warehousing products. The first type handles functions such as locating, extracting, transforming, cleansing, transporting, and loading the data into the data warehouse. The second type is a data management tool—a database engine that stores and manages the data warehouse as well as the metadata. The third type is a data access tool that provides end users with access to analyze the data in the data warehouse. This may include query generators, visualization, EIS, OLAP, and data mining capabilities.

Data Warehouse Development Approaches

Many organizations need to create the data warehouses used for decision support. Two competing approaches are employed. The first approach is that of Bill Inmon, who is often called "the father of data warehousing." Inmon supports a top-down development approach that adapts traditional relational database tools to the development needs of an enterprise-wide data warehouse, also known as the EDW approach. The second approach is that of Ralph Kimball, who proposes a bottom-up approach that employs dimensional modeling, also known as the data mart approach.

Knowing how these two models are alike and how they differ helps us understand the basic data warehouse concepts (e.g., see Breslin, 2004). Table 8.3 compares the two approaches. We describe these approaches in detail next.

TABLE 8.3 Contrasts Between the Data Mart and EDW Development Approaches

Effort	Data Mart Approach	EDW Approach
Scope	One subject area	Several subject areas
Development time	Months	Years
Development cost	$10,000 to $100,000+	$1,000,000+
Development difficulty	Low to medium	High
Data prerequisite for sharing	Common (within business area)	Common (across enterprise)
Sources	Only some operational and external systems	Many operational and external systems
Size	Megabytes to several gigabytes	Gigabytes to petabytes
Time horizon	Near-current and historical data	Historical data
Data transformations	Low to medium	High
Update frequency	Hourly, daily, weekly	Weekly, monthly
Technology		
Hardware	Workstations and departmental servers	Enterprise servers and mainframe computers
Operating system	Windows and Linux	Unix, Z/OS, OS/390
Databases	Workgroup or standard database servers	Enterprise database servers
Usage		
Number of simultaneous users	10s	100s to 1,000s
User types	Business area analysts and managers	Enterprise analysts and senior executives
Business spotlight	Optimizing activities within the business area	Cross-functional optimization and decision making

Sources: Adapted from J. Van den Hoven, "Data Marts: Plan Big, Build Small," in *IS Management Handbook,* 8th ed., CRC Press, Boca Raton, FL, 2003; and T. Ariyachandra and H. Watson, "Which Data Warehouse Architecture Is Most Successful?" *Business Intelligence Journal,* Vol. 11, No. 1, First Quarter 2006, pp. 4–6.

THE INMON MODEL: THE EDW APPROACH Inmon's approach emphasizes top-down development, employing established database development methodologies and tools, such as entity-relationship diagrams (ERD), and an adjustment of the spiral development approach. The EDW approach does not preclude the creation of data marts. The EDW is the ideal in this approach because it provides a consistent and comprehensive view of the enterprise. Murtaza (1998) presented a framework for developing EDW.

THE KIMBALL MODEL: THE DATA MART APPROACH Kimball's data mart strategy is a "plan big, build small" approach. A data mart is a subject-oriented or department-oriented data warehouse. It is a scaled-down version of a data warehouse that focuses on the requests of a specific department, such as marketing or sales. This model applies dimensional data modeling, which starts with tables. Kimball advocated a development methodology that entails a bottom-up approach, which in the case of data warehouses means building one data mart at a time.

WHICH MODEL IS BEST? There is no one-size-fits-all strategy to data warehousing. An enterprise's data warehousing strategy can evolve from a simple data mart to a complex data warehouse in response to user demands, the enterprise's business requirements, and the enterprise's maturity in managing its data resources. For many enterprises, a data mart is frequently a convenient first step to acquiring experience in constructing and managing a data warehouse while presenting business users with the benefits of better access to their data; in addition, a data mart commonly indicates the business value of data warehousing. Ultimately, obtaining an EDW is ideal (see Application Case 8.5). However, the development of individual data marts can often provide many benefits along the way toward developing an EDW, especially if the organization is unable or unwilling to invest in a large-scale project. Data marts can also demonstrate feasibility and success in providing benefits. This could potentially lead to an investment in an EDW. Table 8.4 summarizes the most essential characteristic differences between the two models.

APPLICATION CASE 8.5
HP Consolidates Hundreds of Data Marts into a Single EDW

In December 2005, HP planned to consolidate its 762 data marts around the world into a single EDW. HP took this approach to gain a superior sense of its own business and to determine how best to serve its customers. Mark Hurd, HP's president and chief executive, stated that "there was a thirst for analytic data" inside the company that had unfortunately led to the creation of many data marts. Those data silos were very expensive to design and maintain, and they did not produce the enterprise-wide view of internal and customer information that HP wanted. In mid-2006, HP started to consolidate the data in the data marts into the new data warehouse. All the disparate data marts will ultimately be eliminated.

Sources: Adapted from C. Martins, "HP to Consolidate Data Marts into Single Warehouse," *Computerworld,* December 13, 2005; C. Martins, "HP to Consolidate Data Marts into Single Warehouse," *InfoWorld,* December 13, 2005; and C. Martins, "HP to Consolidate Data Marts into One Warehouse," December 14, 2005.

TABLE 8.4 Essential Differences Between Inmon's and Kimball's Approaches

Characteristic	Inmon	Kimball
Methodology and Architecture		
Overall approach	Top-down	Bottom-up
Architecture structure	Enterprise-wide (atomic) data warehouse "feeds" departmental databases	Data marts model a single business process, and enterprise consistency is achieved through a data bus and conformed dimensions
Complexity of the method	Quite complex	Fairly simple
Comparison with established development methodologies	Derived from the spiral methodology	Four-step process; a departure from relational database management system (RDBMS) methods
Discussion of physical design	Fairly thorough	Fairly light
Data Modeling		
Data orientation	Subject or data driven	Process oriented
Tools	Traditional (entity-relationship diagrams [ERD], data flow diagrams [DFD])	Dimensional modeling; a departure from relational modeling
End-user accessibility	Low	High
Philosophy		
Primary audience	IT professionals	End users
Place in the organization	Integral part of the corporate information factory	Transformer and retainer of operational data
Objective	Deliver a sound technical solution based on proven database methods and technologies	Deliver a solution that makes it easy for end users to directly query the data and still get reasonable response times

Sources: Adapted from M. Breslin, "Data Warehousing Battle of the Giants: Comparing the Basics of Kimball and Inmon Models," *Business Intelligence Journal,* Vol. 9, No. 1, Winter 2004, pp. 6–20; and T. Ariyachandra and H. Watson, "Which Data Warehouse Architecture Is Most Successful?" *Business Intelligence Journal,* Vol. 11, No. 1, First Quarter 2006.

Additional Data Warehouse Development Considerations

Some organizations want to completely outsource their data warehousing efforts. They simply do not want to deal with software and hardware acquisitions, and they do not want to manage their information systems. One alternative is to use hosted data warehouses. In this scenario, another firm—ideally, one that has a lot of experience and expertise—develops and maintains the data warehouse. However, there are security and privacy concerns with this approach. See Technology Insights 8.1 for some details.

Data Warehouse Structure: The Star Schema

A typical data warehouse structure is shown in Figure 8.1. Many variations on data warehouse architecture are possible; the most important one is the star schema. The data warehouse design is based on the concept of dimensional modeling. **Dimensional modeling** is a retrieval-based system that supports high-volume query access. The star schema is the means by which dimensional modeling is implemented. A star schema contains a central fact table surrounded by several **dimension tables** (Adamson, 2009). The fact table contains a large number of rows that correspond to observed facts. A fact table contains the attributes needed to perform decision analysis, descriptive attributes used for query reporting, and foreign keys to link to dimension tables. The decision analysis attributes consist of performance measures, operational metrics, aggregated measures, and all

TECHNOLOGY INSIGHTS 8.1   Hosted Data Warehouses

A hosted data warehouse has nearly the same, if not more, functionality as an onsite data warehouse, but it does not consume computer resources on client premises. A hosted data warehouse offers the benefits of BI minus the cost of computer upgrades, network upgrades, software licenses, in-house development, and in-house support and maintenance.

A hosted data warehouse offers the following benefits:

- Requires minimal investment in infrastructure
- Frees up capacity on in-house systems
- Frees up cash flow
- Makes powerful solutions affordable
- Enables powerful solutions that provide for growth
- Offers better quality equipment and software
- Provides faster connections
- Enables users to access data from remote locations
- Allows a company to focus on core business
- Meets storage needs for large volumes of data

Despite its benefits, a hosted data warehouse is not necessarily a good fit for every organization. Large companies with revenue upward of $500 million could lose money if they already have underused internal infrastructure and IT staff. Furthermore, companies that see the paradigm shift of outsourcing applications as loss of control of their data are not prone to use a business intelligence service provider (BISP). Finally, the most significant and common argument against implementing a hosted data warehouse is that it may be unwise to outsource sensitive applications for reasons of security and privacy.

Sources: Partly adapted from M. Thornton and M. Lampa, "Hosted Data Warehouse," *Journal of Data Warehousing,* Vol. 7, No. 2, 2002, pp. 27–34; and M. Thornton, "What About Security? The Most Common, but Unwarranted, Objection to Hosted Data Warehouses," *DM Review,* Vol. 12, No. 3, March 18, 2002, pp. 30–43.

the other metrics needed to analyze the organization's performance. In other words, the fact table primarily addresses what the data warehouse supports for decision analysis.

Surrounding the central fact tables (and linked via foreign keys) are dimension tables. The dimension tables contain classification and aggregation information about the central fact rows. Dimension tables contain attributes that describe the data contained within the fact table; they address how data will be analyzed. Dimension tables have a one-to-many relationship with rows in the central fact table. Some examples of dimensions that would support a product fact table are location, time, and size. The star schema design provides extremely fast query-response time, simplicity, and ease of maintenance for read-only database structures. According to Raden (2003), setting up a star schema for real-time updating could be a straightforward approach, as long as a few rules are followed. We show an example star schema in Figure 8.9.

The **grain** (also known as granularity) of a data warehouse defines the highest level of detail that is supported. The grain indicates whether the data warehouse is highly summarized or also includes detailed transaction data. If the grain is defined too high, then the warehouse may not support detail requests to **drill down** into the data. Drill-down analysis is the process of probing beyond a summarized value to investigate each of the detail transactions that comprise the summary. A low level of granularity will result in more data being stored in the warehouse. Larger amounts of detail may affect the performance of queries by making the response times longer. Therefore, during the scoping of a data warehouse project, it is important to identify the level of granularity that will be needed. See Tennant (2002) for a discussion of granularity issues in metadata.

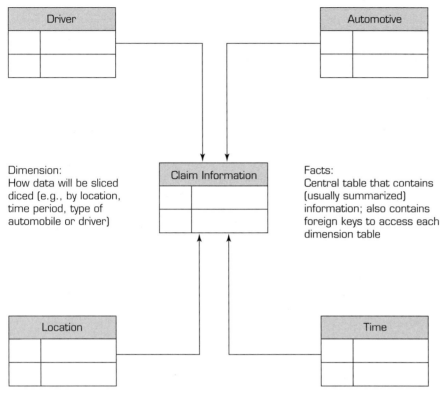

FIGURE 8.9   Star Schema

Data Warehousing Implementation Issues

Implementing a data warehouse is generally a massive effort that must be planned and executed according to established methods. However, the project lifecycle has many facets, and no single person can be an expert in each area. Here we discuss specific ideas and issues as they relate to data warehousing. Inmon (2006) provided a set of actions that a data warehouse systems programmer may use to tune a data warehouse.

Reeves (2009) and Solomon (2005) provided some guidelines regarding the critical questions that must be asked, some risks that should be weighed and some processes that can be followed to help ensure a successful data warehouse implementation. He compiled a list of 11 major tasks that could be performed in parallel:

1. Establishment of service-level agreements and data-refresh requirements
2. Identification of data sources and their governance policies
3. Data quality planning
4. Data model design
5. ETL tool selection
6. Relational database software and platform selection
7. Data transport
8. Data conversion
9. Reconciliation process
10. Purge and archive planning
11. End-user support

Following these guidelines should increase an organization's chances for success. Given the size and scope of an enterprise-level data warehouse initiative, failure to anticipate these issues greatly increases the risks of failure.

Hwang and Xu (2005) conducted a major survey of data warehousing success issues. The results established that data warehousing success is a multifaceted construct, and Hwang and Xu proposed that a data warehouse be constructed while keeping in mind the goal of improving user productivity. Extremely significant benefits of doing so include prompt information retrieval and enhanced quality information. The survey results also indicated that success hinges on factors of different dimensions.

People want to know how successful their BI and data warehousing initiatives are in comparison to those of other companies. Ariyachandra and Watson (2006a) proposed some benchmarks for BI and data warehousing success. Watson et al. (1999) researched data warehouse failures. Their results showed that people define a "failure" in different ways, and this was confirmed by Ariyachandra and Watson (2006a). The Data Warehousing Institute (**tdwi.org**) has developed a data warehousing maturity model that an enterprise can apply in order to benchmark its evolution. The model offers a fast means to gauge where the organization's data warehousing initiative is now and where it needs to go next. The maturity model consists of six stages: prenatal, infant, child, teenager, adult, and sage. Business value rises as the data warehouse progresses through each succeeding stage. The stages are identified by a number of characteristics, including scope, analytic structure, executive perceptions, types of analytics, stewardship, funding, technology platform, change management, and administration. See Eckerson et al. (2009) and Eckerson (2003) for more details.

Saunders (2009) provided an easy-to-understand cooking analogy to developing data warehouses. Weir (2002) specifically described some of the best practices for implementing a data warehouse, which include the following guidelines:

- The project must fit with corporate strategy and business objectives.
- There must be complete buy-in to the project by executives, managers, and users.
- It is important to manage user expectations about the completed project.
- The data warehouse must be built incrementally.
- Adaptability must be built in.
- The project must be managed by both IT and business professionals.
- A business–supplier relationship must be developed.
- Only load data that have been cleansed and are of a quality understood by the organization.
- Do not overlook training requirements.
- Be politically aware.

Data warehouse projects have many risks. Most of them are also found in other IT projects, but data warehousing risks are more serious because data warehouses are expensive, large-scale projects. Each risk should be assessed at the inception of the project. Adelman and Moss (2001) described some of these risks, including the following:

- No mission or objective
- Quality of source data unknown
- Skills not in place
- Inadequate budget
- Lack of supporting software
- Source data not understood
- Weak sponsor
- Users not computer literate
- Political problems or turf wars

- Unrealistic user expectations
- Architectural and design risks
- Scope creep and changing requirements
- Vendors out of control
- Multiple platforms
- Key people leaving the project
- Loss of the sponsor
- Too much new technology
- Having to fix an operational system
- Geographically distributed environment
- Team geography and language culture

Practitioners have unearthed a wealth of mistakes that have been made in the development of data warehouses. Watson et al. (1999) discussed how such mistakes could lead to data warehouse failures (also see Barquin et al., 1997). Turban et al. (2006) listed the following reasons for failure: cultural issues being ignored, inappropriate architecture, unclear business objectives, missing information, unrealistic expectations, low levels of data summarization, and low data quality.

When developing a successful data warehouse, it is important to carefully consider the following issues:

- ***Starting with the wrong sponsorship chain.*** You need an executive sponsor who has influence over the necessary resources to support and invest in the data warehouse. You also need an executive project driver, someone who has earned the respect of other executives, has a healthy skepticism about technology, and is decisive but flexible. You also need an IS/IT manager to head up the project.
- ***Setting expectations that you cannot meet.*** You do not want to frustrate executives at the moment of truth. Every data warehousing project has two phases: Phase 1 is the selling phase, in which you internally market the project by selling the benefits to those who have access to needed resources. Phase 2 is the struggle to meet the expectations described in Phase 1. For a mere $1 million to $7 million, hopefully, you can deliver.
- ***Engaging in politically naive behavior.*** Do not simply state that a data warehouse will help managers make better decisions. This may imply that you feel they have been making bad decisions until now. Sell the idea that they will be able to get the information they need to help in decision making.
- ***Loading the warehouse with information just because it is available.*** Do not let the data warehouse become a data landfill. This would unnecessarily slow down the use of the system. There is a trend toward real-time computing and analysis. Data warehouses must be shut down to load data in a timely way.
- ***Believing that data warehousing database design is the same as transactional database design.*** In general, it is not. The goal of data warehousing is to access aggregates rather than a single or a few records, as in transaction-processing systems. Content is also different, as is evident in how data are organized. DBMS tend to be nonredundant, normalized, and relational, whereas data warehouses are redundant, not normalized, and multidimensional.
- ***Choosing a data warehouse manager who is technology oriented rather than user oriented.*** One key to data warehouse success is to understand that the users must get what they need, not advanced technology for technology's sake.
- ***Focusing on traditional internal record-oriented data and ignoring the value of external data and of text, images, and, perhaps, sound and***

video. Data come in many formats and must be made accessible to the right people at the right time and in the right format. They must be cataloged properly.

- *Delivering data with overlapping and confusing definitions.* Data cleansing is a critical aspect of data warehousing. It includes reconciling conflicting data definitions and formats organization-wide. Politically, this may be difficult because it involves change, typically at the executive level.
- *Believing promises of performance, capacity, and scalability.* Data warehouses generally require more capacity and speed than is originally budgeted for. Plan ahead to scale up.
- *Believing that your problems are over when the data warehouse is up and running.* DSS/BI projects tend to evolve continually. Each deployment is an iteration of the prototyping process. There will always be a need to add more and different data sets to the data warehouse, as well as additional analytic tools for existing and additional groups of decision makers. High energy and annual budgets must be planned for because success breeds success. Data warehousing is a continuous process.
- *Focusing on ad hoc data mining and periodic reporting instead of alerts.* The natural progression of information in a data warehouse is: (1) Extract the data from legacy systems, cleanse them, and feed them to the warehouse; (2) support ad hoc reporting until you learn what people want; and (3) convert the ad hoc reports into regularly scheduled reports.

  This process of learning what people want in order to provide it seems natural, but it is not optimal or even practical. Managers are busy and need time to read reports. Alert systems are better than periodic reporting systems and can make a data warehouse mission critical. Alert systems monitor the data flowing into the warehouse and inform all key people who have a need to know as soon as a critical event occurs.

Sammon and Finnegan (2000) revealed the outcome of a study of four mature users of data warehousing technology. Their practices were captured in an outline of 10 organizational requisites for applying data warehousing. Organizations can use this representation to internally evaluate the chances of the success of a data warehousing project and to recognize the parts that need attention prior to beginning implementation. A summary of their prerequisites model is as follows:

- A business-driven data warehousing initiative
- Executive sponsorship and commitment
- Funding commitment based on realistically managed expectations
- A project team
- Attention to source data quality
- A flexible enterprise data model
- Data stewardship
- A long-term plan for automated data extraction methods/tools
- Knowledge of data warehouse compatibility with existing systems
- Hardware/software proof of concept

Wixom and Watson (2001) defined a research model for data warehouse success that identified seven important implementation factors that can be categorized into three criteria (i.e., organizational issues, project issues, and technical issues):

1. Management support
2. Champion
3. Resources
4. User participation

5. Team skills
6. Source systems
7. Development technology

In many organizations, a data warehouse will be successful only if there is strong senior management support for its development and if there is a project champion. Although this would likely be true for any IT project, it is especially important for a data warehouse. The successful implementation of a data warehouse results in the establishment of an architectural framework that may allow for decision analysis throughout an organization and in some cases also provides comprehensive SCM by granting access to an organization's customers and suppliers. The implementation of Web-based data warehouses (called *Webhousing*) has facilitated ease of access to vast amounts of data, but it is difficult to determine the hard benefits associated with a data warehouse. Hard benefits are defined as benefits to an organization that can be expressed in monetary terms. Many organizations have limited IT resources and must prioritize projects. Management support and a strong project champion can help ensure that a data warehouse project will receive the resources necessary for successful implementation. Data warehouse resources can be a significant cost, in some cases requiring high-end processors and large increases in direct-access storage devices (DASD). Web-based data warehouses may also have special security requirements to ensure that only authorized users have access to the data.

User participation in the development of data and access modeling is a critical success factor in data warehouse development. During data modeling, expertise is required to determine what data are needed, define business rules associated with the data, and decide what aggregations and other calculations may be necessary. Access modeling is needed to determine how data are to be retrieved from a data warehouse, and it assists in the physical definition of the warehouse by helping to define which data require indexing. It may also indicate whether dependent data marts are needed to facilitate information retrieval. The team skills needed to develop and implement a data warehouse include in-depth knowledge of the database technology and development tools used. Source systems and development technology, as mentioned previously, reference the many inputs and the processes used to load and maintain a data warehouse.

Application Case 8.6 presents an excellent example for a large-scale implementation of an integrated data warehouse in the insurance industry.

APPLICATION CASE 8.6

A Large Insurance Company Integrates Its Enterprise Data with AXIS

A large U.S. insurance company developed an integrated data management and reporting environment to provide a unified view of the enterprise performance and risk, and to take a new strategic role in planning and management activities of the large number of business units.

XYZ Insurance company (the actual name is not revealed) and its affiliated companies constitute one of the world's largest financial services organizations. Incorporated a century ago, XYZ Insurance has grown and diversified to become a leading provider of domestic property and casualty insurance, life

insurance, retirement savings, asset management, and strategic investment services. Today the firm is an industry powerhouse with over $150 billion in statutory assets, over $15 billion in annual revenue, 20,000+ employees, and more than 100 companies operating under the XYZ Insurance umbrella.

Problem

For most of its years in business, the growing family of XYZ Insurance companies enjoyed considerable independence and autonomy. Over time, as the enterprise got bigger, such a decentralized management style produced an equally diverse reporting and decision-making environment. With no common view of enterprise performance, corporate reporting was shortsighted, fragmented, slow, and often inaccurate. The burden of acquiring, consolidating, cleaning, and validating basic financial information crippled the organization's ability to support management with meaningful analysis and insight.

In order to address the pressing needs for integration, in January 2004 XYZ Insurance launched a needs analysis initiative, which resulted in a shared vision for having a unified data management system. The integrated system, called AXIS, was envisioned to be capable of supporting enterprise-level planning, capital management, risk assessment, and managerial decision making with state-of-the-art reporting and analytical services that were timely, accurate, and efficient.

Solution

XYZ Insurance decided to develop AXIS using a best-of-breed approach. As opposed to buying all of the components from a single vendor, it chose the best fit for each module as determined by the needs analysis. The following tools/vendors were selected:

- The data warehouse: The AXIS environment has a hub-and-spoke architecture with a Teradata data warehouse at the center.
- Extraction, transportation, integration, and metadata management: All data movement from originating systems into the AXIS environment (and between systems within AXIS) is handled by Informatica PowerCenter.
- Reporting and analysis: Virtually all reporting and analytical functionality in the AXIS

environment is provided through a suite of Hyperion tools that includes Essbase, Planning, Reporter, Analyzer, and Intelligence.
- Master data management: Reference data hierarchies and dimensions and business rules for interface translation and transformation are developed and maintained using master data management software from Kalido.

Results

Implementing the AXIS environment was a monumental undertaking, even for an organization with XYZ Insurance's resources. More than 200 operational source system interfaces had to be created. At its peak, the development team employed 280 people (60% from internal IT and the business department and 40% external contractors) who dedicated 600,000 man-hours to the project. The system with full functionality was released in April 2006.

By standardizing the information assets along with the technology base and supporting processes, XYZ Insurance was able to consolidate much of the labor-intensive transactional and reporting activities. That freed up people and resources for more strategic, high-value contributions to the business. Another benefit is that business units across the organization now have consistent and accurate operating information on which to base their decisions. Probably the most important benefit of the AXIS environment is its ability to turn XYZ Insurance into an agile enterprise. Because they have access to corporate level data in a timely manner, the business units can react to changing conditions (address problems and take advantage of opportunities) accurately and rapidly.

Source: Teradata, "A Large US-based Insurance Company Masters Its Finance Data," Teradata Industry Solutions, **teradata.com/t/WorkArea/DownloadAsset.aspx?id=4858** (accessed July 2009).

Massive Data Warehouses and Scalability

In addition to flexibility, a data warehouse needs to support scalability. The main issues pertaining to scalability are the amount of data in the warehouse, how quickly the warehouse is expected to grow, the number of concurrent users, and the complexity of user queries. A data warehouse must scale both horizontally and vertically. The warehouse will grow as a function of data growth and the need to expand the warehouse to support new business functionality. Data growth may be a result of the addition of current cycle data (e.g., this month's results) and/or historical data.

Hicks (2001) described huge databases and data warehouses. Wal-Mart is continually increasing the size of its massive data warehouse. Wal-Mart is believed to use a warehouse with hundreds of terabytes of data to study sales trends and track inventory and other tasks. IBM recently publicized its 50-terabyte warehouse benchmark (IBM, 2009). The U.S. Department of Defense is using a 5-petabyte data warehouse and repository to hold medical records for 9 million military personnel. Because of the storage required to archive its news footage, CNN also has a petabyte-sized data warehouse.

Given that the size of data warehouses is expanding at an exponential rate, scalability is an important issue. Good scalability means that queries and other data-access functions will grow (ideally) linearly with the size of the warehouse. See Rosenberg (2006) for approaches to improve query performance. In practice, specialized methods have been developed to create scalable data warehouses. Scalability is difficult when managing hundreds of terabytes or more. Terabytes of data have considerable inertia, occupy a lot of physical space, and require powerful computers. Some firms use parallel processing, and others use clever indexing and search schemes to manage their data. Some spread their data across different physical data stores. As more data warehouses approach the petabyte size, better and better solutions to scalability continue to be developed.

Hall (2002) also addressed scalability issues. AT&T is an industry leader in deploying and using massive data warehouses. With its 26-terabyte data warehouse, AT&T can detect fraudulent use of calling cards and investigate calls related to kidnappings and other crimes. It can also compute millions of call-in votes from TV viewers selecting the next American Idol.

For a sample of successful data warehousing implementations, see Edwards (2003). Jukic and Lang (2004) examined the trends and specific issues related to the use of offshore resources in the development and support of data warehousing and BI applications. Davison (2003) indicated that IT-related offshore outsourcing had been growing at 20 to 25 percent per year. When considering offshoring data warehousing projects, careful consideration must be given to culture and security (for details, see Jukic and Lang, 2004).

Section 8.6 Review Questions

1. List the benefits of data warehouses.
2. List several criteria for selecting a data warehouse vendor, and describe why they are important.
3. Does a bottom-up data warehouse development approach use an enterprise data model?
4. Describe the major similarities and differences between the Inmon and Kimball data warehouse development approaches.
5. List the different types of data warehouse architectures.

8.7 REAL-TIME DATA WAREHOUSING

Data warehousing and BI tools traditionally focus on assisting managers in making strategic and tactical decisions. Increased data volumes and accelerating update speeds are fundamentally changing the role of the data warehouse in modern business. For many businesses, making fast and consistent decisions across the enterprise requires more than a traditional data warehouse or data mart. Traditional data warehouses are not business critical. Data are commonly updated on a weekly basis, and this does not allow for responding to transactions in near-real-time.

More data, coming in faster and requiring immediate conversion into decisions, means that organizations are confronting the need for real-time data warehousing. This is because decision support has become operational, integrated BI requires closed-loop analytics, and yesterday's ODS will not support existing requirements.

In 2003, with the advent of real-time data warehousing, there was a shift toward using these technologies for operational decisions. **Real-time data warehousing (RDW)**, also known as **active data warehousing (ADW)**, is the process of loading and providing data via the data warehouse as they become available. It evolved from the

EDW concept. The active traits of an RDW/ADW supplement and expand traditional data warehouse functions into the realm of tactical decision making. People throughout the organization who interact directly with customers and suppliers will be empowered with information-based decision making at their fingertips. Even further leverage results when an ADW provides information directly to customers and suppliers. The reach and impact of information access for decision making can positively affect almost all aspects of customer service, SCM, logistics, and beyond. E-business has become a major catalyst in the demand for active data warehousing (see Armstrong, 2000). For example, online retailer Overstock.com, Inc. (**overstock.com**), connected data users to a real-time data warehouse. At Egg plc, the world's largest purely online bank, a customer data warehouse is refreshed in near-real-time. See Application Case 8.7.

APPLICATION CASE 8.7
Egg Plc Fries the Competition in Near-Real-Time

Egg plc (**egg.com**) is the world's largest online bank. It provides banking, insurance, investments, and mortgages to more than 3.6 million customers through its Internet site. In 1998, Egg selected Sun Microsystems to create a reliable, scalable, secure infrastructure to support its more than 2.5 million daily transactions. In 2001, the system was upgraded to eliminate latency problems. This new customer data warehouse (CDW) used Sun, Oracle, and SAS software products. The initial data warehouse had about 10 terabytes of data and used a 16-CPU server. The system provides near-real-time data access. It provides data warehouse and data mining services to internal users, and it provides a requisite set of customer data to the customers themselves. Hundreds of sales and marketing campaigns are constructed using near-real-time data (within several minutes). And better, the system enables faster decision making about specific customers and customer classes.

Sources: Compiled from "Egg's Customer Data Warehouse Hits the Mark," *DM Review,* Vol. 15, No. 10, October 2005, pp. 24–28; Sun Microsystems, "Egg Banks on Sun to Hit the Mark with Customers," September 19, 2005, **sun.com/smi/Press/sunflash/2005-09/sunflash.20050919.1.xml** (accessed April 2006); and ZD Net UK, "Sun Case Study: Egg's Customer Data Warehouse," **whitepapers.zdnet.co.uk/0,39025945,60159401p-39000449q,00.htm** (accessed June 2009).

As business needs evolve, so do the requirements of the data warehouse. At this basic level, a data warehouse simply reports what happened. At the next level, some analysis occurs. As the system evolves, it provides prediction capabilities, which lead to the next level of operationalization. At its highest evolution, the ADW is capable of making events happen (e.g., activities such as creating sales and marketing campaigns or identifying and exploiting opportunities). See Figure 8.10 for a graphic description of this evolutionary process. A recent survey on managing evolution of data warehouses can be found in Wrembel (2009).

Teradata Corp. provides the baseline requirements to support an EDW. It also provides the new traits of active data warehousing required to deliver data freshness, performance, and availability and to enable enterprise decision management (see Figure 8.11 for an example).

An ADW offers an integrated information repository to drive strategic and tactical decision support within an organization. With real-time data warehousing, instead of extracting operational data from an OLTP system in nightly batches into an ODS, data are assembled from OLTP systems as and when events happen and are moved at once into the data warehouse. This permits the instant updating of the data warehouse and the elimination of an ODS. At this point, tactical and strategic queries can be made against the RDW to use immediate as well as historical data.

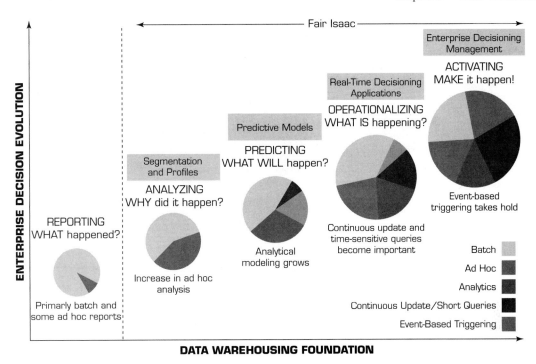

FIGURE 8.10 Enterprise Decision Evolution *Source:* Courtesy of Teradata Corporation. Used with permission.

According to Basu (2003), the most distinctive difference between a traditional data warehouse and an RDW is the shift in the data acquisition paradigm. Some of the business cases and enterprise requirements that led to the need for data in real time include the following:

- A business often cannot afford to wait a whole day for its operational data to load into the data warehouse for analysis.
- Until now, data warehouses have captured snapshots of an organization's fixed states instead of incremental real-time data showing every state change and almost analogous patterns over time.
- With a traditional hub-and-spoke architecture, keeping the metadata in sync is difficult. It is also costly to develop, maintain, and secure many systems as opposed to one huge data warehouse so that data are centralized for BI/BA tools.
- In cases of huge nightly batch loads, the necessary ETL setup and processing power for large nightly data warehouse loading might be very high, and the processes might take too long. An EAI with real-time data collection can reduce or eliminate the nightly batch processes.

Despite the benefits of an RDW, developing one can create its own set of issues. These problems relate to architecture, data modeling, physical database design, storage and scalability, and maintainability. In addition, depending on exactly when data are accessed, even down to the microsecond, different versions of the truth may be extracted and created, which can confuse team members. For details, refer to Basu (2003) and Terr (2004).

Real-time solutions present a remarkable set of challenges to BI activities. Although it is not ideal for all solutions, real-time data warehousing may be successful if the organization develops a sound methodology to handle project risks, incorporate proper planning, and focus on quality assurance activities. Understanding the common challenges and applying best practices can reduce the extent of the

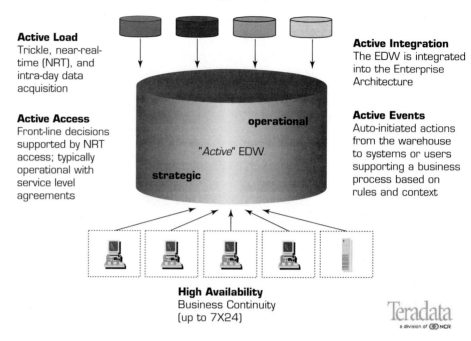

"*Active*" is Enterprise Data Warehousing plus any of these active elements:

Active Load
Trickle, near-real-time (NRT), and intra-day data acquisition

Active Access
Front-line decisions supported by NRT access; typically operational with service level agreements

Active Integration
The EDW is integrated into the Enterprise Architecture

Active Events
Auto-initiated actions from the warehouse to systems or users supporting a business process based on rules and context

operational

"*Active*" EDW

strategic

High Availability
Business Continuity
(up to 7X24)

Teradata
a division of NCR

FIGURE 8.11 The Teradata Active EDW *Source:* Courtesy of Teradata Corporation.

problems that are often a part of implementing complex data warehousing systems that incorporate BI/BA methods. Details and real implementations are discussed by Burdett and Singh (2004) and Wilk (2003). Also see Akbay (2006) and Ericson (2006).

See Technology Insights 8.2 for some details on how the real-time concept evolved. The flight management dashboard application at Continental Airlines (see the end of chapter application case) illustrates the power of real-time BI in accessing a data warehouse for use in face-to-face customer interaction situations. The operations staff uses the real-time system to identify issues in the Continental flight network. As another example, UPS invested $600 million so it could use real-time data and processes. The investment was expected to cut 100 million delivery miles and save 14 million gallons of fuel annually by managing its real-time package-flow technologies (see Malykhina, 2003). Table 8.5 compares traditional and active data warehousing environments.

Real-time data warehousing, near-real-time data warehousing, zero-latency warehousing, and *active data warehousing* are different names used in practice to describe the same concept. Gonzales (2005) presented different definitions for ADW. According to Gonzales, ADW is only one option that provides blended tactical and strategic data on demand. The architecture to build an ADW is very similar to the corporate information factory architecture developed by Bill Inmon. The only difference between a corporate information factory and an ADW is the implementation of both data stores in a single environment. However, an SOA based on XML and Web services provides another option for blending tactical and strategic data on demand.

One critical issue in real-time data warehousing is that not all data should be updated continuously. This may certainly cause problems when reports are generated in real time, because one person's results may not match another person's. For example, a company using Business Objects Web Intelligence noticed a significant problem with real-time

TECHNOLOGY INSIGHTS 8.2   The Real-Time Realities of Active Data Warehousing

By 2003, the role of data warehousing in practice was growing rapidly. Real-time systems, though a novelty, were the latest buzz, along with the major complications of providing data and information instantaneously to those who need them. Many experts, including Peter Coffee, *eWeek*'s technology editor, believe that real-time systems must feed a real-time decision-making process. Stephen Brobst, CTO of the Teradata division of NCR, indicated that active data warehousing is a process of evolution in how an enterprise uses data. *Active* means that the data warehouse is also used as an operational and tactical tool. Brobst provided a five-stage model that fits Coffee's experience (2003) of how organizations "grow" in their data utilization (see Brobst et al., 2005). These stages (and the questions they purport to answer) are reporting (What happened?), analysis (Why did it happen?), prediction (What will happen?), operationalizing (What is happening?), and active warehousing (What do I want to happen?). The last stage, active warehousing, is where the greatest benefits may be obtained. Many organizations are enhancing centralized data warehouses to serve both operational and strategic decision making.

Sources: Adapted from P. Coffee, "'Active' Warehousing," *eWeek*, Vol. 20, No. 25, June 23, 2003, p. 36; and Teradata Corp., "Active Data Warehousing," **teradata.com/t/page/87127/index.html** (accessed April 2006).

---

intelligence. Real-time reports produced at slightly different times differ (see Peterson, 2003). Also, it may not be necessary to update certain data continuously (e.g., course grades that are 3 or more years old).

Real-time requirements change the way we view the design of databases, data warehouses, OLAP, and data mining tools, because they are literally updated concurrently while queries are active. But the substantial business value in doing so has been demonstrated, so it is crucial that organizations adopt these methods in their business processes. Careful planning is critical in such implementations.

TABLE 8.5 Comparison of Traditional and Active Data Warehousing Environments

Traditional Data Warehouse Environment	Active Data Warehouse Environment
Strategic decisions only	Strategic and tactical decisions
Results sometimes hard to measure	Results measured with operations
Daily, weekly, monthly data currency acceptable; summaries often appropriate	Only comprehensive detailed data available within minutes is acceptable
Moderate user concurrency	High number (1,000 or more) of users accessing and querying the system simultaneously
Highly restrictive reporting used to confirm or check existing processes and patterns; often uses predeveloped summary tables or data marts	Flexible ad hoc reporting, as well as machine-assisted modeling (e.g., data mining) to discover new hypotheses and relationships
Power users, knowledge workers, internal users	Operational staffs, call centers, external users

Sources: Adapted from P. Coffee, "'Active' Warehousing," *eWeek*, Vol. 20, No. 25, June 23, 2003, p. 36; and Teradata Corp., "Active Data Warehousing," **teradata.com/t/page/87127/index.html** (accessed April 2006).

Section 8.7 Review Questions

1. What is an RDW?
2. List the benefits of an RDW.
3. What are the major differences between a traditional data warehouse and an RDW?
4. List some of the drivers for RDW.

8.8 DATA WAREHOUSE ADMINISTRATION AND SECURITY ISSUES

Data warehouses provide a distinct competitive edge to enterprises that effectively create and use them. Due to its huge size and its intrinsic nature, a data warehouse requires especially strong monitoring in order to sustain satisfactory efficiency and productivity. The successful administration and management of a data warehouse entails skills and proficiency that go past what is required of a traditional database administrator (DBA). A **data warehouse administrator (DWA)** should be familiar with high-performance software, hardware, and networking technologies. He or she should also possess solid business insight. Because data warehouses feed BI systems and DSS that help managers with their decision-making activities, the DWA should be familiar with the decision-making processes so as to suitably design and maintain the data warehouse structure. It is particularly significant for a DWA to keep the existing requirements and capabilities of the data warehouse stable while simultaneously providing flexibility for rapid improvements. Finally, a DWA must possess excellent communications skills. See Benander et al. (2000) for a description of the key differences between a DBA and a DWA.

Security and privacy of information are main and significant concerns for a data warehouse professional. The U.S. government has passed regulations (e.g., the Gramm-Leach-Bliley privacy and safeguards rules, the Health Insurance Portability and Accountability Act of 1996 [HIPAA]) instituting obligatory requirements in the management of customer information. Hence, companies must create security procedures that are effective yet flexible to conform to numerous privacy regulations. According to Elson and LeClerc (2005), effective security in a data warehouse should focus on four main areas:

1. Establishing effective corporate and security policies and procedures. An effective security policy should start at the top, with executive management, and should be communicated to all individuals within the organization.
2. Implementing logical security procedures and techniques to restrict access. This includes user authentication, access controls, and encryption technology.
3. Limiting physical access to the data center environment.
4. Establishing an effective internal control review process with an emphasis on security and privacy.

See Technology Insights 8.3 for a description of Ambeo's important software tool that monitors security and privacy of data warehouses. Finally, keep in mind that accessing a data warehouse via a mobile device should always be performed cautiously. In this instance, data should only be accessed as read-only.

In the near term, data warehousing developments will be determined by noticeable factors (e.g., data volumes, increased intolerance for latency, the diversity and complexity of data types) and less noticeable factors (e.g., unmet end-user requirements for dashboards, balanced scorecards, master data management, information quality). Given these drivers, Moseley (2009) and Agosta (2006) suggested that data warehousing trends will lean toward simplicity, value, and performance.

TECHNOLOGY INSIGHTS 8.3   Ambeo Delivers Proven Data Access Auditing Solution

Since 1997, Ambeo (**ambeo.com**; now Embarcadero Technologies, Inc.) has deployed technology that provides performance management, data usage tracking, data privacy auditing, and monitoring to *Fortune* 1000 companies. These firms have some of the largest database environments in existence. Ambeo data access auditing solutions play a major role in an enterprise information security infrastructure.

The Ambeo technology is a relatively easy solution that records everything that happens in the databases, with low or zero overhead. In addition, it provides data access auditing that identifies exactly who is looking at data, when they are looking, and what they are doing with the data. This real-time monitoring helps quickly and effectively identify security breaches.

Sources: Adapted from "Ambeo Delivers Proven Data Access Auditing Solution," *Database Trends and Applications,* Vol. 19, No. 7, July 2005; and Ambeo, "Keeping Data Private (and Knowing It): Moving Beyond Conventional Safeguards to Ensure Data Privacy," **am-beo.com/why_ambeo_white_papers.html** (accessed May 2009).

Section 8.8 Review Questions

1. What steps can an organization take to ensure the security and confidentiality of customer data in its data warehouse?
2. What skills should a DWA possess? Why?

8.9 RESOURCES, LINKS, AND THE TERADATA UNIVERSITY NETWORK CONNECTION

The use of this chapter and most other chapters in this book can be enhanced by the tools described in the following sections.

Resources and Links

We recommend looking at the following resources and links for further reading and explanations:

- The Data Warehouse Institute (**tdwi.com**)
- *DM Review* (**dmreview.com**)
- DSS Resources (**dssresources.com**)

Cases

All major MSS vendors (e.g., MicroStrategy, Microsoft, Oracle, IBM, Hyperion, Cognos, Exsys, Fair Isaac, SAP, Information Builders) provide interesting customer success stories. Academic-oriented cases are available at the Harvard Business School Case Collection (**harvardbusinessonline.hbsp.harvard.edu**), Business Performance Improvement Resource (**bpir.com**), Idea Group Publishing (**idea-group.com**), Ivy League Publishing (**ivylp.com**), ICFAI Center for Management Research (**icmr.icfai.org/casestudies/icmr_case_studies.htm**), KnowledgeStorm (**knowledgestorm.com**), and other sites. For additional case resources, see Teradata University Network (**teradatauniversitynetwork.com**). For data warehousing cases, we specifically recommend the following from the Teradata University Network (**teradatauniversitynetwork.com**): "Continental Airlines Flies High with Real-Time Business Intelligence," "Data Warehouse Governance at Blue

Cross and Blue Shield of North Carolina," "3M Moves to a Customer Focus Using a Global Data Warehouse," "Data Warehousing Supports Corporate Strategy at First American Corporation," "Harrah's High Payoff from Customer Information," and "Whirlpool." We also recommend the Data Warehousing Failures Assignment, which consists of eight short cases on data warehousing failures.

Vendors, Products, and Demos

A comprehensive list of vendors, products, and demos is available at *DM Review* (**dmreview.com**). Vendors are listed in Table 8.2. Also see **technologyevaluation.com**.

Periodicals

We recommend the following periodicals:

- *Baseline* (**baselinemag.com**)
- *Business Intelligence Journal* (**tdwi.org**)
- *CIO* (**cio.com**)
- *CIO Insight* (**cioinsight.com**)
- *Computerworld* (**computerworld.com**)
- *Decision Support Systems* (**elsevier.com**)
- *DM Review* (**dmreview.com**)
- *eWeek* (**eweek.com**)
- *InfoWeek* (**infoweek.com**)
- *InfoWorld* (**infoworld.com**)
- *InternetWeek* (**internetweek.com**)
- *Management Information Systems Quarterly* (*MIS Quarterly*; **misq.org**)
- *Technology Evaluation* (**technologyevaluation.com**)
- *Teradata Magazine* (**teradata.com**)

Additional References

For additional information on data warehousing, see the following.

- C. Imhoff, N. Galemmo, and J. G. Geiger. (2003). *Mastering Data Warehouse Design: Relational and Dimensional Techniques.* New York: Wiley.
- D. Marco and M. Jennings. (2004). *Universal Meta Data Models.* New York: Wiley.
- J. Wang. (2005). *Encyclopedia of Data Warehousing and Mining.* Hershey, PA: Idea Group Publishing.

For more on databases, the structure on which data warehouses are developed, see the following:

- R. T. Watson. (2006). *Data Management,* 5th ed. New York: Wiley.

The Teradata University Network (TUN) Connection

TUN (**teradatauniversitynetwork.com**) provides a wealth of information and cases on data warehousing. One of the best is the Continental Airlines case, which we require you to solve in a later exercise. Other recommended cases are mentioned earlier in this chapter. At TUN, if you click the Courses tab and select Data Warehousing, you will see links to many relevant articles, assignments, book chapters, course Web sites, PowerPoint presentations, projects, research reports, syllabi, and Web seminars. You will also find links to active data warehousing software demonstrations. Finally, you will see links to Teradata (**teradata.com**), where you can find additional information, including excellent data warehousing success stories, white papers, Web-based courses, and the online version of *Teradata Magazine*.

Chapter Highlights

- A data warehouse is a specially constructed data repository where data are organized so that they can be easily accessed by end users for several applications.
- Data marts contain data on one topic (e.g., marketing). A data mart can be a replication of a subset of data in the data warehouse. Data marts are a less expensive solution that can be replaced by or can supplement a data warehouse. Data marts can be independent of or dependent on a data warehouse.
- An ODS is a type of customer-information-file database that is often used as a staging area for a data warehouse.
- Data integration comprises three major processes: data access, data federation, and change capture. When

these three processes are correctly implemented, data can be accessed and made accessible to an array of ETL and analysis tools and data warehousing environments.
- ETL technologies pull data from many sources, cleanse them, and load them into a data warehouse. ETL is an integral process in any data-centric project.
- Real-time or active data warehousing supplements and expands traditional data warehousing, moving into the realm of operational and tactical decision making by loading data in real time and providing data to users for active decision making.
- The security and privacy of data and information are critical issues for a data warehouse professional.

Key Terms

active data warehousing
    (ADW) *359*
data integration *342*
data mart *330*
data warehouse (DW)
    329
data warehouse
    administrator
    (DWA) *364*

dependent data mart *330*
dimension table *351*
dimensional modeling *351*
drill down *352*
enterprise application
    integration (EAI) *343*
enterprise data
    warehouse
    (EDW) *330*

enterprise information
    integration (EII) *344*
extraction,
    transformation, and
    load (ETL) *344*
grain *352*
independent data
    mart *330*
metadata *332*

oper mart *330*
operational data store
    (ODS) *330*
real-time data
    warehousing
    (RDW) *359*

Questions for Discussion

1. Compare data integration and ETL. How are they related?
2. What is a data warehouse, and what are its benefits? Why is Web accessibility important with a data warehouse?
3. A data mart can replace a data warehouse or complement it. Compare and discuss these options.
4. Discuss the major drivers and benefits of data warehousing to end users.
5. List the differences and/or similarities between the roles of a database administrator and a data warehouse administrator.
6. Describe how data integration can lead to higher levels of data quality.

7. Compare the Kimball and Inmon approaches toward data warehouse development. Identify when each one is most effective.
8. Discuss security concerns involved in building a data warehouse.
9. Investigate current data warehouse development implementation through offshoring. Write a report about it. In class, debate the issue in terms of the benefits and costs, as well as social factors.

Exercises

TERADATA STUDENT NETWORK (TSN) AND OTHER HANDS-ON EXERCISES

1. Consider the case describing the development and application of a data warehouse for Coca-Cola Japan (a summary appears in Application Case 8.4), available at the DSS Resources Web site, **dssresources.com/cases/**

cocacolajapan/index.html. Read the case and answer the nine questions for further analysis and discussion.
2. Read the Ball (2005) article and rank-order the criteria (ideally for a real organization). In a report, explain how important each criterion is and why.
3. Explain when you should implement a two- or three-tiered architecture when considering developing a data warehouse.

4. Read the full Continental Airlines case (summarized in the end-of-chapter case) at **teradatastudentnetwork.com** and answer the questions.

5. At **teradatastudentnetwork.com**, read and answer the questions to the case "Harrah's High Payoff from Customer Information." Relate Harrah's results to how airlines and other casinos use their customer data.

6. At **teradatastudentnetwork.com**, read and answer the questions of the assignment "Data Warehousing Failures." Because eight cases are described in that assignment, the class may be divided into eight groups, with one case assigned per group. In addition, read Ariyachandra and Watson (2006a), and for each case identify how the failure occurred as related to not focusing on one or more of the reference's success factor(s).

7. At **teradatastudentnetwork.com**, read and answer the questions with the assignment "Ad-Vent Technology: Using the MicroStrategy Sales Analytic Model." The MicroStrategy software is accessible from the TUN site. Also, you might want to use Barbara Wixom's PowerPoint presentation about the MicroStrategy software ("Demo Slides for MicroStrategy Tutorial Script"), which is also available at the TUN site.

8. At **teradatastudentnetwork.com**, watch the Web seminars titled "Real-Time Data Warehousing: The Next Generation of Decision Support Data Management" and "Building the Real-Time Enterprise." Read the article "Teradata's Real-Time Enterprise Reference Architecture: A Blueprint for the Future of IT," also available at this site. Describe how real-time concepts and technologies work and how they can be used to extend existing data warehousing and BI architectures to support day-to-day decision making. Write a report indicating how real-time data warehousing is specifically providing competitive advantage for organizations. Describe in detail the difficulties in such implementations and operations and describe how they are being addressed in practice.

9. At **teradatastudentnetwork.com**, watch the Web seminars "Data Integration Renaissance: New Drivers and Emerging Approaches," "In Search of a Single Version of the Truth: Strategies for Consolidating Analytic Silos," and "Data Integration: Using ETL, EAI, and EII Tools to Create an Integrated Enterprise." Also read the "Data Integration" research report. Compare and contrast the presentations. What is the most important issue described in these seminars? What is the best way to handle the strategies and challenges of consolidating data marts and spreadsheets into a unified data warehousing architecture? Perform a Web search to identify the latest developments in the field. Compare the presentation to the material in the text and the new material that you found.

10. Consider the future of data warehousing. Perform a Web search on this topic. Also, read these two articles: L. Agosta, "Data Warehousing in a Flat World: Trends for 2006," *DM Direct Newsletter,* March 31, 2006; and J. G. Geiger, "CIFe: Evolving with the Times," *DM Review,* November 2005, pp. 38–41. Compare and contrast your findings.

11. Access **teradatastudentnetwork.com**. Identify the latest articles, research reports, and cases on data warehousing. Describe recent developments in the field. Include in your report how data warehousing is used in BI and DSS.

TEAM ASSIGNMENTS AND ROLE-PLAYING PROJECTS

1. Kathryn Avery has been a DBA with a nationwide retail chain (Big Chain) for the past 6 years. She has recently been asked to lead the development of Big Chain's first data warehouse. The project has the sponsorship of senior management and the CIO. The rationale for developing the data warehouse is to advance the reporting systems, particularly in sales and marketing, and, in the longer term, to improve Big Chain's CRM. Kathryn has been to a Data Warehousing Institute conference and has been doing some reading, but she is still mystified about development methodologies. She knows there are two groups—EDW (Inmon) and architected data marts (Kimball)—that have equally robust features.

Initially, she believed that the two methodologies were extremely dissimilar, but as she has examined them more carefully, she isn't so certain. Kathryn has a number of questions that she would like answered:

a. What are the real differences between the methodologies?

b. What factors are important in selecting a particular methodology?

c. What should be her next steps in thinking about a methodology?

Help Kathryn answer these questions. (This exercise was adapted from K. Duncan, L. Reeves, and J. Griffin, "BI Experts' Perspective," *Business Intelligence Journal,* Vol. 8, No. 4, Fall 2003, pp. 14–19.)

2. Jeet Kumar is the administrator of data warehousing at a big regional bank. He was appointed 5 years ago to implement a data warehouse to support the bank's CRM business strategy. Using the data warehouse, the bank has been successful in integrating customer information, understanding customer profitability, attracting customers, enhancing customer relationships, and retaining customers.

Over the years, the bank's data warehouse has moved closer to real time by moving to more frequent refreshes of the data warehouse. Now, the bank wants to implement customer self-service and call center applications that require even fresher data than is currently available in the warehouse.

Jeet wants some support in considering the possibilities for presenting fresher data. One alternative is to entirely commit to implementing real-time data warehousing. His ETL vendor is prepared to assist him make this change. Nevertheless, Jeet has been informed about

EAI and EII technologies and wonders how they might fit into his plans.

In particular, he has the following questions:

a. What exactly are EAI and EII technologies?

b. How are EAI and EII related to ETL?

c. How are EAI and EII related to real-time data warehousing?

d. Are EAI and EII required, complementary, or alternatives to real-time data warehousing?

Help Jeet answer these questions. (This exercise was adapted from S. Brobst, E. Levy, and C. Muzilla, "Enterprise Application Integration and Enterprise Information Integration," *Business Intelligence Journal,* Vol. 10, No. 2, Spring 2005, pp. 27–32.)

3. Interview administrators in your college or executives in your organization to determine how data warehousing could assist them in their work. Write up a proposal describing your findings. Include cost estimates and benefits in your report.

4. Go through the list of data warehousing risks described in this chapter and find two examples of each in practice.

5. Access **teradata.com** and read the white papers "Measuring Data Warehouse ROI" and "Realizing ROI: Projecting and Harvesting the Business Value of an Enterprise Data Warehouse." Also, watch the Web-based course "The ROI Factor: How Leading Practitioners Deal with the Tough Issue of Measuring DW ROI." Describe the most important issues described in them. Compare these issues to the success factors described in Ariyachandra and Watson (2006a).

6. Read the article K. Liddell Avery and Hugh J. Watson, "Training Data Warehouse End-users," *Business Intelligence Journal,* Vol. 9, No. 4, Fall 2004, pp. 40–51 (which is available at **teradatastudentnetwork.com**). Consider the different classes of end users, describe their difficulties, and discuss the benefits of appropriate training for each group.

Have each member of the group take on one of the roles and have a discussion about how an appropriate type of data warehousing training would be good for each of you.

INTERNET EXERCISES

1. Search the Internet to find information about data warehousing. Identify some newsgroups that have an interest in this concept. Explore ABI/INFORM in your library, e-library, and Google for recent articles on the topic. Begin with **tdwi.com**, **technologyevaluation.com**, and the major vendors: **teradata.com**, **sas.com**, **oracle.com**, and **ncr.com**. Also check **cio.com**, **dmreview.com**, **dssresources.com**, and **db2mag.com**.

2. Survey some ETL tools and vendors. Start with **fairisaac.com** and **egain.com**. Also with **dmreview .com**.

3. Contact some data warehouse vendors and obtain information about their products. Give special attention to vendors that provide tools for multiple purposes, such as Cognos, Software A&G, SAS Institute, and Oracle. Free online demos are available from some of these vendors. Download a demo or two and try them. Write a report describing your experience.

4. Explore **teradata.com** for developments and success stories about data warehousing. Write a report about what you have discovered.

5. Explore **teradata.com** for white papers and Web-based courses on data warehousing. Read the former and watch the latter. (Divide up the class so that all the sources are covered.) Write up a report on what you have discovered.

6. Find recent cases of successful data warehousing applications. Go to data warehouse vendors' sites and look for cases or success stories. Select one and write a brief summary to present to your class.

END OF CHAPTER APPLICATION CASE
Continental Airlines Flies High with Its Real-Time Data Warehouse

As business intelligence (BI) becomes a critical component of daily operations, real-time data warehouses that provide end users with rapid updates and alerts generated from transactional systems are increasingly being deployed. Real-time data warehousing and BI, supporting its aggressive Go Forward business plan, have helped Continental Airlines alter its industry status from "worst to first" and then from "first to favorite." Continental Airlines is a leader in real-time BI. In 2004, Continental won the Data Warehousing Institute's Best Practices and Leadership Award.

Problem(s)

Continental Airlines was founded in 1934, with a single-engine Lockheed aircraft in the Southwestern United States. As of 2006, Continental was the fifth largest airline in the United States and the seventh largest in the world. Continental has the broadest global route network of any U.S. airline, with more than 2,300 daily departures to more than 227 destinations.

Back in 1994, Continental was in deep financial trouble. It had filed for Chapter 11 bankruptcy protection twice and was heading for its third, and probably final, bankruptcy. Ticket sales were hurting because performance on factors that are important to customers was dismal, including a low percentage of on-time departures, frequent baggage arrival problems, and too many customers turned away due to overbooking.

Solution

The revival of Continental began in 1994, when Gordon Bethune became CEO and initiated the Go Forward plan, which consisted of four interrelated parts to be implemented simultaneously. Bethune targeted the need to improve customer-valued performance measures by better understanding customer needs as well as customer perceptions of the value of services that were and could be offered. Financial management practices were also targeted for a significant overhaul. As early as 1998, the airline had separate databases for marketing and operations, all hosted and managed by outside vendors. Processing queries and instigating marketing programs to its high-value customers were time-consuming and ineffective. In additional, information that the workforce needed to make quick decisions was simply not available. In 1999, Continental chose to integrate its marketing, IT, revenue, and operational data sources into a single, in-house EDW. The data warehouse provided a variety of early, major benefits.

As soon as Continental returned to profitability and ranked first in the airline industry in many performance metrics, Bethune and his management team raised the bar by escalating the vision. Instead of just performing best, they wanted Continental to be their customers' favorite airline. The Go Forward plan established more actionable ways to move from first to favorite among customers. Technology became increasingly critical for supporting these new initiatives. In the early days, having access to historical, integrated information was sufficient. This produced substantial strategic value. But it became increasingly imperative for the data warehouse to provide real-time, actionable information to support enterprise-wide tactical decision making and business processes.

Luckily, the warehouse team had expected and arranged for the real-time shift. From the very beginning, the team had created an architecture to handle real-time data feeds into the warehouse, extracts of data from legacy systems into the warehouse, and tactical queries to the warehouse that required almost immediate response times. In 2001, real-time data became available from the warehouse, and the amount stored grew rapidly. Continental moves real-time data (ranging from to-the-minute to hourly) about customers, reservations, check-ins, operations, and flights from its main operational systems to the warehouse. Continental's real-time applications include the following:

- Revenue management and accounting
- Customer relationship management (CRM)
- Crew operations and payroll
- Security and fraud
- Flight operations

Results

In the first year alone, after the data warehouse project was deployed, Continental identified and eliminated over $7 million in fraud and reduced costs by $41 million. With a $30 million investment in hardware and software over 6 years, Continental has reached over $500 million in increased revenues and cost savings in marketing, fraud detection, demand forecasting and tracking, and improved data center management. The single, integrated, trusted view of the business (i.e., the single version of the truth) has led to better, faster decision making.

Continental is now identified as a leader in real-time BI, based on its scalable and extensible architecture, practical decisions on what data are captured in real time, strong relationships with end users, a small and highly competent data warehouse staff, sensible weighing of strategic and tactical decision support requirements, understanding of the synergies between decision support and operations, and changed business processes that use real-time data. (For a sample output screen from the Continental system, see **teradata.com/t/page/139245/**.)

Questions for the Case

1. Describe the benefits of implementing the Continental Go Forward strategy.
2. Explain why it is important for an airline to use a real-time data warehouse.
3. Examine the sample system output screen at **teradata.com/t/page/139245/**. Describe how it can assist the user in identifying problems and opportunities.
4. Identify the major differences between the traditional data warehouse and a real-time

data warehouse, as was implemented at Continental.

5. What strategic advantage can Continental derive from the real-time system as opposed to a traditional information system?

Sources: Adapted from H. Wixom, J. Hoffer, R. Anderson-Lehman, and A. Reynolds, "Real-Time Business Intelligence: Best Practices at Continental Airlines," *Information Systems Management Journal,* Winter 2006, pp. 7–18; R. Anderson-Lehman, H. Watson, B. Wixom, and J. Hoffer, "Continental Airlines Flies High with Real-Time Business Intelligence," *MIS Quarterly Executive,* Vol. 3, No. 4, December 2004, pp. 163–176

(available at **teradatauniversitynetwork.com**); H. Watson, "Real Time: The Next Generation of Decision-Support Data Management," *Business Intelligence Journal,* Vol. 10, No. 3, 2005, pp. 4–6; M. Edwards, "2003 Best Practices Awards Winners: Innovators in Business Intelligence and Data Warehousing," *Business Intelligence Journal,* Fall 2003, pp. 57–64; R. Westervelt, "Continental Airlines Builds Real-Time Data Warehouse," August 20, 2003, **searchoracle .techtarget.com**; R. Clayton, "Enterprise Business Performance Management: Business Intelligence + Data Warehouse = Optimal Business Performance," *Teradata Magazine,* September 2005, **teradata.com/t/page/139245/**; and The Data Warehousing Institute, "2003 Best Practices Summaries: Enterprise Data Warehouse," 2003, **tdwi.org/display.aspx?ID=6749**.

References

Adamson, C. (2009). *The Star Schema Handbook: The Complete Reference to Dimensional Data Warehouse Design.* Hoboken, NJ: Wiley.

Adelman, S., and L. Moss. (2001, Winter). "Data Warehouse Risks." *Journal of Data Warehousing,* Vol. 6, No. 1.

Agosta, L. (2006, January). "The Data Strategy Adviser: The Year Ahead—Data Warehousing Trends 2006." *DM Review,* Vol. 16, No. 1.

Akbay, S. (2006, Quarter 1). "Data Warehousing in Real Time." *Business Intelligence Journal,* Vol. 11, No. 1.

Ambeo. "Keeping Data Private (and Knowing It): Moving Beyond Conventional Safeguards to Ensure Data Privacy." **am-beo.com/why_ambeo_white_papers.html** (accessed May 2009).

Ambeo. (2005, July). "Ambeo Delivers Proven Data Access Auditing Solution." *Database Trends and Applications,* Vol. 19, No. 7.

Anthes, G. H. (2003, June 30). "Hilton Checks into New Suite." *Computerworld,* Vol. 37, No. 26.

Ariyachandra, T., and H. Watson. (2005). "Key Factors in Selecting a Data Warehouse Architecture." *Business Intelligence Journal,* Vol. 10, No. 2.

Ariyachandra, T., and H. Watson. (2006a, January). "Benchmarks for BI and Data Warehousing Success." *DM Review,* Vol. 16, No. 1.

Ariyachandra, T., and H. Watson. (2006b). "Which Data Warehouse Architecture Is Most Successful?" *Business Intelligence Journal,* Vol. 11, No. 1.

Armstrong, R. (2000, Quarter 3). "E-nalysis for the E-business." *Teradata Magazine Online,* **teradata.com**.

Ball, S. K. (2005, November 14). "Do You Need a Data Warehouse Layer in Your Business Intelligence Architecture?" **datawarehouse.ittoolbox.com/documents/industry-articles/do-you-need-a-data-warehouse-layer-in-your-business-intelligencearchitecture-2729** (accessed June 2009).

Barquin, R., A. Paller, and H. Edelstein. (1997). "Ten Mistakes to Avoid for Data Warehousing Managers." In R. Barquin and H. Edelstein (eds.). *Building, Using, and Managing the Data Warehouse.* Upper Saddle River, NJ: Prentice Hall.

Basu, R. (2003, November). "Challenges of Real-Time Data Warehousing." *DM Review.*

Bell, L. D. (2001, Spring). "MetaBusiness Meta Data for the Masses: Administering Knowledge Sharing for Your Data Warehouse." *Journal of Data Warehousing,* Vol. 6, No. 2.

Benander, A., B. Benander, A. Fadlalla, and G. James. (2000, Winter). "Data Warehouse Administration and Management." *Information Systems Management,* Vol. 17, No. 1.

Bonde, A., and M. Kuckuk. (2004, April). "Real World Business Intelligence: The Implementation Perspective." *DM Review,* Vol. 14, No. 4.

Breslin, M. (2004, Winter). "Data Warehousing Battle of the Giants: Comparing the Basics of Kimball and Inmon Models." *Business Intelligence Journal,* Vol. 9, No. 1.

Brobst, S., E. Levy, and C. Muzilla. (2005, Spring). "Enterprise Application Integration and Enterprise Information Integration." *Business Intelligence Journal,* Vol. 10, No. 2.

Brody, R. (2003, Summer). "Information Ethics in the Design and Use of Metadata." *IEEE Technology and Society Magazine,* Vol. 22, No. 2.

Brown, M. (2004, May 9–12). "8 Characteristics of a Successful Data Warehouse." *Proceedings of the Twenty-Ninth Annual SAS Users Group International Conference* (SUGI 29). Montreal, Canada.

Burdett, J., and S. Singh. (2004). "Challenges and Lessons Learned from Real-Time Data Warehousing." *Business Intelligence Journal,* Vol. 9, No. 4.

Coffee, P. (2003, June 23). "'Active' Warehousing." *eWeek,* Vol. 20, No. 25.

Cooper, B. L., H. J. Watson, B. H. Wixom, and D. L. Goodhue. (1999, August 15–19). "Data Warehousing Supports Corporate Strategy at First American Corporation." SIM International Conference, Atlanta.

Cooper, B. L., H. J. Watson, B. H. Wixom, and D. L. Goodhue. (2000). "Data Warehousing Supports Corporate

Strategy at First American Corporation." *MIS Quarterly,* Vol. 24, No. 4, pp. 547–567.

Dasu, T., and T. Johnson. (2003). *Exploratory Data Mining and Data Cleaning.* New York: Wiley.

Davison, D. (2003, November 14). "Top 10 Risks of Offshore Outsourcing." META Group Research Report, now Gartner, Inc., Stamford, CT.

Devlin, B. (2003, Quarter 2). "Solving the Data Warehouse Puzzle." *DB2 Magazine.*

Dragoon, A. (2003, July 1). "All for One View." *CIO.*

Eckerson, W. (2003, Fall). "The Evolution of ETL." *Business Intelligence Journal,* Vol. 8, No. 4.

Eckerson, W. (2005, April 1). "Data Warehouse Builders Advocate for Different Architectures." *Application Development Trends.*

Eckerson, W., R. Hackathorn, M. McGivern, C. Twogood, and G. Watson. (2009). "Data Warehousing Appliances." *Business Intelligence Journal,* Vol. 14, No. 1, pp. 40–48.

Edwards, M. (2003, Fall). "2003 Best Practices Awards Winners: Innovators in Business Intelligence and Data Warehousing." *Business Intelligence Journal,* Vol. 8, No.4.

"Egg's Customer Data Warehouse Hits the Mark." (2005, October). *DM Review,* Vol. 15, No. 10, pp. 24–28.

Elson, R., and R. LeClerc. (2005). "Security and Privacy Concerns in the Data Warehouse Environment." *Business Intelligence Journal,* Vol. 10, No. 3.

Ericson, J. (2006, March). "Real-Time Realities." *BI Review.*

Furtado, P. (2009). "A Survey of Parallel and Distributed Data Warehouses." *International Journal of Data Warehousing and Mining,* Vol. 5, No. 2, pp. 57–78.

Golfarelli, M., and Rizzi, S. (2009). *Data Warehouse Design: Modern Principles and Methodologies.* San Francisco: McGraw-Hill Osborne Media.

Gonzales, M. (2005, Quarter 1). "Active Data Warehouses Are Just One Approach for Combining Strategic and Technical Data." *DB2 Magazine.*

Hall, M. (2002, April 15). "Seeding for Data Growth." *Computerworld,* Vol. 36, No. 16.

Hicks, M. (2001, November 26). "Getting Pricing Just Right." *eWeek,* Vol. 18, No. 46.

Hoffer, J. A., M. B. Prescott, and F. R. McFadden. (2007). *Modern Database Management,* 8th ed. Upper Saddle River, NJ: Prentice Hall.

Hwang, M., and H. Xu. (2005, Fall). "A Survey of Data Warehousing Success Issues." *Business Intelligence Journal,* Vol. 10, No. 4.

IBM. (2009). *50 Tb Data Warehouse Benchmark on IBM System Z.* Armonk, NY: IBM Redbooks.

Imhoff, C. (2001, May). "Power Up Your Enterprise Portal." *E-Business Advise.*

Inmon, W. H. (2005). *Building the Data Warehouse,* 4th ed. New York: Wiley.

Inmon, W. H. (2006, January). "Information Management: How Do You Tune a Data Warehouse?" *DM Review,* Vol. 16, No. 1.

Jukic, N., and C. Lang. (2004, Summer). "Using Offshore Resources to Develop and Support Data Warehousing Applications." *Business Intelligence Journal,* Vol. 9, No. 3.

Kalido. "BP Lubricants Achieves BIGS, Key IT Solutions." **keyitsolutions.com/asp/rptdetails/report/95/cat/1175/** (accessed August 2009).

Kalido. "BP Lubricants Achieves BIGS Success." **kalido.com/collateral/Documents/English-US/CS-BP%20BIGS.pdf** (accessed August 2009).

Karacsony, K. (2006, January). "ETL Is a Symptom of the Problem, Not the Solution." *DM Review,* Vol. 16, No. 1.

Kassam, S. (2002, April 16). "Freedom of Information." *Intelligent Enterprise,* Vol. 5, No. 7.

Kay, R. (2005, September 19). "EII." *Computerworld,* Vol. 39, No. 38.

Kelly, C. (2001, June 14). "Calculating Data Warehousing ROI." *SearchSQLServer.com Tips.*

Malykhina, E. (2003, January 3). "The Real-Time Imperative." *Information Week,* Issue 1020.

Manglik, A., and V. Mehra. (2005, Winter). "Extending Enterprise BI Capabilities: New Patterns for Data Integration." *Business Intelligence Journal,* Vol. 10, No. 1.

Martins, C. (2005, December 13). "HP to Consolidate Data Marts into Single Warehouse." *Computerworld.*

Matney, D. (2003, Spring). "End-User Support Strategy." *Business Intelligence Journal,* Vol. 8, No. 2.

McCloskey, D. W. (2002). *Choosing Vendors and Products to Maximize Data Warehousing Success.* New York: Auerbach Publications.

Mehra, V. (2005, Summer). "Building a Metadata-Driven Enterprise: A Holistic Approach." *Business Intelligence Journal,* Vol. 10, No. 3.

Moseley, M. (2009). "Eliminating Data Warehouse Pressures with Master Data Services and SOA." *Business Intelligence Journal,* Vol. 14, No. 2, pp. 33–43.

Murtaza, A. (1998, Fall). "A Framework for Developing Enterprise Data Warehouses." *Information Systems Management,* Vol. 15, No. 4.

Nash, K. S. (2002, July). "Chemical Reaction." *Baseline.*

Orovic, V. (2003, June). "To Do & Not to Do." *eAI Journal.*

Parzinger, M. J., and M. N. Frolick. (2001, July). "Creating Competitive Advantage Through Data Warehousing." *Information Strategy,* Vol. 17, No. 4.

Peterson, T. (2003, April 21). "Getting Real About Real Time." *Computerworld,* Vol. 37, No. 16.

Raden, N. (2003, June 30). "Real Time: Get Real, Part II." *Intelligent Enterprise.*

Reeves, L. (2009). *Manager's Guide to Data Warehousing.* Hoboken, NJ: Wiley.

Romero, O., and A. Abelló. (2009). "A Survey of Multidimensional Modeling Methodologies." *International Journal of Data Warehousing and Mining,* Vol. 5, No. 2, pp. 1–24.

Rosenberg, A. (2006, Quarter 1). "Improving Query Performance in Data Warehouses." *Business Intelligence Journal,* Vol. 11, No. 1.

Sammon, D., and P. Finnegan. (2000, Fall). "The Ten Commandments of Data Warehousing." *Database for Advances in Information Systems,* Vol. 31, No. 4.

Sapir, D. (2005, May). "Data Integration: A Tutorial." *DM Review,* Vol. 15, No. 5.

Saunders, T. (2009). "Cooking Up a Data Warehouse." *Business Intelligence Journal,* Vol. 14, No. 2, pp. 16–22.

Schwartz, K. D. "Decisions at the Touch of a Button." *Teradata Magazine,* **teradata.com/t/page/117774/index.html** (accessed June 2009).

Schwartz, K. D. (2004, March). "Decisions at the Touch of a Button." *DSS Resources,* pp. 28–31. **dssresources.com/cases/coca-colajapan/index.html** (accessed April 2006).

Sen, A. (2004, April). "Metadata Management: Past, Present and Future." *Decision Support Systems,* Vol. 37, No. 1.

Sen, A., and P. Sinha (2005). "A Comparison of Data Warehousing Methodologies." *Communications of the ACM,* Vol. 48, No. 3.

Solomon, M. (2005, Winter). "Ensuring a Successful Data Warehouse Initiative." *Information Systems Management Journal.*

Songini, M. L. (2004, February 2). "ETL Quickstudy." *Computerworld,* Vol. 38, No. 5.

Sun Microsystems. (2005, September 19). "Egg Banks on Sun to Hit the Mark with Customers." **sun.com/smi/Press/sunflash/2005-09/sunflash.20050919.1.xml** (accessed April 2006; no longer available online).

Tannenbaum, A. (2002, Spring). "Identifying Meta Data Requirements." *Journal of Data Warehousing,* Vol. 7, No. 2.

Tennant, R. (2002, May 15). "The Importance of Being Granular." *Library Journal,* Vol. 127, No. 9.

Teradata Corp. "A Large US-based Insurance Company Masters Its Finance Data." **teradata.com/t/WorkArea/DownloadAsset.aspx?id=4858** (accessed July 2009).

Teradata Corp. "Active Data Warehousing." **teradata.com/t/page/87127/index.html** (accessed April 2006).

Teradata Corp. "Coca-Cola Japan Puts the Fizz Back in Vending Machine Sales." **teradata.com/t/page/118866/index.html** (accessed June 2009).

Teradata. "Enterprise Data Warehouse Delivers Cost Savings and Process Efficiencies." **teradata.com/t/resources/case-studies/NCR-Corporation-eb4455/** (accessed June 2009).

Terr, S. (2004, February). "Real-Time Data Warehousing: Hardware and Software." *DM Review,* Vol. 14, No. 2.

Thornton, M. (2002, March 18). "What About Security? The Most Common, but Unwarranted, Objection to Hosted Data Warehouses." *DM Review,* Vol. 12, No. 3, pp. 30–43.

Thornton, M., and M. Lampa. (2002). "Hosted Data Warehouse." *Journal of Data Warehousing,* Vol. 7, No. 2, pp. 27–34.

Turban, E., D. Leidner, E. McLean, and J. Wetherbe. (2006). *Information Technology for Management,* 5th ed. New York: Wiley.

Vaduva, A., and T. Vetterli. (2001, September). "Metadata Management for Data Warehousing: An Overview." *International Journal of Cooperative Information Systems,* Vol. 10, No. 3.

Van den Hoven, J. (1998). "Data Marts: Plan Big, Build Small." *Information Systems Management,* Vol. 15, No. 1.

Watson, H., J. Gerard, L. Gonzalez, M. Haywood, and D. Fenton. (1999). "Data Warehouse Failures: Case Studies and Findings." *Journal of Data Warehousing,* Vol. 4, No. 1.

Watson, H. J. (2002). "Recent Developments in Data Warehousing." *Communications of the ACM,* Vol. 8, No. 1.

Watson, H. J., D. L. Goodhue, and B. H. Wixom. (2002). "The Benefits of Data Warehousing: Why Some Organizations Realize Exceptional Payoffs." *Information & Management,* Vol. 39.

Weir, R. (2002, Winter). "Best Practices for Implementing a Data Warehouse." *Journal of Data Warehousing,* Vol. 7, No. 1.

Wilk, L. (2003, Spring). "Data Warehousing and Real-Time Computing." *Business Intelligence Journal,* Vol. 8, No. 2.

Wixom, B., and H. Watson. (2001, March). "An Empirical Investigation of the Factors Affecting Data Warehousing Success." *MIS Quarterly,* Vol. 25, No. 1.

Wrembel, R. (2009). "A Survey of Managing the Evolution of Data Warehouses." *International Journal of Data Warehousing and Mining,* Vol. 5, No. 2, pp. 24–56.

ZD Net UK. "Sun Case Study: Egg's Customer Data Warehouse." **whitepapers.zdnet.co.uk/0,39025945,60159401p-39000449q,00.htm** (accessed June 2009).

Zhao, X. (2005, October 7). "Meta Data Management Maturity Model," *DM Direct Newsletter.*

9

Business Performance Management

LEARNING OBJECTIVES

1 Understand the all-encompassing nature of business performance management (BPM)
2 Understand the closed-loop processes linking strategy to execution
3 Describe some of the best practices in planning and management reporting
4 Describe the difference between performance management and measurement

5 Understand the role of methodologies in BPM
6 Describe the basic elements of the balanced scorecard and Six Sigma methodologies
7 Describe the differences between scorecards and dashboards
8 Understand some of the basics of dashboard design

Business performance management (BPM) is an outgrowth of decision support systems (DSS), enterprise information systems (EIS), and business intelligence (BI). From a market standpoint, it was over 25 years in the making. As with decision support, BPM is more than just a technology. It is an integrated set of processes, methodologies, metrics, and applications designed to drive the overall financial and operational performance of an enterprise. It helps enterprises translate their strategies and objectives into plans, monitor performance against those plans, analyze variations between actual results and planned results, and adjust their objectives and actions in response to this analysis.

This chapter examines the processes, methodologies, metrics, and systems underlying BPM. Because BPM is distinguished from DSS and BI by its focus on strategy and objectives, the chapter begins with an exploration of the notions of enterprise strategy and execution and the gap that often exists between them. The specific sections are:

9.1 Opening Vignette: Double Down at Harrah's
9.2 Business Performance Management (BPM) Overview
9.3 Strategize: Where Do We Want to Go?
9.4 Plan: How Do We Get There?
9.5 Monitor: How Are We Doing?

9.6 Act and Adjust: What Do We Need to Do Differently?

9.7 Performance Measurement

9.8 BPM Methodologies

9.9 BPM Technologies and Applications

9.10 Performance Dashboards and Scorecards

9.1 OPENING VIGNETTE: DOUBLE DOWN AT HARRAH'S

Harrah's Entertainment, Inc., is the largest gaming company in the world and has been in operation since 1937. For most of its history, it has enjoyed financial success and unprecedented growth. In 2000, it had 21 hotel-casinos in 17 markets across the United States, employed over 40,000 people, and served over 19 million customers. By 2008, those numbers had risen to 51 hotel-casinos on 6 continents, 85,000 employees, and over 40 million customers. Much of Harrah's growth is attributable to savvy marketing operations and customer service, as well as its acquisition strategy.

Problem

Besides being a leader in the gaming industry, Harrah's has been a long-time leader in the business intelligence and performance management arena. Unlike its competitors, Harrah's has generally avoided investing vast sums of money in lavish hotels, shopping malls, and attractions. Instead, it has operated on the basis of a business strategy that focuses on "knowing their customers well, giving them great service, and rewarding their loyalty so that they seek out a Harrah's casino whenever and wherever they play" (Watson and Volonino, 2001). The execution of this strategy has involved creative marketing, innovative uses of information technology, and operational excellence.

The strategy actually started back in the late 1990s when Harrah's hired Gary Loveman as its chief operating officer (COO). Today, Loveman is Harrah Entertainment's chairman, president, and chief executive officer. Prior to joining Harrah's, Loveman had been an associate professor at the Harvard University Graduate School of Business Administration, with extensive experience in retail marketing and service management. When he arrived at Harrah's he was given the task of turning Harrah's into a "market-driven company that would build customer loyalty" (Swabey, 2007). At the time, Harrah's actually had little choice. Harrah's didn't have the capital to build new luxury casinos and entertainment centers, a strategy being pursued by its rivals like the Bellagio. Instead, it decided to maximize its ROI by understanding its customers' behavior and preferences. It reasoned that in the highly competitive gaming market, the need to attract and retain customers is critical to business success, because customer loyalty and satisfaction can make or break a company. Attraction and retention require more than opulent accommodations and surroundings. Instead, the goal should be to persuade gamblers to spend a greater share at Harrah's properties.

Because it had a couple of year's worth of loyalty card data, Harrah's already knew a lot about its customers (Swabey, 2007). But focus groups revealed what management suspected— they might have cards, but they weren't loyal. Nearly 65 percent of their gambling expenditures went elsewhere. The first step was to find out who its customers were. The analysis revealed two facts: (1) over 80 percent of revenues came from over 25 percent of customers and (2) most of the customers were "average folks" (middle-aged or seniors) and not the high rollers attracted by the luxury hotels (Shill and Thomas, 2005). How could Harrah's collect, utilize, and leverage data, analysis, and findings of this type to maximize the lifetime value of a customer?

Solution

Harrah's answer was Total Gold, a patented customer loyalty program that is now known as the Total Rewards program. Not only did the program serve to reward customers with cash and comps for their gaming and other activities at any of Harrah's properties, but, more important, it provided Harrah's with a vast collection of high volume, real-time transaction data regarding its customers and their behaviors. The data is collected via the Total Rewards card which is used to record guest activities of all sorts (e.g., purchases at restaurants and wins and losses from any type of gaming activity).

The data is fed to a centralized data warehouse. Staff at any of Harrah's properties can access the data. The data warehouse forms the base of a "closed-loop" marketing system that enables Harrah's to clearly define the objectives of its marketing campaigns, to execute and monitor those campaigns, and to learn what types of campaigns provide the highest return for particular types of customers. The overall result is that Harrah's has established a "differentiated loyalty and service framework to continuously improve customer service interactions and business outcomes" (Stanley, 2006). The system also acts as a real-time feed to Harrah's operational systems, which can impact the experience of customers while they gamble and participate in other activities at Harrah's properties.

Results and a New Problem

Harrah's Total Rewards loyalty card program and closed-loop marketing system has produced substantial returns over the past decade, including (Watson and Volonino, 2001):

- A brand identity for Harrah's casinos
- An increase in customer retention worth several million dollars
- An increase in the number of customers who play at more than one Harrah's property, increasing profitability by millions of dollars
- A high internal rate of return on its information technology investments

The bottom line is that customers' discretionary spending versus their competitors has increased substantially from year-to-year, resulting in hundreds of millions of dollars in additional revenue.

The system has won a number of awards (e.g., TDWI Best Practices Award) and has been the subject of many case studies. It has been recognized as the "most spectacularly successful example of analytics in action today" (Swabey, 2007). Of course, awards and accolades are no guarantee of future success, especially in the face of a global economic downturn.

For the 10 years leading up to the end of 2007, the U.S. gaming industry had the highest performing equity index of any industry in America (Knowledge@W.P. Carey, 2009). The past 2 years have been a different story. Once thought to be immune to economic downturns, the gaming industry has suffered substantially from the collapse of the capital markets and the world economy. In cities like Las Vegas, not only have hotel occupancy rates declined, but the average spend per visitor has also dwindled. The plight of many casinos remains precarious, because they relied on huge amounts of debt to build newer and bigger hotel-casino projects and lacked the reserves to handle declining revenues.

Unlike its competitors, Harrah's has never had an "edifice" complex (Shill and Thomas, 2005). Yet, like its competitors, Harrah's still faces substantial economic problems. In the first 3 months of 2009, it posted operating losses of $127 million, although this was an improvement over 2008. In the first 3 months of 2008, it had operating losses of $270 million. In 2008, Harrah's also doubled its debt load (to the tune of $24 billion) when it was taken private in January 2008 by the equity firms Apollo Management and TPG Capital. Today, its debt load has left it facing potential bankruptcy.

So, even though Harrah's has had an award-winning performance management system in place for years and is a recognized leader in the use of data and predictive analytics, it still confronts the same strategic problems and economic issues that its "lesser equipped" competitors face.

Harrah's has continued to rely on its marketing campaigns to boost demand. Additionally, it has instituted a number of initiatives designed to reduce its debt and to cut costs. In December 2008, Harrah's completed a debt-exchange deal that reduced its overall debt by $1.16 billion, and it is in the midst of another debt-reduction and maturity-extension program involving $2.8 million in notes. Like most other gaming companies, it laid off 1,600 workers in Las Vegas, cut managers' pay, and suspended 401K contributions during the downturn. It delayed the completion of 660 more rooms at Caesar's Palace, although it is still working on a new convention center at Caesar's, which has had strong bookings.

Management has also been encouraged by the results of an "efficiency-management" process pioneered by Toyota called Lean Operations Management. Lean Operations Management is a performance management framework focused primarily on efficiency rather than effectiveness. Harrah's has launched pilot programs at several properties and plans to roll it out company-wide in 2009.

Questions for the Opening Vignette

1. Describe Harrah's marketing strategy. How does Harrah's strategy differ from its competitors?
2. What is Harrah's Total Rewards program?
3. What are the basic elements of Harrah's closed-loop marketing system?
4. What were the results of Harrah's marketing strategy?
5. What economic issues does Harrah's face today? Could the Total Rewards system be modified in any way to handle these issues?

What We Can Learn from This Vignette

For a number of years, Harrah's closed-loop marketing system enabled it to execute a strategy that clearly differentiated it from its competitors. The system also provided the means to monitor key indicators of operational and tactical importance. One of the problems with the system is that it is predicated on the assumption of growing, or at least stable, demand. What it could not do, at least in the short run, was predict drastically reduced or nonexistent demand or fundamental changes in the economy. As Loveman, Harrah's CEO, has said, "We are not experiencing a recession, but a fundamental restructuring of financial interaction that we have grown accustomed to over a very long period of time. And it's not at all clear yet where that's going."

Sources: Compiled from Knowledge@W.P. Carey, "High-Rolling Casinos Hit a Losing Streak," March 2, 2009, **knowledge.wpcarey.asu.edu/article.cfm?articleid=1752#** (accessed July 2009); S. Green, "Harrah's Reports Loss, Says LV Properties Hit Hard," *Las Vegas Sun,* March 13, 2009, **lasvegassun.com/news/2009/mar/13/harrahs-reports-loss-says-lv-properties-hit-hard** (accessed July 2009); W. Shill and R. Thomas, "Exploring the Mindset of the High Performer," *Outlook Journal,* October 2005, **accenture.com/Global/Research_and_Insights/Outlook/By_Issue/Y2005/ExploringPerformer.htm** (accessed July 2009); T. Stanley, "High-Stakes Analytics," *InformationWeek,* February 1, 2006, **informationweek.com/shared/printableArticle.jhtml?articleID=177103414** (accessed July 2009); P. Swabey, "Nothing Left to Chance," *Information Age,* January 18, 2007, **information-age.com/channels/information-management/features/272256/nothing-left-to-chance.thtml** (accessed July 2009); and H. Watson and L. Volonino, "Harrah's High Payoff from Customer Information," *The Data Warehousing Institute Industry Study 2000—Harnessing Customer Information for Strategic Advantage: Technical Challenges and Business Solutions,* January 2001, **terry.uga.edu/~hwatson/Harrahs.doc** (accessed June 2009).

9.2 BUSINESS PERFORMANCE MANAGEMENT (BPM) OVERVIEW

As this chapter will show, Harrah's closed-loop marketing system has all the hallmarks of a performance management system. Essentially, the system allowed Harrah's to align its strategies, plans, analytical systems, and actions in such as way that it substantially improved its performance. Harrah's recent experience also shows that successful performance also requires a broad focus, as opposed to a narrow one (e.g. just on marketing or customer loyalty), as well as the ability to question and explore assumptions, especially during times of uncertainty. Organizations need to adapt constantly if they are to achieve sustained success. An organization's performance management processes are the principal mechanism for assessing the impact of change and tuning the business in order to survive and prosper (Axson, 2007).

BPM Defined

In the business and trade literature, performance management has a number of names, including corporate performance management (CPM), enterprise performance management (EPM), strategic enterprise management (SEM), and business performance management (BPM). CPM was coined by the market analyst firm Gartner (**gartner.com**). EPM is a term associated with Oracle's PeopleSoft offering by the same name. SEM is the term that SAP (**sap.com**) uses. In this chapter, BPM is used rather than the other terms, because the term was originally coined by the BPM Standards Group and is still used by the BPM Forum. The term **business performance management (BPM)** refers to the business processes, methodologies, metrics, and technologies used by enterprises to measure, monitor, and manage business performance. It encompasses three key components (*BPM Magazine,* 2009):

- A set of integrated, closed-loop management and analytic processes, supported by technology, that address financial as well as operational activities
- Tools for businesses to define strategic goals and then measure and manage performance against those goals
- A core set of processes, including financial and operational planning, consolidation and reporting, modeling, analysis, and monitoring of key performance indicators (KPIs), linked to organizational strategy

BPM and BI Compared

BPM is an outgrowth of BI and incorporates many of its technologies, applications, and techniques. When BPM was first introduced as a separate concept, there was confusion about the differences between BPM and BI. Was it simply a new term for the same concept? Was BPM the next generation of BI, or were there substantial differences between the two? The confusion still persists today for the following reasons:

- BPM is promoted and sold by the same companies that market and sell the BI tools and suites.
- BI has evolved so that many of the original differences between the two no longer exist (e.g., BI used to be focused on departmental rather than enterprise-wide projects).
- BI is a crucial element of BPM.

The term *BI* now describes the technology used to access, analyze, and report on data relevant to an enterprise. It encompasses a wide spectrum of software, including ad hoc querying, reporting, online analytical processing (OLAP), dashboards, scorecards, search, visualization, and more. These software products started as stand-alone tools, but BI software vendors have incorporated them into their BI suites.

BPM has been characterized as "BI + Planning," meaning that BPM is the convergence of BI and planning on a unified platform—the cycle of plan, monitor, and analyze (Calumo Group, 2009). The processes that BPM encompasses are not new. Virtually every medium and large organization has processes in place (e.g., budgets, detailed plans, execution, and measurement) that feed back to the overall strategic plan, as well as the operational plans. What BPM adds is a framework for integrating these processes, methodologies, metrics, and systems into a unified solution.

BI practices and software are almost always part of an overall BPM solution. BPM, however, is not just about software. BPM is an enterprise-wide strategy that seeks to prevent organizations from optimizing local business at the expense of overall corporate performance. BPM is not a "one-off" project or departmentally focused. Instead, BPM is an ongoing set of processes that, if done correctly, impacts an organization from top to bottom. Critical to the success of BPM is alignment throughout an organization. It "helps users take action in pursuit of their 'common cause': achieving performance targets, executing company strategy, and delivering value to stakeholders" (Tucker and Dimon, 2009).

This is not to say that a BI project cannot be strategically oriented, centrally controlled, or impact a substantial part of an organization. For example, the Transportation Security Administration (TSA) uses a BI system called the Performance Information System (PIMS) to track passenger volumes, screener performance (attribution, absenteeism, overtime, and injuries), dangerous items, and total passenger throughput

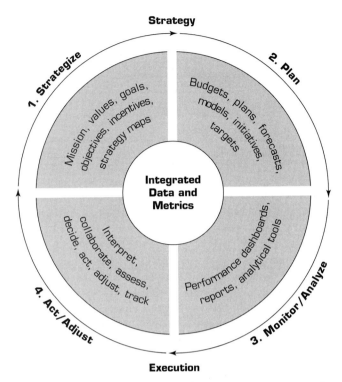

FIGURE 9.1 BPM Cycle   *Source:* W. Eckerson, "Performance Management Strategies: How to Create and Deploy Performance Management Strategies," *TDWI Best Practices Report*, 2009.

(Henschen, 2008). The system is built on BI software from MicroStrategy (**microstrategy .com**) and is used by over 2,500 "power users" on a daily basis and 9,500 casual users on a weekly basis. The information in PIMS is critical to the operation of the TSA and in some cases is mandated by Congress. It is used by TSA employees from the top of the agency to the bottom and reduced agency costs by approximately $100 million for fiscal year 2007–2008. Clearly, the system has strategic and operational importance. However, it is not a BPM system.

The primary distinction is that a BPM system is strategy driven. It encompasses a closed-loop set of processes that link strategy to execution in order to optimize business performance (see Figure 9.1). The loop implies that optimum performance is achieved by setting goals and objectives (i.e., strategize), establishing initiatives and plans to achieve those goals (i.e., plan), monitoring actual performance against the goals and objectives (i.e., monitor), and taking corrective action (i.e., act and adjust). In Sections 9.3 through 9.6, each of these major processes is examined in detail.

Section 9.2 Review Questions

1. Define *BPM*.
2. How does BPM differ from BI? How are they the same?
3. Briefly describe TSA's PIMS system.
4. List the major BPM processes.

9.3 STRATEGIZE: WHERE DO WE WANT TO GO?

For the moment, imagine that you are a distance runner and are in the process of training for an upcoming event. In preparation, suppose your coach said to you, "I haven't thought much about the race. I'm not even sure what the distance is, but I think you should just go out and run for 8 hours a day until race day. Things will work out in the end." If a coach said this, you would think your coach was nuts. Obviously, for your training plan to make sense, you would need to know what race you were running (e.g., is it a marathon, a half marathon, 10 miler) and what sort of time you were shooting for (e.g., a top-5 finish with a time of 2 hours, 10 minutes). You would also need to know what your strengths and weaknesses were in order to determine whether the goal was realistic and what sorts of things you would need to work on to achieve your goal (e.g., trouble with finishing speed over the last few miles of a race).

You would be surprised at the number of companies that operate much like the coach, especially during uncertain and challenging times. The general refrain is something like, "Setting a strategy and developing a formal plan is too slow and inflexible. You need actions that are far bolder and more attuned to the unique nature of our time. If you take the time to define your goals, set your priorities, develop your strategies, and manage your outcomes, someone will beat you to the finish line." However, without specific goals or objectives, it is difficult to evaluate alternative courses of action. Without specific priorities, there is no way to determine how to allocate resources among the alternatives selected. Without plans, there is no way to guide the actions among those working on the alternatives. Without analysis and evaluation, there is no way to determine which of the opportunities are succeeding or failing. Goals, objectives, priorities, plans, and critical thinking are all part of a well-defined strategy.

Strategic Planning

The term *strategy* has many definitions. To add to the confusion, it is also often used in combination with a variety of other terms, such as *strategic vision* and *strategic focus*. Regardless of the differences in meaning, they all address the question "Where do we want to go in the future?" For most companies, the answer to this question is provided in a strategic plan. You can think of a strategic plan as a map, detailing a course of action for moving an organization from its current state to its future vision.

Typically, strategic plans start at the top and begin with an enterprise-wide view. From there, strategic plans are created for the company's business units or functional units. The following tasks are quite common to the strategic planning process, regardless of the level at which the planning is done—enterprise-wide, business unit, or functional unit:

1. ***Conduct a current situation analysis.*** This analysis reviews the company's current situation ("Where are we?") and establishes a baseline, as well as key trends, for financial performance and operational performance.
2. ***Determine the planning horizon.*** Traditionally, organizations produce plans on a yearly basis, with the planning horizon running 3 to 5 years. In large part, the time horizon is determined by the volatility and predictability of the market, product life cycles, the size of the organization, the rate of technological innovation, and the capital intensity of the industry. The more volatile, the less predictable, the shorter the life cycles, the smaller the organization, the faster the rate of innovation, and the less the capital intensity, the shorter the planning horizon.
3. ***Conduct an environment scan.*** An environment scan is a standard strengths, weaknesses, opportunities, and threats (SWOT) assessment of the company. It identifies and prioritizes the key customer, market, competitor, government, demographic, stakeholder, and industry factors potentially or actually affecting the company.
4. ***Identify critical success factors.*** **Critical success factors (CSF)** delineate those things that an organization must excel at to be successful in its market space. For a product-focused company, product quality and product innovation are examples of CSF. For a low-cost provider such as Wal-Mart, distribution capabilities are a CSF.

5. *Complete a gap analysis.* Like the environment scan, a gap analysis is used to identify and prioritize the internal strengths and weaknesses in an organization's processes, structures, and technologies and applications. The gaps reflect what the strategy actually requires and what the organization actually provides.

6. *Create a strategic vision.* An organization's **strategic vision** provides a picture or mental image of what the organization should look like in the future—the shift in its products and markets. Generally, the vision is couched in terms of its strategy focus and identifies the as-is state and the desired state.

7. *Develop a business strategy.* The challenge in this step is to produce a strategy that is based on the data and information from the previous steps and is consistent with the strategic vision. Common sense tells us that the strategy needs to exploit the organization's strengths, take advantage of its opportunities, address weaknesses, and respond to threats. The company needs to ensure that the strategy is internally consistent, that the organizational culture is aligned with the strategy, and that sufficient resources and capital are available to implement the strategy.

8. *Identify strategic objectives and goals.* A strategic plan that fails to provide clear directions for the operational and financial planning process is incomplete. Before an operational or financial plan can be established, strategic objectives must be established and refined into well-defined goals or targets. A **strategic objective** is a broad statement or general course of action that prescribes targeted directions for an organization. Before a strategic objective can be linked to an operational plan or a financial plan, it should be converted into a well-defined goal or target. A **strategic goal** is a quantification of an objective for a designated period of time. For example, if an organization has an objective of improving return on assets (ROA) or increasing overall profitability, these objectives need to be turned into quantified targets (e.g., an increase of ROA from 10 to 15 percent or an increase in profit margin from 5 to 7 percent) before the organization can begin to detail the operational plans needed to achieve these targets. Strategic goals and targets guide operational execution and allow progress to be tracked against overall objectives.

The Strategy Gap

It's one thing to create a long-term strategy and another to execute it. Over the past couple of decades a number of surveys have highlighted the gap that routinely exists in many organizations between their strategic plans and the execution of those plans. Recent surveys of senior executives by the Monitor Group (Kaplan and Norton, 2008) and the Conference Board (2008) pinpointed "strategy execution" as the executive's number 1 priority. Similarly, statistics from the Palladium Group (Norton, 2007) suggest that 90 percent of organizations fail to execute their strategies successfully. The reasons for the "strategy gap" are varied, although many studies pinpoint one of four reasons:

1. *Communication.* In many organizations, a very small percentage of the employees understand the organization's strategy. The Palladium Group (Norton, 2007) put the figure at less than 10 percent. On the one hand, it is difficult, if not impossible, for employees to make decisions and act in accordance with the strategic plan if they have never seen nor heard the plan. On the other hand, even when the plan is communicated, the strategy often lacks clarity, so that no one is quite sure whether their actions are in line or at variance with the plan.

2. *Alignment of rewards and incentives.* Linking pay to performance is important for successful execution. However, incentive plans are often linked to short-term financial results, not to the strategic plan or even to the strategic initiatives

articulated in the operational plan. Maximizing short-term gains leads to less than rational decision making. Again, the Palladium Group (Norton, 2007) indicated that 70 percent of organizations failed to link middle management incentives to their strategy.

3. **Focus.** Management often spends time on the periphery of issues rather than concentrating on the core elements. Hours can be spent debating line items on a budget, with little attention given to the strategy, the linkage of the financial plan to the strategy, or the assumptions underlying the linkage. The Palladium Group (Norton, 2007) suggested that in many organizations 85 percent of managers spend less than 1 hour per month discussing strategy.

4. **Resources.** Unless strategic initiatives are properly funded and resourced, their failure is virtually assured. The Palladium Group (Norton, 2007) found that less than 40 percent of organizations tied their budgets to their strategic plans.

Section 9.3 Review Questions

1. Why does a company need a well-formulated strategy?
2. What are the basic tasks in the strategic planning process?
3. What are some of the sources of the gap between formulating a strategy and actually executing the strategy?

9.4 PLAN: HOW DO WE GET THERE?

When operational managers know and understand the *what* (i.e., the organizational objectives and goals), they will be able to come up with the *how* (i.e., detailed operational and financial plans). Operational and financial plans answer two questions. What tactics and initiatives will be pursued to meet the performance targets established by the strategic plan? What are the expected financial results of executing the tactics?

Operational Planning

An **operational plan** translates an organization's strategic objectives and goals into a set of well-defined tactics and initiatives, resource requirements, and expected results for some future time period, usually, but not always, a year. In essence, an operational plan is like a project plan that is designed to ensure that an organization's strategy is realized. Most operational plans encompass a portfolio of tactics and initiatives. The key to successful operational planning is integration. Strategy drives tactics, and tactics drive results. Basically, the tactics and initiatives defined in an operational plan need to be directly linked to key objectives and targets in the strategic plan. If there is no linkage between an individual tactic and one or more strategic objectives or targets, management should question whether the tactic and its associated initiatives are really needed at all. The BPM methodologies discussed in Section 9.8 are designed to ensure that these linkages exist.

Operational planning can be either tactic-centric or budget-centric (see Axson, 2007). In a *tactic-centric* plan, tactics are established to meet the objectives and targets established in the strategic plan. Conversely, in a *budget-centric* plan, a financial plan or budget is established that sums to the targeted financial values. Best practice organizations use tactic-centric operational planning. This means that they begin the operational planning process by defining the alternative tactics and initiatives that can be used to reach a particular target. For example, if a business is targeting a 10 percent growth in profit margin (i.e., the ratio of the difference between revenue and expenses divided by revenue), the business will first determine whether it plans to increase the margin by increasing revenues, by reducing expenses, or some combination of both. If it focuses on revenues, then the question will become whether it plans to enter new markets or increase sales to existing markets, whether it plans to enhance existing products or introduce new products, or some combination of these. The alternate scenarios and associated initiatives have to be weighed in terms of their overall risk, resource requirements, and financial viability. Online File W9.1 discusses the steps used in making decisions among the various scenarios.

Financial Planning and Budgeting

In most organizations, resources tend to be scarce. If they were not, organizations could simply throw people and money at their opportunities and problems and overwhelm the competition. Given the scarcity of resources, an organization needs to put its money and people where its strategies and linked tactics are. An organization's strategic objectives and key metrics should serve as top-down drivers for the allocation of an organization's tangible and intangible assets. While continuing operations clearly need support, key resources should be assigned to the most important strategic programs and priorities. Most organizations use their budgets and compensation programs to allocate resources. By implication, both of these need to be carefully aligned with the organization's strategic objectives and tactics in order to achieve strategic success.

The best way for an organization to achieve this alignment is to base its financial plan on its operational plan or, more directly, to allocate and budget its resources against specific tactics and initiatives. For example, if one of the tactics is to develop a new sales channel, budgeted revenues and costs need to be assigned to the channel rather than simply having costs assigned to particular functional units, such as marketing and R&D. Without this type of tactical resource planning, there is no way to measure the success of those tactics and hence the strategy. This type of linkage helps organizations avoid the problem of "random" budget cuts that inadvertently affect associated strategies. Tactic-based budgeting ensures that the link between particular budget-line items and particular tactics or initiatives is well established and well known.

The financial planning and budgeting process has a logical structure that typically starts with those tactics that generate some form of revenue or income. In organizations that sell goods or services, the ability to generate revenue is based on either the ability to directly produce goods and services or acquire the right amount of goods and services to sell. After a revenue figure has been established, the associated costs of delivering that level of revenue can be generated. Quite often, this entails input from several departments or tactics. This means the process has to be collaborative and that dependencies between functions need to be clearly communicated and understood. In addition to the collaborative input, the organization also needs to add various overhead costs, as well as the costs of the capital required. This information, once consolidated, shows the cost by tactic as well as the cash and funding requirements to put the plan into operation.

Section 9.4 Review Questions

1. What is the goal of operational planning?
2. What is tactic-centric planning? What is budget-centric planning?
3. What is the primary goal of a financial plan?

9.5 MONITOR: HOW ARE WE DOING?

When the operational plan and financial plans are under way, it is imperative that the performance of the organization be monitored. A comprehensive framework for monitoring performance should address two key issues: what to monitor and how to monitor. Because it is impossible to look at everything, an organization needs to focus on monitoring specific issues. After the organization has identified the indicators or measures to look at, it needs to develop a strategy for monitoring those factors and responding effectively.

In Sections 9.7 and 9.8, we examine in detail how to determine what should be measured by a BPM system. For the moment, we simply note that the "what" is usually defined by the CSF and the goals or targets established in the strategic planning process. For example, if an instrument manufacturer has a specified strategic objective of increasing the overall profit margin of its current product lines by 5 percent annually over the next 3 years, then the organization needs to monitor the profit margin throughout the year to see whether it is trending toward the targeted annual rate of 5 percent. In the same vein, if this company plans to introduce a new product every quarter for the next two years, the organization needs to track new product introduction over the designated time period.

Diagnostic Control Systems

Most companies use what is known as a *diagnostic control system* to monitor organizational performance and correct deviations from present performance standards. This is true even for those organizations that do not have formal BPM processes or systems. A **diagnostic control system** is a cybernetic system, meaning that it has inputs, a process for transforming the inputs into outputs, a standard or benchmark against which to compare the outputs, and a feedback channel to allow information on variances between the outputs and the standard to be communicated and acted upon. Virtually any information system can be used as a diagnostic control system if it is possible to (1) set a goal in advance, (2) measure outputs, (3) compute or calculate absolute or relative performance variances, and (4) use the variance information as feedback to alter inputs and/or processes to bring performance back in line with present goals and standards. The key elements of a diagnostic control system are depicted in Figure 9.2. Balanced scorecards, performance dashboards, project monitoring systems, human resources systems, and financial reporting systems are all examples of systems that can be used diagnostically.

An effective diagnostic control system encourages *management by exception.* Instead of constantly monitoring a variety of internal processes and target values and comparing actual results with planned results, managers receive regularly scheduled exception reports. Measures that are aligned with expectations receive little attention. If, however, a significant variation is identified, then—and only then—managers need to invest time and attention to investigate the cause of the deviation and initiate appropriate remedial action.

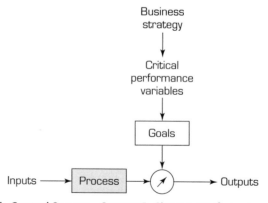

FIGURE 9.2 Diagnostic Control System *Source:* R. Simons, *Performance Measurement and Control Systems for Implementing Strategy,* p. 207, Prentice Hall, Upper Saddle River, NJ, 2002.

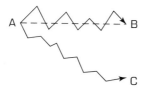

FIGURE 9.3 Operational Variance or Strategic Issue?

Pitfalls of Variance Analysis

In many organizations, the vast majority of the exception analysis focuses on negative variances when functional groups or departments fail to meet their targets. Rarely are positive variances reviewed for potential opportunities, and rarely does the analysis focus on assumptions underlying the variance patterns. Consider, for a moment, the two paths depicted in Figure 9.3. In this figure, the dashed line from A to B represents planned or targeted results over a specified period of time. Recognizing that there will be minor deviations from the plan, we might expect the actual results to deviate slightly from the targeted results. When the deviation is larger than expected, this is typically viewed as an operational error that needs to be corrected. At this point, managers usually direct their employees to do whatever it takes to get the plan back on track. If revenues are below plan, they are chided to sell harder. If costs are above plan, they are told to stop spending.

However, what happens if our strategic assumptions—not the operations—are wrong? What if the organization needs to change strategic directions toward point C rather than continuing with the original plan? As Application Case 9.1 exemplifies, the results of proceeding on the basis of fallacious assumptions can be disastrous. The only way to make this sort of determination is to monitor more than actual versus targeted performance. Whatever diagnostic control system is being used needs to track underlying assumptions, cause-and-effect relationships, and the overall validity of the intended strategy. Consider, for instance, a growth strategy that is focused on the introduction of a new product. This sort of strategy is usually based on certain assumptions about market demand or the availability of parts from particular suppliers. As the strategy unfolds, management needs to monitor not only the revenues and costs associated with the new product but also variations in the market demand or availability of parts or any other key assumptions.

APPLICATION CASE 9.1

Discovery-Driven Planning: The Coffee Wars

For the last couple of years, Starbucks, Dunkin Donuts, and McDonald's have been locked in a battle to capture the specialty coffee market. For Starbucks and Dunkin Donuts, a major part of the battle revolves around the growth in the number of stores. This is not an issue for McDonald's, because it already has a worldwide presence.

Since 2000, Starbucks has been opening stores at a "remarkable pace." Its store count went from just over 3,000 stores in 2000 to approximately 15,000 stores in 2007. The underlying assumption was that there was pent up demand for specialty coffee and

unless it opened new stores to service this demand its competitors would. One of these competitors was Dunkin Donuts. In 2007, Dunkin Donuts decided to expand its franchises both in numbers and geographical reach. Prior to 2007, most of Dunkin Donuts' 5,000 franchises were in the Northeast (Weier, 2007). Its new goal was to increase to 15,000 franchises worldwide. Unlike Starbucks, Dunkin Donuts does not own its stores. Instead, it relies on individuals to apply for franchises, to pay a franchise fee after the approval process, and pay royalties from ongoing operations.

To help keep track of its progress toward its franchise goal, Dunkin Donuts instituted a new dashboard-type software application that would tell it where deals were stalling, whether there were any deals in close proximity to one another, what the average cycle time was for closing a franchise deal, and the average size of the deals (Weier, 2007). Suppose that Dunkin Donuts found that the average cycle time was longer than expected or that the deals were stalling. What would its response be?

Given Dunkin Donuts sunk costs in its strategy, the first responses would certainly revolve around increasing the cycle time or determining why the deals were stalling. Its last response would probably be to question the whole strategy of opening new franchises and the underlying assumption about pent-up demand. This is certainly what happened to Starbucks.

Starbucks continued to open stores at a rapid rate even in the face of substantial decline in comparative-store sales, which measures how fast sales are growing at stores open at least a year (Wailgum, 2008). Starbucks' first response to the issue was to focus on the decline in sales. In 2007, it announced a set of strategic initiatives aimed at addressing the problem. It was going to move to new blends of coffees, replace existing espresso machines with new equipment, institute a customer rewards program, and open a new Web site. It was not until January 2008 that Starbucks realized that it needed to modify its growth strategy. Essentially, the new stores were cannibalizing sales at existing outlets. In response, Starbucks scaled back its growth plans, lowered its yearly targets for new store openings, retracted its long-term goal of opening 40,000 stores, and began closing unprofitable locations in the United States.

Discovery-Driven Planning

When a major company like Starbucks or Dunkin Donuts embarks on an enterprise-wide growth strategy, considerable effort is made to ensure that everyone is on board. When things go astray, a variety of biases often come into play, directly and indirectly putting pressure on employees to stick to the plan at all costs. Especially, in very competitive, well-publicized circumstances of this sort, there is a tendency for companies to experience:

- *Confirmation bias.* Embracing new information that confirms existing assumptions and rejecting information that challenges them.

- *Recency bias.* Forgetting that key assumptions were made in the first place, making it difficult to interpret or learn from unfolding experiences.
- *Winner's bias.* Overvaluing winning in competitive situations, even when the price exceeds the prize.
- *Social or political bias.* Sticking to a "public" plan, rather than admitting either ignorance or a mistake.

Part of the problem is that conventional planning processes of the sort used by Starbucks and Dunkin Donuts provide little in the way of probing or analyzing the underlying assumptions on which the plan is based. As an alternative to conventional planning, McGrath and MacMillan (2009) suggested that companies use discovery-driven planning. With most growth strategies, the outcomes are initially uncertain and unpredictable. They also rest on a variety of critical assumptions that will certainly change as the plan unfolds. As the strategic plan unfolds, the key is to reduce the "assumption-to-knowledge" ratio (turning assumptions into facts). This is the focus of discovery-driven planning. *Discovery-driven planning* (DDP) offers a systematic way to uncover problematic assumptions that otherwise remain unnoticed and unchallenged. It is called *discovery-driven* because as plans evolve new data are uncovered and new potentials are discovered.

DDP consists of a series of steps. Some are similar to conventional planning (e.g., establishing a growth strategy), whereas others are not. In the context of this discussion, three steps distinguish DDP from conventional planning:

1. *Reverse financials.* The first step is to use a set of financial documents to model how all the various assumptions in a plan affect one another and to determine as information is gained whether the plan is gaining traction or is at risk.
2. *Deliverables specification.* The second step is to lay out all the activities required to produce, sell, service, and deliver the product or service to the customer. Together, these activities represent the allowable costs.
3. *Assumption checklist.* All of the activities required to build a business rest on key assumptions. In this step, a written checklist

of each of the assumptions associated with the project deliverables laid out in step 2 is created.

Suppose you plan to open an upscale French restaurant and your goal is to break even the first year of operation (based on $2 million in sales). One question to ask is, "Is this a realistic sales number?" More specifically, "What activities would it take to generate $2 million in sales and do these activities make sense?"

One way to answer these questions is to consider the number of customers your restaurant will need to serve on a yearly basis and how much they will have to spend on average when they dine at your restaurant. In terms of the average spend per person, you could make a guess about the types of courses in an average meal (e.g., an appetizer, entrée) and the average cost of those courses, or you could look at the average bill at comparable restaurants. So, for instance, maybe the average meal at other high-end French restaurants in your region of the country is $120 to $150 per person.

Given these figures, you would need to serve somewhere between 13,333 and 16,667 customers a year, or between 44 and 56 customers a night. The question is: Do these figures make sense? Are they too optimistic? If so, you might need to adjust your goals. No matter what the answers are, you would still need to lay out all the other activities and associated costs needed to meet your specific goals.

Once a new growth plan is under way, DDP helps identify key checkpoints and assumption checklists that enable a company to assess not only their current performance but also the ongoing validity of the assumptions on which the plan was and is based. If Starbucks had employed DDP, they might have discovered the flaws in their growth strategy earlier.

Sources: Compiled from R. McGrath and I. MacMillan, *Discovery-Driven Growth*, Cambridge, MA, Harvard University Press, 2009; T. Wailgum, "How IT Systems Can Help Starbucks Fix Itself," *CIO*, January 25, 2008, **cio.com/article/176003/How_IT_Systems_Can_Help_Starbucks_Fix_Itself** (accessed July 2009); M. Weier, "Dunkin' Donuts Uses Business Intelligence in War Against Starbucks," *InformationWeek*, April 16, 2007.

Section 9.5 Review Questions

1. What are the critical questions that a monitoring framework answers?
2. What are the key elements of a diagnostic control system?
3. What is management by exception?
4. What is one of the major pitfalls of variance analysis, from a managerial perspective?

9.6 ACT AND ADJUST: WHAT DO WE NEED TO DO DIFFERENTLY?

Whether a company is interested in growing its business or simply improving its operations, virtually all strategies depend on new projects—creating new products, entering new markets, acquiring new customers or businesses, or streamlining some process. Most companies approach these new projects with a spirit of optimism rather than objectivity, ignoring the fact that most new projects and ventures fail. What is the chance of failure? Obviously, it depends on the type of project (Slywotsky and Weber, 2007). Hollywood movies have around a 60 percent chance of failure. The same is true for mergers and acquisitions. IT projects fail at the rate of 70 percent. For new food products, the failure rate is 80 percent. For new pharmaceutical products it is even higher, around 90 percent. Overall, the rate of failure for most new projects or ventures runs between 60 and 80 percent.

A project can fail in a number of different ways, ranging from considering too few options or scenarios, failing to anticipate a competitor's moves, ignoring changes in the economic or social environment, inaccurately forecasting demand, or underestimating the investment required to succeed, just to name a few of the possibilities. This is why it is critical for a company to continually monitor its results, analyze what has happened, determine why it has happened, and adjust its actions accordingly.

Reconsider Harrah's closed-loop marketing system discussed in the opening vignette. The system is depicted in Figure 9.4. As the figure indicates, the process has five basic steps:

1. The loop begins by *defining* quantifiable objectives of a marketing campaign or test procedure in the form of expected values or outcomes for customers who are in the experimental test group versus those in the control groups. The campaign is designed to provide the right offer and message at the right time. The selection of customers and their treatments are based on their prior experiences with Harrah's.

2. Next, the campaign or test is *executed*. The campaign is designed to provide the right offer and message at the right time. The selection of particular customers and the treatments they receive are based on their prior experiences with Harrah's.

3. Each customer's response to the campaign is *tracked*. Not only are response rates measured, but other metrics are as well, such as revenues generated by the incentive and whether the incentive induced a positive change in behavior (e.g., increased frequency of visit, profitability of the visit, or cross-play among the various casinos).

4. The effectiveness of a campaign is *evaluated* by determining the net value of the campaign and its profitability relative to other campaigns.

5. Harrah's *learns* which incentives have the most effective influence on customer behavior or provide the best profitability improvement. This knowledge is used to continuously refine its marketing approaches.

Over the years, Harrah's has run literally thousands of these tests. Although all five steps are critical, it is the fact that Harrah's is continually analyzing and adjusting its strategy to produce optimal results that sets it apart from its competitors.

Like Harrah's, most organizations spend an enormous amount of money and time developing plans, collecting data, and generating management reports. However, most of

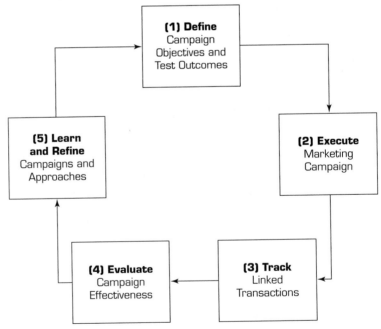

FIGURE 9.4 Harrah's Closed-Loop Marketing Model   *Source:* H. Watson and L. Volonino, "Harrah's High Payoff from Customer Information," *The Data Warehousing Institute Industry Study 2000–Harnessing Customer Information for Strategic Advantage: Technical Challenges and Business Solutions,* January 2001. **terry.uga.edu/~hwatson/Harrahs.doc** (accessed June 2009).

these organizations pale in comparison when it comes to performance management practices. As research from the Saxon Group has suggested (Axson, 2007):

> Most organizations are trying to manage increasingly volatile and complex processes with management practices that are more than half a century old. Detailed five year strategic plans, static annual budgets, calendar-driven reporting, and mind numbing detailed financial forecasts are largely ineffective tools for managing change, uncertainty, and complexity, yet for many organizations they remain the foundation for the management process.

The Saxon Group consulting firm is headed by David Axson, who was formerly with the Hackett Group, a global strategic advisory firm who is a leader in best practice advisory, benchmarking, and transformation consulting services. Axson has personally participated in well over 300 benchmarking studies. Between mid-2005 and mid-2006, the Saxon Group conducted surveys or working sessions with over 1,000 financial executives from North America, Europe, and Asia in an effort to determine the current state of the art with respect to business management. Companies from all major industry groups were represented. Approximately 25 percent of the companies had annual revenues of less than $500 million, 55 percent between $500 million and $5 billion, and 20 percent in excess of $5 billion.

The following is a summary of the Saxon Group's findings (Axson, 2007):

- Only 20 percent of the organizations utilized an integrated performance management system, although this was up from less than 10 percent just 5 years prior.
- Fewer than 3 out of 10 companies developed plans that clearly identified the expected results of major projects or initiatives. Instead, they focused on the wrong things. Financial plans did not show the expected costs and benefits of each initiative nor did they identify the total investment involved. Tactical plans failed to describe major initiatives to be undertaken.
- More than 75 percent of the information reported to management was historic and internally focused; less than 25 percent was predictive of the future or focused on the marketplace.
- The average knowledge worker spent less than 20 percent of his or her time focused on the so-called higher-value analytical and decision support tasks. Basic tasks such as assembling and validating data needed for higher-valued tasks consumed most of the average knowledge worker's time.

The overall impact of the planning and reporting practices of the average company was that management had little time to review results from a strategic perspective, decide what should be done differently, and act on the revised plans. The fact that there was little tie between a company's strategy, tactics, and expected outcomes (Axson, 2007):

> . . . leaves many organizations dangerously exposed when things do not turn out exactly as projected—which is most of the time. Without a clear understanding of the cause-and-effect relationships between tactics and objectives, you can have little confidence that today's actions will produce tomorrow's desired results. Best practice organizations do not necessarily develop better predictions or plans; however, they are far better equipped to quickly identify changes or problems, diagnose the root causes, and take corrective action.

Section 9.6 Review Questions

1. Why do 60 to 80 percent of all new projects or ventures fail?
2. Describe the basic steps in Harrah's closed-loop model.

3. According to the Saxon Group's research results, what are some of the performance management practices of the average company?

4. Why do few companies have time to analyze their strategic and tactical results and take corrective action based on this analysis?

9.7 PERFORMANCE MEASUREMENT

Underlying BPM is a performance measurement system. According to Simons (2002), **performance measurement systems**:

> Assist managers in tracking the implementations of business strategy by comparing actual results against strategic goals and objectives. A performance measurement system typically comprises systematic methods of setting business goals together with periodic feedback reports that indicate progress against goals.

All measurement is about comparisons. Raw numbers are rarely of little value. If you were told that a salesperson completed 50 percent of the deals he or she was working on within a month, that would have little meaning. Now, suppose you were told that the same salesperson had a monthly close rate of 30 percent last year. Obviously, the trend is good. What if you were also told that the average close rate for all salespeople at the company was 80 percent? Obviously, that particular salesperson needs to pick up the pace. As Simons's definition suggests, in performance measurement, the key comparisons revolve around strategies, goals, and objectives.

KPIs and Operational Metrics

There is a difference between a "run of the mill" metric and a "strategically aligned" metric. The term **key performance indicator (KPI)** is often used to denote the latter. A KPI represents a strategic objective and measures performance against a goal. According to Eckerson (2009), KPIs are multidimensional. Loosely translated, this means that KPIs have a variety of distinguishing features, including:

- *Strategy.* KPIs embody a strategic objective.
- *Targets.* KPIs measure performance against specific targets. Targets are defined in strategy, planning, or budget sessions and can take different forms (e.g., achievement targets, reduction targets, absolute targets).
- *Ranges.* Targets have performance ranges (e.g., above, on, or below target).
- *Encodings.* Ranges are encoded in software, enabling the visual display of performance (e.g., green, yellow, red). Encodings can be based on percentages or more complex rules.
- *Time frames.* Targets are assigned time frames by which they must be accomplished. A time frame is often divided into smaller intervals to provide performance mileposts.
- *Benchmarks.* Targets are measured against a baseline or benchmark. The previous year's results often serve as a benchmark, but arbitrary numbers or external benchmarks may also be used.

A distinction is sometimes made between KPIs that are "outcomes" and those that are "drivers." Outcome KPIs—sometimes known as *lagging indicators*—measure the output of past activity (e.g., revenues). They are often financial in nature, but not always. Driver KPIs—sometimes known as *leading indicators* or *value drivers*—measure activities that have a significant impact on outcome KPIs (e.g., sales leads).

In some circles, driver KPIs are sometimes called *operational KPIs*, which is a bit of an oxymoron (Hatch, 2008). Most organizations collect a wide range of operational metrics. As the name implies, these metrics deal with the operational activities and performance of a company. The following list of examples illustrates the variety of operational areas covered by these metrics:

- ***Customer performance.***   Metrics for customer satisfaction, speed and accuracy of issue resolution, and customer retention.
- ***Service performance.***   Metrics for service-call resolution rates, service renewal rates, SLA compliance, delivery performance, and return rates.
- ***Sales operations.***   New pipeline accounts, sales meetings secured, conversion of inquiries to leads, and average call closure time.
- ***Sales plan/forecast.***   Metrics for price-to-purchase accuracy, purchase order-to-fulfillment ratio, quantity earned, forecast-to-plan ratio, and total closed contracts.

Whether an operational metric is strategic or not depends on the company and its use of the measure. In many instances, these metrics represent critical drivers of strategic outcomes. For instance, Hatch (2008) recalls the case of a mid-tier wine distributor that was being squeezed upstream by the consolidation of suppliers and downstream by the consolidation of retailers. In response, it decided to focus on four operational measures: on-hand/on-time inventory availability, outstanding "open" order value, net-new accounts, and promotion costs and return on marketing investment (ROMI). The net result of its efforts was a 12 percent increase in revenues in 1 year. Obviously, these operational metrics were key drivers. However, as described in the following section, in many cases companies simply measure what is convenient with minimal consideration as to why the data is being collected. The result is a significant waste of time, effort, and money.

Problems with Existing Performance Measurement Systems

If you were to survey most companies today, you would have a hard time finding a company that would not claim that it had a performance measurement system (as opposed to a performance management system). The most popular system in use is some variant of Kaplan and Norton's balanced scorecard (BSC). Various surveys and benchmarking studies indicate that anywhere from 50 to over 90 percent of all companies have implemented some form of a BSC at one time or another. For example, every year since 1993 Bain & Company (Rigby and Bilodeau, 2009) has surveyed a broad spectrum of international executives to determine which management tools are in widespread use. The 2008 survey results were based on responses from over 1,400 executives. According to the survey, 53 percent of the companies indicated they were currently using a BSC. In most of these sorts of surveys, when the same executives are asked to describe their BSC, there seems to be some confusion about what constitutes "balance." There is no confusion for the originators of the BSC, Kaplan and Norton (1996):

> Central to the BSC methodology is a holistic vision of a measurement system tied to the strategic direction of the organization. It is based on a four-perspective view of the world, with financial measures supported by customer, internal, and learning and growth metrics.

Yet, as the Saxon Group found, the overwhelming majority of performance measures are financial in nature (65%), are focused on lagging indicators (80%), and are internal rather than external in nature (75%). What these companies really have is a "scorecard"— a set of reports, charts, and specialized displays that enable them to compare actual results with planned results for a miscellaneous collection of measures.

Calendar-driven financial reports are a major component of most performance measurement systems. This is no surprise. First, most of these systems are under the purview of the finance department. Second, most organizations (Saxon puts it at 67%) view the planning process as a financial exercise that is completed annually. Third, most executives place little faith in anything except financial or operational numbers. Research indicates that executives value a variety of different types of information (e.g., financial, operational, market, customer), but they think that outside the financial or operational arenas, most of the data are suspect, and they are unwilling to bet their jobs on the quality of that information.

The drawbacks of using financial data as the core of a performance measurement system are well known. Among the limitations most frequently cited are:

- Financial measures are usually reported by organizational structures (e.g., research and development expenses) and not by the processes that produced them.
- Financial measures are lagging indicators, telling what happened, not why it happened or what is likely to happen in the future.
- Financial measures (e.g., administrative overhead) are often the product of allocations that are not related to the underlying processes that generated them.
- Financial measures are focused on the short term and provide little information about the longer term.

Financial myopia is not the only problem plaguing many of the performance measurement systems in operation today. Measurement overload and measurement obliquity are also major problems confronting the current crop of systems.

It is not uncommon to find companies proudly announcing that they are tracking 200 or more measures at the corporate level. It is hard to imagine trying to drive a car with 200 dials on the dashboard. Yet, we seem to have little trouble driving companies with 200 dials on the corporate dashboard, even though we know that humans have major difficulty keeping track of more than a handful of issues and that anything else is simply shoved to the side. This sort of overload is exacerbated by the fact that companies rarely retire the measures they collect. If some new data or request for data comes along, it is simply added to the list. If the number of measures is 200 today, it will be 201 tomorrow, and 202 the day after that. Even though plans change and opportunities and problems come and go with increasing frequency, little effort is made to determine whether the list of measures being tracked is still applicable to the current situation.

For many of the measures being tracked, management lacks direct control. Michael Hammer (2003) called this the *principle of obliquity*. On the one hand, measures such as earnings per share (EPS), return on equity (ROE), profitability, market share, and customer satisfaction need to be monitored. On the other hand, these measures can only be pursued in an oblique fashion. What can be controlled are the actions of individual workers or employees. Unfortunately, the impact of any individual action on a corporate strategy or business unit strategy is negligible. What is required to tie the critical with the controllable is a strategic business model or methodology that starts at the top and links corporate goals and objectives all the way down to the bottom-level initiatives being carried out by individual performers.

Effective Performance Measurement

A number of books provide recipes for determining whether a collection of performance measures is good or bad. Among the basic ingredients of a good collection are the following:

- Measures should focus on key factors.
- Measures should be a mix of past, present, and future.
- Measures should balance the needs of shareholders, employees, partners, suppliers, and other stakeholders.
- Measures should start at the top and flow down to the bottom.
- Measures need to have targets that are based on research and reality rather than be arbitrary.

Online File W9.2 provides a more detailed methodology and a set of templates for making the determination.

As the section on KPIs notes, although all of these characteristics are important, the real key to an effective performance measurement system is to have a good strategy. Measures need to be derived from the corporate and business unit strategies and from an analysis of the key business processes required to achieve those strategies. Of course, this is easier said than done. If it were simple, most organizations would already have effective performance measurement systems in place, but they do not.

Application Case 9.2, which describes the Web-based KPI scorecard system at Expedia.com, offers insights into the difficulties of defining both outcome and driver KPIs and the importance of aligning departmental KPIs with overall company objectives.

APPLICATION CASE 9.2

Expedia.com's Customer Satisfaction Scorecard

Expedia, Inc., is the parent company to some of the world's leading travel companies, providing travel products and services to leisure and corporate travelers in the United States and around the world. It owns and operates a diversified portfolio of well-recognized brands, including Expedia.com, Hotels.com, Hotwire.com, TripAdvisor, Egencia, Classic Vacations, and a range of other domestic and international businesses. The company's travel offerings consist of airline flights, hotel stays, car rentals, destination services, cruises, and package travel provided by various airlines, lodging properties, car rental companies, destination service providers, cruise lines, and other travel product and service companies on a stand-alone and package basis. It also facilitates the booking of hotel rooms, airline seats, car rentals, and destination services from its travel suppliers. It acts as an agent in the transaction, passing reservations booked by its travelers to the relevant airline, hotel, car rental company, or cruise line. Together, these popular brands and innovative businesses make Expedia, Inc., the largest online travel agency in the world, the third largest travel company in the United States, and the fourth largest travel company in the world. Its mission is to become the largest and most profitable seller of travel in the world, by helping everyone everywhere plan and purchase everything in travel.

Problem

Customer satisfaction is key to Expedia's overall mission, strategy and success. Because Expedia.com is an online business, the customer's shopping experience is critical to Expedia's revenues. The online shopping experience can make or break an online business. It is also important that the customer's shopping experience is mirrored by a good trip experience. Because the customer experience is critical, all customer issues need to be tracked, monitored, and resolved as quickly as possible. Unfortunately, a few years back, Expedia lacked visibility into the "voice of the customer." It had no uniform way of measuring satisfaction, of analyzing the drivers of satisfaction, or of determining the impact of satisfaction on the company's profitability or overall business objectives.

Solution

Expedia's problem was not lack of data. The Customer Satisfaction group at Expedia knew that it had lots of data. In all, there were 20 disparate databases with 20 different owners. Originally, the group charged one of its business analysts with the task of pulling together and aggregating the data from these various sources into a number of key measures for satisfaction. The business analyst spent 2 to 3 weeks every month pulling and aggregating the data, leaving virtually no time for analysis. Eventually, the group realized that it wasn't enough to aggregate the data. The data needed to be viewed in the context of strategic goals, and individuals had to take ownership of the results.

To tackle the problem, the group decided it needed a refined vision. It began with a detailed analysis of the fundamental drivers of the department's performance and the link between this performance and Expedia's overall goals. Next, the group converted these drivers and links into a scorecard. This process involved three steps:

1. ***Deciding how to measure satisfaction.*** This required the group to determine which measures in the 20 databases would be useful for demonstrating a customer's level of satisfaction. This became the basis for the scorecards and KPIs.
2. ***Setting the right performance targets.*** This required the group to determine whether KPI targets had short-term or long-term payoffs. Just because a customer was satisfied with his or her online experience, does not mean that the customer was satisfied with the vendor providing the travel service.
3. ***Putting data into context.*** The group had to tie the data to ongoing customer satisfaction projects.

Figure 9.5 provides a technical overview of the system. The various real-time data sources are fed into a main database (called the Decision Support Factory). In the case of the Customer Satisfaction group, these include customer surveys, CRM systems, interactive voice response (IVR) systems, and other customer-service systems. The data in the DSS Factory are loaded on a daily basis into several data marts and multidimensional cubes. Users can access the data in a variety of ways that are relevant to their particular business needs.

Benefits

Ultimately, the Customer Satisfaction group came up with 10 to 12 objectives that linked directly to Expedia's corporate initiatives. These objectives were, in turn, linked to more than 200 KPIs within the Customer Satisfaction group. KPI owners can build, manage, and consume their own scorecards, and managers and executives have a transparent view of how well actions are aligning with the strategy. The scorecard also provides the Customer Satisfaction group with the ability to drill down into the data underlying any of the trends or patterns observed. In the past, all of this would have taken weeks or months to do, if it was done at all. With the scorecard, the Customer Service group can immediately see how well it is doing with respect to the KPIs, which, in turn, are reflected in the group's objectives and the company's objectives.

As an added benefit, the data in the system not only support the Customer Satisfaction group, but also other business units in the company. For example, a frontline manager can analyze airline expenditures on a market-by-market basis to evaluate negotiated

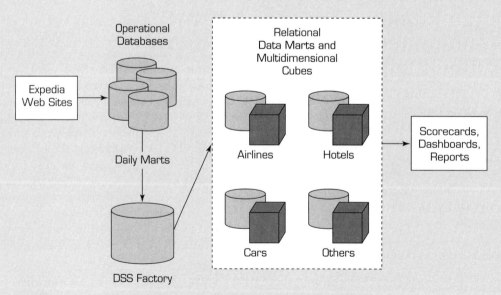

FIGURE 9.5 Expedia Scorecarding System

contract performance or determine the savings potential for consolidating spending with a single carrier. A travel manager can leverage the business intelligence to discover areas with high volumes of unused tickets or offline bookings and devise strategies to adjust behavior and increase overall savings.

Sources: Compiled from Microsoft, "Expedia: Scorecard Solution Helps Online Travel Company Measure the Road to Greatness," April 12, 2006, **microsoft.com/casestudies/Case_Study_Detail.aspx?CaseStudyID=49076** (accessed July 2009); R. Smith, "Expedia-5 Team Blog: Technology," April 5, 2007, **expedia-team5.blogspot.com** (accessed July 2009).

Section 9.7 Review Questions

1. What is a performance measurement system?
2. What is a KPI, and what are its distinguishing characteristics?
3. How does a KPI differ from an operational metric?
4. What are some of the drawbacks of relying solely on financial metrics for measuring performance?
5. What is the principle of obliquity?
6. What are some of the characteristics of a "good" collection of performance measures?

9.8 BPM METHODOLOGIES

There is more to performance measurement than simply keeping score. An effective performance measurement system should help do the following:

- Align top-level strategic objectives and bottom-level initiatives.
- Identify opportunities and problems in a timely fashion.
- Determine priorities and allocate resources based on those priorities.
- Change measurements when the underlying processes and strategies change.
- Delineate responsibilities, understand actual performance relative to responsibilities, and reward and recognize accomplishments.
- Take action to improve processes and procedures when the data warrant it.
- Plan and forecast in a more reliable and timely fashion.

A holistic or systematic performance measurement framework is required to accomplish these aims, as well as others. Over the past 40 or more years, various systems have been proposed. Some of them, such as activity-based costing (ABC) or management, are financially focused. Others, such as total quality management (TQM), are process oriented. In the discussion that follows, we examine two widely used approaches that support the basic processes underlying BPM: the balanced scorecard (see **thepalladiumgroup.com**) and Six Sigma (see **motorola.com/motorolauniversity.jsp**).

Balanced Scorecard (BSC)

Probably the best-known and most widely used performance management system is the balanced scorecard (BSC). Kaplan and Norton first articulated this methodology in their *Harvard Business Review* article "The Balanced Scorecard: Measures That Drive Performance," which appeared in 1992. A few years later, in 1996, these same authors produced a groundbreaking book—*The Balanced Scorecard: Translating Strategy into Action*—that documented how companies were using the BSC to not only supplement their financial measures with nonfinancial measures, but also to communicate and implement their strategies. Over the past few years, BSC has become a generic term (much like Coke or Xerox) that is used to represent virtually every type of scorecard application and implementation, regardless of whether it is balanced or strategic. In response to this bastardization of the term, Kaplan and Norton released a new book in 2000, *The Strategy-Focused Organization: How Balanced Scorecard Companies Thrive in the New Business Environment.* This book was designed to reemphasize the strategic nature of the BSC methodology. This was followed a few years later, in 2004, by *Strategy Maps: Converting Intangible Assets into Tangible Outcomes*, which describes a detailed process for linking strategic objectives to operational tactics and initiatives. Finally, their latest book, *The Execution Premium*, published in 2008, focuses on the strategy gap—linking strategy formulation and planning with operational execution.

THE MEANING OF BALANCE   From a high-level viewpoint, the **balanced scorecard (BSC)** is both a performance measurement and a management methodology that helps translate an organization's financial, customer, internal process, and learning and growth objectives and targets into a set of actionable initiatives. As a measurement methodology, BSC is designed to overcome the limitations of systems that are financially focused. It does this by translating an organization's vision and strategy into a set of interrelated financial and nonfinancial objectives, measures, targets, and initiatives. The nonfinancial objectives fall into one of three perspectives:

- *Customer.*   These objectives define how the organization should appear to its customers if it is to accomplish its vision.
- *Internal business process.*   These objectives specify the processes the organization must excel at in order to satisfy its shareholders and customers.
- *Learning and growth.*   These objectives indicate how an organization can improve its ability to change and improve in order to achieve its vision.

Basically, the three perspectives form a simple causal chain with "learning and growth" driving "internal business process" change which produces "customer" outcomes that are responsible for reaching a company's "financial" objectives. A simple chain of this sort is exemplified in Figure 9.6.

In BSC, the term *balance* arises because the combined set of measures are supposed to encompass indicators that are:

- Financial and nonfinancial
- Leading and lagging
- Internal and external
- Quantitative and qualitative
- Short term and long term

ALIGNING STRATEGIES AND ACTIONS   As a strategic management methodology, BSC enables an organization to align its actions with its overall strategies. BSC accomplishes this task through a series of interrelated steps. The specific steps that are involved vary from one book to the next. In their latest rendition, Kaplan and Norton (2008) lay out a six-stage process:

1. *Developing and formulating a strategy.*   Develop and clarify the organization's mission, values, and vision; identify through strategic analysis the internal and external forces impacting the strategy; and define the organization's strategic direction, specifying where and how the organization will compete.
2. *Planning the strategy.*   Convert statements of strategic direction into specific objectives, measures, targets, initiatives, and budgets that guide actions and align the organization for effective strategy execution.
3. *Aligning the organization.*   Ensure that business unit and support unit strategies are in line with the corporate strategy and that employees are motivated to execute the strategy.

4. **Planning the operations.** Ensure that the changes required by the strategy are translated into changes in operational processes and that resource capacity, operational plans, and budgets reflect the directions and needs of the strategy.

5. **Monitoring and learning.** Determine through formal operational review meetings whether short-term financial and operational performance are in line with specified targets and through strategy review meetings whether the overall strategy is being executed successfully.

6. **Testing and adapting the strategy.** Determine through strategy testing and adapting meetings whether the strategy is working, whether fundamental assumptions are still valid, and whether the strategy needs to be modified or adapted over time.

On the surface, these steps are very similar to the closed-loop BPM cycle depicted in Figure 9.1. This should not be a surprise, because the BSC methodology is a BPM methodology. However, one thing that distinguishes the BSC methodology from other methodologies is its use of two innovative tools that are unique to the methodology—strategy maps and balanced scorecards.

Strategy maps and balanced scorecards work hand-in-hand. A **strategy map** delineates the process of value creation through a series of cause-and-effect relationships among the key organizational objectives for all four BSC perspectives—financial, customer, process, and learning and growth. A balanced scorecard tracks the actionable measures and targets associated with the various objectives. Together, they help companies translate, communicate, and measure their strategies.

Figure 9.6 displays a strategy map and balanced scorecard for a fictitious company. It also includes the portfolio of initiatives designed to help the organization achieve its targets. From the map, we can see that the organization has four objectives across the four BSC perspectives. Like other strategy maps, this one begins at the top with a financial objective (i.e., increase net income). This objective is driven by a customer objective (i.e., increase customer retention). In turn, the customer objective is the result of an internal process objective (i.e., improve call center performance). The map continues down to the bottom of the hierarchy, where the learning objective is found (e.g., reduce employee turnover).

Each objective that appears in a strategy map has an associated measure, target, and initiative. For example, the objective "increase customer retention" might be measured by

	Strategy Map: Linked Objectives	Balanced Scorecard: Measures and Targets		Strategic Initiatives: Action Plans
Financial	Increase Net Income	Net income growth	Increase 25%	
Customer	Increase Customer Retention	Maintenance retention rate	Increase 15%	Change licensing and maintenance contracts
Process	Improve Call Center Performance	Issue turnaround time	Improve 30%	Standardized call center processes
Learning and Growth	Reduce Employee Turnover	Voluntary turnover rate	Reduce 25%	Salary and bonus upgrade

FIGURE 9.6 Strategy Map and Balanced Scorecard

"maintenance retention rate." For this measure, we might be targeting a 15 percent increase over last year's figures. One of the ways of accomplishing this improvement is by changing (simplifying) licensing and maintenance contracts.

Overall, strategy maps like the one in Figure 9.6 represent a hypothetical model of a segment of the business. When specific names (of people or teams) are assigned to the various initiatives, the model serves to align the bottom-level actions of the organization with the top-level strategic objectives. When actual results are compared with targeted results, a determination can be made about whether the strategy that the hypothesis represents should be called into question or whether the actions of those responsible for various parts of the hypothesis need to be adjusted.

The strategy map shown in Figure 9.6 is relatively simple and straightforward and only represents a segment of the business. Most strategy maps are more complex and cover a broader range of objectives. Because of these complexities, Kaplan and Norton have recently introduced the concept of "strategic themes." "Strategic themes split a strategy into several distinct value-creating processes." Each **strategic theme** represents a collection of related strategic objectives. For example, in Figure 9.6 this collection of objectives might be labeled "customer management." If the fictitious company represented by Figure 9.6 was also trying to increase net income by acquiring a competitor, then it might have a theme of "mergers and acquisitions." The idea behind strategic themes is to simplify the processes of formulating, executing, tracking, and adjusting a strategy.

Six Sigma

Since its inception in the mid-1980s, Six Sigma has enjoyed widespread adoption by companies throughout the world. For the most part, it has not been used as a performance management methodology. Instead, most companies use it as a process improvement methodology that enables them to scrutinize their processes, pinpoint problems, and apply remedies. In recent years, some companies, such as Motorola, have recognized the value of using Six Sigma for strategic purposes. In these instances, Six Sigma provides the means to measure and monitor key processes related to a company's profitability and to accelerate improvement in overall business performance. Because of its focus on business processes, Six Sigma also provides a straightforward way to address performance problems after they are identified or detected.

SIX SIGMA DEFINED   The history of Six Sigma dates to the late 1970s, although many of its ideas can be traced to earlier quality initiatives (see **en.wikipedia.org/wiki/Six_Sigma**). The term *Six Sigma* was coined by Bill Smith, an engineer at Motorola. In fact, Six Sigma is a federally registered trademark of Motorola. In the late 1970s and early to mid-1980s, Motorola was driven to Six Sigma by internal and external pressures. Externally, it was being beaten in the marketplace by competitors who were able to produce higher-quality products at a lower price. Internally, when a Japanese firm took over a U.S. Motorola factory that manufactured Quasar televisions and was able to produce TV sets with 1/20 the number of defects produced under regular operating procedures, Motorola executives had to admit that their quality was not good. In response to these pressures, Motorola's CEO, Bob Galvin, led the company down a quality path called Six Sigma. Since that time, hundreds of companies around the world, including General Electric, Allied Signal, DuPont, Ford, Merrill Lynch, Caterpillar, and Toshiba, have used Six Sigma to generate billions of dollars of top-line growth and bottom-line earnings improvement.

In Six Sigma, a business is viewed as a collection of processes. A *business process* is a set of activities that transform a set of inputs, including suppliers, assets, resources (e.g., capital, material, people), and information into a set of outputs (i.e., goods or services) for another person or process. Table 9.1 lists some categories of business processes that can affect overall corporate performance.

TABLE 9.1   Categories of Business Processes
Accounting and measurements
Administrative and facility management
Audits and improvements
Business planning and execution
Business policies and procedures
Global marketing and sales
Information management and analysis
Leadership and profitability
Learning and innovation
Maintenance and collaboration
Partnerships and alliances
Production and service
Purchasing and supply-chain management
Recruitment and development
Research and development

Source: P. Gupta, *Six Sigma Business Scorecard*, 2nd ed., McGraw Hill Professional, New York, 2006.

Sigma, σ, is a letter in the Greek alphabet that statisticians use to measure the variability in a process. In the quality arena, *variability* is synonymous with the number of defects. Generally, companies have accepted a great deal of variability in their business processes. In numeric terms, the norm has been 6,200 to 67,000 defects per million opportunities (DPMO). For instance, if an insurance company handles 1 million claims, then under normal operating procedures 6,200 to 67,000 of those claims would be defective (e.g., mishandled, have errors in the forms). This level of variability represents a 3- to 4-sigma level of performance. To achieve a Six Sigma level of performance, the company would have to reduce the number of defects to no more than 3.4 DPMO. Therefore, **Six Sigma** is a performance management methodology aimed at reducing the number of defects in a business process to as close to 0 DPMO as possible.

THE DMAIC PERFORMANCE MODEL   Six Sigma rests on a simple performance improvement model known as DMAIC. Like BPM, **DMAIC** is a closed-loop business improvement model, and it encompasses the steps of defining, measuring, analyzing, improving, and controlling a process. The steps can be described as follows:

1. ***Define.***   Define the goals, objectives, and boundaries of the improvement activity. At the top level, the goals are the strategic objectives of the company. At lower levels—department or project levels—the goals are focused on specific operational processes.
2. ***Measure.***   Measure the existing system. Establish quantitative measures that will yield statistically valid data. The data can be used to monitor progress toward the goals defined in the previous step.
3. ***Analyze.***   Analyze the system to identify ways to eliminate the gap between the current performance of the system or process and the desired goal.
4. ***Improve.***   Initiate actions to eliminate the gap by finding ways to do things better, cheaper, or faster. Use project management and other planning tools to implement the new approach.
5. ***Control.***   Institutionalize the improved system by modifying compensation and incentive systems, policies, procedures, manufacturing resource planning (MRP), budgets, operation instructions, or other management systems.

For new processes, the model that is used is called *DMADV* (define, measure, analyze, design, and verify). Traditionally, DMAIC and DMADV have been used primarily with operational issues. However, nothing precludes the application of these methodologies to strategic issues such as company profitability.

LEAN SIX SIGMA   In recent years there has been a focus on combining the Six Sigma methodology with the methodology known as **Lean Manufacturing**, *Lean Production,* or simply as *Lean* (see **en.wikipedia.org/wiki/Lean_manufacturing** for a summary of the methodology). The early concepts of lean date back to Henry Ford's use of mass production based on work flow. More recently, the concept has been associated with the production processes used by Toyota (which are known as the Toyota Production System). The term *Lean Production* was coined in 1988 by John Krafcik in an article entitled the "Triumph of the Lean Production System" published in the *Sloan Management Review* (Krafcik 1988) and based on his master's thesis at the Sloan School of Management at MIT. Before his stint at MIT, Krafcik was a quality engineer at a joint project between Toyota and General Motors.

Six Sigma and Lean Production both deal with quality. The two methodologies are compared in Table 9.2.

As Table 9.2 indicates, Lean focuses on the elimination of waste or non-value-added activities, whereas Six Sigma focuses on reducing the variation or improving the consistency of a process. From a Lean perspective, waste (or "muda") comes in a variety of forms (Six Sigma Institute, 2009):

- Overproduction ahead of demand
- Waiting for the next process step of information
- Transporting materials unnecessarily
- Over- and non-value-added processing
- Inventory that is more than bare minimum
- Unnecessary motion by employees
- Producing nonconforming parts

Lean can be applied to any sort of production or workflow, not just manufacturing. The goal is to examine the flow in order to eliminate waste. The following are some examples of waste that can arise in handling customer requests or complaints at a call center:

- Overproduction—sending all information to everyone
- Waiting—people waiting for information
- Transportation—call transfers to many operators
- Processing—excessive approvals for information release
- Inventory—caller awaiting to be answered
- Motion—retrieving printed instruction manual
- Defect—errors in information provided to callers

TABLE 9.2   Comparison of Lean Production with Six Sigma

Feature	Lean	Six Sigma
Purpose	Remove waste	Reduce variation
Focus	Flow focused	Problem focused
Approach	Many small improvements	Removing root causes
Performance measure	Reduced flow time	Uniform output
Results	Less waste with increased efficiency	Less variation with consistent output

Source: Compiled from P. Gupta, *Six Sigma Business Scorecard,* 2nd ed., McGraw-Hill Professional, New York, 2006.

What Lean adds to Six Sigma is speed (Poppendieck, 2009). It does this by eliminating non-value-added steps. Once the process flow consists only of value-added steps, Six Sigma can be used to ensure that those steps are performed as consistently as possible. For instance, in the call center example once the appropriate steps for retrieving printed instructions (motion) are identified, the next step would be to determine how the steps could be carried out in a consistent manner.

THE PAYOFF FROM SIX SIGMA   Six Sigma experts and pundits are quick to praise the methodology and point to companies such as General Electric (GE) and Honeywell as proof of its value. Jack Welch, the former CEO of GE who instituted the program back in 1995, publically stated that "Six Sigma helped drive operating margins to 18.9 percent in 2000 from 14.8 percent four years earlier." More recently, an earnings announcement from Caterpillar Inc. (2009) indicated that it will realize $3 billion in savings from its Six Sigma program. Others have pointed to companies like Home Depot as evidence that Six Sigma can also fail (Richardson, 2007). Home Depot's well-publicized adoption of Six Sigma was driven by its former CEO Robert Nardelli, who came from GE. When Home Depot's fortunes started to wane and it lost ground to its archrival Lowes, Nardelli departed the company and claims were made that Six Sigma hadn't panned out as promised. In the same vein, opponents of Six Sigma have noted that the framework works well if a company is solely interested in manufacturing efficiency. It does not work well if a company is interested in driving growth through innovation (Hindo, 2007). A statement by a Honeywell spokesman provides a more balanced view of the overall debate when he noted that "Six Sigma is not the end all be all. It is simply a set of process tools. We would never suggest that a company's performance is solely linked to the adoption of these tools" (Richardson, 2007).

Six Sigma is no different from any other business initiative. You make plans and develop metrics to evaluate the progress. When the deployment is not going as expected, you make adjustments. The following can dramatically increase the success of Six Sigma (Wurtzel, 2008):

- ***Six Sigma is integrated with business strategy.***   Six Sigma techniques are powerful in reducing process variation. Today, an increasing number of companies are implementing a Six Sigma approach to business excellence as part of the business strategy.
- ***Six Sigma supports business objectives.***   Successful deployments are based on some major business challenge or risk that the company can overcome only through Six Sigma. Identifying the challenge means all the company's business leaders are clear about why the company is adopting strategies based on Six Sigma principles.
- ***Key executives are engaged in the process.***   A company must involve all key business leaders in helping to design its Six Sigma deployment. Managers will never fully support Six Sigma if they view it as taking away from their resources rather than adding capability and helping them become more successful in achieving their goals; nor will they actively support it if they think it is eating up vital budgetary allotments rather than setting the stage for significant financial payback.
- ***Project selection process is based on value potential.***   The most effective Six Sigma companies have a rigorous project selection process driven by an evaluation of how much shareholder value a project can generate. It can be characterized as a trade-off decision comparing value delivered to effort expended.
- ***There is a critical mass of projects and resources.***   Some companies start their deployments by training a handful of people and launching a few "demonstration" projects. Others ramp-up for immediate corporate-wide deployment, training hundreds of Black Belts and launching dozens of projects within the first 6 months. In this context a Black Belt refers to an employee who is trained or certified in Six Sigma

and who devotes 100 percent of his or her time to the execution of a Six Sigma project. Either approach is workable, but for every company there is a critical level of Six Sigma effort.

- ***Projects-in-process are actively managed.*** Given that most companies want to generate measurable, significant results within 6 months or a year, the tendency is to push as many projects into the Lean Six Sigma deployment as possible. It is better to focus on getting a few high-potential projects done right than to just flood the workplace with dozens of less-important projects. With the right resources working on the right projects, learning and results are maximized by short cycle times.

- ***Team leadership skills are emphasized.*** Use of Six Sigma does involve some technical skills—the ability to process and analyze data, for example. But good leadership skills are even more important. This emphasis on leadership also relates to how a company chooses people to fill Black Belt roles. Placing the most promising people in the Black Belt role is painful at first, yet it yields fast results and a rapid transformation of the organization.

- ***Results are rigorously tracked.*** Six Sigma results should "pay as you go" and be confirmed by objective parties. Too many companies discount the necessity of having a reliable means to judge project results and impact, or they underestimate the difficulty in creating such a system. As a deployment is planned, a company must think in terms of leading measurements or key performance indicators of the potential financial results. At a minimum, project cycle times and project values must be measured on a regular basis and to gain an understanding of the level of variation in these numbers.

In an effort to increase the probability of success of their Six Sigma initiatives, some companies, such as Motorola and Duke University Hospital, have combined these initiatives with the BSC initiatives. In this way, their quality initiatives are directly tied to their strategic objectives and targets. In the same vein, Gupta (2006) developed a hybrid methodology called Six Sigma Business Scorecard that directly ties the process improvement aspects of Six Sigma to the financial perspective of the BSC. The benefits and structure of this combination are discussed in Technology Insights 9.1.

TECHNOLOGY INSIGHTS 9.1   BSC Meets Six Sigma

A recent book by Praveen Gupta (2006) entitled *Six Sigma Business Scorecard* provides a summary of the differences between the balanced scorecard and Six Sigma methodologies. This summary is shown in Table 9.3. In a nutshell, BSC is focused on improving strategy, whereas Six Sigma is focused on improving process.

Because of these differences, most companies have treated their BSC and Six Sigma implementations as separate initiatives. However, according to Stan Elbaum, senior vice president of research at Aberdeen Group in Boston, these are complementary programs. The true benefits of each cannot be achieved unless the two are integrated (Leahey, 2005). The BSC approach enables companies to quickly and accurately identify critical performance weaknesses and uncover opportunities for improvement and growth. What BSC has a hard time doing is showing how to fix the performance problems. In contrast, Six Sigma projects often flounder because project teams "bounce all over the organization looking for performance weaknesses or focusing attention on areas where improvements will yield only marginal returns" (Leahy, 2005, p. 48). The methodologies are complementary because BSC provides the strategic context for targeted improvement initiatives and Six Sigma can dig down to the underlying causes of a performance shortfall and provide solutions for closing the gap between targets and results.

A while back, a survey (Docherty, 2005) of companies that had adopted BSC or Six Sigma programs revealed that nearly half the programs had failed to break even in the first 3 years of adoption, but those that made them work had achieved substantial financial benefit. The

TABLE 9.3 Comparison of Balanced Scorecard and Six Sigma

Balanced Scorecard	Six Sigma
Strategic management system	Performance measurement system
Relates to the longer-term view of the business.	Provides snapshot of business's performance and identifies measures that drive performance toward profitability.
Designed to develop balanced set of measures.	Designed to identify a set of measurements that impact profitability.
Identifies measurements around vision and values.	Establishes accountability for leadership for wellness and profitability.
Critical management processes are to clarify vision/strategy, communicate, plan, set targets, align strategic initiatives, and enhance feedback.	Includes all business processes, management and operational.
Balances customer and internal operations without a clearly defined leadership role.	Balances management and employees' roles; balances costs and revenue of heavy processes.
Emphasizes targets for each measurement.	Emphasizes aggressive rate of improvement for each measurement, irrespective of target.
Emphasizes learning of executives based on the feedback.	Emphasizes learning and innovation at all levels based on the process feedback. Enlists all employees' participation.
Focuses on growth.	Focuses on maximizing profitability.
Heavy on strategic content.	Heavy on execution for profitability.
Management system consisting of measures.	Measurement system based on process management.

Source: Based on P. Gupta, *Six Sigma Business Scorecard,* 2nd ed., McGraw-Hill Professional, New York, 2006.

companies with the biggest net returns were those that had found a way to integrate the two methods. Integration was achieved by doing the following:

- ***Translating their strategy into quantifiable objectives.*** This was done by mapping the strategy and using a scorecard to monitor the associated metrics.
- ***Cascading objectives through the organization.*** They broke enterprise-wide goals into lower-level operational objectives by applying the causal reasoning underlying Six Sigma.
- ***Setting targets based on the voice of the customer.*** They used BSC and Six Sigma together to ensure that operational targets would directly impact customer expectations.
- ***Implementing strategic projects using Six Sigma.*** They used Six Sigma to drive improvements in product and process quality.
- ***Executing processes in a consistent fashion to deliver business results.*** They viewed the organization from a process perspective. Six Sigma was used to control process variation, and process measures were included in their BSC.

Companies that have successfully combined the two methodologies say that they can't understand why an organization would want to do one without the other. However, they also advise that it takes about a year to provide the necessary workforce training and to overcome existing cultural and organizational barriers.

Sources: Compiled from P. Gupta, *Six Sigma Business Scorecard,* 2nd ed., McGraw-Hill Professional, New York, 2006; P. Docherty, "From Six Sigma to Strategy Execution," 2005, **i-solutionsglobal.com/secure/ FromSixSigmaToStrateg_AAC8C.pdf** (accessed July 2009); and T. Leahy, "The One-Two Performance Punch." *Business Finance,* February 2005, **businessfinancemag.com/magazine/archives/article.html? articleID=14364** (accessed July 2009).

Section 9.8 Review Questions

1. What are the characteristics of an effective performance measurement system?
2. What are the four perspectives in BSC?
3. What does the term *balanced* refer to in BSC?
4. How does a BSC align strategies and actions?
5. What is a strategy map?
6. What is a strategic theme?
7. What does Six Sigma refer to?
8. What are the basic processes in the DMAIC model?
9. Compare Lean Production with Six Sigma.
10. What are some of the ways that the success of Six Sigma implementations is improved?
11. Compare BSC with Six Sigma.
12. How can BSC and Six Sigma be integrated?

9.9 BPM TECHNOLOGIES AND APPLICATIONS

At the beginning of this chapter, we defined *BPM* as an umbrella term covering the processes, methodologies, metrics, and technologies used by enterprises to measure, monitor, and manage business performance. Sections 9.3 through 9.8 examined the process, metrics, and methodologies. This section briefly describes the remaining element—the supporting technologies and applications. The discussion is brief, because many of the underlying technologies are covered by other chapters in the book (e.g., Chapter 8 on data warehousing).

BPM Architecture

The term **system architecture** refers to both the logical and physical design of a system. The *logical design* entails the functional elements of a system and their interactions. The *physical design* specifies how the logical design is actually implemented and deployed across a specific set of technologies, such as Web browsers, application servers, communication protocols, databases, and the like. From a physical standpoint, any particular BPM solution or implementation is likely to be quite complex. From a logical standpoint, they are usually quite simple. Logically speaking, a BPM system consists of three basic parts, or layers (see Figure 9.7). Included are:

- *BPM applications.* This layer supports the BPM processes used to transform user interactions and source data into budgets, plans, forecasts, reports, analysis, and the like. The particular applications used from one BPM implementation to the next will vary from organization to organization, depending on their specific needs and strategic focus. Any BPM solution should be flexible and extensible enough to allow an organization to find its own path, including decisions about which applications to include and when to roll them out. Practically speaking, however, there are some BPM applications that are used quite frequently. These applications are discussed momentarily.
- *Information hub.* Most BPM systems require data and information from a variety of source systems (e.g., ERP or CRM systems). The data and information can be accessed in a number of ways. However, in a well-designed BPM system, the data from these systems are usually mapped to and stored at a central location, typically a data warehouse or data mart.
- *Source systems.* This layer represents all of the data sources containing information fed into the BPM information hub. For most large enterprises this will include financial and other operational data from a variety of enterprise systems. Complete solutions will also access key external information, such as industry trends and competitor intelligence, to provide deeper context and insight into company performance. Rarely are source data accessed directly by the BPM applications. Typically, an ETL application, EAI application, or Web Services are used to move or connect the data to the information hub.

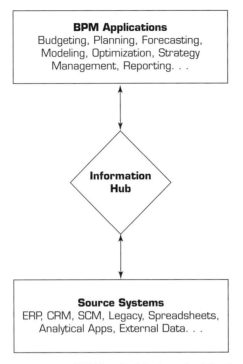

FIGURE 9.7 BPM Logical System Architecture

BPM APPLICATIONS In BPM, a wide variety of applications is needed to cover the closed-loop processes running from strategic planning to operational planning and budgeting to monitoring to adjustment and action. Despite the breadth of the processes, the industry analyst group Gartner contends that the majority of the processes can be handled by the following applications (see Chandler et al., 2009):

1. ***Strategy management.*** Strategy management applications provide a packaged approach to support strategic planning, modeling, and monitoring to improve corporate performance, accelerate management decision making, and facilitate collaboration. These solutions are usually tied to strategy maps or methodologies, such as the balanced scorecard. Strategy management can encompass capabilities for the following:

   - Creation and evaluation of high-level business plans using a "base case plus" or "initiative-based" approach, along with scenario modeling.
   - Initiative/goal management using project-management-like tools to enable responsible managers to execute specific tasks related to a strategy.
   - Scorecards and strategy maps to record strategies, objectives, and tasks; measure performance; and provide a collaborative environment for effective, enterprise-wide communication.
   - Dashboards (or cockpits) to aggregate and display metrics and KPIs so they can be examined at a glance before further exploration via additional BI tools.

   BPM suites should, at the very least, provide dashboard capabilities to help display performance information in a way that is easily understood by users. However, more-sophisticated organizations are implementing strategy maps (linked frameworks of KPIs) using scorecard software to link BPM to other aspects of PM. Strategy management is, therefore, becoming an increasingly important aspect of BPM suites.

2. ***Budgeting, planning, and forecasting.*** These applications support the development of all aspects of budgets, plans, and forecasts. They encompass short-term financially focused budgets, longer-term plans, and high-level strategic plans. These

applications should deliver workflow capabilities to manage budget/plan creation, submission, and approval, and they provide the facility to dynamically create forecasts and scenarios. They should also support the development of an enterprise-wide planning model that links operational plans to financial budgets. In addition, they must be capable of sharing data with domain-specific applications, such as supply-chain planning.

3. *Financial consolidation.* This type of application enables organizations to reconcile, consolidate, summarize, and aggregate financial data based on different accounting standards and federal regulations. These applications are a fundamental part of BPM because they create the audited, enterprise-level view of financial information that must be shared with other BPM applications to analyze variance from targets.

4. *Profitability modeling and optimization.* These applications include activity-based costing (ABC) applications that determine and allocate costs at a highly granular level and activity-based management applications that provide capabilities to enable users to model the impact on profitability of different cost and resource allocation strategies. Some applications have moved beyond the traditional ABC focus to enable revenue to be allocated in addition to costs for model packaging, bundling, pricing, and channel strategies.

5. *Financial, statutory, and management reporting.* BPM applications require specialized reporting tools that can format output as structured financial statements. They may also need to support specific generally accepted accounting principles (GAAP) presentation rules, such as U.S. GAAP or international financial reporting standards. They also include visualization techniques that are specifically designed to support the analysis of variance from budgets or targets, such as hyperbolic trees.

Commercial BPM Suites

The BPM market consists of those software companies offering suites with at least three of the core BPM applications (i.e., budgeting, planning, and forecasting; profitability modeling and optimization; scorecarding; financial consolidation; and statutory and financial reporting). According to estimates by Gartner (Chandler et al., 2009), the commercial software market for BPM suites in 2007 was approximately $1.8 billion in license fees and maintenance revenue. This represented a 19 percent increase from 2006. In contrast, the research firm International Data Corporation (IDC) estimated that the BPM application market was approximately $2 billion in 2007 and was expected to grow to $3.2 billion in 2012 (Vessette and McDonough, 2008). This is a growth rate of over 10 percent per annum.

The primary driver for this growth is that users continue to replace spreadsheet-based applications with more-robust analytics. BPM is relevant to every organization, regardless of industry sector, because all organizations need analytics (e.g., profitability analysis and performance to financial planning), as well as the management information (e.g., financial management reports, budgets, and statutory reports) to support the CFO and finance team and to deliver management information to the leadership team, which is one of the main areas of focus for BPM.

Over the past 3 to 4 years, the biggest change in the BPM market has been the consolidation of the BPM vendors. A few years back, the BPM market was dominated by the pure-play vendors Hyperion, Cognos, and SAS. This was before Oracle acquired Hyperion, IBM acquired Cognos, and SAP acquired Business Objects. Today, the market is dominated by the mega-vendors, including Oracle Hyperion, IBM Cognos, and SAP Business Objects. These mega-vendors, along with Infor and SAS, account for 70 percent of the BPM market.

TABLE 9.4 Gartner's Magic Quadrant

	Vision	
Execution	**Limited**	**Strong**
Strong	Challengers	Leaders
Limited	Niche	Visionaries

As they do with a number of the software markets that they follow, Gartner has established a *magic quadrant* for vendors of CPM suites (see Chandler et al., 2009). The quadrant positions companies in terms of their ability to execute (as a company) and the completeness of their visions. The combination of the two dimensions results in four categories of companies. Table 9.4 shows the CPM software vendors in each category. According to Gartner, Oracle Hyperion, SAP Business Objects, and IBM Cognos are all in the Leaders quadrant. This simply validates the fact that the mega-vendors lead the BPM market.

The fact that a suite is required to have at least three of the basic BPM applications in order to be considered for Gartner's magic quadrant means that the various suites provide similar sorts of capabilities. Table 9.5 provides a summary of the various applications associated with the three BPM suites in the Leaders quadrant.

TABLE 9.5 BPM Applications Provided by SAP, Oracle, and IBM

BPM Application	SAP Business Objects Enterprise Performance Management	Oracle Hyperion Performance Management	IBM Cognos BI and Financial Performance Management
Strategy Management	Strategy Management	Strategic Finance, Performance Scorecard	BI Scorecarding, BI Analysis
Budgeting, Planning, and Forecasting	Business Planning and Consolidation	Planning	Planning
Financial Consolidation	Financial Consolidation, Intercompany Reconciliation	Financial Management	Controller
Profitability Modeling and Optimization	Profitability and Cost Management	Profitability and Cost Management	
Financial, Statutory, and Management Reporting	Business Objects BI, XBRL Publishing	Performance Scorecard	BI Reporting, BI Scorecarding, BI Dashboards
Other BPM Applications	Spend Performance Management, Supply Chain Performance Management	Capital Asset Planning, Workforce Planning, Integrated Operational Planning	
Data Management Applications	Financial Information Management	Financial Data Quality Management, Data Relationship Management	DecisionStream

Sources: Compiled from **sap.com/solutions/sapbusinessobjects/large/enterprise-performance-management/index.epx** (accessed July 2009); **oracle.com/appserver/business-intelligence/hyperion-financial-performance-management/hyperion-financial-performance-management.html** (accessed July 2009); **ibm.com/software/data/cognos** (accessed July 2009).

Section 9.9 Review Questions

1. What is a logical system architecture?
2. What are the three key elements of a BPM architecture?
3. Describe the major categories of BPM applications.
4. What major change has occurred in the BPM market in the last 3 to 4 years?
5. What are the basic categories in Gartner's magic quadrant? Who are some of the vendors in the various categories?

9.10 PERFORMANCE DASHBOARDS AND SCORECARDS

Scorecards and dashboards are common components of most, if not all, performance management systems, performance measurement systems, and BPM suites. **Dashboards** and **scorecards** both provide visual displays of important information that is consolidated and arranged on a single screen so that information can be digested at a single glance and easily explored. A typical dashboard is shown in Figure 9.8. This particular dashboard displays a variety of KPIs for a hypothetical software company that produces specialized charting and visual display components for software developers. The company sells its products over the Web and uses banner ads placed at a handful of sites to drive traffic to the main Web page. From the dashboard, it is easy to see that the banner ad placed on "The Code House" site is driving the most traffic to its site and that "The Code House" has the highest percentage of click-throughs per impression (which in this case shows that every 100 times the software company's banner ad is displayed on "The Code House" site a little over two of the visitors will click the banner ad). Overall, the banner pipeline indicates that there have been over 205 million impressions. These have resulted in 2.2 million visits to the main page followed by 1.2 visits to the product pages and

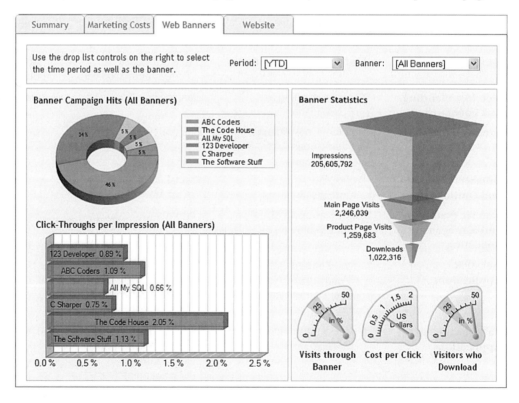

FIGURE 9.8 Sample Dashboard *Source:* Dundas Software, **dundas.com/Gallery/Flash/ Dashboards/index.aspx** (accessed July 2009).

eventually 1 million downloads. Finally, the gauges indicate that the percentage increase year-to-date (YTD) in "visits through banner(s)" and "visitors who download(ed)" have exceeded their targets (i.e., they are above shaded zones), and the cost-per-click is about $0.80. This particular dashboard enables end users to see the differences in the banner statistics and the metrics on the gauges by time period or product (the dropdowns on the upper right).

Dashboards Versus Scorecards

In the trade journals, the terms *dashboard* and *scorecard* are used almost interchangeably, even though as we saw in Table 9.4 the various BPM vendors usually offer separate dashboard and scorecard applications. Although dashboards and scorecards have much in common, there are differences between the two. On the one hand, executives, managers, and staff use scorecards to monitor strategic alignment and success with strategic objectives and targets. As noted, the best known example is the BSC. On the other hand, dashboards are used at the operational and tactical levels. Managers, supervisors, and operators use operational dashboards to monitor detailed operational performance on a weekly, daily, or even hourly basis. For example, this type of dashboard might be used to monitor production quality. In the same vein, managers and staff use tactical dashboards to monitor tactical initiatives. For example, this type of dashboard might be used to monitor a marketing campaign or sales performance.

Dashboard Design

Dashboards are not a new concept. Their roots can be traced at least to the EIS of the 1980s. Today, dashboards are ubiquitous. For example, a few years back Forrester Research estimated that over 40 percent of the largest 2,000 companies in the world use the technology (Ante and McGregor, 2006). The Dashboard Spy Web site (**dashboardspy.com/about**) provides further evidence of their ubiquity. The site contains descriptions and screenshots of thousands of BI dashboards, scorecards, and BI interfaces used by businesses of all sizes and industries, nonprofits, and government agencies. One of the more recent dashboards covered by the site—New York City's Citywide Performance Reporting System—is described in detail in the case at the end of the chapter.

According to Eckerson (2006), a well-known expert on BI in general and dashboards in particular, the most distinctive feature of a dashboard is its three layers of information:

1. ***Monitoring.*** Graphical, abstracted data to monitor key performance metrics.
2. ***Analysis.*** Summarized dimensional data to analyze the root cause of problems.
3. ***Management.*** Detailed operational data that identifies what actions to take to resolve a problem.

Because of these layers, dashboards pack of lot of information into a single screen. According to Few (2005), "The fundamental challenge of dashboard design is to display all the required information on a single screen, clearly and without distraction, in a manner that can be assimilated quickly." Online File W9.3 details part of this challenge. For the most part, dashboards display quantitative measures of what's going on. To speed assimilation of the numbers, the numbers need to be placed in context. This can be done by comparing the numbers of interest to other baseline or target numbers, by indicating whether the numbers are good or bad, by denoting whether a trend is better or worse, and by using specialized display widgets or components to set the comparative and evaluative contexts.

One way to place numbers in context is through comparison. By itself, a number has little meaning. If someone tells you that a company's sales revenue was $20 million for the past quarter, it is hard to determine what that means in terms of the company's performance. However, if someone tells you that the company budgeted $25 million for the quarter or that last year it made $30 million for the same quarter, this puts the numbers in a different light. Given these comparisons, you could probably surmise that the company's performance is not where the company wants it to be. Some of the common comparisons that are typically made in a BPM system include comparisons against past values, forecasted values, targeted values, benchmark or average values, multiple instances of the same measure, and the values of other measures (e.g., revenues vs. costs). In Figure 9.8, the various KPIs are set in context by comparing them with targeted values, the revenue figure is set in context by comparing it with marketing costs, and the figures for the various stages of the sales pipeline are set in context by comparing one stage with another.

Even with comparative measures, it is important to specifically point out whether a particular number is good or bad and whether it is trending in the right direction. Without these sorts of evaluative designations, it can be time-consuming to determine the status of a particular number or result. Typically, either specialized visual objects (e.g., traffic lights) or visual attributes (e.g., color coding) are used to set the evaluative context. Again, for the dashboard in Figure 9.8, color coding is used with the gauges to designate whether the KPI is good or bad, and green up arrows are used with the various stages of the sales pipeline to indicate whether the results for those stages are trending up or down and whether up or down is good or bad. Although not used in this particular example, additional colors—red and orange, for instance—could be used to represent other states on the various gauges.

What to Look for in a Dashboard

Although performance dashboards and standard performance scorecards differ, they do share some of the same characteristics. First, they both fit within the larger BPM or performance measure system. This means that their underlying architecture is the BI or performance management architecture of the larger system. Second, all well-designed dashboards and scorecards possess the following characteristics (Novell, 2009):

- They use visual components (e.g., charts, performance bars, sparklines, gauges, meters, stoplights) to highlight, at a glance, the data and exceptions that require action.
- They are transparent to the user, meaning that they require minimal training and are extremely easy to use.
- They combine data from a variety of systems into a single, summarized, unified view of the business.
- They enable drill-down or drill-through to underlying data sources or reports, providing more detail about the underlying comparative and evaluative context.
- They present a dynamic, real-world view with timely data refreshes, enabling the end user to stay up-to-date with any recent changes in the business.
- They require little, if any, customized coding to implement, deploy, and maintain.

Section 9.10 Review Questions

1. What are the major differences between a scorecard and a dashboard?
2. What distinguishes an operational dashboard from a tactical dashboard?
3. What layers of information are provided by a dashboard?
4. What criteria are important in selecting the particular display widgets to use with particular metrics on a dashboard?
5. What are the characteristics of a well-designed dashboard?

Chapter Highlights

- BPM refers to the processes, methodologies, metrics, and technologies used by enterprises to measure, monitor, and manage business performance.
- BPM is an outgrowth of BI, and it incorporates many of its technologies, applications, and techniques.
- BI has become the term describing the technology used to access, analyze, and report on data relevant to an enterprise.
- BI practices and software are almost always part of an overall BPM solution.
- The primary difference between BI and BPM is that BPM is always strategy driven.
- BPM encompasses a closed-loop set of processes that link strategy to execution in order to optimize business performance.
- The key processes in BPM are strategize, plan, monitor, act, and adjust.
- Strategy answers the question "Where do we want to go in the future?"
- Decades of research highlight the gap between strategy and execution.
- The gap between strategy and execution is found in the broad areas of communication, alignment, focus, and resources.
- Operational and tactical plans address the question "How do we get to the future?"
- The tactics and initiatives defined in an operational plan need to be directly linked to key objectives and targets in the strategic plan.
- An organization's strategic objectives and key metrics should serve as top-down drivers for the allocation of the organization's tangible and intangible assets.
- Monitoring addresses the question of "How are we doing?"
- BSC, performance dashboards, project monitoring systems, human resources systems, and financial reporting systems are all examples of diagnostic control systems.
- Most monitoring focuses on negative variances and pays little attention to underlying assumptions or strategies.
- Conventional planning suffers from a number of biases, including confirmation, recency, winner's, and social or political biases.
- Discovery-driven planning provides a way to systematically uncover problematic assumptions that otherwise remain unnoticed or unchallenged in the planning and monitoring processes.
- The failure rate for new projects and ventures runs between 60 and 80 percent.

- The overall impact of the planning and reporting practices of the average company is that management has little time to review results from a strategic perspective, decide what should be done differently, and act on the revised plans.
- Performance measurement systems assist managers in tracking the implementation of business strategy by comparing actual results against strategic goals and objectives.
- The drawbacks of using financial data as the core of a performance measurement system are well known.
- There is a difference between a "run of the mill" metric and a "strategically aligned" metric.
- Performance measures need to be derived from the corporate and business unit strategies and from an analysis of the key business processes required to achieve those strategies.
- Probably the best-known and most widely used performance management system is the BSC.
- Central to the BSC methodology is a holistic vision of a measurement system tied to the strategic direction of the organization.
- As a measurement methodology, BSC is designed to overcome the limitations of systems that are financially focused.
- Calendar-driven financial reports are a major component of most performance measurement systems.
- As a strategic management methodology, BSC enables an organization to align its actions with its overall strategies.
- In BSC, strategy maps provide a way to formally represent an organization's strategic objectives and the causal connections among them.
- Most companies use Six Sigma as a process improvement methodology that enables them to scrutinize their processes, pinpoint problems, and apply remedies.
- Six Sigma is a performance management methodology aimed at reducing the number of defects in a business process to as close to zero DPMO as possible.
- Six Sigma uses DMAIC, a closed-loop business improvement model that involves the steps of defining, measuring, analyzing, improving, and controlling a process.
- In recent years, there has been a focus on combining the Six Sigma methodology with the Lean strategy.
- Lean focuses on the elimination of waste or non-value-added activities, whereas Six Sigma focuses on reducing the variation or improving the consistency of a process.

- Substantial performance benefits can be gained by integrating BSC and Six Sigma.
- The standard BPM architecture is multilayered and consists of BPM applications, an information hub, and data from a variety of source systems.
- The major BPM applications include strategy management; budgeting, planning, and forecasting; financial consolidation; profitability analysis and optimization; and financial, statutory, and management reporting.
- Over the past 3 to 4 years, the biggest change in the BPM market has been the consolidation of the BPM vendors.

- Scorecards and dashboards are common components of most, if not all, performance management systems, performance measurement systems, and BPM suites.
- Although scorecards and dashboards both provide visual displays of performance, there are significant differences between them.
- The most distinctive feature of a dashboard is its three layers: monitoring, analysis, and management.
- The fundamental challenge of dashboard design is to display all the required information on a single screen, clearly and without distraction, in a manner that can be assimilated quickly.

Key Terms

balanced scorecard (BSC) *396*
business performance management (BPM) *378*
critical success factor (CSF) *380*

dashboard *408*
diagnostic control system *384*
DMAIC *399*
key performance indicator (KPI) *390*
Lean Manufacturing *400*

operational plan *382*
performance measurement system *390*
scorecard *408*
Six Sigma *399*
strategic goal *381*

strategic objective *381*
strategic theme *398*
strategic vision *381*
strategy map *397*
system architecture *404*

Questions for Discussion

1. SAP uses the term *strategic enterprise management* (SEM), Cognos uses the term *corporate performance management* (CPM), and Hyperion uses the term *business performance management* (BPM). Are they referring to the same basic ideas? Provide evidence to support your answer.

2. BPM encompasses five basic processes: strategize, plan, monitor, act, and adjust. Select one of these processes and discuss the types of software tools and applications that are available to support it. Figure 9.1 provides some hints. Also, refer to Bain & Company's list of management tools for assistance (**bain.com/management_tools/home.asp**).

3. Select a public company of interest. Using the company's 2008 annual report, create three strategic financial objectives for 2009. For each objective, specify a strategic goal or target. The goals should be consistent with the company's 2008 financial performance.

4. Netflix's strategy of moving to online video downloads has been widely discussed in a number of articles that can be found online. What are the basic objectives of Netflix's strategy? What are some of the major assumptions underlying the strategy? Given what you know about discovery-driven planning, do these assumptions seem reasonable?

5. In recent years, the Beyond Budgeting Round Table (BBRT; **bbrt.org**) has called into question traditional budgeting practices. A number of articles on the Web discuss the BBRT's position. In the BBRT's view, what is

wrong with today's budgeting practices? What does the BBRT recommend as a substitute?

6. Describe how a BSC fits the description of a diagnostic control system.

7. Distinguish performance management and performance measurement.

8. The EFQM "excellence model" provides an alternative performance measurement and management framework. First, what does EFQM stand for? Second, using materials from the Web, discuss the major tenets of the framework. Compare the framework to BSC and Six Sigma.

9. Create a measure for some strategic objective of interest (you can use one of the objectives formulated in Discussion Question 3). For the selected measure, complete the measurement template found in Table W9.2.1 in the online file for this chapter.

10. Create a strategy for a hypothetical company, using the four perspectives of the BSC. Express the strategy as a series of strategic objectives. Produce a strategy map depicting the linkages among the objectives.

11. Compare and contrast the DMAIC model with the closed-loop processes of BPM.

12. In addition to SAP, Oracle, and IBM, SAS, Infor, and Exact Software appear in Gartner's magic quadrant (Table 9.4). What terms do these companies use to describe their BPM suites. Compare and contrast their offerings in terms of BPM applications and functionality.

Exercises

TERADATA STUDENT NETWORK (TSN) AND OTHER HANDS-ON EXERCISES

1. Go to **teradatastudentnetwork.com**. Select the "Articles" content type. Browse down the list of articles and locate one entitled "Business/Corporate Performance Management: Changing Vendor Landscape and New Market Targets." Based on the article, answer the following questions
   a. What is the basic focus of the article?
   b. What are the major "take aways" from the article?
   c. In the article, which organizational function and role are most intimately involved in CPM?
   d. Which applications are covered by CPM?
   e. How are these applications similar to or different from the applications covered by Gartner's CPM?
   f. What is GRC, and what is its link to corporate performance?
   g. What are some of the major acquisitions that occurred in the CPM marketplace over the last couple of years?
   h. Select two of the companies discussed by the article (not SAP, Oracle, or IBM). What are the CPM strategies of each of the companies? What do the authors think about these strategies?

2. Go to **teradatastudentnetwork.com**. Select the "Case Studies" content type. Browse down the list of cases and locate one entitled "Real-Time Dashboards at Western Digital." Based on the article, answer the following questions:
   a. What is VIS?
   b. In what ways is the architecture of VIS similar to or different from the architecture of BPM?
   c. What are the similarities and differences between the closed-loop processes of BPM and the processes in the OODA decision cycle?
   d. What types of dashboards are in the system? Are they operational or tactical, or are they actually scorecards? Explain.
   e. What are the basic benefits provided by WD's VIS and dashboards?
   f. What sorts of advice can you provide to a company that is getting ready to create its own VIS and dashboards?

3. Go to Stephen Few's blog the Perceptual Edge (**perceptualedge.com**). Go to the section of "Examples." In this section, he provides critiques of various dashboard examples. Read a handful of these examples. Now go to **dundas.com**. Select the "Gallery" section of the site. Once there, click the "Digital Dashboard" selection. You will be shown a variety of different dashboard demos. Run a couple of the demos.
   a. What sorts of information and metrics are shown on the demos? What sorts of actions can you take?
   b. Using some of the basic concepts from Few's critiques, describe some of the good points and bad design points of the demos.

4. Develop a prototype dashboard to display the financial results of a public company. The prototype can be on paper or use Excel. Use data from the 2008 annual plans of two public companies to illustrate the features of your dashboard.

TEAM ASSIGNMENTS AND ROLE-PLAYING

1. Virtually every BPM/CPM vendor provides case studies on their Web sites. As a team, select two of these vendors (you can get their names from the Gartner or AMR lists). Select two case studies from each of these sites. For each, summarize the problem the customer was trying to address, the applications or solutions implemented, and the benefits the customer received from the system.

2. Go to the Dashboard Spy Web sitemap for executive dashboards (**enterprise-dashboard.com/sitemap**). The site provides a number of examples of executive dashboards. As a team, select a particular industry (e.g., health care, banking, airlines). Locate a handful of example dashboards for that industry. Describe the types of metrics found on the dashboards. What types of displays are used to provide the information? Using what you know about dashboard design, provide a paper prototype of a dashboard for this information.

INTERNET EXERCISES

1. A survey conducted by Economist Intelligence Unit and reported in S. Taub, "Closing the Strategy-to-Performance Gap," *CFO Magazine*, February 22, 2005 (**cfo.com/article. cfm/3686974?f=related**), explores the relationship between strategy development and execution. Based on the survey, which is more important for performance management—strategy development or execution? What reasons do respondents give for poor execution? In what ways do respondents think they can improve performance?

2. Go to the NYC Citywide Performance Report site (**nyc.gov/html/ops/cpr/html/home/home**). The performance reports are organized by "Themes" (see this case at the end of the chapter). Use the site to answer the following questions:
   a. How many performance indicators are there for the whole city? For community service? For education?
   b. Overall, how many of the indicators are improving or are stable? Declining?
   c. How many of the education performance indicators are improving or stable? Declining?
   d. Select "Citywide Themes" (on the upper left). One of the themes is "Social Services." Select this theme. Now select "View the performance report for Social Services." How many social service indicators are there? How many are declining by more than 10 percent? What are some of these indicators that are declining? How can NYC use this specific information to address the problem tracked by the performance indicator?

3. One of the more famous BSCs is the one created by Southwest Airlines to manage its business. An earlier article by Anthes provides a strategy map of the system (see

computerworld.com/action/article.do?command=
viewArticleBasic&articleId=78512). Retrieve the article. Using the strategy map, describe this segment of
Southwest's strategy. What major measures and targets is
Southwest using to track its performance against its strategic objectives? Based on what you know about today's
economy in general and the airline industry specifically,
do you think this strategy will work in today's world?

4. Annually, TDWI (The Data Warehouse Institute) identifies
and honors companies that have demonstrated excellence
(i.e., best practices) in developing, deploying, and maintaining business intelligence and data warehousing applications. Go to the Web page with the 2008 winners
(**tdwi.org/research/display.aspx?id=9000**). What categories does TDWI honor? Who were some of the winners?
What were some of the reasons that they won their particular award?

5. A number of Web sites provide examples and directions
for creating executive dashboards and executive balanced
scorecards. Using some of the capabilities described by
these sites, create an Excel prototype of each.

6. A recent white paper titled "Business Intelligence and
Enterprise Performance Management: Trends for Midsize
Companies" by Oracle (see **oracle.com/appserver/busi-
ness-intelligence/hyperion-financial-performance-
management/docs/bi-epm-trends-for-emerging-busi-
nesses.pdf**) compares the BI and performance management
practices of middle-sized and large-sized companies. First,
in the survey, what is a middle-sized company? Second,
what sorts of practices are they surveying? Based on
the survey results, what are some of the similarities and
differences between the practices of the two types of
companies? What conclusions and advice do they give to
vendors?

END OF CHAPTER APPLICATION CASE

Tracking Citywide Performance

Massive systems produce massive amounts of metrics. The challenge is to determine how to slice the
data in ways that benefit users rather than confuse
them, especially when the users have a wide variety
of experiences with information technologies. This
was one of the major issues facing New York City
when it decided to develop its Citywide Performance
Reporting (CPR) Online System, an interactive dashboard providing agencies and citizens with "user-
friendly access to the most critical performance
indicators for every city agency, with monthly
updates and automatic evaluation of trends within
specified program areas."

Development of CPR

CPR is part of NYCStat (**nyc.gov/html/ops/nycstat/
html/home/home.shtml**). NYCStat is New York
City's one-stop-shop for all essential data,
reports, and statistics related to city services.
NYCStat provides access to a wide variety of
performance-related information, including citywide
and agency-specific information, 311-related data,
and interactive mapping features for selected
performance data and quality-of-life indicators.

CPR was launched in February 2008. Initial
plans for CPR were developed by the Mayor's Office
of Operations in concert with the Department of
Information Technology and Communications

(DoITT) in mid-2005 (NYCStat, 2009). The project
had three components:

- *Performance management application.* A
backend computer system providing a single
point of access for agencies to input data.
- *Analytics tool/dashboard.* The frontend
system to provide standardized reporting format with drill-down capabilities, performance
summaries, and trend graphics.
- *Data definition.* Review and identification
of the topics measures and critical indicators to
be included in the CPR system for 44 mayorial
agencies.

Development of these components continued
through July 2007. At this time, the system was
opened to the 44 agencies and the mayor's office for
review. At the end of the summer, Mayor Bloomberg
directed that the system be made available to the
public through the city's NYC.gov Web site as soon as
possible. Subsequent work on the system focused on
making the dashboard as easy and flexible as possible for public use. The system was finally opened on
February 14, 2008, as part of the release of the
Preliminary Fiscal 2008 Mayor's Management Report.

Refining Metrics

CPR is an offshoot of the Mayor's Management
Report (MMR), an annual evaluation of the city's

agencies that measures 1,000 performance indicators, including everything from grade school test scores to the time it takes to fix a pothole. Rather than simply providing an online version of the MMR, the CPR required the agencies to take a fresh look at the services they were delivering and how best to measure the outcomes of those services. Initially, this resulted in thousands of measures, many of which did not exist at the time. Eventually, the list of initial measures was reduced to 525 critical measures. The majority of these measures represent final outcomes of services that directly impact the city's residents. This is why the decision was made to open up the system to the public.

In addition to refining the measures, other key decisions had to be made. Because data was available by month, year-to-date, and full year, choices had to be made about how to best slice and dice the data and make comparisons across the various periods. Decisions also had to be made on how to measure and present trends and performance against preset targets—designating the desired direction of each measure and thresholds for good and bad performance. Finally, because the total number of measures and agencies was so large and none of the public was likely to be familiar with each of the individual agencies, the presentation and navigation needed to be simplified. The developers decided to categorize the measures into eight citywide "themes" that captured the way that the city government serves the people who work and live in New York City. The themes included: citywide administration, community services, economic development and business affairs, infrastructure, education, legal affairs, public safety, and social services.

Impact of CPR

From the viewpoint of the mayor's office, CPR improves performance management in three ways—accountability, transparency, and accessibility. It does this by providing the following capabilities (NYCStat, 2009):

- Tracks performance for the most important "outcome" measures that directly reflect how the lives of the public are affected by city government.
- Measures performance by comparing current data to prior data for the year before, thereby holding agencies accountable for year-over-year improvements.
- Highlights agency performance through graphs and color coding, making positive or negative performance trends immediately obvious.
- Drill-down capability, allowing users to review comparative trends over a 5-year period.
- Aggregates important measures into citywide themes, which cut across agency silos and disciplines to reveal the overall picture about city government performance.
- Updates each measure monthly, quarterly, or annually so that the most recent data is always available.
- Offers the ability to download data in a variety of formats for more detailed review and analysis.
- Provides detailed information about each measure, including an explanation of what the measure means, its reporting frequency, and other useful details.

In March 2009, the CPR system was recognized by the Ash Institute for Democratic Governance and Innovation at the JFK School of Government at Harvard University as one of the Top 50 Government Innovations for the year (*New York Non-Profit Press,* 2009).

Lessons Learned

According to Sarlin, "It is interesting to see how government agencies at all levels are implementing best practices to be more run like a business." In the case of New York City's Mayor's Office of Operations you might expect this, because Mayor Bloomberg comes from the world of business, more specifically, the world of real-time financial information (see **bloomberg.com**). However, other government agencies have announced online dashboards even though they have virtually no connection with business. For instance, the new U.S. CIO Vivek Kundra recently announced the U.S. Federal IT Dashboard, which provides public access to data reported to the Office of Management and Budget (OMB), including general information on over 7,000 federal IT investments and detailed data for nearly 800 of these investments classified as "major." Mr. Kundra has spent his entire career in government positions.

These efforts suggest that business may be able to learn quite a bit from these initiatives.

These government dashboard initiatives demonstrate the following (Buytendijk, 2008):

- ***Transparency makes a difference.*** These initiatives provide widespread, public access to large collections of performance data. Many businesses could learn from the depth and breadth of the information these agencies are sharing.
- ***Importance of collaboration.*** Many BI projects suffer from a silo approach, with different departments doing their own dashboards or scorecards. Each department may realize a short-term ROI. However, the combination will be suboptimal and is not likely to lead to an overall ROI. Both the CPR dashboard and the federal IT dashboard show that it is possible to create an organization-wide initiative spanning multiple domains.
- ***Continuous improvement.*** CPR is based on trends, not targets. This means that the performance indicators are aimed at continuous improvement instead of static goals. It sets a good example for how an operational or tactical dashboard should look.

Questions for the Case

1. What are the major components of the CPR dashboard?
2. How many agencies were involved in the definition and implementation of the CPR dashboard?
3. What were the major steps used in defining and implementing the CPR?
4. What role did "themes" play in the CPR dashboard?
5. What are the major capabilities of the CPR dashboard?
6. What can businesses learn from a government initiative like the CPR?

Sources: Compiled from NYCStat, "CPR Fact Sheet," Mayor's Office of Operations, February 2009, **nyc.gov/html/ops/cpr/ downloads/pdf/cpr_fact_sheet.pdf** (accessed July 2009); B. Sarlin, "Mayor Unveils Web Database Tracking Performance," *New York Sun*, February 15, 2008, **nysun.com/new-york/ mayor-unveils-web-database-tracking-performance/71347/ ?print=5119866421** (accessed July 2009); F. Buytendijk, "The Mother of All Accountability Tools," February 20, 2008, **blogs.oracle.com/frankbuytendijk/2008/02/the_mother_ of_all_ accountabili.htm** (accessed July 2009); *New York Non-Profit Press*, "Eight NYC Programs Among 50 Selected for National Honors," March 31, 2009, **nynp.biz/index.php/ breaking-news/620-eight-nyc-programs-among-50-selected-for-national-honors-** (accessed July 2009); J. Hiner, "U.S. Federal IT Dashboard is a Great Example of How to Promote IT," July 1, 2009, **blogs.zdnet.com/BTL/?p=20157** (accessed July 2009).

References

Ante, S., and J. McGregor. (2006, February 13). "Giving the Boss the Big Picture." *BusinessWeek.* **businessweek .com/magazine/content/06_07/b3971083.htm** (accessed July 2009).

Axson, D. (2007). *Best Practices in Planning and Performance Management: From Data to Decisions.* New York: Wiley.

Buytendijk, F. (2008, February 20). "The Mother of All Accountability Tools." **blogs.oracle.com/frankbuytendijk/ 2008/02/the_mother_of _all_accountabili.html** (accessed July 2009).

Calumo Group. (2009, January 30). "Planning on Microsoft BI Platform." **calumo.com/newsblog** (accessed June 2009).

Caterpillar. (2009, September). "Caterpillar Inc. Announces 2Q 2009 Results." *Caterpillar Press Release.* **cat.com/cda/ components/fullArticleNoNav?m=37523&x=7&id= 1654623** (accessed September 2009).

Chandler, N., N. Rayner, J. Van Decker, and J. Holincheck. (2009, April 30). "Magic Quadrant for Corporate Performance Management Suites." *Gartner RAS Core Research Note G00165786.* **mediaproducts.gartner.com/reprints/ oracle/article51/article51.html** (accessed July 2009).

Colbert, J. (2009, June). "Captain Jack and the BPM Market: Performance Management in Turbulent Times." *BPM Magazine.* **bmpmag.net/mag/captain_jack_bpm** (accessed July 2009).

Conference Board. (2008, December 2). "Weakening Global Economy and Growing Financial Pressures Are Increasing CEO Concerns." Press Release. **conference board.org/ utilities/pressDetail.cfm? press_id =3529** (accessed July 2009).

Docherty, P. (2005). "From Six Sigma to Strategy Execution." **i-solutionsglobal.com/secure/FromSix Sigma ToStrateg_AAC8C.pdf** (accessed July 2009).

Eckerson, W. (2006). *Performance Dashboards.* Hoboken, NJ: Wiley.

Eckerson, W. (2009). "Performance Management Strategies: How to Create and Deploy Effective Metrics." *TDWI Best*

Practices Report. **tdwi.org/research/display.aspx? ID=9390** (accessed July 2009).

Few, S. (2005, Winter). "Dashboard Design: Beyond Meters, Gauges, and Traffic Lights." *Business Intelligence Journal.*

Green, S. (2009, March 13). "Harrah's Reports Loss, Says LV Properties Hit Hard." *Las Vegas Sun.* **lasvegassun.com/ news/2009/mar/13/harrahs-reports-loss-says-lv-properties-hit-hard** (accessed July 2009).

Gupta, P. (2006). *Six Sigma Business Scorecard,* 2nd ed. New York: McGraw-Hill Professional.

Hammer, M. (2003). *Agenda: What Every Business Must Do to Dominate the Decade.* Pittsburgh, PA: Three Rivers Press.

Hatch, D. (2008, January). "Operational BI: Getting 'Real Time' about Performance." *Intelligent Enterprise.* **intelligent enterprise.com/showArticle.jhtml?articleID=205920233** (accessed July 2009).

Henschen, D. (2008, September). "Special Report: Business Intelligence Gets Smart." **intelligententerprise.com/ showArticle.jhtml?articleID=210500374** (accessed July 2009).

Hindo, B. (2007, June 11). "At 3M: A Struggle between Efficiency and Creativity." *BusinessWeek.* **business week .com/magazine/content/07_24/b4038406.htm?chan= top+news_top+news+index_best+of+bw** (accessed July 2009).

Hiner, J. (2009, July 1). "U.S. Federal IT Dashboard Is a Great Example of How to Promote IT." **blogs.zdnet.com/ BTL/?p=20157** (accessed July 2009).

Kaplan, R., and D. Norton. (1992, January–February). "The Balanced Scorecard—Measures That Drive Performance." *Harvard Business Review*, pp. 71–79.

Kaplan, R., and D. Norton. (1996). *The Balanced Scorecard: Translating Strategy into Action.* Cambridge, MA: Harvard University Press.

Kaplan, R., and D. Norton. (2000). *The Strategy-Focused Organization: How Balanced Scorecard Companies Thrive in the New Business Environment.* Boston: Harvard Business School Press.

Kaplan, R., and D. Norton. (2004). *Strategy Maps: Converting Intangible Assets into Tangible Outcomes.* Boston, MA: Harvard Business School Press.

Kaplan, R., and D. Norton. (2008). *Execution Premium.* Boston, MA: Harvard Business School Press.

Knowledge@W.P. Carey. (2009, March 2). "High-Rolling Casinos Hit a Losing Streak." **knowledge.wpcarey.asu.edu/article .cfm?articleid=1752#** (accessed July 2009).

Krafcik, J. (1988, Fall). "Triumph of the Lean production system." *Sloan Management Review.*

Leahy, T. (2005, February). "The One-Two Performance Punch." *Business Finance.* **businessfinancemag.com/ magazine/archives/article.html?articleID=1436** (accessed July 2009).

McGrath, R., and I. MacMillan. (2009). *Discovery-Driven Growth.* Boston: Harvard Business School Press.

Microsoft. (2006, April 12). "Expedia: Scorecard Solution Helps Online Travel Company Measure the Road to Greatness." **microsoft.com/casestudies/Case_Study_Detail.aspx? CaseStudyID=49076** (accessed July 2009).

Nagel, B. (2005). "Balanced Scorecard and Six Sigma: Complementary Tools to Advance the Leadership Agenda." Palladium White Paper. **bscol.com/pdf/Final_BSC_Six_Sigma_ Article-Nagel_v2.pdf** (accessed July 2009).

New York Non-Profit Press. (2009, March 31). "Eight NYC Programs Among 50 Selected for National Honors." **nynp.biz/index.php/breaking-news/620-eight-nyc-programs-among-50-selected-for-national-honors-** (accessed July 2009).

Norton, D. (2007). "Strategy Execution—A Competency That Creates Competitive Advantage." The Palladium Group. **thepalladiumgroup.com/KnowledgeObject Repository/Norton_StrategyExeccreatescompeti tiveadvWP.pdf** (accessed July 2009).

Novell. (2009, April). "Executive Dashboards Elements of Success." Novell White Paper. **novell.com/rc/docrepository/public/ 37/basedocument.2009-03-23.4871823014/Executive Dashboards_Elements_of_Success_White_ Paper_en .pdf** (accessed July 2009).

NYCStat. (2009, February). "CPR Fact Sheet." Mayor's Office of Operations. **nyc.gov/html/ops/cpr/downloads/ pdf/cpr_fact_sheet.pdf** (accessed July 2009).

Person, R. (2009). *Balanced Scorecards and Operational Dashboards with Microsoft Excel.* New York: Wiley.

Poppendieck, LLC. (2009). "Why the Lean in Six Sigma." **poppendieck.com/lean-six-sigma.htm** (accessed July 2009).

Richardson, K. (2007, January 4). "The Six Sigma Factor for Home Depot." *Wall Street Journal Online.* **sukimcin tosh.com/articles/WSJJan4.pdf** (accessed July 2009).

Rigby, D., and B. Bilodeau. (2009). "Management Tools and Trends 2009." Bain & Co. **bain.com/management_ tools/Management_Tools_and_Trends_2009 _Global _Results.pdf** (accessed July 2009).

Sarlin, B. (2008, February 15). "Mayor Unveils Web Database Tracking Performance." *New York Sun.* **nysun.com/new-york/mayor-unveils-web-database-trackingperformance/ 71347/?print=5119866421** (accessed July 2009).

Shill, W., and R. Thomas. (2005, October). "Exploring the Mindset of the High Performer." *Outlook Journal.* **accenture.com/Global/Research_and_Insights/ Outlook/By_Issue/Y2005/ExploringPerformer.htm** (accessed July 2009).

Simons, R. (2002). *Performance Measurement and Control Systems for Implementing Strategy.* Upper Saddle River, NJ: Prentice Hall.

Six Sigma Institute. (2009). "Lean Enterprise." **sixsigmainstitute .com/lean/index_lean.shtml** (accessed August 2009).

Slywotzky, A., and K. Weber. (2007). *The Upside: The 7 Strategies for Turning Big Threats into Growth Breakthroughs.* New York: Crown Publishing.

Smith, R. (2007, April 5). "Expedia-5 Team Blog: Technology." **expedia-team5.blogspot.com** (accessed July 2009).

Stanley, T. (2006, February 1). "High-Stakes Analytics." *Information Week.* **informationweek.com/shared/printable Article.jhtml?articleID=177103414** (accessed July 2009).

Swabey, P. (2007, January 18). "Nothing Left to Chance." *Information Age.* **information-age.com/channels/information-management/features/272256/nothing-left-to-chance.thtml** (accessed July 2009).

Tucker, S., and R. Dimon. (2009, April 17). "Design to Align: The Key Component in BPM Success. *BPM Magazine.* **bpmmag.net/mag/design-to-align-key-component-in-bpm-success-0417** (accessed July 2009).

Vessette, D., and B. McDonough. (2008, November). "Worldwide Business Analytics Software 2008–2012 Forecast and 2007 Vendor Shares." IDC Doc # 214904. **sas.com/news/analysts/idc_ba_1108.pdf** (accessed July 2009).

Wailgum, T. (2008, January 25). "How IT Systems Can Help Starbucks Fix Itself." *CIO.* **cio.com/article/176003/How_IT_Systems_Can_Help_Starbucks_Fix_Itself** (accessed July 2009).

Watson, H., and L. Volonino. (2001, January). "Harrah's High Payoff from Customer Information." *The Data Warehousing Institute Industry Study 2000—Harnessing Customer Information for Strategic Advantage: Technical Challenges and Business Solutions.* **terry.uga.edu/~hwatson/Harrahs.doc** (accessed July 2009).

Weier, M. (2007, April 16). "Dunkin' Donuts Uses Business Intelligence in War Against Starbucks." *Information Week.*

Wurtzel, M. (2008, June 13). "Reasons for Six Sigma Deployment Failures." *BPM Institute.* **bpminstitute.org/articles/article/article/reasons-for-six-sigma-deployment-failures.html** (accessed July 2009).

IV

Collaboration, Communication, Group Support Systems, and Knowledge Management

LEARNING OBJECTIVES FOR PART IV

1 Understand the concepts and process of groupwork

2 Describe how IT-based collaboration and communication support groupwork in general and decision making in particular

3 Understand the fundamental principles and capabilities of groupware and group support systems (GSS)

4 Describe the fundamental principles and capabilities of knowledge management (KM)

5 Describe tools of KM and how they relate to decision support

6 Relate KM, collaboration, and communication to each other

Millions of people and thousands of organizations worldwide use the decision support and business intelligence (BI) concepts and tools described in Chapters 1 through 9 to successfully support their decision making. However, individual decision makers do not work in a vacuum. Typically, groups (or teams) of people work and make decisions together. Very effective computerized methods have evolved to support the complex situations and different settings of work groups. Part IV describes collaborative computing in several situations and settings, supporting people in one room and supporting people in different locations (see Chapter 10). The principles of KM are the subject of Chapter 11.

Group decision support systems (GDSS) were the first specialized form of collaborative decision making supported by computers. Today, many group support system (GSS) technologies can facilitate electronic meetings, including virtual meetings. Many organizations now routinely use GSS, even in asynchronous modes (i.e., different times and different places), usually over the Web, for either direct or indirect support of decision making. Similarly, KM can be considered a form of enterprise-wide collaborative computing paradigm that identifies and makes available the needed knowledge of an organization in a meaningful form to anyone, anyplace, and anytime. The Web is the platform that enables most collaborative support systems, including sharing of data, information, and knowledge and making decisions.

Collaborative Computer-Supported Technologies and Group Support Systems

LEARNING OBJECTIVES

1 Understand the basic concepts and processes of groupwork, communication, and collaboration

2 Describe how computer systems facilitate communication and collaboration in an enterprise

3 Explain the concepts and importance of the time/place framework

4 Explain the underlying principles and capabilities of groupware, such as group support systems (GSS)

5 Understand the concepts of process gain, process loss, task gain, and task loss and explain how GSS introduces, increases, or decreases each of them

6 Describe indirect support for decision making, especially in synchronous environments

7 Become familiar with the GSS products of the major vendors, including Lotus, Microsoft, WebEx, and Groove

8 Understand the concept of GDSS and describe how to structure an electronic meeting in a decision room

9 Describe the three settings of GDSS

10 Describe specifically how a GDSS uses parallelism and anonymity and how they lead to process/task gains and losses

11 Understand how the Web enables collaborative computing and group support of virtual meetings

12 Describe the role of emerging technologies in supporting collaboration

13 Define *creativity* and explain how it can be facilitated by computers

People work together, and groups make most of the complex decisions in organizations. The increase in organizational decision-making complexity increases the need for meetings and groupwork. Supporting groupwork, where team members may be in different locations and working at different times, emphasizes the important aspects of communications, computer-mediated collaboration, and work methodologies. Group support is a critical aspect of decision support systems (DSS). Effective computer-supported group support systems have evolved to increase gains and decrease losses in task performance and underlying processes. In addition, creativity is an important element of decision making that collaborative computing can nurture and enhance. The sections of this chapter are as follows:

10.1 Opening Vignette: Procter & Gamble Drives Ideation with Group Support Systems
10.2 Making Decisions in Groups: Characteristics, Process, Benefits, and Dysfunctions
10.3 Supporting Groupwork with Computerized Systems
10.4 Tools for Indirect Support of Decision Making
10.5 Integrated Groupware Suites
10.6 Direct Computerized Support for Decision Making: From Group Decision Support Systems to Group Support Systems
10.7 Products and Tools for GDSS/GSS and Successful Implementation
10.8 Emerging Collaboration Support Tools: From VoIP to Wikis
10.9 Collaborative Efforts in Design, Planning, and Project Management
10.10 Creativity, Idea Generation, and Computerized Support

10.1 OPENING VIGNETTE: PROCTER & GAMBLE DRIVES IDEATION WITH GROUP SUPPORT SYSTEMS

In a room in West Chester, Ohio, ideas are born that touch nearly all of us. It is the legendary Procter & Gamble "Gym," where people across the company gather both physically and virtually to brainstorm new products, solve problems, or build better teams.

Three billion times a day, Procter and Gamble (P&G) brands touch the lives of people around the world. In 1837, what began as a small, family-operated soap-and-candle company (by two brother-in-laws; James Gamble and William Procter) grew into one of the largest consumer goods providers in the world. With over 138,000 employees working in over 80 countries, providing products and services to consumers in over 180 countries, P&G is truly an exceptional global business success story. From the kitchen to the bathroom and beyond, P&G has one of the largest and strongest portfolios of brands, including Pampers, Tide, Pantene, Folgers, Ariel, Always, Bounty, Pringles, Charmin, Downy, Iams, Crest, Duracell, Gillette, Actonel, and Olay.

Problem

Continuous introduction of profitable, convenient, high-quality products that change the daily lives of consumers is an essential part of conducting business in the consumer goods industry. Staying competitive in an environment that is characterized by the constantly changing needs and wants of consumers requires companies to be effective and efficient in how they manage their products and processes. The idea is to meet and exceed customers' expectations by creating new and improved products, which has been the case for many consumer goods companies in the past. However, companies have become increasingly vocal about the poor returns on their investments in product innovation, especially in the current economic conditions. The need for more efficient ways to design and produce truly innovative products has never been more important. To address this challenge, and potentially turn it into a competitive advantage, P&G wanted to reinvent its new-product innovation processes.

Solution

The solution was a computer-mediated group support system that not only makes the innovation process faster, but much, much better. P&G called its new innovation infrastructure the "innovation Gym." The company's innovation Gym, located near its Cincinnati headquarters, now serves as an incubator for a wide range of innovations. Established by chairman and CEO A. G. Lafley, the facility and the infrastructure bring together employees and consumers for true collaboration and innovation.

The company's focus on consumer needs and innovative product design has paid off. *BusinessWeek* named P&G number seven on its "World's Most Innovative Companies List" in 2007. The same year, the Wharton School of Business gave P&G its "Consumer Goods Technology Award."

P&G has been using GroupSystems to support effective collaboration and brainstorming. The tool is an interactive, Web-based solution that helps teams generate ideas, make decisions, and take collective actions in areas such as product R&D, finance, marketing, human resources, and more. P&G facilitators leverage ThinkTank (GroupSystems software product for team-based collaboration) in the Gym and elsewhere with same-place, same-time groups, as well as same-time, different-place teams.

"ThinkTank is a key tool in my interactive toolbox," said Rick Gregory, Section Head, Innovation Evangelist. "I might combine ThinkTank with a custom music playlist, the right setting, facilitation templates, Post-It notes, big paper, and hula hoops."

Internal "clients" come to P&G's facilitation team for assistance in planning and executing meetings. Facilitators often recommend that groups use ThinkTank, which not only expedites and enriches outcomes, but also reduces the time facilitators spend preparing post-meeting documentation.

Facilitators use ThinkTank's Categorizer function to brainstorm ideas, and then the Organize feature to group them into common "buckets." The solution helps build consensus among groups by identifying areas of disagreement, encouraging focused discussions, and facilitating iterative voting to narrow down lists further.

Results

Following are among the most pronounced benefits of using computer-supported collaboration tools (e.g., ThinkTank) at P&G's Gym:

- ***The power of anonymity.***   ThinkTank adds an important dynamic that typically was missing from physical, and even virtual, meetings—anonymity. Participants can type in their comments and ideas into the ThinkTank interface and vote on issues without identifying themselves. Teresa Parry, Innovation Guide, finds this to be particularly beneficial when meetings involve sensitive subject matter or hierarchies. "The anonymity breaks down barriers between titles because it's completely anonymous," Parry said. "I see it as a breakthrough tool when there's tension or sensitive topics within groups." Because participants type in their ideas, ThinkTank also encourages them to share comments in more complete thoughts. This results in more complete documentation after the meeting.

- ***Fast ideation.***   Parry also sees ThinkTank as a solution for expediting ideation (i.e., new idea creation). Participants contribute ideas quickly and build on them easily, until they reach consensus through ThinkTank's voting process. For instance, to address a pressing issue about product claims, one group at P&G had just 1 day to produce solution alternatives. Using ThinkTank, Parry helped them capture ideas, elaborate on pros and cons of each idea, and arrive at a narrowed list of potential solutions. "My internal client was thrilled with the outcome of her meeting. It exceeded her expectations in terms of quantity of information for the amount of time spent," she said. "ThinkTank is certainly faster than using Post-It notes in terms of capturing ideas and allowing people to build off each other's ideas. Meetings with ThinkTank take much less time than any other alternatives."

- ***Reducing post-meeting busywork.***   Client satisfaction aside, ThinkTank also saves busywork and time for P&G facilitators. As a service, the Gym provides complete post-meeting documentation for its clients. With ThinkTank, participant contributions serve as the documentation for meetings. That means no painstaking transcription at the end of sessions or frustration in trying to read someone else's handwriting. "ThinkTank probably saves three hours of post-meeting work, on average," Parry said. "It's a complete record of the session in one place. That means we get information back to the client faster."

In an organization like P&G, where creativity and speed are the makings of competitive advantage, a group support system like ThinkTank brings out the best in an organization's people faster than ever before.

Questions for the Opening Vignette

1. What led P&G to implement group support systems?
2. What are the pros and cons of using computer-mediated collaboration systems?

3. What is innovation Gym? What is it used for, and who uses it?

4. What are the benefits of the innovation Gym? Can you think of other benefits that are not mentioned in the vignette?

5. Who are the "internal clients" that the vignette refers to? How can they benefit from the Gym?

6. Discuss the difficulties associated with sharing and collaboration in two processes, one with computer-mediated technology and the other without.

What We Can Learn from This Vignette

The opening vignette illustrates how teams that are properly supported by collaborative technologies and procedures can achieve incredible results. The fast pace of today's economy requires companies to innovate, and to do so rapidly and continuously. Group support systems (such as the one referred to in the opening vignette, ThinkTank by GroupSystems) make it possible to bring forth the best ideas from people of different status and backgrounds. As problems become increasingly more complex, computer-mediated group support systems that facilitate brainstorming, idea generation, and decision making are progressively becoming an integral part of the corporate life.

Sources: GroupSystems, "ThinkTank Drives Ideation in Procter & Gamble's 'Innovation Gym,'" **groupsystems .com/resources/custom/PDFs/case-studies/Procter%20and%20Gamble%20Case%20Study.pdf** (accessed June 2009); Procter & Gamble, **pg.com/company**.

10.2 MAKING DECISIONS IN GROUPS: CHARACTERISTICS, PROCESS, BENEFITS, AND DYSFUNCTIONS

Managers and other knowledge workers continuously make decisions, design and manufacture products, develop policies and strategies, create software systems, and so on. When people work in groups (i.e., teams), they perform groupwork (i.e., teamwork). **Groupwork** refers to work done by two or more people together.

Characteristics of Groupwork

The following are some of the functions and characteristics of groupwork:

- A group performs a task (sometimes decision making, sometimes not).
- Group members may be located in different places.
- Group members may work at different times.
- Group members may work for the same organization or for different organizations.
- A group can be permanent or temporary.
- A group can be at one managerial level or span several levels.
- It can create synergy (leading to process and task gains) or conflict.
- It can generate productivity gains and/or losses.
- The task may have to be accomplished very quickly.
- It may be impossible or too expensive for all the team members to meet in one place, especially when the group is called for emergency purposes.
- Some of the needed data, information, or knowledge may be located in many sources, some of which may be external to the organization.
- The expertise of nonteam members may be needed.
- Groups perform many tasks; however, groups of managers and analysts frequently concentrate on decision making.
- The decisions made by a group are easier to implement if supported by all (or at least most) members.

The Group Decision-Making Process

Even in hierarchical organizations, decision making is usually a shared process. A group may be involved in a decision or in a decision-related task, such as creating a short list of acceptable alternatives or choosing criteria for evaluating alternatives and prioritizing them. The following activities and processes characterize meetings:

- The decision situation is important, so it is advisable to make it in a group in a meeting.
- A meeting is a joint activity engaged in by a group of people typically of equal or nearly equal status.
- The outcome of a meeting depends partly on the knowledge, opinions, and judgments of its participants and the support they give to the outcome.
- The outcome of a meeting depends on the composition of the group and on the decision-making process the group uses.
- Differences in opinions are settled either by the ranking person present or, often, through negotiation or arbitration.
- The members of a group can be in one place, meeting face-to-face, or they can be a **virtual team,** in which case they are in different places while in a meeting.
- The process of group decision making can create benefits as well as dysfunctions.

The Benefits and Limitations of Groupwork

Some people endure meetings (the most common form of groupwork) as a necessity; others find them to be a waste of time. Many things can go wrong in a meeting. Participants may not clearly understand their goals, they may lack focus, or they may have hidden agendas. Many participants may be afraid to speak up, while a few may dominate the discussion. Misunderstandings occur through different interpretations of language, gesture, or expression. Table 10.1 provides a comprehensive list of factors that can hinder the effectiveness of a meeting (Nunamaker, 1997). Besides being challenging, teamwork is also expensive. A meeting of several managers or executives may cost thousands of dollars per hour in salary costs alone. In one study, Panko (1994) analyzed the cost of meetings at *Fortune* 500 companies. According to his study, there were more than 11 million formal meetings per day in the United

---

TABLE 10.1 Difficulties Associated with Groupwork

• Waiting to speak	• Wrong composition of people
• Dominating the discussion	• Groupthink
• Fear of speaking	• Poor grasp of problem
• Fear of being misunderstood	• Ignored alternatives
• Inattention	• Lack of consensus
• Lack of focus	• Poor planning
• Inadequate criteria	• Hidden agendas
• Premature decisions	• Conflict of interests
• Missing information	• Inadequate resources
• Distractions	• Poorly defined goals
• Digressions	

States and more than 3 billion meetings per year. Managers spent about 20 percent of their time in formal meetings of five people or more and up to 85 percent of their time communicating.

Groupwork may have both potential benefits (process gains) and potential drawbacks (process losses). **Process gains** are the benefits of working in groups. The unfortunate dysfunctions that may occur when people work in groups are called **process losses**. Examples of each are listed in Technology Insights 10.1.

TECHNOLOGY INSIGHTS 10.1   Benefits of Working in Groups and Dysfunctions of the Group Process

Benefits of Working in Groups (Process Gains)	Dysfunctions of the Group Process (Process Losses)
• It provides learning. Groups are better than individuals at understanding problems.	• Social pressures of conformity may result in **groupthink** (i.e., people begin to think alike and do not tolerate new ideas; they yield to *conformance pressure*).
• People readily take ownership of problems and their solutions. They take responsibility.	• It is a time-consuming, slow process (i.e., only one member can speak at a time).
• Group members have their egos embedded in the decision, so they are committed to the solution.	• There can be lack of coordination of the meeting and poor meeting planning.
• Groups are better than individuals at catching errors.	• Inappropriate influences (e.g., domination of time, topic, or opinion by one or few individuals; fear of contributing because of the possibility of *flaming*).
• A group has more *information* (i.e., knowledge) than any one member. Group members can combine their knowledge to create new knowledge. More and more creative alternatives for problem solving can be generated, and better solutions can be derived (e.g., through *stimulation*).	• There can be a tendency for group members to either dominate the agenda or rely on others to do most of the work (free-riding).
• A group may produce *synergy* during problem solving. The effectiveness and/or quality of groupwork can be greater than the sum of what is produced by independent individuals.	• Some members may be afraid to speak up.
• Working in a group may stimulate the creativity of the participants and the process.	• There can be a tendency to produce compromised solutions of poor quality.
• A group may have better and more precise communication working together.	• There is often nonproductive time (e.g., socializing, preparing, waiting for latecomers; i.e., *air-time fragmentation*).
• Risk propensity is balanced. Groups moderate high-risk takers and encourage conservatives.	• There can be a tendency to repeat what has already been said (because of failure to remember or process).
	• Meeting costs can be high (e.g., travel, participation time spent).
	• There can be incomplete or inappropriate use of information.
	• There can be too much information (i.e., information overload).
	• There can be incomplete or incorrect task analysis.
	• There can be inappropriate or incomplete representation in the group.
	• There can be attention blocking.
	• There can be concentration blocking.

Improving the Meeting Process

Meetings can be very effective if the participants recognize what can go wrong and try to improve the process of conducting a meeting. Researchers have developed methods for improving the processes of groupwork; that is, increasing some of the benefits of meetings and eliminating or reducing some of the losses (see Duke Corporate Education, 2005). Some of these methods are known as group dynamics. Two representative methods are the **nominal group technique (NGT)** and the **Delphi method**. NGT is a group decision-making method whereby each participant provides his or her opinions and corresponding explanations individually prior to the group discussion and elaboration. The main goal is to eliminate groupthink by allowing everybody to contribute their original opinions. The Delphi method is a qualitative opinion-polling methodology that uses anonymous questionnaires. The repetitive process followed in the Delphi method has been shown to be effective for eliciting information from a panel of independent experts about complex and/or sensitive problems. These methods are among the early manual approaches to supporting groupwork; see Lindstone and Turoff (1975) for details. **blogs.techrepublic.com.com/10things/?p=263** provides 10 ways to make meetings more effective.

The limited success of manual methods such as NGT and the Delphi method have led to attempts to use information technology to support group meetings. (Today, both NGT and Delphi are supported by computers in some organizations.)

Section 10.2 Review Questions

1. Define *groupwork*.
2. List five characteristics of groupwork.
3. Describe the process of a group meeting for decision making.
4. Describe five potential gains of group meetings.
5. Describe five potential losses from group meetings.

10.3 SUPPORTING GROUPWORK WITH COMPUTERIZED SYSTEMS

When people work in teams, especially when the members are in different locations and may be working at different times, they need to communicate, collaborate, and access a diverse set of information sources in multiple formats. This makes meetings, especially virtual ones, complex, with a greater chance for process losses. It is important to follow a certain process for conducting meetings. Computerized support can help, as was the case for P&G in the opening vignette. Other reasons for support are cost savings, expedited decisions, the need to support virtual teams, the need for external experts, and improving the decision-making process.

Groupwork may require different levels of coordination (Nunamaker, 1997). Sometimes a group may operate at the individual work level, with members making individual efforts that require no coordination. As with a team of sprinters representing a country participating in a 100-meter dash, group productivity is simply the best of the individual results. Other times group members may interact at the coordinated work level. At this level, as with a team in a relay race, the work requires careful coordination between otherwise independent individual efforts. Sometimes a team may operate at the concerted work level. As in a rowing race, teams working at this level must make a continuous concerted effort to be successful. Different mechanisms support groupwork at different levels of coordination.

Almost all organizations, small and large, are using some computer-based communication and collaboration methods and tools to support people working in teams or groups. For example, Johnson Controls has cut production costs by $20 million with a collaboration portal that integrates supplier applications (see Hall, 2002). Lockheed

Martin won a $19 billion contract on the basis of its collaboration capabilities (see Konicki, 2001). P&G generates innovative ideas more rapidly, making it more competitive in the consumer products market (see opening case).

An Overview of Group Support Systems (GSS)

For groups to collaborate effectively, appropriate communication methods and technologies are needed. The Internet and its derivatives (i.e., intranets and extranets) are the infrastructures on which much communication for collaboration occurs. The Web supports intra- and interorganizational collaborative decision making through collaboration tools and access to data, information, and knowledge from inside and outside the organization.

Intra-organizational networked decision support can be effectively supported by an intranet. People within an organization can work with Internet tools and procedures through enterprise information portals. Specific applications can include important internal documents and procedures, corporate address lists, e-mail, tool access, and software distribution.

An *extranet* links people in different organizations. For example, several automobile manufacturers have involved their suppliers and dealers in extranets to help them to deal with inventories and customer complaints (see **covisint.com**). Other extranets are used to link teams together to design products when several different suppliers must collaborate on design and manufacturing techniques. Many Web-based collaborative configurations and tools are available, such as the one described in the opening vignette. Other examples are Autodesk's Architectural Studio and CoCreate's OneSpace, which allow several designers to work together simultaneously. An interesting use of computer-mediated groupwork to fight crime is summarized in Application Case 10.1.

APPLICATION CASE 10.1

GSS Boosts Innovation in Crime Prevention

According to crime statistics, most homicides are solved within days; about 90 percent of murder victims knew the perpetrator. But when cases are more complex, solving them requires a methodical, in-depth investigation.

For the Hertfordshire Constabulary, the police department for the County of Hertfordshire, United Kingdom, takes a collaborative approach to solving homicides and the causes of crimes. Hertfordshire County, just north of London, is home to 1.1 million people, and sees about 15 homicides and 50 road deaths annually.

The department brings together detectives, administrators, and forensic scientists to uncover new ideas, ask questions, and propose theories. When the department wanted to take a closer look at cold cases and devise ways to reduce overall homicide rates, it was concerned that hierarchies would get in the way of true brainstorming and prevent desired breakthroughs.

"Conventional, group-based oral discussion lets two to three people have more influence than is fair," said Detective Chief Superintendent (DCS) Chris Miller. "And it's very difficult to get all agencies together physically."

Collaboration Nets New Ideas

Hertfordshire Constabulary turned to Steve Bather of Realise (Europe) Limited for help in conducting collaborative meetings. A GroupSystems partner, Realise uses GroupSystems' ThinkTank to bring dynamic collaboration to workshops, conference facilitation, and team building. Realise worked with Hertfordshire to define issues and identify the best approach. "It was the perfect opportunity to use GroupSystems' ThinkTank solution," said Steve Bather. "ThinkTank opens up groups to new ideas, radical discussion, and breakthrough thinking—which was needed in both cold case murder reviews and multi-agency homicide reduction workshops."

Cold Case Murder Reviews

For cold case murder reviews, Hertfordshire brings together all parties for a 1-day session. First, a detective briefs the group on a case or problem. Then Realise introduces ThinkTank with an ice-breaker activity. Every participant has his or her own access to ThinkTank, often from different locations, either on computers provided by Realise or the Constabulary's own computers.

During the initial brainstorm of ideas and questions, all submissions remain anonymous. That anonymity gives participants the ability to contribute freely and submit all the questions, ideas, insights, and theories they have. They are encouraged to input the most obvious ideas they might assume the lead team has already considered as well as more far-out ideas. All participants and perspectives are given a "voice" through the ThinkTank technology.

ThinkTank elicits dozens of ideas in minutes from all parties simultaneously, rather than a few people dominating conversation. Every idea has the potential for further discussion instead of being discounted by outspoken individuals. The group then reviews all facts and theories, further developing groups of ideas into lines of inquiry.

"Using ThinkTank, we get a lot of work out of a lot of people quickly," Miller said. "People are actively engaged in the process and everyone's voice is heard." Using ThinkTank's prioritization and voting features, participants then rank and rate the lines of inquiry. They take into consideration the potential impact on the case and ease of investigation. The outcome: A ranked list of options for the lead detective to pursue.

"There is a new commitment, energy and focus on a smaller number of viable options," Bather said. Before concluding, the group identifies next steps, who should own those steps, expectations, and timeframes. At the end of the workshop, Realise taps ThinkTank for instant reporting to publish the session outcomes. The reports can also be edited to generate summary data valuable to senior management, the victim's family, the press or for legal progress reporting.

Homicide Reduction Strategies

Hertfordshire Constabulary has also engaged Think-Tank and Realise to encourage collaboration at intra- and interagency meetings focused on specific types of homicide (e.g., alcohol-related homicides, road deaths, domestic violence, knife crimes). Relevant agencies attend the day-long discussion supported by ThinkTank to seek a better understanding of the conditions that trigger different types of incidents.

The groups of up to 60 participants brainstorm, discuss, prioritize, and jointly develop strategies to mitigate serious incidents and homicides. Toward the end of the workshop, the participants are invited to commit to a small number of pragmatic strategies they feel will maximize the outcome. With diligent commitment and effective follow-up, the County implemented a number of solutions and strategies—as a result, there has been a reduction in homicides in the county.

Senior detectives now apply this approach to live investigations, learning reviews, and coordination of multiple teams. The Constabulary elicits more ideas from participants, more quickly; ensures that complete team thinking is included and that all voices are heard; and captures and processes all information collaboratively.

Reducing and Solving Crimes

As a result, the Constabulary has refreshed a number of complex cold cases, triggered by new theories raised in ThinkTank workshops. Further diligent police detective work helped build new cases that were brought to prosecution and resolution.

The multi-agency homicide reduction workshops also resulted in proactive new ways of preventing alcohol-related crimes in three county towns. The pilot schemes were so successful that the approach was extended to other major cities and towns in the county. Over the same period, Hertfordshire saw a 33 percent decrease in grievous bodily harm and a 22 percent reduction in actual bodily harm.

The homicide reduction team also won an award for "Innovation in Crime Prevention." "With ThinkTank, we're identifying causes and effects of homicides with a view toward developing a process internally and with partner agencies to reduce the likelihood that incidents might lead to murder," Miller said.

Sources: Group Systems, "Hertfordshire County, UK, Earns 'Innovation in Crime Prevention' Award; GroupSystems Success Story: Hertfordshire Constabulary," **groupsystems.com/documents/ case_studies/hertfordshire.pdf** (accessed August 2009).

Computers have been used for several decades to facilitate groupwork and group decision making. Lately, collaborative tools have received even greater attention due to their increased capabilities and ability to save money (e.g., on travel cost) as well as their ability to expedite decision making. Such computerized tools are called groupware.

Groupware

Many computerized tools have been developed to provide group support. These tools are called **groupware** because their primary objective is to support groupwork. Groupware tools can support decision making directly or indirectly, and they are described in the remainder of this chapter. For example, generating creative solutions to problems is a direct support. Some e-mail programs, chat rooms, instant messaging (IM), and teleconferencing provide indirect support.

Groupware provides a mechanism for team members to share opinions, data, information, knowledge, and other resources. Different computing technologies support groupwork in different ways, depending on the purpose of the group, the task, and the time/place category in which the work occurs.

Time/Place Framework

The effectiveness of a collaborative computing technology depends on the location of the group members and on the time that shared information is sent and received. DeSanctis and Gallupe (1987) proposed a framework for classifying IT communication support technologies. In this framework, communication is divided into four cells, which are shown together with representative computerized support technologies in Figure 10.1. The four cells are organized along the two dimensions time and place.

When information is sent and received almost simultaneously, the communication is **synchronous (real time).** Telephones, IM, and face-to-face meetings are examples of synchronous communication. **Asynchronous** communication occurs when the receiver gets the information at a different time than it was sent, such as in e-mail. The senders and the receivers can be in the same room or in different places.

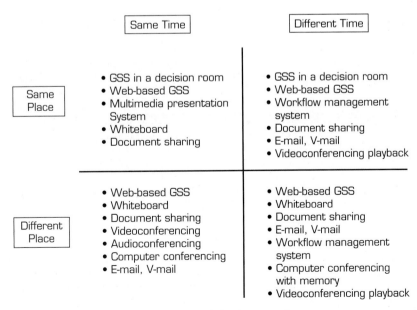

FIGURE 10.1 The Time/Place Framework for Groupwork

As shown in Figure 10.1, time and place combinations can be viewed as a four-cell matrix, or framework. The four cells of the framework are as follows:

- ***Same time/same place.*** Participants meet face-to-face in one place at the same time, as in a traditional meeting or decision room. This is still an important way to meet, even when Web-based support is used, because it is sometimes critical for participants to leave the office to eliminate distractions.
- ***Same time/different place.*** Participants are in different places, but they communicate at the same time (e.g., with videoconferencing).
- ***Different time/same place.*** People work in shifts. One shift leaves information for the next shift.
- ***Different time/different place (any time, any place).*** Participants are in different places, and they also send and receive information at different times. This occurs when team members are traveling, have conflicting schedules, or work in different time zones.

Groups and groupwork (also known as *teams* and *teamwork*) in organizations are proliferating. Consequently, groupware continues to evolve to support effective groupwork, mostly for communication and collaboration.

What Computers Can and Cannot Do

Modern Web-based information technologies provide an inexpensive, fast, capable, and reliable means of supporting communications. But computers cannot support all communication areas. (See Technology Insights 10.2 for some unsupported aspects of

---

TECHNOLOGY INSIGHTS 10.2 Unsupported Aspects of Communication

Communication can be problematic in general because computerized communication methods do not transmit most of our nonverbal cues, which are important in establishing the richer meaning of a message by adding context. A large part of what we mean (perhaps exceeding 50%) is conveyed via nonverbal cues. Facial expressions, body language, voice tone, expression, inflection, touching, and distance are but a few. (For example, it is possible to fairly accurately determine who will win a U.S. presidential election by measuring the average rate of each candidate's eye blinking. The one who blinks the least has won every election from the Kennedy–Nixon contest in 1960 through 2000. Jay Aronson used this method in analyzing the third debate of the 2000 U.S. presidential election to predict the winner correctly.) Cross-cultural aspects and language subtleties are not easily transmitted through computer-mediated communication channels.

Emoticons were a first attempt to include nonverbal cues in text-based e-mail. For example, in the emoticon system, the characters :) are a happy face called a "smiley," and writing your message in all capital letters means you are SHOUTING! These have been updated into icons in IM software.

Some aspects of communication, such as the frequency of touching and the interpersonal distance between participants, are difficult to capture through technology. However, video technology can show facial expressions and some body language. Researchers are attempting to develop collaborative systems that capture more of this imprecise nature of human communication that makes the meaning of the message received more precise. They are also developing output devices (e.g., robot faces that can reflect mood) to do the same. Other devices are being developed to interpret facial cues, voice changes, and body movement.

Sources: D. Ferber, "The Man Who Mistook His Girlfriend for a Robot," *Popular Science,* September 2003, **popsci.com/scitech/article/2003-08/man-who-mistook-his-girlfriend-robot** (accessed June 2009); and D. Rosenbergm and J. A. A. Sillince, "Verbal and Nonverbal Communication in Computer Mediated Settings," *International Journal of Artificial Intelligence in Education,* Vol. 11, 2000.

communication.) Networked computer systems, such as the Internet, intranets, extranets, and proprietary private networks, are the enabling platforms that support communication.

Next, we examine representative tools that support decision making indirectly.

Section 10.3 Review Questions

1. Why do companies use computers to support groupwork?
2. Define and provide simple examples to three coordination levels in groupwork.
3. Describe the components of the time/place framework.
4. What limitation do computers have in terms of supporting groupwork?

10.4 TOOLS FOR INDIRECT SUPPORT OF DECISION MAKING

A large number of tools and methodologies are available to facilitate e-collaboration, communication, and decision support. The following sections present the major tools that support decision making indirectly.

Groupware Tools

Groupware products provide a way for groups to share resources and opinions. Groupware implies the use of networks to connect people, even if they are in the same room. Many groupware products are available on the Internet or an intranet to enhance the collaboration of a large number of people worldwide (e.g., see Henrie, 2004). Also, groupware tools are available in Microsoft Windows and Office 2007.

The features of groupware products that support commutation, collaboration, and coordination are listed in Table 10.2. What follows are brief definitions of some of those features.

SYNCHRONOUS VERSUS ASYNCHRONOUS PRODUCTS   Notice that the features in Table 10.2 may be synchronous, meaning that communication and collaboration are done in real time, or asynchronous, meaning that communication and collaboration are done by the participants at different times. Web conferencing and IM as well as Voice over IP (VoIP) are associated with synchronous mode. Methods that are associated with asynchronous modes include e-mail, wikilogs, and online workspaces, where participants can collaborate, for example, on joint designs or projects, but work at different times. Vignette, Inc. (**vignette.com**), Groove Networks (**groove.net**), and Google Docs (**docs.google.com**) allow users to set up online workspaces for storing, sharing, and collaboratively working on different types of documents. According to Henrie (2004), many of the tools offered by vendors are converging. This is occurring due to new and more advanced technologies, such as Web 2.0, VoIP, and AJAX.

Groupware products are either stand-alone products that support one task (such as videoconferencing) or integrated kits that include several tools. In general, groupware technology products are fairly inexpensive and can easily be incorporated into existing information systems.

VIRTUAL MEETING SYSTEMS   The advancement of Web-based systems opens the door for improved, electronically supported **virtual meetings**, where members are in different locations and even in different countries. For example, online meetings and presentation tools are provided by **webex.com**, **gotomeeting.com**, **wimba.com**, and **facilitate.com**.

The events of September 11, 2001, and the economic slowdown of 2001 through 2003 helped to make virtual meetings more popular (e.g., see Bray, 2004; and Powell et al., 2004). It is difficult for companies to ignore reported cost savings, such as the $4 million per

TABLE 10.2   Groupware Products and Features

General (can be either synchronous or asynchronous)

- Built-in e-mail, messaging system
- Browser interface
- Joint Web-page creation
- Sharing of active hyperlinks
- File sharing (graphics, video, audio, or other)
- Built-in search functions (by topic or keyword)
- Workflow tools
- Use of corporate portals for communication, collaboration, and search
- Shared screens
- Electronic decision rooms
- Peer-to-peer networks

Synchronous (same time)

- Instant messaging (IM)
- Videoconferencing, multimedia conferencing
- Audioconferencing
- Shared whiteboard, smart whiteboard
- Instant video
- Brainstorming
- Polling (voting), and other decision support (consensus builder, scheduler)

Asynchronous (different times)

- Workspaces
- Threaded discussions
- Users can receive/send e-mail, SMS
- Users can receive activity notification alerts, via e-mail or SMS
- Users can collapse/expand discussion threads
- Users can sort messages (by date, author, or read/unread)
- Auto responder
- Chat session logs
- Bulletin boards, discussion groups
- Use of blogs, wikis, and wikilogs
- Collaborative planning and/or design tools
- Use of bulletin boards

month that IBM reported it saved just from cutting travel-related meeting expenses (Callaghan, 2002). In addition, improvements in supporting technology, reductions in the price of the technology, and the acceptance of virtual meetings as a respected way of doing business are fueling their growth.

Virtual meetings are supported by a variety of groupware tools, as discussed in the remainder of this section. We begin our discussion with the support provided by real-time support tools.

Real-Time Collaboration Tools

The Internet, intranets, and extranets offer tremendous potential for real-time and synchronous interaction for people working in groups. *Real-time collaboration (RTC)* tools help companies bridge time and space to make decisions and collaborate on projects. RTC tools support synchronous communication of graphical and text-based information. These tools are also being used in distance learning, virtual classroom, personnel training, product demonstrations, customer support, e-commerce, and sales applications. RTC tools can be purchased as stand-alone tools or used on a subscription basis (as offered by several vendors). One such vendor is WebEx (described later in this chapter), which provides a comprehensive software tool for real-time collaboration (see Application Case 10.2 for a representative example).

APPLICATION CASE 10.2

Catalyst Maintains an Edge with WebEx

Catalyst Software Solutions (**catalystss.com**) develops software-based automation solutions for pharmacies and long-term care facilities. The company's products help manage the distribution of complex medication regimens from pharmacies to health care facilities, creating an auditable trail for improved efficiency and greater patient safety. Catalyst has solidified distribution agreements with health care giant McKesson and pharmacy automation provider Parata and is moving forward with a North American rollout of its software solutions.

Problem

From the beginning, Catalyst needed a way to communicate effectively with key software developers on the other side of the continent. "Relying solely on phone calls for our conversations with the East Coast development team just led to frustration," explains Harvinder Johal, vice president of sales. "We were trying to open the lines of communication between our developers and our clinical experts, but we found that process very challenging without the help of an online meeting tool." As the company moved forward with marketing its products, similar challenges emerged whenever Johal and his team attempted to explain Catalyst's software solutions over the phone. "We quickly realized that the only way to get people excited was to show them a demo," he continues. "This is a complex product, and it's difficult to explain without visual aids. So we began looking for an effective way to demonstrate just how innovative our software really is."

Solution

With WebEx Meeting Center, Johal found a cost-effective means for Catalyst to enhance collaboration and extend the company's sales reach. "We looked at other solutions, but WebEx just offered a great product in terms of market presence, reliability, and ease of use," he says. "Once we began using Meeting Center, we never really looked back. I mean, why change something that's working so well?"

When Johal makes contact with a prospective customer, he first asks a few questions about that customer's needs. Based on the response to those questions, he proceeds with a loosely structured Web demonstration addressing the customer's unique concerns while showing how Catalyst's solutions can help any long-term care facility achieve greater efficiency. "Once our prospects see just how much we have to offer, they're totally on board with us," he says. "It's amazing what a difference a real-time demo can make with this product."

As Catalyst's online demos began to build a larger customer base, Johal and his team found that customer support was becoming a more pressing need. "We needed a way to provide high-level remote support to all of our customers—many of whom are not tech-savvy." By turning to WebEx Support Center Remote Support, Catalyst was able to provide desktop-sharing functionality to a rapidly growing customer base, helping ensure the successful implementation of the company's solutions at sites across North America.

Results

By using Meeting Center, Johal and his team have significantly shortened the company's sales cycle. WebEx enables Catalyst's salespeople to deliver customized, richly interactive demos while devoting less time to customer contact and spending less money on travel. "You can engage in multiple phone conversations just trying to explain our products," Johal says. "But with WebEx, we're able to shorten the explanation process and get on with selling. This tool makes it possible for me to reach out to a prospect on the other side of the continent as if I'm standing in the same room. That means I can win more clients on first contact, which was practically unheard of before. I can't even imagine how much time it's saved us."

WebEx technology enables Catalyst to maintain an edge among much larger competitors in the health care field. "A lot of these technology companies have been around for decades. They're deeply entrenched all over North America," Johal says. "Now we can compete directly with those companies despite having a much smaller physical presence." Although many factors have contributed to Catalyst's success—namely the development of an innovative product that has generated huge demand—Johal admits that much of the company's sales growth would have been difficult to achieve without WebEx technology. "We're still a young company, but fortunately everything's falling into place for us," he says. "And there's no doubt in my mind that we wouldn't be where we are without WebEx."

Sources: WebEx, "Catalyst Maintains an Edge Among Much Larger Competitors with WebEx," **webex.com/pdf/cs_Catalyst.pdf** (accessed June 2009); and Catalyst Software Solutions, **catalystss.com** (accessed June 2009).

ELECTRONIC TELECONFERENCING   **Teleconferencing** is the use of electronic communication to enable two or more people at different locations to have a simultaneous conference. It is the simplest infrastructure for supporting a virtual meeting. Several types of teleconferencing are possible. The oldest and simplest is a telephone conference call, wherein several people talk to each other from three or more locations. The biggest disadvantage of this method is that it does not allow for face-to-face communication. Also, participants in one location cannot see graphs, charts, and pictures at other locations. Although the latter disadvantage can be overcome by using faxes, this is a time-consuming, expensive, and frequently poor-quality process. One solution is video teleconferencing, in which participants can see each other as well as documents.

VIDEO TELECONFERENCING   In **video teleconferencing (videoconferencing)**, participants in one location can see participants at other locations. Dynamic pictures of the participants can appear on a large screen and/or on a desktop computer. Originally, videoconferencing was the transmission of live, compressed TV sessions between two or more points. Today, videoconferencing is a digital technology capable of linking various types of computers across networks. When conferences are digitized and transmitted over networks, they become computer applications.

With videoconferencing, participants can share data, voice, pictures, graphics, and animation. Data can also be sent along with voice and video. Such **data conferencing** makes it possible to work on documents and to exchange computer files during videoconferences. This allows several geographically dispersed groups to work on the same project and to communicate by video simultaneously.

Videoconferencing offers various benefits. For example, it improves employee productivity, cuts travel costs, conserves the time and energy of key employees, and increases the speed of business processes (e.g., product development, contract negotiation, customer service). It also improves the efficiency and frequency of communications and saves an electronic record of a meeting, enabling specific parts of a meeting to be reconstructed for future purposes. Videoconferencing also makes it possible to hold classes at different locations. Finally, videoconferencing can be used to conduct meetings with business partners as well as to interview candidates for employment.

WEB CONFERENCING *Web conferencing* is conducted on the Internet for as few as two and for as many as thousands of people. It allows users to simultaneously view something on their computer screens, such as a sales presentation in Microsoft PowerPoint or a product drawing; interaction takes place via messaging or a simultaneous phone teleconference. Web conferencing is much less expensive than videoconferencing because it runs over the Internet. An example of an application of Web conferencing is banks in Alaska that use video kiosks in sparsely populated areas instead of building branches that would be underutilized. A video kiosk operates on a bank's intranet and provides videoconferencing equipment for face-to-face interactions. A variety of other communication tools, such as online polls, whiteboards, and question-and-answer boards may also be used. Such innovations can be used to educate staff members about a new product line or technology, to amplify a meeting with investors, or to walk a prospective client through an introductory presentation. People can use Web conferencing to view presentations, seminars, and lectures and to collaborate on documents.

Web conferencing is becoming very popular. Almost all Web conferencing products provide whiteboarding and polling features and allow users to give presentations and demos and share applications. Popular Web conferencing products are Microsoft's Windows Meeting Space, Centra's EMeeting, Genesys' Meeting Center, Citrix's GoToMeeting, Wimba's Collaboration Suite, and WebEx's Meeting Center.

INTERACTIVE WHITEBOARDS Whiteboards are a type of groupware. Computer-based whiteboards work like real-world whiteboards with markers and erasers, except for one big difference: Instead of one person standing in front of a meeting room drawing on the whiteboard, all participants can join in. Throughout a meeting, each user can view and draw on a single document that is "pasted" onto the electronic whiteboard on a computer screen. Users can save digital whiteboarding sessions for future use. Some whiteboarding products let users insert graphics files that the group can annotate.

SCREEN SHARING In collaborative work, team members are frequently in different locations. By using **screen-sharing** software, group members can work on the same document, which is shown on the PC screen of each participant. For example, two authors can work on a single manuscript. One may suggest a correction and execute it so that the other author can view the change. Collaborators can work together on the same spreadsheet or on the resultant graphics. Changes can be made by using the keyboard or by touching the screen. This capability can expedite the design of products, the preparation of reports and bids, and the resolution of conflicts.

Groove Networks (**groove.net**, now part of Microsoft) offers a special screen-sharing capability. Its product enables the joint creation and editing of documents on a PC. (See the discussion of Groove later in this chapter.)

INSTANT VIDEO The spread of IM and Internet telephony has naturally led to the idea of linking people via both voice and audio. Called instant video, the idea is a kind of video chat room. Instant video allows users to chat in real time and to see the person(s) with whom they are meeting. A simple way to do this is to add video cameras to the participants' computers. A more sophisticated and better-quality approach is to integrate an existing online videoconferencing service with IM software, creating a service that offers the online equivalent of a videophone.

This idea is still in the early stages. One instant video pioneer is CUworld (**cuworld.com**). Here is how its CUworld software works: Users gets free CUworld software that can compress and decompress video signals sent over an online connection. To start a conference, a user sends a request to an online buddy via IM. The CUworld software goes to the directory of the IM service to determine the Internet addresses of the users' connections, and, using the Web addresses, the computers of the video participants are linked directly via the Internet. A videoconference can then begin.

Instant video sounds like a good product, but no one knows for sure how commercially viable it will be.

Support of Asynchronous Communication

Asynchronous communication is supported mainly by e-mail and short message service (SMS) wireless messages. In the past few years, we have seen an increase in other tools that are not subject to spam. The two major tools, blogs and wikis, are discussed in Section 10.8. Other tools not discussed here are online bulletin (discussion) groups, auto responders, and workflow and interactive portals.

A major new asynchronous tool is the online workspace (see Henrie, 2004).

ONLINE WORKSPACES   Online (electronic) workspaces are online screens that allow people to share documents, files, project plans, calendars, and so on in the same online place, though not necessarily at the same time. An online workspace is an extension of screen sharing, which was developed mainly for synchronous collaboration. An example is Intraspect from Vignette Corp., which allows users to set up workspaces for sharing and storing documents and other unstructured data. Another example is Microsoft's SharePoint, which allows employees to create Web sites, invite coworkers to join discussions, and post documents. Groove Networks sells an online workspace especially suited to users who are frequently outside a company's firewalls. Finally, CollabNet, Inc., offers an online workspace specifically to support collaboration of software developers.

Section 10.4 Review Questions

1. List the major groupware tools and divide them into synchronous and asynchronous types.
2. Describe the various types of electronic teleconferencing, including Web-based conferencing.
3. Describe whiteboards and screen sharing.
4. Describe instant video.
5. Describe the online workspace.

10.5   INTEGRATED GROUPWARE SUITES

Because groupware technologies are computer based and have the objective of supporting groupwork, it makes sense to integrate them among themselves and/or with other computer-based technologies. A software suite is created when several products are integrated into one system. Integrating several technologies can save time and money for users. For example, Polycom, Inc. (**polycom.com**), in an alliance with software developer Lotus, developed an integrated desktop videoteleconferencing product that uses Lotus Notes. Using this integrated system, publisher Reader's Digest has built several applications that have videoconferencing capabilities. Groupware suites provide seamless integration.

Groupware typically contains capabilities for at least one of the following: **electronic brainstorming** (i.e., brainstorming supported by computers), electronic conferencing or meetings, scheduling of meetings, calendaring, planning, conflict resolution, model building, videoconferencing, electronic document sharing (e.g., screen sharing, whiteboards, liveboards), voting, and organizational memory. Some groupware—such as Lotus Notes (**ibm.com**), Windows Meeting Space (**microsoft.com**), Groove (**groove.net**, now part of Microsoft), WebEx (**webex.com**), and ThinkTank (**groupsystems.com**)— support a fairly comprehensive range of activities. These products are known as *suites* and are described next.

Lotus Notes (IBM Collaboration Software)

Lotus Notes (**ibm.com/software/lotus**) was the first widely used groupware (see Langley, 2004). Lotus Notes enables collaboration by letting users access and create shared information through specially programmed Notes documents. Notes provides online collaboration capabilities through Web conferencing on demand, work group e-mail, distributed databases, bulletin whiteboards, text editing, (electronic) document management, workflow capabilities, consensus building, voting, ranking, and various application-development tools, all integrated into one environment with a graphical menu-based user interface. Notes fosters a virtual corporation and creates interorganizational alliances. Notes broadens personal information management (PIM) data to supported mobile or wireless devices, including PDAs, pagers, and mobile phones, and makes available online access to critical business information using mobile devices. It also supports a variety of Web browsers on Linux as well as Microsoft Windows, while providing security features to help protect business-critical information. The software integrates presence awareness and IM to assist in collaboration with colleagues without launching a separate application and gives mobile workers the convenience of working while disconnected from the network.

Although increased competition is cutting into its market share, there are millions of Notes users in thousands of organizations. Many applications have been programmed directly in Lotus Notes (e.g., Learning Space, a courseware package that supports distance learning). Lotusphere is IBM's conferencing software with its Workplace platform, which is integrated with Domino server. Workplace Builder allows nontechnical business users to create applications based on templates. For companies that have fewer than 1,000 employees, IBM offers Lotus Domino Express. For examples, see success stories at IBM (2006).

Microsoft Windows Meeting Space and Live Meeting

Microsoft Windows Meeting Space is a real-time collaboration package that includes whiteboarding (i.e., support of relatively free-form graphics to which all participants can contribute simultaneously), application sharing (of any Microsoft Windows application document), remote desktop sharing, file transfer, text chat, data conferencing, and desktop audio- and videoconferencing. This application sharing is a vast improvement over what was called whiteboarding in the early 1990s. The Windows Meeting Space client is included in the Windows operating system. Microsoft also offers a hosted Web conferencing product for Web conferencing called Live Meeting.

Groove Networks

Groove Virtual Office is a product from Groove (**groove.net**; now a Microsoft company). It is an end-user application for secure discussions, file sharing, projects, and meetings. The software supports seamless shared project documents, allows work between project team members inside and outside an organization, and enables communication about project status and such, live virtual meetings, allocation and tracking of action items and tasks, and access to the latest project information (online or offline).

Used alone or with Groove Enterprise Servers and Hosted Services, Groove Workspace enables spontaneous, online–offline collaboration that reduces project costs and speeds time-to-market for products and services. The Groove Outliner tool is an open-ended brainstorming tool that allows shared space members to build structured hierarchical lists of videos and concepts. Groove's Sketchpad enhances collaboration on drawings and designs. The Groove peer-collaboration platform works across corporate firewalls and requires no special configuration or IT administration. A very functional demo version (with no videoconferencing, however) is available for download. Although it takes a while to structure a first meeting and download all files to users, it is definitely an inexpensive, useful peer-to-peer package. A screenshot of a Groove Outliner session is shown in Figure 10.2.

WebEx Meeting Center and PlaceWare Conference Center

WebEx Meeting Center (**webex.com**) is pay-per-use groupware. It provides a low-cost, simplified way to hold electronic meetings over the Web. WebEx contains all the features you need to run a meeting. WebEx Meeting Center integrates data, voice, and video within a standard Web browser for real-time meetings over the Internet from any desktop, laptop, or wireless handheld device. WebEx delivers active and interactive presentations, allows real-time collaboration with remote coworkers and partners, enhances demonstration of products and services, and assists in document management by allowing viewing, annotation, and editing of documents in real time. Spontaneous Q&A sessions can be held, and closer relationships are built through interactive meetings with customers and partners from an individual's desktop. WebEx contains all the tools needed to share documents or opinions. WebEx Meeting Center is a fully hosted solution, enabling the

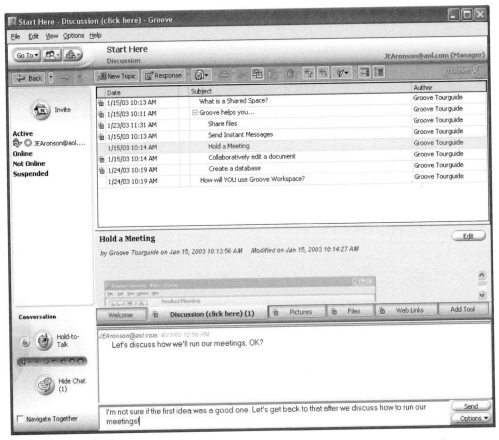

FIGURE 10.2 A Screenshot of Groove Outliner Session   *Source:* Grove Networks screen shot. Reprinted with permission of Microsoft Corporation.

initiation of online meetings that require no IT staff involvement, and it has very low startup costs. The WebEx MediaTone Network also provides fast communication for videoconferencing. For an interesting case with a savings of $6 million, see Smith (2004). Finally, MeetMeNow is designed specifically for the support of data with integrated audio.

The PlaceWare Conference Center (**main.placeware.com/services/pw_ conference_ctr.cfm**), now a subsidiary of Microsoft, provides Live Meeting and is capable of supporting multiple presenters and concurrent meetings, with up to 2,500 participants per session. It is used to conduct product launches, sales demonstrations, training sessions, and more. Live Meeting is easily integrated with existing productivity tools (e.g., sessions can be scheduled quickly through a Microsoft Outlook calendar). The collaborative experience is enhanced through added features such as live polling, audience feedback, and mood indicators. PlaceWare also offers a virtual classroom, a distance-learning environment for training and seminars (**main.placeware.com/services/ virtual_corp_training_orgs.cfm**).

GroupSystems

GroupSystems (**groupsystems.com**) MeetingRoom was one of the first comprehensive same time/same place electronic meeting packages. The follow-up product, GroupSystems OnLine, offered similar capabilities, and it ran in asynchronous mode (anytime/anyplace) over the Web (MeetingRoom ran only over a local area network [LAN]). GroupSystems latest product is ThinkTank, which is a suite of tools that significantly shortens cycle time for brainstorming, strategic planning, product development, problem solving, requirements gathering, risk assessments, team decision makings, and other collaborations. ThinkTank moves face-to-face or virtual teams through customizable processes toward their goals faster and more effectively than its predecessors. ThinkTank offers the following capabilities:

- ThinkTank builds in the discipline of an agenda, efficient participation, workflow, prioritization, and decision analysis.
- ThinkTank's anonymous brainstorming for ideas and comments is an ideal way to capture the participants' creativity and experience.
- ThinkTank Web 2.0's enhanced user interface ensures that participants do not need prior training to join, so they can focus 100 percent on solving problems and making decisions.
- With ThinkTank, all of the knowledge shared by participants is captured and saved in documents and spreadsheets and automatically converted to the meeting minutes and made available to all participants at the end of the session.

A pioneer in the field, GroupSystems' products have been used in many academic studies to establish the foundation (both theoretical as well as empirical) for future generations of GDSS/GSS tools. See Section 10.8 for a more detailed description of the ThinkTank collaboration software suite.

Other Vendors

Another specialized product is eRoom (now owned by EMC/Documentum at **software .emc.com**). This comprehensive Web-based suite of tools can support a variety of collaboration scenarios. Yet another product is Team Expert Choice (EC11), which is an add-on product for Expert Choice (**expertchoice.com**). It has limited decision support capabilities, mainly supporting one-room meetings. Wimba (**wimba.com**) is a collaboration tool suite that primarily focuses on educational applications (e.g., distance learning). Application Case 10.3 summarizes an exemplary use of Wimba collaboration suite in higher education.

APPLICATION CASE 10.3

Wimba Extends Classrooms at CSU, Chico

For years, instructors at California State University, Chico, have taught classes that meet face-to-face but simultaneously have students logged in remotely via Wimba Classroom. These remote students are able to hear and see the teacher via audio and video. A student assistant monitors the online learners, records the live class, and even passes the remote students' questions to the instructor, thereby creating a full classroom experience for both the in-person and remote students.

Wimba is a leading provider of collaborative learning software solutions to the higher education and K–12 markets. Since its inception almost a decade ago, Wimba has focused on education and is committed to harnessing the most powerful element of teaching—the human element—so that facial expressions, vocal intonations, hand gestures, real-time discussion, creativity, and passion can be conveyed in the online learning environment.

Connecting with distance students is nothing new to Chico. Located in northern California with more than 1,000 faculty supporting 16,000 students, CSU, Chico, is one the nation's most technically savvy institutions. Since it started offering distance education classes via satellite in 1975 with the goal of reaching its many graduate students who juggle school, work, and home life, universities within the CSU system and throughout the country have regarded Chico as an innovator. For example, instructional designers and instructors at CSU,

Chico, created the first regularly used rubric that measures the effectiveness of online instruction.

When it comes to capturing the activities that occur in a face-to-face class, most schools typically rely on hardware-based lecture-capture systems. These systems usually require a significant hardware investment and an advanced in-class setup in order to record the instructor's voice and movements while also capturing the visual materials the lecturer presents to the class. However, these lecture-capture systems do not allow students to log in remotely. Today, schools like Chico regularly utilize virtual classrooms to capture in-class activities for later viewing as well as to stream the classes live to make them available to remote students in real time. This expands a school's enrollment capabilities by increasing the number of students who can take (and review) any particular class.

As demand for online education increases, the education community will do what it takes to meet students' needs, and innovative schools like Chico will often pave the way. Distance education is no longer a niche, but a way of life for many educational institutions throughout the world. As traditional distance learning becomes increasingly less functional, more novel and practical solutions will emerge.

Sources: Wimba, "Lecture Capture via Wimba Classroom at California State University, Chico," **wimba.com/assets/resources/wimbaSpotlight_CSUChicoLECTURE.pdf** (accessed June 2009); CSU Chico blog, **blogs.csuchico.edu/tlp/?p=297** (accessed June 2009).

Conclusions About Groupware Suites

Successful **enterprise-wide collaboration systems** such as Lotus Notes/Domino can be expensive to develop and operate. To obtain the full benefits of such groupware, a well-trained, full-time support staff is required to develop applications and operate the system. In contrast, Groove is relatively inexpensive and provides easy-to-use and easy-to-set-up collaboration for an organization.

Industry reports estimate that all forms of groupware (e.g., audioconferencing, videoconferencing, data conferencing, Web-based conferencing) have become a more established part of the corporate decision-making process. The collaboration software market is growing rapidly. This growth is driven by time and money savings due to reduced travel and by organizational decentralization and globalization.

Electronic meeting services such as WebEx Meeting Center (**webex.com**), PlaceWare Conference Center (**main.placeware.com/services/pw_conference_ctr.cfm**), and

Verizon Conferencing (**e-meetings.mci.com**) enable anyone to hold a meeting for a rental fee.

Section 10.5 Review Questions

1. What is an integrated collaboration suite?
2. Describe Lotus Notes/Domino and its major capabilities.
3. Describe Microsoft's collaboration products.
4. What is unique about Groove?
5. Describe the process of renting a place for a virtual meeting, using companies such as WebEx.

10.6 DIRECT COMPUTERIZED SUPPORT FOR DECISION MAKING: FROM GROUP DECISION SUPPORT SYSTEMS TO GROUP SUPPORT SYSTEMS

Decisions are made at many meetings, some of which are called in order to make one specific decision. For example, the federal government meets periodically to decide on the short-term interest rate. Directors may be elected at shareholder meetings, organizations allocate budgets in meetings, a company decides on which candidate to hire, and so on. Although some of these decisions are complex (as was the case for P&G), others can be controversial, as in resource allocation by a city government. Process gains and dysfunctions can be significantly large in such situations; therefore, computerized support has often been suggested to mitigate these complexities (see Duke Corporate Education, 2005; and Powell et al., 2004). These computer-based support systems have appeared in the literature under different names, including *group decision support systems* (GDSS), *group support systems* (GSS), *computer-supported collaborative work* (CSCW), and *electronic meeting systems* (EMS). These systems are the subject of this section.

Group Decision Support Systems (GDSS)

During the 1980s, researchers realized that computerized support to managerial decision making needed to be expanded to groups because major organizational decisions are made by groups such as executive committees, special task forces, and departments. The result was the creation of group decision support systems (see Powell et al., 2004).

A **group decision support system (GDSS)** is an interactive computer-based system that facilitates the solution of semistructured or unstructured problems by a group of decision makers. The goal of GDSS is to improve the productivity of decision-making meetings by speeding up the decision-making process and/or by improving the quality of the resulting decisions.

The following are the major characteristics of a GDSS:

- Its goal is to support the process of group decision makers by providing automation of subprocesses, using information technology tools.
- It is a specially designed information system, not merely a configuration of already-existing system components. It can be designed to address one type of problem or a variety of group-level organizational decisions.
- It encourages generation of ideas, resolution of conflicts, and freedom of expression. It contains built-in mechanisms that discourage development of negative group behaviors, such as destructive conflict, miscommunication, and groupthink.

The first generation of GDSS was designed to support face-to-face meetings in a decision room. Today, support is provided mostly over the Web to virtual groups. The group can meet at the same time or at different times by using e-mail, sending documents, and reading transaction logs. GDSS is especially useful when controversial decisions have to be made (e.g., resource allocation, determining which individuals to lay off). GDSS applications require a facilitator when done in one room or a coordinator or leader when done using virtual meetings.

GDSS can improve the decision-making process in various ways. For one, GDSS generally provide structure to the planning process, which keeps the group on track, although some applications permit the group to use unstructured techniques and methods for **idea generation**. In addition, GDSS offer rapid and easy access to external and stored information needed for decision making. GDSS also support parallel processing of information and idea generation by participants and allow asynchronous computer discussion. They make possible larger meetings that would otherwise be unmanageable; having a larger group means that more complete information, knowledge, and skills will be represented in the meeting. Finally, voting can be anonymous, with instant results, and all information that passes through the system can be recorded for future analysis (producing *organizational memory*).

Initially, GDSS were limited to face-to-face meetings. To provide the necessary technology, a special facility (i.e., room) was created. Also, groups usually had a clearly defined, narrow task, such as allocation of scarce resources or prioritization of goals in a long-range plan.

Over time, it became clear that support teams' needs were broader than that supported by GDSS. For example, as indicated in the opening vignette, a task is not a single decision, but rather a broad challenge that includes several goals and many decisions, some of which are unknown at the project's initiation. Furthermore, it became clear that what was really needed was support for virtual teams, both in different place/same time and different place/different time situations. Also, it became clear that teams needed indirect support in most decision-making cases (e.g., help in searching for information or collaboration) rather than direct support for the decision making. Although GDSS expanded to virtual team support, they were unable to meet all the other needs. Thus, a broader term, *GSS*, was created. We use the terms interchangeably in this book.

Group Support Systems

A **group support system (GSS)** is any combination of hardware and software that enhances groupwork either in direct or indirect support of decision making. GSS is a generic term that includes all forms of collaborative computing. GSS evolved after information technology researchers recognized that technology could be developed to support the many activities normally occurring at face-to-face meetings (e.g., idea generation, consensus building, anonymous ranking).

A complete GSS is still considered a specially designed information system, but since the mid-1990s many of the special capabilities of GSS have been embedded in standard productivity tools. For example, Microsoft Windows Meeting Space Client is part of the Windows XP operating system. Most GSS are easy to use because they have a Windows-based graphical user interface (GUI) or a Web browser interface. Most GSS are fairly general and provide support for activities such as idea generation, conflict resolution, and voting. Also, many commercial products have been developed to support only one or two aspects of teamwork (e.g., videoconferencing, idea generation, screen sharing, wikis).

An **electronic meeting system (EMS)** is a form of GSS that supports anytime/anyplace meetings. Group tasks include, but are not limited to, communication, planning of a meeting, idea generation, problem solving, issue discussion, negotiation, conflict resolution, and collaborative group activities, such as document preparation and sharing. EMS may include desktop videoconferencing, whereas, in the past, GSS did not. However, there is a blurring between these two concepts, so today they should be considered synonymous.

GSS settings range from a group meeting at a single location for solving a specific problem to virtual meetings conducted in multiple locations and held via telecommunication channels for the purpose of addressing a variety of problem types. Continuously adopting new and improved methods, GSS are building up their capabilities to effectively operate in both asynchronous as well as synchronous modes.

GSS can be considered in terms of the common group activities that can benefit from computer-based support: information retrieval, including access of data values from an existing database and retrieval of information from other group members; information sharing, the display of data for the whole group on a common screen or at group members' workstations for viewing; and information use, the application of software technology (e.g., modeling packages, specific application programs), procedures, and group problem-solving techniques for reaching a group decision (e.g., see Technology Insights 10.3). In addition, creativity in problem solving (discussed in Section 10.10) can be enhanced via GSS.

How GDSS (or GSS) Improve Groupwork

The goal of GSS is to provide support to meeting participants to improve the productivity and effectiveness of meetings by streamlining and speeding up the decision-making process (i.e., efficiency) or by improving the quality of the results (i.e., effectiveness). GSS attempts to increase process and task gains and decrease process and task losses. Overall, GSS have been successful in doing just that (see Holt, 2002); however, some process and task gains may decrease, and some process and task losses may increase. Improvement is achieved by providing support to group members for the generation and exchange of ideas, opinions, and preferences. Specific features such as **parallelism** (i.e., the ability of participants in a group to work simultaneously on a task, such as brainstorming or voting) and anonymity produce this improvement. The following are some specific GDSS support activities:

- GDSS support parallel processing of information and idea generation (parallelism).
- GDSS enable the participation of larger groups with more complete information, knowledge, and skills.
- GDSS permit the group to use structured or unstructured techniques and methods.

TECHNOLOGY INSIGHTS 10.3   Modeling in Group Decision Making: EC11 for Groups

Based on the analytic hierarchy process (AHP) decision-making methodology implemented as Expert Choice (see Chapter 4), EC11 for Groups helps group members define objectives, goals, criteria, and alternatives and then organize them into a hierarchical structure. Using PCs, participants compare and prioritize the relative importance of the decision variables. EC11 for Groups then synthesizes the group's judgments to arrive at a conclusion and allows individuals to examine how changing the weighting of their criteria affects the outcome.

EC11 for Groups imitates the way people naturally make decisions: gathering information, structuring the decision, weighing the variables and alternatives, and reaching a conclusion. It supports the decision process. The group structures an AHP decision hierarchy for the problem as members perceive it; members provide the judgments, and members make the decision. A decision portal provides team members with models they can use to evaluate objectives and alternatives from their desktops.

Sources: Partly adapted from Expert Choice, **expertchoice.com** (accessed June 2009); and DSS Resources, "Expert Choice Unveils Latest Enterprise Portfolio Analysis Solutions," July 12, 2004, **dssresources.com/ news/80.php** (accessed May 2009).

- GDSS offer rapid, easy access to external information.
- GDSS allow parallel computer discussions.
- GDSS help participants frame the big picture.
- Anonymity allows shy people to contribute to the meeting (i.e., get up and do what needs to be done).
- Anonymity helps prevent aggressive individuals from driving a meeting.
- GDSS provide for multiple ways to participate in instant, anonymous voting.
- GDSS provide structure for the planning process to keep the group on track.
- GDSS enable several users to interact simultaneously (i.e., conferencing).
- GDSS record all information presented at a meeting (i.e., organizational memory).

A collaborative decision support system is summarized in Application Case 10.4. For more GSS success stories, look for sample cases at vendors' Web sites. As you will see, in many of these cases, collaborative computing led to dramatic process improvements and cost savings, as was the case in the opening vignette.

APPLICATION CASE 10.4

Collaborative Problem Solving at KUKA

A supplier in the field of robot technology is using an enterprise social software and wiki solution to streamline, record, and share information. KUKA Systems, with more than 6,000 employees worldwide, has deployed Traction's TeamPage technology to collaboratively identify, track, manage, and report on issues across various project groups. The ultimate goal is to make smarter decisions faster.

Tom Woodman, enterprise applications manager at KUKA Systems, says,

Prior to using TeamPage, status quo at KUKA was to assemble all stakeholders in time-consuming meetings where we would work through an Excel worksheet listing open issues. I needed a transparent way to raise and discuss the issues affecting enterprise systems and to enable as many interested parties to follow along in the discussion as possible. I also needed a place to capture the results of these discussions. TeamPage helped us document what wasn't working, collaborate around potential solutions and turn on a dime to fix them. Then, it helped us spread the word about those improvements to the rest of the company very quickly. As a byproduct, we are also able to meet compliance requirements, because auditors can easily review the issues and determine if there are any that would need further scrutiny from a financial reporting point of view.

According to Traction, the solution at KUKA Systems helps pull people together to better understand the issues they face—both within and across departments—and get them involved in solving problems.

Coming from a base of a nuts and bolts intranet, KUKA is in a position to deploy TeamPage further as the substance of an Enterprise 2.0 intranet. Over time, TeamPage may take the role of the departmental intranet as well as the primary wiki for managing the playbook (standard operating procedures) and content, supporting organization-wide continuous improvement and encouraging the contribution of ideas and suggestions.

Sources: Traction Software, Inc., "Customer Success Stories: KUKA Systems," **traction.tractionsoftware.com/traction/ read?proj=Public&edate=all&sectionid=customersoverview& normaledate=all*1%2d1&sort=2&title=Customers&stickypar ams=sectionid,normaledate,sort,title&type=single&rec=1653** (accessed June 2009); and *KMWorld,* "Collaborative Problem Solving at KUKA," **kmworld.com/Articles/News/KM-In-Practice/Collaborative-problem-solving-at-KUKA—53813.aspx** (accessed June 2009).

Note that the computer-mediated generation of a large number of ideas does not necessarily mean that electronic brainstorming is better than manual/verbal brainstorming. As a matter of fact, Dennis and Reinicke (2004) proved that the opposite may be true. It may very well depend on the circumstances. More research is needed to identify and explain the related factors.

Facilities for GDSS

There are three options for deploying GDSS/GSS technology: (1) as a special-purpose decision room, (2) as a multiple-use facility, and (3) as Internet or intranet-based groupware, with clients running wherever the group members are.

DECISION ROOMS The earliest GDSS were installed in expensive, customized, special-purpose facilities called **decision rooms** (or electronic meeting rooms) with PCs and large public screens at the front of each room. The original idea was that only executives and high-level managers would use the facility. The software in a special-purpose electronic meeting room usually runs over a LAN, and these rooms are fairly plush in their furnishings. Electronic meeting rooms can be constructed in different shapes and sizes. A common design includes a room equipped with 12 to 30 networked PCs, usually recessed into the desktop (for better participant viewing). A server PC is attached to a large-screen projection system and connected to the network to display the work at individual workstations and aggregated information from the facilitator's workstation. Breakout rooms equipped with PCs connected to the server, where small subgroups can consult, are sometimes located adjacent to the decision room. The output from the subgroups can also be displayed on the large public screen.

Some organizations (e.g., universities, large companies, government agencies) still use electronic decision rooms, and these rooms support same time/same place meetings. One Ohio school district even built a portable facility in a bus (the driver's seat turns around to become the facilitator's seat). However, there is still a need and a desire for groups to meet face-to-face. A facility like this can conveniently provide videoconferencing for communication with outsiders or team members who cannot attend the meeting. It may also supply other groupware as well as function as a fairly expensive computer lab. Decision rooms have been found especially useful when the decision topic is controversial (e.g., resource allocation or long-range planning), and the decision support can provide excellent results. For an example, see Application Case 10.5 and customer success stories at **groupsystems.com**.

APPLICATION CASE 10.5

Eastman Chemical Boosts Creative Processes and Saves $500,000 with Groupware

Problem

Eastman Chemical Co. (**eastman.com**) wanted to use creative problem-solving sessions to process ideas. Team members would present problems in a face-to-face meeting using flip charts and sticky notes to come up with better solutions, but organizing and studying the notes took far too long. The company needed more ideas and better methods to meet customers' needs. Traditional methods were not effective. The process was extremely unproductive and time-consuming.

Solution

Eastman Chemical chose GroupSystems to support its problem-solving process meetings. Here's how the meetings work now. First, participants define the problem and frame it. Then partici-pants brainstorm ideas to develop potential solu-tions to the problem, trying for "outside-the-box" thinking using creativity techniques. Recently, some 400 ideas were generated by nine people in a 2-hour session through parallelism. After catego-rizing similar items, the team establishes common decision criteria to choose the top three ideas, using the Alternative Analysis tool. Results are then copied into an Excel spreadsheet to develop an action plan.

Eastman ran 100 research and development managers through collaborative sessions to deter-mine top strategies. They defined 8 opportunities, with an action plan for the top 3—after generating 2,200 ideas!

Results

Henry Gonzales, manager of the polymer technology core competency group at Eastman, stated, "We found that with GroupSystems, we had more unusual ideas, a richer pool to choose from, and we got to the point a lot faster. I did a study and calculated that the software saved 50 percent of people's time, and projected a cost savings of over $500,000 for the 12 people during a year's time." Consequently, Eastman Chemical bought a second site license and upgraded to another facility so that more people could use the groupware.

Sources: Adapted from GroupSystems, "Eastman Chemical—Creativity and Team Center," **groupsystems.com/resource-center/customersandcases/CorporateCaseStudies/Eastman-Case-Study** (accessed August 2006); and **eastman.com** (accessed February 2006).

MULTIUSE FACILITIES A multiuse facility can also be constructed for GSS. This is sometimes a general-purpose computer lab or computer classroom that is also a less elegant but equally useful GDSS or GSS room. For example, at the Terry College of Business of The University of Georgia, Sanford Hall has a 48-seat lab/computer classroom with GroupSystems' MeetingRoom installed. This room "triples" as a distance-learning classroom, because it contains the latest academic videoconferencing software and hardware. Because a decision room is rarely used 100 percent of the time for groupwork, making such a room a multiuse room is an effective way to lower or share costs.

INTERNET/INTRANET-BASED SYSTEMS Since the late 1990s, the most common approach to GSS facilities has been to use Web- or intranet-based groupware that allows group members to work from any location at any time (e.g., Lotus Notes, Groove, WebEx, PlaceWare, GroupSystems, Windows Meeting Space). This groupware often includes audioconferencing and videoconferencing. The availability of relatively inexpensive groupware (for purchase or for rent), combined with the power and low cost of capable PCs, makes this type of system very attractive. Some groupware vendors, notably Groove, run in peer-to-peer mode, where each person works on a copy of the entire conference so that only differences among the files need to be transmitted. This capability makes this approach even more attractive.

WHICH GSS FACILITY TO USE? For the first and second options, a trained facilitator is necessary to coordinate and facilitate the meetings. The group leader works with the facilitator to structure the meeting. The success of a GSS session depends largely on the quality, activities, and support of the facilitator. For the third option, a coordinator is needed, but the required facilitating skills are much lower.

The high cost of constructing a facility and finding an experienced facilitator, and the need to have participants connect from other locations at any time, have reduced the need for the first two approaches. Therefore, the third option is most frequently used today. However, time deadlines are generally needed for each phase of an anytime/anyplace meeting. (The deadlines are set to allow for time zones and travel.) A problem for non–face-to-face meetings is that participants want to see the people with whom they are working. Some systems have access to still pictures, and others use videoconferencing to enhance some meeting aspects by showing the faces of the participants and sometimes their body language.

In Table 10.3, we provide a list of collaborative computing/GSS and Web impacts. Next, we describe some of the features and structure of a comprehensive GSS, using GroupSystems' ThinkTank as an example.

Section 10.6 Review Questions

1. Define *GDSS* and list the limitations of the initial GDSS software.
2. Define *GSS* and list its benefits.
3. Define *EMS*.

TABLE 10.3 Collaborative Computing/GSS and Web Impacts

Collaborative Computing/GSS	Web Impacts	Impacts on the Web
Collaboration	• Provides a consistent, friendly GUI for client units	• Enables improvements in management, hardware, software, and infrastructure, due mainly to collaboration in (Web-based) CASE and other systems analysis and design tools
	• Provides convenient, fast access to team members	• Enables improvements in site design and development methods
	• Provides improved collaboration tools	• Allows simultaneous Web surfing (e.g., Groove)
	• Enables access to data/information/ knowledge on servers	
	• Enables document sharing	
	• Enables anytime/anywhere collaboration	
	• Enables collaboration between companies, customers, and vendors	
Communication	• Provides improved, fast communication among group members and links to data/information/knowledge sources	Same as above
	• Makes audio- and videoconferencing a reality, especially for individuals not using a local area network (LAN)	
Decision room	• Provides a consistent, friendly GUI for clients	Same as above
	• Supports communication	
	• Provides access to Web-based tools	
	• Enables room design teams to collaborate to provide dramatic improvements in facilities	
Mixed-mode facility	Same as above	Same as above
Colocated team facility (members in different locations)	• Provides fast connections to enable real-time collaboration	Same as above

4. List process gain improvements made by GSS.
5. Define *decision room*.
6. Describe a GSS multiuse facility.
7. Describe Web-based GSS.
8. Why is the third option for a GDSS facility the most popular?

10.7 PRODUCTS AND TOOLS FOR GDSS/GSS AND SUCCESSFUL IMPLEMENTATION

Products and tools designed specifically to support meetings that deal with decision support may appear in groupware products or in special suites, such as that of ThinkTank (by GroupSystems). ThinkTank, GroupSystems' latest product suite, combines MeetingRoom and GroupSystems OnLine into a single software suite that offers capabilities to facilitate both same time/same place face-to-face meetings and same time/different place virtual meetings. Before we describe the software products, let's first take a look at how to get ready to use them.

Organizing a GSS Session

Face-to-face, same time/same place electronic meetings generally follow a common progression. First, the group leader meets with the facilitator to plan the meeting (this is critically important), select the software tools, and develop an agenda. Second, the participants meet in the decision room, and the leader poses a question or problem to the group. Third, the participants type their ideas or comments (i.e., brainstorm), and the results are displayed publicly. Because the participants can see on their own monitors what others are typing, they can provide comments or generate new ideas. Fourth, the facilitator, using idea organization software, searches for common themes, topics, and ideas and organizes them into rough categories (i.e., key ideas) with appropriate comments; new research is attempting to automate this part of the electronic meeting. The results are publicly displayed. Fifth, the leader starts a discussion, either verbal or electronic. The participants next prioritize the ideas. Sixth, the top 5 or 10 topics are sent to idea-generation software following a discussion. The process (idea generation, idea organization, prioritization) can be repeated or a final vote can be taken. The major activities of a typical GDSS session are listed in Technology Insights 10.4.

It is important to remind participants of where they are in the group meeting process and to keep them focused on long-term tasks. Other issues include security (to protect valuable information from theft), universal access (i.e., from home or other sites), folder invitations and information (i.e., participants must be invited to participate in meeting segments), information about the participants (i.e., on virtual business cards), indication of who is on the system (to alleviate feelings of loneliness), and facilitator controls (i.e., to start and stop sessions, to restrict access to activities).

An pictorial overview of the tools and their relationship to the major GSS activities is provided in Figure 10.3.

Planning the session is one of the most critical issues. Facilitators must provide incentives and develop investment in the outcome, communicate often and explicitly, assign roles and tasks with accountability, and be explicit in goal and activity communication. To illustrate this process, let's look at GroupSystems and its product suite, ThinkTank.

ThinkTank by GroupSystems

ThinkTank is a Web 2.0 application for group collaboration. Accessed through an Internet browser, ThinkTank can be used (mainly for brainstorming—identifying, organizing, prioritizing, evaluating, and documenting ideas) in real time or offline to

TECHNOLOGY INSIGHTS 10.4   The Standard GSS Process

The following are the major steps in the GSS process:

- **Idea generation.** This exploratory step looks at the problem and attempts to develop creative ideas about its important features (or alternative solutions in a problem-solving session). The ideas can have anything to do with the problem; they can be potential solutions, criteria, or mitigating factors. An electronic brainstorming tool is appropriate; its output is a list of ideas. Typical time for this step is 30 to 45 minutes.
- **Idea organization.** An idea-organizing tool groups the many ideas generated (possibly hundreds) into a list of key issues. The output of this stage is a list of a few key ideas (about 1 for every 20 original ideas) with the supporting details. Typical time for this step is 45 to 90 minutes.
- **Prioritization.** At this stage, the key ideas are prioritized. A voting tool can be appropriate (Neumann, 2004); its output is a prioritized list of ideas and details. Typical time for this step is 10 to 20 minutes.
- **Additional idea generation.** New ideas are generated based on the prioritization of the key ideas. A brainstorming tool that provides structure, such as a topic commentator tool, is appropriate here. The ideas generated are typically focused on solutions. This stage's output may consist of up to 20 ideas for each of the original key ideas.

This process continues in iterations until a final idea is selected as a solution to the problem that prompted the meeting or a few solutions are identified to be investigated in more depth. Some meetings are oriented toward decision making. Others are exploratory in nature and are focused on generating ideas to pursue in follow-up meetings or individual work. Often, a GDSS meeting takes longer than an unsupported meeting, but participants are generally more thorough in their brainstorming and analysis, and they feel that they have made a better decision by using the system.

---

support face-to-face or virtual-team meeting activities. Each meeting is a unique ThinkTank session that contains all the information about the meeting, including the session leader, date/time of the session, location, agenda, attendees, attendee rights, supporting documents, meeting notes, and outcomes.

Every ThinkTank session has a session leader. The session leader creates the session, defining the title, purpose, start and stop date/time, attendee rights, and agenda. The leader controls the purpose, workflow, and activities of a session by defining a session agenda. A ThinkTank session agenda may be created from either a blank session workspace or from one of the several predefined agendas, called ThinkTank Templates. Supporting documents and other Web-based materials may be linked to a session in order to better organize a meeting. A session agenda is built using any number or combination of the following session activities:

- **Action planner.** Define and collaborate on tasks, assign task ownership, and establish timelines and next steps.
- **Alternative analysis.** Use multiple criteria to establish priorities, make decisions, and gain consensus.
- **Break.** Create a session workflow pause for taking a break during your session.
- **Categorizer.** Brainstorm and organize ideas, issues, and other discussion items.
- **Placeholder.** Add a spot in the agenda for introductions, lunch, or other non–ThinkTank activities.
- **Rank order vote.** Prioritize items based on a single criterion.
- **Survey.** Build and conduct robust opinion surveys.

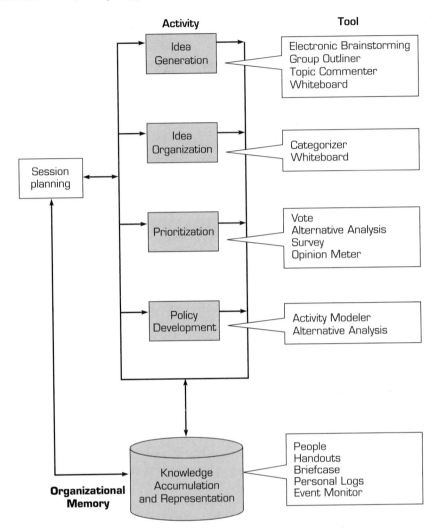

FIGURE 10.3 Typical GSS Activities and Related Tools

To build a session agenda, the leader selects the desired activities, and then drags and drops them onto the agenda workspace. A screenshot of ThinkTank is shown in Figure 10.4. Once the session setup is complete, the leader invites the participants and conducts the meeting.

GroupSystems is the most mature and most popular provider of group decision support tools, but several other companies provide interesting GSS software packages. Table 10.4 lists some of these tools. Free evaluation versions, which are often fully functional products with limited activation time, often are available.

GSS Success Factors

The success of a GSS depends mostly on its results. A system succeeds if it cuts costs (especially travel costs), supports participants in making better decisions, and/or increases productivity substantially. In order to succeed, a GSS needs many of the usual information system success factors: organizational commitment, an executive sponsor, an operating sponsor, user involvement and training, a user-friendly interface, and so on. If the organizational culture does not readily support face-to-face collaboration, then it must be changed

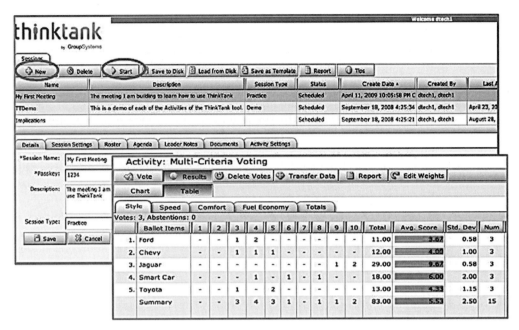

FIGURE 10.4   A Screenshot from ThinkTank Collaboration Suite   *Source:* GroupSystems.com

to do so before a GSS is introduced. Otherwise, the system will not be used, and it will be deemed a failure. This is also a critical issue in knowledge management (see Chapter 11), which involves collaboration at the enterprise level. Having a dedicated, well-trained, personable facilitator is also critical. The GSS must have the correct tools to support the organization's groupwork and must include parallelism and anonymity to provide process and task gains. Good planning is also a key to running successful meetings, including electronic meetings. If anything, bad planning might make a group believe that the GSS is to blame for its poor performance. Finally, GSS must demonstrate cost savings, either through a more effective and efficient meeting process or through reduced travel costs. Tangible results are necessary, but not sufficient; a collaborative culture is necessary.

TABLE 10.4   GDSS Tools

Tool	Company	Web Site
AnyZing	Zing Technologies	**anyzing.com**
Facilitate	Facilitate	**facilitate.com**
Groove	Microsoft	**office.microsoft.com/groove**
Grouputer	Grouputer Solutions	**grouputer.com**
Lotus Notes & Domino	Lotus Software (IBM)	**ibm.com/software/lotus/**
MeetingDragon.com	MeetingDragon	**meetingdragon.com**
TeamPage	Traction Software	**tractionsoftware.com**
TeamWorks	TeamWorks	**teamworks.si**
ThinkTank	GroupSystems	**groupsystems.com**
WebIQ	ynSyte	**webiq.net**
Metallon*	Metallon	**metallon.org**
CoFFEE*	Coffee Soft	**sourceforge.net/projects/coffee-soft**

* Free and/or open source software product.

CRAFTING A COLLABORATIVE CULTURE   Collaboration is about people; however, a collaboration tool will not change their attitudes. Technology provides support to the solution. It is also important to motivate the users to really use the new system. The managers must create a work environment that supports collaboration. According to Agrew (2000), this involves three simple steps:

1. ***Know what you want.***   Get team members to articulate their definition of success (or performance). This is part of the team-building process. For example, at Boeing-Rocketdyne, the team created a formal contract indicating goals and how the team would function.

2. ***Determine resource constraints.***   These include everything from the geographic distribution of team members to reporting relationships to motivations. Each constraint limits the possible tools the team can use.

3. ***Determine what technologies can be used to overcome resource constraints.***   It is important to keep in mind business needs rather than fun, new, or convenient technologies. For example, videoconferencing and detailed product and code design work require high-bandwidth connections.

When all this is determined, it is necessary to set up group sessions with good facilitation to guide and train the participants in the tools used. For more on cultural aspects and international perspectives, see de Vreede and Ackermann (2005).

Implementation Issues for Online Collaboration

This chapter has presented numerous online collaboration issues of different sorts. In addition, a few implementation issues must be addressed when planning online collaboration. First, to connect business partners an organization needs an effective collaborative environment. Such an environment is provided by groupware suites such as Lotus Notes/Domino or Cybozu Share360 (**cybozu.com**). Another issue is the need to connect collaborative tools with file management products on an organization's intranet. Two products that offer such connection capabilities are the WiredRed server and client (**wiredred.com**) and the eRoom server (**software.emc.com**).

Another important issue in collaboration is automatic language translation. This is required for global teams in which not all the participants speak the same language. For discussion on this, see Chapter 13 and Transclick (**transclick.com**).

In addition, to create a truly collaborative environment protocols are needed for easy integration of different applications and to standardize communication. One such protocol is WebDAV (Web Distributed Authoring and Versioning; see **webdav.org**).

An example of a tool that facilitates collaboration administration is Vignette Collaboration 7.0. For administrators, the tool supports clustering and eases administration of user access policies through improved mapping to corporate directories. The tool also enables the display, storage, and search of any Unicode-supported language. Also available is integration with Microsoft's Live Communications Server for presence awareness and IM.

Finally, note that online collaboration is not a panacea for all occasions or all situations. Many times, a face-to-face meeting is a must. People sometimes need the facial cues and the physical closeness that no computer system can currently provide. (A technology called pervasive computing attempts to remove some of these limitations by interpreting facial cues.)

Section 10.7 Review Questions

1. List the steps of organizing a GDSS session.
2. List GroupSystems' major products.
3. List some success factors of GDSS/GSS.
4. How can a company create a collaborative culture?
5. List three implementation issues of GDSS/GSS.

10.8 EMERGING COLLABORATION TOOLS: FROM VOIP TO WIKIS

A large number of new collaborative tools have appeared on the market in the past few years. Representative examples are presented here.

Voice over IP

Voice over IP (VoIP) refers to communication systems that transmit voice calls over Internet Protocol (IP)–based networks. Corporations are moving their phone systems to Internet standards to cut costs and boost efficiency. VoIP is also known as **Internet telephony**. Free Internet telephony software is available from **pc-telephone.com**. Most browsers provide for VoIP capabilities. The browsers enable you to receive telephone calls initiated on the Internet (with a microphone and special VoIP software, which may be provided with the sender's browser). VoIP is helping educational institutions, as discussed in Technology Insights 10.5.

THE BENEFITS OF VOIP According to a Siemens Communication (**communications .USA.Siemens.com**), VoIP communications offer the following benefits:

For the business:

- Allows chief information officers to explore different deployment options for company's communications needs
- Lowers total cost of ownership through voice/data convergence
- Lowers operational costs through use of integrated applications

---

TECHNOLOGY INSIGHTS 10.5   VoIP System Helps Increase Productivity and Enhance Learning Experiences at the State University of New York

The Cortland campus of the State University of New York (SUNY) was one of two winners recognized at the EDUCAUSE 2003 annual conference. The award honors innovative programs or practices that improve network infrastructure and architecture, integration, and quality of service on a campus or within an educational system and that positively affect a campus community or significant subcommunity.

The university chose a Cisco IP Communications system (a popular VoIP system) to replace its traditional private branch exchange (PBX)–based voice network and a shared 10-megabit-per-second Ethernet data network. The new converged network includes 700 Cisco IP phones that work with 3,000 existing analog phones connected via Cisco VG-248 IP gateways.

Daniel Sidebottom, director or Administrative Computing Services at SUNY, stated that the return-on-investment (ROI) analysis for the IP communications system anticipated a return on the technology investment in less than 1 year.

The new system helps university faculty, staff, and students communicate more effectively and provides applications to enhance the academic experience. For example, university faculty and students are able to use streaming video, file sharing, and other high-bandwidth applications, adding considerable value to the curricula as well as driving operational effectiveness. The combined voice and data network features a single call center system to support the admissions and financial aid offices to better serve students, parents, and others who need information and assistance. The solution delivers streamlined voice, data communications, and video to the entire campus and strengthens SUNY Cortland's mission to provide students with the opportunity to develop and use technology in their studies.

Sources: Compiled from T. Spangler, "Cisco to Replace VoIP Tools," *Baseline,* October 1, 2005; and J. A. Pirani, "Implementing an IP-Based Voice, Data and Video an SUNY Cortland," 2005, **educause.edu/ECAR/ ImplementinganIPbasedVoiceData/155115** (accessed June 2009).

- Reduces hardware requirements on the server side for certain applications (e.g., VoIP)
- Provides a holistic approach to security, enhanced by encryption, and identity management
- Helps streamline workflows by empowering companies to communications-enable different business processes
- Enables optimized conferencing tools to replace business travel

For the user:

- Eliminates unwanted interruptions and unproductive actions by intelligently filtering communications
- Provides access to real-time presence information, which helps decisions get made faster
- Initiates ad hoc conferencing/collaboration sessions without the need to prearrange separate audio- or videoconferencing bridges
- Enables participation in conferencing sessions quickly and easily via a variety of mobile devices

Collaborative Workflow

Collaborative workflow refers to software products that address project-oriented and collaborative types of processes. They are administered centrally yet are capable of being accessed and used by workers from different departments and even from different physical locations. The goal of collaborative workflow tools is to empower knowledge workers. The focus of an enterprise solution for collaborative workflow is on allowing workers to communicate, negotiate, and collaborate within an integrated environment. Some leading vendors of collaborative workflow applications are Lotus, EpicData, FileNet, and Action Technologies.

Web 2.0

The term *Web 2.0* refers to what is perceived to be the second generation of Web development and Web design. It is characterized as facilitating communication, information sharing, interoperability, user-centered design, and collaboration on the World Wide Web. It has led to the development and evolution of Web-based communities, hosted services, and novel Web applications. Example Web 2.0 applications include social-networking sites (e.g., LinkedIn, Facebook, MySpace), video-sharing sites (e.g., YouTube, Flickr, MyVideo), wikis, blogs, mashups, and folksonomies.

Web 2.0 sites typically include the following features/techniques, identified by the acronym SLATES:

- *Search.*   The ease of finding information through keyword search.
- *Links.*   Ad hoc guides to other relevant information.
- *Authoring.*   The ability to create content that is constantly updated by multiple users. In wikis, the content is updated in the sense that users undo and redo each other's work. In blogs, content is updated in that posts and comments of individuals are accumulated over time.
- *Tags.*   Categorization of content by creating tags. Tags are simple, one-word, user-determined descriptions to facilitate searching and avoid rigid, premade categories.
- *Extensions.*   Powerful algorithms leverage the Web as an application platform as well as a document server.
- *Signals.*   RSS technology is used to rapidly notify users of content changes.

Wikis

A **wiki** is a piece of server software available at a Web site that allows users to freely create and edit Web page content through a Web browser. (The term *wiki* means "quick" or "to hasten" in the Hawaiian language; e.g., "Wiki Wiki" is the name of the shuttle bus in Honolulu International Airport.) A wiki supports hyperlinks and has a simple text syntax for creating new pages and cross-links between internal pages on-the-fly. It is especially suited for collaborative writing.

Wikis are unusual among group communication mechanisms in that they allow the organization of the contributions to be edited as well as the content itself. The term *wiki* also refers to the collaborative software that facilitates the operation of a wiki Web site.

A wiki enables documents to be written collectively in a very simple markup, using a Web browser. A single page in a wiki is referred to as a "wiki page," and the entire body of pages, which are usually highly interconnected via hyperlinks, is "the wiki"; in effect, it is a very simple, easy-to-use database. For further details, see **en.wikipedia.org/wiki/Wiki** and **wiki.org**.

Wikis come in many shapes and formats, one of which is a wikilog.

WIKILOG   A wikilog (or wikiblog) is an extension of a blog, which is usually created by an individual (or maybe a small group). It may also have a discussion board. A **wikilog** is essentially a blog that allows everyone to participate as a peer (a combination of wikis and blogs, also known as a *bliki*). Anyone may add, delete, or change content. It is like a loose-leaf notebook with a pencil and eraser left in a public place. Anyone can read it, scrawl notes, tear out a page, and so on. Creating a wikilog is a collaborative process. Information added to a wiki can be changed or deleted by anyone (although many wikis preserve previous copies of posted contributions in the background). Unlike protected Web pages, content added to a wiki is at the editorial mercy of the wiki's other participants. For further details, see **usemod.com/cgi-bin/mb.pl?WikiLog**.

COMMERCIAL ASPECTS OF WIKIS AND THEIR DERIVATIVES   Because wikis are a relatively new technology, it is difficult to assess their commercial potential. However, the research firm Gartner Group predicts that wikis will become mainstream collaboration tools in at least 50 percent of companies by 2009 (see **WikiThat.com**, 2009). In addition to being used for collaboration, wikis can replace e-mail because wikis are open source, spam-free communication tools. The benefits of the technology are demonstrated in the DrKW application case at the end of this chapter. A major vendor of wiki commercialization is Socialtext (**socialtext.com**).

Collaboration Hubs

One of the most popular forms of B2B e-commerce is the **collaboration hub**, which is used by members of a supply chain to improve effectiveness between manufacturing companies, their suppliers, and contract producers by reducing inventory, improving flexibility, and increasing supply-chain transparency through the Internet. For details, see Turban et al. (2009).

Collaborative Networks

Traditionally, collaboration took place among supply-chain members, frequently those that were close to each other (e.g., a manufacturer and its distributor, a distributor and a retailer). Even if more partners were involved, the focus was on the optimization of information and product flow between existing nodes in the traditional supply chain. Advanced approaches, such as collaborative planning, forecasting, and replenishment (CPFR; see Section 10.9), do not change this basic structure.

Traditional collaboration results in a vertically integrated supply chain. However, Web technologies can fundamentally change the shape of the supply chain, the number of players in it, and their individual roles. In a collaborative network, partners at any point in the network can interact with each other, bypassing traditional partners. Interaction may occur among several manufacturers or distributors, as well as with new players, such as software agents that act as aggregators, business-to-business (B2B) exchanges, or logistics providers. For discussion and examples, see Turban et al. (2009) and **logility.com**.

Corporate (Enterprise) Portals

A corporate (enterprise) portal is a gateway to a corporate Web site that enables communication, collaboration, and access to company information. A **corporate portal** is a personalized, single point of access through a Web browser to critical business information located inside and outside an organization. In contrast with commercial portals such as Yahoo! and MSN, which are gateways to general information on the Internet, corporate portals provide a single point of access to information and applications available on the Internet, intranets, and extranets of a specific organization. Several types of corporate portals facilitate communication and collaboration.

Section 10.8 Review Questions

1. Describe *VoIP* and list its advantages.
2. Define *collaborative workflow*.
3. Define *wiki* and *wikilog*.
4. Define *collaborative hub*.
5. Define *corporate (enterprise) portal*.

10.9   COLLABORATIVE EFFORTS IN DESIGN, PLANNING, AND PROJECT MANAGEMENT

Three major collaborative efforts are in the areas of joint design, collaborative planning, and project management.

Collaborative Design and Product Development

Collaborative product development involves the use of product design and development techniques across multiple companies to improve product launch success and reduce cost and time to market. During product development, engineering and design drawings can be shared over a secure network among the contract firm, testing facility, marketing firm, and downstream manufacturing and service companies. Other techniques include sharing specifications, test results, design changes, and using online prototyping to obtain customer feedback. Development costs can be reduced by tightly integrating and streamlining communication channels.

Example: Reduction of Product Development Time: Caterpillar, Inc.

Caterpillar, Inc. (**caterpillar.com**), is a multinational heavy-machinery manufacturer. In the traditional mode of operation, cycle time along the supply chain was long because the process involved paper-document transfers among managers, salespeople, and technical staff. To solve the problem, Caterpillar connected its engineering and manufacturing divisions with its active suppliers, distributors, overseas factories, and customers through an extranet-based global collaboration system. By means of the collaboration system, a request for a customized tractor component, for example, can be transmitted from a customer to a Caterpillar dealer and on to designers and suppliers, all in a very short time. Customers can use the extranet to retrieve and modify detailed order information while the vehicle is still on the assembly line. Remote collaboration capabilities between the customer and product developers have decreased cycle time delays caused by rework time. Suppliers are also connected to the system, so they can deliver materials or parts directly to Caterpillar's repair shops or directly to the customer, if appropriate. The system is also used for expediting maintenance and repairs.

For comprehensive coverage of collaborative virtual design environments, see Manninen (2004). For an example of how Procter & Gamble's creative minds collaborate on designing its new consumer products using GroupSystems' ThinkTank, refer to the opening vignette.

Collaborative Planning Along the Supply Chain

Collaborative planning is designed to synchronize production and distribution plans and product flows, optimize resource utilization over an expanded capacity base, increase customer responsiveness, and reduce inventories. In collaborative planning, business partners—manufacturers, suppliers, distribution partners, and others—create the initial demand (or sales) forecasts, provide changes as necessary, and share information (e.g., actual sales, their own forecasts). Thus, all parties work according to a unified schedule aligned to a common view and all have access to order and forecast performance that is globally visible through electronic links. Schedule, order, and product changes trigger immediate adjustments to all parties' schedules. CPFR is an industry project in this area.

THE CPFR PROJECT   **Collaborative planning, forecasting, and replenishment (CPFR)** is an industry-wide project in which suppliers and retailers collaborate in planning and demand forecasting in order to ensure that members of the supply chain will have the right amount of raw materials and finished goods when they need them. When implementing a CPRF project, the collaborators agree on a standard process, shown in Figure 10.5. The process ends with an order forecast. CPFR provides a standard framework for collaborative planning. Retailers and vendors determine the "rules of engagement," such as how often and at what level information will be provided. Typically, they share greater amounts of more detailed information, such as promotion schedules and item point-of-sale history, and use store-level expectations as the basis for all forecasts.

The idea of CPFR is to improve demand forecasting for all the partners in the supply chain and then communicate forecasts, using information-sharing applications (already developed by technology companies such as Manugistics, Oracle, and i2 Technologies). For the retailer, collaborative forecasting means fewer out-of-stocks and resultant lost sales and less stored inventory. For the manufacturer, collaborative forecasting means fewer expedited shipments, optimal inventory levels, and optimally sized production runs.

Besides working together to develop production plans and forecasts for stock replenishment, suppliers and retailers also coordinate the related logistics activities (such as shipment or warehousing), using a common language standard and new information methodologies.

A 2002 survey (see Bradley, 2002) found that 67 percent of 43 large food, beverage, and consumer products companies were researching, piloting, or implementing CPFR. About half of the respondents who were looking at CPFR said they planned to go ahead with their initiatives. However, CPFR is not the answer for all trading partners or all types of stock-keeping units (SKUs). According to Tim Paydos, a vice president of marketing at Syncra Systems, CPFR has generated the highest payback with either highly promoted or seasonal goods, whose inventories historically have often been misaligned with demand. "If I'm going to make the investment in CPFR," noted Paydos, "I want to do it with the products with the greatest return" (Bradley, 2002).

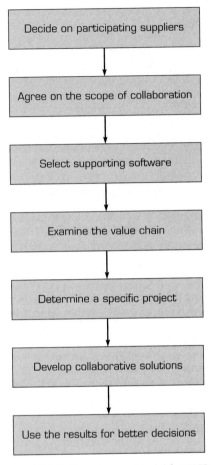

FIGURE 10.5 A Process Model for CPFR

The CPFR strategy has been driven by Wal-Mart and various benchmarking partners. After a successful pilot between Wal-Mart and Warner-Lambert involving Listerine products, a Voluntary Interindustry Commerce Standards (VICS) subcommittee was established to develop the proposed CPFR standard for the participating retailing industries (i.e., Wal-Mart's suppliers). Ace Hardware Corp. and Sears have had interesting applications of CPFR, as discussed in Application Case 10.6.

CPFR can be used with company-centric B2B, sell-side, or buy-side marketplaces. For more on the benefits of CPFR, see **vics.org/committees/cpfr**.

VENDOR-MANAGED INVENTORY With **vendor-managed inventory (VMI)**, retailers make their suppliers responsible for determining when to order and how much to order. The retailer provides the supplier with real-time information (e.g., point-of-sale data), inventory levels, and a threshold below which orders are to be replenished. The reorder quantities also are predetermined and usually recommended by the supplier. By using this approach, the retailer is no longer burdened with inventory management, demand forecasting becomes easier, the supplier can see the potential need for an item before the item is ordered, there are no purchase orders, inventories are kept low, and stockouts occur infrequently. This method was initiated by Wal-Mart in the 1980s and was supported by an electronic data interchange (EDI). Today, it can be supported by CPFR and special software.

VMI software solutions are provided by Sockeye Solutions, Cactus Communications, and JDA Software. For details, see Bury (2004).

For other innovative collaborative solutions to supply-chain problems, see **logility.com**.

Collective Intelligence

Wikipedia, Google, and Threadless are well-known examples of large, loosely organized groups of people working together electronically in surprisingly effective ways. These new modes of organizing work have been described with a variety of terms—*radical decentralization, crowd-sourcing, wisdom of crowds, peer production,* and *wikinomics.* The most popular of these terms is probably *collective intelligence,* which is defined very broadly as groups of individuals doing things collectively that seem intelligent (Malone et al., 2009).

Collective intelligence (CI) is a shared intelligence that emerges from the intentional cooperation, collaboration, and/or coordination of many individuals. CI appears in a wide variety of forms in humans, animals, bacteria, and computer networks. The study of CI may be considered a subfield of sociology, business, computer science, mass communications, and mass behavior. Collective intelligence is also referred to as *symbiotic intelligence.* A simple taxonomy of CI is illustrated in Figure 10.6, where the main branches of CI are shown as cognition, cooperation, and coordination (**en.wikipedia.org/wiki/Collective_intelligence**).

CI can also be defined as a form of networking enabled by the rise of communications technology, namely the Internet. Web 2.0 has enabled interactivity; thus, users are able to generate their own content. CI draws on this to enhance the social pool of

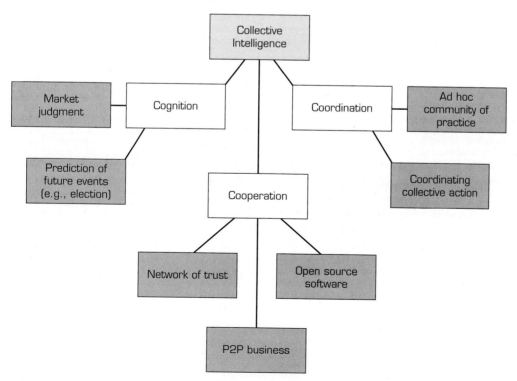

FIGURE 10.6   A Simple Taxonomy for Collective Intelligence   *Source:* **en.wikipedia.org/wiki/Collective_intelligence**

existing knowledge. In order for CI to happen, four features are needed (Tapscott and Williams, 2007):

- *Openness.* During the early stages of communications technology, people and companies were reluctant to share ideas and intellectual property. The reason for this was the idea that these resources provided the edge over competitors. Today, people and companies tend to loosen these resources and reap benefits from doing so. Sharing of ideas through collaboration leads to product and process improvements.
- *Peering.* This is a form of horizontal organization with the capacity to create information, knowledge, technology, and physical products. One example is Linux, an open source system. Users are free to modify and develop the system provided that they make their changes and improvements available to others. Participants in this form of collective intelligence have different motivations for contributing, but the result is improvement of a product or service. Most believe that peering succeeds because it leverages self-organization—a style of production that works more effectively than hierarchical management for certain tasks.
- *Sharing.* This principle has been the subject of debate for many, with the question being, "Should there be no laws against distribution of intellectual property?" Research has shown that more and more companies are sharing some information, while maintaining a degree of control over potential and critical patents. Companies have come to realize that if they limit access to all their intellectual property, they are shutting out possible extension opportunities. Limited sharing has allowed some companies to expand their market knowledge and bring products to market more quickly.
- *Acting globally.* The emergence of communications technology has prompted the rise of global companies, especially in the form of e-commerce. As the influence of the Internet is widespread, a globally integrated company has no geographic boundaries. Such a company also has global connections, allowing it to gain access to new markets, ideas, and technology. Therefore it is important for firms to stay globally competitive or they will face a declining rate of clientele.

Examples of CI projects are emerging. The best-known collective intelligence projects are political parties, which mobilize large numbers of people to form policy, select candidates, and finance and run election campaigns. Military units, trade unions, and corporations are focused on more narrow concerns but would satisfy some definitions of CI—the most rigorous definition would require a capacity to respond to very arbitrary conditions without orders or guidance from "law" or "customers" that tightly constrain actions. Other examples of CI include the following:

- *Wikipedia.* Wikipedia is an online encyclopedia that can be altered by virtually anyone at any time. The concept behind Wikipedia is often termed *wikinomics*. It is a new force that is bringing people together on the Internet to create a giant repository of information. Wikinomics blurs the lines between consumer and producer, leading to the terms *produser* and *prosumer*.
- *Videogames.* Games such as The Sims, Halo, and Second Life are nonlinear and depend on collective intelligence for expansion. This way of sharing is gradually evolving and influencing the mindset of the current and future generations.
- *Online advertising.* Companies like BootB (**bootb.com**) and DesignBay (**designbay.com**) are using collective intelligence in order to bypass traditional marketing and creative agencies.
- *Learner-generated context.* Learner-generated context occurs when a group of users collaboratively marshals available resources to create an ecology that meets their needs, often in relation to the coconfiguration, cocreation, and codesign of a learning space that enables learners to create their own context. In this sense, learner-generated

contexts represent an ad hoc community that facilitates the coordination of collective action in a network of trust.

- ***Animal behavior.*** Ant societies exhibit more intelligence than any other animal except for humans, if we measure intelligence in terms of technology. Ant societies are able to do agriculture, in fact several different forms of agriculture. Some ant societies maintain livestock of various forms; for example, some ants keep and care for aphids for "milking." Leaf cutter ants care for fungi and carry leaves to feed the fungi.

Even though the concept is counterintuitive, CI works. But why? A group of researchers from MIT is looking for answers to this question. Malone et al. (2009) proposed a framework to identify the underlying building blocks of CI. The key questions suggested by the researchers were:

- Who is performing the task? (crowd, specific group, random, etc.)
- Why are they doing it? (money, love, glory, etc.)
- What is being accomplished? (create, decide, predict, etc.)
- How is it being done? (cooperation, collaboration, coordination, etc.)

Additional information on collective intelligence can be found at the Web site of the Center for Collective Intelligence at MIT (**cci.mit.edu/**).

Project Management

Developing large-scale projects requires collaboration among a large number of units and individuals inside and outside an organization. Effective and efficient communication and collaboration is a must. Application Case 10.6 offers an example of how one company is doing it effectively.

APPLICATION CASE 10.6

CPFR Initiatives at Ace Hardware and Sears

Ace Hardware Corp. (**acehardware.com**), based in Oak Brook, Illinois, is a chain of 5,100 independently owned stores that sell everything from 10-penny nails to toasters. In 1999, Ace implemented a CPFR process, using its buy-side private exchange, to achieve more intelligent relationships with its suppliers. This platform creates and executes a single, shared demand forecast, allowing Ace to increase revenue while reducing costs.

Ace began using CPFR with a single supplier, Henkel Consumer Adhesives, a manufacturer of duct tape, adhesives, and other do-it-yourself home and office products. During the first year of implementation, the two companies improved forecast accuracy by 10 percent, lowered distribution costs by 28 percent, lowered freight costs by 18 percent, increased annual sales by 9 percent, and increased employee productivity by more than 20 percent.

Since then, Ace has implemented CPFR initiatives with several dozen suppliers, including Black & Decker, Rust-Oleum, Master Lock, and Sherwin-Williams. More accurate forecasts and seasonal profiles ensure that products are available when consumers want to buy them. Improved service levels, increased sales, and decreased supply-chain costs have combined to make Ace Hardware more competitive.

To improve efficiency and effectiveness of inventory management with its major suppliers, Sears (**sears.com**) is using CPFR software from GNX (**gnx.com**). The system enables total supply-chain visibility. The first experiment was with all major tire vendors (e.g., Michelin, Goodyear, Sumitomo). Using this software, all partners collaborated weekly about optimal replenishment and inventory plans to minimize stock, maximize customer service level, and optimize transport. Each week's actual and forecast sales information was refreshed for more than 500 SKUs related to tires. The initial results of the pilot project were so successful that Sears is implementing the program with all its strategic partners.

Sources: Compiled from D. Buss, "CPFR Initiative Allows Ace to Boost Revenue While Cutting Costs," *Stores,* September 2002; and H. L. Richardson, "The Ins & Outs of VMI," *Logistics Today,* Vol. 45, No. 3, 2004.

Example: Pfizer's Computer-Aided Document Management and Collaborative System

The process of bringing a new drug to market may take 6 to 10 years, and fewer than 10 percent of drugs actually make it. Food and Drug Administration (FDA) approval, which is the final step, takes 18 to 24 months. The U.S. government is putting pressure on drug manufacturers to collaborate with the FDA to cut this step to 12 months. To do so, Pfizer developed a special system called Electronic Submission Navigator (ESUB) that has the following capabilities:

- Provides a global view of the status of a trial or application process.
- Enhances Pfizer's competitive advantage by linking drug researchers around the world; ESUB has attracted business partners, including other drug manufacturers seeking to forge strategic alliances with Pfizer to help market and distribute their drugs.
- Enables Pfizer to penetrate world markets much more quickly by filing concurrent submissions in different countries.
- Gives the company the ability to deliver five new drugs every 12 months—the fastest rate in the industry.
- Allows portable review with a full-featured system, which is important because the FDA frequently uses outside consultants.

For details, see Blodgett (2000) and **pfizer.com**.

Section 10.9 Review Questions

1. Define *CPFR* and describe its process.
2. Define *VMI.*
3. Describe the benefits of collaboration to project management.

10.10   CREATIVITY, IDEA GENERATION, AND COMPUTERIZED SUPPORT

A major task in the decision-making/problem-solving process is generation of alternative courses of action. Knowledge and experience can help in this task, but new and innovative ideas are frequently needed. These can be achieved via creativity and idea generation.

Creativity

Creativity is the human trait that leads to the production of acts, items, and instances of novelty and the achievement of creative products. Creativity is complex. Personality-related creativity traits include inventiveness, independence, individuality, enthusiasm, and flexibility, and these traits have been assessed through the widely used Torrance Tests of Creative Thinking (TTCT; e.g., Cramond, 1995). However, researchers have established that creativity can be learned and improved and is not as strongly dependent on individual traits as originally thought. Innovative companies recognize that creativity may not necessarily be the result of having traits (i.e., being a genius) as much as the result of being in an idea-nurturing work environment (e.g., see Gatignon et al., 2002).

After a problem is formulated, potential criteria and alternatives must be identified. Creative ideas generally lead to better solutions. In brainstorming, there are some specific creativity measures: the quantitative (number of ideas) and qualitative (quality of ideas) components. Both can be positively affected by the use of software that concentrates on idea generation and evaluation of creative solutions to problems.

When creativity is unleashed, it can dramatically enhance productivity and profitability in the long run. Creativity is important in problem solving (see Handzic and Cule, 2002), and thus it is critical to develop computerized support systems for it.

Creativity and innovation can be stimulated by a number of environmental factors. An environment that meets the "serious play" criterion is part of the process. Stimulation by other creative people in the environment can push a group forward. How? Some stimulation can come directly from exciting ideas developed as a consequence of association (i.e., synergy) among creative people (e.g., during brainstorming). This can be done, for example, by presenting a person with a string of related (even distantly related) concepts. Some stimulation may even come from friction among employees. Research suggests that some dissatisfaction and discomfort is a must to spark innovation. A manager should not hire people like himself or herself, because their differences cause stimulation; for example, in brainstorming, differences broaden the viewpoints (see Sutton, 2001). As Malhotra et al. (2001) stated, "Innovation, most often, comes from the collaboration of individuals from a cross-section of disciplines, inside and outside of an organization."

A number of association methods have been proposed and empirically proven to be effective in stimulating creativity. And viewing ideas in a different frame (e.g., outside the box, from different angles) can stimulate creativity (see von Oech, 2002; and Creative Think, at **creativethink.com**). Next, we discuss creativity and innovation in the context of idea generation and electronic brainstorming.

Idea Generation Through Electronic Brainstorming

Idea generation methods and techniques have been adopted to enhance the creativity of both individuals and groups. Idea generation software (e.g., electronic brainstorming) helps to stimulate the free flow of turbulent creative thinking: ideas, words, pictures, and concepts set loose with fearless enthusiasm, based on the principle of synergy (i.e., association). Some packages are designed to enhance the creative thought process of the human mind and can be used to create new product ideas, marketing strategies, promotional campaigns, names, titles, slogans, or stories, or they can be used just for brainstorming.

Bombarding the user with many ideas is a key feature of idea-generating GDSS software. This is critical, because it helps the user move away from an analytic mode and into a creative mode. Psychological research indicates that people tend to anchor their thoughts early on, using their first ideas as springboards for others. Therefore, subsequent ideas may not be significantly new, but simply minor variations of the original idea. Because brainstorming software is free of human subjectivity, it can help broaden the thinking platform and encourage truly unique ideas to emerge.

By definition, idea generation in GDSS is a collaborative effort. One person's idea triggers another's ideas, which trigger even more ideas (in idea chains developed by association). With collaborative computing-support tools (e.g., GDSS), the individuals do all the thinking, and the software system encourages them to proceed. The technology is an anonymous, safe way to encourage participants to voice opinions that they might be reluctant to express in a more conventional setting. By building on each other's ideas, people can obtain creative insights they did not have before, based on associations with existing ideas and with their memories. There is a percolation effect as ideas work their way through the process. Associations trigger memories that can activate creativity. The exchange of information (i.e., learning) can lead to increases in output and creativity. A variety of relatively inexpensive idea-generation packages is on the market. Under the right electronic brainstorming conditions, more ideas and ideas that are more creative overall can be generated. A number of different conditions have been explored.

Generally, if the right approach is used in electronic brainstorming, more ideas and more creative ideas are generated. But a word of caution is in order: Sometimes a group may experience a process gain in the number of ideas and the number of creative ideas but also experience a process loss resulting from information overload or lack of group well-being and member support (see Dennis and Reinicke, 2004). The results of each idea-generation session can be stored in the organizational memory so that results can be carried over from one meeting to another to enhance the creativity of more people.

What if an individual needs to brainstorm alone? Methods are available for enhancing individual brainstorming. Satzinger et al. (1999) developed a simulated brainstorming package to help individuals trigger more creative responses when brainstorming alone. They compared the impact of a simulator that randomly generates ideas to an individual decision maker with an individual decision maker not using a simulator in brainstorming. The participants using the simulator generated more ideas and more creative ideas than the others.

Loosely related to brainstorming, cognitive maps (e.g., Banxia's Decision Explorer) can help an individual or a group understand a messy problem, develop a common frame, and enhance creativity. A cognitive map shows how concepts relate to each other, thus helping users organize their thoughts and ideas. In this way, they can visualize the problem they are trying to solve (see **banxia.com**).

Creativity-Enhancing Software

Although electronic brainstorming enhances creativity, it is primarily human beings who produce the results. In the following subsections, we describe software and methods (other than brainstorming) that enhance human creativity by actually performing some of the creative tasks of a human being. Some of these systems actually exhibit creative behavior.

COMPUTER PROGRAMS THAT EXHIBIT CREATIVE BEHAVIOR   For several decades, people have attempted to write computer programs that exhibit intelligent behavior. A major characteristic of intelligent behavior is creativity. Can computers be creative?

Intelligent agents (i.e., smartbots) can function as facilitators in GDSS. Chen et al. (1995) described an experiment in which an intelligent agent assisted in idea convergence. The agent's performance was comparable to that of a human facilitator in identifying important meeting concepts, but it was inferior in generating precise and relevant concepts. However, the agent was able to complete its task faster than its human counterparts. This concept is in its infancy but has potential for supporting Web-based GDSS, where the facilitator cannot be available on a 24/7 basis.

Rasmus (1995) described three creativity tools. The first one is called Copycat, a program that seeks analogies in patterns of letters. Identifying patterns is the essence of intelligence. Copycat, consisting of several intelligent agents, can find analogies to strings of letters (e.g., find an analogy for transforming aabc to aabd). This ability can be generalized to other problems that require conceptual understanding and the manipulation of objects. The capability of the program to anticipate the meaning of the transformation and find analogous fits provides evidence that computers can mimic a human being's ability to create analogies. The second system, Tabletop, is also capable of finding analogies. A third system, AARON, is a sophisticated art drawing program that has resulted from 15 years of research. Its developer, Harold Cohen, created a comprehensive knowledge base to support AARON. Similar computer programs have been developed to write poems and music and create works in other media. The increased knowledge base, processing speed, and storage now available enable such programs to create artwork of good quality.

ELECTRONIC IDEA GENERATION FOR PROBLEM SOLVING   Goldfire (from Invention Machine Corp., **invention-machine.com**) is an intelligent partner that accelerates technical innovation. Goldfire's semantic processing technology reads, understands, and extracts key concepts from company databases, intranets, and the Internet. The software reads content, creates a problem solution tree (i.e., knowledge index), and delivers an abstract listing of the technical content in relevant documents. Goldfire uses scientific and engineering knowledge as the foundation for its semantic algorithms to accelerate new product and process design innovations.

Goldfire is based on the theory of inventive problem solving (TRIZ—a Russian acronym). TRIZ was first developed by Genrich Altshuller and his colleagues in Russia in 1946 (Altshuller Institute for TRIZ Studies, 2006). More than 2 million patents were examined, classified by level of inventiveness, and analyzed to look for the following innovation principles:

- Problems and solutions are repeated across industries and sciences.
- Patterns of technical evolution are repeated across industries and sciences.
- Innovations may successfully use scientific effects outside the field where they were developed.

The TRIZ creative process is described on the Web sites of *The TRIZ Journal* (**triz-journal.com**) and Ideation International (**ideationtriz.com**).

SOFTWARE THAT FACILITATES HUMAN CREATIVITY   Several software packages can help stimulate creativity. Some have very specific functions, and others use word associations or questions to prompt users to take new, unexplored directions in their thought patterns. This activity can help users break cyclic thinking patterns, get past mental blocks, or overcome procrastination. Such software can use several different approaches to release the user's flow of ideas. Creative WhackPack is an example of this type of software.

Creative Think (**creativethink.com**) provides the Creative WhackPack, a deck of 64 cards that "whack" you out of habitual thought patterns and let you look at your problem in a new way. The cards ("a physical package") are designed to stimulate the imagination. Fortunately, all 64 illustrated cards are up and running on the Web site (as software); you can click the Give Me Another Creative Whack button to select one at random.

Section 10.10 Review Questions

1. Define *creativity*.
2. Relate creativity to collaboration and problem solving.
3. List software categories of creativity enhancement.
4. Describe software programs that exhibit intelligent behavior.

Chapter Highlights

- People collaborate in their work (called *groupwork*). Groupware (i.e., collaborative computing software) supports groupwork.
- Group members may be in the same organization or may span organizations; they may be in the same location or in different locations; they may work at the same time or at different times.
- The time/place framework is a convenient way to describe the communication and collaboration patterns of groupwork. Different technologies can support different time/place settings.
- Working in groups may result in many benefits, including improved decision making.
- Meetings have some limitations and dysfunctions. Computerized support can help.
- When people work in teams, especially when the members are in different locations and may be working at different times, they need to communicate, collaborate, and access a diverse set of information sources in multiple formats.

- Communication can be synchronous (i.e., same time) or asynchronous (i.e., sent and received in different times).
- Groupware refers to software products that provide collaborative support to groups (including conducting meetings).
- Groupware can support decision making/problem solving directly or can provide indirect support by improving communication between team members.
- Collaborative computing is known by a number of terms, including groupware, GSS, GDSS, and CSCW.
- Groups and groupwork (i.e., teams and teamwork) are proliferating in organizations. Consequently, groupware continues to evolve to support effective groupwork.
- The Internet (Web), intranets, and extranets support decision making through collaboration tools and access to data, information, and knowledge.
- An extranet links a work group from several different organizations. A common situation is to use the extranet and groupware in managing a supply chain involving several collaborative organizations.

- People may work together and communicate and collaborate at the same time or at different times and in the same place or in different places.
- Groupware for direct support such as GDSS typically contains capabilities for electronic brainstorming, electronic conferencing or meeting, group scheduling, calendaring, planning, conflict resolution, model building, videoconferencing, electronic document sharing, stakeholder identification, topic commentator, voting, policy formulation, and enterprise analysis.
- Groupware can support anytime/anyplace groupwork.
- A GSS is any combination of hardware and software that facilitates meetings. Its predecessor, GDSS, provided direct support to decision meetings, usually in a face-to-face setting.
- GDSS attempt to increase process and task gains and reduce process and task losses of groupwork.
- Parallelism and anonymity provide several GDSS gains.
- GDSS may be assessed in terms of the common group activities of information retrieval, information sharing, and information use.

- GDSS can be deployed in an electronic decision room environment, in a multipurpose computer lab, or over the Web.
- Web-based groupware is the norm for anytime/anyplace collaboration.
- GDSS for same time/same place meetings generally follow these steps: (1) planning, (2) question posing, (3) brainstorming, (4) idea organization, (5) discussion and idea prioritization, and (6) more idea generation.
- Internet telephony, or VoIP, is an efficient communications media with many applications that facilitate collaboration.
- Creativity is a complex concept that is used to generate alternative courses of actions in decision making.
- Creativity can be learned and fostered with good managerial techniques and a supportive environment.
- Idea generation (i.e., electronic brainstorming) allows participants to generate and share ideas simultaneously and anonymously.
- Human creativity can be supported with idea generation (i.e., electronic brainstorming) systems.
- Creativity software programs use association and "thinking outside the box" to trigger new concepts.

Key Terms

asynchronous *429*
collaboration hub *455*
collaborative planning, forecasting, and replenishment (CPFR) *457*
corporate (enterprise) portal *456*
data conferencing *434*
decision room *445*
Delphi method *426*
electronic brainstorming *436*

electronic meeting system (EMS) *442*
enterprise-wide collaboration system *440*
group decision support system (GDSS) *441*
group support system (GSS) *442*
groupthink *425*
groupware *429*
groupwork *423*
idea generation *442*

Internet telephony *453*
nominal group technique (NGT) *426*
online (electronic) workspace *436*
parallelism *443*
process gain *425*
process loss *425*
screen sharing *435*
synchronous (real-time) *429*
teleconferencing *434*

vendor-managed inventory (VMI) *458*
video teleconferencing (videoconferencing) *434*
virtual meeting *431*
virtual team *424*
Voice over IP (VoIP) *453*
wiki *455*
wikilog *455*

Questions for Discussion

1. How does groupware attain its primary objective?
2. What is nonverbal communication? Explain why it is important in human-to-human interaction. What methods are currently being used to incorporate nonverbal communication into collaborative computing?
3. Explain why it is useful to describe groupwork in terms of the time/place framework.
4. Describe the kinds of support that groupware can provide to decision makers.

5. Explain why most groupware is deployed today over the Web.
6. Compare GDSS and noncomputerized group decision making.
7. Explain why meetings can be so inefficient. Given this, explain how effective meetings can be run.
8. Discuss the details of process gains (i.e., benefits) of groupwork.
9. Discuss the details of process losses (i.e., dysfunctions) of groupwork.

10. Explain how GDSS can increase some of the benefits of collaboration and decision making in groups and eliminate or reduce some of the losses.

11. The original term for group support system (GSS) was group decision support system (GDSS). Why was the word *decision* dropped? Does this make sense? Why or why not?

12. Discuss how parallelism and anonymity can produce improvements in group processes.

13. Describe the three technologies through which GSS is deployed. What are the advantages and disadvantages of each?

14. Explain in detail what creativity is and how it relates to decision support.

15. Explain how GSS can support creativity.

16. Explain how idea generation (i.e., electronic brainstorming) works.

17. Can computers be creative? Why or why not? Discuss.

18. Discuss the benefits of CPFR to retailers and suppliers.

19. Discuss the improvements to supply-chain management that result from using CPFR and VMI.

20. Explain the potential benefits of wikis to a director of marketing.

21. Discuss the benefits of VoIP as a facilitator of communication.

22. Discuss the benefits of collaborative design.

23. Discuss the benefits of CPFR and relate it to decision support.

Exercises

TERADATA STUDENT NETWORK (TSN) AND OTHER HANDS-ON EXERCISES

1. Make a list of all the communications methods (both work and personal) you use during your day. Which are the most effective? Which are the least effective? What kind of work or activity does each communications method enable?

2. Investigate the impact of turning off every communication system in a firm (i.e., telephone, fax, television, radio, all computer systems). How effective and efficient would the following types of firms be: airline, bank, insurance company, travel agency, department store, grocery store? What would happen? Do customers expect 100 percent uptime? (When was the last time a major airline's reservation system was down?) How long would it be before each type of firm would not be functioning at all? Investigate what organizations are doing to prevent this situation from occurring.

3. Read Application Case 10.6 ("CPFR Initiatives at Ace Hardware and Sears") and answer the following questions:
   a. What motivated Ace to try CPFR?
   b. Describe how Ace deployed its CPFR system.
   c. Can you guess the common characteristics of the suppliers Ace used first?
   d. Why did Sears start using CPFR with tires?
   e. What are the benefits of CPFR to Sears and to its suppliers?

4. Investigate how researchers are trying to develop collaborative computer systems that portray or display nonverbal communication factors.

5. For each of the following software packages, check the trade literature and the Web for details and explain how computerized collaborative support system capabilities are included: Groove, GroupSystems OnLine, Windows Meeting Space, and WebEx.

6. From your own experience or from the vendor's information, list all the major capabilities of Lotus Notes and explain how it can be used to support decision making.

7. Compare Simon's four-phase decision-making model (see Chapters 1 and 2) to the steps in using GDSS.

TEAM ASSIGNMENTS AND ROLE-PLAYING

1. Access **groove.net**. Download the demo software to each group member's computer and use it to brainstorm and vote on a specific problem or issue. When brainstorming, think broadly. Did you feel comfortable with the software? Why or why not?

2. Access the Web site of a for-lease Web-based groupware service (e.g., MeetMeNow at WebEx). Describe what features it offers and how they could help the members of a group work together. If the site offers a free trial, have your group try it out and report your experience to the class.

3. Some GDSS researchers are concerned with the cross-cultural effects of computer system use. This is especially important in GDSS where opinions are entered and synthesized by meeting participants at different places around the globe. Examine the literature and write a report on the major issues of how GDSS provide either process gains or process losses in multicultural electronic meeting settings.

4. Access a demo version of a GSS (e.g., Groove, WebEx, Windows Meeting Space) on the Web. Use the system for a meeting of your group to solve a group assignment for any of your courses (check with your instructor). Explain why you did or did not feel comfortable with the software.

5. Prepare a study of all the major Web conferencing software—Centra EMeeting, Genesys Meeting Center, GoToMeeting.com, WebEx Meeting Center, Microsoft Live Meeting, and Oracle.

6. Go to **ifip-dss.org** and find recent material on GSS. At this site, also look at the June 2006 conference proceedings on creativity and innovation in decision support. Prepare a report on your findings.

7. A major claim in favor of wikis is that they can replace e-mail, eliminating its disadvantages (e.g., spam). Go to **socialtext.com** and review such claims. Find other supporters of switching to wikis. Then find counter arguments and conduct a debate on the topic.

8. Go to **ibm.com/software** and find information on the Workplace family of products. Identify all the products that

facilitate collaboration and list their major capabilities. Make sure to check Lotusphere and Lotus Domino Express.

INTERNET EXERCISES

1. Search the Internet to identify sites that describe methods for improving meetings. Investigate ways that meetings can be made more effective and efficient.
2. Go to **groupsystems.com** and identify its current GSS products. List the major capabilities of those products.
3. Go to the Expert Choice Web site (**expertchoice.com**) and find information about the company's group support products and capabilities. Team Expert Choice is related to the concept of the AHP described in Chapter 4. Evaluate this product in terms of decision support. Do you think that key-pad use provides process gains or process losses? How and why? Also prepare a list of the product analytical capabilities. Examine the free trial. How can it support groupwork?
4. Identify five real-world GSS success stories at vendor Web sites (using at least three different vendors). Describe them. How did GSS software and methods contribute to the successes? What common features do they share? What different features do individual successes have?
5. Go to **creativethink.com** with a problem in mind that you are trying to solve (e.g., selecting a graduate school or a job). Click the Give Me Another Whack button to enhance your thinking. Try a few whacks to see if they can help you. Do they?
6. For one of the creativity software packages described in the text, go to the company's Web site, download and try out a demo, and describe your experience in a report. Include what you liked and didn't like and what you found useful and didn't find useful.
7. Go to **groove.net**, **collabnet.com**, and the sites of other vendors that provide workspace products. Summarize the capabilities of each product.
8. Go to **logility.com**. Review collaborative products that optimize supply chains.
9. Go to **software.emc.com/products/software_az/eroom_enterprise.htm?hlnav=T** and find the product's capabilities. Write a report.

END OF CHAPTER APPLICATION CASE

Dresdner Kleinwort Wasserstein Uses Wiki for Collaboration

Dresdner Kleinwort Wasserstein (DrKW) is the international investment banking arm of Dresdner Bank. Based in Europe, DrKW provides a range of capital markets and advisory services, and it employs approximately 6,000 people worldwide. Because of the large number of employees, their geographic distribution, and the diversity of cultures, it became necessary to provide a range of collaborative tools, from blogs and wikis to IM, chat, and audio/video-conferencing in order to allow people to move between modes, depending on which was most appropriate at the time. DrKW installed a primitive open source wiki in 1997. The company reviewed Socialtext products in March 2004 and ran a small pilot on the hosted service in July 2004. Based on the pilot, DrKW decided to upgrade to Socialtext Enterprise, which was installed in the third quarter of 2004.

DrKW chose Socialtext because the company was willing to work with DrKW on better authentication, permissioning, and sharing of information and communication among silos as well as the vendor, and it understood the necessity for information to flow across multiple forms of communications. Because DrKW is highly regulated, everything must be recordable, archivable, searchable, and retrievable.

Usage and Benefits

The information strategy team was the first group to use Socialtext on a hosted service. Because its work needed structure, skills were geographically dispersed, and publication and collaboration at an individual level gained many capabilities through the Socialtext workspace. The team uses it as a communications tool, a collective discussion tool, and as a storehouse for documents and information.

The user-centered design (UCD) team incorporated usability into external-facing applications used across all business lines. The wiki allows all team members to upload information more easily, which encourages collaboration and transparency by making the sharing of e-mail conversations and other ideas uncomplicated. UCD also uses the wiki to help explain what user-centered design is and why it is important to the wider DrKW community as well as to share presentations, documents, and reports.

One of the most important roles of the wiki is to track project development so that the team and management know what progress has been made, regardless of individual geographic locations, and to raise the team's awareness about what each person is doing, the status of each project, and what actions should follow.

In 2004, the equity financing team was one of the largest users of the wiki. This unit deals with loans, equity swaps, and so on. It began using the wiki workspace to eliminate the cumbersome number of e-mails, to view the development of business plans, and to store commonly used information. The team also created an open forum where anyone can post views, comments, and questions on given subjects, publish and share white papers and bulletins, coordinate sales and marketing activities, and organize important team tasks.

The e-capital London team develops back-end applications for the digital markets business line and supports a number of legacy systems. It uses Socialtext to share and develop new system specifications and product overviews and to help with documentation. The wiki provides an instantly editable collaboration platform that simplifies the publication process. The version history function is useful for product specs, where it is important to retain a complete audit trail.

Socialtext also enables individuals to edit the intranet quickly and easily. For example, it is helping build an internal glossary that defines company jargon through employees doing similar jobs. The Wikipedia-style usage cuts down the training time and costs of new hires because it helps them understand internal and external jargon more quickly and easily. It also simplifies the roles of people writing in other locations and languages. Eventually, the wiki will be used for informal training, which will encourage its use.

Questions for the Case

1. What capabilities of a wiki are not available in e-mail?
2. Describe the applications of wikis in finance and operations.
3. How does DrKW's wiki increase employee productivity?
4. How does DrKW's wiki help with foreign languages and training?

Sources: Socialtext, "Dresdner Kleinwort Wasserstein (DrKW)," 2004, **social-text.com/customers/customerdrkw/** (accessed June 2009); and "E-mail Is So Five Minutes Ago," *BusinessWeek* Online, November, 28, 2005, **business-week.com/magazine/content/05_48/b3961120.htm** (accessed June 2009).

References

Agrew, M. (2000, July 10). "Collaboration on the Desktop." *InformationWeek.*

Altshuller Institute for TRIZ Studies. (2006). **aitriz.org** (accessed July 2009).

Bradley, P. (2002, April). "CPFR Gaining Converts." *Logistics.*

Bray, R. (2004). "Virtual Meetings: The New Business Travel: Business Travel Briefing." *Financial Times.*

Bury, S. (2004). "Vendor-Managed Inventory." *Purchasing B2B,* Vol. 46, No. 3.

Buss, D. (2002, September). "CPFR Initiative Allows Ace to Boost Revenue While Cutting Costs." *Stores.*

Callaghan, D. (2002, June 26). "IBM: E-Meetings Save $ Million a Month." *eWeek.*

Chen, H., et al. (1995). "Intelligent Meeting Facilitation Agents: An Experiment on GroupSystems." **ai.bpa.arizona.edu/papers/tool95/tool95.html** (accessed June 2009).

Cramond, B. (1995). "The Torrance Tests of Creative Thinking: From Design Through Establishment of Predictive Validity." In R. F. Subotnik and K. D. Arnold (eds.). *Beyond Terman: Contemporary Studies of Giftedness and Talent.* Norwood, NJ: Ablex Publishing Co., pp. 229–254.

de Vreede, G., and F. Ackermann. (2005, July). "International Perspectives in Group Decision and Negotiation Research." *Group Decision and Negotiation.*

Dennis, A. R., and B. A. Reinicke. (2004, March). "Beta vs. VHS and the Acceptance of Electronic Brainstorming Technology." *MIS Quarterly.*

DeSanctis, G., and R. B. Gallupe. (1987). "A Foundation for the Study of Group Decision Support Systems." *Management Science,* Vol. 33, No. 5.

Duke Corporate Education. (2005). *Building Effective Teams.* Chicago: Dearborn Trade Publications.

"E-mail Is So Five Minutes Ago." (2005, November, 28). *BusinessWeek* Online. **business-week.com/magazine/content/05_48/b3961120.htm** (accessed June 2009).

Ferber, D. (2003, September). "The Man Who Mistook His Girlfriend for a Robot." *Popular Science.* **popsci.com/scitech/article/2003-08/man-who-mistook-his-girlfriend-robot** (accessed June 2009).

Gatignon, H., M. L. Tushman, W. Smith, and P. Anderson. (2002, September). "A Structural Approach to Assessing Innovation: Construct Development of Innovation Locus, Type and Characteristics." *Management Science,* Vol. 48, No. 9.

GroupSystems. "Hertfordshire County, UK, Earns 'Innovation in Crime Prevention' Award" GroupSystems Success Story: Hertfordshire Constabulary. **groupsystems.com/resources/custom/PDFs/case-tudies/Hertfordshire%20Case%20Study.pdf** (accessed June 2009).

GroupSystems. "Eastman Chemical—Creativity and Team Center." **groupsystems.com/resource-center/custom ersandcases/CorporateCaseStudies/Eastman-Case-Study** (accessed August 2006).

GroupSystems. "ThinkTank Drives Ideation in Procter & Gamble's 'Innovation Gym.'" **groupsystems.com/re sources/custom/PDFs/case-studies/Procter%20and%20Gamble %20Case%20Study.pdf** (accessed June 2009).

Hall, M. (2002, July 1). "Decision Support Systems." *Computerworld,* Vol. 36, No. 27.

Henrie, K. S. (2004, July). "All Together Now." *CIO Insight.*

Holt, K. (2002, August 5). "Nice Concept: Two Days' Work in a Day." *Meeting News,* Vol. 26, No. 11.

IBM. (2006). "Case Studies for Lotus Software." **ibm.com/ software/success/cssdb.nsf/topstoriesFM?OpenForm& Site=lotus** (accessed June 2009).

KMWorld. "Collaborative Problem Solving at KUKA." **kmworld .com/Articles/News/KM-In-Practice/Collaborative-problem-solving-at-KUKA—53813.aspx** (accessed June 2009).

Konicki, S. (2001, November 12). "Collaboration Is the Cornerstone of $19B Defense Contract." *InformationWeek.*

Langley, N. (2004, March 23). "Notes Users Can Spread Their Skills." *ComputerWeekly.*

Li, J., P. Zhang, and J. Cao, (2009). "External Concept Support for Group Support Systems Through Web Mining." *Journal of the American Society for Information Science & Technology,* Vol. 60, No 5, pp. 1057–1070.

Lin, C., A. C. P. Liu, M-L. Hsu, and J-C. Wu. (2008). "Pursuing Excellence in Firm Core Knowledge Through Intelligent Group Decision Support System." *Industrial Management & Data Systems,* Vol. 108, No. 3, pp. 277–287.

Lindstone, H., and M. Turroff. (1975). *The Delphi Method: Technology and Applications.* Reading, MA: Addison-Wesley.

Malhotra, A., A. Majchrzak, R. Carman, and V. Lott. (2001, June). "Radical Innovation Without Collocation: A Case Study at Boeing-Rocketdyne." *MIS Quarterly,* Vol. 25, No. 2.

Malone, T. W., R. Laubacher, and C. N. Dellarocas. (2009). "Harnessing Crowds: Mapping the Genome of Collective Intelligence." MIT Sloan Research Paper No. 4732-09. **ssrn.com/abstract=1381502**.

Manninen, M. (2004). *Rich Interaction Model for Game and Virtual Environment Design.* Academic Dissertation, Department of Information Processing Science, University of Oulu. **herkules.oulu.fi/isbn9514272544/isbn95142 72544.pdf** (accessed June 2009).

Neumann, P. (2004). "Special Issue: The Problems and Potentials of Electronic Voting Systems." *Communications of the ACM,* Vol. 47, No. 10, pp. 28–30.

Nunamaker, J. F., R. O. Briggs, D. D. Mittleman, D. T. Vogel, and P. A. Balthazard. (1997). "Lessons from a Dozen Years of Group Support Systems Research: A Discussion of Lab and Field Findings." *Journal of Management Information Systems,* Vol. 13, pp. 163–207.

Panko, R. R. (1994). "Managerial Communication Patterns." *Journal of Organizational Computing,* Vol. 2, No. 1, pp. 95–122.

Pirani, J. A. (2005). "Implementing an IP-Based Voice, Data and Video Converged Network at SUNY Cortland." **educause.edu/ECAR/ImplementinganIPbasedVoice Data/155115** (accessed June 2009).

Powell, A., G. Piccoli, and B. Ives. (2004, Winter). "Virtual Teams: A Review of Current Literature and Directions for Future Research." *Data Base.*

Rasmus, D. W. (1995). "Creativity and Tools." *PC AI,* Pt. 1: May/June; Pt. 2: July/August; Pt. 3: September/October.

Richardson, H. L. (2004). "The Ins & Outs of VMI." *Logistics Today,* Vol. 45, No. 3.

Rosenbergm, D., and J. A. A. Sillince. (2000). "Verbal and Nonverbal Communication in Computer Mediated Settings." *International Journal of Artificial Intelligence in Education,* Vol. 11.

Satzinger, J. W., M. J. Garfield, and M. Nagasundaram. (1999, Spring). "The Creative Process: The Effects of Group Memory on Individual Idea Generation." *Journal of Management Information Systems,* Vol. 15, No. 4.

Smith, C. (2004, March 26). "Emerson Saves $6 Million with WebEx Web Conferencing Services." **webex.com/pr/ pr287.html** (accessed August 2006).

Socialtext. (2004). "Dresdner Kleinwort Wasserstein (DrKW)." **social-text.com/customers/customerdrkw/** (accessed June 2009).

Spangler, T. (2005, October 1). "Cisco to Replace VoIP Tools." *Baseline.*

Sutton, R. I. (2001, October). "The Creativity Dilemma." *CIO Insight.*

Tapscott, D., and A. D. Williams. (2007). *Wikinomics: How Mass Collaboration Changes Everything.* New York: Penguin.

Traction Software, Inc. "Customer Success Stories: KUKA Systems." **traction.tractionsoftware.com/traction/ read?proj=Public&edate=all&sectionid=customers overview&normaledate=all*1%2d1&sort=2&title=Cust omers&stickyparams=sectionid,normaledate,sort,title &type=single&rec=1653** (accessed June 2009).

Turban, E., D. King, and J. Lang. (2009). *Introduction to Electronic Commerce,* 2nd ed. Upper Saddle River, NJ: Prentice Hall.

von Oech, R. (2002). *Expect the Unexpected or You Won't Find It: A Creativity Tool Based on the Ancient Wisdom of Heraclitus.* San Francisco: Berrett-Koehler.

WebEx. "Catalyst Maintains an Edge Among Much Larger Competitors with WebEx." **webex.com/pdf/cs_Catalyst .pdf** (accessed June 2009).

WikiThat.com. (2009). "Collection of Wiki Articles." **wikithat .com/wiki_that/** (accessed June 2009).

Wimba. "Lecture Capture via Wimba Classroom at California State University, Chico." **wimba.com/assets/resources/wimba Spotlight_CSUChicoLECTURE.pdf** (accessed June 2009).

11

Knowledge Management

LEARNING OBJECTIVES

1 Define knowledge and describe the different types of knowledge

2 Describe the characteristics of knowledge management

3 Describe organizational learning and its relationship to knowledge management

4 Describe the knowledge management cycle

5 Describe the technologies that can be used in a knowledge management system (KMS)

6 Describe different approaches to knowledge management

7 Describe the activities of the chief knowledge officer and others involved in knowledge management

8 Describe the role of knowledge management in organizational activities

9 Describe ways of evaluating intellectual capital in an organization

10 Describe how KMS are implemented

11 Describe the roles of people, process, and technology in knowledge management

12 Describe the benefits and drawbacks of knowledge management initiatives

13 Describe how knowledge management can revolutionize the way an organization functions

In this chapter, we describe the characteristics and concepts of knowledge management. In addition, we explain how firms use information technology (IT) to implement KM systems and how these systems are transforming modern organizations. Knowledge management, although conceptually ancient, is a relatively new business philosophy. The goal of knowledge management is to identify, capture, store, maintain, and deliver useful knowledge in a meaningful form to anyone who needs it, anyplace and anytime, within an organization. Knowledge management is about sharing and collaborating at the organization level. Knowledge management has the potential to revolutionize the way we share expertise, make decisions, and conduct business, as discussed in the following sections:

11.1 Opening Vignette: MITRE Knows What It Knows Through Knowledge Management
11.2 Introduction to Knowledge Management
11.3 Organizational Learning and Transformation

11.4 Knowledge Management Activities

11.5 Approaches to Knowledge Management

11.6 Information Technology (IT) in Knowledge Management

11.7 Knowledge Management Systems Implementation

11.8 Roles of People in Knowledge Management

11.9 Ensuring the Success of Knowledge Management Efforts

11.1 OPENING VIGNETTE: MITRE KNOWS WHAT IT KNOWS THROUGH KNOWLEDGE MANAGEMENT

Since knowledge management (KM) first bubbled up in the mid-1990s, many organizations have tried and failed to reap its benefits. Certain enterprises never gave up on the promise of KM. MITRE, operator of three federally funded research and development centers, is one of them. Starting with the MITRE's Information Infrastructure (MII) project in 1996, over the past 13 years it has built a comprehensive KM environment through experimentation and internal sponsorship. The company fosters a knowledge-sharing culture to bring its extensive expertise to bear on customer needs.

The MITRE Corporation was founded in 1958 to address the government's need to create the Semi-Automated Ground Environment (SAGE), an integrated system to defend the United States against the threat of Soviet air attacks. Since then, MITRE has been serving as an objective, nonprofit corporation whose mission is to serve U.S. interests by creating solutions to pervasive, cross-organizational problems facing the federal government in civil aviation, tax administration, and national security. Its mission statement reads: "As a public interest company, in partnership with the government, MITRE addresses issues of critical national importance, combining systems engineering and information technology to develop innovative, viable solutions that make a difference." Frequently, this means enabling innovation, integration, and collaboration within and across public sector agencies, requiring efficient and effective knowledge management.

Problem

MITRE has more than 6,000 employees distributed globally (principally throughout the United States but extending to Europe and the Far East) and includes both technical and mission or operational experts. With 60 percent of its employees having more than 20 years of experience and approximately two-thirds having advanced degrees, leveraging expertise is imperative. MITRE has extensive human assets who often are in positions as trusted advisors to the U.S. government. Regular interaction among technical and domain experts distributed throughout headquarters and sponsor-collocated units enables rapid and high-quality creation of "solutions that make a difference."

It is common for large, knowledge-intensive corporations to develop a culture of silos, each with its own pocket of knowledge. Over time, these silos start to function like rivals, compromising an organization's abilities. This is what MITRE was experiencing that led to the MII initiative in 1996. The main challenge for MITRE was to create an environment so that staff could tap each others' experience to address the requirements of a large number of complex research projects. In addition, demand for MITRE's services continued to increase in size and complexity, while its budget stayed relatively the same. MITRE had to find a way to eliminate the barriers between the knowledge pockets and leverage its knowledge assets to the fullest. MITRE had to develop into a *culture of sharing*.

Solution

As an early attempt at knowledge management, MII was implemented and released to the corporation in 1996. The central element of the system was the knowledge locator (a phonebook-like functionality that pulls together extensive information about the knowledge-workers and makes them available in a single Web page). Since then, MITRE has been experimenting with a number of knowledge management initiatives.

Figure 11.1 illustrates a comprehensive approach to knowledge management (similar to the one adopted at MITRE), which can be viewed as integrating strategies, processes, and technologies that enable the enterprise to acquire, create, share, and make actionable knowledge needed to achieve its mission. As Figure 11.1 illustrates, core knowledge management processes such as the creation, sharing, and application of knowledge are performed within the context of corporate

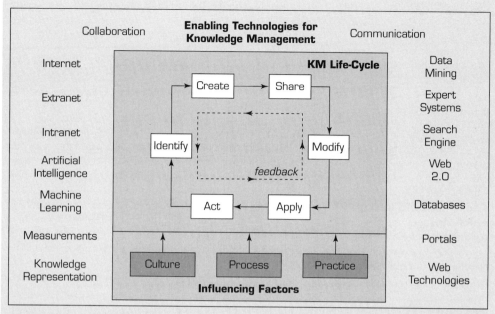

FIGURE 11.1   MITRE's Holistic Approach to Knowledge Management   *Source:* Mark T. Maybury, "Knowledge Management at the MITRE Corporation," 2003, **mitre.org/ work/tech_papers/ tech_papers_03/maybury_knowledge/KM_MITRE.pdf** (accessed June 2009).

processes, practices, and culture. They are supported by a number of enabling technologies, such as intranets, information push/pull, data mining, expert finding, expert practice databases, knowledge mapping, and so on.

MITRE's knowledge management strategy aims to enhance its operations by leveraging internal and external expertise and assets, supporting exchange of knowledge among individuals and groups (e.g., via technical exchange meetings), facilitating knowledge reuse through capturing and sharing knowledge assets (e.g., lessons learned databases), and transferring knowledge captured explicitly in knowledge assets back to people (knowledge internalization). It also includes capture of knowledge from people to create tangible knowledge assets and internalization of knowledge within staff. MITRE's director of knowledge management serves as a corporate steward of the strategy, which is shared among the supporting and line organizations. This extends to business unit knowledge management champions, who help stimulate KM initiatives.

Results

Although MITRE's size and budget are restricted by the government, KM enables it to deliver more work faster to its customers. Since 1995, MITRE has invested millions of dollars in a variety of KM systems; in return, it has reaped an order-of-magnitude ROI in reduced operations cost and improved productivity. According to corporate executives, before the KM initiatives MITRE was successful at what it was doing, but now, with KM, they are very successful, because they can leverage the collective knowledge of the company for every project. KM systems embody MITRE's mission statement—"solutions that make a difference" which has become "the way of life" for them. Recognizing the value of KM, MITRE is constantly looking for ways to improve its *culture of sharing* by empowering people, streamlining processes, and advancing technologies.

Questions for the Opening Vignette

1. What is MITRE, and why is KM critical to its success?
2. What problems led to MITRE's explorations of KM solutions?

3. Describe MITRE's holistic approach to KM. Discuss the value of individual layers and concepts. Is there anything in this approach that you do not agree with?
4. Describe the benefits of MITRE's KM systems. Can you think of other benefits (tangible or intangible) that are not mentioned in the case?
5. Explain how new Internet technologies (such as Web 2.0) can further enable the KM system at MITRE.

What We Can Learn from This Vignette

At large corporations like MITRE where knowledge is the core enabling asset, maximum leverage of intellectual capital is imperative. In its early years, MITRE was not structured in a way that encouraged knowledge sharing, and what little sharing there was generally took place in an unsystematic, informal way. As demand for its services increased, MITRE felt the need to better utilize its intellectual assets and started to develop KM systems. Over time, MITRE's organizational culture changed from the "culture of silos" to the "culture of sharing" as a number of successful KM initiatives and systems were developed. As the case illustrates, knowledge management is not a single task or project, but rather a continuous process of many tasks and projects. Corporate success will increasingly hinge on an organization's ability to turn knowledge management into its way of life.

Sources: R. Swanborg, "Mitre's Knowledge Management Journey," *CIO,* February 2009; and M. T. Maybury, "Knowledge Management at the MITRE Corporation," 2003, **mitre.org/work/tech_papers/ tech_ papers_03/maybury_knowledge/KM_MITRE.pdf** (accessed June 2009).

11.2 INTRODUCTION TO KNOWLEDGE MANAGEMENT

Knowledge management is a broad discipline that is defined and explained in the following section.

Knowledge Management Concepts and Definitions

The opening vignette illustrates the importance and value of identifying an organization's knowledge assets and sharing them throughout the organization. In a series of initiatives, MITRE developed KM systems to leverage its intellectual assets, or **intellectual capital**—the valuable knowledge of its employees. MITRE's culture was transformed through the deployment of KM systems, leading to significantly lower operating costs, higher efficiency, and more collaboration throughout the organization. Although their worth is difficult to measure, organizations recognize the value of their intellectual assets. Fierce global competition drives companies to better use their intellectual assets by transforming themselves into organizations that foster the development and sharing of knowledge.

With roots in organizational learning and innovation, the idea of KM is not new (see Ponzi, 2004; and Schwartz, 2006). However, the application of IT tools to facilitate the creation, storage, transfer, and application of previously uncodifiable organizational knowledge is a new and major initiative in many organizations. Successful managers have long used intellectual assets and recognized their value. But these efforts were not systematic, nor did they ensure that knowledge gained was shared and dispersed appropriately for maximum organizational benefit. Knowledge management is a process that helps organizations identify, select, organize, disseminate, and transfer important information and expertise that are part of the organization's memory and that typically reside within the organization in an unstructured manner. **Knowledge management (KM)** is the systematic and active management of ideas, information, and knowledge residing in an organization's employees. The structuring of knowledge enables effective and efficient problem solving, dynamic learning, strategic planning, and decision making. KM initiatives focus on identifying knowledge, explicating it in such a way that it can be shared in a formal manner, and leveraging its value through reuse. The information technologies that make KM available throughout an organization are referred to as *KM systems* (see Holsapple, 2003a, 2003b; Park and Kim, 2006; Sedighi, 2006; and Zhang and Zhao, 2006).

Through a supportive organizational climate and modern IT, an organization can bring its entire organizational memory and knowledge to bear on any problem, anywhere in the world, and at any time (see Bock et al., 2005). For organizational success, knowledge, as a form of capital, must be exchangeable among persons, and it must be able to grow. Knowledge about how problems are solved can be captured so that KM can promote organizational learning, leading to further knowledge creation.

Knowledge

Knowledge is very distinct from data and information (see Figure 11.2). Data are facts, measurements, and statistics; information is organized or processed data that is timely (i.e., inferences from the data are drawn within the time frame of applicability) and accurate (i.e., with regard to the original data) (Kankanhalli et al., 2005). **Knowledge** is information that is contextual, relevant, and actionable. For example, a map that gives detailed driving directions from one location to another could be considered data. An up-to-the-minute traffic bulletin along the freeway that indicates a traffic slowdown due to construction several miles ahead could be considered information. Awareness of an alternative, back-road route could be considered knowledge. In this case, the map is considered data because it does not contain current relevant information that affects the driving time and conditions from one location to the other. However, having the current conditions as information is useful only if you have knowledge that enables you to avert the construction zone. The implication is that knowledge has strong experiential and reflective elements that distinguish it from information in a given context.

Having knowledge implies that it can be exercised to solve a problem, whereas having information does not carry the same connotation. An ability to act is an integral part of being knowledgeable. For example, two people in the same context with the same information may not have the same ability to use the information to the same degree of success. Hence, there is a difference in the human capability to add value. The differences in ability may be due to different experiences, different training, different perspectives, and other factors. Whereas data, information, and knowledge may all be viewed as assets of an organization, knowledge provides a higher level of meaning about data and information. It conveys meaning and hence tends to be much more valuable, yet more ephemeral.

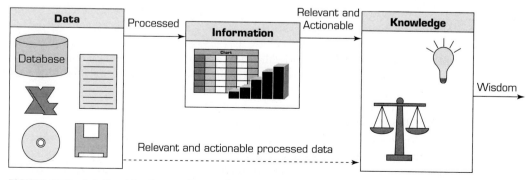

FIGURE 11.2 Relationships Among Data, Information, and Knowledge

Unlike other organizational assets, knowledge has the following characteristics (see Gray, 1999):

- ***Extraordinary leverage and increasing returns.***   Knowledge is not subject to diminishing returns. When it is used, it is not decreased (or depleted), rather it is increased (or improved). Its consumers can add to it, thus increasing its value.
- ***Fragmentation, leakage, and the need to refresh.***   As knowledge grows, it branches and fragments. Knowledge is dynamic; it is *information in action*. Thus, an organization must continually refresh its knowledge base to maintain it as a source of competitive advantage.
- ***Uncertain value.***   It is difficult to estimate the impact of an investment in knowledge. There are too many intangible aspects that cannot be easily quantified.
- ***Value of sharing.***   It is difficult to estimate the value of sharing one's knowledge or even who will benefit most from it.

Over the past few decades, the industrialized economy has been going through a transformation from being based on natural resources to being based on intellectual assets (see Alavi, 2000; and Tseng and Goo, 2005). The **knowledge-based economy** is a reality (see Godin, 2006). Rapid changes in the business environment cannot be handled in traditional ways. Firms are much larger today than they used to be, and, in some areas, turnover is extremely high, fueling the need for better tools for collaboration, communication, and knowledge sharing. Firms must develop strategies to sustain competitive advantage by leveraging their intellectual assets for optimal performance (e.g., in the National Basketball Association; see Berman et al., 2002). Competing in the globalized economy and markets requires quick response to customer needs and problems. To provide service, managing knowledge is critical for consulting firms spread out over wide geographical areas and for virtual organizations (see Application Case 11.1).

There is a vast amount of literature about what knowledge and knowing mean in epistemology (i.e., the study of the nature of knowledge), the social sciences, philosophy, and psychology. Although there is no single definition of what knowledge and KM specifically mean, the business perspective on them is fairly pragmatic. Information as a resource is not always valuable (i.e., information overload can distract from what is important); knowledge as a resource is valuable because it focuses attention back toward what is important (see Carlucci and Schiuma, 2006; and Hoffer et al., 2002). Knowledge implies an implicit understanding and experience that can discriminate between its use and misuse. Over time, information accumulates and decays, whereas knowledge evolves. Knowledge is dynamic in nature. This implies, though, that today's knowledge may well become tomorrow's ignorance if an individual or organization fails to update knowledge as environmental conditions change. For more on the potential drawbacks of managing and reusing knowledge, see Section 11.9.

The term *intellectual capital,* often used as a synonym for knowledge, implies that there is a financial value to knowledge. Not all intellectual capital can be classified as knowledge. Brand and customer are aspects of intellectual capital, but in today's marketplace the most significant and valuable aspect of intellectual capital is indeed knowledge in all its forms (see Ariely, 2006). Although intellectual capital is difficult to measure, some industries have tried. For example, in 2000 the value of the intellectual capital of the property-casualty insurance industry was estimated to be between $270 billion and $330 billion (see Mooney, 2000).

Knowledge evolves over time with experience, which puts connections among new situations and events in context. Given the breadth of the types and applications of knowledge, we adopt the simple and elegant definition that knowledge is information in action.

APPLICATION CASE 11.1

KM at Consultancy Firms

Knowledge has become one of the most highly valued commodities in the modern economy, and as a consequence we may be witnessing the emergence of a knowledge-based economy. In this new economy, knowledge-intensive firms play a key role. Consultancy firms are typically defined as being knowledge-intensive because knowledge is considered to assume greater importance than all other forms of input. Their main assets are said to stem from the knowledge and competence of their personnel, and, like other knowledge-intensive firms, they tend to produce results based on the capacity and expertise of their employees.

For such organizations, the ability to develop and exploit knowledge faster than their competitors is a key component of their competitive success. The management of this crucial resource therefore forms a core function for consultancies, because such employee/organizational knowledge must be continuously managed and enhanced in order to retain existing advantages and create new ventures. Following are a few factors that make it imperative for consultancy firms to develop very effective KM programs:

- Consultancy implies leveraging high levels of contextual knowledge for others.
- Consultancy firms deal with difficult, often unique, problems of their clients.
- Solving challenging problems requires deep knowledge and experience on the part of the consultants.
- Consultants constantly move to other cases/projects, thus developing experience-based inimitable knowledge that not only helps in solving problems but also assists in dealing with all stakeholders (e.g.., clients, coworkers, managers). in an optimal and balanced manner.
- Consultancy companies tend to have high employee turnover rates. Consultants experience burnout from dealing constantly with challenging problems; frequently readjusting to different environments, people, and cultures; and travel demands. Many receive better offers from other companies because of their invaluable problem-solving skills. Others want a more routine lifestyle where they can spend more time with their families.

Even though consultancy companies are prime targets for KM studies, substantial gaps remain in our understanding of the ways in which they manage their intellectual capital. This may be attributed to the fact that they not only use such mechanisms to manage their own knowledge, but also to solve clients' KM problems. Hence, many consultancy companies treat their KM strategies as trade secrets that make them win client contracts.

Donnelly (2008) conducted a comparative study of the KM practices deployed by a multinational consultancy firm. He utilized a case study approach of one of the "Big Four" consultancy firm's business operations in the United Kingdom and The Netherlands. As many of the largest multinational consultancies in the world originated in the US/UK and have expanded internationally in order to meet the needs of their multinational clients, they are likely to have transferred management practices across their operations. Furthermore, indigenous consultancies are often thought to replicate their practices in order to emulate their success and to avoid uncertainty or the risk of being out of step with their US/UK competitors.

In both the United Kingdom and The Netherlands, the firm used four principal mechanisms to diffuse employee/organizational knowledge:

- Team-based interaction (to share partially tacit knowledge)
- Electronic libraries/databases and intranet-based knowledge forums (to share mostly explicit knowledge)
- A coach–apprentice training model (to share pure tacit knowledge)
- Network relationships (to develop know-who knowledge)

Despite these mechanisms, the firm was found to face a number of strong obstacles in attempting to impart knowledge at both the local and national/international levels:

- The firm was highly dependent upon the willingness of its employees to allow their knowledge to be codified.
- Hierarchical relations were found to inhibit knowledge sharing between members at different levels within the firm.

- "Knowledge hoarding" occurred. Because knowledge was linked to power and an individual's position in networks and the firm, employees were reluctant to share their knowledge.
- Competitive tensions were a problem. Some of the firm's employees indicated that they did not wish to lose their "edge" by sharing their knowledge, because it could reduce firm dependency, client demand, and chargeability rates, and, therefore, the likelihood of achieving promotion.
- Information leakage was a concern, because valuable knowledge could be leaked to competitors within and outside the firm.
- There was a fear of criticism in that errors could be identified by colleagues or superiors.
- Time pressure was a problem. Knowledge sharing was a nonchargeable activity and, therefore, had to be accommodated in a finite amount of nonchargeable time or otherwise accomplished in an individual's own unpaid time.
- There was employee apathy toward the firm's knowledge forums/databases.
- There was a lack of rewards associated with knowledge sharing.

According to the study participants, the most significant of these obstacles was knowledge hoarding (i.e., a premeditated attempt to hide knowledge for individual purposes). Certain employees were real gurus who were quite productive in their tasks and yet very protective of their knowledge. They keep it, especially the really technical stuff, because they don't want it abused. If you have special technical planning which will save companies lots of money, you'll want to protect it because if exposed it would lose its value. Rather than leveraging their knowledge capabilities across the entire organization, individuals retained their knowledge because such intellectual capital was said to be synonymous with status and power. Consequently, key items of information were retained by knowledgeable individuals in order to give themselves a competitive advantage over their colleagues.

In summary, consultancy firms are not much different than other knowledge-intensive businesses in that they seek to continuously improve their knowledge management practices by paying due attention to people, processes, and technology-related issues.

Sources: Based on R. Donnelly, "The Management of Consultancy Knowledge: An Internationally Comparative Analysis," *Journal of Knowledge Management*, Vol. 12, No. 3, 2008, pp. 71–83; and M. R. Haas and M. T. Hansen, "When Using Knowledge Can Hurt Performance: The Value of Organizational Capabilities in a Management Consulting Company," *Strategic Management Journal*, Vol. 26, No. 1, 2005, pp. 1–24.

Explicit and Tacit Knowledge

Polanyi (1958) first conceptualized the difference between an organization's explicit and tacit knowledge. **Explicit knowledge** deals with more objective, rational, and technical knowledge (e.g., data, policies, procedures, software, documents). **Tacit knowledge** is usually in the domain of subjective, cognitive, and experiential learning; it is highly personal and difficult to formalize. Alavi and Leidner (2001) provided a taxonomy (see Table 11.1), where they defined a spectrum of different types of knowledge, going beyond the simple binary classification of explicit versus tacit. However, most KM research has been (and still is) debating over the dichotomous classification of knowledge.

Explicit knowledge comprises the policies, procedural guides, white papers, reports, designs, products, strategies, goals, mission, and core competencies of an enterprise and its IT infrastructure. It is the knowledge that has been codified (i.e., documented) in a form that can be distributed to others or transformed into a process or strategy without requiring interpersonal interaction. For example, a description of how to process a job application would be documented in a firm's human resources policy manual. Explicit knowledge has also been called **leaky knowledge** because of the ease with which it can leave an individual, a document, or an organization due to the fact that it can be readily and accurately documented (see Alavi, 2000).

Tacit knowledge is the cumulative store of the experiences, mental maps, insights, acumen, expertise, knowhow, trade secrets, skill sets, understanding, and learning that an organization has, as well as the organizational culture that has embedded in it the past

TABLE 11.1   **Taxonomy of Knowledge**

Knowledge Type	Definition	Example
Tacit	Knowledge is rooted in actions, experience, and involvement in specific context.	Best means of dealing with specific customer
Cognitive tacit:	Mental models	Individual's belief on cause-effect relationships
Technical tacit:	Know-how applicable to specific work	Surgery skills
Explicit	Articulated, generalized knowledge	Knowledge of major customers in a region
Individual	Created by and inherent in the individual	Insights gained from completed project
Social	Created by and inherent in collective actions of a group	Norms for intergroup communication
Declarative	Know-about	What drug is appropriate for an illness
Procedural	Know-how	How to administer a particular drug
Causal	Know-why	Understanding why the drug works
Conditional	Know-when	Understanding when to prescribe the drug
Relational	Know-with	Understanding how the drug interacts with other drugs
Pragmatic	Useful knowledge for an organization	Best practices, treatment protocols, case analyses, post mortems

and present experiences of the organization's people, processes, and values. Tacit knowledge, also referred to as *embedded knowledge* (see Tuggle and Goldfinger, 2004), is usually either localized within the brain of an individual or embedded in the group interactions within a department or a branch office. Tacit knowledge typically involves expertise or high skill levels.

Sometimes tacit knowledge could easily be documented but has remained tacit simply because the individual housing the knowledge does not recognize its potential value to other individuals. Other times, tacit knowledge is unstructured, without tangible form, and therefore difficult to codify. It is difficult to put some tacit knowledge into words. For example, an explanation of how to ride a bicycle would be difficult to document explicitly and thus is tacit. Successful transfer or sharing of tacit knowledge usually takes place through associations, internships, apprenticeship, conversations, other means of social and interpersonal interactions, or even simulations (see Robin, 2000). Nonaka and Takeuchi (1995) claimed that intangibles such as insights, intuitions, hunches, gut feelings, values, images, metaphors, and analogies are the often-overlooked assets of organizations. Harvesting these intangible assets can be critical to a firm's bottom line and its ability to meet its goals. Tacit knowledge sharing requires a certain context or situation in order to be facilitated because it is less commonly shared under normal circumstances (see Shariq and Vendelø, 2006).

Historically, management information systems (MIS) departments have focused on capturing, storing, managing, and reporting explicit knowledge. Organizations now recognize the need to integrate both types of knowledge in formal information systems. For centuries, the mentor–apprentice relationship, because of its experiential nature, has been a slow but reliable means of transferring tacit knowledge from individual to individual. When people leave an organization, they take their knowledge with them. One critical goal of knowledge management is to retain the valuable knowhow that can so easily and quickly leave an organization. **Knowledge management systems (KMS)** refer to the use of modern IT (e.g., the Internet, intranets, extranets, Lotus Notes, software filters, agents, data warehouses, Web 2.0) to systematize, enhance, and expedite intra- and interfirm KM.

KM systems are intended to help an organization cope with turnover, rapid change, and downsizing by making the expertise of the organization's human capital widely accessible. They are being built, in part, because of the increasing pressure to maintain a well-informed, productive workforce. Moreover, they are built to help large organizations provide a consistent level of customer service, as illustrated in Application Case 11.2. For more on the basics of knowledge and the economy, see Ahlawat and Ahlawat (2006) and Holsapple (2003a, 2003b).

APPLICATION CASE 11.2

Cingular Calls on Knowledge

How do you make sure that each of your customer service agents at 22 call centers nationwide can answer virtually any question asked by one of your 22 million clients? That was the challenge faced by Cingular Wireless (**cingular.com**), a major mobile communications provider based in Atlanta (now a part of AT&T wireless services).

Cingular Wireless turned to KM to accomplish this massive task. Cingular benchmarked KM solutions of technology oriented companies, such as Dell and Microsoft. Steve Mullins, vice president of customer experience for Cingular Wireless, and Monica Browning, Cingular's director of knowledge management, met with several KM software vendors to learn how their tools operate. "We thought about how [the knowledge management software] would integrate with what we envisioned the future desktop to look like," said Mullins. "This system would be the foundation for what we use throughout all of our departments."

Following a review of KM solutions used by other companies, Cingular chose eService Suite by ServiceWare (**serviceware.co.jp**). ServiceWare's decision integrity department helped Cingular put together a basis for proving the software's return on investment. To ensure successful implementa-

tion of the system, Cingular embarked on a campaign to obtain the support of everyone involved, from senior executives to each call center agent who would use the system. A pilot program was initiated in technical support departments at three call centers.

To help manage the organizational changes that accompany a shift to knowledge management, Cingular enlisted the help of leading consulting firms Cap Gemini Ernst & Young and Innovative Management Solutions.

A major issue in developing the KMS involved capturing knowledge and storing it in the system. Cingular accomplished this by combining the efforts of its employees and an external authoring group from Innovative Management Solutions. Cingular divided the process into phases. This made it possible to populate the knowledge base with technical support information, common topics, information on rate plans, and so on. Browning estimated that it took about 4 months for the knowledge repository to be ready for the first group of users.

The Cingular KMS uses complex (artificial intelligence–based) algorithms to process natural language queries and provide customer service agents with lists of the most likely answers to their questions. The software also determines the relevance of possible answers by ranking them partly on exact text and phrase matching. In addition, the system can match synonyms and assign additional weight to certain expressions. The system attempts to provide even more focused solutions by retrieving answers from the pool of knowledge that is relevant to a particular user and his or her profile.

Understanding that knowledge must grow and evolve, Cingular encourages users to contribute their expertise to the system. The software can automatically record a sequence of steps that an agent took to find a correct solution to a certain problem and give the agent an option to provide additional feedback.

Cingular realized that ensuring validity and integrity of the knowledge stored and distributed by the KMS is one of the key factors of the system's success. To that end, the company has a knowledge management team that is responsible for monitoring, maintaining, and expanding the system. The team consists of about 25 full-time employees based in Cingular's Atlanta headquarters. The knowledge management team works closely with various departments of the company and subject-matter experts to ensure that the knowledge base has the right answers in a user-friendly format at the right time. In addition, the team reviews contributions to the knowledge base made by the agents and makes appropriate changes or additions to the knowledge base.

Cingular's clients are often the ultimate beneficiaries of the company's knowledge. That is why Cingular plans to bring its knowledge closer to its customers by extending the KMS online and to retail stores. Customers will be able to access instructions on using wireless services and features, handsets, and other devices that Cingular carries, as well as troubleshooting tips.

Sources: Adapted from J. O'Herron, "Building the Bases of Knowledge," *Call Center Magazine*, January 2003; and Cingular Wireless Benefits Knowledge Management Web Site, 2005, **mergeagency.com/case_study.php?id=23** (accessed April 2006).

Section 11.2 Review Questions

1. Define *knowledge management* and describe its purposes.
2. Distinguish between knowledge and data.
3. Describe the knowledge-based economy.
4. Define *tacit knowledge* and *explicit knowledge*.
5. Define *KMS* and describe the capabilities of KMS.

11.3 ORGANIZATIONAL LEARNING AND TRANSFORMATION

Knowledge management is rooted in the concepts of organizational learning and organizational memory. When members of an organization collaborate and communicate ideas, teach, and learn, knowledge is transformed and transferred from individual to individual (see Bennet and Bennet, 2003; and Jasimuddin et al., 2006).

The Learning Organization

The term **learning organization** refers to an organization's capability of learning from its past experience. Before a company can improve, it must first learn. Learning involves an interaction between experience and competence. In communities of practice, these are tightly related. Communities of practice provide not only a context for newcomers to learn but also a context for new insights to be transformed into knowledge (see Wenger, 2002). We discuss communities of practice later in this chapter.

To build a learning organization, three critical issues must be tackled: (1) meaning (determining a vision of what the learning organization is to be), (2) management (determining how the firm is to work), and (3) measurement (assessing the rate and level of learning). A learning organization is one that performs five main activities well: solving problems systematically, experimenting creatively, learning from past experience, learning from the best practices of others, and transferring knowledge quickly and efficiently throughout the organization (see Vat, 2006). For example, Best Buy deliberately and successfully structured its KM efforts around creating a learning organization where it captured best practices (see Brown and Duguid, 2002).

Organizational Memory

A learning organization must have an **organizational memory** and a means to save, represent, and share its organizational knowledge. Estimates vary, but it is generally believed that only 10 to 20 percent of business data are actually used. Organizations "remember" the past in their policies and procedures. Individuals ideally tap into this memory for both explicit and tacit knowledge when faced with issues or problems to be solved. Human intelligence draws from the organizational memory and adds value by creating new knowledge. A KMS can capture the new knowledge and make it available in its enhanced form. See Nevo and Wand (2005) and Jennex and Olfman (2003).

Organizational Learning

Organizational learning is the development of new knowledge and insights that have the potential to influence an organization's behavior. It occurs when associations, cognitive systems, and memories are shared by members of an organization (see Schulz, 2001). Learning skills include the following (see Garvin, 2000):

- Openness to new perspectives
- Awareness of personal biases
- Exposure to unfiltered data
- A sense of humility

Establishing a corporate memory is critical for success (see Hinds and Aronson, 2002). IT plays a critical role in organizational learning, and management must place emphasis on this area to foster it (see Ali et al., 2006; Craig, 2005; Davenport and Sena, 2003; and O'Leary, 2003).

Because organizations are becoming more virtual in their operations, they must develop methods for effective organizational learning. Modern collaborative technologies can help in KM initiatives. Organizational learning and memory depend less on technology than on people issues, as we describe next.

Organizational Culture

An organization's ability to learn, develop memory, and share knowledge is dependent on its culture. *Culture* is a pattern of shared basic assumptions (see Kayworth and Leidner, 2003; and Schein 1999). Over time, organizations learn what works and what doesn't work. As the lessons become second nature, they become part of the **organizational culture**. New employees learn the culture from their mentors, along with knowhow.

The impact of corporate culture on an organization is difficult to measure. However, strong culture generally produces strong, measurable bottom-line results: net income, return on invested capital, and yearly increases in stock price (see Hibbard, 1998). For example, Buckman Laboratories, a pharmaceutical firm, measures culture impact by sales of new products. Buckman undertook to change its organizational culture by making knowledge sharing part of the company's core values. After instituting a knowledge-sharing initiative, sales of products less than 5 years old rose to 33 percent of total sales, up from 22 percent (see Hibbard, 1998; also see Martin, 2000). Sharing initiatives and proper motivation are critical for the success of knowledge management. This is especially tricky in the public sector. However, an organizational culture that does not foster sharing can severely cripple a KM effort (see Alavi et al., 2005/2006; Hinds and Aronson, 2002; Jones et al., 2006; and Riege, 2005).

Encouraging employees to use a KMS, both for contributing knowledge and for seeking knowledge, can be difficult. Riege (2005) reviewed past studies and identified a number of possible reasons that people do not like to share knowledge:

- General lack of time to share knowledge and time to identify colleagues in need of specific knowledge
- Apprehension or fear that sharing may reduce or jeopardize people's job security
- Low awareness and realization of the value and benefit of the knowledge others possess
- Dominance in sharing explicit over tacit knowledge, such as knowhow and experience that requires hands-on learning, observation, dialogue, and interactive problem solving
- Use of a strong hierarchy, position-based status, and formal power
- Insufficient capture, evaluation, feedback, communication, and tolerance of past mistakes that would enhance individual and organizational learning effects
- Differences in experience levels
- Lack of contact time and interaction between knowledge sources and recipients
- Poor verbal/written communication and interpersonal skills
- Age differences
- Gender differences
- Lack of a social network
- Differences in education levels
- Ownership of intellectual property due to fear of not receiving just recognition and accreditation from managers and colleagues
- Lack of trust in people because they may misuse knowledge or take unjust credit for it
- Lack of trust in the accuracy and credibility of knowledge due to the source
- Differences in national culture or ethnic backgrounds and values and beliefs associated with it

Sometimes a technology project fails because the technology does not match the organization's culture. (This is a much deeper issue than having a poor fit between the technology and the task and hand; see McCarthy et al., 2001.) This is especially true for KMS, because they rely so heavily on individuals contributing their knowledge. Most KMS that fail in practice do so because of organizational culture issues (see Zyngier, 2006).

Successful organizations are often characterized by their ability to manage risk associated with technology projects. Risk management and KM are not mutually exclusive management practices. They often overlap in the way that they contextualize the organizational practices. Application Case 11.3 provides a good example of how a large organization like NASA blends the two management practices for their mutual benefit.

APPLICATION CASE 11.3

NASA Blends KM with Risk Management

The mission of NASA's Exploration Systems Mission Directorate (ESMD) is to develop a sustained human presence on the Moon; to promote exploration, commerce, and U.S. preeminence in space; and to serve as a stepping stone for the future exploration of Mars and other destinations. In order to achieve its mission, ESMD initiated efforts to integrate knowledge management and risk management with measurable results. The idea behind the initiative was to not only learn lessons from past programs, such as Apollo, the Space Shuttle, and the International Space Station, but also to generate and share new knowledge in the form of engineering design, operations, and management best practices through ongoing activities and risk management procedures. The underlying assumption was that risks highlight potential "knowledge gaps" that might be mitigated through one or more KM practices and artifacts. These same risks also provide a cueing function for the collection of knowledge, particularly on technical or programmatic challenges that might occur again.

In a fast-paced, resource-constrained environment, ESMD must budget its assets carefully to mitigate risks, while simultaneously capturing and transferring knowledge about risk. To accomplish this, ESMD risk and knowledge management practitioners use a set of interrelated risk and KM processes, including:

- **Pause and Learn (PaL).** The idea behind PaL is to create "learning events" at major milestones in the lifecycle of a lengthy project. Key characteristics of PaL includes (1) an informal, facilitated roundtable discussion, (2) a "not for attributions" approach where judgments about success or failure are withheld, (3) a clear narrow focus on a particular project phase, (4) participation of all who are involved, and (5) a timely approach, where PaL is conducted during the execution of a project 's phases.
- **Knowledge-based risks (KBRs).** ESMD tightly couples continuous risk management and lessons learned to form an active collection of KBRs. By definition, a KBR can be a pertinent lessons learned record, converted to a risk record; or an ESMD risk, with lessons on how the risk was identified and mitigated over time appended to the risk record.
- **Web-enabled high-performance teams.** Given the inherent problems in managing an organizational structure as complex as ESMD, with work spread across all NASA centers, a wiki-type collaboration medium was found

to be an excellent fit. This way, ESMD teams are empowered to collaborate on documents, manage calendars, locate process and expertise information, and, most important, learn from each other.

- **Knowledge-sharing forums.** Knowledge-sharing forums at ESMD range from simple "brown bag" lunch seminars to larger conferences. Events include ESMD alumni events, in which past participants in NASA projects discuss experiences and lessons learned; knowledge-sharing seminars and workshops, where senior project leaders share their insights; and other events that bring together project leaders from across NASA, private industry, and other government agencies.
- **Experience-based training.** Case studies, both internal and external to ESMD, are used to capture and transfer relevant and contextual information to management and the workforce.

A combination of these practices provides ESMD with a menu of options to enhance risk-informed decision making in a measurable fashion. ESMD has been careful not to overemphasize information technology in its approach, which in the past resulted in several "IT junkyards."

The Vision for Space Exploration program provides ESMD personnel with exciting opportunities and formidable challenges. To reduce risk and apply knowledge more effectively, ESMD is integrating its risk and knowledge management practices and systems in a comprehensive manner that will accomplish more with less bureaucracy. The goal is not compliance with detailed processes and procedures, but rather compliance with intent—the intent to learn and share and to probe multiple aspects of risks, so that ESMD's missions have the best possible chances of success.

Sources: D. Lengyel, "Blending KM with Risk Management at NASA," *Knowledge Management Review*, Vol. 10, No. 6, 2008, pp. 8–9; and NASA's Exploration Systems Mission Directorate (ESMD) Implementation Plan, **nasa.gov/pdf/187112main_eip_web.pdf** (accessed June 2009).

Section 11.3 Review Questions

1. Define *learning organization* and identify the characteristics of learning organizations.
2. Define *organizational memory*.
3. Describe organizational learning.
4. Define *organizational culture* and relate it to knowledge management.

11.4 KNOWLEDGE MANAGEMENT ACTIVITIES

This section describes several major activities that take place in knowledge management projects.

Knowledge Management Initiatives and Activities

Given the changing dynamics of the global marketplace and the increasingly intense competition, organizations need to leverage intellectual resources in order to reduce the loss of intellectual capital due to people leaving the company, as well as to reduce costs by decreasing the number of times the company has to repeatedly solve the same problem. IDC estimated that the cost for an organization of 1,000 knowledge workers to find existing knowledge they need, to waste time searching for nonexistent knowledge, and to re-create knowledge that is available but cannot be located can be more than $6 million per year (see Weiss et al., 2004). In addition, knowledge has been recognized as the single most important source for generating value in the modern company (see Weir, 2004). For instance, companies can use business intelligence (BI) to reveal opportunities and then create revenue-generating programs to exploit them. In some highly skilled professions, such as medicine, retaining and using knowledge of best practices are critical in life-and-death situations (see Lamont, 2003a). It is precisely these types of difficulties that have led to the systematic attempt to manage knowledge (see Compton 2001; and Holsapple 2003a, 2003b). Between early 2001 and early 2003, U.S. firms laid off 3.6 million workers (not including retirements). Nineteen percent of baby boomers in executive, administrative, or managerial positions are expected to retire by 2008. When people leave an organization, their knowledge assets leave with them; as Taylor (2001) said, "Intellectual capital has legs."

A KPMG Peat Marwick survey of European firms in 1998 found that almost half of the companies reported having suffered a significant setback due to losing key staff. Similarly, a Cranfield University survey conducted in the same year found that the majority of responding firms believed that much of the knowledge they needed existed inside the organization but that finding and leveraging it were ongoing challenges.

Most KM initiatives have one of three aims: (1) to make knowledge visible, mainly through maps, yellow pages, and hypertext; (2) to develop a knowledge-intensive culture; or (3) to build a knowledge infrastructure. These aims are not mutually exclusive, and, indeed, firms may attempt all three as part of a knowledge management initiative.

Several activities or processes surround the management of knowledge. These include the creation of knowledge, the sharing of knowledge, and the seeking and use of knowledge. Various terms have been used to describe these processes. More important than any particular label assigned to a knowledge activity is having an understanding of how knowledge flows through an organization (see Wenger et al., 2002).

Knowledge Creation

Knowledge creation is the generation of new insights, ideas, or routines. Nonaka (1994) described knowledge creation as an interplay between tacit and explicit knowledge and as a growing spiral as knowledge moves among the individual, group, and organizational levels. The four modes of knowledge creation are socialization, externalization, internalization, and combination. The socialization mode refers to the conversion of tacit knowledge to new tacit knowledge through social interactions and shared experience among organization members (e.g., mentoring). The combination mode refers to the creation of new explicit knowledge by merging, categorizing, reclassifying, and synthesizing existing explicit knowledge (e.g., statistical analyses of market data). The other two modes involve interactions and conversion between tacit and explicit knowledge.

Externalization refers to converting tacit knowledge to new explicit knowledge (e.g., producing a written document describing the procedures used in solving a particular client's problem). Internalization refers to the creation of new tacit knowledge from explicit knowledge (e.g., obtaining a novel insight through reading a document). For further information, see Wickramasinghe (2006).

Knowledge Sharing

Knowledge sharing is the willful explication of one person's ideas, insights, solutions, experiences (i.e., knowledge) to another individual either via an intermediary, such as a computer-based system, or directly. However, in many organizations, information and knowledge are not considered organizational resources to be shared but individual competitive weapons to be kept private. Organizational members may share personal knowledge with trepidation; they perceive that they are of less value if their knowledge is part of the organizational public domain. Research in organizational learning and knowledge management suggests that some facilitating conditions include trust, interest, and shared language (see Hanssen-Bauer and Snow, 1996); fostering access to knowledgeable members (see Brown and Duguid, 1991); and a culture marked by autonomy, redundancy, requisite variety, intention, and fluctuation (see King, 2006).

Knowledge Seeking

Knowledge seeking, also referred to as *knowledge sourcing* (see Gray and Meisters, 2003), is the search for and use of internal organizational knowledge. Lack of time or lack of reward may hinder the sharing of knowledge, and the same is true of knowledge seeking. Individuals may sometimes prefer to not reuse knowledge if they feel that their own performance review is based on the originality or creativity of their ideas. Such was the case for marketing employees in a global consumer goods organization described in Alavi et al. (2003).

Individuals may engage in knowledge creation, sharing, and seeking with or without the use of IT tools. For example, storytelling (described in Chapter 2 as a decision-making technique) is an ancient approach to transmitting and gathering knowledge. Nuances of how a story is told cue the gatherer as to importance and detail. Storytelling may be considered a form of verbal best practices. See Gamble and Blackwell (2002) and Reamy (2002) for details on how storytelling is used in knowledge management.

We next describe several common approaches to knowledge management.

Section 11.4 Review Questions

1. Why do companies need knowledge management initiatives?
2. Describe the process of knowledge creation.
3. What are the characteristics of knowledge sharing?
4. Define *knowledge seeking* (or sourcing).

11.5 APPROACHES TO KNOWLEDGE MANAGEMENT

The two fundamental approaches to knowledge management are the process approach and the practice approach (see Table 11.2). We next describe these two approaches as well as hybrid approaches.

The Process Approach to Knowledge Management

The **process approach** to knowledge management attempts to codify organizational knowledge through formalized controls, processes, and technologies (see Hansen et al., 1999). Organizations that adopt the process approach may implement explicit policies

TABLE 11.2   The Process and Practice Approaches to Knowledge Management

	Process Approach	**Practice Approach**
Type of knowledge supported	Explicit knowledge—codified in rules, tools, and processes	Mostly tacit knowledge—unarticulated knowledge not easily captured or codified
Means of transmission	Formal controls, procedures, and standard operating procedures, with heavy emphasis on information technologies to support knowledge creation, codification, and transfer of knowledge	Informal social groups that engage in storytelling and improvisation
Benefits	Provides structure to harness generated ideas and knowledge Achieves scale in knowledge reuse Provides spark for fresh ideas and responsiveness to changing environment	Provides an environment to generate and transfer high-value tacit knowledge
Disadvantages	Fails to tap into tacit knowledge May limit innovation and forces participants into fixed patterns of thinking	Can result in inefficiency Abundance of ideas with no structure to implement them
Role of information technology (IT)	Requires heavy investment in IT to connect people with reusable codified knowledge	Requires moderate investment in IT to facilitate conversations and transfer of tacit knowledge

Source: Compiled from M. Alavi, T. R. Kayworth, and D. E. Leidner, "An Empirical Examination of the Influence of Organizational Culture on Knowledge Management Practices," *Journal of Management Information Systems,* Vol. 22, No. 3, 2006, pp. 191–224.

governing how knowledge is to be collected, stored, and disseminated throughout the organization. The process approach frequently involves the use of IT, such as intranets, data warehousing, knowledge repositories, decision support tools, and groupware (see Ruggles, 1998) to enhance the quality and speed of knowledge creation and distribution in the organization. The main criticisms of the process approach are that it fails to capture much of the tacit knowledge embedded in firms and it forces individuals into fixed patterns of thinking (see Kiaraka and Manning, 2005). This approach is favored by firms that sell relatively standardized products that fill common needs. Most of the valuable knowledge in these firms is fairly explicit because of the standardized nature of the products and services. For example, a kazoo manufacturer has minimal product changes or service needs over the years, and yet there is steady demand and a need to produce the item. In these cases, the knowledge is typically static in nature.

Even large firms that use tacit knowledge, such as Cap Gemini Ernst & Young, have invested heavily to ensure that the process approach works efficiently. The 250 people at Cap Gemini Ernst & Young's Center for Business Knowledge manage an electronic repository and help consultants find and use information. Specialists write reports and analyses that many teams can use. Each of Cap Gemini Ernst & Young's more than 40 practice areas has a staff member who helps codify and store documents. The resulting area databases are linked through a network (see Hansen et al., 1999). Naturally, people-to-documents is not the only way consultants in firms such as Cap Gemini Ernst & Young and Accenture share knowledge; they talk with one another as well. But they do place a high degree of emphasis on the codification strategy (see Hansen et al., 1999).

The Practice Approach to Knowledge Management

In contrast to the process approach, the **practice approach** to knowledge management assumes that a great deal of organizational knowledge is tacit in nature and that formal controls, processes, and technologies are not suitable for transmitting this type of understanding. Rather than build formal systems to manage knowledge, the focus of this approach is to build the social environments or communities of practice necessary to facilitate the sharing of tacit understanding (see Hansen et al., 1999; Leidner et al., 2006; and Wenger and Snyder, 2000). These communities are informal social groups that meet regularly to share ideas, insights, and best practices. This approach is typically adopted by companies that provide highly customized solutions to unique problems. For these firms, knowledge is shared mostly through person-to-person contact. Collaborative computing methods (e.g., group support systems [GSS], e-mail) help people communicate. The valuable knowledge for these firms is tacit in nature, which is difficult to express, capture, and manage. In this case, the environment and the nature of the problems being encountered are extremely dynamic. Because tacit knowledge is difficult to extract, store, and manage, the explicit knowledge that points to how to find the appropriate tacit knowledge (i.e., people contacts, consulting reports) is made available to an appropriate set of individuals who might need it. Consulting firms generally fall into this category. Firms adopting the codification strategy implicitly adopt the network storage model in their initial KMS (see Alavi, 2000).

The challenge for firms that adopt the personalization strategy, and hence the network storage model, is to develop methods to make the valuable tacit knowledge explicit, capture it, and contribute it to and transfer it from a **knowledge repository** in a KMS. Several major consulting firms are developing methods to do so. They store pointers to experts within the KMS, but they also store the tips, procedures, and best practices, as well as the context in which they work. To make their personalization strategies work, firms such as Bain invest heavily in building networks of people and communications technology, such as telephone, e-mail, and videoconferencing. They also commonly have face-to-face meetings (see Hansen et al., 1999).

In reality, a KM initiative can, and usually does, involve both approaches. Process and practice are not mutually exclusive. Alavi et al. (2003) described the case of an organization that began its KM effort with a large repository but evolved the KM initiative into a community-of-practice approach that existed side-by-side with the repository. In fact, community members would pass information from the community forum to the organizational repository when they felt that the knowledge was valuable outside their community. Application Case 11.4 illustrates how Texaco successfully manages its knowledge by using the practice approach.

APPLICATION CASE 11.4

Texaco Drills for Knowledge

Texaco (**texaco.com**), a company that pumps over a million barrels of oil a day, has discovered a new source of power: the collective knowledge and expertise of its 18,000 employees in 150 countries around the world. Texaco believes that connecting people who have questions with people who have answers gives it the power to work faster and more efficiently.

At Texaco, managing knowledge is a critical business challenge. John Old, Texaco's knowledge guru, approaches this challenge with a strategy that leverages human connections. Old has stated that knowledge, by its nature, is contextual; thus, systems that simply allow people to record what they know are ineffective. He strongly believes that a successful KM solution must recognize the importance of human connections.

Texaco uses technology to help people build personal relationships and share knowledge. One of the systems at work at Texaco is PeopleNet, a search engine for employees on the company's intranet. Employees who have questions can use PeopleNet to review profiles of their colleagues who might have the right answers. Texaco discovered that having biographies and pictures of its employees online makes it possible to establish credibility and trust between people who have not met each other. And it is trust that makes effective knowledge transfer possible.

Another tool that Texaco uses to connect its employees is a software system called Knowledge Mail from Tacit Knowledge Systems. This software analyzes e-mail sent and received by employees to help them make good contacts with colleagues who work on the same issues.

John Old has spoken of several important lessons that Texaco has learned while managing knowledge.

He pointed out that people are more eager to share knowledge when they are united by a clear, specific, and measurable business purpose. Knowledge sharing becomes even more successful when they trust each other and see direct benefits that can be derived from the knowledge exchange. In addition, it is important to give people enough time to reflect on what they know and what they need to learn.

Texaco's approach to KM has provided many positive results. The knowledge management efforts help Texaco's employees successfully resolve numerous issues, ranging from adjusting oil well pumps to deciding whether to enter into new lines of business.

Sources: Compiled from F. Warner, "He Drills for Knowledge," *Fast Company,* September 2001; and D. Drucker, "Theory Doesn't Equal Practice," Internetweek.com, January 29, 2001, **internetweek.cmp.com/newslead01/lead012901.htm** (accessed April 2006).

Hybrid Approaches to Knowledge Management

Many organizations use a hybrid of the process and practice approaches. Early in the development process, when it may not be clear how to extract tacit knowledge from its sources, the practice approach is used so that a repository stores only explicit knowledge that is relatively easy to document. The tacit knowledge initially stored in the repository is contact information about experts and their areas of expertise. Such information is listed so that people in the organization can find sources of expertise (e.g., the process approach). From this start, best practices can eventually be captured and managed so that the knowledge repository will contain an increasing amount of tacit knowledge over time. Eventually, a true process approach may be attained. But if the environment changes rapidly, only some of the best practices will prove useful. Regardless of the type of KMS developed, a storage location for the knowledge (i.e., a knowledge repository) of some kind is needed.

The J.D. Edwards intranet-based Knowledge Garden helps its consultants share best practices (i.e., practice approach) and find subject experts (i.e., process approach) who can help them solve problems faster and more consistently. The application codifies the company's knowledge base, using Site Server taxonomies, and delivers personalized updates automatically based on user needs (see Microsoft, 2000).

Hansen et al. (1999) indicated that firms that attempted to straddle the two strategies (i.e., to use about half of each) in their knowledge management efforts have generally failed. Management consulting firms run into serious trouble when they straddle the strategies. When firms use either strategy exclusively, they also run into trouble. The most successful efforts involve about an 80/20 split in the strategies. With the practice approach, there is a need to provide some codified knowledge in a repository so that people can access it on an as-needed basis. With the process approach, it is necessary to provide access to knowledge contributors, because additional advice and explanations might prove useful or even necessary.

Certain highly skilled, research-oriented industries exhibit traits that require nearly equal efforts with both approaches. For example, Koenig (2001) argued that the pharmaceutical firms in which he has worked require about a 50/50 split. We suspect that industries that require both a lot of engineering effort (i.e., how to create products) and heavy-duty research effort (where a large percentage of research is unusable) would fit the 50/50 hybrid category. Ultimately, any knowledge that is stored in a knowledge repository must be reevaluated; otherwise, the repository will become a knowledge landfill.

For more examples of similar strategies and practices, see Gamble and Blackwell (2002) and Martin (2000). Technology Insights 11.1 provides an interesting bidirectional model to KM.

TECHNOLOGY INSIGHTS 11.1   KM: A Demand-Led Business Activity

According to Murray (2002), one of the main reasons that today's businesses are not able to derive real benefits from their KM efforts is that they view KM as a supply-side issue, believing that the acquisition of knowledge automatically produces benefits. He argued that KM should be more of a demand-side initiative as opposed to a supply-side automation process. Figure 11.3 shows a high-level process model to knowledge management.

The conventional way of interpreting the model is to read it from left to right, as a supply-side value chain. The process starts with basic data and progresses through the stages, each one progressively yielding more value, culminating in worthy business results. The closer to the left (the data end), the emphasis is more on automation and technology; toward the right (the result end), the emphasis is more on people and decision making.

The DIKAR (Data-Information-Knowledge-Action-Results) model in the left to right mode is useful in identifying, collecting, and storing data and information assets of the organization in a systematic manner. It is a technology-driven approach to automate the process of knowledge accumulation from what is available in organizational memory. The assumption is that once you have compiled the data, information, and knowledge (because you are able to do so with automated means), you will be able to figure out a way to productively use it for specific business actions. Unfortunately, establishing the seemingly simple connection between the accumulated knowledge assets and the necessary business actions is not a trivial task. Because of the vast variety of business situations, the knowledge nuggets that the decision maker needs to initiate the right action for a specific situation may not be in the right form to be recognized or often may not even

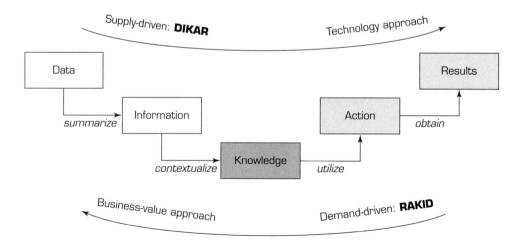

FIGURE 11.3 Bidirectional KM Process Model   *Source:* Peter Murray, "Knowledge Management as a Sustained Competitive Advantage," *Ivey Business Journal*, March/April 2002, pp. 71–76.

exist in the knowledge repository. Therefore, investing in a DIKAR type knowledge management model may not generate significant return on investment to be viable.

The RAKID (Results-Action-Knowledge-Information-Data) model in the right to left mode aims to mitigate the shortcoming of the DIKAR model. RAKID starts with the business question "Given our desired results, what actions are needed to achieve them?" Once identified, the next question is "Given the identified set of actions, what do we need to know to effectively perform these actions?" That is, what knowledge nuggets are needed to identify and execute these actions? Once the necessary knowledge assets are identified, then the information and data sources are identified and processed to generate them. This way, only the necessary knowledge assets are generated to take the right actions to achieve the desired results. This process consumes fewer organizational resources and hence results in better return on investment for KM efforts.

Sources: Based on P. Murray, "Knowledge Management as a Sustained Competitive Advantage," *Ivey Business Journal,* March/April 2002, pp. 71–76; and M. W. McElroy, *The New Knowledge Management: Complexity, Learning, and Sustainable Innovation,* Burlington, MA: Butterworth-Heinemann, p. 145.

Best Practices

Best practices are the activities and methods that the most effective organizations use to operate and manage various functions. Chevron, for example, recognizes four levels of best practices (see O'Dell et al., 1998):

1. A good idea that is not yet proven but makes intuitive sense.
2. A good practice, an implemented technique, a methodology, a procedure, or a process that has improved business results.
3. A local best practice, a best approach for all or a large part of the organization based on analysis of hard data. In other words, the scope within the organization of the best practice is identified: Can it be used in a single department or geographical region, or can it be used across the organization or anywhere in between?
4. An industry best practice, similar to the third level but using hard data from industry.

Historically, the first knowledge repositories simply listed best practices and made them available within the firm. Now that knowledge repositories are electronic and Web accessible, they can have wide-ranging impact on the use of knowledge throughout a firm. For example, Raytheon has successfully used best practices to merge three distinct corporate cultures. See O'Dell and Grayson (2003) and O'Dell et al. (2003) for more on best practices.

Knowledge Repositories

A knowledge repository is neither a database nor a knowledge base in the strictest sense of the terms. Rather, a knowledge repository stores knowledge that is often text based and has very different characteristics. It is also referred to an organizational knowledge base. Do not confuse a knowledge repository with the knowledge base of an expert system. They are very different mechanisms: A knowledge base of an expert system contains knowledge for solving a specific problem. An organizational knowledge base contains all the organizational knowledge.

Capturing and storing knowledge are the goals for a knowledge repository. The structure of the repository is highly dependent on the types of knowledge it stores. The repository can range from simply a list of frequently asked (and obscure) questions and solutions, to a listing of individuals with their expertise and contact information, to detailed best practices for a large organization. Figure 11.4 shows a comprehensive KM architecture designed around an all-inclusive knowledge repository (Delen and Hawamdeh, 2009).

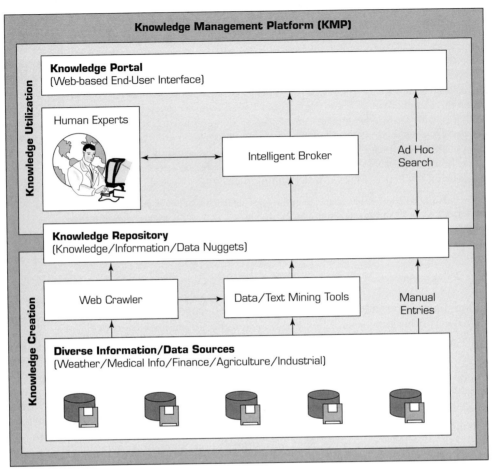

FIGURE 11.4 A Comprehensive View of a Knowledge Repository   *Source:* D. Delen, and S.S. Hawamdeh, "A Holistic Framework for Knowledge Discovery and Management," *Communications of the ACM,* Vol. 52, No. 6, 2009, pp. 141–145.

Developing a Knowledge Repository

Most knowledge repositories are developed using several different storage mechanisms, depending on the types and amount of knowledge to be maintained and used. Each has strengths and weaknesses when used for different purposes within a KMS. Developing a knowledge repository is not an easy task. The most important aspects and difficult issues are making the contribution of knowledge relatively easy for the contributor and determining a good method for cataloging the knowledge. "One of the biggest hurdles in putting a formalized knowledge management structure to collaborative systems is making the structure as seamless as possible," said to Terry Jordan, vice president of marketing for Hyperwave (**hyperwave.com**). "You really have to make the process painless, or you lose all of the knowledge that you are trying to capture because people don't want to have to go through an enormous number of steps" (Zimmermann, 2003b). The users should not be involved in running the storage and retrieval mechanisms of the knowledge repository. Typical development approaches include developing a large-scale Internet-based system or purchasing a formal electronic document management system or a knowledge management suite. The structure and development of the knowledge repository are a function of the specific technology used for the KMS.

Measuring the success of a knowledge repository system is a tricky affair; the repository is only as good as the information stored in it and the willingness of the target users to use it. Also, it is critical that the value of the repository be measured or estimated and that it continually be re-estimated, because the value is sure to fluctuate when knowledge reuse occurs and newer information is collected (see Qian and Bock, 2005).

Section 11.5 Review Questions

1. Describe the process approach to knowledge management.
2. Describe the practice approach to knowledge management.
3. Why is a hybrid approach to KM desirable?
4. Describe best practices as they relate to knowledge management.
5. Define *knowledge repository* and describe how to create one.

11.6 INFORMATION TECHNOLOGY (IT) IN KNOWLEDGE MANAGEMENT

The two primary functions of IT in knowledge management are retrieval and communication. IT also extends the reach and range of knowledge use and enhances the speed of knowledge transfer. Networks facilitate collaboration in KM.

The KMS Cycle

A functioning KMS follows six steps in a cycle (see Figure 11.5). The reason for the cycle is that knowledge is dynamically refined over time. The knowledge in a good KMS is never finished because the environment changes over time, and the knowledge must be updated to reflect the changes. The cycle works as follows:

1. *Create knowledge.*   Knowledge is created as people determine new ways of doing things or develop knowhow. Sometimes external knowledge is brought in. Some of these new ways may become best practices.
2. *Capture knowledge.*   New knowledge must be identified as valuable and be represented in a reasonable way.
3. *Refine knowledge.*   New knowledge must be placed in context so that it is actionable. This is where human insights (i.e., tacit qualities) must be captured along with explicit facts.
4. *Store knowledge.*   Useful knowledge must be stored in a reasonable format in a knowledge repository so that others in the organization can access it.
5. *Manage knowledge.*   Like a library, a repository must be kept current. It must be reviewed to verify that it is relevant and accurate.
6. *Disseminate knowledge.*   Knowledge must be made available in a useful format to anyone in the organization who needs it, anywhere and anytime.

As knowledge is disseminated, individuals develop, create, and identify new knowledge or update old knowledge, which they replenish in the system (see Allard, 2003; and Gaines, 2003).

Knowledge is a resource that is not consumed when used, although it can age (e.g., driving a car in 1900 was different from driving one now, but many of the basic principles still apply). Knowledge must be updated. Thus, the amount of knowledge grows over time.

Components of KMS

Knowledge management is more a methodology applied to business practices than a technology or a product. Nevertheless, IT is crucial to the success of every KMS. IT enables knowledge management by providing the enterprise architecture on which it is

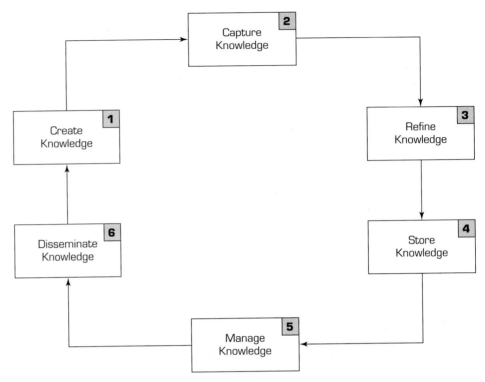

FIGURE 11.5 The Knowledge Management Cycle

built. KMS are developed using three sets of technologies: communication, collaboration, and storage and retrieval.

Communication technologies allow users to access needed knowledge and to communicate with each other—especially with experts. E-mail, the Internet, corporate intranets, and other Web-based tools provide communication capabilities. Even fax machines and telephones are used for communication, especially when the practice approach to knowledge management is adopted.

Collaboration technologies provide the means to perform groupwork. Groups can work together on common documents at the same time (i.e., synchronous) or at different times (i.e., asynchronous); they can work in the same place or in different places. Collaboration technologies are especially important for members of a community of practice working on knowledge contributions. Other collaborative computing capabilities, such as electronic brainstorming, enhance groupwork, especially for knowledge contribution. Additional forms of groupwork involve experts working with individuals trying to apply their knowledge; this requires collaboration at a fairly high level. Other collaborative computing systems allow an organization to create a virtual space so that individuals can work online anywhere and at any time (see Van de Van, 2005).

Storage and retrieval technologies originally meant using a database management system (DBMS) to store and manage knowledge. This worked reasonably well in the early days for storing and managing most explicit knowledge—and even explicit knowledge about tacit knowledge. However, capturing, storing, and managing tacit knowledge usually requires a different set of tools. Electronic document management systems and specialized storage systems that are part of collaborative computing

TABLE 11.3   Knowledge Management Technologies and Web Impacts

Knowledge Management	Web Impacts	Impacts on the Web
Communication	Consistent, friendly graphical user interface (GUI) for client units Improved communication tools Convenient, fast access to knowledge and knowledgeable individuals Direct access to knowledge on servers	Knowledge captured and shared is used in improving communication, communication management, and communication technologies.
Collaboration	Improved collaboration tools Enables anywhere/anytime collaboration Enables collaboration between companies, customers, and vendors Enables document sharing Improved, fast collaboration and links to knowledge sources Makes audio- and videoconferencing a reality, especially for individuals not using a local area network	Knowledge captured and shared is used in improving collaboration, collaboration management, and collaboration technologies (i.e., GSS).
Storage and retrieval	Consistent, friendly GUI for clients Servers provide for efficient and effective storage and retrieval of knowledge	Knowledge captured and shared is utilized in improving data storage and retrieval systems, database management/ knowledge repository management, and database and knowledge repository technologies.

systems fill this void. These storage systems have come to be known as knowledge repositories.

We describe the relationship between these knowledge management technologies and the Web in Table 11.3.

Technologies That Support Knowledge Management

Several technologies have contributed to significant advances in knowledge management tools. Artificial intelligence, intelligent agents, knowledge discovery in databases, eXtensible Markup Language (XML), and Web 2.0 are examples of technologies that enable advanced functionality of modern KMS and form the basis for future innovations in the knowledge management field. Following is a brief description of how these technologies are used in support of KMS.

ARTIFICIAL INTELLIGENCE In the definition of knowledge management, artificial intelligence (AI) is rarely mentioned. However, practically speaking, AI methods and tools are embedded in a number of KMS, either by vendors or by system developers. AI methods can assist in identifying expertise, eliciting knowledge automatically and semi-automatically, interfacing through natural language processing, and intelligently searching through intelligent agents. AI methods—notably expert systems, neural networks, fuzzy logic, and intelligent agents—are used in KMS to do the following:

- Assist in and enhance searching knowledge (e.g., intelligent agents in Web searches)
- Help establish knowledge profiles of individuals and groups
- Help determine the relative importance of knowledge when it is contributed to and accessed from the knowledge repository
- Scan e-mail, documents, and databases to perform knowledge discovery, determine meaningful relationships, glean knowledge, or induce rules for expert systems
- Identify patterns in data (usually through neural networks)
- Forecast future results by using existing knowledge
- Provide advice directly from knowledge by using neural networks or expert systems
- Provide a natural language or voice command–driven user interface for a KMS

INTELLIGENT AGENTS Intelligent agents are software systems that learn how users work and provide assistance in their daily tasks. There are other kinds of intelligent agents as well (see Chapter 14). Intelligent agents can help in KMS in a number of ways. Typically, they are used to elicit and identify knowledge. The following are some examples:

- IBM (**ibm.com**) offers an intelligent data-mining family, including Intelligent Decision Server (IDS), for finding and analyzing massive amounts of enterprise data.
- Gentia (Planning Sciences International, **gentia.com**) uses intelligent agents to facilitate data mining with Web access and data warehouse facilities.

Combining intelligent agents with enterprise knowledge portals is a powerful technique that can deliver to users exactly what they need to perform their tasks. The intelligent agent learns what the user prefers to see and how the user organizes it. Then the intelligent agent takes over to provide that information at the desktop, just as a good administrative assistant would.

KNOWLEDGE DISCOVERY IN DATABASES Knowledge discovery in databases (KDD) is a process used to search for and extract useful information from volumes of documents and data. It includes tasks such as knowledge extraction, data archaeology, data exploration, data pattern processing, data dredging, and information harvesting. All these activities are conducted automatically and allow quick discovery, even by nonprogrammers. Data and document mining is ideal for eliciting knowledge from databases, documents, e-mail, and so on. Data are often buried deep within very large databases, data warehouses, text documents, or knowledge repositories, all of which may contain data, information, and knowledge gathered over many years. (For more on data mining, see Chapter 7.)

AI methods are useful data-mining tools that include automated knowledge elicitation from other sources. Intelligent data mining discovers information within databases, data warehouses, and knowledge repositories that queries and reports cannot effectively reveal. Data-mining tools find patterns in data and may even (automatically) infer rules from them. Patterns and rules can be used to guide decision making and forecast the effects of decisions. KDD can also be used to identify the meaning of data or text, using knowledge management tools that scan documents and e-mail to build an expertise profile of a firm's employees. Data mining can speed up analysis by providing needed knowledge.

Extending the role of data mining and knowledge discovery techniques for knowledge externalization, Bolloju et al. (2002) proposed a framework for integrating knowledge management into enterprise environments for next-generation decision support systems (DSS). Their framework includes model marts and model warehouses where **model marts** are analogous to data marts and **model warehouses** are analogous to data warehouses (refer to Chapter 8). They act as repositories of knowledge created by using knowledge-discovery techniques on past decision instances stored in data marts and data warehouses. The model marts and model warehouses capture operational and historical decision models, similar to the data in data marts and data warehouses. For example, a model mart can store decision rules corresponding to problem-solving knowledge of different decision makers in a particular domain, such as loan approvals in a banking environment.

This integrated framework accommodates different types of knowledge transformations. Systems built around this framework are expected to enhance the quality of support provided to decision makers; support knowledge management functions such as acquisition, creation, exploitation, and accumulation; facilitate discovery of trends and patterns in the accumulated knowledge; and provide means for building up organizational memory.

EXTENSIBLE MARKUP LANGUAGE (XML)   eXtensible Markup Language (XML) enables standardized representations of data structures so that data can be processed appropriately by heterogeneous systems without case-by-case programming. This method suits e-commerce applications and supply-chain management (SCM) systems that operate across enterprise boundaries. XML can not only automate processes and reduce paperwork, it can also unite business partners and supply chains for better collaboration and knowledge transfer. XML-based messages can be taken from back-end repositories and fed out through the portal interface and back again. A portal that uses XML allows the company to communicate better with its customers, linking them in a virtual demand chain where changes in customer requirements are immediately reflected in production plans. Wide adoption of XML can pretty much solve the problem of integrating data from disparate sources. Due to its potential to tremendously simplify systems integration, XML may become the universal language that all portal vendors embrace (see Ruber, 2001).

WEB 2.0   Recent years have seen a shift in how people use the World Wide Web. The Web has evolved from a tool for disseminating information and conducting business to a platform for facilitating new ways of information sharing, collaboration, and communication in the digital age. A new vocabulary has emerged, as mashups, social networks, media-sharing sites, RSS, blogs, and wikis have come to characterize the genre of interactive applications collectively known as Web 2.0. These technologies are expected to give knowledge management a strong boost by making it easy and natural for everyone to share knowledge over the Web.

In a recent blog posting, Davenport (2008) characterized Web 2.0 (and its reflection to the enterprise world, Enterprise 2.0) as "new, new knowledge management." One of the bottlenecks for knowledge management practices has been the difficulty for nontechnical people to natively share their knowledge. Therefore, the ultimate value of Web 2.0 is its ability to foster greater responsiveness, better knowledge capture and sharing, and ultimately, more effective collective intelligence.

Section 11.6 Review Questions

1. Describe the KMS cycle.
2. List and describe the components of KMS.
3. Describe how AI and intelligent agents support knowledge management.
4. Relate XML to knowledge management and to knowledge portals.

11.7 KNOWLEDGE MANAGEMENT SYSTEMS IMPLEMENTATION

The challenge with KMS is to identify and integrate the three essential components—communication technologies, collaboration technologies, and storage and retrieval technologies—to meet the knowledge management needs of an organization. The earliest KMS were developed with networked technology (i.e., intranets), collaborative computing tools (i.e., groupware), and databases (for the knowledge repository). They were constructed from a variety of off-the-shelf IT components. Many organizations, especially large management consulting firms such as Accenture and J.D. Edwards, developed their knowledge architecture with a set of tools that provided the three technology types. Collaborative computing suites such as Lotus Notes/Domino and GroupSystems OnLine provide many KMS capabilities. Other systems were developed by integrating a set of tools from a single or multiple vendors. For example, J.D. Edwards (an Oracle company) used a set of loosely integrated Microsoft tools and products to implement its Knowledge Garden KMS, as did KPMG. In the early 2000s, KMS technology evolved to integrate the three components into a single package. These packages include enterprise knowledge portals and knowledge management suites.

Knowledge Management Products and Vendors

Technology tools that support KM are called **knowware**. Most knowledge management software packages include one or more of the following tools: collaborative computing tools, knowledge servers, enterprise knowledge portals, electronic document management systems, knowledge harvesting tools, search engines, and knowledge management suites. Many packages provide several tools because they are necessary in an effective KMS. For example, most electronic document management systems also include collaborative computing capabilities.

KMS can be purchased in whole or in part from one of numerous software development companies and enterprise information system (EIS) vendors, they can be acquired through major consulting firms, or they can be outsourced to an application service provider (ASP). All three alternatives are discussed later in this chapter. *KMWorld* publishes a "buyers' guide" in every April edition.

SOFTWARE DEVELOPMENT COMPANIES AND EIS VENDORS Software development companies and EIS vendors offer numerous knowledge management packages, from individual tools to comprehensive knowledge management suites. The variety of knowware that is readily available on the market allows companies to find tools that meet their unique KM needs. We next review some software packages and their vendors in each of the seven knowware categories identified earlier.

Collaborative Computing Tools Collaboration tools, or groupware, were the first tools used to enhance tacit knowledge transfer within an organization. One of the earliest collaborative computing systems, GroupSystems, provides many of the tools that support groupwork, including tools for electronic brainstorming and idea categorization. Lotus Notes/Domino provides an enterprise-wide collaborative environment. Other collaboration tools include MeetingPlace (Latitude), QuickPlace (Lotus Development Corp.), eRoom (eRoom Technology Inc.), Groove Networks (**groove.net**), and Microsoft Office Live Meeting (Microsoft). For more details, see Chapter 10.

KNOWLEDGE SERVERS A knowledge server contains the main knowledge management software, including the knowledge repository, and provides access to other knowledge, information, and data. Examples of knowledge servers include the Hummingbird Knowledge Server, the Intraspect Software Knowledge Server, the Hyperwave Information Server, the Sequoia Software XML Portal Server, and Autonomy's Intelligent Data Operating Layer (IDOL) Server. Autonomy's IDOL Server connects people to content, content to content, and people to people through modules that enable organizations to integrate various personalization, collaboration, and retrieval features. The server provides a knowledge repository—a central location for searching and accessing information from many sources, such as the Internet, corporate intranets, databases, and file systems—thereby enabling the efficient distribution of time-sensitive information. The server seamlessly extends and integrates with the company's e-business suite, allowing rapid deployment applications that span the enterprise and can even leverage AI-assisted technology to harvest knowledge assets.

Enterprise Knowledge Portals **Enterprise knowledge portals (EKP)** are the doorways into many KMS. They have evolved from the concepts underlying EIS, GSS, Web browsers, and DBMS. Using EKP is an ideal way to configure a KMS. Most EKP combine data integration, reporting mechanisms, and collaboration, while a server handles document and knowledge management. An enterprise information portal is a virtual place on a network of online users. The portal aggregates each user's total information needs: data and documents, e-mail, Web links and queries, dynamic feeds from the network, and shared calendars and task lists.

When enterprise information portals first entered the market, they did not have knowledge management features. Now most do; hence, they are now called EKP. Leading portal vendors include Autonomy, Corechange, DataChannel, Dataware, Epicentric, Glyphica, Intraspect, Hummingbird, InXight, KnowledgeTrack, IBM/Lotus, Knowmadic, OpenText, Plumtree, Portera, Sequoia Software, Verity, and Viador. Database vendors such as Microsoft, Oracle, and Sybase also sell knowledge portals.

The KnowledgeTrack Knowledge Center offers integrated business-to-business functions and can scale from dot-coms to large enterprises. Knowledge Center can be built into the enterprise architecture instead of simply sitting on top, the way most intranet portals do. The Knowledge Center integrates with external data sources, including enterprise resource planning (ERP), online analytical processing (OLAP), and customer relationship management (CRM) systems. IT also supports communities of practice and enables them for large-project management, allowing information to be shared among all the extended enterprise value chains.

Electronic Document Management (EDM) **Electronic document management (EDM)** systems use the document in electronic form as the collaborative focus of work. EDM systems allow users to access needed documents, generally via a Web browser over a corporate intranet. EDM systems enable organizations to better manage documents and workflow for smoother operations. They also allow collaboration on document creation and revision.

Many KMS use an EDM system as the knowledge repository. There is a natural fit in terms of the purpose and benefits of the two. Pfizer uses a large-scale document management system to handle the equivalent of truckloads of paper documents of drug approval applications passed between Pfizer and the Food & Drug Administration (FDA), its regulating agency. This EDM system dramatically cut the time required for FDA submission and review, making Pfizer more competitive in getting new and effective drugs to market (Blodgett, 2000).

Systems such as DocuShare (Xerox Corporation) and Lotus Notes (Lotus Development Corporation) allow direct collaboration on a common document. Some other EDM systems include EDMS (Documentum, Inc.), Enterprise Work Management (Eastman Software, Inc.), FYI (Identitech), The Discovery Suite (FileNet Corp.), Livelink

(Open Text Corp.), PageKeeper Pro (Caere Corp.), Pagis Pro (ScanSoft, Inc.), Xpedio (IntraNet Solutions), and CaseCentral.com (Document Repository, Inc.).

A new approach to EDM, called **content management systems (CMS)**, is changing the way documents and their content are managed. A CMS produces dynamic versions of documents and automatically maintains the "current" set for use at the enterprise level. With the explosion of Web-based materials, organizations need a mechanism to provide content that is consistent and accurate across the enterprise. EDM systems, EKP, and other CMS fill that need. The goal is to provide large numbers of knowledge workers with access to large amounts of unstructured text (see Sullivan, 2001). An IDC survey of attendees at the *KMWorld* 2001 Conference and Exposition indicated that 63 percent of all respondents had or planned to implement CMS, while 59 percent rated CMS as very to critically important (see Feldman, 2002). Also see Bankes (2003) and Lamont (2003b).

A subset of CMS is business rules management. New software tools and systems, such as Ilog JRules and Blaze Advisor, have been developed to handle these smaller chunks of content.

Knowledge Harvesting Tools   Tools for capturing knowledge unobtrusively are helpful because they allow a knowledge contributor to be minimally (or not at all) involved in the knowledge-harvesting efforts. Embedding this type of tool in a KMS is an ideal approach to knowledge capture. Tacit Knowledge Systems' Knowledge-mail is an expertise-location software package that analyzes users' outgoing e-mail to parse subject expertise. It maintains a directory of expertise and offers ways to contact experts while maintaining privacy controls for them. Autonomy's ActiveKnowledge performs a similar analysis on e-mail and other standard document types. Intraspect Software's Knowledge Server monitors an organization's group memory; captures the context of its use, such as who used it, when, for what, how it was combined with other information, and what people said about it, and then makes the information available for sharing and reuse. KnowledgeX by KnowledgeX, Inc., and a number of other products provide similar functionality.

Search Engines   Search engines perform one of the essential functions of knowledge management—locating and retrieving necessary documents from vast collections accumulated in corporate repositories. Companies such as Google, Verity, and Inktomi offer a wide selection of search engines capable of indexing and cataloging files in various formats as well as of retrieving and prioritizing relevant documents in response to user queries.

Knowledge Management Suites   Knowledge management suites are complete out-of-the-box knowledge management solutions. They integrate the communications, collaboration, and storage technologies into a single convenient package. A knowledge management suite must access internal databases and other external knowledge sources, so some integration is required to make the software truly functional. IBM/Lotus offers an extensive range of knowledge management products, including the Domino platform, QuickPlace and Sametime, Discovery Server and Learning Space, and the WebSphere portal. See Application Case 11.5 to learn how Commerce Bank implemented a KMS based on the IBM/Lotus platform. Several vendors also provide fairly comprehensive sets of tools for knowledge management initiatives, including Dataware Knowledge Management Suite and KnowledgeX by KnowledgeX, Inc. Autonomy Knowledge Management Suite offers document categorization and workflow integration. Microsoft provides central components of knowledge management solutions and is working on developing an encompassing knowledge management framework. Some EIS vendors, such as SAP, PeopleSoft, and Oracle, are developing knowledge management—related technologies as a platform for business applications. Siebel Systems is repositioning itself as a business-to-employee knowledge management platform. Using a knowledge management suite is a powerful approach to developing a KMS because it has one user interface and one data repository, and it is from one vendor.

APPLICATION CASE 11.5

Knowledge Management: You Can Bank on It at Commerce Bank

Commerce Bank is a $15.4 billion financial institution that is quickly growing to become a dominant player in the financial services market of Philadelphia and southern New Jersey. During its 30 years of existence, it has developed a network of 214 branches and has made ambitious plans for continuous growth. Commerce Bank calls itself "America's Most Convenient Bank." It lives up to that name by maintaining a strong banking network and by empowering each branch to make business decisions in an effort to better meet the needs of its customers.

While undergoing explosive growth, Commerce Bank encouraged its associates to learn all about its customers and the right ways to service them. However, the company realized that its most important asset, knowledge, was locked away in the file cabinets and in the heads of its associates. To support this initiative, Commerce Bank needed to tap into that knowledge and find a way to train employees consistently and conveniently across the entire branch network.

The first step for new employees is Commerce University, a boot camp where they are instilled with the fundamentals of customer service. However, the program covers only a few of the range of issues that an associate might encounter.

The need for knowledge management at Commerce Bank was apparent. Jack Allison, vice president of systems development, said,

> We had folks in administration that could spend 70 percent of their time answering calls and clarifying answers for branches. At times, we could wait weeks or months for the right answer to certain questions. Knowing that training may not give answers for every scenario, we needed to give associates a tool that could help them find any answer to any topic at any time. We have so many regulations and products; we needed a way to give our employees all the knowledge to process these.

Commerce Bank envisioned a solution—a workflow-based KMS that could provide instant answers to questions for the bank's employees and online customers. To make this vision a reality, Commerce chose to develop a system based on IBM's Lotus Notes, which the bank has been using since 1995. Using IBM's Domino server, the Lotus Notes client, and an application development tool kit, Commerce Bank created a full-fledged KMS, called Wow Answer Guide.

Introduced in 2000, Wow Answer Guide provides a central repository of knowledge about all bank transactions. It helps employees learn a process and respond to customer inquiries, and it stores information electronically. In addition, the system allows employees to register for the bank's continuing education courses.

The complete Wow Answer Guide contains more than 400 applications, and Commerce plans to add even more, such as a CRM system. The flexibility of the platform simplifies the application-development process and allows the addition of new features and the expansion of functionality with minimal investments of time and effort.

"[The Wow Answer Guide] is especially good for the green associate or veteran who is still learning how to process a new product," said Allison. "We don't want our associates on a scavenger hunt to get the correct information."

Commerce Bank realized that knowledge management would be beneficial not only to the bank's employees but also to its clients. "We wanted to put information in our customers' hands so they could conduct [online] transactions with confidence," said Allison. In the summer of 2000, Commerce Bank deployed a new version of Wow Answer Guide that empowered the bank's online customers.

Knowledge management at Commerce Bank proved to be an effective investment. According to Allison, the application has saved the bank $20,000 per week, or approximately $1 million a year. In fact, the bank achieved a return on investment within a month of launching Wow Answer Guide.

By drawing on the power of the Domino platform, Commerce Bank created workflow-based applications that streamline internal knowledge sharing and route data and information to the appropriate employees within the organization. This dramatically reduces the completion time for approval-intensive transactions, improves the bank's capacity, and minimizes labor costs.

Sources: Adapted from D. Amato-McCoy, "Commerce Bank Manages Knowledge Profitably," *Bank Systems & Technology,* January 2003; and "Knowledge Infusion Helps Commerce Bank Experience Big Pay Off with Talent Management Initiative," October 19, 2005, **onlypun-jab.com/money/fullstory-insight-money+finance-newsID-9368.html** (accessed April 2006).

KNOWLEDGE MANAGEMENT CONSULTING FIRMS All the major consulting firms (e.g., Accenture, Cap Gemini Ernst & Young, Deloitte & Touche, KPMG, PWC) have massive internal knowledge management initiatives. Usually, these become products after they succeed internally and provide assistance in establishing KMS and measuring their effectiveness. Consulting firms also provide some direct, out-of-the-box proprietary systems for vertical markets. Most of the major management consulting firms define their knowledge management offerings as services. For more on consulting firm activities and products, see McDonald and Shand (2000).

KNOWLEDGE MANAGEMENT ASPS ASPs have evolved as a form of KMS outsourcing on the Web. There are many ASPs for e-commerce on the market. For example, Communispace is a high-level ASP collaboration system that focuses on connecting people to people (not just people to documents) to achieve specific objectives, regardless of geographic, time, and organizational barriers. As a hosted ASP solution, Communispace is easy to rapidly deploy within organizations. Unlike conventional KMS that organize data and documents or chat rooms, where people simply swap information, Communispace contains a rich assortment of interactions, activities, and tools that connect people to the colleagues who can best help them make decisions, solve problems, and learn quickly. Communispace is designed to build trust online; it attempts to make a community self-conscious about taking responsibility for its actions and knowledge. Its climate component helps participants measure and understand how people are feeling about the community. Its Virtual Café gives dispersed employees a way to meet and learn about each other through pictures and profiles.

A recent trend among ASPs is to offer a complete KM solution, including a knowledge management suite and the consulting to set it up, as Communispace does.

Integration of KMS with Other Business Information Systems

Because a KMS is an enterprise system, it must be integrated with other enterprise and information systems in an organization. Obviously, when it is designed and developed it cannot be perceived as an add-on application. It must be truly integrated into other systems. Through the structure of the organizational culture (which is changed, if necessary), a KMS and its activities can be directly integrated into a firm's business processes. For example, a group involved in customer support can capture its knowledge to provide help on customers' difficult problems. In this case, help-desk software would be one type of package to integrate into a KMS, especially into the knowledge repository.

Because a KMS can be developed on a knowledge platform/server consisting of communication, collaboration, and storage technologies, and because most firms already have many such tools and technologies in place, it is often possible to develop a KMS in the organization's existing tools (e.g., Lotus Notes/Domino). Or, an EKP can provide universal access and an interface into all of an individual's relevant corporate information and knowledge. In this case, the KMS effort would provide the linkage for everyone into the entire EIS.

INTEGRATION OF KMS WITH DSS/BI SYSTEMS KMS typically do not involve running models to solve problems. This is typically done in DSS/BI systems. However, because a KMS provides help in solving problems by applying knowledge, part of the solution may involve running models. A KMS can integrate into a set of models and data, and it can activate them if a specific problem calls for it. Also, the knowhow and best practice application of models can be stored in a KMS.

INTEGRATION OF KMS WITH AI KM has a natural relationship with AI methods and software, although knowledge management, strictly speaking, is not an AI method. KM and AI can be integrated in a number of ways. For example, if the knowledge stored in a KMS is to be represented and used as a sequence of if-then-else rules, an expert system becomes part of the KMS (see Rasmus, 2000). An expert system could also assist a user in identifying how to apply a chunk of knowledge in the KMS. Natural language processing assists the computer in understanding what a user is searching for. Artificial neural networks help to understand text to determine the applicability of a specific chunk of knowledge as it applies to a particular problem. They are also used to enhance search engines. The most common integration of AI and KM is in identifying and classifying expertise by examining e-mail messages and documents. These include AI-based tools, such as ActiveNet and Knowledge-mail from Tacit Software, Inc. (**tacit.com**), and Categorizer from Inxight Software (**inxight.com**).

Much work is being done in the field of AI relating to knowledge engineering; tacit-to-explicit knowledge transfer; and knowledge identification, understanding, and dissemination. Companies are attempting to realign these technologies and the resultant products with knowledge management. The AI technologies most often integrated with KM are intelligent agents, expert systems, neural networks, and fuzzy logic. Several specific methods and tools are described earlier in this chapter.

INTEGRATION OF KMS WITH DATABASES AND INFORMATION SYSTEMS Because a KMS uses a knowledge repository, sometimes constructed out of a database system or an EDM system, it can automatically integrate to this part of the firm's information system. As data and information updates are made, the KMS can use them. As described earlier in this chapter, KMS also attempt to glean knowledge from documents and databases through AI methods, in a process known as KDD. This knowledge is then represented textually within the knowledge repository described earlier.

INTEGRATION OF KMS WITH CRM SYSTEMS CRM systems help users in dealing with customers. One aspect is the help-desk notion described earlier. But CRM goes much deeper than that. It can develop usable profiles of customers and predict their needs so that an organization can increase sales and better serve its clients. A KMS can certainly provide tacit knowledge to people who use CRM directly in working with customers.

INTEGRATION WITH SCM SYSTEMS The supply chain is often considered to be the logistics end of a business. If products do not move through the organization and go out the door, the firm will fail. It is therefore important to optimize the supply chain and manage it properly. A new set of software called *SCM systems* attempts to do so. SCM can benefit from integration with KMS because there are many issues and problems in the supply chain that require the company to combine tacit and explicit knowledge. Accessing such knowledge directly improves supply-chain performance.

INTEGRATION OF KMS WITH CORPORATE INTRANETS AND EXTRANETS Communication and collaboration tools and technologies are necessary for KMS to function. A KMS is not simply integrated with the technology of intranets and extranets; it is typically developed on them as the communications platform. Extranets are specifically designed to enhance the collaboration of a firm with its suppliers and sometimes with customers. If a firm can integrate its KMS into its intranets and extranets, not only will knowledge flow more freely, both from a contributor and to a user (either directly or through a knowledge repository), but the firm can also capture knowledge directly, with little user involvement, and can deliver it when the system thinks that a user needs knowledge.

Section 11.7 Review Questions

1. Define *knowware*.
2. Describe the major categories of knowledge management tools.

3. Define *EKP.*
4. Define *EDM* and relate it to knowledge management and to CMS.
5. Describe tools for knowledge harvesting.
6. List the major systems that are frequently integrated with KMS.

11.8   ROLES OF PEOPLE IN KNOWLEDGE MANAGEMENT

Managing a KMS requires great effort. As with any other IT, getting it started, implemented, and deployed requires a champion's effort. Many issues of management, people, and culture must be considered to make a KMS a success. In this section, we address those issues. Managing the knowledge repository typically requires a full-time staff (similar to a reference library staff). This staff examines, structures, filters, catalogs, and stores knowledge so that it is meaningful and can be accessed by the people who need it. The staff assists individuals in searching for knowledge and performs environmental scanning: If they identify specific knowledge that an employee or a client might need, they send it directly to whoever needs it, thus adding value to the organization. (This is standard procedure for Accenture knowledge management personnel.) Finally, the knowledge repository staff may create communities of practice (see the case at the end of the chapter) to gather individuals with common knowledge areas to identify, filter, extract, and contribute knowledge to a knowledge repository.

Most of the issues concerning the success, implementation, and effective use of a KMS are people issues. And because a KMS is an enterprise-wide effort, many people are involved. They include the chief knowledge officer (CKO), the CEO, the other officers and managers of the organization, members and leaders of communities of practice, KMS developers, and KMS staff. Each person or group has an important role in either the development, management, or use of a KMS. By far, the CKO has the most visible role in a KMS effort, but the system cannot succeed unless the roles of all the players are established and understood. And the team must consist of the right people, possessing the appropriate level of experience, to take on the various roles (see Riege, 2005).

The Chief Knowledge Officer

Knowledge management projects that involve establishing a knowledge environment conducive to the transfer, creation, or use of knowledge attempt to build cultural receptivity. These attempts are centered on changing the behavior of the firm to embrace the use of knowledge management. Behavior-centric projects require a high degree of support and participation from the senior management of the organization to facilitate their implementation. Most firms developing KMS have created a knowledge management officer—a **chief knowledge officer (CKO)**—at the senior level. The objectives of the CKO's role are to maximize the firm's knowledge assets, design and implement KM strategies, effectively exchange knowledge assets internally and externally, and promote system use. The CKO is responsible for developing processes that facilitate knowledge transfer.

According to Duffy (1998), a CKO must do the following:

- Set knowledge management strategic priorities.
- Establish a knowledge repository of best practices.
- Gain a commitment from senior executives to support a learning environment.
- Teach information seekers how to ask better and smarter questions.
- Establish a process for managing intellectual assets.
- Obtain customer satisfaction information in near real time.
- Globalize knowledge management.

The CKO is responsible for defining the area of knowledge within the firm that will be the focal point, based on the firm's mission and objectives (see Davis, 1998). The CKO is responsible for standardizing the enterprise-wide vocabulary and controlling the knowledge directory. This is critical in areas that must share knowledge across departments, to ensure uniformity. The CKO must get a handle on the company's repositories of research, resources, and expertise, including where they are stored and who manages and accesses them (e.g., perform a knowledge audit). Then the CKO must encourage pollination among disparate workgroups with complementary resources (see McKeen and Staples, 2003).

The CKO is responsible for creating an infrastructure and cultural environment for knowledge sharing. He or she must assign or identify (and encourage/motivate) the knowledge champions within the business units. The CKO's job is to manage the content the champions' groups produce, continually add to the knowledge base, and encourage colleagues to do the same. Successful CKOs should have the full and enthusiastic support of their managers and of top management. Ultimately, the CKO is responsible for the entire knowledge management project while it is under development and then for management of the system and the knowledge after it is deployed.

A CKO needs a range of skills to make knowledge management initiatives succeed. These attributes are indispensable, according to CKOs and consultants (see Flash, 2001):

- Interpersonal communication skills to convince employees to adopt cultural changes
- Leadership skills to convey the knowledge management vision and passion for it
- Business acumen to relate knowledge management efforts to efficiency and profitability
- Strategic thinking skills to relate knowledge management efforts to larger goals
- Collaboration skills to work with various departments and persuade them to work together
- The ability to institute effective educational programs
- An understanding of IT and its role in advancing knowledge management

The CEO, Officers, and Managers of the Organization

Briefly, the CEO is responsible for championing a knowledge management effort. He or she must ensure that a competent and capable CKO is found and that the CKO can obtain all the resources (including access to people with knowledge sources) needed to make the project a success. The CEO must also gain organization-wide support for contributions to and use of the KMS. The CEO must also prepare the organization for the cultural changes that are about to occur. Support is the critical responsibility of the CEO. The CEO is the primary change agent of the organization.

The officers generally must make available to the CKO the resources needed to get the job done. The chief financial officer (CFO) must ensure that the financial resources are available. The chief operating officer (COO) must ensure that people begin to embed knowledge management practices into their daily work processes. There is a special relationship between the CKO and chief information officer (CIO). Usually, the CIO is responsible for the IT vision of the organization and for the IT architecture, including databases and other potential knowledge sources. The CIO must cooperate with the CKO in making these resources available. KMS are expensive propositions, and it is wise to use existing systems if they are available and capable.

Managers must also support the knowledge management effort and provide access to sources of knowledge. In many KMS, managers are an integral part of the communities of practice.

Communities of Practice

The success of many KMS has been attributed to the active involvement of the people who contribute to and benefit from using the knowledge. Consequently, communities of practice have appeared within organizations that are serious about their knowledge management efforts. A **community of practice (COP)** is a group of people in an organization with a common professional interest. Ideally, all the KMS users should each be in at least one COP. Properly creating and nurturing COP is one key to KMS success (see Liedtka, 2002; and Wenger, 2002).

COP are where the organizational culture shift really happens when developing and deploying KMS. A supportive culture must be developed for a KMS to succeed (see Wenger, 2002; and Wenger et al., 2002). In Application Case 11.6, we describe how Xerox Corp. successfully generated improved practices and cost savings through COP.

APPLICATION CASE 11.6

Online Knowledge Sharing at Xerox

In the early 1990s, Xerox had a nationwide database that contained information that could be used to fix its copiers, fax machines, and high-speed printers. However, the information was not readily available to the 25,000 service and field employees and engineers who repaired the machines at customer sites. Satisfaction with customer service was low.

The engineers at Xerox's Palo Alto Research Center (PARC) spent 6 months observing repair personnel, watching how they worked, noting what their frustrations were, and identifying what kind of information they needed. They determined that the repair personnel needed to share their knowledge with their peers. PARC engineers developed Eureka, an online knowledge-sharing system created to assist the service people with time-consuming and complicated repair problems.

Ray Everett, program manager for Eureka, described the powerful impact the program has had on service, "You went from not knowing how to fix something to being able to get the answer instantly. Even better, you could share any solutions you found with your peers around the globe within a day, as opposed to the several weeks it used to take."

Since its inception in 1996, Eureka has been implemented in 71 countries. It has helped solve 350,000 problems and has saved $3 million to $4 million in parts and labor every year. The system is available to all of Xerox's service engineers via notebook computers and is accessed through the Internet. Product fixes (50,000 of them), documentation updates, and product-update bulletins are delivered over the Web. Individual service employees and engineers can enter into the system possible new solutions to problems. A solution appears in Eureka, giving credit to the author and noting the service employee's country of origin. An alert about a new solution is sent to validators who test the solution; if it works consistently, it is sent to all engineers via Eureka updates.

Since 2004, Eureka has been designed to work over wireless Internet connections. Eureka is a constantly evolving and growing system that connects and shares the collective knowledge of Xerox's service force.

One of Eureka's guiding principles is, "We should never create the same solution twice. If a solution already exists, it should be used rather than recreating a new solution. In addition, we should focus on continuously improving existing solutions." Eureka! It works!

Sources: Compiled from S. Barth, "Knowledge as a Function of X," *Knowledge Management,* February 2000; and S. L. Roberts-Witt, "The @HP Way," *Portals Magazine,* November 2002.

In a sense, a COP owns the knowledge that it contributes because it manages the knowledge on its way into the system and must approve modifications to it. The COP is responsible for the accuracy and timeliness of the knowledge it contributes and for identifying its potential use. A number of researchers have investigated how successful COP form and function. In Table 11.4, we illustrate the many ways that COP add value to an organization through KM efforts. Basically, COP make organizations run smoothly because they enable knowledge flow. Informed people make better decisions. People who are involved are happier at work. Wenger et al. (2002) recommended seven design

TABLE 11.4 How Communities of Practice Add Value to an Organization

Name of Added Value	Attributes That Create Value
Creation of higher-quality knowledge	• Diversity in membership and less emphasis on hierarchical status reduce the likelihood of groupthink.
	• Limited requirements for formal reporting allow people to perform riskier brainstorming.
	• A reflection process at the end of a meeting consolidates learning.
Fewer surprises and plan revisions	• Broad participation diffuses knowledge across business units.
	• Openness of interaction format results in effective conflict resolution.
Greater capacity in dealing with unstructured problems	• Work occurs under a set of superordinate goals, not task goals.
	• The sponsoring organization accepts a self-evolving community role.
	• Knowledge leaders can emerge based on issues instead of by assignment to a team or roles within a team.
More effective knowledge sharing among business and corporate staff units	• Voluntary participation implies higher motivation, leading to faster, deeper learning internalization.
	• Trust increases due to indeterminate life span and long-term relationships.
Improved likelihood of implementing joint goals	• The community yields greater external validity because it exists externally to the formal organizational structure.
	• The community has more influence than an individual, given the organizational level of the community members.
More effective individual development and learning	• Group learning is more effective than individual learning.
	• The community's development process embodies learning opportunities through practice.

Source: Based on Table 5.2 in "Strategic Community: Adding Value to the Organization," in E. L. Lesser, M. A. Fontaine, and J. A. Slusher (eds.), *Knowledge and Communities,* Butterworth-Heinemann, Woburn, MA, 2000, p. 77.

principles for successful COP. Each of these facilitates knowledge creation and use. We describe them in Technology Insights 11.2.

Storck and Hill (2002) investigated one of the earliest COP at Xerox. When established at Xerox, the COP was a new organizational form. The word *community* captured the sense of responsible, independent action that characterized the group, which continued to function within the standard boundaries of the large organization. Management sponsored the community but did not mandate it. Community members were volunteers. We list and describe the six key principles that support COP at Xerox in Table 11.5. Brailsford (2001) described how Hallmark Cards built its COP and made similar discoveries to those at Xerox. For more on COP, see Barth (2000a), Brown and Duguid (2002), Lesser and Prusak (2002), McDermott (2002), Smith and McKeen (2003), Storck and Hill (2002), and Wenger (2002).

KMS Developers

KMS developers are the team members who actually develop the system. They work for the CKO. Some are organizational experts who develop strategies to promote and manage

> ### TECHNOLOGY INSIGHTS 11.2   Seven Principles for Designing Successful COP
>
> Here are seven ways to encourage vibrant COP in an organization:
>
> 1. **Design for evolution.**   COP are organic, and many organizational factors influence their direction. Plan carefully. One does not so much manage a community as shepherd it.
> 2. **Open a dialogue between inside and outside.**   Good community design requires an understanding of the community's potential to develop and steward knowledge, but it often takes an outside perspective to help members see possibilities. The COP should not close in on itself.
> 3. **Invite different levels of participation.**   There are typically three main levels of community participation. The first is a small core of people who actively participate in discussions. As the COP matures, this group evolves into the leadership. The next level is the active group. These members attend meetings regularly and participate occasionally in the community forums but not as regularly or as intensely as the core group. A large portion of the COP is peripheral and rarely participates. Do not exclude these people. They often use the knowledge generated. The key to good community participation, and a healthy degree of movement between levels, is to design community activities that allow participants at all levels to feel like full members.
> 4. **Develop public and private spaces.**   The heart of a community is the web of relationships among community members, and private space is necessary to get the relationships to grow.
> 5. **Focus on value.**   Because participation is generally voluntary, a COP must provide value. Communities must create events, activities, and relationships that help their potential value emerge and enable them to discover new ways to harvest it rather than determine expected value in advance.
> 6. **Combine familiarity and excitement.**   Vibrant communities supply divergent thinking and activity. Routine activities provide stability for relationship building.
> 7. **Create a rhythm for the community.**   There is a tempo associated with the members' interactions. This rhythm is the strongest indicator of its life and potential. The COP should contain a balance between large- and small-group sessions and between idea-sharing forums and tool-building projects. The rhythm will evolve with the community, but it is important to find the right one at each stage.
>
> *Sources:* Compiled from E. Wenger, R. McDermott, and W. M. Snyder, *Cultivating Communities of Practice,* Harvard Business School Press, Boston, 2002; and E. Wenger, R. McDermott, and W. M. Snyder. "It Takes a Community," *CIO,* May 15, 2002.

the organizational culture shift. Others are involved in system software and hardware selection, programming, testing, deployment, and maintenance. Still others are initially involved in training users. Eventually, the training function moves to the KMS staff.

KMS Staff

Enterprise-wide KMS require a full-time staff to catalog and manage the knowledge. This staff is either located at the firm's headquarters or dispersed in knowledge centers throughout the organization. Most large consulting firms have more than one knowledge center.

Earlier in this chapter we described the function of the staff as being similar to that of reference librarians. However, KMS staff actually do much more. Some members are functional area experts who are now cataloging and approving knowledge contributions and pushing the knowledge out to clients and employees whom they believe can use the knowledge. These functional experts may also work in a liaison role with the functional areas of the COP. Others work with users to train them on the system or help them with their searches. Still others work on improving the system's performance by identifying better methods with which to manage knowledge. For example, Cap Gemini Ernst &

TABLE 11.5 **The Six Key Principles Supporting Communities of Practice at Xerox**

Community Characteristic	Actions
Interaction format	Consists of meetings, collaborative computing, interaction structure, e-mail, etc.
Organizational culture	Leverages common training, experience, and vocabulary.
	Facilitates working around constraints.
Mutual interest	Builds commitment and promotes continuous improvement of processes.
Individual and collective learning	Recognizes and rewards knowledge contribution and use, leverages knowledge, and provides a culture of knowledge sharing.
Knowledge sharing	Embeds knowledge sharing into work practices.
	Reinforces with immediate feedback the value of knowledge sharing.
Community processes and norms	Builds trust and identity.
	Minimizes linkage to the formal control structure.
	Motivates the community to establish its own governance processes.

Source: Based on J. Storck and P. A. Hill, "Knowledge Diffusion Through Strategic Communities," *Sloan Management Review,* Vol. 41, No. 2, Winter 2000.

Young has 250 people managing the knowledge repository and assisting people in finding knowledge at its Center for Business Knowledge. Some staff members disseminate knowledge, and others are liaisons with the 40 practice areas. They codify and store documents in their areas of expertise (see Hansen et al., 1999).

Section 11.8 Review Questions

1. Describe the role of the CKO.
2. What other managers are involved with knowledge management?
3. Describe COP and relate them to knowledge management.
4. What is the importance of COP in organizations?

11.9 ENSURING THE SUCCESS OF KNOWLEDGE MANAGEMENT EFFORTS

Although there are many cases of knowledge management success, there are also many cases of failure. Let's look at the reasons behind success or failure.

Knowledge Management Success Stories

Organizations can gain several benefits from implementing a knowledge management strategy. Tactically, they can accomplish some or all of the following: reduce loss of intellectual capital due to people leaving the company; reduce costs by decreasing the number of times the company must repeatedly solve the same problem and by achieving economies of scale in obtaining information from external providers; reduce redundancy of knowledge-based activities; increase productivity by making knowledge available more quickly and easily; and increase employee satisfaction by enabling greater personal development and empowerment. The best reason of all may be a strategic need to gain a competitive advantage in the marketplace.

Many factors are necessary for knowledge management to succeed. For example, Gold et al. (2001) described how a knowledge infrastructure consisting of technology, structure, and culture, along with a knowledge process architecture of acquisition, conversion, application, and protection, are essential "preconditions" for effective knowledge management. The situation in an organization must be right in order for a KM effort to succeed. See O'Dell et al. (2003), Smith and McKeen (2003), and Firestone and McElroy (2005) for more KM successes. Technology Insights 11.3 is about an annual study for identifying and recognizing the most admired knowledge enterprises.

A good example of how proper analysis and implementation of knowledge management projects can help a large broadcasting corporation manage their most valuable assets (knowledge, that is) is provided in Application Case 11.7.

TECHNOLOGY INSIGHTS 11.3 MAKE: Most Admired Knowledge Enterprises

MAKE is an annual study administered by Teleos—an independent knowledge management and intellectual capital research firm—in association with the MAKE network to identify the best practitioners of knowledge management. A panel of global *Fortune* 500 senior executives and internationally recognized knowledge management and/or intellectual capital experts collaborate to choose the Global MAKE winners. The panel rates organizations against the MAKE framework of eight key knowledge performance dimensions that are deemed to be the visible drivers of competitive advantage. These eight key knowledge performance dimensions are:

1. Creating a corporate knowledge-driven culture
2. Developing knowledge workers through senior management leadership
3. Fostering innovation
4. Maximizing enterprise intellectual capital
5. Creating an environment for collaborative knowledge sharing
6. Facilitating organizational learning
7. Delivering value based on stakeholder knowledge
8. Transforming enterprise knowledge into stockholder/stakeholder value

The winners of the 11th annual MAKE study were announced in December 2008. For the second year in a row, McKinsey & Company was named the overall Global MAKE winner. Following is the list of all winners of the 2008 Global MAKE competition:

1. McKinsey & Company
2. Google
3. Royal Dutch Shell
4. Toyota
5. Wikipedia
6. Honda
7. Apple
8. Fluor
9. Microsoft
10. PricewaterhouseCoopers
11. Ernst & Young
12. IBM
13. Schlumberger
14. Samsung Group
15. BP
16. Unilever

17. Accenture
18. Tata Group
19. Infosys Technologies
20. APQC

According to Rory Chase, managing director of Teleos, these organizations have been recognized as global leaders in effectively transforming enterprise knowledge into wealth-creating ideas, products, and solutions. They are building portfolios of intellectual capital and intangible assets that will enable them to outperform their competitors now and in the future. Some of the findings of the 2008 Global MAKE study included:

- Knowledge-driven organizations significantly outperform their competitors. For the 10-year period 1997–2007, the total return to shareholders (TRS) for the publicly traded 2008 Global MAKE Winners was over twice that of the *Fortune* 500 company median.
- The capability to innovate and maximize enterprise intellectual capital is seen as *the competitive advantage* across a wide range of business sectors.
- As a result of globalization, most key business sectors will have only three to five global leaders by 2010.

Sources: A. Thomas, "The Global MAKE Awards—2008," Project Management Tips, 2009, **pmtips.net/make-awards-2008** (accessed June 2009); and The MAKE Network, **knowledgebusiness.com** (accessed June 2009).

APPLICATION CASE 11.7

The British Broadcasting Corporation Knowledge Management Success

The British Broadcasting Corporation (BBC) runs on knowledge. When Euan Semple became chief knowledge manager at the BBC, he recognized that the BBC was in fact all about knowledge. Instead of developing a large-scale, expensive KMS, Semple opted to focus on a network-based, conversationally oriented system that matched the way the BBC functions—as a social network. Semple focused on the social network and how he could best make it connect smoothly and effectively. His first tool was the Talk.Gateway bulletin board. By late 2005, 8,000 users (out of 25,000 employees) were performing some 450,000 page views per month.

BBC employees use Talk.Gateway to ask questions and get answers. Knowledge moves rapidly, and Talk.Gateway also generates knowledge. Executives watch it to identify the first signs of problems. In one case, the BBC's director general, Greg Dyke, resigned because of errors in the reporting of the death of an Iraqi arms expert. There was a flood of activity on the bulletin board when this happened.

The next project was Connect, a people finder. People enter their expertise and interests so others can find them. When someone needed to translate a document into Dutch, more than 25 names popped up (zeker!). And, through Connect, COP can and do form. More than 200 interest groups have formed that span the BBC's organizational charts, breaking down silos and spreading knowledge. A blogging server went online next; some of the blogs are by individuals and others are by interest groups. Wikis have been developed as well.

These systems represent a significant shift from conventional information management and afford the possibility of speedy, effective communication among dispersed individuals and groups in modern, complex organizations. These social networking tools enable new, modern forms of collaboration. High-tech and large budgets are not necessary to attain knowledge management success. What is necessary is for the KMS and the organization's culture to have a good fit. At the BBC, it meant connecting people together through effective social networking tools.

Sources: Adapted from D. Weinberger, "The BBC's Low-Tech Knowledge Management," *KMWorld,* September 2005; E. Semple, "Social Networking at the BBC," Online Information 2005 Conference, December 1, 2005; "The Knowledge: Euan Semple," *Inside Knowledge,* Vol. 8, No. 9, June 16, 2005.

While interest in KMS remains strong, few stand-alone KMS applications are available. In many cases, as described earlier, KMS are integrated with other enterprise systems or are modules attached to ERP, BI, or CRM systems. Furthermore, very few companies maintain separate organizational knowledge bases. They keep knowledge in a data warehouse or in knowledge bases of specific applications. A relatively new stand-alone application is known as an *expert location system*.

EXPERT LOCATION SYSTEMS Companies know that IT can be used to find experts. People who need help can post their problem on a corporate intranet and ask for help. Similarly, companies can ask for advice on how to exploit an opportunity. IBM frequently uses this method. Sometimes it obtains hundreds of useful ideas within a few days. It is a kind of brainstorming. The problem with this approach is that it may take days to get answers, if answers are even provided, and the answers may not be from the top experts. Therefore, companies employ expert location systems.

Expert location systems are interactive computerized systems that help employees find and connect with colleagues who have the expertise required for specific problems—whether they are across the country or across the room—in order to solve specific, critical business problems in seconds. Such software is made by companies such as AskMe and Tacit Knowledge Systems, Inc. These systems work by exploring knowledge bases for either an answer to the problem (if it exists there) or to locate qualified experts. The process includes the following steps:

1. An employee submits a question to the expert location system.
2. The software searches its database to see if an answer to the question already exists. If it does, the information (e.g., research reports, spreadsheets) is returned to the employee. If an answer does not exist, the software searches documents and archived communications for an "expert."
3. When a qualified candidate is located, the system asks if he or she is able to answer a question from a colleague. If so, the expert submits a response. If the candidate is unable to answer (perhaps he or she is in a meeting or otherwise indisposed), the person can elect to pass on the question. The question is then routed to the next appropriate candidate until one responds.
4. After the response is sent, it is reviewed for accuracy and sent back to the person who entered the query. At the same time, it is added to the knowledge database. This way, if the question comes up again, it will not be necessary to seek real-time assistance.

Application Case 11.8 demonstrates how an expert location system works for the U.S. government.

APPLICATION CASE 11.8

How the U.S. Department of Commerce Uses an Expert Location System

The U.S. Commercial Service Division at the Department of Commerce (DOC) conducts approximately 200,000 counseling sessions a year, involving close to $40 billion in trade. The division employs many specialists who frequently need to do research or call on experts to answer questions posed by U.S. corporations.

For example, in May 2004 a U.S.–based software company called Brad Anderson, a DOC specialist, for advice. The software company wanted to close a deal with a customer in Poland, but the buyer wanted to charge the U.S. company a 20 percent withholding tax, a tax it attributed to Poland's recent admission into the European Union (EU). Was the tax legitimate?

To find out, Anderson turned to the DOC Insider, an expertise location system (from AskMe). After typing in his question, Anderson first found some documents that were related to his query, but they did not explain the EU tax code completely. Anderson next asked the system to search the 1,700-strong Commercial Service for a live expert, and, within seconds, he was given a list of 80 people in the DOC who might be able to help him. Of those, he chose the six people he felt were most qualified and then forwarded his query.

Before the DOC Insider was in place, Anderson says, it would have taken him about 3 days to find an answer to the question. "You have to make many phone calls and deal with time zones," he said. Thanks to the expert location system, however, he had three responses within minutes and a complete answer within an hour, and the sale went through the following morning. Anderson estimated that he now uses the system for roughly 40 percent of the work he does.

The DOC Insider is an invaluable tool. Anderson said that the tool is vital enough to provide it to other units at the agency. In the first 9 months the system was in place, it saved more than 1,000 labor-hours.

Sources: Compiled from D. D'Agostino, "Expertise Management: Who Knows About This?" *CIO Insight,* July 1, 2004; and P. Fox, "Using IT to Tap Experts' Know-How," March 15, 2004, **computerworld.com/softwaretopics/software/apps/story/0,10801,91174,00.html** (accessed June 2009).

Nowadays, one of the most significant differentiators for successful firms is the way they deal with their customers. As the competition increased, firms looked for the real difference makers, which led to better customer service. Technology Insights 11.4 summarizes the key KM success factors for improved customer service.

TECHNOLOGY INSIGHTS 11.4 Six Keys to KM Success for Customer Service

The role of customer service has probably never been more challenging—yet more critical—for the success (or mere survival) of an organization. Customer service is one of the few real differentiators that businesses can sustain over time. Companies that are winning in today's business environment are the ones providing exceptional customer service by using knowledge to empower contact center agents and foster self-service interactions. Compiled from hundreds of best practices, the following six factors are among the most important for KM implementations:

1. **Quantify value.** Assessing expected and realized return on investment (ROI) before and after the deployment helps justify the initial investment as well as ongoing maintenance of the knowledgebase (KB), while elevating your visibility as a value creator for your business. It is critical that the metrics used are aligned with business objectives. For instance, if your main business goal is to increase up-sell and cross-sell through knowledge-enabled contextual offers, reduction in call-handle times will be a conflicting metric. Keep in mind that KM delivers positive ROI in areas such as:
   - Increase in first-time fixes and revenue through up-sell and cross-sell
   - Reduction in escalations, transfers, repeat calls, call-handle times, training time, unwarranted product returns, field visits, and staff wage premiums
2. **Build the right team.** Successful KM implementations start with the right team for knowledge capture and creation. Therefore, build a cross-functional team that can bring an all-inclusive approach to knowledge creation. A best-practice team typically includes the following:
   - *Lead expert.* Individual who decides how the knowledge base will be organized, which topics will be covered, the roles of various team members, and plans for maintenance and use.
   - *Users.* High-performance contact center agents who provide invaluable suggestions.
   - *Knowledge authors.* Individuals who are trained to use knowledge authoring tools.
   - *Project manager.* Person who keeps the project moving on the right track.
3. **Avoid the "Swiss cheese" syndrome.** Ambitious deployments almost always result in a knowledge base that is solid in certain aspects, but full of holes (like a slice of Swiss

cheese) in many other places. This is a recipe for failure, because if users cannot find the answers, or get inadequate or wrong answers, they will quickly stop using the system. Therefore, one should focus on depth and quality rather than breadth. For instance, if an enterprise sells printers, scanners, and copiers, the best approach would be to cover one product line thoroughly first, then move on to the others.

4. **Maintain velocity.** A classic mistake in KM implementations is not making midcourse adjustments to keep the project on track. Best practices suggest that if the deployment appears to be falling behind schedule, it is better to narrow the scope of the knowledge base and finish it on schedule. In fact, it is better to widen the scope later to expand the benefits of the deployment. As a rough guide, a typical enterprise deployment should not take more than 3 months after the initial planning, with three or four full-time people engaged. Deployment includes software installation, knowledge gathering, and testing both the quality of the knowledge base and system performance.

5. **Balance "ivory tower knowledge" with "street smarts."** Enterprises often make the mistake of relying solely on internally focused domain experts who rarely speak to customers. It is sometimes difficult for experts to get down to the level of ordinary customers who may not know technical terms, such as whether their mutual fund is "no load," "frontloaded," or "back-loaded." Using jargon in questions posed by agents or self-service systems is a guaranteed way to increase escalations and customer attrition. A best practices–based solution would be to find contributors who are both technically competent and not too far from customer contact. Successful customer service depends as much on the questions posed to customers as the answers.

6. **Provide flexible content access.** People have different ways of finding information or the same person may use different methods based on the situation. A flexible approach to information access dramatically improves user adoption and ROI. For instance, novice agents, whether they are in-house or outsourced, may find it difficult to wade through hundreds of search hits to find the right answer, but they may fare better if they are guided through a dialog, powered by an inference engine. In contrast, experienced agents may prefer to quickly process search hits. It is better to provide users with multiple ways to access information, including FAQ, browse, search, and guided help. The key here is to make sure that the knowledge base remains completely integrated and that there are no content silos.

Source: A. Roy, "Knowledge Management for 'Stand-Out' Customer Service: Six Best Practices from the Global 2000," in "Best Practices in KM for Customer Service," a supplement to *KMWorld,* April 2009, No. 8–9.

Knowledge Management Valuation

In general, companies take either an asset-based approach to knowledge management valuation or an approach that links knowledge to its applications and business benefits (see Skyrme and Amidon, 1998). The former approach starts by identifying intellectual assets and then focuses management's attention on increasing their value. The second uses variants of a balanced scorecard, where financial measures are balanced against customer, process, and innovation measures. Among the best-developed measurement methods in use are the balanced scorecard approach (see Kestelyn, 2002; and Zimmermann, 2003a), Skandia's Navigator, Stern Stewart's economic value added (EVA), M'Pherson's inclusive valuation methodology, the return on management ratio, and Levin's knowledge-capital measure. Lunt (2001) described how Duke Children's Hospital, Hilton, and Borden improved performance across their enterprises through the balanced scorecard approach, leading to better customer service. See Skyrme and Amidon (1998) for details on how these measures work in practice.

Another method of measuring the value of knowledge is to estimate its price if it were offered for sale. Most firms are reluctant to sell knowledge unless they are expressly in the business of doing so. Generally, a firm's knowledge is an asset that has competitive value, and if it leaves the organization, the firm loses its competitive advantage. However, the knowledge and access to the knowledge can be priced at a value, making it worth a firm's while to sell. For example, American Airlines' Decision Technologies Corp. grew from a small internal analysis team in the 1970s. Initially, the team was created to solve problems and provide decision support only to American Airlines. As it grew, it became an independent corporation within AMR Corp., and it began to provide consulting systems to other airlines, including American's competitors. The major consulting firms are in the business of selling expertise. Therefore, their knowledge management efforts, which began as internal systems, evolved into quite valuable systems that their clients use on a regular basis. Clearly, the same knowledge can be sold repeatedly.

Success indicators with respect to knowledge management are similar to those for assessing the effectiveness of other business-change projects. They include growth in the resources attached to the project, growth in the volume of knowledge content and usage, the likelihood that the project will survive without the support of a particular individual or individuals, and some evidence of financial return either for the knowledge management activity itself or for the entire organization.

FINANCIAL METRICS FOR KNOWLEDGE MANAGEMENT VALUATION Even though traditional accounting measures are incomplete for measuring knowledge management, they are often used as a quick justification for a knowledge management initiative. ROI is reported to range from 20:1 for chemical firms to 4:1 for transportation firms, with an average of 12:1, based on the knowledge management projects with which one consulting firm has been involved (see Abramson, 1998).

In order to measure the impact of knowledge management, experts recommend focusing knowledge management projects on specific business problems that can be easily quantified. When the problems are solved, the value and benefits of the system become apparent (see MacSweeney, 2002).

At Royal Dutch/Shell, the ROI was explicitly documented: The company invested $6 million in a KMS in 1999, and within 2 years it obtained $235 million in reduced costs and new revenues (see King, 2001). HP offers another example of documented financial returns. Within 6 months of launching its @HP company-wide portal in October 2000, HP realized a $50 million return on its initial investment of $20 million. This was largely due to a reduction in volume of calls to internal call centers and to the new paperless processes (see Roberts-Witt, 2002).

The financial benefit might be perceptual, rather than absolute, but it need not be documented in order for a KMS to be considered a success.

NONFINANCIAL METRICS FOR KNOWLEDGE MANAGEMENT VALUATION Traditional methods of financial measurement may fall short when measuring the value of a KMS, because they do not consider intellectual capital an asset. Therefore, it is necessary to develop procedures for valuing the intangible assets of an organization as well as to incorporate models of intellectual capital that in some way quantify innovation and the development and implementation of core competencies.

When evaluating intangibles, there are a number of new ways to view capital. In the past, only customer goodwill was valued as an asset. Now the following are included as well:

- *External relationship capital.* This is a measure of how an organization links with its partners, suppliers, customers, and regulators.
- *Structural capital.* This type of capital is based on systems and work processes that leverage competitiveness, such as information systems.
- *Human capital.* People have individual capabilities, knowledge, skills, and so on.
- *Social capital.* This is the quality and value of relationships with the larger society.
- *Environmental capital.* This is the value of relationships with the environment.

For example, a knowledge management initiative that Partners HealthCare System, Inc., undertook has not resulted in quantifiable financial benefits, but it has greatly increased the company's social capital. The KMS that Partners implemented for physicians reduced the number of serious medication errors by 55 percent at some of Boston's most prestigious teaching hospitals. Calculating ROI for such a system is an extremely difficult proposition, which is why only a small fraction of hospitals use similar systems. Although Partners is unable to determine how the system affects its bottom line, it is willing to justify the costs based on the system's benefits to society (see Melymuka, 2002). For more on knowledge management valuation, see Kankanhalli and Tan (2005), Chen (2005), Conway (2003), Hanley and Malafsky (2003), Smith and McKeen (2003), Stone and Warsone (2003), and Zimmermann (2003a).

Knowledge Management Failures

No system is infallible. There are many cases of KMS failing. Estimates of knowledge management failure rates range from 50 to 70 percent, where a failure is interpreted to mean that all the major objectives were not met by the effort (Ambrosio, 2000). Failures typically happen when the knowledge management effort mainly relies on technology and does not address whether the proposed system will meet the needs and objectives of the organization and its individuals (see Swan et al., 2000; Barth, 2000b; Berkman, 2001; Malhotra, 2003; McDermott, 2002; Roberts-Witt, 2000; and Sviokla, 2001). Other issues include lack of commitment (this occurred at a large Washington, D.C., constituent lobbying organization) and the failure to provide reasonable incentive for people to use the system (as occurred at Pillsbury Co.; see Barth, 2000b). The disasters of September 11, 2001, might have been avoided or lessened; therefore, in the United States, the Department of Homeland Security is making a massive effort to integrate its sources of knowledge (see Matthews, 2002). Soo et al. (2002) pointed out several knowledge traps that can lead to failure. We describe these in Technology Insights 11.5. Barth (2000b) described several important knowledge management initiatives that failed miserably. Finally, Roberts-Witt (2002) outlined how enterprises implementing portals can and do fail.

Knowledge management projects are among the most risky organizational endeavors. Success requires not only cutting-edge enablers of information technology, but also proper culture of knowledge sharing. While success of these projects brings positive improvements, their failures may also be devastating (see Application Case 11.9 for a representative example).

TECHNOLOGY INSIGHTS 11.5 KM Myths

Sometimes the intimate understanding of a complex concept (e.g., knowledge management) requires not only knowing what the concept is but also what it is not. Following are some myths associated with KM:

- ***Knowledge management is a fad.*** There are pessimists who think that KM is a new fashionable term prone to disappear soon. In fact, in today's business environment knowledge management is one of the most important tools for success. Knowing what you know and what you need to know cannot be a fad.
- ***Knowledge management is a new concept.*** Most people argue that knowledge management as a concept has been around for as long as human history. What is new is the way in which it is being managed using serious, systematic, and orderly means.
- ***Knowledge management is mere technology.*** Knowledge management is about people, relationships, and working together as a synergized entity. Technology is just an enabler to store and disseminate the knowledge assets. If the behavioral means that make people share knowledge are not present, there really is not anything to store and

disseminate. The vast majority of KM efforts have failed because they have been treated as IT projects, ignoring the most important part—the human aspects.

- ***Knowledge management and data warehousing are essentially the same.*** Data warehousing implies a repository of data, not knowledge. Even though data warehousing is essential for KM (as an enabling technology), it falls short on representing the behavioral characteristics of KM.

- ***Knowledge management is another form of reengineering.*** Reengineering is a one-time attempt at introducing radical change to organizational processes to improve efficiency. KM, in contrast, is an ongoing effort of enhancing organizational processes to better identify, store, and disseminate knowledge to whomever and whenever it is needed to improve an organization's competitive posture.

- ***Knowledge management is a part of data management.*** The idea behind this myth is that because data is being collected throughout the organization, it should also be converted into information and knowledge so that when it is needed it can be readily available. This, supply-driven approach to KM is shortsighted because knowledge is context sensitive and volatile. Instead, demand-driven KM, where the needed knowledge determines the nature of the knowledge acquisition and dissemination process, produces significant benefits.

- ***It is a "no-brainer" to share what you know.*** People do not want to share what they know, because they are what they know. In general, only secure people who are assured of the potential benefits of sharing willingly share their knowledge. Sharing has a lot to do with a corporate culture where sharing is not only respected and encouraged, but also properly rewarded.

Source: E. Awad and H. M. Ghaziri, *Knowledge Management,* Prentice Hall, Upper Saddle River, NJ, 2004.

APPLICATION CASE 11.9
When KMS Fail, They Can Fail in a Big Way

Accenture was a pioneer in organization-wide knowledge management efforts. Even though Accenture devoted significant resources to its global KMS, it simply failed at being effective in capturing and disseminating knowledge throughout the organization. Since the early 1990s, Accenture has spent over $500 million on IT and employees to support its global knowledge management strategy. And it continues to support it. In a study of its efforts, researchers discovered that it just was not working as well as it could have. One major problem was cultural. Accenture did not take into consideration local or regional challenges at a reasonable level. For example, the firm was totally unsuccessful in getting its East Asian consultants to contribute to the system because managers never demonstrated appreciation for these efforts. Accenture also apparently did not handle cross-cultural challenges well. Finally, because this was a global effort, the needs of local offices were totally subsumed.

Some of this can be explained by a recent research study. In an examination of five well-documented knowledge management failures, it was discovered that knowledge management failure factors fall into four categories: technology, culture, content, and project management. Clearly, Accenture had culture-based problems.

Other famous knowledge management failures include those of Ford and Firestone. When the tires started blowing out on the Ford Explorer, it cost the company $1.25 billion. In this case, the knowledge was available; it was just not integrated in a way that allowed stakeholders to access and analyze it. International police agencies historically have not effectively shared knowledge; therefore, terrorist activities, such as those that led to the events of September 11, 2001, continue. Today, despite the fact that much can be learned from failures, it is difficult to extract information about them from most organizations.

Sources: Partly adapted from Y. Park and D. Y. Choi, "The Shortcomings of a Standardized Global Knowledge Management System: The Case Study of Accenture," *Academy of Management Executive,* Vol. 19, No. 2, May 2005, pp. 81–85; and S. Patton, "Putting the Pieces Together," *Darwin,* February 2002.

Factors That Lead to Knowledge Management Success

To increase the probability of success of knowledge management projects, companies must assess whether there is a strategic need for knowledge management in the first place. The next step is to determine whether the current process of dealing with organizational knowledge is adequate and whether the organization's culture is ready for procedural changes. Only when these issues are resolved should the company consider technology infrastructure and decide whether a new system is needed. When the right technological solution is chosen, it becomes necessary to properly introduce it to the entire organization and to gain the participation of every employee (see Kaplan, 2002). It is important not to rely too heavily on technology to succeed (Jacob and Ebrahimpur, 2001). Typically, a knowledge management effort is only about 10 to 20 percent technology. The rest of the effort is organizational. While implementing knowledge management projects, one should try to avoid the common traps, some of which are described in Technology Insights 11.6.

TECHNOLOGY INSIGHTS 11.6   Knowledge Management Traps

A recent study of the knowledge management practices of six firms identified several knowledge traps into which even the best firms fell. These can help show the way to avoid failure in knowledge management efforts. The following lessons were learned:

- *Formal databases must be treated as strategic tools rather than mere storage facilities.* Sometimes database systems are perceived as too complicated to use, so they are underused. Strategic information is overlooked because it is too difficult to get to. The organization must make it possible to get to the information and to really capture and codify knowledge.
- *Managing formal database systems per se does not equate to knowledge management.* Databases are important for capturing information, but a strong, informal network is necessary for good access. Also, databases are only one component of a KMS. When textual data are stored, we really consider this a knowledge repository, not a database.
- *Informal networking is an important source of knowledge, but overreliance on it can be detrimental.* Even though informal channels often contain critical information, there is an inherent risk that informal interactions may be too dependent on chance. Lack of structure can lead to knowledge loss.
- *Structure is important.* To reduce the susceptibility of informal networking to randomness, it should be made more structured.
- *Senior management may not know the true state of their firm's KMS.* There is a distinct difference between the perceptions of senior managers and junior managers in their views of the effectiveness of their KMS. This is mainly because the senior managers do not actively use the system, while junior managers do. The attitudes of senior managers may not be the best measure of the success of a KMS.
- *You can't teach an old dog new tricks.* Generally, older managers do not absorb new training well.
- *Unless carefully managed, knowledge is a dark power.* It is difficult to determine how to generate knowledge that is truly useful for an organization. Organizational factors may hinder the capture and free distribution of knowledge. Trust is critical.
- *Creativity in problem solving is the main driver of new knowledge creation and innovation.* However, creativity must be supported by appropriate mechanisms. Resources must be provided to help employees be creative. Often, lack of time hinders individuals. They may be expected to contribute and use knowledge in a KMS, while not diminishing any other aspect of their jobs.

Sources: C. Soo, T. Devinney, D. Midgley, and A. Dering, "Knowledge Management: Philosophy, Processes, and Pitfalls," *California Management Review,* Summer 2002, Vol. 44, No. 4, pp. 129–150; and Y. Malhotra, "Why Knowledge Management Systems Fail?" 2004, **brint.org/WhyKMSFail.htm** (accessed June 2009).

Major factors that lead to knowledge management project success (adapted from Davenport et al., 1998) include the following:

- A link to a firm's economic value, to demonstrate financial viability and maintain executive sponsorship.
- A technical and organizational infrastructure on which to build.
- A standard, flexible knowledge structure to match the way the organization performs work and uses knowledge. Usually, the organizational culture must change to effectively create a knowledge-sharing environment.
- A knowledge-friendly culture that leads directly to user support.
- A clear purpose and language, to encourage users to buy into the system. Sometimes simple, useful knowledge applications need to be implemented first.
- A change in motivational practices, to create a culture of sharing.
- Multiple channels for knowledge transfer, because individuals have different ways of working and expressing themselves. The multiple channels should reinforce one another. Knowledge transfer should be easily accomplished and as unobtrusive as possible.
- A level of process orientation to make a knowledge management effort worthwhile. In other words, new, improved work methods can be developed.
- Nontrivial motivational methods, such as rewards and recognition, to encourage users to contribute and use knowledge.
- Senior management support is critical to initiate a project, provide resources, help identify important knowledge on which the success of the organization relies, and market the project.

Effective knowledge sharing and learning require cultural change within the organization, new managerial practices, senior management commitment, and technological support. The organizational culture must shift to a culture of sharing. This should be handled through strong leadership at the top and by providing knowledge management tools that truly make people's jobs better. As far as encouraging system use and knowledge sharing goes, people must be properly motivated to contribute knowledge. The mechanism for doing so should be part of their jobs, and their salaries should reflect this. People must also be motivated to use the knowledge in the KMS. Again, this should be part of their jobs and their reward structures.

As more companies develop knowledge management capabilities, some of the ground rules are becoming apparent. Success depends on a clear strategic logic for knowledge sharing, the choice of appropriate infrastructure (technical or nontechnical), and an implementation approach that addresses the typical barriers: motivation to share knowledge, resources to capture and synthesize organizational learning, and ability to navigate the knowledge network to find the right people and data.

Potential Drawbacks of KMS

Although managing knowledge has many positive outcomes, as discussed in examples throughout this chapter, it would be shortsighted to not consider the potential negative outcomes associated with reusing knowledge. Henfridsson and Söderholm (2000) analyzed the situation that Mrs. Fields Gifts faced. Mrs. Fields grew remarkably fast and successfully during the early 1980s. A key aspect of the company's strategy was to provide expertise directly from the headquarters to every store. As the number of stores increased, the only feasible way to achieve direct control was through the use of information systems designed to mimic the decision making of the real Debbi Fields. Systems placed in each store would input data (e.g., temperature, day of the week, date); the system would process them and output instructions telling the store manager, say, how many cookies of each type to bake each hour. In essence, the software provided each store manager with explicit directions for planning each day's production, sales, and labor scheduling, along with inventory control and ordering. Because of the well-functioning computer systems, which in principle were systems designed to make the company's tacit knowledge available to all stores, Mrs. Fields was able to successfully function with few managerial levels. However, Mrs. Fields was very slow to respond as the market began to change and consumers became more health conscious. By embedding so much knowledge into systems that were incapable of adaptation, the organization tied itself to a certain way of doing things and failed to engage in knowledge creation (i.e., failed to pick up the signals in the environment that might have suggested a change in strategy or product focus). By the early 1990s, the company had fallen into bankruptcy. The situation at Mrs. Fields illustrates that while organizations may achieve significant short-term gains through KMS, they must not neglect the creative process of new knowledge creation, lest they find themselves applying yesterday's solutions to tomorrow's problems.

Closing Remarks on Knowledge Management

For millennia, we have known about the effective use of knowledge and how to store and reuse it. Intelligent organizations recognize that knowledge is an intellectual asset, perhaps the only one that grows over time, and, when harnessed effectively, can sustain competition and innovation. Organizations can use IT to perform true knowledge management. Leveraging an entire organization's intellectual resources can have tremendous financial impact.

With knowledge management, the definition is clear, the concepts are clear, the methodology is clear, the challenges are clear and surmountable, the benefits are clear and can be substantial, and the tools and technology—though incomplete and somewhat expensive—are viable. Key issues are organizational culture, executive sponsorship, and measurement of success. Technological issues are minimal compared to these. Knowledge management is not just another expensive management fad. Knowledge management is a new paradigm for how we work.

Section 11.9 Review Questions

1. Describe the need for measuring the success of KMS.
2. What are the issues in knowledge management valuation?
3. List some financial (tangible) metrics of knowledge management.
4. List some intangible (nonfinancial) metrics of knowledge management.
5. List failure factors associated with knowledge management.
6. List success factors associated with knowledge management.
7. What are the potential drawbacks of KMS?
8. Describe expert location systems.

Chapter Highlights

- Knowledge is different from information and data. Knowledge is information that is contextual, relevant, and actionable.
- Knowledge is dynamic in nature. It is information in action.
- Tacit (i.e., unstructured, sticky) knowledge is usually in the domain of subjective, cognitive, and experiential learning; explicit (i.e., structured, leaky) knowledge deals with more objective, rational, and technical knowledge, and it is highly personal and difficult to formalize.
- A learning organization has an organizational memory and a means to save, represent, and share it.

- Organizational learning is the development of new knowledge and insights that have the potential to influence behavior.
- The ability of an organization to learn, develop memory, and share knowledge is dependent on its culture. Culture is a pattern of shared basic assumptions.
- Knowledge management is a process that helps organizations identify, select, organize, disseminate, and transfer important information and expertise that typically reside within the organization in an unstructured manner.
- The fastest, most effective and powerful way to manage knowledge assets is through the systematic transfer of best practices.

- Knowledge management requires a major transformation in organizational culture to create a desire to share (i.e., give and receive) knowledge and a commitment to knowledge management at all levels of the firm.
- The knowledge management model involves the following cyclical steps: create, capture, refine, store, manage, and disseminate knowledge.
- The CKO is primarily responsible for changing the behavior of the firm to embrace the use of knowledge management and then managing the development operation of a KMS.
- A COP provides pressure to break down the cultural barriers that hinder knowledge management efforts.
- Knowledge management is an effective way for an organization to leverage its intellectual assets.
- It is difficult to measure the success of a KMS. Traditional methods of financial measurement fall short because they do not consider intellectual capital an asset.
- Two knowledge management approaches are the process approach and the practice approach.

- The two strategies used for knowledge management initiatives are the personalization strategy and the codification strategy.
- The two storage models used for knowledge management projects are the repository storage model and the network storage model.
- Standard knowledge management initiatives involve the creation of knowledge bases, active process management, knowledge centers, collaborative technologies, and knowledge webs.
- A KMS is generally developed using three sets of technologies: communication, collaboration, and storage.
- A variety of technologies can make up a KMS, including the Internet, intranets, data warehousing, decision support tools, and groupware. Intranets are the primary vehicles for displaying and distributing knowledge in organizations.
- Knowledge management is not just another expensive management fad. It is a new paradigm for the way we work.

Key Terms

best practices *491*

chief knowledge officer (CKO) *504*

community of practice (COP) *506*

content management system (CMS) *500*

electronic document management (EDM) *499*

enterprise knowledge portal (EKP) *499*

expert location system *512*

explicit knowledge *478*

intellectual capital *474*

knowledge *475*

knowledge-based economy *476*

knowledge discovery in databases (KDD) *496*

knowledge management (KM) *474*

knowledge management system (KMS) *480*

knowledge repository *488*

knowware *498*

leaky knowledge *478*

learning organization *481*

model mart *497*

model warehouse *497*

organizational culture *482*

organizational learning *482*

organizational memory *482*

practice approach *488*

process approach *486*

tacit knowledge *478*

Questions for Discussion

1. Why is the term *knowledge* so difficult to define?
2. Describe and relate the different characteristics of knowledge to one another.
3. Explain why it is important to capture and manage knowledge.
4. Compare and contrast tacit knowledge and explicit knowledge.
5. Explain why organizational culture must sometimes change before knowledge management is introduced.
6. How does knowledge management attain its primary objective?
7. How can employees be motivated to contribute to and use KMS?
8. What is the role of a knowledge repository in knowledge management?
9. Explain the importance of communication and collaboration technologies to the processes of knowledge management.

10. Explain why firms adopt knowledge management initiatives.
11. Explain how the wrong organizational culture can reduce the effectiveness of knowledge management.
12. Explain the role of the CKO in developing a KMS. What major responsibilities does he or she have?
13. What is meant by a culture of knowledge sharing?
14. Discuss the factors related to knowledge management success.
15. Why is it so difficult to evaluate the impacts of knowledge management?
16. Explain how the Internet and related technologies (e.g., Web browsers, intranets) enable knowledge management.
17. List the three top technologies most frequently used for implementing KMS and explain their importance.
18. Explain the role of a community of practice.
19. Describe an EKP and explain its significance.

Exercises

TERADATA STUDENT NETWORK (TSN) AND OTHER HANDS-ON EXERCISES

1. Make a list of all the knowledge management methods you use during your day (work and personal). Which are the most effective? Which are the least effective? What kinds of work or activities does each knowledge management method enable?

2. Investigate the literature for information on the position of CKO. Find out what percentage of firms with knowledge management initiatives have CKOs and identify their responsibilities.

3. Investigate the literature for new measures of success (metrics) for knowledge management and intellectual capital. Write a report based on your findings.

4. Describe how each of the key elements of a knowledge management infrastructure can contribute to its success.

5. Based on your own experience or on the vendor's information, list the major capabilities of a particular knowledge management product and explain how it can be used in practice.

6. Describe how to ride a bicycle, drive a car, or make a peanut butter and jelly sandwich. Now have someone else try to do it based solely on your explanation. How can you best convert this knowledge from tacit to explicit (or can't you)?

7. Examine the top five reasons that firms initiate KMS and investigate why they are important in a modern enterprise.

8. Read the article by E. Berkman titled "Don't Lose Your Mind Share," available at **cio.com/archive/100100/mindshare.html**. Describe the major problems that Hill and Knowlton faced in February 1999 and what Ted Graham did to solve them.

9. Read *How the Irish Saved Civilization* by Thomas Cahill (New York: Anchor, 1996) and describe how Ireland became a knowledge repository for Western Europe just before the fall of the Roman Empire. Explain in detail why this was important for Western civilization and history.

10. Examine your university, college, or company and describe the roles that the faculty, administration, support staff, and students have in the creation, storage, and dissemination of knowledge. Explain how the process works. Explain how technology is currently used and how it could potentially be used.

TEAM ASSIGNMENTS AND ROLE-PLAYING

1. Compare and contrast the capabilities and features of electronic document management with those of collaborative computing and of KMS. Each team should represent one type of system.

2. Search the Internet for knowledge management products and systems and create categories for them. Assign one vendor to each team. Describe the categories you created and justify them.

3. Consider a decision-making project in industry for this course or from another class or from work. Examine some typical decisions in the project. How would you extract the knowledge you need? Can you use that knowledge in practice? Why or why not?

4. Read the article by A. Genusa titled "Rx for Learning," available at **cio.com/archive/020101/tufts.html,** which describes Tufts University Medical School's experience with knowledge management. Determine how these concepts and such a system could be implemented and used at your college or university. Explain how each aspect would work, or if it would not work, explain why it would not.

INTERNET EXERCISES

1. How does knowledge management support decision making? Identify products or systems on the Web that help organizations accomplish knowledge management. Start with **brint.com** and **knowledgemanagement.com**. Try one out and report your findings to the class.

2. Try the KPMG Knowledge Management Framework Assessment Exercise at **kmsurvey.londonweb.net** and assess how well your university (or company) is doing with knowledge management. Are the results accurate? Why or why not?

3. Search the Internet to identify sites that deal with knowledge management. Start with **google.com**, **kmworld.com**, **kmmag.com**, and **km-forum.org**. How many did you find? Categorize the sites based on whether they are academic, consulting firms, vendors, and so on. Sample one of each and describe the main focus of the site.

4. Identify five real-world knowledge management success stories by searching vendor Web sites (use at least three different vendors). Describe them. How did KMS methods contribute to their success? What features do they share? What different features do individual successes have?

5. Search the Internet for vendors of knowledge management suites, EKP, and out-of-the-box knowledge management solutions. Identify the major features of each product (use three from each) and compare and contrast their capabilities.

6. Access the Microsoft Web site and investigate the current capabilities of its knowledge management initiative.

END OF CHAPTER APPLICATION CASE

Siemens Keeps Knowledge Management Blooming with ShareNet

Siemens AG, a $73 billion electronics and electrical engineering conglomerate, produces everything from light bulbs to x-ray machines, power-generation equipment, and high-speed trains. During its 156-year history, Siemens has become one of the world's largest and most successful corporations. Siemens is well known for the technical brilliance of its engineers, but much of their knowledge used to be unavailable to other employees. Facing pressures to maximize the benefits of corporate membership of each business unit, Siemens AG needed to learn how to leverage the knowledge and expertise of its 460,000 employees worldwide.

Solution

The roots of knowledge management at Siemens go back to 1996, when a number of people in the corporation who had an interest in knowledge management (KM) formed a community of interest. They researched the subject, learned what was being done by other companies, and determined how KM could benefit Siemens. Without suggestion or encouragement from senior executives, midlevel employees in Siemens business units began creating repositories, communities of practice, and informal knowledge-sharing techniques. By 1999, Siemens AG's central board confirmed the importance of KM to the entire company by creating an organizational unit that would be responsible for the worldwide deployment of knowledge management.

Siemens's movement toward KM has presented several challenges to the company, the most notable of which are technological and cultural. At the heart of Siemens's technical solution to knowledge management is a Web site called ShareNet, which combines elements of a database repository, a chat room, and a search engine. Online entry forms allow employees to store information they think might be useful to colleagues. Other Siemens employees are able to search the repository or browse by topic and then contact the authors for more information, using one of the available communication channels. In addition, the system lets employees post alerts when they have an urgent question. Although knowledge management implementation at Siemens involved establishing a network to collect, categorize, and share information using databases and intranets, Siemens realized that IT was only the tool that enabled knowledge management. Randall Sellers, director of knowledge management for the Americas Region of Siemens, stated, "In my opinion, the technology or IT role is a small one. I think it's 20 percent IT and 80 percent change management—dealing with cultural change and human interfaces."

Siemens has used a three-pronged effort to convince employees that it is important to participate in the exchange of ideas and experiences and to share what they know. The challenge is managing the people who manage the knowledge. It has to be easy for them to share, or they won't. Siemens has assigned 100 internal evangelists around the world to be responsible for training, answering questions, and monitoring the system. Siemens's top management has shown its full support for the KM projects, and the company is providing incentives to overcome employees' resistance to change. When employees post documents to the system or use the knowledge, Siemens rewards them with "shares" (similar to frequent-flyer miles). An employee's accumulation of shares can be exchanged for things such as consumer electronics or discounted trips to other countries. However, the real incentive of the system is much more basic. Commission-driven salespeople have already learned that the knowledge and expertise of their colleagues available through ShareNet can be indispensable in winning lucrative contracts. Employees in marketing, service, research and development, and other departments are also willing to participate and contribute when they realize that the system provides them with useful information in a convenient way.

ShareNet has undergone tremendous growth, which has resulted in several challenges for Siemens. The company strives to maintain a balance between global and local knowledge initiatives as well as between KM efforts that support the entire company and those that help individual business units. Furthermore, Siemens works to prevent ShareNet from becoming so overloaded with knowledge that it becomes useless. A group is assigned to monitor the system and remove trivial and irrelevant content.

Results

ShareNet has evolved into a state-of-the-art Web-based knowledge management system (KMS) that stores and catalogs volumes of valuable knowledge, makes it available to every employee, and enhances global collaboration. Numerous companies, including Intel, Philips Electronics, and Volkswagen, studied ShareNet before setting up their own KMS. Teleos, an independent knowledge management research company, has acknowledged Siemens as one of the most admired knowledge enterprises worldwide for 5 years in a row.

Siemens has realized a variety of quantifiable benefits afforded by knowledge management. For example, in April 1999, the company developed a portion of ShareNet to support the Information & Communications Networks Group, at a cost of $7.8 million. Within 2 years, the tool helped to generate $122 million in additional sales.

Ultimately, knowledge management may be one of the major tools that will help Siemens prove that large, diversified conglomerates can work and that being big might even be an advantage in the information age.

Questions for the Case

1. How did the Siemens KMS evolve?
2. How does Siemens view knowledge (i.e., intellectual) assets?
3. What does "leveraging expertise" mean? How did Siemens do this? Explain how this relates to Siemens's high return on investment.
4. Describe the benefits of the Siemens ShareNet KMS.
5. Explain the culture transformation as it occurred at Siemens. Include in your answer how the various constituencies bought into the system.
6. Explain how Internet and Web technologies enabled the Siemens KMS.

Sources: Adapted from G. S. Vasilash, "447,000 Heads Are Better Than One," *Automotive Design & Production,* June 2002; "Business: Electronic Glue," *The Economist,* June 2, 2001; S. Williams, "The Intranet Content Management Strategy Conference," *Management Services,* September 2001; M. Santosus, "How Siemens Keeps KM Blooming," *In the Know at CIO.com,* February 2003, **cio.com/research/ knowledge/edit/k021003_bloom.html**.

References

Abramson, G. (1998, June 15). "Measuring Up." *CIO.*

Ahlawat, S. S., and S. Ahlawat. (2006, March). "Competing in the Global Knowledge Economy: Implications for Business Education." *Journal of American Academy of Business,* Vol. 8, No. 1.

Alavi, M. (2000). "Managing Organizational Knowledge." Chapter 2 in W. R. Zmud (ed.). *Framing the Domains of IT Management: Projecting the Future.* Cincinnati, OH: Pinnaflex Educational Resources.

Alavi, M., T. Kayworth, and D. Leidner. (2003). "An Empirical Investigation of the Impact of Organizational Culture on KM Initiatives." Working paper. Waco, TX: Baylor University.

Alavi, M., T. Kayworth, and D. Leidner (2005/2006). "An Empirical Examination of the Influence of Organizational Culture on Knowledge Management Practice." *Journal of Management Information Systems,* Vol. 22, No. 3.

Alavi, M., and D. Leidner. (1999, February). "Knowledge Management Systems: A Descriptive Study of Key Issues, Challenges, and Benefits." *Communications of the AIS.*

Alavi, M., and D. Leidner. (2001). "Knowledge Management and Knowledge Management Systems: Conceptual Foundations and Research Issues." *MIS Quarterly,* Vol. 25, No. 1, pp. 107–136.

Ali, I., L. Warne, and C. Pascoe. (2006). "Learning in Organizations." In D. G. Schwartz (ed.). *Encyclopedia of Knowledge Management.* Hershey, PA: Idea Group Reference.

Allard, S. (2003). "Knowledge Creation." Chapter 18 in C. W. Holsapple (ed.). *Handbook of Knowledge Management: Knowledge Matters,* Vol. 1. Heidelberg: Springer-Verlag.

Amato-McCoy, D. (2003, January). "Commerce Bank Manages Knowledge Profitably." *Bank Systems & Technology.*

Ambrosio, J. (2000, July 3). "Knowledge Management Mistakes." *Computerworld,* Vol. 34, No. 27.

Ariely, G. (2006). "Intellectual Capital and Knowledge Management." In D. G. Schwartz (ed.). *Encyclopedia of Knowledge Management.* Hershey, PA: Idea Group Reference.

Awad, E., and H. M. Ghaziri. (2004). *Knowledge Management.* Upper Saddle River, NJ: Prentice Hall.

Bankes, A. (2003, April). "Taking on the Challenge of ECM." *KMWorld,* Special Supplement.

Barth, S. (2000a, February). "Knowledge as a Function of X." *Knowledge Management.*

Barth, S. (2000b, October). "KM Horror Stories." *Knowledge Management.*

Bennet, D., and A. Bennet. (2003). "The Rise of the Knowledge Organization." Chapter 1 in C. W. Holsapple (ed.). *Handbook of Knowledge Management: Knowledge Matters,* Vol. 1. Heidelberg: Springer-Verlag.

Berkman, E. (2001, April 1). "When Bad Things Happen to Good Ideas." *Darwin.*

Berman, S. L., J. Down, and C. W. L. Hill. (2002). "Tacit Knowledge as a Source of Competitive Advantage in the National Basketball Association." *Academy of Management Journal,* Vol. 45, No. 1.

Blodgett, M. (2000, February 1). "Prescription Strength." *CIO.*

Bock, G.-W., R. Zmud, Y. Kim, and J. Lee. (2005). "Behavioural Intention Formation in Knowledge Sharing: Examining the Roles of Extrinsic Motivators, Social Psychological Forces and Organizational Climate." *MIS Quarterly Journal,* Vol. 29, No. 1.

Bolloju, N., M. Khalifa, and E. Turban. (2002, June). "Integrating Knowledge Management into Enterprise Environments for the Next Generation of Decision Support." *Decision Support Systems,* Vol. 33.

Brailsford, T. W. (2001, September/October). "Building a Knowledge Community at Hallmark Cards." *Research Technology Management,* Vol. 44, No. 5.

Brown, J. S., and P. Duguid. (1991). "Organizational Learning and Communities-of-Practice: Toward a Unified View of Working, Learning, and Innovation." *Organization Science,* Vol. 2, No. 1.

Brown, J. S., and P. Duguid. (2002). "Organizational Learning and Communities of Practice: Toward a Unified View of Working, Learning, and Innovation." Chapter 7 in E. L. Lesser, M.A. Fontaine, and J.A. Slusher (eds.). *Knowledge and Communities.* Woburn, MA: Butterworth-Heinemann.

Carlucci, D., and G. Schiuma. (2006). "Knowledge Asset Value Spiral: Linking Knowledge Assets to Company's Performance." *Knowledge and Process Management,* Vol. 13, No. 1.

Chen, A. N. K. (2005, June). "Assessing Value in Organizational Knowledge Creation: Consideration for Knowledge Workers." *MIS Quarterly,* Vol. 29, No. 2.

Compton, J. (2001, July). "Climbing Out of the Abyss." *Knowledge Management.*

Conway, S. (2003). "Valuing Knowledge Management Behaviors: Linking KM Behaviors to Strategic Performance Measures." Chapter 24 in C. W. Holsapple (ed.). *Handbook of Knowledge Management: Knowledge Matters,* Vol. 1. Heidelberg: Springer-Verlag.

Craig, C. R. (2005). "Purchasing Social Responsibility and Firm Performance: The Key Mediating Roles of Organizational Learning and Supplier Performance." *International Journal of Physical Distribution & Logistics Management,* Vol. 35, No. 3.

D'Agostino, D. (2004, July 1). "Expertise Management: Who Knows About This?" *CIO Insight.*

Davenport, D. (2008). "Enterprise 2.0: The New, New Knowledge Management?" **discussionleader.hbsp.com/ davenport/2008/02/enterprise_20_the_new_new_ know_1.html** (accessed June 2009).

Davenport, D., and M. Sena. (2003). "Technologies for Knowledge Derivation." Chapter 40 in C. W. Holsapple (ed.). *Handbook of Knowledge Management: Knowledge Directions,* Vol. 2. Heidelberg: Springer-Verlag.

Davenport, T., D. W. DeLong, and M. C. Beers. (1998, Winter). "Successful Knowledge Management Projects." *Sloan Management Review,* Vol. 39, No. 2.

Davis, M. (1998, Fall). "Knowledge Management." *Information Strategy: The Executive's Journal.*

Delen, D., and S. S. Hawamdeh (2009). "A Holistic Framework for Knowledge Discovery and Management." *Communications of the ACM,* Vol. 52, No. 6, pp. 141–145.

Donnelly, R. (2008). "The Management of Consultancy Knowledge: An Internationally Comparative Analysis." *Journal of Knowledge Management,* Vol. 12, No. 3, pp. 71–83.

Drucker, D. (2001, January 29). "Theory Doesn't Equal Practice." *Internetweek.com.* **internetweek.cmp.com/ newslead01/lead012901.htm** (accessed April 2006).

Duffy, D. (1998, November). "Knowledge Champions." *CIO.*

Feldman, S. (2002, June). "What Technologies Are KM Professionals Buying?" *KMWorld.*

Firestone, J. M., and M. W. McElroy. (2005, April). "Doing Knowledge Management." *The Learning Journal,* Vol. 12, No. 2.

Flash, C. (2001, May). "Who Is the CKO?" *Knowledge Management.*

Gaines, B. (2003). "Organizational Knowledge Acquisition." Chapter 16 in C. W. Holsapple (ed.). *Handbook of Knowledge Management: Knowledge Matters.* Heidelberg: Springer.

Gamble, P., and J. Blackwell. (2002). *Knowledge Management: A State-of-the-Art Guide.* London: Kogan Page.

Garvin, D. A. (2000). *Learning in Action.* Boston: Harvard Business School Press.

Godin, B. (2006). "Knowledge-Based Economy: Conceptual Framework or Buzzword." *The Journal of Technology Transfer,* Vol. 31, No. 1.

Gold, A. H., A. Malhotra, and A. H. Segars. (2001, Summer). "Knowledge Management: An Organizational Capabilities Perspective." *Journal of MIS,* Vol. 18, No. 1.

Gray, P. (1999). "Tutorial on Knowledge Management." *Proceedings of the Americas Conference of the Association for Information Systems,* Milwaukee.

Gray, P., and D. Meisters. (2003). "Knowledge Sourcing Effectiveness." Working paper. Pittsburgh: University of Pittsburgh.

Hanley, S., and G. Malafsky. (2003). "A Guide for Measuring the Value of Knowledge Management Investments." Chapter 49 in C. W. Holsapple (ed.). *Handbook of Knowledge Management: Knowledge Directions,* Vol. 2. Heidelberg: Springer-Verlag.

Hansen, M., et al. (1999, March/April). "What's Your Strategy for Managing Knowledge?" *Harvard Business Review*, Vol. 77, No. 2.

Hanssen-Bauer, J., and C. C. Snow. (1996, July/August). "Responding to Hypercompetition: The Structure and Process of a Regional Learning Network." *Organization Science*.

Henfridsson, O., and A. Söderholm. (2000). "Barriers to Learning: On Organizational Defenses and Vicious Circles in Technological Adoption." *Accounting, Management and Information Technologies*, Vol. 10, No. 1, pp. 33–51.

Hibbard, J. (1998, September 21). "Cultural Breakthrough." *InformationWeek*.

Hinds, R. S., and J. E. Aronson. (2002, August). "Developing the Requisite Organizational, Attitudinal, and Behavioral Conditions for Effective Knowledge Management." *Proceedings of the Americas Conference for Information Systems*, Dallas, TX.

Hoffer, J., M. Prescott, and F. McFadden. (2002). *Modern Database Management*, 6th ed. Upper Saddle River, NJ: Prentice Hall.

Holsapple, C. W. (ed.). (2003a). *Handbook of Knowledge Management: Knowledge Matters*, Vol. 1. Heidelberg: Springer-Verlag.

Holsapple, C. W. (ed.). (2003b). *Handbook of Knowledge Management: Knowledge Directions*, Vol. 2. Heidelberg: Springer-Verlag.

Jacob, M., and G. Ebrahimpur. (2001). "Experience vs. Expertise: The Role of Implicit Understandings of Knowledge in Determining the Nature of Knowledge Transfer in Two Companies." *Journal of Intellectual Capital*, Vol. 2, No. 1.

Jasimuddin, S. M., N. A. D. Connell, and J. H. Klein. (2006). "Understanding Organizational Memory." In D. G. Schwartz (ed.). *Encyclopedia of Knowledge Management*. Hershey, PA: Idea Group Reference.

Jennex, M., and L. Olfman. (2003). "Organizational Memory and Its Management." Chapter 11 in C. W. Holsapple (ed.). *Handbook of Knowledge Management: Knowledge Matters*, Vol. 1. Heidelberg: Springer-Verlag.

Jones, M. C., M. Cline, and S. Ryan. (2006, January). "Exploring Knowledge Sharing in ERP Implementation: An Organizational Culture Framework." *Decision Support Systems*, Vol. 41, No. 2.

Kankanhalli, A., and B. C. Y. Tan. (2005). "Knowledge Management Metrics: A Review and Directions for Future Research." *International Journal of Knowledge Management*, Vol. 1, No. 2.

Kankanhalli, A., B. C. Y. Tan, and K. K. Wei. (2005, March). "Contributing Knowledge to Electronic Knowledge Repositories: An Empirical Investigation." *MIS Quarterly*, Vol. 29, No. 1.

Kaplan S. (2002, July 15). "KM the Right Way." *CIO*.

Kayworth, T., and D. Leidner. (2003). "Organizational Culture as a Knowledge Resource." Chapter 12 in C. W. Holsapple (ed.). *Handbook of Knowledge Management: Knowledge Matters*, Vol. 1. Heidelberg: Springer-Verlag.

Kestelyn, J. (2002, July 28). "Microsoft's New Methodology Will Further Validate Balanced Scorecards." *Intelligent Enterprise*.

Kiaraka, R. N., and K. Manning. (2005). "Managing Organizations through a Process-Based Perspective: Its Challenges and Rewards." *Knowledge and Process Management*, Vol. 12, No. 4.

King, J. (2001, July/August). "Shell Strikes Knowledge Gold." *Computerworld*.

King, W. R. (2006). "Knowledge Sharing." In D. G. Schwartz (ed.). *Encyclopedia of Knowledge Management*. Hershey, PA: Idea Group Reference.

"Knowledge: Euan Semple." (2005, June 16). *Inside Knowledge*, Vol. 8, No. 9.

Koenig, M. (2001, September). "Codification vs. Personalization." *KMWorld*.

Lamont, J. (2003a, April). "Prognosis Good for KM in Patient Treatment and Diagnostics." *KMWorld*.

Lamont, J. (2003b, May). "Dynamic Taxonomies: Keeping Up with Changing Content." *KMWorld*.

Leidner, D., M. Alavi, and T. Kayworth. (2006). "The Role of Culture in Knowledge Management: A Case Study of Two Global Firms." *International Journal of eCollaboration*, Vol. 2, No. 1.

Lengyel, D. (2008). "Blending KM with Risk Management at NASA." *Knowledge Management Review*, Vol. 10, No. 6, pp. 8–9.

Lesser, E., and L. Prusak. (2002). "Communities of Practice, Social Capital and Organizational Knowledge." Chapter 8 in E. L. Lesser, M. A. Fontaine, and J. A. Slusher (eds.). *Knowledge and Communities*. Woburn, MA: Butterworth-Heinemann.

Lesser, E. L., M. A. Fontaine, and J. A. Slusher (eds.). (2000). *Knowledge and Communities*. Woburn, MA: Butterworth-Heinemann.

Liedtka, J. (2002). "Linking Competitive Advantage with Communities of Practice." Chapter 9 in E. L. Lesser, M. A. Fontaine, and J. A. Slusher. (eds.). *Knowledge and Communities*. Woburn, MA: Butterworth-Heinemann.

Lunt, P. (2001, July). "Know the Score." *Customer Support Management*.

MacSweeney, G. (2002, June). "The Knowledge Management Payback." *Insurance & Technology*.

Malhotra, Y. (2003). "Why Knowledge Management Systems Fail: Enablers and Constraints of Knowledge Management in Human Enterprises." Chapter 30 in C. W. Holsapple (ed.). *Handbook of Knowledge Management: Knowledge Matters*, Vol. 1. Heidelberg: Springer-Verlag.

Martin, B. (2000). "Knowledge Management Within the Context of Management: An Evolving Relationship." *Singapore Management Review*, Vol. 22, No. 2.

Matthews, W. (2002, April 25). "Knowledge Management's Worst Nightmare." *Federal Computer Week*.

Maybury, M. T. (2003). "Knowledge Management at the MITRE Corporation." **mitre.org/work/tech_papers/tech_papers_03/maybury_knowledge/KM_MITRE.pdf** (accessed June 2009).

McCarthy, R. V., K. Mazouz, and J. E. Aronson. (2001, August). "Measuring the Validity of Task-Technology Fit for Knowledge Management Systems." *Proceedings of the America's Conference on Information Systems* (AMCIS 2001), Boston.

McDermott, R. (2002). "Why Information Technology Inspired but Cannot Deliver Knowledge Management." Chapter 2 in E. L. Lesser, M. A. Fontaine, and J. A. Slusher. (eds.). *Knowledge and Communities.* Woburn, MA: Butterworth-Heinemann.

McDonald, M., and D. Shand. (2000, March). "Request for Proposal: A Guide to KM Professional Services." *Knowledge Management.*

McKeen, J., and S. Staples. (2003). "Knowledge Managers: Who Are They and What Do They Do?" Chapter 2 in C. W. Holsapple (ed.). *Handbook of Knowledge Management: Knowledge Matters,* Vol. 1. Heidelberg: Springer-Verlag.

Melymuka, K. (2002, July 22). "Taking Projects to the Extreme." *Computerworld,* Vol. 36, No. 30.

Microsoft. (2000). "Microsoft Windows Media Adopted by J.D. Edwards & Co. as Corporate Communication Solution." Microsoft.com, February 14, 2000. **microsoft.com/Presspass/ press/2000/feb00/jdedwardspr.mspx** (accessed August 2006).

Mooney, S. F. (2000, December 18–25). "P-C 'Knowledge Capital' Can Be Measured." *National Underwriter,* Vol. 104, Nos. 51–52.

Murray, P. (2002, March/April). "Knowledge Management as a Sustained Competitive Advantage," *Ivey Business Journal,* pp. 71–76.

Nevo, D., and Y. Wand. (2005). "Organizational Memory Information Systems: A Transactive Memory Approach." *Decision Support Systems,* Vol. 39, No. 4.

Nonaka, I. (1994). "A Dynamic Theory of Organizational Knowledge Creation." *Organization Science,* Vol. 5, pp. 14–37.

Nonaka, I., and H. Takeuchi. (1995). *The Knowledge-Creating Company: How Japanese Companies Create the Dynamics of Innovation.* New York: Oxford University Press.

O'Dell, C., and C. J. Grayson. (2003). "Identifying and Transferring Internal Best Practices." Chapter 31 in C. W. Holsapple (ed.). *Handbook of Knowledge Management: Knowledge Matters,* Vol. 1. Heidelberg: Springer-Verlag.

O'Dell, C., C. J. Grayson, Jr., and N. Essaides. (1998). *If Only We Knew What We Know: The Transfer of Internal Knowledge and Best Practice.* New York: The Free Press.

O'Dell, C., F. Hasanali, C. Hubert, K. Lopez, P. Odem, and C. Raybourn. (2003). "Successful KM Implementations: A Study of Best Practice Organizations." Chapter 51 in C. W. Holsapple (ed.). *Handbook of Knowledge Management: Knowledge Directions,* Vol. 2. Heidelberg: Springer-Verlag.

O'Herron, J. (2003, January). "Building the Bases of Knowledge." *Call Center Magazine.*

O'Leary, D. (2003). "Technologies for Knowledge Storage and Assimilation." Chapter 34 in C. W. Holsapple (ed.).

Handbook of Knowledge Management: Knowledge Directions, Vol. 2, Heidelberg: Springer-Verlag.

Park, Y., and D. Y. Choi. (2005, May). "The Shortcomings of a Standardized Global Knowledge Management System: The Case Study of Accenture." *Academy of Management Executive,* Vol. 19, No. 2, pp. 81–85.

Park, Y. T., and S. Kim. (2006, May/June). "Knowledge Management Systems for Fourth Generation R&D: KNOWVATION." *Technovation,* Vol. 26, Nos. 5, 6.

Patton, S. (2002, February). "Putting the Pieces Together." *Darwin.*

Polanyi, M. (1958). *Personal Knowledge.* Chicago: University of Chicago Press.

Ponzi, L. J. (2004). "Knowledge Management: Birth of a Discipline." In M. E. D. Koenig and T. K. Srikantaiah (eds.). *Knowledge Management Lessons Learned: What Works and What Doesn't.* Medford, NJ: Information Today.

Qian, Z., and G. W. Bock. (2005). "An Empirical Study on Measuring the Success of Knowledge Repository Systems." *System Sciences.*

Rasmus, D. W. (2000, March/April). "Knowledge Management: More Than AI but Less Without It." *PC AI,* Vol. 14, No. 2.

Reamy, T. (2002, July/August). "Imparting Knowledge Through Storytelling." *KMWorld,* Vol. 11, No. 7.

Riege, A. (2005). "Three Dozen Knowledge-Sharing Barriers Managers Must Consider." *Journal of Knowledge Management,* Vol. 9, No. 3.

Roberts-Witt, S. L. (2000, October). "Portal Pitfalls." *Knowledge Management.*

Roberts-Witt, S. L. (2002, November). "The @HP Way." *Portals Magazine.*

Robin, M. (2000, March). "Learning by Doing." *Knowledge Management.*

Roy, A. (2009, April). "Knowledge Management for 'Stand-Out' Customer Service: Six Best Practices from the Global 2000." In "Best Practices in KM for Customer Service," a supplement to *KMWorld,* No. 8–9.

Ruber, P. (2001). "Build a Dynamic Business Portal with XML." *Knowledge Management.*

Ruggles, R. (1998). "The State of the Notion: Knowledge Management in Practice." *California Management Review,* Vol. 40, No. 3.

Schein, E. (1999). *The Corporate Culture Survival Guide.* San Francisco: Jossey-Bass.

Schulz, M. (2001, August). "The Uncertain Relevance of Newness: Organizational Learning and Knowledge Flows." *Academy of Management Journal,* Vol. 44, No. 4.

Schwartz, D. G. (ed.). (2006). *Encyclopedia of Knowledge Management.* Hershey, PA: Idea Group Reference.

Sedighi, A. (2006, January/February). "An Indispensable Guide to Knowledge Management Systems." *IEEE Software,* Vol. 23, No. 1.

Semple, E. (2005, December 1). "Social Networking at the BBC." Online Information 2005 Conference.

Shariq, S. G., and M. T. Vendelø. (2006). "Tacit Knowledge Sharing." In D. G. Schwartz (ed.). *Encyclopedia of Knowledge Management.* Hershey, PA: Idea Group Reference.

Skyrme, D. J., and D. M. Amidon. (1998, January/ February). "New Measures of Success." *Journal of Business Strategy,* Vol. 19, No. 1.

Smith, H., and J. McKeen. (2003). "Creating and Facilitating Communities of Practice." Chapter 20 in C. W. Holsapple (ed.). *Handbook of Knowledge Management: Knowledge Matters,* Vol. 1. Heidelberg: Springer-Verlag.

Soo, C., T. Devinney, D. Midgley, and A. Dering. (2002, Summer). "Knowledge Management: Philosophy, Processes, and Pitfalls." *California Management Review,* Vol. 44, No. 4.

Stone, D., and S. Warsone. (2003). "Does Accounting Account for Knowledge?" Chapter 11 in C. W. Holsapple (ed.). *Handbook of Knowledge Management: Knowledge Matters,* Vol. 1. Heidelberg: Springer-Verlag.

Storck, J., and P. A. Hill. (2002). "Knowledge Diffusion Through Strategic Communities." Chapter 5 in E. L. Lesser, M. A. Fontaine, and J. A. Slusher. (eds.). *Knowledge and Communities.* Woburn, MA: Butterworth-Heinemann.

Sullivan, D. (2001). "5 Principles of Intelligent Content Management." *Intelligent Enterprise.*

Sviokla, J. J. (2001, February 15). "Knowledge Pays." *CIO.*

Swan, J., M.. Robertson, and S. Newell. (2000, January). "Knowledge Management—When Will People Management Enter the Debate?" *Proceedings of the 33rd HICSS,* Vol. 3. Los Alamitos, CA: IEEE Computer Society Press.

Swanborg, R. (2009, February). "Mitre's Knowledge Management Journey." *CIO.*

Taylor, C. (2001, March 12). "Intellectual Capital." *Knowledge Management,* Vol. 35, No. 11.

Tseng, C., and J. Goo. (2005). "Intellectual Capital and Corporate Value in an Emerging Economy: Empirical Study of Taiwanese Manufacturers." *R&D Management,* Vol. 35, No. 2.

Tuggle, F. D., and W. E. Goldfinger (2004). "A Methodology for Mining Embedded Knowledge from Process Maps." *Human Systems Management,* Vol. 23, No. 1.

Van de Van, A. H. (2005, June). "Running in Packs to Develop Knowledge-Intensive Technologies." *MIS Quarterly,* Vol. 29, No. 2.

Vat, K. H. (2006, April–June). "Developing a Learning Organization Model for Problem-Based Learning: The Emergent Lesson of Education from the IT Trenches." *Journal of Cases on Information Technology,* Vol. 8, No. 2.

Warner, F. (2001, September). "He Drills for Knowledge." *Fast Company.*

Weinberger, D. (2005, September). "The BBC's Low-Tech Knowledge Management." *KMWorld.*

Weir, J. (2004). "Bringing Structure to the Unstructured." *KMWorld.*

Weiss, L. M., M. M. Capozzi, and L. Prusak. (2004). "Learning from the Internet Giants." *MIT Sloan Management Review,* Vol. 45, No. 4.

Wenger, E. (2002). *Communities of Practice: Learning, Meaning, and Identity.* New York: Cambridge University Press.

Wenger, E., R. McDermott, and W. M. Snyder. (2002). *Cultivating Communities of Practice.* Boston: Harvard Business School Press.

Wenger, E. C., and W. M. Snyder. (2000, January/ February). "Communities of Practice: The Organizational Frontier." *Harvard Business Review,* pp. 139–145.

Wickramasinghe, N. (2006). "Knowledge Creation." In D. G. Schwartz (ed.). *Encyclopedia of Knowledge Management.* Hershey, PA: Idea Group Reference.

Zhang, D. S., and J. L. Zhao. (2006, January–March). "Knowledge Management in Organizations." *Journal of Database Management,* Vol. 17, No. 1.

Zimmermann, K. A. (2003a, April). "Can You Measure Return on Knowledge?" *KMWorld.*

Zimmermann, K. A. (2003b, May). "Happy Together: Knowledge Management and Collaboration Work Hand-in-Hand to Satisfy the Thirst for Information." *KMWorld.*

Zyngier, S. (2006). "Knowledge Management Governance." In D. G. Schwartz (ed.). *Encyclopedia of Knowledge Management.* Hershey, PA: Idea Group Reference.

V

Intelligent Systems

1 Understand the foundations, definitions, and capabilities of artificial intelligence (AI)

2 Learn what expert systems are and understand how expert systems (ES) are used to develop intelligent decision support systems (DSS)

3 Understand how case-based reasoning (CBR) is used to develop intelligent systems

4 Understand how genetic algorithms (GA) are used to develop intelligent systems

5 Understand how fuzzy logic (FL) can be used to develop intelligent systems

6 Understand how support vector machines (SVM) are used to develop intelligent systems

7 Learn what intelligent software agents (ISA) are and understand how they can be used to develop intelligent systems

In this part, we focus on using artificial intelligence techniques to develop intelligent systems for decision support. These systems include **rule-based expert systems (ES)** and a new generation of advanced intelligent systems that use artificial neural networks, support vector machines, genetic algorithms, case-based reasoning, and intelligent software agent techniques. In this part, we first present an overview of artificial intelligence followed by a detailed explanation of rule-based expert systems (in Chapter 12). Chapter 13 describes advanced intelligent systems that are commonly used in the commercial world, including support vector machines, case-based reasoning, genetic algorithms, fuzzy logic, and intelligent software agents.

12

Artificial Intelligence and Expert Systems

LEARNING OBJECTIVES

1 Understand the concept and evolution of artificial intelligence

2 Understand the importance of knowledge in decision support

3 Describe the concept and evolution of rule-based expert systems (ES)

4 Understand the architecture of rule-based ES

5 Learn the knowledge engineering process used to build ES

6 Explain the benefits and limitations of rule-based systems for decision support

7 Identify proper applications of ES

8 Learn about tools and technologies for developing rule-based DSS

In addition to the use of data and mathematical models, some managerial decisions require qualitative information and the judgmental knowledge that resides in the minds of human experts. Therefore, it is necessary to find effective ways to incorporate such information and knowledge into decision support systems (DSS). A system that integrates knowledge from experts is commonly called a knowledge-based decision support system (KBDSS) or an intelligent decision support system (IDSS). A KBDSS can enhance the capabilities of decision support not only by supplying a tool that directly supports a decision maker, but also by enhancing various computerized DSS environments. The foundation for building such systems is the techniques and tools that have been developed in the area of artificial intelligence—rule-based expert systems being the primary one. This chapter introduces the essentials of artificial intelligence and provides a detailed description of expert systems.

12.1   Opening Vignette: A Web-Based Expert System for Wine Selection
12.2   Concepts and Definitions of Artificial Intelligence
12.3   The Artificial Intelligence Field
12.4   Basic Concepts of Expert Systems
12.5   Applications of Expert Systems
12.6   Structure of Expert Systems

12.7   Knowledge Engineering
12.8   Problem Areas Suitable for Expert Systems
12.9   Development of Expert Systems
12.10 Benefits, Limitations, and Critical Success Factors of Expert Systems
12.11 Expert Systems on the Web

12.1   OPENING VIGNETTE: A WEB-BASED EXPERT SYSTEM FOR WINE SELECTION

MenuVino, Inc., a Web-based wine retailer, has developed several online knowledge automation expert systems to provide expert advice on wine selection. The systems analyze a Web site visitor's individual flavor preferences to develop a personal taste profile in order to recommend wines that the customer is more likely to enjoy. The systems also match wines to particular meals as well as to food-related details such as ingredients, preparation methods, sauces, and so on. The expert knowledge embedded into the system allows gastronomic specification along with the combination of ingredients to be used collectively in determining very detailed matching of specific wines to specific meals. The advising expert systems are part of a commercial site aimed at matching users with their ideal wines.

Problem

Selecting the right wine for a given situation requires significant amount of expertise. People often buy a wine without knowing its taste, whether it suits their taste preferences, or if it is in harmony with the intended meal or occasion. Most nonexperts pick a wine based on price (higher is better!) and high-level classification (red for meat and white for fish, etc.). Beyond this simple classification schema, most people are clueless what it is that they are buying. Everyone agrees that it is preferable to savor the wines we genuinely like and appreciate. However, it is difficult to form an opinion unless you have tasted them all, which is an impossible proposition if you are buying them over the Web. Tastes are very personal to individuals, and to discover yours may be difficult even if you have the opportunity to try them all. Even then, they tend to change based on other factors such as the occasion, meal, mood, and so on.

Solution

Using the knowledge of many wine experts, MenuVino developed an expert system that mimics the advising one would receive from a guru. In fact, since it encompasses the knowledge of many experts, it may provide even better recommendations than a single human expert. The MenuVino Web-based expert system was developed with Exsys Knowledge Automation systems, which capture "deep" expert knowledge in a very complex area. The system uses Corvid's MetaBlock approach for probabilistic product selection. The user interface is run with the Corvid Servlet Runtime, which builds graphical and attractive HTML screens to ask questions and interact with the users. The system runs in both French and English.

MenuVino's expert advisor has two main functions: taste profiling and pairing of wines with food. The taste profile subsystems emulate the conversation a person would have with a wine expert (or sommelier). The taste-profiler portion of the expert system aims to identify the user's personal preferences. Using the interactive features of the Corvid expert system shell, it asks expert questions to reveal particular characteristics of the user. Once the user profile is established, the system recommends appropriate wines in different price ranges. The system also allows price limitation and feedback opportunities.

The pairing subsystem recommends the best wines for different flavor combinations. Finding a wine that will complement a meal is difficult unless you are a professional cook or a wine expert. The pairing subsystem incorporates many different types of food, their ingredients, and cooking methods. Hundreds of ingredients, condiments, and styles of preparation cover most of occidental cuisine. Want to know the ideal wine to go with braised kangaroo marinated in Bourgogne mustard and rice wine vinegar—you'll find it here (Domaine André, Mireille et Stéphane Tissot En Barberon 2004, Red). Maybe you prefer broiled sea bream in lime with coriander salt and grey pepper (Pétale de Rose côtes-de-provence rosé 2005, Rosé). This level of detail and granularity can recommend the ideal wines for most any type of meal.

Results

MenuVino provides visitors with a Web-based expert system where the knowledge and experience of wine experts is embedded into an interactive information system. It built a Web-based expert system that not only advises the user on wine selection but that also acts as an educational tool capable of democratizing and facilitating the discovery of wine. As MenuVino says, "Here, you are home. Take a seat at our table. You may be surprised, even amazed. Do not hesitate to participate. We appreciate the interaction, and all your requests will be taken in consideration . . . MenuVino—Wine has never been so simple." As good as it sounds, do not take our word for it! Try it yourself. Go to **menuvino.tv**, register as a new user for free, run the system, and get expert wine advice.

Questions for the Opening Vignette

1. Describe MenuVino's motivation for developing the Web-based expert system.
2. Do you think that expert systems are a good fit for this application domain? Explain. What other application domains may have similar needs?
3. What major difficulties might emerge in the process of developing such an expert system? How can they be overcome?
4. How is the system described in this case different from traditional DSS tools and techniques described in previous chapters?
5. Can you think of alternative tools, technologies, or solutions to the problem described in the case? How do they compare to the presented expert system solution?

What We Can Learn from This Vignette

With the help of artificial intelligence (especially with expert systems), many different types of specialized knowledge and experience can be extracted and represented in a computer. When the experts and expertise are hard to find, such an automated system can be very useful. This case presented a typical application of an expert system where the knowledge of wine experts is embedded into a Web-based information system so that it can be readily used by the non-experts. Making such specialized knowledge accessible to many users in an automated and interactive environment has great potential to boost the utility and profitability of many business applications.

Sources: Exsys, "MenuVino—Wine Advisor," **www.exsys.com/winkPDFs/CommercialOnline WineAdvisors.pdf** (accessed June 2009); and MenuVino, Inc., **menuvino.tv/gouts.php** (accessed June 2009).

12.2 CONCEPTS AND DEFINITIONS OF ARTIFICIAL INTELLIGENCE

The opening vignette illustrates that in some situations the support that can be offered by data and data-driven models may be insufficient. With regards to wine selection, support was provided by rule-based expert systems to substitute for human expertise by providing the necessary knowledge in the form of an automated and interactive information system. In addition to rule-based expert systems, several other technologies can be used to support decision situations where expertise is required. Most of these technologies use qualitative (or symbolic) knowledge rather than numeric and/or mathematical models to provide the needed support; hence, they are referred to as **knowledge-based systems (KBS)**. The overarching field of study that encompasses these technologies and underlying applications is called *artificial intelligence*.

Artificial Intelligence (AI) Definitions

Artificial intelligence (AI) is an area of computer science. Even though the term has many different definitions, most experts agree that AI is concerned with two basic ideas: (1) the study of human thought processes (to understand what intelligence is) and

(2) the representation and duplication of those thought processes in machines (e.g., computers, robots).

One well-publicized, classic definition of AI is "behavior by a machine that, if performed by a human being, would be called intelligent." Rich and Knight (1991) provided a thought-provoking definition: "Artificial intelligence is the study of how to make computers do things at which, at the moment, people are better."

A well-known application of artificial intelligence is the chess program called Deep Blue, developed by a research team at IBM (see Application Case 12.1). The system beat the famous world champion, Grand Master Garry Kasparov, in a game that usually only highly intelligent people can win.

APPLICATION CASE 12.1

Intelligent System Beats the Chess Grand Master

Games are a classic application domain for intelligent systems. An extremely successful system is the computer chess program developed by IBM. In 1997, Deep Blue, a computer system armed with artificial intelligence, beat 34-year-old Russian World Chess Champion Garry Kasparov in a six-game match. This was the first time that a computer demonstrated intelligence in an area that requires human intelligence.

The system ran on an IBM RS/6000 SP machine that was capable of examining 200 million moves per second—or 50 billion positions—in the 3 minutes allocated for a single move in a chess game. A six-person design team led by Chung-Jen Tan designed a hybrid heuristic and brute-force search model to assess the values of different moves.

In February 2003, another human–computer match between Garry Kasparov and Deep Junior, a three-time computer chess champion programmed by Air Ban and Shay Bushinsky in Israel, ended in a 3–3 tie. This further confirmed that the knowledge captured in the computer chess program could be as powerful as that of the best human player. In 2004, a computer–computer match between Deep Junior and Fritz ended in a draw. Fritz is an intelligent system designed by German scientists that can execute 350,000 operations per second.

Although these computer victories do not imply that computer intelligence will prevail, they do indicate the potential of artificial intelligence, particularly in the area of intelligent decision support. Computers armed with intelligent reasoning capabilities could help managers minimize risks and maximize performance.

Sources: IBM Research, "Deep Blue Overview," **research.ibm.com/ deepblue/** (accessed June 2009); and *ChessBase News,* "Kasparov vs. Deep Junior Ends in 3-3," February 8, 2003, **chessbase.com/ newsdetail.asp?newsid=782** (accessed June 2009).

To understand what artificial intelligence is, we need to examine those abilities that are considered to be signs of intelligence:

- Learning or understanding from experience
- Making sense out of ambiguous or contradictory messages
- Responding quickly and successfully to a new situation (i.e., different responses, flexibility)
- Using reasoning in solving problems and directing conduct effectively
- Dealing with perplexing situations
- Understanding and inferring in a rational way
- Applying knowledge to manipulate the environment
- Thinking and reasoning
- Recognizing and judging the relative importance of different elements in a situation

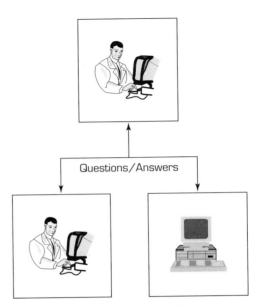

FIGURE 12.1   A Pictorial Representation of the Turing Test

Alan Turing designed an interesting test to determine whether a computer exhibits intelligent behavior; the test is called the **Turing test**. According to this test, a computer can be considered smart only when a human interviewer cannot identify the computer while conversing with both an unseen human being and an unseen computer (see Figure 12.1).

In the next section, we discuss the major characteristics of artificial intelligence.

Characteristics of Artificial Intelligence

Although the ultimate goal of AI is to build machines that mimic human intelligence, the capabilities of current commercial AI technologies are far from exhibiting any significant success in reaching this goal. Nevertheless, AI programs are continuously improving, and they increase productivity and quality by automating many tasks that require human intelligence. Artificial intelligence techniques usually have the features described in the following sections.

SYMBOLIC PROCESSING   Symbolic processing is an essential characteristic of AI, as reflected in the following definition: **Artificial intelligence (AI)** is the branch of computer science that deals primarily with symbolic, non-algorithmic methods of problem solving. This definition focuses on two characteristics:

- *Numeric versus symbolic.*   Computers were originally designed specifically to process numbers (i.e., numeric processing). However, people tend to think symbolically; our intelligence is based, in part, on our mental ability to manipulate symbols rather than just numbers. Although symbolic processing is at the core of AI, this does not mean that AI cannot use numbers and math but rather that the emphasis in AI is on the manipulation of symbols.
- *Algorithmic versus heuristic.*   An algorithm is a step-by-step procedure that has well-defined starting and ending points and is guaranteed to find the same solution to a specific problem. Most computer architectures readily lend themselves to this type of step-by-step approach. Many human reasoning processes however tend to be non-algorithmic; in other words, our mental activities consist of more than just following logical, step-by-step procedures. Rather, human thinking relies more on rules, opinions, and gut feelings, learned from previous experiences.

HEURISTICS **Heuristics** are intuitive knowledge, or rules of thumb, learned from experience. AI deals with ways of representing knowledge using symbols with heuristics methods for processing information. By using heuristics, we do not have to rethink completely what to do every time we encounter a similar problem. For example, when a salesperson plans to visit clients in different cities, a popular heuristic is to visit the next nearest one (i.e., the nearest-neighbor heuristic). Many AI methods use heuristics to reduce the complexity of problem solving.

INFERENCING As an alternative to merely using individual heuristics, AI also includes reasoning (or inferencing) capabilities that can build higher-level knowledge using existing knowledge represented as heuristics in the form of rules. *Inference* is the process of deriving a logical outcome from a given set of facts and rules.

MACHINE LEARNING Learning is an important capability for human beings; it is one of the features that separate humans from other creatures. AI systems do not have the same learning capabilities that humans have; rather, they have simplistic learning capabilities (modeled after the human learning methods) called machine learning. Machine learning allows computer systems to monitor and sense their environmental factors and adjust their behavior to react to changes. Technically speaking, machine learning is a scientific discipline that is concerned with the design and development of algorithms that allow computers to learn based on data coming from sensors or databases. Many machine-learning techniques exist for developing intelligent information systems, some of the most popular ones are described in this part.

Section 12.2 Review Questions

1. What is artificial intelligence?
2. What are the major capabilities of artificial intelligence?
3. What are the major characteristics of artificial intelligence?
4. What are heuristics? Give an example.

12.3 THE ARTIFICIAL INTELLIGENCE FIELD

The field of AI is quite broad. In this section, we introduce its evolution, compare artificial intelligence with natural intelligence, and provide an overview of several major applications.

Evolution of Artificial Intelligence

The evolution of artificial intelligence includes five major stages. Figure 12.2 shows the evolution from 1960 onward until now.

The major event that triggered the wave of artificial intelligence is believed to be the Dartmouth Meeting. A group of computer scientists gathered at Dartmouth College to discuss the great potential of computer applications in 1956. They were confident that, given their enormous computing power, computers would be able to solve many complex problems and outperform human beings in many areas. At that time, scientists had little understanding of the complexity of human intelligence and were overly optimistic about what computers could achieve. Many solutions created at that time were primitive, and hence the stage is called the naïve solutions stage.

After several years of trial and error, scientists started focusing on developing more effective problem-solving methods, such as knowledge representation schemes, reasoning strategies, and effective search heuristics. Because the primary feature of this

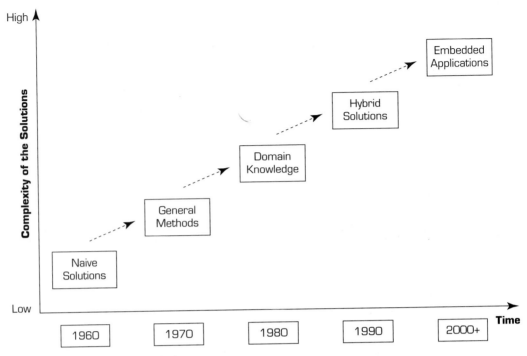

FIGURE 12.2 Stages of AI Evolution

stage was the development of general-purpose methods, it is called the general methods stage.

After building enough general-purpose methods, people started applying them to real-world applications. The applications at this stage were different from the first stage in that people already knew that it was difficult to program how to solve commonsense problems into a computer. Therefore, most applications were targeted at a narrowly defined domain with specialized knowledge. These kinds of systems are called expert or knowledge-based systems. Acquisition of expert knowledge played a key role in the development of such systems. We call this the domain knowledge stage.

After 1990, more advanced problem-solving methods were developed, and there was a strong need to integrate multiple techniques and solve problems in multiple domains. Hybrid systems, such as integrations of rule-based and case-based systems and integrations of ANN and genetic algorithms become necessary. We call this the multiple integration stage.

Since 2000, the trend has been to embed various intelligent components into popular applications. Intelligent systems and robotics continue to spread into everyday use, from video games and business rules to homeland security. The systems we are dealing with today are much smarter than earlier systems. The applications of embedded AI systems are the primary features of the embedded applications stage.

The use of artificial intelligence in BI and DSS has advantages and limitations. See Technology Insights 12.1 for a brief comparison of artificial and natural intelligence.

Applications of Artificial Intelligence

Artificial intelligence is a collection of concepts and ideas that are related to the development of intelligent systems. These concepts and ideas may be developed in different areas and be applied to different domains. In order to understand the scope of AI, therefore, we need to

TECHNOLOGY INSIGHTS 12.1   Artificial Intelligence Versus Natural Intelligence

The potential value of artificial intelligence can be better understood by contrasting it with natural, or human, intelligence. AI has several important advantages over natural intelligence:

- AI is more permanent. Natural intelligence is perishable from a commercial standpoint, in that workers can change their place of employment or forget information. However, AI is permanent as long as the computer systems and programs remain unchanged.
- AI offers ease of duplication and dissemination. Transferring a body of knowledge from one person to another usually requires a lengthy process of apprenticeship; even so, expertise can seldom be duplicated completely. However, when knowledge is embedded in a computer system, it can easily be transferred from that computer to any other computer on the Internet or on an intranet.
- AI can be less expensive than natural intelligence. There are many circumstances in which buying computer services costs less than having corresponding human power carry out the same tasks. This is especially true when knowledge is disseminated over the Web.
- AI, being a computer technology, is consistent and thorough. Natural intelligence is erratic because people are erratic; they do not always perform consistently.
- AI can be documented. Decisions made by a computer can be easily documented by tracing the activities of the system. Natural intelligence is difficult to document. For example, a person may reach a conclusion but at some later date may be unable to re-create the reasoning process that led to that conclusion or to even recall the assumptions that were part of the decision.
- AI can execute certain tasks much faster than a human can.
- AI can perform certain tasks better than many or even most people.

Natural intelligence does have some advantages over AI, such as the following:

- Natural intelligence is truly creative, whereas AI is uninspired. The ability to acquire knowledge is inherent in human beings, but with AI knowledge must be built into a carefully constructed system constrained by a large number of assumptions.
- Natural intelligence enables people to benefit from and use sensory experience directly in a synergistic way, whereas most AI systems must work with numeric and/or symbolic inputs in a sequential manner with predetermined representational forms.

---

see a group of areas that may be called the AI family. Figure 12.3 shows the major branches of AI applications. These applications are built on the foundation of many disciplines and technologies, including computer science, philosophy, electrical engineering, management science, psychology, and linguistics. A sample of representative application areas of AI is briefly described next.

EXPERT SYSTEMS   The term *expert system* was derived from the term *knowledge-based expert system*. An **expert system (ES)** is an information system that uses human knowledge captured in a computer to solve problems that ordinarily require human expertise and reasoning. Later sections of this chapter provide more details on ES.

NATURAL LANGUAGE PROCESSING   **Natural language processing (NLP)** (as described in detail in Chapter 7) is a collection of technologies aimed to provide necessary mechanisms to enable computers and computer users to communicate with each other using native human language. These technologies aim to provide a conversational type of interface between the human and the machine, in contrast to the traditional interfaces where a

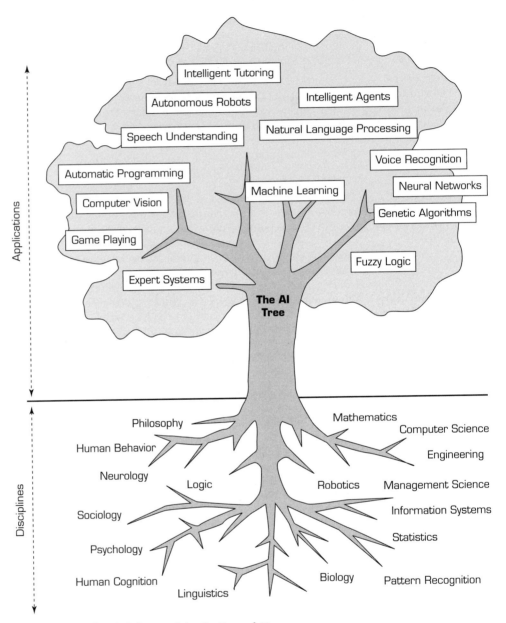

FIGURE 12.3 The Disciplines and Applications of AI

programming language that consists of computer jargon, syntax, and commands is used. NLP includes two main subfields:

- *Natural language understanding* involves the use of technology to enable computers to comprehend (i.e., "understand") human language (syntax as well as semantics) much the same way that a human being does. Here, the ultimate goal is to have computers truly understand human language.

- *Natural language generation* involves the use of technology to enable computers to produce and express ordinary human language. Here, the ultimate goal is to have people understand computers by having them converse in human languages.

Much of the success of NLP is exemplified in text-mining systems, where unstructured text documents are successfully processed (recognized, understood, and interpreted) for acquisition of new knowledge (see Chapter 7 for more details).

SPEECH (VOICE) UNDERSTANDING   **Speech (voice) understanding** is the recognition and understanding of spoken language by a computer. Applications of this technology have become increasingly popular. For instance, many companies have now adopted this technology in their call centers (see Application Case 12.2). An interesting application of speech understanding is the Literacy Innovation that Speech Technology Enables (LISTEN), developed at Carnegie Mellon University, which provides a pleasant and automated environment to improve literacy by listening to children read aloud (try it at **cs.cmu.edu/~listen**).

APPLICATION CASE 12.2
Automatic Speech Recognition in Call Centers

More and more companies are using automated speech recognition technology for interacting with customers. This is particularly popular in call centers. In the United States alone, more than 50,000 call centers spend more than $90 billion dealing with customers' requests. With human operators costing around $1 per minute to maintain, speech recognition offers an enormous opportunity to companies to lower their costs and become more competitive. If done properly (by using smart technologies such as expert systems), such an automated process can also improve customer satisfaction by providing answers to their questions in a timely manner.

Charles Schwab, a U.S. discount stockbroker, introduced the first speech system for retail brokering in 1996. That year, the number of new accounts with the company increased by 41 percent, and the call centers took 97 million calls. An automated attendant in this system can understand 15,000 names of individual equities and funds, takes up to 100,000 calls per day, and is 93 percent accurate in identifying queries the first time they are made. Costs have been cut to $1 per call, down from $4 to $5 per call.

Hotel chain Wyndham International has used speech automation technology to develop intelligent agents with conversational skills to handle advanced customer service calls at Wyndham's call center. Having fast access to all database records, such an intelligent agent (enhanced with conversational skills) is often capable of resolving customer issues more accurately in a fraction of time, compared to its human counterpart.

In 2004, U.S. companies spent $480 million on speech-enabled self-service technology (SESST). By the end of this decade, over 1 billion speech-enabled service centers are expected to be in operation, replacing functions currently taking place in call centers in India and some other developing nations around the world. A call serviced through speech automation costs approximately 15 to 25 percent of the cost of a call handled by an agent in India. Voice technology is destined to have a significant impact on the outsourcing of call centers.

Sources: Adapted from "Just Talk to Me," *The Economist Technology Quarterly,* December 8, 2001; and P. Gooptu, "Threat to Call Centers: Voice Automation!" November 23, 2004, **rediff .com/money/2004/nov/23bpo.htm** (accessed June 2009).

ROBOTICS AND SENSORY SYSTEMS   Sensory systems, such as vision systems, tactile systems, and signal-processing systems, when combined with AI, define a broad category of systems generally called *robots*. A **robot** is an electromechanical device that can be programmed to perform manual tasks. The Robotics Institute of America formally defines a *robot* as "a reprogrammable multifunctional manipulator designed to move materials, parts, tools, or specialized devices through variable programmed motions for the performance of a variety of tasks" (Currie, 1999).

An "intelligent" robot has some kind of sensory apparatus, such as a camera, that collects information about the robot's surroundings and its operations. The intelligent part of the robot allows it to interpret the collected information and to respond and adapt to changes in its environment rather than just follow prespecified instructions. A recent report described the humanoid HRP-2 robots, named Promets, developed by the National Institute of Advanced Industrial Science and Technology in Japan, an excellent example of today's robotic technology. These robots are designed to respond to verbal instructions to perform certain tasks, such as moving chairs or turning on a TV, and they are capable of capturing three-dimensional images of objects and locating them through an infrared sensor (see Yamaguchi, 2006). A Reuters report indicated that Toyota intends to sell service robots by 2010 (Reuters, 2005).

COMPUTER VISION AND SCENE RECOGNITION   **Visual recognition** is a form of computer intelligence where the digitized representation of visual information (received from one or more sensors, such as a camera, radar, an infrared or ultrasound machine, etc.) is used to accurately recognize the underlying object. The output information (recognition of the object) is then used to perform operations such as robotic movement, conveyor speed, and rerouting of out-of-spec products passing through a production line.

The basic objective of computer vision is to interpret scenarios rather than to identify individual pictures. Interpreting scenarios is defined in different ways, depending on the application and the context of the scenario. For example, in interpreting pictures taken by a satellite, it may be sufficient to identify regions of crop damage. In another example, a robot vision system can be designed to identify assembly components so that the robot can correctly affix them to the item being assembled.

INTELLIGENT COMPUTER-AIDED INSTRUCTION   **Intelligent computer-aided instruction (ICAI)** refers to machines that can tutor humans. To a certain extent, such a machine can be viewed as an expert system enhanced with the knowledge of a human expert. However, the major objective of an ES is to render advice, whereas the purpose of an ICAI is to teach. Therefore, the structure of an ordinary ES needs to be tweaked to make it behave like a teacher as opposed to an advisor.

Computer-assisted instruction, which has been in use for many years, brings the power of a computer to bear on the educational process. Now AI methods are being applied to the development of ICAI systems in an attempt to create computerized tutors that shape their teaching techniques to fit the learning patterns of individual students. These are known as **intelligent tutoring systems (ITS)**, many of which have been implemented on the Web. An application can be found in Lopez et al. (2003).

AUTOMATIC PROGRAMMING   Writing computer programs has always been a tedious and error-prone task. Automatic programming allows computers to automatically generate computer programs, usually based on specifications that are higher level and that are easier for humans to specify than ordinary programming languages. Automatic programming occurs with the help of AI techniques embedded within integrated development environments (IDE).

NEURAL COMPUTING   **Neural computing** (or neural networks) describes a set of mathematical models that simulate the way a human brain functions. Such models have been implemented in flexible, easy-to-use software packages such as NeuroSolutions (**nd.com**), BrainMaker (**calsci.com**), and NeuroShell (**wardsystems.com**). The applications of neural networks in business are abundant. We discussed neural computing and its wide range of applications in Chapter 6.

GAME PLAYING   Game playing was one of the very early application areas that AI researchers studied. It is an excellent area for investigating new AI strategies and heuristics because the outcomes are rather easy to demonstrate and measure. The success of Deep Blue (described in Application Case 12.1) is a good example of successful AI-based game development.

LANGUAGE TRANSLATION Automated translation uses computer programs to translate words and sentences from one language to another without much interpretation by humans. For example, you can use Babel Fish Translation, available at **world.altavista.com**, to try more than 20 different combinations of language translation. Similarly, you can also use Google's free tool to translate between 41 different languages (**translate.google.com**).

FUZZY LOGIC **Fuzzy logic** is a technique for processing imprecise linguistic terms. It extends the notions of logic beyond simple true/false statements to allow for partial (or even continuous) truths. Inexact knowledge and imprecise reasoning are important aspects of expertise in applying common sense to decision-making situations. In fuzzy logic, the value of true or false is replaced by the degree of set membership. For example, in the traditional Boolean logic, a person's credit record is either good or bad. In fuzzy logic, the credit record may be assessed as both good and bad, but with different degrees. See Chapter 13 and Tanaka and Niimuara (2007) for more details.

GENETIC ALGORITHMS Genetic algorithms are among the advanced search techniques that resemble the natural process of evolution (i.e., the survival of the fittest). For a specific problem, the solution template is formulated as a "chromosome" structure that contains groups, or genes (often represented with sequences of 0s and 1s), representing the values of decision variables. The genetic algorithm starts with a randomly generated population of solutions (a collection of chromosomes) and then by identifying and using the best solutions (based on a fitness function) it reproduces future generations using genetic operators (e.g., mutation and crossover). The recursive process of "evolution" continues until a satisfactory solution or some other stopping criterion is reached. See Goldberg (1994) for an excellent introduction to genetic algorithms. Ghanea-Hercock and Ghanea-Hercock (2003) discussed Java implementation of the algorithm, and Chapter 13 provides a more descriptive explanation of genetic algorithms.

INTELLIGENT AGENTS **Intelligent agents (IA)** are relatively small programs that reside (and run continuously) in a computer environment to perform certain tasks automatically and autonomously. An intelligent agent runs in the background of a computer, monitors the environment, and reacts to certain triggering conditions based on the knowledge embedded into it. A good example of an intelligent software agent is a virus detection program. It resides on your computer, scans all incoming data, and removes found viruses automatically while learning new virus types and detection methods. Intelligent agents are applied in personal digital assistants (PDAs), e-mail servers, news filtering and distribution, appointment handling, e-commerce, and automated information gathering. See Application Case 12.3 for an example and Chapter 13 for more details on this rapidly popularized AI application area.

APPLICATION CASE 12.3

Agents for Travel Planning at USC

Planning business trips is a tedious task that includes selecting a flight, reserving a hotel, and possibly reserving a car. When a schedule is set, many other decisions must be made, based on past experiences, such as whether driving to the airport or taking a taxi. The time and effort required to make more informed decisions usually outweigh the cost. Schedules can change, prices can decrease after purchasing a ticket, flight delays can result in missed connections, and hotel rooms and rental cars can be given away because of late arrivals. All these contingencies add stress for the traveler.

To address these issues, the University of Southern California (USC) developed an integrated travel planning and monitoring system called Travel Assistant. The system provides the user with the information necessary to make an informed travel plan. It uses information agents to provide information for planning and monitoring agents to trace any changes in the original plan. An information agent takes a particular information request, navigates to the appropriate Web site, extracts information from the Web site, and then returns the information as an XML document for processing.

Monitoring agents are built on top of the information agents and keep track of the status of the schedule. If any information (e.g., cancellation or delay of the flight) that might cause schedule changes is found, the agents send a message to the user. These agents perform their tasks at regular intervals. These agents can send messages about flight delays, flight cancellations, reductions in airfares, and about availability of earlier flights. They can also send faxes to a hotel.

An intelligent agent project that supports travel and tourism planning was also conducted at RMIT University in Australia. Their system was said to support mobile applications running on PDAs, cell phones, and other personal devices.

Sources: Adapted from C. Knoblock, "Agents for Gathering, Integrating, and Monitoring Information for Travel Planning," *IEEE Intelligent Systems,* Vol. 17, No. 6, 2003; and L. Mathies, L. Padgham, and B. Q. Vo, "Agent Based Travel and Tourism Planning," *Proceedings of the Autonomous Agents and Multiagent Systems Conference,* Utrecht University, the Netherlands, July 25–29, 2005.

Section 12.3 Review Questions

1. What are the major advantages of artificial intelligence over natural intelligence?
2. What are the major disadvantages of artificial intelligence compared to natural intelligence?
3. What are the major characteristics of artificial intelligence?
4. Describe an artificial intelligence application.
5. What technology can help move call centers that have been outsourced to other countries back to the United States?
6. Define *natural language processing* and describe an NLP application.
7. Define *speech recognition* and discuss one application of the technology.
8. Define *intelligent agent* and describe one application of the technology.

12.4 BASIC CONCEPTS OF EXPERT SYSTEMS

Expert systems (ES) are computer-based information systems that use expert knowledge to attain high-level decision performance in a narrowly defined problem domain. MYCIN, developed at Stanford University in the early 1980s for medical diagnosis, is the most well-known ES application. ES has also been used in taxation, credit analysis, equipment maintenance, help desk automation, environmental monitoring, and fault diagnosis. ES has been popular in large and medium-sized organizations as a sophisticated tool for improving productivity and quality (see Nedovic and Devedzic, 2002; and Nurminen et al., 2003).

The basic concepts of ES include how to determine who experts are, the definition of expertise, how expertise can be extracted and transferred from a person to a computer, and how the expert system should mimic the reasoning process of human experts. We describe these concepts in the following sections.

Experts

An **expert** is a person who has the special knowledge, judgment, experience, and skills to put his or her knowledge in action to provide sound advice and to solve complex problems in a narrowly defined area. It is an expert's job to provide knowledge about how he or she performs a task that a KBS will perform. An expert knows which facts are important and also understands and explains the dependency relationships among those facts. In diagnosing a problem with an automobile's electrical system, for example, an expert mechanic knows that a broken fan belt can be the cause for the battery to discharge.

There is no standard definition of *expert*, but decision performance and the level of knowledge a person has are typical criteria used to determine whether a particular person is an expert. Typically, experts must be able to solve a problem and achieve a performance level that is significantly better than average. In addition, experts are relative (and not absolute). An expert at a time or in a region may not be an expert in another time or region. For example, an attorney in New York may not be a legal expert in Beijing, China. A medical student may be an expert compared to the general public but may not be considered an expert in brain surgery. Experts have expertise that can help solve problems and explain certain obscure phenomena within a specific problem domain. Typically, human experts are capable of doing the following:

- Recognizing and formulating a problem
- Solving a problem quickly and correctly
- Explaining a solution
- Learning from experience
- Restructuring knowledge
- Breaking rules (i.e., going outside the general norms), if necessary
- Determining relevance and associations
- Declining gracefully (i.e., being aware of one's limitations)

Expertise

Expertise is the extensive, task-specific knowledge that experts possess. The level of expertise determines the performance of a decision. Expertise is often acquired through training, reading, and experience in practice. It includes explicit knowledge, such as theories learned from a textbook or in a classroom, and implicit knowledge, gained from experience. The following is a list of possible knowledge types:

- Theories about the problem domain
- Rules and procedures regarding the general problem domain
- Heuristics about what to do in a given problem situation
- Global strategies for solving these types of problems
- Metaknowledge (i.e., knowledge about knowledge)
- Facts about the problem area

These types of knowledge enable experts to make better and faster decisions than non-experts when solving complex problems.

Expertise often includes the following characteristics:

- Expertise is usually associated with a high degree of intelligence, but it is not always associated with the smartest person.
- Expertise is usually associated with a vast quantity of knowledge.
- Expertise is based on learning from past successes and mistakes.
- Expertise is based on knowledge that is well stored, organized, and quickly retrievable from an expert who has excellent recall of patterns from previous experiences.

Features of ES

ES must have the following features:

- ***Expertise.***   As described in the previous section, experts differ in their level of expertise. An ES must possess expertise that enables it to make expert-level decisions. The system must exhibit expert performance with adequate robustness.
- ***Symbolic reasoning.***   The basic rationale of artificial intelligence is to use symbolic reasoning rather than mathematical calculation. This is also true for ES. That is,

knowledge must be represented symbolically, and the primary reasoning mechanism must be symbolic. Typical symbolic reasoning mechanisms include backward chaining and forward chaining, which are described later in this chapter.

- **Deep knowledge.**   Deep knowledge concerns the level of expertise in a knowledge base. The knowledge base must contain complex knowledge not easily found among nonexperts.
- **Self-knowledge.**   ES must be able to examine their own reasoning and provide proper explanations as to why a particular conclusion was reached. Most experts have very strong learning capabilities to update their knowledge constantly. ES also need to be able to learn from their successes and failures as well as from other knowledge sources.

The development of ES is divided into two generations. Most first-generation ES use if-then rules to represent and store their knowledge. The second-generation ES are more flexible in adopting multiple knowledge representation and reasoning methods. They may integrate fuzzy logic, neural networks, or genetic algorithms with rule-based inference to achieve a higher level of decision performance. A comparison between conventional systems and ES is given in Table 12.1. A simple scenario of ES usage is given in Technology Insights 12.2.

TABLE 12.1   **Comparison of Conventional Systems and Expert Systems**

Conventional Systems	Expert Systems
Information and its processing are usually combined in one sequential program.	The knowledge base is clearly separated from the processing (inference) mechanism (i.e., knowledge rules are separated from the control).
The program does not make mistakes (programmers or users do).	The program may make mistakes.
Conventional systems do not (usually) explain why input data are needed or how conclusions are drawn.	Explanation is a part of most ES.
Conventional systems require all input data. They may not function properly with missing data unless planned for.	ES do not require all initial facts. ES can typically arrive at reasonable conclusions with missing facts.
Changes in the program are tedious (except in DSS).	Changes in the rules are easy to make.
The system operates only when it is completed.	The system can operate with only a few rules (as the first prototype).
Execution is done on a step-by-step (algorithmic) basis.	Execution is done by using heuristics and logic.
Large databases can be effectively manipulated.	Large knowledge bases can be effectively manipulated.
Conventional systems represent and use data.	ES represent and use knowledge.
Efficiency is usually a major goal.	
Effectiveness is important only for DSS.	Effectiveness is the major goal.
Conventional systems easily deal with quantitative data.	ES easily deal with qualitative data.
Conventional systems use numeric data representations.	ES use symbolic and numeric knowledge representations.
Conventional systems capture, magnify, and distribute access to numeric data or information.	ES capture, magnify, and distribute access to judgment and knowledge.

TECHNOLOGY INSIGHTS 12.2 Sample Session of a Rule-Based ES

A rule-based ES contains rules in its knowledge base. The rules are used to generate questions for the user. The user's responses allow the system to provide recommendations. Suppose that you have an ES that recommends notebook computers based on a customer's needs. The following is a possible consultation session:

1. What is your primary task to be performed on the notebook computer?
   ☐ Word processing
   ☐ Communications
   ☐ Multimedia applications
   Answer: 1 (click the first checkbox)

2. Where are you going to use the notebook most often?
   ☐ In the office
   ☐ While traveling
   Answer: 2 (click the second checkbox)

3. What is your budget range?
   ☐ Below $1K
   ☐ Between $1K and $2K
   ☐ Above $2K
   Answer: 2 (click the second checkbox)

System recommendation: You should consider buying a Dell Latitude X1.

Reasons: It is light (2.5 pounds) and more suitable for your word processing and travel needs; it is also priced at $1,950, which fits your budget.

Of course, ES are not exact replicas of the real experts. Compared to real experts, they have advantages and shortcomings. Table 12.2 shows a simple comparison between human experts and ES on several key features.

TABLE 12.2 Differences Between Human Experts and Expert Systems

Features	Human Experts	Expert Systems
Mortality	Yes	No
Knowledge transfer	Difficult	Easy
Knowledge documentation	Difficult	Easy
Decision consistency	Low	High
Unit usage cost	High	Low
Creativity	High	Low
Adaptability	High	Medium
Knowledge scope	Broad	Narrow
Knowledge type	Common sense and technical	Technical
Knowledge content	Experience	Rules and symbolic models

APPLICATION CASE 12.4
Expert System Helps in Identifying Sport Talents

In the world of sports, recruiters are constantly looking for new talent and parents want to identify the sport that is the most appropriate for their child. Identifying the most plausible match between a person (characterized by a large number of unique qualities and limitations) and a specific sport is anything but a trivial task. Such a matching process requires adequate information about the specific person (i.e., values of certain characteristics), as well as the deep knowledge of what this information should include (i.e., the types of characteristics). In other words, expert knowledge is what is needed in order to accurately predict the right sport (with the highest success possibility) for a specific individual.

It is very hard (if not impossible) to find the true experts for this difficult matchmaking problem. Because the domain of the specific knowledge is divided into various types of sports, the experts have in-depth knowledge of the relevant factors only for a specific sport (that they are an expert of), and beyond the limits of that sport they are not any better than an average spectator. In an ideal case, you would need experts from a wide range of sports brought together into a single room to collectively create a matchmaking decision. Because such a setting is not feasible in the real world, one might consider creating it in the computer world using expert systems. Because expert systems are known to incorporate knowledge from multiple experts, this situation seems to fits well with an expert system type solution.

In a recent publication Papic et al. (2009) reported on an expert system application for the identification of sports talents. Tapping into the knowledge of a large number of sports experts, they have built a knowledge base of a comprehensive set of rules that maps the expert-driven factors (e.g., physical and cardiovascular measurement, performance test, skill assessments) to different sports. Taking advantage of the inexact representation capabilities of fuzzy logic, they managed to incorporate the exact natural reasoning of the expert knowledge into their advising system.

The system was built as a Web-based DSS using the ASP.NET development platform. Once the system development was completed, it was tested for verification and validation purposes. The system's prediction results were evaluated by experts using real cases collected from the past several years. Comparison was done between the sport proposed by the expert system and the actual outcome of the person's sports career. Additionally, the expert system output and the human expert suggestions were compared using a large number of test cases. All tests showed high reliability and accuracy of the developed system.

Sources: V. Papic, N. Rogulj, and V. Pletina, "Identification of Sport Talents Using a Web-oriented Expert System with a Fuzzy Module," *Expert Systems with Applications*, Vol. 36, 2009, pp. 8830–8838; and N. Rogulj, V. Papic, and V. Pletina, "Development of the Expert System for Sport Talents Detection," *WSEAS Transactions on Information Science and Applications*, Vol. 9, No. 3, 2006, pp. 1752–1755.

Section 12.4 Review Questions

1. What is an ES?
2. Explain why we need ES.
3. What are the major features of ES?
4. What is expertise? Provide an example.
5. Define *deep knowledge* and give an example of it.

12.5 APPLICATIONS OF EXPERT SYSTEMS

ES have been applied to many business and technological areas to support decision making. Application Case 12.5 shows a few real-world applications of ES. Table 12.3 shows some representative ES and their application domains.

APPLICATION CASE 12.5

Sample Applications of ES

ES can have many applications. The following are a few examples.

Customer Support at Logitech

Logitech is one of the largest vendors of mouse devices and Web cameras in the world. Because the company offers many different models of these tools, customer support is a major challenge. To take advantage of the Internet and technologies in intelligent systems, Logitech deploys an interactive knowledge portal to provide Web-based self-help customer support to its QuickCam customers in North America. The noHold Knowledge Platform emulates the way a human would interact with a customer, allows the user to ask questions or describe problems in natural language, and carries on an intelligent conversation with the user until it has enough information to provide an accurate answer.

China's Freight Train System

An ES was developed in China to allocate freight cars and determine what and how much to load on each car. The ES is integrated with the existing MIS and is distributed to many users.

Electricity Market Forecaster

EnvaPower developed an electricity market forecasting system, called MarketMonitor, that uses AI techniques to gather, synthesize, and analyze a large number of factors that may affect the consumption of electricity.

Rule-Based Engine for Mobile Games

In reaction to the rapid growth in mobile devices and entertainment needs, a group of researchers in the United Kingdom is creating a rule-based AI engine that can support the development of games on mobile devices. The system allows downloadable games to have AI components so that they can become more intelligent.

SEI Investment's Financial Diagnosis System

SEI Investment uses business rules management technologies to create an enabling platform for delivering "financial wellness" solutions to its clients. The system includes rules for regulatory and application checks, transaction management governance, and automation of transactions without human interruption.

Sources: "Logitech Deploys Online Customer Support," *Expert Systems,* November 2001; G. Geng, B. Zhang, J. Zhu, and C. H. Zhong, "Applying AI to Railway Freight Loading," *Expert Systems with Applications,* January 1999; and L. Hall, A. Gordon, R. James, and L. Newell, "A Lightweight Rule-Based AI Engine for Mobile Games," *ACM SIG International Conference on Advances in Computer Entertainment Technologies,* 2004.

TABLE 12.3 **Sample Applications of Expert Systems**

Expert System	Organization	Application Domain
Classical Applications		
MYCIN	Stanford University	Medical diagnosis
XCON	DEC	System configuration
Expert Tax	Coopers & Lybrand	Tax planning
Loan Probe	Peat Marwick	Loan evaluation
La-Courtier	Cognitive Systems	Financial planning
LMOS	Pacific Bell	Network management
PROSPECTOR	Stanford Research Institute	Discovery of new mineral deposits
New Applications		
Fish-Expert	North China	Disease diagnosis in fish
HelpDeskIQ	BMC Remedy	Help desk management
Authorete	Haley	Business rule automation
eCare	CIGNA	Insurance claims
SONAR	NSAD	Stock market monitoring

Classical Applications of ES

Early ES applications, such as DENDRAL for molecular structure identification and MYCIN for medical diagnosis, were primarily in the science domain. XCON for configuration of the VAX computer system at Digital Equipment Corp. (a major producer of minicomputers around 1990 that was later taken over by Compaq) was a successful example in business.

DENDRAL The DENDRAL project was initiated by Edward Feigenbaum in 1965. It used a set of knowledge- or rule-based reasoning commands to deduce the likely molecular structure of organic chemical compounds from known chemical analyses and mass spectrometry data.

DENDRAL proved to be fundamentally important in demonstrating how rule-based reasoning could be developed into powerful knowledge engineering tools and led to the development of other rule-based reasoning programs at the Stanford Artificial Intelligence Laboratory (SAIL). The most important of those programs was MYCIN.

MYCIN MYCIN is a rule-based ES that diagnoses bacterial infections of the blood. It was developed by a group of researchers at Stanford University in the 1970s. By asking questions and backward chaining through a rule base of about 500 rules, MYCIN can recognize approximately 100 causes of bacterial infections, which allows the system to recommend effective drug prescriptions. In a controlled test, its performance was rated to be equal that of human specialists. The reasoning and uncertainty processing methods used in MYCIN are pioneers in the area and have generated long-term impact in ES development.

XCON XCON, a rule-based system developed at Digital Equipment Corp., used rules to help determine the optimal system configuration that fit customer requirements. The system was able to handle a customer request within 1 minute that typically took the sales team 20 to 30 minutes. With the ES, service accuracy increased to 98 percent, from a manual approach with an accuracy of 65 percent, saving millions of dollars every year.

Newer Applications of ES

More recent applications of ES include risk management, pension fund advising, business rule automation, automated market surveillance, and homeland security.

CREDIT ANALYSIS SYSTEMS ES have been developed to support the needs of commercial lending institutions. ES can help a lender analyze a customer's credit record and determine a proper credit line. Rules in the knowledge base can also help assess risk and risk-management policies. These kinds of systems are used in over one-third of the top 100 commercial banks in the United States and Canada.

PENSION FUND ADVISORS Nestlé Foods Corporation has developed an ES that provides information on an employee's pension fund status. The system maintains an up-to-date knowledge base to give participants advice concerning the impact of regulation changes and conformance with new standards. A system offered on the Internet at the Pingtung Teacher's College in Taiwan has functions that allow participants to plan their retirement through a what-if analysis that calculates their pension benefits under different scenarios.

AUTOMATED HELP DESKS BMC Remedy (**remedy.com**) offers HelpDeskIQ, a rule-based help desk solution for small businesses. This browser-based tool enables small businesses to deal with customer requests more efficiently. Incoming e-mails automatically pass into HelpDeskIQ's business rule engine. The messages are sent to the proper technician, based on defined priority and status. The solution assists help desk technicians in resolving problems and tracking issues more effectively.

HOMELAND SECURITY   PortBlue Corp. (**portblue.com/pub/solutions-homeland-security**) has developed an ES for homeland security. It is designed to assess terrorist threats and provide (1) an assessment of vulnerability to terrorist attack, (2) indicators of terrorist surveillance activity, and (3) guidance for managing interactions with potential terrorists. Similarly, the U.S. Internal Revenue Service uses intelligent systems to detect irregular international financial information and to block possible money laundering and terrorist financing.

MARKET SURVEILLANCE SYSTEMS   The National Association of Security Dealers (NASD) has developed an intelligent surveillance system called Securities Observation, New Analysis, and Regulations (SONAR) that uses data mining, rule-based inference, knowledge-based data representation, and NLP to monitor the stock markets and futures markets for suspicious patterns. The system generates 50 to 60 alerts per day for review by several groups of regulatory analysts and investigators (Goldberg et al., 2003).

BUSINESS PROCESS REENGINEERING SYSTEMS   Reengineering involves the exploitation of information technology to improve business processes. KBS are used in analyzing the workflow for business process reengineering. For example, Gensym's System Performance Analysis Using Real-Time Knowledge-based Simulation (SPARKS) can help model the formal and informal knowledge, skills, and competencies that must be embedded in a reengineered system. SPARKS has three components: a process flow model, a resource model, and work volumes and descriptions.

Areas for ES Applications

As indicated in the preceding examples, ES have been applied commercially in a number of areas, including the following:

- *Finance.*   Finance ES include insurance evaluation, credit analysis, tax planning, fraud prevention, financial report analysis, financial planning, and performance evaluation.
- *Data processing.*   Data processing ES include system planning, equipment selection, equipment maintenance, vendor evaluation, and network management.
- *Marketing.*   Marketing ES include customer relationship management, market analysis, product planning, and market planning.
- *Human resources.*   Examples of human resources ES are human resources planning, performance evaluation, staff scheduling, pension management, and legal advising.
- *Manufacturing.*   Manufacturing ES include production planning, quality management, product design, plant site selection, and equipment maintenance and repair.
- *Homeland security.*   Homeland security ES include terrorist threat assessment and terrorist finance detection.
- *Business process automation.*   ES have been developed for help desk automation, call center management, and regulation enforcement.
- *Health care management.*   ES have been developed for bioinformatics and other health care management issues.

Now that you are familiar with a variety of different ES applications, it is time to look at the internal structure of an ES and how the goals of the ES are achieved.

Section 12.5 Review Questions

1. What is MYCIN's problem domain?
2. Name two applications of ES in finance and describe their benefits.
3. Name two applications of ES in marketing and describe their benefits.
4. Name two applications of ES in homeland security and describe their benefits.

12.6 STRUCTURE OF EXPERT SYSTEMS

ES can be viewed as having two environments: the development environment and the consultation environment (see Figure 12.4). An ES builder uses the **development environment** to build the necessary components of the ES and to populate the knowledge base with appropriate representation of the expert knowledge. A nonexpert uses the **consultation environment** to obtain advice and to solve problems using the expert knowledge embedded into the system. These two environments can be separated at the end of the system development process.

The three major components that appear in virtually every ES are the knowledge base, the inference engine, and the user interface. In general, though, an ES that interacts with the user can contain the following additional components:

- Knowledge acquisition subsystem
- Blackboard (workplace)
- Explanation subsystem (justifier)
- Knowledge-refining system

Currently, most ES do not contain the knowledge refinement component. A brief description of each of these components follows.

Knowledge Acquisition Subsystem

Knowledge acquisition is the accumulation, transfer, and transformation of problem-solving expertise from experts or documented knowledge sources to a computer program

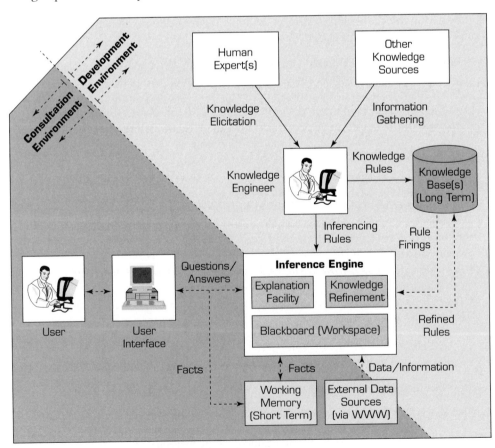

FIGURE 12.4 Structure/Architecture of an Expert System

for constructing or expanding the knowledge base. Potential sources of knowledge include human experts, textbooks, multimedia documents, databases (public and private), special research reports, and information available on the Web.

Currently, most organizations have collected a large volume of data, but the organization and management of organizational knowledge are limited. Knowledge acquisition deals with issues such as making tacit knowledge explicit and integrating knowledge from multiple sources.

Acquiring knowledge from experts is a complex task that often creates a bottleneck in ES construction. In building large systems, a knowledge engineer, or knowledge elicitation expert, needs to interact with one or more human experts in building the knowledge base. Typically, the **knowledge engineer** helps the expert structure the problem area by interpreting and integrating human answers to questions, drawing analogies, posing counterexamples, and bringing conceptual difficulties to light.

Knowledge Base

The **knowledge base** is the foundation of an ES. It contains the relevant knowledge necessary for understanding, formulating, and solving problems. A typical knowledge base may include two basic elements: (1) facts that describe the characteristics of a specific problem situation (or *fact base*) and the theory of the problem area and (2) special heuristics or rules (or *knowledge nuggets*) that represent the deep expert knowledge to solve specific problems in a particular domain. Additionally, the inference engine can include general-purpose problem-solving and decision-making rules (or *meta-rules*—rules about how to process production rules).

It is important to differentiate between the knowledge base of an ES and the knowledge base of an organization. The knowledge stored in the knowledge base of an ES is often represented in a special format so that it can be used by a software program (i.e., an expert system shell) to help users solve a particular problem. The organizational knowledge base, however, contains various kinds of knowledge in different formats (most of which is represented in a way that it can be consumed by people) and may be stored in different places. The knowledge base of an ES is a special case and only a very small subset of an organization's knowledge base.

Inference Engine

The "brain" of an ES is the inference engine, also known as the *control structure* or the *rule interpreter* (in rule-based ES). This component is essentially a computer program that provides a methodology for reasoning about information in the knowledge base and on the blackboard to formulate appropriate conclusions. The inference engine provides directions about how to use the system's knowledge by developing the agenda that organizes and controls the steps taken to solve problems whenever a consultation takes place. It is further discussed in Section 12.7.

User Interface

An ES contains a language processor for friendly, problem-oriented communication between the user and the computer, known as the **user interface**. This communication can best be carried out in a natural language. Due to technological constraints, most existing systems use the graphical or textual question-and-answer approach to interact with the user.

Blackboard (Workplace)

The **blackboard** is an area of working memory set aside as a database for description of the current problem, as characterized by the input data. It is also used for recording intermediate results, hypotheses, and decisions. Three types of decisions can be recorded on the blackboard: a plan (i.e., how to attack the problem), an agenda (i.e., potential actions awaiting execution), and a solution (i.e., candidate hypotheses and alternative courses of action that the system has generated thus far).

Consider this example. When your car fails to start, you can enter the symptoms of the failure into a computer for storage in the blackboard. As the result of an intermediate hypothesis developed in the blackboard, the computer may then suggest that you do some additional checks (e.g., see whether your battery is connected properly) and ask you to report the results. This information is also recorded in the blackboard. Such an iterative process of populating blackboard with values of hypotheses and facts continues until the reason of the failure is identified.

Explanation Subsystem (Justifier)

The ability to trace responsibility for conclusions to their sources is crucial both in the transfer of expertise and in problem solving. The **explanation subsystem** can trace such responsibility and explain the ES behavior by interactively answering questions such as these:

- Why was a certain question asked by the ES?
- How was a certain conclusion reached?
- Why was a certain alternative rejected?
- What is the complete plan of decisions to be made in reaching the conclusion? For example, what remains to be known before a final diagnosis can be determined?

In most ES, the first two questions (why and how) are answered by showing the rule that required asking a specific question and showing the sequence of rules that were used (fired) to derive the specific recommendations, respectively.

Knowledge-Refining System

Human experts have a **knowledge-refining system**; that is, they can analyze their own knowledge and its effectiveness, learn from it, and improve on it for future consultations. Similarly, such evaluation is necessary in expert systems so that a program can analyze the reasons for its success or failure, which could lead to improvements resulting in a more accurate knowledge base and more effective reasoning.

The critical component of a knowledge refinement system is the self-learning mechanism that allows it to adjust its knowledge base and its processing of knowledge based on the evaluation of its recent past performances. Such an intelligent component is not yet mature enough to appear in many commercial ES tools but is being developed in experimental ES at several universities and research institutions.

APPLICATION CASE 12.6

A Fashion Mix-and-Match Expert System

In today's highly competitive marketplace, fashion clothing retail businesses are looking for ways to meet and exceed customers' needs and wants. One strategy that is becoming a routine part of fashion retail businesses is providing customers with mix-and-match expert advice. Customers who like a particular article of clothing are often interested in other items that would fashionably go with it. Such advice enhances customer satisfaction (and loyalty) and also improves sales.

The mix-and-match recommendations are usually provided by individual sales personnel who have the necessary knowledge and experience in the latest fashion trends as well as on the available clothing items in the inventory. Good advisors are either hard to find or are prohibitively expensive for many smaller retailers. The characteristics of this problem resemble those addressed by many successful ES applications. By eliciting and representing the mix-and-match knowledge in the form of production rules, a capable expert system can be created.

Wong et al. (2009) developed an interesting ES to automate fashion mix-and-match advising. The fashion mix-and-match ES was developed to provide customers with professional and systematic mix-and-match recommendations automatically. Based on knowledge acquired from fashion designers, the system emulates the advising decisions on apparel coordination. A set of attributes of apparel coordination were identified and formulated, and their corresponding importance was defined according to the designers' opinions. Wong and colleagues devised a *fashion coordination satisfaction index* that uses a

fuzzy screening approach to represent the degree of coordination between pairs of apparel articles.

In order to automatically recognize clothing items, they proposed an item-level RFID system. When a customer picks a clothing item, the automated mix-and-match ES detects it via RFID and accesses the store database to query the characteristics that it needs to know about the item. The inference mechanism then takes over to advise on clothing items that match with the selection and the customer's taste. Their experimental results demonstrated that the proposed system can generate effective mix-and-match recommendations. The system has been integrated with a smart dressing system used in a fashion store in Hong Kong.

Source: W. K. Wong, X. H. Zeng, W. M. R. Au, P. Y. Moka, and S. Y. S. Leung, "A Fashion Mix-and-Match Expert System for Fashion Retailers Using a Fuzzy Screening Approach," *Expert Systems with Applications*, Vol. 36, 2009, pp. 1750–1764.

Section 12.6 Review Questions

1. Describe the ES development environment.
2. List and define the major components of an ES.
3. What are the major activities performed in the ES blackboard (workplace)?
4. What are the major roles of the explanation subsystem?
5. Describe the difference between a knowledge base of an ES and an organizational knowledge base.

12.7 KNOWLEDGE ENGINEERING

The collection of intensive activities encompassing the acquisition of knowledge from human experts (and other information sources) and conversion of this knowledge into a repository (commonly called a *knowledge base*) are called **knowledge engineering**. The term *knowledge engineering* was first defined in the pioneering work of Feigenbaum and McCorduck (1983) as the art of bringing the principles and tools of artificial intelligence research to bear on difficult application problems requiring the knowledge of experts for their solutions. Knowledge engineering requires cooperation and close communication between the human experts and the knowledge engineer to successfully codify and explicitly represent the rules (or other knowledge-based procedures) that a human expert uses to solve problems within a specific application domain. The knowledge possessed by human experts is often unstructured and not explicitly expressed. A major goal of knowledge engineering is to help experts articulate *how they do what they do* and to document this knowledge in a reusable form.

Knowledge engineering can be viewed from two perspectives: narrow and broad. According to the narrow perspective, knowledge engineering deals with the steps necessary to build expert systems (i.e., knowledge acquisition, knowledge representation, knowledge validation, inferencing, and explanation/justification). Alternatively, according to the broad perspective, the term describes the entire process of developing and maintaining any intelligent systems. In this book, we use the narrow definition. Following are the five major activities in knowledge engineering:

- ***Knowledge acquisition.*** Knowledge acquisition involves the acquisition of knowledge from human experts, books, documents, sensors, or computer files. The knowledge may be specific to the problem domain or to the problem-solving procedures, it may be general knowledge (e.g., knowledge about business), or it may be metaknowledge (knowledge about knowledge). (By *metaknowledge,* we mean information about how experts use their knowledge to solve problems and about problem-solving procedures in general.) Byrd (1995) formally verified that knowledge acquisition is the bottleneck in ES development today; thus, much theoretical and applied research is still being conducted in this area. An analysis of more than 90 ES applications and their knowledge acquisition techniques and methods is available in Wagner et al. (2003).
- ***Knowledge representation.*** Acquired knowledge is organized so that it will be ready for use, in an activity called knowledge representation. This activity involves preparation of a knowledge map and encoding of the knowledge in the knowledge base.
- ***Knowledge validation.*** Knowledge validation (or verification) involves validating and verifying the knowledge (e.g., by using test cases) until its quality is acceptable. Test results are usually shown to a domain expert to verify the accuracy of the ES.
- ***Inferencing.*** This activity involves the design of software to enable the computer to make inferences based on the stored knowledge and the specifics of a problem. The system can then provide advice to nonexpert users.
- ***Explanation and justification.*** This step involves the design and programming of an explanation capability (e.g., programming the ability to answer questions such as why a specific piece of information is needed by the computer or how a certain conclusion was derived by the computer).

Figure 12.5 shows the process of knowledge engineering and the relationships among the knowledge engineering activities. Knowledge engineers interact with human experts or collect documented knowledge from other sources in the knowledge acquisition stage. The acquired knowledge is then coded into a representation scheme to create a knowledge base. The knowledge engineer can collaborate with human experts or use test cases to verify and validate the knowledge base. The validated knowledge can be used in a knowledge-based system to solve new problems via machine inference and to explain the generated recommendation. Details of these activities are discussed in the following sections.

Knowledge Acquisition

Knowledge is a collection of specialized facts, procedures, and judgment usually expressed as rules. Knowledge can come from one or from many sources, such as books, films, computer databases, pictures, maps, stories, news articles, and sensors, as well as from human experts. Acquisition of knowledge from human experts (often called *knowledge elicitation*) is arguably the most valuable and most challenging task in knowledge acquisition. The classical knowledge elicitation methods, which are also called *manual methods*, include interviewing (i.e., structured, semistructured, unstructured), tracking the reasoning process, and observing. Because these manual methods are slow, expensive, and sometimes inaccurate, the ES community has been developing semi-automated and fully automated means to acquire knowledge. These

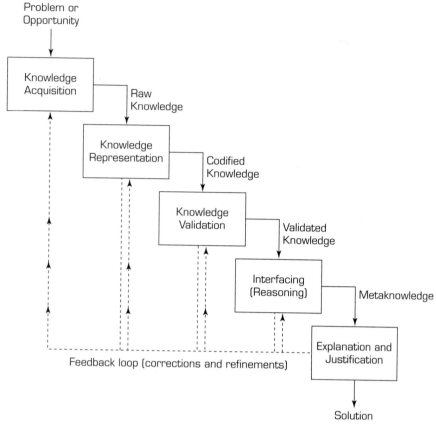

FIGURE 12.5   The Process of Knowledge Engineering

techniques, which rely on computers and AI techniques, aim to minimize the involvement of the knowledge engineer and the human experts in the process. Despite its disadvantages, in real-world ES projects the traditional knowledge elicitation techniques still dominate.

TECHNOLOGY INSIGHTS 12.3   Difficulties in Knowledge Acquisition

Acquiring knowledge from experts is not an easy task. The following are some factors that add to the complexity of knowledge acquisition from experts and its transfer to a computer:

- Experts may not know how to articulate their knowledge or may be unable to do so.
- Experts may lack time or may be unwilling to cooperate.
- Testing and refining knowledge are complicated.
- Methods for knowledge elicitation may be poorly defined.
- System builders tend to collect knowledge from one source, but the relevant knowledge may be scattered across several sources.
- System builders may attempt to collect documented knowledge rather than use experts. The knowledge collected may be incomplete.
- It is difficult to recognize specific knowledge when it is mixed up with irrelevant data.
- Experts may change their behavior when they are observed or interviewed.
- Problematic interpersonal communication factors may affect the knowledge engineer and the expert.

TABLE 12.4 Advantages and Shortcomings of Using Multiple Experts

Advantages	Shortcomings
• On average, multiple experts make fewer mistakes than a single expert.	• Fear on the part of some domain experts of senior experts or a supervisor (i.e., lack of confidentiality).
• Elimination of the need for finding and using the world-class expert (who is difficult to identify and acquire).	• Compromising solutions generated by a group with conflicting opinions.
• Wider domain than a single expert.	• Groupthink.
• Synthesis of expertise.	• Dominating experts (i.e., controlling, not letting others speak).
• Enhanced quality due to synergy among experts.	• Wasted time in group meetings and scheduling difficulties.

A critical element in the development of an ES is the identification of experts. The usual approach to mitigate this problem is to build ES for a very narrow application domain in which expertise is more clearly defined. Even then, there is a very good chance that one might find more than one expert with different (sometime conflicting) expertise. In such situations, one might choose to use multiple experts in the knowledge elicitation process. Some of the advantages and shortcomings of using multiple experts are listed in Table 12.4.

Four possible scenarios, or configurations, can be used when working with multiple experts (see O'Leary, 1993; and Rayham and Fairhurst, 1999): individual experts, primary and secondary experts, small groups, and panels. Each is described in the following list:

- **Individual experts.** In this case, several experts contribute knowledge individually. Using multiple experts in this manner relieves the knowledge engineer of the stress associated with multiple expert teams. However, this approach requires that the knowledge engineer have a means of resolving conflicts and handling multiple lines of reasoning.
- **Primary and secondary experts.** A primary expert may be responsible for validating information retrieved from other domain experts. Knowledge engineers may initially consult the primary expert for guidance in domain familiarization, refinement of knowledge acquisition plans, and identification of potential secondary experts.
- **Small groups.** Several experts may be consulted together and asked to provide agreed-upon information. Working with small groups of experts allows the knowledge engineer to observe alternative approaches to the solution of a problem and the key points made in solution-oriented discussions among experts.
- **Panels.** To meet goals for verification and validation of ongoing development efforts, a program may establish a council of experts. The members of the council typically meet together at times scheduled by the developer for the purpose of reviewing knowledge base development efforts, content, and plans. In many cases, the functionality of the ES is tested against the expertise of such a panel.

Knowledge Verification and Validation

Knowledge acquired from experts needs to be evaluated for quality, including evaluation, validation, and verification. These terms are often used interchangeably. We use the definitions provided by O'Keefe et al. (1987):

- *Evaluation* is a broad concept. Its objective is to assess an ES's overall value. In addition to assessing acceptable performance levels, it analyzes whether the system would be usable, efficient, and cost-effective.

- *Validation* is the part of evaluation that deals with the performance of the system (e.g., as it compares to the expert's). Simply stated, validation is building the right system (i.e., substantiating that a system performs with an acceptable level of accuracy).
- *Verification* is building the system right or substantiating that the system is correctly implemented to its specifications.

In the realm of ES, these activities are dynamic because they must be repeated each time the prototype is changed. In terms of the knowledge base, it is necessary to ensure that the right knowledge base (i.e., that the knowledge is valid) is used. It is also essential to ensure that the knowledge base has been constructed properly (i.e., verification).

Knowledge Representation

Once validated, the knowledge acquired from experts or induced from a set of data must be represented in a format that is both understandable by humans and executable on computers. A variety of knowledge representation methods is available: production rules, semantic networks, frames, objects, decision tables, decision trees, and predicate logic. Next we explain the most popular method—production rules.

PRODUCTION RULES   **Production rules** are the most popular form of knowledge representation for expert systems. Knowledge is represented in the form of condition/action pairs: IF this condition (or premise or antecedent) occurs, THEN some action (or result or conclusion or consequence) will (or should) occur. Consider the following two examples:

- If the stop light is red AND you have stopped, THEN a right turn is okay.
- If the client uses purchase requisition forms AND the purchase orders are approved and purchasing is separate from receiving AND accounts payable AND inventory records, THEN there is strongly suggestive evidence (90 percent probability) that controls to prevent unauthorized purchases are adequate. (This example from an internal control procedure includes a probability.)

Each production rule in a knowledge base implements an autonomous chunk of expertise that can be developed and modified independently of other rules. When combined and fed to the inference engine, the set of rules behaves synergistically, yielding better results than the sum of the results of the individual rules. In some sense, rules can be viewed as a simulation of the cognitive behavior of human experts. According to this view, rules are not just a neat formalism to represent knowledge in a computer; rather, they represent a model of actual human behavior.

KNOWLEDGE AND INFERENCE RULES   Two types of rules are common in artificial intelligence: knowledge and inference. **Knowledge rules**, or *declarative rules,* state all the facts and relationships about a problem. **Inference rules**, or *procedural rules,* offer advice on how to solve a problem, given that certain facts are known. The knowledge engineer separates the two types of rules: Knowledge rules go to the knowledge base, whereas inference rules become part of the inference engine. For example, assume that you are in the business of buying and selling gold. The knowledge rules might look like this:

Rule 1: IF an international conflict begins, THEN the price of gold goes up.

Rule 2: IF the inflation rate declines, THEN the price of gold goes down.

Rule 3: IF the international conflict lasts more than 7 days and IF it is in the Middle East, THEN buy gold.

Inference rules contain rules about rules and thus are also called meta-rules. They pertain to other rules (or even to themselves). Inference (procedural) rules may look like this:

Rule 1: IF the data needed are not in the system, THEN request them from the user.

Rule 2: IF more than one rule applies, THEN deactivate any rules that add no new data.

Inferencing

Inferencing (or reasoning) is the process of using the rules in the knowledge base along with the known facts to draw conclusions. Inferencing requires some logic embedded in a computer program to access and manipulate the stored knowledge. This program is an algorithm that, with the guidance of the inferencing rules, controls the reasoning process and is usually called the **inference engine**. In rule-based systems, it is also called the *rule interpreter*.

The inference engine directs the search through the collection of rules in the knowledge base, a process commonly called *pattern matching*. In inferencing, when all of the hypotheses (the "IF" parts) of a rule are satisfied, the rule is said to be fired. Once a rule is fired, the new knowledge generated by the rule (the conclusion or the validation of the THEN part) is inserted into the memory as a new fact. The inference engine checks every rule in the knowledge base to identify those that can be fired based on what is known at that point in time (the collection of known facts), and keeps doing so until the goal is achieved. The most popular inferencing mechanisms for rule-based systems are forward and backward chaining:

- **Backward chaining** is a goal-driven approach in which you start from an expectation of what is going to happen (i.e., hypothesis) and then seek evidence that supports (or contradicts) your expectation. Often, this entails formulating and testing intermediate hypotheses (or subhypotheses).
- **Forward chaining** is a data-driven approach. We start from available information as it becomes available or from a basic idea, and then we try to draw conclusions. The ES analyzes the problem by looking for the facts that match the IF part of its IF-THEN rules. For example, if a certain machine is not working, the computer checks the electricity flow to the machine. As each rule is tested, the program works its way toward one or more conclusions.

FORWARD AND BACKWARD CHAINING EXAMPLE Here we discuss an example involving an investment decision about whether to invest in IBM stock. The following variables are used:

A = Have $10,000

B = Younger than 30

C = Education at college level

D = Annual income of at least $40,000

E = Invest in securities

F = Invest in growth stocks

G = Invest in IBM stock (the potential goal)

Each of these variables can be answered as true (yes) or false (no).

We assume that an investor has $10,000 (i.e., that A is true) and that she is 25 years old (i.e., that B is true). She would like advice on investing in IBM stock (yes or no for the goal). Our knowledge base includes the following five rules:

R1: IF a person has $10,000 to invest and she has a college degree,

THEN she should invest in securities.

R2: IF a person's annual income is at least $40,000 and she has a college degree,
   THEN she should invest in growth stocks.

R3: IF a person is younger than 30 and she is investing in securities,
   THEN she should invest in growth stocks.

R4: IF a person is younger than 30,
   THEN she has a college degree.

R5: IF a person wants to invest in a growth stock,
   THEN the stock should be IBM.

These rules can be written as follows:

R1: IF A and C, THEN E.
R2: IF D and C, THEN F.
R3: IF B and E, THEN F.
R4: IF B, THEN C.
R5: IF F, THEN G.

Backward Chaining   Our goal is to determine whether to invest in IBM stock. With backward chaining, we start by looking for a rule that includes the goal (G) in its conclusion (THEN) part. Because R5 is the only one that qualifies, we start with it. If several rules contain G, then the inference engine dictates a procedure for handling the situation. This is what we do:

1. Try to accept or reject G. The ES goes to the assertion base to see whether G is there. At present, all we have in the assertion base is A is true. B is true. Therefore, the ES proceeds to step 2.
2. R5 says that if it is true that we invest in growth stocks (F), then we should invest in IBM (G). If we can conclude that the premise of R5 is either true or false, then we have solved the problem. However, we do not know whether F is true. What shall we do now? Note that F, which is the premise of R5, is also the conclusion of R2 and R3. Therefore, to find out whether F is true, we must check either of these two rules.
3. We try R2 first (arbitrarily); if both D and C are true, then F is true. Now we have a problem. D is not a conclusion of any rule, nor is it a fact. The computer can either move to another rule or try to find out whether D is true by asking the investor for whom the consultation is given if her annual income is above $40,000. What the ES does depends on the search procedures used by the inference engine. Usually, a user is asked for additional information only if the information is not available or cannot be deduced. We abandon R2 and return to the other rule, R3. This action is called *backtracking* (i.e., knowing that we are at a dead end, we try something else; the computer must be preprogrammed to handle backtracking).
4. Go to R3; test B and E. We know that B is true because it is a given fact. To prove E, we go to R1, where E is the conclusion.
5. Examine R1. It is necessary to determine whether A and C are true.
6. A is true because it is a given fact. To test C, it is necessary to test R4 (where C is the conclusion).
7. R4 tells us that C is true (because B is true). Therefore, C becomes a fact (and is added to the assertion base). Now E is true, which validates F, which validates our goal (i.e., the advice is to invest in IBM).

Note that during the search, the ES moved from the THEN part to the IF part, back to the THEN part, and so on (see Figure 12.6 for a graphical depiction of the backward chaining).

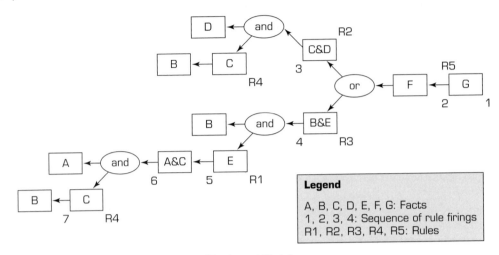

FIGURE 12.6 A Graphical Depiction of Backward Chaining

Forward Chaining   Let us use the same example we examined in backward chaining to illustrate the process of forward chaining. In forward chaining, we start with known facts and derive new facts by using rules having known facts on the IF side. The specific steps that forward chaining would follow in this example are as follows (also see Figure 12.7 for a graphical depiction of this process):

1. Because it is known that A and B are true, the ES starts deriving new facts by using rules that have A and B on the IF side. Using R4, the ES derives a new fact C and adds it to the assertion base as true.
2. R1 fires (because A and C are true) and asserts E as true in the assertion base.
3. Because B and E are both known to be true (they are in the assertion base), R3 fires and establishes F as true in the assertion base.
4. R5 fires (because F is on its IF side), which establishes G as true. So the ES recommends an investment in IBM stock. If there is more than one conclusion, more rules may fire, depending on the inferencing procedure.

INFERENCING WITH UNCERTAINTY   Although uncertainty is widespread in the real world, its treatment in the practical world of artificial intelligence is very limited. One could argue that

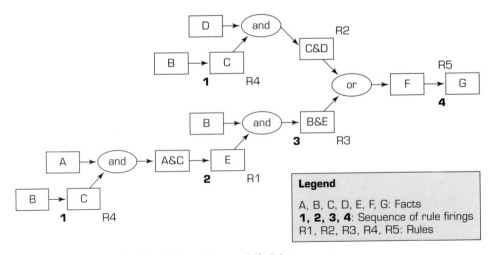

FIGURE 12.7 A Graphical Depiction of Forward Chaining

because the knowledge provided by experts is often inexact an ES that mimics the reasoning process of experts should represent such uncertainty. ES researchers have proposed several methods to incorporate uncertainty into the reasoning process, including probability ratios, the Bayesian approach, fuzzy logic, the Dempster–Shafer theory of evidence, and the theory of certainty factors. Following is a brief description of the theory of certainty factors, which is the most commonly used method to accommodate uncertainty in ES.

The **theory of certainty factors** is based on the concepts of belief and disbelief. The standard statistical methods are based on the assumption that an uncertainty is the probability that an event (or fact) is true or false, whereas certainty theory is based on the *degrees of belief* (not the calculated probability) that an event (or fact) is true or false.

Certainty theory relies on the use of certainty factors. **Certainty factors (CF)** express belief in an event (or a fact or a hypothesis) based on the expert's assessment. Certainty factors can be represented by values ranging from 0 to 100; the smaller the value the lower the probability that the event (or fact) is true or false. Because certainty factors are not probabilities, when we say that there is a certainty value of 90 for rain, we do not mean (or imply) any opinion about no rain (which is not necessarily 10). Thus, certainty factors do not have to sum up to 100.

Combining Certainty Factors   Certainty factors can be used to combine estimates by different experts in several ways. Before using any ES shell, you need to make sure that you understand how certainty factors are combined. The most acceptable way of combining them in rule-based systems is the method used in EMYCIN. In this approach, we distinguish between two cases, described next.

Combining Several Certainty Factors in One Rule   Consider the following rule with an AND operator:

IF inflation is high, CF = 50 (A)

　　AND unemployment rate is above 7 percent, CF = 70 (B)

　　AND bond prices decline, CF = 100 (C),

THEN stock prices decline.

For this type of rule, all IFs must be true for the conclusion to be true. However, in some cases, there is uncertainty as to what is happening. Then the CF of the conclusion is the minimum CF on the IF side:

$$CF(A, B, C) = minimum[CF(A), CF(B), CF(C)]$$

Thus, in our case, the CF for stock prices to decline is 50 percent. In other words, the chain is as strong as its weakest link.

Now look at this rule with an OR operator:

IF inflation is low, CF = 70 percent

　　OR bond prices are high, CF = 85,

THEN stock prices will be high.

In this case, it is sufficient that only one of the IFs is true for the conclusion to be true. Thus, if both IFs are believed to be true (at their certainty factor), then the conclusion will have a CF with the maximum of the two:

$$CF (A \text{ or } B) = maximum [CF (A), CF (B)]$$

In our case, CF must be 85 for stock prices to be high. Note that both cases hold for any number of IFs.

Combining Two or More Rules   Why might rules be combined? There may be several ways to reach the same goal, each with different certainty factors for a given set of facts. When we have a knowledge-based system with several interrelated rules, each of which makes the same conclusion but with a different certainty factor, each rule can be viewed as a piece of evidence that supports the joint conclusion. To calculate the certainty factor (or the confidence) of the conclusion, it is necessary to combine the evidence. For example, let us assume that there are two rules:

> R1: IF the inflation rate is less than 5 percent,
>
> > THEN stock market prices go up (CF = 0.7).
>
> R2: IF the unemployment level is less than 7 percent,
>
> > THEN stock market prices go up (CF = 0.6).

Now let us assume a prediction that during the next year, the inflation rate will be 4 percent and the unemployment level will be 6.5 percent (i.e., we assume that the premises of the two rules are true). The combined effect is computed as follows:

$$CF(R1, R2) = CF(R1) + CF(R2) \times [1 - CF(R1)]$$

$$= CF(R1) + CF(R2) - [CF(R1) \times CF(R2)]$$

In this example, given CF(R1) = 0.7 and CF(R2) = 0.6

$$CF(R1, R2) = 0.7 + 0.6 - [(0.7) \times (0.6)] = 0.88$$

If we add a third rule, we can use the following formula:

$$CF(R1, R2, R3) = CF(R1, R2) + CF(R3) \times [1 - CF(R1, R2)]$$

$$= CF(R1, R2) + CF(R3) - [CF(R1, R2) \times CF(R3)]$$

In our example:

> R3: IF bond price increases,
>
> > THEN stock prices go up (CF = 0.85)

$$CF(R1, R2, R3) = 0.88 + 0.85 - [(0.88) \times (0.85)] = 0.982$$

Note that CF(R1,R2) was computed earlier as 0.88. For a situation with more rules, we can apply the same formula incrementally.

Explanation and Justification

A final feature of expert systems is their interactivity with users and their capacity to provide an explanation consisting of the sequence of inferences that were made by the system in arriving at a conclusion. This feature offers a means of evaluating the integrity of the system when it is to be used by the experts themselves. Two basic types of explanations are the why and the how. Metaknowledge is knowledge about knowledge. It is a structure within the system using the domain knowledge to accomplish the system's problem-solving strategy. This section deals with different methods used in ES for generating explanations.

Human experts are often asked to explain their views, recommendations, or decisions. If ES are to mimic humans in performing highly specialized tasks, they, too, need to justify and explain their actions. An explanation is an attempt by an ES to clarify its reasoning, recommendations, or other actions (e.g., asking a question). The part of an ES that provides explanations is called an *explanation facility* (or *justifier*). The explanation facility has several purposes:

- Make the system more intelligible to the user.
- Uncover the shortcomings of the rules and knowledge base (i.e., debugging of the systems by the knowledge engineer).
- Explain situations that were unanticipated by the user.
- Satisfy psychological and social needs by helping the user feel more assured about the actions of the ES.
- Clarify the assumptions underlying the system's operations to both the user and the builder.
- Conduct sensitivity analyses. (Using the explanation facility as a guide, the user can predict and test the effects of changes on the system.)

Explanation in rule-based ES is usually associated with a way of tracing the rules that are fired during the course of a problem-solving session. This is about the closest to a real explanation that today's systems come, given that their knowledge is usually represented almost exclusively as rules that do not include basic principles necessary for a human-type explanation. Though many explanations have been proposed, in the following section we provide brief descriptions for the two most common types: the why and the how explanations.

WHY EXPLANATIONS   A user poses a typical "why?" question to a computer after the computer asks the user to provide some information. For example, using our earlier investment example, we might have the following dialogue:

COMPUTER: What is your annual income?

CLIENT: Why? (Why do you need to know?)

COMPUTER: R2; meaning "In checking R2, I need to know whether your income is above $40,000. If this is true, I will conclude that because you have a college degree, you should invest in growth stocks."

HOW EXPLANATIONS   A user poses a typical "how?" question when he or she would like to know how a certain conclusion or recommendation was reached. Simple systems are limited to the final conclusion. More complex systems can handle intermediate conclusions as well. The system can explain why a certain rule was fired; that is, it shows the chain of rules used to reach the conclusion. In the investment problem, the how explanation might look like this:

COMPUTER: Invest in IBM stocks.

CLIENT: How? (How was the conclusion reached?)

COMPUTER: R5–R3–R7–R4; meaning "Given that you have $10,000 to invest and you are younger than 30, then according to R4, you have a college degree. If this is the case, then according to R1, you should invest in securities. For a young investor like you, according to R3, you should invest in growth stocks if you are going to invest at all. Finally, according to R5, if you need to invest in growth stocks, then IBM is your best bet."

The why and how explanations often show the rules as they were programmed and not in a natural language. However, some systems have the capability to present these rules in natural language.

Section 12.7 Review Questions

1. State two production rules that can represent the knowledge of repairing your car.
2. Describe how ES perform inference.
3. Describe the reasoning procedures of forward chaining and backward chaining.
4. List the three most popular methods to deal with uncertainty in ES.
5. Why do we need to incorporate uncertainty in ES solutions?
6. What are the ways by which ES justify their knowledge?

12.8 PROBLEM AREAS SUITABLE FOR EXPERT SYSTEMS

ES can be classified in several ways. One way is by the general problem areas they address. For example, diagnosis can be defined as "inferring system malfunctions from observations." *Diagnosis* is a generic activity performed in medicine, organizational studies, computer operations, and so on. The generic categories of ES are listed in Table 12.5. Some ES belong to two or more of these categories. A brief description of each category follows:

- *Interpretation systems.* Systems that infer situation descriptions from observations. This category includes surveillance, speech understanding, image analysis, signal interpretation, and many kinds of intelligence analyses. An interpretation system explains observed data by assigning them symbolic meanings that describe the situation.
- *Prediction systems.* These systems include weather forecasting; demographic predictions; economic forecasting; traffic predictions; crop estimates; and military, marketing, and financial forecasting.
- *Diagnostic systems.* These systems include medical, electronic, mechanical, and software diagnoses. Diagnostic systems typically relate observed behavioral irregularities to underlying causes.
- *Design systems.* These systems develop configurations of objects that satisfy the constraints of the design problem. Such problems include circuit layout, building design, and plant layout. Design systems construct descriptions of objects in various relationships with one another and verify that these configurations conform to stated constraints.
- *Planning systems.* These systems specialize in planning problems, such as automatic programming. They also deal with short- and long-term planning in areas such as project management, routing, communications, product development, military applications, and financial planning.

TABLE 12.5 Generic Categories of Expert Systems

Category	Problem Addressed
Interpretation	Inferring situation descriptions from observations
Prediction	Inferring likely consequences of given situations
Diagnosis	Inferring system malfunctions from observations
Design	Configuring objects under constraints
Planning	Developing plans to achieve goals
Monitoring	Comparing observations to plans and flagging exceptions
Debugging	Prescribing remedies for malfunctions
Repair	Executing a plan to administer a prescribed remedy
Instruction	Diagnosing, debugging, and correcting student performance
Control	Interpreting, predicting, repairing, and monitoring system behaviors

- **Monitoring systems.** These systems compare observations of system behavior with standards that seem crucial for successful goal attainment. These crucial features correspond to potential flaws in the plan. There are many computer-aided monitoring systems for topics ranging from air traffic control to fiscal management tasks.
- **Debugging systems.** These systems rely on planning, design, and prediction capabilities for creating specifications or recommendations to correct a diagnosed problem.
- **Repair systems.** These systems develop and execute plans to administer a remedy for certain diagnosed problems. Such systems incorporate debugging, planning, and execution capabilities.
- **Instruction systems.** Systems that incorporate diagnosis and debugging subsystems that specifically address students' needs. Typically, these systems begin by constructing a hypothetical description of the student's knowledge that interprets her or his behavior. They then diagnose weaknesses in the student's knowledge and identify appropriate remedies to overcome the deficiencies. Finally, they plan a tutorial interaction intended to deliver remedial knowledge to the student.
- **Control systems.** Systems that adaptively govern the overall behavior of a system. To do this, a control system must repeatedly interpret the current situation, predict the future, diagnose the causes of anticipated problems, formulate a remedial plan, and monitor its execution to ensure success.

Not all the tasks usually found in each of these categories are suitable for ES. However, thousands of decisions do fit into these categories.

APPLICATION CASE 12.7

Monitoring Water Quality with Sensor-Driven Expert Systems

Environmental concerns are becoming increasingly more important around the world. Constant monitoring of environmental conditions is a challenging task, but a necessary one. If the authorities and organizations involved in the management of environmental resources were able to examine quantitative and qualitative parameters related to environmental conditions, they then might be able to predict undesirable situations and to draw conclusions about adverse trends, enabling them to take countermeasures to prevent catastrophes in a timely fashion.

Hatzikos et al. (2007) described an environmental expert system that monitors seawater quality and pollution in northern Greece through a sensor network called Andromeda. The expert system monitors data collected by sensors at local monitoring stations and reasons about the suitability of water for various uses, such as swimming and cultivation of fish. The sensor data is collected periodically (at different parts of the sea) and transmitted to the evaluation system via a wireless network. The sensors transmit data on the following to the expert system:

- pH
- Temperature
- Conductance
- Salinity
- Dissolved oxygen
- Turbidity

The expert system uses fuzzy logic (see Chapter 13) to infer about the combination of the sensor input values to identify certain environmental conditions and to create and disseminate appropriate alerts. Authorities hope that the expert system will help them make decisions in their battles against water pollution, which is vital for public health and the local economy.

Source: E. V. Hatzikos, N. Bassiliades, L. Asmanis, and I. Vlahavas, "Monitoring Water Quality Through a Telematic Sensor Network and a Fuzzy Expert System," *Expert Systems,* Vol. 24, No. 3, 2007, pp. 143–161.

Section 12.8 Review Questions

1. Describe a sample ES application for prediction.
2. Describe a sample ES application for diagnosis.
3. Describe a sample ES application for the rest of the generic ES categories.

12.9 DEVELOPMENT OF EXPERT SYSTEMS

The development of ES is a tedious process and typically includes defining the nature and scope of the problem, identifying proper experts, acquiring knowledge, selecting the building tools, coding the system, and evaluating the system.

Defining the Nature and Scope of the Problem

The first step in developing an ES is to identify the nature of the problem and to define its scope. Some domains may not be appropriate for the application of ES. For example, a problem that can be solved by using mathematical optimization algorithms is often inappropriate for ES. In general, rule-based ES are appropriate when the nature of the problem is qualitative, knowledge is explicit, and experts are available to solve the problem effectively and provide their knowledge.

Another important factor is to define a feasible scope. The current technology is still very limited and is capable of solving relatively simple problems. Therefore, the scope of the problem should be specific and reasonably narrow. For example, it may be possible to develop an ES for detecting abnormal trading behavior and possible money laundering, but it is not possible to use an ES to determine whether a particular transaction is criminal.

Identifying Proper Experts

After the nature and scope of the problem have been clearly defined, the next step is to find proper experts who have the knowledge and are willing to assist in developing the knowledge base. No ES can be designed without the strong support of knowledgeable and supportive experts. A project may identify one expert or a group of experts. A proper expert should have a thorough understanding of problem-solving knowledge, the role of ES and decision support technology, and good communication skills.

Acquiring Knowledge

After identifying helpful experts, it is necessary to start acquiring decision knowledge from them. The process of eliciting knowledge is called *knowledge engineering*. The person who is interacting with experts to document the knowledge is called a *knowledge engineer*.

Knowledge acquisition is a time-consuming and risky process. Experts may be unwilling to provide their knowledge for various reasons. First, their knowledge may be proprietary and valuable. Experts may not be willing to share their knowledge without a reasonable payoff. Second, even though an expert is willing to share, certain knowledge is tacit, and the expert may not have the skill to clearly dictate the decision rules and considerations. Third, experts may be too busy to have enough time to communicate with the knowledge engineer. Fourth, certain knowledge may be confusing or contradictory in nature. Finally, the knowledge engineer may misunderstand the expert and inaccurately document knowledge.

The result of knowledge acquisition is a knowledge base that can be represented in different formats. The most popular one is if-then rules. The knowledge may also be represented as decision trees or decision tables. The knowledge in the knowledge base must be evaluated for its consistency and applicability.

Selecting the Building Tools

After the knowledge base is built, the next step is to choose a proper tool for implementing the system. There are three different kinds of development tools, as described in the following sections.

GENERAL-PURPOSE DEVELOPMENT ENVIRONMENT The first type of tool is general-purpose computer languages, such as C++, Prolog, and LISP. Most computer programming languages support the if-then statement. Therefore, it is possible to use C++ to develop an ES for a particular problem domain (e.g., disease diagnosis). Because these programming languages do not have built-in inference capabilities, using them in this way is often very costly and time consuming. Prolog and LISP are two languages for developing intelligent systems. It is easier to use them than to use C++, but they are still specifically designed for professional programmers and are not very friendly. For recent Web-based applications, Java and computer languages that support Web services (such as the Microsoft .NET platform) are also useful.

ES SHELLS The second type of development tool, the **expert system (ES) shell**, is specifically designed for ES development. An ES shell has built-in inference capabilities and a user interface, but the knowledge base is empty. System development is therefore a process of feeding the knowledge base with rules elicited from the expert.

A popular ES shell is the Corvid system developed by Exsys (**exsys.com**). The system is an object-oriented development platform that is composed of three types of operations: variables, logic blocks, and command blocks. Variables define the major factors considered in problem solving. Logic blocks are the decision rules acquired from experts. Command blocks determine how the system interacts with the user, including the order of execution and the user interface. Figure 12.8 shows a screenshot of a logic block that shows the decision rules. More products are available from business rules management vendors, such as Haley (**haley.com**), ILOG (**ilog.com**), and LPA's VisiRule (**lpa.co.uk/vsr.htm**), which is based on a general-purpose tool called Micro-Prolog.

TAILORED TURN-KEY SOLUTIONS The third tool, a tailored turn-key tool, is tailored to a specific domain and can be adapted to a similar application very quickly. Basically, a tailored turn-key tool contains specific features often required for developing applications in a particular domain. This tool must adjust or modify the base system by tailoring the user interface or a relatively small portion of the system to meet the unique needs of an organization. For example, both Haley and ILOG offer various tailor-made solutions for insurance, medical, scheduling, and homeland security applications.

CHOOSING AN ES DEVELOPMENT TOOL Choosing among these tools for ES development depends on a few criteria. First, you need to consider the cost benefits. Tailored turn-key solutions are the most expensive option. However, you need to consider the total cost, not just the cost of the tool. Second, you need to consider the technical functionality and flexibility of the tool; that is, you need to determine whether the tool provides the function you need and how easily it allows the development team to make necessary changes. Third, you need to consider the tool's compatibility with the existing information infrastructure in the organization. Most organizations have many existing applications, and the tool must be compatible with those applications and needs to be able to be integrated as part of the entire information infrastructure. Finally, you need to consider the reliability of the tool and vendor support. The vendor's experiences in similar domains and training programs are critical to the success of an ES project.

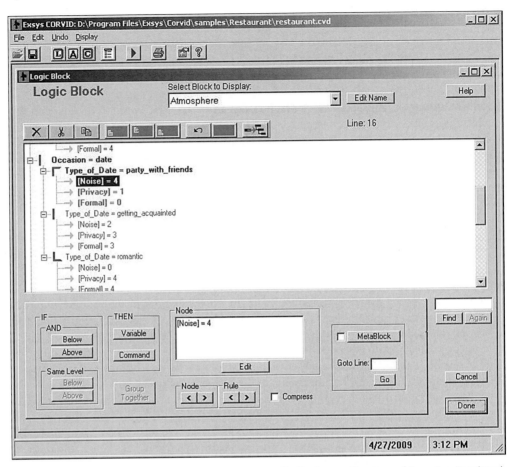

FIGURE 12.8 A Screenshot from Corvid Expert System Shell *Source:* Courtesy of Exsys Inc. Reprinted with permission.

Coding the System

After choosing a proper tool, the development team can focus on coding the knowledge based on the tool's syntactic requirements. The major concern at this stage is whether the coding process is efficient and properly managed to avoid errors. Skilled programmers are helpful and important.

Evaluating the System

After an ES system is built, it must be evaluated. Evaluation includes both verification and validation. Verification ensures that the resulting knowledge base contains knowledge exactly the same as that acquired from the expert. In other words, verification ensures that no error occurred at the coding stage. Validation ensures that the system can solve the problem correctly. In other words, validation checks whether the knowledge acquired from the expert can indeed solve the problem effectively.

Section 12.9 Review Questions

1. Describe the major steps in developing rule-based ES.
2. What are the necessary conditions for a good expert?
3. Compare three different types of tools for developing ES.
4. List the criteria for choosing a development tool.
5. What is the difference between verification and validation of an ES?

12.10 BENEFITS, LIMITATIONS, AND CRITICAL SUCCESS FACTORS OF EXPERT SYSTEMS

Thousands of ES are in use today in almost every industry and in every functional area. For example, Eom (1996) prepared a comprehensive survey of about 440 operational ES in business. His survey revealed that many ES have a profound impact, shrinking the time for tasks from days to hours, minutes, or seconds, and that nonquantifiable benefits include improved customer satisfaction, improved quality of products and services, and accurate and consistent decision making. ES in finance and in engineering applications are described in Nedovic and Devedzic (2002) and Nurminen et al. (2003). For many firms, ES have become indispensable tools for effective management, but the application of ES may also have limitations. In this section, we outline the major benefits and limitations of this technology.

Benefits and Limitations of ES

The use of ES can create benefits and at the same time incur limitations, as explained in the following sections.

BENEFITS OF ES   The following are some of the benefits of ES:

- *Increased output and productivity.* ES can work faster than humans can. For example, the classic XCON enabled Digital Equipment Corp. to increase the throughput of its popular VAX minicomputers configuration orders fourfold.
- *Decreased decision-making time.* Using the recommendations of an ES, a human can make decisions much faster. For example, American Express can now make charge approval decisions in less than 5 seconds, compared to about 3 minutes before implementation of an ES. This property is important in supporting frontline decision makers who must make quick decisions while interacting with customers.
- *Increased process and product quality.* ES can increase quality by providing consistent advice and reducing the size and rate of errors. For example, XCON reduced the error rate of configuring computer orders from 35 to 2 percent and then even less, thus improving the quality of the minicomputers.
- *Reduced downtime.* Many operational ES are used for diagnosing malfunctions and prescribing repairs. By using ES, it is possible to reduce machine downtime significantly. For example, on an oil rig 1 day of lost time can cost as much as $250,000. A system called DRILLING ADVISOR was developed to detect malfunctions in oil rigs. This system saved a considerable amount of money for the company by significantly reducing downtime.
- *Capture of scarce expertise.* The scarcity of expertise becomes evident in situations in which there are not enough experts for a task, the expert is about to retire or leave the job, or expertise is required over a broad geographic area. For example, more than 30 percent of all requests for authorization of benefits are approved automatically through eCare, enabling CIGNA Behavioral Health to handle more requests with its existing staff.
- *Flexibility.* ES can offer flexibility in both the service and manufacturing industries.
- *Easier equipment operation.* An ES makes complex equipment easier to operate. For example, Steamer was an early ES used to train inexperienced workers to operate complex ship engines. Another example is an ES developed for Shell Oil Company to train people to use complex computer program routines.
- *Elimination of the need for expensive equipment.* Often, a human must rely on expensive instruments for monitoring and control. ES can perform the same

tasks with lower-cost instruments because of their ability to investigate the information provided more thoroughly and quickly.

- *Operation in hazardous environments.* Many tasks require humans to work in hazardous environments. An ES can allow humans to avoid such environments. They can enable workers to avoid hot, humid, or toxic environments, such as a nuclear power plant that has malfunctioned. This feature is extremely important in military conflicts.

- *Accessibility to knowledge and help desks.* ES make knowledge accessible, thus freeing experts from routine work. People can query systems and receive useful advice. One area of applicability is the support of help desks, such as the HelpDeskIQ system offered by BMC Remedy.

- *Ability to work with incomplete or uncertain information.* In contrast to conventional computer systems, ES can, like human experts, work with incomplete, imprecise, and uncertain data, information, or knowledge. The user can respond with "don't know" or "not sure" to one or more of the system's questions during a consultation, and the ES can produce an answer, although it may not be a certain one.

- *Provision of training.* ES can provide training. Novices who work with ES become more and more experienced. The explanation facility can also serve as a teaching device, as can notes and explanations that can be inserted into the knowledge base.

- *Enhancement of problem solving and decision making.* ES enhance problem solving by allowing the integration of top experts' judgment into the analysis. For example, an ES called Statistical Navigator was developed to help novices use complex statistical computer packages.

- *Improved decision-making processes.* ES provide rapid feedback on decision consequences, facilitate communication among decision makers on a team, and allow rapid response to unforeseen changes in the environment, thus providing a better understanding of the decision-making situation.

- *Improved decision quality.* ES are reliable. They do not become tired or bored, call in sick, or go on strike, and they do not talk back to the boss. ES also consistently pay attention to all details and do not overlook relevant information and potential solutions, thereby making fewer errors. In addition, ES provide the same recommendations to repeated problems.

- *Ability to solve complex problems.* One day, ES may explain complex problems whose solutions are beyond human ability. Some ES are already able to solve problems in which the required scope of knowledge exceeds that of any one individual. This allows decision makers to gain control over complicated situations and improve the operation of complex systems.

- *Knowledge transfer to remote locations.* One of the greatest potential benefits of ES is its ease of transfer across international boundaries. An example of such a transfer is an eye care ES for diagnosis and recommended treatment, developed at Rutgers University in conjunction with the World Health Organization. The program has been implemented in Egypt and Algeria, where serious eye diseases are prevalent but eye specialists are rare. The PC program is rule based and can be operated by a nurse, a physician's assistant, or a general practitioner. The Web is used extensively to disseminate information to users in remote locations. The U.S. government, for example, places advisory systems about safety and other topics on its Web sites.

- *Enhancement of other information systems.* ES can often be found providing intelligent capabilities to other information systems. Many of these benefits lead to improved decision making, improved products and customer service, and a sustainable strategic advantage. Some may even enhance an organization's image.

PROBLEMS AND LIMITATIONS OF ES Available ES methodologies may not be straightforward and effective, even for many applications in the generic categories. The following problems have slowed the commercial spread of ES:

- Knowledge is not always readily available.
- It can be difficult to extract expertise from humans.
- The approach of each expert to a situation assessment may be different, yet correct.
- It is difficult, even for a highly skilled expert, to abstract good situational assessments when under time pressure.
- Users of ES have natural cognitive limits.
- ES work well only within a narrow domain of knowledge.
- Most experts have no independent means of checking whether their conclusions are reasonable.
- The vocabulary, or jargon, that experts use to express facts and relations is often limited and not understood by others.
- Help is often required from knowledge engineers who are rare and expensive, and this could make ES construction costly.
- Lack of trust on the part of end users may be a barrier to ES use.
- Knowledge transfer is subject to a host of perceptual and judgmental biases.
- ES may not be able to arrive at conclusions in some cases. For example, the initial fully developed XCON system could not fulfill about 2 percent of the orders presented to it. Human experts must step in to resolve these problems.
- ES, like human experts, sometimes produce incorrect recommendations.

The Web is a major facilitator of ES that overcomes several of these limitations. The ability to disseminate ES to the masses makes them more cost-effective. Consequently, more money can be spent on better systems.

Gill (1995) discovered that only about one-third of all commercial ES studied survived over a 5-year period. The short-lived nature of so many systems was generally not attributable to failure to meet technical performance or economic objectives. Instead, managerial issues—such as lack of system acceptance by users, inability to retain developers, problems in transitioning from development to maintenance, and shifts in organizational priorities—appeared to be the most significant factors resulting in long-term ES disuse. Proper management of ES development and deployment can resolve most of these issues in practice.

These limitations clearly indicate that some ES fall short of generally intelligent human behavior. Although there is no recent follow-up research, the rapid progress of information technology can reduce the possibility of failure, and several of these limitations will diminish or disappear with technological improvements over time.

Critical Success Factors for ES

Several researchers have investigated the reasons ES succeed and fail in practice. As with many MIS, a number of studies have shown that the level of managerial and user involvement directly affects the success level of MIS, specifically ES. However, these factors alone are not sufficient to guarantee success, and the following issues should also be considered:

- The level of knowledge must be sufficiently high.
- Expertise must be available from at least one cooperative expert.
- The problem to be solved must be mostly qualitative (fuzzy) and not purely quantitative (otherwise, a numeric approach should be used).
- The problem must be sufficiently narrow in scope.

- ES shell characteristics are important. The shell must be of high quality and naturally store and manipulate the knowledge.
- The user interface must be friendly for novice users.
- The problem must be important and difficult enough to warrant development of an ES (but it need not be a core function).
- Knowledgeable system developers with good people skills are needed.
- The impact of ES as a source of end-user job improvement must be considered.
- The impact should be favorable. End-user attitudes and expectations must be considered.
- Management support must be cultivated.
- End-user training programs are necessary.
- The organizational environment should favor adoption of new technology.
- The application must be well-defined and structured, and it should be justified by strategic impact.

Managers attempting to introduce ES technology should establish end-user training programs, demonstrating its potential as a business tool. As part of the managerial support effort, the organizational environment should favor new technology adoption.

Section 12.10 Review Questions

1. Describe the major benefits of using ES.
2. Describe some of the limitations of ES.
3. Describe the critical success factors of ES.

12.11 EXPERT SYSTEMS ON THE WEB

The relationship between ES and the Internet and intranets can be divided into two categories. The first is the use of ES on the Web. In this case, the Web supports ES (and other AI) applications. The second is the support ES (and other AI methods) give to the Web.

One of the early reasons for ES development was its potential to provide knowledge and advice to large numbers of users. Because the Web enables knowledge to be disseminated to many people, the cost per user becomes small, making ES very attractive. However, according to Eriksson (1996), attaining this goal has proven to be very difficult. Because advisory systems are used infrequently, they need a large number of users to justify their construction. As a result, very few ES disseminate knowledge to many users.

The widespread availability and use of the Internet and intranets provide the opportunity to disseminate expertise and knowledge to mass audiences. By implementing ES (and other intelligent systems) as knowledge servers, it becomes economically feasible and profitable to publish expertise on the Web. ES running on servers can support a large group of users who communicate with the system over the Web. In this way, user interfaces based on Web protocols and the use of browsers provide access to the knowledge servers. This implementation approach is described in Eriksson (1996). If you go to the Web site of Exsys (**exsys.com**), you can try the Banner with Brains, which integrates ES capabilities into a Web banner (see Application Case 12.8). Another example is a rule-based system for intelligent online dialogue, developed by German scholars (see Application Case 12.9). Gensym (**gensym.com**) offers a real-time supporting tool called G2 that has been applied to many mission-critical domains, such as chemical, oil, gas, and process manufacturing.

APPLICATION CASE 12.8

Banner with Brains: Web-Based ES for Restaurant Selection

Selecting a restaurant for dating or business in a foreign city has never been easier, thanks to the availability of services over the Web and support from expert systems. At **exsys.com**, you can try a demo system that integrates an ES with a banner. All interactions occur through the banner.

The ES is familiar with restaurants in Albuquerque. When you need to find a restaurant, the system asks about the occasion and the type of food you desire. The preference data is then fed to a spreadsheet of information on the various restaurants. The system creates a probabilistic ranking of the restaurants that meet your needs. It then weighs various factors, based on the specified occasion, and displays up to five restaurants. It also explains why it recommends these restaurants. This kind of application will become increasingly popular in the future.

Sources: Exsys, "Corvid Restaurant Selection Knowledge Automation Expert System," **exsys.com/Demos/Restaurant/ restaurant_demo.html** (accessed June 2009); and G. Adomavicius and A. Tuzhilin, "Toward the Next Generation of Recommender Systems: A Survey of the State-of-the-Art and Possible Extensions," *IEEE Transactions on Knowledge and Data Engineering*, Vol. 17, No. 6, June 2005.

APPLICATION CASE 12.9

Rule-Based System for Online Consultation

A group of German scientists took advantage of the convenience of the Internet to offer a Web-based online consultation system for intelligent dialogue in assisting and conducting interviews. Traditionally, interviews are conducted face-to-face or over the telephone. The new system is used by a university to interview applicants and assess their chances of being admitted and by companies to screen job applicants. The system consists of a rule-based knowledge base that can dynamically adjust the questions to ask, based on user responses to previous questions. The system can also be used to support social workers in interacting with their clients online.

Sources: S. Mertens, M. Rosu, and Y. Erdani, "An Intelligent Dialogue for Online Rule-Based Expert Systems," 9th International Conference on Intelligent User Interface, January 13–16, 2004; and **expertise2go.com** (accessed March 2006).

ES can be transferred over the Web not only to human users, but also to other computerized systems, including DSS, robots, and databases. Other ES Web support possibilities include system construction. Here, collaboration between builders, experts, and knowledge engineers can be facilitated by Internet-based groupware. This can reduce the cost of building ES. Knowledge acquisition costs can be reduced, for example, in cases in which there are several experts or in which the expert is in a different location from the knowledge engineer. Knowledge maintenance can also facilitate the use of the Internet, which is also helpful to users.

Finally, the Web can greatly support the spread of multimedia-based ES. Such systems, called *intellimedia systems*, support the integration of extensive multimedia applications and ES. Such systems can be very helpful for remote users, such as those in the tourism industry (see Stabb et al., 2002) and in remote equipment failure diagnosis.

The other aspect of the ES–Internet relationship is the support that ES and other AI technologies can provide to the Internet and intranets. The major contributions of AI to the Internet and intranets are summarized in Table 12.6.

Information about the relationships among ES, intelligent agents, and other AI and the Internet is readily available on the Internet. For example, the Web sites of *PC AI* magazine

TABLE 12.6 AI/ES and Web Impacts

Aspects	Impacts from the Web	Impacts on the Web
Knowledge acquisition	Experts in different areas can collaborate over the Internet.	Knowledge of Web operations and activities can be acquired and managed for sharing and use.
	Knowledge acquisition can be done at different times to fit the schedules of different experts.	
	Knowledge acquired from different experts can be shared on the Internet to stimulate discussion for enhancement.	
Expert systems development	Collaborative design of expert systems by a geographically distributed team becomes possible.	ES can be designed to support Web activities, automatic services, and better performance.
	Outsourcing of the design effort becomes feasible.	
	ES evaluation can be done remotely.	
	The Web provides a unified multimedia user interface for easy system integration.	
	Web services provide an improved platform for designing ES.	
Expert systems consultation	Users in remote areas can use the system to solve problems.	Applications of ES are available for Web browsing and monitoring.
	Expertise can easily be disseminated to a large body of users.	

(**pcai.com**) and the American Association for Artificial Intelligence (**aaai.org**) provide sets of hyperlinks to related Web sites. University of Maryland, Baltimore County (**agents .umbc.edu**) provides a collection of resources on intelligent agents. In the future, more applications on the Internet will be available; particularly those that provide automated decision making and real-time decision support (see Technology Insights 12.4).

Section 12.11 Review Questions

1. What are the benefits of deploying an ES on the Web?
2. How can an ES help a decision maker use the Web to find relevant information?
3. Visit **exsys.com** and run two of the demo systems. Describe each system.

TECHNOLOGY INSIGHTS 12.4 Automated and Real-Time Decision Systems

A technology called automated decision systems (ADS) is taking off, and it embodies the best attributes of artificial intelligence and business analytics. ADS are based on business rules, somewhat similar to ES, and, like other DSS technologies, they often involve statistical or algorithmic analysis of data. The main differences between the rules in ADS and the rules in ES are in the way they are created and used. The rules in ES are determined based on the experiences of domain experts and are executed collectively by an inference engine. In contrast, the rules in ADS are often created from historical data using advanced business analytics techniques and are used individually to trigger an automatic decision for a routine business situation. ADS typically make decisions in real-time after weighing all the data and relevant business rules for a particular case (ES can also be used to make real-time decisions, but often through a consultation session with the end user). Sometimes ADS incorporate business process management information, leading some observers to classify them as "smart business process management" systems.

The most salient characteristic of these systems is that they actually make a decision, such as what price to charge a particular customer, whether to grant a loan or an insurance policy, which delivery truck to reroute, or what drug to prescribe to a diabetic patient. In many cases, their decisions are made without any human intervention at all; in others—sometimes for legal or ethical reasons—they work alongside a human expert, such as a doctor. For the most part, these systems are used for decisions that must be made frequently and very rapidly, using information available online. The decision domains are relatively highly structured, with well-understood decision factors.

"Real time" can be looked at from both business and technology perspectives. From the business perspective, "real time" signifies that the users require rapid responses to customer requests. From the technology perspective, "real time" means that the system needs to have enough power to respond quickly to a user request.

Real-time ES are widely used for environmental protection and chemical processes. For example, RTXPS is a real-time ES designed for online dynamic decision support, mission-critical command, and control and communication tasks such as (1) emergency management for technological and environmental hazards, including early warning for events such as floods, toxic or oil spills, tsunamis, landslides, and so on; and (2) complex control and assessment tasks, including coordination of first response, recovery, restoration, and cleanup operations (see **ess.co.at/RTXPS/**).

Sources: C. White, "Intelligent Business Strategies: Near Real-Time and Automated Decision Making," *DM Review Magazine,* October 2002; and T. Davenport, "Decision Evolution," *CIO Magazine,* October 2004.

Chapter Highlights

- Artificial intelligence (AI) is a discipline that investigates how to build computer systems to perform tasks that can be characterized as intelligent.
- The major characteristics of AI are symbolic processing, the use of heuristics instead of algorithms, and the application of inference techniques.
- AI has several major advantages over people: It is permanent, it can be easily duplicated and disseminated, it can be less expensive than human intelligence, it is consistent and thorough, and it can be documented.
- Natural (human) intelligence has advantages over AI: It is creative, it uses sensory experiences directly, and it reasons from a wide context of experiences.
- Knowledge, rather than data or information, is the major focus of AI.
- Major areas of AI include expert systems, natural language processing, speech understanding, intelligent robotics, computer vision, fuzzy logic, intelligent agents, intelligent computer-aided instruction, automatic programming, neural computing, game playing, and language translation.
- Expert systems (ES) are the most often applied AI technology. ES attempt to imitate the work of experts. They capture human expertise and apply it to problem solving.

- For an ES to be effective, it must be applied to a narrow domain, and the knowledge must include qualitative factors.
- Natural language processing investigates techniques that allow users to communicate with computers in a natural language. It includes text-based and voice-based natural language user interfaces.
- An intelligent robot is a computer-based program or machine that can respond to changes in its environment. Most of today's robots do not have the same capabilities as human beings have, but they are improving rapidly.
- Intelligent tutoring systems use AI to help users learn. Artificial intelligence can improve training and teaching.
- The power of an ES is derived from the specific knowledge it possesses, not from the particular knowledge representation and inference schemes it uses.
- Expertise is task-specific knowledge acquired through training, reading, and experience.
- ES technology can transfer knowledge from experts and documented sources to the computer and make it available for use by nonexperts.
- The major components of an ES are the knowledge acquisition subsystem, knowledge base, inference

engine, user interface, blackboard, explanation sub-system, and knowledge-refinement subsystem.

- The inference engine provides reasoning capability for an ES.
- ES inference can be done by using forward chaining or backward chaining.
- Knowledge engineers are professionals who know how to capture the knowledge from an expert and structure it in a form that can be processed by the computer-based ES.
- ES development process includes defining the nature and scope of the problem, identifying proper experts, acquiring knowledge, selecting the building tools, coding the system, and evaluating the system.
- ES are popular in a number of generic categories: interpretation, prediction, diagnosis, design, planning, monitoring, debugging, repair, instruction, and control.

- The ES shell is an ES development tool that has the inference engine and building blocks for the knowledge base and the user interface. Knowledge engineers can easily develop a prototype system by entering rules into the knowledge base.
- ES have many benefits. The most important are improvement in productivity or quality, preservation of scarce expertise, enhancement of other systems, ability to cope with incomplete information, and provision of training.
- Many ES failures are caused by nontechnical problems, such as lack of managerial support and poor end-user training.
- Although there are several technical limitations to the use of ES, some of them will disappear with improved technology.
- Some ES provide advice in a real time.
- ES and AI provide support to the Internet and intranets.

Key Terms

artificial intelligence (AI) *534*
backward chaining *558*
blackboard *551*
certainty factors (CF) *561*
consultation environment *550*
development environment *550*
expert *542*
expert system (ES) *537*
expert system (ES) shell *567*
expertise *543*

explanation subsystem *552*
forward chaining *558*
fuzzy logic *541*
heuristics *535*
inference engine *558*
inferences rules *557*
intelligent agent (IA) *541*
intelligent computer-aided instruction (ICAI) *540*
intelligent tutoring system (ITS) *540*

knowledge acquisition *550*
knowledge base *551*
knowledge engineer *551*
knowledge engineering *553*
knowledge rules *557*
knowledge-based system (KBS) *532*
knowledge-refining system *552*
natural language processing (NLP) *537*
neural computing *540*
production rules *557*

robot *539*
rule-based expert systems *529*
speech (voice) understanding *539*
theory of certainty factors *561*
Turing test *534*
user interface *551*
visual recognition *540*

Questions for Discussion

1. Compare numeric and symbolic processing techniques and give an example to illustrate their differences.
2. Do you agree with the statement that using speech communication as the user interface could increase people's willingness to use ES? Why or why not?
3. It is said that powerful computers, inference capabilities, and problem-solving heuristics are necessary but not sufficient for solving real problems. Explain.
4. Explain how the Web improves the benefit–cost ratio of ES and enables systems that otherwise are not justifiable.
5. Explain the relationship between the development environment and the consultation (i.e., runtime) environment.
6. Explain the difference between forward chaining and backward chaining and describe when each is most appropriate.

7. What kind of mistakes might ES make and why? Why is it easier to correct mistakes in ES than in conventional computer programs?
8. Review the limitations of ES discussed in this chapter. From what you know, which of these limitations are the most likely to still be limitations in the year 2100? Why?
9. An ES for stock investment is developed and licensed for $1,000 per year. The system can help identify the most undervalued securities on the market and the best timing for buying and selling the securities. Will you order a copy as your investment advisor? Explain why or why not.
10. Given the current status of the Web, discuss how it is changing the availability of ES and how it is being used to embed expertise in other systems.

Exercises

TERADATA STUDENT NETWORK (TSN) AND OTHER HANDS-ON EXERCISES

1. Go to **teradatastudentnetwork.com** and search for stories about Chinatrust Commercial Bank's (CTCB's) use of the Teradata Relationship Manager and its reported benefits. Study the functional demo of the Teradata Relationship Manager to answer the following questions:

   a. What functions in the Teradata Relationship Manager are useful for supporting the automation of business rules? In CTCB's case, identify a potential application that can be supported by rule-based ES and solicit potential business rules in the knowledge base.

   b. Access Haley and compare the Teradata Relationship Manager and Haley's Business Rule Management System. Which tool is more suitable for the application identified in the previous question?

2. We list 10 categories of ES applications in the chapter. Find 20 sample applications, 2 in each category, from the various functional areas in an organization (i.e., accounting, finance, production, marketing, and human resources).

TEAM ASSIGNMENTS AND ROLE-PLAYING

1. Download Exsys' Corvid tool for evaluation. Identify an expert (or use one of your teammates) in an area where experience-based knowledge is needed to solve problems, such as buying a used car, selecting a school and major, selecting a job from many offers, buying a computer, diagnosing and fixing computer problems, etc. Go through the knowledge-engineering process to acquire the necessary knowledge. Using the evaluation version of the Corvid tool, develop a simple expert system application on the expertise area of your choice. Report on your experiences in a written document; use screenshots from the software as necessary.

2. Search to find applications of artificial intelligence and ES. Identify an organization with which at least one member of your group has a good contact who has a decision-making problem that requires some expertise (but is not too complicated). Understand the nature of its business and identify the problems that are supported or can potentially be supported by rule-based systems. Some examples include selection of suppliers, selection of a new employee, job assignment, computer selection, market contact method selection, and determination of admission into graduate school.

3. Identify and interview an expert who knows the domain of your choice. Ask the expert to write down his or her knowledge. Choose an ES shell and build a prototype system to see how it works.

INTERNET EXERCISES

1. Go to **exsys.com** to play with the restaurant selection example in its demo systems. Analyze the variables and rules contained in the example's knowledge base.

2. In 1995, there were about 2,000 Web sites related to AI. Today, there are substantially more. Do a search at Google and describe how many Web sites you find. Categorize the first 20 into groups, or if you used a search engine that grouped them, what groups did you find?

3. Search the Internet using the keyword expert systems and describe what you find. List the first five applications in your search results and compare their differences.

4. Access the Web site of the American Association for Artificial Intelligence (**aaai.org**). Examine the workshops it has offered over the past year and list the major topics related to intelligent systems.

5. Search online to find a few ES development tools not listed in the chapter. Classify them into different categories.

END OF CHAPTER APPLICATION CASE

Business Rule Automation at Farm Bureau Financial Services

Financial service is a major area for ES because the process involves a number of complicated rules. Farm Bureau is a 60-year-old comprehensive financial services provider that offers a broad range of innovative products. With the 2003 merger of three Farm Bureau insurance companies into Farm Bureau Financial Services, the new management team believed that technology would enable the organization to improve the business processes

each of the entities had performed in the past. One area the carrier sought to improve was underwriting, and it turned to a rule-based system that would eliminate many of the tasks previously required of underwriters.

"Farm Bureau's goal was to get the carrier's business rules out of the legacy code so the rules would be more manageable," explained Brett Clausen, vice president of the property/casualty companies for Farm Bureau. "The question we asked ourselves initially was 'How could we use this tool to achieve speed to market while at the same time underwriting more effectively and efficiently?'" Farm Bureau identified several benefits it expected to gain with rule-based underwriting. That list included reduction in workloads, better policy issuance times, improved consistency in underwriting risks, adaptable response to market regulatory changes, expense reduction, underwriters being able to focus more on exposures that create a higher liability to the company, and the ability to better manage and monitor results.

The benefits of using rule-based systems are quite clear. "Our challenge early on was a lot of our policies going through were being reviewed," Clausen said. "There was a very low percentage—about 10 percent to 12 percent—of transactions that were going through without being reviewed. We've increased that now to more than 60 percent of transactions going through without being reviewed."

With such an increase, Clausen pointed out that it was easy to see how many rules had changed in the past 2 years. The cautious pace allowed users to identify the business rules that were important and had an impact on business results and to eliminate some of the rules that didn't have an impact on decision making. "We wanted to be conservative and targeted 20 percent as a good pass-through rate," he said. "That would give us the ability to step back and look at what rules were firing and what rules were not firing." Audits were conducted to make sure the policies that were passing through without being looked at were quality business and also to ensure that a policy that the carrier normally would not have written didn't get through.

"We were pleased with that initial juncture, and then we started looking at the rules again," Clausen said. It wasn't hard for Farm Bureau's underwriters and customer service representatives to reexamine the rules because the results of those rules were showing up in their workload. As a result, Farm Bureau has reduced its transaction time by about 75 percent, Clausen claimed. "The amount of transactions that are coming through is phenomenal," he said. "In 2005, we had about 450,000 transactions come through our automated underwriting rules base. Roughly 250,000 of those passed without being looked at. When you look at the impact that has on the human resource perspective, getting our underwriters to focus on where we want them to focus, and our customer service representatives to focus on building relationships with our policyholders, that's a major step."

Questions for the Case

1. Describe the role of business rules at Farm Bureau and explain why those rules are very important.
2. Describe the benefits of using the rule-based system at Farm Bureau and explain why the system can generate these benefits.
3. Evaluate potential tools for implementing such a rule-based system and list the criteria that you would use in tool selection.
4. Find a proper application outside the financial services domain (such as manufacturing or retailing) and evaluate whether a rule-based system will generate the same level of benefits as those in the Farm Bureau system and explain why.

Sources: Compiled from R. Hyle, "Business Rules Streamline Underwriting for Farm Bureau Financial Services," *Tech Decisions,* February 2006; and **fbfs.com** (accessed March 2009).

References

Adomavicius, G., and A. Tuzhilin. (2005, June). "Toward the Next Generation of Recommender Systems: A Survey of the State-of-the-Art and Possible Extensions." *IEEE Transactions on Knowledge and Data Engineering,* Vol. 17, No. 6.

Byrd, T. A. (1995). "Expert Systems Implementation: Interviews with Knowledge Engineers." *Industrial Management and Data Systems,* Vol. 95, No. 10, 67–75.

ChessBase News. (2003, February 8). "Kasparov vs. Deep Junior Ends in 3-3." **chessbase.com/newsdetail.asp? newsid=782** (accessed June 2009).

Currie, A. (1999). "The History of Robotics." **faculty.ucr.edu/ ~currie/roboadam.htm** (accessed September 2006).

Davenport, T. (2004, October). "Decision Evolution." *CIO Magazine.*

Eom, S. B. (1996, September/October). "A Survey of Operational Expert Systems in Business (1980–1993)." *Interfaces,* Vol. 26, No. 5.

Eriksson, H. (1996, June). "Expert Systems as Knowledge Servers." *IEEE Expert.*

Feigenbaum, E., and P. McCorduck. (1983). *The Fifth Generation.* Reading, MA: Addison-Wesley.

Geng, G., B. Zhang, J. Zhu, and C. H. Zhong. (2002, May). "Applying AI to Railway Freight Loading." *Expert Systems with Applications.*

Ghanea-Hercock, R., and R. K. Ghanea-Hercock. (2003). *Applied Evolutionary Algorithms in Java.* New York: Springer-Verlag.

Gill, T. G. (1995, March). "Early Expert Systems: Where Are They Now?" *MIS Quarterly,* Vol. 19, No. 1.

Goldberg, D. E. (1994, March). "Genetic and Evolutionary Algorithms Come of Age." *Communications of the ACM,* Vol. 37, No. 3.

Goldberg, H., D. Kirkland, D. Lee, P. Shyr, and D. Thakker. (2003). "The NASD Securities Observation, News Analysis & Regulation System (SONAR)."*Proceedings of the Fifteenth Conference on Innovative Applications of Artificial Intelligence, AAAI,* pp. 11–18.

Gooptu, P. (2004, November 23). "Threat to Call Centers: Voice Automation!" **rediff.com/money/2004/nov/23bpo.htm** (accessed June 2009).

Hall, L., A. Gordon, R. James, and L. Newell. (2004). "A Lightweight Rule-Based AI Engine for Mobile Games." *ACM SIG International Conference on Advances in Computer Entertainment Technologies.*

Hatzikos, E. V., N. Bassiliades, L. Asmanis, and I. Vlahavas. (2007). "Monitoring Water Quality Through a Telematic Sensor Network and a Fuzzy Expert System." *Expert Systems,* Vol. 24, No. 3, pp. 143–161.

IBM Research. "Deep Blue Overview." **research.ibm.com/ deepblue/** (accessed June 2009).

"Just Talk to Me." (2001, December 8). *The Economist Technology Quarterly.*

Knoblock, C. (2003). "Agents for Gathering, Integrating, and Monitoring Information for Travel Planning." *IEEE Intelligent Systems,* Vol. 17, No. 6.

Lopez, M. A., C. H. Flores, and E. G. Garcia. (2003). "An Intelligent Tutoring System for Turbine Startup Training of Electronic Power Plant Operators." *Expert Systems with Applications,* Vol. 24, No. 1.

Mathies, L., L. Padgham, and B. Q. Vo. (2005, July 25–29). "Agent Based Travel and Tourism Planning." *Proceedings of the Autonomous Agents and Multiagent Systems Conference,* Utrecht University, the Netherlands.

Nedovic, L., and V. Devedzic. (2002). "Expert Systems in Finance: A Cross-Section of the Field." *Expert Systems with Applications,* Vol. 23, No. 1.

Nurminen, J., O. Karonen, and K. Hätönen. (2003). "What Makes Expert Systems Survive Over 10 Years: Empirical Evaluation of Several Engineering Applications." *Expert Systems with Applications,* Vol. 24, No. 1.

O'Keefe, R. M., O. Balci, and E. P. Smith. (1987, Winter). "Validating Expert System Performance." *IEEE Expert.*

O'Leary, D. E. (1993, March/April). "Determining Differences in Expert Judgment: Implications for Knowledge Acquisition and Validation." *Decision Sciences,* Vol. 24, No. 2.

Papic, V., N. Rogulj, and V. Pleština. (2009). "Identification of Sport Talents Using a Web-oriented Expert System with a Fuzzy Module." *Expert Systems with Applications,* Vol. 36, pp. 8830–8838.

Rayham, A. F. R., and M. C. Fairhurst. (1999, February). "Enhancing Multiple Expert Decision Combination Strategies Through Exploration of a Priori Information Sources." *IEEE Proceedings—Vision, Image and Signal Processing,* Vol. 146, No. 1.

Reuters. (2005, June 2). "Toyota Aims to Sell Service Robots by 2010?" **robots.net/article/1517.html** (accessed March 2006).

Rich, E., and K. Knight. (1991). *Artificial Intelligence,* 2nd ed. New York: McGraw-Hill.

Rogulj, N., V. Papic, and V. Pleština. (2006). "Development of the Expert System for Sport Talents Detection." *WSEAS Transactions on Information Science and Applications,* Vol. 9, No. 3, pp. 1752–1755.

Stabb, S., H. Werther, F. Ricci, A. Zipf, U. Gretzel, D. Fesenmaier, C. Paris, and C. Knoblock. (2002, November/December). "Intelligent Systems for Tourism." *IEEE Intelligent Systems,* Vol. 17, No. 6.

Tanaka, K., and T. Niimuara. (2007). *An Introduction to Fuzzy Logic for Practical Applications.* New York: Springer.

Wagner, W. P., J. R. Otto, and Q. B. Chung. (2003)."The Impact of Problem Domains and Knowledge Acquisition Techniques: A Content Analysis of P/OM Expert System Case Studies." *Expert Systems with Applications,* Vol. 24, pp. 79–86.

White, C. (2002, October). "Intelligent Business Strategies: Near Real-Time and Automated Decision Making," *DM Review Magazine.*

Wong, W. K., X. H. Zeng, W. M. R. Au, P. Y. Moka, and S. Y. S. Leung. (2009). "A Fashion Mix-and-Match Expert System for Fashion Retailers Using a Fuzzy Screening Approach." *Expert Systems with Applications,* Vol. 36, pp. 1750–1764.

Yamaguchi, M. (2006, January 27). "Japanese Lab Develops Robot for Errands." The Associated Press.

13

Advanced Intelligent Systems

LEARNING OBJECTIVES

1 Understand machine-learning concepts

2 Know the concepts behind and applications of case-based reasoning systems

3 Know the concepts behind and applications of genetic algorithms

4 Understand fuzzy logic and its application in designing intelligent systems

5 Understand the concepts behind support vector machines and their applications in developing advanced intelligent systems

6 Understand the concepts behind intelligent software agents and their use, capabilities, and limitations in developing advanced intelligent systems

7 Explore integrated intelligent support systems

In addition to rule-based expert systems, several other advanced techniques are available for designing intelligent information systems. These include case-based reasoning systems, genetic algorithms, fuzzy logic and fuzzy inference systems, support vector machines, and intelligent agents. A case-based reasoning system contains a large repository of historical cases that represents unique past experiences. Genetic algorithms mimic the natural process of evolution to help find solutions to complex problems. Fuzzy logic (and fuzzy inference systems) creates a bridge between symbolic reasoning and mathematical calculation to improve decision performance in uncertain problem situations. Support vector machines are becoming increasingly more popular prediction systems for complex real-world problems. Intelligent software agents are the key enabling technology for the next generation of intelligent information systems distributed over the Internet. The concepts and motivating applications of these advanced techniques are described in this chapter, which is organized into the following sections:

13.1 Opening Vignette: Machine Learning Helps Develop an Automated Reading Tutoring Tool
13.2 Machine-Learning Techniques
13.3 Case-Based Reasoning
13.4 Genetic Algorithms and Developing GA Applications
13.5 Fuzzy Logic and Fuzzy Inference Systems
13.6 Support Vector Machines
13.7 Intelligent Agents
13.8 Developing Integrated Advanced Systems

13.1   OPENING VIGNETTE: MACHINE LEARNING HELPS DEVELOP AN AUTOMATED READING TUTORING TOOL

Literacy is the ability to identify, understand, interpret, create, and communicate printed materials associated with varying contexts. The United Nations recognizes literacy as a human right, noting that basic education, of which literacy is the key learning tool, was recognized as a human right over 50 years ago in the Universal Declaration of Human Rights. However, a significantly large number of people are illiterate—they cannot read or write. Researchers are seeking creative ways to apply information, communication, and machine-learning technologies to address reading and literacy-related developmental challenges in the world.

Problem

In order to reduce and potentially eliminate illiteracy via automated means, it is necessary to understand what makes learning to read an easy and effective process. To date, experts believe that guided oral reading greatly enhances word identification and comprehension in context. Ample evidence suggests that one of the major differences between good and poor readers is the amount of time they spend reading. Poor readers are unlikely to practice on their own. Students who need the most practice spend the least amount of time actually reading. Poor readers tend to reread the same easy stories over and over. Building on the foundational understanding of reading, researchers from Carnegie Mellon University are developing automated reading tutors using a combination of machine-learning techniques.

Solution

The project, called LISTEN (Literacy Innovation that Speech Technology ENables), is an interdisciplinary research effort at Carnegie Mellon University's Machine Learning Department aimed at developing a novel tool to improve literacy—an automated reading tutor that displays a story on a computer screen and listens to children read it aloud. To provide a pleasant, authentic experience in assisted reading, the reading tutor lets the child choose from a menu of high-interest stories from *Weekly Reader* and other sources, including user-authored stories. The reading tutor employs Carnegie Mellon's Sphinx-II speech recognizer to analyze the student's oral reading. The reading tutor intervenes when the reader makes mistakes, gets stuck, clicks for help, or is likely to encounter difficulty. The reading tutor responds with proper assistance by employing an interactive process modeled after expert reading teachers, but adapted to the enhanced capabilities and ordinary limitations of the computer technology.

Results

Even though it is not yet a commercial product, the reading tutor is being used by hundreds of children as part of studies to test its effectiveness. Thousands of hours of usage logged at multiple levels of detail, including millions of words read aloud, provide unique opportunities for improvement of advanced machine-learning methods and their applications in education.

Speech-recognition-based, computer-guided oral reading has demonstrated usability, user acceptance, and assistive effectiveness. Even with barely 20 minutes of use per day, successive versions of the reading tutor have produced substantially higher comprehension gains than current conventional intervention practices in controlled studies lasting several months. To ensure that results were due to the reading tutor intervention, researchers compared different treatments within the same classrooms and randomized treatment assignment, stratifying by pretest scores within class. They have computed effect size as the difference in gains between the reading tutor and current practice, divided by the average standard deviation in gains of the two groups. Effect sizes for passage comprehension were substantial compared to other studies.

Why does the reading tutor improve comprehension? Theoretically, students who recognize words effortlessly can devote more attention to comprehension, and the relationship between the rate of oral reading and reading comprehension is strong throughout the early education years. The cognitive load imposed by word identification before it has become a mentally automatic process consumes limited mental resources, such as attention and short-term memory, needed to comprehend the sentence and its relationship to the surrounding context. Automated tools like the reading tutor enhance reading efficiency by addressing these theoretical pointers.

Using a combination of machine-learning techniques, including speech recognition, natural language processing, expert knowledge representation, and an inference engine, the LISTEN project has demonstrated what is possible with these cutting-edge information technologies. The LISTEN project team is now taking reading tutor to developing countries in Africa to test its larger viability and to help improve global literacy. The underlying research for the LISTEN project has been supported by NSF (under the IERI and ITR programs), and is currently being supported by the U.S. Department of Education's Institute of Educational Sciences under Grants, and by the Heinz Endowments.

Questions for the Opening Vignette

1. What is literacy and why does it have a global importance?
2. How can information systems help in overcoming illiteracy?
3. What types of machine-learning technologies can be used in improving reading skills?
4. What do you think are the characteristics of an expert reading tutor that should be closely represented in an automated computer tool like the reading tutor?

What We Can Learn from This Vignette

Machine learning is a collection of advanced technologies commonly used to solve complex real-world problems. The opening vignette demonstrates the utility of machine-learning techniques as they apply to developing an automated reading tutor to fight illiteracy. Specifically, the LISTEN project used speech recognition, natural language processing, expert knowledge representation, and an inference engine to create an automated tutor, which was modeled after the ideal learning process guided by the expert reading tutors. In fact, testing demonstrated that the automated reading tutor met and often exceeded the effectiveness and efficiency of the traditional intervention techniques.

Sources: A. Mills-Tettey, J. Mostow, M. B. Dias, T. M. Sweet, S. M. Belousov, M. F. Dias, and H. Gong, "Improving Child Literacy in Africa: Experiments with an Automated Reading Tutor," *Third IEEE/ACM International Conference on Information and Communication Technologies and Development* (ICTD2009), April 17–19, 2009, pp. 129–138; and "Educational Data Mining of Students' Interactions with a Reading Tutor That Listens at Carnegie Mellon University," **cs.cmu.edu/~listen/** (accessed June 2009).

13.2 MACHINE-LEARNING TECHNIQUES

Machine-learning techniques enable computers to acquire knowledge (i.e., learn) from data that reflects the historical happenings. They overcome deficiencies of manual knowledge acquisition techniques by automating the learning process.

Machine-Learning Concepts and Definitions

Attempts at discovering knowledge to solve problems have been made for generations, starting long before the computer age. Some examples are statistical models, such as regression and forecasting; management science models, such as those for inventory level determination and resource allocation; and financial models, such as those for make-versus-buy decisions and equipment-replacement methods. Unfortunately, such methods are often limited to processing quantifiable and well-known factors. When problems are complex and factors are both quantitative and qualitative, standard models cannot solve them; additional, deeper, richer knowledge is needed.

Many organizations use neural networks to support complex decision making. Neural networks (see Chapter 6) can identify patterns from which they generate recommended courses of action. Because such networks learn from past experience to improve their own performance, they are members of a technology family called *machine learning*. **Machine learning** is a family of artificial intelligence technologies that is primarily concerned with the design and development of algorithms that allow computers to learn based on historical data. It is different in several ways from the conventional knowledge-acquisition methods described in Chapter 11. Knowledge acquisition from human experts often suffers from an expert's unwillingness or inability to provide accurate knowledge, whereas machine learning is an attempt to implicitly induce expert knowledge from historical cases and decisions. In other words, instead of asking the experts to articulate their knowledge, the learning module of the system is able to identify interesting patterns from the historical data available in the organizational database.

Although machine learning is considered to be a part of artificial intelligence, it is closely related to many other fields, including statistics, probability theory, management science, pattern recognition, adaptive control, and theoretical computer science.

Learning

Learning is a process of self-improvement and thus an important feature of intelligent behavior. Understanding learning is a critical part of artificial intelligence (and machine learning), because it is an investigation of the basic principles that underlie intelligence. Machine learning is essential to providing intelligent management support systems (MSS) with self-enhancement capabilities.

Human learning is a combination of many complicated cognitive processes, including induction, deduction, analogy, and other special procedures related to observing and/or analyzing different situations. Machine-learning techniques are very similar to human learning techniques, largely due to the fact that they are modeled after the human learning processes (as we currently understand them). The following are relevant observations on how learning relates to intelligent systems:

- Automated learning systems demonstrate intriguing learning behaviors, some of which (e.g., chess- and checkers-playing programs) can actually challenge the performance of human experts.
- Although artificial intelligence sometimes matches human-level learning capabilities, it is not able to learn as well as humans or in the same way that humans do (e.g., checkers-playing programs learn quite differently from humans).
- There is no claim that machine learning can be applied in a truly creative way, although some automated systems can handle cases to which they have never been exposed. Simulated creativity is an intensely studied artificial intelligence topic (see the Imagination Engines, Inc., Web site, at **imagination-engines.com**).
- Automated learning systems are not anchored in any formal bedrock; thus, their implications are not well understood. Many systems have been tested exhaustively, but exactly why they succeed or fail is not clear.
- A common thread running through most artificial intelligence approaches to learning (distinguishing them from non–artificial-intelligence approaches to learning) is the manipulation of symbols rather than mere numeric information.

Machine-Learning Methods

Machine learning has three major categories: supervised learning, unsupervised learning, and reinforcement learning. **Supervised learning** is a process of inducing knowledge from a set of observations whose outcomes are known. For example, say we induce a set of rules from historical loan-evaluation data. Because the decisions on these loan cases are known, we can test how the induced model performs when it is applied to these historical cases.

Unsupervised learning is used to discover knowledge from a set of data whose outcomes are unknown. A typical application is to classify customers into several different profiles or lifestyles. Before the classification, we do not know how many different kinds of profiles or lifestyles are available, nor do we know which customer belongs to a particular profile or lifestyle.

Another style of learning that lies somewhat in between the supervised and unsupervised approaches is reinforcement learning. **Reinforcement learning** is not as popular as the other two types, due to the fact that it is not as matured and its applicability is limited to a small set of real-world situations. An example of reinforcement learning would be to learn which of several possible actions a robot should execute at every stage in an ongoing sequence of experiences given only the final outcome of its actions. This differs from supervised learning in that there is not a set of historical cases from which to learn; the machine learns as it experiences new situations. It differs from unsupervised learning because there is not a natural grouping of things. This type of learning is successfully applied to learning to play backgammon, autonomous search robots, and controlling the flight of helicopters. Borrowing terms from psychological learning theory, the good-result or bad-result information is called a *reward* or a *reinforcement*, and hence this style of learning is called *reinforcement learning* or *trial-and-error learning*. Figure 13.1 shows a simplistic taxonomy of machine learning with exemplary methods listed under each category.

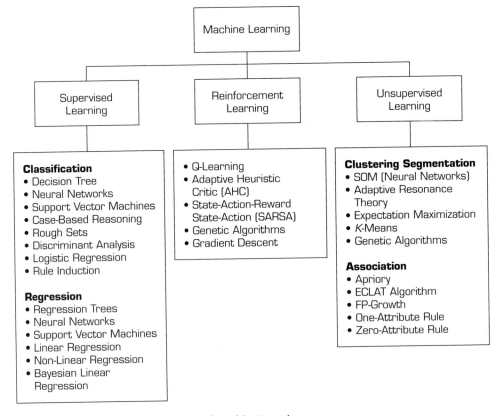

FIGURE 13.1 A Simplified Taxonomy of Machine Learning

Section 13.2 Review Questions

1. Define *machine learning*.
2. What is learning?
3. What are the differences between supervised learning and unsupervised learning?
4. List several techniques for supervised learning and unsupervised learning.
5. List five machine-learning methods.

13.3 CASE-BASED REASONING

The basic premise of machine learning is that there are data that preserve and delineate previous decision experiences. These experience-based records are usually called *cases*. They may be used either as direct references to support similar decisions in the future or to induce rules or decision patterns (i.e., generalized decision models). The former, called **case-based reasoning (CBR)**, or **analogical reasoning**, adapts solutions used to solve old problems for use in solving new problems. The latter, called **inductive learning**, allows the computer to examine historical cases and generate rules (or other generalized knowledge representations) that can be used to solve new problems (of similar nature) or that can be deployed for automating a decision support process that repeatedly deals with a specific class of problems (e.g., evaluating loan applications). In this section, we describe the concept of CBR and its applications to intelligent management support systems.

The Basic Idea of CBR

CBR is based on the premise that new problems are often similar to previously encountered problems, and, therefore, past successful solutions may be of use in solving the current situation. Cases are often derived from legacy databases, thereby converting existing organizational information assets into exploitable knowledge repositories. CBR is particularly applicable to problems in which the domain is not understood well enough to build a robust generalized model-based prediction system using rules, equations, or other numeric and/or symbolic formulations. CBR is commonly used for diagnosis-type (or, more generally speaking, for classification-type) tasks, such as determining the nature of a machine failure from the observable attributes and prescribing a fix based on the successful solutions found in the past history of similar occurrences.

The foundation of CBR is a repository (or library) of cases called a *case base* that contains a number of previous cases for decision making. For an overview, see Shiu and Pal (2004). CBR has proved to be an extremely effective approach for problems in which existing rules are inadequate (see Watson, 2002). In fact, because experience is an important ingredient in human expertise, CBR is thought to be a more psychologically plausible model of the reasoning of an expert than a rule-based model. A theoretical comparison of the two models is summarized in Table 13.1. According to Riesbeck and Schank (1989), the use of this approach is justified by the fact that human thinking does not use logic (or reasoning from first principles), but is basically a processing of the right information being retrieved at the right time. Thus, the central problem is the identification of pertinent information whenever needed.

The Concept of a Case in CBR

A *case* is the primary knowledge element in a CBR application. It is a combination of the problem features and proper business actions associated with each situation. These features and actions may be represented in natural language or in a specific structured format (e.g., objects).

TABLE 13.1   Comparison of CBR and Rule-Based Systems

Criterion	Rule-Based Reasoning	Case-Based Reasoning
Knowledge unit	Rule	Case
Granularity	Fine	Coarse
Knowledge acquisition units	Rules, hierarchies	Cases, hierarchies
Explanation mechanism	Backtrack of rule firings	Precedent cases
Characteristic output	Answer and confidence measure	Answer and precedent cases
Knowledge transfer across problems	High if backtracking; low if deterministic	Low
Speed as a function of knowledge base size	Exponential if backtracking; linear if deterministic	Logarithmic if index tree is balanced
Domain requirements	Domain vocabulary	Domain vocabulary
	Good set of inference rules	Database of example cases
	Either few rules or rules apply sequentially	Stability (a modified good solution is probably still good)
	Domain mostly obeys rules	Many exceptions to rules
Advantages	Flexible use of knowledge	Rapid knowledge acquisition
	Potentially optimal answers	Explanation by examples
Disadvantages	Possible errors due to misfit rules and problem parameters	Suboptimal solutions
		Redundant knowledge base
	Black-box answers	Computationally expensive
		Long development time

Source: Based on a discussion with Marc Goodman, Cognitive Systems, Inc., in 1995.

Kolodner (1993) classified cases into three categories—ossified cases, paradigmatic cases, and stories—based on their different characteristics and the different ways of handling them. **Ossified cases** appear very often and are quite standard. They can be generalized into rules or other forms of knowledge through inductive learning. **Paradigmatic cases** contain certain unique features that cannot be generalized. They need to be stored and indexed in a case base for future reference. **Stories** are special cases that contain rich contents and special features with deep implications. Figure 13.2 shows the way the three types of cases can be handled. CBR is particularly well designed for processing paradigmatic cases that cannot be properly handled by rule-based reasoning.

The Process of CBR

CBR can be formalized as a four-step process:

1. *Retrieve.*   Given a target problem, retrieve from a library of past cases the most similar cases that are relevant to solving the current case.
2. *Reuse.*   Map the solution from the previous case to the target problem. Reuse the best old solution to solve the current case.
3. *Revise.*   Having mapped the previous solution to the target situation, test the new solution in the real world (or a simulation) and, if necessary, revise the case.
4. *Retain.*   After the solution has been successfully adapted to the target problem, store the resulting experience as a new case in the **case library**.

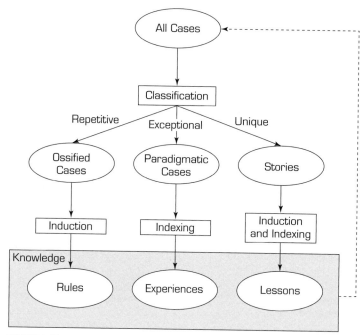

FIGURE 13.2   Deriving Knowledge from Different Types of Cases

The process of using CBR is shown graphically in Figure 13.3. Boxes represent processes, and ovals represent knowledge structure.

A detailed description of the reasoning process and recent applications can be found in Humphreys et al. (2003). An examination of case libraries in problem solving is available in Hernandez-Serrano and Jonassen (2003).

Example: Loan Evaluation Using CBR

Let's consider a possible scenario of CBR in loan evaluation. When a new case is received, the system builds a set of features to represent it. Let's assume that the applicant is a 40-year-old married man, with a $50,000 annual income job in a midsize manufacturing company. The set of features is [age = 40, marriage = yes, salary = 50,000, employer = midsize, industry = manufacturing]. The system goes to the case base to find similar cases. Suppose the system finds the following three similar cases:

John = [age = 40, marriage = yes, salary = 50,000, employer = midsize, industry = bank]

Ted = [age = 40, marriage = yes, salary = 45,000, employer = midsize, industry = manufacturing]

Larry = [age = 40, marriage = yes, salary = 50,000, employer = small, industry = retailing]

If John and Ted performed well in paying their loans, and if Larry was unable to pay back due to company bankruptcy, then the system can recommend that the loan be approved because John and Ted, who are more similar to the new applicant (four of the five attributes are the same), were able to pay back without problems. Larry is considered less similar to the new applicant (only three of the five attributes are the same) and hence is less useful for reference.

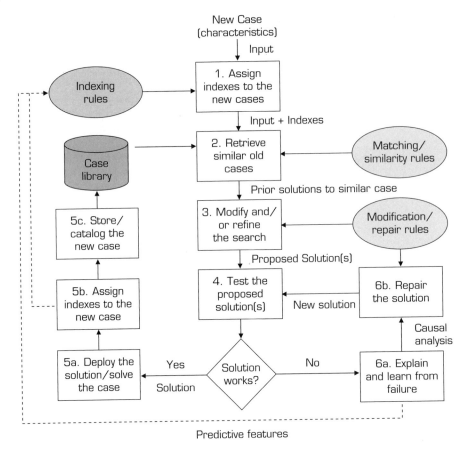

FIGURE 13.3 The Case-Based Reasoning Process

Benefits and Usability of CBR

CBR makes learning much easier and the recommendations more sensible. Many applications of CBR have been implemented. For example, Shin and Han (2001) reported an application of CBR to corporate bond rating. Hastings et al. (2002) applied CBR to rangeland management. Humphreys et al. (2003) described an application of CBR to evaluate supplier environment-management performance. Park and Han (2002) applied CBR to bankruptcy prediction. Khan and Hoffmann (2003) reported the development of a case-based recommendation system without the involvement of human knowledge engineers. Finally, Pham and Setchi (2003) applied CBR to design adaptive product manuals.

The following are the advantages of using CBR:

- Knowledge acquisition is improved. It is easier to build, simpler to maintain, and less expensive to develop and support knowledge acquisition.
- System development time is faster than when using manual knowledge acquisition.
- Existing data and knowledge are leveraged.
- Complete formalized domain knowledge (as required with rules) is not required.
- Experts feel better discussing concrete cases (not general rules).
- Explanation becomes easier. Rather than showing many rules, a logical sequence can be shown.

- Acquisition of new cases is easy (i.e., can be automated).
- Learning can occur from both successes and failures.

Issues and Applications of CBR

CBR can be used on its own or it can be combined with other reasoning paradigms. Several implementations of CBR systems combine rule-based reasoning (RBR) in order to address limitations such as accuracy in case indexing and adaptation.

Table 13.2 describes CBR applications in different fields. For a comprehensive CBR Web site, see **ai-cbr.org**, maintained by the University of Kaiserslautern in Germany. It contains applications, demos, and research material.

Designers must give careful thought to the following issues and questions regarding case-based implementation:

- What makes up a case? How can we represent case memory?
- Automatic case-adaptation rules can be very complex.
- How is memory organized? What are the indexing rules?
- The quality of the results is heavily dependent on the indexes used.
- How does memory function in relevant information retrieval?
- How can we perform efficient searching (i.e., knowledge navigation) of the cases?
- How can we organize (i.e., cluster) the cases?
- How can we design the distributed storage of cases?
- How can we adapt old solutions to new problems? Can we simply adapt the memory for efficient querying, depending on context? What are the similarity metrics and the modification rules?
- How can we factor errors out of the original cases?

TABLE 13.2 Case-Based Reasoning Application Categories and Examples

Category	Examples
Electronic commerce	Intelligent product catalog searching, intelligent customer support, and sales support
Web and information search	Catalogs, case-based information retrieval in construction, and skill profiling in electronic recruitment
Planning and control	Conflict resolution in air traffic control and planning of bioprocess recipes in the brewing industry
Design	Conceptual building design aid, conceptual design aid for electromechanical devices, and very large-scale integration (VLSI) design
Reuse	Reuse of structural design calculation documents, reuse of object-oriented software, and reuse assistant for engineering designs
Diagnosis	Prediction of blood alcohol content, online troubleshooting and customer support, and medical diagnosis
Reasoning	Heuristic retrieval of legal knowledge, reasoning in legal domains, and computer-supported conflict resolution through negotiation or mediation

- How can we learn from mistakes? That is, how can we repair and update the case base?
- The case base may need to be expanded as the domain model evolves, yet much analysis of the domain may be postponed.
- How can we integrate CBR with other knowledge representations and inferencing mechanisms?
- Are there better pattern-matching methods than the ones we currently use?
- Are there alternative retrieval systems that match the CBR schema?

Since 1995, increasing evidence has shown positive results for the use of CBR in solving practical problems (see Lee and Kim, 2002; and Luu et al., 2003). Application Case 13.1 summarizes a successful application of CBR in selecting songs that a community of listeners are most likely to enjoy.

APPLICATION CASE 13.1

A CBR System for Optimal Selection and Sequencing of Songs

Although digital distribution of media over the Internet has revolutionized the way we buy and share music, the way we listen to songs in shared environments (e.g., Internet radio) has not changed. Often a large group of people with similar tastes listen to a unique stream of music in the virtual world without contributing any feedback on the nature and sequence of selections. This is true of the real world as well; for instance, in a music club a DJ may be too busy selecting and mixing songs to check listener feedback, and radio broadcasters find it difficult to meet the tastes of all of their listeners. Beyond the technical difficulties, intrinsic representational challenges make it difficult to develop recommendation and personalization techniques for music.

Information retrieval systems (such as search engines) use keyword extraction to represent subject matter (e.g., documents, customer comments/reviews, business transactions) for indexing and retrieval, but comparable processes for audio artifacts are still a subject of much research. One method would be to rely on human input for content description, but this would be a laborious and knowledge-intensive process. Automated collaborative filtering (ACF) as part of a case-based reasoning (CBR) system is often proposed as a technique to ease the difficulties of knowledge elicitation with regards to music (Hayes, 2003).

Baccigalupo and Plaza (2007) developed an interactive social framework to overcome the unidirectional music selection problem with the goal of improving audience satisfaction. They proposed a unique group-based Web radio architecture called Poolcasting, where the music played on a channel is not preprogrammed but influenced in real time by the current audience. In this architecture, users can submit explicit preferences via a Web interface, they can request new songs to be played, evaluate scheduled songs, and send feedback about recently played ones. The main issue in such a system is how to guarantee fairness to the members of the audience with respect to the songs that are broadcasted. To address this issue, they have implemented a CBR system that schedules songs for each channel that combines both musical requirements (such as variety and continuity) and listeners' preferences. In order to remain fair in the presence of concurrent preferences, they used a strategy that favors those listeners who were less satisfied with recently played songs.

The CBR system that they have developed uses the following three steps to accomplish the Web radio song-scheduling task:

1. **Retrieval.** In this process, a subset of songs is identified from the music pool of the specific channel (e.g., easy listening, classical jazz). The songs are either recommended by an audience member via the Web interface or they are songs that have not been played recently and are musically associated with the last song scheduled to play.

2. Reuse. This process takes the output of the retrieval process (the retrieved set) and ranks the songs by taking into account the preferences of current listeners, giving more importance to those listeners who are less satisfied with the music recently played on that channel. The song that best matches the following four properties (which are used as the similarity measures) is scheduled as the next song:

a. **Variety.** No song or artist should be repeated closely on a channel.

b. **Continuity.** Each song should be musically associated with the song it follows.

c. **Satisfaction.** Each song should match the musical preferences of the current listeners, or at least of most of them.

d. **Fairness.** The more a listener is unsatisfied with the songs recently streamed, the more the listener's preferences should influence the selection of the next songs that will be played, so that nobody in the audience will be left out.

3. Revision. While a song is playing on a channel, the Web interface displays the title, artist, cover art, and remaining time. Listeners are asked to rate whether they like the song or not. Listeners can evaluate the songs played on the channel by providing positive or negative feedback, which, in turn, increases or decreases the degree of association of this song with the previous one. The assumption is that if a user rates a song played on a channel positively, then he or she likes that song and/or the song fits in the sequence of music programmed for that channel. Using this feedback, Poolcasting updates both the

listeners' preference models and the musical knowledge about song associations.

This collective approach to music scheduling shifts the paradigm from a classical monolithic approach where "one controls, many listen" toward a new decentralized scheduling approach where "many control, many listen." The developers attest that the system has generated very satisfactory results for both passive users (who provide nothing more than their implicit preferences) as well as active users (who provide constant feedback along with their preferences). Initial results of the system also showed that users enjoyed the songs and discovered new music that was not included in their preference lists, crediting the success of the system that intelligently associates songs of similar flavor using a multidimensional similarity measure.

Case-based reasoning made it possible to overcome many of the surmountable obstacles in developing such an advanced music recommendation system where the composition of audience is dynamically changing (new listeners are being added while some are leaving the channel). Using a fine balance between desirable properties for a radio channel (e.g., variety, continuity) and community preferences (satisfaction and fairness) the Poolcasting system seems to deliver on its promise. In fact, the article summarizing the system has received the best application paper award at the Seventh International Conference on Case-Based Reasoning in Belfast, Ireland, in 2007.

Sources: C. Baccigalupo and E. Plaza, "A Case-Based Song Scheduler for Group Customized Radio," *Proceedings of the Seventh International Conference on Case-Based Reasoning (ICCBR),* Belfast, Northern Ireland, UK: Springer, 2007; and C. Hayes, "Smart Radio: Building Community-Based Internet Music Radio," Ph.D. dissertation, University of Dublin, Ireland, 2003.

Success Factors for CBR Systems

CBR systems exhibit some unique properties that, if properly managed and implemented, can lead to very successful systems. Klahr (1997) described the following seven principles for a successful CBR strategy:

1. **Determine specific business objectives.** Every software project should have a business focus. Call center and help desk environments have great potential for CBR methods.

2. **Understand your end users and customers.** A successful case base directly supports the end user. The case base (i.e., knowledge) must be at the level of expertise of the end users. Shortcuts should be provided for more knowledgeable end users.

3. **Design the system appropriately.**   This includes understanding the problem domain and types of information the case base will provide and recognizing system and integration requirements.

4. **Plan an ongoing knowledge-management process.**   The knowledge in the case base must be updated as new cases arise (i.e., to avoid gaps in the case base) or as new products or services are delivered (i.e., as new content is added).

5. **Establish achievable returns on investment (ROI) and measurable metrics.**   Develop a level of acceptable ROI (e.g., 5–13 percent is being achieved in the field) and a means to measure it (e.g., 20 fewer phone calls, with a 13 percent larger customer base handled; or the ability to handle four times more questions than under the manual system).

6. **Plan and execute a customer-access strategy.**   The strength of CBR is that it can be put into the hands of customers, even over the Web, thus providing service 24 hours every day (e.g., Broderbund Software's Gizmo Trapper). This empowers customers to obtain the assistance they need when they need it. It also further broadens the use of the system, which helps in identifying exceptions and updating the case base. This is a key component of success.

7. **Expand knowledge generation and access across the enterprise.**   Just as knowledge is made available to customers, internal customers who are in direct contact with external customers may be able to provide helpful feedback and knowledge.

Tools for Building CBR

CBR systems are usually built with the help of special tools, and often with the help of experienced consultants. Some representative tools are listed in Table 13.3.

TABLE 13.3   Representative CBR Tools

Vendor	Product	URL
AcknoSoft	KATE	**acknosoft.com**
Atlantis Aerospace	SpotLight	**ai-cbr.org/tools/spotlight.html**
Brightware	ART*Enterprise	**firepond.com/**
Casebank Technologies	SpotLight	**casebank.com**
Esteem Software	ESTEEM	**ai-cbr.org/tools/esteem.html**
Inductive Solutions	CasePower	**inductive.com**
Inference	k-commerce (formerly CBR Express)	**inference.com**
Intelligent Electronics	TechMate	**ai-cbr.org/tools/techmate.html**
Intellix	KnowMan	**intellix.com**
ServiceSoft	Knowledge Builder & Web Adviser	**ai-cbr.org/tools/servicesoft.html**
tecInno GmbH	CBR-Works	**tecinno.com**
TreeTools	HELPDESK-3	**treetools.com.br**
The Haley Enterprise	The Easy Reasoner, CPR, & Help!CPR	**haley.com**

Sources: AI-CBR, **ai-cbr.org** (accessed June 2009); and *PC AI,* special issue, "Intelligent Web Applications & Agents," Vol. 19, No. 2, 2005.

AI-CBR Web site (**ai-cbr.org**) provides details and links for numerous CBR tools and applications. Although this site is no longer actively maintained, it still offers plenty of basic information and leads to additional resources. The site offers information on applied CBR, actual case bases for download, a searchable bibliography, and even a virtual library.

A comprehensive CBR toolkit is available from LPA (**lpa.co.uk/cbr.htm**). It includes modules for source selection, construction of an input query, record retrieval, and reordering of retrieved records. It also includes source code examples and an example of a CBR application.

Section 13.3 Review Questions

1. What is CBR? What problems is CBR most suitable for?
2. Describe the four steps of the CBR process.
3. List five benefits of CBR.
4. Comment on the current and future usability of CBR.
5. List three success factors of CBR.

13.4 GENETIC ALGORITHMS AND DEVELOPING GA APPLICATIONS

Genetic algorithms (GA) are a part of global search techniques used to find approximate solutions to optimization-type problems that are too complex to be solved with traditional optimization methods (which are guaranteed to produce the best solution to a specific problem). Genetic algorithms have been successfully applied to a wide range of highly complex real-world problems, including vehicle routing (see Baker and Syechew, 2003), bankruptcy prediction (see Shin and Lee, 2002), and Web searching (see Nick and Themis, 2001).

Genetic algorithms are a part of the machine-learning family of methods under artificial intelligence. Because they cannot guarantee the truly optimal solution, genetic algorithms are considered to be heuristic methods. Genetic algorithms are sets of computational procedures that conceptually follow the steps of the biological process of evolution. That is, better and better solutions evolve from the previous generation of solutions until an optimal or near-optimal solution is obtained.

Genetic algorithms (also known as **evolutionary algorithms**) demonstrate self-organization and adaptation in much the same way that biological organisms do by following the chief rule of evolution, *survival of the fittest*. The method improves the solutions by producing offspring (i.e., a new collection of feasible solutions) using the best solutions of the current generation as "parents." The generation of offspring is achieved by a process modeled after biological reproduction whereby mutation and crossover operators are used to manipulate genes in constructing newer and "better" chromosomes. Notice that a simple analogy between genes and decision variables and between chromosomes and potential solutions underlies the genetic algorithm terminology.

Example: The Vector Game

To illustrate how genetic algorithms work, we describe the classical Vector game (see Walbridge, 1989). This game is similar to MasterMind. As your opponent gives you clues about how good your guess is (i.e., the outcome of the fitness function), you create a new solution, using the knowledge gained from the recently proposed solutions and their quality.

DESCRIPTION OF THE VECTOR GAME Vector is played against an opponent who secretly writes down a string of six digits (in a genetic algorithm, this string consists of a *chromosome*). Each digit is a decision variable that can take the value of either 0 or 1. For example, say that the secret number that you are to figure out is 001010. You must try to guess this number as quickly as possible (with the least number of trials). You present a sequence of digits (a guess) to your opponent, and he or she tells you how many of the digits (but not which ones) you guessed are correct (i.e., the fitness function or quality of your guess). For example, the guess 110101 has no correct digits (i.e., the score = 0). The guess 111101 has only one correct digit (the third one, and hence the score = 1).

DEFAULT STRATEGY: RANDOM TRIAL AND ERROR   There are 64 possible six-digit strings of binary numbers. If you pick numbers at random, you will need, on average, 32 guesses to obtain the right answer. Can you do it faster? Yes, if you can interpret the feedback provided to you by your opponent (a measure of the goodness or fitness of your guess). This is how a genetic algorithm works.

IMPROVED STRATEGY: USE OF GENETIC ALGORITHMS   The following are the steps in solving the Vector game with genetic algorithms:

1. Present to your opponent four strings, selected at random. (Select four arbitrarily. Through experimentation, you may find that five or six would be better.) Assume that you have selected these four:

   (A)   110100; score = 1 (i.e., one digit guessed correctly)
   (B)   111101; score = 1
   (C)   011011; score = 4
   (D)   101100; score = 3

2. Because none of the strings is entirely correct, continue.
3. Delete (A) and (B) because of their low scores. Call (C) and (D) parents.
4. "Mate" the parents by splitting each number as shown here between the second and third digits (the position of the split is randomly selected):

   (C)   01:1011
   (D)   10:1100

   Now combine the first two digits of (C) with the last four of (D) (this is called crossover). The result is (E), the first offspring:

   (E)   011100; score = 3

   Similarly, combine the first two digits of (D) with the last four of (C). The result is (F), the second offspring:

   (F)   101011; score = 4

   It looks as though the offspring are not doing much better than the parents.
5. Now copy the original (C) and (D).
6. Mate and crossover the new parents, but use a different split. Now you have two new offspring, (G) and (H):

   (C)   0110:11
   (D)   1011:00
   (G)   0110:00; score = 4
   (H)   1011:11; score = 3

   Next, repeat step 2: Select the best "couple" from all the previous solutions to reproduce. You have several options, such as (G) and (C). Select (G) and (F). Now duplicate and crossover. Here are the results:

   (F)   1:01011
   (G)   0:11000
   (I)   111000; score = 3
   (J)   001011; score = 5

You can also generate more offspring:

(F) 101:011
(G) 011:000
(K) 101000; score = 4
(L) 011011; score = 4

Now repeat the processes with (J) and (K) as parents, and duplicate the crossover:

(J) 00101:1
(K) 10100:0
(M) 001010; score = 6

That's it! You have reached the solution after 13 guesses. Not bad compared to the expected average of 32 for a random-guess strategy.

Terminology of Genetic Algorithms

A genetic algorithm is an iterative procedure that represents its candidate solutions as strings of genes called **chromosomes** and measures their viability with a fitness function. The fitness function is a measure of the objective to be obtained (i.e., maximum or minimum). As in biological systems, candidate solutions combine to produce offspring in each algorithmic iteration, called a *generation*. The offspring themselves can become candidate solutions. From the generation of parents and children, a set of the fittest survive to become parents that produce offspring in the next generation. Offspring are produced using a specific genetic reproduction process that involves the application of crossover and mutation operators. Along with the offspring, some of the best solutions are also migrated to the next generation (a concept called **elitism**) in order to preserve the best solution achieved up until the current iteration. Following are brief definitions of these key terms:

- *Reproduction.* Through **reproduction**, genetic algorithms produce new generations of potentially improved solutions by selecting parents with higher fitness ratings or by giving such parents a greater probability of being selected to contribute to the reproduction process.

- *Crossover.* Many genetic algorithms use a string of binary symbols (each corresponding to a decision variable) to represent chromosomes (potential solutions), as was the case in the Vector game described earlier. **Crossover** means choosing a random position in the string (e.g., after the first two digits) and exchanging the segments either to the right or the left of that point with those of another string's segments (generated using the same splitting schema) to produce two new offspring.

- *Mutation.* This genetic operator was not shown in the Vector game example. **Mutation** is an arbitrary (and minimal) change in the representation of a chromosome. It is often used to prevent the algorithm from getting stuck in a local optimum. The procedure randomly selects a chromosome (giving more probability to the ones with better fitness value) and randomly identifies a gene in the chromosome and inverses its value (from 0 to 1 or from 1 to 0), thus generating one new chromosome for the next generation. The occurrence of mutation is usually set to a very low probability (0.1 percent).

- *Elitism.* An important aspect in genetic algorithms is to preserve a few of the best solutions to evolve through the generations. That way, you are guaranteed to end up with the best possible solution for the current application of the algorithm. In practice, a few of the best solutions are migrated to the next generation.

How Do Genetic Algorithms Work?

Figure 13.4 is a flow diagram of a typical genetic algorithm process. The problem to be solved must be described and represented in a manner amenable to a genetic algorithm. Typically, this means that a string of 1s and 0s (or other more recently proposed complex representations) are used to represent the decision variables, the collection of which represents a potential solution to the problem. Next, the decision variables are mathematically and/or symbolically pooled into a *fitness function* (or *objective function*). The fitness function can be one of two types: maximization (something that is more is better, such as profit) or minimization (something that is less is better, such as cost). Along with the fitness function, all of the constraints on decision variables that collectively dictate whether a solution is a feasible one should be demonstrated. Remember that only feasible solutions can be a part of the solution population. Infeasible ones are filtered out before finalizing a generation of solutions in the iterations process. Once the representation is complete, an initial set of solutions is generated (i.e., the initial population). All infeasible solutions are eliminated, and fitness functions are computed for the feasible ones. The solutions are rank-ordered based on their fitness values; those with better fitness values are given more probability (proportional to their relative fitness value) in the random selection process.

A few of the best solutions are migrated to the next generation. Using a random process, several sets of parents are identified to take part in the generation of offspring.

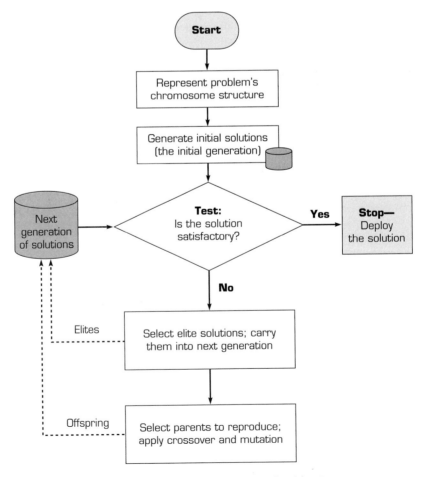

FIGURE 13.4 A Flow Diagram of a Typical Genetic Algorithm Process

Using the randomly selected parents and the genetic operators (i.e., crossover and mutation), offspring are generated. The number of potential solutions to generate is determined by the population size, which is an arbitrary parameter set prior to the evolution of solutions. Once the next generation is constructed, the solutions go through the evaluation and generation of new populations for a number of iterations. This iterative process continues until a good enough solution is obtained (an optimum is not guaranteed), no improvement occurs over several generations, or the time/iteration limit is reached.

As mentioned, a few parameters must be set prior to the execution of the genetic algorithm. Their values are dependent on the problem being solved and are usually determined through trial and error:

- Number of initial solutions to generate (i.e., the initial population)
- Number of offspring to generate (i.e., the population size)
- Number of parents to keep for the next generation (i.e., elitism)
- Mutation probability (usually a very low number, such as 0.1 percent)
- Probability distribution of crossover point occurrence (generally equally weighted)
- Stopping criteria (time/iteration based or improvement based)
- The maximum number of iterations (if the stopping criteria are time/iteration based)

Sometimes these parameters are set and frozen beforehand, or they can be varied systematically while the algorithm is running for better performance. For more information on the GA process, please see Niettinen et al. (1999) and Grupe and Jooste (2004).

Example: The Knapsack Problem

The knapsack problem is a conceptually simple optimization problem that can be solved directly using analytical methods. Even so, it is ideal for illustrating a genetic algorithm approach. Say that you are going on an overnight hike and have a number of items that you could take along. Each item has a weight (in pounds) and a benefit or value to you on the hike (say, in U.S. dollars), and you can take one, at most, of each item (sorry, no partial items allowed—it's all or nothing). There is a capacity limit on the weight you can carry (only one constraint, but there can be several measures and capacities, including volume, time, etc.). The knapsack problem has many important applications, including determining what items to carry on a space shuttle mission. For our example, there are seven items, numbered 1 through 7, with respective benefits and weights as follows:

Item	1	2	3	4	5	6	7
Benefit	5	8	3	2	7	9	4
Weight	7	8	4	10	4	6	4

The knapsack holds a maximum of 22 pounds. The string 1010100, with a total benefit or fitness of $7 + 4 + 4 = 15$, can represent a solution of items 1, 3, and 5.

We set up the problem in an Excel worksheet, where we represent a solution as a string of seven 1s and 0s and the fitness function as the total benefit, which is the sum of the gene values in a string solution multiplied by their respective benefit coefficients. The method generates a set of random solutions (i.e., initial parents), uses the objective function (i.e., total benefit) for the fitness function, and selects parents randomly to create generations of offspring through crossover and mutation operations. Selection is statistically based on the parents' fitness values. Higher values are more likely to be selected than lower ones. In Figure 13.5, we show the best solution found by Evolver, an easy-to-use Excel add-in genetic algorithm package (from Palisade Corp., **palisade.com**; demo available online).

Another interesting example of using a genetic algorithm is the shortest-tracks-route example provided by Grupe and Jooste (2004).

Limitations of Genetic Algorithms

According to Grupe and Jooste (2004), the following are among the most important limitations of genetic algorithms:

- Not all problems can be framed in the mathematical manner that genetic algorithms demand.
- Development of a genetic algorithm and interpretation of the results requires an expert who has both the programming and statistical/mathematical skills demanded by the genetic algorithm technology in use.
- It is known that in a few situations the "genes" from a few comparatively highly fit (but not optimal) individuals may come to dominate the population, causing it to converge on a local maximum. When the population has converged, the ability of the genetic algorithm to continue to search for better solutions is effectively eliminated.
- Most genetic algorithms rely on random number generators that produce different results each time the model runs. Although there is likely to be a high degree of consistency among the runs, they may vary.

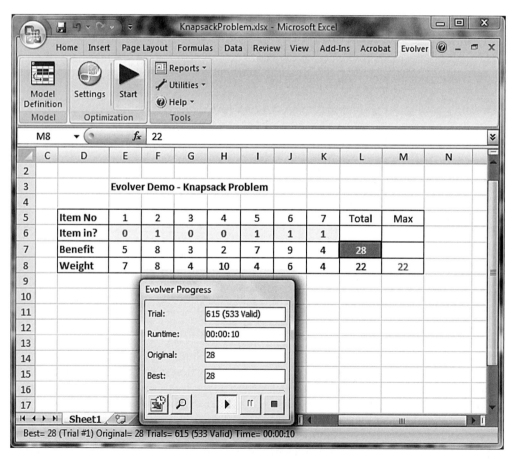

FIGURE 13.5   Evolver's Solution to the Knapsack Problem Example

- Locating good variables that work for a particular problem is difficult. Obtaining the data to populate the variables is equally demanding.
- Selecting methods by which to evolve the system requires thought and evaluation. If the range of possible solutions is small, a genetic algorithm will converge too quickly on a solution. When evolution proceeds too quickly, thereby altering good solutions too quickly, the results may miss the optimum solution.

Genetic Algorithm Applications

Genetic algorithms are a type of machine learning for representing and solving complex problems. They provide a set of efficient, domain-independent search heuristics for a broad spectrum of applications, including the following:

- Dynamic process control
- Induction of optimization of rules
- Discovery of new connectivity topologies (e.g., neural computing connections, neural network design)
- Simulation of biological models of behavior and evolution
- Complex design of engineering structures
- Pattern recognition
- Scheduling
- Transportation and routing
- Layout and circuit design
- Telecommunication
- Graph-based problems

A genetic algorithm interprets information that enables it to reject inferior solutions and accumulate good ones, and thus it learns about its universe. Genetic algorithms are also suitable for parallel processing.

Over the past two decades, the number of successful business applications of genetic algorithms has increased. For example, since 1993 Channel 4 television (England) has been using a genetic algorithm embedded in an ES to schedule its commercials to maximize revenues (see **xpertrule.com**). In another example, a team of researchers at the Electrotechnical Laboratory (ETL) in Japan developed a hardware-implemented genetic algorithm on a central processing unit (CPU) chip that minimizes the impact of imperfect clock cycles in integrated-circuit fabrication variations. Increasing the chip yield rate from 2.9 percent to 51.1 percent cleared the path toward inexpensive gigahertz clock rate CPUs for PCs (see Johnson, 1999).

Examples of genetic algorithms applied to real problems include those for assembly-line balancing (see Application Case 13.2), facility layout, machine and job shop scheduling, production planning, industrial packing and cutting, task assignment for satellites, construction scheduling with limited resources, utility pricing, personnel planning, sawmill board-cut selection, scheduling of ship maintenance for a large fleet, Web searches (see Nick and Themis, 2001), routing based on the traveling salesperson problem (see Baker and Syechew, 2003), design and improvement of water-distribution systems and similar networks, determination of creditworthiness, and aircraft design. Several other applications are listed in Grupe and Jooste (2004).

Genetic algorithms are often used to improve the performance of other artificial intelligence methods, such as ES or neural networks. In neural networks, genetic algorithms dynamically adjust to find the optimal network weights (see Kuo and Chen, 2004). The integration of multiple intelligent methods is discussed in Section 13.8. For a genetic algorithm environment for the Internet, see Tan et al. (2005).

APPLICATION CASE 13.2

Genetic Algorithms Schedule Assembly Lines at Volvo Trucks North America

The buyer of a Volvo 770 trailer cab has dozens of choices: engine size, paint color, fabric, woodgrain finish, stereo, suspension, axles, bumpers, pneumatic systems, transmissions, and so on. When the cost is more than $100,000 and the time to be spent in the cab is about 2,000 hours a year, the buyer should have plenty of options. This leads to millions of configurations Volvo can use to build a truck. When a specific truck is to be built, all the tools and parts must be available, but this is difficult to schedule with so many possible combinations.

Gus Riley is responsible for scheduling the assembly line at Volvo's million-square-foot factory in Dublin, Virginia. He must cope with hundreds of constraints. Until 1995, Riley solved this operations research problem by eyeballing the production requirements for each week (on the average output of 550 trucks per week) and sorting color-coded punch cards, each representing one truck and its characteristics that might affect scheduling. It took 4 days to construct a week's schedule, and there were always bottlenecks as conditions changed on the factory floor.

In August 1996, Volvo installed OptiFlex (from i2 Technologies), which uses genetic algorithms to evolve a good schedule from a sequence of so-so schedules. Jeffrey Herrmann, a vice president at i2 Technologies, explained, "You tell it what the

production at the end of a period should be and then you go have a cup of coffee." The program randomly devises 100 feasible solutions and ranks them according to cost, labor constraints, materials availability, and productivity. Then the program connects parts of good schedules to parts of other ones in an effort to find even better solutions.

The offspring of these genetic pairings are thrown into the pool, which is evaluated and ranked again. The pool is always kept at 100 by deleting poorer solutions. Running through roughly five iterations per second, OptiFlex comes up with maybe not the best possible schedule, but a good one, in minutes.

Each Wednesday, Riley feeds in data to make the weekly schedule 5 weeks out. He eyeballs it and tinkers with it by tightening some constraints and loosening others. He catches errors in data entry. OptiFlex, running on a PC connected to the factory network, accepts corrections and quickly generates new solutions. Creating a schedule takes only 1 day instead of 4. And reworking the schedule because of unforeseen events, such as customers changing their minds about features or broken equipment, takes only minutes.

Sources: Adapted from S. S. Rao, "Evolution at Warp Speed," *Forbes*, January 12, 1998, pp. 82–83; and "Job-Shop Scheduling at the Volvo Truck Plant," CNN Interactive, November 6, 1998 (no longer available online).

Because the kernels of genetic algorithms are pretty simple, it is not difficult to write computer codes to implement them. For better performance, software packages are available. A brief description of some of the available software programs is provided in Technology Insights 13.1.

TECHNOLOGY INSIGHTS 13.1   Genetic Algorithm Software

Several genetic algorithm codes are available for fee or for free (try searching the Web for research and commercial sites). In addition, a number of commercial packages offer online demos. Representative commercial packages include Microsoft Solver and XpertRule GenAsys, an ES shell with an embedded genetic algorithm (see **xpertrule.com**). Genetic algorithms are also related to artificial life scenarios, such as John Conway's Game of Life (e.g., Stephen Stuart's Java implementation at **tech.org/~stuart/life**). Also see the predictive suite from Predictive Dynamix, Inc. (**predictivedynamix.com**)

Evolver (from Palisade Corp., **palisade.com**) is an optimization add-in for Excel. It uses an innovative genetic algorithm to quickly solve complex optimization problems in finance, scheduling, manufacturing, and so on. See the example in Figure 13.6.

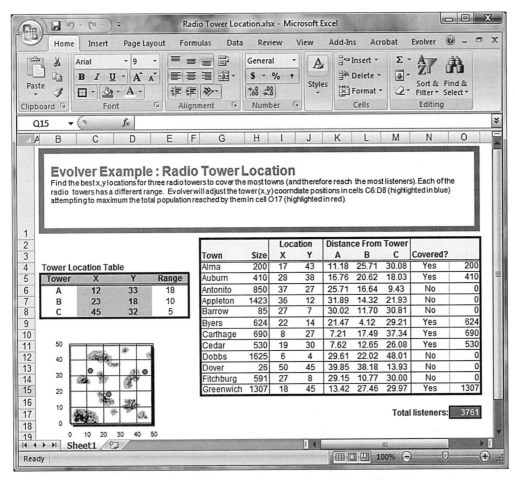

FIGURE 13.6 Evolver Finds Solutions to Optimization Problems Using Genetic Algorithms
Source: Palisade.com.

Section 13.4 Review Questions

1. Define *genetic algorithm*.
2. Describe the evolution process in genetic algorithms. How is it similar to biological evolution?
3. Describe the major genetic algorithm operators.
4. List major areas of genetic algorithm application.
5. Describe in detail three genetic algorithm applications.
6. Describe the capability of Evolver as an optimization tool.

13.5 FUZZY LOGIC AND FUZZY INFERENCE SYSTEMS

Fuzzy logic deals with reasoning that is approximate rather than precise, which intimately resembles the kind of uncertainty and partial information that today's decision makers are constantly being exposed to in real-world situations. In contrast to binary logic, also known as *crisp logic*, the variables represented with fuzzy logic can have membership values other than just 0 or 1 (or true/false, yes/no, black/white, etc.). The term *fuzzy logic* emerged from the development of the theory of fuzzy sets by Lotfi Zadeh (1965). This technique, which uses the mathematical theory of **fuzzy sets**, simulates the process of human reasoning by allowing the computer to process information that is less precise, which is quite contrary to the foundation of conventional computer logic. The thinking behind this approach is that decision making is not always a matter of "black or white" or "true or false"; it often involves tones of gray and varying degrees of truth. In fact, creative decision-making processes are usually unstructured, playful, contentious, and rambling.

Fuzzy logic can be useful because it is an effective way to describe human perceptions of many decision-making problems in situations that are not 100 percent true or false. Many control and decision-making problems do not easily fit into the strict true/false situation required by mathematical models, and when they are forced into such binary logic representation they tend to suffer from lack of representational integrity and inaccurate reasoning. A good description of fuzzy logic and its applications can be found in Tanaka and Niimura (2007) and at the Stanford Encyclopedia of Philosophy (**plato.stanford.edu/entries/logic-fuzzy/**).

Example: Fuzzy Set for a Tall Person

Let's look at an example of a fuzzy set that describes a tall person. If we survey people to define the minimum height a person must attain before being considered tall, the answers could range from 5 to 7 feet (1 foot is about 30 cm, 1 inch is 2.54 cm). The distribution of answers might look like this:

Height	Proportion Voted For
5'10"	0.05
5'11"	0.10
6'	0.60
6'1"	0.15
6'2"	0.10

Suppose that Jack's height is 6 feet. From probability theory, we can use the cumulative probability distribution and say that there is a 75 percent chance that Jack is tall. In fuzzy logic, we say that Jack's degree of membership in the set of tall people is 0.75. The difference is that in probability terms Jack is perceived as either tall or not tall, and we are not completely sure whether he is tall. In contrast, in fuzzy logic, we agree that Jack is more or less tall. Then we can assign a membership function to show the relationship of Jack to the set of tall people (i.e., the fuzzy logic set):

<Jack, 0.75 = Tall>

In contrast to certainty factors, which include two values (e.g., the degrees of belief and disbelief), fuzzy sets use a spectrum of possible values called *belief functions*. We express our belief that a particular item belongs to a set through a membership function, as shown in Figure 13.7. At a height of 69 inches, a person starts to be considered tall, and at 74 inches, he or she is definitely tall. Between 69 and 74 inches, the person's membership function value varies from 0 to 1. Likewise, a person has a membership function value in the set of short people and medium-height people, depending on his or her height. The medium range spans both the short and tall ranges, so a person has a belief of potentially being a member of more than one fuzzy set at a time. This is a critical strength of fuzzy sets: They lack crispness, yet they are consistent in their logic.

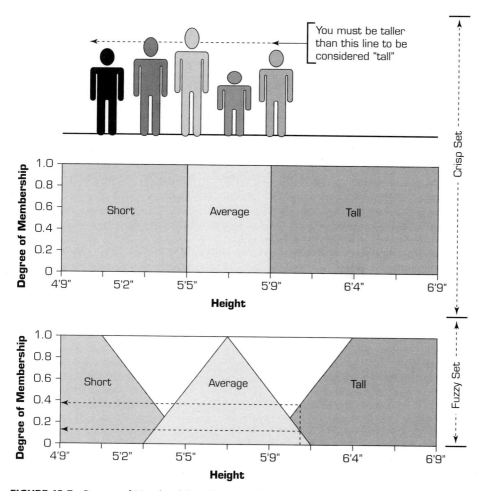

FIGURE 13.7 Degree of Membership in Fuzzy Logic and in Crisp Logic

The application of fuzzy logic to managerial decision support has recently been gaining momentum despite the fact that it is complex to develop, requires considerable computing power, and is difficult to explain to users. However, thanks to increasing computational power and software, this situation has been changing since the 1990s.

Fuzzy Inference System

A fuzzy inference system (or *fuzzy expert system*) is essentially an expert system where the knowledge is represented in the form of fuzzy rules. Fuzzy inference is the process of formulating the mapping between a given set of inputs and an output using fuzzy logic. The process of fuzzy inference involves three main components: membership functions, logical operators, and fuzzy if-then rules. Different values of variables are represented with membership functions as opposed to crisp values (e.g., the value "tall" of the variable height can be represented with a trapezoidal function with some specific parameter). The rules are represented using fuzzy variable values (e.g., IF a person is *tall*, THEN his odds of becoming a basketball player are *high*). The logical operators are then used to combine and consolidate the fuzzy variables in order to reach the most accurate conclusion.

The fuzzy inference system comprises four steps. First, the crisp inputs provided by the user (a human or a machine) are converted into their fuzzy representations using their respective fuzzy membership functions. The *fuzzified* inputs are then presented to the inference engine to fire the fuzzy rules. The outcome of the fuzzy rules is then combined to form a fuzzy output using logic operators. In the last step, the fuzzy output is converted back into crisp values using an operation called **defuzzification.** This four-step process, along with a simple example of determining what percent tip to leave at a restaurant, is shown in Figure 13.8 (this example is adopted from the MathWork's fuzzy logic toolbox tutorial). As can be seen, the crisp inputs (service quality and food quality—each represented with a number between 0 and 10) are pushed through the fuzzy inference system (firing three fuzzy rules) to ultimately generate a crisp output (percent tip to leave).

Fuzzy Logic Applications

Fuzzy logic is difficult to apply when people supply the membership information. The problems range from linguistic vagueness to difficulty in supplying the definitions needed. Fuzzy logic is being used extensively in the area of consumer products, where the input is provided by sensors rather than by people. Fuzzy logic in consumer products is sometimes called *continuous logic* (after all, who wants a fuzzy camcorder?). Fuzzy logic provides smooth motion in consumer products. It is also appropriate for subway control systems and for other motor controls and navigation (see Ross, 2004).

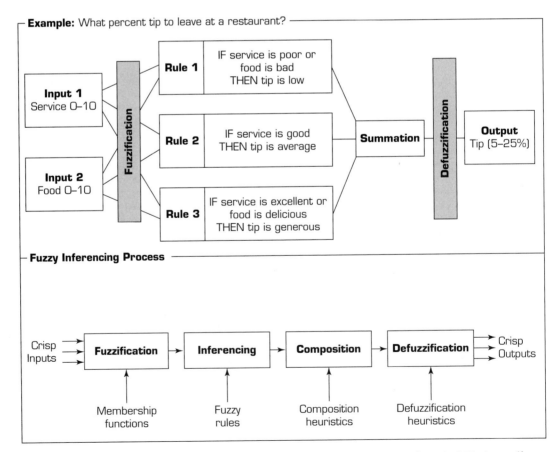

FIGURE 13.8 The Fuzzy Inference System for the Tipping Problem *Source:* Based on MathWork.com (from Mathlab Fuzzy Logic Toolbox Tutorial).

FUZZY LOGIC APPLICATIONS FOR MANUFACTURING AND MANAGEMENT Fuzzy logic applications are well known in consumer products such as air conditioners, antilock brakes, toasters, cameras, camcorders, dishwashers, and microwaves. Fuzzy logic has also been applied to the following industrial and managerial areas:

- Selection of stocks to purchase
- Data retrieval
- Inspection of beverage cans for printing defects
- Matching of golf clubs to customers' swings
- Risk assessment
- Control of the amount of oxygen in cement kilns
- Accuracy and speed increases in industrial quality-control applications
- Sorting problems in multidimensional spaces
- Enhancement of models involving queuing (i.e., waiting lines)
- Managerial decision-support applications
- Project selection
- Environmental control in buildings
- Control of the motion of trains
- Paper mill automation
- Space shuttle vehicle orbiting
- Regulation of water temperature in shower heads

FUZZY LOGIC APPLICATIONS IN BUSINESS Many fuzzy logic applications in the area of controls and automation have been reported. We next provide three examples of fuzzy logic applications in business.

Example 1: Fuzzy Strategic Planning Hall (1987) developed STRATASSIST, a fuzzy ES that helps small- to medium-sized firms plan strategically for a single product. During a consultation, STRATASSIST asks questions in five strategic, competitive areas that a firm should consider in evaluating its strengths and weaknesses:

- Threat of new entries to the industry
- Threat of substitute products
- Buyer group power (i.e., consumers' power)
- Supplier group power
- Rivalry in the industry

Each question asks the user to rate the firm in each of these competitive areas. STRATASSIST feeds the answers into its fuzzy knowledge base, which consists of rules such as the following:

IF the importance of personal service in the distribution of your product is high,

THEN strategic action should be to distribute the firm's product or service through small, flexible, local units.

Hall used uncommonly rigorous experimental design procedures to test STRATASSIST's effectiveness. He asked MBA students to develop strategic plans for a fictional company. One-third of the students used STRATASSIST output in their planning, one-third used answers to the questions in the five strength/weakness areas, and one-third worked without STRATASSIST. Twelve expert judges from academia and industry rated the students' plans. The students who used STRATASSIST were judged to have formulated significantly better strategies than the others. See Dwinnell (2002) for additional applications of fuzzy logic in strategic decision making.

Example 2: Fuzziness in Real Estate   In conducting property appraisals, it is necessary to use judgment to generate estimates. Experience and intuition are essential factors. Some of the needed estimates are land value, value of buildings, building replacement costs, and the amount the building has appreciated. Then it is necessary to review sales of comparable properties, decide what is relevant, and, finally, estimate the net income. Most of these data are fuzzy. See Bagnoli and Smith (1998) for fuzzy logic applications in real estate.

Example 3: A Fuzzy Bond-Evaluation System   The value of bonds depends on factors such as company profitability, assets, and liability; market volatility; and possibly fluctuations in foreign exchange and risk. There is considerable fuzziness in factors such as foreign exchange risk. Chorafas (1994) constructed a fuzzy logic system that helps in making decisions about investing in bonds. The results indicate superior values over an average noncomputerized bond evaluation.

New applications of fuzzy logic are continually being developed because of its effectiveness. For examples, a fuzzy logic system was proposed for terrorist detection (see Cox, 2001). For other applications, see Liao (2003) and Xu and Xu (2003).

Software companies in this field include Rigel Corp. (**rigelcorp.com/flash.htm**) and Inform Software (**informusa.com/fuzzy/index.htm**).

Section 13.5 Review Questions

1. Define *fuzzy logic* and describe its characteristics.
2. What are the basic premises behind the fuzzy logic approach?
3. What are the major advantages of fuzzy logic? What are its major limitations?
4. List some nonbusiness applications of fuzzy logic.
5. List some business applications of fuzzy logic.

13.6   SUPPORT VECTOR MACHINES

Support vector machines (SVM) are one of the most popular machine-learning techniques. They belong to the family of generalized linear models, which achieve a classification or regression decision based on the value of the linear combination of input features. Because of their architectural similarities, SVM are also closely associated with feedforward-type artificial neural networks.

Using historical data along with supervised learning algorithms, SVM generate mathematical functions to map input variables to desired outputs for classification and/or regression prediction problems. For classification problems, nonlinear kernel functions are often used to transform the input variables (inherently representing highly complex nonlinear relationships) to a high-dimensional feature space in which the input data become more separable (i.e., linearly separable) compared to the original input space. Then, the maximum-margin hyperplanes are constructed to optimally separate different classes from each other based on the given training dataset. A **hyperplane** is a geometric concept commonly used to describe the separation surface between different classes of things within a multidimensional space. In SVM, two parallel hyperplanes usually are constructed on each side of the separation space with the aim of maximizing the distance between them. It is assumed that the larger the distance between these two parallel hyperplanes, the lower the generalization error (and hence the greater the prediction accuracy) of the classifier will be.

In addition to their solid mathematical foundation in statistical learning theory, SVM have demonstrated highly competitive performance in numerous real-world applications, including medical diagnosis, bioinformatics, face recognition, financial predictions, and text mining, which has established SVM as one of the most popular tools for knowledge discovery and data mining.

Similar to artificial neural networks, SVM possess the well-known ability of being universal approximators of any multivariate function to any desired degree of accuracy. Therefore, they are of particular interest to modeling highly nonlinear, complex systems and decision situations.

How Does SVM Work?

Generally, many linear hyperplanes are able to separate data into multiple subsections, each belonging to a specific class. However, only one hyperplane achieves maximum separation. Following a machine-learning process, SVM *learns* from the historic cases (represented as data points) to build a mathematical model that can optimally assign the data instances into respective classes. If there are only two dimensions, the data may be separated with a line; however, most real-world problems have data points in more than two dimensions. In that case, we are interested in separating the data into classes by an $n - 1$ dimensional hyperplane. Though this may be seen as a typical form of linear classifier, the goal is to achieve the maximum separation (margin) between the two (or more) classes. As Figure 13.9a illustrates, the squares and circles (the two classes represented in a two-dimensional space) can be separated from each other using a number of lines (e.g., L_1, L_2, L_3). SVM aims to pick a hyperplane so that the distance from the hyperplane to the nearest data point is maximized. Now, if such a hyperplane exists, it is clearly of interest to the modeler and is known as the *maximum-margin hyperplane*, and such a linear classifier is called a *maximum-margin classifier* (see Figure 13.9b).

Implementation

The parameters of the maximum-margin hyperplane are derived by solving the quadratic optimization problem. This is a highly complex and laborious task, and several specialized algorithms have been developed to quickly solve the quadratic optimization problem. These algorithms mostly rely on heuristics that break the problem down into smaller, more-manageable chunks and solve them at that granular level. One well-known algorithm is Platt's sequential minimal optimization (SMO), which breaks the problem down into two-dimensional subproblems that can be solved analytically (Platt 1998), eliminating the need for a burdensome iterative numeric procedure such as the conjugate gradient method.

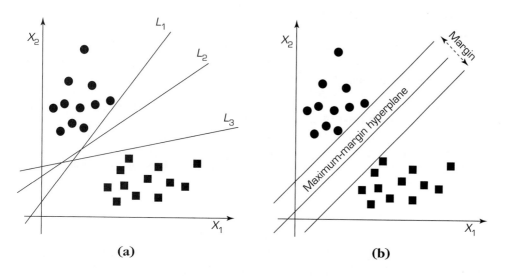

FIGURE 13.9   Many Linear Classifiers (Hyperplanes) May Separate the Data

Kernel Trick

In machine learning, the **kernel trick** is a method for using a linear classifier algorithm to solve a nonlinear problem by mapping the original nonlinear observations onto a higher-dimensional space, where the linear classifier is subsequently used; this makes a linear classification in the new space equivalent to nonlinear classification in the original space. In SVM, kernel trick allows us to construct a decision surface that is linear in the feature space (i.e., higher-dimensional space) while it is inherently nonlinear in the original input space. Such a transformation is done by using Mercer's theorem, which states that any continuous, symmetric, positive semidefinite kernel function can be expressed as a dot product in a high-dimensional space.

The kernel trick transforms any algorithm that exclusively depends on the dot product between two vectors. Wherever a dot product is used, it is replaced with the kernel function. Thus, a linear algorithm can easily be transformed into a nonlinear algorithm. This nonlinear algorithm is equivalent to the linear algorithm operating in the higher-dimensional space. However, because kernels are used, the higher-dimensional space function is never explicitly computed, hence the name *kernel trick*. This is desirable, because the high-dimensional space may be an infinite-dimensional one (as is the case when the kernel is a Gaussian).

Although the origin of the term *kernel trick* is not known, it was first published by Aizerman et al. (1964). Since then, it has been applied to several kinds of algorithms in machine learning and statistics, including neural networks, support vector machines, principal components analysis, Fisher's linear discriminant analysis, and variety of clustering methods.

The Process of Building SVM

Due largely to the better classification results, SVM have become a popular technique for classification-type problems. Even though people consider them to be easier to use than artificial neural networks, users who are not familiar with the intricacies of SVM often get unsatisfactory results. What follows is a simple recipe (a step-by-step process) to develop SVM-based prediction models that are more likely to produce better results:

1. Preprocess the data.
   a. Scrub the data.
   - Deal with the missing values.
   - Deal with the presumably erroneous values.
   - Deal with the noisy data.

   b. Transform the data.
   - Numerisize the data
   - Normalize the data

2. Develop the model.
   a. Select the **kernel type** (RBF is often a natural choice).
   b. Determine the kernel parameters based on the selected kernel type (e.g., C and γ for RBF). This is a difficult decision, because there is no universally optimal choice here. One should consider using cross-validation and experimentation to determine the most appropriate values for these parameters.
   c. If the results are satisfactory, finalize the model, otherwise change the kernel type and/or kernel parameters to achieve the desired accuracy level.

3. Extract and deploy the model.

For clarification purposes, a pictorial representation of the recipe is depicted in Figure 13.10. A brief description for some of the important steps (and substeps) of this process follows.

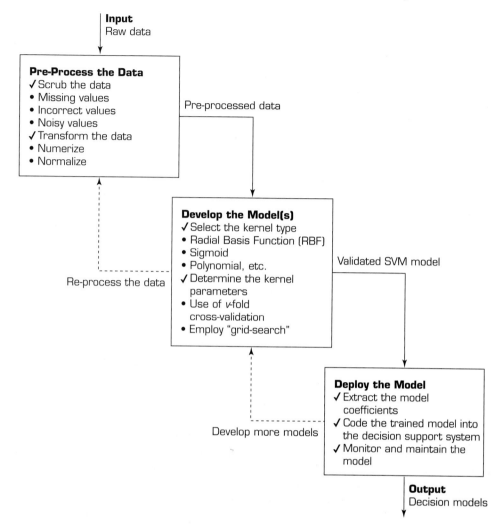

FIGURE 13.10 A Three-Step Process Description for SVM Model Development

NUMERISIZING THE DATA Similar to ANN, SVM also require that each data instance be represented as a vector of real numbers. Hence, if there are categorical attributes, they need to be converted into numeric data representations. It is often recommended to use m pseudo-variables to represent an m-category attribute. To represent a unique value, only one of the m numbers (corresponding to the value) is set to 1, and others are set to 0. For example, a three-category attribute such as {red, green, blue} can be represented as {0,0,1}, {0,1,0}, and {1,0,0}.

NORMALIZING THE DATA Again, similar to ANN, SVM want the input data to be normalized prior to the training process. The main advantage of normalizing (or scaling) the data is to avoid attributes in greater numeric ranges dominating those in smaller numeric ranges. Another advantage is to avoid numerical burden during the iterative calculations. Because kernel values usually depend on the inner products of feature vectors (e.g., the linear kernel and the polynomial kernel), large attribute values might cause calculation and rounding problems. It is recommended to linearly scale each attribute to the range [−1, +1] or [0, 1]. Of course, we have to use the same method to scale the testing data before they are presented to the trained model.

SELECT THE KERNEL MODEL   Although there are only four common kernels mentioned in this section, we must decide which one to try first. Then, the penalty parameter C and kernel parameters are chosen. According to the SVM literature, in the absence of compelling reasons, RBF is the reasonable first choice. The RBF kernel nonlinearly maps samples into a higher-dimensional space, so it can (unlike the linear kernel) handle the case when the relations between class labels and attributes are nonlinear. Furthermore, the linear kernel is a special case of RBF, such that the linear kernel with a penalty parameter C has the same performance as the RBF kernel with the corresponding parameters (C, γ). The second reason is the number of hyperparameters, which influences the complexity of model selection. The polynomial kernel has more hyperparameters than the RBF kernel. Finally, the RBF kernel has fewer numerical difficulties.

Two parameters must be set when using RBF kernels: C and γ. It is not known beforehand which C and γ are the best for one specific prediction problem; consequently, some kind of model selection (parameter search) must be done. The goal is to identify good (C, γ) so that the classifier can accurately predict unknown data (i.e., testing data). Note that it may not be useful to achieve high training accuracy (i.e., classifiers accurately predict training data whose class labels are indeed known). Therefore, a common way is to separate training data into two parts, one of which is considered unknown in training the classifier. Then the prediction accuracy on this set can more precisely reflect the performance on classifying unknown data.

An improved version of this procedure is cross-validation. In v-fold cross-validation, we first divide the training set into v subsets of equal size. Sequentially, one subset is tested using the classifier trained on the remaining $v - 1$ subsets. Thus, each instance of the whole training set is predicted once so that the cross-validation accuracy is the percentage of data that are classified correctly. The cross-validation procedure can prevent the overfitting problem.

Another recommendation for dealing with the overfitting problem is a "grid search" on C and γ using cross-validation. Basically pairs of (C, γ) are tried and the one with the best cross-validation accuracy is picked. Exponentially growing sequences of C and γ is a practical method to identify good parameters (e.g., $C = 2 - 5, 2 - 3, \ldots, 215$, $\gamma = 2 - 15, 2 - 13, \ldots, 23$). Grid search is straightforward, but it seems brainless. Several advanced methods can save computational cost by, for example, approximating the cross-validation rate. However, there are two motivations why the simple grid-search approach is preferable: (1) it provides an exhaustive search of all possible options, and (2) it does not take much longer than more sophisticated heuristic search techniques. In some situations, the proposed procedure is not good enough, so other techniques, such as feature selection, may be needed. Such issues are beyond our consideration here. Our experience indicates that the simple grid-search-based SVM procedure explained above works well for data that do not have very many features. If there are thousands of attributes, it may be best to choose a subset of them before giving the data to SVM.

Applications of SVM

SVM are the most widely used kernel-learning algorithms for a wide range of classification and regression problems. According to Haykin (2009), in the machine-learning literature SVM represent the state-of-the-art by virtue of their excellent generalization performance, superior prediction power, ease of use, and rigorous theoretical foundation. Testimony to this claim is a number of recently published research articles where the results of SVM are compared against other prediction methods.

DIAGNOSING NERVE DISEASE   Polat et al. (2009) compared several classifier algorithms, including the C4.5 decision tree classifier, the least squares support vector machine (LS-SVM), and the artificial immune recognition system (AIRS) for diagnosing macular and optic nerve diseases from electroretinography signal patterns. Electroretinography signal patterns were obtained from 106 subjects who had optic nerve and/or macular disease.

In order to show the unbiased test performance of the classifier algorithms, a number of measures were used, including classification accuracy, receiver operating characteristic curves, sensitivity and specificity values, a confusion matrix, and 10-fold cross-validation. The classification results obtained were 81.82, 85.9, and 100 percent for the AIRS classifier, C4.5 decision tree classifier, and the LS-SVM classifier, respectively, using a 10-fold cross-validation methodology. The study showed that the SVM classifier was significantly better than the other two classifiers in correctly diagnosing macular and optic nerve diseases. It has also proven to be a robust and efficient classifier system.

IDENTIFYING THE WINNER OF COMPETITIVE EVENTS   Use of predictive modeling for the identification of winners in competitive events (e.g., games, races, elections) has been an interesting and exceptionally challenging problem for researchers and practitioners alike. A study by Lessmann et al. (2009) used prediction modeling to identify the winners at horse races. The goal of such modeling is to appraise the informational efficiency of betting markets. The prevailing approach involves forecasting the runners' finish positions by means of discrete or continuous-response regression models. However, theoretical considerations and empirical evidence suggest that the information contained within finish positions might be unreliable, especially among minor placements. Lessmann et al. proposed a classification-based modeling paradigm to alleviate this problem that relied only on data distinguishing winners and losers. To assess its effectiveness, an experiment was conducted using data from a UK racetrack. The results demonstrated that their SVM-based classification model compared favorably with the state-of-the-art alternatives and confirmed the reservations of relying on rank-ordered finishing data. Simulations conducted to further explore the origin of the model's success evaluated the marginal contribution of its constituent parts.

ANALYZING METABOLITE CONCENTRATIONS   *Metabolomics,* the systematic study of the unique chemical fingerprints that specific cellular processes leave behind, is an emerging field that is providing invaluable insight into physiological processes. It is an effective tool to investigate disease diagnosis or conduct toxicological studies by observing changes in metabolite concentrations in various biological fluids.

Traditionally, multivariate statistical analysis has been employed with nuclear magnetic resonance (NMR) or mass spectrometry (MS) data to determine differences between groups (e.g., diseased versus healthy individuals). Mahadevan et al. (2008) thought it might be possible to build distinctive predictive models based on a set of training data that are able to predict whether new data falls into a specific class. They obtained metabolomic data by performing NMR spectroscopy on urine samples obtained from healthy subjects (both male and female) and patients suffering from *Streptococcus* pneumonia, a human pathogenic bacterium recognized as a major cause of pneumonia. They compared the performance of traditional partial-least-squared discriminant analysis (PLS-DA) to support SVM on two case studies: (1) a case where nearly complete distinction can be seen (healthy versus pneumonia) and (2) a case where distinction was more ambiguous (male versus female). They showed that SVM were superior to PLS-DA in both cases in terms of predictive accuracy using the least number of features. SVM were able to generate more robust models with better predictive accuracy with fewer features when compared to PLS-DA.

Support Vector Machines Versus Artificial Neural Networks

The development of ANN followed a heuristic path, with applications and extensive experimentation preceding theory. In contrast, the development of SVM involved sound theory first, followed by implementation and experiments. A significant advantage of SVM is that although ANN can suffer from multiple local minima, the solution to an SVM is global and unique. Two additional advantages of SVM are that they have a simple geometric interpretation and give a sparse solution. Unlike ANN, the computational complexity of SVM does not depend on the dimensionality of the input space. ANN use empirical risk minimization, whereas SVM use structural risk minimization. The reason that SVM often outperform ANN in practice is that they deal with the biggest problem with ANN in that SVM are less prone to overfitting.

Benefits of SVM

The following are some of the major benefits of SVM:

- They differ radically from comparable approaches, such as neural networks. SVM always find a global minimum, and their simple geometric interpretation provides fertile ground for further investigation.
- Because the SVM approach "automatically" solves the network complexity problem, the size of the hidden layer is obtained as the result of the quadratic programming procedure. Hidden neurons and support vectors correspond to each other, so the center problems of the RBF network are also solved, because the support vectors serve as the basis function centers.
- In problem situations where linear decision hyperplanes are not feasible, an input space is mapped into a feature space (corresponding to the hidden layer in ANN models), resulting in a nonlinear classifier.
- SVM, after the learning stage, create the same type of decision hypersurfaces as do some well-developed and popular ANN classifiers. Note that the training of these diverse models is different. However, after the successful learning stage, the resulting decision surfaces are identical.
- Unlike conventional statistical and neural network methods, the SVM approach does not attempt to control model complexity by limiting the number of features.
- Classical learning systems such as neural networks suffer from their theoretical weakness (e.g., backpropagation usually converges only to locally optimal solutions). SVM can provide a significant improvement.
- In contrast to neural networks, SVM automatically select their model size (by selecting the support vectors).
- The absence of local minima from the algorithms marks a major departure from traditional systems such as neural networks.
- Although the weight decay term is an important aspect for obtaining good generalization in the context of neural networks for regression, the margin plays a somewhat similar role in classification problems.
- In comparison with traditional multilayer perceptron neural networks that suffer from the existence of multiple local minima solutions, convexity is an important and interesting property of nonlinear SVM classifiers.

Disadvantages of SVM

SVM are not immune to problems and limitations. Following are some of the most commonly observed ones:

- One of the biggest limitations of SVM lies in the choice of the kernel. Determination of the best kernel type for a specific dataset may require a laborious trial-and-error approach, especially when the dataset is rather large with a lot of variables.
- Speed and size are a problem, both in training and testing. SVM models tend to take more time to develop, compared to their counterparts.
- Development of discrete data is a time-consuming and tedious task.
- The optimal design for multiclass SVM classifiers is an ongoing research effort.
- Although SVM have good generalization performance, they can be abysmally slow in test phase, making them less desirable for situations requiring a quick response.
- Another important practical question that remains unsolved is the optimal selection of the kernel function parameters.
- From a practical point of view, perhaps the most serious problem with SVM is the high algorithmic complexity and extensive memory requirements of the quadratic optimization programming in large-scale modeling tasks.

Section 13.6 Review Questions

1. Define *support vector machines* and describe their characteristics.
2. How does SVM work? What types of problems can SVM be applied to?
3. What are the steps in building SVM solutions?
4. What are the major advantages of SVM? What are its major limitations?
5. List and discuss some applications of SVM.

13.7 INTELLIGENT AGENTS

An **intelligent agent (IA)** is an autonomous computer program that observes and acts upon an environment and directs its activity toward achieving specific goals. Intelligent agents may have the ability to learn by using and expanding the knowledge embedded into them. Intelligent agents are powerful tools for overcoming the most critical burden of the Internet—information overload—and making e-commerce a viable organizational tool. In the following sections, we provide definitions and discuss the capabilities of this promising agent technology.

Intelligent Agents: A Brief History and Definitions

The term *agent* is derived from the concept of agency, referring to employing someone to act on one's behalf. A human agent represents a person and interacts with others to accomplish a predefined task.

The concept of agents goes surprisingly far back. More than 60 years ago, Vannevar Bush envisioned a machine called a *memex*. He imagined the memex assisting humans to manage and process huge amounts of data and information. In the 1950s, John McCarthy developed *Advice Taker*, a software robot that would navigate the networks of information that would develop in the future (see McCarthy, 1958). Advice Taker's similarity to today's agents is amazing. Given a task by a human user, the robot autonomously takes the necessary steps to perform the task or asks for advice from the user when it gets stuck. The futuristic prototypes of intelligent personal agents, such as Apple's *Phil* and Microsoft's *Bob*, perform complicated tasks for their users, following the functionality first laid out by McCarthy in Advice Taker. Current trends in IA research are in mobility, intelligence, multiagent networks, and collaboration.

Several names have been used to describe intelligent agents, including *software agents, wizards, software daemons, softbots* (for "intelligent software robots"), or simply *bots*. These terms sometimes refer to different types of agents or agents with different capabilities and intelligence levels. Throughout this chapter and this book, we use the terms *intelligent agent, software agent,* and *intelligent software agent* interchangeably.One of the most common examples of learning agents was the Office Assistant found in Microsoft Office 2003 and previous editions. This agent automatically popped up to offer assistance when it "sensed" that the user was in need of help. Presumably, using some sort of machine-learning techniques, they can offer assistance on a timely manner as they observe and learn from the user's computer activities over time.

Daemon was a popular term for an intelligent agent in the early stages of IA development. Daemons are small computer programs that run in the background and take action by alerting the user of certain situations when certain prespecified conditions have been met. An example is the X Window program *xbiff*. This program monitors a user's incoming e-mail and indicates via an icon whether the user has any unread messages. Virus detection agents and e-mail inbox management agents are similar examples. The term *bot*, an abbreviation for "robot," has become a common substitute for the term *agent*. Bots have been given specific prefixes, based on their use. Typical bots include chatterbots, docbots, hotbots, jobbots, knowbots, mailbots, musicbots, shopbots, spiderbots, and spambots.

Intelligent agent can be defined in a number of ways, and each definition seems to explicate the definer's perspective. Here are some examples:

- According to IBM, *intelligent agents* are software entities that carry out some set of operations on behalf of a user or another program, with some degree of independence or autonomy, and in so doing, employ some knowledge or representation of the user's goals or desires (Knapik and Johnson, 1998).
- According to Maes (1995), a well-known researcher from MIT, *autonomous agents* are computational systems that inhabit some complex dynamic environment, sense and act autonomously in that environment, and by doing so realize a set of goals or tasks for which they are designed.
- According to Wooldridge (2009), an *agent* is a computer system that is situated in some environment and that is capable of autonomous action in that environment in order to meet its design objectives. Intelligent agents continuously perform three functions: perceive the dynamic conditions in the environment, act to affect certain conditions in the environment, and reason to interpret perceptions, solve problems, draw inferences, and determine actions.
- According to Hess et al. (2002), an *intelligent agent* is a software implementation of a task in a specified domain, on behalf or in lieu of an individual or another agent. The implementation contains homeostatic goal(s), persistence, and reactivity to the degree that the implementation (1) will persist long enough to carry out the goal(s) and (2) will reach sufficiently within its domain to allow the goal(s) to be met and to know that fact.
- Franklin and Graesser (1996) defined *autonomous agent* as a system situated within and part of an environment that senses the environment and acts on it, over time, in pursuit of its own agenda, so as to affect what it senses in the future.

These definitions from different perspectives point out some of the commonalities and differences in the characteristics and capabilities of agents.

Intelligent agents often are associated with the following features (Wooldridge, 2009; Stenmark, 1999):

- ***Reactiveness.*** Intelligent agents are able to perceive their environment and respond in a timely fashion to changes that occur in it in order to satisfy their design objectives.

- ***Proactiveness.***   Intelligent agents are able to exhibit goal-directed behavior by taking the initiative in order to satisfy their design objectives.
- ***Sociability.***   Intelligent agents are capable of interacting with other agents (and possibly humans) in order to satisfy their design objectives.
- ***Autonomy.***   Intelligent agents must have control over their own actions and be able to work and launch actions independently of the user or other actors.
- ***Intelligence.***   Intelligent agents must learn from their experiences to continually get better at achieving their design objectives.

Components of an Agent

Intelligent agents are autonomous computer programs that are generally associated with the following components:

- ***Owner.***   The owner is the user name, parent process name, or master agent name. Intelligent agents can have several owners. Either humans or the process itself can spawn agents (e.g., a stockbroker or the brokerage process using intelligent agents) to monitor prices, and other intelligent agents can spawn their own supporting agents.
- ***Author.***   The author is the development owner, service, or master agent. Intelligent agents can be created by people or processes and then supplied as templates for users to personalize.
- ***Account.***   An intelligent agent must have an anchor to an owner's account and an electronic address for tracing and billing purposes.
- ***Goal.***   A clear statement of successful agent task completion is necessary, as are metrics for determining a task's point of completion and the value of the results. Measures of success can include simple completion of a transaction within the boundaries of the stated goal or a more complex measure. Often agents have recurring tasks that last indefinitely.
- ***Subject description.***   The subject description details the agent's purpose and attributes. These attributes provide the boundaries of the agent, task, possible resources to call on, and class of need (e.g., stock purchase price, airline ticket price).
- ***Creation and duration.***   The creation and duration are the time dependent attributes associated with an agent that describe when an instance of an agent should be created and when it should be terminated.
- ***Background.***   Intelligent agents are to run in the background, pursuing specific tasks without interfering with the ordinary activities of the operating system.
- ***Intelligent subsystem.***   An intelligent subsystem, such as a rule-based ES or a neural computing system, provides the agent's learning capabilities.

Characteristics of Intelligent Agents

In most cases, an agent is designed to accomplish a single task. A single task could be searching the Internet to find where and when certain items are auctioned, or it might be filtering e-mail to identify and categorize them into different groups. Although more advanced agents are capable of doing multiple tasks, it is likely that many future (and recent) agent systems will really be multiagent networks, a collection of agents, each handling a simple task (Wooldridge, 2009).

Although there is no single commonly accepted definition for the term *intelligent agent,* several traits and abilities that many people think of when they discuss intelligent agents can be considered their major characteristics. The following sections describe these traits and abilities.

AUTONOMY (EMPOWERMENT) An agent has **autonomy**; that is, it is capable of acting on its own or of being empowered. An agent must be able to make decisions on its own as a result of being goal oriented, collaborative, and flexible. It must be able to alter its course of behavior when it meets an obstacle and find ways around the impediment. Maes (1995) pointed out that regular computers respond only to direct manipulation, but with the advent of agents users are able to give open-ended commands to their electronic agents in order to get work done. For example, an agent should be able to accept high-level requests and decide on its own where and how to carry out each request. In the process, the agent should be able to ask clarification questions and modify requests instead of blindly obeying commands.

Autonomy implies that an agent takes initiative and exercises control over its own actions by having the following characteristics:

- *Goal oriented.* The agent should accept high-level requests indicating what a human wants, and it should be responsible for deciding how and where to satisfy the requests. Hess et al. (2000) referred to these goals as *homeostatic goal(s)*.
- *Collaborative.* The agent should not blindly obey commands but be able to modify requests, ask clarification questions, or even refuse to satisfy certain requests.
- *Flexible.* Actions are not scripted; an agent should be able to dynamically choose which actions to invoke, and in what sequence, in response to the state of its external environment.
- *Self-starting.* Unlike standard programs directly invoked by a user, an agent should sense changes in its environment and decide when to act.

The autonomy capability is also based on an agent's intelligence, mobility, and **interactivity** attributes, which are described later.

COMMUNICATION AND COLLABORATION (INTERACTIVITY) Many agents are designed to interact with other agents, humans, or software programs. This is a critical ability in view of the narrow repertoire of any single agent. Instead of making a single agent conduct several tasks, a network of agents can be used to handle complex tasks. Thus, there is a need for agent communication and collaboration. Agents communicate by following certain communication languages and standards, such as ACL (agent communication language) and KQML (knowledge query and manipulation language) (Bradshaw, 1997; Jennings et al., 1998).

AUTOMATING REPETITIVE TASKS (CONSISTENCY) An agent is usually designed to perform a narrowly defined task, which it can do over and over without getting bored or sick or going on strike; and if it is an intelligent agent, it gets better at it.

REACTING TO SITUATIONS (REACTIVITY) Agents perceive their environment—which may be the physical world, a user via a graphical user interface, a collection of other agents, the Internet, or perhaps all of these combined—and respond in a timely fashion to changes that occur in it. This means agents can recognize changes in their environment.

BEING PROACTIVE Agents do not simply act in response to their environment. They are able to exhibit goal-directed behavior by taking autonomous initiatives. They observe, interpret, and act on situations when the right conditions develop.

HAVING TEMPORAL CONTINUITY An agent should be a continuously running process, not a one-shot deal that terminates after completing a series of predetermined steps. The program can also be temporarily inactive (or semi-active), waiting for something to occur.

DEVELOPING PERSONALITY   For an agent to be effective, it must develop its own personality much the same way that human agents do, so that they are believable and capable of interacting with human users.

OPERATING IN THE BACKGROUND (MOBILITY)   An agent must be able to work out of sight, within the realm of cyberspace or other computer systems, without the constant attention of its user (or "master"). Some developers use the terms *remote execution* and *mobile agents* in referring to this attribute. In the Internet environment, an agent may need mobility to work on different machines (called a *mobile agent*). A mobile agent can transport itself across different system architectures and platforms, and it is far more flexible than agents that cannot. Many e-commerce agents are mobile.

LEARNING FROM EXPERIENCE (INTELLIGENCE)   Currently, the majority of agents are not truly intelligent because they cannot learn; only some agents can learn. For an intelligent agent, learning goes beyond mere rule-based reasoning (see Chapter 12), because the agent is expected to learn and behave autonomously. Although many in the artificial intelligence community argue that few people want agents that learn by "spying" on their users, the ability to learn often begins with the ability to observe users and predict their behavior.

Agents may be confused with objects and ES. A summary of their differences is provided in Technology Insights 13.2.

TECHNOLOGY INSIGHTS 13.2   Intelligent Agents, Objects, and ES

Objects and agents are similar in that they are both designed for independent operation, but they differ in some important ways. *Objects* are computational entities that encapsulate a state, are able to perform actions or methods on that state, and communicate through message passing. The major difference between objects and agents is that agents have clear intentions and goals. In other words, after receiving a message an object in a computer program receives the message and must act. An agent, however, may choose not act if the request is not consistent with its goal. The distinction has been nicely summarized in the slogan "Objects do it for free; agents do it because they want to."

To summarize, the differences between objects and agents include the following:

- Agents embody a stronger notion of autonomy than objects; in particular, they decide for themselves whether to perform an action on request from another agent.
- Agents are capable of flexible (e.g., reactive, proactive, social) behavior, and the standard model of objects has nothing to say about these types of behavior.
- A multiagent system is inherently multithreaded in that each agent is assumed to have at least one thread of control.

Agents often are considered a realization of small ES over the Internet. Although both incorporate domain knowledge to automate decision making, agents and ES differ in the following respects:

- Classic ES are not coupled to the environment in which they act; rather, they act through a user as a middleman. Agents can actively search for information in the environment in which they reside.
- ES are not generally capable of reactive and proactive behavior.
- ES are not generally equipped with social ability in the sense of cooperation, coordination, and negotiation.

Sources: Compiled from M. Wooldridge, *An Introduction to Multiagent Systems,* Wiley, New York, 2002; and P. Ciancarini, *Agent-Oriented Software Engineering,* Springer, New York, 2001.

Why Use Intelligent Agents?

In *Future Shock* (1970), Alvin Toffler warned of an impending flood—not of water but of information. He predicted that people would become so inundated with data that they would become paralyzed and unable to choose between options. His prediction has become a reality.

Information overload is one of the unintended by-products of the modern information age. Managers and other decision makers cannot be expected to examine every document that crosses their desks, be aware of every relevant datum recorded in databases, read every article in the magazines and journals to which they subscribe, or even look at all the e-mail that hits their computer mailboxes. According to the Gartner Group (Desouza, 2002):

- The amount of data collected by large enterprises doubles every year.
- Knowledge workers can analyze only about 5 percent of this data.
- Most of knowledge workers' efforts are spent in trying to discover important patterns in the data (60% or more), a much smaller percentage is spent determining what these patterns mean (20% or more), and very little time (10% or less) is spent actually doing something about the patterns.
- Information overload reduces our decision-making capabilities by as much as 50 percent.

The real crisis started to develop with the emergence of the Internet. The Internet contains a collection of information-generating and -replicating machines. Thousands of new systems and even more new users bring new sources of data onto the Web every minute. It can be an overwhelming experience to log on for the first time, because so many resources are immediately available. Experienced users look for ways to filter the data so that they can make sense out of the streams of information found online. Search engines and directories help with the winnowing process, but even they bring up volumes of data, much of which is only loosely tied to the decision maker's immediate concerns. In addition, search engines rarely discriminate between copies of the same information offered through different sources, so replication adds to the pile of useless information. Despite all this, managers are expected to take into account key business information and consistently make accurate decisions.

A major value of intelligent agents is that they are able to assist in searching through all the data. They save time by making decisions about what is relevant to the user. With these agents at work, a competent user's decision-making ability is enhanced with information rather than paralyzed by too much input. Agents are artificial intelligence's answer to a need created by computers (e.g., Nwana and Ndumu, 1999).

Information access and navigation are today's major applications of intelligent agents, but there are several other reasons this technology is expected to grow rapidly. For example, intelligent agents can improve computer network management and security, support e-commerce, empower employees, and boost productivity and quality (see Papazoglou, 2001; and Vlahavas et al., 2002). The advantage of agents can be even greater when a wireless computing environment is involved. Agents can handle many routine activities that need to be done quickly.

The main reasons for the success of agents can be summarized as follows:

- ***Supporting the knowledge worker.*** There is a need for increased support for tasks performed by knowledge workers, especially in decision making. Timely and knowledgeable decisions made by these professionals greatly increase their effectiveness and the success of their businesses in the marketplace.
- ***Empowering frontline decision makers.*** In a call center, there is a need to empower employees interacting with customers. Similarly, salespeople in the field

need the latest and greatest information to close sales. These can be achieved by using intelligent agents.

- *Automating repetitive office activities.* There is a pressing need to automate tasks performed by administrative and clerical personnel in functions such as sales or customer support to reduce labor costs and increase office productivity.
- *Assisting ordinary personal activity.* In a fast-paced society, time-strapped people need new ways to minimize the time spent on routine personal tasks such as booking airline tickets so that they can devote more time to professional activities.
- *Searching and retrieving.* It is not possible to directly manipulate a distributed database system in an e-commerce setting with millions of data objects. Users nowadays rely on agents for the tasks of searching, collecting, consolidating, and comparing relevant data records. These agents perform the tedious, time-consuming, repetitive tasks so that only the relevant information is delivered to the requester for better decision making.
- *Replicating domain expertise.* It is advisable to model mission-critical expertise and make it widely available to who may need it within the organization. Examples of expert software agents could be models of real-world agents, such as translators, lawyers, mentors, mechanics, advisors, stockbrokers, tutors, and even doctors.

An agent can perform a number of management-oriented tasks, including the following: advise, alert, broadcast, browse, critique, distribute, enlist, empower, explain, filter, guide, identify, match, monitor, navigate, negotiate, organize, present, query, remind, report, retrieve, schedule, search, secure, solicit, sort, store, suggest, summarize, teach, translate, and watch.

In short, software agents can improve an end user's productivity by performing a variety of tasks. The most important of these are gathering information, filtering it, and providing it to the people who need it to make accurate and timely decisions.

Classification of Intelligent Agents

Agents can be classified in different ways. Some popular classifications are by application type and by characteristics. Other classifications are based on control structure, computational environment, and programming language.

CLASSIFICATION BY APPLICATION TYPE Franklin and Graesser (1996) used a taxonomic tree to classify autonomous agents (see Figure 13.11). Relevant to managerial decision making is the category of computational agents, software agents, and task-specific agents. They can be further differentiated by the nature of applications, as specified below.

Organizational and Personal Agents Organizational agents execute tasks on behalf of a business process or computer application. Personal agents perform tasks on behalf of individual users. For example, corporate use of agent monitoring software is becoming a key component in the drive to cut support costs and increase computer productivity. Intelligent agents can search through e-mail messages for certain keywords. Depending on what keywords are contained in a message, the agent automatically sends out answers based on FAQ files. A company can use such an agent to help customers obtain answers to their questions quickly (e.g., **egain.com** and **brightware.com**). Another example of an organizational intelligent agent is an automatic e-mail sorting system. When a new message comes in, it is automatically routed to the right file and folder. Personal agents

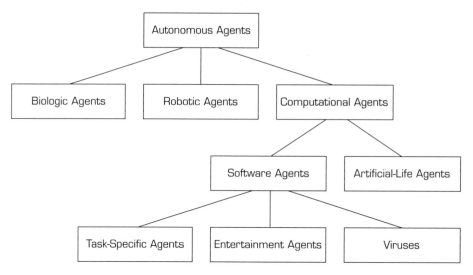

FIGURE 13.11   A Taxonomic Tree to Classify Autonomous Agents

are very powerful. They allow users to go directly to the information they want on the Internet, saving time for busy people.

Private and Public Agents   A private (or personal) agent works for only one user who creates it. Public agents are created by a designer for the use of anybody who has access to the application, network, or database.

Software Agents and Intelligent Agents   According to Lee et al. (1997), truly intelligent agents must be able to learn and exhibit high-level autonomy. However, most Internet and e-commerce agents do not exhibit these characteristics yet, at least not at the level that they are expected. Therefore, they are often called **software agents**. The second generation of Internet and e-commerce being developed today includes more and more agents with learning capabilities (see **media.mit.edu/research/groups/ software-agents**).

Another classification by Wooldridge (2002) included the following different categories:

- Agents for workflow and business process management
- Agents for distributed sensing
- Agents for retrieval and management
- Agents for e-commerce
- Agents for human–computer interaction
- Agents for virtual environments
- Agents for social simulation

CLASSIFICATION BY CHARACTERISTICS   Of the various characteristics of agents, three are of special importance: agency, intelligence, and mobility.

Agency is the degree of autonomy and authority vested in an agent and can be measured, at least qualitatively, by the nature of the interaction between the agent and other entities in the system. At a minimum, an agent must run asynchronously. The degree of agency is enhanced if an agent represents a user in some way. An advanced agent can interact with other entities, such as data, applications, or services. Even more advanced agents collaborate and negotiate with other agents.

Intelligence is the degree of reasoning and learned behavior; it is an agent's ability to accept the user's statement of goals and carry out the tasks delegated to it. At a minimum, there can be some statements of preferences, perhaps in the form of rules, with an inference engine or some other reasoning mechanism to act on these preferences. Higher levels of intelligence include a user model or some other form of understanding and reasoning about what a user wants done and planning the means to achieve this goal. Farther out on the intelligence scale are systems that learn and adapt to their environment, both in terms of the user's objectives and in terms of the resources available to the agent. Such a system, like a human assistant, might discover new relationships, connections, or concepts independently of the human user and exploit them in anticipating and satisfying user needs.

Mobility is the degree to which agents themselves travel through a network. Some agents may be static, either residing on the client machine (e.g., to manage a user interface) or initiated at the server. Mobile scripts can be composed on one machine and shipped to another for execution in a suitably secure environment; in this case, the program travels before execution, so no state data need be attached. Finally, agents can be mobile with state, transporting from machine to machine in the middle of execution and carrying accumulated state data with them. Such agents can be viewed as mobile objects, which travel to agencies, where they can present their credentials and obtain access to services and data managed by the agencies. Agencies can also serve as brokers or matchmakers, bringing together agents with similar interests and compatible goals and providing a meeting point at which they can interact safely.

Mobile agents can move from one Internet site to another and send data to and retrieve data from the user, who can focus on other work in the meantime. This can be very helpful to a user. For example, if users want to continuously monitor an electronic auction that takes a few days (e.g., at eBay), they would essentially have to be online continuously for days. Software applications that automatically watch auctions and stocks are readily available. For example, a mobile agent travels from site to site, looking for information on a certain stock, as instructed by the user. If the stock price hits a certain level, or if there is news about the stock, the agent alerts the user. What is unique about a mobile agent is that it is a software application that moves on its own to different computers to execute (see Murch and Johnson, 1999).

Nonmobile agents can be defined by two dimensions, intelligence (x-axis) and agency (y-axis) (see Figure 13.12), and mobile agents are defined in a three-dimensional space (with the addition of mobility, z-axis). For example, in Figure 13.12, we see that the definition of an intelligent agent becomes stronger as it improves on agency and intelligence dimensions. The absence of intelligence would result in a dumb software agent, whereas the absence of agency would result in an expert system. Mobility is an additional dimension that helps define mobile or immobile/fixed agents.

Leading Intelligent Agent Research Programs

Following are among the most famous research programs that deal with advancing the theory and application of intelligent agents. Web sites of these programs provide ample resources and slightly different perspectives to the ever more popular world of intelligent agents and their uses in the real-world applications.

- IBM (**research.ibm.com/iagents**)
- Carnegie Mellon University (**cs.cmu.edu/~softagents/index.html**)
- MIT (**agents.media.mit.edu**)
- University of Maryland, Baltimore County (**agents.umbc.edu**)
- University of Massachusetts (**dis.cs.umass.edu**)
- University of Liverpool (**csc.liv.ac.uk/research/agents**)
- University of Melbourne (**agentlab.unimelb.edu.au**)
- Multiagent Systems Blog (**multiagent.com**)
- Sample of Commercial Agents/Bots (**botspot.com**)

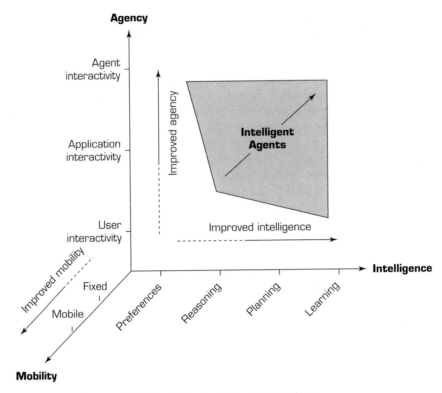

FIGURE 13.12   Scope of Intelligent Agents in Three Dimensions

Section 13.7 Review Questions

1. Define *intelligent agents*. Why are there so many different definitions and names for intelligent agents?
2. What are the main features of intelligent agents?
3. Describe the major components of intelligent agents.
4. List and briefly comment on different categories of agents.
5. Describe the differences between software agents and intelligent agents.

13.8   DEVELOPING INTEGRATED ADVANCED SYSTEMS

Neural computing, expert systems, case-based reasoning, genetic algorithms, fuzzy logic, support vector machines, and intelligent agents are excellent tools for dealing with today's complex problems. Each of these methods handles complexity and ambiguity differently, and these technologies can often be blended to use the best features of each to achieve even more impressive results. For example, a combination of neural computing and fuzzy logic can result in synergy that improves representation, generalization, fault tolerance, and adaptability.

Integrated intelligent systems have a variety of real-world applications. These include the system described in the opening vignette, where voice recognition and natural language processing were combined with inference engines to develop automated reading tutors. Other integrated intelligent systems include a supplier-selection system that uses fuzzy logic and neural networks (Golmohammadi et al., 2009); a clustering system that uses neural networks and fuzzy logic to identify different muscle movements (Karlik et al., 2009); the United Technologies Carrier product-reliability system that integrates a rule-based system and a neural network

(Deng and Tsacle, 2000); a construction-price estimation tool that integrates an ES and a neural network (Li and Love, 1999); a forecasting tool that integrates genetic algorithms and fuzzy logic (Li and Kwan, 2003); and a prediction and optimization system for a ceramic-casting process that integrates neural networks and fuzzy logic (Kuo and Chen, 2004). Many similar examples can be found with Web searches as well as on digital library databases. The sections that follow show a few examples of integration of multiple intelligent technologies.

Fuzzy Neural Networks

Fuzzy neural networks combine fuzzy logic with artificial neural networks (ANN). The integration can occur either way; fuzzy logic can help develop more expressive ANN or ANN can help develop efficient fuzzy logic applications. The input (as well as output) variables can be processed by the fuzzy logic (using fuzzy membership functions) prior to entering them into the ANN for training. This step is commonly called **fuzzification**. The neural network uses the fuzzified input (as well as the output) variables to derive a model that represents the natural imprecision inherent in the system. Once the model is built, the exact pre- and post-transformation required takes place in the production system (the actual use with unknown cases); that is, the crisp inputs are fuzzified, pushed through the trained ANN, and then the output is *defuzzified* to generate an actionable crisp output. The output of the ANN model can further become an input to another intelligent system.

From the other perspective, ANN can be used to represent fuzzy membership functions for within a fuzzy inference system. One of the criticisms of fuzzy logic is the difficulty in determining the fuzzy membership functions. Because ANN are capable of extracting highly nonlinear functions from historical datasets, they can (and often are) used to perform the membership function representation task when developing fuzzy inference systems. Similar types of integration can also be applied to fuzzy decision trees and fuzzy expert systems (see fuzzy inference systems in Section 13.5). Application Case 13.3 offers a good example of combining fuzzy logic with ANN to address the international stock selection problem.

APPLICATION CASE 13.3

International Stock Selection

An international investment company uses a combination of fuzzy logic and ANN—FuzzyNet—to forecast the expected returns from stocks, cash, bonds, and other investment options so that an optimal allocation of funds can be determined. Because the company invests in global markets, it must first determine the creditworthiness of various countries. This is accomplished by leveraging historical data to estimate future performances on key socioeconomic metrics/ratios. The system then selects specific stocks, based on company, industry, and overall economic data. The final stock portfolio must be adjusted according to the forecast of foreign exchange rates, interest rates, along with other macroeconomic factors, which are handled by an integrated multistep analysis system. The highly integrated conceptual architecture of the underlying system, shown in Figure 13.13, employs the following technologies:

- *Expert system.* Built based the knowledge of human experts, this system provides the necessary help for both country and stock selection (i.e., rule-based expert system).
- *Neural network.* A trained neural network provides necessary forecasting using the data being captured and stored in the database.

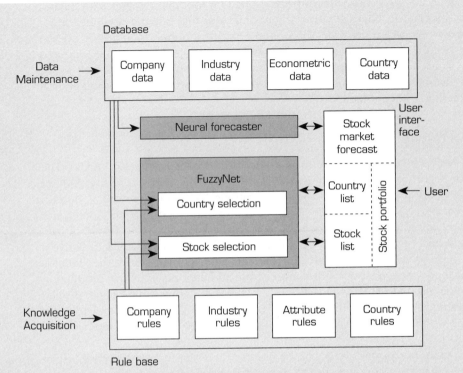

FIGURE 13.13 The Conceptual Architecture of FuzzyNet *Source:* F. Wong et al., "Neural Networks, Genetic Algorithms, and Fuzzy Logic for Forecasting," *Proceedings, International Conference on Advanced Trading Technologies,* New York, July 1992, p. 48. Adapted, with permission, from *Financial Analysts Journal,* January/February 1992. Copyright 1992. Association for Investment Management and Research, Charlottesville, VA.

• *Fuzzy logic.* The fuzzy logic component supports the assessment of factors for which there are no exact data or knowledge. For example, the credibility of rules in the rule base is given only as a probability. Therefore, the conclusion of the rule can be expressed either as a probability or as a fuzzy membership function value.

The rule base feeds into FuzzyNet along with data from the database. FuzzyNet is composed of three modules: a membership function generator (MFG), a fuzzy information processor (FIP), and a backpropagation neural network (BPN). The modules are interconnected, and each performs a different task in the decision process. The integrated system has addressed a very complex real-world investment problem very efficiently.

Source: F. Wong et al., "Neural Networks, Genetic Algorithms, and Fuzzy Logic for Forecasting," *Proceedings, International Conference on Advanced Trading Technologies,* New York, July 1992.

Genetic Algorithms for Decision Rules and Neural Networks

Genetic algorithms can be used for production-rule discovery in large databases. Once a good set of rules is discovered, it can be fed into a conventional expert system (as part of its knowledge base) or as part of some other intelligent system.

A typical way to integrate genetic algorithms with neural networks is to use genetic algorithms to search for optimal values of different network parameters, such as the number of hidden layers, the number of neurons on each layer, the learning rate, the momentum parameter, and/or the weights associated with the network connections. A good genetic algorithm implementation can automate the experimental process of training, thereby significantly reducing the time and effort needed to obtain a good ANN model. Cao and Parry (2009) developed earnings-per-share forecasting models that combined the power of genetic algorithms with the expressive modeling capabilities of neural networks for better prediction results. Kim and Han (2003) developed an integrated system using neural networks and genetic algorithms to conduct activity-based costing. Wang (2003) presented an integrated intelligent method for modeling an electrical discharge machining (EDM) process.

By using several advanced technologies, it is possible to handle a broader range of information and solve more complex problems (see Application Case 13.4). This concept is valid not only in cutting-edge technologies, but also in any integration of decision models.

APPLICATION CASE 13.4
Hybrid ES and Fuzzy Logic System Dispatches Trains

The Carajás line in Brazil is one of the busiest railway routes and leading carriers of iron ore in the world. The 892-kilometer-long single-track line connects São Luís harbor with the Carajás iron ore mine in the state of Pará in the Amazon. The line has become even busier because a unique real-time knowledge-based system is increasing its productivity and reducing its operating costs, without compromising safety.

Train dispatchers try to keep the trains running safely all day and all night while attempting to maximize the amount of iron ore transported per day, economize on fuel consumption, and minimize train delays. For over 10 years, paper and pencil were used to solve this difficult task.

An innovative, rule-based ES that uses fuzzy logic has transformed the culture of the train operations. Operational rules are used directly in the ES. Fuzzy logic techniques analyze train movements and help the operators make the best possible decisions (e.g., priorities of trains). The module that generates the initial train-movement plans has helped increase the volume of iron ore transported by about 15 percent while saving about 1.6 liters of fuel per 1,000 metric tons of ore transported. With system improvements, further gains are expected.

Sources: Modified from P. Vieira and F. Gomide, "Computer-Aided Train Dispatch," *IEEE Spectrum*, July 1996, Vol. 33, No. 7, pp. 51–53; and R. Santos, J. A. Meech, and L. Ramos, "Thickener Operations at Carajás Using a Fuzzy Logic Controller," *Proceedings of the 6th International Fuzzy Systems Association World Congress*, IFSA-95, Sao Paulo, Brazil, July 1995.

Section 13.8 Review Questions

1. What is a fuzzy neural network? Give an example of an application of a fuzzy neural network.
2. Describe how genetic algorithms can be integrated with other intelligent methods and provide a sample application.
3. What are the pros and cons of integrating intelligent systems?

Chapter Highlights

- Machine learning is a family of methods whereby machines acquire knowledge for problem solving through historical cases.
- Machine-learning methods can be classified into supervised, unsupervised, and reinforcement learning. Supervised learning derives knowledge from cases whose outcomes are known; unsupervised learning derives knowledge from cases whose outcomes are unknown; and reinforcement learning derives knowledge from the outcomes of its immediate actions.
- Popular machine-learning methods include case-based reasoning, neural networks, support vector machines, genetic algorithms, cluster analysis, and fuzzy logic.
- CBR is based on experience with similar situations. The attributes of an existing case are compared with critical attributes derived from cases stored in a case library.

- Cases in CBR include ossified cases, paradigmatic cases, and stories. Different types of cases must be handled differently to maximize the effect of learning.
- CBR has advantages over rule-based reasoning in that it can capture expert knowledge, better explain decisions, and build incremental learning capabilities.
- Genetic algorithms are search techniques that emulate the natural process of biological evolution. They utilize three basic operations: reproduction, crossover, and mutation.
- Reproduction is a process that creates the next-generation population based on the performance of different cases in the current population.
- Crossover is a process that allows elements in different cases to be exchanged to search for a better solution.
- Mutation is a process that changes an element in a case to search for a better solution.
- Fuzzy logic deals with the kind of uncertainty that is inherently human in nature. It allows numeric data to be converted into linguistic terms, such as *young* or *good*, for symbolic processing.
- Fuzzy logic can be combined with other techniques, such as rule induction and neural networks, to achieve better performance.
- A fuzzy inference system is essentially an expert system where the knowledge is represented in the form of fuzzy rules.
- Fuzzy inference involves three main components: membership functions, logical operators, and fuzzy if-then rules.
- Development of a fuzzy inference system is a four-step process: fuzzification, inferencing, summation, and defuzzification.
- Support vector machines (SVM) are among the most popular machine-learning techniques. They are used for both classification and regression-type prediction problems.
- SVM belong to the family of generalized linear models, which achieves a classification or regression decision based on the value of the linear combination of input features.
- SVM represent the state-of-the-art by virtue of their excellent generalization performance, superior prediction power, ease of use, and rigorous theoretical foundation.
- Compared to ANN, support vector machines always find the optimal mode, and their simple geometric interpretation provides fertile ground for further investigation.
- An intelligent agent is an autonomous computer program that observes and acts upon an environment and directs its activity toward achieving specific goals.
- Intelligent agents have the ability to learn by using and expanding the knowledge embedded into them.
- *Intelligent agent* can be defined in a number of different ways based on the definer's perspective.
- Intelligent agents are often associated with the following features: reactiveness, proactiveness, sociability, autonomy, and intelligence.
- Autonomy is the most important characteristic of intelligent agents, making them capable of acting on their own or of being empowered.
- Intelligent agents are often used to ease information overload.
- Integrated systems where more than one machine-learning technique is used synergistically can solve even more complex problems.
- Integration of machine-learning techniques can mitigate the problems with each method while improving problem-solving capabilities.

Key Terms

agency *620*
analogical reasoning *585*
autonomy *616*
case library *586*
case-based reasoning (CBR) *585*
chromosome *595*
crossover *595*
defuzzification *604*
elitism *595*

evolutionary algorithm *593*
fuzzification *623*
fuzzy logic *601*
fuzzy set *601*
genetic algorithm *593*
hyperplane *606*
inductive learning *585*
information overload *618*
integrated intelligent system *622*

intelligence *620*
intelligent agent (IA) *613*
interactivity *616*
kernel trick *608*
kernel type *608*
learning *583*
machine learning *583*
mobility *621*
mutation *595*
ossified case *586*

paradigmatic case *586*
reinforcement learning *584*
reproduction *595*
software agent *620*
story *586*
supervised learning *583*
support vector machine (SVM) *606*
unsupervised learning *584*

Questions for Discussion

1. Machine learning is a discipline that investigates how computers can learn from existing data. Scholars disagree about whether machines can really learn. Some insist that computers do not learn and are only taught by humans. Do you agree? Why or why not?

2. CBR produces new decisions based on past cases. Advocates claim that the process can capture the experiences of experts and alleviate problems of knowledge acquisition from human experts in rule-based systems. Do you agree? Why or why not?

3. How can an investor use genetic algorithms to make a fortune in the stock market? Can a system based on a genetic algorithm perform better than one based on a neural network? Why or why not?

4. Describe three advantages of fuzzy reasoning and provide an example to support each.

5. Discuss the advantages and disadvantages of integrating multiple methods for developing complex intelligent systems. Describe all the possible integrations among CBR, ANN, genetic algorithms, fuzzy logic, and rule-based systems and assess their feasibility.

6. Discuss the logic of combining natural language processing, voice recognition, and expert systems.

7. Discuss the pros and cons of SVM as they compare to ANN.

8. For what types of problems are SVM most appropriate? Discuss your choices in the context of requirements of those problem scenarios.

9. Why is the use of intelligent agents increasing exponentially?

10. Why are there so many different names and definitions for intelligent agents? Does this help or hurt the development of the technology? Explain.

Exercises

TERADATA STUDENT NETWORK (TSN) AND OTHER HANDS-ON EXERCISES

1. Access **home.earthlink.net/~dwaha/research/case-based-reasoning.html**. Examine the latest CBR research and demo software. How is CBR different from rule-based concepts? Try some reasoning software, compare that method to rule-based inferencing, and write about your experience in a report.

2. Identify a newsgroup that is interested in SVM. Post a question regarding recent successful applications of SVM and see what feedback you get. What are the latest concerns and questions in the emerging field of SVM?

3. Express the following statements in terms of fuzzy sets:
   a. The chance for rain today is 80 percent. (Rain? No rain?)
   b. Mr. Smith is 60 years old. (Young?)
   c. The salary of the president of the United States is $250,000 per year. (Low? High? Very high?)
   d. The latest survey of economists indicates that they believe that the recession will bottom out in April (20%), in May (30%), or in June (22%).

4. You are trying to identify a specific number in the set 1–16. You can ask questions such as, "Is this number in the set 1–8?" The answer can be only yes or no. In either case, you continue to ask more questions until you identify the number.
   a. How many questions are needed in the worst and the best possible cases to identify such a number?
   b. Is this problem suitable for parallel processing? Why or why not?

5. Relate the problem in Exercise 4 to a solution using a genetic algorithm.

6. Compare the effectiveness of genetic algorithms against standard methods for problem solving, as described in the literature. How effective are genetic algorithms?

7. Solve the knapsack problem from Section 13.4 manually, and then solve it using Evolver. Try another code (find one on the Web). Finally, develop your own genetic algorithm code in Visual Basic, C++, or Java.

8. Many companies induce employees and customers to use self-service functions such as updating their own addresses or finding the balance in their banking accounts. Explain how the technologies described in this chapter can facilitate this type of self-service.

TEAM ASSIGNMENTS AND ROLE-PLAYING

1. Identify a real-world application problem that is suitable for CBR and develop a plan for crafting an intelligent system that integrates case-based and rule-based approaches.

2. Examine the marketplace for consumer products that incorporate fuzzy logic (sometimes this feature is called *continuous logic*). Try some of the products available in your area. Determine the advantages and disadvantages (if any) of these products over their nonfuzzy counterparts.

3. Survey your class by having everyone write down a height representing tall, medium, and short for men and for women. Tally the results and determine what is meant by tall, medium, and short in a fuzzy way. Create the membership functions in these sets and examine the results.

4. Join the artificial intelligence discussion group at **groups.yahoo.com/group/pcai/join**. Trace postings on the topics of this chapter over the past 2 years. Prepare a report about your findings.

5. Go to **solver.com/gabasics.htm** and **palisade.com/evolver/**. Compare Solver and Evolver in terms of using genetic algorithms to solve problems.

6. Investigate the status of text-to-speech technology (e.g., **naturalreaders.com**) and speech-to-text technology (Avoke STX, from **bbn.com**), as well as the combination of both (**naturalvoices.att.com** and **ivoice.com**). Write a report about your findings.

7. Research the area of knowledge discovery with support vector machines. Find studies that compare and contrast SVM with other prediction models.

8. Identify cutting-edge intelligent agent applications on the Web. Classify the agents. Are they intelligent and/or mobile?

9. Search and find an integrated intelligent system. Identify the roles of the individual technologies. Propose extensions to the system to make it even better.

INTERNET EXERCISES

1. Search the Web for games and simulations that are based on genetic algorithms. Be sure to try out J. J. Merelo's MasterMind (**kal-el.ugr.es/mastermind.html**) and M. S. Miller's Manna Mouse (**caplet.com/MannaMouse.html**). Write a report on your findings.

2. Access *PC AI*'s Web site (**pcai.com**). Search for vendors of fuzzy logic, genetic algorithms, neural networks, and integrated intelligent systems used in business. Examine definitions and vendors. What is new in these areas?

3. CBR has been used lately for data mining. Explore the Web to find vendors and research literature about this topic.

4. Search online to find vendors of genetic algorithms and investigate the business applications of their products. What kinds of applications are most prevalent?

5. Examine fuzzy logic vendor Web sites and identify the kinds of problems to which fuzzy logic is currently being applied. Find a demo version of a system and try it out. Report your findings to the class.

6. Access the Web and electronic journal databases in your library to find at least three reports on the use of integrated intelligent methods for intelligent decision support. Evaluate whether the applications are feasible in the real world.

7. Go to **lpa.co.uk/cbr.htm** and find information about LPA's intelligent products. Write a one-page summary. Also, find information at the LPA Web site about products for the other systems described in this chapter. View the demos. Write a short report about your findings.

8. Go to **voiceingov.org/blog** and **fluencyvoice.com** and identify three applications of each technology. Write a summary about your findings.

9. Go to **lec.com** and **languageweaver.com** and review all their translation products. Write a report about your findings.

10. Go to **palisade.com** and examine the capabilities of Evolver. Write a summary about your findings.

11. Find three journal articles describing successful implementation of prediction systems with SVM. In a report, summarize the nature of the problem and the proposed or implemented solution. Make sure to express your critical comments.

12. Conduct a search (Web, library databases, etc.) to identify a real-world application of a multiagent system. Comment on the necessity and usefulness of such a system. Provide extensions and/or alternative designs to address the same application needs.

END OF CHAPTER APPLICATION CASE

Improving Urban Infrastructure Management with Case-Based Reasoning

Problem

Like many other cities, the city of Verdun (Quebec, Canada) is attempting to rehabilitate its infrastructure. The city is attempting different strategies to restore the quality of the environment, to manage its many large and complex systems of services (e.g., education, social services), and to maintain and rehabilitate its existing infrastructure. The problem is that in order to do all these things the city needs more resources than it has—a typical problem in almost all cities.

One of the many areas that require attention in Verdun is citizens' requests and complaints, which need to be addressed by city employees in different departments, such as the Department of Public Works. In addition to actions that result from citizen complaints and reports from employees, action may result from reports from sensors and other devices that monitor city infrastructure (e.g., water level in a pumping station). Here we examine the area of complaints management in the Department of Public Works.

Solution

An information system was constructed to handle the complaint management system for Verdun's Department of Public Works. This system presents the sequential and parallel procedures to determine the immediate action needed to resolve new complaints. Each time a complaint (or an alert recorded by sensors) is received, the system follows certain steps before it resolves the problem. Those steps can be disaggregated into seven major categories, where many people and software components intervene, such as databases, knowledge bases, model-based systems, and intelligent decision support systems (IDSS).

At the core of the IDSS is an intelligent technology called case-based reasoning (CBR), a technology that uses a repository (or library) of knowledge about historical problems, situations, actions, and solutions (some good and some bad). The CBR system includes a mechanism to manage that knowledge, such as knowledge storage, retrieval, and presentation. The technology helps manage and analyze each complaint, using similar historical complaints. The system classifies each complaint and then prioritizes it automatically, using CBR. The system then routes the complaint to the proper place for resolution. Each complaint may go through up to four analyses. The analyses consider legal, financial, and other constraints.

When a complaint is routed to a department, a solution (resolution) needs to be generated. The CBR automatically proposes solutions, based on past experience (i.e., comparison of case characteristics). The CBR tries to see if a past solution will solve the new problem. The computer may present several possible solutions to a manager. This is an interactive process between the user and the CBR. Finally, the manager considers priorities against the available resources.

Results

Verdun's system can find similarities between current complaints and previous complaints/calls to the Department of Public Works. Also, the system can find complaints of the same type that occur in the same area at the same time. This kind of complaint analysis helps diminish the number of interventions. Case retrieval is based first on the type similarity and then on geographic similarity. When a case has been solved, it is automatically added to the case library—the knowledge base of a CBR system.

Verdun's CBR-based system helped improve the delivery, performance, and coordination of most municipal services. Complaints are now resolved much faster than before, often with fewer resources.

Questions for the Case

1. Explain how CBR supports, rather than replaces, managers in the Verdun system.
2. Describe the CBR process in the Verdun system.
3. What were the specific capabilities and benefits of the CBR in the Verdun system?
4. Why are historical cases a good knowledge source?
5. Could an expert system (ES) be used instead of CBR? Why or why not?

Sources: Compiled from A. Quintero, D. Konare, and S. Pierre, "Decision-Aid to Improve Organizational Performance," *European Journal of Operations Research*, May 2005; and F. Burstein and H. Linger, "Supporting Post-Fordist Work Practices: A Knowledge Management Framework for Supporting Knowledge Work," *Information Technology & People*, September 2003.

References

Baccigalupo, C., and E. Plaza. (2007). "A Case-Based Song Scheduler for Group Customized Radio." *Proceedings of the Seventh International Conference on Case-Based Reasoning* (ICCBR), Belfast, Northern Ireland, UK: Springer.

Bagnoli, C., and H. C. Smith. (1998). "The Theory of Fuzzy Logic and Its Application to Real Estate Valuation." *Journal of Real Estate Research*, Vol. 16, No. 2.

Baker, B. M., and M. A. Syechew. (2003). "A Genetic Algorithm for the Vehicle Routing Problem." *Computers and Operations Research*, Vol. 30.

Burstein, F., and H. Linger. (2003, September). "Supporting Post-Fordist Work Practices: A Knowledge Management Framework for Supporting Knowledge Work." *Information Technology & People*.

Cao, Q., and M. E. Parry. (2009). "Neural Network Earnings per Share Forecasting Models: A Comparison of Backward Propagation and the Genetic Algorithm." *Decision Support Systems*, Vol. 47, No. 1, pp. 32–43.

Chorafas, D. N. (1994). *Chaos Theory in the Financial Markets*. Chicago: Probus Publishing.

Ciancarini, P. (2001). *Agent-Oriented Software Engineering*. New York: Springer.

Cox, E. (2001). "Building Intelligent Business Applications with Semantic Nets and Business Rules." *PC AI*, Vol. 15, No. 1.

Deng, P. S., and E. G. Tsacle. (2000). "Coupling Genetic Algorithm and Rule-Based Systems for Complex Decisions." *Expert Systems with Applications*, Vol. 19, No. 3.

Desouza, K. C. (2002). *Managing Knowledge with Artificial Intelligence: An Introduction with Guidelines for Nonspecialists.* Westport, CT: Quorum Books, p. 8.

Dettmer, R. (2003, June). "It's Good to Talk [Speech Technology for On-Line Services Access]." *IEE Review.*

Dubois, D., E. Hüllermeier, and H. Prade. (2003). "On the Representation of Fuzzy Rules in Terms of Crisp Rules." *Information Sciences,* Vol. 151.

Dwinnell, W. (2002, March/April). "Putting Fuzzy Logic to Work: An Intro to Fuzzy Logic." *PC AI.*

Golmohammadi, D., R. C. Creese, and H. Valian. (2009). "Neural Network Application for Supplier Selection." *International Journal of Product Development,* Vol. 8, No. 3, pp. 252–261.

Grupe, F. H., and S. Jooste. (2004, March). "Genetic Algorithms: A Business Perspective." *Information Management and Computer Security.*

Grupe, F. H., R. Urwiler, and N. K. Ramarapu. (1998). "The Application of Case-Based Reasoning to the Software Development Process." *Information and Software Technology,* Vol. 40, No. 9.

Hall, N. (1987). "A Fuzzy Decision Support System for Strategic Planning." In E. Sanchez and L. Zadeh (eds.). *Approximate Reasoning in Intelligent Systems, Decision, and Control.* Oxford, UK: Pergamon Press.

Hastings, J., K. Branting, and J. Lockwood. (2002). "CARMA: A Case-Based Rangeland Management Adviser." *AI Magazine.*

Hayes, C. (2003). *Smart Radio: Building Community-Based Internet Music Radio.* Ph.D. Dissertation, University of Dublin, Ireland, UK.

Haykin, S. (2009). *Neural Networks and Learning Machines.* Upper Saddle River, NJ: Pearson.

Hernandez-Serrano, J., and D. H. Jonassen. (2003). "The Effect of Case Libraries on Problem Solving." *Journal of Computer-Assisted Learning,* Vol. 19, No. 1.

Humphreys, P., R. T. McIvor, and F. T. S Chan. (2003). "Using Case-Based Reasoning to Evaluate Supplier Environmental Management Performance." *Expert Systems with Applications,* Vol. 25.

Johnson, R. C. (1999, August 16). "Genetic Algorithms Adapt Fast ICs to Fab Variations." *Electronic Engineering Times,* No. 1074.

Karlik, B., Y. Koçyigit, and M. Korürek. (2009). "Differentiating Types of Muscle Movements Using a Wavelet-based Fuzzy Clustering Neural Network." *Expert Systems,* Vol. 26, No. 1, pp. 49–57.

Khan, A. S., and A. Hoffmann. (2003). "Building a Case-Based Recommendation Systems Without a Knowledge Engineer." *Artificial Intelligence in Medicine,* Vol. 27, No. 2.

Kim, K., and I. Han. (2003). "Application of a Hybrid Algorithm and Neural Network Approach in Activity-Based Costing." *Expert Systems with Applications,* Vol. 24, No. 1.

Klahr, P. (1997, January/February). "Getting Down to Cases." *PC AI.*

Kolonder, J. (1993). *Case-Based Reasoning.* Mountain View, CA: Morgan Kaufmann.

Kuo, R. J., and C. A. Chen. (2004). "A Decision Support System for Order Selection in Electronic Commerce Based on Fuzzy Neural Network Supported by Real-Coded Genetic Algorithm." *Expert Systems with Applications.*

Lee, J. K., and J. K. Kim. (2002). "A Case-Based Reasoning Approach for Building a Decision Model." *Expert Systems,* Vol. 19, No. 3.

Lessmann, E., M-C. Sung, and J. E. V. Johnson. (2009). "Identifying Winners of Competitive Events: A SVM-based Classification Model for Horserace Prediction." *European Journal of Operational Research,* Vol. 196, No. 2, pp. 569–580.

Li, H., and P. E. D. Love. (1999, March). "Combining Rule-Based Expert Systems and Artificial Neural Networks for Mark-Up Estimation." *Construction Management and Economics,* Vol. 17, No. 2.

Li, J., and R. S. K. Kwan. (2003). "A Fuzzy Genetic Algorithm for Driver Scheduling." *European Journal of Operational Research,* Vol. 147.

Liao, T. W. (2003). "Classification of Welding Flaw Types with Fuzzy Expert Systems." *Expert Systems with Applications,* Vol. 25, No. 1.

Luu, D. T., S. T. Ng, and S. E. Chen. (2003). "A Case-Based Procurement Advisory System for Construction." *Advances in Engineering Software,* Vol. 34, No. 7.

Mahadevan, S., S. L. Shah, T. J. Marrie, and C. M. Slupsky. (2008). "Analysis of Metabolomic Data Using Support Vector Machines." *Analytical Chemistry,* Vol. 80, No. 19, pp. 7562–7770.

Marling, C., M. Sqalli, E. Rissland, H. Munoz-Avila, and D. Aha. (2002, Spring). "Case-Based Reasoning Integrations." *AI Magazine,* pp. 69–86.

Miller, T. W. (2005). *Data and Text Mining: A Business Applications Approach.* Upper Saddle River, NJ: Prentice Hall.

Mills-Tettey, A., J. Mostow, M. B. Dias, T. M. Sweet, S. M. Belousov, M. F. Dias, and H. Gong. (2009, April 17–19). "Improving Child Literacy in Africa: Experiments with an Automated Reading Tutor." *Third IEEE/ACM International Conference on Information and Communication Technologies and Development* (ICTD2009), pp. 129–138.

Mitchell, T. M., R. M. Keller, and S. T. Kedar-Cabelli. (1986). "Explanation-Based Generalization: A Unifying View." *Machine Learning,* No. 1.

Nick, Z., and P. Themis. (2001). "Web Search Using a Genetic Algorithm." *IEEE Internet Computing,* Vol. 5, No. 2.

Niettinen, K., et al. (1999). *Recent Advances in Genetic Algorithms.* New York: Wiley.

Oracle. (2006). "New to Voice Technology." **oracle.com/technology/tech/wireless/beginner/voice.html?_template5/ocom/t** (accessed March 2006).

Park, C., and I. Han. (2002). "A Case-Based Reasoning with the Feature Weights Derived by Analytic Hierarchy Process for Bankruptcy Prediction." *Expert Systems with Applications,* Vol. 23, No. 3.

Pham, D. T., and R. M. Setchi. (2003). "Case-Based Generation of Adaptive Product Manuals." *Journal of Engineering Manufacturing,* Vol. 217, No. 3.

Polat, K., S. Kara, A. Güven, and S. Günes. (2009). "Comparison of Different Classifier Algorithms for Diagnosing Macular and Optic Nerve Diseases." *Expert Systems,* Vol. 26, No. 1, pp. 22–31.

Quintero, A., D. Konare, and S. Pierre. (2005, May). "Decision-Aid to Improve Organizational Performance." *European Journal of Operations Research.*

Rao, S. S. (1998, January 12). "Evolution at Warp Speed." *Forbes,* pp. 82–83.

Riesbeck, C. K., and R. L. Schank. (1989). *Inside Case-Based Reasoning.* Hillsdale, NJ: Erlbaum Associates.

Ross, T. J. (2004). *Fuzzy Logic with Engineering Applications,* 2nd ed. New York: Wiley.

Santos, R., J. A. Meech, and L. Ramos. (1995, July). "Thickener Operations at Carajás Using a Fuzzy Logic Controller." *Proceedings of the 6th International Fuzzy Systems Association World Congress,* IFSA-95, Sao Paulo, Brazil.

Scheiner, M. (2003, July). "Neiman Marcus Uses Natural Language Search to Boost Online Sales." *Customer Relationship Management.*

Shin, K., and I. Han. (2001). "A Case-Based Approach Using Inductive Indexing for Corporate Bond Rating." *Decision Support Systems,* Vol. 42.

Shin, K., and Y. Lee. (2002). "A Genetic Algorithm Application in Bankruptcy Prediction Modeling." *Expert Systems with Applications,* Vol. 23, No. 3.

Shiu, S., and S. K. Pal. (2004, March). *Foundations of Soft Case-Based Reasoning.* New York: Wiley Interscience.

Sullivan, D. (2001, August 31). "5 Principles of Intelligent Content Management." *Intelligent Enterprise.*

Tan, K. C., M. L. Wong, and W. Peng. (2005, April). "A P2P Genetic Environment for the Internet." *Communications of the ACM.*

Tanaka, K., and T. Niimura. (2007). *An Introduction to Fuzzy Logic for Practical Applications.* New York: Springer.

Vieira, P., and F. Gomide. (1996, July). "Computer-Aided Train Dispatch." *IEEE Spectrum,* Vol. 33, No. 7, pp. 51–53.

Walbridge, C. T. (1989, June). "Genetic Algorithms: What Computers Can Learn from Darwin." *Technology Review.*

Wang, Y. (2003). "Using Genetic Algorithm Models to Solve Course Scheduling Problems." *Expert Systems with Applications,* Vol. 25, No. 1.

Watson, I. (2002). *Applying Knowledge Management: Techniques for Building Corporate Memories.* San Francisco: Morgan Kauffman.

Wong, F. (1992, July). "Neural Networks, Genetic Algorithms, and Fuzzy Logic for Forecasting." *Proceedings, International Conference on Advanced Trading Technologies,* New York.

Wooldridge, M. (2002). *An Introduction to Multiagent Systems.* New York: Wiley.

Xu, J. X., and X. Xu. (2003, January 1). "A New Fuzzy Logic Learning Control Scheme for Repetitive Trajectory Tracking Problems." *Fuzzy Sets and Systems.*

Zadeh, L. (1965). "Fuzzy Sets." *Information and Control,* Vol. 8, pp. 338–353.

Implementing Decision Support Systems and Business Intelligence

LEARNING OBJECTIVES FOR PART VI

1 Explore some of the emerging technologies that offer interesting application and development opportunities for management support systems in general and business intelligence in particular. These include RFID, virtual worlds, social networking, Web 2.0, reality mining, and cloud computing.

2 Describe personal, organizational, and societal impacts of MSS

3 Learn about major ethical and legal issues of MSS implementation

This part consists of only one chapter, Chapter 14. The primary purpose of this chapter is to introduce several emerging technologies that will provide new opportunities for application and extension of business intelligence techniques and management support systems. This part also briefly explores the individual, organizational, and societal impacts of these technologies, especially the ethical and legal issues in MSS implementation. After describing many of the emerging technologies or application domains, we will focus on organizational issues.

Management Support Systems: Emerging Trends and Impacts

LEARNING OBJECTIVES

1 Explore some of the emerging technologies that may impact MSS

2 Know how RFID data analysis can help improve supply-chain management and other operations

3 Describe how massive data acquisition techniques can enable reality mining

4 Describe how virtual-world technologies can be used for decision support and the associated advantages and disadvantages

5 Describe how virtual-world applications can result in additional data for BI applications

6 Describe the potential of cloud computing in business intelligence

7 Understand Web 2.0 and its characteristics as related to MSS

8 Understand social networking concepts, selected applications, and their relationship to BI

9 Describe organizational impacts of MSS

10 Learn the potential impacts of MSS on individuals

11 Describe societal impacts of MSS

12 List and describe major ethical and legal issues of MSS implementation

This chapter introduces several emerging technologies that are likely to have major impacts on the development and use of business intelligence applications. Many other interesting technologies are also emerging, but we have focused on some trends that have already been realized and others that are about to impact MSS further. Using a crystal ball is always a risky proposition, but this chapter provides a framework for analysis of emerging trends. We introduce and explain some emerging technologies, explore their current applications, and conclude with their relationship to MSS. We then discuss the organizational, personal, legal, ethical, and societal impacts of support systems that may affect their implementation. We close the chapter with a case that updates the widely acclaimed use of BI at Continental Airlines. This case was also introduced at the end of Chapter 8. This chapter contains the following sections:

14.1 Opening Vignette: Coca-Cola's RFID-Based Dispenser Serves a New Type of Business Intelligence
14.2 RFID and New BI Application Opportunities
14.3 Reality Mining

14.4 Virtual Worlds

14.5 The Web 2.0 Revolution

14.6 Virtual Communities

14.7 Online Social Networking: Basics and Examples

14.8 Cloud Computing and BI

14.9 The Impacts of Management Support Systems: An Overview

14.10 Management Support Systems Impacts on Organizations

14.11 Management Support Systems Impacts on Individuals

14.12 Automating Decision Making and the Manager's Job

14.13 Issues of Legality, Privacy, and Ethics

14.14 Resources, Links, and the Teradata University Network Connection

14.1 OPENING VIGNETTE: COCA-COLA'S RFID-BASED DISPENSER SERVES A NEW TYPE OF BUSINESS INTELLIGENCE

Coca-Cola, the soft-drink giant based in Atlanta, Georgia, wanted to develop a way to increase sales and find a cheaper way to test new products. During the summer of 2009, the company installed new self-serve soft-drink dispensers with RFID technology in selected fast-food restaurants in California, Georgia, and Utah, and plans to eventually distribute the dispensers nationwide. The new dispensers, called Freestyle, hold up to 30 flavor cartridges, which enable customers to create 100 different drinks, including sodas, juices, teas, and flavored waters. Each beverage requires only a few drops of flavoring. Customers use the dispensers by choosing a brand and flavoring options on the dispenser's LCD panel, which runs on the Windows CE operating system.

The RFID technology will allow Coca-Cola to test new drink flavors and concepts, observe what flavors and combinations customers are choosing, identify regional preferences, and keep track of the amounts they are drinking. By being able to use the flavors in multiple combinations through the dispensers, the company can see what new combinations are most popular and then produce them for other markets. This process saves Coca-Cola money. Previously, it would bottle new products and send them out to various markets. Sometimes the products were canceled after only a year or two because they did not gain in popularity.

The RFID technology will also help individual restaurants keep track of when it is time to order new cartridges, thus increasing inventory accuracy, and determine what flavors are most popular so that they know which ones to stock. Individual restaurants are able to view reports concerning beverage consumption created from the data collected from the RFID system and reorder products by using an e-business portal developed by Coca-Cola. The technology even allows them to see what beverages are most popular at different times of the day.

The RFID technology in this case works by a RFID chip being placed on each flavor cartridge and an RFID reader being located in the dispenser. Each night, the information recorded is sent to Coca-Cola's SAP data warehouse system at its Atlanta headquarters via a private Verizon wireless network. Microsoft System Center Configuration Manager for Mobile Devices runs at the Coca-Cola headquarters and controls the dispensers through the wireless network. Additionally, Coca-Cola can use the wireless network to send instructions for new mix combinations to the dispensers and to shut down recalled cartridges instantly nationwide.

Questions for the Opening Vignette

1. What is the benefit of RFID for reducing inventory in this case?
2. How would a restaurant benefit from having RFID-enabled syrup cartridges?
3. What benefit would a customer derive from the new dispenser?
4. What issues might impact the widespread acceptance of this dispenser?

What We Can Learn from This Vignette

This short vignette illustrates the potential of new technologies when innovative uses are developed by creative minds. Most of the technologies described in this chapter are nascent and have yet to see widespread adoption. Therein lies the opportunity to create the next "killer" application. For example, use of RFID is beginning to grow, with each company exploring its use in supply chains, retail stores, manufacturing, or service operations. The vignette illustrates that with the right combination of ideas, networking, and applications, it is possible to develop creative technologies that have the potential to impact a company's operations in multiple ways.

Source: Based on M. H. Weier, "Coke's RFID-Based Dispensers Redefine Business Intelligence," *Information Week,* June 6, 2009, **informationweek.com/story/showArticle.jhtml?articleID= 217701971** (accessed July 2009).

14.2 RFID AND NEW BI APPLICATION OPPORTUNITIES[1]

With a June 2003 mandate that its top 100 suppliers place RFID tags on pallets and cases shipped to stores in the Dallas, Texas, region, Wal-Mart jumpstarted a 50-year-old technology that, until the mandate, had found limited (but successful) use in a variety of niche areas. Since that announcement, the RFID industry has blossomed. The Department of Defense soon followed with its own mandate; Target, Albertson's, and Best Buy, among others, quickly followed suit. Initial efforts focused on the largest suppliers in the retail supply chain (e.g., Procter & Gamble, Gillette, Kraft), but have now spread to include smaller retail suppliers—Wal-Mart's next 200 largest suppliers began shipping tagged products in January 2006.

RFID is a generic technology that refers to the use of radio frequency waves to identify objects. Fundamentally, RFID is one example of a family of automatic identification technologies, which also include the ubiquitous barcodes and magnetic strips. Since the mid-1970s, the retail supply chain (and many other areas) has used barcodes as the primary form of automatic identification. The potential advantages of RFID have prompted many companies (led by large retailers such as Wal-Mart, Target, and Albertson's) to aggressively pursue this technology as a way to improve their supply chain, and thus reduce costs and increase sales.

How does RFID work? In its simplest form, an RFID system consists of a tag (attached to the product to be identified), an interrogator (i.e., reader), one or more antennae attached to the reader, and a computer (to control the reader and capture the data). At present, the retail supply chain has primarily been interested in using passive RFID tags. *Passive tags* receive energy from the electromagnetic field created by the interrogator (e.g., a reader) and backscatter information only when it is requested. The passive tag will remain energized only while it is within the interrogator's magnetic field.

In contrast, *active tags* have a battery on board to energize them. Because active tags have their own power source, they don't need a reader to energize them; instead they can initiate the data transmission process on their own. On the positive side, active tags have a longer read range, better accuracy, more complex rewritable information storage, and richer processing capabilities (Moradpour and Bhuptani, 2005). On the negative side, due to the battery, active tags have a limited lifespan, are larger in size than passive tags, and are more expensive. Currently, most retail applications are designed and operated with passive tags. Active tags are most frequently found in defense or military systems, yet they also appear in technologies such as EZ Pass, where tags are linked to a prepaid account, enabling drivers to pay tolls by driving past a reader rather than stopping to pay at a tollbooth (U.S. Department of Commerce, 2005).

---

[1] This section is adapted from our own research conducted in collaboration with Dr. Bill Hardgrave of the University of Arkansas and director of the RFID Research Center.

The most commonly used data representation for RFID technology is the Electronic Product Code (EPC), which is viewed by many in the industry as the next generation of the Universal Product Code (UPC) (most often represented by a barcode). Like the UPC, the EPC consists of a series of numbers that identifies product types and manufacturers across the supply chain. The EPC code also includes an extra set of digits to uniquely identify items.

Currently, most RFID tags contain 96 bits of data in the form of serialized global trade identification numbers (SGTIN) for identifying cases or serialized shipping container codes (SSCC) for identifying pallets (although SGTINs can also be used to identify pallets). The complete guide to tag data standards can be found on EPCglobal's Web site (**epcglobalinc.org**). EPCglobal, Inc., is a subscriber-driven organization of industry leaders and organizations focused on creating global standards for the EPC to support the use of RFID.

As illustrated in Figure 14.1, tag data, in its purest form, is a series of binary digits. This set of binary digits can then be converted to the SGTIN decimal equivalent. As shown, an SGTIN is essentially a UPC (UCC-14, for shipping-container identification) with a serial number. The serial number is the most important difference between the 14-digit UPC used today and the SGTIN contained on an RFID tag. With UPCs, companies can identify the product family to which a case belongs (e.g., 8-pack Charmin tissue), but they cannot distinguish one case from another. With an SGTIN, each case is uniquely identified. This provides visibility at the case level, rather than the product-family level.

One of the applications of the massive amounts of data that are generated by RFID is in supply-chain management (Delen, Hardgrave, and Sharda, 2007). Figure 14.2 represents the typical functions performed in a distribution center (DC) and in a retail store with respect to the flow of materials between these supply units. In a DC, the primary functions are receiving, put-away, picking, and shipping. Receiving is the collection of all the activities related to the orderly receipt of materials/goods, inspection for quantity and quality, and dispersion of the received goods to storage/put-away and/or to cross-docking for immediate shipment (Tompkins et al., 2002).

Typically, the following sequence of operations happens once a truck backs up to the receiving door: (1) unloading the contents of the trailer; (2) verification of the receipt of goods against expected delivery (purchase order); (3) sorting of the damaged goods and documentation of the discrepancy in count and/or product type to be settled later; (4) if needed, application of labels to the pallets, cases, or items so that units can be tracked inside the warehouse; and (5) sorting of goods for put-away or cross-dock based on current demand and schedule.

Most suppliers put a tag on a product as it leaves their facility. As a product moves from the supplier to the retail DC and then on to the retail outlet, it passes through a number of RFID-read locations. Readers capture and record the case's tag data as it passes

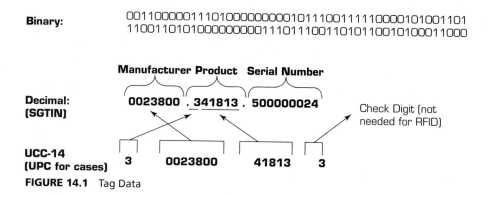

FIGURE 14.1 Tag Data

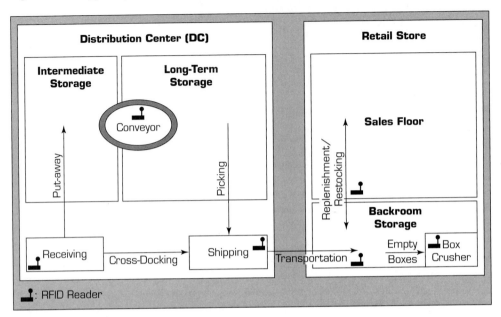

FIGURE 14.2 Operations and Related Functions of a Typical Retail System

through these points. The key read points in a generic distribution center are indicated in Figure 14.2. As product is delivered to the distribution center, read portals (created by stationary readers and antennae on each side of the delivery door) capture the pallet and case data. At this point, Wal-Mart and other retailers do not expect to see 100 percent of the individual cases on a pallet. Rather, they expect to read a pallet tag and several of the cases. They do expect to read 100 percent of the cases after they are removed from the pallet (Hardgrave and Miller, 2006).

The product is stored in the distribution center for an indeterminate amount of time, then individual cases are moved through the distribution center (e.g., put on a conveyor system for sorting or cross-docked in full-pallet format) to the proper shipping doors, which contain read portals similar to the receiving doors. The actual reads for a single case may vary depending on the type of product (e.g., bagged pet foods are not placed on conveyors) and the type of DC it enters (refrigerated/grocery DCs are different from general merchandise; e.g., grocery DCs have stretch-wrap machines where readers can be placed, but do not have conveyors) (Alexander et al., 2003). Often, a case may not even follow the prescribed route.

As a representative example, Table 14.1 traces the actual movements of a single case of product (SGTIN: 0023800.341813.500000024) from its arrival at the distribution center to its end of life at the box crusher. This particular case of product arrived at distribution center 123 on August 4, was put on the conveyor system on August 9, and departed shortly thereafter. (For readability, only one read per portal per event is shown; duplicate reads at a single portal were removed.) It arrived at store 987 about 12 hours after leaving the DC, went almost immediately to the sales floor, returned from the sales floor about 5 hours later, and was put in the backroom where it stayed until the following day, where it once again went to the sales floor, returned about 45 minutes later, and then went to the box crusher for ultimate disposal. This product mostly follows the prescribed route, but veers off course toward the end as it goes out to the sales floor and back again on two separate occasions.

What can the snippet of data from Table 14.1 tell us (as one simple instance of RFID data)? If we examine the data closely, it offers up several insights.

TABLE 14.1 Sample RFID Data

Location	EPC	Date/Time	Reader
DC 123	0023800.341813.500000024	08-04-05 23:15	Inbound
DC 123	0023800.341813.500000024	08-09-05 7:54	Conveyor
DC 123	0023800.341813.500000024	08-09-05 8:23	Outbound
ST 987	0023800.341813.500000024	08-09-05 20:31	Inbound
ST 987	0023800.341813.500000024	08-09-05 20:54	Sales floor
ST 987	0023800.341813.500000024	08-10-05 1:10	Sales floor
ST 987	0023800.341813.500000024	08-10-05 1:12	Backroom
ST 987	0023800.341813.500000024	08-11-05 15:01	Sales floor
ST 987	0023800.341813.500000024	08-11-05 15:47	Sales floor
ST 987	0023800.341813.500000024	08-11-05 15:49	Box crusher

First, knowing the dates/times of movement is important for ensuring such things as freshness of the product, tracking recalls, or getting products to the stores in a timely manner (especially for time-sensitive products). For example, consider the situation faced by companies offering promotions on their products. Advertising (local, national) is generally launched to promote the products, and the fate of the product is determined in the first few days after the promotion begins. If the product is not on the shelf in a timely manner, sales may suffer. Gillette has used RFID to determine whether stores have stocked their shelves with particular items for a particular promotion. They found that in those stores that used RFID to move a product from the backroom to the shelf before a promotion started, sales were 48 percent higher than those that did not move the product in a timely manner (Evans, 2005). RFID provided the data, and the insight, needed.

Second, the data provides insight into the backroom process of moving freight to the sales floor. In the example provided in Table 14.1, we see that the product moved to the sales floor twice. Perhaps the first time it was taken out it did not fit on the shelf and was returned to the backroom. The second time it went out it fit on the shelf. This "unnecessary case cycle" raises several questions. Moving the product out to the sales floor and back unnecessarily wastes precious human resources, and the more times a product is handled, the higher the chances are that it will be damaged. Also, why did the product make two trips to the sales floor? If the product was not needed until August 11 (the day it fit on the shelf), why was it delivered to the store on August 10? This could signal a problem with the forecasting and replenishment system. Or, perhaps a worker placed a manual order for the product when it wasn't needed. If so, why was the manual order placed? It could be that the product was in the backroom, but was not visible or easy to find. Rather than taking the time to look for it, the worker manually ordered the product. While the product was in transit, another worker found the product in the backroom and stocked the shelf. When the manually ordered product arrived, it would not fit on the shelf and an unnecessary trip (for the manually ordered product) was created. How can RFID help in this situation? When a worker attempts to place a manual order, the system can check to see if a case currently exists in the backroom (as determined by a backroom read). If a case exists, the system could help the worker find the case by using a handheld or portable RFID reader.

Third, it provides a precise indication of how long it took the product to move through the supply chain and the exact time between each of the key read points—on a case-by-case basis! This type of insight has never before been possible. Lead times are generally estimated based upon the movement of large quantities of product families through the system. Also, visibility at the store level was not possible before RFID. This visibility requires developing the appropriate measures to be able to determine the distribution center performance. Delen, Hardgrave, and Sharda (2007) proposed several performance measures to capture this visibility.

RFID can also be used by companies to improve either the efficiency or effectiveness of various existing processes by incremental process change. For example, early evidence suggested that RFID can reduce the amount of time to receive product at a warehouse (Katz, 2006). Instead of scanning each case of product individually with a barcode scanner, RFID tagged product can be read automatically at a receiving-door portal. Gillette reported a reduction in pallet-receiving time at its distribution center from 20 to 5 seconds due to RFID and its tag-at-source strategy (Katz, 2006). The process of receiving was not drastically changed (i.e., forklifts unloaded the product as before). The only change was eliminating the need to manually scan the product. Thus, the process became more efficient. Processes can also be made more effective. For example, Wal-Mart found a 26 percent reduction in out-of-stocks by using RFID data to generate better lists of products to be replenished (Hardgrave et al., 2006). The shelf replenishment process was not changed, but improved by the use of RFID. Wal-Mart has also reduced the number of unnecessary manual orders by 10 percent; thus, making the ordering and forecasting system more effective (Sullivan, 2005). RFID is also being used in receiving to reduce the number of errors, which improves inventory accuracy, ultimately leading to better forecasting and replenishment.

RFID data have been used in many other related applications. For example, perishable goods present some of the biggest challenges for supply-chain management due to the high number of variants with different perishability characteristics, requirements to account for the flow of goods in some supply chains, and large volumes of goods handled over long distances. Although food represents a major portion of the perishables portfolio, many other products, including fresh-cut flowers, pharmaceuticals, cosmetics, and auto parts, among others, require strict environmental controls to retain their quality. Due to the extremely large volumes of goods handled, the likelihood for problems increases (Sahin et al., 2007). The elimination of even a small percentage of spoilage, for example, adds up to a significant improvement to the supply chain. Therefore, the optimal management of the perishables supply chain is of paramount importance to businesses in this market segment.

The success of today's highly volatile perishables supply chains depends on the level (and the timeliness) of product visibility. Visibility should provide answers to the questions of "where is my product?" and "what is the condition of my product?" Already, several companies have begun experimenting with RFID for perishables. Consider the following examples:

- Samworth Brothers Distribution (UK; sandwiches, pastries, etc.) has implemented real-time temperature monitoring in its trucks (Swedberg, 2006a).
- Fresh Express uses RFID to look at flow-through of the product coupled with expiration dates (Intel, 2007).
- Starbucks uses temperature tracking for food-preparation products going to retail outlets (Swedberg, 2006b).
- Sysco uses RFID to check load conditions without opening doors (Collins, 2005).
- A regional restaurant chain (700 restaurants) uses RFID-based temperature monitoring to determine conditions of beef patties, eggs, onions, and so on (Banker, 2005).
- TNT uses RFID to monitor temperature profiles of products moving from Singapore to Bangkok (Bacheldor, 2006).

Another example of use of RFID in supply chains is in managing product quality. Studies using sensor-based RFID tags in refrigerated trucks carrying food items revealed that the temperature did not remain uniform as assumed. Indeed, it varied rather widely

(Delen, Hardgrave, and Sharda, 2009). As a product moves through the supply chain, the environment can change, affecting the product quality and safety. RFID-enabled environmental sensors provide insight into the changing environmental conditions experienced by the product and provide the data necessary to determine to what extent those changes affect the quality or safety of the product. Without sensors, one can get various single-point estimations of the environmental conditions (e.g., temperature at the time of loading, temperature at time of delivery), but not have visibility between these points. In the sample applications, temperatures varied by position on the pallet (e.g., top, middle, bottom), by load configuration (i.e., the position of the pallets), by container type, by product type, and by packaging material (e.g., corrugated box versus plastic tote). The obvious impact of many variables suggests that continuous environmental monitoring is necessary to fully understand the conditions at the pallet and/or case level. Overall, RFID-enabled (temperature) sensors worked well. The sensors provided tremendous insights into the conditions faced by the product as it passed through the supply chain—insight that is not possible with single-point estimations.

The opening vignette included a very interesting emerging application that includes an innovative use of RFID and business intelligence. The overall lesson is that RFID technology generates massive amounts of data that can be analyzed to achieve great insights into a company's environment, a major purpose for the very existence of business intelligence and decision support. The next section illustrates another emerging opportunity for business intelligence arising from massive data being collected.

Section 14.2 Review Questions

1. What is RFID?
2. What kinds of data are read/recorded through RFID?
3. What can a company learn by reading RFID at a distribution center?
4. Search online for applications of RFID in health care, entertainment, and sports.

14.3 REALITY MINING

Just as RFID generates major data streams ripe for further analysis through BI technologies that can assist in decision making, another massive data source is emerging, along with the technologies to make sense of the data. Indeed, a new name has been given to this type of data mining—**reality mining**. Eagle and Pentland (2006) appear to have been the first to use this term. Alex (Sandy) Pentland of MIT and Tony Jebara of Columbia University have a company called Sense Networks (**sensenetworks.com**) that focuses on the development of reality-mining applications. The material in this section is adapted and included with permission from Sense Networks.

Many devices in use by consumers and businesspeople are constantly sending out their location information. Cars, buses, taxis, mobile phones, cameras, and personal navigation devices all transmit their locations thanks to network-connected positioning technologies such as GPS, WiFi, and cell tower triangulation. Millions of consumers and businesses use location-enabled devices for finding nearby services, locating friends and family, navigating, tracking of assets and pets, dispatching, and engaging in sports, games, and hobbies. This surge in location-enabled services has resulted in a massive database of historical and real-time streaming location information. It is, of course, scattered and by itself not very useful. Reality mining builds on the idea that these datasets could provide remarkable real-time insight into aggregate human activity trends.

By analyzing and learning from these large-scale patterns of movement, it is possible to identify distinct classes of behaviors in specific contexts, called "tribes" (Eagle and Pentland, 2006). Macrosense is an application platform developed by Sense Networks that takes the data being generated by all of these mobile devices and, after spatial and time-based cleaning, applies proprietary clustering algorithms to these massive datasets to classify the incoming data streams as belonging to different types of customers/clients/etc. This approach allows a business to better understand its customer patterns and also to make more informed decisions about promotions, pricing, and so on.

Sense Networks is now adapting this general technology to help consumers find people with similar interests. This application is called Citysense. Figure 14.3 includes a map of an area of San Francisco. It is best seen in color at **sensenetworks.com/citysense .php**, but even the black-and-white image shows that it is possible to learn where people are going at this particular time. Each dot represents the presence of people and animates to show patterns of how people group and move around the city over time. Sense Networks' core analytical platform, Macrosense is also able to analyze the aggregate information shown in Citysense to cluster users and identify tribes. Macrosense is able to identify which tribes are where by sampling the distribution of tribes at any given place and

FIGURE 14.3 Citysense Example

time, making it possible to infer what it means when a user is there at that place and time. For example, rock clubs and hip-hop clubs each retain distinct tribal distributions. When a user is out at night, Macrosense learns their preferred tribe distribution from time spent in these places. Sense Networks says that in future releases of Citysense tribes will be included, and when users visit other cities, they will be able to see hotspots recommended on the basis of this distribution and combined with overall activity information.

Users who go to rock clubs will see rock club hotspots, whereas users who frequent hip-hop clubs will see hip-hop hotspots, and those who go to both will see both. The question "Where is everybody like me right now?" is thus answered for these users—even in a city they have never visited before. Simulating the real world via the use of tribes makes it possible to provide personalized services to each user without collecting personally identifiable information.

By applying algorithms that reduce the dimensionality of location data, reality mining can characterize places according to the activity and movement between them. From massive amounts of high-dimensional location data, these algorithms uncover trends, meaning, and relationships to eventually produce human understandable representations. It then becomes possible to use such data to automatically make intelligent predictions and find important matches and similarities between places and people. Loecher et al. (2009) provided some details of their algorithms. Essentially, activity information as recorded through cell phone data is used to study the behavioral links between places in the real world. This also takes into account the time of the day, because one group of people may go to one location for work in the morning; however, an entirely different group of people may frequent the same location at night because of a nightclub nearby. Due to the temporal sensitivity of the number and type of people frequenting a place (which can be far more dynamic than a static Web page on the Internet), the raw data describing places in the real world requires a staggering number of dimensions.

According to the material provided by Sense Networks, it attributes 487,500 dimensions to every place in a city. The dimensions are based on the movement of people in and out of that place over time, and the places those people visit before and afterward. Their "Minimum Volume Embedding" algorithms reduce the dimensionality of location and temporal data to two dimensions while retaining over 90 percent of the information. This allows for visualizations of data that allow humans to better understand key dimensions to extract key relationships in the flow of people in a city, such as the flow of those shopping, commuting to and from work, or socializing. In addition, they also employ historical data combined with demographic, weather, and other variables. Once a broad understanding of the spatial behaviors in a city is available, companies can leverage the continuously updating clusters to better understand their own customers from sparse location data, discover trends in aggregate consumer behavior for correlation with financial indicators, and predict demand for services and places.

One key concern in employing these technologies is the loss of privacy. If someone can track the movement of a cell phone, the privacy of that customer is a big issue. But Sense Networks claims that it only needs to gather aggregate flow information, not individually identifiable information, to be able to place someone in a tribe.

See the Sense Networks Web site (**sensenetworks.com**) for the latest developments in this area. The technology is evolving fast. Baker (2009) and a recent story in *Economist* (2009) highlighted some of the possible applications of reality mining for business government. For example, a British company called Path Intelligence (**pathintelligence.com**) has developed a system called FootPath that ascertains how people move within a city or even within a store. All of this is done by automatically tracking movement without any cameras recording the movement visually. Such analysis can help determine the best layout for products or even public transportation options. The automated data collection enabled through capture of cell phone and WiFi hotspot access points presents an interesting new dimension in nonintrusive market research data collection and, of course, microanalysis of such massive datasets.

Section 14.3 Review Questions

1. Define *reality mining*.
2. What types of data are used in reality mining?
3. Briefly describe how the data are used to create profiles of users.
4. What other applications can you imagine if you were able to access cell phone location data? Do a search on location-enabled services.

14.4 VIRTUAL WORLDS

Virtual worlds have existed for a long time in various forms, including stereoscopes, Cinerama, simulators, computer games, and head-mounted displays. For our purposes, **virtual worlds** are defined as artificial worlds created by computer systems in which the user has the impression of being immersed. The intention is to achieve a feeling of tele-presence and participation from a distance. Current popular virtual worlds include Second Life (**secondlife.com**), Google Lively (**lively.com**), and EverQuest (**everquest.com**). A good overview of the technologies, applications, and social and organization issues of virtual worlds can be found at Wikipedia (**en.wikipedia.org/wiki/Virtual_world**). In these virtual worlds, trees move with the wind, water flows down a stream, birds chirp in the trees, and trucks roar in the street. Users create digital characters called *avatars* that interact, walk, and talk with other computer-generated individuals, in computer-generated landscapes. Some even run global businesses.

Real-world institutions ranging from universities and businesses to governmental organizations are increasingly incorporating virtual worlds into their strategic marketing initiatives. Virtual worlds are becoming an important channel for reaching a wider consumer base, as well as for "seeing" the customers and interacting with them in a way that was not possible a few years ago. Concepts such as virtual currencies often allow participants to buy or sell virtual goods or services, such as attire or training. Virtual worlds provide rich and enhanced modes of advertising that can be immersive or absorptive, active or passive. The advertising can include audio and video in addition to text, enhancing product knowledge and customers' purchase intentions. Although studies on the use of online avatars in marketing are few, some evidence suggests that avatars and virtual representations may positively influence trust and online purchasing intention, because they simulate experiences customers have in real stores (Stuart, 2007). However, not all real-world attributes can be experienced virtually, because not all of the human senses, such as "taste" can be digitized and presented on a computer monitor (Tsz-Wai, Gabriele, and Blake, 2007).

Second Life can be an effective business tool. Managers can exploit Second Life today for real-world decision support. According to John Brandon, in a *Computerworld* article (2007) on the top business sites in Second Life:

> What makes the IBM presence even more interesting, though, is what takes place behind closed doors. Regular 'brainstorming' meetings with clients have produced interesting ideas, such as a grocer that would sell items in Second Life and have them delivered to homes, and a fuel company that would hold regular training sessions for employees—which would not be open to the public.

The use of Second Life for decision support needs to be carefully planned. Professor Dan Power wrote a column some time back on the advantages and disadvantages of virtual worlds for decision support. See Technology Insights 14.1 for excerpts from that column.

TECHNOLOGY INSIGHTS 14.1   Second Life as a Decision Support Tool

Major advantages of using Second Life for decision support:

1. ***Easy access and low cost.***   The client is a free download and people can participate without paying a membership fee. The client is still evolving, and the new voice client is in testing by the community, so the software may need to be downloaded every few weeks with updates. The software requires a high-speed Internet connection, a fast microprocessor, a good video/graphics card, 512MB or more RAM, and hard drive space for the many files in the download.

2. ***Experienced and dedicated designer/builders.***   A quick visit to Second Life showcases the possibilities and the wonders that are still to come. Second Life has few restrictions and provides broad and flexible content authoring experiences for developers. The quantity of available objects, textures, and scripts to reuse is impressive, and designers are available to create custom avatars, buildings, and products. If you can make a rough sketch, a good builder can create a prototype quickly. If supplied with the floor plans and dimensions, a builder can replicate your factory or, given enough time, replicate an entire city.

3. ***Tools and venues for communications-driven decision support.***   Tools include streaming video, streaming voice, PowerPoint, agenda and meeting management tools, chat recorders, and even name tags for avatars. **DecisionSupportWorld.com** has some resources related to venues with Second Life links.

4. ***A large, dedicated user base.***   It doesn't cost much to "hire" people/avatars to work for you in Second Life. The pay is in Linden dollars, and you can easily hire employees from more than 50 countries. Companies like Manpower are in Second Life and can help sort out employment issues. Second Life is an easy way for a company to "go global." Also, many of the users have great computing skills.

5. ***Impression management and creativity enhancement.***   Avatars look like whatever the user wants. Anonymity has some advantages for certain types of decision support. Second Life breaks down barriers to creative thinking and frees the imagination. Some people are reluctant to use videoconferencing because of concerns about how they will appear; with Second Life, users can consciously manage the impressions they create during meetings, events, and activities.

6. ***Time compression.***   A day in Second Life is 4 hours long. People connect quickly and teleport from venue to venue. Second Life operates around the clock. The 7/24/365 nature of Second Life can speed up activities and change users' time perceptions.

7. ***Easy data integration from real life using RSS feeds.***   The possibilities for integrating data from various Web sources into Second Life are expanding rapidly.

8. ***Encourages active participation and experiential learning.***   People experience Second Life, and those experiences impact real life. A Second Life meeting can be both enjoyable and memorable. A walk through a virtual factory can help people understand what it will be like when built.

Major disadvantages of using Second Life for decision support:

1. ***Learning time and training costs.***   Company executives are generally unfamiliar with Second Life and the learning curve is at least 8 hours to gain a basic comfort level. A good coach can make the learning process much easier for an "newbie" manager.

2. ***Distractions are numerous.***   Second Life is a big virtual space with a lot going on, from shopping to sex, from sunning at the beach to skiing, from dancing under the stars at the Romantic Starlight Ballroom to a live music performance at the Second Life synagogue. Some of the distractions are very pleasant, but they create the possibility that employees will be playing when they should be working. Also, companies will need disclaimers, and HR will need to review policies on sexual harassment.

3. ***Pranksters and spam are common.***   All sorts of crazy people are floating around Second Life with too much time to waste. Many of them devise pranks and engage in nasty activities, from defacing buildings to harassing worshippers at a synagogue or conference attendees. Some of conference venues now have security staff or restrict access based on a land-based access list. Security of many types is an issue.

4. ***Technology problems persist.***   Some technology problems include slow responses, lags in resizing objects, the need to empty cache memory following crashes (which do happen), and frequent software updates.

5. ***Chat is a very slow communication tool.***   The new voice client will speed up interaction of people in Second Life, but chat will still have a use, especially with the automatic translators for multilanguage communication. Voice interaction will be invaluable for Second Life meetings.

6. ***Resistance to use.***   Second Life is not like anything most executives have experienced, and there will be resistance to using this technology. It is easy to view Second Life as a game and to overlook the real-world decision support possibilities.

7. ***Addiction.***   Some people have become addicted to using Second Life and spend hours on the system, becoming sleep deprived and neglecting real-life activities. Company HR personnel will need to monitor the behavior and attitudes of employees who are heavy users of tools like Second Life.

Source: D. Power, "What Are the Advantages and Disadvantages of Using Second Life for Decision Support?" *DSS News,* Vol. 8, No. 15, July 29, 2007, **dssresources.com/newsletters/195.php** (accessed July 2009).

Although virtual worlds are becoming interesting tools for businesses and consumers, some short-term technical and practical considerations have kept them from gaining widespread acceptance. For example, participation in most of these virtual environments requires downloading of a "plug-in." Although it is just a matter of downloading and installing (usually) free software, many businesses and government organizations prohibit any kind of software downloads on employees' computers. This limits the use of these services to a select few employees, typically those in IT.

However, despite a few limitations, consumer applications of virtual worlds are growing at a fast pace. One of the coauthors of this book (Sharda) has been involved in virtual world applications for tradeshows. *Tradeshow* is only one of numerous terms describing a temporary market event, held at some interval, where a large number of potential buyers (attendees) and sellers (exhibitors) interact for the purpose of learning about new goods and services. Tradeshows such as book shows, technology shows, and human resource shows (career fairs) are held worldwide throughout the year.

Physical tradeshows allow face-to-face interactions, the richest form of communication. Disadvantages of traditional tradeshows include restricted geographic reach, limited operating hours, high cost of participation, and the need to get maximum exposure through the strategic location of exhibition stands. To gain more value from tradeshow participation, many show participants now use technologies such as virtual worlds to gain more visibility. Some information technology tools mimic the specific activities of tradeshows. For example, it is common today to use Webinars, presentations, lectures, or seminars that are transmitted over the Web (Good, 2005). These tools typically offer a one-way communication from presenter to audience, but can be interactive, with the ability to give, receive, and discuss information between the presenter and the audience. However, Webinars typically do not deliver the content, stakeholder information, and lead data available to an exhibitor at a traditional tradeshow.

Virtual world technology may be useful in replicating a tradeshow participation experience by organizing virtual events that can extend the reach of the event to include many more attendees and perhaps even more exhibitors. A virtual tradeshow is held in cyberspace and may be viewed as an extension of the physical exhibition or in lieu of a physical event. It replicates many of the information exchange, communication, and community-gathering aspects of a physical event. A virtual tradeshow thus has an event orientation and is capable of supporting information exchange among various exhibitors and numerous attendees. Its structure often includes a virtual exhibit hall that users enter by permission and with specific capabilities, to either attend and view virtual tradeshow displays or to build virtual booths to exhibit information, just as they would at a trade fair in a convention center. The virtual tradeshow may have other components, such as a virtual Web conference, a collection of Web seminars, or other educational presentations. Visitors fill out an online registration form to create an online badge before entering the virtual exhibit hall to visit various booths. The virtual booths often look like real-world tradeshow booths, with desks and displays that users can relate to easily. Detailed tracking mechanisms enable organizers to record and analyze the flow of traffic in the virtual tradeshow. Virtual tradeshows can serve as international tradeshows, business matchmakers, procurement fairs, and product launches. The experience also translates well for other applications, such as virtual job fairs, virtual benefits fairs, online employee networks, distributor fairs, and venture capital fairs. This recognition of the synergies between virtual worlds and tradeshows has been employed by some virtual tradeshow companies. One of these is **iTradeFair.com**. An example virtual booth is shown in Figure 14.4.

In traditional tradeshows, there are no standard rules for designing the booth. Good booth design focuses on the product and ways to increase the number of visitors coming to the booth. In virtual worlds, the technology platforms provide exhibitors with tools to develop professional-looking virtual booths. The booth-builder software puts control of the booth's contents in the exhibitors' hands, so they can customize everything to their satisfaction. Through a very easy-to-use browser-based interface, the exhibitor can create and edit any of the booth's contents, even during the event. In a physical event, this would be very disruptive and expensive. Using "Booth Skins," the exhibitor picks from a library of skins and graphical images. At a tradeshow, color has one of the biggest influences on the human psyche (Siskind, 2005) and ties the display to the product. The booth-builder system allows exhibitors to pick colors that match their corporate colors and culture. In addition, they can

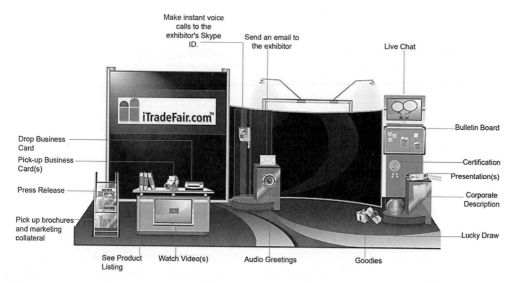

FIGURE 14.4 Sample of a Virtual Booth

add signs and graphics that match the brand. Sound can be added to enhance the visitors' experience. This is also the component where all other relevant information is entered, for example, specific literature, videos, presentations, giveaways at the booth, phone numbers that are connected when an attendee requests a call, and so on.

The trade fair participant goes to a specific virtual tradeshow homepage. The participant first visits a virtual exhibit floor. On the virtual exhibit floor, the participant can select a virtual booth and gather information or engage in live interaction and information dissemination. Technologies enable communication through features such as chat, Web callback, fax, and e-mail. Participants have access to community-building features such as online discussion boards and online live-chat forums that allow many-to-many collaboration for discussion and debate, followed by online surveys, and a search engine for searches based on keyword and state. Participants can experience a virtual pressroom with press releases from various virtual booths. Special speakers or guests can communicate through video-streamed keynote Webcasts. Attendees can also interact with each other through a chat room. Although this enables the event attendees to exchange information in a same-time, different-place mode, it is not as media rich as the avatar visibility experience through Second Life.

Thousands of attendees can visit a virtual tradeshow, possibly visiting hundreds of booths each. Attendees register through a simple set of forms, different for each virtual show. The virtual show producer sets the access policy for the event and allows participation after certain registration conditions have been met. This process gives the producer the opportunity to ensure that appropriate, qualified attendees participate. In the same way that a magazine collects additional demographics for free subscriptions, the registration may prompt attendees for additional information, which the producer may choose to make mandatory or voluntary. The virtual tradeshow platform allows attendees to customize their visit at a virtual event. They can take advantage of personalized services, such as creating their own itinerary to guide them through the show floor, or by creating, printing, and e-mailing a notepad with notes made during visits to booths. These features mimic the experience of an attendee at a physical event.

One of the main reasons for exhibitors to participate in trade fairs is to acquire new leads and contacts. In a virtual show, exhibitors can receive attendee leads in real time. A generic attendee report (similar to traditional show attendee lists) containing every registered attendee is available to all exhibitors through the event producer. Exhibitors can also access detailed traffic reports of all attendees who visit their virtual booth. Attendees visiting the booth can drop a business card. A record of all attendees who drop off their digital business card is available. The report includes all attendees' names, titles, and relevant contact information and whether the attendee has requested additional information on any products and services, the company in general, or employment opportunities. A comprehensive "Booth Footprints Report" is available on all registered attendees who view an exhibitor's virtual booth. This report provides insight into what is of interest to each specific visitor. For obvious privacy and security purposes, all reports are under controlled access. But such reports provide a wealth of information to the tradeshow producers and exhibitors and can be analyzed through business intelligence technologies.

As described in this section, virtual worlds provide an opportunity to offer decision support capabilities in a novel way. In the next few years we will see a further expansion of immersive decision support capabilities. In addition, such environments (e.g., iTradeFair.com's virtual tradeshows) generate massive amounts of data about users' activities and participation in online activities. These massive datasets can be analyzed through BI technologies to better understand customer behavior and customize products/services or the technology environments. Sections 14.2 through 14.4 have described three technologies that enable large-scale data collection and the possibilities of the analysis of such massive datasets.

Section 14.4 Review Questions

1. What is a virtual world?
2. What are the advantages and disadvantages of providing decision support through virtual worlds?
3. What activities of a physical tradeshow can be experienced in a virtual event? Which ones cannot be replicated?
4. What type of data analysis might you perform on data about users in a specific virtual-world setting (e.g., a company island in Second Life, a virtual tradeshow booth)?

14.5 THE WEB 2.0 REVOLUTION

Web 2.0 is the popular term for describing advanced Web technologies and applications, including blogs, wikis, RSS, mashups, user-generated content, and social networks. A major objective of Web 2.0 is to enhance creativity, information sharing, and collaboration.

One of the most significant differences between Web 2.0 and the traditional Web is the greater collaboration among Internet users and other users, content providers, and enterprises. As an umbrella term for an emerging core of technologies, trends, and principles, Web 2.0 is not only changing what is on the Web, but also how it works. Web 2.0 concepts have led to the evolution of Web-based virtual communities and their hosting services, such as social networking sites, video-sharing sites, and more. Many believe that companies that understand these new applications and technologies—and apply the capabilities early on—stand to greatly improve internal business processes and marketing. Among the biggest advantages is better collaboration with customers, partners, and suppliers, as well as among internal users.

Representative Characteristics of Web 2.0

The following are representative characteristics of the Web 2.0 environment:

- The ability to tap into the collective intelligence of users. The more users contribute, the more popular and valuable a Web 2.0 site becomes.
- Data is made available in new or never-intended ways. Web 2.0 data can be remixed or "mashed up," often through Web service interfaces, much the way a dance-club DJ mixes music.
- Web 2.0 relies on user-generated and user-controlled content and data.
- Lightweight programming techniques and tools let nearly anyone act as a Web site developer.
- The virtual elimination of software-upgrade cycles makes everything a *perpetual beta* or work-in-progress and allows rapid prototyping, using the Web as an application development platform.
- Users can access applications entirely through a browser.
- An architecture of participation and *digital democracy* encourages users to add value to the application as they use it.
- A major emphasis on social networks and computing.
- Strong support of information sharing and collaboration.
- Rapid and continuous creation of new business models.

Other important features of Web 2.0 are its dynamic content, rich user experience, metadata, scalability, open source basis, and freedom (net neutrality).

Most Web 2.0 applications have a rich, interactive, user-friendly interface based on Ajax or a similar framework. Ajax (Asynchronous JavaScript and XML) is an effective and efficient Web development technique for creating interactive Web applications. The intent is to make Web pages feel more responsive by exchanging small amounts of data with the server behind the scenes so that the entire Web page does not have to be reloaded each time the user makes a change. This is meant to increase the Web page's interactivity, loading speed, and usability.

Web 2.0 Companies and New Business Models

A major characteristic of Web 2.0 is the global spreading of innovative Web sites and startup companies. As soon as a successful idea is deployed as a Web site in one country, other sites appear around the globe. This section presents some of these sites. For example, approximately 120 companies specialize in providing Twitter-like services in dozens of countries. An excellent source for material on Web 2.0 is Search CIO's *Executive Guide: Web 2.0* (see **searchcio.techtarget.com/general/0,295582,sid19_gci1244339,00.html#glossary**).

A new business model that has emerged from Web 2.0 is the accumulation of the "power of the crowd." The potential of such a business model is unlimited. For example, Wikia (**wikia.com**) is working on community-developed Web searches. If they can create a successful one, Google will have a challenger.

Many companies provide the technology for Web 2.0, and dozens of firms have emerged as providers of infrastructure and services to social networking. A large number of startups appeared in 2005–2008. For a guide to the 25 hottest Web 2.0 companies and the powerful trends that are driving them see **money.cnn.com/magazines/business2/business2_archive/2007/03/01/8401042/index.htm**.

Section 14.5 Review Questions

1. Define *Web 2.0*.
2. List the major characteristics of Web 2.0.
3. What new business model has emerged from Web 2.0?

14.6 VIRTUAL COMMUNITIES

A *community* is a group of people with common interests who interact with one another. A **virtual (Internet) community** is one in which the interaction takes place over a computer network, mainly the Internet. Virtual communities parallel typical physical communities, such as neighborhoods, clubs, or associations, but people do not meet face-to-face. Instead, they meet online. A virtual community is a social network organized around a common interest, idea, task, or goal; members interact across time, geographic location, and organizational boundaries to develop personal relationships. Virtual communities offer several ways for members to interact, collaborate, and trade (see Table 14.2). Many physical communities have Web sites to support Internet-related activities that supplement physical activities.

Characteristics of Traditional Online Communities and Their Classification

Many thousands of communities exist on the Internet, and the number is growing rapidly. Pure-play Internet communities may have thousands, or even hundreds of millions, of members. MySpace grew to 100 million members in just 1 year. This is one major difference from traditional purely physical communities, which usually are smaller. Another difference is that offline communities frequently are confined to one geographic location, whereas only a few online communities are geographically confined. For more information on virtual communities, see **en.wikipedia.org/wiki/Virtual_community**.

TABLE 14.2 Elements of Interaction in a Virtual Community

Category	Element
Communication	Bulletin boards (discussion groups)
	Chat rooms/threaded discussions (string Q&A)
	E-mail and instant messaging and wireless messages
	Private mailboxes
	Newsletters, "netzines" (electronic magazines)
	Blogging, wikis, and mushups
	Web postings
	Voting
Information	Directories and yellow pages
	Search engine
	Member-generated content
	Links to information sources
	Expert advice
EC element	Electronic catalogs and shopping carts
	Advertisements
	Auctions of all types
	Classified ads
	Bartering online

TYPES OF COMMUNITIES   Some popular categories of communities with examples follow. Table 14.3 lists additional types of communities.

Public Versus Private Communities   Communities can be designated as *public*, meaning that their membership is open to anyone. The owner of the community may be a privately held corporation or a public one. Most of the social networks, including MySpace and Facebook belong to the public category.

In contrast, *private* communities belong to a company, an association, or a group of companies and their membership is limited to people who meet certain requirements (e.g., work for a particular employer or work in a particular profession). Private communities may be internal (e.g., only employees can be members) or external.

Example: IBM's Virtual Universe Community   This is a private, internal community of over 5,500 individuals (as of January 2009) who are active in virtual worlds. It was launched in 2006 with the goal of moving IBM into a range of new and profitable industries, from the creation of IBM mainframes for virtual worlds to 24-hour virtual service desks staffed by avatars.

Internal and External Private Communities   *Internal private communities* exist within organizations. Such communities include employees, retirees, suppliers, and customers who share a common interest. The focus of such communities is on knowledge sharing, collaboration, expert location, and knowledge creation. Companies such as Pfizer, FedEx, Caterpillar, Wells Fargo, and IBM have such communities.

External private communities include one organization and its business partners, government agencies, and prospects. The participants share information on a variety of issues. For example, customers may collaborate around product issues. External private

TABLE 14.3 Types of Virtual Communities

Community Type	Description
Transaction and other business activities	Facilitate buying and selling (e.g., **ausfish.com.au**). Combine an information portal with an infrastructure for trading. Members are buyers, sellers, intermediaries, etc., who are focused on a specific commercial area (e.g., fishing).
Purpose or interest	No trading, just exchange of information on a topic of mutual interest. Examples: Investors consult The Motley Fool (**fool.com**) for investment advice; rugby fans congregate at the Fans Room at **nrl.com.au**; music lovers go to **mp3.com**.
Relations or practices	Members are organized around certain life experiences. Examples: **ivillage.com** caters to women and **seniornet.com** is for senior citizens. Professional communities also belong to this category. For example, **isworld.org** is a space for information systems faculty, students, and professionals.
Fantasy	Members share imaginary environments. Examples: sport fantasy teams at **espn.com**; GeoCities members can pretend to be medieval barons at **dir.yahoo.com/Recreation/games/role_playing_games/titles**. See **games.yahoo.com** for many more fantasy communities.
Social networks	Members communicate, collaborate, create, share, form groups, entertain, and more. MySpace (**myspace.com**) is the leader.
Virtual worlds	Members use avatars to represent them in a simulated 3D environment where they can play, conduct business, socialize, and fantasize. See Second Life (**secondlife.com**).

communities have fewer restrictions with regard to participation and security than do internal communities. External communities are used for collaboration, market research, product innovation, or improved customer and suppliers support.

Example: A Virtual World Community In 2008, Sony launched a virtual community service for its PlayStation 3 (PS3) videogame network with 8 million members. The 3D service called Home allows users to create avatars, decorate homes, and interact and socialize with other users in a virtual world. Sony considers this an important part of the game-playing experience. Avatars can interact with each other, and users can play games with friends at a virtual arcade. The community is regional due to language and cultural considerations. As an extension, the service allows downloading of content and movies to PS3.

Other Classifications of Virtual Communities Virtual communities can be classified in several other ways. One possibility is to classify the members as *traders, players, just friends, enthusiasts,* or *friends in need.* A more common classification recognizes six types of Internet communities: (1) transaction, (2) purpose or interest, (3) relations or practices, (4) fantasy, (5) social networks, and (6) virtual worlds. For issues of participation and design of communities, see **en.wikipedia.org/wiki/Virtual_community**.

Section 14.6 Review Questions

1. Define *virtual (Internet) communities* and describe their characteristics.
2. List the major types of virtual communities.
3. Distinguish between private and public communities.
4. Distinguish between internal and external communities.

14.7 ONLINE SOCIAL NETWORKING: BASICS AND EXAMPLES

Social networking is built on the idea that there is structure to how people know each other and interact. The basic premise is that social networking gives people the power to share, making the world more open and connected. Although social networking is usually practiced in social networks such as MySpace and Facebook, aspects of it are also found in Wikipedia and YouTube.

We first define *social networks* and then look at some of the services they provide and their capabilities.

A Definition and Basic Information

A *social network* as a place where people create their own space, or homepage, on which they write blogs (Web logs); post pictures, videos, or music; share ideas; and link to other Web locations they find interesting. In addition, members of social networks can tag the content they create and post it with keywords they choose themselves, which makes the content searchable. The mass adoption of social networking Web sites points to an evolution in human social interaction.

THE SIZE OF SOCIAL NETWORK SITES   Social network sites are growing rapidly, with some having over 100 million members. The typical annual growth of a successful site is 40 to 50 percent in the first few years and 15 to 25 percent thereafter. For a list of the major sites, including user counts, see **en.wikipedia.org/wiki/List_of_social_networking_websites**.

SOCIAL NETWORK ANALYSIS SOFTWARE   **Social network analysis (SNA) software** is used to identify, represent, analyze, visualize, or simulate network nodes (e.g., agents, organizations, or knowledge) and edges (relationships) from various types of input data (relational and nonrelational), including mathematical models of social networks. Various input and output file formats exist.

Network analysis tools enable researchers to investigate representations of networks of different forms and different sizes, from small (e.g., families, project teams) to very large. Visual representations of social networks are popular and important to understand network data and to convey the results of the analysis.

Some of the representative tools that enable such presentations are:

- Business-oriented social network tools such as InFlow and NetMiner
- Social Networks Visualizer, or SocNetV, which is a Linux-based open source package

For details, see **en.wikipedia.org/wiki/Social_network_analysis_software**. Social networking is strongly related to mobile devices and networks.

Mobile Social Networking

Mobile social networking refers to social networking where members converse and connect with one another using cell phones or other mobile devices. A current trend for social networking Web sites such as MySpace and Facebook is to offer mobile services. Some social networking sites offer mobile-only services (e.g., Brightkite, and Fon11).

There are two basic types of mobile social networks. The first type is companies that partner with wireless carriers to distribute their communities via the default start pages on cell phone browsers. For example, users can access MySpace via AT&T's wireless network. The second type is companies that do not have such carrier relationships (also known as "off deck") and rely on other methods to attract users. Examples of this second type include MocoSpace (**mocospace.com**) and Mobikade (**mkade.com**).

Windows Live Spaces Mobile can be viewed on mobile devices with limited screen size and slow data connections. It allows users to browse and add photos, blog entries, and comments directly from their mobile devices. However, it has also introduced several other features to improve the user experience with handheld devices. For more information on Windows Live Spaces Mobile, see **mobile.spaces.live.com** and **en.wikipedia.org/wiki/Windows_Live_Spaces_Mobiles**.

Mobile social networking is much more popular in Japan, South Korea, and China than it is in the West, generally due to better mobile networks and data pricing (flat rates are widespread in Japan). The explosion of mobile Web 2.0 services and companies means that many social networks can be based from cell phones and other portable devices, extending the reach of such networks to the millions of people who lack regular or easy access to computers.

With the current software that is available, interactions within mobile social networks are not limited to exchanging simple text messages on a one-to-one basis. In many cases, they are evolving toward the sophisticated interactions of Internet virtual communities.

MOBILE ENTERPRISE NETWORKS   Several companies have developed (or fully sponsor) mobile-based social networks. For example, in 2007 Coca-Cola created a social network that could only be accessed by cell phones in an attempt to lure young people to its sodas and other products.

MOBILE COMMUNITY ACTIVITIES   In many mobile social networks, users can use their mobile devices to create their profiles, make friends, participate in chat rooms, create chat rooms, hold private conversations, and share photos, videos, and blogs. Some companies provide wireless services that allow their customers to build their own mobile community and brand it (e.g., Sonopia at **sonopia.com**).

Mobile video sharing, which is sometimes combined with photo sharing, is a new technological and social trend. Mobile video-sharing portals are becoming popular (e.g., see **myubo.com** and **myzenplanet.com**). Many social networking sites are offering mobile features. For example, MySpace has partnership agreements with a number of U.S. wireless providers to support its MySpace Mobile service. Similarly, Facebook is available in both the United States and Canada via a number of wireless carriers. Bebo has joined forces with O2 Wireless in the United Kingdom and Ireland. This phenomenon is just the next step in the race to establish access to social networking sites across multiple mediums. Some argue that these deals do more to sell mobile phones than to promote the social networking sites; however, the social networks are more than happy to collect the residual attention.

Major Social Network Services: Facebook and Orkut

Now that you are familiar with social network services, let's take a closer look at some of the most popular ones.

FACEBOOK: THE NETWORK EFFECT   Facebook (**facebook.com**), which was launched in 2004 by former Harvard student Mark Zuckerberg, is the second-largest social network service in the world, with more than 200 million active users worldwide as of April 2009. When Zuckerberg first created Facebook, he had very strong social ambitions and wanted to help people connect to others on the Web.

A primary reason why Facebook has expanded so rapidly is the network effect—more users means more value. As more users become involved in the social space, more people are available to connect with. Initially, Facebook was an online social space for college and high school students that automatically connected students to other students at the same school. However, Facebook realized that it could only keep college and university users for 4 years. In 2006, Facebook opened its doors to anyone age 13 or older with a valid e-mail address. Expanding to a global audience has enabled Facebook to compete directly with MySpace.

Today, Facebook has a number of applications that support photos, groups, events, marketplaces, posted items, and notes. Facebook also has an application called "People You May Know," which helps users connect with people they might know. More applications are being added constantly. A special feature on Facebook is the News Feed, which enables users to track the activities of friends in their social circles. For example, when a user changes his or her profile, the updates are broadcast to others who subscribe to the feed. Users can also develop their own applications or use any of the millions of Facebook applications that have been developed by other users.

ORKUT: EXPLORING THE VERY NATURE OF SOCIAL NETWORKING SITES Orkut (**orkut .com**) was the brainchild of a Turkish Google programmer of the same name. Orkut was to be Google's homegrown answer to MySpace and Facebook. Orkut follows a format similar to that of other major social networking sites: a homepage where users can display every facet of their personal life they desire using various multimedia applications.

A major highlight of Orkut is the individual power afforded to those who create their own groups and forums, which are called "communities." Who can join and how posts are edited and controlled lies solely in the hands of the creator of each community. Moderating an Orkut community is comparable to moderating ones' own Web site, given the authority the creator possesses with regard to design and control of content. Orkut users gain substantial experience with Web 2.0 tools, creating an enormous wave of online proficiency, which is sure to contribute to the development of the online environment.

Orkut recognizes that it is the users who dictate the content of their chosen social networking site. Given this, Orkut has adapted in a number of interesting ways. First, it is adding more languages, expanding the Hindi, Bengali, Marathi, Tamil, and Telugu sites, which expands the popularity of the site and improves user control over the site. Second, Orkut greets its users on their national and religious holidays with fun features. For example, it wished Indian users a Happy Diwali (**en.wikipedia.org/wiki/Diwali**) by providing a feature that allowed users to redesign their personal site with Diwali-themed colors and decorations.

Implications of Business and Enterprise Social Networks

Although advertising and sales are the major EC activities in public social networks, there are emerging possibilities for commercial activities in business-oriented networks such as LinkedIn and in enterprise social networks.

Recognizing the opportunities, many software vendors are developing Web tools and applications to support enterprise social networking. For example, IBM Lotus is encouraging its 5,000-plus solution providers who are working with Notes/Domino, Sametime, and other Lotus software to add Lotus Connections to their product lineups, building applications based on social networking technology.

Representative areas and examples of enterprise social networking follow.

FINDING AND RECRUITING WORKERS Most of the public social networks, especially the business-oriented ones, facilitate recruiting and job finding (see Hoover, 2007). For example, recruiting is a major activity at LinkedIn and was the driver for the site's development. To be competitive, companies must look at the global market for talent, and they can use global social networking sites to find it. Large companies are using their in-house social networks to find in-house talent for vacant positions. Application Case 14.1 illustrates one such application that combines BI and social networking.

APPLICATION CASE 14.1

Using Intelligent Software and Social Networking to Improve Recruiting Processes

The Internet has made advertising and applying for jobs online a much simpler process. However, sometimes with simplicity comes complexity. The challenge now for some large companies is how to cost-effectively manage the online recruiting process, because online ads are attracting large numbers of applicants. For example, Infosys now receives in excess of 1 million job applications each year to fill about 9,000 positions. It might sound like a good problem to have too many applicants, but companies are finding that there is often a poor match between the skills and attributes they require and the many hundreds of applications received. Thus, despite attracting a lot of applicants, they often still suffer from a shortage of good applications. Furthermore, how can a company be sure it is accessing and attracting the very best talent in a particular field? Some interesting new developments are changing the way companies may address these issues.

Trovix (a Monster.com company) offers a service to companies based on its award-winning HR software, which uses embedded intelligence to help manage the entire recruitment process. Trovix argues that its tools Trovix Recruit and Trovix Intelligent Search can emulate human decision makers and assess a candidate's amount, depth, relevance, and recency of work experience, education, and the like. The software presents in rank order the best candidates to fit an advertised position. Other features enable tracking of applicants, reporting, and communications. A number of institutions are using this service, including Stanford University, which needs to fill thousands of positions each year. Trend Micro adopted Trovix and was able to screen 700 applicants and list the top 10 in about 20 minutes. The accuracy is probably no better than manual processing, but the software can screen applicants in a much shorter period of time.

A slightly more personal approach is available through some of the social networking sites, which offer support for companies to locate the best talent for a particular position. Sites such as Jobster (**jobster.com**) and LinkedIn (**linkedin.com**) rely more on a networking approach. Jobs posted on Jobster, for example, are linked to other job sites, to blogs, to user groups, to university alumni sites, and so on. People who are part of the social network are encouraged to recommend others who might be suited to a particular job, irrespective of whether they are actively seeking new work. In this way, a company looking to recruit the best talent has its job advertised much more widely and may benefit from word-of-mouth recommendations and referrals. For example, LinkedIn offers prospective employers a network of more than 8 million people across 130 industries, meaning much larger exposure for job vacancies and a much larger talent pool to seek referrals from. Sites such as Jobster can also track where applicants come from, helping companies adopt better recruitment strategies and thus achieve better returns from their investments in seeking the best staff.

Sources: Adapted from J. McKay, "Where Did Jobs Go? Look in Bangalore," *Gazette.com*, March 21, 2004, **post-gazette.com/pg/04081/288539.stm** (accessed July 2009); and "Trovix Makes Good at Stanford University: Premier Educational Institution Turns to Intelligent Search Provider for Recruiting Top Talent," March 8, 2006, **trovix.com/about/press/050806.jsp** (accessed July 2009).

MANAGEMENT ACTIVITIES AND SUPPORT Applications in this category are related to supporting managerial decision making based on analysis of data collected in social networks. Some typical examples include identifying key performers, locating experts and finding paths to access them, soliciting ideas and possible solutions to complex problems, and finding and analyzing candidates for management succession planning. For example, Deloitte Touche Tohmatsu set up a social network to assist its human resources managers in downsizing and regrouping teams. Hoover's has established a social network that uses Visible Path's technology to identify target business users for relationship building and to reach specific users. The Advances in Social Network Analysis and Mining conference on the use of data mining in social networks (July 2009 in Athens, Greece) has been dedicated to the topic.

TRAINING Several companies use enterprise social networking, and virtual worlds in particular, for training purposes. For example, Cisco is trying to use its virtual campus in Second Life for product training and executive briefings. IBM runs management and customer interaction training sessions in Second Life, too.

KNOWLEDGE MANAGEMENT AND EXPERT LOCATION Applications in this category include activities such as knowledge discovery, creation, maintenance, sharing, transfer, and dissemination. An elaborate discussion on the role of discussion forums, blogs, and wikis for conversational knowledge management can be found in Wagner and Bolloju (2005). Other examples of these applications include expert discovery and mapping communities of expertise.

Consider the following examples of social networking for knowledge management and expert location:

- Innocentive (**innocentive.com**), a social network with over 150,000 participating scientists, specializes in solving science-related problems (for cash rewards).
- Northwestern Mutual Life created an internal social network where over 7,000 financial representatives share captured knowledge (using Awareness.com blogging software).
- Caterpillar created a knowledge network system for its employees, and it even markets the software to other companies.

Companies also are creating *retiree corporate social networks* to keep retirees connected with each other and with the organization. These people possess huge amounts of knowledge that can be tapped for productivity increases and problem solving (e.g., Alumni Connect from SelectMinds). With 64 million people retiring within the next few years (per the Conference Board), preserving their knowledge is critical.

ENHANCING COLLABORATION Collaboration in social networking is done both internally, among employees from different units working in virtual teams for example, and externally, when working with suppliers, customers, and other business partners. Collaboration is done mostly in forums and other types of groups and by using wikis and blogs. For details on collaboration in social networks, see Coleman and Levine (2008).

USING BLOGS AND WIKIS WITHIN THE ENTERPRISE The use of these tools is expanding rapidly. Jefferies (2008) reports on a study that shows that 71 percent of the best-in-class companies use blogs and 64 percent use wikis for the following applications:

- Project collaboration and communication (63%)
- Process and procedure documentation (63%)
- FAQs (61%)
- E-learning and training (46%)
- Forums for new ideas (41%)
- Corporate-specific dynamic glossary and terminology (38%)
- Collaboration with customers (24%)

The term *Web 2.0* was coined by O'Reilly Media in 2004 to refer to a supposed second generation of Internet-based services that let people generate and control content using tools such as wikis, blogs, social networks, and folksonomies (see O'Reilly, 2005). Recognizing the potential of Web 2.0, researchers at the MIT Center for Digital Business (Brynjolfsson and McAfee, 2007) and Harvard Business School (McAfee, 2006; Cross et al., 2005) extended the Web 2.0 concept into *Enterprise 2.0* (the use of Web 2.0 within the enterprise), asserting that the Web 2.0 tools create a collaborative platform that reflects the way knowledge work is really and naturally done. These tools have the potential to enhance communication and collaboration and aid in virtual team decision-making processes (Turban et al., 2009).

USING TWITTER TO GET A PULSE OF THE MARKET   Twitter is a new social networking site that enables friends to keep in touch and follow what others are saying. An analysis of "tweets" can be used to determine how well a product /service is doing in the market. For example, Rui et al. (2009) used "tweets" to predict box office success of movies during a weekend (**sloanreview.mit.edu/business_insight/articles/2009/5/5152/follow-the-tweets/**).

Section 14.7 Review Questions

1. Define *social network.*
2. List some major social network sites.
3. Describe the global nature of social networks.
4. Describe mobile social networking.
5. Identify Facebook's major strategic issues (e.g., look at the marketing efforts at **insidefacebook.com** and at **facebook.com**).
6. Much of Facebook's early success was due to the close affiliation of its members' networks. How does Facebook expand into new markets without losing what originally made the site popular and alienating existing users?

14.8   CLOUD COMPUTING AND BI

Another emerging technology trend that business intelligence users should be aware of is cloud computing. Wikipedia (**en.wikipedia.org/wiki/cloud_computing**) defines **cloud computing** as "a style of computing in which dynamically scalable and often virtualized resources are provided over the Internet. Users need not have knowledge of, experience in, or control over the technology infrastructures in the cloud that supports them." This definition is broad and comprehensive. In some ways, cloud computing is a new name for many previous related trends: utility computing, application service provider grid computing, on-demand computing, *software as a service* (SaaS), and even older centralized computing with dumb terminals. But the term *cloud computing* originates from a reference to the Internet as a "cloud" and represents an evolution of all of previous shared/centralized computing trends. The Wikipedia entry also recognizes that cloud computing is a combination of several information technology components as services. For example, *infrastructure as a service* (IaaS) refers to providing computing *platforms as a service* (PaaS), as well as all of the basic platform provisioning, such as management administration, security, and so on. It also includes SaaS, which includes applications to be delivered through a Web browser while the data and the application programs are on some other server.

Although we do not typically look at Web-based e-mail as an example of cloud computing, it can be considered a basic cloud application. Typically, the e-mail application stores the data (e-mail messages) and the software (e-mail programs that let us process and manage e-mails). The e-mail provider also supplies the hardware/software and all the basic infrastructure. As long as the Internet is available, one can access the e-mail application from anywhere in the Internet cloud. When the application is updated by the e-mail provider (e.g., when Yahoo! updated its e-mail application), it becomes available to all the customers without them downloading any new programs. Thus, any Web-based general application is in a way an example of a cloud application. Another example of a general cloud application is Google Docs & Spreadsheets. This application allows a user to create text documents or spreadsheets that are stored on Google's servers and are available to the users anywhere they have access to the Internet. Again, no programs need to be installed, "the application is in the cloud." The storage space is also "in the cloud."

A very good general business example of cloud computing is Amazon.com's Web Services. Amazon.com has developed an impressive technology infrastructure for e-commerce as well as for business intelligence, customer relationship management, and supply-chain management. It has built major data centers to manage its own operations. However, through Amazon.com's cloud services, many other companies can employ these very same facilities to gain advantages of these technologies without a similar investment. Like other cloud-computing services, a user can subscribe to any of the facilities on a pay-as-you-go basis. This model of letting someone else own the hardware and software but making use of the facilities on a pay-per-use basis is the cornerstone of cloud computing. A number of companies offer cloud-computing services, including Salesforce.com, IBM, Sun Microsystems, Microsoft (Azure), Google, and Yahoo!

Cloud computing, like many other IT trends, has resulted in new offerings in business intelligence. White (2008) and Trajman (2009) provided examples of BI offerings related to cloud computing. Trajman identified several companies offering cloud-based data warehouse options. These options permit an organization to scale up its data warehouse and pay only for what it uses. Companies offering such services include 1010data, LogiXML, and Lucid Era. These companies offer feature extract, transform, and load capabilities as well as advanced data analysis tools. These are examples of SaaS as well as *data as a service* (DaaS) offerings. Other companies, such as Elastra and Rightscale, offer dashboard and data management tools that follow the SaaS and DaaS models, but they also employ IaaS from other providers, such as Amazon.com or Go Grid. Thus, the end user of a cloud-based BI service may use one organization for analysis applications that, in turn, uses another firm for the platform or infrastructure.

These types of cloud-based offerings are continuing to grow in popularity. A major advantage of these offerings is the rapid diffusion of advanced analysis tools among the users, without significant investment in technology acquisition. However, a number of concerns have been raised about cloud computing, including loss of control and privacy, legal liabilities, cross-border political issues, and so on. Nonetheless, cloud computing is an important initiative for a BI professional to watch.

Section 14.8 Review Questions

1. Define *cloud computing*. How does it relate to PaaS, SaaS, and IaaS?
2. Give examples of companies offering cloud services.
3. How does cloud computing affect business intelligence?

14.9 THE IMPACTS OF MANAGEMENT SUPPORT SYSTEMS: AN OVERVIEW

Management support systems are important factors in the information, Web, and knowledge revolution. This is a cultural transformation with which most people are only now coming to terms. Unlike the slower revolutions of the past, such as the Industrial Revolution, this revolution is taking place very quickly and affecting every facet of our lives. Inherent in this rapid transformation are a host of managerial, economic, and social issues. According to Gartner Group, the MSS share of the computer industry, including embedded systems and BI, is expected to grow at a 37.5 percent compound annual growth rate, and the MSS impact may be substantial (reported by Labat, 2006).

Separating the impact of MSS from that of other computerized systems is a difficult task, especially because of the trend toward integrating, or even embedding, MSS with other computer-based information systems. Very little published information is available about the impact of pure MSS technologies, because the techniques are frequently integrated with other information systems and their benefits are mostly intangible. Another problem in assessing the impacts of MSS is rapid changes in MSS implementation. Thus, some of our discussion must relate to computer systems in general. We recognize, however, that MSS technologies have some unique implications, which are highlighted throughout the remainder of this chapter.

MSS can have both micro and macro implications. Such systems can affect particular individuals and jobs, and they can also affect the work structures of departments and units within an organization. They can also have significant long-term effects on total organizational structures, entire industries, communities, and society as a whole (i.e., a macro impact).

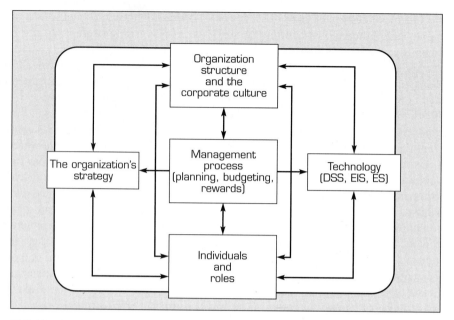

FIGURE 14.5 A Framework for Organizational and Societal Impacts of Artificial Intelligence Technology

Figure 14.5 presents a framework that shows the high-level architecture of an MSS. Such a system stays in equilibrium as long as all of its parts are unchanged. If there is a major change in one of the parts or in the relevant environment, the change is likely to affect some of the other parts. The major change stimuli relevant to MSS are usually *strategy* and *technology*, especially when BI or ES are introduced.

Computer technology has already changed our world, and much more change is anticipated. In addition to the effect on individuals, there are significant societal effects. The following are some of the major areas of social impact:

- Changing role of home-bound people
- Computer crime and fraud
- Consumers
- The digital divide
- Employment levels
- Opportunities for the disabled
- Quality of life
- Work in hazardous environments

One of the major changes now occurring is the emergence of the Web and its impact on MSS. Another is the relationship of decision support and knowledge management. Both are related to the organizational transformation.

The impact of computers and MSS technology can be divided into three general categories: organizational, individual, and societal. In each of these, computers have had many impacts. We cannot possibly consider all of them in this chapter, so in the next sections we touch upon topics we feel are most relevant to MSS.

Section 14.9 Review Questions

1. How can MSS affect particular individuals and jobs or the work structure of departments and units within an organization?
2. How can MSS affect organizational structures, entire industries, communities, and society as a whole?
3. What are the major stimuli for change in the MSS environment?
4. List some of the major social impacts of MSS.

14.10   MANAGEMENT SUPPORT SYSTEMS IMPACTS ON ORGANIZATIONS

Of the many organizational impacts, the following sections describe those that are closely related to MSS.

New Organizational Units

One change in organizational structure is the possibility of creating a management support department, a BI department (unit), an artificial intelligence department, or a knowledge management department in which MSS play a major role. This special unit can be combined with or replace a quantitative analysis unit, or it can be a completely new entity.

Some large corporations have separate decision support units or departments. For example, many major banks have such departments in their financial services divisions. Mead Corp., for example, has a special corporate DSS applications department, although it is integrated with other enterprise activities. Many companies have small decision support or BI/data warehouse units. For example, Continental Airlines (see the closing case at the end of this chapter) reportedly has a group of 14 data warehouse analysts supporting the rest of the organization (Wixon et al., 2008).

These types of departments are usually involved in training in addition to consulting and application development activities. A number of firms have created knowledge management departments (or units), headed by a chief knowledge officer (CKO). Others have empowered a chief technology officer over BI, intelligent systems, and e-commerce applications.

Growth of the BI industry has resulted in the formation of new units within IT provider companies. For example, IBM recently announced formation of a new business unit focused on analytics. This group includes units in business intelligence, optimization models, data mining, and business performance.

There is also consolidation through acquisition of specialized software companies by major IT providers. For example, IBM acquired ILOG, an optimization software company. Oracle acquired Hyperion some time back. Finally, there are also collaborations to enable companies to work cooperatively in some cases while also competing elsewhere. For example, SAS and Teradata announced a collaboration in 2007 to let Teradata users develop BI applications using SAS analytical modeling capabilities.

Organizational Culture

Organizational culture can affect the diffusion rate of technology and can be influenced by it. For example, the use of Lotus Notes changed the organizational climate of a large CPA firm by making employees more cooperative and willing to share information and use computers. In addition, virtual teams can meet anytime and anyplace. People can join a virtual team for as long as the project lasts or whenever their expertise is needed. When a project is completed, the team can disband. For changes in organizational culture due to MSS, see Watson et al. (2000).

Automated decision support (ADS) applications can empower lower-level frontline employees, giving them more autonomy. They may also reduce the size of organizations and change the organization's culture.

Restructuring Business Processes and Virtual Teams

In many cases, it is necessary to restructure business processes before introducing new information technologies. For example, before IBM introduced e-procurement, it restructured all related business processes, including decision making, searching inventories, reordering, and shipping. When a company introduces a data warehouse and BI, the information flows and related business processes (e.g., order fulfillment) are likely to change. Such changes are often necessary for profitability, or even survival. Restructuring is especially necessary when major IT projects such as ERP or BI are undertaken. Sometimes an organization-wide, major restructuring is needed, and then it is referred to as *reengineering*. Reengineering involves changes in structure, organizational culture, and processes. In a case in which an entire (or most of an) organization is involved, the process is referred to as **business process reengineering (BPR)**.

Several concepts of BPR greatly change organizational structure and mode of operation: team-based organization, mass customization, empowerment, and telecommuting. Therefore, in some cases, MSS may be used extensively as an enabler. MSS also play a major role in BPR (see El Sawy, 2001). MSS allow business to be conducted in different locations, providing flexibility in manufacturing; permit quicker delivery to customers; and support rapid, paperless transactions among suppliers, manufacturers, and retailers.

ES can enable organizational changes by providing expertise to nonexperts. An example is shown in Figure 14.6. The upper part of the figure shows a bank before reengineering. A customer who needed several services had to go to several departments. The bank kept multiple records and provided the customer with several monthly statements. The reengineered bank is shown in the lower part. A customer now makes contact with only one person, an account manager, who is supported by an ES. The new arrangement is less expensive, and customers save time and receive only one statement.

Related to organizational structure is the creation of virtual teams whose members are in different locations. Intelligent systems and ADS systems support these employees.

SIMULATION MODELING AND ORGANIZATIONAL RESTRUCTURING   It may be difficult to carry out restructuring and its planning and analysis even with a computer spreadsheet. For this reason, consultants and IT specialists are turning to an expanding class of products called *business simulation tools*. Many of these programs let users set up flowcharts to diagram the movement of resources through manufacturing or other business processes. El Sawy (2001) provided a comprehensive description of how to use simulation modeling for BPR.

The Impacts of ADS Systems

As indicated in Chapter 1 and other chapters, ADS systems, such as those for pricing, scheduling, and inventory management, are spreading rapidly, especially in industries such as airlines, retailing, transportation, and banking (see Davenport and Harris, 2005). These systems will probably have the following impacts:

- Reduction of middle management
- Empowerment of customers and business partners
- Improved customer service (e.g., faster reply to requests)
- Increased productivity of help desks and call centers

Other Organizational Impacts

Several other organizational impacts can be attributed to MSS. As described throughout this book, MSS are expected to increase productivity, speed, customer satisfaction, quality, and supply-chain improvements. This results in strategic advantage. Much of this comes about in integrated systems in which a DSS or an ES is a component. For a comprehensive description of the benefits of the introduction of data warehouses and BI, see Watson et al. (2000).

The impact goes beyond one company or one supply chain, however. Entire industries are affected. The use of profitability models and optimization are reshaping retailing, real estate, banking, transportation, airlines, and car rental agencies, among other industries. For more on organizational issues, see Mora (2002).

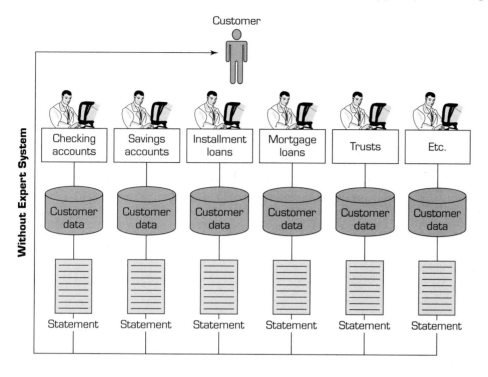

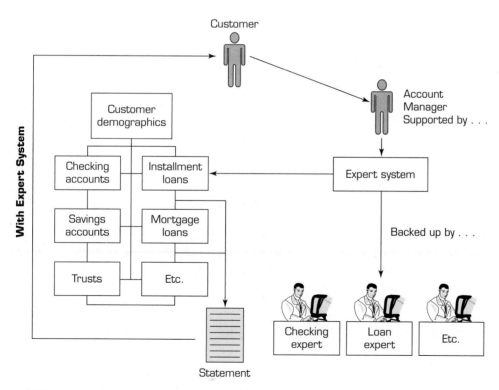

FIGURE 14.6   Restructuring a Bank with an ES

14.11   MANAGEMENT SUPPORT SYSTEMS IMPACTS ON INDIVIDUALS

MSS can affect individuals in various ways. What is considered to be a benefit to one individual may be a curse to another. What is an added stress today can be a relief tomorrow. Related to this is the use of computers and MSS by managers (e.g., see Elbeltagi et al., 2005). Representative areas where MSS may affect individuals, their perceptions, and behaviors are described next.

Job Satisfaction

Although many jobs may be substantially enriched by MSS, other jobs may become more routine and less satisfying. For example, more than 35 years ago, Argyris (1971) predicted that computer-based information systems would reduce managerial discretion in decision making and lead to managers being dissatisfied. A study by Ryker and Ravinder (1995) showed that IT has had a positive effect on four of the five core job dimensions: identity, significance, autonomy, and feedback. No significant effect was found on skill variety. In their study about ADS, Davenport and Harris (2005) found that employees using ADS systems, especially those who are empowered by the systems, were more satisfied with their jobs.

Inflexibility, Dehumanization, Stress, and Anxiety

A common criticism of traditional data-processing systems is their negative effects on people's individuality. Such systems are criticized as being impersonal: They may dehumanize and depersonalize activities that have been computerized because they reduce or eliminate the human element that was present in noncomputerized systems. Some people feel a loss of identity; they feel like just another number. On the bright side, one of the major objectives of MSS is to create flexible systems and interfaces that allow individuals to share their opinions and knowledge and work together with computers. Despite all these efforts, some people are still afraid of computers, so they are stressed; others are mostly afraid of their employers watching what they do on the computer.

JOB STRESS AND ANXIETY   An increase in workload and/or responsibilities can trigger job stress. Although computerization has benefited organizations by increasing productivity, it has also created an ever-increasing and changing workload on some employees—many times brought on by downsizing and redistributing entire workloads of one employee to another. Some workers feel overwhelmed and begin to feel anxious about their jobs and their performance. These feelings of anxiety can adversely affect their productivity. Management must alleviate these feelings by redistributing the workload among workers or conducting appropriate training.

One of the negative impacts of the information age is information anxiety. This disquiet can take several forms, such as frustration with the inability to keep up with the amount of data present in our lives. The following are some other forms of information anxiety:

- Frustration with not being able to master computers as well as others.
- Frustration with the quality of information available on the Web. This information is frequently not up-to-date or is incomplete.

- Frustration due to having too many online sources of information.
- Frustration due to guilt associated with not being better informed or being informed too late (e.g., "How come everyone else knew before we did?").

Constant connectivity afforded through mobile devices, e-mail, and instant messaging creates its own challenges and stress. Research on e-mail response strategies (**iris .okstate.edu/REMS**) includes many examples of studies conducted to recognize such stress. Constant alerts about incoming e-mails lead to interruptions, which eventually result in loss of productivity (and then an increase in stress). Systems have been developed to provide decision support to determine how often a person should check his or her e-mail (see Gupta and Sharda, 2009).

Cooperation of Experts

Human experts who are planning to give their knowledge to an organizational or to a problem-specific knowledge base may have reservations. Consider the following examples of thoughts that might enter an expert's mind:

- The computer may take my knowledge and replace me.
- The computer may make me less important.
- Why should I tell the computer my secrets? What will I gain?
- The computer may reveal that I am not as great an expert as people think.

This kind of thinking may cause the expert not to cooperate or even to give incorrect knowledge to the computer. To deal with such situations, management should motivate (and possibly compensate) the experts.

Section 14.11 Review Questions

1. How can MSS affect job satisfaction?
2. In what ways may MSS affect inflexibility, dehumanization, stress, and anxiety?
3. Describe the issue of experts' cooperation in MSS.

14.12 AUTOMATING DECISION MAKING AND THE MANAGER'S JOB

Computer-based information systems have had an impact on the jobs of managers for about five decades. However, this impact was felt mainly at the lower- and middle-managerial levels. Since 2000, MSS have been affecting almost everyone, including top managers.

The most important task of managers is making decisions. MSS technologies can change the manner in which many decisions are made and can consequently change managers' jobs. The impacts of MSS on decision making are numerous; the most common areas are discussed next.

The Effect of MSS on Managers' Activities and Their Performance

According to Perez-Cascante et al. (2002), an ES/DSS was found to improve the performance of both existing and new managers as well as other employees. It helped managers gain more knowledge, experience, and expertise, and it consequently enhanced the quality of their decision making.

Many managers report that computers have finally given them time to get out of the office and into the field. (BI can save an hour a day for every user.) They have also found that they can spend more time planning activities instead of putting out fires because they can be alerted to potential problems well in advance, thanks to intelligent agents, ES, and other analytical tools.

Another aspect of the managerial challenge lies in the ability of MSS to support the decision-making process in general and strategic planning and control decisions in particular. MSS could change the decision-making process and even decision-making styles. For example, information gathering for decision making is completed much more quickly when MSS are in use. Enterprise information systems are extremely useful in supporting strategic management (see Liu et al., 2002). Artificial intelligence technologies are now used to improve external environmental scanning of information. As a result, managers can change their approach to problem solving (see Huber, 2003). Research indicates that most managers tend to work on a large number of problems simultaneously, moving from one to another as they wait for more information on their current problem (see Mintzberg et al., 2002). MSS tend to reduce the time required to complete tasks in the decision-making process and eliminate some of the nonproductive waiting time by providing knowledge and information. Therefore, managers work on fewer tasks during each day but complete more of them. The reduction in startup time associated with moving from task to task could be the most important source of increased managerial productivity.

Another possible impact of MSS on the manager's job could be a change in leadership requirements. What are now generally considered good leadership qualities may be significantly altered by the use of MSS. For example, face-to-face communication is frequently replaced by e-mail, wikis, and computerized conferencing; thus, leadership qualities attributed to physical appearance could become less important.

Even if managers' jobs do not change dramatically, the methods managers use to do their jobs will. For example, an increasing number of CEOs no longer use computer intermediaries; instead, they work directly with computers and the Web. When voice recognition is of high quality, we may see a real revolution in the way managers use computers.

The following are some potential impacts of MSS on managers' jobs:

- Less expertise (experience) is required for making many decisions.
- Faster decision making is possible because of the availability of information and the automation of some phases in the decision-making process.
- Less reliance on experts and analysts is required to provide support to top executives; managers can do it by themselves with the help of intelligent systems.
- Power is being redistributed among managers. (The more information and analysis capability they possess, the more power they have.)
- Support for complex decisions makes them faster to make and of better quality.
- Information needed for high-level decision making is expedited or even self-generated.
- Automation of routine decisions or phases in the decision-making process (e.g., for frontline decision making and using ADS) may eliminate some managers.

Can Managers' Jobs Be Fully Automated?

The generic decision-making process involves specific tasks (e.g., identifying problems, finding possible solution alternatives, forecasting consequences, evaluating alternatives). This process can be fairly lengthy, which is bothersome for a busy manager. Automation of certain tasks can save time, increase consistency, and enable better decisions to be made (see Davenport and Harris, 2005). Thus, the more tasks we automate in the process, the better. However, is it possible to completely automate the manager's job?

In general, it has been found that the job of middle managers is the most likely job to be automated. Midlevel managers make fairly routine decisions, which can be fully automated. Managers at lower levels do not spend much time on decision making.

Instead, they supervise, train, and motivate nonmanagers. Some of their routine decisions, such as scheduling, can be automated; other decisions that involve behavioral aspects cannot. However, even if we completely automate their decisional role, we could not automate their jobs. The Web provides an opportunity to automate certain tasks done by frontline employees; this empowers them, thus reducing the workload of approving managers. The job of top managers is the least routine and therefore the most difficult to automate. For further discussion, see Huber (2003).

Section 14.12 Review Questions

1. List the impacts of MSS on decision making.
2. List the impacts of MSS on other managerial tasks.
3. Explain the issues related to completely automating managers' jobs.

14.13 ISSUES OF LEGALITY, PRIVACY, AND ETHICS

Several important legal, privacy, and ethical issues are related to MSS. Here we provide only representative examples and sources.

Legal Issues

The introduction of MSS, and especially of ES, may compound a host of legal issues already relevant to computer systems. For example, questions concerning liability for the actions of advice provided by intelligent machines are just beginning to be considered. The issue of computers as a form of unfair competition in business was raised in the 1990s, with the well-known dispute over the practices of airline reservation systems.

In addition to resolving disputes about the unexpected and possibly damaging results of some MSS, other complex issues may surface. For example, who is liable if an enterprise finds itself bankrupt as a result of using the advice of an MSS? Will the enterprise itself be held responsible for not testing the system adequately before entrusting it with sensitive issues? Will auditing and accounting firms share the liability for failing to apply adequate auditing tests? Will the software developers of intelligent systems be jointly liable? Consider the following specific legal issues:

- What is the value of an expert opinion in court when the expertise is encoded in a computer?
- Who is liable for wrong advice (or information) provided by an ES? For example, what happens if a physician accepts an incorrect diagnosis made by a computer and performs an act that results in the death of a patient?
- What happens if a manager enters an incorrect judgment value into an MSS and the result is damage or a disaster?
- Who owns the knowledge in a knowledge base?
- Should royalties be paid to experts who provide knowledge to an ES or a knowledge base? If so, how much should they receive?
- Can management force experts to contribute their expertise?

Privacy

Privacy means different things to different people. In general, **privacy** is the right to be left alone and the right to be free from unreasonable personal intrusions. Privacy has long been a legal, ethical, and social issue in many countries. The right to privacy is recognized today in every state of the United States and by the federal government, either by statute or by common law. The definition of *privacy* can be interpreted quite broadly. However, the following two rules have been followed fairly closely in past court decisions: (1) The right of privacy is not absolute. Privacy must be balanced against the needs of society. (2) The public's right to know is superior to the individual's right to privacy. These two rules show why it is difficult, in some cases, to determine and enforce privacy regulations (see Peslak, 2005). Privacy issues online have their own characteristics and policies. One area where privacy may be jeopardized is discussed next. For privacy and security issues in the data warehouse environment, see Elson and LeClerc (2005).

COLLECTING INFORMATION ABOUT INDIVIDUALS   The complexity of collecting, sorting, filing, and accessing information manually from numerous government agencies was, in many cases, a built-in protection against misuse of private information. It was simply too expensive, cumbersome, and complex to invade a person's privacy. The Internet, in combination with large-scale databases, has created an entirely new dimension of accessing and using data. The inherent power in systems that can access vast amounts of data can be used for the good of society. For example, by matching records with the aid of a computer, it is possible to eliminate or reduce fraud, crime, government mismanagement, tax evasion, welfare cheating, family-support filching, employment of illegal aliens, and so on. However, what price must the individual pay in terms of loss of privacy so that the government can better apprehend criminals? The same is true on the corporate level. Private information about employees may aid in better decision making, but the employees' privacy may be affected. Similar issues are related to information about customers.

THE WEB AND INFORMATION COLLECTION   The Internet offers a number of opportunities to collect private information about individuals. Here are some of the ways it can be done:

- By reading an individual's newsgroup postings
- By looking up an individual's name and identity in an Internet directory
- By reading an individual's e-mail
- By wiretapping wireline and wireless communication lines and listening to employees
- By conducting surveillance on employees
- By asking an individual to complete Web site registration
- By recording an individual's actions as he or she navigates the Web with a browser, using cookies or spyware

The implications for online privacy are significant. The ability of law enforcement agencies to authorize installation of pen registers and trap-and-trace devices has increased. The U.S. PATRIOT Act also broadens the government's ability to access student information and personal financial information without any suspicion of wrongdoing by attesting that the information likely to be found is pertinent to an ongoing criminal investigation (see Electronic Privacy Information Center, 2005).

Two effective tools for collecting information about individuals are cookies and spyware. Single-sign-on facilities that let a user access various services from a provider are beginning to raise some of the same concerns as cookies. Such services (Google, Yahoo!, MSN) let consumers permanently enter a profile of information along with a password and use this information and password repeatedly to access services at multiple sites. Critics say that such services create the same opportunities as cookies to invade an individual's privacy.

The use of artificial intelligence technologies in the administration and enforcement of laws and regulations may increase public concern regarding privacy of information.

These fears, generated by the perceived abilities of artificial intelligence, will have to be addressed at the outset of almost any artificial intelligence development effort.

Fortunately, individuals can take steps to improve their privacy. Tynan (2002) provides 34 tips that show how to do it.

MOBILE USER PRIVACY   Many users are unaware of the private information being tracked through mobile PDA or cell phone use. For example, Sense Networks' models are built using data from cell phone companies that track each phone as it moves from one cell tower to another, from GPS-enabled devices that transmit users' locations, and from PDAs transmitting information at WiFi hotspots. Sense Networks claims that it is extremely careful and protective of users' privacy, but it is interesting to note how much information is available through just the use of a single device.

HOMELAND SECURITY AND INDIVIDUAL PRIVACY   Using MSS technologies such as mining and interpreting the content of telephone calls, taking photos of people in certain places and identifying them, and using scanners to view your personal belongings are considered by many as an invasion of privacy. However, many people recognize that MSS tools are effective and efficient means to increase security, even though the privacy of many innocent people is compromised.

The U.S. government applies analytical technologies on a global scale in the war on terrorism. In the first year and a half after September 11, 2001, supermarket chains, home improvement stores, and other retailers voluntarily handed over massive amounts of customer records to federal law enforcement agencies, almost always in violation of their stated privacy policies. Many others responded to court orders for information, as required by law. The U.S. government has a right to gather corporate data under legislation passed after September 11, 2001. The FBI now mines enormous amounts of data, looking for activity that could indicate a terrorist plot or crime.

Privacy issues abound. Because the government is acquiring personal data to detect suspicious patterns of activity, there is the prospect of improper or illegal use of the data. Many see such gathering of data as a violation of citizens' freedoms and rights. They see the need for an oversight organization to "watch the watchers," to ensure that the Department of Homeland Security does not mindlessly acquire data. Instead, it should acquire only pertinent data and information that can be mined to identify patterns that potentially could lead to stopping terrorists' activities. This is not an easy task.

Ethics in Decision Making and Support

Several ethical issues are related to MSS. A comprehensive overview of ethics in problem formulation and decision making is provided by Chae et al. (2005), who suggested the model of ethical problem formulation that is shown in Figure 14.7.

Representative ethical issues that could be of interest in MSS implementations include the following:

- Electronic surveillance
- Ethics in DSS design (see Chae et al., 2005)
- Software piracy
- Invasion of individuals' privacy (discussed earlier)
- Use of proprietary databases
- Use of intellectual property such as knowledge and expertise
- Exposure of employees to unsafe environments related to computers

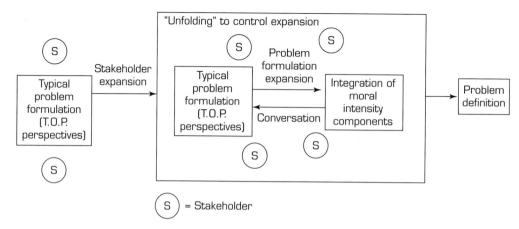

FIGURE 14.7 A Model of Ethical Problem Formulation

- Computer accessibility for workers with disabilities
- Accuracy of data, information, and knowledge
- Protection of the rights of users
- Accessibility to information
- Use of corporate computers for non-work-related purposes
- How much decision making to delegate to computers

Personal values constitute a major factor in the issue of ethical decision making. For a comprehensive study, see Fritzsche (1995). The study of ethical issues in MSS is complex because of its multidimensionality (see Chae et al., 2005). Therefore, it makes sense to develop frameworks to describe ethics processes and systems. Mason et al. (1995) explained how technology and innovation expand the size of the domain of ethics and discuss a model for ethical reasoning that involves four fundamental focusing questions: Who is the agent? What action was actually taken or is being contemplated? What are the results or consequences of the act? Is the result fair or just for all stakeholders? They also described a hierarchy of ethical reasoning in which each ethical judgment or action is based on rules and codes of ethics, which are based on principles, which in turn are grounded in ethical theory. For more on ethics in decision making, see Murali (2004).

NON-WORK-RELATED USE OF THE INTERNET Employees are tempted to use e-mail and the Web for non-work-related purposes. In some companies, this use is tremendously out of proportion with the work-related uses (see Anandarajan, 2002). The problem has several dimensions. For example, e-mail can be used to harass other employees or to pose a legal threat to a company. It can also be used to conduct illegal gambling activity (e.g., betting on results of a football game). Some employees may use corporate e-mail to advertise their own businesses. Using other corporate computing facilities for private purposes may be problematic, too. Last but not least is the time employees waste surfing non-work-related Web sites during working hours.

Section 14.13 Review Questions

1. List some legal issues of MSS.
2. Describe privacy concerns in MSS.
3. Explain privacy concerns on the Web.
4. List ethical issues in MSS.
5. Describe an ethical framework for MSS.

14.14 RESOURCES, LINKS, AND THE TERADATA UNIVERSITY NETWORK CONNECTION

The use of this chapter and most other chapters in this book can be enhanced by the tools described in the following section.

1. **Teradatastudentnetwork.com** has a case study on Continental Airlines (the subject of this chapter's closing case) and on MYCIN, an expert system mentioned in Chapter 12 and in discussion questions below.
2. Virtual events are gaining popularity. Many companies such as Polycom, Cisco, and Microsoft define their virtual events in terms of business meetings. These companies' Web sites include information about their offerings.
3. Companies such as **iTradefair.com** also offer white papers and case studies describing benefits and issues with virtual trade fairs.
4. **Sensenetworks.com** describes the company's adaptation of clustering algorithms to identifying tribes based upon the movement of customers.

Chapter Highlights

- RFID data can provide useful analytics for supply-chain management and performance measurement. Sensor-based RFID can help analyze product conditions within a supply chain.
- Virtual worlds provide new immersive experiences for decision support and replicate many of the features of physical gatherings.
- Location information from mobile phones and PDAs can be used to create profiles of user behavior and movement. Such location information can enable users to find other people with similar interests and advertisers to customize their promotions.
- Analysis of large-scale data being gathered offers new opportunities for data mining.
- Web 2.0 is about the innovative application of existing technologies. Web 2.0 has brought together the contributions of millions of people and has made their work, opinions, and identity matter.
- User-created content is a major characteristic of Web 2.0, as is the emergence of social networking.
- Virtual communities create new types of business opportunities.
- Large Internet communities enable the sharing of content, including text, videos, and photos, and promote online socialization and interaction.
- Business-oriented social networks concentrate on business issues both in one country and around the world (e.g., recruiting, finding business partners). Business-oriented social networks include LinkedIn and Xing.
- Cloud computing offers the possibility of using software, hardware, platform, and infrastructure, all on a service-subscription basis. Cloud computing enables a more scalable investment on the part of a user.

- Cloud-computing-based BI services offer organizations the latest technologies without significant upfront investment.
- MSS can affect organizations in many ways, as stand-alone systems or integrated among themselves or with other computer-based information systems.
- MSS could reduce the need for supervision by providing more guidelines to employees electronically.
- The impact of MSS on individuals varies; it can be positive, neutral, or negative.
- Management should motivate experts to contribute their knowledge to knowledge bases.
- Serious legal issues may develop with the introduction of intelligent systems; liability and privacy are the dominant problem areas.
- In one view, intelligent systems and other MSS will cause massive unemployment because of increased productivity, lower required skill levels, and impacts on all sectors of the economy.
- In another view, intelligent systems and other MSS will increase employment levels, because automation makes products and services more affordable and so demand increases. The process of disseminating automation is slow enough to allow the economy to adjust to intelligent technologies.
- Many positive social implications can be expected from MSS. These range from providing opportunities to disabled people to leading the fight against terrorism. Quality of life, both at work and at home, is likely to improve as a result of MSS.
- Managers need to plan for the MSS of the future so as to be ready to make the most of them.

Key Terms

business process
    reengineering (BPR)
    662
cloud computing *658*

mobile social
    networking *653*
privacy *667*
reality mining *641*

RFID *636*
social network
    analysis (SNA)
    software *653*

virtual (Internet)
    community *650*
virtual worlds *644*
Web 2.0 *649*

Questions for Discussion

1. What are the potential benefits and challenges of using RFID in supply-chain management?
2. Given that RFID data streams are large but only include basic tracking information, how would you derive useful information from these streams? You may want to read Delen, Hargrave, and Sharda (2007).
3. What are the benefits and issues of using virtual worlds for decision support?
4. If you had an opportunity to participate in a virtual career fair, what factors would motivate and inhibit your participation?
5. "Location-tracking-based profiling (reality mining) is powerful but also poses privacy threats." Comment.
6. Is cloud computing "just an old wine in a new bottle"? How is it similar to other initiatives? How is it different?
7. What are the major characteristics of Web 2.0? What are some of the advantages of Web 2.0 applications?
8. Discuss the use of virtual communities to do business on the Internet.
9. How can wikis be used to facilitate knowledge management?
10. Discuss the relationship between mobile devices and social networking.
11. Some say that MSS in general, and ES in particular, dehumanize managerial activities, and others say they do not. Discuss arguments for both points of view.
12. The U.S. Department of Transportation in a large metropolitan area has an ES that advises an investigator about

whether to open an investigation of a reported car accident. (This system, which includes 300 rules, was developed by T. J. Nagy at George Washington University.) Discuss the following questions:
  a. Should the people involved in an accident be informed that a machine is deciding the future of an investigation?
  b. What are some of the potential legal implications of this?
  c. In general, what do you think of such a system?
13. Diagnosing infections and prescribing pharmaceuticals are the weak points of many practicing physicians (according to E. H. Shortliffe, one of the developers of MYCIN). It seems, therefore, that society would be better served if MYCIN (and other ES, see Chapter 12) were used extensively, but few physicians use ES. Answer the following questions:
  a. Why do you think ES are little used by physicians?
  b. Assume that you are a hospital administrator whose physicians are salaried and report to you. What would you do to persuade them to use ES?
  c. If the potential benefits to society are so great, can society do something that will increase doctors' use of ES?
14. Discuss the potential benefits of integrating KMS into a DSS.
15. Discuss the potential impacts of ADS systems on various types of employees and managers.

Exercises

TERADATA STUDENT NETWORK (TSN) AND OTHER HANDS-ON EXERCISES

1. Go to **teradatstudentnetwork.com** and search for case studies. Read the Continental Airlines cases written by Hugh Watson and his colleagues. What new applications can you imagine with the level of detailed data an airline can capture today.
2. Also review the MYCIN case at **teradatastudentnetwork .com.** What other similar applications can you envision?
3. At **teradatastudentnetwork.com,** go to podcasts library. Find podcasts of pervasive BI submitted by Hugh Watson. Summarize the points made by the speaker.

TEAM ASSIGNMENTS AND ROLE-PLAYING

1. Item-level RFID tagging will be useful to retail stores as well as to customers. Stores already use RFID to track inventory more accurately. Customers could use RFID to locate items more easily, possibly even using a within-store GPS to find an item. However, RFID does have some potential privacy issues. Form two groups. One group will argue for RFID adoption and the other group will argue against it.
2. Search the Web for "virtual trade shows." Form two teams arguing for and against the use of virtual worlds in business applications.

3. Location-tracking-based clustering provides the potential for personalized services but challenges for privacy. Divide the class in two parts to argue for and against applications such as Citysense.

4. Each group is assigned to a social network that features business activities (e.g., LinkedIn, Xing, Facebook, Second Life). Each group will then register with **hellotxt.com** to find out what is going on in the site with regard to recent business activities. Write a report and make a class presentation.

   With Hello TXT, you log on to the site and enter your text message into the dashboard. You then select the sites you want to update with your new status message, and Hello TXT does the rest, reaching out to your various pages to add your new status message. It is a great centralized way to keep all your various profiles as up-to-date as possible, and it is designed to update your LinkedIn status by answering the question "What are you working on?"

5. As a group, sign in to **secondlife.com** and create an avatar. Each group member is assigned to explore a certain business area (e.g., virtual real estate, educational activities, diplomatic island). Make sure the avatar interacts with other people's avatars. Write a report.

6. Enter **facebook.com** and **myspace.com** and find out how 10 well-known corporations use the sites to conduct commercial activities. Also, compare the functionalities of the two sites.

7. Several hospitals are introducing or considering the introduction of an intelligent bedside assistant that provides physicians and staff with a patient's medical record database for diagnosis and prognosis. The system supplies any information required from the patient's medical records, makes diagnoses based on symptoms, and prescribes medications and other treatments. The system includes an ES as well as a DSS. The system is intended to eliminate some human error and improve patient care. You are a hospital administrator and are very excited about the benefits for the patients. However, when you called a staff meeting, the following questions were raised: What if the system malfunctions? What if there is an undetected error in the program or the rules? The system, once implemented, takes full responsibility for patient care because physicians rely on it. A loss of data or an error in the program may lead to disaster. For example, suppose there is a bug in the database program, and, as a result, a critical piece of information is missing from the patient's record. A physician who relies on the system could prescribe a drug on the basis of incomplete data. The consequence of this mistake could be life threatening. Another possibility is that some of the rules in the knowledge base might not be accurate for all patients. Would you implement such a system? Why or why not?

8. Read Chae et al. (2005). Summarize all the ethical issues described there and then find examples in each area.

9. Divide the class into two sections: those who believe that BI will replace business analysts, and those who oppose the idea. Conduct a debate.

10. Identify ethical issues related to managerial decision making. Search the Internet, join chat rooms, and read articles from the Internet. Prepare a report on your findings.

11. There has been considerable talk about the impact of the Internet on society. Concepts such as *global village, Internet community, digital divide, Internet society,* and the like are getting much attention. Search the Internet and prepare a short report on the topic. How does this concept relate to managerial decision making?

12. Search the Internet to find examples of how intelligent systems (especially ES and intelligent agents) facilitate activities such as empowerment, mass customization, and teamwork.

13. Investigate the American Bar Association's Technology Resource Center (**abanet.org/tech/ltrc/techethics .html**) and **nolo.com**. What are the major legal and societal concerns and advances addressed there? How are they being dealt with?

14. Explore several sites related to health care (e.g., **WebMD .com**, **who.int**). Find issues related to MSS and privacy. Write a report on how these sites improve health care.

15. Go to **computerworld.com** and find five legal issues related to BI and MSS.

INTERNET EXERCISES

1. Enter the *RFID Journal* Web site (**rfidjournal.com**). List at least two applications related to supply-chain management and two applications in one of the following areas: health care, education, entertainment, law enforcement.

2. Enter **blog.itradefair.com**. What are some of the interesting applications of virtual trade fairs?

3. Enter **youtube.com**. Search for videos on cloud computing. Watch at least two. Summarize your findings.

4. Enter **sensenetworks.com**. Review the Citysense application and media reports about it. Write a report on what you learned.

5. Enter the Web site of a social network service (e.g., **myspace .com** or **facebook.com**). Build a homepage. Add a chat room and a message board to your site using the free tools provided. Describe the other capabilities available. Make at least five new friends.

6. Enter **pandora.com**. Find out how you can create and share music with friends. Why is this a Web 2.0 application?

7. Enter **smartmobs.com**. Go to blogroll. Find three blogs related to Web 2.0 and summarize their major features.

8. Enter **mashable.com** and review the latest news regarding social networks and network strategy. Right a report.

9. Access Hof's "My Virtual Life" (2008) at **businessweek .com/print/magazine/content/06_18/b3982001.htm? chang=g1** and meet the seven residents in the slide show. Prepare a table that shows the manner in which they make money, the required skills, and the reason they do it in Second Life.

10. Identify two virtual worlds (other than Second Life).

11. Enter **secondlife.com** and find any islands that relate to BI and decision support. Write a report on what they offer.

12. Enter **yedda.com** and explore its approach to knowledge sharing.

END OF CHAPTER APPLICATION CASE

Continental Continues to Score with Data Warehouse

We started this book with an opening vignette from a Teradata success story. This last case is from a similar success story, also covered in Chapter 8. Continental's success with using a data warehouse to improve its revenue management, customer service operations, and so on has been widely reported (Anderson et al., 2004; Watson et al., 2006). Wixom et al. (2008) have studied on Continental's continued success and interesting new uses of its data warehouse. Although these are not futuristic uses, these cases suggest the potential for what can be done to continue to exploit investments in BI technologies.

Wixom and colleagues had studied the use of data warehouses at Continental in the late 1990s. They recently returned to the company and conducted follow-up interviews with the users and developers of the data warehouse. They learned that the data warehouse has become an integral part of the airline's operations, helping it make strategic and tactical decisions. When a system becomes part of the daily operations, it indicates a different level of acceptance in a company's culture. It also usually means that the number of users may grow substantially. The warehouse now supports over 50 subject areas and more than 1,400 users writing ad hoc queries to generate business intelligence to make better decisions. In the following sections, reproduced (and adapted) with the authors' permission, a few new uses are highlighted (Wixom et al., 2008):

Tax Department, London

In the United Kingdom, Continental must pay a departure tax for passengers who leave the UK on Continental flights. Each month, employees in the London office calculated this departure tax by manually reviewing the records for every passenger who traveled out of London, and the employees submitted the appropriate amount to the government. If passengers are passing through the UK in less than 24 hours, they are exempt from the tax, but the manual process could not always identify those individuals. Thus, Continental regularly overpaid the departure tax, which equated to a $300,000 annual cost for the airline. Last year, several members of the Continental London office were visiting Houston for routine training, which included a presentation by the warehouse group. During the presentation, the London employees noticed that data in the warehouse potentially could identify passengers who were exempt from the departure tax. They approached the warehouse team to build a specialized application. Now, the group runs a monthly query to the warehouse, prints out a report with an accurate departure tax amount, and submits the report. The application eliminates significant time and overpayment.

Flight Performance

Prior to the data warehouse, Continental Operations built and managed their own information and reporting systems. The systems support staff was very small; when a support employee went on vacation or was sick, systems were put on hold until the person returned to work. Eventually, management mandated a move to the warehouse to improve continuity of the support operations. Steve Hayes, a manager within this operations support group, has leveraged the warehouse for his area in significant ways. For example, he has built a real-time status application that communicates up-to-the-minute performance statistics on how the airline is operating. And, when Jet Blue and American Airlines were criticized for incidents that involved stranding passengers in planes for long periods of time (Cummings, 2006; Zeller, 2007), Hayes was able to adapt his application, and help Continental avoid similar situations. Continental's old process for detecting these kinds of events was manual and time consuming. Hayes explains, "You had to hunt and peck through flight logs. In the middle of a snow storm, you don't have time to do that." Once Operations identified the need to monitor planes on the tarmac, Steve added an alert to the real time performance statistics application. Now, flights that sit on the ground away from a gate for at least 2 hours immediately appear on the screen. In real-time, Operations can work to get those flights off the ground, or get them back to the gate in a timely manner.

The warehouse also has helped streamline Operations reporting processes. In the past, Continental manually tracked the reasons for flight delays (e.g., weather, part failure); there are about a hundred delay codes. Sometimes stations forgot to record the reason for delay, so Operations regularly ran a query on the legacy system, downloaded the results into Excel, e-mailed the results to the general managers, who would then fill in the blanks and send information back by e-mail or telex. According to Hayes, "It would take forever to track down the information and update the codes into the legacy system." Using the warehouse, Hayes built an application one weekend that automatically lists flights that need delay codes for each station. The general manager now directly logs into the application, clicks on a flight, and enters the delay code. The new process eliminates multiple steps, and creates much more accurate results. Hayes explains that this situation is representative of how he now can quickly develop simple applications or application enhancements using the data warehouse that have high impact on Operations processes.

These examples are just two of the many new uses of the data warehouse at Continental. Wixom et al. (2008) describe many others and also list the following as facilitators in continuing success of BI at Continental:

- A common data foundation
- "Open data" philosophy
- A culture of data
- Personnel who are business–IT hybrids

Questions for the Case

1. Visit **teradatastudentnetwork.com** and learn more about Continental's experiences in data warehouses. Summarize your reading.
2. Wixom et al. call Continental's work with business intelligence a journey rather than a destination. Comment.
3. What other new applications of data warehouses can you imagine at an airline?
4. The case summary includes two example applications of BI at an airline. Can you relate these applications to your own organization's domain?
5. Comment on the list of facilitating success factors for a mature data warehouse.

Sources: Adapted from R. Anderson-Lehman, H. J. Watson, B. H. Wixom, and J. Hoffer, "Continental Airlines Flies High with Real-Time Business Intelligences," *MIS Quarterly Executive,* Vol. 3, No. 4, 2004, pp. 163–176; C. Cummings, "Passengers Stuck on Plane Over 8 Hours," *The Dallas Morning News,* December 30, 2006; H. J. Watson, B. H. Wixom, J. Hoffer, J. Anderson-Lehman, and A. M. Reynolds, "Real-Time Business Intelligence: Best Practices at Continental Airlines," *Information Systems Management,* Vol. 23, No. 1, 2006, pp. 7–19; B. H. Wixom, H. J. Watson, A. M. Reynolds, and J. A. Hoffer, "Continental Airlines Continues to Soar with Business Intelligence," *Information Systems Management,* Vol. 25, No. 2, March 1, 2008, pp. 102–112; T. Zeller, "Held Hostage on the Tarmac: Time for a Passenger Bill of Rights?" *The New York Times,* February 16, 2007.

References

Alexander, K., T. Gilliam, K. Gramling, M. Kindy, D. Moogimane, M. Schultz, and M. Woods. (2003). "Focus on the Supply Chain: Applying Auto-ID within the Distribution Center." White paper, Auto-ID Center, MIT, Massachusetts.

Anandarajan, M. (2002, January). "Internet Abuse in the Workplace." *Communications of the ACM.*

Anderson-Lehman, R., H. J. Watson, B. H. Wixom, and J. Hoffer. (2004). "Continental Airlines Flies High with Real-Time Business Intelligences." *MIS Quarterly Executive,* Vol. 3, No. 4, pp. 163–176.

Argyris, C. (1971, February). "Management Information Systems: The Challenge to Rationality and Emotionality." *Management Science,* Vol. 17, No. 6.

Bacheldor, B. (2006, October). "TNT Uses RFID to Track Temperatures of Sensitive Goods." *RFID Journal.*

Baker, S. (2009, February 26). "Mapping a New, Mobile Internet." *BusinessWeek.* **businessweek.com/magazine/content/09_10/b4122042889229.htm** (accessed July 2009).

Banker, S. (2005, September). "Achieving Operational Excellence in the Cold Chain." *ARC Brief.* **sensitech.com/PDFs/coldchain_info/achieving_xcellence_CC.pdf** (accessed September 2009).

Brandon, J. (2007, May 2). "The Top Eight Corporate Sites in Second Life." *Computerworld,* **computerworld.com/s/article/9018238/The_top_eight_corporate_sites_in_Second_Life** (accessed July 2009).

Brynjolfsson, E., and A. P. McAfee. (2007, Spring). "Beyond Enterprise." *MIT Sloan Management Review*, pp. 50–55.

Chae, B., D. B. Paradice, J. F. Courtney, and C. J. Cagle. (2005, August). "Incorporating an Ethical Perspective into Problem Formulation." *Decision Support Systems,* Vol. 40.

Coleman, D., and S. Levine. (2008). *Collaboration 2.0.* Cupertino, CA: Happy About Info.

Collins, J. (2005, June). "Sysco Gets Fresh with RFID." *RFID Journal.*

Cross, R., J. Liedtka, and L. Weiss. (2005, March). "A Practical Guide to Social Networks." *Harvard Business Review.*

Cummings, C. (2006, December 30). "Passengers Stuck on Plane Over 8 Hours." *The Dallas Morning News.*

Davenport, T. H., and J. G. Harris. (2005, Summer). "Automated Decision Making Comes of Age." *MIT Sloan Management Review.*

Delen, D., B. Hardgrave, and R. Sharda. (2007, September/October). "RFID for Better Supply-Chain Management Through Enhanced Information Visibility." *Production and Operations Management*, Vol. 16, No. 5, pp. 613–624.

Delen, D., B. Hardgrave, and R. Sharda. (2009). "Promise of RFID-based Sensors in the Perishables Supply Chain." IRIS working paper OSU.

Eagle, N., and A. Pentland. (2006). "Reality Mining: Sensing Complex Social Systems." *Personal and Ubiquitous Computing.* Vol. 10, No. 4, pp. 255–268.

Economist. (2009, June 4). "Sensors and Sensitivity." **economist.com/sciencetechnology/tq/displayStory.cfm?story_id=13725679** (accessed July 2009).

El Sawy, O. (2001). *Redesigning Enterprise Processes for E-Business.* New York: McGraw-Hill.

Elbeltagi, I., N. McBride, and G. Hardaker. (2005, April–June). "Evaluating the Factors Affecting DSS Usage by Senior Managers in Local Authorities in Egypt." *Journal of Global Information Management.*

Electronic Privacy Information Center. (2005). "The U.S.A. PATRIOT Act." **epic.org/privacy/terrorism/usapatriot/** (accessed July 2009).

Elson, R. J., and R. LeClerc. (2005, Summer). "Security and Privacy Concerns in the Data Warehouse Environment." *Business Intelligence Journal.*

Evans, B. (2005). "Business Technology: Implementing RFID Is a Risk Worth Taking." *Information Week's RFID Insights.* **informationweek.com/news/mobility/RFID/showArticle.jhtml?articleID=164302282** (accessed July 2009).

Fritzsche, D. (1995, November). "Personal Values: Potential Keys to Ethical Decision Making." *Journal of Business Ethics*, Vol. 14, No. 11.

Good, R. (2005). "What Is Web Conferencing?" **master-newmedia.org/reports/webconferencing/guide/what_is_web_conferencing.htm** (accessed July 2009).

Gupta, A., and R. Sharda. (2009). "SIMONE: A Simulator for Interruptions and Message Overload in Network Environments." *International Journal of Simulation and Process Modeling*, Vol. 4, Nos. 3/4, pp. 237–247.

Hardgrave, B. C., M. Waller, and R. Miller. (2006). "RFID Impact on Out of Stocks? A Sales Velocity Analysis." White paper, RFID Research Center, Information Technology Research Institute, Sam M. Walton College of Business, University of Arkansas. **itrc.uark.edu** (accessed July 2009).

Hof, R. D. (2008, May 1). "My Virtual Life." *BusinessWeek.*

Hoover, J. N. (2007, February 26). "Enterprise 2.0." *Information Week.*

Huber, G. (2003). *The Necessary Nature of Future Firms.* San Francisco: Sage.

Intel. (2007). "Early RFID Adopters Seize the Initiative." White paper. **www.intel.com/cd/00/00/33/74/337466_337466.pdf** (accessed September 2009).

Jefferies, A. (2008, October 30). "Sales 2.0: Getting Social About Selling." *CRM Buyer.*

Katz, J. (2006, February). "Reaching the ROI on RFID." *IndustryWeek.* **industryweek.com/ReadArticle.aspx?ArticleID=11346** (accessed July 2009).

Labat, A. (2006). "ESL Lives Up to Its Early Promise in Embedded Systems Design." *Chip Design Magazine.* **chipdesignmag.com/display.php?articleId=397** (accessed July 2009).

Liu, S., J. Carlsson, and S. Nummila. (2002, July). "Mobile E-Services: Creating Added Value for Working Mothers." *Proceedings DSI AGE 2002*, Cork, Ireland.

Loecher, M., D. Rosenberg, and T. Jebara. (2009). "Citysense: Multiscale Space Time Clustering of GPS points and Trajectories." *Joint Statistical Meeting 2009.*

Mason, R. O., F. M. Mason, and M. J. Culnan. (1995). *Ethics of Information Management.* Thousand Oaks, CA: Sage.

McAfee, A. P. (2006). "Enterprise 2.0: The Dawn of Emergent Collaboration." *MIT Sloan Management Review*, Vol. 47, No. 3, pp. 21–29.

McKay, J. (2004, March 21). "Where Did Jobs Go? Look in Bangalore." *Gazette.com.* **post-gazette.com/pg/04081/288539.stm** (accessed July 2009).

McKnight, W. (2005, February). "Building BI: Will BI Replace the Business Analyst." *DM Review.*

McNurlin, B. C., and R. H. Sprague, Jr. (2006). *Information Systems Management in Practice*, 7th ed. Upper Saddle River, NJ: Prentice Hall.

Mintzberg, H., et al. (2002). *The Strategy Process*, 4th ed. Upper Saddle River, NJ: Prentice Hall.

Mora, M. (2002, October/December). "Management and Organizational Issues for Decision Making Support Systems." *Information Resources Management Journal*, Special Issue.

Moradpour, S., and M. Bhuptani. (2005). "RFID Field Guide: Deploying Radio Frequency Identification Systems." New York: Sun Microsystems Press.

Murali, D. (2004, December 2). "Ethical Dilemmas in Decision Making." *BusinessLine.*

O'Reilly, T. (2005, September 30). "What Is Web 2.0?" *O'Reillynet.com* **oreilly.com/web2/archive/what-is-web-20.html** (accessed July 2009).

Perez-Cascante, L. P., M. Plaisent, L. Maguiraga, and P. Bernard. (2002, October–December). "The Impact of Expert Decision Support Systems on the Performance of New Employees." *Information Resources Management Journal.*

Peslak, A. P. (2005, January–March). "Internet Privacy Policies." *Information Resources Management Journal.*

Power, D. J. (2007, July 29). "What Are the Advantages and Disadvantages of Using Second Life for Decision Support?" *DSS News,* Vol. 8, No. 15, **dssresources.com/faq/index .php?action=artikel&id=138** (accessed July 2009).

Ryker, R., and N. Ravinder. (1995, October). "An Empirical Examination of the Impact of Computer Information Systems on Users." *Information and Management,* Vol. 29, No. 4.

Sahin, E., M. Z. Babaï, Y. Dallery, and R. Vaillant. (2007). "Ensuring Supply Chain Safety Through Time Temperature Integrators." *The International Journal of Logistics Management.* Vol. 18, No. 1, pp. 102–124.

Siskind, B. (2005). *Powerful Exhibit Marketing, The Complete Guide to Successful Tradeshows, Conferences and Consumer Shows.* New York: Wiley.

Stuart, B. (2007). "Virtual Worlds as a Medium for Advertising." *SIGMIS Database,* Vol. 38, No. 4, pp. 45–55.

Sullivan, L. (2005, October). "Wal-Mart RFID Trial Shows 16% Reduction in Product Stock-Outs." *InformationWeek.* **informationweek.com/story/showArticle.jhtml?artic leID=172301246** (accessed July 2009).

Swedberg, C. (2006a, October). "Samworth Keeps Cool with RFID." *RFID Journal.* **rfidjournal.com/article/ articleview/2733/** (accessed September 2009).

Swedberg, C. (2006b, December). "Starbucks Keeps Fresh with RFID." *RFID Journal.* **rfidjournal.com/article/ articleview/2890/** (accessed September 2009).

Tompkins, J. A., J. A. White, Y. A. Bozer, and J. M. A. Tanchoco. (2002). *Facilities Planning,* 3rd ed. New York: Wiley.

Trajman, O. (2009, March 5). "Business Intelligence in the Clouds." *InfoManagement Direct.* **information-management .com/infodirect/2009_111/10015046-1.html** (accessed July 2009).

Tsz-Wai, L., P. Gabriele, and I. Blake. (2007). "Marketing Strategies in Virtual Worlds." *SIGMIS Database,* Vol. 38, No. 4, pp. 77–80.

Turban, E., A. P. J. Wu, and T.-P. Liang. (2009). "The Potential Role of Web 2.0 Tools in Virtual Teams Decision Making and Negotiation: An Exploratory Study." Working paper National Sun Yat-sen University, Kaohsiung, Taiwan.

Tynan, D. (2002, June). "How to Take Back Your Privacy (34 Steps)." *PC World.*

U.S. Department of Commerce. (2005). "Radio Frequency Identification: Opportunities and Challenges in Implementation." Department of Commerce, pp. 1–38.

Wagner, C., and N. Bolloju. (2005). "Supporting Knowledge Management in Organizations with Conversational Technologies: Discussion Forums, Weblogs, and Wikis." *Journal of Database Management,* Vol. 16, No. 2.

Watson, H. J., B. H. Wixom, and D. L. Goodhue. (2000, Winter). "The Effects of Technology-Enabled Business Strategy at First American Corporation." *Organization Dynamics.*

Watson, H. J., B. H. Wixom, J. Hoffer, J. Anderson-Lehman, and A. M. Reynolds. (2006). "Real-Time Business Intelligence: Best Practices at Continental Airlines." *Information Systems Management,* Vol. 23, No. 1, pp. 7–19.

Weier, M. H. (2009, June 6). "Coke's RFID-Based Dispensers Redefine Business Intelligence." *Information Week.* **informationweek.com/story/showArticle.jhtml?arti cleID=217701971** (accessed July 2009).

White, C. (2008, July 30). "Business Intelligence in the Cloud: Sorting Out the Terminology." *BeyeNetwork.* **b-eye-network.com/channels/1138/view/8122** (accessed July 2009).

Wikipedia. (2009). "Cloud Computing." **en.wikipedia.org/ wiki/Cloud_computing** (accessed July 2009).

Wixom, B. H., H. J. Watson, A. M. Reynolds, and J. A. Hoffer. (2008, March 1). "Continental Airlines Continues to Soar with Business Intelligence." *Information Systems Management,* Vol. 25, No. 2, pp. 102–112.

Zeller, T. (2007, February 16). "Held Hostage on the Tarmac: Time for a Passenger Bill of Rights?" *The New York Times.*

GLOSSARY

active data warehousing *See* real-time data warehousing.

ad hoc DSS A DSS that deals with specific problems that are usually neither anticipated nor recurring.

ad hoc query A query that cannot be determined prior to the moment the query is issued.

adaptive resonance theory (ART) An unsupervised learning method created by Stephen Grossberg. ART is a neural network architecture that is aimed at being brainlike in unsupervised mode.

agency The degree of autonomy vested in a software agent.

algorithm A step-by-step search in which improvement is made at every step until the best solution is found.

analog model An abstract, symbolic model of a system that behaves like the system but looks different.

analogical reasoning The process of determining the outcome of a problem by using analogies. It is a procedure for drawing conclusions about a problem by using past experience.

analytic hierarchy process (AHP) A modeling structure for representing *multicriteria* (multiple goals, multiple objectives) *problems*—with sets of criteria and alternatives (choices)—commonly found in business environments.

analytical models Mathematical models into which data are loaded for analysis.

analytical techniques Methods that use mathematical formulas to derive an optimal solution directly or to predict a certain result, mainly in solving structured problems.

analytics The science of analysis.

application service provider (ASP) A software vendor that offers leased software applications to organizations.

Apriori algorithm The most commonly used algorithm to discover association rules by recursively identifying frequent itemsets.

area under the ROC curve A graphical assessment technique for binary classification models where the true positive rate is plotted on the *Y*-axis and false positive rate is plotted on the *X*-axis.

artificial intelligence (AI) The subfield of computer science concerned with symbolic reasoning and problem solving.

artificial neural network (ANN) Computer technology that attempts to build computers that operate like a human brain. The machines possess simultaneous memory storage and work with ambiguous information. Sometimes called, simply, a *neural network*. *See* neural computing.

association A category of data mining algorithm that establishes relationships about items that occur together in a given record.

asynchronous Occurring at different times.

authoritative pages Web pages that are identified as particularly popular based on links by other Web pages and directories.

automated decision support (ADS) A rule-based system that provides a solution to a repetitive managerial problem. Also known as *enterprise decision management (EDM)*.

automated decision system (ADS) A business rule-based system that uses intelligence to recommend solutions to repetitive decisions (such as pricing).

autonomy The capability of a software agent acting on its own or being empowered.

axon An outgoing connection (i.e., terminal) from a biological neuron.

backpropagation The best-known learning algorithm in neural computing where the learning is done by comparing computed outputs to desired outputs of training cases.

backward chaining A search technique (based on if-then rules) used in production systems that begins with the action clause of a rule and works backward through a chain of rules in an attempt to find a verifiable set of condition clauses.

balanced scorecard (BSC) A performance measurement and management methodology that helps translate an organization's financial, customer, internal process, and learning and growth objectives and targets into a set of actionable initiatives.

best practices In an organization, the best methods for solving problems. These are often stored in the knowledge repository of a knowledge management system.

blackboard An area of working memory set aside for the description of a current problem and for recording intermediate results in an expert system.

black-box testing Testing that involves comparing test results to actual results.

bootstrapping A sampling technique where a fixed number of instances from the original data is sampled (with replacement) for training and the rest of the dataset is used for testing.

bot An intelligent software agent. Bot is an abbreviation of robot and is usually used as part of another term, such as knowbot, softbot, or shopbot.

business (or system) analyst An individual whose job is to analyze business processes and the support they receive (or need) from information technology.

business analytics (BA) The application of models directly to business data. Business analytics involve using DSS tools, especially models, in assisting decision makers. It is essentially OLAP/DSS. *See* business intelligence (BI).

business intelligence (BI) A conceptual framework for decision support. It combines architecture, databases (or data warehouses), analytical tools, and applications.

business network A group of people who have some kind of commercial relationship; for example, sellers and buyers, buyers among themselves, buyers and suppliers, and colleagues and other colleagues.

business performance management (BPM) An advanced performance measurement and analysis approach that embraces planning and strategy.

business process reengineering (BPR) A methodology for introducing a fundamental change in specific business processes. BPR is usually supported by an information system.

case library The knowledge base of a case-based reasoning system.

case-based reasoning (CBR) A methodology in which knowledge or inferences are derived from historical cases.

categorical data Data that represent the labels of multiple classes used to divide a variable into specific groups.

certainty A condition under which it is assumed that future values are known for sure and only one result is associated with an action.

certainty factors (CF) A popular technique for representing uncertainty in expert systems where the belief in an event (or a fact or a hypothesis) is expressed using the expert's unique assessment.

chief knowledge officer (CKO) The person in charge of a knowledge management effort in an organization.

choice phase The third phase in decision making, in which an alternative is selected.

chromosome A candidate solution for a genetic algorithm.

classification Supervised induction used to analyze the historical data stored in a database and to automatically generate a model that can predict future behavior.

clickstream analysis The analysis of data that occur in the Web environment.

clickstream data Data that provide a trail of the user's activities and show the user's browsing patterns (e.g., which sites are visited, which pages, how long).

cloud computing Information technology infrastructure (hardware, software, applications, platform) that is available as a service, usually as virtualized resources.

clustering Partitioning a database into segments in which the members of a segment share similar qualities.

cognitive limits The limitations of the human mind related to processing information.

collaboration hub The central point of control for an e-market. A single collaboration hub (c-hub), representing one e-market owner, can host multiple collaboration spaces (c-spaces) in which trading partners use c-enablers to exchange data with the c-hub.

collaborative filtering A method for generating recommendations from user profiles. It uses preferences of other users with similar behavior to predict the preferences of a particular user.

collaborative planning, forecasting, and replenishment (CPFR) A project in which suppliers and retailers collaborate in their planning and demand forecasting to optimize the flow of materials along the supply chain.

community of practice (COP) A group of people in an organization with a common professional interest, often self-organized, for managing knowledge in a knowledge management system.

complexity A measure of how difficult a problem is in terms of its formulation for optimization, its required optimization effort, or its stochastic nature.

confidence In association rules, the conditional probability of finding the RHS of the rule present in a list of transactions where the LHS of the rule already exists.

connection weight The weight associated with each link in a neural network model. Neural networks learning algorithms assess connection weights.

consultation environment The part of an expert system that a non-expert uses to obtain expert knowledge and advice. It includes the workplace, inference engine, explanation facility, recommended action, and user interface.

content management system (CMS) An electronic document management system that produces dynamic versions of documents and automatically maintains the current set for use at the enterprise level.

content-based filtering A type of filtering that recommends items for a user based on the description of previously evaluated items and information available from the content (e.g., keywords).

corporate (enterprise) portal A gateway for entering a corporate Web site. A corporate portal enables communication, collaboration, and access to company information.

corpus In linguistics, a large and structured set of texts (now usually stored and processed electronically) prepared for the purpose of conducting knowledge discovery.

CRISP-DM A cross-industry standardized process of conducting data mining projects, which is a sequence of six steps that starts with a good understanding of the business and the need for the data mining project (i.e., the application domain) and ends with the deployment of the solution that satisfied the specific business need.

critical success factors (CSF) Key factors that delineate the things that an organization must excel at to be successful in its market space.

crossover The combination of parts of two superior solutions by a genetic algorithm in an attempt to produce an even better solution.

cube A subset of highly interrelated data that is organized to allow users to combine any attributes in a cube (e.g., stores, products, customers, suppliers) with any metrics in the cube (e.g., sales, profit, units, age) to create various two-dimensional views, or *slices*, that can be displayed on a computer screen.

customer experience management (CEM) Applications designed to report on the overall user experience by detecting Web application issues and problems, by tracking and resolving business process and usability obstacles, by reporting on site performance and availability, by enabling real-time alerting and monitoring, and by supporting deep-diagnosis of observed visitor behavior.

dashboard A visual presentation of critical data for executives to view. It allows executives to see hot spots in seconds and explore the situation.

data Raw facts that are meaningless by themselves (e.g., names, numbers).

data conferencing Virtual meeting in which geographically dispersed groups work on documents together and exchange computer files during videoconferences.

data cube A two-dimensional, three-dimensional, or higher-dimensional object in which each dimension of the data represents a measure of interest.

data integration Integration that comprises three major processes: data access, data federation, and change capture. When these three processes are correctly implemented, data can be accessed and made accessible to an array of ETL, analysis tools, and data warehousing environments.

data integrity A part of data quality where the accuracy of the data (as a whole) is maintained during any operation (such as transfer, storage, or retrieval).

data mart A departmental data warehouse that stores only relevant data.

data mining A process that uses statistical, mathematical, artificial intelligence, and machine-learning techniques to extract and identify useful information and subsequent knowledge from large databases.

data quality (DQ) The holistic quality of data, including their accuracy, precision, completeness, and relevance.

data visualization A graphical, animation, or video presentation of data and the results of data analysis.

data warehouse (DW) A physical repository where relational data are specially organized to provide enterprise-wide, cleansed data in a standardized format.

data warehouse administrator (DWA) A person responsible for the administration and management of a data warehouse.

database A collection of files that are viewed as a single storage concept. The data are then available to a wide range of users.

database management system (DBMS) Software for establishing, updating, and querying (e.g., managing) a database.

deception detection A way of identifying deception (intentionally propagating beliefs that are not true) in voice, text, and/or body language of humans.

decision analysis Methods for determining the solution to a problem, typically when it is inappropriate to use iterative algorithms.

decision making The action of selecting among alternatives.

decision room An arrangement for a group support system in which PCs are available to some or all participants. The objective is to enhance groupwork.

decision style The manner in which a decision maker thinks and reacts to problems. It includes perceptions, cognitive responses, values, and beliefs.

decision support systems (DSS) A conceptual framework for a process of supporting managerial decision making, usually by modeling problems and employing quantitative models for solution analysis.

decision tables Conveniently organized information and knowledge in a systematic, tabular manner, often prepared for further analysis.

decision tree A graphical presentation of a sequence of interrelated decisions to be made under assumed risk. This technique classifies specific entities into particular classes based upon the features of the entities; a root followed by internal nodes, each node (including root) is labeled with a question, and arcs associated with each node cover all possible responses.

decision variable A variable in a model that can be changed and manipulated by the decision maker. Decision variables correspond to the decisions to be made, such as quantity to produce, amounts of resources to allocate, etc.

defuzzification The process of creating a crisp solution from a fuzzy logic solution.

Delphi method A qualitative forecasting methodology that uses anonymous questionnaires. It is effective for technological forecasting and for forecasting involving sensitive issues.

demographic filtering A type of filtering that uses the demographic data of a user to determine which items may be appropriate for recommendation.

dendrite The part of a biological neuron that provides inputs to the cell.

dependent data mart A subset that is created directly from a data warehouse.

descriptive model A model that describes things as they are.

design phase The second decision-making phase, which involves finding possible alternatives in decision making and assessing their contributions.

development environment The part of an expert system that a builder uses. It includes the knowledge base and the inference engine, and it involves knowledge acquisition and improvement of reasoning capability. The knowledge engineer and the expert are considered part of the environment.

diagnostic control system A cybernetic system that has inputs, a process for transforming the inputs into outputs, a standard or benchmark against which to compare the outputs, and a feedback channel to allow information on variances between the outputs and the standard to be communicated and acted on.

digital divide The gap between those who have and those who do not have the ability to use technology.

dimension table A table that addresses *how* data will be analyzed.

dimensional modeling A retrieval-based system that supports high-volume query access.

directory A catalog of all the data in a database or all the models in a model base.

discovery-driven data mining A form of data mining that finds patterns, associations, and relationships among data in order to uncover facts that were previously unknown or not even contemplated by an organization.

distance measure A method used to calculate the closeness between pairs of items in most cluster analysis methods. Popular distance measures include Euclidian distance (the ordinary distance between two points that one would measure with a ruler) and Manhattan distance (also called the rectilinear distance, or taxicab distance, between two points).

distributed artificial intelligence (DAI) A multiple-agent system for problem solving. DAI involves splitting a problem into multiple cooperating systems to derive a solution.

DMAIC A closed-loop business improvement model that includes these steps: defining, measuring, analyzing, improving, and controlling a process.

document management systems (DMS) Information systems (e.g., hardware, software) that allow the flow, storage, retrieval, and use of digitized documents.

drill-down The investigation of information in detail (e.g., finding not only total sales but also sales by region, by product, or by salesperson). Finding the detailed sources.

DSS application A DSS program built for a specific purpose (e.g., a scheduling system for a specific company).

dynamic models Models whose input data are changed over time (e.g., a 5-year profit or loss projection).

effectiveness The degree of goal attainment. Doing the right things.

efficiency The ratio of output to input. Appropriate use of resources. Doing things right.

electronic brainstorming A computer-supported methodology of idea generation by association. This group process uses analogy and synergy.

electronic document management (EDM) A method for processing documents electronically, including capture, storage, retrieval, manipulation, and presentation.

electronic meeting systems (EMS) An information technology-based environment that supports group meetings (groupware), which may be distributed geographically and temporally.

elitism A concept in genetic algorithms where some of the better solutions are migrated to the next generation in order to preserve the best solution.

end-user computing Development of one's own information system. Also known as *end-user development*.

Enterprise 2.0 Technologies and business practices that free the workforce from the constraints of legacy communication and productivity tools such as e-mail. Provides business managers with access to the right information at the right time through a Web of interconnected applications, services, and devices.

enterprise application integration (EAI) A technology that provides a vehicle for pushing data from source systems into a data warehouse.

enterprise data warehouse (EDW) An organizational-level data warehouse developed for analytical purposes.

enterprise decision management (EDM) *See* automated decision support (ADS).

enterprise information integration (EII) An evolving tool space that promises real-time data integration from a variety of sources, such as relational databases, Web services, and multidimensional databases.

enterprise knowledge portal (EKP) An electronic doorway into a knowledge management system.

enterprise-wide collaboration system A group support system that supports an entire enterprise.

entropy A metric that measures the extent of uncertainty or randomness in a data set. If all the data in a subset belong to just one class, then there is no uncertainty or randomness in that data set, and therefore the entropy is zero.

environmental scanning and analysis A process that involves conducting a search for and an analysis of information in external databases and flows of information.

evolutionary algorithm A class of heuristic based optimization algorithms modeled after the natural process of biological evolution, such as genetic algorithms and genetic programming.

expert A human being who has developed a high level of proficiency in making judgments in a specific, usually narrow, domain.

expert location system An interactive computerized system that helps employees find and connect with colleagues who have expertise required for specific problems—whether they are across the county or across the room—in order to solve specific, critical business problems in seconds.

expert system (ES) A computer system that applies reasoning methodologies to knowledge in a specific domain to render advice or recommendations, much like a human expert. An ES is a computer system that achieves a high level of performance in task areas that, for human beings, require years of special education and training.

expert system (ES) shell A computer program that facilitates relatively easy implementation of a specific expert system. Analogous to a DSS generator.

expert tool user A person who is skilled in the application of one or more types of specialized problem-solving tools.

expertise The set of capabilities that underlines the performance of human experts, including extensive domain knowledge, heuristic rules that simplify and improve approaches to problem solving, metaknowledge and metacognition, and compiled forms of behavior that afford great economy in a skilled performance.

explanation subsystem The component of an expert system that can explain the system's reasoning and justify its conclusions.

explanation-based learning A machine-learning approach that assumes that there is enough existing theory to rationalize why one instance is or is not a prototypical member of a class.

explicit knowledge Knowledge that deals with objective, rational, and technical material (e.g., data, policies, procedures, software, documents). Also known as *leaky knowledge*.

extraction The process of capturing data from several sources, synthesizing them, summarizing them, determining which of them are relevant, and organizing them, resulting in their effective integration.

extraction, transformation, and load (ETL) A data warehousing process that consists of extraction (i.e., reading data from a database), transformation (i.e., converting the extracted data from its previous form into the form in which it needs to be so that it can be placed into a data warehouse or simply another database), and load (i.e., putting the data into the data warehouse).

facilitator (in a GSS) A person who plans, organizes, and electronically controls a group in a collaborative computing environment.

forecasting Predicting the future.

forward chaining A data-driven search in a rule-based system.

functional integration The provision of different support functions as a single system through a single, consistent interface.

fuzzification A process that converts an accurate number into a fuzzy description, such as converting from an exact age into categories such as young and old.

fuzzy logic A logically consistent way of reasoning that can cope with uncertain or partial information. Fuzzy logic is characteristic of human thinking and expert systems.

fuzzy set A set theory approach in which set membership is less precise than having objects strictly in or out of the set.

genetic algorithm A software program that learns in an evolutionary manner, similar to the way biological systems evolve.

geographic information system (GIS) An information system capable of integrating, editing, analyzing, sharing, and displaying geographically referenced information.

Gini index A metric that is used in economics to measure the diversity of the population. The same concept can be used to determine the purity of a specific class as a result of a decision to branch along a particular attribute/variable.

global positioning systems (GPS) Wireless devices that use satellites to enable users to detect the position on earth of items (e.g., cars or people) the devices are attached to, with reasonable precision.

goal seeking Asking a computer what values certain variables must have in order to attain desired goals.

grain A definition of the highest level of detail that is supported in a data warehouse.

graphical user interface (GUI) An interactive, user-friendly interface in which, by using icons and similar objects, the user can control communication with a computer.

group decision support system (GDSS) An interactive computer-based system that facilitates the solution of semi-structured and unstructured problems by a group of decision makers.

group support system (GSS) Information systems, specifically DSS, that support the collaborative work of groups.

groupthink In a meeting, continual reinforcement of an idea by group members.

groupware Computerized technologies and methods that aim to support the work of people working in groups.

groupwork Any work being performed by more than one person.

heuristic programming The use of heuristics in problem solving.

heuristics Informal, judgmental knowledge of an application area that constitutes the rules of good judgment in the field. Heuristics also encompasses the knowledge of how to solve problems efficiently and effectively, how to plan steps in solving a complex problem, how to improve performance, and so forth.

hidden layer The middle layer of an artificial neural network that has three or more layers.

hub One or more Web pages that provide a collection of links to authoritative pages.

hybrid (integrated) computer system Different but integrated computer support systems used together in one decision-making situation.

hyperlink-induced topic search (HITS) The most popular publicly known and referenced algorithm in Web mining used to discover hubs and authorities.

hyperplane A geometric concept commonly used to describe the separation surface between different classes of things within a multidimensional space.

hypothesis-driven data mining A form of data mining that begins with a proposition by the user, who then seeks to validate the truthfulness of the proposition.

iconic model A scaled physical replica.

idea generation The process by which people generate ideas, usually supported by software (e.g., developing alternative solutions to a problem). Also known as *brainstorming*.

implementation phase The fourth decision-making phase, involving actually putting a recommended solution to work.

independent data mart A small data warehouse designed for a strategic business unit or a department.

inductive learning A machine-learning approach in which rules are inferred from facts or data.

inference engine The part of an expert system that actually performs the reasoning function.

information overload An excessive amount of information being provided, making processing and absorbing tasks very difficult for the individual.

influence diagram A diagram that shows the various types of variables in a problem (e.g., decision, independent, result) and how they are related to each other.

influences rules In expert systems, a collection of if-then rules that govern the processing of knowledge rules acting as a critical part of the inferencing mechanism.

information Data organized in a meaningful way.

information gain The splitting mechanism used in ID3 (a popular decision-tree algorithm).

institutional DSS A DSS that is a permanent fixture in an organization and has continuing financial support. It deals with decisions of a recurring nature.

integrated intelligent systems A synergistic combination (or hybridization) of two or more systems to solve complex decision problems.

intellectual capital The know-how of an organization. Intellectual capital often includes the knowledge that employees possess.

intelligence A degree of reasoning and learned behavior, usually task or problem-solving oriented.

intelligence phase The initial phase of problem definition in decision making.

intelligent agent (IA) An expert or knowledge-based system embedded in computer-based information systems (or their components) to make them smarter.

intelligent computer-aided instruction (ICAI) The use of AI techniques for training or teaching with a computer.

intelligent database A database management system exhibiting artificial intelligence features that assist the user or designer; often includes ES and intelligent agents.

intelligent tutoring system (ITS) Self-tutoring systems that can guide learners in how best to proceed with the learning process.

interactivity A characteristic of software agents that allows them to interact (communicate and/or collaborate) with each other without having to rely on human intervention.

intermediary A person who uses a computer to fulfill requests made by other people (e.g., a financial analyst who uses a computer to answer questions for top management).

intermediate result variable A variable that contains the values of intermediate outcomes in mathematical models.

Internet telephony *See* Voice over IP (VoIP).

interval data Variables that can be measured on interval scales.

inverse document frequency A common and very useful transformation of indices in a term-by-document matrix that reflects both the specificity of words (document frequencies) as well as the overall frequencies of their occurrences (term frequencies).

iterative design A systematic process for system development that is used in management support systems (MSS). Iterative design involves producing a first version of MSS, revising it, producing a second design version, and so on.

kernel methods A class of algorithms for pattern analysis that approaches the problem by mapping highly nonlinear data into a high dimensional feature space, where the data items are transformed into a set of points in a Euclidean space for better modeling.

kernel trick In machine learning, a method for using a linear classifier algorithm to solve a nonlinear problem by mapping the original nonlinear observations onto a higher-dimensional space, where the linear classifier is subsequently used; this makes a linear classification in the new space equivalent to nonlinear classification in the original space.

kernel type In kernel trick, a type of transformation algorithm used to represent data items in a Euclidean space. The most commonly used kernel type is the radial basis function.

key performance indicator (KPI) Measure of performance against a strategic objective and goal.

k-fold cross-validation A popular accuracy assessment technique for prediction models where the complete dataset is randomly split into k mutually exclusive subsets of approximately equal size. The classification model is trained and tested k times. Each time it is trained on all but one fold and then tested on the remaining single fold. The cross-validation estimate of the overall accuracy of a model is calculated by simply averaging the k individual accuracy measures.

knowledge Understanding, awareness, or familiarity acquired through education or experience; anything that has been learned, perceived, discovered, inferred, or understood; the ability to use information. In a knowledge management system, knowledge is information in action.

knowledge acquisition The extraction and formulation of knowledge derived from various sources, especially from experts.

knowledge audit The process of identifying the knowledge an organization has, who has it, and how it flows (or does not) through the enterprise.

knowledge base A collection of facts, rules, and procedures organized into schemas. A knowledge base is the assembly of all the information and knowledge about a specific field of interest.

knowledge discovery in databases (KDD) A machine-learning process that performs rule induction or a related procedure to establish knowledge from large databases.

knowledge engineer An artificial intelligence specialist responsible for the technical side of developing an expert system. The knowledge engineer works closely with the domain expert to capture the expert's knowledge in a knowledge base.

knowledge engineering The engineering discipline in which knowledge is integrated into computer systems to solve complex problems that normally require a high level of human expertise.

knowledge management The active management of the expertise in an organization. It involves collecting, categorizing, and disseminating knowledge.

knowledge management system (KMS) A system that facilitates knowledge management by ensuring knowledge flow from the person(s) who knows to the person(s) who needs to know throughout the organization; knowledge evolves and grows during the process.

knowledge repository The actual storage location of knowledge in a knowledge management system. A knowledge repository is similar in nature to a database but is generally text oriented.

knowledge rules A collection of if-then rules that represents the deep knowledge about a specific problem.

knowledge-based economy The modern, global economy, which is driven by what people and organizations know rather than only by capital and labor. An economy based on intellectual assets.

knowledge-based system (KBS) Typically, a rule-based system for providing expertise. A KBS is identical to an expert system, except that the source of expertise may include documented knowledge.

knowledge-refining system A system that is capable of analyzing its own performance, learning, and improving itself for future consultations.

knowware Technology tools that support knowledge management.

Kohonen self-organizing feature map A type of neural network model for machine learning.

leaky knowledge *See* explicit knowledge.

lean manufacturing Production methodology focused on the elimination of waste or non-value-added features in a process.

learning A process of self-improvement where the new knowledge is obtained through a process by using what is already known.

learning algorithm The training procedure used by an artificial neural network.

learning organization An organization that is capable of learning from its past experience, implying the existence of an organizational memory and a means to save, represent, and share it through its personnel.

learning rate A parameter for learning in neural networks. It determines the portion of the existing discrepancy that must be offset.

linear programming (LP) A mathematical model for the optimal solution of resource allocation problems. All the relationships among the variables in this type of model are linear.

linguistic cues A collection of numerical measures extracted from the textual content using linguistic rules and theories.

link analysis The linkage among many objects of interest is discovered automatically, such as the link between Web pages and referential relationships among groups of academic publication authors.

literature mining A popular application area for text mining where a large collection of literature (articles, abstracts, book excerpts, and commentaries) in a specific area is processed using semi-automated methods in order to discover novel patterns.

machine learning The process by which a computer learns from experience (e.g., using programs that can learn from historical cases).

management science (MS) The application of a scientific approach and mathematical models to the analysis and solution of managerial decision situations (e.g., problems, opportunities). Also known as *operations research* (OR).

management support system (MSS) A system that applies any type of decision support tool or technique to managerial decision making.

mathematical (quantitative) model A system of symbols and expressions that represent a real situation.

mathematical programming An optimization technique for the allocation of resources, subject to constraints.

mental model The mechanisms or images through which a human mind performs sense-making in decision making.

metadata Data about data. In a data warehouse, metadata describe the contents of a data warehouse and the manner of its use.

metasearch engine A search engine that combines results from several different search engines.

middleware Software that links application modules from different computer languages and platforms.

mobile agent An intelligent software agent that moves across different system architectures and platforms or from one Internet site to another, retrieving and sending information.

mobile social networking Members converse and connect with one another using cell phones or other mobile devices.

mobility The degree to which agents travel through a computer network.

model base A collection of preprogrammed quantitative models (e.g., statistical, financial, optimization) organized as a single unit.

model base management system (MBMS) Software for establishing, updating, combining, and so on (e.g., managing) a DSS model base.

model building blocks Preprogrammed software elements that can be used to build computerized models. For example, a random-number generator can be employed in the construction of a simulation model.

model mart A small, generally departmental repository of knowledge created by using knowledge-discovery techniques on past decision instances. Model marts are similar to data marts. *See* model warehouse.

model warehouse A large, generally enterprise-wide repository of knowledge created by using knowledge-discovery techniques on past decision instances. Model warehouses are similar to data warehouses. *See* model mart.

momentum A learning parameter in backpropagation neural networks.

MSS architecture A plan for organizing the underlying infrastructure and applications of an MSS project.

MSS suite An integrated collection of a large number of MSS tools that work together for applications development.

MSS tool A software element (e.g., a language) that facilitates the development of an MSS or an MSS generator.

multiagent system A system with multiple cooperating software agents.

multidimensional analysis (modeling) A modeling method that involves data analysis in several dimensions.

multidimensional database A database in which the data are organized specifically to support easy and quick multidimensional analysis.

multidimensional OLAP (MOLAP) OLAP implemented via a specialized multidimensional database (or data store) that summarizes transactions into multidimensional views ahead of time.

multidimensionality The ability to organize, present, and analyze data by several dimensions, such as sales by region, by product, by salesperson, and by time (four dimensions).

multiple goals Refers to a decision situation in which alternatives are evaluated with several, sometimes conflicting, goals.

mutation A genetic operator that causes a random change in a potential solution.

natural language processing (NLP) Using a natural language processor to interface with a computer-based system.

neural computing An experimental computer design aimed at building intelligent computers that operate in a manner modeled on the functioning of the human brain. *See* artificial neural network (ANN).

neural (computing) networks A computer design aimed at building intelligent computers that operate in a manner modeled on the functioning of the human brain.

neural network *See* artificial neural network (ANN).

neuron A cell (i.e., processing element) of a biological or artificial neural network.

nominal data A type of data that contains measurements of simple codes assigned to objects as labels, which are not measurements. For example, the variable *marital status* can be generally categorized as (1) single, (2) married, and (3) divorced.

nominal group technique (NGT) A simple brainstorming process for nonelectronic meetings.

normative model A model that prescribes how a system should operate.

nucleus The central processing portion of a neuron.

numeric data A type of data that represent the numeric values of specific variables. Examples of numerically valued variables include age, number of children, total household income (in U.S. dollars), travel distance (in miles), and temperature (in Fahrenheit degrees).

object A person, place, or thing about which information is collected, processed, or stored.

object-oriented model base management system (OOMBMS) An MBMS constructed in an object-oriented environment.

online analytical processing (OLAP) An information system that enables the user, while at a PC, to query the system, conduct an analysis, and so on. The result is generated in seconds.

online (electronic) workspace Online screens that allow people to share documents, files, project plans, calendars, and so on in the same online place, though not necessarily at the same time.

oper mart An operational data mart. An oper mart is a small-scale data mart typically used by a single department or functional area in an organization.

operational data store (ODS) A type of database often used as an interim area for a data warehouse, especially for customer information files.

operational models Models that represent problems for the operational level of management.

operational plan A plan that translates an organization's strategic objectives and goals into a set of well-defined tactics and initiatives, resource requirements, and expected results.

optimal solution A best possible solution to a modeled problem.

optimization The process of identifying the best possible solution to a problem.

ordinal data Data that contains codes assigned to objects or events as labels that also represent the rank order among them. For example, the variable *credit score* can be generally categorized as (1) low, (2) medium, and (3) high.

organizational agent An agent that executes tasks on behalf of a business process or computer application.

organizational culture The aggregate attitudes in an organization concerning a certain issue (e.g., technology, computers, DSS).

organizational knowledge base An organization's knowledge repository.

organizational learning The process of capturing knowledge and making it available enterprise-wide.

organizational memory That which an organization knows.

ossified case A case that has been analyzed and has no further value.

paradigmatic case A case that is unique that can be maintained to derive new knowledge for the future.

parallel processing An advanced computer processing technique that allows a computer to perform multiple processes at once, in parallel.

parallelism In a group support system, a process gain in which everyone in a group can work simultaneously (e.g., in brainstorming, voting, ranking).

parameter *See* uncontrollable variable (parameter).

part-of-speech tagging The process of marking up the words in a text as corresponding to a particular part of speech (such as nouns, verbs, adjectives, adverbs, etc.) based on a word's definition and context of its use.

pattern recognition A technique of matching an external pattern to a pattern stored in a computer's memory (i.e., the process of classifying data into predetermined categories). Pattern recognition is used in inference engines, image processing, neural computing, and speech recognition.

perceptron An early neural network structure that uses no hidden layer.

performance measurement system A system that assists managers in tracking the implementations of business strategy by comparing actual results against strategic goals and objectives.

personal agent An agent that performs tasks on behalf of individual users.

physical integration The seamless integration of several systems into one functioning system.

polysemes Words also called *homonyms*, they are syntactically identical words (i.e., spelled exactly the same) with different meanings (e.g., *bow* can mean "to bend forward," "the front of the ship," "the weapon that shoots arrows," or "a kind of tied ribbon").

portal A gateway to Web sites. Portals can be public (e.g., Yahoo!) or private (e.g., corporate portals).

practice approach An approach toward knowledge management that focuses on building the social environments or communities of practice necessary to facilitate the sharing of tacit understanding.

prediction The act of telling about the future.

predictive analysis Use of tools that help determine the probable future outcome for an event or the likelihood of a situation occurring. These tools also identify relationships and patterns.

predictive analytics A business analytical approach toward forecasting (e.g., demand, problems, opportunities) that is used instead of simply reporting data as they occur.

principle of choice The criterion for making a choice among alternatives.

privacy In general, the right to be left alone and the right to be free of unreasonable personal intrusions. Information privacy is the right to determine when, and to what extent, information about oneself can be communicated to others.

private agent An agent that works for only one person.

problem ownership The jurisdiction (authority) to solve a problem.

problem solving A process in which one starts from an initial state and proceeds to search through a problem space to identify a desired goal.

process approach An approach to knowledge management that attempts to codify organizational knowledge through formalized controls, processes, and technologies.

process gain In a group support system, improvements in the effectiveness of the activities of a meeting.

process loss In a group support system, degradation in the effectiveness of the activities of a meeting.

processing element (PE) A neuron in a neural network.

production rules The most popular form of knowledge representation for expert systems where atomic pieces of knowledge are represented using simple if-then structures.

prototyping In system development, a strategy in which a scaled-down system or portion of a system is constructed in a short time, tested, and improved in several iterations.

public agent An agent that serves any user.

quantitative software package A preprogrammed (sometimes called *ready-made*) model or optimization system. These packages sometimes serve as building blocks for other quantitative models.

query facility The (database) mechanism that accepts requests for data, accesses them, manipulates them, and queries them.

rapid application development (RAD) A development methodology that adjusts a system development lifecycle so that parts of the system can be developed quickly, thereby enabling users to obtain some functionality as soon as possible. RAD includes methods of phased development, prototyping, and throwaway prototyping.

RapidMiner A popular, open-source, free-of-charge data mining software suite that employs a graphically enhanced user interface, a rather large number of algorithms, and a variety of data visualization features.

ratio data Continuous data where both differences and ratios are interpretable. The distinguishing feature of a ratio scale is the possession of a nonarbitrary zero value.

real-time data warehousing The process of loading and providing data via a data warehouse as they become available.

real-time expert system An expert system designed for online dynamic decision support. It has a strict limit on response time; in other words, the system always produces a response by the time it is needed.

reality mining Data mining of location-based data.

recommendation system (agent) A computer system that can suggest new items to a user based on his or her revealed preference. It may be content based or use collaborative filtering to suggest items that match the preference of the user. An example is Amazon.com's "Customers who bought this item also bought . . ." feature.

regression A data mining method for real-world prediction problems where the predicted values (i.e., the output variable or dependent variable) are numeric (e.g., predicting the temperature for tomorrow as 68°F).

reinforcement learning A sub-area of machine learning that is concerned with learning-by-doing-and-measuring to maximize some notion of long-term reward. Reinforcement learning differs from supervised learning in that correct input/output pairs are never presented to the algorithm.

relational database A database whose records are organized into tables that can be processed by either relational algebra or relational calculus.

relational model base management system (RMBMS) A relational approach (as in relational databases) to the design and development of a model base management system.

relational OLAP (ROLAP) The implementation of an OLAP database on top of an existing relational database.

reproduction The creation of new generations of improved solutions with the use of a genetic algorithm.

result (outcome) variable A variable that expresses the result of a decision (e.g., one concerning profit), usually one of the goals of a decision-making problem.

RFID A generic technology that refers to the use of radio frequency waves to identify objects.

risk A probabilistic or stochastic decision situation.

risk analysis A decision-making method that analyzes the risk (based on assumed known probabilities) associated with different alternatives.

robot A machine that has the capability of performing manual functions without human intervention.

rule-based system A system in which knowledge is represented completely in terms of rules (e.g., a system based on production rules).

SAS Enterprise Miner A comprehensive, and commercial data mining software tool developed by SAS Institute.

satisficing A process by which one seeks a solution that will satisfy a set of constraints. In contrast to optimization, which seeks the best possible solution, satisficing simply seeks a solution that will work well enough.

scenario A statement of assumptions and configurations concerning the operating environment of a particular system at a particular time.

scorecard A visual display that is used to chart progress against strategic and tactical goals and targets.

screen sharing Software that enables group members, even in different locations, to work on the same document, which is shown on the PC screen of each participant.

search engine A program that finds and lists Web sites or pages (designated by URLs) that match some user-selected criteria.

self-organizing A neural network architecture that uses unsupervised learning.

semantic Web An extension of the current Web, in which information is given well-defined meanings, better enabling computers and people to work in cooperation.

semantic Web services An XML-based technology that allows semantic information to be represented in Web services.

SEMMA An alternative process for data mining projects proposed by the SAS Institute. The acronym "SEMMA" stands for "sample, explore, modify, model, and assess."

sensitivity analysis A study of the effect of a change in one or more input variables on a proposed solution.

sentiment analysis The technique used to detect favorable and unfavorable opinions toward specific products and services using a large numbers of textual data sources (customer feedback in the form of Web postings).

sequence discovery The identification of associations over time.

sequence mining A pattern discovery method where relationships among the things are examined in terms of their order of occurrence to identify associations over time.

sigmoid (logical activation) function An S-shaped transfer function in the range of 0 to 1.

simple split Data is partitioned into two mutually exclusive subsets called a *training set* and a *test set* (or *holdout set*). It is common to designate two-thirds of the data as the training set and the remaining one-third as the test set.

simulation An imitation of reality in computers.

singular value decomposition (SVD) Closely related to principal components analysis, reduces the overall dimensionality of the input matrix (number of input documents by number of extracted terms) to a lower dimensional space, where each consecutive dimension represents the largest degree of variability (between words and documents).

Six Sigma A performance management methodology aimed at reducing the number of defects in a business process to as close to zero defects per million opportunities (DPMO) as possible.

social media The online platforms and tools that people use to share opinions, experiences, insights, perceptions, and various media, including photos, videos, music, with each other.

social network analysis (SNA) The mapping and measuring of relationships and information flows among people, groups, organizations, computers, and other information- or knowledge-processing entities. The nodes in the network are the people and groups, whereas the links show relationships or flows between the nodes. SNAs provide both visual and a mathematical analyses of relationships.

software agent A piece of autonomous software that persists to accomplish the task it is designed for (by its owner).

software-as-a-service (SaaS) Software that is rented instead of sold.

speech (voice) understanding An area of artificial intelligence research that attempts to allow computers to recognize words or phrases of human speech.

SPSS PASW Modeler A very popular, commercially available, comprehensive data, text, and Web mining software suite developed by SPSS (formerly Clementine).

staff assistant An individual who acts as an assistant to a manager.

static models Models that describe a single interval of a situation.

status report A report that provides the most current information on the status of an item (e.g., orders, expenses, production quantity).

stemming A process of reducing words to their respective root forms in order to better represent them in a text mining project.

stop words Words that are filtered out prior to or after processing of natural language data (i.e., text).

story A case with rich information and episodes. Lessons may be derived from this kind of case in a case base.

strategic goal A quantified objective that has a designated time period.

strategic models Models that represent problems for the strategic level (i.e., executive level) of management.

strategic objective A broad statement or general course of action that prescribes targeted directions for an organization.

strategic theme A collection of related strategic objectives, used to simplify the construction of a strategic map.

strategic vision A picture or mental image of what the organization should look like in the future.

strategy map A visual display that delineates the relationships among the key organizational objectives for all four balanced scorecard perspectives.

Structured Query Language (SQL) A data definition and management language for relational databases. SQL front ends most relational DBMS.

suboptimization An optimization-based procedure that does not consider all the alternatives for or impacts on an organization.

summation function A mechanism to add all the inputs coming into a particular neuron.

supervised learning A method of training artificial neural networks in which sample cases are shown to the network as input, and the weights are adjusted to minimize the error in the outputs.

support The measure of how often products and/or services appear together in the same transaction; that is, the proportion of transactions in the dataset that contain all of the products and/or services mentioned in a specific rule.

support vector machines (SVM) A family of generalized linear models, which achieve a classification or regression decision based on the value of the linear combination of input features.

synapse The connection (where the weights are) between processing elements in a neural network.

synchronous (real time) Occurring at the same time.

system architecture The logical and physical design of a system.

system development lifecycle (SDLC) A systematic process for the effective construction of large information systems.

tacit knowledge Knowledge that is usually in the domain of subjective, cognitive, and experiential learning. It is highly personal and difficult to formalize.

tactical models Models that represent problems for the tactical level (i.e., midlevel) of management.

teleconferencing The use of electronic communication that allows two or more people at different locations to have a simultaneous conference.

term–document matrix (TDM) A frequency matrix created from digitized and organized documents (the corpus) where the columns represent the terms while rows represent the individual documents.

text mining The application of data mining to nonstructured or less structured text files. It entails the generation of meaningful numeric indices from the unstructured text and then processing those indices using various data-mining algorithms.

theory of certainty factors A theory designed to help incorporate uncertainty into the representation of knowledge (in terms of production rules) for expert systems.

threshold value A hurdle value for the output of a neuron to trigger the next level of neurons. If an output value is smaller than the threshold value, it will not be passed to the next level of neurons.

tokenizing Categorizing a block of text (token) according to the function it performs.

topology The way in which neurons are organized in a neural network.

transformation (transfer) function In a neural network, the function that sums and transforms inputs before a neuron fires. It shows the relationship between the internal activation level and the output of a neuron.

trend analysis The collecting of information and attempting to spot a pattern, or *trend*, in the information.

Turing test A test designed to measure the "intelligence" of a computer.

uncertainty In expert systems, a value that cannot be determined during a consultation. Many expert systems can accommodate uncertainty; that is, they allow the user to indicate whether he or she does not know the answer.

uncontrollable variable (parameter) A factor that affects the result of a decision but is not under the control of the decision maker. These variables can be internal (e.g., related to technology or to policies) or external (e.g., related to legal issues or to climate).

unstructured data Data that does not have a predetermined format and is stored in the form of textual documents.

unsupervised learning A method of training artificial neural networks in which only input stimuli are shown to the network, which is self-organizing.

user interface The component of a computer system that allows bidirectional communication between the system and its user.

user interface management system (UIMS) The DSS component that handles all interaction between users and the system.

user-developed MSS An MSS developed by one user or by a few users in one department, including decision makers and professionals (i.e., knowledge workers, e.g., financial analysts, tax analysts, engineers) who build or use computers to solve problems or enhance their productivity.

utility (on-demand) computing Unlimited computing power and storage capacity that, like electricity, water, and telephone services, can be obtained on demand, used, and reallocated for any application and that are billed on a pay-per-use basis.

vendor-managed inventory (VMI) The practice of retailers making suppliers responsible for determining when to order and how much to order.

video teleconferencing (videoconferencing) Virtual meeting in which participants in one location can see participants at other locations on a large screen or a desktop computer.

virtual (Internet) community A group of people with similar interests who interact with one another using the Internet.

virtual meeting An online meeting whose members are in different locations, possibly even in different countries.

virtual team A team whose members are in different places while in a meeting together.

virtual worlds Artificial worlds created by computer systems in which the user has the impression of being immersed.

visual interactive modeling (VIM) *See* visual interactive simulation (VIS).

visual interactive simulation (VIS) A simulation approach used in the decision-making process that shows graphical animation in which systems and processes are presented dynamically to the decision maker. It enables visualization of the results of different potential actions.

visual recognition The addition of some form of computer intelligence and decision making to digitized visual information, received from a machine sensor such as a camera.

voice of customer (VOC) Applications that focus on "who and how" questions by gathering and reporting direct feedback from site visitors, by benchmarking against other sites and offline channels, and by supporting predictive modeling of future visitor behavior.

voice (speech) recognition Translation of human voice into individual words and sentences that are understandable by a computer.

Voice over IP (VoIP) Communication systems that transmit voice calls over Internet Protocol (IP)–based networks. Also known as *Internet telephony*.

voice portal A Web site, usually a portal, that has an audio interface.

voice synthesis The technology by which computers convert text to voice (i.e., speak).

Web 2.0 The popular term for advanced Internet technology and applications, including blogs, wikis, RSS, and social bookmarking. One of the most significant differences between Web 2.0 and the traditional World Wide Web is greater collaboration among Internet users and other users, content providers, and enterprises.

Web analytics The application of business analytics activities to Web-based processes, including e-commerce.

Web content mining The extraction of useful information from Web pages.

Web crawlers An application used to read through the content of a Web site automatically.

Web mining The discovery and analysis of interesting and useful information from the Web, about the Web, and usually through Web-based tools.

Web services An architecture that enables assembly of distributed applications from software services and ties them together.

Web structure mining The development of useful information from the links included in Web documents.

Web usage mining The extraction of useful information from the data being generated through Web page visits, transactions, and so on.

WEKA A popular, free-of-charge, open-source suite of machine-learning software written in Java, developed at the University of Waikato.

what-if analysis A process that involves asking a computer what the effect of changing some of the input data or parameters would be.

wiki A piece of server software available in a Web site that allows users to freely create and edit Web page content, using any Web browser.

wikilog A Web log (blog) that allows people to participate as peers; anyone can add, delete, or change content.

work system A system in which humans and/or machines perform a business process, using resources to produce products or services for internal or external customers.

INDEX

Page numbers followed by an f, t, or W represent figures, tables, and Web pages respectively.

AARON, 464
Academic text mining applications, 300–302
Accenture, 487, 498, 502, 504, 511, 517
Accuracy metrics for classification models, 218t
Ace Hardware Corp., 458, 461, 467
Acting globally in collective intelligence (CI), 460
Action planner as session activity, 449
Active (real time) data warehousing, 330, 359–364
Active DSS, 105
Active tags in RFID, 636
Acxiom's PersonicX, 21, 23
Adaptive resonance theory (ART), 255
Adaptive Resonance Theory (ART) networks, 274
Ad hoc DSS, 82, 84
Ad-hoc queries, 17–18, 22
Agency, 620
Agility support, 10
AI. See Artificial intelligence (AI)
AIS SIGDS classification, 79–81, 82
AJAX, 431
Algorithms, 58, 168–169, 169f
    decision tree, 220–221
    evolutionary, 626
    genetic, 541, 593–601
    ID3, 199, 221
    learning, 252, 253f
    in reality mining, 643
    well-known, 221
Alicebot.org, 103
Alternate analysis as session activity, 449
Alter's output classification, 82
Altshuller Institute for TRIZ Studies, 465
Amazon.com, 102, 194, 317, 658, 659
American Airlines, 91, 140, 515, 674
Ammunition Requirements Calculator (ARC), 76
Analogical reasoning, 585
Analog model, 44
Analytical models, 44n, 97
Analytical search techniques, 168
Analytical techniques, 58
Analytic hierarchy process (AHP), 165–166, 443
ANN. See Artificial neural network (ANN)
Apple, 102, 315, 510, 613
Application service providers (ASPs), 108
Apriori, 203, 227–228, 227f
Area under the ROC curve, 219f
Artificial intelligence (AI)
    beats chess grand master, 533
    capabilities, 19
    characteristics of, 534–535
    definitions of, 532–533
    field applications, 535–542
    integrating with KMS, 502–503
    vs. natural, 537
    signs of intelligence and, 533–534
Artificial intelligence (AI) field, evolution of, 535–536, 536f
Artificial neural network (ANN), 80, 97, 106, 241–283
    applications of, 273–276

architectures, 251–253
black box testing by using sensitivity analysis, 264–267
biological and artificial, 246–248, 246f, 247f
concepts of, basic, 245
data mining classification, 220
data mining methods, 192
elements of, 248–249
gambling referenda predicted by using, 242–244
Hopfield networks, 272–273, 273f
information processing (See Network information processing)
knowledge-based artificial neural networks (KBANN), 276
Kohonen's self-organizing feature maps (SOM), 270–272
vs. logistic regression, 269t
Microsoft's mail delivery helped by, 254
network-based systems, developing (See Neural network-based systems, developing)
neural network-based systems, developing, 259–264
sample project, 267–270, 268f
telecommunications fraud reduced by using, 248
Artificial neurons, 245
Association rule mining, 225–228
Associations
    in artificial neural networks (ANN), 274
    defined, 200, 203
    in text mining, 308
    See also Association rule mining
Asynchronous communication, 429, 436
Asynchronous products, 431, 432t
Attributes, 220
Auctions, model-based, 136–138
Audio data, 198
Authoritative pages, 314
Autodesk's Architectural Studio, 427
Automated decision-making (ADM), technology, 47
Automated decision support (ADS), 661, 662, 665–667
Automated decision system (ADS), 13–15, 15f
Automated help desks, 548
Automatic programming in AI field, 540
Automatic sensitivity analysis, 159
Automatic summarization, 295
Autonomy, 616
Axons, 245

Babel Fish Translation, 541
Back-error propagation, 258–259, 258f
Backpropagation, 258–259, 258f
Backtracking, 559
Backward chaining, 558–559, 560f
Bag-of-words used in text mining, 292
Black box testing by using sensitivity analysis, 264–267
Banking, 204
Banner with Brains, 572, 573
Bayesian classifiers, 220

Best Buy, 103, 482, 636
Best Matching Unit (BMU), 271–272
BI. See Business intelligence (BI)
Binary digits in RFID, 637
Bing, 102
Biomedical text mining applications, 299–300
Blackboard (workplace), 551–552
Black-box syndrome, 265
Blending problem, 157
Bliki, 455
Blind searching, 170
Blogs, 436, 454, 657
Bots, W3.1.22
Bounded rationality, 55
Brainstorming, electronic, 436, 463–464
Branch, 220
Break as session activity, 449
Break-even point, goal seeking analysis used to compute, 160
Budgeting, 22
Building, process of, 610
Business activity monitoring (BAM), 60, 62, 63, 330–331
Business analytics (BA), 20, 21, 78, 97
Business intelligence (BI), 19
    advanced models used in, 78
    analytic applications, business value of, 24t
    application areas of, common, 22
    architecture of, 20, 20f
    benefits of, 22
    business analytics, 20–21
    business performance management, 22
    data mining for, 190–239
    data warehousing, 20
    definitions of, 19, 75
    DSS-BI connection, 23–24
        (See also DSS/BI)
    DSS evolving into, 18
    history and evolution of, 19–20, 19f
    management support system, 24–25
    origins and drivers of, 23
    styles of, 22
    tool vendors, 228
    user interface, 22
Business intelligence service provider (BISP), 352
Business Objects, 348t
Business Performance Improvement Resource, 180, 365
Business performance management (BPM), 20, 22, 330
Business Pressures–Responses–Support model, 5–7, 6t
Business process management (BPM), 60, 62, 63, 103
Business process reengineering (BPR), 662

California Scientific Software, 254, 263, 281
Camp Fire USA, 109, 128
Candidate generation, 227
Capacities, 154
Cap Gemini Ernst & Young, 480, 487, 502, 508–509
Capital One, 194
Carnegie Mellon University, 102, 539, 581, 621

CART, 192, 221, 228, 229t
Case-based reasoning (CBR), 220, 585–593
Case library, 586
Catalog design, 226
Catalyst Software Solutions, 433–434
Categorical data, 198, 208–209
Categorization in text mining applications, 289
Categorizer as session activity, 449
Caterpillar, Inc., 456–457
Cell phones
    call-by-call services, 238
    mobile enterprise networks and, 654
    mobile social networking and, 653–654
    mobile user privacy and, 669
Centroid, 225
Certainty, decision making under, 147, 148
Certainty factors (CF), 561–562
Channel optimization, 22
Chief executive officer (CEO), 505
Chief financial officer (CFO), 505
Chief information officer (CIO), 505
Chief knowledge officer (CKO), 504–505
Chief operating officer (COO), 505
Chi-squared automatic interaction detector (CHAID), 221
ChoiceAnalyst application, 167, 168f
Choice phase of decision-making process, 46, 47t, 58, 62
Chromosome, 595
Cingular Wireless, 480–481
Cisco, 453, 657
Classification, 201–202
    in artificial neural networks (ANN), 274
    assessment methodologies, 216–217, 216–223
    matrix, 217, 217f
    techniques, 220
    in text mining, 307
Class label, 220
Clementine, 199, 228, 229t, 230, 312, 318
Clickstream analysis, 316
Client/server data warehousing, 330
Cloud computing, 658–659
Cluster analysis for data mining, 223–225
Clustering
    in artificial neural networks (ANN), 274
    defined, 202
    function of, 200
    goal of, 202
    in text mining, 289, 307–308
    See also Cluster analysis for data mining
Clusters, 223
Coca-Cola, 106, 238, 347, 367, 635, 654
Cognitive limits, 10
Cognos, 84, 125, 365, 406, 412
Collaboration hubs, 455
Collaborative computing tools, 498–502
Collaborative design and product development, 456–457
Collaborative networks, 455–456

Collaborative planning, forecasting, and replenishment (CPFR). *See* CPFR.
Collaborative planning along supply chain, 457–459
Collaborative workflow, 454
Collective intelligence (CI), 459–461
Community of practice (COP), 505–507, 507t, 508, 509t
Complete enumeration, 170
Complexity in simulation, 172
Compound DSS, 79
Comprehensive database in data warehousing process, 334
Computer-based information system (CBIS), 75, 96
Computer hardware and software. *See* Hardware; Software
Computerized decision support system
  direct, 441–448
  Gorry and Scott-Morton classical framework, 11–13
  indirect, 431–436
  reasons for using, 9–11
  for semistructured problems, 15
  for structured decisions, 13–15 (*See also* Automated decision system (ADS))
  for unstructured decisions, 15
Computer-supported collaboration tools
  benefits of using, 422
  collaboration hubs, 455
  collaborative networks, 455–456
  collaborative workflow, 454
  corporate (enterprise) portals, 456
  for decision making (*See* Computerized decision support system)
  groupware suites (*See* Groupware suites, integrated)
  Voice over IP (VoIP), 453–454
  Web 2.0, 454
  wikis, 455
Computer-supported collaborative work (CSCW), 441
Computer vision, 540
Concepts, defined, 290
Conceptual methodology, 16
Condition-based maintenance, 205
Confidence gap, 177
Confidence metric, 226–227
Confusion matrix, 217, 217f
Connection weights, 250
Constraints, 146, 154, 302
Consultation environment used in ES, 550
Continental Airlines, 369–370, 674–675
Contingency table, 217, 217f
Continuous probability distributions, 174, 175t
Control system, 565
Corporate intranets and extranets, 503
Corporate performance management (CPM), 22
Corporate portals, 22
Corporate (enterprise) portals, 456
Corpus, 290, 303
CPFR, 457–458, 458f, 461
Creativity, 462–464
Creativity enhancing software, 464–465
Credibility assessment (deception detection), 297–299, 298f, 299t
Credit analysis system, 548
CRISP-DM, 207–213, 207f
Cross-Industry Standard Process for Data Mining. *See* CRISP-DM

Cross-marketing, 226
Cross-selling, 226
Cross-validation accuracy (CVA), 219
Cube analysis, 22
Customer attrition, 24t
Customer experience management (CEM), 320–321
Customer profitability, 24t
Customer relationship management (CRM), 43, 60, 62, 63, 142, 204, 503
Customer segmentation, 24t
Customer service success in KMS, 513–514
Custom-made DSS system, 84–85
CUworld, 435–436

DARPA, 287–288, W3.1.12–11
Dashboard, 22, W9.3.1–2
Data
  access and integration, W3.1.9, W3.1.11
  best practices for, W3.1.9
  defined, 197
  Extraction, transformation, and load (ETL), W3.1.11
  integrity, W3.1.9
  problems, W3.1.6–7
  quality, W3.1.6–8
  quality action plan, W3.1.8
  raw, methods for collecting, W3.1.5
Data archeology, 196
Data as a service (DaaS), 659
Database
  commercial services, W3.1.14
  defined, 90–91
  document-based, W3.1.21
  external data, W3.1.2–4
  integrating with KMS, 503, W3.1.9
  intelligent, W3.1.21
  internal data, W3.1.2–3
  multimedia-based, W3.1.19–20
  nature and sources of data, W3.1.2–3
  organization and structures, W3.1.17–18
  personal data and knowledge, W3.1.4
Database management system (DBMS), 86, 88t, 92, 337, W3.1.16
Data cleanup tools, 94
Data collection and preparation in ANN, 261
Data conferencing, 434
Data directory, 93
Data dredging, 196
Data extraction, 92, 334
Data in RFID, 638–640, 639t
Data integration, 94–95
  in data warehousing, 342–344
  software, W3.1.13
  via XML, W3.1.12
Data loading in data warehousing process, 334
Data management, improved, 10
Data management subsystem, 89–95, 90f
Data marts, 330
Data migration tools, 337
Data mining, 190–239
  applications, 204–207
  artificial neural network (ANN) for (*See* Artificial neural network (ANN))
  associations used in, 203
  as blend of multiple disciplines, 197f
  in cancer research, 213–214
  characteristics of, 196–197, 197f

classification of tasks used in, 200, 201–202, 201f
  clustering used in, 202–203
  commercial uses of, 194–195
  data extraction capabilities of, 92
  data in, 197–199, 197f
  definitions of, 21, 196
  DSS templates provided by, 85
  hypothesis- or discovery-driven, 204
  intelligent system in, 106
  law enforcement's use of, 199–200
  methods, 216–228
  myths and blunders, 233–234
  names associated with, 196
  patterns identified by, 200
  prediction used in, 191–193, 201
  process, 207–215
  recent popularity of, 194
  software tools, 228–233
  term origin, 194
  time-series forecasting used in, 203
  using predictive analytics tools, 23
  visualization used in, 203
Data modeling *vs.* analytical models, 44n
Data organization, 91–92
Data-oriented DSS, 17–18
Data preparation, 209–211, 209f, 211t
Data processing, 209–211, 209f, 211t
Data quality, 93–94
Data (information) quality management, 94
Data security, 95
Data sources in data warehousing process, 334
Data warehouse (DW), 10, 20, 86
  Continental's success using, 674–675
  defined, 329
  development, 346–359
  drill down in, 352
  grain of, 352
  hosted, 452
  See also Data warehousing
Data warehouse administrator (DWA), 364–365
Data Warehouse Institute, 365
Data warehouse vendors, 348–349, 348t
Data warehousing, 20, 23, 326–371
  additional references, 366
  architectures, 335–342
  characteristics of, 329–330
  components of, major, 334
  cost savings and process efficiencies delivered by, 331–332
  data integration in, 342–346
  data marts in, 330
  DirectTV thrives by using, 327–328
  DWA and security issues in, 364–365
  enterprise data warehouse (EDW) in, 330–331
  extraction, transformation, and load (ETL) and, 332, 344–346, 345f
  First American Corporation supported by, 333
  implementation, 353–358
  metadata in, 330, 332–333
  operational data store (ODS) in, 330
  process, 333–334, 334f
  real-time, 330, 359–364
  vendors, products, and demos, 366
  See also Data warehouse (DW)
The Data Warehousing Institute (TDWI), 30, 64, 93, 125, 348t, 354, 365, 376, 414
Date/time data, 198

DB2 Information Integrator, 95
Debugging system, 565
Deception detection, 297–299, 298f, 299t
Decisional managerial roles, 7, 8t
Decision analysis, 161–165
Decision automation system (DAS), 13–14
Decision makers, 43
Decision making
  under certainty, 147, 148
  characteristics of, 41
  decision makers in, 43
  decision style in, 42–43
  definition of, working, 41–42
  disciplines, 42
  managerial, 7–9
  models (*See* Decision-making models)
  multicriteria, with pairwise comparisons, 165–167
  and problem solving, 42
  problem solving and, 42
  under risk, 147, 148–149
  and risk management, 67–68
  under uncertainty, 147, 148
  vendors, products, and demos, 64
  zones of, 148–149, 148f
Decision-making models
  analog, 44
  benefits of, 45
  classifying, 98
  components of, 98
  defined, 44
  design variables in, 50–51
  iconic (scale), 44
  Kepner-Tregoe method, 47
  mathematical (quantitative), 45
  mental, 44–45
  Simon's four-phase model, 45–47, 47t
Decision-making process, phases of, 45–48, 46f
Decision modeling, using spreadsheets, 39–40
Decision rooms, 445
Decision style, 42–43
Decision support in decision making, 59–63, 59f
Decision support matrix, 12f, 13
Decision support system (DSS)
  applications, 75–76
  architecture of, 17, 18f
  in business intelligence, 18
  capabilities of, overall, 87t
  characteristics and capabilities of, 77–79, 77f
  classifications of, 79–85
  components of, 85–87, 88t
  configurations of, 74
  definition and concept of, 16
  description of, 75–76
  DSS-BI connection, 23–24 (*See also* DSS/BI)
  hardware for, 107–108
  for health care, 71–74
  for managing inventory, example of, 16–17
  Miller's *MIS Cases,* 126
  modeling language: Planners Lab, 108–125
  references, additional, 31
  singular and plural of, 2n
  as specific application, 17
  spreadsheet-based (*See* Spreadsheets)
  types of, 17–18
  as umbrella term, 16–17

Decision support system (DSS)
  (*Continued*)
  users of, 89t, 106–107
  vendors, products, and demos, 31
  work system view of, 25
  See also Computerized decision
    support system
Decision tables, 162
Decision trees, 192, 220–222
Decision variables, 146, 154, 162
Deep Blue (chess program), 533, 541
Defuzzification, 626
Dell, 336, 348t, 480
Delphi method, 426
Delta error, 255
DeltaMaster, 229t
DENDRAL, 548
Dendrites, 245
Dependent data mart, 330
Dependent variables, 146
Descriptive models, 54–55
Design phase of decision-making
  process, 46, 47t, 50–58
  alternatives, developing
    (generating), 55–56
  decision support for, 60–62
  descriptive models used in, 54–55
  design variables used in, 50–51
  errors in decision making, 57
  normative models used in, 51–53
  outcomes, measuring, 56
  principle of choice, selecting, 51
  risk, 56–57
  satisficing, 55
  scenarios, 57
  suboptimization approach to, 53–54
Design system, 564
Development environment used
  in ES, 550
Diagnostic system, 564
Dialog generation and management
  system, 100–101
Dictionary, 305
Digital cockpits, 22
DIKAR (Data-Information-
  Knowledge-Action-Results)
  model, 490–491, 490f
Dimensional modeling, 351–352
Dimensional reduction, 210
Dimension tables, 351–352
Directory, data, 93
DirecTV, 327–328, 329
Discovery-driven data mining, 204
Discrete probability distributions,
  174, 175t
Discretization, 202
Disseminator, 8t
Disturbance handler, 8t
DNA microarray analysis, 299
Document management systems
  (DMS), W3.1.14
Drill down data warehouse, 352
DRILLING ADVISOR, 569
DSS. *See* Decision support
  system (DSS)
DSS/BI
  database management systems in,
    W3.1.16
  defined, 24
  emerging technologies and
    technology trends, 28
  hybrid support system, 27–28
  integrating with KMS, 502
  models in, 44–45
  tools and techniques used in, 26, 26t
  tools-Web connection, 27
DSS/ES, 105
DSS Resources, 64, 125, 365
Dynamic model, 143

ECHELON surveillance system, 297
Eclat algorithm, 203, 227
E-commerce site design, 226
Economic order quantity (EOQ), 53
E-learning simulation applications, 176
Electroencephalography, 104
Electronic brainstorming, 436, 463–464
Electronic document management
  (EDM), 499–500
Electronic idea generation for
  problem solving, 464–465
Electronic meeting system (EMS),
  441, 442
Electronic Product Code (EPC), 637
Electronic Submission Navigator
  (ESUB), 462
Electronic teleconferencing, 434
Elitism, 626
E-mail, 436, 658, 665
Embedded knowledge, 478–479
Emotiv, 104
End-user modeling tool, 149, 150f
Enterprise application integration
  (EAI), 343–344
Enterprise data house cleaning, W3.1.13
Enterprise data warehouse (EDW),
  330–331, 349, 349t, 350, 351t
Enterprise information integration
  (EII), 95, 332, 344
Enterprise information system (EIS),
  43, 62, 63, 76
  capabilities of, Web tools for, 102,
    108
  integration issues, 95
software development companies
  and, 498
Enterprise knowledge portals
  (EKP), 499
Enterprise Miner, 228, 229, 229t, 230
Enterprise reporting, 22
Enterprise resource management
  (ERM), 43
Enterprise resource planning (ERP),
  43, 62, 63
Enterprise 2.0, 657
Entertainment industry, 206
Entity extraction, 295
Entity identification, 295
Entity-relationship diagrams (ERD), 350
Entrepreneur, 8t
Entropy, 222
Environmental scanning and
  analysis, 141
ERoom server, 439, 452, 498
EService Suite, 480
Ethics in decision making and
  support, 669–670
Evolutionary algorithm, 626
Executive information system (EIS),
  18, 19
Experience-based training, 484
Expert, defined, 542–543
Expert Choice (EC11), 64, 66,
  165–166, 439, 443
Expertise, 543
Expertise Transfer System (ETS), 81
Expert location system, 512
Expert-support system, 105
  Expert system (ES), 28, 80, 81, 82,
    105–106, 108, 542–546
  in AI field, 537
  applications of, 546–549
  benefits of, 569–570
  vs. conventional system, 544t
  critical success factors for, 571–572
  development of, 566–568
  expertise and, 543
  experts in, 542–543
  features of, 543–544

generic categories of, 564t
vs. human experts, 545t
monitoring water quality with, 565
problem areas suitable for, 564–565
problems and limitations of, 571
rule-based, 545, 573
structure of, 550–553
used in identifying sport
  to talent, 546
on Web, 572–574, 574t
Expert system (ES) shell, 567, 568
Expert tool users, 107
Explanation and justification, 554
Explanation-based learning, 626
Explanation facility (or justifier), 563
Explanations, why and how, 563
Explanation subsystem in ES, 552
Explicit knowledge, 478
Exsys, 125, 365, 567, 572, 573, 577
Exsys Corvid, 106
EXtensible Markup Language (XML),
  91–92, 95, 339, 497
External data, 91
Extraction, transformation, and load
  (ETL), 92, 332, 344–346, 345f,
  W3.1.11
Extraction of data, 92
Extranets, 427, 433, 503

Facebook, 454, 651, 653, 654–655, 673
Facial cues, 452
Facilitate, 431, 451t
Facilitators (in GSS), 107
Fair Isaac Business Science, 64, 125,
  229t, 365
Feedforward-backpropagation
  paradigm, 248
  See also Backpropagation
Figurehead, 8t
Financial consolidation, 22
Financial market predictions, 274
Folksonomies, 454
FootPath, 644
Forecasting (predictive analytics),
  142–143
Foreign language reading/writing,
  295–296
Forest CoverType dataset, W6.1.1–6
Forward chaining, 558–559, 560f
Forward-thinking companies, 319
FP-Growth algorithm, 203, 227
Frame, 55
Fraud detection/prevention, 24t, 275
Frequent-terms report, 302
Fuzzy inference systems, 603–604
Fuzzy logic, 541, 601–603, 604–606
Fuzzy neural networks, 623
Fuzzy set, 626

G. Pierce Wood Memorial Hospital
  (GPW), W3.1.19
Gambling referenda predicted by
  using ANN, 242–244
Game playing in AI field, 540–541
Garbage in/garbage out (GIGO), 93
Gartner Group, 289, 455, 618, 659
GATE, 312
GDSS/GSS and successful
  implementation, products and
  tools for, 448–452
  collaborative culture in, crafting, 452
  GDSS tools, 451t
  GSS procedure, standard, 449
  GSS session agenda,
    448, 449–450, 450f
  GSS success factors, 450–452
  GSS Web impacts, 447t
  online collaboration, issues
    for, 452

using ThinkTank by GroupSystems,
  448–450, 451f
General methods stage, 536
General Motors, 130–131, 176, 177, 400
General-purpose development
  environment, 567
General reporting, 22
Genetic algorithms, 220, 541, 593–601
Genoa project, 287
Geographical information system
  (GIS), 22, 139, 143, 178
Gini index, 221
Global Information Systems (GIS), 331
Global MAKE study, 511
Goal seeking analysis, 159–161
Google Docs & Spreadsheets, 431, 658
Google Lively, 644
Gorry and Scott-Morton classical
  framework, 11–13
Government and defense, 205
GPS, 60, 641, 669
GPSS/PC (Minuteman Software), 178
Grain of data warehouse, 352
Graphical user interface (GUI), 86
Groove Networks, 431, 435,
  436–438, 451t
Group decision support system
  (GDSS), 419, 441–445
  benefits of, 441–442
  characteristics of, 441
  collaborative problem solving
    at KUKA, 444
  defined, 441
  facilities for, 445–447
  groupwork improved by, 443–444
  limitations of, 442
  support activities in, 443–444
  See also GDSS/GSS and successful
    implementation, products and
    tools for
Group support system (GSS), 28, 43,
  55, 56, 60, 62, 419, 442–445
  collaboration capabilities of,
    102, 105
  in crime prevention, 427–428
  defined, 80, 84, 442
  facilitators in, 107
  settings, 443
  See also GDSS/GSS and successful
    implementation, products and
    tools for
GroupSystems, 439, 451t
Groupware, 431
  defined, 429
  products and features, 432t
  tools, 431–432, 432t
Groupware suites, integrated, 436–441
  capabilities of, 436–437
  conclusions about, 440–441
  eRoom, 439
  Groove Networks, 437–438, 438f
  GroupSystems, 437, 439
  Lotus Notes (IBM collaboration
    software), 437
  Microsoft Windows Meeting Space
    and Live Meeting, 437
  PlaceWare Conference Center,
    439, 440
  Team Expert Choice (EC11), 439
  WebEx Meeting Center, 438–439, 440
  Wimba, 439–440
Groupwork
  benefits and limitations of, 424–425
  characteristics of, 423
  computerized system used
    to support, 426–431
  defined, 423
  difficulties associated with, 424t
  group decision-making process, 424

group support system at P&G, 421–423
meeting process, improving, 426

Hardware
data mining used in, 205
for DSS, 107–108
for DSS user interfaces, 103–104
Harrah's Entertainment, Inc., 64, 142–143, 368, 375–377, 388
Heuristic programming, 170
Heuristics, defined, 170
Heuristic searching, 170–171
Heuristics in AI, 535
Hewlett-Packard Company (HP), 39–40, 80, 178, 185–186, 323–324, 327, 348t, 350
Hidden layer, 249, 249f, 251
Holdout set, 218
Holsapple and Whinston's classification, 82
Homeland security, 206, 549, W3.1.12–11
Homonyms, 290
Hopfield networks, 272–273, 273f
Hosted data warehouse (DW), 452
How explanations, 563
HP. See Hewlett-Packard Company (HP)
Hub, 315
Hybrid approaches to KMS, 489–490
Hybrid (integrated) support system, 27–28
Hyperion Solutions, 125, 348t, 406, 661
Hyperlink-induced topic search (HITS), 315
Hyperplane, 606
Hypothesis-driven data mining, 204

IBM
Cognos, 228
DB2, 337
Deep Blue (chess program), 533, 541
Domino, 451t, 452
ILOG acquisition, 661
InfoSphere Warehouse, 312
Intelligent Decision Server (IDS), 496
Intelligent Miner, 229t
Intelligent Miner Data Mining Suite, 312
Lotus Development Corp., 498, 499
Lotus Domino Express, 437
Lotus Notes, 436–437, 451t, 452
Lotusphere, 437
sentiment analysis approach developed by, 295
Virtual Universe Community, 651
WebSphere portal, 102
Workplace Builder, 437
Iconic (scale) model, 44
IData Analyzer, 229t
Idea generation, 449, 464–465
Idea organization in GSS process, 449
ID3, 199, 221
Image data, 198
Implementation
defined, 59
phase of decision-making process, 46, 47t, 58–59, 62–63
Independent data mart, 330
Indices represented in TDM, 305–306
Individual DSS, 84
Inductive learning, 585
Inference, 592
Inference engine, 551, 558
Inferencing, 554, 558
in AI, 535
backward chaining, 558–559, 560f
combining two or more rules, 562

forward chaining, 558–559, 560f
with uncertainty, 560–561
Influence diagrams, 145, W4.1.1–3
Informational managerial roles, 7, 8t
Information Builders, 64, 125, 365
Information extraction in text mining applications, 289, 295
Information gain, 221–222
Information harvesting, 196
Information overload, 585, W3.1.2–4
Information retrieval, 295
Information system, integrating with KMS, 503
Information technology (IT) in knowledge management, 493–498
Information warfare, 206
Infrastructure as a service (IaaS), 658
Inmon, Bill, 340, 349, 350, 351
Inmon model (EDW approach), 330–331, 349, 349t, 350, 351t
Input/output (technology) coefficients, 154
Insightful Miner, 229t
Instant messaging (IM), 429, 431, 435–436, 437, 452
Instant video, 435–436
Institute Readiness Program (READY), 55
Institutional DSS, 82
Instruction system, 565
Insurance, 205
Integrated data warehousing, 329
Integrated intelligent system, 585
Intellectual capital, 476
Intelligence phase of decision-making process, 46, 47t, 48–50, W2.1–7
Intelligent agents (IA), 464, 496, 613–622
autonomy, 616
being proactive, 616
characteristics of, 615
classification by characteristics, 620–621
classification of, 619–620
communication and collaboration (interactivity), 616
components of an angel, 615
experienced learning, 617
having temporal continuity, 616–617
history and definitions, 613–615
operating in the background (mobility), 617
personality, developing, 617
reasons for using, 618
repetitive tasks, automating, 616
research programs, 621–622
Intelligent agents (IA) in AI field, 541
Intelligent computer-aided instruction (ICAI), 540
Intelligent decision support system (IDSS), 530
Intelligent DSS, 105
Intelligent Miner, 229t
Intelligent system, 105–106
Intelligent tutoring system (ITS), 540
Intellimedia system, 573
Interactive Financial Planning System (IFPS), 110
Interactive whiteboards, 435
Intermediary, 107
Intermediate result variables, 147
Internal data, 91
International Assignment Profile (IAP), 106
Internet
data provided over, 91
GDSS facilities, 446
non-work-related use of, 670

as real-time collaboration tool, 433
virtual communities, 650–652
Internet telephony, 435
Interpersonal managerial roles, 7, 8t
Interpretation system, 564
Interval data, 198
Intranets, 433, 446, 503
Inverse document frequency, 306
IT/software products for simulation, 176

Jackknifing, 219
Java, 97, 98, 100, 104, 106, 108

KDD (knowledge discovery in databases), 215
Kernel methods, 626
Key performance indicators, 22
K-fold cross-validation, 218–219
Kimball model (data mart approach), 349, 349t, 350, 351t
K-means clustering algorithm, 225
Knowledge
acquisition, 554–558
characteristics of, 476
creation, 485–486
data, information, and, 475, 475f
defined, 475
explicit, 478
leaky, 478
seeking, 486
sharing, 486
tacit, 478–479
taxonomy of, 479t
Knowledge acquisition in ES, 550–551
Knowledge and inference rules, 557–558
Knowledge-based artificial neural networks (KBANN), 276
Knowledge-based decision support system (KBDSS), 530
Knowledge-based DSS, 105
Knowledge-based economy, 476
Knowledge-based management system (KBMS), 86, 89t, 105–106
Knowledge-based modeling, 143
Knowledge-based risks (KBRs), 484
Knowledge-based system (KBS), 532
Knowledge base in ES, 551
Knowledge discovery in databases (KDD), 215, 496–497
Knowledge discovery in textual databases. See Text mining
Knowledge elicitation, 554
Knowledge engineer, 566
Knowledge engineering, 553–564, 566
Knowledge extraction, 196
See also Data mining
Knowledge extraction methods, 289, 307–308
Knowledge Garden, 489
Knowledge harvesting tools, 500
Knowledge Mail, 489
Knowledge management ASPS, 502
Knowledge management consulting firms, 502
Knowledge management suites, 500
Knowledge management system (KMS), 43, 60, 62, 86, 331, 471–524, 480
approaches to, 486–490
best practices in, 491
Cingular Wireless and, 480–481
concepts and definitions, 474–475
at consultancy firms, 477–478
DIKAR model used in, 490–491, 490f
drawbacks of, potential, 519–520
failures, 516–517
initiatives and activities, 485
knowledge management valuation, 514–516

knowledge repository in, 488, 491–493, 492f
learning organization in, 481–482
MITRE's MII project and, 472–474
myths, 516–517
NASA's ESMD and, 483–484
organizational culture in, 482–483
organizational learning in, 482
organizational memory in, 482
Rakid model used in, 490f, 491
roles of people in (See Knowledge management system (KMS), roles of people in)
successes, 511–524
at Texaco, 488–489
text-oriented DSS vs. KBMS, 105
traps, 518
See also Knowledge
Knowledge management system (KMS), implementation of, 498–504
integration, 502–503
products and vendors, 498–502
Knowledge management system (KMS), roles of people in, 504–509
Knowledge Miner, 229t
Knowledge nuggets (KN), 81
Knowledge-refining system in ES, 552
Knowledge repository, 488, 491–493, 492f
Knowledge representation, 554, 557–558
KnowledgeSeeker, 228
Knowledge servers, 499
Knowledge-sharing forums, 484
Knowledge validation, 554
Kohonen's self-organizing feature maps (SOM), 270–272
KXEN (Knowledge eXtraction ENgines), 229t

Language Technologies Institute, 102
Language translation, 103, 452
Language translation in AI field, 541
Laptop computers, 63
Latent semantic indexing, 291, 306–307
Law enforcement, 206
Leader, 8t
Leaf node, 220
Leaky knowledge, 478
Learner-generated context, 460–461
Learning algorithms, 252, 253f, 262, 271–272
Learning in artificial neural network (ANN), 253–259
algorithms, 252, 253f
backpropagation, 258–259, 258f
how a network learns, 256–258
learning rate, 257
momentum, 257
process of, 255, 256f
supervised and unsupervised, 254–255, 257t
taxonomy of, 253f
Learning organization, 481–482
Learning rate, 257
Leave-one-out, 219
Left-hand side (LHS) products and/or service, 226–227
Legal issues in MSS, 667
Liaison, 8t
Lindo Systems, Inc., 149, 156, 180, 184
Linear programming (LP)
allocation problems, 153, 154
assumptions of, 153
blending problem in, 157, W4.2.1–3
characteristics of, 153
formulation and terminology, 157, W4.2.5–6

Linear programming (LP)
(*Continued*)
mathematical programming and, 152–153, 157
modeling in, example of, 154–157, 156f
modeling system, 157
product-mix problem, 154
Linguistic cues, 299t
Link analysis, 203
LinkedIn, 454, 655, 656, 673
Linux, 437
Literature mining, 309
Loan application approvals, 274–275
Lockheed Martin Space Systems Company, 140–141, 426–427
Logistics, 204–205
Lotus Notes. *See* IBM
Lotus Software. *See* IBM

Machine-learning techniques, 582–585
Machine translation, 295
Macrosense, 641–643
Magnetic resonance spectroscopy (MRS), 276
Management control, 13
Management information system (MIS), 13, 16, 480
Management science (MS), 13
Management support system (MSS), 634–675
automatic decision making and the manager's job, 665–667
cloud computing and BI, 658–659
customer success stories and, 125–126
decision support system hardware and, 107
decision support system user and, 106–107
defined, 24
ethics in decision making and support, 669–670
impacts of, 659–660
legal issues, 667
modeling, 139–145
privacy, 643–644, 667–669
reality mining, 641–644
RFID and new BI application opportunities, 636–641
social networking, online, 653–658
user interface and, 100, 101
virtual communities, 650–652
virtual worlds, 644–649
Web 2.0 revolution, 649–650
Managerial performance, 7
Manual methods, 555
Manufacturing, 205
Market-basket analysis.
See Association rule mining
Marketing text mining applications, 296–297
Market surveillance system, 549
MARS, 228, 229t
Mashups, 454
Massively parallel processing (MPP), 95
Mathematical (quantitative) model, 45, 140, 145–147
Mathematical programming, 152–153, 156
Megaputer, 228, 263, 301
PolyAnalyst, 179, 228, 229t
Text Analyst, 312
WebAnalyst, 318
Mental model, 44–45
Message feature mining, 297–299, 298
Metadata in data warehousing, 330, 332–333, 334

Microsoft
Agent technology, 103
Enterprise Consortium, 229, 230–231
Excel, 151–152, 151f, 152f, 230, W4.5.1 (*See also* Spreadsheets)
Live Communications Serve, 452
Live Meeting, 437, 439
Outlook Calendar, 439
PowerPoint, 435
SharePoint, 436
System Center Configuration Manager for Mobile Devices, 635
Windows, 437
Windows-based GUI, 442
Windows Live Spaces Mobile, 654
Windows Meeting Space, 435, 437, 442
Windows XP, 442
See also Groove Networks; SQL
MicroStrategy Corp., 22, 64, 84, 125, 179, 228, 365, 379
Middleware tools in data warehousing process, 334
Mind-reading platforms, 104
Mintzberg's 10 managerial roles, 8t
MIT, 621, 641, 657
MITRE, 287–288, 472–474, 473f
Mix-and-match recommendations in ES, 552–553
Mobile community activities, 654
Mobile enterprise networks, 654
Mobile social networking, 653–654
Model base, 96–97
Model base management system (MBMS), 86, 88t, 99, 100, 179–180
Modeling and analysis
certainty, uncertainty, and risk, 147–149
decision analysis, 161–165
goal seeking analysis, 159–161, 161f
management support system (MSS) modeling, 139–145
mathematical models for decision support, 145–147
mathematical program optimization, 152–157 (*See also* Linear programming (LP))
Miller's *MIS Cases*, 181
model-based auctions, 136–138
model base management, 179–180
multicriteria decision making with pairwise comparisons, 165–168
of multiple goals, 157–158
problem-solving search methods, 168–171, 169f
quantitative software packages, 179
sensitivity analysis, 158–159
simulation, 171–177
with spreadsheets, 149–152 (*See also under* Spreadsheets)
vendors, products, and demos, 181
visual active simulation, 177–179
what-if analysis, 159, 160f
See also individual headings
Model libraries, 144
Model management subsystem, components of, 96–100
model base, 96–97
model base management system (MBMS), 86, 88t, 99, 100
model building blocks and routines, 97
model components for building DSS, 97–98
model directory, 99
model execution, integration, and command, 99–100
modeling tools, 98
Model marts, 497

Models/modeling
categories of models, 144t
components of, 146t
for decision-making (*See* Decision-making models)
issues (*See* Models/modeling issues)
languages, 98
mathematical, management science based on, 13
model base (*See* Model base)
model building blocks, 97
model command, 99–100
model components for building DSS, 97–98
model directory, 99
model execution, 99–100
model integration, 99–100
model-oriented DSS, 17
routines, 97
tools, 98
See also Modeling and analysis; Model management subsystem, components of
Models/modeling issues, 141–145
environmental scanning and analysis, 141
forecasting (predictive analytics), 142–143
knowledge-based modeling, 143
model categories, 143
model management, 143
multiple models, 143
trends in, current, 144–145
variable identification, 141–142
Model warehouses, 497
Momentum, 257
Monitor, 8t
Monitoring system, 565
Morphology, 290
Mortgage crisis, 67
MP3 players, 103, 652t
MSN, 456, 668
MSS. *See* Management support system (MSS)
Multicriteria decision analysis, 162
Multicriteria decision making with pairwise comparisons, 165–167
Multicriteria problems, 165
Multidimensional analysis (modeling), 145
Multidimensional cube presentation, 22
Multiple-attribute utility theory, 140
Multiple goals, analysis of, 157–158
Multiple goals, defined, 164
Multiprocessor clusters, 95
Multiuse GDSS facilities, 446
MySpace, 454, 651, 652t, 653, 654, 655, 673
MySpace Mobile, 654
MySQL, 92

Naïve solutions stage, 535
Named-entity recognition, 295
Narrative, 54–55
NASA, 483–484
Natural language generation, 295
Natural language processing (NLP), 103, 105, 292–296
in AI field, 537–539
defined, 292–293
goal of, 292
implementation challenges of, 293
sentiment analysis and, 293, 295
Natural language understanding, 295
Negotiator, 8t
NEOS Server for Optimization, 144
.NET Framework, 108
Network information processing, 249–251

Networks, 246
Neural computing, 245, 540
Neural network, 245
See also Artificial neural network (ANN)
Neural network-based systems, developing, 259–264
data collection and preparation, 261
implementation of ANN, 264
learning algorithm selection, 262
network structure, selection of, 261–262, 262f
network training, 262–263
process of, 259–261, 260f
software, 263
testing, 263–264
Neurodes, 246
Neurons, 245, 246
Nominal data, 198
Nominal group technique (NGT), 426
Nonmathmatical descriptive models, 54
Nonvolatile data warehousing, 329
Norfolk Southern, 3–4
Normative models, 51–53
Notebook computers, 92, 506, 545
Ntellimedia system, 573
Nucleus, 246
Numeric data, 198

Objective function, 154
Objective function coefficients, 154
Object-oriented databases, 91–92
Object-oriented model base management system (OOMBMS), 180
Object-oriented simulation, 175
Objects, defined, 101
OLAP. *See* Online analytical processing (OLAP)
OLTP system, 334, 344–345, 360
1-of-N pseudo variables, 198–199
1-800-Flowers, 195
One-tier architecture, 335–336, 335f, 336f
Online advertising, 460
Online analytical processing (OLAP), 9, 18, 85
vs. advanced spreadsheet software, 151
Analysis Services OLAP engine, 324
ANN and data-induction tools used in, 106
data extraction capabilities of, 92
DSS templates provided by, 85
mathematical (quantitative) models embedded in, 140
Online bulletin (discussion) groups, 436
Online collaboration, implementation issues for, 452
Online transaction processes.
See OLTP system
Openness in collective intelligence (CI), 460
Operational control, 13
Operational data store (ODS), 330
Operational models, 97
Operations research (OR), 13
Optical character recognition, 296
Optimal solution, 153
Optimization, 51, 108
in clustering techniques, 202
in mathematical programming, 152–157
model, spreadsheet-based, 150
of online advertising, 226
Oracle
Business Intelligence Suite, 342
Data Mining (ODM), 229t
Hyperion, 228, 661
XML Data Synthesis, 95

Orange Data Mining Tool, 229t, 230
Orca Visual Simulation Environment (VSE), 178
Ordinal data, 198
Ordinal multiple logistic regression, 198
Organizational culture in KMS, 482–483
Organizational knowledge base, 86
Organizational learning in KMS, 482
Organizational memory, 437, 442, 482
Organizational performance, 7
Organizational support, 84
Ossified case, 586
O2 Wireless, 654
Overall Analysis System for Intelligence Support (OASIS), 297
Overall classifier accuracy, 217

Paradigmatic case, 586
Parallelism, 443
Parallel processing, 249, 337, 353
Parameters, 146
Partitioning, 337
Part-of-speech tagging, 290
PASW Modeler, 199–200, 228, 229, 230
Patent analysis, 291
Pattern analysis, 196
Pattern matching, 558
Pattern recognition, 221, 274
Pattern searching, 196
Pause and Learn (PaL), 484
Peering in collective intelligence (CI), 460
Pension fund advisors, 548
Per class accuracy rates, 217
Performance management, effective, W9.2.1
Personal digital assistants (PDAs), 63, 102, 103, 108, 342, 437, 541
Personal information management (PIM), 437
Personal support, 84
Pervasive computing, 452
Pfizer, 462, 499, 651
Pharmaceutical development, applications for, 177
Placeholder as session activity, 449
Planners Lab, 108–125
    charts, summary of, 121–122, 121f
    components of, 110
    downloading, 110
    Goal Seek scenario, 117–118, 117f
    keywords used in, 122–125
    model assumptions, 111, 111f
    model-building process, 110–111
    model outline and highlighted reserved words, 113f
    Monte Carlo simulation, 114, 115f, 118, 119f, 120
    NORRAND, 122
    playground, chart options in, 114–115, 115f
    startup screen, 111–112, 112f
    TRIRAND, 114, 115f, 122
    tutorial example, 111–120
    validate model option with errors highlighted, 114f
    Variable Tree chart, 118, 119f, 120, 122
    What If variables, 120, 120f
Planning and forecasting, 22
Planning Sciences International, 496
Planning system, 564
Platforms as a service (PaaS), 658
PolyAnalyst, 179, 228, 229t, 301–302
Polysemes, 290
Portfolio of options, W9.1.1
Practice approach to KMS, 487t, 488
Prediction, 200, 201

Prediction system, 564
Predictive analytics, 22, 78, 142
Prioritization in GSS process, 449
Privacy issues in MSS, 667–669
Private data, 91
Probabilistic simulation, 174–175, 175t
Problem classification, 49
Problem decomposition, 49
Problem (or opportunity) identification, 48–49
Problem ownership, 46, 50
Problem solving and decision making, 42
Problem-solving search methods, 168–171, 169f
Process approach to KMS, 486–487, 487t
Process gains, 425
Processing element (PE), 248
Process losses, 425
Procter & Gamble (P&G), 80, 132–133, 139–140, 143, 178, 421–423, 636
Product design, applications for, 177
Production, 176, 205, 557
Product life-cycle management (PLM), 60, 62, 331
Product-mix model formulation, 154, 155, 155f, W4.3.1, W4.4.1–2
Product pricing, 226
Product visibility, RFID and, 640–641
Profitability analysis, 22
Project management, 461–462
Propensity to buy, 24t

Qualitative data, 208–209
Quality support, 10
Quantitative data, 208–209
Quantitative software packages, 179
Query facility, 93
Query-specific clustering, 308
Question answering in text mining applications, 290, 295

Radio frequency identification (RFID), 636–641
    active tags, 636
    binary digits in, 637
    Coca-Cola and, 635–636
    data, 638–640, 639t
    defined, 636
    Electronic Product Code (EPC) used in, 637
    operations and functions of retail system and, 637–638, 638f
    product visibility and, 640–641
    supply-chain management and, 637
    tags, 636–637
    used in Cleveland Museum of Art, 63
RAKID (Results-Action-Knowledge-Information-Data) model, 490f, 491
Rank order vote as session activity, 449
RapidMiner, 229, 230
Ratio data, 7, 198
Ready-made DSS system, 84–85
Reality mining, 30, 641–644
Real-time collaboration (RTC) tools, 433–436
Real-time data warehousing, 330, 359–364
Real-time Online Decision Support System (RODOS), 167
Regression, 216, 274
Reinforcement learning, 586
Relational model base management system (RMBMS), 180
Relational/multidimensional data warehousing, 329
Repair system, 565

Report delivery and alerting, 22
Reproduction, 595
Resource allocator, 8t
Result (outcome) variables, 146, 162
Retailing, 204–205
Retail system, operations and functions of, 637–638, 638f
Retiree corporate social networks, 657
Revenue management, 331
Revenue (or yield) management system (RMS), 14, 142
Revenue optimization system, 14
RFID. See Radio frequency identification (RFID)
Right-hand side (RHS) products and/or service, 226–227
Risk
    analysis, 149
    decision making under, 147, 148–149, 163, 163t
    defined, 56–57
@RISK (Palisade Corp.), 149
Robot/robotics, 539–540
Rotation estimation, 218–219
Rough sets, 220
Ruby on Rails, 108
Rule-based solutions, 14
Rule-based systems, 586t
Rule-induction methods, 106
Rule interpreter, 558

Sales and marketing analysis, 22
Sales/promotion configuration, 226
SAP, 64, 125, 228, 365, 406, 407t, 412, 500
SAS
    enterprise data integration server, 342
    Enterprise Miner, 228, 229, 229t, 230, 324
    Institute, Inc., 214, 228, 324, 342, 348t, 360, 406, 661
    Statistics, 230
    Text Miner, 312, 324
    Web Analytics, 318
Satisficing, 55
Scalability, 95, 358–359
Scatter/gather, 308
Scenarios, 57
Scene recognition, 540
Screen sharing, 435
Search engines, 500
Search methods, problem-solving. See Problem-solving search methods
Search precision, 307–308
Search recall, 307
Sears, 458, 461, 467
Second Life (videogame), 460, 644–646, 648, 657, 673
Securities Observation, New Analysis, and Regulations (SONAR), 549
Securities trading, 205
Security and counterterrorism, 287–288
Security text mining applications, 297–299
Self-organizing network, 255
Semistructured decisions, 13
Semistructured problems, 12, 15
SEMMA, 214–215, 214f
Sense Networks, 30, 641–643, 669
Sensitivity analysis, 58, 158–159, 193
Sensor networks, 103
Sensory system, 539–540
Sentiment analysis, 293, 295
September 11, 2001, 206, 431, 516, 517, 669
Sequence mining, 203
Sequence pattern discovery, 317

Sequential relationship patterns, 200
Sequoia Software, 499
Serial analysis of gene expression (SAGE), 299
Serialized global trade identification numbers (SGTIN), 637
Serialized shipping container codes (SSCC), 637
Service-oriented architectures (SOA), 332
Sharing in collective intelligence (CI), 460
Short message service (SMS), 102–103, 436
Sigmoid (logical activation) function, 251
Sigmoid transfer function, 251
Simon's four phases of decision making. See Decision-making process, phases of
Simple split, 218, 218f
Simulation, 54, 108, 171–177
    advantages of, 172–173
    applications, 176–177
    characteristics of, 172
    decision making in Finnish Air Force by using, 171–172
    defined, 171
    disadvantages of, 173
    examples of, 175–176
    inadequacies in, conventional, 177
    methodology of, 173–174, 174f
    software, 175
    types of, 174–175, 175t
    visual interactive models and DSS, 178–179
    visual interactive simulation (VIS), 177–179
Simultaneous goals, 157
Singular-value decomposition (SVD), 291, 306–307
SLATES (Web 2.0 acronym), 454
Slice-and-dice analysis, 22
SMS. See Short message service (SMS)
Social network analysis (SNA) software, 653
Social networking, online, 653–658
    blogs and wikis used in, 657
    defined, 653
    enhancing collaboration, 657
    expert location, 657
    Facebook, 654–655
    knowledge management, 657
    management activities and support, 656
    mobile (See Mobile social networking)
    Orkut, 655
    retiree corporate social networks, 657
    size of, 653
    training, 657
    workers, finding and recruiting, 655
Social-networking sites, 454
Socialtext, 455, 468–469
Software
    in artificial neural networks (ANN), 263
    creativity enhancing, 464–465
    data mining used in, 205
    development companies and EIS vendors, 498
    development tools, 108
    for DSS user interfaces, 103
    for intelligent system, 105–106
    social network analysis (SNA), 653
    in text mining, 312
    used in data mining, 228–233
    Web usage mining, 318t

Software as a service (SaaS), 658, 659
Solution technique libraries, 144
SOM. *See* Kohonen's self-organizing feature maps (SOM)
SPARKS, 549
Speech-generation technology, 103
Speech recognition, 296
Speech synthesis, 296
Speech (voice) understanding, 539
Spreadsheets
   for ammunition requirements planning for Canadian Army, 76–77
   cloud applications and, 658
   decision modeling using, 39–40
   as end-user modeling tool, 149
   of goal seeking analysis, 161f
   for inventory target setting at P&G, 132–133
   management support system (MSS) modeling with
   model used to create schedules for medical interns, 152–153
   MSS modeling with, 149–152, 150f, 151f
   vs. OLAP, 151
SPRINT, 221
SPSS
   Clementine, 199, 228, 229t, 230
   PASW Modeler, 192f, 199–200, 228, 229, 230
   Statistics, 230
   Text Mining for Clementine, 312
   Web Mining for Clementine, 318
SQL
   query structures, 93
   Server, 337
   Server 2008 Business Intelligence Suite, 229
   Server database, 324
   Server Data Mining, 229t
Staff assistants, 107
Starbucks, 385–387, 640
Star schema, 351–352, 353f
State of nature, 162
Static model, 143
Statistica Data Miner, 228, 229, 229t
Statistical Navigator, 570
Statistica Text Mining, 312
StatSoft, Inc., 228, 238, 270
Statutory reporting, 22
Stemming, 290
Stock-keeping units (SKUs), 457
Stop terms, 290, 305
Stop words, 290, 305
Store design, 226
Story, 586
Strategic models, 96
Strategic planning, 13
Structured problems, 12
Structured processes, 11t, 12
Subject matter expert (SME), 81
Subject-oriented data warehousing, 329
Suboptimization, 53–54
Summarization in text mining applications, 289
Sun Microsystems, 360, 659
Supervised learning, 254–255, 257t
Supply-chain management (SCM), 16, 43, 62, 63, 330
   integrating with KMS, 503
   and RFID, 637
Support metric, 226–227
Support vector machines (SVM), 606–613
   vs. artificial neural networks, 612
   benefits of, 612

building, process of, 608–612, 609
   disadvantages of, 612
   function of, 607
   implementation of, 607
   kernel trick, 608
Survey as session activity, 449
Sybase, 108, 348t, 499
Symbiotic intelligence. *See* Collective intelligence (CI)
Symbolic processing in AI, 534
Symmetric multiprocessing (SMP) system, 95
Synapse, 246
Synchronous communication, 429
Synchronous products, 431, 432t
Synonyms, 290

Tablet computers, 63, 92
Tabletop, 464
Tacit knowledge, 478–479
Tacit Knowledge Systems, 489, 512
Tactical models, 97
Tags, RFID, 636–637
Tailored turn-key solutions, 567
Team Expert Choice (EC11), 439, 443
Teamwork. *See* Groupwork
Teleconferencing, 434–435
Teradata Corp., 64, 84, 228, 327, 337, 339, 347, 348t, 360, 661
Teradata University Network (TUN), 365, 366
Term-by-document matrix (occurrence matrix), 290–291
Term dictionary, 290
Term-document matrix (TDM), 303–307, 304f
Terms, defined, 290
Test set, 218
Text categorization, 307
Text data mining. *See* Text mining
Text mining, 286–324
   applications, 296–302
   bag-of-words used in, 292
   concepts and definitions, 289–291
   HP and, 323–323
   natural language processing (NLP) in, 292–296
   for patent analysis, 291
   research literature survey with, 309
   terms used in, 290
   three-step process, 302–311, 304f
   tools, 312
Text proofing, 296
Text-to-speech, 102–103, 296
Theory of certainty factors, 561
ThinkTank, 427–428, 437, 439, 448–450, 451f, 451t
Three-tier architecture, 335–336, 335f, 336f
Threshold value, 251
Time compression, 172
Time-dependent simulation, 175
Time-independent simulation, 175
Time/place framework, 429–430, 429f
Time pressure, 52
Time-series forecasting, 203, 275
Time variant (time series) data warehousing, 329
Tokenizing, 290
Topic tracking in text mining applications, 289
Topologies, 248
Torrance Tests of Creative Thinking (TTCT), 462
Touch-screen computing, 104
Toyota, 131, 376, 400, 510, 540
Traction Software, 451t

Tradeshows, 646–648
Training set, 218
Transaction-processing system (TPS), 91
Transformation (transfer) function, 251, 251f
Transportation Security Administration (TSA), 378–379
Traumatic brain injury diagnostics, 275
Travel industry, 205
Trend analysis in text mining, 308
Trial-and-error sensitivity analysis, 159
Tribes, 641
TRIZ (Russian acronym), 465
Turing test, 534
Twitter, 658
Two-tier architecture, 335–336, 335f, 336f

Uncertainty, decision making under, 147, 148, 162–163
Uncontrollable variables, 146, 162
Unified Modeling Language (UML), 175
U.S. Department of Homeland Security (DHS), 94, 183, 206, 297, 316, 516, 669, W3.1.12–11
Unstructured data (*vs.* structured data), 290
Unstructured decisions, 13
Unstructured problems, 12, 15
Unstructured processes, 11t, 12
Unstructured text data, 198
Unsupervised learning, 254–255, 257t, 586
USA PATRIOT Act, 206
User-centered design (UCD), 468
User interface
   in DSS, 101–104
   in ES, 551
   subsystem, 86, 100–105
User interface management system (UIMS), 100–101, W3.1.2.1
Users of decision support system (DSS), 89t, 106–107
Utility theory, 140, 158

Variables
   decision, 146, 154, 162
   dependent, 146
   identification of, 141–142
   intermediate result, 147
   result (outcome), 146, 162
   uncontrollable, 146, 162
Vendor-managed inventory (VMI), 458–459
Verity, 499, 500
Verizon, 103, 635
Verizon Conferencing, 441
Videogames, 460
Video-sharing sites, 454
Video teleconferencing, 434–435
Vignette, 431, 436, 452
Virtual booth, 647, 647f
Virtual communities, 650–652
Virtual (Internet) community, 650
Virtual meeting system, 431–432
Virtual reality, 22
Virtual worlds, 644–649
VisSim (Visual Solutions, Inc.), 178–179
Visual inactive modeling (VIM), 177–179
Visual interactive models and DSS, 178–179
Visual interactive problem solving, 177–179
Visual interactive simulation (VIS), 177–179

Visualization, 22, 203, 272
Visualizer, 653
Visual output displays, 103
Visual recognition, 540
Visual simulation, 175
Vivisimo/Clusty, 312
Vodafone New Zealand Ltd., 5–6, 34–35
Voice input (speech recognition), 103
Voice of customer (VOC), 320–321
Voice output (speech-to-text), 103
Voice over IP (VoIP), 431, 453
Voice recognition, 103
Voluntary Interindustry Commerce Standards (VICS), 458

Wal-Mart, 91, 103, 358–359, 380, 458, 636, 638, 640
Web analytics, 97, 319–321
Web-based data warehousing, 329, 336–337, 336f
Web conferencing, 435
Web content mining, 314–315
Web crawlers, 314
Web Distributed Authoring and Versioning (WebDAV), 452
Web-enabled high-performance teams, 484
WebEx Meeting Center, 433–434, 435, 437, 438–439, 440
WebGPSS, 175
Web-HIPRE application, 166
Webhousing, 357
Webinars, 646
Web mining, 314–318
Web site optimization ecosystem, 319–321, 320f, 321f
Web structure mining, 315
Web 2.0, 649–650
   characteristics of, 649–650
   companies and new business models, 650
   defined, 454, 649–650
   features/techniques in, 454
   as new knowledge management, 497
   used in online social networking, 657
Web usage mining, 316–317, 317f, 318t
What-if analysis, 58, 160, 160f
Why explanations, 563
WiFi hotspot access points, 643–644, 669
Wikia, 650
Wikilog, 455
Wikinomics, 460
Wikipedia, 104, 263, 459, 460, 510, 644, 653, 658
Wikis, 436, 454, 468–469, 657
Wimba, 431, 435, 439–440
Word counting, 292
Word frequency, 290
WordStat analysis, 312
Workflow, 436, 454
Work system, 25
Worldwide Customer Services (WCS), 331–332

XCON, 548
Xerox Corporation, 499, 506, 507
XLMiner, 229t
XML Miner, 318

Yahoo!, 102, 169, 263, 315, 456, 659, 668
Yield management, 179, 205
YouTube, 454, 653, 673